Geography of Europe

The map on the following pages features the co North Africa and the Middle East. Like most m bination of physical and political information. natural world—the shapes of landmasses, mou serves as a kind of background or screen onto which projected. Categories of political information commonly featured maps include the location and names of important cities and states, the changing borders of countries and empires, and the routes people traveled as they explored, migrated, traded, and fought with one another.

Europe is one of seven continents; the others are Africa, Asia, North America, South America, Australia, and Antarctica. Europe is bounded in the north by the Arctic Sea, in the west by the Atlantic Ocean, in the south by the Mediterranean Sea, and in the southeast by the Black Sea and the Caspian Sea. Off the mainland but traditionally considered a part of Europe are thousands of islands, from those of the United Kingdom, Ireland, and Iceland in the northwest, to Crete, Sicily, and Sardinia in the southeast.

Europe is quite distinctive in shape. The first thing to notice is that there is no natural border between Europe and Asia. The traditional eastern boundary is the Ural River, but looked at from a purely geographic standpoint, Europe might simply be called western Asia. The second thing to notice is how much of Europe is made up of peninsulas. In fact, Europe itself is one gigantic peninsula, with a coastline equal in distance to one and a half times around the equator (37,877 miles).

North Americans are often surprised to discover the small size of the European continent. The geographic area of France, for example, is less than that of Texas; Britain is similar in size to Alabama. The distance from London to Paris is about the same as from New York to Boston, while the distance from Berlin to Moscow is comparable to that of Chicago to Denver.

Major Peninsulas and Islands There are six major European peninsulas: the Iberian (comprising Portugal and Spain); the Apennine (Italy); the Balkan (Slovenia, Croatia, Bosnia-Herzegovina, Serbia and Montenegro, Albania, Greece, Bulgaria, and Macedonia); the Anatolian (Turkey); the Scandinavian (Norway, Sweden, and Finland); and the Jutland or Danish peninsula. The islands of Iceland, Ireland, and the United Kingdom lie to the Atlantic west, while to the east lie some of the major islands of the Mediterranean, such as Corsica, Sardinia, Sicily, Crete, and Cyprus.

Seas, Lakes, and Rivers Europe's irregular coastline encloses large areas of water into bays, gulfs, and seas. Moving from west to east in the Mediterranean, we have the Tyrrhenian Sea (between Italy and the islands of Sicily, Sardinia, and Corsica), the Adriatic (between Italy and the nations of the western Balkan peninsula), the Ionian (between Italy and Greece), and the Aegean (between Greece and Turkey). The Baltic Sea is bordered on the east (moving clockwise from the north) by Finland, Russia, Estonia, Latvia, Lithuania, Poland, Germany, and Sweden. It is connected by narrow channels to the North Sea, which lies (moving clockwise from the north) between Norway, Denmark, Germany, the Netherlands, and Belgium in the east and south, to the United Kingdom in the north and west. The English Channel separates England and France; the Bay of Biscay lies between southwestern

Elevation
Meters
Feet
4,000
13,120
2,000
6,560
500
1,640
200
656
Sea level
Sea level
Below sea level
Below sea level
National capital
Other city
Reykjavik
ICELAND
Arctic Circle
Faroe Islands (Den.)
Shetland Islands (U.K.)
SWEDE
NORWAY
Oslo
NORTHERN IRELAND
Belfast
Edinburgh
North Sea
IRELAND
Dublin
DENMARK
Copenhagen
Baltic
Kalinir
UNITED KINGDOM
NETHERLANDS
Hamburg
Gdansk
Cardiff
London
Amsterdam
Elbe R.
PO
Berlin
ATLANTIC OCEAN
English Channel
GERMANY
Brussels
Bonn
Leipzig
BELGIUM
Frankfurt
Seine R.
Paris
Luxembourg
LUX.
Prague
Loire R.
Stuttgart
CZECH REPUBLIC
Bay of Biscay
Rhine R.
Munich
FRANCE
Zurich
LIECH.
Vienna
Brati
Bern
Vaduz
Geneva
SWITZ.
ALPS
AUSTRIA
HUN
Lyons
Ljubljana
Milan
Rhône R.
Turin
SLOVENIA
Zagreb
Po R.
CROATIA
Porto
PYRENEES
SAN MARINO
San Marino
BOSNIA & HERZEGOVINA
PORTUGAL
SPAIN
Monaco
Andorra la Vella
ANDORRA
MONACO
APENNINES
Adriatic Sea
Sarajevo
Lisbon
Madrid
Tagus R.
Barcelona
Corsica (Fr.)
Rome
Podgorica
Balearic Islands (Sp.)
ITALY
VATICAN CITY
ALBAN
Naples
Tiranë
Sardinia (It.)
Tyrrhenian Sea
Mediterranean Sea
Gibraltar (U.K.)
Ionia Sea
Rabat
Algiers
Sicily (It.)
MOROCCO
Tunis
ALGERIA
ATLAS MTS.
0
200
400 Km.
400 Mi.
Valletta
MALTA
TUNISIA

70°N
40°E
60°
50°N
40°N
30°
N
URAL MTS.
RUSSIA
Lake Ladoga
St. Petersburg
Astana
Volga R.
Moscow
Ural R.
KAZAKHSTAN
Volga R.
Aral Sea
UZBEKISTAN
Kiev
Kharkov
Dnieper R.
Don R.
Donetsk
Dnepropetrovsk
MOLDOVA
Odessa
Caspian Sea
TURKMENISTAN
Ashgabat
CAUCASUS MTS.
GEORGIA
Tbilisi
Baku
Bucharest
Black Sea
AZERBAIJAN
ARMENIA
Yerevan
Bosporus
Istanbul
AZER.
ANATOLIA
Ankara
Tehran
IRAN
Dardanelles
TURKEY
TAURUS MTS.
ZAGROS MTS.
SYRIA
Nicosia
Baghdad
CYPRUS
Beirut
IRAQ
LEBANON
Damascus

France and northern Spain. The Black Sea, on the southern border of Russia and Ukraine, is connected by two straits—the Bosphorous and the Dardanelles—to the Aegean Sea. The Caspian Sea, bordered in the north by Russia and Kazakhstan, is the world's largest saltwater lake and, at 92 feet below sea level, the lowest point in Europe.

Several of Europe's major rivers flow across the Russian plain. At 2,194 miles, the Volga is the longest river in Europe. Linked by canals and other river systems to the Arctic Ocean in the north and the Baltic Sea in the south, the Volga originates west of Moscow and empties into the Caspian Sea after flowing some 2,194 miles. At 1,777 miles, the Danube is Europe's second longest river and the principal waterway in the central part of the continent. It originates in southern Germany and flows through Austria, Slovakia, Hungary, Croatia, Serbia and Montenegro, Bulgaria, Moldova, Ukraine, and Romania, before reaching the Black Sea. The Rhine river comes next, at 766 miles, winding its way from the Swiss Alps to the Netherlands and the North Sea. Other prominent riverways in Europe include the Elbe (678 miles), which originates in the Czech Republic and passes through Germany before it, too, empties into the North Sea, and the Rhône (505 miles), which runs from Switzerland, through France, and into the Mediterranean Sea. The proximity of most areas of the European landmass to the coastline and to major river systems greatly affected the Continent's history.

Land Regions Despite its relatively small size, the European continent presents a wide range of landforms, from rugged mountains to sweeping plains. These can be separated into four major regions: the Northwest Mountains, the Great European Plain, the Central Uplands, and the Alpine Mountain System. The mountains of the Northwest Region cover most of the region, running through northwestern France, Ireland, northern Great Britain, Norway, Sweden, northern Finland, and the northwest corner of Russia. The Great European Plain covers almost all of the European part of the former Soviet Union, extending from the Arctic Ocean to the Caucasus Mountains. This belt stretches westward across Poland, Germany, Belgium, the western portion of France, and southeastern England. The Central Uplands is a belt of high plateaus, hills, and low mountains. It reaches from the central plateau of Portugal, across Spain, the central highlands of France, to the hills and mountains of southern Germany, the Czech Republic, and Slovakia. The Alpine Mountain System is made up of several mountain ranges, including the Pyrenees between Spain and France, the Alps in southeastern France, northern Italy, Switzerland, and western Austria, and the Apennine range in Italy. Also included are the mountain ranges of the Balkan Peninsula, the Carpathian Mountains in Slovakia and Romania, and the Caucasus Mountains between the Black and Caspian Seas.

When studying the map of Europe, it is important to notice the proximity of Central Asia, the Middle East, and North Africa. Interaction with the peoples and cultures of these regions has had a profound impact on the course of European history.

Western Civilization

A Brief History with Readings

Tenth Edition

Marvin Perry | Joseph R. Peden | Theodore H. Von Laue |
J. Wayne Baker | Pamela Pfeiffer Hollinger

CENGAGE
Learning®

Australia • Brazil • Japan • Korea • Mexico • Singapore • Spain • United Kingdom • United States

CENGAGE Learning

Western Civilization: A Brief History with Readings, Tenth Edition

Executive Editors:
Maureen Staudt
Michael Stranz

Senior Project Development Manager:
Linda deStefano

Marketing Specialist:
Courtney Sheldon

Senior Production/Manufacturing Manager:
Donna M. Brown

Production Editorial Manager:
Kim Fry

Sr. Rights Acquisition Account Manager:
Todd Osborne

Printed in the United States of America

Western Civilization, A Brief History, 10th Edition
Marvin Perry

Library of Congress Control Number: 2011935447

Sources of the Western Tradition, Volume 1:
From Ancient Times to Enlightenment, 7th Edition
Marvin Perry | Joseph R. Peden | Theodore H. Von Laue

The Humanities in the Western Tradition: Ideas and Aesthetics, Volume I:
Ancient to Midieval, 1st Edition
Marvin Perry | J. Wayne Baker | Pamela Pfeiffer Hollinger

Sources of the Western Tradition, Volume 2, 7th Edition
Marvin Perry | Joseph R. Peden | Theodore H. Von Laue

ISBN-13: 978-1-285-12162-8

ISBN-10: 1-285-12162-7

Cengage Learning
5191 Natorp Boulevard
Mason, Ohio 45040
USA
Cengage Learning is a leading provider of customized learning solutions with office locations around the globe, including Singapore, the United Kingdom, Australia, Mexico, Brazil, and Japan. Locate your local office at:
international.cengage.com/region.

Cengage Learning products are represented in Canada by Nelson Education, Ltd.
For your lifelong learning solutions, visit **www.cengage.com/custom.**
Visit our corporate website at **www.cengage.com.**

Brief Contents

Insert:
Western Tradition: From Ancient Times to Present
Marvin Perry

Contents

Maps

Chronologies

Preface

Western civilization is a grand but tragic drama. The West has forged the instruments of reason that make possible a rational comprehension of physical nature and human culture, conceived the idea of political liberty, and recognized the intrinsic worth of the individual. But the modern West, though it has unraveled nature's mysteries, has been less successful at finding rational solutions to social ills and conflicts between nations. Science, a great achievement of the Western intellect, while improving conditions of life, has also produced weapons of mass destruction. Though the West has pioneered in the protection of human rights, it has also produced totalitarian regimes that have trampled on individual freedom and human dignity. Although the West has demonstrated a commitment to human equality, it has also practiced brutal racism.

Despite the value that Westerners have given to reason and freedom, they have shown a frightening capacity for irrational behavior and a fascination with violence and irrational ideologies. And they have willingly sacrificed liberty for security or national grandeur. The world wars and the totalitarian movements of the twentieth century have demonstrated that Western Civilization, despite its extraordinary achievements, is fragile and perishable. Yet the West has also shown a capacity to reassert its best values and traditions.

Western Civilization: A Brief History, Tenth Edition, is an abridged version of *Western Civilization: Ideas, Politics, and Society,* Tenth Edition. Like the longer text, this volume examines those unique patterns of thought and systems of values that constitute the Western heritage. While focusing on key ideas and broad themes, the text also provides economic, political, and social history for students in Western Civilization courses.

The text is written with the conviction that history is not a meaningless tale. Without knowledge of history, men and women cannot fully know themselves, for all human beings have been shaped by institutions and values inherited from the past. Without an awareness of the historical evolution of reason and freedom, the dominant ideals of Western civilization, commitment to these ideals will diminish. Without knowledge of history, the West cannot fully comprehend or adequately cope with the problems that burden its civilization and the world.

In attempting to make sense out of the past, the author has been careful to avoid superficial generalizations that oversimplify historical events and forces and arrange history into too neat a structure. But the text does strive to interpret and synthesize in order to provide students with a frame of reference with which to comprehend the principal events and eras in Western history.

Changes in the Tenth Edition

For the tenth edition, most chapters have been reworked to some extent. The numerous carefully selected modifications and additions significantly enhance the text. Some changes deepen the book's conceptual character; others provide useful and illustrative historical details. The most significant addition in the previous edition was the insertion in every chapter of a primary source that illuminates the narrative. These primary sources are retained in the tenth edition, and we have added questions for analysis of the documents. The Geography of Europe essay at the beginning of the book has been updated. In order to strengthen the organization of the book, we have split the final chapter of the previous edition into two chapters, increasing the total number of chapters from twenty-one to twenty-two.

In Chapter 1, "The Ancient Near East: The First Civilizations," we introduced Sargon's daughter, Enheduanna, the world's oldest known poet. We have also expanded the section on Egyptian religion and inserted material on Egyptian literature. In Chapter 2, "The Hebrews: A New View of God and the Individual," we have expanded the discussion of Hebrew law and strengthened the concluding section, "The Legacy of the Ancient Jews." Several brief insertions enhance the understanding of events and concepts in Chapter 3, "The Greeks: From Myth to Reason." The chapter now includes a discussion of women in the Hellenistic world. The most notable changes in Chapter 4, "Rome: From City-State to World Empire," are fuller discussions of the battle of Cannae, including Roman responses to the disaster, the military accomplishments of Julius Caesar, and the problems of the Late Roman Empire. Chapter 5, "Early Christianity: A World Religion," includes more material on Jesus' life and death and a discussion of the views of early

Christian theorists regarding various sexual matters. The most significant additions to Chapter 6, "The Rise of Europe: Fusion of Classical, Christian, and Germanic Traditions," are expanded treatments of Muhammad and early Islam, the cultural decline in Latin Christendom during the Early Middle Ages, and the thought of Maimonides, the renown Jewish scholar and physician. The impact of the Black Death on European society is given greater coverage in Chapter 7, "The Flowering and Dissolution of Medieval Civilization." In Chapter 9, "Political and Economic Transformation: National States, Overseas Expansion, Commercial Revolution," we have enhanced the discussion of African slavery and the slave trade. Somewhat more attention is given to the philosophes' critique of Christianity in Chapter 10, "Intellectual Transformation: The Scientific Revolution and the Age of Enlightenment."

Chapter 11, "The Era of the French Revolution: Affirmation of Liberty and Equality," contains additional material on the Terror in the Vendée; the discussions of the impact of Napoleon on the reforms of the Revolution and the phenomenon of total war upgrade the end piece, "The Meaning of the French Revolution." The introduction to Chapter 12, "The Industrial Revolution: The Transformation of Society," has been enhanced, and material has been inserted on the difficulties faced by early trade unions. The discussion of the Revolution of 1848 in Germany has been deepened in Chapter 14, "Surge of Liberalism and Nationalism: Revolution, Counterrevolution, and Unification." The next four chapters are largely unchanged. The only addition to Chapter 15, "Thought and Culture in the Mid-Nineteenth Century: Realism, Positivism, Darwinism, and Social Criticism," are brief insertions in the section "Darwinism and Christianity." The only addition to Chapter 16, "Europe in the Late Nineteenth Century: Modernization, Nationalism, Imperialism," is a brief insertion in the section on anti-Semitism. In Chapter 17, "Modern Consciousness: New Views of Nature, Human Nature, and the Arts," we have slightly reinforced the section on Freud, as we have done with the section "War as Celebration" in Chapter 18, "World War I: The West in Despair." Chapter 19, "An Era of Totalitarianism," contains new material on the Nazi state, particularly the German people's adoration of Hitler, and the section on "Existentialism" has been completely restructured. The most noteworthy changes in Chapter 20, "World War II: Western Civilization in the Balance," are found in the end piece, "The Legacy of World War II." There we have added several paragraphs on the impact of the war on women and on the Enlightenment and Christian traditions. The previous edition Chapter 21, "The West in a Global Age," has been split into two chapters: Chapter 21, "Europe After World War II: Recovery, and Realignment, 1945–1989" and Chapter 22, "The Troubled Present." Chapter 21 now contains a much fuller treatment of the origins of the Cold War and the arms race. Chapter 22 aims to be very current. It treats the economic problems confronting the European Union, the status of Al Qaeda, the course of the wars in Iraq and Afghanistan, and the significance of the Arab revolt in early 2011. Finally, some changes have been made in the art essays.

Distinctive Features

This brief edition was prepared for Western Civilization courses that run for one term only; for instructors who like to supplement the main text with primary source readers, novels, or monographs; and for humanities courses in which additional works on literature and art will be assigned. In abbreviating the longer text by about a third, the number of chapters has been reduced from thirty-three to twenty-two. The emphasis on the history of ideas and culture has been retained, but the amount of detail has of necessity been reduced.

The text contains several pedagogical features. Chapter introductions provide comprehensive overviews of key themes and give a sense of direction and coherence to the flow of history. Chronologies at the beginning of most chapters show the sequence of important events discussed in the chapter. Many chapters contain concluding essays that treat the larger meaning of the material. Facts have been carefully selected to illustrate key relationships and concepts and to avoid overwhelming students with unrelated and disconnected data. Each chapter concludes with an annotated bibliography.

This text is published in both single-volume and two-volume editions. Volume I covers the period from the first civilizations in the Near East through the age of Enlightenment in the eighteenth century (Chapters 1–10). Volume II covers the period from the Renaissance and the Reformation to the contemporary age (Chapters 8–22), and incorporates the last three chapters in Volume I: "Transition to the Modern Age: Renaissance and Reformation," "Political and Economic Transformation: National States, Overseas Expansion, Commercial Revolution," and "Intellectual Transformation: The Scientific Revolution and the Age of Enlightenment." Volume II also contains a comprehensive introduction that surveys the ancient world and the Middle Ages; the introduction is designed particularly for students who have not taken the first half of the course.

Ancillaries

We are pleased to introduce an expanded ancillary package that will help students in learning and instructors in teaching.

Instructor's Resources

PowerLecture DVD with ExamView® and JoinIn®. An all-in-one multimedia resource for class preparation, presentation, and testing. The Instructor's Resource Manual, prepared by Jason Ripper, includes instructional objectives, chapter outlines, lecture suggestions, group learning projects, primary source analysis, audiovisual bibliographies, suggested readings, and Internet resources. Microsoft® PowerPoint® slides of lecture outlines, as well as images and maps from the text, can be used as offered or customized by importing personal lecture slides or other material; JoinIn PowerPoint slides with clicker content are also provided. An image library contains .jpg images from the text. The test bank, prepared by Dolores Grapsas, includes key term identification, multiple-choice, essay, and map questions. ExamView, an easy-to-use assessment and tutorial system, allows instructors to create, deliver, and customize tests in minutes. Instructors can build tests with as many as 250 questions using up to twelve question types. Using the complete word-processing capabilities of ExamView, instructors can enter an unlimited number of new questions or edit existing ones.

Companion Website. This website for instructors features all of the free student assets plus an Instructor's Resource Manual (instructional objectives, chapter outlines, lecture suggestions, group learning projects, primary source analysis, audiovisual bibliographies, suggested readings, and Internet resources) and PowerPoint presentations (lecture outlines, images and maps, and JoinIn PowerPoint slides with clicker content). In addition, access to HistoryFinder, a searchable online database with thousands of assets, allows instructors to easily create exciting presentations for their classroom by downloading art, photographs, maps, primary sources, and audio/video clips directly into a Microsoft PowerPoint slide.

WebTutor™ on Blackboard® or WebCT®. With the WebTutor text-specific, preformatted content and total flexibility, instructors can easily create and manage their own custom course website. Instructors can provide virtual office hours, post syllabi, set up threaded discussions, track student progress with the quizzing material, and much more. For students, WebTutor offers real-time access to an interactive eBook and a full array of study tools, including animations and videos that bring the book's topics to life, plus chapter outlines, summaries, learning objectives, glossary flashcards (with audio), practice quizzes, and web links.

CourseMate. Cengage Learning's History CourseMate brings course concepts to life with interactive learning, study tools, and exam preparation tools that support the printed textbook. Use Engagement Tracker to monitor student engagement in the course, and watch student comprehension soar as your class works with the printed textbook and the textbook-specific website. An interactive eBook allows students to take notes, highlight, search, and interact with embedded media (such as quizzes, flashcards, and videos). Access to the History Resource Center, a "virtual reader," provides students with hundreds of primary sources. Learn more at www.cengage.com/coursemate.

Wadsworth Western Civilization Resource Center. Wadsworth's Western Civilization Resource Center gives your students access to a "virtual reader" with hundreds of primary sources including speeches, letters, legal documents and transcripts, poems, maps, simulations, timelines, and additional images that bring history to life, along with interactive assignable exercises. A map feature including Google Earth™ coordinates and exercises will aid in student comprehension of geography and use of maps. Students can compare the traditional textbook map with an aerial view of the location today. It's an ideal resource for study, review, and research. In addition to this map feature, the resource center also provides blank maps for student review and testing.

CourseReader: Western Civilization. This application is Cengage Learning's easy, affordable way to build your own online customizable reader. Through a partnership with Gale, *CourseReader: Western Civilization* searches thousands of primary and secondary sources, readings, and audio and video clips from multiple disciplines. Select exactly and only the material you want your students to work with. Each selection can be listened to (using the "Listen" button) to accommodate varied learning styles. Additionally, an instructor can choose to add his or her own notes to readings to direct students' attention or ask them questions about a particular passage. Each primary source is accompanied by an introduction and questions to help students understand the reading. *CourseReader: Western Civilization* is the perfect complement to any class.

Student Resources

Companion Website. This website provides a variety of resources prepared by Sylvia Gray to help you review for class. These study tools include a glossary, crossword puzzles, short quizzes, essay questions, critical thinking questions, primary sources links, and weblinks.

WebTutor on Blackboard or *WebCT.* WebTutor offers real-time access to an interactive eBook and a full array of study tools, including animations and videos that bring the book's topics to life, plus chapter outlines, summaries, learning objectives, glossary flashcards (with audio), practice quizzes, and weblinks.

CourseMate. The more you study, the better the results. Make the most of your study time by accessing everything you need to succeed in one place. Read your textbook, take notes, review flashcards, watch videos, and take practice quizzes online with CourseMate. In addition, you can access the History Resource Center, a "virtual reader" that provides you with hundreds of primary sources.

Wadsworth Western Civilization Resource Center. Wadsworth's Western Civilization Resource Center gives you access to a "virtual reader" with hundreds of primary sources including speeches, letters, legal documents and transcripts, poems, maps, simulations, timelines, and additional images that bring history to life, along with interactive assignable exercises. A map feature including Google Earth coordinates and exercises will aid in your comprehension of geography and use of maps. You can compare the traditional textbook map with an aerial view of the location today. It's an ideal resource for study, review, and research. In addition to this map feature, the resource center also provides blank maps for student review and testing.

Rand McNally Historical Atlas of Western Civilization, 2e. This valuable resource features over forty-five maps, including maps that highlight classical Greece and Rome; maps documenting European civilization during the Renaissance; maps that follow events in Germany, Russia, and Italy as they led up to World Wars I and II; maps that show the dissolution of Communism in 1989; maps documenting language and religion in the Western world; and maps describing the unification and industrialization of Europe.

Document Exercise. Prepared by Donna Van Raaphorst, Cuyahoga Community College, this is a collection of exercises based around primary sources, available in two volumes.

Music of Western Civilization. Available free to adopters, and for a small fee to students, this CD contains a broad sampling of many important musical pieces of Western civilization.

Writing for College History, 1e. Prepared by Robert M. Frakes, Clarion University, this brief handbook for survey courses in American History, Western Civilization/European History, and World Civilization guides students through the various types of writing assignments they encounter in a history class. Providing examples of student writing and candid assessments of student work, this text focuses on the rules and conventions of writing for the college history course.

The History Handbook, 1e. Prepared by Carol Berkin of Baruch College, City University of New York, and Betty Anderson of Boston University, this book teaches students both basic and history-specific study skills such as how to read primary sources, research historical topics, and correctly cite sources. Substantially less expensive than comparable skill-building texts, *The History Handbook* also offers tips for Internet research and evaluating online sources.

Doing History: Research and Writing in the Digital Age, 1e. This text was prepared by Michael J. Galgano, J. Chris Arndt, and Raymond M. Hyser of James Madison University. Whether you're starting down the path as a history major or simply looking for a straightforward and systematic guide to writing a successful paper, you'll find this text to be an indispensible handbook to historical research. This text's "soup to nuts" approach to researching and writing about history addresses every step of the process, from locating your sources and gathering information to writing clearly and making proper use of various citation styles to avoid plagiarism. You'll also learn how to make the most of every tool available to you—especially the technology that helps you conduct the process efficiently and effectively.

The Modern Researcher, 6e. Prepared by Jacques Barzun and Henry F. Graff of Columbia University, this classic introduction to the techniques of research and the art of expression is used widely in history courses but is also appropriate for writing and research methods courses in other departments. Barzun and Graff thoroughly cover every aspect of research, from the selection of a topic through the gathering, analysis, writing, revision, and publication of findings, presenting the process not as a set of rules but through actual cases that put the subtleties of research in a useful context. Part One covers the principles and methods of research; Part Two covers writing, speaking, and getting one's work published.

Acknowledgments

The author would like to thank the following instructors for their critical reading of sections of the manuscript: Gerard Clock, Borough of Manhattan Community College; P. Scott Corbett, Ventura College; David Head, John Tyler Community College; and Nancy Rupprecht, Middle Tennessee State University. Several of their suggestions were incorporated into the final version.

In preparing this abridgment, I have made extensive use of the chapters written by my colleagues for *Western Civilization: Ideas, Politics, and Society*. Chapter 8, "Transition to the Modern Age: Renaissance and Reformation," and Chapter 9, "Political and Economic Transformation: National States, Overseas Expansion, Commercial Revolution," are based largely on James R. Jacob's and Margaret C. Jacob's chapters in the longer volume. Parts of Chapter 12, "The Industrial Revolution: The Transformation of Society," and of Chapter 16, "Europe in the Late Nineteenth Century: Modernization, Nationalism, Imperialism," are drawn from Myrna Chase's chapters. Material on tsarist Russia and the Soviet Union and the concluding chapter, "The Troubled Present," are based in part on Theodore H. Von Laue's contributions to the larger text. To a lesser or greater extent, my colleagues' material has been abridged, restructured, and rewritten to meet the needs of this volume. Therefore, I alone am responsible for all interpretations and any errors. I wish to thank my colleagues for their gracious permission to use their words and thoughts.

I am also grateful to the staff of Cengage Learning who lent their considerable talents to the project. In particular, I wish to thank Adrienne Zicht, Associate Editor, for her conscientiousness and superb administrative skills and Jane Lee, Senior Content Project Manager, for her careful supervision. Over the years, both Jean Woy, Senior Consulting Editor, who has been affiliated with the book since the first edition, and Nancy Blaine, Senior Sponsoring Editor, with whom I have worked for ten years, continued to recognize and support what I am trying to do—and for this I remain grateful. Although Nancy Blaine is no longer with Cengage Learning, her replacement, Brooke Barbier, has immediately identified with the project—and for this I am also grateful. In addition, I would like to thank Cate Barr, Senior Art Director, for her creativity and artistic vision in updating the cover and interior design for this edition. Three people not part of Cengage Learning made valuable contributions to the project. A special thanks to Karunakaran Gunasekaran at PreMediaGlobal, who managed the overall production with skill and dedication and the copy editor Daniel Nighting for his careful eye for detail. The photo researcher, Wendy Granger from the Bill Smith Group, deserves praise for her fine eye and enthusiasm for the project.

I am especially grateful to my friend of many years, George Bock, who read the manuscript with an eye for organization, major concepts, and essential relationships. As ever, I am grateful to my wife, Phyllis G. Perry, for her encouragement.

M. P.

Part One

The Ancient World: Foundation of the West

to A.D. *500*

Robert Harding Picture Library.

The Acropolis of Athens.

	Politics and Society	Thought and Culture
3000 B.C.	Rise of civilization in Sumer (c. 3200) Union of Upper and Lower Egypt (c. 2900) Rise of Minoan civilization (c. 2600)	Cuneiform writing in Sumer; hieroglyphics in Egypt
2000 B.C.	Rise of Mycenaean civilization (c. 2000) Hammurabi of Babylon builds an empire (1792–1750)	*Epic of Gilgamesh* (c. 1900) Code of Hammurabi (c. 1790) Amenhotep IV and a movement toward monotheism in Egypt (1369–1353) Moses and the Exodus (1200s)
1000 B.C.	Creation of a unified Hebrew monarchy under David (1000–961) Dark Age in Greece (c. 1100–800)	Origins of Phoenician alphabet (1000s) Homer's *Iliad* and *Odyssey* (700s)
500 B.C.	Hellenic Age (c. 800–323) Persian conquest of Near East (550–525) Formation of Roman Republic (509) Persian Wars (499–479) Peloponnesian War (431–404) Conquest of Greek city-states by Philip of Macedonia (338) Conquests of Alexander the Great (336–323) Hellenistic Age (323–30) Roman conquest of Carthage and Hellenistic kingdoms (264–146)	Age of classical prophecy: flowering of Hebrew ethical thought (750–430) Law of the Twelve Tables (450) Rise of Greek philosophy: Ionians, Pythagoreans, Parmenides (500s and 400s) Greek dramatists: Aeschylus, Sophocles, Euripides, Aristophanes (400s) Greek philosophers: Socrates, Plato, Aristotle (400s and 300s) Rise of Hellenistic philosophies: Epicureanism and Stoicism (300s and 200s)
100 B.C.	Political violence and civil wars in Rome (88–31) Assassination of Julius Caesar (44) Octavian takes the title Augustus and becomes first Roman emperor (27) Pax Romana: height of Roman Empire (27 B.C.–A.D. 180)	Roman philosophers during the Republic: Lucretius, Cicero (1st cent.) Rise and spread of Christianity: Jesus (d. A.D. 29); Paul's missionary activity (c. 34–64) Gospel of Mark (c. 66–70) Roman historians, poets, and philosophers during the Pax Romana: Livy, Tacitus, Virgil, Horace, Ovid, Juvenal, Seneca, Marcus Aurelius
200 A.D.	Military anarchy in Rome (235–285) Goths defeat Romans at Adrianople (378) End of Roman Empire in the West (476)	Church fathers: Jerome, Ambrose, Augustine (300s and 400s)

Chapter 1

The Ancient Near East: The First Civilizations

- **Prehistory**
- **The Rise to Civilization**
- **Mesopotamian Civilization**
- **Egyptian Civilization**
- **Empire Builders**
- **The Religious Orientation of the Ancient Near East**

Focus Questions

1. What is meant by the term *civilization*? Under what conditions did it emerge?
2. What did Mesopotamian and Egyptian civilizations have in common? How did they differ?
3. In what ways did mythopoeic thought characterize Near Eastern civilization? How does this type of thinking differ from that of science?
4. What elements of Near Eastern civilization were passed on to Western civilization?

Civilization was not inevitable; it was an act of human creativity. The first civilizations emerged some five thousand years ago in the river valleys of Mesopotamia and Egypt. There, human beings established cities and states, invented writing, developed organized religion, and constructed large-scale buildings and monuments—all characteristics of civilized life. Humanity's rise to civilization was long and arduous. Some 99 percent of human history took place before the creation of civilization, in the vast ages of prehistory. ❖

Prehistory

The period called the Paleolithic Age, or Old Stone Age, began with the earliest primitive, toolmaking human beings who inhabited East Africa some three million years ago. It ended about ten thousand years ago in parts of the Near East when people discovered how to farm. Our Paleolithic ancestors lived as hunters and food gatherers. Because they had not learned how to farm, they never established permanent villages. When their food supplies ran short, they abandoned their caves or tentlike structures of branches and searched for new dwelling places.

Human social development was shaped by this three-million-year experience of hunting and food gathering. For survival, groups of families formed bands consisting of around thirty people; members learned how to plan, organize, cooperate, trust, and share. Hunters assisted one another in tracking and killing game, finding cooperative efforts more successful than individual forays. By sharing their kill and bringing some back to their camp for the rest of the group, they reinforced the social bond. So, too, did women, who gathered nuts, seeds, and fruit for the group. Bands that did not cooperate in the hunt, in food gathering, or in food distribution were unlikely to survive.

Although human progress was very slow during the long centuries of the Paleolithic Age, developments occurred that influenced the future enormously. Paleolithic people developed spoken language and learned how to make and use tools of bone, wood, and stone. With these simple tools, they dug up roots; peeled the bark off trees; trapped, killed, and skinned animals; made clothing; and fashioned fishnets. They also discovered how to control fire, which allowed them to cook their meat and provided warmth and protection.

Like toolmaking and the control of fire, language was a great human achievement. Language enabled individuals to acquire and share with one another knowledge, experiences, and feelings. Thus, language was the decisive factor in the development of culture and its transmission from one generation to the next.

Most likely, our Paleolithic ancestors developed mythic-religious beliefs to explain the mysteries of nature, birth, sickness, and death. They felt that living powers operated within and beyond the world they experienced, and they sought to establish friendly relations with these powers. To Paleolithic people, the elements—sun, rain, wind, thunder, and lightning—were alive. The natural elements were spirits; they could feel and act with a purpose. To appease them, Paleolithic people made offerings. Gradually, there emerged shamans, medicine men, and witch doctors, who, through rituals, trances, and chants, seemed able to communicate with these spirits. Paleolithic people also began the practice of burying their dead, sometimes with offerings, which suggests a belief in life after death.

Between thirty thousand and twelve thousand years ago, Paleolithic people sought out the dark and silent interior of caves, which they probably viewed as sanctuaries, and, with only torches for light, they painted remarkably skillful and perceptive pictures of animals on the cave walls. Even prior to civilization, human beings demonstrated artistic talent and an esthetic sense. When these prehistoric artists drew an animal with a spear in its side, they probably believed that this act would make them successful in hunting; when they drew a herd of animals, they probably hoped that this would cause game to be plentiful.

Some ten thousand years ago, the New Stone Age, or Neolithic Age, began in the Near East. During the Neolithic Age, human beings discovered farming, domesticated animals, established villages, polished stone tools, made pottery, and wove cloth. So important were these achievements that they are referred to as the Neolithic Revolution.

Agriculture and the domestication of animals revolutionized life. Whereas Paleolithic hunters and food gatherers had been forced to use whatever nature made available to them, Neolithic farmers altered their environment to satisfy human needs. Instead of spending their time searching for grains, roots, and berries, women and children grew crops near their homes; instead of tracking animals over great distances, men could slaughter domesticated goats or sheep nearby.

Chronology 1.1 ❖ The Near East

3200 B.C.*	Rise of civilization in Sumer
2900	Union of Upper and Lower Egypt
2686–2181	Old Kingdom: essential forms of Egyptian civilization take shape
2180	Downfall of Akkadian empire
1792–1750	Hammurabi of Babylon brings Akkad and Sumer under his control and fashions a code of laws
1570	Egyptians drive out Hyksos and embark on empire building
1369–1353	Reign of Amenhotep IV: a movement toward monotheism
1200	Fall of Hittite empire
612	Fall of Assyrian empire
604–562	Reign of Nebuchadnezzar: height of Chaldean empire
550–525 B.C.	Persian conquests form a world empire

*Most dates are approximations.

Farming made possible a new kind of community. Since farmers had to live near their fields and could store food for the future, farming led to the rise of permanent settlements.

Villages changed the patterns of life. A food surplus freed some people to devote part of their time to sharpening their skills as basket weavers or toolmakers. The demand for raw materials and the creations of skilled artisans fostered trade, sometimes across long distances, and spurred the formation of trading settlements. An awareness of private property emerged. Hunters had accumulated few possessions, since belongings presented a burden when moving from place to place. Villagers, however, acquired property and were determined to protect it from one another and from outsiders, such as nomadic horsemen, who might raid the village. Hunting bands were egalitarian; generally, no one member had more possessions or more power than another. In farming villages, a ruling elite emerged that possessed wealth and wielded power. Scholars ponder the psychological dimensions of this shift from the hunter's way of life to sedentary farming.

Neolithic people made great strides in technology. By shaping and baking clay, they made pottery containers for cooking and for storing food and water. The invention of the potter's wheel enabled them to form bowls and plates more quickly and precisely. Stone tools were sharpened by grinding them on rock. The discovery of the wheel and the sail improved transportation and promoted trade, and the development of the plow and the ox yoke made tilling the soil easier for farmers.

The Neolithic period also marked the beginning of the use of metals. The first to be used was copper, which was easily fashioned into tools and weapons. Copper implements lasted longer than those of stone and flint, and they could be recast and reshaped if broken. In time, artisans discovered how to make bronze by combining copper and tin in the proper ratio. Bronze was harder than copper, which made a sharper cutting edge possible.

During the Neolithic Age, the food supply became more reliable, village life expanded, and the population increased. Families that acquired wealth gained a higher social status and became village leaders. Religion grew more formal and structured; nature spirits evolved into deities, each with specific powers over nature or human life. Altars were erected in their honor, and ceremonies were conducted by priests, whose power and wealth increased as people gave offerings to the gods. Neolithic society was growing more organized and complex; it was on the threshold of civilization.

Caves of Lascaux, Dordogne, France/The Bridgeman Art Library.

PALEOLITHIC CAVE PAINTING FROM LASCAUX, FRANCE. Produced as part of magical religious rites of hunting, these early paintings display considerable artistic skill.

THE RISE TO CIVILIZATION

What we call *civilization* arose some five thousand years ago in the Near East (in Mesopotamia and Egypt) and then later in East Asia (in India and China). The first civilizations began in cities that were larger, more populated, and more complex in their political, economic, and social structure than Neolithic villages. Because the cities depended on the inhabitants of adjacent villages for their food, farming techniques must have been sufficiently developed to produce food surpluses. Increased production provided food for urban inhabitants, who engaged in nonagricultural occupations; they became merchants, craftsmen, bureaucrats, and priests.

The invention of writing enabled the first civilizations to preserve, organize, and expand knowledge and to pass it on to future generations. It also allowed government officials and priests to conduct their affairs more efficiently. Moreover, civilized societies possessed organized governments, which issued laws and defined the boundary lines of their states. On a scale much larger than Neolithic communities, the inhabitants erected buildings and monuments, engaged in trade and manufacturing, and used specialized labor for different projects. Religious life grew more organized and complex, and a powerful and wealthy priesthood emerged. These developments—cities, specialization of labor, writing, organized government, monumental architecture, and a complex religious structure—differentiate the first civilizations from prehistoric cultures.

Religion was the central force in these primary civilizations. It provided satisfying explanations for the workings of nature, helped ease the fear of death, and justified traditional rules of morality. Law was considered sacred, a commandment of the gods. Religion united people in the common enterprises needed for survival—for example, the construction and maintenance of irrigation works and the storage of food. In addition, the power of rulers, who were regarded either as gods or as agents of the gods, derived from religion.

The emergence of civilization was a great creative act and not merely the inevitable development of agricultural societies. Many communities had learned how to farm, but only a handful made the leap to civilization. How was it possible for Sumerians and Egyptians, the creators of the earliest civilizations, to make this breakthrough? Most scholars stress the relationship between civilizations and river valleys. Rivers deposited fertile silt on adjoining fields, provided water for crops, and served as avenues for trade. But environmental factors alone do not adequately explain the emergence of civilization. What cannot be omitted is the human contribution: capacity for thought and cooperative activity. Before these rivers could be of any value in producing crops, swamps around them had to be drained; jungles had to be cleared; and dikes, reservoirs, and canals had to be built. To construct and maintain irrigation works required the cooperation of large numbers of people, a necessary condition for civilization.

In the process of constructing and maintaining irrigation networks, people learned to formulate and obey rules and developed administrative, engineering, and mathematical skills. The need to keep records stimulated the invention of writing. These creative responses to the challenges posed by nature spurred the early inhabitants of Sumer and Egypt to make the breakthrough to civilization, thereby altering the course of human destiny.

Civilization also had its dark side. Epidemic disease thrived in urban centers, where people lived close together in unsanitary conditions, drinking contaminated water and surrounded by rotting garbage. Slavery was an essential and accepted feature of early civilization. The authority wielded by rulers and their officials and the habits of discipline acquired by the community's members made possible the construction of irrigation works, but these social structures were also harnessed for destructive conflicts between states. Such warfare, which involved managing large numbers of combatants, was far more lethal than the sporadic and generally disorganized acts of violence that had occurred in Neolithic times. A hostile and aggressive attitude toward members of alien groups has plagued human beings since the rise of civilization. Warfare fascinated the people who created the first civilizations. Scribes recounted battle after battle, warrior-kings boasted of their military conquests, and military heroes were held in the highest esteem.

Mesopotamian Civilization

Mesopotamia is the Greek word for "land between the rivers." It was here, in the valleys of the Tigris and Euphrates Rivers, that the first civilization began. The first people to develop an urban civilization in Mesopotamia (modern-day Iraq) were the Sumerians, who colonized the marshlands of the lower Euphrates, which, along with the Tigris, flows into the Persian Gulf.

Through constant toil and imagination, the Sumerians transformed the swamps into fields of barley and groves of date palms. Around 3000 B.C., their hut settlements gradually evolved into twelve independent city-states, each consisting of a city and its surrounding countryside. Among the impressive achievements of the Sumerians were a system of symbol writing *(Cuneiform)** in which pictures for objects and marks for numbers were engraved on clay tablets with a reed stylus to represent ideas; elaborate brick houses, palaces, and temples; bronze tools and weapons; irrigation works; trade with other peoples; an early form of money; religious and political institutions; schools; religious and secular literature; varied art forms; codes of law; medicinal drugs; and a lunar calendar.

The history of Mesopotamia is marked by a succession of conquests. To the north of Sumer lay a Semitic† city called Akkad. About 2350 B.C., the people of Akkad, led by Sargon the Great, a warrior-king, conquered the Sumerian cities. Sargon built the world's first empire, which extended from the Persian Gulf to the Mediterranean Sea. Establishing a pattern that future despotic rulers would emulate, Sargon stationed garrisons in conquered lands and appointed governors and officials to administer the territories, as well as additional bureaucrats to register and parcel out the precious metals, horses, grain, and other commodities exacted from conquered peoples. He also retained a large standing army to quell revolts and to launch new imperialistic ventures. The Akkadians adopted Sumerian cultural forms,

**Cuneiform* is the Latin term for "nail-shaped," which the marks inscribed in clay appeared to represent.

†Semites included Akkadians, Hebrews, Babylonians, Phoenicians, Canaanites, Assyrians, and Aramaeans. Hebrew and Arabic are Semitic languages.

including cuneiform, and spread them beyond the boundaries of Mesopotamia with their conquests. Mesopotamian religion became a blend of Sumerian and Akkadian elements.

Illustrating the confluence of Akkadian and Sumerian culture was Saragon's daughter, Enheduanna, the world's first known poet. Serving as high priestess in the Sumerian city of Ur, Enheduanna wrote numerous poems and hymns to temple deities. In one of her hymns to the Sumerian goddess Ianna, she depicts Ianna as a fierce warrior; in a second, Ianna emerges as an overseer of home and children; and in the third surviving hymn, the poetess appeals to Ianna to help her regain her position as temple priestess after it was taken from her by a male enemy.

In succeeding centuries, the Sumerian cities were incorporated into various kingdoms and empires. The Sumerian language, replaced by a Semitic tongue, became an obscure language known only to priests, and the Sumerians gradually disappeared as a distinct people. But their cultural achievements endured. Akkadians, Babylonians, Elamites, and others adopted Sumerian religious, legal, literary, and artistic forms. The Sumerian legacy served as the basis for a Mesopotamian civilization, which maintained a distinct style for three thousand years.

Religion: The Basis of Mesopotamian Civilization

Religion lay at the center of Mesopotamian life. Every human activity—political, military, social, legal, literary, or artistic—was generally subordinated to an overriding religious purpose. Religion was the Mesopotamians' frame of reference for understanding nature, society, and themselves; it dominated and inspired all other cultural expressions and human activities. Wars between cities, for instance, were interpreted as conflicts between the gods of those cities, and victory ultimately depended on divine favor, not on human effort. Myths—narratives about the activities of the gods—explained the origins of the human species. According to the earliest Sumerian myths, the first human beings issued forth from the earth like plant life, or were shaped from clay by divine craftsmen and granted a heart by the goddess Nammu, or were formed from the blood of two gods sacrificed for that purpose.

The Mesopotamians believed that people were given life so that they could execute on earth the will of the gods in heaven. No important decisions were made by kings or priests without first consulting the gods. To discover the wishes of the gods, priests sacrificed animals and then examined their entrails, or the priests might find their answers in the stars or in dreams.

The cities of Mesopotamia were sacred communities dedicated to serving divine masters, and people hoped that appeasing the gods would bring security and prosperity to their cities. Each city belonged to a particular god, who was the real owner of the land and the real ruler of the city; often a vast complex of temples was built for the god and the god's family.

Supervised by priests, the temple was the heart of the city's life. The temple probably owned most of the land in its city; temple priests collected rents, operated businesses, and received contributions for festivals. Most inhabitants of the city worked for the temple priests as tenant farmers, agricultural laborers, or servants. Anxious to curry favor with the gods and goddesses who watched over the fields, peasants surrendered part of their crops to the temples. Priests coordinated the city's economic activity, supervising the distribution of land, overseeing the irrigation works, and storing food for emergencies. Temple scribes kept records of expenditures and receipts.

The Mesopotamians believed that the gods controlled the entire universe and everything in it. The moon, the sun, and the storm, the city, the irrigation works, and the fields—each was directed by a god. The Mesopotamians saw gods and demons everywhere in nature. There was a god in the fire and another in the river; evil demons stirred up sandstorms, caused disease, and endangered women in childbirth. To protect themselves from hostile powers, Mesopotamians wore charms and begged their gods for help. When misfortune befell them, they attributed it to the gods. Even success was not due to their own efforts, but to the intervention of a god who had taken a special interest in them. Compared with the gods, an individual was an insignificant and lowly creature.

Uncertainty and danger filled life in Mesopotamia. Sometimes, the unpredictable waters of the

Penn Museum object B17694 image 22097.

Wooden Soundbox of a Sumerian Harp, Ur, c. 2600 b.c. The top panel features a heroic figure embracing two man-faced bulls made from shells inlaid in bitumen. Beneath are three panels with various animals carrying food or drink and musical instruments. The theme may depict a fable of some festive celebration or ritual myth.

rivers broke through the dikes, flooding fields, ruining crops, and damaging cities. At other times, an insufficient overflow deprived the land of water, causing crops to fail. Mesopotamia had no natural barriers to invasion. Feeling themselves surrounded by incomprehensible and often hostile forces, Mesopotamians lived in an atmosphere of anxiety that permeated their civilization.

Contributing to this sense of insecurity was the belief that the gods behaved capriciously, malevolently, and vindictively. What do the gods demand of me? Is it ever possible to please them? To these questions Mesopotamians had no reassuring answers, for the gods' behavior was a mystery to mere human beings.

A mood of uncertainty and anxiety, an awareness of the cosmos as unfathomable and mysterious, a feeling of dread about the fragility of human existence and the impermanence of human achievement—these attitudes are as old as the first civilization. The *Epic of Gilgamesh*, the finest work of Mesopotamian literature, masterfully depicts this mood of pessimism and despair. The *Gilgamesh* deals with a profound theme: the human protest against death. Confronted with the reality of his own death, Gilgamesh yearns for eternal life. But he learns that when the gods created human beings, they made death part of their lot. "Where is the man who can clamber to heaven? Only the gods live forever . . . but as for us men, our days are numbered, our occupations are a breath of wind."[1] The Mesopotamians had little to look forward to after death. They believed that they would either be confined to a dreary underworld whose rulers would inflict pain on them or be transformed into spirits, flying about and tormenting the living.

Government, Law, and Economy

Kingship, bestowed on a man by the gods, was the central institution in Mesopotamian society. Unlike Egyptian pharaohs, Mesopotamian kings did not see themselves as gods, but rather as great men selected by the gods to represent them on earth. Gods governed through the kings, who reported to the gods about conditions in their land (which was the gods' property) and petitioned the gods for advice.

The king administered the laws, which came from the gods. The principal collection of laws in ancient Mesopotamia was the famous code of Hammurabi (c. 1792–c. 1750 B.C.), the Babylonian ruler. Unearthed by French archaeologists in 1901–1902, the code has provided invaluable insights into Mesopotamian society. In typical Mesopotamian fashion, Hammurabi claimed that his code rested on the authority of the gods; to violate it was to contravene the divine order.

The code reveals social status and mores in that area and time. Women were subservient to men, although efforts were made to protect women and children from abuse. By making death the penalty for adultery, the code probably sought to preserve family life. Punishments were generally severe—"an eye for an eye and a tooth for a tooth." The code prescribed death for housebreaking, kidnapping, aiding the escape of slaves, receiving stolen goods, and bearing false witness, but being forgiven by the wronged party could mitigate the penalty. For example, a wife who committed adultery could be spared execution if she was pardoned by her husband. Class distinctions were expressed in the code. For example, a person received more severe punishment for harming a noble than for harming a commoner. Government officials who engaged in extortion or bribery were harshly punished. The code's many provisions relating to business transactions underscore the importance of trade to Mesopotamian life.

The economy of Mesopotamian cities depended heavily on foreign and domestic trade. To safeguard it, governments instituted regulations to prevent fraud, and business transactions had to be recorded in writing. Enterprising businessmen set up trading outposts in distant lands, making the Mesopotamians pioneers in international trade.

Mathematics, Astronomy, and Medicine

The Mesopotamians made some impressive advances in mathematics. They devised multiplication and division tables, including even cubes and cube roots. They determined the area of right-angle triangles and rectangles, divided a circle into 360 degrees, and had some understanding of the principles that centuries later would be developed into the Pythagorean theorem and quadratic equations. But the Babylonians, who made the chief contribution in mathematics, barely advanced to the level of devising theories: they did not formulate general principles or furnish proofs for their mathematical operations.

By carefully observing and accurately recording the positions of planets and constellations of stars, Babylonian sky watchers took the first steps in developing the science of astronomy, and they devised a calendar based on the cycles of the moon. As in mathematics, however, they did not form theories to coordinate and illuminate their data. Believing that the position of the stars and planets revealed the will of the gods, astronomers did not examine the heavens to find what we call cause-and-effect connections between the phenomena. Rather, they sought to discover what the gods wanted. With this knowledge, people could organize their political, social, and moral lives in accordance with divine commands, and they could escape the terrible consequences that they believed resulted from ignoring the gods' wishes.

Consistent with their religious worldview, the Mesopotamians believed that gods or demons caused disease. To cure a patient, priest-physicians resorted to magic; through prayers and sacrifices, they attempted to appease the gods and eject the demons from the sick body. Nevertheless, in identifying illnesses and prescribing appropriate remedies, Mesopotamians demonstrated some accurate knowledge of medicine and pharmacology.

Egyptian Civilization

During the early period of Mesopotamian civilization, the Egyptians developed their civilization in the fertile valley of the Nile. Without this mighty river, which flows more than four thousand miles from central Africa northward to the Mediterranean, virtually all Egypt would be a desert. When the Nile overflowed its banks, as it did reliably and predictably, the floodwaters deposited a layer of fertile black earth, which, when cultivated, provided abundant food to support Egyptian civilization. The Egyptians learned how to control the river—a feat that required cooperative effort and ingenuity, as well as engineering and administrative skills. In addition to water and fertile land, the Nile provided an excellent transportation link between Upper (southern) and Lower (northern) Egypt. Natural barriers—mountains, deserts, cataracts (rapids) in the Nile, and the Mediterranean—protected Egypt from attack, allowing the inhabitants to enjoy long periods of peace and prosperity. Thus, unlike Mesopotamians, Egyptians derived a sense of security from their environment.

From the Old Kingdom to the Middle Kingdom

About 2900 B.C., a ruler of Upper Egypt known as Narmer, or Menes, conquered the Nile Delta and Lower Egypt. By 2686 B.C., centralized rule had been firmly established, and great pyramids, tombs for the pharaohs, were being constructed. The pyramids required rigorous central planning to coordinate the tens of thousands of Egyptian laborers drafted to build these immense monuments. During this Pyramid Age, or Old Kingdom (2686–2181 B.C.), royal power reached its height, and the essential forms of Egyptian civilization crystallized.

The Egyptians believed the pharaoh to be both a man and a god, the earthly embodiment of the deity Horus. He was an absolute ruler who kept the irrigation works in order, maintained justice in the land, and expressed the will of heaven. In time, the nobles who served as district governors gained in status and wealth and gradually came to undermine the divine king's authority. The nobles' growing power and the enormous expenditure of Egypt's human and material resources on building pyramids led to the decline of the Old Kingdom. From 2181 to 2040 B.C., a span of time called the First Intermediate Period, rival families competed for the throne, destroying the unity of the kingdom. The civil wars and collapse of the central authority required to maintain the irrigation system cast a pall over the land.

During what is called the Middle Kingdom (2040–1786 B.C.), strong kings reasserted pharaonic rule and reunited the state. The restoration of political stability reinvigorated cultural life, and economic activity revived. Pharaohs extended Egyptian control south over the land of Nubia (modern Sudan), which became a principal source of gold. A profitable trade was carried on with Palestine, Syria, and Crete.

Around 1800 B.C., central authority again weakened. In the era known as the Second Intermediate Period (1786–1570 B.C.), the nobles regained some of their power, the Nubians broke away from Egyptian control, and the Hyksos (a mixture of Semites and Indo-Europeans) invaded Egypt. The Hyksos dominated Egypt for about a hundred years, until the Egyptians drove them out in 1570 B.C. The period of empire building known as the New Kingdom (1570–1085 B.C.) then began.

The basic features of Egyptian civilization had been forged during the Old and Middle Kingdoms. Egyptians looked to the past, convinced that the ways of their ancestors were best. For almost three thousand years, Egyptian civilization sought to retain a harmony with the order of nature instituted at creation. Believing in a changeless universe, the Egyptians did not value change or development—what we call progress—but venerated the institutions, traditions, and authority that embodied permanence.

Religion: The Basis of Egyptian Civilization

Religion was omnipresent in Egyptian life and accounted for the outstanding achievements of Egyptian civilization. Religious beliefs were the basis of Egyptian art, medicine, astronomy, literature, and government. The great pyramids, which took decades to finish, were tombs for the pharaohs, man-gods. Magical utterances pervaded medical practices, for disease was attributed to the gods. Astronomy evolved to determine the correct time for performing religious rites and sacrifices. The earliest examples of literature dealt wholly with religious themes. A sacrosanct monarch, the pharaoh served as an intermediary between the gods and human beings. The Egyptians developed an ethical code, which they believed the gods had approved.

Egyptian polytheism took many forms, including the worship of animals, for the people believed that gods manifested themselves in both human and animal shapes. The Egyptians also believed the great powers in nature—sky, sun,

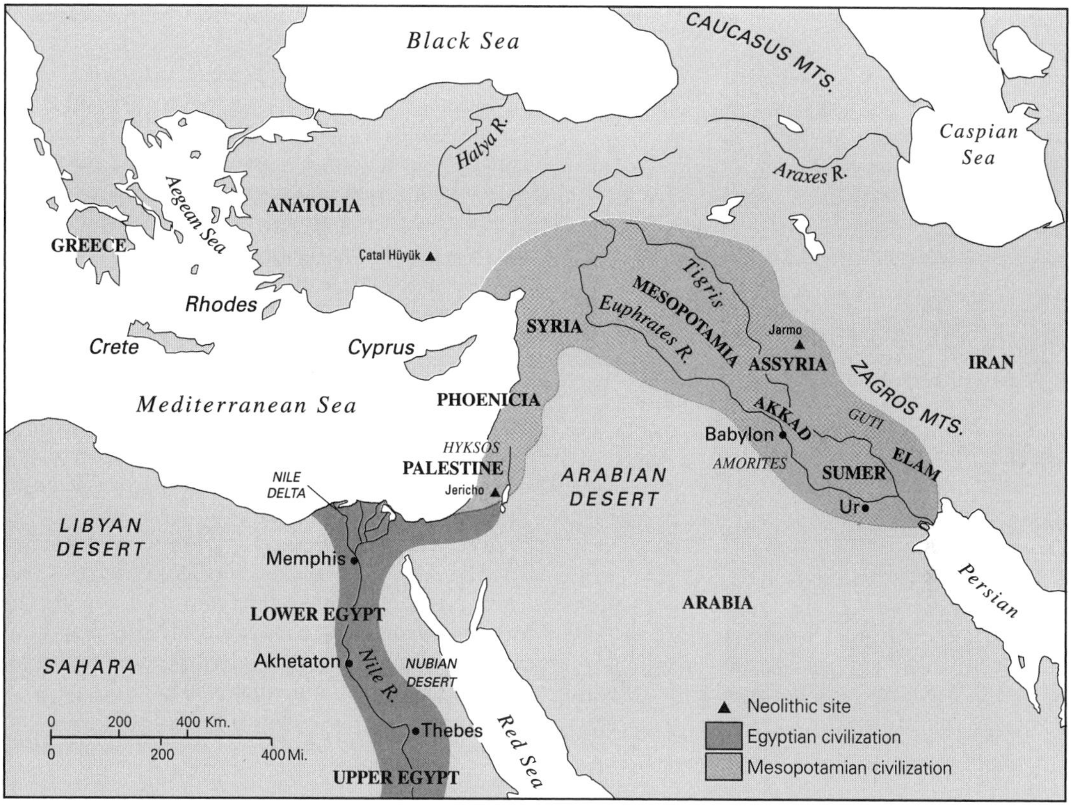

Map 1.1 Mesopotamian and Egyptian Civilizations The first civilizations emerged in river valleys: Mesopotamia in the valleys of the Tigris and Euphrates rivers, Egypt in the Nile valley.

earth, the Nile—to be gods or the abodes of gods. In the heavens alive with gods, the Egyptians found answers to the great problems of human existence. In their temples, Egyptians prayed and dedicated offerings to their gods. During temple rituals, women chanted and played musical instruments.

A crucial feature of Egyptian religion was the afterlife. Through pyramid-tombs, mummification to preserve the dead, and funerary art, the Egyptians showed their yearning for eternity and their desire to overcome death. Mortuary priests recited incantations to ensure the preservation of the dead body and the continuity of existence. Inscribed on the pyramids' interior walls were "pyramid texts," written in *hieroglyphics*—a form of picture writing in which figures, such as crocodiles, sails, eyes, and so forth, represented words or sounds that would be combined to form words. The texts contained fragments from myths, historical annals, and magical lore and provided spells to assist the king in ascending to heaven.

At first, the Egyptians believed that only the pharaoh and the royal family were immortal. In time, the nobility and then commoners claimed that they too could share in the blessings of the "other world." Prayers hitherto reserved for the pharaoh were, for a fee, recited by priests at the burial of commoners. Believing that their deceased relative would intercede with the gods in their behalf, Egyptians wrote letters to these spirits, petitioning them for help with such problems as infertility, inheritance of property, and family quarrels. To the Egyptians, the other world offered

Harvard MFA Expedition. Courtesy, Museum of Fine Arts, Boston.

Pharaoh Mycerinus and His Queen, c. 2525 b.c. Swelling chests and hips idealize the royal couple's humanity, but the cubic feeling of the sculpture and the rigid confidence of the pose proclaim their unquestioned divinity.

the same pleasures as those enjoyed on earth: friends, servants, fishing, hunting, paddling a canoe, picnicking with family members, entertainment by musicians and dancers, and good food. But since earthly existence was not fundamentally unhappy, Egyptians did not long for death.

Divine Kingship

Divine kingship was the basic institution of Egyptian civilization. The Egyptians saw rule by a god-king as the only acceptable political arrangement: it was in harmony with the order of the universe, and it brought justice and security to the nation.

The pharaoh's power extended to all sectors of society. Peasants were drafted to serve in labor corps as miners or construction workers. Foreign trade was a state monopoly, conducted according to the kingdom's needs. As the supreme overlord, the pharaoh oversaw an army of government officials who collected taxes, supervised construction projects, checked the irrigation works, surveyed the land, kept records, conducted foreign trade, and supervised government warehouses, where grain was stored as insurance against a bad harvest. All Egyptians, including the priesthood and standing army, were subservient to the pharaoh, whose word was regarded as a divine ordinance. Most pharaohs took their responsibilities seriously and tried to govern as benevolent protectors of the people.

The pharaoh was seen as ruling in accordance with *Ma'at*, which means "justice, law, right, and truth." To oppose the pharaoh was to violate the universal and divinely ordained order of Ma'at and to bring disorder to society. Because the Egyptians regarded Ma'at, which was established with the creation of the universe, as the right order of nature, they believed that its preservation must be the object of human activity—the guiding norm of the state and the standard by which individuals conducted their lives. Those who did Ma'at and spoke Ma'at would be justly rewarded. Could anything be more reassuring than this belief that divine truth was represented in the person of the pharaoh, who guaranteed and defended the sacred order of the universe?

Science, Mathematics, and Literature

Like the Mesopotamians, the Egyptians made practical advances in the sciences. They demonstrated superb engineering skills in building pyramids and fashioned an effective system of mathematics, including geometry for measurements, which enabled them to solve relatively simple problems. The Egyptians' solar calendar, which allowed them to predict when the Nile would overflow, was more accurate than the Babylonians' lunar calendar.

In the area of medicine, Egyptian doctors were more capable than their Mesopotamian

dgmata/Shutterstock.com

The Great Sphinx at Giza. With the body of a lion and the face of a man, the Sphinx watches over Giza as a testament to the divine kingship of the pharaohs.

counterparts. They could identify illnesses and recognized that uncleanliness encouraged contagion. They also had some knowledge of anatomy and performed operations: circumcision and perhaps the draining of abscessed teeth. But their knowledge of medicine, like that of the Mesopotamians, was handicapped by their belief that supernatural forces caused illnesses. Thus sick people were instructed to recite an incantation designed to free the body from the demon's hold and to perform a ritual act such as being burned with hot irons.

Generally only a small percentage of the population—the elite—was literate. Egyptian literature took a wide variety of forms: hymns and other religious texts; love poems; tales of adventure, romance, and fantasy; and collections of maxims prepared by elderly sages for the benefit of young rulers. Containing hymns, litanies, and other religious texts, the *Book of the Dead* was written to guide a deceased person safely between this world and the afterlife. In the "Judgment Hall," before Osiris and other gods who assisted him, deceased individuals proclaimed, among other things, that they had not robbed, murdered, or uttered evil words.

The New Kingdom and the Decline of Egyptian Civilization

The New Kingdom began in 1570 B.C. with the war of liberation against the Hyksos. This war gave rise to an intense militancy, which found expression in empire building. Aggressive pharaohs conquered territory that extended as far east as the Euphrates River. From its subject states, Egypt acquired tribute and slaves. Conquests led to the expansion of the bureaucracy, the development of a professional army, and the increased power of priests, whose temples—which grew larger and more lavish—shared in the spoils. Foreign slaves acquired from imperial conquests provided much of the labor for the construction of new shrines and temples. The formation of the empire ended Egyptian isolation and accelerated commercial and cultural intercourse with other peoples. During this period, Egyptian art, for example, showed the influence of foreign forms.

A growing cosmopolitanism was paralleled by a movement toward monotheism during the reign of Pharaoh Amenhotep IV (c. 1369–1353 B.C.). Amenhotep sought to replace traditional polytheism with the worship of Aton, a single god of all people, who was represented as the sun disk. Amenhotep took the name Akhenaten ("It is well with Aton") and moved the capital from Thebes to a newly constructed holy city called Akhataten (near modern Tell el Amarna). The city had palaces, administrative centers, and a temple complex honoring Aton. Akhenaten and his wife, Nefertiti, who played a prominent role in his court, dedicated themselves to Aton—the creator of the world, the sustainer of life, and the god of love, justice, and peace. Akhenaten also ordered his officials to chisel out the names of other gods from inscriptions on temples and monuments. With awe, Akhenaten glorified Aton:

> *How manifold are thy works!*
> *They are hidden from man's sight.*
> *O sole god, like whom there is no other.*
> *Thou hast made the earth according to thy*
> *desire.*[2]

AKHENATEN. A bas relief found in Tell el-Amarna shows Akhenaten and his family sacrificing to Aton, the sun god.

Akhenaten's "monotheism" had little impact on the masses of Egyptians, who retained their ancient beliefs, and was resisted by priests, who resented his changes. After Akhenaten's death, a new pharaoh had the monuments to Aton destroyed, along with records and inscriptions bearing Akhenaten's name. The great visionary was now vilified as "the Blasphemer."

The most significant historical questions about Akhenaten are these two: was his religion genuine monotheism, which pushed religious thought in a new direction? And if so, did it influence Moses, who led the Israelites out of Egypt about a century later? These questions have aroused controversy among historians. The principal limitation on the monotheistic character of Atonism is that there were really two gods in Akhenaten's religion: Aton and the pharaoh himself, who was still worshiped as a deity. Nor is there any evidence that Akhenaten influenced the monotheism of Moses. Moreover, the Hebrews never identified their God with the sun or any other object in nature.

Late in the thirteenth century B.C., Libyans, probably seeking to settle in the more fertile land of Egypt, attacked from the west, and the Peoples of the Sea, as unsettled raiders from the Aegean Sea area and Asia Minor were called, launched a series of strikes at Egypt. A weakened Egypt abandoned its empire. In the succeeding centuries, Egypt came under the rule of Libyans, Nubians, Assyrians, Persians, and finally Greeks, to whom Egypt lost its independence in the fourth century B.C.

Egyptian civilization had flourished for nearly two thousand years before it experienced an almost one-thousand-year descent into stagnation, decline, and collapse. During its long history, the Egyptians tried to preserve the ancient forms of their civilization, revealed to them by their ancestors and representing for all time those unchanging values that they believed were the way of happiness.

Empire Builders

The rise of an Egyptian empire during the New Kingdom was part of a wider development in Near Eastern history after 1500 B.C.—the emergence of international empires. Empire building led to the intermingling of peoples and cultural traditions and to the extension of civilization well beyond the river valleys.

One reason for the growth of empires was the migration of peoples known as Indo-Europeans. Originally from a wide area ranging from southeastern Europe to the region beyond the Caspian Sea, Indo-Europeans embarked, around 2000 B.C., on a series of migrations that eventually brought them into Italy, Greece, Asia Minor, Mesopotamia, Persia, and India. From a core Indo-European tongue emerged the Greek, Latin, Germanic, Slavic, Persian, and Sanskrit languages.

Hittites

Several peoples established strong states in the Near East around 1500 B.C.—the Hurrians in northern Mesopotamia, the Kassites in southern Mesopotamia, and the Hittites in Asia Minor. The Hittites wanted to control the trade routes that ran along the Euphrates River into Syria. In the 1300s, the Hittite empire reached its peak. Its leaders ruled Asia Minor and northern Syria, raided Babylon, and challenged Egypt for control of Syria and Palestine.

The Hittites borrowed several features of Mesopotamian civilization, including cuneiform, legal principles, and literary and art forms. Hittite religion blended the beliefs and practices of Indo-Europeans, native inhabitants of Asia Minor, and Mesopotamians. The Hittites were probably the first people to develop a substantial iron industry. Initially, they apparently used iron only for ceremonial and ritual objects and not for tools and weapons. However, because iron ore was more readily available than copper or tin (needed for bronze), after 1200 B.C. iron weapons and tools spread throughout the Near East, although bronze implements were still used. Around 1200 B.C., the Hittite empire fell, most likely to Indo-European invaders from the north.

Small Nations

During the twelfth century B.C., there was a temporary lull in empire building, and this permitted a number of small nations in Syria and Palestine to assert their sovereignty. Three of these peoples—the Phoenicians, the Aramaeans, and the Hebrews*—were originally Semitic desert nomads. The Phoenicians were descendants of the Canaanites, a Semitic people who had settled Palestine around 3000 B.C. The Canaanites who had migrated northwest into what is now Lebanon were called Phoenicians.

Settling in the coastal Mediterranean cities of Tyre, Byblos, Berytus (Beirut), and Sidon, the Phoenicians were naturally drawn to the sea. These daring explorers established towns along the coast of North Africa, on the islands of the western Mediterranean, and in Spain; they became the greatest sea traders of the ancient world. The Phoenicians (or their Canaanite forebears) devised the first alphabet, which was a monumental contribution to writing. Since all words could be represented by combinations of letters, it saved memorizing thousands of diagrams and aided the Phoenicians in transmitting the cultural achievements of the Near East to the western Mediterranean. Adopted by the Greeks, who added vowels, the phonetic alphabet became a crucial component of European languages.

The Aramaeans, who settled in Syria, Palestine, and northern Mesopotamia, performed a role similar to that of the Phoenicians. As great caravan traders, they carried both goods and cultural patterns to various parts of the Near East.

*The Hebrews are discussed in Chapter 2.

The Hebrews and the Persians, for example, acquired the Phoenician alphabet from the Aramaeans.

Assyria

In the ninth century B.C., empire building resumed with the Assyrians, a Semitic people from the region around the upper Tigris River. Although they had made forays of expansion in 1200 and 1100 B.C., the Assyrians began their march to "world" empire three centuries later. In the eighth and seventh centuries, they became a ruthless fighting machine that stormed through Mesopotamia—including Armenia and Babylonia—as well as Syria, Palestine, and Egypt.

The Assyrian king, who was the representative and high priest of the god Ashur, governed absolutely. Nobles appointed by the king kept order in the provinces and collected tribute. The Assyrians improved roads, established messenger services, and engaged in large-scale irrigation projects to facilitate effective administration of their conquered lands and to promote prosperity. They exacted obedience by resorting to terror and by deporting troublemakers from their home territories.

Despite an almost all-consuming concern for war, the Assyrians preserved and spread the culture of the past. They copied and edited the literary works of Babylonia, adopted the old Sumerian gods, and used Mesopotamian art forms. The Assyrian king Ashurbanipal (669–626 B.C.) maintained a great library that housed thousands of clay tablets. After a period of wars and revolts by oppressed subjects weakened Assyria, a coalition of Medes from Iran and Chaldeans, or Neo-Babylonians, sacked the Assyrian capital of Nineveh in 612 B.C., destroying Assyrian power.

Persia: Unifier of the Near East

The destruction of the Assyrian empire made possible the rise of a Chaldean empire that included Babylonia, Assyria, Syria, and Palestine. Under Nebuchadnezzar, who ruled from 604 to 562 B.C., the Chaldean, or Neo-Babylonian, empire reached its height. After Nebuchadnezzar's death, the empire was torn by civil war and threatened by a new power: the Persians, an Indo-European people who had settled in southern Iran. (Iranians today are descendants of the ancient Persians.) Under Cyrus the Great and his son and successor, Cambyses, the Persians conquered all lands between the Nile in Egypt and the Indus River in India. This conquest took twenty-five years, from 550 to 525 B.C.

The Near Eastern conception of absolute monarchy justified by religion reached its culminating expression in the person of the Persian king, who, with divine approval, ruled a vast empire, "the four quarters of the earth." Persian kings developed an effective system of administration—based in part on an Assyrian model—that gave stability and a degree of unity to their extensive territories. The Persian empire was divided into twenty provinces *(satrapies)*, each one administered by a governor *(satrap)* responsible to the emperor. To guard against subversion, the king employed special agents—"the eyes and ears of the emperor"—who supervised the activities of the governors. Persian kings allowed the provincials a large measure of self-rule. They also respected local traditions, particularly in matters of religion, as long as subjects paid their taxes, served in the royal army, and refrained from rebellion.

The empire was bound together by a uniform language, Aramaic (the language of the Aramaeans of Syria), used by government officials and merchants. Aramaic was written in letters based on the Phoenician alphabet. By making Aramaic a universal language, the Persians facilitated written and oral communication within the empire. The empire was further unified by an elaborate network of roads, an efficient postal system, a common system of weights and measures, and an empirewide coinage based on an invention of the Lydians from western Asia Minor.

Besides providing impressive political and administrative unity, the Persians fused and perpetuated the various cultural traditions of the Near East. Persian palaces, for example, boasted the terraces of Babylon, the colonnades of Egypt, the winged bulls that decorated Assyrian palace gates, and the craftsmanship of Median goldsmiths.

The political and cultural universalism of the Persian empire had its counterpart in the emergence of an ethically oriented religion, Zoroastrianism, which contained both monotheistic and dualistic elements and emphasized the individual's capacity to choose between good and evil. Named

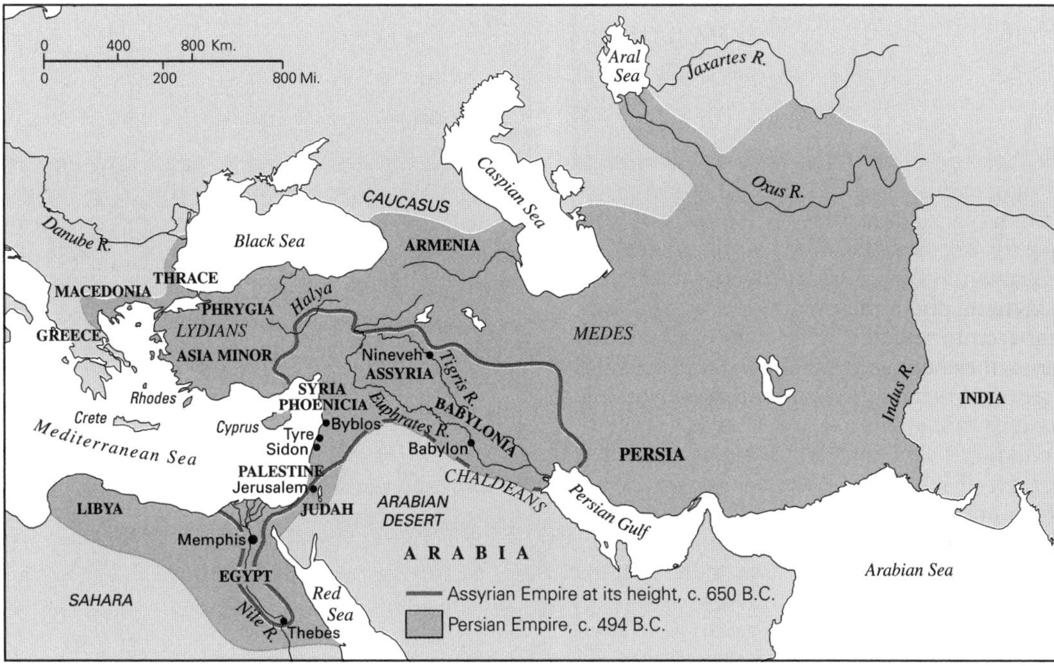

Map 1.2 The Assyrian and Persian Empires In the last part of the sixth century B.C., the Persians established the greatest empire of the ancient Near East, conquering all the lands between the Nile in Egypt and the Indus River in India.

for its founder, the Persian prophet Zoroaster, who probably lived in the sixth century B.C. (although some scholars place him much earlier), this religion taught belief in Ahura Mazda—the Wise Lord—god of light, justice, wisdom, goodness, and immortality. In addition to Ahura Mazda, however, there existed Ahriman, the spirit of darkness, who was evil and destructive; Ahriman was in conflict with the ultimately triumphant Ahura Mazda. People were free to choose whom they would follow. To serve Ahura Mazda, one had to speak the truth and be good to others; the reward for such behavior was eternal life in paradise, the realm of light and goodness. Followers of the evil spirit could be cast into a realm of darkness and torment. In contrast to the traditional religions of the Near East, Zoroastrianism rejected magic, polytheism, and blood sacrifices. Instead, it stressed ethics.

Persia unified the nations of the Near East into a world-state, headed by a divinely appointed king. It also synthesized the region's cultural traditions. Soon it would confront the city-states of Greece, whose political system and cultural orientation differed from those of the Near East.

The Religious Orientation of the Ancient Near East

Religion dominated, suffused, and inspired all features of Near Eastern society: law, kingship, art, and science. In the first civilizations, the deepest thoughts of human beings were expressed in the form of religious myths. Priest-kings or god-kings, their power sanctioned by divine forces, furnished the necessary authority to organize large numbers of people in cooperative ventures. Religion also encouraged and justified wars—including enslavements and massacres—which were seen as conflicts between the gods. Religious beliefs and values served as a powerful social force uniting people into a cohesive community.

A Mythmaking Worldview

A religious, or mythopoeic (mythmaking), view of the world gave Near Eastern civilization its distinctive form and allows us to see it as an organic whole. Mesopotamians and Egyptians inherited from their prehistoric ancestors a great variety of communally produced imagery, rituals, and tales accounting for the origin of the world and human life. With unrestrained imagination, they altered the old myths and elaborated new ones to resolve questions that today we try to answer with science. Mythmaking was humanity's first way of thinking; it was the earliest attempt to explain the beginnings of the universe and human history, to make nature's mysteries and life's uncertainties comprehensible.

Originating in sacred rites, ritual dances, feasts, and ceremonies, myths depicted the deeds of gods, who, in some remote past, had brought forth the world and human beings. Holding that human destiny was determined by the gods, Near Eastern people interpreted their experiences through myths. Mesopotamian myths, for example, attributed personal misfortune and the catastrophes that afflicted a city to supernatural forces displeased with people's behavior. These myths gave Near Eastern people a framework with which to pattern their experiences into a meaningful order, justify their rules of conduct, make nature intelligible, and help them to overcome the uncertainty of existence.

The civilizations of the ancient Near East were based on a way of thinking fundamentally different from the modern scientific outlook. The scientific mind views physical nature as an *it*—inanimate, impersonal, and governed by universal law. The mythmaking mind of the Near East saw every object in nature as a *thou*—personified, alive, with an individual will. It saw gods or demons manipulating things. The world was enchanted, imbued with mysterious spirits. The sun and stars, the rivers and mountains, the wind and lightning were either gods or the dwelling places of gods. Live agents were the forces behind natural events. If a river flooded the region, destroying crops, it was because it wanted to; the river or the gods desired to punish the people. The Babylonians attributed drought to the hot breath of the Bull of Heaven. The drought ended when the gigantic bird Imdugud devoured the bull and covered the sky with the storm clouds in its wings.

The Egyptians believed that Nut, the sky goddess, gave birth to the sun, a deity who sailed west across the celestial sea before descending into his mother's womb to be reborn again in the morning. For the Egyptians, the rising and setting of the sun were not natural occurrences—a celestial body obeying an impersonal law—but a religious drama.

The scientific mind holds that natural objects obey universal rules; hence, the location of planets, the speed of objects, and the onset of a hurricane can be predicted. The mythmaking mind of the ancient Near East attributed all occurrences in nature to the actions of gods, whose behavior was often erratic and unpredictable. Shamans employed magic to protect people from evil supernatural forces that surrounded them. Mythical explanations of nature and human experience made life seem less overwhelming and death less frightening.

Of course, Near Eastern people did engage in rational forms of thought and behavior. They certainly employed reason in building irrigation works, in preparing a calendar, and in performing mathematical operations. Moreover, in their daily life, men and women were often driven by purely pragmatic concerns. Fields had to be planted, goods sold, and household chores attended to. In dealing with these concerns, people did what had to be done in commonsense ways. They planned and prepared; they weighed actions as either beneficial or harmful and behaved accordingly. However, because rational, or logical, thought remained subordinate to a mythic-religious orientation, they did not arrive at a *consistently* and *self-consciously* rational method of inquiring into physical nature and human culture.

Thus, Near Eastern civilization reached the first level in the development of science: observing nature, recording data, and improving technology in mining, metallurgy, and architecture. But it did not advance to the level of self-conscious philosophical and scientific thought—that is, logically deduced abstractions, hypotheses, and generalizations. Mesopotamians and Egyptians did not fashion a body of philosophical and scientific

Primary Source

Mythical Thinking

The mythopoeic mind accounts for causation by personifying inanimate substances. To explain through personification is to seek the "who" behind events, to attribute these events to the will of a god (or to an object suffused with divine presence). Thus, if a river did not rise, it was because it refused to do so; either the river or the gods were angry at the people.

The following excerpts from Mesopotamian literature are examples of personification. Whereas we regard table salt as an ordinary mineral, to the Mesopotamians it was alive, a fellow being. In one passage, a person appeals to salt to end his bewitchment. In the second, an afflicted person who believes himself bewitched calls on fire to destroy his enemies.

O Salt

O Salt, created in a clean place,
For food of gods did *Enlil* [father of the Sumerian gods] destine thee.
Without thee no meal is set out in *Ekur*,
Without thee god, king, lord, and prince do not smell incense.
I am so-and-so, the son of so-and-so,
Held captive by enchantment,
Held in fever by bewitchment.
O Salt, break my enchantment! Loose my spell!
Take from me the bewitchment!—And as My Creator
I shall extol thee.

Scorching Fire

Scorching Fire, warlike son of Heaven,
Thou, the fiercest of thy brethren,
Who like Moon and Sun decidest lawsuits—
Judge thou my case, hand down the verdict.

Burn the man and woman who bewitched me;
Burn, O Fire, the man and woman who bewitched me;
Scorch, O Fire, the man and woman who bewitched me;

Burn them, O Fire;
Scorch them, O Fire;
Take hold of them, O Fire;
Consume them, O Fire;
Destroy them, O Fire.

Questions for Analysis

1. How does mythical thinking differ from scientific thinking?
2. When might the ancient Mesopotamians have turned to the gods for help?

Henri Frankfort et al., *Before Philosophy*, 143, 147.

ideas that were logically structured, discussed, and debated. They had no awareness of general laws that govern particular events. These later developments were the singular achievement of Greek philosophy. It gave a "rational interpretation to natural occurrences which had previously been explained by ancient mythologies. . . . With the study of nature set free from the control of mythological fancy, the way was opened for the development of science as an intellectual system."[3]

Near Eastern Achievements

The Sumerians and the Egyptians demonstrated enormous creativity and intelligence. They built irrigation works and cities, organized governments, charted the course of heavenly bodies, performed mathematical operations, constructed large-scale monuments, engaged in international trade, established bureaucracies and schools, and considerably advanced the level of technology and engineering skills. Without the Sumerian invention of writing—one of the great creative acts in history—what we mean by *civilization* could not have emerged.

Many elements of ancient Near Eastern civilization were passed on to the West. The wheeled vehicle, the plow, and the phonetic alphabet—all important to the development of civilization—derive from the Near East. In the realm of medicine, the Egyptians knew the value of certain drugs, such as castor oil; they also knew how to use splints and bandages. The innovative divisions that gave 360 degrees to a circle and 60 minutes to an hour originated in Mesopotamia. Egyptian geometry and Babylonian astronomy were utilized by the Greeks and became a part of Western knowledge. In Christian art, too, one finds connections to Mesopotamian art forms—for example, the Assyrians depicted winged angel-like beings.

Both the Hebrews and the Greeks borrowed Mesopotamian literary themes. For instance, some biblical stories—the Flood, the quarrel between Cain and Abel, and the Tower of Babel—stem from Mesopotamian antecedents. A similar link exists between the Greek and the earlier Mesopotamian mythologies.

Thus, many achievements of the Egyptians and the Mesopotamians were inherited and assimilated by both the Greeks and the Hebrews, the principal founders of Western civilization. Even more important for an understanding of the essential meaning of Western civilization are the ways in which the Greeks and the Hebrews rejected or transformed elements of the older Near Eastern traditions to create new points of departure for the human mind.

❖ ❖ ❖

Notes

1. *Epic of Gilgamesh*, with an introduction by N. K. Sandars (Baltimore: Penguin Books, 1960), pp. 69, 104.
2. Quoted in John A. Wilson, *The Culture of Ancient Egypt*, p. 227. Copyright © 1951 by University of Chicago Press. All rights reserved. Reprinted by permission.
3. Samuel Sambursky, *The Physical World of the Greeks* (New York: Collier Books, 1962), pp. 18–19.

Suggested Reading

Kuhrt, Amélie, *The Ancient Near East* (1995). An authoritative two-volume history.

Leick, Gwendolyn, *The Babylonians: An Introduction* (2003). An accessible survey.

Saggs, H. W. F., *Civilization Before Greece and Rome* (1989). Focuses on culture and society.

Sherman, David P., ed., *Ancient Egypt* (1997). Leading scholars explore ancient Egyptian culture.

Silverman, David P., ed., *Ancient Egypt* (1997). Clearly written accounts by experts on all phases of ancient Egyptian society.

Snell, Daniel C., *Life in the Ancient Near East* (1997). A synthesis of socioeconomic life.

Strouhal, Eugen, *Life of the Ancient Egyptians* (1992). Daily life of Egyptians; lavishly illustrated.

Tyldesley, Joyce, *Hatchepsut* (1996). A study of the female pharaoh.

von Soden, Wolfram, *The Ancient Orient* (1994). A thematic treatment of ancient Mesopotamian civilization.

Chapter 2

The Hebrews: A New View of God and the Individual

- Early Hebrew History
- God: One, Sovereign, Transcendent, Good
- The Individual and Moral Autonomy
- The Covenant and the Law
- The Hebrew Idea of History
- The Prophets
- The Legacy of the Ancient Jews

Focus Questions

1. In what ways did the Hebrew view of God mark a revolutionary break with Near Eastern thought?
2. How did Hebrew religious thought promote the ideas of moral autonomy?
3. What were the distinguishing features of Hebrew law?
4. What were the unique achievements of the Hebrew prophets?
5. Why are the Hebrews regarded as a principal source of the Western tradition?

Ancient Mesopotamia and Egypt, the birthplaces of the first civilizations, are not the spiritual ancestors of the West; for the origins of the Western tradition we must turn to the Hebrews (Jews) and the Greeks. Both Greeks and Hebrews, of course, absorbed elements of the civilizations of Mesopotamia and Egypt, but what is more significant is how they transformed this inheritance and shaped worldviews that differed markedly from the outlooks of these first civilizations. As Egyptologist John A. Wilson writes,

> *The Children of Israel built a nation and a religion on the rejection of things Egyptian. Not only did they see God as one, but they ascribed to him consistency of concern for man and consistency of justice to man. . . . Like the Greeks, the Hebrews took forms from their great neighbors; like the Greeks, they used those forms for very different purposes.*[1]

In this chapter, we examine one source of the Western tradition, the Hebrews, whose conception of God broke with the outlook of the Near East and whose ethical teachings helped to fashion the Western idea of the dignity of the individual. ❖

Early Hebrew History

The Hebrews (Israelites or Jews) originated in Mesopotamia and migrated to Canaan, a portion of which was later called Palestine.* The Hebrew patriarchs—Abraham, Isaac, and Jacob, so prominently depicted in the Old Testament—were chieftains of seminomadic clans that roamed Palestine and occasionally journeyed to Mesopotamia and Egypt. The early Hebrews absorbed some features of Mesopotamian civilization. For example, there are parallels between biblical law and the Mesopotamian legal tradition. Several biblical stories, including those of the Garden of Eden and the Flood, derive from Mesopotamian sources.

According to Hebrew Scriptures, some Hebrews journeyed from Canaan to Egypt to be herdsmen and farmers, but they eventually became forced laborers for the Egyptians. Fearful of turning into permanent slaves of the pharaoh, the Hebrews yearned for an opportunity to escape. In the thirteenth century B.C., an extraordinary leader called Moses rose among them and was accepted as a messenger of God. Leading the Hebrews in their exodus from Egypt, Moses transformed them during their wanderings in the wilderness of Sinai into a nation, united and uplifted by a belief in Yahweh, the one God.

Some scholars dismiss the Exodus as fiction, arguing that there is no extrabibical evidence for the Exodus or even for the presence of Hebrews in Eygpt; while there are abundant Egyptian hieroglyphics detailing events at the time, none of them refer specifically to Israelites in Egypt. Certainly, say these scholars, the flight of thousands of foreigners would have attracted notice. Moreover, it is highly unlikely that an escape by a large group of slaves could have succeeded when Egypt was at the peak of its power. The biblical account says that Israelites wandered in the Sinai Desert for forty years, but archeologists, who have excavated numerous sites in the Sinai mentioned in the Book of Exodus, have uncovered no traces of Israelite campsites. These scholars, known as biblical minimalists, deny there ever was an Exodus from Egypt. Other scholars reject this position, holding that there is evidence of Asiatic slaves toiling in Egypt, some of whom might have been Hebrews. Moreover, assert these scholars, ancient Hebrew scribes would not have concocted and faithfully preserved such an inglorious history of enslavement unless the biblical account contained a core historical truth along with legend, folklore, and mythic imagery.

The wandering Hebrews returned to Canaan to rejoin other Hebrew tribes that had not migrated to Egypt. The conquest and colonization of Canaan was a gradual process that took many generations. Threatened by the Philistines (originally from the islands of the Aegean Sea and the coast of Asia Minor), the twelve Hebrew tribes united under the leadership of Saul, a charismatic hero, whom they acclaimed as their first king. Under Saul's successor, David, a gifted warrior and poet, the Hebrews (or Israelites) broke the back of Philistine power and subdued neighboring peoples.

David's son Solomon built a royal palace in Jerusalem and beside it a magnificent temple honoring God. Under Solomon, ancient Israel was at the height of its political power and prosperity, but opposition to Solomon's tax policies and his favored treatment of the region of Judah in the south led to the division of the kingdom after his death in 922 B.C. The tribes loyal to Solomon's son belonged to the Kingdom of Judah, whereas the other tribes organized the northern Kingdom of Israel.

*Since there is a paucity of references to the early Hebrews in nonbiblical sources, scholars have to rely almost entirely on the Hebrew Bible for reconstructing much of the history of the ancient Israelites. The divergence of scholarly opinion regarding the Bible's accuracy and reliability creates additional uncertainty for the historian.

Chronology 2.1 ❖ The Hebrews

1250 B.C.	Hebrew exodus from Egypt
1024–1000	Reign of Saul, Israel's first king
1000–961	Creation of a united monarchy under David
961–922	Reign of Solomon; construction of the first temple
750–430	Age of classical prophecy
722	Kingdom of Israel falls to Assyrians
586	Kingdom of Judah falls to Chaldeans; the temple is destroyed
586–539	Babylonian exile
538	Cyrus of Persia allows exiles to return to Judah
515 B.C.	Second temple is dedicated

In 722 B.C., Israel fell to the Assyrians, who deported many Hebrews to other parts of the Assyrian empire. These transplanted Hebrews merged with neighboring peoples and lost their identity as the people who had made a covenant with God. By 586 B.C., the Chaldeans had conquered Judah, destroyed Solomon's temple, devastated the land, and deported several thousand Hebrews to Babylon. This was the darkest moment in the history of the Hebrews. Their state was gone, and neighboring peoples had overrun their land; their holy temple, built during the reign of King Solomon, was in ruins; thousands had died in battle, had been executed or had fled to Egypt and other lands; and thousands more were in exile in Babylon. This exile is known as the Babylonian Captivity.

Still, the Hebrews, now commonly called Jews, survived as a people—a fact that is a marvel of history. Although many of the exiles in Babylon assimilated Babylonian ways, some remained faithful to their God, Yahweh, and to the Law of Moses, and they longed to return to their homeland. Thus, their faith enabled them to endure conquest and exile. When the Persians conquered Babylon, King Cyrus, in 538 B.C., permitted the exiles to return to Judah, now a Persian province, and to rebuild the temple.

The Jews regained their independence in the second century B.C.; however, in the next century their land fell within the Roman orbit. After failed revolutions in the first and second centuries A.D., they became a dispersed people. But they never relinquished their commitment to God and his Law as recorded in the Hebrew Scriptures. Called *Tanak* by Jews (and the Old Testament by Christians), these Scriptures consist of thirty-nine books by several authors who lived in different centuries. Jews call the first five books—Genesis, Exodus, Leviticus, Numbers, and Deuteronomy—the Torah (which originally meant "teaching" or "instruction"). Often the Torah is referred to as the Pentateuch, a Greek word meaning "five books."

The Hebrew Scriptures represent Jewish written and oral tradition dating from about 1250 to 150 B.C. The record of more than a thousand years of ancient Jewish life, they include Jewish laws, wisdom, hopes, legends, and literary expressions. In describing an ancient people's efforts to comprehend the ways of God, the Scriptures emphasize and value the human experience; their heroes are not demigods but human beings. The Scriptures depict human strength as well as weakness. Some passages exhibit cruelty and unseemly revenge against the enemies of Israel and apostates, but others express the highest ethical values.

Compiled by religious devotees, not research historians, the Hebrew Scriptures understandably contain factual errors, imprecisions, and discrepancies. However, they also offer passages of reliable history, and historians find these Scriptures an indispensable source for studying the ancient Near East. Students of literature explore the Old Testament for its poetry, legends, and themes, all of which are an integral part of the Western literary

A Dead Sea Scroll, Judea, Second Century B.C. God's law, as recorded in the Holy Scriptures, still remains a unifying force among Jews. Many ancient Hebrew scrolls were found in caves near the west bank of the Dead Sea beginning in the late 1940s. The scroll depicted here contains the earliest existing copy of a complete Hebrew text of the book of the prophet Isaiah. It barely differs from more modern manuscripts.

tradition. But it is as a work of religious inspiration that the Hebrew Bible attains its profoundest importance. As set forth there, the Hebrew idea of God and his relationship to human beings is one of the foundations of the Western tradition.

God: One, Sovereign, Transcendent, Good

Monotheism, the belief in one God, became the central force in the life of the Hebrews and marked a profound break with Near Eastern religious thought. Near Eastern gods were not truly free; their power was not without limits. Unlike Yahweh, Near Eastern gods were not eternal but were born or created; they issued from some prior realm. They were also subject to biological conditions, requiring food, drink, sleep, and sexual gratification. Sometimes they became ill or grew old or died. When they behaved wickedly, they had to answer to fate, which demanded punishment as retribution; even the gods were subject to fate's power.

The Hebrews regarded God as *fully sovereign*. He ruled all and was subject to nothing. The Hebrews believed that nothing preceded God in time or surpassed him in power. They saw God as eternal and omnipotent, as the source of all in the universe, and as having a supreme will.

Whereas Near Eastern divinities dwelt within nature, the Hebrew God was *transcendent,* above nature and not a part of it. Yahweh was not identified with any natural force and did not dwell in a particular place in heaven or on earth. Since God was the creator and ruler of nature, there was no place for a sun god, a moon god, a god in the river, or a demon in the storm. Nature was God's creation, but was not itself divine. The stars and planets were creations of Yahweh, not divinities or the abodes of divinities. The Hebrews neither regarded them with awe nor worshiped them.

The removal of the gods from nature—the demythicizing of nature—is a necessary prerequisite for scientific thought. But concerned as they were with religion and morality, the Hebrews did not create theoretical science. As testimony to God's greatness, nature inspired them to sing the praises of the Lord; it invoked worship of God, not scientific curiosity. When they gazed at the heavens, they did not seek to discover mathematical relationships but admired God's magnificent handiwork. They did not view nature as a system governed by self-operating physical principles or natural law. Rather, they saw the rising sun, spring rain, summer heat, and winter cold as God intervening in an orderly manner in his creation. The Hebrews, unlike the Greeks, were not philosophical or scientific thinkers. They were concerned with God's will, not the human intellect; with the feelings of the heart, not the power of the mind; with righteous behavior, not abstract thought.

Unlike the Greeks, the Hebrews did not speculate about the origins of all things and the operations of nature; they knew that God had created everything. For the Hebrews, God's existence was based on religious conviction, not on rational inquiry; on revelation, not reason. It was the Greeks, not the Hebrews, who originated self-conscious, systematic, rational thought. But Christianity, born of Judaism, retained the Hebrew view of a transcendent God and the orderliness of his creation concepts that could accommodate Greek science.

The Hebrews also did not speculate about God's nature. They knew only that he was *good* and that he made ethical demands on his people. Unlike Near Eastern gods, Yahweh was not driven by lust or motivated by evil but was "merciful and gracious, long-suffering, and abundant in goodness and truth . . . forgiving inequity and transgression and sin" (Psalm 145:8).[2] In contrast to pagan gods, who were indifferent to human beings, Yahweh was attentive to human needs. By asserting that God was *one, sovereign, transcendent,* and *good,* the Hebrews effected a religious revolution that separated them entirely from the worldview held by the other peoples of the ancient Near East.

The Individual and Moral Autonomy

This new conception of God made possible a new awareness of the individual, who was seen as the culmination and centerpiece of God's creation. Created in the image of God, the human being is unique, qualitatively different from the rest of animate nature. Only the human being has the power of volition, the power to make choices. The Hebrews believed that God, who possessed total freedom himself, had bestowed on his people moral freedom—the capacity to choose between good and evil. Thus, in confronting God, the Hebrews developed an awareness of *self,* or *I:* the individual became conscious of his or her own person, moral autonomy, and personal worth.

Fundamental to Hebrew belief was the insistence that God did not create people to be his slaves. The Hebrews regarded God with awe and humility, with respect and fear, but they did not believe that God wanted people to grovel before him; rather, he wanted them to fulfill their moral potential by freely making the choice to follow or not to follow God's Law. Thus, in creating men and women in his own image, God made them autonomous and sovereign. In God's plan for the universe, human beings were the highest creation, subordinate only to God. Of all his creations, only they had been given the freedom to choose between righteousness and wickedness, between "life and good, and death and evil" (Deuteronomy 30:15). But having the power to choose freely, men and women must bear the responsibility for their choice.

God demanded that the Hebrews have no other gods and that they make no images "nor any manner of likeness, of any thing that is in heaven above, or that is in the earth beneath, . . . thou shalt not bow down unto them nor serve them" (Exodus 20:4–5). The Hebrews believed that the worship of idols deprived people of their freedom and dignity; people cannot be fully human if they surrender themselves to a lifeless idol. Hence, the Hebrews rejected images and all other forms of idolatry. A crucial element of Near Eastern religion was the use of images—art forms that depicted divinities—but the Hebrews believed that God, the Supreme Being, could not be represented by pictures or sculpture fashioned by human hands. The Hebrews rejected entirely the belief that an image possessed divine powers, which could be manipulated for human advantage. Ethical considerations, not myth or magic, were central to Hebrew religious life.

By making God the center of life, Hebrews could become free moral agents; no person, no human institution, and no human tradition could claim their souls. Because God alone was the supreme value in the universe, only he was worthy of worship. Thus, to give ultimate loyalty to a king or a general violated God's stern warning against the worship of false gods. The first concern of the Hebrews was righteousness, not power, fame, or riches, which were only idols and would impoverish a person spiritually and morally.

There was, however, a condition to freedom. For the Hebrews, people were not free to create their own moral precepts, their own standards of right and wrong. Freedom meant voluntary obedience to commands that originated with God. Evil and suffering were not caused by blind fate, malevolent demons, or arbitrary gods; they resulted from people's disregard of God's commandments. The dilemma is that in possessing freedom of choice, human beings are also free to disobey God, to commit sin, which leads to suffering and death. Thus, in the Genesis story, Adam and Eve were punished for disobeying God in the Garden of Eden.

For the Hebrews, to know God was not to comprehend him intellectually, to define him, or to prove his existence; to know God was to be righteous and loving, merciful and just. When men and women loved God, the Hebrews believed, they were uplifted and improved. Gradually, they learned to overcome the worst elements of human nature and to treat people with respect and compassion. The Jews came to interpret the belief that human beings were created in God's image to mean that each individual has a divine spark in him or her, giving every person a unique dignity that cannot be taken away.

Through their devotion to God, the Hebrews asserted the value and autonomy of human beings. Thus, the Hebrews conceived the idea of moral freedom: that each individual is responsible for his or her own actions. These concepts of human dignity and moral autonomy, which Christianity inherited, are at the core of the Western tradition.

The Covenant and the Law

Central to Hebrew religious thought and decisive in Hebrew history was the covenant, God's special agreement with the Hebrew people: if they obeyed his commands, they would "be unto Me a kingdom of priests, and a holy nation" (Exodus 19:6). By this act, the Israelites as a nation accepted God's lordship. Justice was the central theme of Old Testament ethics. The Israelites, liberated from slavery by a righteous and compassionate God, had a moral responsibility to overcome injustice and to care for the poor, the weak, and the oppressed.

The Hebrews came to see themselves as a unique nation, a "chosen people," for God had given them a special honor, a profound opportunity, and (as they could never forget) an awesome responsibility. The Hebrews did not claim that God had selected them because they were better than other peoples or because they had done anything special to deserve God's election. They believed that God had selected them to receive the Law, including the Ten Commandments, so that their nation would set an example of righteous behavior and ultimately make God and his moral commands known to the other nations. This divinely assigned responsibility to be the moral teachers of humanity weighed heavily on the Hebrews.

Israelite law incorporated many elements from Near Eastern legal codes and oral traditions. But by making people more important than property, by expressing mercy toward the oppressed,

Wall Painting from the Synagogue of Dura-Europos, Roman Syria, Early Third Century A.D. Although a strict prohibition of the use of images inhibited representational art among the Hebrews, in Hellenistic times scenes from Hebrew history appeared on the walls and floors of Jewish synagogues. Here the prophet Samuel is depicted anointing David as king of Israel.

and by rejecting the idea that law should treat the poor and the rich differently, Israelite law demonstrated a greater ethical awareness and a more humane spirit than other legal codes of the Near East as the following passage illustrates:

> *Ye shall not steal; neither shall ye deal falsely, nor lie to one another. . . . Thou shalt not oppress thy neighbour nor rob him. . . . Ye shall do no unrighteousness in judgment; thou shalt not respect [be partial to] the person of the poor, nor favour the person of the mighty; but in righteousness shalt thou judge thy neighbor. . . . And if a stranger sojourn with thee in your land, ye shall not do him wrong. The stranger that sojourneth with you shall be unto you as the home born among you, and thou shalt love him as thyself.* (Leviticus 19:11, 13, 15, 33, 34)

While biblical law valued human life and was concerned with human welfare, it also contained provisions that shock us as cruel, for example, ordering the slaughter of the enemy in war, the stoning to death of one's family members who chose to serve other gods, and the execution of homosexuals. Over the centuries, however, there arose an oral and interpretive tradition that made the written law less rigid and led the Hebrews to adapt to changing cultural traditions.

Like other Near Eastern societies, the Jews placed women in a subordinate position. The husband was considered his wife's master, and she often addressed him as a servant or subject would speak to a superior. A husband could divorce his wife, but she could not divorce him. Only when there was no male heir could a wife inherit property from her husband or a daughter from her father. Outside the home, women were not regarded as competent witnesses in court and played a lesser role than men in organized worship.

On the other hand, the Jews also showed respect for women. Wise women and prophetesses like Judith and Deborah were esteemed by the community and consulted by its leaders. Prophets compared God's love for the Hebrews with a husband's love for his wife. Jewish law regarded the woman as a person, not as property. Even female captives taken in war were not to be abused or humiliated. The law required a husband to respect and support his wife and never to strike her. One of the Ten Commandments called for honoring both father and mother.

The Hebrew Idea of History

Their idea of God made the Hebrews aware of the crucial importance of historical time. Holidays commemorating such specific historical events as the Exodus from Egypt, the receiving of the Ten Commandments on Mount Sinai, and the destruction of Solomon's temple kept the past alive and vital. Egyptians and Mesopotamians did not have a similar awareness of the uniqueness of a given event; to them, today's events were repetitions of events experienced by their ancestors. To the Jews, the Exodus and the covenant at Mount Sinai were singular, nonrepetitive occurrences, decisive in shaping their national history. This historical uniqueness and importance of events derived from the idea of a universal God who is profoundly involved in human affairs—a God who cares, teaches, and punishes.

The Jews valued the future as well as the past. Regarding human history as a process leading to a goal, they envisioned a great day when God would establish on earth a glorious age of peace, prosperity, happiness, and human brotherhood. This utopian notion has become deeply embedded in Western thought.

The Hebrews saw history as the work of God; it was a divine drama filled with sacred meaning and moral significance. Historical events revealed the clash of human wills with God's commands. Through history's specific events, God's presence was disclosed and his purpose made known. When the Hebrews suffered conquest and exile, they interpreted these events as divine retribution for violating God's Law and as punishment for their stubbornness, sinfulness, and rebelliousness. For the Hebrews, history also revealed God's compassion and concern. Thus, the Lord liberated Moses and the Israelites at the Red Sea and appointed prophets to plead for the poor and the oppressed. Because historical events revealed God's attitude toward human beings, these events possessed spiritual meaning and therefore were worth recording, evaluating, and remembering.

The Prophets

Jewish history was marked by the emergence of spiritually inspired persons called *prophets,* who felt compelled to act as God's messengers. The prophets believed that God had commanded them to speak and had legitimated their words. The flowering of the prophetic movement—the age of classical, or literary, prophecy—began in the eighth century B.C. Among the prophets were Amos, a shepherd from Judea in the south; his younger contemporary, Hosea, from Israel in the north; Isaiah of Jerusalem; and Jeremiah, who witnessed the siege of Jerusalem by the Chaldeans in the early sixth century B.C. The prophets cared nothing for money or possessions, feared no one, not even the powerful, and preached without invitation. Often emerging in times of social distress and moral confusion, they exhorted the entire nation to make God's moral commands central to its existence and taught that when people forgot God and made themselves the center of all things, they would bring disaster on themselves and their community. The prophets saw national misfortune as an opportunity for penitence and reform.

In attacking oppression, cruelty, greed, and exploitation, the classical prophets added a new dimension to Israel's religious development. These prophets were responding to problems emanating from Israel's changed social structure. A tribal society generally lacks class distinctions, but this situation had been altered by the rise of Hebrew kings, the expansion of commerce, and the

Primary Source

Isaiah and Social Justice

The prophets' insistence that rituals were not the essence of the Law and their passion for righteousness are voiced in the Scriptures by Isaiah of Jerusalem, who lived in the mid-eighth century B.C. Scholars agree that Isaiah of Jerusalem did not write all sixty-six chapters that make up the book of Isaiah. Some material appears to have been written by his disciples and interpreters, and Chapters 40 to 55, which were composed two centuries later, are attributed to a person given the name Second Isaiah. The following verses come from Isaiah of Jerusalem.

11 "What to me is the multitude of your
sacrifices?
says the LORD;
I have had enough of burnt offerings of rams
and the fat of the fed beasts;
I do not delight in the blood of bulls, or of
lambs, or of he-goats . . .
13 Bring no more vain offerings;
incense is an abomination to me.
New moon and sabbath and the calling of
assemblies—
I cannot endure iniquity and solemn
assembly.
14 Your new moons and your appointed feasts
my soul hates;
they have become a burden to me;
I am weary of bearing them.
15 When you spread forth your hands,
I will hide my eyes from you;
even though you make many prayers,
I will not listen;
your hands are full of blood.
16 Wash yourselves; make yourselves clean;
remove the evil of your doings
from before my eyes;
cease to do evil,
17 learn to do good;
seek justice,
defend the fatherless,
plead for the widow.
(Isaiah 1)

Isaiah denounces the rich and the powerful for exploiting the poor.

13 The LORD has taken his place to contend, he
stands to judge his people.
14 The LORD enters into judgement with the
elders and princes of his people:
"It is you who have devoured the
vineyard, the spoil of the poor is in
your houses.
15 What do you mean by crushing my people,
by grinding the face of the poor?"
says the Lord GOD of hosts.
(Isaiah 3)

Question for Analysis

1. Discuss the following statement: for Isaiah, ethical conduct was preferable to ritual acts as a way to worship God.

growth of cities. By the eighth century, there was a significant disparity between the wealthy and the poor. Small farmers in debt to moneylenders faced the loss of their land or even bondage; the poor were often dispossessed by the greedy wealthy. To the prophets, these social evils were religious sins that would bring ruin to Israel. In the name of God, they denounced the greed and pomp of the heartless rich and the hypocrisy of pious Jews who worshiped in the prescribed manner but neglected their social obligations to their neighbor. The purpose of worship and ritual was to instill in human beings a passion for justice. God is compassionate, the prophets insisted. He cares for all, especially the poor, the unfortunate, the suffering, and the defenseless.

Prophets also denounced people whose principal concern was the accumulation of possessions and wealth. These objects are only transient, said Isaiah, "but the word of God will stand forever" (Isaiah 40:8).

Prophets stressed the direct spiritual-ethical encounter between the individual and God. The inner person concerned them more than the outer forms of religious activity. Holding that the essence of the covenant was righteousness, the prophets criticized priests whose commitment to rites and rituals was not supported by a deeper spiritual insight or a zeal for morality in daily life. To the prophets, an ethical sin was far worse than a ritual omission. To live unjustly, to mistreat one's neighbors, to act without compassion—these actions violated God's Law and endangered the entire social order.

The prophets thus helped shape a social conscience that has become part of the Western tradition. They held out the hope that life on earth could be improved, that poverty and injustice need not be accepted as part of an unalterable natural order, and that the individual was capable of elevating himself or herself morally and could respect the dignity of others.

Two tendencies were present in Hebrew thought: parochialism and universalism. Parochial-mindedness stressed the special nature, destiny, and needs of the chosen people, a nation set apart from others. This narrow, tribal outlook was offset by universalism: a concern for all humanity, which found expression in those prophets who envisioned the unity of all people under God. All people were equally precious to God.

The prophets were not pacifists, particularly if a war was being waged against the enemies of Yahweh. But some prophets denounced war as obscene and looked forward to its elimination. They maintained that when people glorify force, they dehumanize their opponents, brutalize themselves, and dishonor God. When violence rules, there can be no love of God and no regard for the individual.

The prophets' universalism was accompanied by an equally profound awareness of the individual and his or her intrinsic worth. Before the prophets, virtually all religious tradition had been produced communally and anonymously. The prophets, however, spoke as fearless individuals who, by affixing their signatures to their thoughts, fully bore the responsibility for their religious inspiration and conviction.

In coming to regard God's Law as a *command to conscience, an appeal to the inner person,* the prophets heightened the awareness of the human personality. They indicated that the individual could not know God by merely following edicts and performing rituals; the individual must experience God. Precisely this *I–Thou* relationship could make the individual fully conscious of self and could deepen and enrich his or her own personality. During the Exodus, the Hebrews were a tribal people who obeyed the Law largely out of awe and group compulsion. By the prophets' time, the Jews appeared to be autonomous individuals who heeded the Law because of a deliberate, conscious inner commitment.

The ideals proclaimed by the prophets helped sustain the Jews throughout their long and often painful historical odyssey, and they remain a vital force for Jews today. Incorporated into the teachings of Jesus, these ideals, as part of Christianity, are embedded in the Western tradition.

The Legacy of the Ancient Jews

For the Jews, monotheism had initiated a process of self-discovery and self-realization unmatched by other peoples of the Near East. The great value that westerners place on the individual and on human dignity derives in part from the ancient Hebrews, who held that man and woman were created in God's image and possessed free will and a conscience answerable to God. Inherited by Christianity, the prophets' teachings constitute the core principles of Western morality, and their command to the power structure not to abuse its authority but to pursue justice continues to inspire reformers.

Throughout the centuries the Jewish Bible, with its view of God, human nature, divine punishment, the pursuit of righteousness, and social justice, has played a pivotal and profound role in Jewish life. Moreover, its significance has transcended the Jewish experience; it is also a cornerstone of Western civilization. Christianity, the essential religion of Western civilization, emerged from ancient Judaism, and the links between the two, including monotheism, moral autonomy, prophetic values, and the Hebrew Scriptures as the Word of God, are numerous and strong. The historical Jesus cannot be understood without examining his Jewish background, and his followers appealed to the Hebrew Scriptures in order to demonstrate the validity of their beliefs. For these reasons, we talk of a Judeo-Christian tradition as an essential component of Western civilization.

The Hebrew vision of a future messianic age, a golden age of peace and social justice, is at the root of the Western idea of progress—that people can build a more just society, that there is a reason to be hopeful about the future. This way of perceiving the world has greatly influenced modern reform movements. People longing to escape from oppression—African Americans in particular—have found inspiration in the Hebrews' deliverance from bondage in Egypt, the theme of Exodus.

In seeking to comprehend their relationship to God, the writers of the Hebrew Scriptures produced a treasury of themes, stories, and models of literary style and craftsmanship that have been a source of inspiration for Western religious thinkers, novelists, poets, and artists to the present day. Historians and archaeologists find the Hebrew Scriptures a valuable source in their efforts to reconstruct Near Eastern history.

❖ ❖ ❖

Notes

1. John A. Wilson, "Egypt—the Kingdom of the 'Two Lands,'" in *At the Dawn of Civilization,* ed. E. A. Speiser (New Brunswick, N.J.: Rutgers University Press, 1964), pp. 267–268. Vol. I in *The World History of the Jewish People.*
2. The Scriptural quotations in this chapter come from *Tanakh: The New JPS Translation According to the Traditional Hebrew Text* (Philadelphia: The Jewish Publication Society, 1985). Copyright © 1985 by the Jewish Publication Society. Used by permission.

Suggested Reading

Anderson, Bernhard, *Understanding the Old Testament,* 2nd ed. (1966). An excellent survey of the Old Testament in its historical setting.

Armstrong, Karen, *A History of God* (1994). Changing views of God from the ancient Hebrews until today.

Boadt, Lawrence, *Reading the Old Testament* (1984). A study of ancient Israel's religious experience by a sympathetic Catholic scholar.

Bright, John, *A History of Israel* (1972). A thoughtful, clearly written survey; the best of its kind.

Dever, William G., *Who Were the Israelites and Where Did They Come From?* (2003). An archeologist explores the controversy regarding biblical accounts of the origins of the Israelites.

Finkelstein, Israel, and Neil Asher Silberman, *The Bible Unearthed: Archeology's New Vision of Ancient Israel and the Origin of Its Sacred Texts* (2001). A provocative treatment of the Bible's reliability.

Grant, Michael, *The History of Ancient Israel* (1984). A lucid account.

Metzger, Bruce M., and Michael D. Coogan, eds., *The Oxford Companion to the Bible* (1993). A valuable reference work.

Shanks, Hershel, ed., *Ancient Israel* (1999). The revised and expanded edition contains authoritative essays on various phases of the history of ancient Israel. Highly recommended.

CourseMate

Go to the CourseMate website at **www.cengagebrain.com** for additional study tools and review materials—including audio and video clips—for this chapter.

Chapter 3

The Greeks: From Myth to Reason

- **Early Aegean Civilizations**
- **Evolution of the City-States**
- **The Decline of the City-States**
- **Philosophy in the Hellenic Age**
- **Art**
- **Poetry and Drama**
- **History**
- **The Hellenistic Age: The Second Stage of Greek Civilization**
- **Hellenistic Thought and Culture**
- **The Greek Achievement: Reason, Freedom, Humanism**

Focus Questions

1. What were the basic features and limitations of Greek democracy?
2. How did Greek political life demonstrate both the best and the worst features of freedom as well as both the capabilities and limitations of reason?
3. Why is the Greek political experience crucial to the shaping of the Western tradition?
4. How did the Pre-Socratic thinkers make the transition from myth to reason?
5. How did the Sophists and Socrates advance the tradition of reason and humanism?
6. What do Plato and Aristotle have in common? How do they differ?
7. How did Greek drama, art, and historiography contribute to the tradition of reason and humanism?
8. What are the basic differences between the Hellenic and Hellenistic Ages?

9. What prescription did each of the Hellenistic philosophies offer for achieving happiness?
10. What is the enduring significance of Stoicism for the modern world?

The Hebrew conception of ethical monotheism, with its stress on human dignity, is one principal source of the Western tradition. The second major source is ancient Greece. Both Hebrews and Greeks absorbed the achievements of Near Eastern civilizations, but they also developed their own distinctive viewpoints and styles of thought, which set them apart from the Mesopotamians and Egyptians. The great achievements of the Hebrews lay in the sphere of religious-ethical thought; those of the Greeks lay in the development of philosophical and scientific thought.

The Greeks conceived of nature as following general rules, not acting according to the whims of gods or demons. They saw human beings as having a capacity for rational thought, a need for freedom, and a worth as individuals. Although the Greeks never dispensed with the gods, they increasingly stressed the importance of human reason and human decisions; they came to assert that reason is the avenue to knowledge and that people—not the gods—are responsible for their own behavior. In this shift of attention from the gods to human beings, the Greeks broke with the mythmaking orientation of the Near East and created the rational, humanist outlook that is a distinctive feature of Western civilization. ❖

Chronology 3.1 ❖ The Greeks

1700–1450 B.C.*	Height of Minoan civilization
1400–1230	Height of Mycenaean civilization
1100–800	Dark Age
c. 700	Homer
750–550	Age of Colonization
594	Solon is given power to institute reforms
507	Cleisthenes broadens democratic institutions
480	Xerxes of Persia invades Greece; Greek naval victory at Salamis
479	Spartans defeat Persians at Plataea, ending Persian Wars
431	Start of Peloponnesian War
404	Athens surrenders to Sparta, ending Peloponnesian War
387	Plato founds a school, the Academy
359	Philip II becomes king of Macedonia
338	Battle of Chaeronea: Greek city-states fall under dominion of Macedonia
335	Aristotle founds a school, the Lyceum
323 B.C.	Death of Alexander the Great

*Most dates are approximations.

Early Aegean Civilizations

Until the latter part of the nineteenth century, historians placed the beginning of Greek (or Hellenic) history in the eighth century B.C. Now it is known that two civilizations preceded Hellenic Greece: the Minoan and the Mycenaean. Although the ancient Greek poet Homer spoke of an earlier Greek civilization in his works, historians had believed that Homer's epics dealt solely with myths and legends, not with a historical past. In 1871, however, a successful German businessman, Heinrich Schliemann, began a search for earliest Greece. In excavating several sites mentioned by Homer, Schliemann discovered tombs, pottery, ornaments, and the remains of palaces of what hitherto had been a lost Greek civilization. The ancient civilization was named after Mycenae, the most important city of the time.

In 1900, Arthur Evans, a British archaeologist, excavating on the island of Crete, southeast of the Greek mainland, unearthed a civilization even older than that of the Mycenaean Greeks. The Cretans, or Minoans, were not Greeks and did not speak a Greek language, but their influence on mainland Greece was considerable and enduring. Minoan civilization lasted about 1,350 years (2600–1250 B.C.) and reached its height during the period from 1700 to 1450 B.C.

The centers of Minoan civilization were magnificent palace complexes, whose construction attested to the wealth and power of Minoan kings. The palaces housed royal families, priests, and government officials and contained workshops that produced decorated silver vessels, daggers, and pottery for local use and for export.

Judging by the archaeological evidence, the Minoans were peaceful. Minoan art generally did not depict military scenes, and Minoan palaces, unlike the Mycenaean ones, had no defensive walls or fortifications. Thus, the Minoans were vulnerable to the warlike Mycenaean Greeks, whose invasion contributed to the decline of Minoan civilization.

Who were these Mycenaeans? Around 2000 B.C., Greek-speaking tribes moved southward into the Greek peninsula, where, together with the pre-Greek population, they fashioned the Mycenaean civilization. In the Peloponnesus, in southern Greece, the Mycenaeans built palaces that were based in part on Cretan models. In these palaces, Mycenaean kings conducted affairs of state, and priests and priestesses performed religious ceremonies. Potters, smiths, tailors, and chariot builders practiced their crafts in the numerous workshops, much like their Minoan counterparts. Mycenaean arts and crafts owed a considerable debt to Crete. A script that permitted record keeping probably also came from Crete.

Mycenaean civilization, which consisted of several small states, each with its own ruling dynasty, reached its height in the period from 1400 to 1230 B.C. Following that, constant warfare among the Mycenaean kingdoms (and perhaps foreign invasions) led to the destruction of the palaces and the abrupt disintegration of Mycenaean civilization about 1100 B.C. But to the later Greek civilization, the Mycenaeans left a legacy of religious forms, pottery making, metallurgy, agriculture, language, a warrior culture and code of honor immortalized in the Homeric epics, and myths and legends that offered themes for Greek drama.

Evolution of the City-States

From 1100 to 800 B.C., the Greek world passed through the Dark Age, an era of transition between a dead Mycenaean civilization and a still-unborn Hellenic civilization. The Dark Age saw the migration of Greek tribes from the barren mountainous regions of Greece to more fertile plains and from the mainland to Aegean islands and the coast of Asia Minor. During this period, the Greeks experienced insecurity, warfare, poverty, and isolation.

After 800 B.C., however, town life revived. Writing again became part of the Greek culture, this time with the more efficient Phoenician script. (Other borrowings from the Near East included artistic imagery and motifs, religious practices, craft skills, and mythological tales that were adapted and transformed by Greek poets.) The population increased dramatically, there was a spectacular rise in the use of metals, and overseas trade expanded. Gradually, Greek cities founded settlements on the islands of the Aegean, along the coast of Asia Minor and the Black Sea, and to the west in Sicily and southern Italy. These colonies, established to relieve overpopulation and land hunger, were independent, self-governing city-states, not possessions of the homeland city-states. During these two hundred years of colonization (750–550 B.C.), trade and industry expanded and the pace of urbanization quickened.

Homer: Shaper of the Greek Spirit

The poet Homer lived during the eighth century B.C., just after the Dark Age. His great epics, the *Iliad* and the *Odyssey*, helped shape the Greek spirit and Greek religion. Homer was the earliest molder of the Greek outlook and character. For centuries, Greek youngsters grew up reciting the Homeric epics and admiring the Homeric heroes, who strove for honor and faced suffering and death with courage.

Homer was a poetic genius who could reveal a human being's deepest thoughts, feelings, and conflicts in a few brilliant lines. His characters, complex in their motives and expressing powerful human emotions—wrath, vengeance, guilt, remorse, compassion, and love—would intrigue and inspire Western writers to the present day.

The *Iliad* deals in poetic form with a small segment of the last year of the Trojan War, which had taken place centuries before Homer's time, during the Mycenaean period. Homer's theme is the wrath of Achilles. In depriving "the swift and excellent" Achilles of his rightful war prize (the captive young woman Briseis), King Agamemnon has insulted Achilles' honor and has violated the solemn rule that warrior heroes treat each other with respect. His pride wounded, Achilles refuses to rejoin Agamemnon in battle against Troy. Achilles plans to affirm his honor by demonstrating that the Greeks need his valor and military prowess. Not until many brave men have been slain, including his dearest friend Patroclus, does Achilles set aside his quarrel with Agamemnon and enter the battle.

Homer employs a *particular* event, the quarrel between an arrogant Agamemnon and a revengeful

Achilles, to demonstrate a *universal* principle: that "wicked arrogance" and "ruinous wrath" will cause much suffering and death. Homer grasps that there is an internal logic to existence. For Homer, says British classicist H. D. F. Kitto, "actions must have their consequences; ill-judged actions must have uncomfortable results."[1] People, and even the gods, operate within a certain unalterable framework; their deeds are subject to the demands of fate, or necessity. With a poet's insight, Homer sensed what would become a fundamental attitude of the Greek mind: there is a universal order to things. Later Greeks would formulate Homer's poetic insight in scientific and philosophical terms.

Heroism, the pursuit of glory and fame, and war's exhilaration are central to the *Iliad*, but Homer is also sensitive to the suffering caused by war. Battlefields littered with dead and maimed warriors fill soldiers with tears. And the grief of widows, orphans, and parents is unremitting.

Homer grasped war's tragic character: it confers honor and dignity on the victorious, but suffering, grief, enslavement, and death on the defeated. And one day, the hero, who had been lauded for his courage and prowess and had brought glory to his family and city, will also perish by the sword. This is his destiny. Homer's insights into life's tragic nature instructed the great Greek dramatists and future Western writers.

In Homer, we also see the origin of the Greek ideal of *aretē,* excellence. The Homeric warrior expresses a passionate desire to assert himself, to demonstrate his worth, and to gain the glory that poets would immortalize in their songs. In the warrior-aristocrat world of Homer, *excellence* was principally interpreted as bravery and skill in battle. Homer's portrayal also bears the embryo of a larger conception of human excellence, one that combines thought with action. A man of true worth, says the wise Phoenix to the stubborn Achilles, is both "a speaker of words and a doer of deeds." In this passage, we find the earliest statement of the Greek educational ideal: the molding of a man who, says classicist Werner Jaeger, "united nobility of action with nobility of mind," who realized "the whole of human potentialities."[2] Thus, in Homer we find the beginnings of Greek humanism—a concern with man and his achievements.

Essentially, Homer's works are an expression of the poetic imagination and mythical thought. However, his view of the eternal order of the world and his conception of the individual striving for excellence form the foundations of the Greek outlook.

Although Homer did not intend his poetry to have any theological significance, his treatment of the gods had important religious implications for the Greeks. In time, his epics formed the basis of the Olympian religion accepted throughout Greece. The principal gods were said to reside on Mount Olympus, and on its highest peak was the palace of Zeus, the chief deity. Religion pervaded daily life, but in time, traditional religion was challenged and undermined by a growing secular and rational spirit.

The Break with Theocratic Politics

From 750 B.C. to the death of Alexander the Great in 323 B.C., Greek society comprised many independent city-states. The city-state based on tribal allegiances was generally the first political association during the early stages of civilization. Moreover, Greece's many mountains, bays, and islands—natural barriers to political unity—favored this type of political arrangement.

The scale of the city-state, or *polis*, was small; most city-states had fewer than 5,000 male citizens. Athens, which was a large city-state, had some 35,000 to 40,000 adult male citizens at its height in the fifth century B.C.; the rest of its population of 350,000 consisted of women, children, resident aliens, and slaves, none of whom could participate in lawmaking. The polis gave individuals a sense of belonging, for its citizens were intimately involved in the political and cultural life of the community.

In the fifth century B.C., at its maturity, the Greeks viewed their polis as the only avenue to the good life—"the only framework within which man could realize his spiritual, moral, and intellectual capacities," in Kitto's words.[3] The mature polis was a self-governing community that expressed the will of free citizens, not the desires of gods, hereditary kings, or priests. In the Near East, religion dominated political activity, and to abide by the mandates of the gods was the ruler's first responsibility. The Greek polis also had begun as a religious institution, in which the citizens sought to maintain an alliance with their deities. Gradually, however, the citizens deemphasized the gods' role in political life and based government not on the magic powers of divine rulers but on human intelligence as expressed through the community. The great innovation that the Greeks introduced into politics and social theory was the principle that law did not derive from gods or divine kings but from the human community. Seers, purported to have supernatural skills, might offer advice but could not override the rulings of the Assembly.

The emergence of rational attitudes did not, of course, spell the end of religion, particularly for the peasants, who retained their devotion to their ancient cults, gods, and shrines. Paying homage to the god of the city remained a required act of patriotism to which Greeks unfailingly adhered. Thus, the religious-mythical tradition never died in Greece but existed side by side with a growing rationalism, becoming weaker as time passed. When Athenian democracy reached its height in the middle of the fifth century B.C., religion was no longer the dominant factor in politics. Athenians had consciously come to rely on human reason, not divine guidance, in their political and intellectual life.

What made Greek political life different from that of earlier Near Eastern civilizations, and also gave it enduring significance, was the Greeks' gradual realization that community problems are caused by human beings and require human solutions. The Greeks also valued free citizenship. An absolute king, a despot who ruled arbitrarily and by decree and who was above the law, was abhorrent to them.

The ideals of political freedom are best exemplified by Athens. But before turning to Athens, let us examine another Greek city, which followed a different political course.

Sparta: A Garrison State

Situated on the Peloponnesian peninsula, Sparta conquered its neighbors, including Messenia, in the eighth century B.C. Instead of selling the Messenians abroad, the traditional Greek way of treating a defeated foe, the Spartans kept them as state serfs, or *helots*. Helots were owned by the state rather than by individual Spartans. Enraged by their enforced servitude, the Messenians, also a Greek people, desperately tried to regain their freedom. After a bloody uprising was suppressed, the fear of a helot revolt became indelibly stamped on Spartan consciousness.

To maintain their dominion over the Messenians, who outnumbered them ten to one, the Spartans—with extraordinary single-mindedness, discipline, and loyalty—transformed their own society into an armed camp. Agricultural labor was performed by helots; trade and crafts were left to the *perioikoi*, conquered Greeks who were free but who had no political rights. The Spartans learned only one craft—soldiering—and were inculcated with only one conception of excellence: fighting bravely for their city, and if needed, dying for it.

The Spartans were trained in the arts of war and indoctrinated to serve the state. Military training for Spartan boys began at age seven; they exercised, drilled, competed, and endured physical hardships. Other Greeks admired the Spartans for their courage, obedience to law, and achievement in molding themselves according to an ideal. Spartan soldiers were better trained and disciplined and were more physically fit than other Greeks. But the Spartans were also criticized for having a limited conception of *aretē*.

Athens: The Rise of Democracy

The contrast between the city-states of Athens and Sparta is striking. Whereas Sparta was a land power and exclusively agricultural, Athens, which was located on the peninsula of Attica near the coast, possessed a great navy and was the commercial leader among the Greeks. The Athenians also were determined to protect their city from enemies, but, unlike the regimented Spartans, they valued political freedom and sought the full development and enrichment of the human personality. Thus, while authoritarian and militaristic Sparta turned culturally sterile, the relatively free and open society of Athens became the cultural leader of Hellenic civilization.

National Archeological Museum/TAPService, Athens.

WRESTLERS: RELIEF FROM A STATUE BASE, ATHENIAN, LATE SIXTH CENTURY B.C. Physical fitness and athletics were highly prized by the Greeks. Poets sang the praise of Olympic champions, and sculptors captured the beauty of athletic physiques for an admiring public.

Greek city-states generally moved through four stages: rule by a king (monarchy), rule by landowning aristocrats (oligarchy), rule by one man who seized power (tyranny), and rule by the people (democracy). During the first stage, monarchy, the king, who derived his power from the gods, commanded the army and judged civil cases.

Oligarchy, the second stage, was instituted in Athens during the eighth century B.C. when aristocrats (*aristocracy* is a Greek word meaning "rule of the best") usurped power from hereditary kings. In the next century, aristocratic regimes experienced a social crisis. Peasants who borrowed from the aristocracy, pledging their lands as security, lost their property and even became enslaved for nonpayment of their debts. Merchants and peasants also protested that the law, which was based on oral tradition and administered exclusively by aristocrats, was unjust. In Athens, the embittered and restless middle and lower classes were granted one concession. In 621 B.C., the aristocrats appointed Draco to draw up a code of law. Although Draco's code let the poor know what the law was and reduced the possibility that aristocratic judges would behave arbitrarily, penalties were extremely severe, and the code provided no relief for the peasants' economic woes. As the poor began to organize and press for the cancellation of their debts and the redistribution of land, Athens was moving toward civil war.

Solon, the Reformer. In 594 B.C., Solon (c. 640–559 B.C.), a traveler and poet with a reputation for wisdom, was elected chief executive. He maintained that the wealthy landowners, through their greed, had disrupted community life and brought Athens to the brink of civil war. Solon initiated a rational approach to the problems of society by deemphasizing the gods' role in human affairs and attributing the city's ills to the specific behavior of individuals; he sought practical remedies for these ills; and he held that written law should be in harmony with *Dikē*, the principle of justice that underlies the human community. The concept of a just city, a unifying principle of Solon's reforms, became a formative ideal of Greek political thought. At the same time, he wanted to instill in Athenians of all classes a sense of working for the common good of the city.

Solon aimed at restoring a sick Athenian society to health by restraining the nobles and improving the lot of the poor. To achieve this goal, he canceled debts, freed Athenians enslaved for debt, and brought back to Athens those who had been sold abroad; however, he refused to confiscate

Map 3.1 The Aegean Basin This map shows major battle sites. Note also the Hellespont, where Xerxes' forces crossed into Greece, and Ionia, the coast of Asia Minor, where Greek philosophy was born.

and redistribute the nobles' land as the extremists demanded. He permitted all classes of free men, even the poorest, to sit in the Assembly, which elected magistrates and accepted or rejected legislation proposed by a new Council of Four Hundred. He also opened the highest offices in the state to wealthy commoners, who had previously been excluded from these positions because they lacked noble birth. Thus, Solon undermined the traditional rights of the hereditary aristocracy and initiated the transformation of Athens from an aristocratic oligarchy into a democracy.

Solon also instituted ingenious economic reforms. Recognizing that the poor soil of Attica was not conducive to growing grain, he urged the cultivation of grapes for wine and the growing of olives, whose oil could be exported. To encourage industrial expansion, he ordered that all fathers teach their sons a trade and granted citizenship to foreign craftsmen who were willing to migrate to Athens. These measures and the fine quality of the native reddish-brown clay allowed Athens to become the leading producer and exporter of pottery. Solon's economic policies transformed Athens into a great commercial center. However, Solon's reforms did not eliminate factional disputes among the aristocratic clans or relieve much of the discontent of the poor.

Pisistratus, the Tyrant. In 546 B.C., Pisistratus (c. 605–527 B.C.), an aristocrat, took advantage of the general instability to become a one-man ruler, driving into exile those who had opposed him. Tyranny thus replaced oligarchy. Tyranny

Greek Warriors. The Greek warriors in this vase painting have weapons and armor very much like those used by the Greeks in the Persian Wars.

occurred frequently in the Greek city-states. Almost always aristocrats themselves, tyrants generally posed as champions of the poor in their struggle against the aristocracy. Pisistratus sought popular support by having conduits constructed to increase the Athenian water supply; like tyrants in other city-states, he gave to peasants land confiscated from exiled aristocrats and granted state loans to small farmers.

Pisistratus' great achievement was the promotion of cultural life. He initiated grand architectural projects, encouraged sculptors and painters, arranged for public recitals of the Homeric epics, and founded festivals, which included dramatic performances. In all these ways, he made culture, formerly the province of the aristocracy, available to commoners. Pisistratus thus launched a policy that eventually led Athens to emerge as the cultural capital of the Greeks.

Cleisthenes, the Democrat. Shortly after Pisistratus' death, a faction headed by Cleisthenes, an aristocrat sympathetic to democracy, assumed leadership. By an ingenious method of redistricting the city, Cleisthenes ended the aristocratic clans' traditional jockeying for the chief state positions, which had caused much divisiveness and bitterness in Athens. Cleisthenes replaced this practice, rooted in tradition and authority, with a new system, rationally planned to ensure that historic allegiance to tribe or clan would be superseded by loyalty to the city as a whole.

Cleisthenes hoped to make democracy the permanent form of government for Athens. The power to govern Athens, he believed, should rest with the male citizens acting as a body and not with aristocratic factions or a tyrant. To safeguard the city against tyranny, he utilized (or perhaps introduced) the practice of *ostracism*. Once a year, Athenians were given the opportunity to inscribe on a fragment of pottery (*ostracon*) the name of anyone who they felt endangered the state. An individual against whom enough votes were cast was ostracized, that is, forced to leave Athens for ten years.

Cleisthenes firmly secured democratic government in Athens. The Assembly, which Solon had opened to all male citizens, was in the process of becoming the supreme authority in the state. But the period of Athenian greatness lay in the future; the Athenians first had to fight a war of survival against the Persian Empire.

The Persian Wars

In 499 B.C., the Ionian Greeks of Asia Minor rebelled against their Persian overlord. Sympathetic to the Ionian cause, Athens sent twenty ships to aid the revolt. Bent on revenge, Darius I, king of Persia, sent a small detachment to Attica. In 490 B.C., on the plains of Marathon, the citizen army of Athens defeated the Persians—for the Athenians, one of the finest moments in their history. Ten years later, Xerxes, Darius' son, organized a huge invasion force—some 250,000 men and more than 500 ships—with the aim of reducing Greece to a Persian province. Setting aside their separatist instincts, many of the city-states united to defend their independence and their liberty. The historian Herodotus viewed the conflict as an ideological clash between Greek freedom and oriental despotism.

The Persians crossed the waters of the Hellespont (Dardanelles) and made their way into northern Greece. Herodotus describes their encounter at the mountain pass of Thermopylae with three hundred Spartans, who, true to their training and ideal of *aretē*, "resisted to the last with their swords if they had them, and if not, with their hands and teeth, until the Persians, coming on from the front over the ruins of the wall and closing in from behind, finally overwhelmed them."[4] Northern Greece fell to the Persians, who continued south, burning a deserted Athens.

When it appeared that the Greeks' spirit had been broken, the Athenian statesman and general Themistocles (c. 527–460 B.C.), demonstrating in military affairs the same rationality that Cleisthenes had shown in political life, lured the Persian fleet into the narrowest entry to the Bay of Salamis. Unable to deploy its more numerous ships in this cramped space, the Persian armada was destroyed by Greek ships. In 479 B.C., a year after the Athenian naval victory at Salamis, the Spartans defeated the Persians in the land battle of Plataea. The inventive intelligence with which the Greeks had planned their military operations and a fierce desire to preserve their freedom—which, the war made them realize, was their distinguishing attribute—had enabled them to defeat the greatest military power the Mediterranean world had yet seen.

The Persian Wars were decisive in the history of the West. The confidence and pride that came with its astonishing victory propelled Athens into a golden age whose achievements were pivotal in the shaping of European culture. But the conflict also roused the Athenian urge for dominance in Greece. The Persian Wars ushered in an era of Athenian imperialism, which had drastic consequences for the future. Immediately after the wars, more than 150 city-states organized a confederation, the Delian League (named after its treasury on the island of Delos), to protect themselves against a renewed confrontation with Persia. Because of its wealth, its powerful fleet, and the restless energy of its citizens, Athens assumed leadership of the Delian League. Athenians consciously and rapaciously manipulated the league for their own economic advantage, seeing no contradiction between imperialism and democracy. Athens forbade member states to withdraw, stationed garrisons on the territory of confederate states, and used the league's treasury to finance public works in Athens. Although member states did receive protection from both pirates and Persians, were not overtaxed, and enjoyed increased trade, they resented Athenian domination. In converting the Delian League into an instrument of Athenian imperialism, Athens may have lost an opportunity to perform a great creative act—the creation of a broad, voluntary confederation which might have forestalled the intercity warfare that gravely weakened Hellenic civilization.

The Mature Athenian Democracy

Athenian imperialism was one consequence of the Persian Wars; another was the flowering of Athenian democracy and culture. The Athenian state was a direct democracy, in which the citizens themselves, not elected representatives, made the laws. In the Assembly, that was open to all adult male citizens and which met some forty times a year, Athenians debated and voted on key issues of state: they declared war, signed treaties, and spent public funds. The lowliest cobbler, as well as the wealthiest aristocrat, had the opportunity to express his opinion in the Assembly, to vote, to speak before and submit motions to the Assembly, to hold the highest public positions, and to receive equal treatment before the law. By the middle of the fifth century, the will of the people, as expressed in the Assembly, was supreme.

The Council of Five Hundred (which had been established by Cleisthenes to replace Solon's Council of Four Hundred) managed the ports, military installations, and other state properties and prepared the agenda for the Assembly.

Because its members were chosen annually by lot and could not serve more than twice in a lifetime, the Council could never supersede the Assembly. Chosen at random, its membership could not become a cabal of the most powerful and ambitious citizens. Some 350 magistrates, also chosen by lot, performed administrative tasks: collecting fines, policing the city, repairing streets, inspecting markets, and so forth. In view of the special competence that their posts required, the ten generals who led the army were not chosen by lot but were elected by the Assembly.

Athens has been aptly described as a government of amateurs: there were no professional civil servants, no professional soldiers and sailors, no state judges, and no elected lawmakers. Ordinary citizens performed the duties of government. Such a system rested on the assumption that the average citizen was capable of participating intelligently in the affairs of state and that he would, in a spirit of civic patriotism, carry out his responsibilities to his city. In Athens of the fifth century B.C., excellence was equated with good citizenship—a concern for the good of the community that outweighs personal aspirations. Indeed, to a surprisingly large number of Athenians, politics was an overriding concern, and they devoted considerable time and thought to civic affairs. Those who allowed private matters to take precedence over the needs of the community were denounced as useless people living purposeless lives.

Athenian democracy achieved its height in the middle of the fifth century B.C. under the leadership of Pericles (c. 495–429 B.C.), a gifted statesman, orator, and military commander. In the opening stage of the monumental clash with Sparta, the Peloponnesian War (431–404 B.C.), Pericles delivered an oration in honor of the Athenian war casualties. The oration, as reported by Thucydides, the great Athenian historian of the fifth century B.C., contains a glowing description of the Athenian democratic ideal:

> *We are called a democracy, for the administration is in the hands of the many and not of the few. But while the law secures equal justice to all alike in their private disputes, the claim of excellence is also recognized; and when a citizen is any way distinguished, he is [selected for] public service . . . as the reward of merit. Neither is poverty a bar, but a man may benefit his country whatever may be the obscurity of his condition. . . . There is no exclusiveness in our public life, and in our private intercourse we are not suspicious of one another, nor angry with our neighbor if he does what he likes; we do not put on sour looks at him which though harmless are unpleasant. . . . [A] spirit of reverence pervades our public acts; we are prevented from doing wrong by respect for authority and for the laws. . . .*[5]

Athenian democracy undoubtedly had its limitations and weaknesses. Modern critics point out that resident aliens were almost totally barred from citizenship and therefore from political participation. Slaves, who constituted about one-fourth of the Athenian population, enjoyed none of the freedoms that Athenians considered so precious. The Greeks regarded slavery as a necessary precondition for civilized life; for some to be free and prosperous, they believed, others had to be enslaved. Slaves were generally prisoners of war or captives of pirates. In Athens, some slaves were Greeks, but most were foreigners. Slaves usually did the same work as Athenian citizens: farming, commerce, manufacturing, and domestic chores. However, those slaves, including preadolescent children, who toiled in the mines suffered a grim fate.

Athenian women were another group denied legal or political rights. Most Greeks, no doubt, agreed with Aristotle, who said: "The male is by nature superior, and the female inferior, and . . . the one rules and the other is ruled."[6] A girl usually was married at fourteen to a man twice her age, and the marriage was arranged by a male relative. The wedding day might be the first time that the young bride saw her future husband. Although either spouse could obtain a divorce, the children remained with the father after the marriage was dissolved. Wives did not dine with their husbands and spent much of their time in the women's quarters.

Athenian women were barred from holding public office and generally could not appear in court without a male representative. They could not act in plays, and when they attended the theater they sat in the rear, away from the men. Greek women received no formal education, although some young women learned to read and write at home. Training in household skills was considered the only education a woman needed. Since it was believed that a woman could not act independently, she was required to have a guardian—normally her father or her husband—who controlled her property and supervised her behavior. Convinced that financial dealings were too difficult for women and that they needed to be protected from strangers, men, not women, did the marketing. When a woman left the house, she was usually accompanied by a male. The Athenian wife was treated as a minor; in effect, she was her husband's ward.

The flaws in Athenian democracy should not cause us to undervalue its extraordinary achievement. The idea that the state represents a community of free, self-governing citizens remains a crucial principle of Western civilization. Athenian democracy embodied the principle of the legal state—a government based not on force but on laws debated, devised, altered, and obeyed by free citizens.

This idea of the legal state could have arisen only in a society that was aware of and respected the rational mind. Just as the Greeks demythicized nature, so too they removed myth from the sphere of politics. Holding that government was something that people create to satisfy human needs, the Athenians regarded their leaders neither as gods nor as priests, but as men who had demonstrated a capacity for statesmanship.

Both democratic politics and systematic political thought originated in Greece. There, people first asked questions about the nature and purpose of the state, rationally analyzed political institutions, speculated about human nature and justice, and discussed the merits of various forms of government. It is to Greece that we ultimately trace the idea of democracy and all that accompanies it: citizenship, constitutions, equality before the law, government by law, reasoned debate, respect for the individual, and confidence in human intelligence.

The Decline of the City-States

Although the Greeks shared a common language and culture, they remained divided politically. A determination to preserve city-state sovereignty prevented the Greeks from forming a larger political grouping that might have prevented the intercity warfare that ultimately cost the city-state its vitality and independence. But the creation of a Pan-Hellenic union would have required a radical transformation of the Greek character, which for hundreds of years had regarded the independent city-state as the only suitable political system.

The Peloponnesian War

Athenian control of the Delian League frightened the Spartans and their allies in the Peloponnesian League. Sparta and the Peloponnesian states decided on war because they saw a dynamic and imperialistic Athens as a threat to their independence. At stake for Athens was control over the Delian League, which gave Athens political power and contributed to its economic prosperity. Neither Athens nor Sparta anticipated the catastrophic consequences that the war would have for Greek civilization.

The war began in 431 B.C. and ended in 404 B.C. When a besieged Athens, with a decimated navy and a dwindling food supply, surrendered, Sparta dissolved the Delian League, left Athens with only a handful of ships, and forced the city to pull down its long walls—ramparts designed to protect it against siege weapons.

The Peloponnesian War shattered the spiritual foundations of Hellenic society. During its course, men became brutalized; cities were sacked and captives murdered; selfish individualism triumphed over civic duty; moderation gave way to extremism; and in several cities, including Athens, politics degenerated into civil war between oligarchs and democrats. Oligarchs, generally from the wealthier segments of Athenian society, wanted to concentrate power in their own hands by depriving the lower classes of political rights. Democrats, generally from the poorer segment of society, sought to preserve the political rights of all adult male citizens. Strife between oligarchs and democrats was quite common in the Greek city-states even before the Peloponnesian War.

The Fourth Century

The Peloponnesian War was the great crisis of Hellenic history. The golden age of Athenian culture came to an end. The city-states never fully recovered from their self-inflicted spiritual wounds. The civic loyalty and confidence that had marked the fifth century waned, and the fourth century was dominated by a new mentality that the leaders of the Age of Pericles would have abhorred. A concern for private affairs superseded devotion to the general good of the polis. Increasingly, professionals, rather than ordinary citizens, administered the tasks of government, and mercenaries began to replace citizen soldiers.

In the fourth century, the quarrelsome city-states formed new systems of alliances and persisted in their ruinous conflicts. While the Greek cities battered one another in fratricidal warfare, a new power was rising in the north—Macedonia. To the Greeks, the Macedonians, a wild mountain people who spoke a Greek dialect and had acquired a sprinkling of Hellenic culture, differed little from other non-Greeks, whom they called barbarians. In 359 B.C., at the age of twenty-three, Philip II (382–336 B.C.) ascended the Macedonian throne. Converting Macedonia into a first-rate military power, he began a drive to become master of the Greeks.

Incorrectly assessing Philip's strength, the Greeks were slow to organize a coalition against Macedonia. In 338 B.C., Philip's forces decisively defeated the Greeks at Chaeronea, and all of Greece was his. The city-states still existed, but they had lost their independence. The world of the small, independent, and self-sufficient polis was drawing to a close, and Greek civilization was taking a different shape.

The Dilemma of Greek Politics

Philip's conquest of the city-states points to fundamental weaknesses of Greek politics. Despite internal crisis and persistent warfare, the Greeks were unable to fashion any other political framework than the polis. The city-state was fast becoming an anachronism, but the Greeks were unable to see that, in a world moving toward larger states and empires, the small city-state could not compete. An unallied city-state, with its small citizen army, could not withstand the powerful military machine that Philip had created. A challenge confronted the city-states: the need to shape some form of political union, a Pan-Hellenic federation, that would end the suicidal internecine warfare, promote economic well-being, and protect the Greek world from hostile states. Because they could not respond creatively to this challenge, the city-states ultimately lost their independence to foreign conquerors.

The waning of civic responsibility among the citizens was another reason for the decline of the city-states. The vitality of the city-state depended on the willingness of its citizens to put aside private concerns for the good of the community. However, although Athens had recovered commercially from the Peloponnesian War, its citizens had suffered a permanent change in character; the abiding devotion to the polis, which had distinguished the Age of Pericles, greatly diminished during the fourth century. The factional strife, the degeneration of politics into personal ambition, the demagoguery, and the fanaticism that Thucydides (see "History" later in the chapter) had described persisted into the fourth century and were aggravated by the economic discontent of the poor. The Periclean ideal of citizenship dissipated as Athenians neglected the community to concentrate on private affairs or sought to derive personal profit from public office. The decline in civic responsibility could be seen in the hiring of mercenaries to replace citizen soldiers and in the indifference and hesitancy with which the Athenians confronted Philip. The Greeks did not respond to the Macedonian threat as they had earlier rallied to fight off the Persian menace because the quality of citizenship had deteriorated.

Greek political life demonstrated the best and worst features of freedom. On the one hand, as Pericles boasted, freedom encouraged active citizenship, reasoned debate, and government by law. On the other, as Thucydides lamented, freedom could degenerate into factionalism, demagoguery, unbridled self-interest, and civil war. Because monarchy deprives people of freedom and self-rule, the Greeks regarded monarchy as a form of government appropriate for uncivilized barbarians. But their political experience showed that free men in a democracy are susceptible to demagogues, will base political decisions on keyed-up emotions rather than on cool reasoning, and are capable of behaving brutally toward political opponents. Moreover, Greek democracy, which valued freedom, was unable to overcome a weakness that afflicts despotic rulers: an incautious attitude toward power that causes the state to overreach itself. Such an attitude demonstrated the self-destructive hubris that Greek moralists warned against. This is how Thucydides interpreted Athens' disastrous Sicilian expedition during the Peloponnesian War. Driven by a mad passion to possess what was beyond their reach, the Athenians brought ruin to their city.

The Athenians, who saw no conflict between imperialism and democracy, considered it natural for stronger states to dominate weaker ones, an attitude that helped to precipitate the destructive Peloponnesian War. A particularly egregious example of this outlook occurred during that war when Athenians decided to invade the island of Melos despite the assurances of the Melians that they represented no threat to Athens. As reported by Thucydides, the Athenian envoys told the Melians that "the strong do what they have the power to do, and the weak accept what they have to accept."[7] When the Melians resisted, the Athenians slaughtered the men, enslaved the women and children, and colonized the territory.

Greek politics also revealed both the capabilities and the limitations of reason. Originally, the polis was conceived as a divine institution, in which the citizen had a religious obligation to obey the law. As the rational and secular outlook became more pervasive, the gods lost their authority. When people no longer regarded law as an expression of sacred traditions ordained by the gods but saw it as a merely human contrivance, respect for the law diminished, weakening the foundations of the society. The results were party conflicts, politicians who scrambled for personal power, and moral uncertainty. Recognizing the danger, conservatives insisted that law must again be conceived as issuing from the gods and the city must again treat its ancient traditions with reverence. Although the Greeks originated the lofty ideal that human beings could regulate their political life according to reason, their history, marred by intercity warfare and internal violence, demonstrates the extreme difficulties involved in creating and maintaining a rational society.

Philosophy in the Hellenic Age

The Greeks broke with the mythopoeic outlook of the Near East and conceived a new way of viewing nature and human society that is the basis of the Western scientific and philosophical tradition. By the fifth century B.C., the Greeks had emancipated thought from myth and gradually applied reason to the physical world and to all human activities. This emphasis on reason marks a turning point for human civilization.

The development of rational thought in Greece was a process, a trend, not a finished achievement. The process began when some thinkers rejected mythical explanations for natural phenomena. The nonphilosophical majority of the people never entirely eliminated the language, attitudes, and beliefs of myth from their life and thought. For them, the world remained controlled by divine forces, which were appeased through cultic practices. Even in the mature philosophy of Plato and Aristotle, mythical modes of thought persisted. What is of immense historical importance, however, is not the degree to which the Greeks successfully integrated the norm of reason, but the fact that they originated this norm, defined it, and consciously applied it to intellectual concerns and social and political life.

The first theoretical philosophers in human history emerged in the sixth century B.C. in the Greek cities of Ionia in Asia Minor. Curious about the essential composition of nature and dissatisfied with earlier creation legends, the Ionians sought physical, rather than mythic-religious, explanations for natural occurrences. In the process, they arrived at a new concept of nature and a new method of inquiry. They maintained that nature was not manipulated by arbitrary and willful gods, nor was it governed by blind chance. The Ionians said that there is an intelligible pattern to nature; that nature contains a hidden structure—principles of order or general laws—that govern phenomena; and that these fundamental rules were ascertainable by the human mind. They implied that the origin, composition, and structure of the world can be investigated rationally and systematically. Thus, in seeking to account for rainbows, earthquakes, and eclipses, the Ionians posited entirely naturalistic explanations that relied on observation, showed an awareness of cause and effect, and excluded the gods. This new outlook marks the beginning of scientific thought.

What conditions enabled the Greeks to make this breakthrough? Perhaps their familiarity with Near Eastern achievements in mathematics and science stimulated their ideas. But this influence should not be exaggerated, says Greek scholar John N. Theodorakopoulos, for Egyptians and Mesopotamians "had only mythological systems of belief and a knowledge of practical matters. They did not possess those pure and crystal-clear products of the intellect which we call science and philosophy. Nor did they have any terminology to describe them."[8] Rooted in mythological thinking, the ancient Near East experienced no eruption of theorizing about nature in pristine philosophical and scientific terms as Greece did beginning in the sixth century B.C.

One can only speculate about why the Greeks achieved this breakthrough. Perhaps the poets' conception of human behavior as subject to universal destiny was extended into the philosophers' belief that nature was governed by law. Perhaps the breakthrough was fostered by the Greeks' freedom from a priesthood and rigid religious doctrines that limited thought. Or perhaps Greek speculative thought was an offspring of the city, because if law governed human affairs, providing balance and order, should not the universe also be regulated by principles of order?

The Cosmologists: A Rational Inquiry into Nature

The first Ionian philosophers are called cosmologists because they sought to discover the underlying principles of the universe: how nature came to be the way it was. They held that some single, eternal, and imperishable substance, which underwent various modifications, gave rise to all phenomena in nature.

Ionian philosophy began with Thales (c. 624–548 B.C.) of Miletus, a city in Ionia. He was a contemporary of Solon of Athens. Concerned with understanding the order of nature, Thales said that water was the basic element, the underlying substratum of nature, and that through some natural process—similar to the formation of ice or steam—water gave rise to everything else in the world.

Thales revolutionized thought because he omitted the gods from his account of the origins of nature and searched for a natural explanation of how all things came to be. Thales also broke with the commonly held belief that earthquakes were caused by Poseidon, god of the sea, and offered instead a naturalistic explanation for these disturbances: that the earth floated on water, and when the water experienced turbulent waves, the earth was rocked by earthquakes.

Anaximander (c. 611–547 B.C.), another sixth-century Ionian, rejected Thales' theory that water was the original substance. He rejected any specific substance and suggested that an indefinite substance, which he called the Boundless, was the source of all things. He believed that from this primary mass, which contained the powers of heat and cold, there gradually emerged a nucleus, the seed of the world. He said that the cold and wet condensed to form the earth and its cloud cover, while the hot and dry formed the rings of fire that we see as the moon, the sun, and the stars. The heat from the fire in the sky dried the earth and shrank the seas. From the warm slime on earth arose life, and from the first sea creatures there evolved land animals, including human beings. Anaximander's account of the origins of the universe and nature understandably contained fantastic elements. Nevertheless, by offering a natural explanation for the origin of nature and life and by holding that nature was lawful, it surpassed the creation myths.

Like his fellow Ionians, Anaximenes, who died about 525 B.C., made the transition from myth to reason. He maintained that a primary substance, air, underlay reality and accounted for the orderliness of nature. Air that was rarefied became fire, whereas wind and clouds were formed from condensed air. If the process of condensation continued, it produced water, earth, and eventually stones. Anaximenes also rejected the old belief that a rainbow was the goddess Iris; instead, he said that the rainbow was caused by the sun's rays falling on dense air.

The Ionians have been called "matter philosophers" because they held that everything issued from a particular material substance. Other thinkers of the sixth century B.C. tried a different approach. Pythagoras (c. 580–507 B.C.) and his followers, who lived in the Greek cities in southern Italy, did not find the nature of things in a particular substance, but rather in mathematical relationships. The Pythagoreans discovered that the intervals in the musical scale can be expressed mathematically. Extending this principle of proportion found in sound to the universe at large, they concluded that the cosmos also contained an inherent mathematical order and harmony. Thus, the Pythagoreans shifted the emphasis from matter to form, from the world of sense perception to the logic of mathematics. The Pythagoreans were also religious mystics who believed in the immortality and transmigration of souls. Consequently, they refused to eat animal flesh, fearing that it contained former human souls.

Parmenides (c. 515–450 B.C.), a native of the Greek city of Elea in southern Italy, argued that the fundamental view of the Ionians that the universe underwent change and development over time was utterly mistaken. In developing his position, Parmenides applied to philosophical argument the logic used by the Pythagoreans in mathematical thinking. In putting forth the proposition that an argument must be consistent and contain no contradictions, Parmenides became the founder of formal logic. Despite appearances, asserted Parmenides, reality—the cosmos and all that is within it—is one, eternal, and unchanging. It is made known not through the senses, which are misleading, but through the mind; not through experience, but through reason. Truth is reached through abstract thought alone. Parmenides' concept of an unchanging reality apprehended by thought alone influenced Plato and is the foundation of metaphysics.

Democritus (c. 460–370 B.C.), from the Greek mainland, renewed the Ionians' concern with the world of matter and reaffirmed their confidence in knowledge derived from sense perception. But he also retained Parmenides' reverence for reason. His model of the universe consisted of two fundamental realities: empty space and an infinite number of atoms. Eternal, indivisible, and imperceptible, these atoms moved in the void. All things consisted of atoms, and combinations of atoms accounted for all change in nature. In a world of colliding atoms, everything behaved according to mechanical principles.

Concepts essential to scientific thought thus emerged in embryonic form with the early Greek philosophers: natural explanations for physical occurrences (Ionians), the mathematical order of nature (Pythagoras), logical proof (Parmenides), and the mechanical structure of the universe (Democritus). By giving to nature a rational, rather than a mythical, foundation and by holding that theories should be grounded in evidence and that one should be able to defend them logically, the early Greek philosophers pushed thought in a new direction. This new approach made possible theoretical thought and the systematization of knowledge—as distinct from the mere observation and collection of data. It also allowed a critical analysis of theories, whereas myths, accepted unconditionally on faith and authority, did not promote discussion and questioning.

This systematization of knowledge extended into several areas. Greek mathematicians, for example, organized the Egyptians' practical experience with land measurements into the logical and coherent science of geometry. They established mathematics as an ordered system based on fundamental premises and necessary connections, and they developed logical procedures for arriving at mathematical proofs. Both Babylonians and Egyptians had performed fairly complex mathematical operations, but unlike the Greeks, they made no attempt to prove underlying mathematical principles. In another area, Babylonian priests had observed the heavens for religious reasons, believing that the stars revealed the wishes of the gods. The Greeks used the data collected by the Babylonians, but not for a religious purpose; rather, they sought to discover the geometric laws that govern the motions of heavenly bodies.

A parallel development occurred in medicine. No Near Eastern medical text explicitly attacked magical beliefs and practices. In contrast, Greek doctors associated with the medical school of Hippocrates (c. 460–c. 377 B.C.) asserted that diseases have a natural, not a supernatural, cause. The following tract on epilepsy, which was considered a sacred disease, illustrates the development of a scientific approach to medicine:

> *I am about to discuss the disease called "sacred." It is not, in my opinion, any more divine or sacred than any other disease,*

> *but has a natural cause, and its supposed divine origin is due to men's inexperience, and to their wonder at its peculiar character. Now . . . men continue to believe in its divine origin because they are at a loss to understand it. . . . My own view is that those who first attributed a sacred character to this malady were like the magicians, purifiers, charlatans, and quacks of our own day; men who claim great piety and superior knowledge. Being at a loss, and having no treatment which would help, they concealed and sheltered themselves behind superstition, and called this illness sacred, in order that their utter ignorance might not be manifest.*[9]

The Sophists: A Rational Investigation of Human Culture

In their effort to understand the external world, the cosmologists had created the tools of reason. These early Greek thinkers were developing a new and profound awareness of the mind's capacity for theoretical thinking. Equally important, they were establishing the mind's autonomy—its ability to inquire into any subject, relying solely on its own power to think. Greek thinkers then turned away from the world of nature and attempted a rational investigation of people and society, dismissing efforts to explain the social world through inherited beliefs about the gods. The Sophists exemplified this shift in focus. They were professional teachers who wandered from city to city teaching rhetoric, grammar, poetry, gymnastics, mathematics, and music. The Sophists insisted that it was futile to speculate about the first principles of the universe, for such knowledge was beyond the grasp of the human mind. Instead, they urged that individuals improve themselves and their cities by applying reason to the tasks of citizenship and statesmanship. The Western humanist tradition owes much to the Sophists, who examined political and ethical problems, cultivated the minds of their students, and invented formal secular education.

The Sophists answered a practical need in Athens, which had been transformed into a wealthy and dynamic imperial state after the Persian Wars. Because the Sophists claimed that they could teach *political aretē*—the skill to formulate the right laws and policies for cities and the art of eloquence and persuasion—they were sought as tutors by politically ambitious young men, especially in Athens.

The Sophists were philosophical relativists; that is, they held that no truth is universally valid. Protagoras, a fifth-century Sophist, said that "man is the measure of all things." By this he meant that good and evil, truth and falsehood are matters of individual judgment; there are no universal standards that apply to all people at all times. Human laws and ethical beliefs have evolved according to a particular community's needs; they are simply human contrivances and conventions, not objective truths or standards written into nature. While not based on moral absolutes, hopefully the city's laws derive from the judgment of wise and good men.

In applying reason critically to human affairs, the Sophists challenged the traditional religious and moral values of Athenian society. Some Sophists taught that speculation about the divine was useless; others went further and asserted that religion was just a human invention to ensure obedience to traditions and laws.

The Sophists also applied reason to law, with the same effect: the undermining of traditional authority. The laws of a given city, they asserted, did not derive from the gods; nor were they based on any objective, universal, and timeless standards of justice and good, for such standards did not exist. The more radical Sophists argued that law was merely something made by the most powerful citizens for their own benefit. This view had dangerous implications: since law rested on no higher principle than might, it need not be obeyed.

Some Sophists combined this assault on law with an attack on the ancient Athenian idea of *sophrosyne*—moderation and self-discipline—because it denied human instincts. Instead of moderation, they urged that people should maximize pleasure and trample underfoot those traditions that restricted them from fully expressing their desires.

In subjecting traditions to the critique of reason, the radical Sophists provoked an intellectual and spiritual crisis. Their doctrines encouraged disobedience to law, neglect of civic duty, and selfish individualism. These attitudes became widespread during and after the Peloponnesian War, dangerously weakening community bonds. Conservatives

Hirmer Verlag Fotoarchiv, München.

The Parthenon, Athens, 447–432 B.C. A masterpiece of the Doric style, the great temple dedicated to Athena Parthenos (the Maiden), the patron goddess of the city, was constructed through the efforts of Pericles. Its cult statue and the sculptural reliefs under its roofline were designed by the outstanding sculptor of the age, Phidias. In post-Hellenistic times, it served as a Christian church and then as a mosque until it was destroyed in 1687. Between 1801 and 1812, the marble reliefs were removed by the Englishman Lord Elgin and now reside in the British Museum in London.

sought to restore the authority of law and a respect for moral values by renewing allegiance to those sacred traditions undermined by the Sophists.

Socrates: Shaping the Rational Individual

Socrates (c. 469–399 B.C.), one of the most extraordinary figures in the history of Western civilization, took a different approach. He attacked the Sophists' relativism, holding that people should regulate their behavior in accordance with universal values. While he recognized that the Sophists taught skills, he felt that they had no insights into questions that really mattered: What is the purpose of life? What are the values by which man should live? How does man perfect his character? Here the Sophists failed, said Socrates; they taught the ambitious to succeed in politics, but persuasive oratory and clever reasoning do not instruct a man in the art of living. According to

PORCH OF THE MAIDENS, ATTIC SCULPTURE FROM THE ACROPOLIS. The architect has incorporated the human form as a functional element in a rationally organized structure. The balance and harmony of the Porch of the Maidens weds humanity with art.

Socrates, the Sophists had attacked the old system of beliefs but had not provided the individual with a constructive replacement.

Socrates' central concern was the perfection of individual human character, the achievement of moral excellence. For Socrates, moral values did not derive from a transcendent God, as they did for the Hebrews. Individuals attained them by regulating their lives according to objective standards arrived at through rational reflection, that is, by making reason the formative, guiding, and ruling agency of the soul. For Socrates, true education meant the shaping of character according to values discovered through the active and critical use of reason.

Socrates wanted to subject all human beliefs and behavior to the scrutiny of reason and in this way remove ethics from the realm of authority, tradition, dogma, superstition, and myth. He believed that reason was the only proper guide to the most crucial problem of human existence—the question of good and evil.

Dialectics. In urging Athenians to think rationally about the problems of human existence, Socrates offered no systematic ethical theory and no list of ethical precepts. What he did supply was a method of inquiry called *dialectics*, or logical discussion. As Socrates used it, a dialectical exchange between individuals or with oneself, a *dialogue,* was the essential source of knowledge. It forced people out of their apathy and smugness and compelled them to examine their thoughts critically; to confront illogical, inconsistent, dogmatic, and imprecise assertions; and to express their ideas in clearly defined terms.

Dialectics demonstrated that the acquisition of knowledge was a creative act. The human mind could not be coerced into knowing; it was not a passive vessel into which a teacher poured knowledge. The dialogue compelled the individual to play an active role in acquiring the ideals and values by which to live. In a dialogue, individuals became thinking participants in a search for knowledge. Through relentless cross-examination, Socrates induced the persons with whom he spoke to explain and justify their opinions rationally, for only thus did knowledge become a part of one's being.

Dialogue implied that reason was meant to be used in relations between human beings and that they could learn from each other, help each other, teach each other, and improve each other. It implied further that the human mind could and should make rational choices. To deal rationally with oneself and others is the distinctive mark of being human.

Condemned to Death. Socrates devoted much of his life to what he believed was his mission, pricking the conscience of uncritical and smug Athenians and persuading them to think critically about how they lived their lives. Through probing questions, he tried to stir people out of their complacency and make them realize how directionless and purposeless their lives were.

For many years, Socrates challenged Athenians without suffering harm, for Athens was generally distinguished by its freedom of speech and thought. However, in the uncertain times during and immediately after the Peloponnesian War, Socrates made enemies. When he was seventy, he was accused of corrupting the youth of the city and of not believing in the city's gods but in other, new divinities. Underlying these accusations was the fear that Socrates was a troublemaker, a subversive who threatened the state by subjecting its ancient and sacred values to the critique of thought.

Socrates denied the charges and conducted himself with great dignity at his trial, refusing to grovel and beg forgiveness. Instead, he defined his creed:

> *If you think that a man of any worth at all ought to . . . think of anything but whether he is acting justly or unjustly, and as a good or a bad man would act, you are mistaken. . . . If you were therefore to say to me, "Socrates, we will not listen to [your accuser]. We will let you go, but on the condition that you give up this investigation of yours, and philosophy. If you are found following these pursuits again you shall die." I say, if you offered to let me go on these terms, I should reply: . . . As long as I have breath and strength I will not give up philosophy and exhorting you and declaring the truth to every one of you whom I meet, saying, as I am accustomed, "My good friend, you are a citizen of Athens . . . are you not ashamed of caring so much for making of money and for fame and prestige, when you neither think nor care about wisdom and truth and the improvement of your soul?"*[10]

Convicted by an Athenian court, Socrates was ordered to drink poison. Had he attempted to appease the jurors, he probably would have been given a light punishment, but he would not disobey the commands of his conscience and alter his principles even under threat of death.

Socrates did not write down his philosophy and beliefs. We are able to construct a coherent account of his life and ideals largely through the works of his most important disciple, Plato.

Plato: The Rational Society

Plato (c. 429–347 B.C.) used his master's teachings to create a comprehensive system of philosophy that embraced both the world of nature and the social world. Many of the problems discussed by Western philosophers for the past two millennia were first raised by Plato. We focus on two of his principal concerns, the theory of Ideas and the theory of the just state.

Theory of Ideas. Socrates had taught that universal standards of right and justice exist and are arrived at through thought. Building on the insights of his teacher, Plato postulated the existence of a higher world of reality, independent of the world of things that we experience every day. This higher reality, he said, is the realm of Ideas, or Forms—unchanging, eternal, absolute, and universal standards of beauty, goodness, justice, and truth.

Truth resides in this world of Forms and not in the world made known through the senses. For example, a person can never draw a perfect square, but the properties of a perfect square exist in the world of Forms. Similarly, the ordinary person derives an opinion of what beauty is only from observing beautiful things; the philosopher, aspiring to true knowledge, goes beyond what he sees and tries to grasp with his mind the Idea of beauty. The ordinary individual lacks a true conception of justice or goodness; such knowledge is available only to the philosopher, whose mind can leap from worldly particulars to an ideal world beyond space and time.

A champion of reason, Plato aspired to study human life and arrange it according to universally valid standards. In contrast to sophistic relativism, he maintained that objective and eternal standards do exist.

The Just State. In adapting the rational legacy of Greek philosophy to politics, Plato constructed a comprehensive political theory. What the Greeks had achieved in practice—the movement away from mythic and theocratic politics—Plato accomplished on the level of thought: the fashioning of a rational model of the state.

Like Socrates, Plato attempted to resolve the problem caused by the radical Sophists: the undermining of traditional values. Socrates had tried to dispel this spiritual crisis through a moral transformation of the individual based on reason, whereas Plato wanted the entire community to conform to rational principles. Plato said that if human beings are to live an ethical life, they must do so as citizens of a just and rational state. In an unjust state, people cannot achieve Socratic wisdom, for their souls will mirror the state's wickedness.

Plato had experienced the ruinous Peloponnesian War and witnessed Socrates' trial and execution. Disillusioned by the corruption of Athenian morality and democratic politics, he concluded that under the Athenian constitution neither the morality of the individual Athenian nor the good of the state could be enhanced. He became convinced that Athens required moral and political reform founded on Socratic philosophy.

In his great dialogue *The Republic*, Plato devised an ideal state based on standards that would rescue his native Athens from the evils that had befallen it. For Plato, the just state could not be founded on tradition (for inherited attitudes did not derive from rational standards) or on the doctrine of might being right (a principle taught by radical Sophists and practiced by Athenian statesmen). A just state, in his view, had to conform to universally valid principles and aim at the moral improvement of its citizens, not at increasing its power and wealth. Such a state required leaders distinguished by their wisdom and virtue rather than by sophistic cleverness and eloquence.

Fundamental to Plato's political theory as formulated in *The Republic* was his criticism of Athenian democracy. An aristocrat by birth and temperament, Plato believed that it was foolish to expect the common man to think intelligently about foreign policy, economics, or other vital matters of state. Yet the common man was permitted to speak in the Assembly and to vote, and he could also be selected by lot for executive office. A second weakness of democracy for Plato was that leaders were chosen and followed for nonessential reasons, such as persuasive speech, good looks, wealth, and family background.

A third danger of democracy was that it could degenerate into anarchy, said Plato. Intoxicated by liberty, the citizens of a democracy could lose all sense of balance, self-discipline, and respect for law: "The citizens become so sensitive that they resent the slightest application of control as intolerable tyranny, and in their resolve to have no master they end up by disregarding even the law, written or unwritten."[11]

As the democratic city falls into disorder, a fourth weakness of democracy will become evident. A demagogue—often a wealthy, handsome war hero of noble birth with an ability to stir the multitude with words—will be able to gain power by promising to plunder the rich to benefit the poor. Increasingly the tyrant throws off all constraints and uses his authority to satisfy his desire for power and possessions. To retain his hold over the state, the tyrant "begins by stirring up one war after another, in order that the people may feel their need of a leader."[12] Because of these inherent weaknesses of democracy, Plato insisted that Athens would be governed properly only when the wisest people, the philosophers, attained power.

Plato rejected the fundamental principle of Athenian democracy: that the ordinary citizen is capable of participating sensibly in public affairs. People would not entrust the care of a sick person to just anyone, said Plato, nor would they allow a novice to guide a ship during a storm. Yet in a democracy, amateurs were permitted to run the government and to supervise the education of the young; no wonder Athenian society was disintegrating. Plato believed that these duties should be performed only by the best people in the city, the philosophers, who would approach human problems with reason and wisdom derived from knowledge of the world of unchanging and perfect Ideas. He asserted that only these possessors of truth would be competent to rule.

Plato divided people into three groups: those who demonstrated philosophical ability should be rulers; those whose natural bent revealed exceptional courage should be soldiers; and those driven by desire, the great masses, should be producers (tradespeople, artisans, or farmers). In *The Republic*, the philosophers were selected by a rigorous system of education that was open to all children. Those not demonstrating sufficient intelligence or strength of character were to be weeded out to become workers or warriors, depending on their natural aptitudes. After many years of education and practical military and administrative experience, the philosophers were to be entrusted with political power. If they had been properly educated, the philosopher-rulers would not seek personal wealth or personal power; their only concern would be pursuing justice and serving the community. The philosophers were to be absolute rulers. Although the people would have lost their right to participate in political decisions, they would have gained a well-governed state whose leaders, distinguished by their wisdom, integrity, and sense of responsibility, sought only the common good. Only thus, said Plato, could the individual and the community achieve well-being.

Plato wanted to rescue the city-state from disintegration by re-creating the community spirit that had vitalized the polis—and he wanted to recreate it not on the basis of mere tradition but on a higher level, with philosophical knowledge. The social and political institutions of Athens, Plato thought, must be reshaped according to permanent and unalterable ideals of truth and justice, and this could be done only when power and wisdom were joined. He aimed to fashion a just individual and a just state by creating conditions that permitted reason to prevail over the appetites, self-interest, and class and party loyalties.

Aristotle: Synthesis of Greek Thought

Aristotle (384–322 B.C.) stands at the apex of Greek thought because he achieved a creative synthesis of the knowledge and theories of earlier thinkers. The range of Aristotle's interests and intellect is extraordinary. He was the leading expert of his time in every field of knowledge, with the possible exception of mathematics.

Aristotle undertook the monumental task of organizing and systematizing the thought of the Pre-Socratics, Socrates, and Plato. He shared with the natural philosophers a desire to understand the physical universe; he shared with Socrates and Plato the conviction that reason was a person's highest faculty and that the polis was the primary formative institution of Greek life.

Critique of Plato's Theory of Ideas. To the practical and empirically minded Aristotle, the Platonic notion of an independent and separate world of Forms beyond space and time seemed contrary to common sense. To comprehend reality, said Aristotle, one should not escape into another world. For him, Plato's two-world philosophy suffered from too much mystery, mysticism, and poetic fancy; moreover, Plato undervalued the world of facts and objects revealed through sight, hearing, and touch, a world that was important to Aristotle. Like Plato, Aristotle desired to comprehend the essence of things and held that understanding universal principles is the ultimate aim of knowledge. But unlike Plato, he did not turn away from the world of things to obtain such knowledge. Possessing a scientist's curiosity to understand nature, Aristotle respected knowledge obtained through the senses.

For Aristotle, the Forms were not located in a higher world outside and beyond phenomena but existed in things themselves. He said that through human experience with such things as men, horses, and white objects the essence of man, horse, and whiteness can be discovered; through reason, the Form of Man, the Form of Horse, and the Form of Whiteness can be determined. These universals, which apply to all men, all horses, and all white things, were for both Aristotle and Plato the true objects of knowledge. For Plato, these Forms existed independently of particular objects: the Forms for men or horses or whiteness or triangles or temples existed, whether or not representations of these Ideas in the form of material objects were made known to the senses. For Aristotle, however, universal Ideas could not be determined without examination of particular things. Whereas Plato's use of reason tended to stress otherworldliness, Aristotle brought philosophy back to earth.

By holding that certainty in knowledge comes from reason alone and not from the senses, Plato was predisposed toward mathematics and metaphysics—pure thought that transcends the world of change and material objects. By stressing the importance of knowledge acquired through the rational examination of sense experience, Aristotle favored the development of empirical sciences—physics, biology, zoology, botany, and other disciplines based on the observation and investigation of nature and the recording of data.

Ethical Thought. Like Socrates and Plato, Aristotle believed that a knowledge of ethics was possible and that it must be based on reason, for this is what distinguishes human beings from other forms of life. In his *Nicomachean Ethics*, the good life is the examined life; it means making intelligent decisions when confronted with specific problems. People achieve happiness when they exercise the distinctively human trait of reasoning, when they apply their knowledge relevantly to life, and when their behavior is governed by intelligence and not by whim, tradition, or authority.

Aristotle recognized, however, that people are not entirely rational and that the passionate element in the human personality can never be eradicated or ignored. According to Aristotle, surrendering completely to desire meant descending to the level of beasts, but denying the passions and living as an ascetic was a foolish and unreasonable rejection of human nature. Aristotle maintained that people could attain virtue, when they avoided extremes of behavior and rationally chose the way of moderation. "Nothing in excess" is the key to Aristotle's ethics.

Political Thought. Aristotle's *Politics* complements his *Ethics*. To live the good life, he said, a person must do so as a member of a political community. Only the polis would provide people with an opportunity to lead a rational and moral existence, that is, to fulfill their human potential. With this assertion, Aristotle demonstrated a typically Greek attitude. Also in typically Greek fashion, Aristotle held that enhancing the good of the community is nobler and more virtuous than doing good for oneself, however worthy the act.

Like Plato, Aristotle presumed that political life could be rationally understood and intelligently directed. He emphasized the importance of the rule of law. He placed his trust in law rather than in individuals, for individuals are subject to unruly passions. Aristotle recognized that at times laws should be altered, but he recommended great caution; otherwise, people would lose respect for law and legal procedure.

Tyranny and revolution, Aristotle said, can threaten the rule of law and the well-being of the citizen. To prevent revolution, the state must maintain "the spirit of obedience to law. . . . Men should not think it slavery to live according to the rule of the constitution, for it is their salvation."[13]

Aristotle held "that the best political community is formed by citizens of the middle class [that is, those with a moderate amount of property], and that those states are likely to be well-administered in which the middle class is large and stronger if possible than the other classes [the wealthy and the poor]." Both the rich, who excel in "beauty, strength, birth, [and] wealth," and the poor, who are "very weak or very much disgraced," find it "difficult to follow rational principles. Of these two the one sort grow into violence and great criminals, the other into rogues and petty rascals." The rich are unwilling "to submit to authority . . . for when they are boys, by reason of the luxury in which they are brought up, they never learn even at school, the habit of obedience." Consequently, the wealthy "can only rule despotically." On the other hand, the poor "are too degraded to command and must be ruled like slaves."[14] Middle-class citizens are less afflicted by envy than the

ZEUS, C. 460 B.C. This bronze statue was found off the Greek coast in 1926. Although its face is still stylized, the athletic body pulsates with life, capturing the essence of Zeus as the omnipotent ruler of the gods.

poor and are more likely than the rich to view their fellow citizens as equals.

ART

The classical age of Greek art spans the years from the end of the Persian Wars (479 B.C.) to the death of Alexander the Great (323 B.C.). During this period, standards were established that would dominate Western art until the emergence of modern art in the late nineteenth century.

Greek art coincided with Greek achievement in all other areas. Like Greek philosophy and politics, it too applied reason to human experience and made the transition from a mythopoeic-religious worldview to a world perceived as orderly and rational. It gradually transformed the supernatural religious themes with which it was at first preoccupied into secular human themes. Classical art was representational—that is, it strove to imitate reality, to represent the objective world realistically as it appeared to the human eye.

Artists carefully observed nature and human beings and sought to achieve an exact knowledge of human anatomy; they tried to portray accurately the body at rest and in motion. They knew when muscles should be taut or relaxed, one hip lower than the other, the torso and neck slightly twisted—in other words, they succeeded in transforming marble or bronze into a human likeness that seemed alive. Yet although it was realistic and naturalistic, Greek art was also idealistic, aspiring to a finer, more perfect representation of what was seen and depicting the essence and form of a thing more truly than the way it actually appeared. Thus, a Greek statue resembled no specific individual but revealed a flawless human form, without wrinkles, warts, scars, or other imperfections.

In achieving an accurate representation of objects and in holding that there were rules of beauty that the mind could discover, the Greek artist employed an approach consistent with the new scientific outlook. The Greek temple, for example, is an organized unity, obeying nature's laws of equilibrium and harmony; classical sculpture captures the basic laws that govern life in motion.

Greek artists exemplified the humanist spirit that characterized all aspects of Greek culture. They made the human form the focal point of attention, and exalted the nobility, dignity, self-assurance, and beauty of the human being.

Poetry and Drama

Like philosophers and artists, Greek poets and dramatists gave expression to the rise of the individual and the emerging humanist values. One of the earliest and best of the Greek poets was Sappho; she lived around 600 B.C., on the island of Lesbos. Sappho established a school to teach music and singing to well-to-do girls and to prepare them for marriage. With great tenderness, Sappho wrote poems of friendship and love.

Pindar (c. 518–438 B.C.) was another Greek lyric poet. In his poem of praise for a victorious athlete, Pindar expressed the aristocratic view of excellence. Although life is essentially tragic—triumphs are short-lived, misfortunes are many, and ultimately death overtakes all—man must still demonstrate his worth by striving for excellence.

The high point of Greek poetry is drama, an art form that originated in Greece. In portraying the sufferings, weaknesses, and triumphs of individuals, Greek dramatists shifted attention from the gods to human beings. Just as a Greek sculptor shaped a clear visual image of the human form, so a Greek dramatist brought the inner life of human beings, their fears and hopes, into sharp focus and tried to find the deeper meaning of human experience. Thus, both art and drama evidenced the growing self-awareness of the individual.

Drama originated in the religious festivals honoring Dionysus, the god of wine and agricultural fertility. A profound innovation in these sacred performances, which included choral songs and dances, occurred in the last part of the sixth century B.C.: Thespis, the first actor known to history, stepped out of the chorus and engaged it in dialogue. By separating himself from the choral group, Thespis demonstrated a new awareness of the individual.

With only one actor and a chorus, however, the possibilities for dramatic action and human conflicts were limited. Then Aeschylus introduced a second actor in his dramas, and Sophocles a third. Dialogue between individuals thus became possible. The Greek actors wore masks, and by changing them, each actor could play several roles in the same performance. This flexibility allowed the dramatists to depict the clash and interplay of human wills and passions on a greater scale. By the middle of the fifth century B.C., tragedies were performed regularly as civic festivals.

A development parallel to Socratic dialectics—dialogue between thinking individuals—occurred in Greek drama. By setting characters in conflict against each other, dramatists showed individuals as active subjects, responsible for their behavior and decisions.

Like the natural philosophers, Greek dramatists saw an inner logic to the universe; they called this logic Fate or Destiny. Both physical and social worlds obeyed laws. When people were stubborn, narrow-minded, arrogant, or immoderate they were punished. The order in the universe required it, said Sophocles:

> *The man who goes his way*
> *Overbearing in the word and deed,*
> *who fears no justice,*
> *Honors no temples of the gods—*
> *May an evil destiny seize him.*
> *And punish his ill-starred pride.*[15]

In being free to make decisions, the dramatists said, individuals have the potential for greatness, but in choosing wrongly and unintelligently they bring disaster to themselves and others.

Also like philosophy, Greek tragedy entailed rational reflection. Tragic heroes were not passive victims of fate. They were thinking human beings who felt a need to comprehend their position, explain the reasons for their actions, analyze their feelings, and respond to their fate with insight.

The essence of Greek tragedy lies in the tragic heroes' struggle against cosmic forces and insurmountable obstacles, which eventually crush them. But what impressed the Greek audience (and impresses us today) was not the vulnerability or weaknesses of human beings, but their courage and determination in the face of these forces.

The three great Athenian tragedians were Aeschylus (525–456 B.C.), Sophocles (c. 496–406 B.C.), and Euripides (c. 485–406 B.C.). Aeschylus believed that the world was governed by divine justice, which could not be violated with impunity; when individuals evinced *hubris* (overweening pride or arrogance), which led them to overstep the bounds of moderation, they had to be punished.

Sophocles maintained that individuals should shape their character in the way a sculptor shapes a form: according to laws of proportion. In his view, when the principles of harmony were violated by immoderate behavior, a person's character would be thrown off balance and misfortune would strike. In *Antigone*, Sophocles raised a question that is timeless: should individual conscience, which is prompted by a higher law, prevail over the laws of the state when the two are in conflict?

The rationalist spirit of Greek philosophy permeated the tragedies of Euripides. Like the Sophists, Euripides subjected the problems of human life to critical analysis and challenged human conventions. His plays carefully scrutinized the role of the gods, women's conflicts, the horrors of war, the power of passion, and the prevalence of human suffering and weakness. Euripides blended a poet's insight with the psychologist's probing to reveal the tangled world of human passions and souls in torment.

Greek dramatists also wrote comedies. Aristophanes (c. 448–c. 380 B.C.), the greatest of the Greek comic playwrights, lampooned Athenian statesmen and intellectuals and censured government policies. Behind Aristophanes' sharp wit lay a deadly seriousness; he sought an end to the ruinous Peloponnesian War and a reaffirmation of traditional values, which the Sophists had undermined.

History

The Mesopotamians and the Egyptians kept annals that purported to narrate the deeds of gods and their human agents, the priest-kings or god-kings. These chronicles, filled with religious sayings, royal records, and boastful accounts of military campaigns, are devoid of critical analysis and interpretation. The Hebrews valued history, but, believing that God acted in human affairs, they did not remove historical events from the realm of religious-mythical thought. The Greeks initiated a different approach to the study of history. For them, history was not a narrative about the deeds of gods, as it was for the Egyptians and Mesopotamians, or the record of God's wrath or benevolence, as it was for the Hebrews; instead, it dealt with human actions and state policies.

As the gods were eliminated from the nature philosophers' explanations for the origins of things in the natural world, mythical elements were also removed from the writing of history. Greek historians asked themselves questions about the deeds of people, based their answers on available evidence, and wrote in prose, the language of rational thought. They not only narrated events but also examined causes.

Herodotus

Often called the "father of history," Herodotus (c. 484–c. 424 B.C.) wrote a history of the Persian Wars. The central theme of this book, entitled *The Histories*, is the contrast between Near Eastern despotism and Greek freedom and the subsequent clash of these two worldviews in the wars. Though Herodotus found much to praise in the Persian Empire, he was struck by a lack of freedom and by what he considered barbarity. He emphasized that the mentality of the free citizen was foreign to the East, where men were trained to obey the ruler's commands absolutely. Not the rule of law but the whim of despots prevailed in the East.

Another theme evident in Herodotus' work was punishment for hubris. In seeking to become king of both Asia and Europe, Xerxes had acted arrogantly; although he behaved as if he were superhuman, "he too was human, and was sure to be disappointed of his great expectations."[16] Like the Greek tragedians, Herodotus drew universal moral principles from human behavior.

In several ways, Herodotus was a historian rather than a teller of tales. First, he asked questions about the past, instead of merely repeating ancient legends; he tried to discover what had

Primary Source

Euripides: *Medea*

The Greek dramatist Euripides applied a keen critical spirit to the great question of individual life versus the demands of society. His play Medea *focuses on a strong-willed woman whose despair at being cast off by her husband leads her to exact a terrible revenge. But in the following passage, Medea might speak for the deepest feelings of any Greek woman.*

It was everything to me to think well of one man,
And he, my own husband, has turned out wholly vile.
Of all things which are living and can form a judgement
We women are the most unfortunate creatures.
Firstly, with an excess of wealth it is required
For us to buy a husband and take for our bodies
A master; for not to take one is even worse.
And now the question is serious whether we take
A good or bad one; for there is no easy escape.
For a woman, nor can she say no to her marriage.
She arrives among new modes of behaviour and manners,
And needs prophetic power, unless she has learnt at home,
How best to manage him who shares the bed with her.
And if we work out all this well and carefully,
And the husband lives with us and lightly bears his yoke,
Then life is enviable. If not, I'd rather die.
A man, when he's tired of the company in his home,
Goes out of the house and puts an end to his boredom
And turns to a friend or companion of his own age.
But we are forced to keep our eyes on one alone.
What they say of us is that we have a peaceful time
Living at home, while they do the fighting in war:
How wrong they are! I would very much rather stand
Three times in the front of battle than bear one child.

Question for Analysis

1. According to this passage, what were the difficulties Greek women faced?

Euripedes, *Medea,* trans. Rex Warner (London: The Bodley Head, 1944), 18.

happened and the motivations behind the actions. Second, he demonstrated at times a cautious and critical attitude toward his sources of information. Third, although the gods appeared in his narrative, they played a far less important role than they did in Greek popular mythology. Nevertheless, by retaining a belief in the significance of dreams, omens, and oracles and by allowing divine intervention, Herodotus fell short of being a thoroughgoing rationalist. His writings contain the embryo of rational history. Thucydides brought it to maturity.

Thucydides

Thucydides (c. 460–c. 400 B.C.) also concentrated on a great political crisis confronting the Hellenic world: the Peloponnesian War. Living in Periclean Athens, whose lifeblood was politics, Thucydides regarded the motives of statesmen and the acts of government as the essence of history. He did not just catalogue facts but sought those general concepts and principles that the facts illustrated. His history was the work of an intelligent mind trying to make sense of his times.

Thucydides applied to the sphere of political history a rationalist empiricism. He strove for factual accuracy and drew conclusions based on a critical analysis of events and motives. He searched for the truth underlying historical events and attempted to present it objectively. Thucydides maintained that a proper analysis of the events of the Peloponnesian War would reveal general principles that govern human behavior and relations between states. He intended his history to be a source of enlightenment for future ages, a possession for all time, because the kinds of behavior that caused the conflict between Sparta and Athens would recur regularly through history, for human nature is unchanging and predictable.

In Thucydides' history, there was no place for myths, for legends, for the fabulous—all hindrances to historical truth. He recognized that a work of history was a creation of the rational mind and not an expression of the poetic imagination. The historian seeks to learn and to enlighten, not to entertain.

Rejecting the notion that the gods interfere in history, Thucydides looked for the social forces and human decisions behind events. Where Herodotus occasionally lapsed into supernatural explanations, Thucydides wrote history in which the gods were absent, and he denied their intervention in human affairs. For Thucydides, history was the work of human beings, and the driving force in history was men's will to power and domination.

In addition to being a historian, Thucydides was also an astute and innovative political thinker with a specific view of government, statesmen, and international relations. He warned against the dangers of extremism unleashed by the strains of war, and he believed that when reason was forsaken, the state's plight would worsen. He had contempt for statesmen who waged war lightly, acting from impulse, reckless daring, and an insatiable appetite for territory. Although Thucydides admired Athens for its democratic institutions, rule of law, sense of civic duty, and cultural achievements, he recognized an inherent danger in democracy: the emergence of demagogues who rise to power by stirring up the populace and abuse their power once in office.

Political scientists, historians, and statesmen still turn to Thucydides for insights into the realities of power politics, the dangers of political fanaticism, the nature of imperialism, the methods of demagogues, and the effects of war on democratic politics.

The Hellenistic Age: The Second Stage of Greek Civilization

Greek civilization, or Hellenism, passed through three distinct stages: the Hellenic Age, the Hellenistic Age, and the Greco-Roman Age. The Hellenic Age began around 800 B.C. with the early city-states, reached its height in the fifth century B.C., and endured until the death of Alexander the Great in 323 B.C. At that time, the ancient world entered the Hellenistic Age, which ended in 30 B.C. when Egypt, the last major Hellenistic state, fell to Rome. The Greco-Roman Age lasted five hundred years, encompassing the period of the Roman Empire up to the collapse of the Empire's western half in the last part of the fifth century A.D.

Although the Hellenistic Age absorbed the heritage of classical (Hellenic) Greece, its style of civilization changed. During the first phase of Hellenism, the polis was the center of political life. The polis gave Greeks an identity, and only within the polis could a Greek live a good and civilized life. With the coming of the Hellenistic Age, this situation changed. Kingdoms and empires eclipsed the city-state in power and importance. Even though cities retained a large measure of autonomy in domestic affairs, they lost their freedom of action in foreign affairs because they were now dominated by monarchs. Monarchy, the essential form of government in the Hellenistic world, had not been admired by the Greeks of the Hellenic Age. They had agreed with Aristotle that monarchy was suitable only for non-Greeks, who lacked the capacity to govern themselves.

Now, however, as a result of Alexander the Great's conquests of the lands between Greece and India, tens of thousands of Greek soldiers, merchants, and administrators settled in eastern lands. Their encounters with the different peoples and cultures of the Near East widened the Greeks' horizon and weakened their ties to their native cities. Because of these changes, the individual had to define a relationship not to the narrow, parochial society

Alinari/Art Resource, N.Y.

Alexander the Great on Horseback. In conquering the lands from Greece to India, Alexander the Great displayed a military genius that would fascinate commanders from Caesar to Napoleon.

of the polis but to the larger world. The Greeks had to examine their place in a world more complex, foreign, and threatening than the polis. They had to fashion a conception of a community that would be more comprehensive than the city-state.

Hellenistic philosophers struggled with these problems of alienation and community. They sought to give people the inner strength to endure in a world where the polis no longer provided security. In this new situation, philosophers no longer assumed that the good life was tied to the affairs of the city. Freedom from emotional stress—not active citizenship and social responsibility—was the avenue to the good life. This pronounced tendency of people to withdraw into themselves and seek release from anxiety and depression helped shape a cultural environment that contributed to the spread and triumph of Christianity in the Greco-Roman Age.

In the Hellenic Age, Greek philosophers had a limited conception of humanity, dividing the world into Greek and barbarian. In the Hellenistic Age, the intermingling of Greeks and peoples of the Near East—the fusion of different ethnic groups and cultures scattered over great distances—caused a shift in focus from the city to the *oikoumene* (the inhabited world); parochialism gave way to cosmopolitanism and universalism as people began to think of themselves as members of a world community. Philosophers came to regard the civilized world as one city, the city of humanity. This new concept was their response to the decline of the city-state and the quest for an alternative form of community.

Alexander the Great

After the assassination of Philip of Macedon in 336 B.C., his twenty-year-old son, Alexander, succeeded to the throne. Alexander inherited a proud and fiery temperament from his mother. From his tutor Aristotle, Alexander gained an appreciation for Greek culture, particularly the Homeric epics. Undoubtedly, the young Alexander was stirred by these stories of legendary heroes, especially Achilles, and their striving for personal glory. He also acquired military skills and qualities of leadership from his father.

Alexander inherited from Philip an overriding policy of state: the invasion of Persia. With an army of thirty-five thousand men, Macedonians and Greeks combined, he crossed into Asia Minor in 334 B.C. and eventually advanced all the way to India. In these campaigns, Alexander proved himself to be a superb strategist and leader of men. Winning every battle, his army carved an empire that stretched from Greece to India.

The world after Alexander differed sharply from the one that existed before he took up the sword. Alexander's conquests brought West and East closer together, marking a new epoch. Alexander himself helped to implement this transformation, whether intentionally or unwittingly. He took a Persian bride, arranged for eighty of his officers and ten thousand of his soldiers to marry Near Eastern women, and planned to incorporate thirty thousand Persian youths into his army. Alexander founded Greek-style cities in Asia, where Greek settlers mixed with the native population.

As Greeks acquired greater knowledge of the Near East, the parochialism of the polis gave way to a world outlook. As trade and travel between West and East expanded, as Greek merchants and soldiers settled in Asiatic lands, and as Greek culture spread to non-Greeks, the distinctions between barbarian and Greek lessened. Although Alexander never united all the peoples in a world-state, his career pushed the world in a new direction, toward a fusion of disparate peoples and the intermingling of cultural traditions.

The Competing Dynasties

In 323 B.C., Alexander, not yet thirty-three years old, died after a sickness that followed a drinking party. After his premature death, his generals engaged in a long and bitter struggle to see who would succeed the conqueror. Since none of the generals or their heirs had enough power to hold together Alexander's vast empire, the wars of succession ended in a stalemate. By 275 B.C., the empire was fractured into three dynasties: the Ptolemies in Egypt, the Seleucids in Asia, and the Antigonids in Macedonia. Macedonia, Alexander's native country, continued to dominate the Greek cities, which periodically tried to break its hold. Later, the kingdom of Pergamum in western Asia Minor emerged as the fourth Hellenistic monarchy.

Rome, a new power, became increasingly drawn into the affairs of the quarrelsome Hellenistic kingdoms. By the middle of the second century B.C., it had imposed its will upon them. From that time on, the political fortunes of the western and eastern Mediterranean were inextricably linked.

Cosmopolitanism

Hellenistic society was characterized by a growing cosmopolitanism—a mingling of peoples and an interchange of cultures. Greek traditions spread to the Near East, and Mesopotamian, Egyptian, Hebrew, and Persian traditions—particularly religious beliefs—moved westward. A growing cosmopolitanism replaced the parochialism of the city-state. Although the rulers of the Hellenistic kingdoms were Macedonians and their high officials and generals were Greeks, the style of government was modeled after that of the ancient oriental kingdoms. In the Hellenic Age, the law had expressed the will of the community, but in this new age of monarchy the kings were the law. To promote loyalty, the Macedonian rulers encouraged the oriental cultic practice of worshiping the king as a god or as a

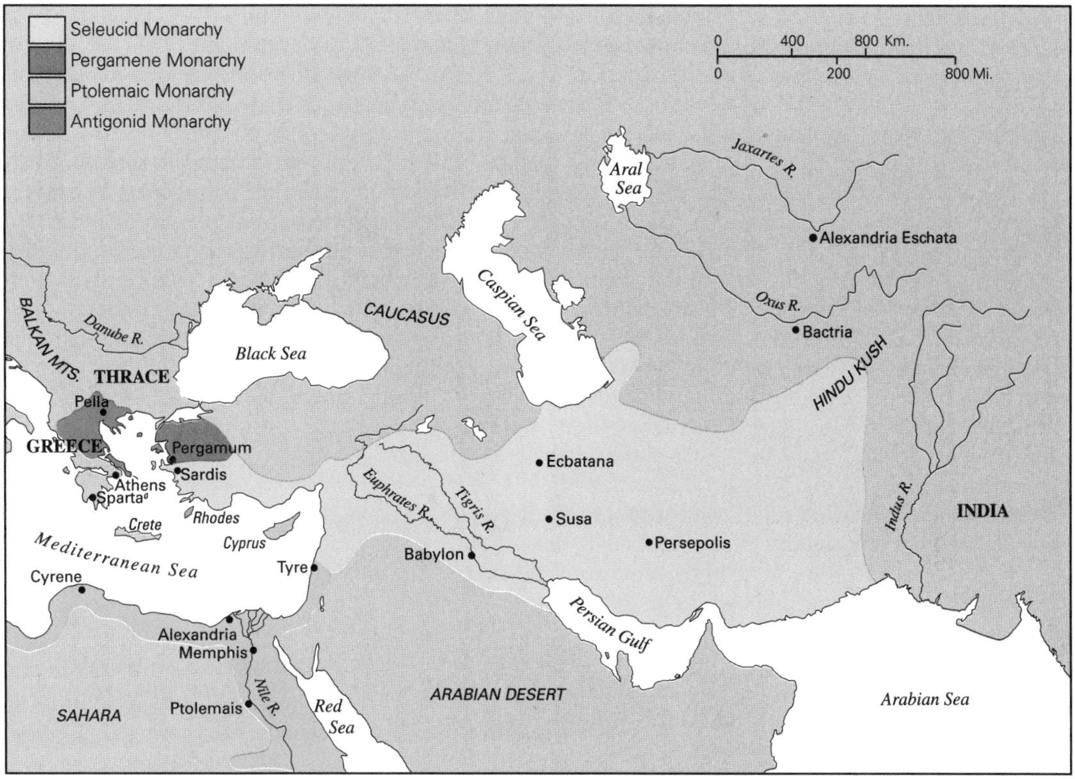

Map 3.2 The Division of Alexander's Empire and the Spread of Hellenism None of Alexander's generals could hold together the vast empire, which fractured into competing dynasties.

representative of the gods. In Egypt, for example, the priests conferred on the Macedonian king the same divine powers and titles traditionally held by Egyptian pharaohs; in accordance with ancient tradition, statues of the divine king were installed in Egyptian temples, suffusing political power with supernatural authority, in marked contrast to the democratic spirit of the Greek Assembly.

Following Alexander's lead, the Seleucids founded cities in the East patterned after the city-states of Greece. The cities, which were often founded to protect trade routes and as fortresses against hostile tribes, adopted the political institutions of Hellenic Greece, including a popular assembly and a council. Hellenistic kings generally did not intervene in the cities' local affairs. Thousands of Greeks settled in these cities, which were Greek in architecture and contained Greek schools, temples, theaters (where performances of classical plays were staged), and gymnasia. Gymnasia were essentially places to exercise, train in sports, and converse, but some had libraries and halls where public lectures and competitions of orators and poets were held. Hellenistic kings brought books, paintings, and statues from Greece to their cities. Hellenistic cities, inhabited by tens of thousands of people from many lands and dominated by a Hellenized upper class, served as centers and agents of Hellenism, which non-Greeks adopted. The cities in Egypt and Syria saw the emergence of a native elite who spoke Greek, wore Greek-style clothing, and adopted Greek customs. *Koine* (or shared language), a form of spoken Greek spread by soldiers, administrators, merchants, teachers, and others, became a common tongue throughout much of the Mediterranean world.

The greatest city of the time and the one most representative of the Hellenistic Age was Alexandria in Egypt, founded by Alexander the Great. Strategically located at one of the mouths of the Nile, Alexandria became a center of commerce and culture. The most populous city of the Mediterranean world, Alexandria at the beginning of the Christian era contained perhaps a million people: Egyptians, Persians, Macedonians, Greeks, Jews, Syrians, and Arabs. The city was an unrivaled commercial center; goods from the Mediterranean world, East Africa, Arabia, and India circulated in its market-places. This cosmopolitan center also attracted poets, philosophers, physicians, astronomers, and mathematicians.

All phases of cultural life were permeated by cultural exchange. Sculpture showed the influence of many lands. Historians wrote world histories, not just local ones. Greek astronomers worked with data collected over the centuries by the Babylonians. The Hebrew Scriptures were translated into Greek for use by Greek-speaking Jews, and some Jewish thinkers, admiring Greek learning, expressed Jewish religious ideas in philosophical terms: God was identified with reason and Moses' Law with the rational order of the universe. Greeks increasingly demonstrated a fascination with oriental religious cults. Philosophers helped to break down the barriers between peoples by asserting that all inhabit a single fatherland.

The spread of Greek civilization from the Aegean to the Indus River gave the Hellenistic world a cultural common denominator, but Hellenization did not transform the East and make it one with the West. Hellenization was limited almost entirely to the cities, and in many urban centers it was often only a thin veneer. Many Egyptians in Alexandria learned Greek, and some assumed Greek names, but for most, Hellenization did not go much deeper. In the countryside, there was not even the veneer of Greek culture. Retaining traditional attitudes, the countryside in the East resisted Greek ways. In the villages, local and traditional law, local languages, and family customs remained unchanged; religion, the most important ingredient of the civilizations of the Near East, also kept its traditional character.

To be sure, Hellenistic society was male dominated, but the status of women did show some improvement over the classical period. Some royal mothers and daughters exercised political power, even if behind the scenes, and royal women had access to great wealth as indicated by their cash contributions to cities. Some nonroyal ladies held important priestly offices, and far more than in the classical era women contributed to high culture as poets, harpists, artists, and architects. Two of the new schools of philosophy, Epicureanism and Cynicism, welcomed female participation.

Hellenistic Thought and Culture

Hellenistic culture rested on a Hellenic foundation, but it also revealed new trends: a heightened universalism and a growing individualism.

History, Art, Science

The leading historian of the Hellenistic Age was Polybius (c. 200–118 B.C.), whose history of the rise of Rome is one of the great works of historical literature. Reflecting the universal tendencies of the Hellenistic Age, Polybius endeavored to explain how Rome had progressed from a city-state to a world conqueror. As a disciple of Thucydides, Polybius sought rational explanations for human events. Like Thucydides, he relied on eyewitness accounts (including his own personal experiences), checked sources, and strove for objectivity.

Hellenistic art, like Hellenistic philosophy, expressed a heightened awareness of the individual. Whereas Hellenic sculpture aimed to depict ideal beauty—the perfect body and face—Hellenistic sculpture, moving from idealism to realism, captured individual character and expression, often of ordinary people. Scenes of daily life were realistically depicted.

During the Hellenistic Age, Greek scientific achievement reached its height. When Alexander invaded Asia Minor, the former student of Aristotle brought along surveyors, engineers, scientists, and historians, who continued with him into Asia. The vast amount of data on botany, zoology, geography, and astronomy collected by Alexander's staff stimulated an outburst of activity. Hellenistic science, says historian Benjamin Farrington, stood "on the threshold of the modern world. When modern science began in the sixteenth century, it took up where the Greeks left off."[17]

Because of its state-supported museum, Alexandria attracted leading scholars and superseded Athens in scientific investigation. The museum contained a library of more than half a million volumes, as well as botanical gardens and an observatory. It was really a research institute, in which some of the best minds of the day studied and worked.

Alexandrian doctors advanced medical skills. They improved surgical instruments and techniques and, by dissecting bodies, added to anatomical knowledge. Through their research, they discovered organs of the body not known until then, made the distinction between arteries and veins, divided nerves into those constituting the motor and the sensory systems, and identified the brain as the source of intelligence. Their investigations brought knowledge of anatomy and physiology to a level that was not significantly improved until the sixteenth century A.D.

Knowledge in the fields of astronomy and mathematics also increased. Eighteen centuries before Copernicus, the Alexandrian astronomer Aristarchus (310–230 B.C.) said that the sun was the center of the universe, that the planets revolved around it, and that the stars were situated at great distances from the earth. But these revolutionary ideas were not accepted, and the belief in an earth-centered universe persisted. In geometry, Euclid, an Alexandrian mathematician who lived around 300 B.C., creatively synthesized earlier developments. Euclid's hundreds of geometric proofs, derived from reasoning alone—his conclusions flowed logically and flawlessly from given assumptions—are a profound witness to the power of the rational mind.

Eratosthenes (c. 275–194 B.C.), an Alexandrian geographer, sought a scientific understanding of the enlarged world. He divided the planet into climatic zones, declared that the oceans are joined, and, with extraordinary ingenuity and accuracy, measured the earth's circumference. Archimedes of Syracuse (287–212 B.C.), who studied at Alexandria, was a mathematician, a physicist, and an ingenious inventor. His mechanical inventions, including war engines, dazzled his contemporaries. However, in typically Greek fashion, Archimedes

Old Market Woman, c. Second Century B.C. Hellenistic genre sculpture depicted people in everyday situations as individuals, rather than as types. This woman's stooped shoulders, weighed down by groceries, also suggest the harsh physical conditions that have worn her down over the years.

dismissed his practical inventions, preferring to be remembered as a theoretician.

Philosophy

Hellenistic thinkers preserved the rational tradition of Greek philosophy, but they also transformed it, for they had to adapt their thought to the requirements of a cosmopolitan society. In the Hellenic Age, the starting point of philosophy was the citizen's relationship to the city; in the Hellenistic Age, the point of departure was the solitary individual's relationship to humanity and the individual's destiny in a complex world. Philosophy tried to deal with the feeling of alienation—of not belonging—resulting from the weakening of the individual's attachment to the polis and sought a conception of community that corresponded to the social realities of a world grown larger. It aspired to make people ethically independent so that they could achieve happiness in a hostile and competitive world. As the philosopher Epicurus said: "Empty are the words of that philosopher who offers no therapy for human suffering. For just as there is no use in medical expertise if it does not give therapy for bodily disease, so too there is no use in philosophy if it does not expel the suffering of the soul."[18] To "expel the suffering of the soul"—to conquer fear and anxiety and to achieve happiness—said Hellenistic philosophers, people must not allow themselves to be troubled by cares and concerns that are ultimately trivial. In striving for tranquillity of mind and relief from conflict, Hellenistic thinkers reflected the general anxiety that pervaded their society.

Epicureanism. Two principal schools of philosophy arose in the Hellenistic world: Epicureanism and Stoicism. In the tradition of Plato and Aristotle, Epicurus (342–270 B.C.) founded a school in Athens at the end of the fourth century B.C. Epicurus broke with the attitude of the Hellenic Age in significant ways. Unlike classical Greek philosophers, Epicurus, reflecting the Greeks' changing relationship to the city, taught the value of passivity and withdrawal from civic life. To him, citizenship was not a prerequisite for individual happiness. Wise persons, said Epicurus, would refrain from engaging in public affairs, for politics is marred by clashing factions and treachery that could deprive them of their self-sufficiency, their freedom to choose and to act. Nor would wise individuals pursue wealth, power, or fame, as the pursuit would only provoke anxiety. For the same reason, wise persons would not surrender to hate or love, desires that distress the soul. They would also try to live justly, because those who behave unjustly are burdened with troubles. Nor could people find happiness if they worried about dying or pleasing the gods.

To Epicurus, dread that the gods punished people in this life and could inflict suffering after death was the principal cause of anxiety. To remove this source of human anguish, he favored a theory of nature that had no place for supernatural intervention in nature or in people's lives. Therefore, he adopted the physics of Democritus, which taught that all things consist of atoms in motion. In a universe of colliding atoms, there could be no higher intelligence ordering things; there was no room for divine activity. Epicurus taught that the gods probably did exist, but that they did not influence human affairs; consequently, individuals could order their own lives.

People could achieve happiness, said Epicurus, when their bodies were "free from pain" and their minds "released from worry and fear." Although Epicurus wanted to increase pleasure for the individual, he rejected unbridled hedonism. Because he believed that happiness must be pursued rationally, he urged avoidance of the merely sensuous pleasures that have unpleasant aftereffects (such as overeating and excessive drinking). In general, Epicurus espoused the traditional Greek view of moderation and prudence. By opening his philosophy to men and women, slave and free, Greek and barbarian, and by separating ethics from politics, Epicurus fashioned a philosophy adapted to the post-Alexandrian world of kingdoms and universal culture.

Stoicism. Around the time when Epicurus founded his school, Zeno (335–263 B.C.) also opened a school in Athens. Zeno's teachings, called Stoicism (because his school was located in the *stoa*, or colonnade), became the most important philosophy in the Hellenistic world. By teaching that the world constituted a single society, Stoicism gave theoretical expression to the world-mindedness of the age. Through its concept of a

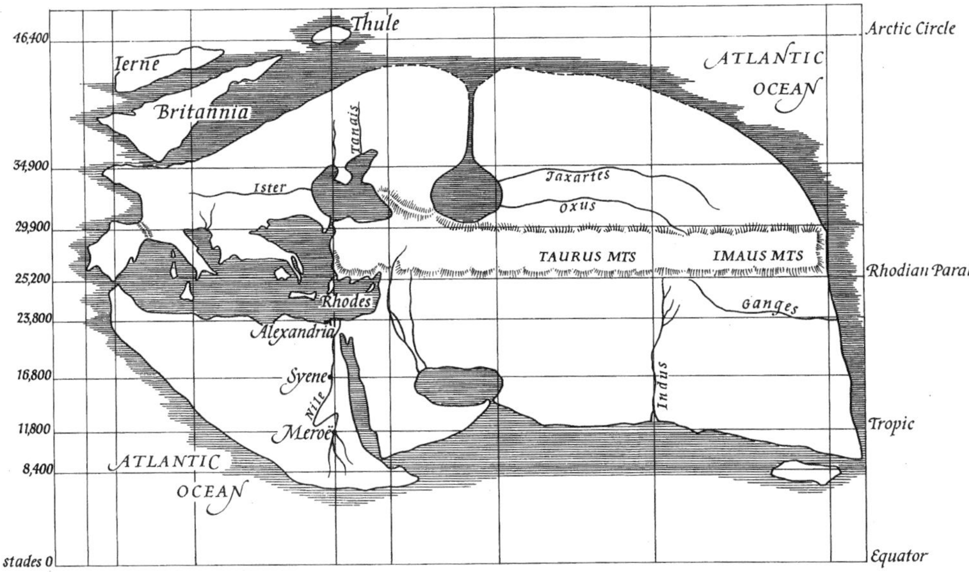

RECONSTRUCTION OF THE MAP OF THE WORLD BY ERATOSTHENES (C. 275–194 B.C.). Geographical knowledge expanded enormously among the Hellenistic Greeks. The first systematic scientific books on geography were credited to Eratosthenes, head of the Alexandrian library, the greatest scientific and humanistic research center in the Hellenistic world. Eratosthenes estimated the circumference of the earth with remarkable accuracy for his time. His map illustrates the limits of the world known to the Greeks. (from John Onians, Art and Thought in the Hellenistic Age [Thames and Hudson, 1979]. Reprinted by permission of Thames and Hudson Ltd.)

world community, the city of humanity, Stoicism offered an answer to the problem of community and alienation posed by the decline of the city-state. By stressing inner strength in dealing with life's misfortunes, it opened an avenue to individual happiness in a world fraught with uncertainty.

At the core of Stoicism was the belief that built into the universe was a principle of order, variously called Divine Reason (Logos), the Divine Fire, God—more an impersonal force than a living being. This ruling principle underlay reality and permeated all things; it ordered the cosmos according to law. The Stoics reasoned that, being part of the universe, people too shared in the Logos that operated throughout the cosmos. Inherent in every human soul, and discovered through reason, the Logos enabled people to act virtuously and intelligently and to comprehend the principles of order that governed nature. This natural law provided human beings with an awareness of what is and is not correct behavior, especially when dealing with other human beings. The virtuous person lived in accordance with natural law, which was the avenue to both virtue and happiness. Natural law alone commanded ultimate obedience. Because reason was common to all, human beings were essentially brothers and fundamentally equal. Reason gave individuals dignity and enabled them to recognize and respect the dignity of others. To the Stoics, all people—Greek and barbarian, free and slave, rich and poor—were fellow human beings, and one law, the law of nature, applied to everyone. What people had in common as fellow human beings far outweighed differences based on culture. Thus the Stoics, like the Hebrews, arrived at the idea of the oneness of humanity.

Like Socrates, the Stoics believed that a person's distinctive quality was the ability to reason and that happiness came from the disciplining of emotions by the rational part of the soul. Also like Socrates, the Stoics maintained that individuals should progress morally and perfect their character. In the Stoic view, wise persons ordered their lives according to the natural law, the law of reason, that underlay the cosmos. This harmony with the Logos would give them the inner strength to resist the torments inflicted by others, by fate, and by their own passionate natures. Self-mastery and inner peace, or happiness, would follow. Such individuals would remain undisturbed by life's misfortunes, for their souls would be their own. Even slaves were not denied this inner freedom; although their bodies were subjected to the power of their masters, their minds still remained independent and free.

Stoicism had an enduring influence on the Western mind. To some Roman political and legal thinkers, the Empire fulfilled the Stoic ideal of a world community, in which people of different nationalities held citizenship and were governed by a worldwide law that accorded with the law of reason, or natural law, operating throughout the universe. Stoic beliefs—that by nature we are all members of one family, that each person is significant, that distinctions of rank and race are of no account, and that human law should not conflict with natural law—were incorporated into Roman jurisprudence, Christian thought, and modern liberalism. There is continuity between the Stoic idea of natural law—a moral order that underlies nature—and the principle of inalienable rights stated in the American Declaration of Independence. In the modern age, the principle of natural law provided theoretical justification for the idea of human rights as the birthright of each individual.

The Greek Achievement: Reason, Freedom, Humanism

Like other ancient peoples, the Greeks warred, massacred, and enslaved; they could be cruel, arrogant, contentious, and superstitious; and they often violated their own ideals. But their achievements were unquestionably of profound historical significance. Western thought essentially begins with the Greeks, who first defined the individual by the capacity to reason. It was the great achievement of the Greek spirit to rise above magic, miracles, mystery, authority, and custom and to discover the procedures and terminology that permit a rational understanding of nature and society. Every aspect of Greek civilization—science, philosophy, art, drama, literature, politics, historical writing—showed a growing reliance on human reason and a diminishing dependence on the gods and mythical thinking.

In Mesopotamia and Egypt, people had no clear conception of their individual worth and no understanding of political liberty. They were not citizens but subjects marching to the command of a ruler whose power originated with the gods. Such royal power was not imposed on an unwilling population; it was religiously accepted and obeyed.

Unlike in the Near East, monarchs were incidental to Hellenic Greek political history, a development that enabled the Greeks to create both civic politics and political freedom. They saw the state as a community of free citizens who made laws that served the common good and in which disputes between citizens were decided by a jury of one's peers, not by the whims of a ruler or his officials. The citizens had no master other than themselves. The Greeks held that men are capable of governing themselves, and they regarded active participation in public affairs as a duty. For the Greeks, the state was a civilizing agent, permitting people to live the good life. Greek political thinkers arrived at a conception of the rational, or legal, state: a state in which law was an expression of reason, not of whim or divine commands; of justice, not of might; of the general good of the community, not of self-interest.

The Greeks also gave to Western civilization a conception of inner, or ethical, freedom. People were free to choose between shame and honor, cowardice and duty, moderation and excess. The idea of ethical freedom reached its highest point with Socrates, who shifted the focus of thought from cosmology to the human being and the moral life. To shape oneself according to ideals known to the mind—to develop into an autonomous and self-directed person—became for the Greeks the highest form of freedom.

During the Hellenistic Age, the Greeks, like the Hebrews earlier, arrived at the idea of universalism, the oneness of humanity. Stoic philosophers taught that all people, because of their ability to reason, are fundamentally alike and can be governed by the same laws. This idea is at the root of the modern principle of natural or human rights, which are the birthright of each individual.

Underlying everything accomplished by the Greeks was a humanist attitude toward life. The Greeks expressed a belief in the worth, significance, and dignity of the individual. They called for the maximum cultivation of human talent, the full development of human personality, and the deliberate pursuit of excellence. In valuing the human personality, the Greek humanists did not approve of living without restraints; they aimed at creating a higher type of man. Such a man would mold himself according to worthy standards and make his life as harmonious and flawless as a work of art. This aspiration required effort, discipline, and intelligence. Despite their lauding of the human being's creative capacities, the Greeks were not naïve about human nature. Rather, intensely aware of the individual's inherent capacity for evil, Greek thinkers repeatedly warned that without the restraining forces of law, civic institutions, moral norms, and character training, society would be torn apart by the savage elements within human nature. But fundamental to the Greek humanist outlook was the belief that human beings could master themselves. Contemporary humanists continue to derive inspiration and guidelines from the literary, artistic, and philosophical creations of the ancient Greeks.

By discovering theoretical reason, by defining political freedom, and by affirming the worth and potential of human personality, the Greeks broke with the past and founded the rational and humanist tradition of the West. "Had Greek civilization never existed," says the poet W. H. Auden, "we would never have become fully conscious, which is to say that we would never have become, for better or worse, fully human."[19]

❖ ❖ ❖

Notes

1. H. D. F. Kitto, *The Greeks* (Baltimore: Penguin Books, 1957), p. 60.
2. Werner Jaeger, *Paideia: The Ideals of Greek Culture,* trans. Gilbert Highet (New York: Oxford University Press, 1945), vol. 1, p. 8.
3. Kitto, *The Greeks*, p. 78.
4. Herodotus, *The Histories,* trans. Aubrey de Sélincourt (Baltimore: Penguin Books, 1954), p. 493.
5. Thucydides, *The Peloponnesian War*, trans. B. Jowett (Oxford: Clarendon Press, 1881), bk. 2, chap. 37.
6. Aristotle, *Politics*, in *Basic Works of Aristotle*, ed., Richard McKeon (New York: Random House, 1941), 1132.
7. Thucydides, *The Peloponnesian War*, trans. Rex Warner (Baltimore: Penguin Books, 1954), p. 360.
8. John N. Theodorakopoulos, "The Origins of Science and Philosophy," in *History of the Hellenic World: The Archaic Period* (University Park: Pennsylvania State University Press, 1975), p. 438.
9. Quoted in George Sarton, *A History of Science* (Cambridge, Mass.: Harvard University Press, 1952), vol. 1, pp. 355–356.
10. Plato, *Apology*, trans. F. J. Church, rev. R. D. Cummings (Indianapolis: Bobbs-Merrill, 1956), secs. 16–17.
11. Plato, *The Republic*, trans. F. M. Cornford (New York: Oxford University Press, 1945), p. 289.
12. Ibid., p. 293.
13. *Politics*, in *Basic Works of Aristotle*, ed. Richard McKeon (New York: Random House, 1941), pp. 1246, 1251.
14. Ibid., pp. 1220–1221.
15. Sophocles, *Oedipus the King*, trans. Bernard M. W. Knox (New York: Washington Square Press, 1959), p. 61.
16. Herodotus, *The Histories*, p. 485.
17. Benjamin Farrington, *Greek Science* (Baltimore: Penguin Books, 1961), p. 301.

18. Quoted in Anthony Gottlieb, *The Dream of Reason* (New York, W. W. Norton, 2000), pp. 283–284.
19. W. H. Auden, ed., *The Portable Greek Reader* (New York: Viking, 1952), p. 38.

Suggested Reading

Boardman, John, et al., *The Oxford History of the Classical World* (1986). Essays on all facets of Greek culture.

Bruhschwig, Jacques, and Geoffrey E. R. Lloyd, eds., *Greek Thought* (2000). Essays dealing with many areas of Greek thought.

Cartledge, Paul, *Alexander the Great* (2004). A recent biography.

Chamoux, François, *Hellenistic Civilizations* (2003). An overview of the period.

Fine, John V. A., *The Ancient Greeks* (1983). An up-to-date, reliable analysis of Greek history.

Gergel, Tania, ed., *Alexander the Great: The Brief Life and Towering Exploits of History's Greatest Conqueror As Told by His Original Biographers* (2004). A convenient anthology of sources.

Gottlieb, Anthony, *The Dream of Reason* (2000). Superb chapters on Greek philosophy.

Grant, Michael, *A Social History of Greece and Rome* (1992). Essays on the rich, the poor, women, slaves, and freedmen and freedwomen.

Hanson, Victor Davis, *A War Like No Other* (2005) A perceptive analysis of the Peloponnesian War.

Koester, Helmut, *Introduction to the New Testament, Volume One: History, Culture, and Religion of the Hellenistic Age* (1982). An intelligent guide.

Levi, Peter, *The Pelican History of Greek Literature* (1985). Sound insights into Greek writers.

Meier, Christian, *Athens: A Portrait of the City in Its Golden Age* (1999). Rich in details and interpretation.

Ober, Joseph, *The Athenian Revolution* (1996). Thoughtful essays on Greek democracy and political theory.

Powell, Anton, ed., *The Greek World* (1995). Essays by authorities on all phases of Greek life.

Stockton, David, *The Classical Athenian Democracy* (1990). The evolution and nature of Greek democracy.

Tripolitis, Antonia, *Religions of the Hellenistic Age* (2002). An excellent survey.

Wallbank, F. W., *The Hellenistic World* (1982). A survey of the Hellenistic world; makes judicious use of quotations from original sources.

CourseMate

Go to the CourseMate website at **www.cengagebrain.com** for additional study tools and review materials—including audio and video clips—for this chapter.

Chapter 4

Rome: From City-State to World Empire

- **Evolution of the Roman Constitution**
- **Roman Expansion to 146 B.C.**
- **Culture in the Republic**
- **The Collapse of the Republic**
- **Augustus and the Foundations of the Roman Empire**
- **The Pax Romana**
- **Signs of Trouble**
- **The Decline of Rome**
- **The Roman Legacy**

Focus Questions

1. What factors enabled the city-state of Rome to conquer Italy and the Mediterranean world?
2. What was the significance of Roman expansion?
3. What were the reasons for the collapse of the Roman Republic?
4. Why is the Pax Romana regarded as one of the finest periods in world history? What continuity is there between the Pax Romana and the Hellenistic Age?
5. How did Roman law evolve? How did it incorporate Stoic principles?
6. What are the reasons for the decline of the Roman Empire?
7. What is Rome's legacy to Western civilization?

Rome's great achievement was to transcend the narrow political orientation of the city-state and to create a world-state that unified the different nations of the Mediterranean world. Regarding the polis as the only means to the good life, the Greeks had not desired a larger political unit and had almost totally excluded foreigners from citizenship. Although Hellenistic philosophers had conceived the possibility of a world community, Hellenistic politics could not shape one. But Rome overcame the limitations of the city-state mentality and developed an empirewide system of law and citizenship. The Hebrews were distinguished by their prophets and the Greeks by their philosophers. The Romans produced no Amos or Isaiah and no Plato or Aristotle; their genius found expression in law and government and in the transmission of the Greek cultural achievement.

Historians divide Roman history into two broad periods. The period of the Republic began in 509 B.C. with the overthrow of the Etruscan monarchy; the period of the Empire began in 27 B.C., when Octavian (Augustus) became in effect the first Roman emperor, ending almost five hundred years of republican self-government. By conquering the Mediterranean world and extending Roman law and, in some instances, citizenship to different nationalities, the Roman Republic transcended the parochialism typical of the city-state. The Republic initiated the trend toward political and legal universalism, which reached fruition in the second period of Roman history, the Empire. ❖

Evolution of the Roman Constitution

By the eighth century B.C., peasant communities existed on some of Rome's seven hills near the Tiber River in central Italy. To the north stood Etruscan cities, and to the south, Greek cities. The more advanced civilizations of both the Etruscans and Greeks were gradually absorbed by the Romans.

The origin of the Etruscans remains a mystery, although some scholars believe that they came from Asia Minor and settled in northern Italy. From them, Romans acquired architectural styles and skills in road construction, sanitation, hydraulic engineering (including underground conduits), metallurgy, ceramics, and portrait sculpture. Etruscan words and names entered the Latin language, and Roman religion absorbed Etruscan gods.

The Etruscans had expanded their territory in Italy during the seventh and sixth centuries B.C., and they controlled the monarchy in Rome. Defeated by Celts, Greeks, and finally Romans, by the third century B.C. the Etruscans ceased to exercise any political power in Italy.

Rome became a republic at the end of the sixth century B.C.—the traditional date is 509 B.C.—when the landowning aristocrats, or patricians, overthrew the Etruscan king. As in the Greek cities, the transition from theocratic monarchy to republic offered possibilities for political and legal growth. In the opening phase of republican history, religion governed the people, dictated the law, and legitimized the rule of the patricians, who regarded themselves as the preservers of sacred traditions. Gradually, the Romans loosened the ties between religion and politics and hammered out a constitutional system that paralleled the Greek achievement of rationalizing and secularizing politics and law. In time, the Romans, like the Greeks, came to view law as an expression of the public will and not as the creation of god-kings, priest-kings, or a priestly caste.

The impetus for the growth of the Roman constitution came from a conflict—known as the Struggle of the Orders—between the patricians and the commoners, or plebeians. At the beginning of the fifth century B.C., the patrician-dominated government consisted of two annually elected executives called consuls, the Centuriate Assembly, and the Senate. Patricians owned most of the land and controlled the army. The two consuls, who came from the nobility, commanded the army, served as judges, and initiated legislation.

The Centuriate Assembly was a popular assembly, but because of voting procedures, it was controlled by the nobility. The Assembly elected consuls and other magistrates and made the laws, which also needed Senate approval. The Senate advised the Assembly but did not itself enact laws; it controlled public finances and foreign policy. Senators either were appointed for life terms by

Chronology 4.1 ❖ Rome

509 B.C.	Expulsion of the Etruscan monarch
287	End of the Struggle of the Orders
264–241	First Punic War: Rome acquires provinces
218–201	Second Punic War: Hannibal is defeated
133–122	Land reforms by the Gracchi brothers; they are murdered by the Senate
88–83	Conflict between Sulla and the forces of Marius; Sulla emerges as dictator
49–44	Caesar is dictator of Rome
27 B.C.	Octavian assumes the title *Augustus* and becomes, in effect, the first Roman emperor; start of the Pax Romana
A.D. 180	Marcus Aurelius dies; end of the Pax Romana
212	Roman citizenship is granted to virtually all free inhabitants of Roman provinces
235–285	Military anarchy; Germanic incursions
285–305	Diocletian tries to deal with the crisis by creating a regimented state
378	Battle of Adrianople: Visigoths defeat the Roman legions
406	Borders collapse, Germanic tribes move into the Empire
476	End of the Roman Empire in the West

the consuls or were former magistrates. The Senate was the principal organ of patrician power.

The tension between patricians and commoners stemmed from plebeian grievances, which included enslavement for debt, discrimination in the courts, prevention of intermarriage with patricians, lack of political representation, and the absence of a written code of laws. Resenting their inferior status and eager for economic relief, the plebeians organized and waged a struggle for political, legal, and social equality.

The plebeians had one decisive weapon: their threat to secede from Rome, that is, not to pay taxes, work, or serve in the army. Realizing that Rome, which was constantly involved in warfare on the Italian peninsula, could not endure without plebeian help, the pragmatic patricians grudgingly made concessions. Thus, the plebeians slowly gained legal equality.

Early in the fifth century, the plebeians won the right to form their own assembly (the Plebeian Assembly, which was later enlarged and called the Tribal Assembly). This assembly could elect tribunes, officials who were empowered to protect plebeian rights. As a result of plebeian pressure, around 450 B.C. the first Roman code of laws was written. Called the Twelve Tables, the code gave plebeians some degree of protection against unfair and oppressive patrician officials, who could interpret customary law in an arbitrary way. Other concessions gained later by the plebeians included the right to intermarry with patricians; access to the highest political, judicial, and religious offices in the state; and the elimination of slavery as payment for debt. In 287 B.C., a date generally recognized as the termination of the plebeian–patrician struggle, laws passed by the Tribal Assembly no longer required the Senate's approval. Now the plebeians had full civil equality and legal protection, and their assembly had full power to enact legislation.

Despite these changes, Rome was still ruled by an upper class. The oligarchy that held power now consisted of patricians and influential plebeians who had joined forces with the old nobility. Marriages between patricians and politically powerful plebeians strengthened this alliance. Generally only wealthy plebeians became tribunes, and they tended to side with the old nobility rather than defend the interests of poor plebeians. By using bribes, the ruling oligarchy maintained control over the Assembly, and the Senate remained a bastion of aristocratic power. Deeming themselves Rome's finest citizens, the ruling oligarchy led Rome during its period of expansion and demonstrated a sense of responsibility and a talent for statesmanship.

During the two-hundred-year Struggle of the Orders, the Romans forged a constitutional system based on civic needs rather than on religious mystery. The essential duty of government ceased to be the regular performance of religious rituals and became the maintenance of order at home and the preservation of Roman might and dignity in international relations. Although the Romans retained the ceremonies and practices of their ancestral religion, public interest, not religious tradition or the prospect of divine punishment, determined the content of law. Public interest was also the standard by which all the important acts of the city were judged. In the opening stage of republican history, law was priestly and sacred, spoken only by priests and known only to men of religious families. Gradually, as law was written, debated, and altered, it became disentangled from religion. Another step in this process of secularization and rationalization occurred when the study and interpretation of law passed from the hands of priests to a class of professional jurists, who analyzed, classified, and systematized it and sought commonsense solutions to legal problems.

The Roman constitution was not a product of abstract thought, nor was it the gift of a great lawmaker, such as the Athenian Solon. Rather, like the unwritten English constitution, the Roman constitution evolved gradually and empirically in response to specific needs. The Romans, unlike the Greeks, were distinguished by practicality and common sense, not by a love of abstract thought. In their pragmatic and empirical fashion, they gradually developed the procedures of public politics and the legal state.

Scala/Art Resource, N.Y.

Statue Portrait, First Century A.D. The Romans valued family, city, and tradition. Here a noble proudly exhibits the busts of his ancestors.

Roman Expansion to 146 B.C.

At the time of the Struggle of the Orders, Rome was also extending its power over the Italian peninsula. Without the civic harmony and stability gained by patrician concessions, it could not have achieved expansion. By 146 B.C., it had become the dominant power in the Mediterranean world.

Roman expansion occurred in three main stages: the uniting of the Italian peninsula, which gave Rome the manpower that transformed it from a city-state into a great power; the collision with Carthage, from which Rome emerged as ruler of the western Mediterranean; and the subjugation of the Hellenistic states, which brought Romans in close contact with Greek civilization. As Rome expanded territorially, its leaders enlarged their vision. Instead of restricting citizenship to people having ethnic kinship, Rome assimilated other peoples into its political community. As law had grown to cope with the earlier grievances of the plebeians, so too it adjusted to the new situations resulting from the creation of a multinational empire. The city of Rome was evolving into the city of humanity—the cosmopolis envisioned by the Stoics.

The Uniting of Italy

During the first stage of expansion, Rome extended its hegemony over Italy, subduing in the process neighboring Latin kinsmen, semicivilized Italian tribes, the once-dominant Etruscans, and Greek city-states in southern Italy. Rome's conquest of Italy stemmed in part from superior military organization, training, and, iron discipline. Copying the Greeks, the Romans organized their soldiers into battle formations; in contrast, their opponents often fought as disorganized hordes, which were prone to panic and flight. Romans also willingly made sacrifices so that Rome might endure. In conquering Italy, they were united by a moral and religious devotion to their city strong enough to overcome social conflict, factional disputes, and personal ambition. Also fueling Roman expansion was an aristocratic ethos that placed the highest value on glory. Demonstrating prowess in war, aristocrats believed, was the finest way to win the esteem of fellow Romans, bring honor to their family, and enhance their own political career.

Despite its army's strength, Rome could not have mastered Italy without the cooperation of other Italian peoples. Like other ancient peoples, Rome plundered, enslaved, and brutalized, at times with great ferocity. But it also endeavored, through generous treatment, to gain the loyalty of conquered people. Some defeated communities retained a measure of self-government but turned the conduct of foreign affairs over to Rome and contributed contingents to the army when Rome went to war. Other conquered people received partial or full citizenship. In extending its dominion over Italy, Rome displayed a remarkable talent for converting former enemies into allies and eventually into Roman citizens. No Greek city had ever envisaged integrating nonnatives into its political community.

The Conquest of the Mediterranean World

When Rome finished unifying Italy, there were five great powers in the Mediterranean area: the Seleucid monarchy in the Near East, the Ptolemaic monarchy in Egypt, the kingdom of Macedonia, Carthage in the western Mediterranean, and the Roman-dominated Italian Confederation. One hundred twenty years later—in 146 B.C.—Rome had subjected the other states to its dominion.

Roman expansion beyond Italy did not proceed according to a set plan. Indeed, some Roman leaders considered involvement in foreign adventures a threat to both Rome's security and its traditional way of life. However, as its interests grew, Rome was drawn into conflicts and, without planning it, acquired an overseas empire.

Shortly after asserting supremacy in Italy, Rome engaged Carthage, the other great power in the western Mediterranean, in a prolonged conflict, the First Punic War (264–241 B.C.). Founded about 800 B.C. by Phoenicians, the North African city of Carthage had become a prosperous commercial center. The Carthaginians had acquired an empire comprising North Africa and coastal regions of southern Spain, Sardinia, Corsica, and western Sicily.

War between the two great powers began because Rome feared Carthage's designs on the northern Sicilian city of Messana. Rome was apprehensive about the southern Italian city-states that were its allies, fearing that Carthage would use Messana either to attack them or to interfere with their trade. Rome decided that the security of

A Roman Warship with Legionnaires on a Relief from the Temple of Fortuna Primigenia, First Century B.C. Roman soldiers fought on sea as well as on land, conquering nations throughout the Mediterranean area during the eras of the Republic and the Empire.

its allies required intervention in Sicily. Although Rome suffered severe losses—including the annihilation of an army that had invaded North Africa and the destruction of hundreds of ships in battle and storms—the Romans never considered anything but a victor's peace. Drawing manpower from loyal allies throughout Italy, Rome finally prevailed over Carthage, which had to surrender Sicily to Rome. Three years later, Rome seized the islands of Corsica and Sardinia from a weakened Carthage. With the acquisition of these territories beyond Italy, which were made into provinces, Rome had the beginnings of an empire.

Carthaginian expansion in Spain precipitated the Second Punic War (218–201 B.C.). Coming from Spain, the Carthaginian army was commanded by Hannibal (247–183 B.C.), whose military genius astounded the ancients. Hannibal led a seasoned army, complete with war elephants for charging enemy lines, across mountain passes so steep and icy that men and animals sometimes lost their footing and fell to their deaths. Some twenty-six thousand men survived the crossing into Italy; fifteen thousand more were recruited from Gallic tribesmen of the Po Valley. At the battle of Cannae (216 B.C.), the Carthaginian forces, in a brilliant encircling maneuver, completely destroyed a Roman army of sixty thousand soldiers—the largest single force Rome had ever put into the field. The butchering by hand of the trapped Roman soldiers lasted for hours.

These were the Republic's worst days. Nevertheless, says the Roman historian Livy, the Romans did not breathe a word of peace. Hannibal could not follow up his victory at Cannae with a finishing blow, for Rome wisely would not allow its army to be lured into another major engagement. Nor did Hannibal possess the manpower to capture the city itself with its formidable fortifications. In addition, most of Rome's Italian allies remained loyal, although many southern Italian cities went over to Hannibal. Rome quickly raised and equipped new legions, even enlisting seventeen-year-olds and promising freedom to slaves and amnesty to criminals who volunteered to serve. To finance the army, taxes were doubled and women surrendered their jewelry to the state.

When Rome invaded North Africa, threatening Carthage, Hannibal was forced to withdraw his troops from Italy in order to defend his homeland. Hannibal, who had won every battle in Italy, was defeated by Scipio Africanus at the battle of Zama in North Africa in 202 B.C. Carthage was compelled to surrender Spain and to give up its elephants and its navy. Sheer determination, vast reserves of manpower, and the state's willingness to garner its wealth to strengthen its legions explain Rome's victory.

The Second Punic War left Rome as the sole great power in the western Mediterranean; it also hastened Rome's entry into the politics of the Hellenistic world. In the year after Cannae, during Rome's darkest ordeal, Philip V of Macedonia entered into an alliance with Hannibal. Fearing that the Macedonian ruler might invade Italy, Rome initiated the First Macedonian War and won it in 205 B.C. To end Macedonian influence in Greece, which Rome increasingly viewed as a Roman protectorate, the Romans fought two other wars with Macedonia. Finally, in 148 B.C., Rome created the province of Macedonia.

Intervention in Greece led to Roman involvement in the Hellenistic kingdoms of the Near East and Asia Minor: Seleucia, Egypt, and Pergamum. The Hellenistic states became client kingdoms of Rome and consequently lost their freedom of action in foreign affairs.

In 146 B.C., the same year that Rome's hegemony over the Hellenistic world was ensured, Rome concluded an unnecessary Third Punic War with Carthage. It had launched this war of annihilation against Carthage in 149 B.C. even though Carthage was by then a second-rate power and no longer a threat to Rome's security. The Romans were driven by old hatreds and the traumatic memory of Hannibal's near-conquest. Rome sold Carthaginian survivors into slavery, obliterated the city, and turned the territory into the Roman province of Africa. Rome's savage and irrational behavior toward a helpless Carthage was an early sign of the deterioration of senatorial leadership; there would be others.

Rome had not yet reached the limits of its expansion, but there was no doubt that by 146 B.C. the Mediterranean world had been subjected to its will. No power could stand up to Rome.

The Consequences of Expansion

Expansion had important consequences for Rome and the Mediterranean world. Thousands of Greeks, many of them educated persons who had been enslaved as a result of Rome's eastern conquests, came to Rome. This influx accelerated the process of Hellenization—the adoption of Greek culture—that had begun earlier through Rome's contact with the Greek cities of southern Italy.

A crucial consequence of expansion was Roman contact with the legal experience of other peoples, including the Greeks. Demonstrating the Roman virtues of pragmatism and common sense, Roman jurists selectively incorporated into Roman law elements of the legal codes and traditions of these nations. Thus, Roman jurists gradually and empirically fashioned the *jus gentium*, the law of nations, or peoples, which eventually was applied throughout the Empire.

Roman conquerors transported to Italy hundreds of thousands of war captives, including Greeks, from all over the Empire. It is estimated that between 80 and 8 B.C., more than two million enslaved aliens were transported to Italy. By the middle of that century, slaves constituted about one-third of Italy's population, compared with about 10 percent before the Second Punic War. The wars of conquest (and piracy) had made the slave trade a vast and lucrative commercial venture. Like the Greeks, Romans considered slavery indispensable for the preservation of civilized life. Roman jurists and intellectuals regarded the division of humanity into masters and slaves as a rule of nature and viewed the slave as an animate tool, an object that produced and served; like other forms of property, slaves could be sold or rented out by their masters. The more fortunate or more

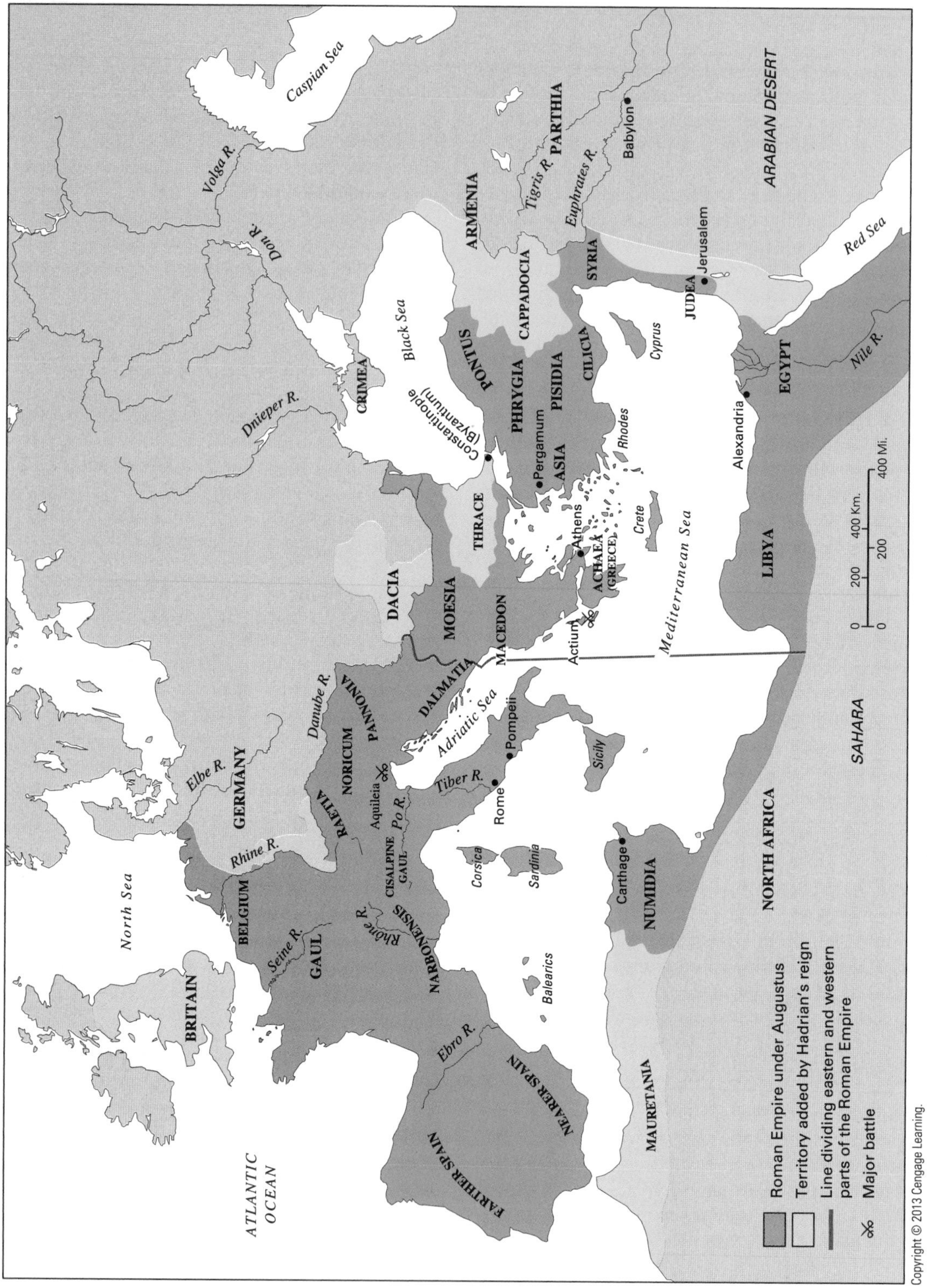

Roman Empire under Augustus
Territory added by Hadrian's reign
Line dividing eastern and western parts of the Roman Empire
Major battle
0 200 400 Km.
0 200 400 Mi.
ATLANTIC OCEAN
North Sea
BRITAIN
BELGIUM
GAUL
Seine R.
Rhine R.
Rhône R.
NARBONENSIS
CISALPINE GAUL
Po R.
GERMANY
Elbe R.
RAETIA
NORICUM
PANNONIA
Danube R.
Aquileia
DALMATIA
Adriatic Sea
Tiber R.
Rome
Pompeii
Corsica
Sardinia
Sicily
Balearics
Ebro R.
NEARER SPAIN
FARTHER SPAIN
MAURETANIA
NUMIDIA
Carthage
NORTH AFRICA
SAHARA
DACIA
MOESIA
MACEDON
Actium
ACHAEA (GREECE)
Athens
THRACE
Crete
Mediterranean Sea
LIBYA
Constantinople (Byzantium)
Pergamum
ASIA
Rhodes
PHRYGIA
PISIDIA
PONTUS
CILICIA
CAPPADOCIA
Black Sea
CRIMEA
Dnieper R.
Don R.
Volga R.
Caspian Sea
ARMENIA
Tigris R.
Euphrates R.
PARTHIA
Babylon
SYRIA
Cyprus
JUDEA
Jerusalem
Alexandria
EGYPT
Nile R.
Red Sea
ARABIAN DESERT

capable slaves worked as craftsmen and servants; the luckless and more numerous toiled, branded and chained, on the growing number of plantations or died early laboring in mines under inhuman conditions. So brutal was their existence that they begged for death, reported a Roman observer. Roman masters often treated their slaves brutally. Torture was common, and masters sexually exploited both male and female slaves for their own pleasure or compelled them to work as prostitutes. Although slave uprisings were not common, their ferocity terrified the Romans. In 135 B.C., slaves in Sicily revolted and captured some key towns, defeating Roman forces before being subdued. In 73 B.C., gladiators, led by Spartacus, broke out of their barracks and were joined by tens of thousands of runaways. Spartacus aimed to escape into Gaul and Thrace, the homelands of many slaves. His slave army defeated Roman armies and devastated southern Italy before the superior might of Rome prevailed. Some six thousand of the defeated slaves were tortured and crucified on the road from Capua to Rome.

Roman governors, lesser officials, and businessmen found the provinces a source of quick wealth; they were generally unrestrained by the Senate, which was responsible for administering the overseas territories. Exploitation, corruption, looting, and extortion soon ran rampant. "No administration in history has ever devoted itself so whole heartedly to fleecing its subjects for the private benefit of its ruling class as Rome of the last age of the Republic," concludes E. Badian.[1] The Roman nobility proved unfit to manage a world empire.

Despite numerous examples of misrule in the provinces, Roman administration had many positive features. Rome generally allowed its subjects a large measure of self-government and did not interfere with religion and local customs. Usually, the Roman taxes worked out to be no higher, and in some instances were lower, than those under previous regimes. Most important, Rome reduced the endemic warfare that had plagued these regions.

◄ *Map 4.1* Roman Conquests During the Republic The conquest of Italy gave Rome the manpower to expand throughout the Mediterranean world. In the Second Punic War, Rome defeated its greatest rival, Carthage.

Culture in the Republic

One of the chief consequences of expansion was greater contact with Greek culture. During the third century B.C., Greek civilization started to exercise an increasing and fruitful influence on the Roman mind. Greek teachers, both slave and free, came to Rome and introduced Romans to Hellenic cultural achievements. As they conquered the eastern Mediterranean, Roman generals began to ship libraries and works of art from Greek cities to Rome. Roman sculpture and painting imitated Greek prototypes. In time, Romans acquired from Greece knowledge of scientific thought, philosophy, medicine, and geography. Roman writers and orators used Greek history, poetry, and oratory as models. Adopting the humanist outlook of the Greeks, the Romans came to value human intelligence and eloquent and graceful prose and poetry. Wealthy Romans retained Greek tutors, poets, and philosophers in their households and sent their sons to Athens to study. Thus, Rome creatively assimilated the Greek achievement and transmitted it to others, thereby extending the orbit of Hellenism. To be sure, some conservative Romans were hostile to the Greek influence, which they felt threatened traditional Roman values that had accounted for Rome's greatness. Cato the Elder (234–149 B.C.) and other Roman moralists denounced Socrates for undermining respect for Athenian law and warned that Greek philosophy might lure Roman youth into similar subversive behavior. Moreover, said these moralists, Greek philosophy, with its endless discussions of abstract themes, contrasted with the virtue most cherished by Romans—*gravitas* or seriousness—which enabled Romans to conduct public affairs effectively. Philosophy seemed designed for a life of leisure and inaction, whereas a virtuous Roman was actively involved in practical civic matters.

Plautus (c. 254–184 B.C.), Rome's greatest playwright, adopted features of fourth- and third-century Greek comedy. His plays had Greek characters and took place in Greek settings; the actors wore the Greek style of dress. But the plays also contained familiar elements that appealed to Roman audiences: scenes of gluttony, drunkenness, womanizing, and the pains of love.

Another playwright, Terence (c. 185–159 B.C.), was originally from North Africa and had been brought to Rome as a slave. His owner, a Roman senator, provided the talented youth with an education and freed him. Terence's humor, restrained and refined, lacked the boisterousness of Plautus that Romans liked, but his style was technically superior.

Catullus (c. 84–c. 54 B.C.), a native of northern Italy, is generally regarded as one of the world's great lyric poets. His father provided him with a gentleman's education. Tormented by an ill-fated love, Catullus wrote memorable poems dealing with passion and its anguish.

The leading Roman Epicurean philosopher, Lucretius (c. 96–c. 55 B.C.), was influenced by the conflict fostered by two generals, Marius and Sulla, which is discussed later in this chapter. Distraught by the seemingly endless strife, Lucretius yearned for philosophical tranquillity. In his work *On the Nature of Things,* Lucretius expressed his appreciation of Epicurus. Like his mentor, Lucretius denounced superstition and religion for fostering psychological distress and advanced a materialistic conception of nature, one that left no room for the activity of gods—mechanical laws, not the gods, governed all physical happenings. To dispel the fear of punishment after death, Lucretius marshaled arguments to prove that the soul perishes with the body. Like Epicurus, he held that the simple life, devoid of political involvement and excessive passion, was the highest good and the path that would lead from emotional turmoil to peace of mind.

Cicero (106–43 B.C.), a leading Roman statesman, was also a distinguished orator, an unsurpassed Latin stylist, and a student of Greek philosophy. His letters, more than eight hundred of which have survived, provide modern historians with valuable insights into the politics of the late Republic. His Senate speeches have served as models of refined rhetoric for all students of the Latin language. Cicero's discussion of such topics as republicanism, citizenship, friendship, virtue, duty, and justice had an enduring influence on Western moral and political thought. Dedicated to republicanism, Cicero sought to prevent one-man rule. He admired the Stoic goal of the self-sufficient sage who sought to accord his life with standards of virtue inherent in nature. He adopted the Stoic belief that natural law governs the universe and applies to all, that all belong to a common humanity, and that reason is the individual's noblest faculty. Stoicism was the most influential philosophy in Rome. Its stress on virtuous conduct and performance of duty coincided with Roman ideals, and its doctrine of a natural law that applies to all nations harmonized with the requirements of a world empire.

In the eighteenth century, the Founding Fathers of the United States praised Cicero's natural law philosophy, which coincided with their belief in inalienable rights; his condemnation of tyranny; and his advocacy of liberty, republicanism, and constitutional government.

The Collapse of the Republic

In 146 B.C., Roman might spanned the Mediterranean world. After that year, the principal concerns of the Republic were no longer foreign invasions but adjusting city-state institutions to the demands of empire and overcoming critical social and political problems at home. The Republic proved unequal to either challenge. Instead of developing a professional civil service to administer the conquered lands, Roman leaders attempted to govern an empire with city-state institutions, which had evolved for a different purpose. The established Roman administration proved unable to govern the Mediterranean world. In addition, Rome's ruling elite showed little concern for the welfare of its subjects. Provincial rule worsened as governors, tax collectors, and soldiers shamelessly exploited the provincials.

During Rome's march to empire, all its classes had demonstrated a magnificent civic spirit in fighting foreign wars. With Carthage and Macedonia no longer threatening Rome, this cooperation deteriorated. Internal dissension tore Rome apart as the ferocious drive for domination, formerly directed against foreign enemies, turned inward against fellow Romans. Civil war replaced foreign war.

Neither the Senate nor its opponents could rejuvenate the Republic. Eventually it collapsed, a victim of class tensions, poor leadership, power-hungry demagogues, and civil war. Underlying all these conditions was the breakdown of social harmony and the deterioration of civic patriotism. The Republic had conquered an empire, only to see the spiritual qualities of its citizens decay. In a high moral tone, the historian Sallust (c. 86–34 B.C.) condemned the breakdown of republican values:

> *Growing love of money, and the lust for power which followed it, engendered every kind of evil. Avarice destroyed honor, integrity, and every other virtue, and instead taught men to be proud and cruel, to neglect religion, and to hold nothing too sacred to sell. Ambition tempted many to be false. . . . At first these vices grew slowly and sometimes met with punishments; later on, when the disease had spread like a plague, Rome changed: her government, once so just and admirable, became harsh and unendurable.*[2]

The Gracchian Revolution

The downhill slide of the Republic began with an agricultural crisis. During the long war with Hannibal in Italy, farms were devastated, and with many Roman soldier-farmers serving in the army for long periods, fields lay neglected. Returning veterans lacked the wealth to restore their land. They were forced to sell their farms to wealthy landowners at low prices.

Another factor that helped to squeeze out the small farm owners was the importation of hundreds of thousands of slaves to work on large plantations, called *latifundia*. This massive use of slave labor was unprecedented in Roman history. Farmers who had formerly increased their meager incomes by working for wages on neighboring large estates were no longer needed. Sinking ever deeper into poverty and debt, they gave up their lands and went to Rome and other cities to seek work. The dispossessed peasantry found little to do in Rome, where there was not enough industry to provide them with employment and where much of the work was done by slaves. The once sturdy and independent Roman farmer, who had done all that his country had asked of him, was becoming part of a vast urban underclass, poor, embittered, and alienated.

In 133 B.C., Tiberius Gracchus (163–133 B.C.), who came from one of Rome's most honored families, was elected tribune. Distressed by the injustice done to the peasantry and recognizing that the Roman army depended on the loyalty of small landowners, Tiberius made himself the spokesman for land reform. He proposed a simple and moderate solution for the problem of the landless peasants: he would revive an old law barring any Roman from using more than 312 acres of the state-owned land obtained in the process of uniting Italy. For many years, the upper class had ignored this law, occupying vast tracts of public land as squatters and treating this land as their own. By enforcing the law, Tiberius hoped to free land for distribution to landless citizens.

Rome's leading families viewed Tiberius as a revolutionary who threatened their property and political authority. They also feared that he was seeking to stir up the poor in order to gain political power for himself. To preserve the status quo, with wealth and power concentrated in the hands of a few hundred families, senatorial extremists killed Tiberius and some three hundred of his followers, dumping their bodies into the Tiber.

The cause of land reform was next taken up by Gaius Gracchus (153–121 B.C.), a younger brother of Tiberius, who was elected tribune in 123 B.C. Gaius aided the poor by reintroducing his brother's plan for land distribution and by enabling them to buy grain from the state at less than half the market price. But like his brother, Gaius aroused the anger of the senatorial class who ordered his murder. A brief civil war raged in Rome, during which Gaius Gracchus (who may have committed suicide) and three thousand of his followers perished.

By killing the Gracchi, the Senate had substituted violence for reason and made murder a means of coping with troublesome opposition. Soon the club and the dagger became common weapons in Roman politics, hurling Rome into an era of political violence that ended with the destruction of the Republic. Although the Senate considered itself the guardian of republican liberty, in reality it was expressing the determination of a few hundred families to retain their control over the state. It is a classic example of a once creative minority clinging tenaciously to power long after it had ceased to govern effectively or to inspire allegiance. In the century after the Gracchi, Roman politics was bedeviled by intrigues, rivalries, personal ambition, and political violence. The Senate behaved like a decadent oligarchy, and the Tribal Assembly, which had become the voice of the urban mob, demonstrated a weakness for demagogues, an openness to bribery, and an abundance of deceit and incompetence. The Roman Republic had passed the peak of its greatness.

Rival Generals

Marius (157–86 B.C.), who became consul in 107 B.C., adopted a military policy that eventually contributed to the wrecking of the Republic. Short of troops for a campaign in Numidia in North Africa, Marius disposed of the traditional property requirement for entrance into the army and filled his legions with volunteers from the urban poor, a dangerous precedent. These new soldiers, disillusioned with Rome, served only because Marius held out the promise of pay, loot, and land grants after discharge. They gave their loyalty not to Rome but to Marius, and they remained loyal to their commander only as long as he fulfilled his promises.

Other ambitious commanders followed the example set by Marius. They saw that a general could use his army to advance his political career—that by retaining the confidence of his soldiers, he could cow the Senate and dictate Roman policy. No longer an instrument of government, the army became a private possession of generals. Seeing its authority undermined by generals appointed by the Assembly, the Senate was forced to seek army commanders who would champion the cause of senatorial rule. In time, Rome would be engulfed in civil wars, as rival generals used their troops to strengthen their political affiliations and to further their own ambitions.

Meanwhile, the Senate continued to deal ineffectively with Rome's problems. When Rome's Italian allies—who had provided the manpower needed to conquer the empire—pressed for citizenship, the Senate refused to make concessions. The Senate's shortsightedness plunged Italy into a terrible war known as the Social War (91–88 B.C.). As war ravaged the peninsula, the Romans reversed their policy and conferred citizenship on the Italians. The unnecessary and ruinous rebellion petered out.

A conflict over who would command an army in the east broke out between Marius and Sulla (138–78 B.C.), who had distinguished himself in the Social War. In this prolonged civil war, Sulla won the first round, capturing the capital. But then Marius and his troops retook Rome and, in a frenzy, lashed out at Sulla's supporters. The killing lasted for five days and nights. Marius died shortly afterward. Sulla quickly subdued Marius's supporters on his return and instituted a terror that far surpassed Marius's violence.

Sulla believed that only rule by an aristocratic oligarchy could protect Rome from future military adventurers and ensure domestic peace. Consequently, he restored the Senate's right to veto acts of the Assembly, limited the power of the tribunes and the Assembly, and, to prevent any march on Rome, reduced the military authority of provincial governors. To make the Senate less oligarchic, he increased its membership to six hundred. Having put through these reforms, Sulla retired.

Julius Caesar

The Senate, however, failed to wield its restored authority effectively. The Republic was still menaced by military commanders who used their troops for their own political advantage, and underlying problems remained unsolved. In 60 B.C., a triumvirate (a ruling group of three) consisting of Julius Caesar (c. 100–44 B.C.), a politician, Pompey, a general, and Crassus, a wealthy banker, conspired to take over Rome. The ablest of the three was Caesar, who descended from an ancient noble family.

Recognizing the importance of a military command as a prerequisite for political prominence, Caesar gained command of the legions in Gaul in 59 B.C. The following year he began the conquest of the part of Gaul outside of Roman control, bringing the future France into the orbit of Greco-Roman culture. The campaign was brilliantly described in his *Commentaries*, although, to be sure, the work was a deliberate attempt to apprise the Roman public of his military prowess. The successful Gallic campaigns and invasion of Britain revealed Caesar's exceptional talent for generalship: he acted decisively, moved troops rapidly, and had excellent rapport with his men. By plundering Gaul, he also acquired a fortune that could be used to further his political career. Indeed, Caesar's victories alarmed the Senate, which feared that the popular general would use his devoted troops and soaring reputation to seize control of the state.

Meanwhile, the triumvirate had fallen apart. In 53 B.C., Crassus had perished with his army in a disastrous campaign against the Parthians in the East. Pompey, who was jealous of Caesar's success and eager to expand his own power, drew closer to the Senate. Supported by Pompey, the Senate ordered Caesar to relinquish his command. Caesar, realizing that without his troops he would be defenseless, decided instead to march on Rome. After he crossed the Rubicon River into Italy in 49 B.C., civil war again ravaged the Republic. Pompey proved no match for so talented a general; the Senate acknowledged Caesar's victory and appointed him to be dictator, a legal office, for ten years.

Caesar realized that republican institutions no longer operated effectively and that only strong and enlightened leadership could permanently end the civil warfare destroying Rome. He fought exploitation in the provinces and generously extended citizenship to more Italians and provincials. To aid the poor in Rome, he began a public works program, which provided employment and beautified the city. He also relocated more than a hundred thousand veterans and members of Rome's lower class to the provinces, where he gave them land.

In February 44 B.C., Rome's ruling class, jealous of Caesar's success and power and afraid of his ambition, became thoroughly alarmed when his temporary dictatorship was converted into a lifelong office. The aristocracy saw this event as the end of senatorial government and their rule, which they equated with liberty, and as the beginning of a hated Hellenistic type of monarchy. On March 15, a group of aristocrats, regarding themselves as defenders of republican traditions and institutions more than four-and-a-half centuries old, assassinated Caesar.

The Republic's Last Years

The assassination of Julius Caesar did not restore republican liberty; rather, it plunged Rome into renewed civil war. Two of Caesar's trusted lieutenants, Mark Antony and Lepidus, joined with Octavian, Caesar's adopted son, and defeated the armies of Brutus and Cassius, conspirators in the plot against Caesar. After Lepidus was forced into political obscurity, Antony and Octavian fought each other, with control of Rome as the prize. In 31 B.C., at the naval battle of Actium in western Greece, Octavian crushed the forces of Antony and his wife, Egypt's Queen Cleopatra. Octavian emerged as master of Rome and four years later became, in effect, the first Roman emperor.

The Roman Republic, which had amassed power to a degree hitherto unknown in the ancient world, was wrecked not by foreign invasion but by internal weaknesses: the degeneration of senatorial leadership and the transformation of political rivalry into violence and terror in which opponents were condemned to death and their property confiscated; the formation of private armies, in which soldiers gave their loyalty to their commander rather than to Rome; the transformation of a self-reliant peasantry into an impoverished and demoralized city rabble; and the deterioration of the ancient virtues that had been the source of the state's vitality. Before 146 B.C., the threat posed by foreign enemies, particularly Carthage, forced Romans to work together for the benefit of the state. This social cohesion broke down when foreign danger had been reduced.

Augustus and the Foundations of the Roman Empire

After Octavian's forces defeated those of Antony and Cleopatra at the battle of Actium, no opponents could stand up to him. The century of civil war, political murder, corruption, and mismanagement had exhausted the Mediterranean world, which longed for order. Like Caesar before him, Octavian recognized that only a strong monarchy could rescue Rome from civil war and anarchy. But, learning from Caesar's assassination, he also knew that republican ideals were far from dead.

To exercise autocratic power openly, like a Hellenistic monarch, would have aroused the hostility of the Roman ruling class, whose assistance and good will Octavian desired.

Octavian demonstrated his political genius by reconciling his military monarchy with republican institutions: he held absolute power without abruptly breaking with a republican past. Magistrates were still elected, and assemblies still met; the Senate administered certain provinces, retained its treasury, and was invited to advise Octavian. With some truth, Octavian could claim that he ruled in partnership with the Senate. By maintaining the facade of the Republic, Octavian camouflaged his absolute power and contained senatorial opposition, which had already been weakened by the deaths of leading nobles in battle or in the purges that Octavian had instituted against his enemies.

In 27 B.C., Octavian shrewdly offered to surrender his power, knowing that the Senate, purged of opposition, would demand that he continue to lead the state. By this act, Octavian could claim to be a legitimate constitutional ruler leading a government of law, not one of lawless despotism, which was hateful to the Roman mentality. In keeping with his policy of maintaining the appearance of traditional republican government, Octavian refused to be called king or even, like Caesar, dictator. Instead, he cleverly disguised his autocratic rule by taking the inoffensive title *princeps* (first citizen); the rule of Octavian and his successors is referred to as the *principate.* The Senate also honored Octavian by conferring on him the semireligious and revered name of *Augustus.*

The reign of Augustus signified the end of the Roman Republic and the beginning of the Roman Empire—the termination of aristocratic politics and the emergence of one-man rule. Despite his introduction of autocratic rule, however, Augustus was by no means a self-seeking tyrant, but a creative statesman. Heir to the Roman tradition of civic duty, he regarded his power as a public trust delegated to him by the Roman people. He was faithful to the classical ideal that the state should promote the good life by protecting civilization from barbarism and ignorance, and he sought to rescue a dying Roman world by restoring political order and reviving the moral values and civic spirit that had contributed to Rome's greatness.

Augustus instituted reforms and improvements throughout the Empire. He reformed the army to guard against the reemergence of ambitious generals like those whose rivalries and private armies had wrecked the Republic. He maintained the loyalty of his soldiers by ensuring that veterans, on discharge, would receive substantial bonuses and land in Italy or in the provinces. For the city of Rome, Augustus had aqueducts and water mains built, bringing water to most Roman homes. He created a fire brigade, which reduced the danger of great conflagrations in crowded tenement districts, and he organized a police force to contain violence. He improved the distribution of free grain to the impoverished proletariat, and he financed the popular gladiatorial combats out of his own funds.

In Italy, Augustus had roads repaired, fostered public works, and arranged for Italians to play a more important role in the administration of the Empire. He earned the gratitude of the provincials by correcting tax abuses and fighting corruption and extortion, as well as by improving the quality of governors and enabling aggrieved provincials to bring charges against Roman officials. An imperial bureaucracy, which enabled talented and dedicated men to serve the state, gradually evolved.

The Pax Romana

The brilliant statesmanship of Augustus inaugurated Rome's greatest age. For the next two hundred years, the Mediterranean world enjoyed the blessings of the *Pax Romana,* the Roman peace. The ancient world had never experienced such a long period of peace, order, efficient administration, and prosperity. Although both proficient and inept rulers succeeded Augustus, the essential features of the Pax Romana persisted.

The Successors of Augustus

The first four emperors who succeeded Augustus were related either to him or to his third wife, Livia. They constituted the Julio-Claudian dynasty, which ruled from A.D. 14 to 68. Although their reigns were marked by conspiracies, summary executions, and assassinations, the essential achievements of Augustus were preserved.

The Julio-Claudian dynasty came to an end when the emperor Nero committed suicide in A.D. 68. Nero had grown increasingly tyrannical and had lost the confidence of the people, the senatorial class, and the generals, who rose in revolt. In the year following his death, anarchy reigned as military leaders competed for the throne. After a bloody civil war, the execution of two emperors, and the suicide of another, Vespasian gained the principate. His reign (A.D. 69–79) marked the beginning of the Flavian dynasty. By having the great Colosseum of Rome constructed for gladiatorial contests, Vespasian earned the gratitude of the city's inhabitants. He also had nationalist uprisings put down in Gaul and Judea.

In Judea, Roman rule clashed with Jewish religious-national sentiments. Recognizing the tenacity with which Jews clung to their faith, the Roman leaders deliberately refrained from interfering with Hebraic religious beliefs and practices. Numerous privileges, such as exemption from emperor worship because it conflicted with the requirements of strict monotheism, were extended to Jews not only in Judea but throughout the Empire. Sometimes, however, the Romans engaged in activities that outraged the Jews. For example, the emperor Caligula (A.D. 37–41) ordered that a golden statue of himself be placed in Jerusalem's temple, the central site and focus of Jewish religious life. To the Jews, this display of a pagan idol in their midst was an abomination. The order was rescinded when the Jews demonstrated their readiness to resist.

Relations between the Jews of Judea and the Roman authorities deteriorated progressively in succeeding decades. Militant Jews, who rejected Roman rule as a threat to the purity of Jewish life, urged their people to take up arms. Feeling a religious obligation to reestablish an independent kingdom in their ancient homeland and unable to reconcile themselves to subjection to hated idolaters, the Jews launched a full-scale war of liberation in A.D. 66. In A.D. 70, after a five-month siege had inflicted terrible punishment on the Jews, Roman armies captured Jerusalem and destroyed the temple.

Vespasian was succeeded by his sons Titus (A.D. 79–81) and Domitian (A.D. 81–96). The reign of Titus was made memorable by the eruption of Mount Vesuvius, which devastated the towns of Pompeii and Herculaneum. After Titus's brief time as emperor, his younger brother Domitian became ruler. Upon crushing a revolt led by the Roman commander in Upper Germany, a frightened Domitian executed many leading Romans. These actions led to his assassination in A.D. 96, ending the Flavian dynasty.

The Senate selected one of its own, Nerva, to succeed the murdered Domitian. Nerva's reign (A.D. 96–98) was brief and uneventful. But he introduced a wise practice that would endure until A.D. 180: he adopted as his son and designated as his heir a man with proven ability, Trajan, the governor of Upper Germany. This adoptive system ensured a succession of competent rulers.

During his rule (A.D. 98–117), Trajan eased the burden of taxation in the provinces, provided for the needs of poor children, and had public works built. With his enlarged army, he conquered Dacia (parts of Romania and Hungary), where he seized vast quantities of gold and silver. He made the territory into a Roman province, adding to the large frontier Rome had to protect. The settlement of the region by many of Trajan's veterans led to its Romanization.

Trajan's successor, Hadrian (A.D. 117–138), strengthened border defenses in Britain and fought the second Hebrew revolt in Judea (A.D. 132–135). After initial successes, including the liberation of Jerusalem, the Jews were again defeated by superior Roman might. The majority of Palestinian Jews were killed, sold as slaves, or forced to seek refuge in other lands. The Romans renamed the province Syria Palestina; they forbade Jews to enter Jerusalem, except once a year; and they encouraged non-Jews to settle the land. Although the Jews continued to maintain a presence in Palestine, they had become a dispossessed and dispersed people.

After Hadrian came another ruler who had a long reign, Antoninus Pius (A.D. 138–161). He introduced humane and just reforms: limits on the right of masters to torture their slaves to obtain evidence and the establishment of the principle that an accused person be considered innocent until proven guilty. During his reign, the Empire remained peaceful and prosperous.

Marcus Aurelius (A.D. 161–180), the next emperor, was also a philosopher; his *Meditations* eloquently expressed Stoic thought. His reign was

Scala/Art Resource, N.Y.

ARCH OF TITUS, C. A.D. 81, CONCRETE FACED WITH MARBLE, ROME. The arch stands at the crest of the Sacred Way to commemorate Titus' successful capture of Jerusalem in A.D. 70. It was dedicated in A.D. 81 by his brother, the Emperor Domitian.

marked by renewed conflict in the East, with the kingdom of Parthia. The Roman legions were victorious in this campaign but brought back from the East an epidemic that decimated the population of the Empire.

From the accession of Nerva in A.D. 96 to the death of Marcus Aurelius in A.D. 180, the Roman Empire was ruled by the "Five Good Emperors." During this period, the Empire was at the height of its power and prosperity, and nearly all its peoples benefited. The four emperors preceding Marcus Aurelius had no living sons, so they resorted to the adoptive system in selecting successors, which served Rome effectively. But Marcus Aurelius chose his own son, Commodus, to succeed him. With the accession of Commodus, a misfit and a megalomaniac, in A.D. 180, the Pax Romana came to an end.

The "Time of Happiness"

The Romans called the Pax Romana the "Time of Happiness." They saw this period as the fulfillment of Rome's mission: the creation of a world-state that provided peace, security, ordered civilization, and the rule of law. Roman legions defended the Rhine–Danube River frontiers from incursions by German tribesmen, held the Parthians at bay in the East, and subdued the few uprisings that occurred. Nerva's adoptive system of selecting emperors provided Rome with internal stability and a succession of exceptionally able emperors. These Roman emperors did not use military force needlessly but fought for sensible political goals. Generals did not wage war recklessly; instead, they tried to limit casualties, avoid risks, and deter conflicts by a show of force. On balance, the Pax Romana was one of the finest periods in world history.

Constructive Rule. Roman rule was constructive. The Romans built roads—some fifty-three thousand miles of roads from Scotland to the Euphrates—improved harbors, cleared forests, drained swamps, irrigated deserts, and cultivated undeveloped lands. The aqueducts they constructed brought fresh water for drinking and bathing to large numbers of people, and the effective sewage systems enhanced the quality of life. Goods were transported over roads made safe by Roman soldiers and across a Mediterranean Sea swept clear of pirates. A wide variety of goods circulated throughout the Empire. A stable currency, generally not subject to depreciation, contributed to the economic well-being of the Mediterranean world.

Scores of new cities sprang up, and old ones grew larger and wealthier. Although these municipalities had lost their power to wage war and had to bow to the will of the emperors, they retained considerable freedom of action in local matters. Imperial troops guarded against civil wars within the cities and prevented warfare between cities—two traditional weaknesses of city life in the ancient world. The municipalities served as centers of Greco-Roman civilization, which spread to the farthest reaches of the Mediterranean, continuing a process initiated during the Hellenistic Age. Citizenship, generously granted, was finally extended to virtually all free men by an edict of A.D. 212.

Improved Conditions for Slaves and Women. Conditions improved for those at the bottom of society, the slaves. At the time of Augustus, slaves may have accounted for a quarter of the population of Italy. But their numbers declined as Rome engaged in fewer wars of conquest. The freeing of slaves also became more common during the Empire. Freed slaves gained citizenship, with most of the rights and privileges of other citizens; their children suffered no legal disabilities whatsoever. During the Republic, slaves had been terribly abused; they were often mutilated, thrown to wild beasts, crucified, or burned alive. Several emperors issued decrees protecting slaves from cruel masters.

The status of women had gradually improved during the Republic. In the early days of the Republic, a woman lived under the absolute authority first of her father and then of her husband. By the time of the Empire, a woman could own property and, if divorced, keep her dowry. A father could no longer force his daughter to marry against her will. Women could make business arrangements and draw up wills without the consent of their husbands. Unlike their Greek counterparts, Roman women were not secluded in their homes but could come and go as they pleased. Upper-class women of Rome also had far greater opportunities for education than those of Greece. The history of the Empire—indeed, Roman history in general—is filled with talented and influential women. Cornelia, the mother of Tiberius and Gaius Gracchus, influenced Roman politics through her sons. Livia, the dynamic wife of Augustus, was often consulted on important matters of state, and during the third century there were times when women controlled the throne.

An Orderly World Community. From Britain to the Arabian Desert, from the Danube River to the sands of the Sahara, some fifty to seventy million people with differing native languages, customs, and histories were united by Roman rule into a world community. Unlike officials of the Republic, when corruption and exploitation in the provinces were notorious, officials of the Empire felt a high sense of responsibility to preserve the Roman peace, institute Roman justice, and spread Roman civilization.

In creating a stable and orderly political community with an expansive conception of citizenship, Rome resolved the problems posed by the limitations of the Greek city-state: civil war, intercity warfare, and a parochial attitude that divided people into Greek and non-Greek. Rome also brought to fruition an ideal of the Greek city-state: the protection and promotion of civilized life. By constructing a world community that broke down barriers between nations, by preserving and spreading Greco-Roman civilization, and by developing a rational system of law that applied to all humanity, Rome completed the trend toward universalism and cosmopolitanism that had emerged in the Hellenistic Age.

Roman Culture and Law During the Pax Romana

During the late Roman Republic, Rome had acquired Greek scientific thought, philosophy, medicine, and geography. Roman writers used Greek models; sharing in the humanist outlook of the Greeks, they valued human intelligence and achievement and expressed themselves in a graceful and eloquent style. The diffusion of Hellenism throughout the Mediterranean world produced a cultural unity among elites that underlay the Pax Romana.

Literature and History. Roman cultural life reached its high point during the reign of Augustus, when Rome experienced the golden age of Latin literature. At the request of Augustus, who wanted a literary epic to glorify the Empire and his role in founding it, Virgil (70–19 B.C.) wrote the *Aeneid*, a masterpiece of world literature. The Aeneid is a literary epic of national glory. The profoundest ideas and feelings expressed in the poem are Roman virtues—patriotism, devotion to the family, duty to the state, and a strong sense of religion. Virgil ascribed to Rome a divine mission

Primary Source

Aelius Aristides: The Blessings of the Pax Romana

In the following reading, Aelius Aristides (A.D 117–187), a Greek intellectual, glowingly praises the Pax Romana in an oration that was probably delivered in Rome. In the tradition of Roman orators, Aristides used hyperbole and exaggeration. Nevertheless, the oration does capture the universalism and cosmopolitanism that characterized the Roman Empire.

But the most marvelous and admirable achievement of all, and the one deserving our fullest gratitude, is this. . . . You alone of the imperial powers of history rule over men who are free. You have not assigned this or that region to [an unscrupulous governor] . . . Just as citizens in an individual city might designate magistrates, so you, whose city is the whole world, appoint governors to protect and provide for the governed, as if they were elective, not to lord it over their charges. As a result, so far from disputing the office as if it were their own, governors make way for their successors readily when their term is up, and may not even await their coming. Appeals to a higher jurisdiction are as easy as appeals from parish to county. . . .

But the most notable and praiseworthy feature of all, a thing unparalleled, is your magnanimous conception of citizenship. All of your subjects (and this implies the whole world) you have divided into two parts: the better endowed and more virile, wherever they may be, you have granted citizenship and even kinship; the rest you govern as obedient subjects. Neither the seas nor expanse of land bars citizenship; Asia and Europe are not differentiated. Careers are open to talent. . . . Rich and poor find contentment and profit in your system; there is no other way of life. Your polity is a single and all-embracing harmony. . . .

. . . [You] established cities in diverse parts. The cities you filled with colonists; you introduced arts and crafts and established an orderly culture. . . . Your military organization makes all others childish. Your soldiers and officers you train to prevail not only over the enemy but over themselves. The soldier lives under discipline daily, and none ever deserts the post assigned him.

You alone are, so to speak, natural rulers. Your predecessors were masters and slaves in turn; as rulers they were counterfeits, and reversed their positions like players in a ball game. . . . You have measured out the world, bridged the rivers, cut roads through mountains, filled the wastes with posting stations, introduced orderly and refined modes of life. . . .

Be all gods and their offspring invoked to grant that this empire and this city flourish forever and never cease until stones float upon the sea and trees forbear to sprout in the springtide. May the great Ruler and his sons be preserved to administer all things well.

Question for Analysis

1. What did Aristides find so admirable in Rome's imperial system?

Moses Hadas, *A History of Rome: From Its Origins to 529 A.D. as Told by the Roman Historians* (Doubleday Anchor Books, 1956), 143–145.

to bring peace and civilized life to the world, and he praised Augustus as a divinely appointed ruler who had fulfilled Rome's mission. The Greeks might be better sculptors, orators, and thinkers, said Virgil, but only the Romans knew how to govern an empire.

> *For other peoples will, I do not doubt,*
> *still cast their bronze to breathe with softer features,*
> *or draw out of the marble living lines, plead causes better,*
> *trace the ways of heaven with wands and tell the rising*
> *constellations; but yours will be the rulership of nations,*
> *remember, Roman, these will be your arts:*
> *to teach the ways of peace to those you conquer, to spare*
> *defeated peoples, to tame the proud.*[3]

In his *History of Rome,* Livy (59 B.C.–A.D. 17) also glorified Roman character, customs, and deeds. He praised Augustus for attempting to revive traditional Roman morality, to which Livy felt a strong attachment. Although Livy was a lesser historian than Thucydides or Polybius, his work was still a major achievement, particularly in its depiction of the Roman character, which helped make Rome great.

Roman writers who excelled in poetry include Horace (65–8 B.C.), the son of a freed slave. He broadened his education by studying literature and philosophy in Athens, and his writings reflect Greek ideals. Horace enjoyed the luxury of country estates, banquets, fine clothes, and courtesans, along with the simple pleasures of mountain streams and clear skies. His poetry touched on many themes—the joy of good wine, the value of moderation, and the beauty of friendship. Unlike Horace, Virgil, or Livy, Ovid (43 B.C.–A.D. 17) did not experience the civil wars during his adult years. Consequently, he was less inclined to praise the Augustan peace. His poetry showed a preference for romance and humor, and he is best remembered for his advice to lovers.

Alinari/Art Resource, N.Y.

BASALT BUST OF LIVIA. Octavian's third wife, Livia (58 B.C.–A.D. 29), was admired for her wisdom and dignity, and the emperor valued her counsel.

The writers who lived after the Augustan age were mostly of a lesser quality than their predecessors. The historian Tacitus (A.D. 55–c. 118) was an exception. Sympathetic to republican institutions, Tacitus denounced Roman emperors and the imperial system in his *Histories* and *Annals.* In *Germania,* he turned his sights on the habits of the Germanic peoples, describing the Germans as undisciplined but heroic, with a strong love of freedom. Another outstanding writer was the satirist Juvenal (A.D. c. 55–138). His works attacked evils of Roman society such as the misconduct of emperors, the haughtiness of the wealthy, the barbaric tastes of commoners, the failures of parents, and the noise, congestion, and poverty of the capital.

Marcus Aurelius, Roman Emperor (A.D. 161–180). In this relief, Marcus Aurelius rides through the Roman Forum in ceremonial triumph, after defending the Empire against barbarian incursions.

Philosophy. Stoicism was the principal philosophy of the Pax Romana, and its leading exponents were Seneca (4 B.C.–A.D. 65), Epictetus (A.D. c. 60–c. 117), and Marcus Aurelius. Perpetuating the rational tradition of Greek philosophy, Rome's early Stoics saw the universe as governed by reason, and they esteemed the human intellect. Like Socrates, they sought the highest good in this world, not in an afterlife, and they envisioned no power above human reason. Moral values were obtained from reason alone. The individual was self-sufficient and depended entirely on rational faculties for knowing and doing good. Stoics valued self-sufficient persons who attained virtue and wisdom by exercising rational control over their lives. The Stoic doctrine that all people, because of their capacity to reason, belong to a common humanity coincided with the requirements of the multinational Roman Empire.

The Stoic conception of God underwent a gradual transformation, reflecting the religious yearnings of the times. For the early Stoics, God was an intellectual necessity, an impersonal principle that gave order to the universe. For later Roman

AQUEDUCT AT PONT DU GARD, NÎMES, FRANCE, 19 B.C. The discovery and use of concrete allowed the Romans to carry out a vast program of public works—roads, bridges, aqueducts, harbor facilities, and fortifications. Without such aqueducts to bring clean water from distant sources, the Roman style of urban life would have been impossible.

Stoics, God had become a moral necessity, comforting and reassuring people. While maintaining the traditional Stoic belief that the individual can attain virtue through unaided reason, Epictetus and Marcus Aurelius came close to seeking God's help to live properly. And Seneca showed an uncommon compassion for slaves and a revulsion for gladiatorial combat. The gap between Greek philosophy and Christianity was narrowing.

Science. The two most prominent scientists during the Greco-Roman Age were Ptolemy, a mathematician, geographer, and astronomer who worked at Alexandria in the second century A.D., and Galen (A.D. c. 130–c. 201), who investigated medicine and anatomy. Ptolemy's thirteen-volume work, *Mathematical Composition*—more commonly known as the *Almagest,* a Greek-Arabic term meaning "the greatest"—summed up antiquity's knowledge of astronomy and became the authoritative text during the Middle Ages. In the Ptolemaic system, a motionless, spherical earth stood in the center of the universe; the moon, sun, and planets moved about the earth in circles or in combinations of circles. The Ptolemaic system was built on a faulty premise, as modern astronomy eventually showed. However, it did work—that is, it provided a model of the universe that adequately accounted for most observed phenomena. The Ptolemaic system was not challenged until the middle of the sixteenth century.

Just as Ptolemy's system dominated astronomy, so the theories of Galen dominated medicine down to modern times. By dissecting both dead and living animals, Galen attempted a rational investigation of the body's working parts. Although his work contains many errors, he made essential contributions to the knowledge of anatomy. Thanks to Arab physicians who preserved his writings during the Middle Ages, Galen's influence continued in the West into early modern times.

Art and Architecture. The Romans borrowed art forms from other peoples, particularly the Greeks, but they borrowed creatively, transforming and enhancing their inheritance. Roman portraiture continued trends initiated during the Hellenistic Age. Imitating Hellenistic models, Roman sculptors realistically carved every detail of a subject's face: unruly hair, prominent nose, lines and wrinkles, a jaw that showed weakness or strength. Sculpture also gave expression to the imperial ideal. Statues of emperors conveyed nobility and authority; reliefs commemorating victories glorified Roman might and grandeur.

The Romans most creatively transformed the Greek inheritance in architecture. The Greek temple was intended to be viewed from the outside; the focus was exclusively on the superbly balanced exterior. By using arches, vaults, and domes, the Romans built structures with large, magnificent interiors. The vast interior, massive walls, and overarching dome of the famous Pantheon, a temple built in the early second century A.D. during the reign of Hadrian, symbolize the power and majesty of the Roman world-state.

Engineering. The Romans excelled at engineering. In addition to amphitheaters and public baths, they built the finest roads in the ancient world. Roman engineers carefully selected routes with an eye for minimizing natural barriers and drainage problems. The great embanked roads constructed during the Empire were designed by military engineers. Stone bridges across rivers, as well as aqueducts that carried water to Roman cities, still survive.

Law. Expressing the Roman yearning for order and justice, law was Rome's great legacy to Western civilization. Roman law passed through two essential stages: the formation of civil law (*jus civile*) and the formation of the law of nations (*jus gentium*). The basic features of the civil law evolved during the two-hundred-year Struggle of the Orders, at the same time as Rome was extending its dominion over Italy. The Twelve Tables, drawn up in the early days of the patrician–plebeian struggle, established written rules of criminal and civil law for the Roman state that applied to all citizens. Over the centuries, the civil law was expanded through statutes enacted by the assemblies and through the legal decisions of jurisdictional magistrates, the rulings of emperors, and the commentaries of professional jurists, who, aided by familiarity with Greek logic, engaged in systematic legal analysis.

During the period of the Republic's expansion outside Italy, contact with the Greeks and other peoples led to the development of the second branch of Roman law, jus gentium, which combined Roman civil law with principles selectively drawn from the legal traditions of Greeks and other peoples. Roman jurists identified the jus gentium with the natural law (*jus naturale*) of the Stoics. The jurists said that a law should accord with rational principles inherent in nature: uniform and universally valid standards that can be discerned by rational people. Serving to bind different peoples together, the law of nations harmonized with the requirements of a world empire and with Stoic ideals. As Cicero pointed out,

> *True law is right reason in agreement with nature; it is of universal application, unchanging and everlasting. And there will not be different laws at Rome and at Athens or different laws now and in the future, but one eternal and unchangeable law will be valid for all nations and all times.*[4]

The law of nations came to be applied throughout the Empire, although it never entirely supplanted local law. In the eyes of the law, a citizen–and by A.D. 212, virtually all free people had been granted citizenship–was not a Syrian or a Briton or a Spaniard, but a Roman.

After the fall of the Western Roman Empire, Roman law fell into disuse in Western Europe. Gradually reintroduced in the twelfth century, it came to form the basis of the common law in all Western lands except Britain and its dependencies. Some provisions of Roman law are readily recognizable in modern legal systems, as the following excerpts illustrate:

> *Justice is a constant, unfailing disposition to give everyone his legal due.*
>
> *No one is compelled to defend a cause against his will.*
>
> *No one suffers a penalty for what he thinks.*
>
> *In the case of major offenses it makes a difference whether something is committed purposefully or accidentally.*
>
> *In inflicting penalties, the age ... of the guilty party must be taken into account.*[5]

Entertainment. Despite its many achievements, Roman civilization presents a paradox. On the one hand, Roman culture and law evidence high standards of civilization. On the other, the Romans institutionalized barbaric practices: battles to the death between armed gladiators and the tormenting and slaughtering of wild beasts. The major forms of entertainment in both the Republic and the Empire were chariot races, wild-animal shows, and gladiatorial combat. Chariot races were gala events in which the most skillful riders and the finest and best-trained stallions raced in an atmosphere of rabid excitement. The charioteers, many of them slaves hoping that victory would bring them freedom, became popular heroes.

The Romans craved brutal spectacles. One form of entertainment pitted wild beasts against each other or against men armed with spears. Another consisted of battles, sometimes to the death, between highly trained gladiators. The gladiators, mainly slaves and condemned criminals, learned their craft at schools run by professional trainers. Some gladiators entered the arena armed with a sword; others, with a trident and a net. The spectators were transformed into a frenzied mob that lusted for blood. If they were displeased with a losing gladiator's performance, they would call for his immediate execution. Over the centuries, these spectacles grew more bizarre and brutal. Hundreds of tigers were set against elephants and bulls; wild bulls tore apart men dressed in animal skins; women battled in the arena; dwarfs fought each other. Few Romans questioned these barbarities, which had become a routine part of daily life. Occasionally, however, thoughtful Romans had strong doubts. After watching a public spectacle, the Stoic philosopher Seneca wrote in disgust: "There is nothing more harmful to one's character than attendance at some spectacle, because vices more easily creep into your soul while you are being entertained. When I return from some spectacle, I am greedier, more aggressive and ... more cruel and inhuman."[6]

Signs of Trouble

Most people in the Mediterranean world welcomed Roman rule and could not conceive of a world without the Empire that brought them peace and security. But even during the Time of Happiness, signs of trouble appeared, and they grew to crisis proportions in the third century. Unrest in Egypt, Gaul, and Judea demonstrated that not all people at all times welcomed the grand majesty of the Roman peace, that localist and separatist tendencies persisted in a universal empire. In the centuries that followed, as Rome staggered under the weight of economic, political, and military difficulties, these native loyalties reasserted themselves. Increasingly, the masses and even the Romanized elite of the cities withdrew their support from the Roman world-state.

Social and Economic Weaknesses

A healthy world-state required empirewide trade to serve as an economic base for political unity, expanding agricultural production to feed the cities, and growing internal mass markets to stimulate industrial production. But the economy of the Empire during the Pax Romana had serious defects. The means of communication and transportation were slow, which hindered long-distance commerce. Many nobles, considering it unworthy for a gentleman to engage in business, chose to squander their wealth rather than invest it in commercial or industrial enterprises. Lacking the stimulus of capital investment, the economy could not expand.

Ultimately, only a small portion of the population—the middle and upper classes of the cities, that is, landlords, whose estates were outside the city, merchants, and administrators—reaped the benefits of the Roman peace. They basked in luxury, leisure, and culture. These privileged classes bought off the urban poor with bread and circuses, but occasionally mass discontent expressed itself in mob violence. Outside the cities, the peasantry—still the great bulk of the population—was exploited to provide cheap food for the city dwellers. An enormous cultural gap existed between town and countryside.

Such a parasitical, exploitative, and elitist social system might function in periods of peace and tranquillity, but could it survive crises? Would the impoverished people of town and country—the overwhelming majority of the population—remain loyal to a state whose benefits barely extended to them and whose sophisticated culture, which they hardly comprehended, virtually excluded them?

Cultural Stagnation and Transformation

Perhaps the most dangerous sign for the future was the spiritual paralysis that crept over the ordered world of the Pax Romana. A weary and sterile Hellenism underlay the Roman peace. The ancient world was going through a transformation of values that foreshadowed the end of Greco-Roman civilization.

During the second century A.D., Greco-Roman civilization lost its creative energies, and the values of classical humanism were challenged by mythic-religious movements. No longer regarding reason as a satisfying guide to life, the educated elite subordinated the intellect to feelings and an unregulated imagination. No longer finding the affairs of this world to have purpose, people placed their hope in life after death. The Roman world was undergoing a religious revolution and was seeking a new vision of the divine.

The application of reason to nature and society was the great achievement of the Greek mind. Yet despite its many triumphs, Greek rationalism never entirely subdued the mythic-religious mentality, which draws its strength from human emotions. The masses of peasants and slaves remained attracted to religious forms. Ritual, mystery, magic, and ecstasy never lost their hold on the ancient world—nor, indeed, have they lost their hold on our own scientific and technological society. During the Hellenistic Age, the tide of rationalism gradually receded, and the nonrational, an ever-present undercurrent, showed renewed vigor. This resurgence of the mythical mentality could be seen in the popularity of the occult, magic, alchemy, and astrology. Burdened by danger and emotional stress, and fearing fate as fixed in the stars, people turned for deliverance to magicians, astrologers, and exorcists.

They also became devotees of the many Near Eastern religious cults that promised personal salvation. The proliferation of Eastern mystery religions was a clear expression of this transformation of classical values. During the Hellenistic era, slaves, merchants, and soldiers brought many religious cults westward from Persia, Babylon, Syria, Egypt, and Asia Minor. The various mystery cults possessed many common features. Converts underwent initiations and were bound by oath to secrecy. The initiates, in a state of rapture, attempted to unite with the deity after first purifying themselves through baptism (sometimes with the blood of a bull), fasting, having their heads shaved, or drinking from a sacred vessel. Communion was achieved by donning the god's robe, eating a sacred meal, or visiting the god's sanctuary. Cultists were certain that their particular savior god would protect them from misfortune and ensure their soul's immortality. More and more people felt that the good life could not be achieved by individuals through their own efforts; they needed outside help.

Like the mystery religions, philosophy reached for something beyond this world in order to edify and comfort the individual. Philosophers eventually sought escape from this world through union with a divine presence greater than human power. In Neo-Platonism, which replaced Stoicism as the dominant school of philosophy in the Late Roman Empire, religious yearnings were transformed into a religious system that transcended reason. Plotinus (A.D. c. 205–c. 270), the most influential spokesman of Neo-Platonism, subordinated philosophy to mysticism and the occult. Plato's philosophy, we have seen, contained both a major and a minor key. The major key stressed

THE COLOSSEUM, ROME, A.D. 70–80. The joint work of the emperor Vespasian and his sons Titus and Domitian, this huge amphitheater was the largest in the ancient world. It was the site of innumerable spectacles, sham sea battles, gladiatorial games, wild beast hunts, and the deaths of Christian martyrs.

a rational interpretation of the human community and called for reforming the polis on the basis of knowledge, whereas the minor key urged the soul to rise to a higher world of reality. Plotinus was intrigued by Plato's otherworldliness.

What Plotinus desired was union with the One, or the Good, sometimes called God—the source of all existence. Plotinus felt that the intellect could neither describe nor understand the One, which transcended all knowing, and that joining with the One required a mystical leap, a purification of the soul that dispensed with logic, evidence, and proof. This vision, which intends the soul to return to its true home, is for Plotinus something greater and more compelling than reason. For Plotinus, philosophy became a religious experience, a contemplation of the eternal. Compared with this union with the divine One, of what value was knowledge of the sensible world or a concern for human affairs? For Plotinus, this world was a sea of tears and troubles from which the individual yearned to escape. Reality was not in this world but beyond it, and the principal goal of life was not comprehension of the natural world or the fulfillment of human potential or the betterment of the human community, but knowledge of the One. Thus, his philosophy broke with the essential meaning of classical humanism.

By the time of the Late Roman Empire, mystery religions intoxicated the masses, and mystical philosophy beguiled the educated elite. Classical civilization was being transformed. Philosophy had become subordinate to religious belief; secular values seemed inferior to religious experience. The earthly city had raised its eyes toward heaven. The culture of the Roman world was moving in a direction in which the quest for the divine was to predominate over all human enterprises.

The Decline of Rome

In the third century A.D., the ordered civilization of the Pax Romana ended. Several elements caused this disruption. The Roman Empire was plunged into military anarchy, raided by Germanic tribes, and burdened by economic dislocations. During these critical times, effective leadership was lacking, for the adoptive system abandoned by Marcus Aurelius was not restored.

Third-Century Crisis

The degeneration of the army was a prime reason for the crisis. During the great peace, the army had remained an excellent fighting force, renowned for its discipline, organization, and loyalty. In the third century, however, there was a marked deterioration in the quality of Roman soldiers. Lacking loyalty to Rome and greedy for spoils, soldiers used their weapons to prey on civilians and to make and unmake emperors. Fearful of being killed by their unruly troops who wanted spoils or of being murdered by a suspicious emperor, generals were driven to seize the throne. Once in power, they had to buy the loyalty of their soldiers and guard against assassination by other generals. From A.D. 235 to 285, military mutiny and civil war raged as legion fought legion. Many emperors were assassinated. The once stalwart army neglected its duty of defending the borders against incursions by Germanic tribes and disrupted the internal life of the Empire.

During the third century, Rome also had to deal with a reborn Persian Empire that forced the Romans to shift large contingents of legions eastward. Taking advantage of the weakened borders and military anarchy, Germanic tribesmen crossed the Rhine—Danube frontier to loot and destroy. The Persian Empire, led by the Sassanid dynasty, attacked and for a while conquered Roman lands in the East. Some sections of the Empire, notably in Gaul, attempted to break away; these moves reflected an assertion of local patriotism over Roman universalism. The "city of mankind" was crumbling.

These eruptions had severe economic repercussions. Cities were pillaged and destroyed, farmlands ruined, and trade disrupted. To obtain funds and supplies for the military, emperors confiscated goods, exacted forced labor, and debased the coinage, causing inflation. These measures brought ruin to the middle class. Invasions, civil war, rising prices, a debased coinage, declining agricultural production, disrupted transportation, and the excessive demands of the state caused economic havoc and famine in the cities. The urban centers of the ancient world, creators and disseminators of high civilization, were caught in a rhythm of breakdown.

Diocletian and Constantine: The Regimented State

The emperors Diocletian (A.D. 285–305) and Constantine (A.D. 306–337) tried to contain the awesome forces of disintegration. At a time when agricultural production was steadily declining, they had to feed the city poor and an expanded army of more than 500,000 strung out over the Empire. They also had to prevent renewed outbreaks of military anarchy, drive the Germans back across the Rhine–Danube frontier, and secure the eastern region against renewed aggression from Persia. Their solution was to tighten the reins of central government and to squeeze more taxes and requisitions out of the citizens. In the process, they transformed Rome into a bureaucratic, regimented, and militarized state that has been described as "a vast prison."

Cities lost their traditional right of local self-government, consolidating a trend started earlier. To ensure continuous production of food and goods, as well as the collection of taxes, the state forced unskilled workers and artisans to hold their jobs for life and to pass them on to their children. For the same reasons, peasants were turned into virtual serfs, bound to the land that they cultivated. An army of government agents was formed to hunt down peasants who fled the land to escape crushing taxes and poverty.

Also frozen into their positions were city officials (*curiales*). They often found it necessary to furnish from their own pockets the difference between the state's tax demands and the amount that they could collect from an already overtaxed population. This system of a hereditary class of tax collectors and of crippling taxes to pay for a vastly expanded bureaucracy and military establishment enfeebled urban trade and industry. Such conditions killed the civic spirit of townspeople, who desperately sought escape. By overburdening urban dwellers with taxes and regulations, Diocletian and Constantine helped to shatter the vitality of city life, on which Roman prosperity and civilization depended. During the Pax Romana, municipal authorities enjoyed considerable autonomy; now the state bureaucracy extended its often onerous and rapacious power everywhere.

Rome was now governed by a highly centralized monarchy that regimented the lives of its subjects. Whereas Augustus had upheld the classical ideal that the commonwealth was a means of fostering the good life for the individual, Diocletian adopted the despotic attitude that the individual lives for the state. To guard against military insurrection, he appointed a loyal general as emperor to govern the western provinces of the Empire while he ruled the eastern regions; although both emperors bore the title Augustus, Diocletian remained superior. Constantine furthered this trend of dividing the Empire into eastern and western halves by building an imperial capital, Constantinople, at the Bosporus, a strait where Asia meets Europe.

Tribal Migrations and Invasions

By imposing some order on what had been approaching chaos, Diocletian and Constantine prevented the Empire from collapsing. Rome had been given a reprieve. But in the last part of the fourth century, the problem of guarding the frontier grew more acute.

The Huns, a nomadic people from Central Asia, swept across the plains of Russia and with their formidable cavalry put pressure on the Visigoths, a Germanic tribe that had migrated into southeastern Europe. Terrified of the Huns, the Goths sought refuge within the Roman Empire. Hoping to increase his manpower and unable to stop the panic-stricken Germans, the emperor Valens permitted them to cross the Danube frontier. But enraged by their mistreatment at the hands of Roman officials, the Visigoths took up arms. In 378, Visigoth cavalry cut to pieces Roman forces in a historic battle at Adrianople. This battle signified that Rome could no longer defend its borders. The Visigoths were on Roman territory to stay, and they now plundered the Balkans at will. The Germanic tribes increased their pressure on the Empire's borders, which finally collapsed at the very end of 406 as Vandals, Alans, Suebi, and other tribes joined the Goths in devastating and overrunning the Empire's western provinces. In 410, the Visigoths looted Rome.

Economic conditions continued to deteriorate. Cities in Britain, Gaul, Germany, and Spain lay abandoned. Other metropolises saw their populations dwindle and production stagnate. The great network of Roman roads was not maintained, and trade in the West almost disappeared or passed into the hands of Greeks, Syrians, and Jews from the East. Everywhere famine, the extortion of taxes by government officials, the proliferation of marauding outlaws driven from their homes by the excessive financial demands imposed by the state bureaucracy, and murderous warfare added to the misery of the Roman populace and the decomposition and fragmentation of the Empire.

In 451, Attila (c. 406–453), called "the Scourge of God," led his Huns into Gaul, where he was defeated by a coalition of Germans and the remnants of the Roman army. He died two years later, having come within a hairsbreadth of turning Europe into a province of a Mongolian empire. But Rome's misfortunes persisted. In 455, Rome was again looted, this time by the Vandals. Additional regions fell under the control of Germanic chieftains. Germanic soldiers in the pay of Rome gained control of the government and dictated the choice of emperor. In 476, German officers overthrew the Roman emperor Romulus and placed a fellow German, Odoacer, on the throne. This act is traditionally regarded as the end of the Roman Empire in the West. By the end of the fifth century, the Western Empire had fragmented into separate Germanic kingdoms.

Reasons for Rome's Decline

What were the underlying causes for the decline and fall of the Roman Empire in the West? Surely no other question has intrigued the historical imagination more than this one. Implicit in the answers suggested by historians and philosophers is a concern for their own civilization. Will it suffer the same fate as Rome?

To analyze so monumental a development as the fall of Rome, some preliminary observations are necessary. First, the fall of Rome was a process lasting hundreds of years; it was not a single event that occurred in A.D. 476. Second, only the western half of the Empire fell. The eastern half—wealthier, more populous, less afflicted with civil wars, and less exposed to barbarian invasions—survived as the Byzantine Empire until the middle of the fifteenth century. Third, no single explanation suffices to account for Rome's decline; multiple forces—internal problems and external threats—operated concurrently to bring about the fall.

The Role of the Germanic Tribes. The pressures exerted by the Germans along an immense frontier aggravated Rome's internal problems. The barbarian attacks left border regions depopulated and impoverished, and expenditures for the military drained the western Empire's resources. The Empire imposed high taxes and labor services on its citizens in order to strengthen the armed forces, causing the overburdened middle and lower classes to hate the imperial government that took so much from them.

Spiritual Considerations. The classical mentality, once brimming with confidence about the potentialities of the individual and the power of the intellect, suffered a failure of nerve. The urban upper class, on whom the responsibility for preserving cosmopolitan Greco-Roman culture traditionally rested, became dissolute and apathetic, no longer taking an interest in public life. The aristocrats secluded themselves behind the walls of their fortified country estates; many did not lift a finger to help the Empire. The townspeople demonstrated their disenchantment by avoiding public service and by rarely organizing resistance forces against the barbarian invaders. Hounded by the state and persecuted by the army, many farmers viewed the Germans as liberators. The great bulk of the Roman citizenry, apathetic and indifferent, simply gave up, despite the fact that they overwhelmingly outnumbered the barbarian hordes.

Political and Military Considerations. The Roman government itself contributed to this spiritual malaise through its increasingly autocratic tendencies, which culminated in the regimented rule of Diocletian and Constantine. The insatiable demands and regulations of the state in the Late Roman Empire sapped the initiative and civic spirit of its citizens. The ruined middle and lower classes withdrew their loyalty. For many, the state had become the enemy, and its administration was hated and feared more than the Germans.

In the Late Roman Empire, the quality of Roman soldiers deteriorated, and the legions failed to defend the borders even though they outnumbered the German invaders. During the third century, the army consisted predominantly of the provincial peasantry. These nonurban, non-Italian, semicivilized soldiers, often the dregs of society, were not committed to Greco-Roman civilization. They had little comprehension of Rome's mission, and at times they used their power to attack the cities and towns. The emperors also recruited large numbers of barbarians into the army to fill its depleted ranks—German tribesmen had served as auxiliaries since Julius Caesar. Ultimately, the army consisted mostly of barbarians, as both legionnaires and officers. Although these Germans made brave soldiers, they too had little loyalty to Greco-Roman civilization and to the Roman state. Moreover, barbarian units serving with the Roman army under their own commanders did not easily submit to traditional discipline or training. This deterioration of the Roman army occurred because many young citizens evaded conscription. No longer imbued with patriotism, they considered military service a servitude to be shunned.

Economic Considerations. Among the economic factors contributing to the decline of the Roman Empire in the west were a decrease in population, failure to achieve a breakthrough in technology, the heavy burden of taxation, and economic decentralization, which abetted political decentralization.

Largely because of war and epidemics, the population of the Empire shrank. This decrease adversely affected the Empire in at least three important ways. First, at the same time as the population was declining, the costs of running the Empire were spiraling, which created a terrible burden for taxpayers. Second, fewer workers were available for agriculture, the most important industry of the Empire. Third, population decline reduced the manpower available for the army, forcing emperors to permit the establishment of Germanic colonies within the Empire's borders to serve as feeders for the army. This situation led to the barbarization of the army.

The failure to expand industry and commerce was another economic reason for the Empire's decline. Instead of expanding industry and trade, towns maintained their wealth by exploiting the countryside. The Roman cities were centers of civilized life and opulence, but they lacked industries. They spent, but they did not produce. Provided with food and entertainment—"bread and circuses"—the unproductive city dwellers, driven out of the labor force by economic stagnation and slavery, were a heavy burden for the state. The towns were dominated by landlords whose estates lay beyond the city and whose income derived from grain, oil, and wine. Manufacturing was rudimentary, confined essentially to textiles, pottery, furniture, and glassware. The methods of production—rarely significantly improved—were simple, the market limited, the cost of transportation high, and agricultural productivity low—the labor of perhaps nineteen peasants was required to support one townsman. Such a fundamentally unhealthy economy could not weather the dislocations caused by uninterrupted warfare and the demands of a mushrooming bureaucracy and the military.

With the barbarians pressing on the borders, the increased military expenditures overstrained the Empire's resources. To pay for the food, uniforms, arms, and armor of the soldiers, taxes were raised, growing too heavy for peasants and townspeople. The state also requisitioned wood and grain and demanded that citizens maintain roads and bridges. The government often resorted to force to collect taxes and exact services. Crushed by these demands, many peasants simply abandoned their farms and sought the protection of large landowners or turned to banditry.

The growth of industries on latifundia, the large, fortified estates owned by wealthy aristocrats, promoted economic decentralization. Producing exclusively for the local market, these estates contributed to the impoverishment of urban centers by reducing the number of customers available to buy goods made in the cities. As life grew more desperate, urban craftsmen and small farmers, made destitute by the state, sought the protection of these large landlords, whose estates grew in size and importance. The growth of latifundia was accompanied by both the decline of cities and the transformation of independent peasants into virtual serfs.

These great estates were also new centers of political power that the imperial government could not curb. A new society was taking shape in the Late Roman Empire. The center of gravity had shifted from the city to the landed estate, from the imperial bureaucrats to the local aristocrats. These developments epitomized the decay of ancient civilization and presaged the Middle Ages.

The Roman Legacy

Rome left the West a rich heritage that has endured for centuries. The idea of a world empire united by a common law and effective government never died. In the centuries following the collapse of Rome, people continued to be attracted to the idea of a unified and peaceful world-state. By preserving and adding to the philosophy, literature, science, and art of ancient Greece, Rome strengthened the foundations of the Western cultural tradition. Latin, the language of Rome, lived on long after Rome perished. The Western church fathers wrote in Latin, and during the Middle Ages, Latin was the language of learning, literature, and law. From Latin came Italian, French, Spanish, Portuguese, and Romanian. Roman law, the quintessential expression of Roman genius, influenced church law and formed the basis of the legal codes of most European states. Finally, Christianity, the core religion of the West, was born within the Roman Empire and was greatly influenced by Roman law (the church's canon law owed much to Roman jurisprudence) and organization (the pope, head of the church and ruling from Rome, was the counterpart of the Roman emperor, and bishoprics were established in regions that coincided with the Empire's administrative structure). The ideal of a single Christian society embracing many different nationalities, so dear to medieval thinkers, was superimposed on the model of the Roman Empire.

❖ ❖ ❖

Notes

1. E. Badian, *Roman Imperialism in the Late Republic* (Ithaca, N.Y.: Cornell University Press, 1971), p. 87.
2. Sallust, *The Conspiracy of Catiline,* trans. S. A. Handford (Baltimore: Penguin Books, 1963), pp. 181–182.
3. From *The Aeneid of Virgil* by Virgil, translated by Allen Mandelbaum, copyright © 1971 by Allen Mandelbaum. Used by permission of Bantam Books, a division of Random House, Inc.
4. Reprinted by permission of the publishers and the Trustees of the Loeb Classical Library® from Cicero: Volume XVI, *De Re Publica,* Loeb Classical Library Vol. 213, translated by Clinton W. Keyes (Cambridge, Mass.: Harvard University Press), p. 211. Copyright © 1928 by the President and Fellows of Harvard College. The Loeb Classical Library® is a registered trademark of the President and Fellows of Harvard College.
5. Excerpted in Naphtali Lewis and Meyer Reinhold, eds., *Roman Civilization, Sourcebook II: The Empire* (New York: Harper & Row, 1966), pp. 535, 539, 540, 547, 548.
6. Seneca, *The Epistles,* trans. Thomas Morell (London: W. Woodfall, 1786), vol. 1, epistle 7.

Suggested Reading

Boardman, John, et al., eds., *The Oxford History of the Classical World* (1986). Essays on all facets of Roman culture.

Boren, H. C., *Roman Society* (1977). A social, economic, and cultural history of the Republic and the Empire; written with the student in mind.

Chambers, Mortimer, ed., *The Fall of Rome* (1963). A valuable collection of readings.

Christ, Karl, *The Romans* (1984). A good survey.

Crawford, M., *The Roman Republic* (1982). A reliable survey with many quotations from original sources.

Dupont, Florence, *Daily Life in Ancient Rome* (1989). Social structure, religion, and notions of time and space.

Errington, R. M., *The Dawn of Empire: Rome's Rise to World Power* (1972). A study of Rome, the reluctant imperialist.

Everitt, Anthony, *Augustus* (2006). A recent biography.

Ferrill, Arthur, *The Fall of the Roman Empire* (1986). A military explanation.

Galinsky, Karl, *Augustan Culture* (1996) Weaves together the history and culture of the period.

Goldsworthy, Adrian, *How Rome Fell* (2009). An important recent study of Rome's decline, paying special attention to Rome's frequent internal wars starting in the third century.

Grant, Michael, *The Fall of the Roman Empire* (1990). A clearly written synthesis.

Harris, William V., *War and Imperialism in Republican Rome 327–70 B.C.* (1992). The motives behind Roman foreign policy.

Heather, Peter, *The Fall of the Roman Empire: A New History of Rome and the Barbarians* (2006). An insightful exploration of the age-old question of Rome's decline.

Holland, Tom, *Rubicon: The Last Years of the Roman Republic* (2003). An accessible account of the death of the Roman Republic.

Jenkyns, Richard, ed., *The Legacy of Rome* (1992). Essays on Rome's impact on Western civilization.

Lewis, Naphtali, and Meyer Reinhold, eds., *Roman Civilization* (1966). A two-volume collection of source readings.

McGeoch, Kevin M., *The Romans* (2004). A comprehensive analysis of Roman society and culture in the Republic and Empire.
Ogilvie, R. M., *Roman Literature and Society* (1980). An introductory survey of Latin literature.
Veyne, Paul, ed., *A History of Private Life* (1987). A discussion of all phases of Roman social life.
Wardman, Alan, *Rome's Debt to Greece* (1976). Roman attitudes toward the Greek world.
White, Lynn, ed., *The Transformation of the Roman World* (1973). A useful collection of essays on the transformation of the ancient world and the emergence of the Middle Ages.

CourseMate

Go to the CourseMate website at **www.cengagebrain.com** for additional study tools and review materials—including audio and video clips—for this chapter.

Chapter 5

Early Christianity: A World Religion

- **The Origins of Christianity**
- **The Spread and Triumph of Christianity**
- **Development of Christian Organization, Doctrine, and Attitudes**
- **Saint Augustine: The Christian Worldview**
- **Christianity and Classical Humanism: Alternative Worldviews**

Focus Questions

1. How did Saint Paul transform a Jewish sect into a world religion?
2. What factors contributed to the triumph of Christianity in the Roman Empire?
3. How was early Christianity influenced by Judaism, Greek philosophy, and Hellenistic mystery religions?
4. What do the worldviews of Christianity and Greco-Roman humanism have in common? Why are they essentially different?

As confidence in human reason and hope for happiness in this world waned in the last centuries of the Roman Empire, a new outlook began to take hold. Evident in philosophy and in the popularity of Near Eastern religions, this viewpoint stressed escape from an oppressive world and communion with a higher reality. Christianity evolved and expanded within this setting of declining classicism and heightening otherworldliness. As one response to a declining Hellenism, Christianity offered a spiritually disillusioned Greco-Roman world a reason for living: the hope of personal immortality. The triumph of Christianity marked a break with classical antiquity and a new stage in the evolution of the West, for there was a fundamental difference between the classical and the Christian concepts of God, the individual, and the purpose of life. ❖

The Origins of Christianity

A Palestinian Jew named Jesus was executed by the Roman authorities during the reign of Tiberius (A.D. 14–37), who had succeeded Augustus. At the time, few people paid much attention to what proved to be one of the most pivotal events in world history. In the quest for the historical Jesus, scholars have stressed the importance of both his Jewishness and the religious ferment that prevailed in Palestine in the first century B.C. Jesus' ethical teachings are rooted in the moral outlook of the Old Testament prophets. Jesus, who prayed as a Jew, taught as a Jew to fellow Jews, and valued Jewish Law and prophetic teachings, could only conceive of himself as a Jew. Hans Küng, the prominent Swiss student of religion, elaborates on this point:

> *Jesus was a Jew, a member of a small, poor, politically powerless nation living at the periphery of the Roman Empire. He was active among Jews and for Jews. His mother Mary, his father Joseph, his family, his followers were Jews. His name was Jewish (Hebrew Yeshu'a). . . . His bible, his worship, his prayers were Jewish. In the situation at that time he could not have thought of any proclamation among the gentiles. His message was for the Jewish people, but for this people in its entirety without any exception. From this basic fact it follows irrevocably that without Judaism there would be no Christianity. The Bible of the early Christians was the "Old Testament." The New Testament Scriptures became part of the bible only by being appended to the Old. The gospel of Jesus Christ everywhere quite consciously presupposes the Torah and the Prophets.*[1]

Judaism in the First Century B.C.

In the first century B.C., four principal social-religious parties, or sects, existed among the Palestinian Jews: Sadducees, Pharisees, Essenes, and Zealots. The religiously conservative Sadducees, composed of the upper stratum of Jewish society—influential landed gentry and hereditary priests, who controlled the temple in Jerusalem—insisted on a strict interpretation of Mosaic Law and the perpetuation of temple ceremonies. Claiming to be the descendants of Sadok, the high priest of Solomon, Sadducees believed that they were maintaining the ancient Hebrew teachings concerning the Torah, which they interpreted literally. Rejecting the concepts of the resurrection of the dead and of an afterlife, they held that God meted out rewards and punishments on earth. Challenging the aristocratic Sadducees, the Pharisees adopted a more flexible attitude toward Mosaic Law; they allowed discussion and varying interpretations of the Law and granted authority to oral tradition—an "oral Torah" that was communicated from one generation to another—as well as to written Scripture. The Pharisees had the support of most of the Jewish nation. All later forms of Judaism developed from the Pharisees. The third religious party, the Essenes, founded by a man they referred to as the "Teacher of Righteousness," established a semi-monastic community near the Dead Sea. In 1947, leather scrolls in hermetically sealed cylinders were found near the Essene community of Qumran, about fourteen miles from Jerusalem, close to the Dead Sea. Dated from between c. 200 B.C. and A.D. 66–70, the "Dead Sea Scrolls" contain the oldest extant Hebrew manuscripts and also documents that are unique to the sect of the Essenes. The fourth sect, the Zealots, demanded that the Jews neither pay taxes to Rome nor acknowledge the authority of the Roman emperor. Devoted patriots, the Zealots engaged in acts of resistance to Rome, which culminated in the great revolt of A.D. 66–70 (see "The Pax Romana" in Chapter 4).

Unlike the Sadducees, the Pharisees believed in life after death. The concept of personal immortality is barely mentioned in the Hebrew Scriptures. A later addition to Hebrew religious thought, probably acquired from Persia, the idea had gained wide acceptance by the time of Jesus. The Essenes, too, believed in the physical resurrection

Chronology 5.1 ❖ Early Christianity

A.D. 29	Crucifixion of Jesus
c. 34–64	Missionary activity of Saint Paul
c. 66–70	Gospel of Mark is written
250–260	Decade of brutal persecution of Christians by the Romans
313	Constantine grants toleration to Christianity
325	Council of Nicaea rules that God and Christ are of the same substance, coequal and coeternal
391–392	Theodosius I prohibits public acts of pagan worship and the public profession of pagan religions; during his reign, Christianity becomes the state religion
430	Death of Saint Augustine
529	Saint Benedict founds monastery at Monte Cassino

of the body but gave this doctrine a more compelling meaning by tying it to the immediate coming of God's kingdom.

Besides the afterlife, another widely recognized idea in the first century B.C. was the belief in the Messiah, a redeemer chosen by God to liberate Israel from foreign rule. In the days of the Messiah, it was predicted, Israel would be free, the exiles would return, and the Jews would be blessed with peace, unity, and prosperity. The Messiah, in contrast to wicked Roman rulers, would govern justly and righteously.

Jesus (c. 4 B.C.–A.D. c. 29) performed his ministry within this context of Jewish religious-national expectations and longings. The hopes of Jesus' early followers stemmed from a lower-class dissatisfaction with the aristocratic Sadducees; the Pharisee emphasis on prophetic ideals and the afterlife; the Essene preoccupation with the end-of-days and belief in the nearness of God and the need for repentance; and a conquered people's yearning for the Messiah, who would liberate their land from Roman rule and establish God's reign.

Jesus: Moral Transformation of the Individual

Jesus himself wrote nothing, and nothing was written about him during his lifetime. In the generations following his death, both Roman and Jewish historians paid him scant attention. Consequently, virtually everything we know about Jesus comes from the Bible's New Testament, which was written decades after Jesus' death by devotees seeking to convey a religious truth and to propagate a faith. Modern historians have rigorously and critically analyzed the New Testament; their analyses have provided some insights into Jesus and his beliefs, though much about him remains obscure.

At around the age of thirty, no doubt influenced by John the Baptist, Jesus began to preach the coming of the reign of God and the need for people to repent—to undergo moral transformation so that they could enter God's kingdom. For Jesus, the coming of the kingdom was imminent; the process leading to its establishment on earth had already begun. A new order would soon emerge, in which God would govern his people righteously and mercifully. Hence, the present moment was critical—a time for spiritual preparedness and penitence—because an individual's thoughts, goals, and actions would determine whether he or she would gain entrance into the kingdom. People had to change their lives radically. They had to eliminate base, lustful, hostile, and selfish feelings; stop pursuing wealth and power; purify their hearts; and show their love for God and their fellow human beings. Like the Hebrew prophets, Jesus saw ethics as the core of Mosaic Law: "So whatever you wish that men would do to you, do so to them; for this is the law and the prophets" (Matthew 7:12). Like the prophets, he denounced injustice and oppression, urged mercy and compassion, and expressed a special concern for the poor and downtrodden.

Although Jesus did not intend to draw away his fellow Jews from their ancestral religion, he was distressed by the Judaism of his day. The rabbis taught the Golden Rule, as well as God's love and mercy for his children, but it seemed to Jesus that these ethical considerations were being undermined by an exaggerated rabbinical concern with ritual, restrictions, and the fine points of the Law. Jesus believed that the center of Judaism had shifted from prophetic values to obeying the rules and prohibitions regulating the smallest details of daily life. (To Jewish leaders, of course, these detailed regulations governing eating, washing, Sabbath observance, family relations, and so forth were God's commands, intended to sanctify all human activities.) To Jesus, such a rigid view of the Law distorted the meaning of prophetic teachings. Rules dealt only with an individual's visible behavior; they did not penetrate to the person's inner being and lead to a moral transformation based on love, compassion, and selflessness. The inner person concerned Jesus, and it was an inner change that he sought. With the fervor of a prophet, he urged a moral transformation of human character through a direct encounter between the individual and God.

Jewish scribes and priests, guardians of the faith, regarded Jesus as a troublemaker who threatened ancient traditions and undermined respect for the Sabbath. Stated succinctly, Jewish leaders believed that Jesus was setting the authority of his person over Mosaic Law—an unpardonable blasphemy in their eyes. They saw him as a false prophet who was leading the people astray. To the Romans who ruled Palestine, Jesus was a political agitator who could ignite Jewish messianic expectations into a revolt against Rome. After Jewish leaders turned Jesus over to the Roman authorities, the Roman procurator, Pontius Pilate, sentenced him to death by crucifixion, a customary punishment for someone guilty of high treason. Jesus' execution was consistent with Roman policy in Judea, for the Romans routinely arrested and executed Jews suspected of inciting unrest against Roman rule. Inscribed on the cross on which he was crucified were the words "King of the Jews," a seemingly clear indication of why Pilate ordered his death. Although it is questionable if Jesus ever intended to challenge Roman authority, Pilate was taking no chances. He wanted to eliminate the popular leader before he might ignite a popular uprising.

Believing that Jesus was an inspired prophet or even the long-awaited Messiah, some Jews had become his followers; the chief of these were the Twelve Disciples. But at the time of Jesus' death, Christianity was still just a small Hebrew sect, with dim prospects for survival. What established the Christian movement and gave it strength was the belief of Jesus' followers that he was raised from the dead on the third day after his burial. The doctrine of the Resurrection made possible the belief in Jesus as divine, a savior-god who had come to earth to show people the way to heaven. For early Christians, Jesus' death and belief in his resurrection took on greater importance than his life. For these Christians, Jesus the savior-god became the center of their emerging church.

There is no evidence that Jesus, who never preached to Gentiles, intended to establish a new church; this was accomplished by his followers. In the years immediately following the Crucifixion, the religion of Jesus was confined almost exclusively to Jews, who could more appropriately be called Jewish-Christians. The word *Christian* derives from a name given Jesus: *Christ* (the Lord's Anointed, the Messiah). Before this new Jewish messianic movement could realize the universal implications of Jesus' teachings and become a world religion, as distinct from a reformist Jewish sect, it had to extricate itself from Jewish ritual, politics, and culture. This achievement was the work of a Hellenized Jew named Saul—known to the world as Saint Paul.

Saint Paul: From a Jewish Sect to a World Religion

Saint Paul (A.D. c. 5–c. 67) came from the Greek city of Tarsus in southeastern Asia Minor. He belonged to the Diaspora, or the "Dispersion"—the millions of Jews living outside Palestine. The non-Jews, or *Gentiles* (from Latin *gens*, or "nation"), who came into contact with Jews of the Diaspora were often favorably impressed by Hebrew monotheism, ethics, and family life. Some Gentiles embraced Hebrew monotheism but refused to adhere to provisions of the Law requiring circumcision and dietary regulations. Among these

Vanni/Art Resource, N.Y.

Christ Gives the Law to Saints Peter and Paul, Fifth Century, Santa Costanza, Rome. This mosaic portrays a haloed, beardless Christ bestowing the law in the manner of an emperor delivering an edict.

Gentiles and the non-Palestinian Jews who were greatly influenced by the Greco-Roman milieu, Jesus' Apostles would find receptive listeners.

At first, Saul persecuted the followers of Jesus, but then he underwent a spiritual transformation and became a follower of Jesus. Serving as a zealous missionary of Jewish Christianity in the Diaspora, Saint Paul preached to his fellow Jews in synagogues. Recognizing that the Christian message applied to non-Jews as well, Paul urged spreading it to the Gentiles. In the process of his missionary activity—and he traveled extensively throughout the Roman Empire—Paul formulated ideas that represented a fundamental break with Judaism and became the heart of this new religion. He taught that the crucified Messiah had suffered and died for humanity's sins; that through Jesus God had revealed himself to all people, both Jews and Gentiles; and that this revelation supplanted God's earlier revelation to the Jewish people. Alone, one was helpless, possessed by sin, unable to overcome one's wicked nature. Jesus was the only hope, said Paul.

In attempting to reach the Gentiles, Saint Paul had to disentangle Christianity from a Jewish sociocultural context. Thus, he held that neither Gentile nor Jewish followers of Jesus were bound by the hundreds of rituals and rules that constitute Mosaic Law. As a consequence of Jesus' coming, Paul insisted, Mosaic regulations hindered missionary activity among the Gentiles.* To Paul, the

*Paul's understanding of Mosaic Law is a matter of controversy. Some scholars argue that he regarded the Law as obsolete and broke with his ancestral faith. Other scholars, arguing that Paul did not forsake the Law, point to a famous passage: "Do we then nullify the law by this faith? Not at all! Rather we uphold the law" (Rom. 3:31). Paul, who continually described himself as a Pharisee, lived an observant life and celebrated Jewish festivals. For these scholars, Paul never stopped revering the Torah, but he taught that Jesus, the Messiah, fulfilled the Torah's higher purpose—the biblical prophecy of the Messiah's coming.

new Christian community was the true fulfillment of Judaism; Jesus' followers were the new Israelites. The Jews regarded their faith as a national religion, bound inseparably with the history of their people. Paul held that Jesus fulfilled not only the messianic aspirations of the Jews, but also the spiritual needs and expectations of all peoples. For Paul, the new Christian community was not a nation, but an *oikoumene,* a world community. To this extent, Christianity shared in the universalism of the Hellenistic Age.

In preaching the doctrine of the risen Savior and insisting that Mosaic Law had been superseded, Paul (whatever his intentions) was breaking with his Jewish roots and transforming a Jewish sect into a new religion. Separating Christianity from Judaism enormously increased its appeal for those non-Jews who were attracted to Hebrew ethical monotheism but repelled by circumcision, dietary rules, and other strict requirements of Mosaic Law. Paul built on the personalism and universalism implicit in the teachings of Jesus (and the Hebrew prophets) to create a religion intended not for a people with its own particular history, culture, and land but for all humanity.

The Spread and Triumph of Christianity

By establishing Christianity's independence from Judaism, Saint Paul made the new religion fit for export to the Greco-Roman world. But its growth was slow. Originating in the first century, Christianity took firm root in the second, grew extensively in the third, and became the official religion of the Roman Empire at the end of the fourth century.

The Appeal of Christianity

The triumph of Christianity was linked to a corresponding decline in the vitality of Hellenism and a shift in cultural emphasis—a movement from reason to emotion and revelation. Offering comforting solutions to the existential problems of life and death, religion demonstrated a greater capacity than reason to stir human hearts. Hellenism had invented the tools of rational thought, but the power of mythical thought was never entirely subdued. By the Late Roman Empire, science and philosophy could not compete with mysticism, myth, and the divine. Mystery cults, which promised personal salvation, were spreading and gaining followers. Neo-Platonists yearned for a mystical union with the One. Astrology and magic, which offered supernatural explanations for the operations of nature, were also popular. This recoil from rational and worldly values helped prepare the way for Christianity. In a culturally stagnating and spiritually troubled Greco-Roman world, Christianity gave a new meaning to life and a new hope to disillusioned men and women.

The Christian message of a divine Savior and a concerned Father, as well as of brotherly love, inspired men and women who were dissatisfied with the world of the here-and-now—who felt no attachment to city or empire, derived no inspiration from philosophy, and suffered from a profound sense of loneliness. Christianity offered the individual what the city and the Roman world-state could not: an intensely personal relationship with God, an intimate connection with a higher world, and membership in a community of the faithful who cared for one another.

Stressing the intellect and self-reliance, Greco-Roman thought did not provide for the emotional needs of the ordinary person. Christianity addressed itself to this defect in the Greco-Roman outlook. The poor, the oppressed, and the slaves were attracted to the personality, life, death, and resurrection of Jesus, his love for all, and his concern for suffering humanity. They found spiritual sustenance in a religion that offered a hand of love and taught that a person need not be well-born, rich, educated, or talented to be worthy, that God draws no distinction between the lowly, poor, and slaves and the mightiest aristocrats. To people burdened with misfortune and terrified by death, Christianity held the promise of eternal life, a kingdom of heaven where they would be comforted by God the Father. Thus, Christianity gave the common person what the aristocratic values of Greco-Roman civilization generally did not: hope, a sense of dignity, and inner strength. By and large, classical philosophy offered little compassion for the sufferer, but the cardinal principle of Christianity was that Jesus had endured earthly torments because of his love for all human beings and that even the lowliest could be redeemed.

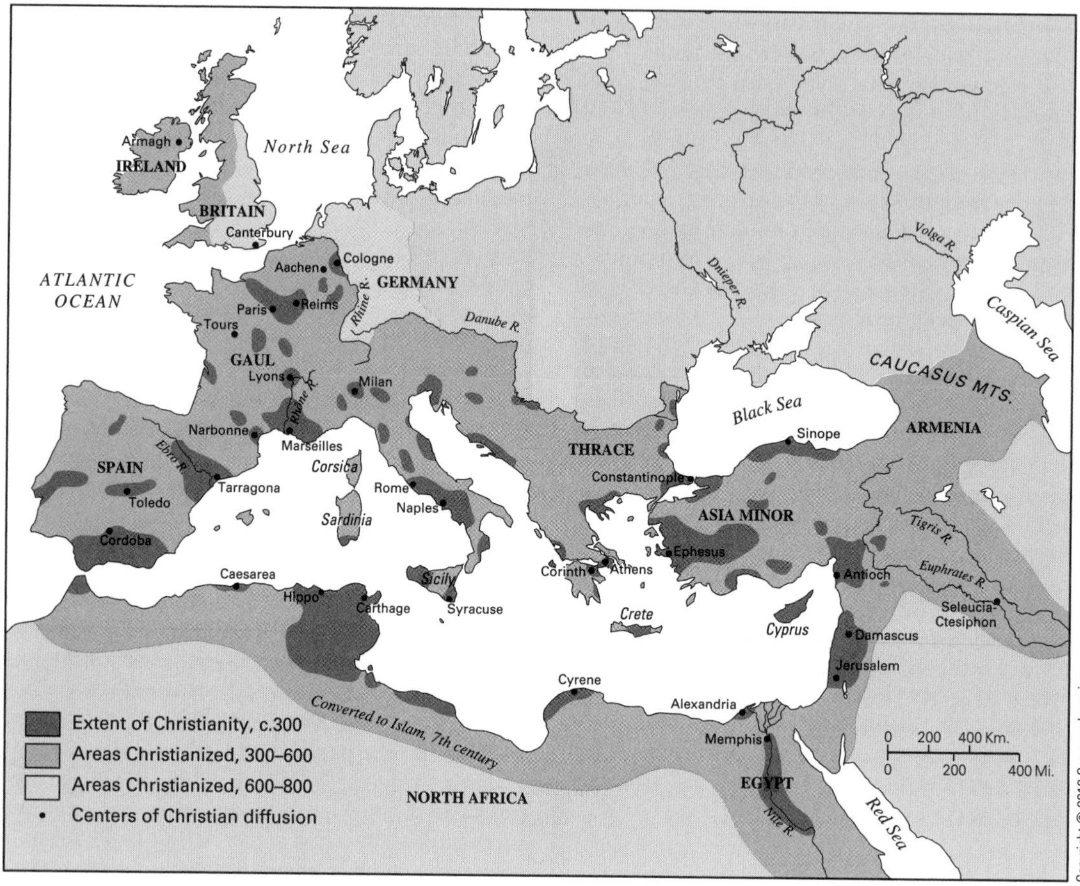

Map 5.1 The Spread of Christianity Aided by dedicated missionaries, Christianity expanded throughout the Mediterranean world and later into Germanic lands.

Christianity succeeded not only through the appeal of its message, but also through the power of its institution, the Christian church, which grew into a strong organization uniting the faithful. For city dwellers, lonely, alienated, and disillusioned with public affairs—stranded mortals groping for a sense of community—the church that called its members "brother" and "sister" filled an elemental need of human beings to belong. The church welcomed women converts, who were often the first to join and brought their menfolk after them. Among the reasons that the church drew women was its command to husbands to treat their wives kindly, remain faithful, and provide for the children. Moreover, in the eyes of God, women were spiritually equal with men. The church won new converts and retained the loyalty of its members by furnishing social services for the poor and infirm, welcoming slaves, criminals, sinners, and other outcasts, and offering a hand of brotherhood and comfort during difficult times.

The ability of an evolving Christianity to assimilate elements from Greek philosophy and even from the mystery religions also contributed in no small measure to its growth. By utilizing Greek philosophy, Christianity was able to present itself in terms intelligible to those versed in Greek learning and thus attract educated people. Converts to Christianity who were trained in philosophy proved to be able defenders of their newly adopted faith. Because some Christian doctrines (the risen savior-god, the virgin and child, life after death, communion with the divine), practices (purification through baptism), and holy days (December 25 was the birth date of the god Mithras) either paralleled or were adopted from the mystery religions, it became relatively easy to win converts from these rivals.

Christianity and Rome

Generally tolerant of religions, the Roman government at first did not significantly interfere with the Christian movement. Indeed, Christianity benefited in many ways from its association with the Roman Empire. Christian missionaries traveled throughout the Empire, over roads and across seas made safe by Roman arms. The common Greek dialect, Koine, spoken in most parts of the Empire, facilitated the missionaries' task. Had the Mediterranean world been fractured into separate and competing states, the spread of Christianity might well have faced an insurmountable obstacle. The universalism of the Roman Empire, which made citizenship available to peoples of many nationalities, prepared the way for the universalism of Christianity, which welcomed membership from all nations. Early Christians grafted onto Rome's imperial mission a spiritual evangelical cause: "Go ye therefore and teach all nations" (Matthew 28:19).[2]

As the number of Christians increased, Roman officials began to fear the Christians as subversives who preached allegiance to God and not to Rome. To many Romans, Christians were disloyal citizens, enemies of the social order: strange people who would not accept the state gods, would not engage in sacrifices to Roman divinities, scorned gladiatorial contests, stayed away from public baths, glorified nonviolence, refused to honor deceased emperors as gods, and worshiped a crucified criminal as Lord. Romans ultimately found in Christians a universal scapegoat for the ills burdening the Empire, such as famines, plagues, and military reverses. Were not these afflictions divine punishment for Christians' refusal to honor ancestral gods and traditions? In an effort to stamp out Christianity, emperors occasionally resorted to persecution. Christians were imprisoned, beaten, starved, burned alive, beheaded, torn apart by wild beasts in the arena for the amusement of the Roman crowd, and crucified. However, the persecutions did not last long enough to extirpate the new religion. Actually, they strengthened the determination of most of the faithful and won new converts, who were awed by the extraordinary courage of the martyrs willingly dying for their faith. Many Christians embraced the opportunity for martyrdom; they believed that they were reenacting the passion of Jesus, who sacrificed himself for humanity.

Unable to crush Christianity by persecution, Roman emperors decided to gain the support of the growing number of Christians within the Empire. In A.D. 313, Constantine, probably genuinely attracted to Christianity, issued the Edict of Milan, granting toleration to Christians. By A.D. 392, Theodosius I had made Christianity the state religion of the Empire and declared the worship of pagan gods illegal. With Christians in power, persecution did not end, but its target had shifted from Christians to pagans, Jews, and Christians with unorthodox views. The polytheistic religions of the Roman world did not claim to possess an exhaustive truth—did not assert that a particular god or a particular form of worship should prevail over all others and that wrongful religious expressions should be rooted out. People were relatively free to select their own credo and engage in their own acts of worship. Christianity, in contrast, possessing an exclusive attitude toward truth, felt compelled to cleanse society of false gods and beliefs and often viewed nonbelievers as wicked enemies of God who deserved punishment. Thus mobs, often driven by fanatic clergy, hurled non-Christian writings into bonfires, destroyed pagan altars and sacred images, and squelched pagan rites and festivals. Emperors, often pushed by the clergy, passed decrees calling for fining, imprisoning, torturing, and executing adherents of pagan cults.

Christianity and Greek Philosophy

Christianity synthesized both the Hebrew and the Greco-Roman traditions. Having emerged from Judaism, it assimilated Hebrew monotheism and prophetic morality and retained the Old

Testament as the Word of God. As the new religion evolved, it also assimilated elements of Greek philosophy. The ability to combine a historic Judaic monotheism, which had many admirers in the Gentile world, with Greek rational philosophy was a crucial reason for Christianity's triumph in the Roman Empire. But there was a struggle between conservatives, who wanted no dealings with pagan philosophy, and those believers who recognized the value of Greek thought to Christianity.

To conservative church fathers—early Christian writers whose works are accepted as authoritative by the Catholic church—classical philosophy was entirely in error because it did not derive from divine revelation. As the final statement of God's truth, Christianity superseded both pagan philosophy and pagan religions. These conservatives feared that studying classical authors would contaminate Christian morality (did not Plato propose a community of wives, and did not the dramatists treat violent passions?) and promote heresy (was not classical literature replete with references to pagan gods?). For these church fathers, there could be no compromise between Greek philosophy and Christian revelation. They considered their life's mission to be preaching the Gospel of Jesus, which required no reinforcement from pagan ideas. For them, faith was more reliable than all the demonstrations of human reason. "What indeed has Athens to do with Jerusalem?" asked Tertullian (A.D. 150–225). "With our faith, we desire no further belief. For this is our faith that there is nothing which we ought to believe besides."[3]

Some church fathers, including several who had a Greek education, resisted this anti-intellectualism. Defending the value of studying classical literature, they maintained that such literature, properly taught, could aid in the moral development of children because it presented many examples of virtuous deeds. Some church fathers claimed that Greek philosophy contained a dim glimmer of God's truth, a pre-Christian insight into divine wisdom. Christ had corrected and fulfilled an insight reached by the philosophical mind. Knowledge of Greek philosophy, they also contended, helped Christians explain their beliefs logically and argue intelligently with pagan critics of Christian teachings.

Utilizing the language and categories of Greek philosophy, Christian intellectuals transformed Christianity from a simple ethical creed into a theoretical system, a theology. This effort to express Christian beliefs in terms of Greek rationalism is referred to as the Hellenization of Christianity.

Greek philosophy enabled Christians to explain rationally God's existence and revelation. Christ was depicted as the divine or incarnate Logos (reason) in human form. Educated believers could argue that the fundamental principles which Greek philosophers saw operating in the universe were established by God the Father. The Stoic teaching that all people are fundamentally equal because they share in universal reason could be formulated in Christian terms: that all are united in Christ. Christians could interpret the church to be the true fulfillment of the Stoic idea of a polity embracing the entire world. Stoic ethics, which stressed moderation, self-control, and brotherhood, was compatible with Christianity. Particularly in Platonism, which drew a distinction between a world perceived by the senses and a higher order—a transcendent world that should be the central concern of human existence—Christian thinkers found a congenial vehicle for expressing Christian beliefs. The perfect and universal Forms, or Ideas, which Plato maintained were the true goal of knowledge and the source of ethical standards, were held by Christians to exist in God's mind.

That Greek philosophy exerted an influence on church doctrine is of immense importance: it meant that rational thought, the priceless achievement of the Greek mind, was not lost. However, the Hellenization of Christianity did not mean the triumph of classicism over Christianity, but rather the reverse: Christianity triumphed over Hellenism. Greek philosophy had to sacrifice its essential autonomy—the ability to think freely—to the requirements of Christian revelation; that is, reason had to fit into a Christian framework and serve faith. Although Christianity made use of Greek philosophy, Christian truth ultimately rested on faith, not reason. And in any conflict between reason and faith, faith would prevail.

Saint Paul Mosaic from the Baptistry of the Arians, Ravenna, Italy. Inspired by Jesus' life and death, Paul taught that Jesus was a resurrected redeemer who held the promise of salvation for both Jews and Gentiles.

Development of Christian Organization, Doctrine, and Attitudes

Early in its history, the church developed along hierarchical lines. Those members of the Christian community who had the authority to preside over the celebration of the Mass—breaking bread and offering wine as Christ had done at the Last Supper—were called either priests or bishops. Gradually, the designation *bishop* was reserved for the one clergyman in the community with the authority to resolve disputes over doctrines and practices. Regarded as the successors to Jesus' Twelve Disciples, bishops supervised religious activities within their regions. In creating a diocese that was supervised by a bishop and had its center in a leading city, the church adapted Roman administrative techniques.

The Primacy of the Bishop of Rome

The bishop of Rome, later to be called the pope, claimed primacy over the other bishops. In developing the case for their supremacy over the church organization, bishops of Rome increasingly referred to the famous New Testament passage in which Jesus says to his disciple Simon (also called Peter): "'And I tell you, you are Peter, and on this rock I will build my church'" (Matthew 16:18). Because *Peter* in Greek means "rock" *(petra),* it was argued that Christ had chosen Peter to succeed him as ruler of the universal church. Since it was commonly accepted that Saint Peter had established a church in Rome and was martyred there, it was argued further that the Roman bishop inherited the power that Christ had passed on to Peter.

The Rise of Monasticism

Some devout Christians committed to living a perfect Christian life were distressed by the wickedness of the world about them, including the moral laxity of those clergy who chased after wealth and pomp. Seeking to escape from the agonies and corruptions of this world, some ardent

Christians withdrew to deserts and mountains in search of spiritual renewal. In their zeal for holiness, they sometimes practiced extreme forms of asceticism: self-flogging, wearing spiked corsets, eating only herbs, or living for years on a column high above the ground. Gradually, colonies of these hermits sprang up, particularly in Egypt; in time, the leaders of these monastic communities drew up written rules that required monks to refrain from bodily abuses and to engage in manual labor.

The monastic ideal spread from East to West. The principal figure in the shaping of monasticism in the West was Saint Benedict (c. 480–c. 543), who founded a monastery at Monte Cassino, Italy, in 529. The Rule of Saint Benedict called for the monks to live in poverty and to study, labor, and obey the abbot, the head of the monastery. Monks were required to pray often, work hard, talk little, and surrender private property. In imposing discipline and regulations, Benedict eliminated the excessive and eccentric individualism of the early monks; he socialized and institutionalized the spiritual impulse that led monks to withdraw from the world. Benedict demonstrated the same genius for administration that the Romans had shown in organizing and governing the Empire. His rule became the standard for monasteries in Western Europe.

The Ascension of Jesus into Heaven: A Miniature Painting, c. 586. In this illustration contained in a manuscript produced by a monk at Saint John's Abbey, Zagba, Mesopotamia, the upper zone of the painting reflects a vision of the prophet Ezekiel (1:3–28). The lower zone shows Jesus' disciples and his mother, Mary, with two angels as witnesses to Jesus' ascension into heaven (Acts 1:7-14).

The Scriptural Tradition and Doctrinal Disputes

The earliest surviving Christian writings are Paul's Epistles, written some twenty-five to thirty years after the death of Jesus. Jesus' sayings and deeds were preserved by word of mouth. Sometime around A.D. 66–70, about forty years after the Crucifixion, Saint Mark formulated the Christian message from this oral tradition and perhaps from some material that had been put in writing earlier. Later, Saint Matthew and Saint Luke, relying heavily on Mark's account, wrote somewhat longer Gospels. The Gospels of Mark, Matthew, and Luke are called *synoptic* because their approach to Jesus is very similar. The remaining Gospel, written by Saint John around A.D. 110, varies significantly from the synoptic Gospels. The synoptic Gospels, the Gospel of Saint John, the Acts of the Apostles, the twenty-one Epistles (including those written by Saint Paul), and Revelation constitute the twenty-seven books of the Christian New Testament. Christians also accepted the Hebrews' Old Testament as God's Word.

The early Christians had a Bible and a clergy to teach it. But the Holy Writ could be interpreted differently by equally sincere believers, and controversies over doctrine threatened the unity of the early church. The most important controversy concerned how people viewed the relationship between God and Christ. Arius (A.D. 250–336), a Greek priest in Alexandria, led one faction. He denied the complete divinity of Christ, one of the basic tenets of the church. To Arius, Christ was more than man but less than God; there was no permanent union between God and Christ; the Father alone was eternal and truly God.

The Council of Nicaea (A.D. 325), the first assembly of bishops from all parts of the Roman world, was called to settle the controversy. The council condemned Arius and ruled that God and Christ were of the same substance, coequal and coeternal. The position adopted at Nicaea became the basis of the Nicene Creed, which remains the official doctrine of the church. Although Arianism, the name given the heresy of Arius, won converts for a time, it eventually died out, helped along by persecution.

Christianity and Society

Although salvation was their ultimate aim, Christians still had to dwell within the world and deal with its imperfections. In the process, Christian thinkers challenged some of the mores of Greco-Roman society and formulated attitudes that would endure for centuries. Influenced by passages in the New Testament that condemned acts of revenge and the shedding of blood, some early Christians refused military service. Others, however, held that in a sinful world, defense of the state was necessary and served in the army without concealment or apology. After Roman emperors professed Christianity, Christians began to serve the government more often. With the barbarians menacing the borders, these Christian officials could not advocate nonviolence. Christian theorists began to argue that under certain circumstances—to punish injustice or to restore peace—war was just. But even such wars must not entail unnecessary violence.

The early Christian view of women was rooted in the patriarchal tradition of Jewish society. Paul subjected the wife to her husband's authority. "Wives, be subject to your husbands, as to the Lord. For the husband is the head of the wife as Christ is the head of the church" (Ephesians 5:22–23). But Paul also held that all are baptized in Christ: "There is neither Jew nor Greek, there is neither slave nor free, there is neither male nor female; for you are all one in Christ Jesus" (Galatians 3:28). Consequently, both sexes were subject to divine law; both men and women possessed moral autonomy. The early church held to strict standards on sexual matters. It condemned adultery and esteemed virginity pledged for spiritual reasons.

Christians waged no war against slavery, which was widely practiced and universally accepted in the ancient world. Paul commanded slaves to obey their masters, and many Christians, including leaders of local churches, were themselves slave owners. While Christians did not try to alter the legal status of slaves, they did teach that slaves, too, were children of God, sought their conversion, urged owners not to treat them harshly, and considered it a virtue for masters to free their slaves. In the modern world, the Christian teaching that all persons are spiritually equal before God would impel some Christians to fight for the abolition of slavery.

Christian theorists condemned sex outside of marriage, adultery, prostitution, homosexuality, and abortion, and insisted that the sex drive should be confined to reproduction, as Clement of Alexandria wrote: "Yet marriage in itself merits esteem and the highest approval, for the Lord wished men to 'be fruitful and multiply.' He did not tell them, however, to act like libertines, nor did He intend them to surrender themselves to pleasure as though born only to indulge in sexual relations. . . . To indulge in intercourse without intending children is to outrage nature."[4]

Christianity and the Jews

The central theme of the New Testament Gospels is love of both God and fellow human beings. But the Gospels also devote considerable attention to the fallen angel, Satan, and the evil demons that inhabit his kingdom. Increasingly, Christians identified opponents—Jews, pagans, and heretics—with Satan and viewed conflicts in a moral context: a struggle between God's faithful and Satan's servants. Over the centuries, the view that they were participants in a cosmic struggle between good

Primary Source

Saint Benedict of Nursia: *The Christian Way of Life*

In the following selection from his monastic book of rules, Saint Benedict of Nursia advises his monks on the attitudes and conduct necessary to live a virtuous Christian life..

What Are the Instruments of Good Works?

In the first place, to love the Lord God with the whole heart, whole soul, whole strength, then his neighbor as himself.

Then not to kill, not to commit adultery, not to steal, not to covet, not to bear false witness, to honor all men, and what anyone would not have done to him, let him not do to another. To deny himself, that he may follow Christ, to chasten the body, to renounce luxuries, to love fasting. To relieve the poor, to clothe the naked, to visit the sick, to bury the dead, to help in tribulation, to console the afflicted.

To make himself a stranger to the affairs of the world, to prefer nothing before the love of Christ, not to give way to anger, not to bear any grudge, not to harbour deceit in the heart, not to forsake charity. Not to swear, lest haply he perjure himself, to utter truth from his heart and his mouth. Not to return evil for evil, not to do injuries, but rather to bear them patiently, to love his enemies, not to curse against those that curse him, but rather to bless them, to endure persecution for righteousness' sake. Not to be proud, not given to wine, not gluttonous, not addicted to sleep, not slothful, not given to murmur, not a slanderer. To commit his hope to God; when he sees anything good in himself to attribute it to God, and not to himself, but let him always know that which is evil is his own doing; and impute it to himself. To fear the day of judgment, to dread hell, to desire eternal life with all spiritual longing, to have the expectation of death every day before his eyes. To watch over his actions at all times, to know certainly that in all places the eye of God is upon him; those evil thoughts which come into his heart to dash to pieces on Christ, and to make them known to his spiritual senior. To keep his lips from evil and wicked discourse, not to be fond of much talking, not to speak vain words or such as provoke laughter, not to love much or violent laughter. To give willing attention to the sacred readings, to pray frequently every day, to confess his past sins to God, in prayer, with tears and groanings; from thence forward to reform as to those sins.

Not to fulfill the desires of the flesh, to hate his own will, in all things to obey the commands of the abbot, even though he himself (which God forbid) should do otherwise, remembering our Lord's commands: "What they say, do; but what they do, do ye not." Not to desire to be called a saint before he is one, but first to be one that he may be truly called one; every day to fulfill the commands of God in his deeds, to love chastity, to hate no one, not to have jealousy or envy, not to love contention, to avoid self-conceit; to reverence seniors, to love juniors, to pray for enemies in the love of Christ, to be reconciled with his adversary, before the going down of the sun, and never to despair of the mercy of God. . . .

Question for Analysis

1. According to Saint Benedict, how should a Christian lead a virtuous life?

Oliver J. Thatcher, ed., *Library of Original Sources* (Milwaukee: University Research Extension, 1907), 4:133–134.

and evil led Christians to demonize adversaries, a practice that exacerbated hatred and justified mistreatment, even massacre. Christian attitudes and behavior toward Jews poignantly illustrate this point.

Numerous links connect early Christianity and Judaism. Jesus himself and his earliest followers, including the Twelve Apostles, were Jews who were faithful to Jewish law. Jesus attended synagogue and frequently quoted the Hebrew scriptures—which to him and his disciples were the authoritative word of God—to support a particular viewpoint. Jesus' message was first spread in synagogues throughout the Roman Empire. Early Christianity's affirmation of the preciousness of the human being created in God's image, its belief that God rules history, its awareness of human sinfulness, its call for repentance, and its appeal to God for forgiveness are rooted in Judaism. The Christian reference to God as a "merciful Father" derives from Jewish prayer. Also rooted in Judaism are the moral norms proclaimed by Jesus in the Sermon on the Mount and on other occasions. For example, "Thou shalt love thy neighbor as thyself" was the motto of the Jewish sage Hillel, a contemporary of Jesus who founded a school. The great value that the Torah places on charity was inherited by Christianity. Jesus' use of parables to convey his teachings, the concept of the Messiah, respect for the Sabbath, the practice of giving alms to the poor, and congregational worship likewise stem from Judaism. And, of course, Christians viewed the Hebrew Scriptures as God's word. A deeper understanding of the New Testament requires knowledge of the Old Testament, for its thought and language permeated the Christian gospels.

However, over the years, particularly after more and more non-Jews became followers of Christ, Christians forgot or devalued this relationship to Judaism, and some thinkers began to show hostility toward Judaism and Jews, which had tragic consequences in later centuries. Several factors fueled this anti-Judaism: resentment against Jews for their refusal to accept Jesus; the polemics of the Jewish establishment against the followers of Jesus; the role in Jesus' death ascribed to Jews by the New Testament; resentment against those Christians who Judaized, that is, continued to observe Jewish festivals and the Jewish Sabbath, to regard the synagogue as holy, and to practice circumcision; and anger that Judaism remained a vital religion, for this undermined the conviction that Christianity was the fulfillment of Judaism and the one true faith.

What made Christian anti-Judaism particularly ominous was the effort of some theologians to demonize the Jewish people. The myth emerged that Jews, murderers of the incarnate God who embodied all that was good, were a cursed nation, children of the Devil, whose suffering was intended by God. Thus Origen (c. 185–c. 251) maintained that "the blood of Jesus [falls] not only upon those who lived then but also upon all generations of the Jewish people following afterwards until the end of the world."[5] In the late fourth century, John Chrysostom described Jews as "inveterate murderers, destroyers, men possessed by the Devil." "[T]hey murder their offspring and immolate them to the devil." The synagogue, he said, was "the domicile of the devil as is also the soul of the Jews." Their rites are "criminal and impure," their religion is "a disease." For the "odious assassination of Christ," there is "no expiation possible, . . . no pardon." Jews will live "under the yoke of servitude without end."[6] Since the Devil was very real to early and medieval Christians, the Jew became identified with evil. Christians developed a mindset, concludes the Reverend Robert A. Everett, that was "unable to see anything positive in Judaism. . . . Judaism and the Jewish people came to have no real value for Christians except as a negative contrast to Christianity."[7] Because of this "teaching of contempt" and the "diabolization of the Jew," the Christian ethic of love did not extend to Jews.

> *[O]nce it is established that God has cursed the Jews, how can one argue that Christians should love them? If Jews have been fated by God to have . . . a long history of suffering, who are Christians to alter their history by doing anything to relieve Jewish suffering? The theology of victimization thus precludes Christian love as a basis of relating to Jews.*[8]

The diabolization of the Jew, which bore no relationship to the actual behavior of Jews or to their highly ethical religion, and the "theology of victimization," which held that the Jews were collectively and eternally cursed for denying Christ, became powerful myths. Over the centuries, these myths poisoned Christians' hearts and minds against Jews, spurring innumerable humiliations, persecutions, and massacres by Christians who believed that their actions were pleasing to God. Alongside this hatred of Jews and antipathy to their suffering, there also evolved the belief that Jews, faithless and perfidious though they were, should be permitted to survive, for their dispersal among the nations was evidence of divine punishment; moreover, one day they would see the light and convert to the true faith.

Saint Augustine: The Christian Worldview

During the early history of Christianity, many learned men, fathers of the church, explained and defended church teachings. Most of the leading early fathers wrote in Greek, but in the middle of the fourth century, three great Latin writers—Saint Jerome, Saint Ambrose, and Saint Augustine—profoundly influenced the course of Christianity in the West.

Saint Jerome (A.D. c. 340–420) wrote about the lives of the saints and promoted the spread of monasticism. But his greatest achievement was the translation of the Old and New Testaments from Hebrew and Greek into Latin. Jerome's text, the common, or Vulgate, version of the Bible, became the official edition of the Bible for the Western church.

Saint Ambrose (A.D. 340–397), bishop of Milan, Italy, instructed the clergy to deal humanely with the poor, the old, the sick, and the orphaned. He urged clerics not to pursue wealth but to practice humility and avoid favoring the rich over the poor. Ambrose sought to defend the autonomy of the church against the power of the state. His dictum that "the Emperor is within the church, not above it" became a cardinal principle of the medieval church.

Erich Lessing/Art Resource, N.Y.

The Ladder of Divine Ascent, Twelfth-Century Icon, St. Catherine's Monastery, Mount Sinai. Monks climbing a ladder to heaven while demons try to prevent them from leaving earth.

The most important Christian theoretician in the Late Roman Empire was Saint Augustine (A.D. 354–430), bishop of Hippo in North Africa and author of *The City of God*. Augustine became the principal architect of the Christian outlook that succeeded a dying classicism.

In 410, when Augustine was in his fifties, Visigoths sacked Rome—a disaster for which the classical consciousness was unprepared. Throughout the Empire, people panicked. Non-Christians blamed the tragedy on Christianity. Even Christians expressed anxiety. Why were the righteous also suffering? Where was the kingdom of God on earth that had been prophesied? In *The City of God*, Augustine maintained that the worldly city could never be the central concern of Christians.

The misfortunes of Rome, therefore, should not distress Christians unduly because the true Christian was a citizen of a heavenly city that could not be pillaged by ungodly barbarians but would endure forever. Compared with God's heavenly city, Rome and its decline were unimportant. What really mattered in history, said Augustine, was not the coming to be or the passing away of cities and empires, but the individual's entrance into heaven or hell.

Augustine did not hold that by his death Christ had opened the door to heaven for all. The majority of humanity remained condemned to eternal punishment, said Augustine; only a handful were blessed with the gift of faith and the promise of heaven. People could not by their own efforts overcome a sinful nature; a moral and spiritual regeneration stemmed not from human will power, but from God's grace. The small number endowed with God's grace constituted the City of God. These people lived on earth as visitors only, for they awaited deliverance to the Kingdom of Christ. Most inhabitants of the earthly city were destined for eternal punishment in hell. A perpetual conflict existed between the two cities and between their inhabitants: one city stood for sin and corruption; the other, for God's truth and perfection.

For Augustine, the highest good was not of this world. Rather, it consisted of eternal life with God. His distinction between this higher world of perfection and a lower world of corruption remained influential throughout the Middle Ages.

Augustine repudiated the distinguishing feature of classical humanism: the autonomy of reason. For him, ultimate wisdom could not be achieved through rational thought alone; reason had to be guided by faith. Without faith, there could be no true knowledge, no understanding. Philosophy had no validity if it did not first accept as absolutely true the existence of God and the authority of his revelation. Thus, Augustine upheld the primacy of faith. But he did not necessarily regard reason as an enemy of faith, and he did not call for an end to rational speculation. What he denied of the classical view was that reason alone could attain wisdom. The wisdom that Augustine sought was Christian wisdom, God's revelation to humanity. The starting point for this wisdom, he said, was belief in God and the Scriptures. To Augustine, secular knowledge for its own sake was of little value; the true significance of knowledge lay in its role as a tool for comprehending God's will. Augustine adapted the classical intellectual tradition to the requirements of Christian revelation.

With Augustine, the human-centered outlook of classical humanism, which for centuries had been undergoing transformation, gave way to a God-centered worldview. The fulfillment of God's will, not the full development of human capacities, became the chief concern of life. *The City of God* encompassed several themes that would concern Christians for centuries: the meaning of history and the place of the individual, the state, and the church in God's plan.

Christianity and Classical Humanism: Alternative Worldviews

Christianity and classical humanism are the two principal components of the Western tradition. The value that modern Western civilization places on the individual derives ultimately from classical humanism and the Judeo-Christian tradition. Classical humanists believed that human worth came from the capacity of individuals to reason and to shape their character and life according to rational standards. Christianity also places great stress on the individual. In the Christian view, God cares for each person; he wants people to behave righteously and to enter heaven; Christ died for all because he loves humanity. Christianity espouses active love and genuine concern for fellow human beings. Without God, people are as Augustine described them: "foul, crooked, sordid, . . . vicious." With God, the human personality can undergo a moral transformation and become loving, good, and free. The idea of a Christian conscience, prompted by God and transcending all other loyalties, reinforces respect for all human beings regardless of cultural and national differences. Also promoting respect for each person is the presupposition of natural equality stemming

CHRIST ENTHRONED. This detail from the funerary sarcophagus of Junius Bassus, dating from A.D. 359, shows Christ sitting on a throne.

from the Christian belief that each individual, regardless of birth, wealth, or talent, is precious to God.

There are striking parallels between Christian and Stoic ethics. Both Stoics and Christians believed that there is an essential "brotherhood of man," that all human beings are related and possess a fundamental dignity. Both urged suppressing wild passions, expressing concern for others, living simply, and heeding the inner voice of conscience that commands human beings to do what is right.

But Christianity and classical humanism also represent two essentially different worldviews. The triumph of the Christian outlook signified a break with the essential meaning of classical humanism; it pointed to the end of the world of antiquity and the beginning of an age of faith, the Middle Ages. With the victory of Christianity, the ultimate goal of life shifted. Life's purpose was no longer to achieve excellence in this world through the full and creative development of human capacities, but to attain salvation in a heavenly city. A person's worldly accomplishments amounted to very little if he or she did not accept God and his revelation. The Christian ideal of the isolated and contemplative monk who rejected the world in order to serve God was alien to the spirit of classical humanism, which valued active citizenship and active participation in worldly activities. Equally foreign to the Greco-Roman mind was another idea introduced by Christianity: the need to escape from a sinful human nature, a consequence of Adam and Eve's defiance of God. This view of a corrupt human nature and an unclean human body, particularly in Augustine's formulation, became deeply embedded in the European mind during the Christian centuries—the Middle Ages.

In the classical view, history had no ultimate end, no ultimate meaning; periods of happiness and misery repeated themselves endlessly. In the Christian view, history is filled with spiritual meaning. It is the profound drama of individuals struggling to overcome their original sin in order to gain eternal happiness in heaven. History began with Adam and Eve's fall and would end when Christ returns to earth, evil is eradicated, and God's will prevails. For the Christian, Christ on the cross was both the central event and a turning point in world history.

Classicism held that there was no authority higher than reason, that individuals had within themselves, through unaided reason, the ability to understand the world and life. Christianity teaches that, without God as the starting point, knowledge is formless, purposeless, and prone to error. Classicism, unlike Judaism or Christianity, possessed no truths or moral precepts revealed by a divine power. Rather, classicism held that ethical standards were expressions of universal reason, laws of nature, which the human mind could discover. Through reason, individuals could discern the norms by which they should regulate their lives. Reason would enable them to govern desires and will; it would show where their behavior was wrong and teach them how to correct it. Because individuals sought what was best for themselves, they would obey the voice of reason. Christianity, on the other hand, maintains that ethical standards emanate from the personal will of God. Without submission to God's commands, people remain wicked forever; the human will, essentially sinful, cannot be transformed by the promptings of reason. Only when individuals turn to God for forgiveness and guidance can they find the inner strength to overcome their sinful nature. People cannot perfect themselves through scientific knowledge; it is spiritual insight and belief in God that they require and that must serve as the first principle of their lives. For classicism, the ultimate good was sought through independent thought and action; for Christianity, the ultimate good comes through knowing, obeying, and loving God.

Although some Christian thinkers dismissed Greek philosophy as erroneous and useless, others respected the Greek intellectual tradition and rejected attempts to eradicate it. Rather, they sought to fit it into a Christian framework—that is, rational inquiry must be guided by and never conflict with Christian teachings. By holding that the mind is limited in its capacity to think for itself and must be guided by faith and clerical authority, Christianity contributed to the waning of the classical tradition in the Late Roman Empire. Nevertheless, by preserving the Greek philosophical tradition—even if it remained subordinate to the Christian outlook—Christian thinkers performed a task of immense historical significance.

Christianity inherited the Hebrew view of the overriding importance of God for humanity: God, who is both Lawgiver and Judge, makes life intelligible and purposeful. For the Christian, God is a living being, loving and compassionate, in whose company one seeks to spend eternity; one knows God essentially through faith and feeling. Although the Greek philosophers had a conception of God, it was not comparable to the God of Hebrews and Christians. For the Greeks, God was a logical abstraction, a principle of order, the prime mover, the first cause, the mind of the universe, pure thought, the supreme good, the highest truth; God was a concept, impersonal, unfeeling, and uninvolved with human concerns. The Greeks approached God through the intellect, not the heart; they neither loved nor worshiped God. In addition, because religion was at the periphery, not the center, of classical humanism, the idea of God did not carry the same significance as it did for Christianity.

Christianity maintained that there was a prescribed way to worship the one true God, that belief in other gods was an abomination, and that nonbelievers (or infidels) and heretics were wicked sinners hated by God. Over the centuries, this outlook sanctioned fanaticism, persecution, and holy war with accompanying massacres—a terrible legacy that constitutes the dark side of monotheism. Unlike the monotheistic faiths—Judaism, Christianity, and Islam—Greek and Roman polytheism had no concepts of martyrdom for the true faith and holy war against the infidel and consistently tolerated many different religious beliefs and practices as long as they did not threaten the state.

In the classical world, the political community was the avenue to justice, happiness, and self-realization. In Christianity, the good life was identified not with worldly achievement but with life eternal, and the ideal commonwealth could only be one that was founded and ruled by Christ. It was entrance into God's kingdom that each person must make the central aim of life. Christian thinkers viewed the state as an inferior community to their own, the church of Christ, with its ties to a spiritual realm, the highest good. Secular power, they held, should submit to ecclesiastical authority. For the next thousand years, this distinction between heaven and earth, this otherworldly, theocentric outlook, would define the Western mentality.

In the Late Roman Empire, when classical values were in decay, Christianity was a dynamic and creative movement. Possessing both institutional and spiritual strength, Christianity survived the fall of Rome. Because it retained elements of Greco-Roman civilization and taught a high morality, Christianity served as a civilizing agent in the centuries that followed Rome's collapse. Indeed, Christianity was the essential shaper of the European civilization that emerged in the Middle Ages.

❖ ❖ ❖

Notes

1. Hans Küng, "Christianity and Judaism," in *Jesus' Jewishness,* ed. James H. Charlesworth (New York: Crossroad, 1991), p. 259.
2. The biblical quotations are from the *Revised Standard Version of the Bible,* copyright © 1946, 1952, and 1971 the National Council of the Churches of Christ in the USA. Used by permission. All rights reserved.
3. Tertullian, "On Prescription Against Heretics," in *The Ante-Nicene Fathers,* ed. Alexander Roberts and James Donaldson (New York: Charles Scribner's Sons, 1918), vol. 3, chap. 7, p. 246.
4. From Clement of Alexandria, *Christ the Educator,* trans. Simon P. Woo, C. P. (New York, Fathers of the Church, 1954), 175.
5. *Origenis, Commentariorum in Evangelium Secundum Matthaeum,* in *Patrologiae Cursus Completus,* series Graeca Prior, ed. J. P. Migne (Paris: Parisiorum, 1862), vol. 13, cols. 1494–1495, pars. 775–776; trans. J. Castora for this volume.
6. Quoted in Edward H. Flannery, *The Anguish of the Jews* (London: Macmillan, 1965), p. 48.
7. Randolph Braham, ed., *The Origins of the Holocaust: Christian Anti-Semitism* (Boulder, Colo.: Social Science Monographs and Institute for Holocaust Studies of the City University of New York, 1986), p. 36.
8. Ibid., p. 37.

Suggested Reading

Armstrong, Karen, *A History of God* (1994). Good material on early Christianity.

Bettenson, Henry, and Chris Maunder, eds., *Documents of the Christian Church* (1999). A new edition of this invaluable reference work.

Chadwick, Henry, *The Early Church* (1967). A survey of early Christianity in its social and ideological context.

Charlesworth, James, ed., *Jesus' Jewishness* (1991). Essays by prominent scholars exploring the Jewish context of early Christianity.

Ferguson, Everett, ed., *Encyclopedia of Early Christianity* (1990). Entries on all aspects of early Christianity.

———, *Backgrounds of Early Christianity* (1993). A clear and thorough examination of the milieu in which Christianity was born.

Grant, Michael, *Jesus* (1977). An examination of the Gospels.

Le Beau, Bryan F., Leonard Greenspoon, and Dennis Hamm, S. J., eds, *The Historical Jesus Through Catholic and Jewish Eyes* (2000). Perceptive essays on Jesus' Jewish background.

Nicholls, William, *Christian Antisemitism* (1993). A Christian scholar analyzes the roots of anti-Judaism.

Perkins, Pheme, *Reading the New Testament* (1978). Introduces the beginning student to the New Testament.

Perry, Marvin, and Frederick M. Schweitzer, eds., *Jewish-Christian Encounters over the Centuries* (1994). Useful essays on Jesus, Paul, the Dead Sea Scrolls, and early Christian anti-Judaism.

Tripolitis, Anton'a, *Religions of the Hellenistic-Roman Age* (2002). An excellent introduction to religious and philosophic movements when Christianity was emerging.

Wilkin, Robert L., *The Christians as the Romans Saw Them* (1984). Pagan reaction to the rise of Christianity.

Wills, Gary, *What Jesus Meant* (2006). A fresh and intriguing reading of the Gospels by an eminent Catholic intellectual.

Part Two

The Middle Ages: The Christian Centuries

500–1400

Coronation of Charlemagne.

Scala/Art Resource, N.Y.

	Politics and Society	Thought and Culture
500	Germanic kingdoms established on former Roman lands (400s and 500s) Saint Benedict founds monastery at Monte Cassino (529) Pope Gregory I sends missionaries to convert the Anglo-Saxons (596)	Boethius, *The Consolation of Philosophy* (523) Law Code of Justinian (529) Byzantine church Hagia Sophia (532–537) Cassiodorus establishes a monastic library at Vivarium (540)
600	Spread of Islam (622–732)	The Koran (610)
700	Charles Martel defeats the Muslims at Tours (732)	Bede, *Ecclesiastical History of the English People* (c. 700) Muslim Golden Age (700s and 800s)
800	Charlemagne crowned emperor of Romans (800) Muslim, Magyar, and Viking invasions of Latin Christendom (9th and early 10th century) Growth of feudalism (800–1100)	Carolingian Renaissance (768–814) Alfred the Great promotes learning in England (871–899)
900	German king Otto I becomes first Holy Roman Emperor (962)	
1000	Split between the Byzantine and Roman churches (1054) Norman conquest of England (1066) Start of First Crusade (1096)	Romanesque style in architecture (1000s and 1100s)
1100	Philip Augustus expands central authority in France (1180–1223) Development of common law and jury system in England (1100s) Pontificate of Innocent III: height of papal power (1198–1216)	Flowering of medieval culture (1100s and 1200s): universities, Gothic architecture, scholastic philosophy, revival of Roman law
1200	Magna Carta (1215) Destruction of Baghdad by Mongols (1258)	Aquinas, *Summa Theologica* (1267–1273)
1300	Hundred Years' War (1337–1453) Black Death (1347–1351) Great Schism of papacy (1378–1417)	Dante, *Divine Comedy* (c. 1307–1321) Chaucer, *Canterbury Tales* (c. 1388–1400)

Chapter 6

The Rise of Europe: Fusion of Classical, Christian, and Germanic Traditions

- **The Medieval East**
- **Latin Christendom in the Early Middle Ages**
- **Feudal Society**
- **Agrarian Society**
- **Economic Expansion During the High Middle Ages**
- **The Rise of States**
- **The Growth of Papal Power**
- **Christians and Jews**

Focus Questions

1. How did Latin Christendom blend Christian, Greco-Roman, and Germanic traditions?
2. What was Byzantium's long-term influence on world history?
3. What does Islam have in common with Christianity? How do they differ?
4. What was the significance of medieval Muslim intellectual life?
5. What conditions led to the rise of feudalism and manorialism?
6. What were the signs of vitality and recovery in European economic, political, and religious life during the High Middle Ages?
7. Why was there a conflict between church and state during the Middle Ages?
8. What prompted lords and commoners to heed the papacy's call for a crusade?

9. What conditions led to the rise of states? What were the essential differences characterizing the development of medieval England, France, and Germany?
10. What factors led to the rise of anti-Semitism during the Middle Ages? How does anti-Semitism demonstrate the power of mythical thinking?

The triumph of Christianity and the establishment of Germanic kingdoms on once Roman lands constituted a new phase in Western history: the end of the ancient world and the beginning of the Middle Ages, a period that spanned a thousand years. In the ancient world, the locus of Greco-Roman civilization was the Mediterranean Sea. The heartland of medieval civilization gradually shifted to the north, to regions of Europe that Greco-Roman civilization had barely penetrated. During the Middle Ages, a common European civilization, Latin Christendom, evolved integrating Christian, Greco-Roman, and Germanic traditions: Christianity was at the center of medieval civilization; Rome, the seat of the papacy, was the spiritual capital and Latin the language of intellectual life; and Germanic customs pervaded social and legal relationships. In the Early Middle Ages (500–1050), the new civilization was struggling to take form; in the High Middle Ages (1050–1300), medieval civilization reached its peak. ❖

THE MEDIEVAL EAST

Three new civilizations based on religion emerged from the ruins of the Roman Empire: Latin Christendom (Western and Central Europe) and two Eastern civilizations, Byzantium and Islam.

Byzantium

Although the Roman Empire in the West fell to the German tribes, the eastern provinces survived. They did so because they were richer, more urbanized, and more populous and because the main Germanic and Hunnish invasions were directed at the western regions. In the eastern parts, Byzantine civilization took shape. Its religion was Christianity; its language and culture Greek; and its machinery of administration Roman. The capital, Constantinople, was a fortress city, perfectly situated to resist attacks from land and sea.

During the Early Middle Ages, Byzantine civilization was economically and culturally far more advanced than that of the Latin West. At a time when few Westerners (Latin Christians) could read or write, Byzantine scholars studied the literature, philosophy, science, and law of ancient Greece and Rome. Whereas trade and urban life had greatly declined in the West, Constantinople was a magnificent Byzantine city of schools, libraries, open squares, and bustling markets.

Over the centuries, many differences developed between the Byzantine church and the Roman church. The pope resisted domination by the Byzantine emperor, and the Byzantines would not accept the pope as head of all Christians. The two churches quarreled over ceremonies, holy days, the display of images, and the rights of the clergy. The final break came in 1054: the Christian church split into the Roman Catholic church in the West and the Eastern (Greek) Orthodox church in the East, a division that still persists.

Political and cultural differences widened the rift between Latin Christendom and Byzantium. In the Byzantine Empire, Greek was the language of religion and intellectual life; in the West, Latin predominated. Latin Christians refused to recognize that the Byzantine emperors were, as they claimed to be, successors to the Roman emperors. Byzantine emperors were absolute rulers who held that God had chosen them to rule and to institute divine will on earth. As successors to the Roman emperors, they claimed to rule all the lands that had once been part of the Roman Empire.

At its height, under Emperor Justinian, who reigned from 527 to 565, the Byzantine Empire included Greece, Asia Minor, Italy, southern Spain, and parts of the Near East, North Africa, and the Balkans. Over the centuries, the Byzantines faced attacks from the Germanic Lombards and Visigoths, Persians, Muslim Arabs, Seljuk Turks, and Latin Christians. The death blow to the empire was dealt by the Ottoman Turks. Originally from Central Asia, they had accepted Islam and had begun to build an empire. They drove the Byzantines from Asia Minor and conquered much of the Balkans. By the beginning of the fifteenth century, the Byzantine Empire consisted of only two small territories in Greece and the city of Constantinople. In 1453, the Ottoman Turks broke through Constantinople's great walls and plundered the city. After more than ten centuries, the Byzantine Empire had come to an end.

During its thousand years, Byzantium had a significant impact on world history. First, it prevented the Muslim Arabs from advancing into Eastern Europe. Had the Arabs broken through Byzantine defenses, much of Europe might have been converted to the new faith of Islam. Another far-reaching development was the codification of the laws of ancient Rome under Justinian. This monumental achievement, the *Corpus Juris Civilis*, preserved Roman law's principles of reason and justice. Today's legal codes in much of Europe and Latin America trace their roots to the Roman law recorded by Justinian's lawyers. The Byzantines also preserved the philosophy, science, mathematics, and literature of ancient Greece.

Contacts with Byzantine civilization stimulated learning in both the Islamic world to the east and Latin Christendom to the west. Speros Vryonis, a student of Byzantine civilization, states: "The Byzantines carried the torch of civilization unextinguished at a time when the barbarous Germanic and Slav tribes had reduced much of Europe to near chaos: and they maintained this high degree of civilization until Western Europe gradually emerged and began to take form."[1] Byzantium exerted an important religious, cultural, and linguistic influence on Latin

Chronology 6.1 ❖ The Early and High Middle Ages

496	Clovis adopts Roman Christianity
596	Pope Gregory I sends missionaries to convert the Anglo-Saxons
732	Charles Martel defeats the Muslims at Tours
768	Charlemagne becomes king of the Franks
800	Charlemagne is crowned emperor of the Romans by Pope Leo III
c. 840s	Height of Viking attacks
962	Otto I crowned emperor of the Romans, beginning the Holy Roman Empire
987	Hugh Capet becomes king of France
1054	Split between the Byzantine and Roman churches
1066	Norman conquest of England
1075	Start of the Investiture Controversy
1096	First Crusade begins
1198–1216	Pontificate of Innocent III: height of the church's power

Romanians, eastern Slavs (Russians and Ukrainians), and southern Slavs (Serbs and Bulgars). From Byzantium, the Slavs acquired legal principles, art forms, and an alphabet (the Cyrillic, based on the Greek) for writing their languages. (On the other hand, the western Slavs—Poles, Czechs, and Slovaks—came under the influence of Latin Christianity and Latin culture.)

Islam

The second civilization to arise after Rome's fall was based on the vital new religion of Islam, which emerged in the seventh century among the Arabs of Arabia. Its founder was Muhammad (c. 570–632), a prosperous merchant in the trading city of Mecca. At times the introspective Muhammad withdrew from worldly affairs and devoted himself to meditation. He began to experience visions, which he interpreted as messages from God. When Muhammad was about forty, he believed that he was visited in his sleep by the angel Gabriel, who ordered him to "recite in the name of the Lord!" Transformed by this experience, Muhammad came to believe that he had been chosen to serve as a prophet, the carrier of God's revelation. Although most desert Arabs worshiped tribal gods, many Arabs in the towns and trading centers, including Muhammad, were familiar with Judaism and Christianity, and some had accepted the idea of one God. Rejecting the many deities of the tribal religions, Muhammad offered the Arabs a new monotheistic faith, Islam, which means "surrender to Allah (God)."

Islamic standards of morality and rules governing daily life are set by the Koran, which Muslims believe contains the words of Allah as revealed to Muhammad. Muslims see their religion as the completion and perfection of Judaism and Christianity; they believe both of these monotheistic predecessors were superseded by Allah's revelation to Muhammad. Muslims regard the ancient Hebrew prophets as messengers of God and value their message of compassion and the oneness of humanity. They also acknowledge Jesus as a great prophet but do not consider him divine and view the Trinity as a form of polytheism. Muslims view Muhammad as the last and greatest of the prophets and see him as entirely human; they worship only Allah, the creator and ruler of heaven and earth,

Hugh Rooney/© Eye Ubiquitous/Corbis.

Mosque of Muhammad Ali, Cairo, Twelfth Century A.D. This mosque was a gathering place for prayer, preaching, and study of the Koran. Mosques were usually rectangular buildings, with arcaded porticos surrounding an open court. Inside, the focal point was an apse facing Mecca from which the local Imam (holy man) led the congregation in prayer. Nearby was a pulpit for preaching and a copy of the Koran on a lectern. In the outer court were pools or fountains for ritual purification. At the Cairo mosque, the fountains were covered by a domed building. Attached to the mosque were minarets for calling the faithful to daily prayers.

a single, all-powerful God who is merciful, compassionate, and just. According to the Koran, on the Day of Judgment unbelievers and the wicked will be dragged into a fearful place of "scorching winds and seething water," and "sinners . . . shall eat . . . [bitter] fruit . . . [and] drink boiling water."[2] Faithful Muslims who have lived virtuously are promised paradise, a garden of bodily pleasures and spiritual delights.

In a little more than two decades, Muhammad united the often feuding Arabian tribes into a powerful force dedicated to Allah and to spreading the Islamic faith. After Muhammad's death in 632, his friend and father-in-law, Abu Bakr, became his successor, or caliph. Regarded as the defender of the faith, whose power derived from Allah, the caliph governed in accordance with Muslim law as defined in the Koran.

The Islamic state was a theocracy, in which government and religion were inseparable; there could be no distinction between secular and spiritual authority. The separation of church and state, which became firmly rooted in the West in modern times, still remains an alien and hated concept for many Muslims. Muslims viewed God as the source of all law and political authority and the caliph as his earthly deputy. Divine law regulated all aspects of human relations. The ruler who did not enforce Koranic law failed in his duties. Thus, Islam was more than a religion; it was also a system of government, society, law, and thought that bound its adherents into an all-encompassing community. The idea of a single society governed by the Koran and aspiring to extend its power over non-Muslims remained deeply embedded in the Muslim mind over the centuries and for some is still a powerful force today.

Christians and Jews who lived in Islamic lands had to accept a subordinate status—they could not bear arms, were assessed a special tax, could be barred from testifying in court against a Muslim, and were required to wear clothing with distinguishing marks—a sign of humiliation. Nevertheless, as "people of the book," Jews and Christians were protected communities, and despite instances of loss of property or life, or both, the two groups generally went about their business and practiced their religions free of persecution. As a rule, Jews were physically safer in Muslim than in Christian lands.

Islam gave the many Arab tribes the unity, discipline, and organization to succeed in their wars of conquest. Under the first four caliphs, who ruled from 632 to 661, the Arabs, with breathtaking speed, overran the Persian Empire, seized some of Byzantium's provinces, and invaded Europe. Muslim warriors believed that they were engaged in a holy war or *jihad* (literally, striving in the path of God), to spread Islam to nonbelievers and that those who died in the jihad were assured a place in paradise. Either by conversion or conquest, maintained Islamic theorists, infidels were destined to submit to Islamic jurisdiction. A desire to escape from the barren Arabian Desert and to exploit the rich Byzantine and Persian lands was another compelling reason for expansion. In the east, Islam's territory eventually extended into India and to the borders of China; in the west, it encompassed North Africa and most of Spain. But the Muslims' northward push lost momentum and was halted in 717 by the Byzantines at Constantinople and in 732 by the Franks at the battle of Tours in central France.

The Arabs who burst into the Byzantine and Persian empires had no tradition of science or philosophy. But they were quick to absorb the learning of others. In the eighth and ninth centuries, under the Abbasid caliphs, Muslim civilization entered its golden age. Islamic civilization creatively integrated Arabic, Byzantine, Persian, and Indian cultural traditions. During the Early Middle Ages, when learning was at a low point in Western Europe, the Muslims forged a high civilization. Muslim science, philosophy, and mathematics rested largely on the achievements of the ancient Greeks. The Muslims acquired Greek learning from the older Persian and Byzantine civilizations, which had kept alive the Greek inheritance. By translating Greek works into Arabic and commenting on them, Muslim scholars performed the great historical task of preserving the philosophical and scientific heritage of ancient Greece. This Greek learning, supplemented by original contributions of Muslim scholars and scientists, was eventually passed on to Christian Europe, a transmission of immense historical significance, as the historian W. Montgomery Watt explains:

> *When one becomes aware of the full extent of Arab experimenting, Arab thinking and Arab writing, one sees that without the Arabs European science and philosophy would not have developed when they did. The Arabs were no mere transmitters of Greek thought, but genuine bearers, who both kept alive the disciplines they had been taught and extended their range. When about 1100 Europeans became seriously interested in . . . science and philosophy . . . (they) had to learn all they could from the Arabs before they themselves could make further advances.*[3]

The Arab empire, stretching from Spain to India, was unified by a common language (Arabic), a common faith, and a common culture. By the eleventh century, however, the Arabs began losing their dominance in the Islamic world. The Seljuk Turks, who had taken Asia Minor from the Byzantines, also conquered the Arabic lands of Syria, Palestine, and much of Persia. Although the Abbasid caliphs remained the religious and cultural leaders of Islam, political power was exercised by Seljuk sultans. In the eleventh and twelfth centuries, the Muslims lost Sicily and most of Spain to Christian knights, and European Crusaders carved out kingdoms in the Near East.

In the thirteenth century, Mongols led by Genghis Khan devastated Muslim lands; in the late fourteenth century, this time led by Tamerlane, they again plundered and massacred their way through Arab territory. After Tamerlane's death in 1404, his empire disintegrated, and its collapse left the way open for the Ottoman Turks.

The Ottoman Empire reached its height in the sixteenth century with the conquest of Egypt, North Africa, Syria, and the Arabian coast. The Ottomans developed an effective system of administration, but they could not restore the cultural brilliance, the thriving trade, or the prosperity that the Muslim world had known under the Abbasid caliphs of Baghdad.

Latin Christendom in the Early Middle Ages

The centuries of cultural greatness of both the Islamic and the Byzantine civilizations enriched the Western world. However, neither Islam nor Byzantium made the breakthroughs in science, technology, philosophy, the arts, economics, and political thought that gave rise to the modern world. That process was the singular achievement of Europe. During the Early Middle Ages (500–1050), Latin Christendom was culturally far behind the two Eastern civilizations, but by the twelfth century it had caught up.

In succeeding centuries, it produced the movements that ushered in the modern age: the Renaissance, the Reformation, the Scientific Revolution, the Age of Enlightenment, the French Revolution, and the Industrial Revolution.

Political, Economic, and Intellectual Transformation

From the sixth to the eighth century, Europeans struggled to overcome the disorder created by the breakup of the Roman Empire and the deterioration of Greco-Roman civilization. In the process, a new civilization, with its own distinctive style, took root. It grew out of the intermingling of Greco-Roman civilization, the Christian outlook, and Germanic traditions. But centuries would pass before it would come to fruition.

In the fifth century, German invaders founded kingdoms in North Africa, Italy, Spain, Gaul, and Britain—lands formerly belonging to Rome. Even before the invasions, the Germans had acquired some knowledge of Roman culture and were attracted to it. Therefore, the new Germanic rulers sought not to destroy Roman civilization but to share in its advantages. For example, Theodoric the Great (476–526), the Ostrogoth ruler of Italy, retained the Roman Senate, government officials, civil service, and schools, and rich aristocratic Roman families continued to hold high government offices. The Burgundians in Gaul and the Visigoths in Spain maintained Roman law for their conquered subjects. All the Germanic kingdoms tried to keep Roman systems of taxation; furthermore, Latin remained the official language of administration.

But the Germanic kingdoms, often torn by warfare, internal rebellion, and assassination, provided a poor political base on which to revive a decadent and dying classical civilization. Most of the kingdoms survived for only a short time and had no enduring impact. An exception to this trend occurred in Gaul and south-central Germany, where the most successful of the Germanic kingdoms was established by the Franks—the founders of the new Europe.

The Roman world was probably too far gone to be rescued, but even if it had not been, the Germans were culturally unprepared to play the role of restorer. By the end of the seventh century, the old Roman lands in Western Europe showed a marked decline in central government, town life, commerce, and learning. Though vigorous and brave, the German invaders were essentially a rural and warrior people, tribal in organization and outlook. Their native culture, which was without cities or written literature, was primitive compared with the literary, philosophical, scientific, and artistic achievements of the Greco-Roman world. The Germans were not equipped to reform the decaying Roman system of administration and taxation or to cope with the economic problems that had burdened the Empire. Nor could they maintain roads and irrigation systems, preserve skills in the arts of stoneworking and glassmaking, or breathe new life into the dying humanist culture.

The distinguishing feature of classical civilization, its vital urban institutions, had deteriorated in the Late Roman Empire. Under the kingdoms created by Germanic chieftains, the shift from an urban to a rural economy accelerated. Although towns did not vanish altogether, they continued to lose control over the surrounding countryside and to decline in wealth and importance. They were the headquarters of bishops, rather than centers of commerce and intellectual life. Italy remained an exception to this general trend. There, Roman urban institutions persisted, even during the crudest period of the Early Middle Ages. Italian cities kept some metal currency in circulation and traded with one another and with Byzantium.

In retreat since the Late Roman Empire, Greco-Roman humanism continued its decline in the centuries immediately following Rome's demise. The old Roman upper classes abandoned their heritage and absorbed the ways of their Germanic conquerors, the Roman schools closed, and Roman law faded into disuse. Aside from clerics, few people could read and write Latin, and even learned clerics were rare. Knowledge of the Greek language in Western Europe was almost totally lost, and the Latin rhetorical style deteriorated. Many literary works of classical antiquity were either lost or neglected. Raids by Germanic tribes and later by Muslims, Magyars, and Vikings devastated libraries. Works by great authors were lost forever. For example, of the hundred dramas written by Sophocles, only seven survived. Gone were attempts to understand the natural world through reason; magic and the occult prevailed among both pagans and Christians. The literature of the seventh century, concerned principally with the lives of saints, was devoid of the humanist themes that had motivated Greek and Roman poets and dramatists. European culture was much poorer than the high civilizations of Byzantium, Islam, and ancient Rome.

During this period of cultural poverty, the few persons who were learned generally did not engage in original thought but rather salvaged and transmitted remnants of classical civilization. In a rudimentary way, they were struggling to create a Christian culture that combined the intellectual tradition of Greece and Rome with the religious teachings of the Christian church.

An important figure in the intellectual life of this transitional period was Boethius (480–c. 525), a descendant of a noble Italian family. Aspiring to rescue the intellectual heritage of antiquity, Boethius translated into Latin some of Aristotle's treatises on logic and wrote commentaries on Aristotle, Cicero, and Porphyry (a Neo-Platonist philosopher). Until the twelfth century, virtually all that Latin Christendom knew of Aristotle came from Boethius's translations and commentaries. Similarly, his work in mathematics, which contains fragments from Euclid, was the main source for the study of that discipline in the Early Middle Ages. In his theological writings, Boethius tried to demonstrate that reason did not conflict with orthodoxy—an early attempt to attain a rational comprehension of belief, or, as he expressed it, to join faith to reason. Boethius's early effort to examine Christian doctrines rationally, a salient feature of medieval philosophy, was to grow to maturity in the twelfth and thirteenth centuries.

Cassiodorus (c. 490–575), another Italian, collected Greek and Latin manuscripts and helped start the monastic practice of copying classical texts. Without this tradition, many key Christian and pagan works would undoubtedly have perished. In Spain, another preserver of ancient works, Isidore of Seville (c. 576–636), compiled an encyclopedia, *Etymologiae*, covering a diversity of topics from arithmetic and furniture to God. Isidore derived his information from many secular and religious sources. Quite understandably, his work contained many errors, particularly in its references to nature. For centuries, though, the *Etymologiae* served as a standard reference work and was found in every monastic library of note.

The translations and compilations made by Boethius, Cassiodorus, and Isidore, the books collected and copied by monks and nuns, and the schools established in monasteries (particularly those in Ireland, England, and Italy) kept intellectual life from dying out completely in the Early Middle Ages.

The Church: Shaper of Medieval Civilization

Christianity was the integrating principle and the church was the dominant institution of the Middle Ages. During the Late Roman Empire, as the Roman state and its institutions decayed, the church gained in power and importance. Its organization grew stronger, and its membership increased. Unlike the Roman state, the church was a healthy and vital organization. The elite of the Roman Empire had severed their commitment to the values of classical civilization, whereas the church leaders were intensely devoted to their faith.

When the Empire collapsed, the church retained the Roman administrative system and preserved elements of Greco-Roman civilization. A unifying and civilizing agent, the church provided people with an intelligible and purposeful conception of life and death. In a dying world, the church was the only institution capable of reconstructing civilized life. Thus, the Christian outlook, rather than the traditions of the German tribes, formed the foundation of medieval civilization. During the course of the Middle Ages, people came to see themselves as participants in a great drama of salvation. There was only one truth: God's revelation to humanity. There was only one avenue to heaven, and it passed through the church. Membership in a universal church replaced citizenship in a universal empire. Across Europe, from Italy to Ireland, a new society centered on Christianity was taking shape.

Monks helped build the foundation of medieval civilization. During the seventh century, intellectual life on the European Continent continued its steady decline. In the monasteries of Ireland

Mosaic, The Court of Justinian, c. a.d. 547. During his long reign, Justinian succeeded in regaining lands in the western Mediterranean that had been conquered by the Germanic invaders. His lasting achievement was the appointment of a commission of scholars to collect and codify Rome's ancient laws and the commentaries of learned jurists.

and England, however, a tradition of learning persisted. Early in the fifth century, Saint Patrick began the conversion of the Irish to Christianity. In Ireland, Latin became firmly entrenched as the language of both the church and scholars at a time when it was in danger of disappearing in many parts of the Continent. Irish monks preserved and cultivated Latin and even preserved some knowledge of Greek, and during their missionary activities, they revived the use of Latin on the Continent. In England, the Anglo-Saxons, both men and women—who converted to Christianity mainly in the seventh century—also established monasteries that kept learning alive. In the sixth and seventh centuries, Irish and Anglo-Saxon monks became the chief agents for converting people in Northern Europe. Thus, monks and nuns made possible a unitary European civilization based on a Christian foundation. By copying and preserving ancient texts, they also kept alive elements of ancient civilization.

During the Early Middle Ages, when cities were in decay, monasteries, whose libraries contained theological works and ancient Latin classics, were the principal cultural centers; they would remain so until the rebirth of towns in the High Middle Ages. Monasteries also offered succor to the sick and the destitute and served as places of refuge for travelers. To the medieval mind, the monks' and nuns' selfless devotion to God, adoption of apostolic poverty, and dedication to prayer and contemplation represented the highest expression of the Christian way of life; it was the finest and most certain path to salvation. It was not uncommon for both men and women, with old age or even death approaching, to take the vows so they might die as monks or nuns.

The Early Middle Ages were a formative period for the papacy, as well as for society in general. A decisive figure in the strengthening of the papacy was Gregory I, known as the Great (590–604). One of the ablest of medieval popes, Gregory used Roman methods of administration to organize papal property effectively in Italy, Sicily, Sardinia, Gaul, and other regions. He strengthened his authority over bishops and monks, dispatched missionaries to England to win over the Anglo-Saxons, and set his sights on an alliance with the Franks. Finally materializing 150 years later, this alliance helped shape medieval history.

The Kingdom of the Franks

From their homeland in the Rhine River valley, the Frankish tribes had expanded into Roman territory during the fourth and fifth centuries. The ruler Clovis united the various Frankish tribes and conquered most of Gaul. In 496, he converted to Roman Christianity. Clovis's conversion to Catholicism was an event of great significance. A number of other German kings had adopted the Arian form of Christianity, which the church had declared heretical. By embracing Roman Christianity, the Franks became a potential ally of the papacy.

Clovis's successors could not maintain control over their lands, and power passed to the mayor of the palace, the king's chief officer. Serving as mayor of the palace from 717 to 741, Charles Martel subjected all Frankish lands to his rule. In addition, at the battle of Tours in 732, he defeated the Muslims. Although the Muslims continued to occupy the Iberian Peninsula, they would advance no farther north into Europe.

Charles Martel was succeeded by his son Pepin the Short, who in 751 deposed the king. With the approval of the papacy and his nobles, Pepin was crowned king by Boniface, a prominent bishop. Two years later, Pope Stephen II anointed Pepin again as king of the Franks and appealed to him to protect the papacy from the Lombards, the last German tribe to invade formerly Roman territory. Pepin crossed into Italy, defeated the Lombards, and turned over captured lands to the papacy. This famous Donation of Pepin made the pope ruler of the territory between Rome and Ravenna, which became known as the Papal States.

The Era of Charlemagne

The alliance between the Franks and the papacy was continued by Pepin's successor, Charlemagne (Charles the Great), who ruled from 768 to 814. Charlemagne continued the Carolingian (the term refers to Charles Martel and his descendants) policy of expanding the Frankish kingdom. He destroyed the Lombard kingdom and declared himself king of the Lombards. He added Bavaria to his kingdom, and after long, terrible wars, he forced the Saxons to submit to his rule and convert to Christianity—thousands were beheaded when they were slow to choose between baptism or execution. He also conquered a region in northern Spain, the Spanish March, which served as a buffer between the Christian Franks and the Muslims in Spain.

Immense difficulties arose in governing the expanded territories. Size seemed an insuperable obstacle to effective government, particularly since Charlemagne's administrative structure, lacking in trained personnel, was primitive by Islamic, Byzantine, or Roman standards. The empire was divided into about 250 counties, administered by counts—nobles who were personally loyal to the ruler and who implemented the king's decisions.

On Christmas Day in Rome in the year 800, Pope Leo III crowned Charlemagne emperor of the Romans. The title signified that the tradition of a world empire still survived, despite the demise of the Western Roman Empire three hundred years earlier. But because the pope crowned Charlemagne, the emperor now had a spiritual responsibility to spread and defend the faith. Thus, Roman universalism was fused with Christian universalism.

The Frankish empire, of course, was only a dim shadow of the Roman Empire. The Franks had no Roman law or Roman legions; there were no cities that were centers of economic and cultural activity; and officials were not trained civil servants with a world outlook but uneducated war chieftains with a tribal viewpoint. Yet Charlemagne's empire did embody the concept of a

Map 6.1 The Carolingian World Resting more on the personal qualities of Charlemagne than on any firm economic or political foundation, the Carolingian empire did not survive the emperor's death in 814.

universal Christian empire—an ideal that would endure throughout the Middle Ages.

The crowning of a German ruler as emperor of the Romans by the head of the church represented the merging of German, Christian, and Roman traditions, which is the essential characteristic of medieval civilization. This blending of traditions was also evident on a cultural plane, for Charlemagne, a German warrior-king, showed respect for classical learning and Christianity, both non-Germanic traditions.

Charlemagne believed that it was his religious duty to raise the educational level of the clergy so that they understood and could properly teach the faith. He also fostered education to train administrators who would be capable of overseeing his empire and royal estates; such men had to be literate. He himself learned Latin and spoke it fluently. To achieve his purpose, Charlemagne gathered some of the finest scholars in Europe. Alcuin of York, England (735–804), was given charge of the palace school attended by Charlemagne and his family, high lords, and youths training to serve the emperor. Throughout Gaul, Alcuin expanded schools and libraries, promoted the copying of ancient manuscripts, and imposed basic literacy standards on the clergy.

The focus of the Carolingian Renaissance—the cultural revival produced by Charlemagne's teachers and scholars—was predominantly Christian: an effort to train clergymen and improve their understanding of the Bible and the writings of the church fathers. This process raised the level of literacy and improved the Latin style. Most important, monastic copyists continued to preserve ancient texts, which otherwise might never have survived. The oldest surviving manuscripts of many Greek and Roman works are Carolingian copies.

Compared with the Greco-Roman past, with the cultural explosion of the twelfth and thirteenth centuries, or with the great Italian Renaissance of the fifteenth century, the Carolingian Renaissance seems slight indeed. But we must bear in mind the cultural poverty that prevailed before the era of Charlemagne. The Carolingian Renaissance reversed the process of cultural decay that characterized much of the Early Middle Ages. Learning would never again fall to the low level it had reached in the centuries following the decline of Rome.

During the era of Charlemagne, a distinct European civilization emerged. It blended the Roman heritage of a world empire, the intellectual achievement of the Greco-Roman mind, Christian otherworldliness, and the customs of the Germanic peoples. This nascent Western European civilization differed from Byzantine and Islamic civilizations, and Europeans were growing conscious of the difference. But the new medieval civilization was still centuries away from its high point, which would be reached in the twelfth and thirteenth centuries.

Charlemagne's empire also engendered the ideal of a unified Latin Christendom: a single Christian community under one government. Over the centuries, the pursuit of this ideal of a Christian world-state, Christendom, would inspire many people, both clergy and laity.

The Breakup of Charlemagne's Empire

After Charlemagne's death in 814, his son, Louis the Pious, inherited the throne. Louis aimed to preserve the empire, but the task was virtually impossible. The empire's strength rested more on Charlemagne's personal qualities than on any firm economic or political foundation. In particular, it never developed an empirewide system of taxation such as had supported the Roman Empire for centuries. Moreover, the empire was simply too large and consisted of too many diverse peoples to be governed effectively. Besides Frankish nobles, who sought to increase their own power at the emperor's expense, Louis had to deal with his own rebellious sons. After Louis died in 840, the empire was divided among the three surviving sons.

The Treaty of Verdun in 843 gave Louis the German the eastern part of the empire, which marked the beginning of Germany; to Charles the Bald went the western part, which was the start of France; and Lothair received the Middle Kingdom, which extended from Rome to the North Sea. This Middle Kingdom would be an area of conflict between France and Germany right into the twentieth century. As central authority waned, large landowners increasingly exercised authority in their own regions. Simultaneous invasions from all directions furthered this movement toward localism and decentralization.

In the ninth and tenth centuries, Latin Christendom was attacked on all sides. From bases in North Africa, Spain, and southern Gaul, Muslims ravaged regions of Southern Europe, even as far as the suburbs of Rome. They deported shiploads of Christians to the slave markets of North Africa. The Magyars, originally from western Asia, had established themselves on the plains of the Danube; their horsemen launched lightning raids into northern Italy, western Germany, and parts of France. Defeated in Germany in 933 and again in 955, the Magyars withdrew to what is now Hungary; they ceased their raids and adopted Christianity.

Still another group of invaders, the Northmen, or Vikings, sailed south from Scandinavia in their long, wooden ships to raid the coasts and river valleys of Western Europe. Villages were devastated, ports were destroyed, monasteries were plundered and their libraries set ablaze, and the population was decimated. Trade came to a standstill, coins no longer circulated, and farms turned into wastelands. Already gravely weakened, the European economy collapsed. The political authority of kings disappeared, and cultural life and learning withered.

These terrible attacks heightened political insecurity and accelerated anew the process of decentralization that had begun with the decline of Rome. During these chaotic times, counts came to regard as their own the land that they administered and defended for their king. At a time when monarchs could no longer guarantee the safety of their subjects, the inhabitants of a district looked on the count or local lord, frequently a former Carolingian official, as their ruler, for his men and fortresses protected them. In their regions, nobles exercised public power formerly held by kings. Europe had entered an age of feudalism, in which the essential unit of government was not a kingdom but a local region, and political power was the private possession of local lords.

Feudal Society

Arising during a period of collapsing central authority, invasion, scanty public revenues, and declining commerce and town life, feudalism attempted to provide some order and security. Feudalism was not a planned system derived logically from general principles, but rather an improvised response to the challenge posed by ineffectual central authority. Feudal practices were not uniform; they differed from locality to locality, and in some regions they barely took root. Although it was only a stopgap means of governing, feudalism did bring some order, justice, and law during an era of breakdown, localism, and transition. It remained the predominant political arrangement until kings reasserted their authority in the High and Late Middle Ages.

Vassalage

Feudal relationships enabled lords to increase their military strength. The need for military support was the principal reason for the practice of vassalage, in which a knight, in a solemn ceremony, pledged loyalty to a lord. This feature of feudalism derived from an ancient German ceremony, during which warriors swore personal allegiance to the head of the war-band. Among other things, the vassal gave military service to his lord and received in return a *fief,* which was usually land. This fief was inhabited by peasants, and the crops that they raised provided the vassal with his means of support.

Besides rendering military assistance and supplying knights, the vassal owed several other obligations to his lord in return for the fief and the lord's protection. These duties included sitting in the lord's court and judging cases, such as the breach of feudal agreements between the lord and his other vassals; providing lodgings when the lord traveled through the vassal's territory; offering a gift when the lord's son was knighted or when his eldest daughter married; and raising a ransom should the lord be captured by an enemy.

Generally, both lord and vassal felt honor-bound to abide by the oath of loyalty. It became an accepted custom for a vassal to renounce his loyalty to his lord if the latter failed to protect the vassal from enemies, mistreated him, or increased his obligations as fixed by the feudal contract. On the other hand, if a vassal did not live up to his obligations, the lord would summon him to his court, where he would be tried for treachery. If found guilty, the vassal could lose his fief and perhaps his life. At times, disputes between vassals and lords erupted into warfare. Because a vassal often held land from more than one lord and sometimes was himself a lord to vassals, situations frequently became awkward, complex, and confusing. On occasion, a vassal had to decide to which lord he owed *liege homage* (prime loyalty).

As feudalism evolved, the king came to be regarded as the chief lord, who had granted fiefs to the great lords, who in turn had divided them into smaller units and regranted them to vassals. Thus, all members of the ruling class, from the lowliest knights to the king, occupied a place in the feudal hierarchy. In theory, the king was the highest political authority and the source of land tenure,

Primary Source

Bishop Adalbero of Laon: The Tripartite Society

Medieval thinkers came to see their society as divided into three different but complementary groups: clergy, lords, and serfs. Each group had its own responsibilities—priests guided the souls of the faithful; lords protected society from its enemies; and the serfs' toil provided sustenance for everyone. Written in about 1020, the following statement by Bishop Adalbero of Laon, France, illustrates the tripartite nature of medieval society.

The community of the faithful is a single body, but the condition of society is threefold in order. For human law distinguishes two classes. Nobles and serfs, indeed, are not governed by the same ordinance. . . . The former are the warriors and the protectors of the churches. They are the defenders of the people, of both great and small, in short, of everyone, and at the same time they ensure their own safety. The other class is that of the serfs. This luckless breed possesses nothing except at the cost of its own labour. Who could, reckoning with an abacus, add up the sum of the cares with which the peasants are occupied, of their journeys on foot, of their hard labours? The serfs provide money, clothes, and food, for the rest; no free man could exist without serfs. Is there a task to be done? Does anyone want to put himself out? We see kings and prelates make themselves the serfs of their serfs; [but in truth] the master, who claims to feed his serf, is fed by him. And the serf never sees an end to his tears and his sighs. God's house, which we think of as one, is thus divided into three; some pray, others fight, and yet others work. The three groups, which coexist, cannot bear to be separated; the services rendered by one are a precondition for the labours of the two others; each in his turn takes it upon himself to relieve the whole. Thus the threefold assembly is none the less united, and it is thus that law has been able to triumph, and that the world has been able to enjoy peace.

Question for Analysis

1. According to Bishop Adalbero, what was the virtue of the tripartite society?

Jacques Le Goff, *Medieval Civilization*, trans. Julia Barrow (Oxford: Blackwell, 1990), 255.

but in actual fact he was often less powerful than many other nobles of the realm. Feudalism declined when kings converted their theoretical powers into actual powers. The decline of feudalism was a gradual process; conflict between the crown and the aristocracy persisted, with varying degrees of intensity, for several centuries, but the future belonged to the centralized state being shaped by kings, not to feudal fragmentation.

Feudal Warriors

Feudal lords viewed manual labor and commerce as degrading for men of their rank. They considered only one vocation worthy: that of warrior. Through combat, the lord demonstrated his valor, earned his reputation, measured his individual worth, derived excitement, added to his wealth, and defended his rights. Warfare gave meaning to his life. During the twelfth century, to relieve the boredom of peacetime, nobles staged gala tournaments in which knights, fighting singly or in teams, engaged each other in battle to prove their skill and courage and to win honor. The feudal glorification of combat became deeply ingrained in Western society and endured into the twentieth century. Over the centuries, a code of behavior, called *chivalry*, evolved for the feudal nobility. A true knight was expected to fight bravely, demonstrate loyalty to his lord, and treat other knights with respect and courtesy.

In time, the church interjected a religious element into the warrior culture of the feudal knight. It sought to use the fighting spirit of the feudal class for Christian ends: knights could assist the clergy in enforcing God's will. Thus, a Christian component was added to the Germanic tradition of loyalty and courage. As a Christian gentleman, a knight was expected to honor the laws of the church and to wield his sword in the service of God.

Regarding the private warfare of lords as lawless violence that menaced social life, the church, in the eleventh century, imposed strictures called the Peace of God and the Truce of God. These restrictions limited feudal warfare to certain days of the week and certain times of the year. Although only partially effective, these religious restraints did offer Christian society some respite from plundering and incessant warfare.

Noblewomen

Feudal society was very much a man's world. In theory, women were deemed to be physically, morally, and intellectually inferior to men. Although the church taught that both men and women were precious to God and that marriage was a sacred rite, clergymen viewed women as evil temptresses who, like the biblical Eve, lured men into sin. Women were subjected to male authority. Fathers arranged the marriages of their daughters. Girls from aristocratic families were generally married at age sixteen or younger to men often twice their age; frequently, aristocratic girls who did not marry had to enter a convent. The wife of a lord was at the mercy of her husband; if she annoyed him, she might expect a beating. But as the lady of the castle, she performed important duties. She assigned tasks to the servants; made medicines; preserved food; taught young girls how to sew, spin, and weave; and, despite her subordinate position, took charge of the castle when her husband was away.

The nunneries provided an outlet for the talents of unmarried noblewomen. Abbesses demonstrated organizational skills in supervising the convent's affairs. Some nuns acquired an education and, like their male counterparts, copied manuscripts and thus preserved the knowledge of the past. The nun Hroswitha (c. 935–c. 1001) of Gandersheim in Saxony, Germany, produced poetry, history, and plays. Inspired by the Roman poet Terence, she wrote six dramas—the first since Roman times—along with a history of German rulers and one of her own convent.

Agrarian Society

Feudalism was built on an economic foundation known as *manorialism*. Although pockets of free peasantry remained, a village community (manor) consisting of serfs bound to the land became the essential agricultural arrangement for much of the Middle Ages. The manorial village was the means of organizing an agricultural society with limited markets and money. Neither the lords who warred nor the clergy who prayed performed economically productive work. Their ways of life were made possible by the toil of serfs.

The origins of manorialism can be traced in part to the Late Roman Empire, when peasants depended on the owners of large estates for protection and security. This practice developed further during the Early Middle Ages, especially during the invasions of Northmen, Magyars, and Muslims in the ninth and tenth centuries. Peasants continued to sacrifice their freedom in exchange for protection; in some cases, they were too weak to resist the encroachments of local magnates. Like feudalism, manorialism was not an orderly system; it consisted of improvised relationships and practices that varied from region to region.

A lord controlled at least one manorial village; great lords might possess hundreds. A small manor had a dozen families; a large one had as many as fifty or sixty. The manorial village was never completely self-sufficient because salt, millstones, and metalware were generally obtained from outside sources. It did, however, constitute a balanced economic setting. Peasants grew grain and raised cattle, sheep, goats, and hogs; blacksmiths, carpenters, and stonemasons did the building and repairing; the village priest cared for the souls of the inhabitants; and the lord defended the manor and administered the customary law. The serf and his family lived in a dismal, one-room cottage that

akg-images.

NOBLEWOMEN. At times, medieval ladies joined their husband's hunting party.

they shared with chickens and pigs. In the center burned a small fire, the smoke escaping through a hole in the roof. In cold weather when the fire was strong, the room was filled with smoke. When it rained, water came through the thatched roof and turned the earth floor into mud. The odor from animal excrement was ever present. Peasants were often held in contempt by lords, and medieval literature routinely depicted them as repulsive creatures—ugly, dirty, cowardly, and uncouth.

When a manor was attacked by another lord, the peasants found protection inside the walls of their lord's house. By the twelfth century, in many places, this building had become a well-fortified stone castle. Peasants generally lived, worked, and died on the lord's estate and were buried in the village churchyard. Few had any contact with the world beyond the village of their birth.

In return for protection and the right to cultivate fields and to pass these holdings on to their children, the serfs owed obligations to their lord, and their personal freedom was restricted in a variety of ways. Bound to the land, they could not leave the manor without the lord's consent. Before a serf could marry, he had to obtain the lord's permission and pay a fee. The lord could select a wife for his serf and force him to marry her. Sometimes, a serf, objecting to the lord's choice, preferred to pay a fine. These rules also applied to the serf's children, who inherited their parents' obligations. In addition to working their allotted land, the serfs had to tend the fields reserved for the lord. Other services exacted by the lord included digging ditches, gathering firewood, building fences, repairing roads and bridges, and sewing clothes. Probably somewhat more than half of a serf's workweek was devoted to fulfilling these labor obligations. Serfs also paid a variety of dues to the lord, including payments for using the lord's mill, bake-oven, and winepress.

Serfs did derive some benefits from manorial relationships. They received protection from brigands and warring nobles, and they possessed customary rights, which the lord generally respected, to cottages and farmlands. If a lord demanded more services or dues than was customary, or if he interfered with their right to cottages or strips of farmland, the peasants might demonstrate their discontent by refusing to labor for the lord. Until the fourteenth century, however, open rebellion was rare because lords possessed considerable military and legal power. The manorial system promoted attitudes of dependency and servility among the serfs; their hopes for a better life were directed toward heaven.

ECONOMIC EXPANSION DURING THE HIGH MIDDLE AGES

Manorialism and feudalism presupposed a hierarchical, organic, and stable social order: clergy who prayed, lords who fought, and peasants who toiled. People believed that society functioned smoothly when all individuals accepted their status and performed their proper role. Consequently, a person's rights, duties, and relationship to law depended on his or her ranking in the social order. To change position was to upset the organic unity of society. And no one, serfs included, should be deprived of the traditional rights associated with his or her rank. This arrangement was justified by the clergy, who maintained that "God himself has willed that among men, some must be lords and some serfs."[4]

During the High Middle Ages (1050–1300), however, the revival of an urban economy and the reemergence of central authority undermined feudal and manorial relationships. By the end of the eleventh century, Europe showed many signs of recovery. The invasions of Magyars and Vikings had ended, and powerful lords and kings imposed greater order in their territories. A period of economic vitality, the High Middle Ages witnessed an agricultural revolution, a commercial revolution, the rebirth of towns, and the rise of an enterprising and dynamic middle class.

An Agricultural Revolution

Important advances were made in agriculture during the Middle Ages. Many of these innovations occurred in the Early Middle Ages but were only gradually adopted and were not used everywhere. In time, however, they markedly increased production. By the end of the thirteenth century, medieval agriculture had reached a technical level far superior to that of the ancient world.

One innovation was a heavy plow that cut deeply into the soil. This new plow enabled farmers to work more quickly and effectively. As a result, they could cultivate more land, including the heavy, moist soils of northern Europe, which had offered too much resistance to the light plow. Another important advance in agricultural technology was the invention of the collar harness. The old yoke harness worked well with oxen, but it tended to choke horses—and horses, because they move faster and have greater stamina than oxen, are more valuable for agricultural work. The widening use of the water mill by the tenth century and the introduction of windmills in the twelfth century saved labor in grinding grain; these inventions replaced ancient hand-worked mills.

The gradual emergence of the three-field system of managing agricultural land, particularly in Northern Europe, increased production. In the old, widely used two-field system, half the land was planted in autumn with winter wheat, while the other half was left fallow to restore its fertility. In the new three-field system, one-third of the land was planted in autumn with winter wheat, a second third was planted the following spring with oats and vegetables, and the last third remained fallow. The advantages of the three-field system were that two-thirds of the land was farmed and only one-third left unused and that the diversification of crops made more vegetable protein available.

Greater agricultural production reduced the number of deaths from starvation and dietary disease and thus contributed to a population increase. Soon the farmlands of a manorial village could not support its growing population. Consequently, peasants had to look beyond their immediate surroundings and colonize trackless wastelands. Lords vigorously promoted this conversion of uncultivated soil into agricultural land because it increased their incomes. Monastic communities also actively engaged in this enterprise. Almost everywhere, peasants were draining swamps, clearing forests, and establishing new villages. Their endeavors during the eleventh and twelfth centuries brought vast areas of Europe under cultivation for the first time. New agricultural land was also acquired through expansion, the most notable example being the organized settlement of lands to the east by German colonists.

The colonizing and cultivation of virgin lands contributed to the decline of serfdom. Lords owned vast tracts of forests and swamps that would substantially increase their incomes if cleared, drained, and farmed. But serfs were often unwilling to move from their customary homes and fields to do the hard labor needed to cultivate these new lands. To lure serfs away from their villages, lords promised them freedom from most or all personal services. In many cases, the settlers fulfilled their obligations to the lord by paying rent rather than by performing services or providing foodstuffs, thus making the transition from serfs to freemen. In time, they came to regard the land as their own.

The improvement in agricultural technology and the colonization of new lands altered the conditions of life in Europe. Surplus food and the increase in population freed people to work at nonfarming occupations, making possible the expansion of trade and the revival of town life.

The Revival of Trade

Expanding agricultural production, the end of Viking attacks, greater political stability, the growth of a considerable money supply, and an increasing population brought about a revival of commerce. During the Early Middle Ages, Italians and Jews kept alive a small amount of long-distance trade between Catholic Europe and the Byzantine and Islamic worlds. In the eleventh century, sea forces of Italian trading cities cleared the Mediterranean of Muslim fleets that preyed on Italian shipping. As in Roman times, goods could circulate once again from one end of the sea to the other. In the twelfth and thirteenth centuries, local, regional, and long-distance trade gained such momentum that some historians describe the period as a commercial revolution that surpassed the commercial activity of the Roman Empire during the Pax Romana. A class of traders emerged, many of them former serfs who started by taking to the road as humble peddlers. Gradually they acquired business contacts in other lands, know-how, and ambition.

Crucial to the growth of trade were international fairs, where merchants and craftspeople set up stalls and booths to display their wares. Because of ever-present robbers, lords provided protection for merchants carrying their wares to and from fairs. Each fair lasted about three to six weeks; then the merchants would move on to another site. The Champagne region in northeastern France was the great center for fairs because the count of Champagne provided protection for merchants both en route and at the fair; judges to guarantee the enforcement of contracts; and the necessary equipment, including covered stalls and accurate scales.

The principal arteries of trade flowed between the eastern Mediterranean and the Italian cities; between Scandinavia and the Atlantic coast; between northern France, Flanders, and England; and from the Baltic Sea in the north to the Black Sea and Constantinople via Russian rivers.

Increased economic activity led to advances in business techniques. Since individual merchants often lacked sufficient capital for large-scale enterprises, groups of merchants formed partnerships. By enabling merchants to pool their capital, reduce their risks, and expand their knowledge of profit-making opportunities, these arrangements furthered commerce. Underwriters insured cargoes; the development of banking and credit instruments made it unnecessary for merchants to carry large amounts of cash. The international fairs not only were centers of international trade, but also served as capital markets for international credit transactions. The arrangements made by fair-going merchants to settle their debts were the origin of the bill of exchange, which allowed one currency to be converted into another. The invention of double-entry bookkeeping gave merchants an overview of their financial situation: the value of their goods and their ready cash. Without such knowledge, no large-scale commercial activity could be conducted on a continuous basis. Another improvement in business techniques was the formation of commercial law, which defined the rules of conduct for debts and contracts.

The Rebirth of Towns

In the eleventh century, towns emerged anew throughout Europe, and in the twelfth, they became active centers of commercial and intellectual life. Towns were a new and revolutionary force—socially, economically, and culturally. A new class of merchants and craftspeople came into being. This new class—the middle class—was made up of those who, unlike the lords and serfs, were not affiliated with the land. The townsman was a new man, with a different value system from that of the lord, the serf, and the clergyman.

One reason for town growth was the increased food supply stemming from advances in agricultural technology. Surplus farm production meant that the countryside could support an urban population of artisans and professionals. Another reason for the rise of urban centers was the expansion of trade. Towns emerged in locations that were natural for trade: seacoasts, riverbanks, crossroads, and market sites; they also sprang up outside fortified castles and monasteries and on surviving Roman sites. The colonies of merchants who gathered at these places were joined by peasants skilled in crafts or willing to work as laborers. Most towns had a small population. The largest ones—Florence, Ghent, and Paris—had between fifty thousand and a hundred thousand inhabitants. Covering only small areas, these walled towns were crowded with people.

Merchants and artisans organized guilds to protect their members from outside competition. The merchant guild in a town prevented outsiders from doing much business. A craftsman new to a town had to be admitted to the guild of his trade before he could open a shop. Competition between members of the same guild was discouraged. To prevent one guild member from making significantly more money than another, a guild required its members to work the same number of hours, pay employees the same wages, produce goods of equal quality, and charge customers a just price. These rules were strictly enforced.

Women took an active part in the economic life of towns, working with men, usually their husbands, in the various crafts—as cobblers, tailors, hatters, bakers, goldsmiths, and so forth. Women brewed beer; made and sold charcoal; sold vegetables, fish, and poultry; and ran inns. In many towns, the wives and widows of master craftsmen were admitted to guilds. These guildswomen had many of the privileges of a master, including the right to train apprentices.

Because many towns were situated on land belonging to lords or on the sites of old Roman towns ruled by bishops, these communities at first came under feudal authority. In some instances, lords encouraged the founding of towns, for urban industry and commerce brought wealth to the region. However, tensions soon developed between merchants, who sought freedom from feudal restrictions since they interfered with the pursuit of financial gain, and lords and bishops, who wanted to preserve their authority over the towns. Townspeople, or burghers, refused to be treated as serfs bound to a lord and liable for personal services and customary dues. The burghers wanted to travel, trade, marry, and dispose of their property as they pleased; they wanted to make their own laws and levy their own taxes. Sometimes by fighting, but more often by payments of money, the townspeople obtained charters from the lords giving them the right to set up their own governing councils. These assemblies passed laws, collected taxes, and formed courts that enforced the laws. Towns became more or less self-governing municipalities, the first since Greco-Roman days.

In a number of ways, towns loosened the hold of lords on serfs. Seeking freedom and fortune, serfs fled to the new towns, where, according to custom, lords could no longer reclaim them after a year and a day. Enterprising serfs earned money by selling food to the townspeople. When they acquired a sufficient sum, they bought their freedom from lords, who needed cash to pay for goods bought from merchants. Lords increasingly began to accept fixed cash payments from serfs in place of labor services or foodstuffs. As serfs met their obligations to lords with money, they gradually became rent-paying tenants and, in time, were no longer bound to the lord's land. The manorial system of personal relations and mutual obligations was disintegrating.

The activities of townspeople made them a new breed; they engaged in business and had money and freedom. Their world was the market rather than the church, the castle, or the manor. Townspeople were freeing themselves from the prejudices both of feudal aristocrats, who considered trade and manual work degrading, and of the clergy, who cursed the pursuit of riches as sordid, shameful, and an obstacle to salvation. The townspeople were critical, dynamic, and progressive—a force for change. Medieval towns nurtured the origins of the *bourgeoisie* (literally, "citizens of the burg," the walled town), the urban middle class, which would play a crucial role in modern European history.

The Rise of States

The revival of trade and the growth of towns were signs of the vitality of Latin Christendom. Another sign of strength was the greater order and security provided by the emergence of states. Aided by educated and trained officials who enforced royal law, tried people in royal courts, and collected royal taxes—all serving to reduce the power of local lords—kings expanded their territory and slowly fashioned strong central governments. These developments laid the foundations of European states. Not all areas followed the same pattern. Whereas England and France achieved a large measure of unity during the Middle Ages, Germany and Italy remained divided into numerous independent territories.

England

In 1066, the Normans—those Northmen who had first raided and then settled in France—conquered Anglo-Saxon England. Normans replaced the Anglo-Saxon aristocracy and ecclesiastical hierarchy. Determined to establish effective control over his new kingdom, William the Conqueror (1027–1087), duke of Normandy, kept a sixth of conquered England for himself. In accordance with feudal practice, he distributed the rest among his Norman nobles, who swore an oath of loyalty to William and provided him with military assistance. But William made certain that no feudal baron had enough land or soldiers to threaten his power. Because he had conquered England in one stroke, his successors did not have to travel the long, painful road to national unity that French monarchs had to take.

To strengthen royal control, William retained some Anglo-Saxon administrative practices. The land remained divided into *shires* (counties) administered by *sheriffs* (royal agents). This structure gave the king control over local government. To determine how much money he could demand, William ordered a vast census to be taken of people and property in every village. These data were compiled in the *Domesday Book,* which listed the number of tenants, cattle, sheep, and pigs and the quantities of farm equipment throughout the realm. Thus, William knew his kingdom's assets better than any other monarch of his day.

A crucial development in shaping national unity was the emergence of common law. During the reigns of Henry I (1100–1135) and Henry II (1154–1189), royal judges traveled to different parts of the kingdom. Throughout England, important cases began to be tried in the king's court rather than in local courts, thereby increasing royal power. The decisions of royal judges were recorded and used as guides for future cases. In this way, a law common to the whole land gradually came to prevail over the customary law of a specific locality. Because common law applied to all England, it served as a force for unity. It also provided a fairer system of justice. Common law remains the foundation of the English legal system and the legal systems of lands settled by English people, including the United States.

Henry II made trial by jury a regular procedure for many cases heard in the king's court, thus laying the foundations of the modern judicial system. Twelve men familiar with the facts of the case appeared before the king's justices and were asked under oath if the plaintiff's statement was true. The justices based their decisions on the answers. Henry II also ordered representatives of a given locality to report under oath to visiting royal judges any local persons who were suspected of murder or robbery. This indictment jury was the ancestor of the modern grand jury system.

King John (1199–1216) inadvertently precipitated a situation that led to another step in the political development of England. Fighting a costly and losing war with the king of France, John coerced his vassals into giving him more and more revenue; he had also punished some vassals without a proper trial. In 1215, the angry barons rebelled and compelled John to fix his seal to a document called the *Magna Carta,* or Great Charter. The Magna Carta is celebrated as the root of the uniquely English respect for basic rights and liberties. Although essentially a feudal document directed against a king who had violated the rights of feudal barons, the Magna Carta stated certain principles that could be interpreted more broadly.

Over the centuries, these principles were expanded to protect the liberties of the English against governmental oppression. The Magna Carta stated that no unusual feudal dues "shall be imposed in our kingdom except by the common consent of our kingdom." In time, this right came to mean that the king could not levy taxes without the consent of Parliament, the governmental body that represents the English people. The Magna Carta also provided that "no freeman shall be taken or imprisoned . . . save by the lawful judgment of his peers or by the law of the land." The barons who drew up the document had intended it to mean that they must be tried by fellow barons. As time passed, these words were regarded as a guarantee of trial by jury for all men, a prohibition against arbitrary arrest, and a command to dispense justice fully, freely, and equally. Implied in the Magna Carta is the idea that the king cannot rule as he pleases but must govern according to the law—that not even the king can violate the law of the nation. Centuries afterward, when Englishmen sought to limit the king's power, they would interpret the Magna Carta in this way.

Anglo-Saxon England had retained the Germanic tradition that the king should consider the advice of the leading men in the land. Later, William the Conqueror continued this practice by seeking the opinions of leading nobles and bishops. In the thirteenth century, it became accepted custom that the king should not decide major issues without consulting these advisers, who assembled in the Great Council. Lesser nobility and townspeople also began to be summoned to meet with the king. These two groups were eventually called the House of Lords (bishops and nobles) and the House of Commons (knights and burghers). Thus, the English Parliament evolved; by the mid-fourteenth century, it had become a permanent institution of government. Frequently in need of money but unable to levy new taxes without the approval of Parliament, the king had to turn to that body for help. Over the centuries, Parliament would use this control over money matters to increase its power. The tradition grew that the power to govern rested not with the king alone, but with the king and Parliament together.

During the Middle Ages, England became a centralized and unified state. The king, however, did not have unlimited power; he was not above the law. The rights of the people were protected by certain principles implicit in the common law and the Magna Carta and by the emergence of Parliament.

France

In the 150 years after Charlemagne's death, the western part of his empire, which was destined to become France, faced terrible ordeals. Charlemagne's heirs fought one another for the crown; the Vikings raided everywhere their ships would carry them; Muslims from Spain plundered the southern coast; and strong lords usurped power for themselves. With the Carolingian family unable to maintain the throne, the great lords bestowed the title of king on one of their own. In 987, they chose Hugh Capet (987–996), the count of Paris. Because many great lords held territories far larger than those of Hugh, the French king did not seem a threat to noble power. But Hugh strengthened the French monarchy by having the lords also elect his son as his co-ruler. This practice continued until it became understood that the crown would remain with the Capetian family.

With the accession of Louis VI (1108–1137), a two-hundred-year period of steadily increasing royal power began. Louis started this trend by successfully subduing the barons in his own duchy. A decisive figure in the expansion of royal power was Philip Augustus (1180–1223). Philip struck successfully at King John of England (of Magna Carta fame), who held more territory as feudal lord in France than Philip did. When William, duke of Normandy in western France, conquered England in 1066, he became ruler of England and Normandy; William's great-grandson Henry II acquired much of southern France through his marriage to Eleanor of Aquitaine (c. 1122–1204) in 1152. Thus, as a result of the Norman Conquest and intermarriage, the destinies of France and England were closely intertwined until the end of the Middle Ages. By stripping King John of most of his French territory (Normandy, Anjou, and much of Aquitaine), Philip trebled the size of his kingdom and became stronger than any French lord.

In the thirteenth century, the power of the French monarch continued to grow. Departing from feudal precedent, Louis IX (1226–1270) issued ordinances for the entire realm without seeking the consent of his vassals. Kings added to their lands through warfare and marriage. They also devised new ways of raising money, including taxing the clergy. A particularly effective way of increasing the monarch's power was by extending royal justice; many cases previously tried in lords' courts were transferred to the king's court.

At the beginning of the fourteenth century, Philip IV (the Fair) engaged in a struggle with the papacy. Seeking to demonstrate that he had the support of his subjects, Philip convened a national assembly—the Estates General—representing the clergy, the nobility, and the townspeople. This assembly would be called again to vote funds for the crown. But unlike the English Parliament, the Estates General never became an important body in French political life, and it never succeeded in controlling the monarch. Whereas the basis for limited monarchy had been established in England, no comparable checks on the king's power developed in France. By the end of the Middle Ages, French kings had succeeded in creating a unified state. But regional and local loyalties remained strong and persisted for centuries.

Germany

After the destruction of Charlemagne's empire, its German territories were broken into large duchies. Following an ancient German practice, the ruling dukes elected one of their own as king. The German king, however, had little authority outside his own duchy. Some German kings tried not to antagonize the dukes, but Otto the Great (936–973) was determined to control them. He entered into an alliance with German bishops and archbishops, who could provide him with fighting men and trained administrators—a policy continued by his successors. In 962, emulating the coronation of Charlemagne, the pope crowned Otto "Emperor of the Romans." (Later the title would be changed to Holy Roman Emperor.)

Otto and his successors wanted to dominate Italy and the pope—an ambition that embroiled the Holy Roman Emperor in a life-and-death struggle with the papacy. The papacy allied itself with the German dukes and the Italian cities, enemies of the emperor. The intervention in papal and Italian politics was the principal reason why German territories did not achieve unity in the Middle Ages.

The Growth of Papal Power

In the High Middle Ages, a growing religious vitality accompanied the economic recovery and increased political stability. It was marked by several developments. Within the church, reform movements attacked clerical abuses, the papacy increased its power, and a holy war against the Muslims drew the Christian community closer together. Furthermore, the church tried with great determination to make society follow divine standards—that is, it tried to shape all institutions and cultural expressions according to a comprehensive Christian outlook.

As the sole interpreters of God's revelation and the sole ministers of his sacraments—sacred rites—the clergy imposed and supervised the moral standards of Christendom. Divine grace was channeled through the sacraments, which could be administered only by the clergy, the indispensable intermediary between the individual and God. On those who resisted its authority, the church could impose the penalty of excommunication—expulsion from the church and denial of the sacraments, without which there could be no salvation.

Gregorian Reform

By the tenth century, the church was Western Europe's leading landholder, owning perhaps a third of the land in Italy and vast properties in other lands. However, the papacy was in no position to exercise commanding leadership over Latin Christendom. The office of pope had fallen under the domination of aristocratic families; they conspired and on occasion murdered in order to place one of their own on the wealthy and powerful throne of Saint Peter. As the papacy became a prize for Rome's leading families, it was not at all unusual for popes themselves to be involved in conspiracies and assassinations. Also weakening the authority of the papacy were local lords, who dominated churches and monasteries by appointing bishops and abbots and by collecting the income from church taxes. These bishops and abbots, appointed by lords for political reasons, lacked the spiritual devotion to maintain high standards of discipline among the priests and monks.

What raised the power of the papacy to unprecedented heights was the emergence of a reform movement, particularly in French and German monasteries. High-minded monks called for a reawakening of spiritual fervor and the elimination of moral laxity among the clergy.

They particularly denounced the concern for worldly goods, the taking of mistresses, and the diminishing commitment to the Benedictine rule. Of the many monasteries that took part in this reform movement, the Benedictine monks of Cluny, in Burgundy, France, were the most influential.

In the middle of the eleventh century, popes came under the influence of the monastic reformers. In 1059, a special synod, convened by the reform-minded Pope Nicholas II, moved to end the interference of Roman nobles and German Holy Roman Emperors in choosing the pope. Henceforth, a select group of clergymen in Rome, called *cardinals,* would be responsible for picking a new pontiff.

The reform movement found its most zealous exponent in the person of Hildebrand, who became Pope Gregory VII in 1073. Gregory insisted that human society was part of a divinely ordered universe governed by God's universal law, and as the supreme spiritual leader of Christendom the pope was charged with the mission of establishing a Christian society on earth. As successor to Saint Peter, the pope had the final word on matters of faith and doctrine. All bishops came under his authority; so too did kings, whose powers should be used for Christian ends. Disobeying the pope, God's viceroy on earth, constituted disobedience to God himself. The pope was responsible for instructing rulers in the proper use of their God-given powers, and kings had a solemn duty to obey these instructions. If the king failed in his Christian duty, the pope could deny him his right to rule. Responsible for implementing God's law, the pope could never take a subordinate position to kings.

Like no other pope before him, Gregory VII made a determined effort to assert the preeminence of the papacy over both the church hierarchy and secular rulers. This determination led to a bitter struggle between the papacy and the German monarch and future Holy Roman Emperor Henry IV. The dispute was a dramatic confrontation between two competing versions of the relationship between secular and spiritual authority.

Through his reforms, Gregory VII intended to improve the moral quality of the clergy and to liberate the church from all control by secular authorities. He forbade priests who had wives or concubines to celebrate Mass, deposed clergy who had bought their offices, excommunicated bishops and abbots who had received their estates from a lay lord, and expelled from the church lay lords who invested bishops with their office. The appointment of bishops, Pope Gregory insisted, should be controlled by the church.

This last point touched off the conflict, called the Investiture Controversy, between King Henry and Pope Gregory. Bishops served a dual function. On the one hand, they belonged to the spiritual community of the church; on the other, as members of the nobility and holders of estates, they were also integrated into the feudal order. Traditionally, emperors had both granted bishops their feudal authority and invested them with their spiritual authority. In maintaining that no lay rulers could confer ecclesiastical offices on their appointees, Pope Gregory threatened Henry's authority.

In earlier times, seeking allies in the conflict with feudal nobility, German kings had made vassals of the upper clergy. In return for a fief, bishops had agreed to provide troops for a monarch in his struggle against the lords. But if kings had no control over the appointment of bishops—in accordance with Pope Gregory's view—they would lose the allegiance, military support, and financial assistance of their most important allies. To German monarchs, bishops were officers of the state who served the throne. Moreover, if they agreed to Gregory's demands, German kings would lose their freedom of action and be dominated by the Roman pontiff. Henry IV regarded Gregory VII as a fanatic who trampled on custom, meddled in German state affairs, and challenged legitimate rulers established by God, thereby threatening to subordinate kingship to the papacy.

With the approval of the German bishops, Henry called for Pope Gregory to descend from the throne of Saint Peter. Gregory in turn excommunicated Henry and deposed him as king. German lands were soon embroiled in a civil war, as German lords used the quarrel to strike at Henry's power. Finally, Henry's troops crossed the Alps, successfully attacked Rome, and installed a new pope, who crowned Henry emperor of the Romans. Gregory died in exile in 1085.

In 1122, the papacy and Emperor Henry V reached a compromise. Bishops were to be elected exclusively by the church and invested with the staff and the ring—symbols of spiritual power—by the archbishop, not the king. This change signified that the bishop owed his role as spiritual leader to the church only. But the king would grant the bishop the scepter, to indicate that the bishop was also the recipient of a fief and the king's vassal, owing feudal obligations to the crown. This compromise, called the Concordat of Worms, recognized the dual function of the bishop as a spiritual leader in the church and a feudal landowner. Similar settlements had been reached with the kings of France and England several years earlier.

The conflict between the papacy and the German rulers continued after the Concordat of Worms—a contest for supremacy between the heir of Saint Peter and the heir of Charlemagne. German monarchs wanted to control the papacy and the prosperous northern Italian cities. When Frederick I (1152–1190), known as Frederick Barbarossa (Red Beard), tried to assert authority over these cities, they resisted. In 1176, the armies of an alliance of Italian cities, supported by the pope, trounced Frederick's forces at the battle of Legnano. The Italian infantry showed that it could defeat knights on horseback, and Frederick was compelled to recognize the independence of the Italian cities. His numerous expeditions to Italy weakened his authority. German princes strengthened themselves at the expense of the monarchy, thereby continuing to preclude German unity.

The Crusades

Like the movement for spiritual renewal associated with the Cluniac reformers, the Crusades—wars to regain the Holy Land from the Muslims—were an outpouring of Christian zeal and an attempt by the papacy to assert its preeminence. Along with the renewal of commerce and the growth of towns, the Crusades signaled the increased vitality and self-confidence of Western Europe. The victims of earlier Muslim attacks, Latin Christians now took the offensive.

The Crusades were also part of a general movement of expansion that took place in Europe during the High Middle Ages. By the middle of the eleventh century, Genoese and Pisans had driven the Muslims from Sardinia. By 1091, Normans from France had taken Sicily from the Muslims and southern Italy from Byzantium. With the support of the papacy, Christian knights engaged in the long struggle to drive the Muslims from Spain; by 1248, after more than two centuries of conflict, only the small southern kingdom of Granada remained in Muslim hands. Germans conquered and colonized lands south of the Baltic coast inhabited by non-Christian Slavs, Balts, and Prussians. German settlers brought with them Christianity and German language and culture. They cleared vast tracts of virgin land for farming and established towns, bishoprics, and monasteries in a region where urban life had been virtually unknown.

Seeking to regain lands taken from Byzantium by the Seljuk Turks, the Byzantine emperor Alexius appealed to the West for mercenaries. Pope Urban II, at the Council of Clermont (in France) in 1095, exaggerated the danger confronting Eastern Christianity and called for a holy crusade against the heathen Turks, whom he accused of defiling and destroying Christian churches. A Christian army, mobilized by the papacy to defend the faith and to regain the Holy Land from nonbelievers, accorded with the papal concept of a just war; it would channel the endemic violence of Europe's warrior class in a Christian direction.

What motivated the knights and others who responded to Urban's appeal? No doubt the Crusaders regarded themselves as armed pilgrims dedicated to rescuing holy places from the hated Muslims. Moreover, Urban declared that participation in a crusade was itself an act of penance, an acceptable way of demonstrating sorrow for sin. To the warrior nobility, a crusade was a great adventure promising land, glory, and plunder, but it was also an opportunity to remit sins by engaging in a holy war. The enthusiasm with which knights became Christian warriors revealed the extent to which Christian principles had permeated the warrior mentality of the nobles.

Stirred by popular preachers, the common people also became gripped by the crusading spirit. The most remarkable of the evangelists was Peter the Hermit. Swayed by this old man's eloquence, thousands of poor people abandoned their villages and joined Peter's march to Jerusalem. After reaching Constantinople, Peter's recruits crossed into Turkish territory, where they were massacred.

An army of Christian knights also departed from Constantinople. In June 1099, three years after leaving Europe, this army stood outside the walls of Jerusalem. Using siege weapons, it broke into the city and slaughtered the Muslim and Jewish inhabitants. Besides capturing Jerusalem, the Crusaders carved out four principalities in the Near East.

Never resigned to the establishment of Christian states in their midst, Muslim leaders called for a jihad, or holy war. In 1144, one of the Crusader states, the County of Edessa, fell to the resurgent forces of Islam. Alarmed by the loss of Edessa, Pope Eugenius II called for the Second Crusade, which was a complete failure.

After 1174, Saladin, a brilliant commander, became the most powerful leader in the Muslim Near East. In 1187, he invaded Palestine, annihilating a Christian army near Nazareth and recapturing Jerusalem. This led to the Third Crusade, in which some of Europe's most prominent rulers took part—Richard I, the Lion-Hearted, of England; Philip Augustus of France; and Frederick Barbarossa of Germany. The Crusaders captured Acre and Jaffa, but Jerusalem remained in Muslim hands.

Pope Innocent III, who called the Fourth Crusade (1202–1204), was enraged by the actions of the Crusaders. They had first attacked the Christian port of Zara, controlled by the king of Hungary, and then looted and defiled churches and massacred Byzantines in Constantinople. This shameful behavior, along with the belief that the papacy was exploiting the crusading ideal to extend its own power, weakened both the crusading zeal of Christendom and the moral authority of the papacy. Other Crusades followed, but the position of the Christian states in the Near East continued to deteriorate. In 1291, almost two centuries after Pope Urban's appeal, the last Christian strongholds in the Near East fell.

The Crusades increased the wealth of the Italian cities that furnished transportation for the Crusaders and benefited from the increased trade with the East. They may have contributed to the decline of feudalism and the strengthening of monarchy because many lords were killed in battle or squandered their wealth financing expeditions to the Holy Land. The Crusades sparked an interest in geography and travel; introduced westerners to new foods, clothing, and architecture; and became a theme in literature. Nevertheless, they did not significantly influence European intellectual progress. The Crusaders had no contact with Muslim centers of learning in the Near East; it was through Spain and Sicily that Muslim learning penetrated Latin Christendom and helped stimulate the cultural awakening of the twelfth and thirteenth centuries. Over the centuries, some have praised the Crusades for inspiring idealism and heroism. Others, however, have castigated the movement for corrupting the Christian spirit and unleashing religious intolerance and fanaticism—including the massacre of Jews in the Rhineland and of Muslims and Jews in Jerusalem—that would lead to strife in future centuries. The Crusades remain a crucial component of the ideology of contemporary Islamic extremists.

Dissenters and Reformers

Freedom of religion is a modern concept; it was totally alien to the medieval outlook. Regarding itself as the possessor and guardian of divine truth, the church felt a profound obligation to purge Christendom of heresy—beliefs that challenged Christian orthodoxy. To the church, heretics had committed treason against God and were carriers of a deadly infection. Heresy was the work of Satan; lured by false ideas, people might abandon the true faith and deny themselves salvation. In the eyes of the church, heretics not only obstructed individual salvation but also undermined the foundations of society.

To compel obedience, the church used its power of excommunication. An excommunicated person could not receive the sacraments or attend church services—fearful punishments in an age of faith. In dealing with a recalcitrant ruler, the church could declare an interdict on his territory, which in effect denied the ruler's subjects the sacraments (although exceptions could be made). The church hoped that the pressure exerted by an aroused populace would compel the offending ruler to mend his ways.

The church also conducted heresy trials. Before the thirteenth century, local bishops were responsible for finding heretics and putting them on trial. In 1233, the papacy established the Inquisition, a court specially designed to fight heresy. The accused were presumed guilty until proven innocent; they were not told the names of their accusers, nor could they have legal defense. To wrest a confession from the accused, torture (which had been sanctioned by Roman law) was permitted. Those who persisted in their beliefs might be turned over to the civil authorities to be burned at the stake.

The Waldensians. Religious dissent in the Middle Ages was often reformist in character. Inspired by the Gospels, reformers criticized the church for its wealth and involvement in worldly affairs. They called for a return to the simpler, purer life of Jesus and the Apostles.

In their zeal to emulate the moral purity and material poverty of the first followers of Jesus, these reform-minded dissenters attacked ecclesiastical authority. The Waldensians, followers of Peter Waldo, a rich merchant of Lyons, were a case in point. In the 1170s, Peter distributed his property to the poor and attracted both male and female supporters. Like their leader, the Waldensians committed themselves to poverty and to preaching the Gospel in the vernacular, or native tongue, rather than in the church's Latin, which many Christians did not understand.

The Waldensians considered themselves true Christians, faithful to the spirit of the apostolic church. Repelled by Waldensian attacks against the immorality of the clergy and by the fact that these laypeople were preaching the Gospel without the permission of ecclesiastical authorities, the church condemned the movement as heretical. Despite persecution, however, the Waldensians continued to survive as a group in northern Italy.

The Cathari. Catharism was the most radical heresy to confront the medieval church. This belief represented a curious mixture of Eastern religious movements that had competed with Christianity in the days of the Roman Empire. Cathari tenets differed considerably from those of the church. The Cathari believed in an eternal conflict between the forces of the god of good and those of the god of evil. Because the evil god, whom they identified with the God of the Old Testament, had created the world, this earthly home was evil. The soul, spiritual in nature, was good, but it was trapped in wicked flesh.

The Cathari taught that, since the flesh is evil, Christ would not have taken a human form; hence, he could not have suffered on the cross or have been resurrected. Nor could God have issued forth from the evil flesh of the Virgin. According to Catharism, Jesus was not God but an angel. In order to enslave people, the evil god created the church, which demonstrated its wickedness by pursuing power and wealth. Repudiating the church, the Cathari organized their own ecclesiastical hierarchy.

The center for the Catharist heresy was southern France, where a strong tradition of protest against the moral laxity and materialism of the clergy existed. When the Cathari did not submit to peaceful persuasion, Innocent III called on kings and lords to exterminate Catharism with the sword before the infection spread throughout Europe. Lasting from 1208 to 1229, the war against the Cathari was marked by brutality and fanaticism. Under Innocent's successor, Dominican and Franciscan inquisitors completed the task of exterminating them virtually to the last person, a horrendous slaughter that some refer to as medieval genocide.

The Franciscans and the Dominicans. Driven by a zeal for reform, devout laypeople condemned the clergy for moral abuses. Sometimes their piety and resentment exploded into heresy; at other times it was channeled into movements that served the church. Such was the case with the two great orders of friars, the Franciscans and the Dominicans.

Like Peter Waldo, Saint Francis of Assisi (c. 1181–1226) came from a wealthy merchant family. After undergoing an intense religious experience, Francis abandoned his possessions and devoted his life to imitating Christ. Dressed as a beggar, he wandered into villages and towns, preaching, healing, and befriending the poor, the helpless, the sick, and even lepers, whom everyone feared to approach. The saintly Francis soon attracted disciples, called Little Brothers, who followed in their leader's footsteps.

As the Franciscans grew in popularity, the papacy exercised greater control over their activities. In time, the order was transformed from a spontaneous movement of inspired laymen into an organized agent of papal policy. The Franciscans served the church as teachers and missionaries in Eastern Europe, North Africa, the Near East, and China. The papacy set aside Francis's prohibition against the Brothers owning churches, houses, and lands corporately. His desire to keep the movement a lay order was abandoned when the papacy granted the Brothers the right to hear confession. Francis's opposition to formal learning as irrelevant to preaching Gospel love was rejected when the movement began to urge university education for its members. Those who protested against these changes as a repudiation of Francis's spirit were persecuted, and a few were even burned at the stake as heretics.

The Dominican order was founded by Saint Dominic (c. 1170–1221), a Spanish nobleman who had preached against the Cathari in southern France. Believing that those who were well versed in Christian teaching could best combat heresy, Dominic, unlike Francis, insisted that his followers engage in study. Eventually, the Dominicans became some of the leading theologians in the universities. Like the Franciscans, they went out into the world to preach the Gospel and to proselytize. Dominican friars became the chief operators of the Inquisition. For their zeal in fighting heresy, they were known as the hounds of the Lord.

Innocent III: The Apex of Papal Power

During the pontificate of Innocent III (1198–1216), papal theocracy reached its zenith. More than any earlier pope, Innocent made the papacy the center of European political life; in the tradition of Gregory VII, he forcefully asserted the theory of papal monarchy. As head of the church, Vicar of Christ, and successor of Saint Peter, Innocent claimed the authority to intervene in the internal affairs of secular rulers when they threatened the good order of Christendom. According to Innocent, the pope, "lower than God but higher than man . . . judges all and is judged by no one."[5]

Innocent applied these principles of papal supremacy in his dealings with the princes of Europe. When King Philip Augustus of France repudiated Ingeborg of Denmark the day after their wedding and later divorced her to marry someone else, Innocent placed an interdict on France to compel Philip to take Ingeborg back. For two decades, Innocent III championed Ingeborg's cause, until she finally became the French queen. When King John of England rejected the papal candidate for archbishop of Canterbury, Stephen Langton, Innocent first laid an interdict on the country. Then he excommunicated John, who expressed his defiance by confiscating church property and by forcing many bishops into exile. However, when Innocent urged Philip Augustus of France to invade England, John backed down.

Innocent called the Fourth Crusade against the Muslims and a crusade against the heretical Cathari. The culminating expression of Innocent's supremacy was the Fourth Lateran Council, convened in 1215. Comprising some twelve hundred clergy and representatives of secular rulers, the council issued several far-reaching decrees. It maintained that the Eastern Orthodox church was subordinate to the Roman Catholic church. It prohibited the state from taxing the clergy and declared laws detrimental to the church null and void. It also made bishops responsible for ferreting out heretics in their dioceses and ordered secular authorities to punish convicted heretics. Furthermore, the council insisted on high standards of behavior for the clergy and required each Catholic to confess his or her sins to a priest at least once a year and to perform the prescribed penance. Through this directive, the church tightened its control over the conscience of Europe. The council also decreed that in the sacrament of the Eucharist the body and blood of Christ are actually present in the bread and wine used in the sacrament. This meant that the priest at the altar was God's agent in the performance of a wondrous miracle.

Christians and Jews

In their relations with heretics, pagans, and Muslims, medieval Christians demonstrated a narrow and hostile attitude that ran counter to the Gospel message that all human beings were children of God and that Christ had suffered for all humanity. Muslims were seen, in the words of Pope Urban II, as a "vile breed," "infidels," and "enemies of God."

Medieval Christians also showed hatred for Jews—a visibly alien group in a society dominated by the Christian worldview. The First Crusade was a turning point for medieval Jews. Until then there were few instances of organized violence against Jewish communities. If we are warring against God's enemies, reasoned zealous crusaders, why not annihilate the Lord's enemies living in our midst? In 1096, bands of crusaders, proclaiming that they were seeking vengeance against "Christ-killers," slaughtered Jews in French and German towns. The Crusaders were often aided by townspeople driven by hateful images of Jews and eager to seize Jewish property. The venomous hatred of Jews unleashed by the First Crusade triggered other massacres during the Middle Ages, at times fomented by the clergy. Viewing the Jews as possessions to be exploited, kings and lords taxed and fined them relentlessly and periodically expelled Jews from their territories in order to confiscate their property. In 1290, Jews were expelled from England, and in 1306, from France. Between 1290 and 1293, expulsions, massacres, and forced conversions led to the virtual disappearance of a centuries-old Jewish community life in southern Italy. In Germany, savage riots periodically led to the torture and murder of Jews. In 1348–1349, when the Black Death (see "The Fourteenth Century: An Age of Adversity" in Chapter 7) raged across Europe, Jews were accused of spreading the plague by poisoning well water; thousands of Jews were burned alive in Basel, Freiburg, Strasbourg, Mainz, and other towns.

Several factors contributed to anti-Jewish feelings during the Middle Ages. To medieval Christians, the refusal of the Jews to embrace Christianity was an act of wickedness, particularly since the church taught that the coming of Christ had been prophesied by the Old Testament. Related to this prejudice was the portrayal of the Crucifixion in the Gospels. In the minds of medieval Christians, the crime of deicide—the killing of God—eternally tainted the Jews as a people; medieval Christians viewed Jews as dangerous sinners rejected by God and deserving of ceaseless punishment. Christian theologians taught they were to remain forever in subjection to Christians. It was just such a view that led town magistrates and princes periodically to confiscate Jewish property, sometimes after burning the helpless Jews alive in a public spectacle. The flames of hatred were fanned by the absurd allegation that Jews, made bloodthirsty by the spilling of Christ's blood, tortured and murdered Christians, particularly children, to obtain blood for ritual purposes. This blood libel was widely believed and incited numerous riots that led to the murder, torture, and expulsion of countless Jews, despite the fact that some popes and emperors condemned the charge as groundless.

The role of Jews as moneylenders also provoked animosity toward them. Increasingly excluded from international trade and most professions, barred from the guilds, and in many areas barred from landholding as well, Jews found that virtually the only means of livelihood open to them was moneylending. This activity, which was in theory forbidden to Christians, aroused the hatred of the individual peasants, clergy, lords, and kings who did the borrowing.

The policy of the church toward the Jews was that they should not be harmed but that they should live in humiliation, a fitting punishment for their act of deicide and continued refusal to embrace Christianity. Thus, the Fourth Lateran Council barred Jews from public office, required them to wear a distinguishing badge on their clothing as a symbol of their degradation, and ordered them to remain off the streets during Christian festivals. Christian art, literature, and religious instruction depicted the Jews in a derogatory manner, often identifying them with the Devil, who was very real and very terrifying to medieval Christians. Such people deserved no mercy, reasoned medieval Christians. Indeed, nothing was too bad for them. Because Jews were seen as evil allies of Satan engaged in a diabolical plot against God and Christendom, Jew-hatred was regarded as an expression of Christian virtue. Deeply etched into the minds and hearts of Christians, the distorted image of the Jew as a contemptible creature persisted in the European mentality into the twentieth century.

Despite their precarious position, medieval Jews maintained their faith, expanded their tradition of biblical and legal scholarship, and developed a flourishing Hebrew literature. The work of Jewish translators, doctors, and philosophers contributed substantially to the flowering of medieval culture in the High Middle Ages.

The foremost Jewish scholar of the Middle Ages was Moses ben Maimon (1135–1204), also called by the Greek name Maimonides. He

ANTI-SEMITISM. Holding the Jews responsible for the Black Death, Christians committed mass murder. In Basel, several hundred Jews were herded into a wooden house and burned to death. Some six thousand Jews were burned alive in Mainz. Flames consumed another two thousand in a huge pyre outside Strasbourg, and their property was distributed to the local townspeople. In this picture depicting the slaughter of the Jews of Strasbourg, the townspeople evidently enjoy the spectacle.

was born in Cordoba, Spain, then under Muslim rule. After his family emigrated from Spain, Maimonides went to Egypt, where he became physician to the sultan. During his lifetime, Maimonides achieved fame as a philosopher, theologian, mathematician, and physician. He was recognized as the leading Jewish sage of his day, and his writings were respected by Christian and Muslim thinkers as well. Like Christian and Muslim philosophers, Maimonides sought to harmonize faith with reason, to reconcile the Hebrew Scriptures and the Talmud (Jewish biblical commentary) with Greek philosophy. In his writings on ethical themes, Maimonides demonstrated piety, wisdom, and humanity, as when he discussed charity. He held that the highest form of charity was helping someone who has fallen on bad times to become self-supporting by finding him work or providing him with a gift or loan to get started again. Just below that was helping a poor person in such a way that neither the recipient nor the donor knows each other.

❖ ❖ ❖

Notes

1. Speros Vryonis, Jr., *Byzantium and Europe* (New York: Harcourt, Brace & World, 1967), p. 193.
2. The Koran, trans. N. J. Dawood (Baltimore: Penguin Books, 1961), pp. 108–109.
3. W. Montgomery Watt, *The Influence of Islam on Medieval Europe* (Edinburgh: Edinburgh University Press, 1972), p. 43.
4. Quoted in V. H. H. Green, *Medieval Civilization in Western Europe* (New York: St. Martin's Press, 1971), p. 35.
5. Excerpted in Brian Tierney, ed., *The Crisis of Church and State, 1050–1300* (Englewood Cliffs, N.J.: Prentice-Hall, 1964), p. 132.

Suggested Reading

Chazan, Robert, *Medieval Stereotypes and Modern Antisemitism* (1997). The deterioration of the image of the Jew in the High Middle Ages.

Collins, Roger, *Medieval Europe 300–1000* (1999). Comprehensive and clearly written.

Dawson, Christopher, *The Making of Europe* (1957). Stresses the role of Christianity in shaping European civilization.

Esposito, John L., ed., *The Oxford History of Islam* (1999). Essays by scholars on Islamic history and culture.

Fossier, Robert, ed., *The Cambridge Illustrated History of the Middle Ages 950–1250* (1997). Essays by scholars on the High Middle Ages.

Gies, Frances, and Joseph Gies, *Women in the Middle Ages* (1978). The narrative weaves in valuable quotations from medieval sources.

———, *Life in a Medieval Castle* (1974). The castle as the center of medieval life; passages from journals, songs, and account books permit medieval people to speak for themselves.

Herrin, Judith, *The Formation of Christendom* (1987). The transition from antiquity to the Middle Ages.

Holmes, George, ed., *The Oxford History of Medieval Europe* (1988). Essays by several scholars; good opening essay on transformation of the Roman world.

Lewis, Bernard, *The Arabs in History* (1966). A valuable survey.

Madden, Thomas F., ed., *Crusades: The Illustrated History* (2004). Useful essays on the various Crusades and their legacy.

Mango, Cyril, ed., *The Oxford History of Byzantium* (2002). Essays by scholars on Byzantine history and culture.

McCall, Andrew, *The Medieval Underworld* (2004). Acounts of witches, heretics, homosexuals and others on the margin of society.

Shahar, Shulamith, *The Fourth Estate* (1983). Women in the Middle Ages.

Spufford, Peter, *Power and Profit: The Merchant in Medieval Europe* (2002) A detailed study replete with interesting accounts.

Tyerman, Christopher, *Fighting for Christendom: Holy War and the Crusades* (2004). Includes insightful discussion of how the Crusades are perceived by Christians, Muslims, and Jews today.

Zacour, Norman, *An Introduction to Medieval Institutions* (1969). Comprehensive essays on all phases of medieval society.

Chapter 7

The Flowering and Dissolution of Medieval Civilization

- **Revival of Learning**
- **The Medieval Worldview**
- **Philosophy, Science, and Law**
- **Literature**
- **Architecture**
- **The Fourteenth Century: An Age of Adversity**
- **The Decline of the Papacy**
- **Breakup of the Thomistic Synthesis**
- **The Middle Ages and the Modern World: Continuity and Discontinuity**

Focus Questions

1. What conditions contributed to the revival of learning during the High Middle Ages?
2. What were scholastic philosophers trying to accomplish?
3. How does the medieval view of the universe differ from the modern view?
4. How did religion pervade much of the medieval philosophy, science, literature, art, and architecture?
5. Why is the fourteenth century described as an age of adversity?
6. What led to the decline of the medieval papacy? What is the historical significance of this development?

7. What is the legacy of the Middle Ages to the modern world?
8. How does the characteristic outlook of the Middle Ages differ from that of the modern age?

Europe in the High Middle Ages showed considerable vitality. The population increased, long-distance trade revived, new towns emerged, states started to take shape, and papal power grew. The culminating expression of this recovery and resurgence was the cultural flowering in philosophy, the visual arts, and literature. Creative intellects achieved on a cultural level what the papacy accomplished on an institutional level: the integration of life around a Christian viewpoint. The High Middle Ages saw the restoration of some of the learning of the ancient world, the rise of universities, the emergence of an original form of architecture (the Gothic), and the erection of an imposing system of thought, called *scholasticism*. Medieval theologian-philosophers fashioned Christian teachings into an all-embracing philosophy that represented the spiritual essence and the distinctive style of medieval civilization. They perfected what Christian thinkers in the Roman Empire had initiated and what the learned men of the Early Middle Ages had been groping for: a synthesis of Greek philosophy and Christian revelation. ❖

Chronology 7.1 ❖ The High and Late Middle Ages

c. 1100	Revival of the study of Roman law at Bologna
1163	Start of the construction of the Cathedral of Notre Dame
1267–1273	Saint Thomas Aquinas writes *Summa Theologica*
1309–1377	Babylonian Captivity: the popes, all French, reside at Avignon and are influenced by the French monarchy
c. 1321	Dante completes *Divine Comedy*
1337–1453	Hundred Years' War between England and France
1347–1351	Black Death reaches Italian ports and ravages Europe
1377	Pope Gregory XI returns the papacy to Rome
1378–1417	Great Schism: Christendom has two and then three popes
1415	The battle of Agincourt: Henry V of England defeats the French; Jan Hus, a Bohemian religious reformer, is burned at the stake
1453	The English are driven from France, except Calais; the end of the Hundred Years' War
1460	Pope Pius II condemns the Conciliar Movement as heretical

Revival of Learning

In the late eleventh century, Latin Christendom began to experience a cultural revival; all areas of life showed vitality and creativeness. In the twelfth and thirteenth centuries, a rich civilization with a distinctive style united the educated elite in the lands from Britain to Sicily. Gothic cathedrals, an enduring testament to the creativity of the religious impulse, were erected throughout Europe. Universities sprang up in several cities. Roman authors were again read and their style imitated. The quality of written Latin—the language of the church, learning, and education—improved, and secular and religious poetry, both in Latin and in the vernacular, abounded. Roman law emerged anew in Italy, spread to Northern Europe, and regained its importance (lost since Roman times) as worthy of study and scholarship. Some key works of ancient Greece were translated into Latin and studied in universities. Employing the rational tradition of Greece, men of genius harmonized Christian doctrines and Greek philosophy.

Several conditions contributed to this cultural explosion, known as the Twelfth-Century Awakening. As attacks of Vikings, Muslims, and Magyars ended and kings and great lords imposed more order and stability, people found greater opportunities for travel and communication. The revival of trade and the growth of towns created a need for literacy and provided the wealth required to support learning. Increasing contact with Islamic and Byzantine cultures in Spain, Sicily, and Italy led to the translation into Latin of ancient Greek works preserved by these Eastern civilizations. By preserving Greek philosophy and science—and by producing creative commentaries on these classical works—Islamic civilization acted as a bridge between antiquity and the cultural revival of the High Middle Ages. The Twelfth-Century Awakening was also prompted by the legacy of the Carolingian Renaissance, whose cultural lights had dimmed but never wholly vanished in the period of disorder after the dissolution of Charlemagne's empire.

In the Early Middle Ages, the principal educational centers were the monastic schools. During the twelfth century, cathedral schools in towns gained importance. Their teachers, paid a stipend by a local church, taught grammar, rhetoric, and logic. However, the chief expression of expanding intellectual life was the university, a distinct creation of the Middle Ages. The first universities were not planned but grew spontaneously. They developed as students, eager for knowledge, gathered around prominent teachers. The renewed importance of Roman law for business and politics, for example, drew students to Bologna to study with acknowledged masters.

University students attended lectures, prepared for examinations, and earned degrees. They studied grammar, rhetoric, logic, arithmetic, geometry, astronomy, medicine, music, and, when ready, church law and theology, which was considered the queen of the sciences. The curriculum relied heavily on Latin translations of ancient texts, chiefly the works of Aristotle. Students in mathematics and astronomy read Latin translations of Euclid and Ptolemy, while those in medicine studied the works of two great medical men of the ancient world, Hippocrates and Galen.

Universities performed a crucial function in the Middle Ages. Students learned the habit of reasoned argument. Universities trained professional secretaries and lawyers, who administered the affairs of church, state, and the growing cities. These institutions of learning also produced theologians and philosophers, who shaped the climate of public opinion. Since the curriculum and the texts studied were essentially the same in all lands, the learning disseminated by universities tightened the cultural bonds that united Christian Europe. Medieval universities established in the West a tradition of learning that has never died. There is direct continuity between the universities of our own day and medieval centers of learning.

God as Architect of the Universe, French Old Testament Miniature Painting, Thirteenth Century. To the medieval Christian, God was the creator of the world. The universe had a known hierarchical order, a "great chain of being" extending from God downward to the lowest form of being.

The Medieval Worldview

A distinctive worldview, based essentially on Christianity, evolved during the Middle Ages. This outlook differed from both the Greco-Roman and the modern scientific and secular views of the world. In the Christian view, not the individual but the Creator determined what constituted the good life. Thus, reason that was not illuminated by revelation was either wrong or inadequate, for God had revealed the proper rules for the regulation of individual and social life. Ultimately, the good life was not of this world but came from a union with God in a higher world. This Christian belief, as formulated by the church, made life and death purposeful and intelligible; it dominated the thought of the Middle Ages.

The Universe: Higher and Lower Worlds

Medieval thinkers sharply differentiated between spirit and matter, between a realm of grace and an earthly realm, between a higher world of perfection and a lower world of imperfection. Moral values derived from the higher world, which was also the final destination for the faithful. Two sets of laws operated in the medieval universe, one for the heavens and one for the earth. The cosmos was a giant ladder, with God at the summit; earth, composed of base matter, stood at the bottom, just above hell, where farthest from God dwelled Satan, his evil spirits, and the souls of the damned.

From Aristotle and Ptolemy, medieval thinkers inherited the theory of an earth-centered universe—the *geocentric theory*—which they imbued with Christian meaning. The geocentric theory held that revolving around the motionless earth at uniform speeds were seven transparent spheres, in which were embedded the seven "planets"—the moon, Mercury, Venus, the sun, Mars, Jupiter, and Saturn. (Because Earth did not move, it was not considered a planet.) A sphere of fixed stars—that is, the stars stayed in a constant relationship to one another—enclosed this planetary system. Above the firmament of the stars were the three heavenly spheres. The outermost, the Empyrean Heaven, was the abode of God and the Elect. Through the sphere below—the Prime Mover—God transmitted motion to the planetary spheres. Beneath this was the lowest sphere, the invisible Crystalline Heaven.

An earth-centered universe accorded with the Christian idea that God had created the universe for men and women and that salvation was the primary aim of life. Because God had created people in his image, they deserved this central position in the universe. Although they might be living at the bottom rung of the cosmic ladder, only they, of all living things, had the capacity to ascend to heaven, the realm of perfection.

Also acceptable to the Christian mentality was the sharp distinction drawn by Aristotle between the world above the moon and the one below it. Aristotle held that terrestrial bodies were made of four elements: earth, water, air, and fire. Celestial bodies, which occupied the region above the moon, were composed of a fifth element, ether—too clear, too pure, and too perfect to be found on earth. The planets and stars existed in a world apart; they were made of the divine ether and followed celestial laws, which did not apply to earthly objects. Whereas earthly bodies underwent change—ice converting to water, a burning log converting to ashes—heavenly objects were incorruptible, immune to all change. Unlike earthly objects, they were indestructible.

Heavenly bodies also followed different laws of motion from earthly objects. Aristotle said that it was natural for celestial bodies to move eternally in uniform circles, such motion being considered a sign of perfection. According to Aristotle, it was also natural for heavy bodies (stone) to fall downward and for light objects (fire, smoke) to move upward toward the celestial world; the falling stone and the rising smoke were finding their natural place in the universe.

The Individual: Sinful but Redeemable

At the center of medieval belief was the idea of a perfect God and a wretched and sinful human being. God, who had conceived and created the universe, had given Adam and Eve freedom to choose; rebellious and presumptuous, they had used their freedom to disobey God. In doing so, they made evil an intrinsic part of the human personality. But God, who had not stopped loving human beings, showed them the way out of sin. God became man and died so that human beings might be saved. Men and women were weak, egocentric, and sinful. With God's grace, they could overcome their sinful nature and gain salvation; without grace, they were utterly helpless.

The medieval individual's understanding of self stemmed from a comprehension of the universe as a hierarchy instituted by and culminating in God. On earth, the basest objects were lifeless stones, devoid of souls. Higher than stones were plants, endowed with a primitive type of soul that allowed reproduction and growth. Still higher were animals, which had the capacity for motion and sensation. The highest of the animals were human beings; unlike other animals, they could grasp some part of universal truth. Far superior to them were the angels, who apprehended God's truth without difficulty. At the summit of this graduated universe (the Great Chain of Being) was God, who was pure Being, without limitation, and the source of all existence. God's revelation reached down to humanity through the hierarchical order. From God, revelation passed to the angels, who were also arranged

The Art of the Ancient World and the Middle Ages

The art of the classical period (c. fifth century B.C.) was important not only to the ancient Greeks but also to the Romans and to later generations, from the Renaissance to the postmodern period of the late twentieth century. Through the ages, classical art has been kept alive—adopted, adapted, altered, and appreciated—by artists and craftspeople. Why has the classical style remained at the forefront of artistic endeavor?

The classical period has given us the first works of the Western world to represent the human form with accuracy. The body itself was the sculptors' subject. Their aim was to shape their marble so as to make a general and schematic figure lifelike. Classical sculpture has been a powerful learning device for aspiring artisans from Michelangelo to nineteenth-century artists such as Auguste Rodin. Ancient sculptures—and plaster casts made from them—have been used as teaching tools by educators since the Renaissance. Learning to draw from casts of ancient works was the traditional first step in an artist's education; even many abstract artists of the twentieth century had a solid grounding in works of the classical period.

Praxiteles: Hermes with Young Dionysus, c. 350 B.C. Praxiteles (fl. 375–330 B.C.) is renowned for the quality of his marble sculpture, such as the *Hermes with Young Dionysus,* considered one of his finest works. The statue has many of the attributes that distinguish classical sculpture at its best. The stance is relaxed: an S-curve takes the weight off of one leg and shifts it to the opposite hip. This *contrapposto* or counterbalanced pose draws attention to every part of the god's body. The sculpture is so realistic and fluid that viewers might forget they are looking at marble. How does this work express the humanistic outlook of classical Greece? (Olympia Museum/Bridgeman Art Library.)

Hellenistic Sculpture: *The Laocoön,* Second Century B.C. This Hellenistic sculpture, attributed to three artists, depicts the suffering, anguish, and death of the mythological Laocoön and his sons as divine retribution for his having broken an oath. It presents an interesting contrast to earlier Hellenic art, which was characteristically harmonious and serene. What statement does the shape and arrangement of the figures in the group seem to be making about human destiny? How does it differ from the usual approach of Hellenic art in portraying the human figure? (Museo Pio Clementino, Vatican Museums, Vatican State/Scala/Art Resource.)

Detail of Pompeian Wall Fresco: Lady Playing the Cithara. Upon the removal of lava and ash from Pompeii, a first-century Roman city appeared, providing historians with data on the daily life of almost twenty centuries ago. What does this fresco scene disclose about the state of Roman culture and the lives of Roman matrons?

Apse Mosaic: Justinian and Attendants, Church of San Vitale, Ravenna. Emperor Justinian, who ruled Byzantium from 527 to 565, appears in this mosaic as a symbol of Christ rather than as an ordinary ruler on earth. The golden halo and the presence of exactly twelve attendants, reminiscent of the Twelve Apostles, confirm this impression. The way in which an artist depicts the human figure reveals a lot about past cultures. What can we learn about Byzantium by comparing the portrayal of Justinian with that of the Roman matron playing the cithara on the previous page? (Scala/Art Resource, N.Y.)

Byzantine School: *Enthroned Madonna and Child,* Thirteenth Century. During the thirteenth century, the Byzantine style, characterized by a blending of the art of Byzantium and the Catholic West, emerged in Italy. An excellent example of this fusion is evident in the *Enthroned Madonna and Child,* probably painted by a Greek artist working in Italy. What is typically Byzantine about this work is the richness of color and the use of gold in the background and in the Madonna's robes. The faces of the figures, the high-backed wooden throne, the halos decorated with floral patterns, and the full-length image of the Virgin on her throne show an Italian influence. Why is Mary seated on a throne? How would a medieval viewer interpret this painting? (National Gallery of Art, Washington, D.C., Gift of Mrs. Otto H. Kahn, 1940.)

April from *Les trés riches heures* of Jean, Duke of Berry. This page from a beautifully illustrated volume of prayers, which was made during 1413 through 1416, is one of the paintings of months appearing in the nobleman's book. What does this scene reveal about the lifestyle of nobles, both men and women?
(Giraudon/Art Resource, N.Y.)

Domenico Veneziano (c. 1410–1461): *Madonna and Child with Saints*, c. 1445. This Florentine master painted the altar panel (6' 7-1/2" × 6' 11-7/8") in a new style, called *sacra conversazione* (sacred conversation). The enthroned Madonna and child are framed by architectural elements and flanked by the formal, solemn figures of saints, who seem to converse with her or between themselves, or even with the onlooker. Saint John, to the left of the child and the Madonna, gazes out of the painting as he points to them, in effect directing the onlooker's eyes. In his color scheme, Domenico uses sunlight and spots of bright primary colors, along with pastels, to present a glowing scene. What elements in the painting indicate that it is an Early Renaissance work? (Alinari/Art Resource, N.Y.)

Hubert or Jan van Eyck: ***The Last Judgment*****, c. 1420–1425.** The major concern of medieval people was the salvation of their souls. At the Last Judgment, the good would be drawn to heaven while the damned would be sealed in hell. In *The Last Judgment*, the Flemish artist van Eyck depicts this final division in graphic detail. How does the relationship between man and the divine portrayed by van Eyck differ from the classical humanism of ancient Greek art? (Copyright © 1996 by The Metropolitan Museum of Art, Fletcher Fund, 1933.)

Bildarchiv Preussischer Kulturbesitz/Art Resource, N.Y.

School of Bologna Manuscript Illumination. The core of the medieval curriculum included the *trivium* and the *quadrivium*. Students mastered grammar, rhetoric, and dialectic—the "three ways" (trivium)—and then proceeded to mathematics, geometry, astronomy, and music (quadrivium). The technique of teaching was the *disputatio*, or oral disputation between master and student.

hierarchically. From the angels, the truth reached men and women; it was grasped first by prophets and apostles and then by the multitudes. Thus, all things in the universe, from God to angels to men and women to the lowest earthly objects, occupied a place peculiar to their nature and were linked by God in a great, unbroken chain.

Medieval individuals derived a sense of security from this hierarchical universe, in which the human position was clearly defined. True, they were sinners who dwelt on a corruptible earth at the bottom of the cosmic hierarchy. But they could ascend to the higher world of perfection above the moon. As children of God, they enjoyed the unique distinction that each human soul was precious; all Christians commanded respect unless they were heretics. (A heretic forfeited dignity and could be justly executed.)

Medieval thinkers also arranged knowledge in a hierarchical order: knowledge of spiritual things surpassed all worldly knowledge, all human sciences. To know what God wanted of the individual was the summit of self-knowledge and permitted entry into heaven.

Philosophy, Science, and Law

Medieval philosophy, or scholasticism, applied reason to revelation. It explained and clarified Christian teachings by means of concepts and principles of logic derived from Greek philosophy. Scholastics tried to show that the teachings of faith, although not derived from reason, were not contrary to reason, that logic could confirm the truth of church dogma. They tried to prove through reason what they already held to be true through faith. For example, the existence of God and the immortality of the soul, which every Christian accepted as articles of faith, could also, they thought, be demonstrated by reason. In struggling to harmonize faith with reason, medieval thinkers constructed an extraordinary synthesis of Christian revelation and Greek rationalism.

The scholastic masters used reason not to challenge but to serve faith: to elucidate, clarify, and buttress it. They did not break with the central concern of Christianity: earning God's grace and achieving salvation. Although this goal could be realized solely by faith, scholastic thinkers insisted that a science of nature did not obstruct the pursuit of grace and that philosophy could assist the devout in contemplating God. They did not reject those Christian beliefs that were beyond the grasp of human reason and therefore could not be deduced by rational argument. Instead, they held that such truths rested entirely on revelation and were to be accepted on faith. To medieval thinkers, reason did not have an independent existence but ultimately had to acknowledge a suprarational, superhuman standard of truth; Greek philosophy had to be interpreted to accord with Christian revelation. These thinkers wanted rational thought to be directed by faith for Christian ends and guided by scriptural and ecclesiastical authority. Ultimately, faith had the final word.

Not all Christian thinkers welcomed the use of reason. Regarding Greek philosophy as an enemy of faith (would not reason lead people to question belief in miracles?), a fabricator of heresies (would not reason encourage disbelief in essential church teachings?), and an obstacle to achieving communion of the soul with God (would not a deviation from church teachings, under the influence of pagan philosophy, deprive people of salvation?), conservative theologians opposed the application of reason to Christian revelation. In a sense, the conservatives were right. By giving renewed vitality to Greek thought, medieval philosophy nurtured a powerful force that would eventually shatter the medieval concepts of nature and society and weaken Christianity. Modern Western thought was created by thinkers who refused to subordinate reason to Christian authority. Reason proved a double-edged sword: it both ennobled and undermined the medieval worldview.

Saint Anselm and Abelard

An early scholastic, Saint Anselm (1033–1109) was abbot of the Benedictine monastery of Le Bec in Normandy. He used rational argument to serve the interests of faith. Like Augustine before him and other thinkers who followed him, Anselm said that faith was a precondition for understanding. Without belief there could be no proper knowledge. He developed a philosophical proof for the existence of God. Anselm argued as follows: We can conceive of no being greater than God. But if God were to exist only in thought and not in actuality, his greatness would be limited; he would be less than perfect. Hence, he exists.

Anselm's motive and method reveal something about the essence of medieval philosophy. He does not begin as a modern might: "If it can be proven that God exists, I will adopt the creed of Christianity; if not, I will either deny God's existence (atheism) or reserve judgment (agnosticism)." Rather, Anselm accepts God's existence as an established fact because he believes what Holy Scripture says and what the church teaches. He then proceeds to employ logical argument to demonstrate that God can be known not only through faith, but also through reason. He would never use reason to subvert what he knows to be true by faith. This attitude would generally characterize later medieval thinkers, who also applied reason to faith.

As a young teacher of theology at the Cathedral School of Notre Dame, Peter Abelard (1079–1142) acquired a reputation for brilliance and combativeness. His tragic affair with Héloise, whom he tutored and seduced, has become one of the great romances in Western literature. Abelard's most determined opponent, Bernard of Clairvaux, accused him of using the method of dialectical argument to attack faith. To Bernard, a monk and mystic, subjecting revealed truth to critical analysis was fraught with danger. Hearkening to Bernard's powerful voice, the church condemned Abelard and confined him to a monastery for the rest of his days.

Abelard believed that it was important to apply reason to faith and that careful and constant questioning led to wisdom. In *Sic et Non* (Yes and No), he took 150 theological issues and, by presenting passages from the Bible and the church

Primary Source

Peter Abelard: The Synthesis of Reason and Faith

In the cathedral school at Paris, Peter Abelard brilliantly taught dialectics, a method of logical analysis, as applied to the Bible and the writings of early Christian thinkers. In his book Sic et Non *(Yes and No), Abelard listed some 150 questions on which the early church authorities had taken differing positions over the centuries. He suggested that these issues could be resolved by the careful application of the dialectical method to the language of the texts.*

Although he never intended to challenge the Christian faith, Abelard raised, with his critical scrutiny, fears that the dialectical approach would undermine faith and foster heresy, and he was forced to quit his teaching post. Nevertheless, the new scholastic, rationalistic approach swept the schools of Europe. In the following reading, Abelard describes the critical use of rational methods in textual analysis.

We must be careful not to be led astray by attributing views to the [Church] Fathers which they did not hold. This may happen if a wrong author's name is given to a book or if a text is corrupt. For many works are falsely attributed to one of the Fathers to give them authority, and some passages even in the Bible are corrupt through the errors of copyists. . . . We must be equally careful to make sure that an opinion quoted from a Father was not withdrawn or corrected by him in the light of later and better knowledge. . . . Again the passage in question may not give the Father's own opinion, but that of some other writer whom he is quoting. . . .

We must also make a thorough inquiry when different decisions are given on the same matter under canon [church] law. We must discover, whether it is meant to grant an indulgence or exhort to some perfection. In this way we may clear up the apparent contradiction. . . . If the opinion is a definitive judgment, we must determine whether it is of general application or directed to a particular case. . . . The when and why of the order must also be considered because what is allowed at one time is often forbidden at another, and what is often laid down as the strict letter of the law may be sometimes moderated by a dispensation. . . .

Furthermore we customarily talk of things as they appear to our bodily senses and not as they are in actual fact. So judging by what we see we say it is a starry sky or it is not, and that the sun is hot or has no heat at all, when these things though variable in appearance are ever constant. Can we be surprised, then, that some matters have been stated by the Fathers as opinions rather than the truth? Then again many controversies would be quickly settled if we could be on our guard against a particular word used in different senses by different authors. . . .

By collecting contrasting divergent opinions I hope to provoke young readers to push themselves to the limit in the search for truth, so that their wits may be sharpened by their investigation. It is by doubting that we come to investigate, and by investigating that we recognise the truth.

Questions for Analysis

1. Describe the methods of literary analysis promoted by Peter Abelard.
2. Why did Abelard's new method of textual analysis create so much controversy?

Excerpted in David Ayerst and A. S. S. Fisher, eds. *Records of Christianity*, Vol. 2, *Christendom* (Oxford: Blackwell, 1977), 196–197.

fathers, showed that there were conflicting opinions. He suggested that the divergent opinions of authorities could be reconciled through proper use of dialectics. But like Anselm before him, Abelard did not intend to refute traditional church doctrines. Reason would buttress, not weaken, the authority of faith. He wrote after his condemnation in 1141: "I will never be a philosopher, if this is to speak against St. Paul; I would not be an Aristotle if this were to separate me from Christ. . . . I have set my building on the cornerstone on which Christ has built his Church. . . . I rest upon the rock that cannot be moved."[1]

Saint Thomas Aquinas: The Synthesis of Faith and Reason

The introduction into Latin Christendom of the major works of Aristotle created a dilemma for religious authorities. Aristotle's comprehensive philosophy of nature and man, a product of human reason alone, conflicted in many instances with essential Christian doctrine. Whereas Christianity taught that God created the universe at a specific point in time, Aristotle held that the universe was eternal. Nor did Aristotle believe in the personal immortality of the soul, another cardinal principle of Christianity.

Some church officials feared that the dissemination of Aristotle's ideas and the use of Aristotelian logic would endanger faith. At various times in the first half of the thirteenth century, they forbade teaching the scientific works of Aristotle at the University of Paris. But because the ban did not apply throughout Christendom and was not consistently enforced in Paris, Aristotle's philosophy continued to be studied. Rejecting the position of conservatives, who insisted that philosophy would contaminate faith, Saint Thomas Aquinas (c. 1225–1274) upheld the value of human reason and natural knowledge. Aquinas taught at Paris and in Italy. His greatest work, *Summa Theologica,* is a systematic exposition of Christian thought and the crowning expression of the medieval attempt to integrate Aristotle with Christianity.

Can the teachings of faith conflict with the evidence of reason? For Aquinas, the answer was emphatically no. Since both faith and reason came from God, they were not in competition with each other but, properly understood, supported each other and formed an organic unity. Consequently, reason should not be feared, for it was another avenue to God. Because there was an inherent agreement between true faith and correct reason—they both ultimately stemmed from God—contradictions between them were only a misleading appearance. Although philosophy had not yet been able to resolve the dilemma, for God no such contradictions existed. In heaven, human beings would attain complete knowledge, as well as complete happiness. While on earth, however, they must allow faith to guide reason; they must not permit reason to oppose or undermine faith.

Thus, in exalting God, Aquinas also paid homage to human intelligence, proclaimed the value of rational activity, and asserted the importance of physical reality discovered through human senses. Consequently, he prized the natural philosophy of Aristotle. Correctly used, Aristotelian thought would assist faith. Aquinas's great effort was to synthesize Aristotelianism with the divine revelation of Christianity. That the two could be harmonized he had no doubt. He made use of Aristotelian categories in his five proofs of God's existence. In his first proof, for example, Aquinas argued that a thing cannot move itself. Whatever is moved must be moved by something else, and that by something else again. "Therefore, it is necessary to arrive at a first mover, moved by no other; and this everyone understands to be God."[2]

Aquinas upheld the value of reason. To love the intellect was to honor God and not to diminish the truth of faith. He had confidence in the power of the rational mind to comprehend most of the truths of revelation, and he insisted that in nontheological questions about specific things in nature—those questions not affecting salvation—people should trust only reason and experience. Thus, Aquinas gave new importance to the empirical world and to scientific speculation and human knowledge.

Traditionally medieval thinkers maintained that knowledge derived from the natural world was an obstacle to true knowledge. Aquinas altered this tradition by affirming the importance of knowledge of the social order and the physical world. He gave human reason and worldly knowledge a new dignity. Thus, the City of Man was not merely a sinful place from which people tried to escape in order to enter God's city; it was worthy of investigation and understanding. But Aquinas remained a medieval thinker, for he always maintained that secular knowledge should be supervised and corrected by revealed truth, and he never questioned the truth of the medieval Christian view of the world and the individual.

Science

During the Early Middle Ages, few scientific works from the ancient world were available to Western Europeans. Scientific thought was at its lowest ebb since its origination more than a thousand years earlier in Greece. In contrast, both the Islamic and Byzantine civilizations preserved and, in some instances, added to the legacy of Greek science. In the High Middle Ages, however, many ancient texts were translated from Greek and Arabic into Latin and entered Latin Christendom for the first time. Spain, where Christian and Muslim civilizations met, was one of the two principal centers of translation. The other was Sicily, which had been controlled by Byzantium up to the last part of the ninth century and then by Islam until Christian Normans completed the conquest of the island by 1091.

In the thirteenth and fourteenth centuries, a genuine scientific movement did occur. Impressed with the naturalistic and empirical approach of Aristotle, some medieval schoolmen spent time examining physical nature. Among them was the Dominican Albert the Great (Albertus Magnus, c. 1206–1280). Born in Germany, he studied at Padua and taught at the University of Paris, where Thomas Aquinas was his student. Albert devoted himself to editing and commenting on the vast body of Aristotle's works.

While retaining the Christian emphasis on God, revelation, the supernatural, and the afterlife, Albert (unlike many earlier Christian thinkers) considered nature a valid field for investigation. In his writings on geology, chemistry, botany, and zoology, Albert, like Aristotle, displayed a respect for the concrete details of nature, utilizing them as empirical evidence. Albert stressed the value of knowledge derived from experience with nature,

Millefleurs Tapestry: Two Musicians, School of the Loire, France, c. 1500. The courtly love tradition, in which women were worshiped and untouchable, inspired poetry. Troubadours sang this poetry, which expressed a changing attitude toward women. By inviting poets to their courts and writing poetry themselves, noblewomen actively influenced the rituals and literature of courtly love.

sought rational explanations for natural occurrences, and held that theological debates should not stop scientific investigations.

Other scholars in the scientific movement included Robert Grosseteste (c. 1175–1253), the chancellor of Oxford University. He insisted that mathematics was necessary in order to understand the physical world, and he carried out experiments on the refraction of light. Another Englishman, the monk and philosopher Roger Bacon (c. 1214–1294), foreshadowed the modern attitude of using science to gain mastery over nature. Bacon valued the study of mathematics and read Arabic works on the reflection and refraction of light. Among his achievements were experiments in optics and the observation that light travels much faster than sound. His description of the anatomy of the vertebrate eye and optic nerves was the finest of that era, and he recommended dissecting the eyes of pigs and cows to obtain greater knowledge of the subject.

Medieval scholars did not make the breakthrough to modern science. They retained the belief that the earth was at the center of the universe and that different sets of laws operated on earth and in the heavens. They did not invent analytic geometry or calculus or arrive at the concept of inertia—all crucial for modern science. Moreover, medieval science was never wholly removed from a theological setting.

Medieval scholars and philosophers did, however, advance knowledge about optics, the tides, and mechanics. They saw the importance of mathematics for interpreting nature, and they performed some experiments. By translating and commenting on ancient Greek and Arabic works, medieval scholars provided future ages with ideas to reflect on and to surpass, a necessary precondition for the emergence of modern science. Medieval thinkers also developed an anti-Aristotelian physics, which some historians of science believe influenced Galileo, the creator of modern mechanics, more than two centuries later.

Recovery of Roman Law

During the Early Middle Ages, Western European law essentially consisted of Germanic customs, some of which had been put into writing. Some elements of Roman law endured as custom and practice, but the formal study of Roman law had disappeared. The late eleventh and twelfth centuries saw the revival of Roman law, particularly in Bologna, Italy. Irnerius lectured on the *Corpus Juris Civilis,* codified by Byzantine jurists in the sixth century, and made Bologna the leading center for the study of Roman law. Irnerius and his students employed the methods of organization and logical analysis that scholastic theologians used in studying philosophical texts.

Unlike traditional Germanic law, which was essentially tribal and parochial, Roman law assumed the existence of universal principles that could be grasped by the human intellect and expressed in the law of the state. Roman jurists had systematically and rationally structured the legal experience of the Roman people. The example of Roman law stimulated medieval jurists to organize their own legal tradition. Intellectuals increasingly came to insist on both a rational analysis of evidence and judicial decisions based on rational procedures. Law codes compiled in parts of France and Germany and in the kingdom of Castile were influenced by the recovery of Roman law.

Literature

Medieval literature was written both in Latin and in the vernacular. Much of medieval Latin literature consisted of religious hymns and dramas depicting the life of Christ and saints. In their native tongues, medieval writers created different forms of poetry: *chansons de geste,* the *roman,* and *troubadour* songs, which emerged during the High Middle Ages.

The French chansons de geste—epic poems of heroic deeds that had first been told orally—were written in the vernacular of northern France. These poems dealt with Charlemagne's battles against the Muslims, with rebellious nobles, and with feudal warfare. The finest of these epic poems, *The Song of Roland,* expressed the feudal ethic—loyalty to one's lord and devotion to Christianity were the highest virtues and treachery an unpardonable crime. Roland, Charlemagne's nephew who was killed in a battle with the Muslims, is idolized as the brave Christian knight who battles God's enemies. He is a warrior of heroic proportions and great physical prowess, who is loyal to God, the King, and his knightly entourage. The *Nibelungenlied,* the best expression of the heroic epic in Germany, is often called "the *Iliad* of the Germans." Like its French counterpart, it dealt with heroic feats.

The roman—a blending of old legends, chivalric ideals, and Christian concepts—combined love with adventure, war, and the miraculous. Among the romans were the tales of King Arthur and his Round Table. Circulating by word of mouth for centuries, these tales spread from the British Isles to France and Germany. In the twelfth century, they were put into French verse.

Another form of medieval poetry, which flourished particularly in Provence, in southern France, dealt with the romantic glorification of women. Sung by troubadours, many of them nobles, the

The Triumph of St. Thomas Aquinas: Wall Painting, the Spanish Chapel, Church of Santa Maria Novella, Florence, Fourteenth Century. In a church built by his fellow Dominican friars, the saint, theologian, and philosopher Thomas Aquinas sits enthroned expounding Christian theology illustrated by the principles of Aristotle. This painting is by Taddeo Gaddi, a pupil of the master painter Giotto.

courtly love poetry expressed a changing attitude toward women. Although medieval men generally regarded women as inferior and subordinate, courtly love poetry ascribed to noble ladies superior qualities of virtue. To the nobleman, the lady became a goddess worthy of all devotion, loyalty, and worship. He would honor her and serve her as he did his lord; for her love he would undergo any sacrifice.

Noblewomen actively influenced the rituals and literature of courtly love. They often invited poets to their courts and wrote poetry themselves. They demanded that knights treat them with gentleness and consideration and that knights dress neatly, bathe often, play instruments, and compose (or at least recite) poetry. To prove worthy of his lady's love, a knight had to demonstrate patience, charm, bravery, and loyalty. By devoting himself to a lady, it was believed, a knight would ennoble his character.

Courtly love did not involve a husband–wife relationship but rather a noble's admiration of and yearning for another woman of his class. Among nobles, marriages were arranged for political and economic reasons. The rituals of courtly love expanded the skills and refined the tastes of the noble. The rough warrior acquired wit, manners, charm, and skill with words. He was becoming a courtier and a gentleman.

The greatest literary figure of the Middle Ages was Dante Alighieri (1265–1321) of Florence. Dante appreciated the Roman classics and wrote not just in Latin, the traditional language of intellectual life, but in Italian, his native tongue. In this respect, he anticipated the Renaissance (see Chapter 8). In the tradition of the troubadours, Dante wrote poems to his beloved Beatrice.

In *The Divine Comedy,* Dante synthesized the various elements of the medieval outlook and summed up, with immense feeling, the medieval understanding of the purpose of life. Written while Dante was in exile, *The Divine Comedy* describes the poet's journey through hell, purgatory, and paradise. Dante arranges hell into nine concentric circles; in each region, sinners are punished in proportion to their earthly sins. The poet experiences all of hell's torments—burning sand, violent storms, darkness, and fearful monsters that whip, claw, bite, and tear sinners apart. The ninth circle, the lowest, is reserved for Lucifer and traitors. Lucifer has three faces, each a different color, and two batlike wings. In each mouth he gnaws on one of the greatest traitors in history: Judas Iscariot, who betrayed Jesus, and Brutus and Cassius, who assassinated Caesar. Those condemned to hell are told: "All hope abandon, ye who enter in." In purgatory, Dante meets sinners who, although they undergo punishment, will eventually enter paradise. In paradise, an abode of light, music, and gentleness, the poet, guided by Beatrice, meets the great saints and the Virgin Mary. For an instant, he glimpses the Vision of God. In this mystical experience, the aim of life is realized.

Another masterpiece of the Middle Ages is *The Canterbury Tales* of Geoffrey Chaucer (c. 1340–1400), written in the vernacular. Chaucer chose as his theme twenty-nine pilgrims en route from London to the religious shrine at Canterbury. In describing the pilgrims, Chaucer displayed humor, charm, an understanding of human nature, and a superb grasp of the attitudes of the English. Few writers have pictured their times better.

Architecture

Two styles of architecture evolved during the Middle Ages: Romanesque and Gothic. The Romanesque style dominated the eleventh century and the greater part of the twelfth. In imitation of ancient Roman structures, Romanesque buildings had massive walls that supported stone barrel-and-groin vaults with rounded arches. The thick walls were needed to hold up the great weight of the roofs. The walls left few spaces for windows, and so little light entered the interior. However, the development of the pointed arch permitted supports that lessened the bearing pressure of the roof on the walls. This new style, called Gothic, allowed buildings to have lofty, vaulted ceilings and huge windows, which permitted sunlight to flood the interiors. The Romanesque building produced an impression of massive solidity; Gothic buildings created an illusion of lightness and soaring energy and an upward reach to the heavens.

The magnificently designed stained-glass windows and complex sculptural decoration of Gothic cathedrals depicted scenes from the Bible and the lives of saints—as well as scenes from daily life—for the worshipers, many of whom were illiterate. The reduction of wall space, which allowed these massive glass illustrations, was made possible by the flying buttresses on the buildings' exteriors. These great arcs of masonry carry the weight and thrust of the stone vaults out to the exterior walls.

The Gothic style was to remain vigorous until the fifteenth century, spreading from France to England, Germany, Spain, and beyond. Revived from time to time thereafter, it has proved to be one of the most enduring styles in Western art and architecture.

Scala/Art Resource, N.Y.

The Romanesque Nave of the Cathedral of St. Sernin, Toulouse. The nave is covered by a stone barrel vault, replacing earlier wooden roofs, which were susceptible to fire. The columns, thick walls, and small windows were required structurally to bear the great weight of the roof vaulting. Little light penetrated the interior.

The Fourteenth Century: An Age of Adversity

By the fourteenth century, Latin Christendom had experienced more than 250 years of growth. On the economic level, agricultural production had expanded, commerce and town life had revived, and the population had increased. On the political level, kings had become more powerful, bringing greater order and security to large areas. On the religious level, the papacy had demonstrated its strength as the spiritual leader of Christendom, and the clergy had been reformed. On the cultural level, a unified worldview, blending faith and reason, had been forged.

During the Late Middle Ages (roughly the fourteenth century), however, Latin Christendom was afflicted with severe problems. The earlier increases in agricultural production did not continue. Limited use of fertilizers and limited knowledge of conservation exhausted the topsoil. From 1301 to 1314, there was a general shortage of food, and from 1315 to 1317, famine struck Europe. People subsisted by scavenging. On roads and in villages, the deceased and those dying of starvation remained unattended. Throughout the century, starvation and malnutrition were widespread.

Adding to the economic crisis was the Black Death, or bubonic plague, a bacillus carried by fleas on black rats. The disease probably first struck Mongolia in 1331–1332, and from there it crossed into Russia. Carried back from Black Sea ports, the plague reached Sicily in 1347 and then spread swiftly throughout much of Europe through human contact. Some historians contend that the Black Death may have consisted of two diseases, the bubonic plague and anthrax, which was transmitted by eating meat from diseased cattle. The first onslaught lasted until 1351, and other serious outbreaks occurred in later decades. The crowded cities and towns, where sewage made rats more fecund, had the highest mortality rate, as much as 60 percent. Perhaps twenty million people—about one-quarter to one-third of the European population—perished in the worst disaster in recorded history caused by natural forces. Contemporaries viewed the plague as divine punishment for humanity's sins.

Overwhelmed by terror, people abandoned their sick children, spouses, and parents. Panic-stricken people drifted into debauchery, lawlessness, and

Roger Viollet/Getty Images.

The Gothic Nave and Choir of Notre Dame Cathedral, Paris, Twelfth Century. The Gothic nave is wider than the Romanesque nave because pointed arches can bridge a wider space and carry a roof with less heavy vaulting. The walls are raised higher, are thinner, and are punctured with larger open spaces for windows than were possible in Romanesque buildings. The weight of the roof and walls is born by "flying buttresses," stone arched supports external to the walls.

frenzied forms of religious life. Confidence in the church declined as many priests fled, depriving the sick of spiritual comfort and the dying of last rites. Organized bands of flagellants marched from region to region, beating themselves and each other with sticks and whips in a desperate effort to appease God, who they believed had cursed them with the plague. Expressing the pervasive gloom and pessimism of these times, art concentrated on morbid scenes of decaying flesh, open graves laden with worm-eaten corpses—even the Madonna was represented as a corpse being eaten by snakes and frogs—dances of death, and the torments of hell. Sometimes, this hysteria was directed against Jews, who were accused of causing the plague by poisoning wells. Terrible massacres of Jews, often by mass burnings, occurred despite the pleas of the papacy.

The millions of deaths caused production of food and goods to plummet. However, depopulation was a boon for surviving artisans, who found opportunities and higher wages in depopulated towns desperate for skilled workers. A diminishing labor pool also benefited peasants, who were able to attain lighter burdens from strapped lords, and free peasants who toiled as day laborers demanded higher wages The combination of lower agricultural prices and increasing wages hurt aristocratic landowners. As their agricultural income lessened, nobles tried to make peasants bear the brunt of the crisis. Economic and social tensions, some of them antedating the Black Death, escalated into rebellions. Each rebellion had its own specific causes, but a general pattern characterized the uprisings in the countryside. When kings and lords, breaking with customary social relationships, imposed new and onerous regulations, the peasants rose in defense of their traditional rights.

In 1323, the lords' attempt to reimpose old manorial obligations infuriated the free peasants of Flanders, whose condition had improved in earlier decades. The Peasants' Revolt lasted five bloody years. In 1358, French peasants took up arms in protest against the plundering of the countryside by soldiers. Perhaps twenty thousand peasants died in the uprising known as the *Jacquerie*. In 1381, English peasants revolted, angered over legislation that tied them to the land and imposed new taxes. Like the revolts in Flanders and France, the uprising in England failed. To the landed aristocracy, the peasants were sinners attacking a social system ordained by God. Possessing superior might, the nobility suppressed the peasants, sometimes with savage cruelty.

Social unrest also afflicted towns. The wage earners of Florence (1378), the weavers of Ghent (1382), and the poor of Paris (1382) rose up against the ruling oligarchies. These revolts were generally initiated not by the poorest and most downtrodden but by those who had made some gains and were eager for more. The rebellions of the urban poor were crushed just like the peasant uprisings.

Compounding the adversity was the series of conflicts known as the Hundred Years' War (1337–1453). Because English kings ruled parts of France, conflicts between the two monarchies were common. In the opening phase of the war, the English inflicted terrible defeats on French knights at the battles of Crécy (1346) and Poitiers (1356). Using longbows, which allowed them to shoot arrows rapidly, English archers cut down wave after wave of charging French cavalry. The war continued on and off throughout the fourteenth century. During periods of truce, gangs of unemployed soldiers roamed the French countryside killing and stealing, actions that precipitated the Jacquerie, the peasant uprising.

After the battle of Agincourt (1415), won by the English under Henry V, the English controlled most of northern France. It appeared that England would shortly conquer France and join the two lands under one crown. At this crucial moment in French history, a young, illiterate peasant girl, Joan of Arc (1412–1431), helped rescue France. Believing that God commanded her to drive the English out of France, Joan rallied the demoralized French troops, leading them in battle. In 1429, she liberated the besieged city of Orléans. Later she was captured and imprisoned by the English, and in 1431 she was condemned as a heretic and a witch by a handpicked church court and was burned at the stake. Inspired by Joan's death, the French drove the English from all French territory except the port of Calais.

During the Hundred Years' War, French kings introduced new taxes, which added substantially to their incomes. These monies furnished them with the means to organize a professional army of well-paid and loyal troops. By evoking a sense of pride and oneness in the French people, the war also contributed to a growing, but still incomplete, national unity. The English, too, emerged from the war with a greater sense of solidarity, and Parliament, because it had to finance the war, gained in stature. However, the war had horrendous consequences for the French peasants. Thousands of farmers were killed, and valuable farmland was destroyed by English armies and marauding bands of mercenaries. In a portentous development, the later stages of the Hundred Years' War saw the use of gunpowder and heavy artillery.

The Decline of the Papacy

The principal sign of the decline of medieval civilization in the Late Middle Ages was the waning authority and prestige of the papacy. In the High Middle Ages, the papacy had been the dominant institution in Christendom, but in the Late Middle Ages, its power weakened. The medieval ideal of a unified Christian commonwealth guided by the papacy was shattered. Papal authority declined in the face of the growing power of kings, who championed the parochial interests of states. As the pope became more embroiled in European politics, papal prestige and the pope's capacity to command diminished. Many pious Christians felt that the pope was behaving more like a secular ruler than like an Apostle of Christ. Political theorists and church reformers further undermined papal authority.

Conflict with France

Philip IV of France (1285–1314) taxed the church in his land to raise revenue for war. In doing so, he disregarded the church prohibition against the taxing of its property without papal permission. In 1296, in the bull *Clericis Laicos,* Pope Boniface VIII (1294–1303) decreed that kings and lords who imposed taxes on the clergy and the clergy who paid them would be excommunicated. Far from bowing to the pope's threat, Philip acted forcefully to assert his authority over the church in his kingdom. Boniface backed down from his position, declaring that the French king could tax the clergy in times of national emergency. Thus, the matter was resolved to the advantage of the state.

A second dispute had more disastrous consequences for Boniface. Philip tried and imprisoned a French bishop despite Boniface's warning that this was an illegal act and a violation of church law and tradition, which held that the church, not the state, must judge the clergy. Philip summoned the first meeting of the Estates General to gain the backing of the nation. Shortly afterward, Boniface threatened to excommunicate Philip. The outraged monarch raided the papal summer palace at Anagni in September 1303 and captured the pope. Although Boniface was released, this

The Jacquerie. Enraged French peasants attack the castle of a lord.

shocking event proved too much for him, and a month later he died.

Boniface's two successors, Benedict XI (1303–1304) and Clement V (1305–1314), tried to conciliate Philip. In particular, Clement decided to remain at Avignon, a town on the southeastern French frontier, where he had set up a temporary residence.

From 1309 to 1377, a period known as the Babylonian Captivity, the popes were all French and resided in Avignon, not Rome. During this time, the papacy, removed from Rome and deprived of revenues from the Papal States in Italy, was often forced to pursue policies favorable to France. The growing antipapalism among the laity further damaged the papal image. Laypeople were repelled by the luxurious style of living at Avignon and by the appointment of high churchmen to lands where they did not know the language and showed little concern for the local population. Criticism of the papacy increased. The conflict between Boniface and Philip provoked a battle of words between proponents of papal supremacy and defenders of royal rights.

The most important critique of clerical intrusion into worldly affairs was *The Defender of the Peace* (1324) by Marsiglio of Padua (c. 1290–c. 1343). Marsiglio held that the state ran according to its own principles, which had nothing to do with religious commands originating in a higher realm. Religion dealt with a supranatural world and with principles of faith that could not be proved by reason, wrote Marsiglio. Politics, on the other hand, dealt with the natural world and the affairs of the human community. Political thinkers should not try to make the earthly realm conform to articles of faith. For Marsiglio, the state was self-sufficient; it needed no instruction from a higher authority. Thus, Marsiglio denied the essential premises of medieval papal political theory: that the pope, as God's vicar, was empowered to guide kings; that the state, as part of a divinely ordered world, must conform to and fulfill supranatural ends; and that the clergy were above the laws of the state. Marsiglio viewed the church as a spiritual institution with no temporal power. Marsiglio's concept of an autonomous state that did not answer to clerical authority anticipated modern political thought.

The Great Schism and the Conciliar Movement

Pope Gregory XI returned the papacy to Rome in 1377, ending the Babylonian Captivity. But the papacy was to endure an even greater humiliation: the Great Schism. Elected pope in 1378, Urban VI abused and imprisoned a number of cardinals. Fleeing from Rome, the cardinals declared that the election of Urban had been invalid and elected Clement VII as the new pope. Refusing to step down, Urban excommunicated Clement, who responded in kind. To the utter confusion and anguish of Christians throughout Europe, there were now two popes: Urban ruling from Rome and Clement from Avignon.

Prominent churchmen urged the convening of a general council—the Council of Pisa—to end the disgraceful schism, which obstructed the papacy from performing its sacred duties. Held in 1409 and attended by hundreds of churchmen, the Council of Pisa deposed both Urban and Clement and elected a new pope. Neither deposed pope recognized the council's decision, so Christendom then had three popes. A new council was called at Constance in 1414. In the struggle that ensued, each of the three popes either abdicated or was deposed in favor of an appointment by the council. In 1417, the Great Schism ended.

During the first half of the fifteenth century, church councils met at Pisa (1409), Constance (1414–1418), and Basel (1431–1449) in order to end schism, combat heresy, and reform the church. The Conciliar Movement attempted to transform the papal monarchy into a constitutional system, in which the pope's power would be regulated by a general council. Supporters of the movement held that the papacy could not reform the church as effectively as a general council representing the clergy. But the Conciliar Movement ended in failure. As the Holy Roman Emperor and then the French monarch withdrew support from the councils, the papacy regained its authority over the higher clergy. In 1460, Pope Pius II condemned the Conciliar Movement as heretical.

Deeply embroiled in European power politics, the papacy often neglected its spiritual and moral responsibilities. Many devout Christians longed for a religious renewal, a return to simple piety. The papacy barely heard this cry for reform. Its failure to provide creative leadership for reform made possible the Protestant Reformation of the sixteenth century. By splitting Christendom into Catholic and Protestant, the Reformation destroyed forever the vision of a Christian world commonwealth guided by Christ's vicar, the pope.

Fourteenth-Century Heresies

Another threat to papal power and to the medieval ideal of a universal Christian community guided by the church came from radical reformers who questioned the function and authority of the entire church hierarchy. These heretics in the Late Middle Ages were forerunners of the Protestant Reformation.

The two principal dissenters were the Englishman John Wycliffe (c. 1320–1384) and the Bohemian (Czech) Jan Hus (c. 1369–1415). By stressing a personal relationship between the individual and God and by claiming that the Bible itself, rather than church teachings, was the ultimate Christian authority, Wycliffe challenged the fundamental position of the medieval church: that the avenue to salvation passed through the church alone. He denounced the wealth of the higher clergy and sought a return to the spiritual purity and material poverty of the early church.

To Wycliffe, the wealthy, elaborately organized hierarchy of the church was unnecessary and wrong. The splendidly dressed and propertied bishops had no resemblance to the simple people who first followed Christ. Indeed, these worldly bishops, headed by a princely and tyrannical pope, were really anti-Christians, the "fiends of Hell." Wycliffe wanted the state to confiscate church property and the clergy to embrace poverty. By denying that priests changed the bread and wine of communion into the substance of the body and blood of Christ, Wycliffe rejected the sacramental power of the clergy. The church, in response, deprived the Lollards—an order of poor priests that spread Wycliffe's teachings—of their priestly functions.

Wycliffe's ideas were enthusiastically received by Czech reformers in Bohemia led by Jan Hus. Like Wycliffe, Hus advocated vernacular translations of the Bible, which would be accessible to common people, and upbraided the upper clergy for their luxury and immorality.

Although both movements were declared heretical and some of Wycliffe's followers and Hus were burned at the stake, the church could not crush the dissenters' followers or eradicate their teachings. To some extent, the doctrines of the Reformation would parallel the teachings of Wycliffe and Hus.

Breakup of the Thomistic Synthesis

In the Late Middle Ages, the papacy lost power as kings, political theorists, and religious dissenters challenged papal claims to supreme leadership. The great theological synthesis constructed by the scholastic theologians of the twelfth and thirteenth centuries was also breaking down. The process of fragmentation seen in the history of the church took place in philosophy as well.

Thomas Aquinas' system was the culmination of the scholastic attempt to show the basic agreement of philosophy and religion. In the fourteenth century, a number of thinkers cast doubt on the possibility of synthesizing Aristotelianism and Christianity, that is, reason and faith. Denying that reason could demonstrate the truth of Christian doctrines with certainty, philosophers tried to separate reason from faith. Whereas Aquinas had said that reason proved or clarified much of revelation, fourteenth-century thinkers asserted that the basic propositions of Christianity were not open to rational proof. Whereas Aquinas had held that faith supplemented and perfected reason, some philosophers were now proclaiming that reason often contradicted faith.

To be sure, this new outlook did not urge abandoning faith in favor of reason. Faith had to prevail in any conflict with reason because faith rested on God, the highest authority in the universe. But the relationship between reason and revelation was altered. Articles of faith, it was now held, had nothing to do with reason; they were to be believed, not proved. Reason was not an aid to theology but a separate sphere of activity. This new attitude snapped the link between reason and faith that Aquinas had so skillfully forged. The scholastic synthesis was disintegrating.

The chief proponent of this new outlook was William of Ockham (c. 1285–1349). In contrast to Aquinas, Ockham insisted that natural reason could not prove God's existence, the soul's immortality, or any other essential Christian doctrine. Reason could say only that God probably exists and that he probably endowed human beings with an immortal soul; it could not prove these propositions with certainty. The tenets of faith were beyond the reach of reason, said Ockham; there was no rational foundation to Christianity. For Ockham, reason and faith did not necessarily complement each other as they did for Aquinas; it was neither possible nor helpful to join reason to faith. He did not, however, seek to undermine faith—only to disengage it from reason.

In the process of proclaiming the authority of faith, Ockham also furthered the use of reason to comprehend nature. Ockham's approach, separating natural knowledge from religious dogma, made it easier to explore the natural world empirically, without fitting it into a religious framework. Ockham thus is a forerunner of the modern mentality, which is characterized by the separation of reason from religion and by an interest in the empirical investigation of nature.

The Middle Ages and the Modern World: Continuity and Discontinuity

Medieval civilization began to decline in the fourteenth century, but no era of cultural stagnation, economic collapse, and social transformation comparable to the three centuries following Rome's fall descended on Europe; its economic and political institutions and technological skills had grown too strong. Instead, the waning of the Middle Ages opened up possibilities for another stage in Western civilization: the modern age.

The modern world is linked to the Middle Ages in innumerable ways. European cities, the middle class, the state system, English common law, universities—all had their origins in the Middle Ages. During medieval times, important advances were made in business practices, including partnerships, systematic bookkeeping, and the bill of exchange, which paved the way for modern banking. By translating and commenting on the writings of Greek and Arabic thinkers, medieval scholars preserved a priceless intellectual heritage, without which the modern mind could never have evolved. In addition, numerous strands connect the thought of the scholastics and that of early modern philosophers.

Feudal traditions lasted long after the Middle Ages. Up until the French Revolution, for instance, French aristocrats enjoyed special privileges and exercised power over local government. In England, the aristocracy controlled local government until the Industrial Revolution transformed English society in the nineteenth century. Retaining the medieval ideal of the noble warrior, aristocrats continued to dominate the officer corps of European armies through the nineteenth century and even into the twentieth. Aristocratic notions of duty, honor, loyalty, and courtly love have endured into our own day.

During the Middle Ages, Europeans began to take the lead over the Muslims, the Byzantines, the Chinese, and all other peoples in the use of technology. Medieval technology and inventiveness stemmed in part from Christianity, which taught that God had created the world specifically for human beings to subdue and exploit. Consequently, medieval people tried to employ animal power and laborsaving machinery to relieve human drudgery. Moreover, Christianity taught that God was above nature, not within it, so Christians faced no spiritual obstacle to exploiting nature—unlike, for instance, the Hindus. In contrast to classical humanism, the Christian outlook did not consider manual work degrading; even monks combined it with study.

The Christian stress on the sacred worth of the individual (each person had an immortal soul that was God's concern), on human equality (differences in rank and birth were of no account to God on Judgment Day), and on the higher law of God (divine precepts had a greater pull on conscience than did the state's laws) has never ceased to influence Western civilization. Even though in modern times the various Christian churches have not often taken the lead in political and social reform, the ideals identified with the Judeo-Christian tradition have become part of the Western heritage. As such, they have inspired social reformers who may no longer identify with their ancestral religion.

Believing that God's Law was superior to state or national decrees, medieval philosophers provided a theoretical basis for opposing tyrannical kings who violated Christian principles. The idea that both the ruler and the ruled are bound by a higher law would, in a secularized form, become a principal element of modern liberal thought.

Feudalism also contributed to the history of liberty. According to feudal custom, the king, as a member of the feudal community, was duty-bound to honor agreements made with his vassals. Lords possessed personal rights, which the king was obliged to respect. Resentful of a king who ran roughshod over customary feudal rights, lords also negotiated contracts with the crown, such as the famous Magna Carta, to define and guard their customary liberties. To protect themselves from the arbitrary behavior of a king, feudal lords initiated what came to be called *government by consent* and the *rule of law.*

During the Middle Ages, then, there gradually emerged the idea that law was not imposed on inferiors by an absolute monarch but required the collaboration of the king and his subjects; that the king, too, was bound by the law; and that lords had the right to resist a monarch who violated agreements. A related phenomenon was the rise of representative institutions, with which the king was expected to consult on the realm's affairs. The most notable such institution was the British Parliament; although subordinate to the king, it became a permanent part of the state. Later, in the seventeenth century, Parliament would successfully challenge royal authority. Thus, continuity exists between the feudal tradition of a king bound by law and the modern practice of limiting the authority of the head of state.

Although the elements of continuity are clear, the characteristic outlook of the Middle Ages is as different from that of the modern age as it was from the outlook of the ancient world. Religion—which often expressed a disdain for earthly pursuits and a preoccupation with the world to come—was the integrating feature of the Middle Ages, whereas science and secularism—a preoccupation with worldly life—determine the modern outlook. The period from the Italian Renaissance of the fifteenth century through the eighteenth-century Age of Enlightenment constituted a gradual breaking away from the medieval worldview: a rejection of the medieval conception of nature, the individual, and the purpose of life. The transition from medieval to modern was neither sudden nor complete, for there are no sharp demarcation lines separating historical periods. While many distinctively medieval ways endured into the sixteenth, seventeenth, and even eighteenth centuries, these centuries saw as well the rise of new intellectual, political, and economic forms that marked the emergence of modernity.

Medieval thought began with the existence of God and the truth of his revelation as interpreted by the church, which set the standards and defined the purposes for human endeavor. The medieval mind rejected the fundamental principle of Greek philosophy: the autonomy of reason. Without the guidance of revealed truth, reason was seen as feeble. Philosophical inquiry was permissible only if the mind arrived at clerically approved conclusions.

Scholastics engaged in genuine philosophical speculation, but they did not allow philosophy to challenge the basic premises of their faith. Unlike either ancient or modern thinkers, medieval schoolmen ultimately believed that reason alone could not provide a unified view of nature or society. A rational soul had to be guided by a divine light. To understand the natural world properly, it was necessary to know its relationship to the higher world. The discoveries of reason had to accord with Scripture as interpreted by the church. In medieval thought, says the historian-philosopher Ernst Cassirer,

> *neither science nor morality, neither law nor state, can be erected on its own foundations. Supernatural assistance is always needed to bring them to true perfection. . . . Reason is and remains the servant of revelation; within the sphere of natural intellectual and psychological forces, reason leads toward, and prepares the ground for, revelation.*[3]

In the modern view, both nature and the human intellect are self-sufficient. Nature is a mathematical system that operates without miracles or any other form of divine intervention. To comprehend nature and society, the mind needs no divine assistance; it accepts no authority above reason. The modern mentality finds it unacceptable to reject the conclusions of science on the basis of clerical authority and revelation or to ground politics, law, or economics on religious dogma. It refuses to settle public issues by appeals to religious belief, which is now seen as a strictly private concern.

Rejecting the medieval division of the universe into higher and lower realms and superior and inferior substances, the modern view postulates the uniformity of nature and of nature's laws: the cosmos knows no privilege of rank; heavenly bodies follow the same laws of nature as earthly objects. Space is geometric and homogeneous, not hierarchical, heterogeneous, and qualitative. The universe is no longer conceived of as finite and closed but is seen as infinite, and its operations are explained mathematically. The modern thinker studies mathematical law and chemical composition, not grades of perfection. Spiritual meaning is not sought in an examination of the material world. Roger Bacon, for example, described seven coverings of the eye and then concluded that God had fashioned the eye in this manner in order to express the seven gifts of the Spirit. This way of thinking is alien to the modern outlook. So, too, is the medieval belief that natural disasters, such as plagues and famines, are God's punishments for people's sins.

The outlook of the modern West also broke with the rigid division of medieval society into three orders: clergy, nobles, and commoners. The intellectual justification for this arrangement, as expressed by the English prelate John of Salisbury (c. 1115–1180), has been rejected

Bibliothèque Royale de Belgique.

WISDOM URGES MEDIEVAL SCHOLARS FORWARD. During the Middle Ages, Europeans made considerable advances in technology. The astrolabe, quadrant, sundials, and mechanical clocks shown here exemplify medieval technical skills.

by modern Westerners: "For inferiors owe it to their superiors to provide them with service, just as the superiors in their turn owe it to their inferiors to provide them with all things needful for their protection and succor."[4] Opposing the feudal principle that an individual's obligations and rights are a function of his or her rank in society, the modern view stresses equality of opportunity and equal treatment under the law. It rejects the idea that society should be guided by clergy, who are deemed to possess a special wisdom; by nobles, who are entitled to special privileges; and by monarchs, who are thought to receive their power from God.

The modern West has also rejected the personal and customary character of feudal law. As the modern state developed, law assumed an impersonal and objective character. For example, if a lord demanded more than the customary forty days of military service, a vassal might refuse to comply because he would see the lord's request as an unpardonable violation of custom and agreement, as well as an infringement on his liberties. In the modern state, with a constitution and a representative assembly, if a new law increasing the length of military service is passed, it merely replaces the old law. People do not refuse to obey it because the government has broken faith or violated custom.

In the modern world, the individual's relationship to the universe has been radically transformed. Medieval people lived in a geocentric universe that was finite in space and time. The universe was small, enclosed by a sphere of stars, beyond which were the heavens. The universe, it was believed, was some four thousand years old, and, in the not-too-distant future, Christ would return and human history would end. People in the Middle Ages knew why they were on earth and what was expected of them; they never doubted that heaven would be their reward for living a Christian life. Preparation for heaven was the ultimate aim of life.

This comforting medieval vision is alien to the modern outlook. Today, in a universe more than thirteen billion years old, in which the earth is a tiny speck floating in an endless cosmic ocean, where life evolved over tens of millions of years, many Westerners no longer believe that human beings are special children of God; that heaven is their ultimate goal; that under their feet is hell, where grotesque demons torment sinners; and that God is an active agent in human history. To many intellectuals, the universe seems unresponsive to people's religious supplications, and life's purpose is sought within the limits of earthly existence. Science and secularism have driven Christianity and faith from their central position to the periphery of human concerns.

In the nineteenth and twentieth centuries, Christian thinkers lamented the waning of faith. Distressed by all-consuming secularism, crude materialism, and vicious class and national antagonisms, these thinkers attributed the ills of the modern West to a diminishing commitment to Christianity and called for spiritual renewal. Some of them, looking back nostalgically to the Middle Ages when life had an overriding religious purpose and few doubted the truth of Christian teachings, contended that the modern West would benefit from a reaffirmation of those Christian concerns and values that had energized medieval society.

The modern outlook developed gradually in the period from the Renaissance to the eighteenth-century Age of Enlightenment. Mathematics rendered the universe comprehensible. Economic and political thought broke free of the religious frame of reference. Science became the great hope of the future. The thinkers of the Enlightenment wanted to liberate humanity from superstition, ignorance, and traditions that could not pass the test of reason. They saw themselves as emancipating culture from theological dogma and clerical authority. Rejecting the Christian idea of a person's inherent sinfulness, they held that the individual was basically good and that evil resulted from faulty institutions, poor education, and bad leadership. Thus, the concept of a rational and free society in which individuals could realize their potential slowly emerged.

❖ ❖ ❖

Notes

1. Quoted in David Knowles, *The Evolution of Medieval Thought* (New York: Vintage Books, 1964), p. 123.
2. Thomas Aquinas, *Summa Theologica,* Pt. 1, question 2, art. 3. Excerpted in Anton C. Pegis, ed., *Introduction to Saint Thomas Aquinas* (New York: Modern Library, 1948), p. 25.
3. Ernst Cassirer, *The Philosophy of the Enlightenment* (Boston: Beacon Press, 1955), p. 40.
4. John of Salisbury, *Policraticus,* trans. John Dickinson (New York: Russell & Russell, 1963), pp. 243–244.

Suggested Reading

Baldwin, John W., *The Scholastic Culture of the Middle Ages* (1971). A useful introductory survey.

Bonner, Anthony, ed., *Songs of the Troubadours* (1972). Collection of troubadour poetry.

Cantor, Norman F., *In the Wake of the Plague: The Black Death and the World It Made* (2001). A readable and current synthesis of latest scholarship.

Colish, Marcia L., *Medieval Foundations of the Western Intellectual Tradition 400–1400* (1997). Valuable insights into many areas of medieval thought and culture.

Copleston, F. C., *A History of Medieval Philosophy* (1974). A lucid, comprehensive survey of medieval philosophy.

Flanagan, Sabina, *Hildegard of Bingen* (1989). A biography of a remarkable medieval woman who distinguished herself as a mystic, poet, and naturalist.

Gilson, Etienne, *Reason and Revelation in the Middle Ages* (1966). A superb brief exposition of the medieval philosophical tradition.

Gimpel, Jean, *The Cathedral Builders* (1984). The financial, political, and spiritual forces behind the building of cathedrals.

Haren, Michael, *Medieval Thought: The Western Intellectual Tradition from Antiquity to the Thirteenth Century* (1992). A solid introduction.

Lerner, Robert E., *The Age of Adversity* (1968). A short, readable survey of the fourteenth century.

Nirenberg, David, *Communities of Violence: Persecution of Minorities in the Middle Ages* (1996). Focuses on medieval beliefs that triggered violent attacks minorities.

Ozment, Steven E., *The Age of Reform, 1250–1550* (1980). An intellectual and religious history of late medieval and Reformation Europe.

Pegg, Mark Gregory, *A Most Holy War: The Albigensian Crusade and the Battle for Christendom* (2008). A gripping narrative of medieval mass murder.

Pieper, Josef, *Scholasticism* (1964). Written with intelligence and grace.

Piltz, Anders, *The World of Medieval Learning* (1981). A clearly written, informative survey of medieval education and learning.

Wolff, Philippe, *The Cultural Awakening* (1968). A readable survey of medieval thought.

Part Three

The Rise of Modernity: From the Renaissance to the Enlightenment

1350–1789

Galileo's Telescope.

	Politics and Society	Thought and Culture
1300	Hundred Years' War (1337–1453)	Italian Renaissance begins (c. 1350)
1400	War of Roses in England (1455–1485) Rule of Ferdinand and Isabella in Spain (1469–1516) Charles VIII of France (1483–1498) Henry VII, beginning of Tudor dynasty in England (1485–1509) Columbus reaches America (1492)	Early Renaissance artists and architects: Brunelleschi, Masaccio, van Eyck Printing with movable type (c. 1450) Humanists: Valla, Pico della Mirandola Late Renaissance artists: Botticelli, Leonardo da Vinci, Michelangelo, Raphael, Bellini, Giorgione, Titian Renaissance spreads to Northern Europe (late 15th and early 16th cent.)
1500	Henry VIII of England (1509–1547) Francis I of France (1515–1547) Charles V, Holy Roman Emperor (1519–1556) Henry VIII of England breaks with Rome (1529–1536) Council of Trent (1545–1563) Peace of Augsburg in Germany (1555) Philip II of Spain (1556–1598) Elizabeth I of England (1558–1603) Religious wars in France (1562–1598) Revolt of the Netherlands from Spain (1566–1609) Defeat of Spanish Armada (1588)	Humanists: Castiglione, Erasmus, Montaigne, Rabelais, More, Cervantes, Shakespeare Machiavelli, *The Prince* (1513) Luther writes his *Ninety-Five Theses* (1517) Copernicus, *On the Revolution of the Heavenly Spheres* (1543)
1600	Thirty Years' War (1618–1648) English Revolution (1640–1660, 1688–1689) Louis XIV of France (1643–1715) Peter the Great of Russia (1682–1725)	Scientists: Kepler, Galileo, Newton Philosophers: Bacon, Descartes, Hobbes, Locke
1700	War of Spanish Succession (1702–1714) War of Austrian Succession (1740–1748) Frederick the Great of Prussia (1740–1786) Maria Theresa of Austria (1740–1780) Seven Years' War (1756–1763) American Declaration of Independence (1776) American Revolution (1776–1783) Beginning of French Revolution (1789)	Enlightenment thinkers: Voltaire, Montesquieu, Rousseau, Diderot, Hume, Adam Smith, Thomas Jefferson, Kant

Chapter 8

Transition to the Modern Age: Renaissance and Reformation

- **Italy: Birthplace of the Renaissance**
- **The Renaissance Outlook**
- **Renaissance Art**
- **The Spread of the Renaissance**
- **The Renaissance and the Modern Age**
- **Background to the Reformation: The Medieval Church in Crisis**
- **The Lutheran Revolt**
- **The Spread of the Reformation**
- **The Catholic Response**
- **The Reformation and the Modern Age**

Focus Questions

1. What conditions gave rise to the Italian Renaissance?
2. What is the historical significance of Renaissance humanism?
3. How did Machiavelli's political thought mark a break with the medieval outlook?
4. What are the general features of Renaissance art?
5. Why is the Renaissance considered a departure from the Middle Ages and the beginning of modernity?

6. How did Luther's theology mark a break with the church? Why did many Germans become followers of Luther?
7. How did the Reformation contribute to the shaping of the modern world?

From the Italian Renaissance of the fifteenth century through the Age of Enlightenment of the eighteenth century, the outlook and institutions of the Middle Ages disintegrated and distinctly modern forms emerged. The radical change in European civilization affected every level of society. On the economic level, commerce and industry expanded greatly, and capitalism largely replaced medieval forms of economic organization. On the political level, central government grew stronger at the expense of feudalism. On the religious level, the rise of Protestantism fragmented the unity of Christendom. On the social level, middle-class townspeople, increasing in number and wealth, began to play a more important role in economic and cultural life. On the cultural level, the clergy lost its monopoly over learning, and the otherworldly orientation of the Middle Ages gave way to a secular outlook in literature and the arts. Theology, the queen of knowledge in the Middle Ages, surrendered its crown to science, and reason, which had been subordinate to revelation, asserted its independence.

Many of these tendencies manifested themselves dramatically during the Renaissance (1350–1600). The word *renaissance* means "rebirth," and it is used to refer to the attempt by artists and thinkers to recover and apply the ancient learning and standards of Greece and Rome. During the Renaissance, individuals showed an increasing concern for worldly life and self-consciously aspired to shape their destinies, an attitude that is the key to modernity.

To be sure, the Renaissance was not a complete and abrupt break with the Middle Ages. Many medieval ways and attitudes persisted. Nevertheless, the view that the Renaissance represents the birth of modernity has much to recommend it. Renaissance writers and artists themselves were aware of their age's novelty. They looked back on the medieval centuries as a "Dark Age" that followed the grandeur of ancient Greece and Rome, and they believed that they were experiencing a rebirth of cultural greatness. Renaissance artists and writers were fascinated by the cultural forms of Greece and Rome; they sought to imitate classical style and to capture the secular spirit of antiquity. In the process, they broke with medieval artistic and literary forms. They valued the full development of human talent and expressed a new excitement about the possibilities of life in this world. This outlook represents a break with the Middle Ages and the emergence of modernity.

The Renaissance, then, was an age of transition. It saw the rejection of certain elements of the medieval outlook, the revival of classical cultural forms, and the emergence of distinctly modern attitudes. This rebirth began in Italy during the fourteenth century and gradually spread north and west to Germany, France, England, and Spain during the late fifteenth and sixteenth centuries.

The Renaissance was one avenue to modernity; another was the Reformation. By dividing Europe into Catholic and Protestant, the Reformation ended medieval religious unity. It also accentuated the importance of the individual person, a distinctive feature of the modern outlook. It stressed individual conscience rather than clerical authority, insisted on a personal relationship between each man or woman and God, and called attention to the individual's inner religious capacities. ❖

Italy: Birthplace of the Renaissance

The city-states of northern Italy that spawned the Renaissance were developed urban centers where people had the wealth, freedom, and inclination to cultivate the arts and to enjoy the fruits of worldly life. In Italy, moreover, reminders of ancient Rome's grandeur were visible everywhere: Roman roads, monuments, and manuscripts intensified the Italians' links to their Roman past. Northern Italian city-states had developed into flourishing commercial and banking centers and had monopolized trade in the Mediterranean during the twelfth and thirteenth centuries. The predominance of business and commerce within these city-states meant that the feudal nobility, which held the land beyond the city walls, played a much less important part in government than it did elsewhere in Europe. By the end of the twelfth century, these city-states had adopted a fairly uniform pattern of republican self-government built around the office of a chief magistrate.

This republicanism proved precarious, however. During the fourteenth and early fifteenth centuries, republican institutions in one city after another toppled, giving way to rule by despots. The city-states had come to rely on mercenary troops, whose leaders, the notorious *condottieri*—unschooled in and owing no loyalty to the republican tradition—simply seized power during emergencies.

Florence, the leading city of the Renaissance, held out against the trend toward despotism for a long time. But by the mid-fifteenth century, even Florentine republicanism was giving way before the intrigues of a rich banking family, the Medici. They had installed themselves in power in the 1430s with the return of Cosimo de' Medici from exile. Cosimo's grandson, Lorenzo the Magnificent, completed the destruction of the republican constitution in 1480 when he managed to set up a government staffed by his supporters.

New ways of life developed within the Italian city-states. Prosperous businesspeople played a leading role in the political and cultural life of the city. With the expansion of commerce and industry, the feudal values of birth, military prowess, and a fixed hierarchy of lords and vassals decayed

Chronology 8.1 ❖ The Renaissance and the Reformation

1304–1374	Petrarch, "father of humanism"
c. 1445	Johann Gutenberg invents movable metal type
1513	Machiavelli writes *The Prince*
1517	Martin Luther writes his *Ninety-Five Theses* and the Reformation begins
1520	Pope Leo X excommunicates Luther
1524–1526	German peasants revolt
1529	English Parliament accepts Henry VIII's Reformation
1534	Henry VIII is declared head of the Church of England; King Francis I of France declares Protestants to be heretics; Ignatius Loyola founds the Society of Jesus; Anabaptists, radical reformers, capture Münster in Westphalia
1535	Sir Thomas More, English humanist and author of *Utopia*, is executed for treason
1536–1564	Calvin leads the Reformation in Geneva
1545–1563	Council of Trent
1555	Peace of Augsburg

in favor of ambition and individual achievement, whether at court, in the counting house, or inside the artist's studio.

Art served as a focus of civic pride and patriotism. Members of the urban upper class—patricians—became patrons of the arts, providing funds to support promising artists and writers. Just as they contended on the battlefield, rulers competed for art and artists to bolster their prestige. The popes, too, heaped wealth on artists to enhance their own flagging prestige. They became the most lavish patrons of all, as the works of Michelangelo and Raphael testify.

Some women of wealthy and noble Italian families were educated in classical languages and literature and served as patrons of the arts. Thus, Isabella d'Este, wife of the ruler of a small state in northern Italy, knew Latin and Greek, collected books, and displayed works of artists that she had commissioned.

The result of this new patronage by popes and patricians was an explosion of artistic creativity. The amount, and especially the nature, of this patronage also helped shape both art and the artist. Portraiture became a separate genre for the first time since antiquity and was developed much further than ever before. Patrician rivalry and insecurity of status, fed by the Renaissance ethic of individual achievement and reward, produced a scramble for honor and reputation. This pursuit fostered the desire to be memorialized in a painting if not in a sculpture. Distinguished portrait painters and sculptors were in great demand.

The great artists emerged as famous men by virtue of their exercise of brush and chisel. In the Middle Ages, artists had been regarded as craftsmen who did lowly (manual) labor and who as a result were to be accorded little if any status. Indeed, for the most part they remained anonymous. But the unparalleled Renaissance demand for art brought artists public recognition.

The Renaissance Outlook

Increasingly, a secular outlook came to dominate Renaissance society. Intrigued by the active life of the city and eager to enjoy the worldly pleasures

Alinari/Art Resource, N.Y.

The School of Athens, by **Raphael (1483–1520).** The ancient Greek philosophers, with Plato and Aristotle at the center, are depicted here, assembled in classical grandeur. Painted to decorate the Vatican, the papal palace in Rome, the picture exudes the Renaissance reverence for classical antiquity and reflects the widely held view that ancient philosophy represented a foreshadowing of Christianity and was essentially in harmony with it.

that their money could obtain, wealthy merchants and bankers moved away from the medieval preoccupation with salvation. Reviving the Greco-Roman view that the complete individual is a political animal who participates actively in civil affairs, many Renaissance figures were critical of monastic withdrawal and asceticism and of the scholastics' purely contemplative life. To be sure, the urban elite were neither nonbelievers nor atheists, but, more and more, religion had to compete with worldly concerns. Consequently, members of the urban upper class paid religion less heed or at least did not allow it to interfere with their quest for the full life. The challenge and pleasure of living well in this world seemed more exciting than the promise of heaven. This outlook found concrete expression in Renaissance art and literature.

Individualism was another hallmark of the Renaissance. In contrast to medieval thinkers, who emphasized the Christian belief in human weakness, sinfulness, and dependency, Renaissance figures revived the classical confidence in human capacities and extolled the infinite possibilities of individual life. The urban elite sought to assert their own personalities, demonstrate their unique talents, and gain recognition for their accomplishments. Traditional feudal values of birth and place in a fixed hierarchy were superseded by the desire for individual achievement. Individual worth was interpreted far more broadly than it had been by feudal lords, who had equated worth with military prowess. Renaissance Italy produced a distinctive human type, the "universal man": a many-sided person who not only showed mastery of the ancient classics, an appreciation of and even talent for the visual arts, and a concern for the day-to-day affairs of his city, but also aspired to mold his life into a work of art. Disdaining Christian humility, Renaissance individuals took pride in their talents and worldly accomplishments—"I can work miracles," said the great Leonardo da Vinci. Renaissance artists portrayed the individual character of human beings, captured the rich diversity of human personality, produced the first portraits since Roman times, and affixed their signatures to their works. Renaissance writers probed their own feelings and manifested a self-awareness that characterizes the modern outlook. This new outlook, however, applied almost exclusively to an elite—princes, courtiers, court ladies, wealthy urban families, and exceptionally talented artists and writers.

In later centuries, as the secular outlook gathered strength, it focused even more intently on the individual. It led to the conviction that the individual should be freed from domination by otherworldly concerns, theological dogma, and ecclesiastical authority and should concentrate on the full development of human talents and on improving the quality of earthly existence.

During the Renaissance, the secular spirit and the concern with the individual found expression in the intellectual movement called humanism and in a political theory that separated politics from Christian principles.

Humanism

Humanism, the most characteristic intellectual movement of the Renaissance, was an educational and cultural program based on the study of ancient Greek and Roman literature. The humanist attitude toward antiquity differed from that of medieval scholars, who had taken pains to fit classical learning into a Christian worldview. Renaissance humanists did not subordinate the classics to the requirements of Christian doctrines. Rather, they valued ancient literature for its own sake—for its clear and graceful style and for its insights into human nature. From the ancient classics, humanists expected to learn much that could not be provided by medieval writings: for instance, how to live well in this world and how to perform one's civic duties. For the humanists, the classics were a guide to the good life, the active life. To achieve self-cultivation, to write well, to speak well, and to live well, it was necessary to know the classics. In contrast to scholastic philosophers, who used Greek philosophy to prove the truth of Christian doctrines, Italian humanists used classical learning to nourish their new interest in a worldly life. Whereas medieval scholars were familiar with only some ancient Latin writers, Renaissance humanists restored to circulation every Roman work that could be found. Similarly, knowledge of Greek was very rare in Latin Christendom during the Middle Ages, but Renaissance humanists increasingly cultivated the study of Greek in order to read Homer, Demosthenes, Plato, and other ancients in the original.

Although predominantly a secular movement, Italian humanism was not un-Christian. True, humanists often treated moral problems in a purely secular manner. Yet in dealing with religious and theological issues, they did not challenge Christian belief or question the validity of the Bible. They did, however, attack scholastic philosophy for its hairsplitting arguments and preoccupation with trivial matters. They stressed instead a purer form of Christianity based on the direct study of the Bible and the writings of the church fathers.

One of the early humanists, sometimes called the father of humanism, was Petrarch (1304–1374). Petrarch and his followers carried the recovery of the classics further through their systematic attempt to discover the classical roots of medieval Italian rhetoric. Petrarch's own efforts to learn Greek were largely unsuccessful, but he advanced humanist learning by encouraging his students to master the ancient tongue. Petrarch was particularly drawn to Cicero, the ancient Roman orator. Following Cicero's example, he maintained that education should consist not only of learning and knowing things but also of learning how to communicate one's knowledge and

Primary Source

Leonardo Bruni: Study of Greek Literature and a Humanist Educational Program

Leonardo Bruni (1374–1444) was a Florentine humanist who extolled both intellectual study and active involvement in public affairs, an outlook called civic humanism. In this excerpt from his History of His Own Times in Italy, *Bruni expresses the humanist's love for ancient Greek literature and language.*

Love for Greek Literature

Then first came a knowledge of Greek, which had not been in use among us for seven hundred years. Chrysoloras the Byzantine,[1] a man of noble birth and well versed in Greek letters, brought Greek learning to us. When his country was invaded by the Turks, he came by sea, first to Venice. The report of him soon spread, and he was cordially invited and besought and promised a public stipend, to come to Florence and open his store of riches to the youth. I was then studying Civil Law,[2] but . . . I burned with love of academic studies, and had spent no little pains on dialectic and rhetoric. At the coming of Chrysoloras I was torn in mind, deeming it shameful to desert the law, and yet a crime to lose such a chance of studying Greek literature; and often with youthful impulse I would say to myself: "Thou, when it is permitted thee to gaze on Homer, Plato and Demosthenes,[3] and the other [Greek] poets, philosophers, orators, of whom such glorious things are spread abroad, and speak with them and be instructed in their admirable teaching, wilt thou desert and rob thyself? Wilt thou neglect this opportunity so divinely offered? For seven hundred years, no one in Italy has possessed Greek letters; and yet we confess that all knowledge is derived from them. How great advantage to your knowledge, enhancement of your fame, increase of your pleasure, will come from an understanding of this tongue? There are doctors of civil law everywhere; and the chance of learning will not fail thee. But if this one and only doctor of Greek letters disappears, no one can be found to teach thee." Overcome at length by these reasons, I gave myself to Chrysoloras with such zeal to learn, that what through the wakeful day I gathered, I followed after in the night, even when asleep.

Questions for Analysis

1. Why was it so important to Leonardo Bruni to learn to read Greek?
2. Who are the ancient Greek thinkers whom Bruni singles out for special praise?

[1]Chrysoloras (c. 1355–1415), a Byzantine writer and teacher, introduced the study of Greek literature to the Italians, helping open a new age of Western humanistic learning.
[2]Civil Law refers to the Roman law as codified by Emperor Justinian in the early sixth century A.D. and studied in medieval law schools.
[3]Demosthenes (384–322 B.C.) was an Athenian statesman and orator whose oratorical style was much admired by Renaissance humanists.

Henry Osborn Taylor, *Thought and Expression in the Sixteenth Century* (New York: Frederick Ungar, 1930), 1, 36–37.

how to use it for the public good. Therefore, the emphasis in education should be on rhetoric and moral philosophy—wisdom combined with eloquence. This was the key to virtue in the ruler, the citizen, and the republic. Petrarch helped to make Ciceronian values dominant among the humanists. His followers set up schools to inculcate the new Ciceronian educational ideal.

Implicit in the humanist educational ideal was a radical transformation of the Christian idea of human beings. According to the medieval (Augustinian) view, men and women, because of their sinful nature, were incapable of attaining excellence through their own efforts. They were completely subject to divine will. In contrast, the humanists, recalling the classical Greek concept of human beings, made the achievement of excellence through individual striving the end not only of education but of life itself. Moreover, because individuals were capable of this goal, it was their duty to pursue it as the end of life. The pursuit was not effortless; indeed, it took extraordinary energy and skill.

People, then, were deemed capable of excellence in every sphere and duty-bound to make the effort. This emphasis on human creative powers was one of the most characteristic and influential doctrines of the Renaissance. A classic expression of it is found in the *Oration on the Dignity of Man* (1486) by Giovanni Pico della Mirandola (1463–1494). Man, said Pico, has the freedom to shape his own life. Pico has God say to man: "We have made you a creature" such that "you may, as the free and proud shaper of your own being, fashion yourself in the form you may prefer."[1]

An attack on the medieval scholastics was also implicit in the humanist educational ideal. Humanists accused scholastics of corrupting the Latin style of ancient Rome and of dealing with useless questions. This humanist emphasis on the uses of knowledge offered a stimulus to science and art.

So hostile were the humanists to things scholastic and medieval that they reversed the prevailing view of history. According to the Christian view, history was a simple unfolding of God's will and providence. The humanists, however, stressed the importance of human actions and human will in history—the importance of people as active participants in the shaping of events. They characterized the epoch preceding their own as a period of decline from classical heights—a dark age—and saw their own time as a period of rebirth, representing the recovery of classical wisdom and ideals. Thus, the humanists invented the notion of the Middle Ages as the period separating the ancient world from their own. To the humanists, then, we owe the current periodization of history into ancient, medieval, and modern. The humanists' view also contained an element of today's idea of progress: they dared to think that they, "the moderns," might even surpass the ancient glories of Greece and Rome.

The humanist emphasis on historical scholarship yielded a method of critical inquiry that could help to undermine traditional loyalties and institutions. Medieval thinkers generally did not relate a text to its times but accepted it uncritically as an authoritative work of wisdom. In contrast, Renaissance humanists approached ancient civilization with a critical attitude; they studied texts in a historical context and examined them for authenticity and accuracy. The work of Lorenzo Valla (c. 1407–1457) provides the clearest example of this trend. Educated as a classicist, Valla trained the guns of critical scholarship on the papacy in his most famous work, *Declamation Concerning the False Decretals of Constantine*. The papal claim to temporal authority rested on a document that purported to verify the so-called Donation of Constantine, through which the Emperor Constantine, when he moved the capital of the Roman Empire to Constantinople in the fourth century, had given the pope dominion over the entire Western Empire. But Valla proved that the document was based on an eighth-century forgery because the language at certain points was unknown in Constantine's time and did not come into use until much later.

Also embedded in the humanist reevaluation of individual potential was a new appreciation of the moral significance of work. For the humanist, the honor, fame, and even glory bestowed by one's city or patron for meritorious deeds were the ultimate rewards for effort. The humanist pursuit of praise and reputation became something of a Renaissance cult.

A Revolution in Political Thought

By turning away from the religious orientation of the Middle Ages and discussing the human condition in secular terms, Renaissance humanists

Scala/Art Resource, N.Y.

Niccolò Machiavelli (1469–1527). Machiavelli looked back to the ancient Roman republic for his ideals and spent his life serving the city-state of Florence, but as the author of *The Prince*, his name became a byword for atheism and deceit. *Machiavellian* is still used to describe an unscrupulous politician.

opened up new possibilities for thinking about political and moral problems. Niccolò Machiavelli (1469–1527), a keen observer of Italian politics, saw the Italian city-states, ruled by men whose authority rested solely on their cunning and effective use of force, as a new phenomenon. He recognized that traditional political theory, concerned with ideal Christian ends, could not adequately explain it. Italian princes made no effort to justify their policies on religious grounds; war was endemic, and powerful cities took over weaker ones; diplomacy was riddled with intrigue, betrayal, and bribery. In such a tooth-and-claw world—where political survival depended on alertness, cleverness, and strength—medieval theorists, who expected the earthly realm to accord with standards revealed by God, seemed utterly irrelevant. Machiavelli simply wanted rulers to understand how to preserve and expand the state's power. In his book *The Prince*, he expounded a new political theory—one that had no place for Christian morality but coincided with the emerging modern secular state. He himself was aware that his study of statecraft in the cold light of reason, free of religious and moral illusions, represented a new departure.

For Machiavelli, survival was the state's overriding aim; it transcended any concern with moral or religious values and the interests of individual subjects. Removing questions of good and evil from the political realm, Machiavelli maintained that the prince may use any means to save the state when its survival is at stake. Successful princes, he contended, have always been indifferent to moral and religious considerations—a lesson of history that rulers ignore at their peril. Thus, if the situation warrants it, the prince can violate agreements with other rulers, go back on his word with his subjects, and resort to cruelty and terror.

Machiavelli broke with the distinguishing feature of medieval thought: the division of the universe into the higher world of the heavens and a lower earthly realm. To this extent, he did for politics what Galileo accomplished a century later for physics. Medieval thinkers believed that rulers derived their power from God and had a religious obligation to govern in accordance with God's commands. Rejecting completely this otherworldly, theocentric orientation, Machiavelli ascribed no divine origin or purpose to the state. He saw it as a natural entity; politics had nothing to do with God's intent or with moral precepts originating in a higher world. Machiavelli's significance as a political thinker rests on the fact that he removed political thought from a religious frame of reference and viewed the state and political behavior in the detached and dispassionate manner of a scientist. In secularizing and rationalizing political philosophy, he initiated a trend of thought that we recognize as distinctly modern.

Renaissance Art

The essential meaning of the Renaissance is conveyed through its art, particularly architecture, sculpture, and painting. Renaissance examples

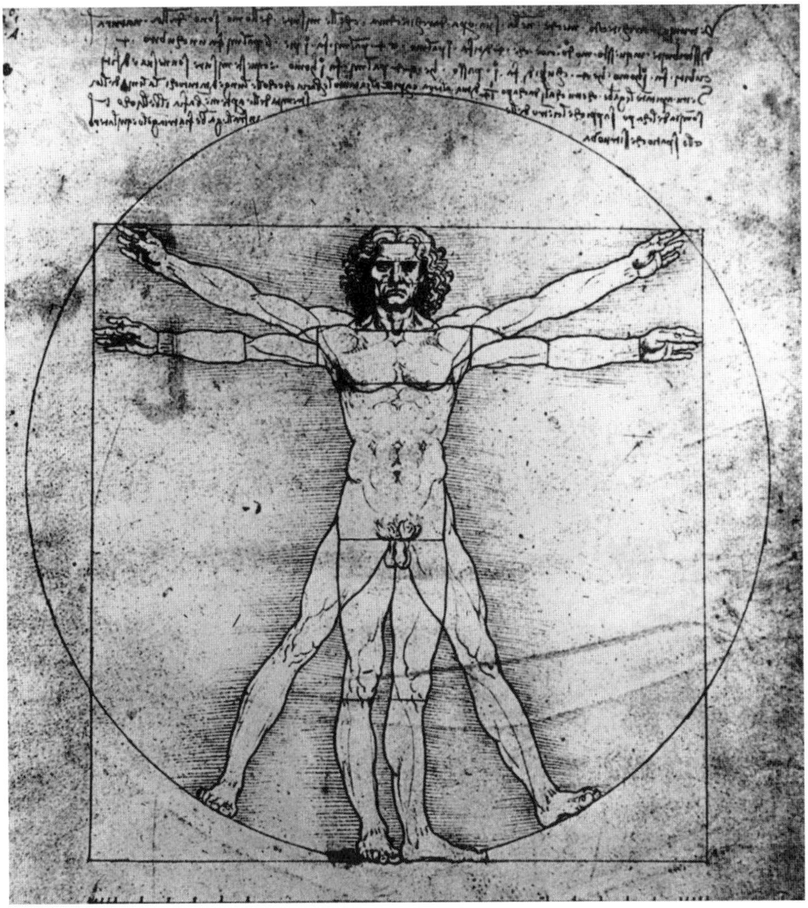

Hulton Archive/Handout/Getty Images.

Leonardo da Vinci, *The Proportions of Man*. Leonardo was fascinated by the human body. In his notebook, his written observations are accompanied by this marvelous drawing of the body, conceived and framed with realism and proportion.

of all three art forms reflect a style that stressed proportion, balance, and harmony. These artistic values were achieved through a new, revolutionary conceptualization of space and spatial relations. To a considerable extent, Renaissance art also reflects the values of Renaissance humanism: a return to classical models in architecture, to the rendering of the nude figure, and to a heroic vision of human beings.

Medieval art served a religious function: the world was a veil merely hinting at the other perfect and eternal world. Renaissance artists continued to utilize religious themes, but they shattered the dominance of religion over art by shifting attention from heaven to the natural world and to the human being. Renaissance artists depicted the human qualities of men and women and celebrated the beauty and grace of the human form. The reference was less to the other world and more to this world, and people were treated as creatures who found their spiritual destiny as they fulfilled their human one. Renaissance artists also developed a new conception of visual space, which resulted in a naturalistic, three-dimensional rendering of the real world. It was a quantitative space in which the artist, employing reason and mathematics, portrayed the essential form of the object in perspective, as it would appear to the human eye. Thus, at its most distinctive, Renaissance art represents a conscious revolt against the art of the Middle Ages. This revolt produced revolutionary discoveries that served as the foundation of Western art up to the twentieth century.

In art, as in literature, the Florentines played a leading role in this esthetic transformation. They, more than anyone else, were responsible for the way artists saw and drew for centuries and for the way most Western people still see or want to see. The first major contributor to Renaissance painting was the Florentine painter Giotto (c. 1276–1337). Borrowing from Byzantine painting, he created figures delineated by alterations in light and shade. He also developed several techniques of perspective, representing three-dimensional figures and objects on two-dimensional surfaces so that they appear to stand in space. Giotto's figures look remarkably alive. They are drawn and arranged in space to tell a story, and their expressions and the illusion of movement they convey heighten the dramatic effect. Giotto's best works were *frescoes*, wall paintings painted while the plaster was still wet, or *fresh*. Lionized in his own day, Giotto had no immediate successors, and his ideas were not taken up and developed further for almost a century.

By the early fifteenth century, the revival of classical learning had begun in earnest. In Florence, it had its artistic counterpart among a circle of architects, painters, and sculptors who sought to revive classical art. The leader of this group was an architect, Filippo Brunelleschi (1377–1446). He designed churches reflecting classical models. To him we also owe a scientific discovery of the first importance in the history of art: the rules of perspective. Giotto had revived the ancient technique of foreshortening; Brunelleschi completed the discovery by rendering perspective in mathematical terms. His devotion to ancient models and his new tool of mathematical perspective set the stage for the further development of Renaissance painting. Brunelleschi's young Florentine friend Masaccio (1401–1428) took up the challenge. Faithful to the new rules of perspective, Masaccio was also concerned with painting statuesque figures and endowing his paintings with a grandeur and simplicity whose inspiration was classical. Perspective came with all the force of religious revelation.

In his work *On Painting*, Leon Battista Alberti (1404–1472), a humanist, scholar, and art theoretician, brought the Renaissance trend toward perspectival art to a summation by advancing the first mathematical theory of artistic perspective. By defining visual space and the relationship between the object and the observer in mathematical terms, Renaissance art and artistic theory helped to pave the way for the development of the modern scientific approach to nature, which later found expression in the astronomy of Copernicus and the physics of Galileo.

Renaissance artists were dedicated to representing things as they are, or at least as they are seen to be. Part of the inspiration for this was also classical. The ancient ideal of beauty was the beautiful nude. Renaissance admiration for ancient art meant that for the first time since the fall of Rome artists studied anatomy; they learned to draw the human form by having models pose for them, a practice fundamental to artistic training to this day. Another member of Brunelleschi's circle, the Florentine sculptor Donatello (1386–1466), also showed renewed interest in the human form.

The great Renaissance artists included Leonardo da Vinci (1452–1519), Michelangelo Buonarroti (1475–1564), and Raphael Santi (1483–1520). All of them were closely associated with Florence. Leonardo was a scientist and engineer as well as a great artist. He was an expert at fortifications and gunnery, an inventor, an anatomist, and a naturalist. Bringing careful observation of nature to his paintings, he combined it with powerful psychological insight to produce works of unsurpassed genius, though few in number. Among his most important paintings are *The Last Supper* and *La Gioconda*, or the *Mona Lisa*. The *Mona Lisa* is an example of an artistic invention of Leonardo's—what the Italians call *sfumato*. Leonardo left the outlines of the face a little vague and shadowy; this freed it of any wooden quality that more exact drawing would impart, and thus made it more lifelike and mysterious.

Michelangelo's creation of artistic harmony derived from a mastery of anatomy and drawing. His model in painting came from sculpture: his paintings are sculpted drawings. He was, of course, a sculptor of the highest genius whose approach to his art was poetic and visionary. Instead of trying to impose form on marble, he thought of sculpting as releasing the form from the rock. Among his greatest sculptures are *David*, *Moses*, and *The Dying Slave*. Michelangelo was also an architect; patronized by the pope, he designed the dome of the new Saint Peter's Basilica in Rome. But perhaps his most stupendous work was the ceiling of the Sistine Chapel in the Vatican, commissioned by Pope Julius II. In four years, working with little assistance, Michelangelo covered the empty space with the most monumental sculpted pictures ever painted, pictures that summarize the Old Testament story. *The Creation of Adam* is the most famous of these superlative frescoes.

Raphael, the last of these three artistic giants, is especially famous for the sweetness of his Madonnas. But he was capable of painting other subjects and conveying other moods, as his portrait of his patron, *Pope Leo X with Two Cardinals*, reveals.

THE SPREAD OF THE RENAISSANCE

Aided by the invention of printing, the Renaissance spread to Germany, France, England, and Spain in the late fifteenth and sixteenth centuries. In its migration northward, Renaissance culture adapted itself to conditions different from those in Italy—particularly the strength of lay piety. For example, the Brethren of the Common Life was a lay movement emphasizing education and practical piety. Intensely Christian and at the same time anticlerical, the people in such lay movements found in Renaissance culture tools for sharpening their wits against the clergy—not to undermine the faith, but rather to restore it to its apostolic purity.

Thus, northern humanists, like those in Italy, were profoundly devoted to ancient learning. But nothing in northern humanism compares with the non-Christian trend of the Italian Renaissance. The northerners were chiefly interested in the question of what constituted original Christianity. They sought a model in the light of which they might reform the corrupted church of their own time.

***Giovanni Arnolfini and His Bride*, by Jan van Eyck (c. 1390–1441).** This painting uses the new technique of perspective and draws a careful and idealized portrait of a prosperous married couple in their bedroom. It depicts a world that values privacy, sober prosperity, and intimacy of a certain kind: he stares out at us, while she looks deferentially at him.

Humanism outside Italy was less concerned with the revival of classical values than with the reform of Christianity and society through a program of Christian humanism. The Christian humanists cultivated the new arts of rhetoric and history, as well as the classical languages—Latin, Greek, and Hebrew. But the ultimate purpose of these pursuits was more religious than it had been in Italy, where secular interests predominated. Northern humanists used humanist scholarship and language to satirize and vilify medieval scholastic Christianity and to build a purer, more Scriptural Christianity. The discovery of accurate biblical texts, it was hoped, would lead to a great religious awakening. Protestant reformers, including Martin Luther, relied on humanist scholarship.

Erasmian Humanism

To Erasmus (c. 1466–1536) belongs the credit for making Renaissance humanism an international movement. He was educated in the Netherlands by the Brethren of the Common Life, which was one of the most advanced religious movements of the age, combining mystical piety with rigorous humanist pedagogy. Erasmus traveled throughout Europe as a humanist educator and biblical scholar. Like other Christian humanists, he trusted the power of words and used his pen to attack scholastic theology and clerical abuses and promote his philosophy of Christ. His weapon was satire, and his *Praise of Folly* and *Colloquies* won him a reputation for acid wit vented at the expense of conventional religion.

True religion, Erasmus argued, does not depend on dogma, ritual, or clerical power. Rather, it is revealed clearly and simply in the Bible and therefore is directly accessible to all people, from the wise and great to the poor and humble. Erasmian humanism stressed toleration, kindness, and respect for human rationality.

This clear but quiet voice was drowned out by the storms of the Reformation, and the Erasmian emphasis on the individual's natural capacities succumbed to a renewed emphasis on human sinfulness and dogmatic theology. Erasmus was caught in the middle and condemned on all sides; for him, the Reformation was both a personal and a historical tragedy. He had worked for peace and unity, only to experience a spectacle of war and fragmentation. Erasmian humanism, however, survived these horrors as an ideal, and during the next two centuries, whenever thinkers sought toleration and rational religion, they looked back to Erasmus for inspiration.

French and English Humanism

François Rabelais (c. 1494–c. 1553), a former monk, exemplified the humanist spirit in France. In response to religious dogmatism, he asserted the essential goodness of the individual and the right to enjoy the world rather than being bound by the fear of a punishing God. His folk-epic *Gargantua and Pantagruel* celebrates earthly life and earthly enjoyments, expresses an appreciation for secular learning and a confidence in human nature, and attacks monastic orders and clerical education for stifling the human spirit.

According to Rabelais, once freed from dogmatic theology, with its irrelevant concerns, and narrow-minded clergy, who deprived them of life's joys, people could, by virtue of their native goodness, build a paradise on earth and disregard the one dreamed up by theologians. In *Gargantua and Pantagruel*, Rabelais imagined a monastery where men and women spend their lives "not in laws, statutes, or rules, but according to their own free will and pleasure." They slept and ate when they desired and learned to "read, write, sing, play upon several musical instruments, and speak five or six . . . languages and compose in them all very quaintly." They observed only one rule: "do what thou wilt."[2]

The most influential humanist of the early English Renaissance was Sir Thomas More (1478–1535), who studied at Oxford. His impact came from both his writing and his career. Trained as a lawyer, he was a successful civil servant and member of Parliament. His most famous book is *Utopia*, the first major utopian treatise to be written in the West since Plato's *Republic* and one of the most original works of the entire Renaissance. Many humanists had attacked private wealth as the principal source of pride, greed, and human cruelty. However, only More carried this insight to its ultimate conclusion: in *Utopia*, he called for the elimination of private property. He had too keen a sense of human weakness to think that people could become perfect, but he used *Utopia* to call attention to contemporary abuses and to suggest radical reforms.

More succeeded Cardinal Wolsey as lord chancellor under Henry VIII. But when the king broke with the Roman Catholic church, More resigned, unable to reconcile his conscience with the king's rejection of papal supremacy. Three years later, in July 1535, More was executed for treason because he refused to swear an oath acknowledging the king's ecclesiastical supremacy.

William Shakespeare (1564–1616), widely considered the greatest playwright the world has ever produced, gave expression to conventional Renaissance values: honor, heroism, and the struggle against fate and fortune. But there is nothing conventional about Shakespeare's treatment of characters possessing these virtues. His greatest plays, the tragedies (*King Lear*, *Julius Caesar*, and others), explore a common theme: men, even heroic men, despite virtue, are able to overcome their human weaknesses only with the greatest difficulty, if at all. What fascinated Shakespeare was the contradiction between the Renaissance image of nobility, which is often the self-image of Shakespeare's heroes, and human beings' capacity for evil and self-destruction. The plays are thus intensely human, but so much so that humanism fades into the background; art transcends doctrine to represent life itself.

The Renaissance and the Modern Age

The Renaissance, then, marks the birth of modernity in the conception of the individual. Central to this birth was a bold new view of human nature that departed from the medieval view: individuals in all endeavors are not constrained by a destiny imposed by God from the outside but are free to make their own destiny, guided only by the example of the past, the force of present circumstances, and the drives of their own inner nature. Set free from theology, individuals were seen as the products, and in turn the shapers, of history; their future would be the work of their own free will.

Within the Italian city-states where the Renaissance was born, rich merchants were at least as important as the church hierarchy and the old nobility. Commercial wealth and a new politics produced a new culture that relied heavily on ancient Greece and Rome. This return to antiquity also entailed a rejection of the Middle Ages as dark, barbarous, and rude. The humanists clearly preferred the secular learning of ancient Greece and Rome to the clerical learning of the more recent past. The reason for this was obvious: the ancients had the same worldly concerns as the humanists; the scholastics did not.

The revival of antiquity by the humanists did not mean, however, that they identified completely with it. The revival itself was done too self-consciously for that. In the very act of looking back, the humanists differentiated themselves from the past and recognized that they were different. They were in this sense the first modern historians, because they could study and appreciate the past for its own sake and, to some degree, on its own terms.

In the works of Renaissance artists and thinkers, the world was, to a large extent, depicted and explained without reference to a higher supernatural realm of meaning and authority. This is clearly seen in Machiavelli's analysis of politics. Renaissance humanism exuded a deep confidence in the capacities of able people, instructed in the wisdom of the ancients, to understand and change the world.

This new confidence was closely related to another distinctive feature of the Renaissance: the cult of the individual. Both prince and painter were motivated in part by the desire to display their talents and to satisfy their ambitions. This individual striving was rewarded and encouraged by the larger society of rich patrons and calculating princes, which valued ability. Gone was the medieval Christian emphasis on the virtue of self-denial and the sin of pride. Instead, the Renaissance placed the highest value on self-expression and self-fulfillment—on the realization of individual potential, especially of the gifted few. The Renaissance fostered an atmosphere in which talent, even genius, was allowed to flourish.

To be sure, the Renaissance image of the individual and the world, bold and novel, was the exclusive prerogative of a small, well-educated urban elite and did not reach down to include the masses. Nevertheless, the Renaissance set an example of what people might achieve in art and architecture, taste and refinement, education and urban culture. In many fields, the Renaissance set the cultural standards of the modern age.

Background to the Reformation: The Medieval Church in Crisis

The Renaissance had revitalized European intellectual life and in the process discarded the medieval preoccupation with theology. Similarly, the Reformation marked the beginning of a new religious outlook. The Protestant Reformation, however, did not originate in the elite circles of humanistic scholars. Rather, it was sparked by Martin Luther (1483–1546), an obscure German monk and brilliant theologian. Luther started a rebellion against the church's authority that in less than one decade shattered the religious unity of Christendom. Begun in 1517, the Reformation dominated European history throughout much of the sixteenth century.

The Roman Catholic church, centered in Rome, was the one European institution that transcended geographic, ethnic, linguistic, and national boundaries. For centuries, it had extended its influence into every aspect of European society and culture. As a result, however, its massive wealth and power appeared to take precedence over its commitment to the search for holiness in this world and salvation in the next. Encumbered by wealth, addicted to international power, and protective of their own interests, the clergy, from the pope down, became the focus of a storm of criticism, starting in the Late Middle Ages.

In the fourteenth century, as kings increased their power and as urban centers with their sophisticated laity grew in size and number, people began to question the authority of the international church and its clergy. Political theorists rejected the pope's claim to supremacy over kings. The central idea of medieval Christendom—a Christian commonwealth led by the papacy—increasingly fell into disrepute. Theorists argued that the church was only a spiritual body, and therefore its power did not extend to the political realm. They said that the pope had no authority over kings, that the state needed no guidance from the papacy, and that the clergy were not above secular law. During the late fourteenth century, Latin Christendom witnessed the first systematic attacks ever launched against the church. Church corruption—such as the selling of indulgences (see the upcoming section on "The Break with Catholicism"), nepotism (the practice of appointing one's relatives to offices), the pursuit of personal wealth by bishops, and the sexual indulgence of the clergy—was nothing new. What was new and startling was the willingness of both educated and uneducated Christians to attack these practices publicly.

Thus, the Englishman John Wycliffe and the Bohemian Jan Hus (see "Fourteenth-Century Heresies" in Chapter 7), both learned theologians, denounced the wealth of the clergy as a violation of Christ's precepts and attacked the church's authority at its root by arguing that the church did not control an individual's destiny. They maintained that salvation depends not on participating in the church's rituals or receiving its sacraments but on accepting God's gift of faith.

Wycliffe's and Hus's efforts to initiate reform coincided with a powerful resurgence of religious feeling in the form of mysticism. Late medieval mystics sought an immediate and personal communication with God, and such experiences inspired them to advocate concrete reforms aimed at renewing the church's spirituality. The church hierarchy inevitably regarded mysticism with some suspicion, for if individuals could experience God directly, they would seemingly have little need for the church and its rituals. In the fourteenth century, these mystical movements seldom became heretical. But in the sixteenth and seventeenth centuries, radical reformers often found in Christian mysticism a powerful alternative to institutional control and even to the need for a priesthood.

With the advent of Lutheranism, personal faith, rather than adherence to the practices of the church, became central to the religious life of European Protestants. Renaissance humanists had sought to reinstitute the wisdom of ancient times; Protestant reformers wanted to restore the spirit of early Christianity, in which faith seemed purer, believers more sincere, and clergy uncorrupted by luxury and power. By the 1540s, the Roman Catholic church had initiated its own internal reformation, but it came too late to stop the movement toward Protestantism in Northern and Western Europe.

The Lutheran Revolt

The Protestant Reformation of the sixteenth century ushered in a spiritual revolution that had a great impact on the Western world. This reformation was precipitated and largely defined by the Augustinian monk Martin Luther. Luther had no intention of founding a new church or overthrowing the political and ecclesiastical order of his native Germany. Rather, it was a search to resolve his own spiritual crisis that led to the permanent schism within the church. In his youth, Luther at first fulfilled his father's wish and studied law, but at the age of twenty-one, he suddenly abandoned his legal studies to enter the Augustinian monastery at Erfurt. Luther began his search for spiritual and personal identity, and therefore for salvation, within the strict confinement and discipline of the monastery. He pursued his theological studies there and prepared for ordination.

Erich Lessing/Art Resource, N.Y.

***Portrait of Martin Luther,* by Lucas Cranach the Elder (1529).** Martin Luther was both a dour and thoughtful man with great determination.

The Break with Catholicism

As he studied and prayed, Luther grew increasingly terrified by the possibility of his damnation. As a monk, he sought union with God, and he understood the church's teaching that salvation depended on faith, works (meaning acts of charity, prayer, fasting, and so on), and grace—God's influence and favor, which sanctify and regenerate human life. He participated in the sacraments of the church, which, according to its teaching, were intended to give grace. Indeed, after his ordination, Luther administered the sacraments. Yet he still felt the weight of his sins, and nothing the church could offer seemed to relieve that burden. Seeking solace and salvation, Luther increasingly turned to reading the Bible. Two passages seemed to speak directly to him: "For therein is the righteousness of God revealed from faith to faith: as it is written, 'He who through faith is righteous shall live'" (Romans 1:17); and "They are justified by his grace as a gift, through the redemption which is in Christ Jesus" (Romans 3:24).[3] In these two passages, Luther found, for the first time in his adult life, some hope for his own salvation. Faith, freely given by God through Christ, enables the recipient to receive salvation.

The concept of salvation by faith alone provided an answer to Luther's spiritual quest. Practicing such good works as prayer, fasting, pilgrimages, and participation in the Mass and the other sacraments had never brought Luther peace of mind. He concluded that no amount of good works, however necessary for maintaining the Christian community, would bring salvation. Through reading the Bible and through faith alone the Christian could find the meaning of earthly existence. For Luther, the true Christian was a courageous figure who faced the terrifying quest for salvation armed only with the hope that God had granted him or her the gift of faith. This new Christian served others not to trade good works for salvation but solely to fulfill the demands of Christian love.

The starting point for the Reformation was Luther's attack in 1517 on the church's practice of selling indulgences. The church taught that some individuals go directly to heaven or hell, while others go to heaven only after spending time in purgatory—a period of expiation necessary for

The Granger Collection, New York.

ICONOCLAST JURY. In the sixteenth century, reformers tore out the statues and stained glass in Protestant churches, arguing that decoration distracts from the Bible and the Word of God. To this day, Protestant churches remain less decorated than Catholic ones.

those who have sinned excessively in this life but who have had the good fortune to repent before death. To die in a state of mortal sin meant to writhe in hell eternally. Naturally, people worried about how long they might have to suffer in purgatory. Indulgences were intended to remit portions of that time and were granted to individuals by the church for their prayers, attendance at Mass, and almost any acts of charity—including monetary offerings to the church. This last good work was the most controversial, since it could easily appear that people were buying their way into heaven.

In the autumn of 1517, a Dominican friar named John Tetzel was selling indulgences in the area near Wittenberg. Luther launched his attack on Tetzel and the selling of indulgences by tacking on the door of the Wittenberg castle church his *Ninety-Five Theses*. Luther's theses (propositions) challenged the entire notion of selling indulgences not only as a corrupt practice but also as based on a theologically unsound assumption—namely, that salvation can be earned by good works.

At the heart of Luther's argument in the *Ninety-Five Theses* and in his later writings was the belief that the individual achieves salvation through inner religious feeling, a sense of contrition for sins, and a trust in God's mercy—that church attendance, fasting, pilgrimages, charity, and other good works did not earn salvation. The church, in contrast, held that *both* faith and good works were necessary for salvation. Luther further insisted that every individual could discover the meaning of the Bible unaided by the clergy; the church, however, maintained that only the clergy could read and interpret the Bible properly. Luther argued that in matters of faith there was no difference between the clergy and the laity, for each person could receive faith directly and freely from God. But the church held that the clergy were intermediaries between individuals and God and that, in effect, Christians reached eternal salvation through the clergy. For Luther, no priest, no ceremony, and no sacrament could mediate between the Creator and his creatures. Hope lay only in a personal relationship between the individual and God, as expressed through faith in God's mercy and grace. By declaring that clergy and church rituals do not hold the key to salvation, Luther rejected the church's claim that it alone offered men and women the way to eternal life.

Recognizing that he might be in danger if he continued to preach without a protector, Luther appealed for support to the prince of his district, Frederick, the elector of Saxony. The elector was a powerful man in international politics—one of seven lay and ecclesiastical princes who chose the Holy Roman Emperor. Frederick's support convinced church officials, including the pope, that this monk would have to be dealt with cautiously. When the pope finally acted against Luther in 1520, it was too late; Luther had been given the needed time to promote his views. He proclaimed that the pope was the Antichrist and that the church was the "most lawless den of robbers, the most shameless of all brothels, the very kingdom of sin, death and Hell."[4] When the papal bull excommunicating him was delivered, Luther burned it.

No longer members of the church, Luther and his followers established congregations for the purpose of Christian worship. Christians outside the church needed protection, and in 1520 Luther published the *Address to the Christian Nobility of the German Nation*. In it he appealed to the emperor and the German princes to reform the church and to cast off their allegiance to the pope, who, he argued, had used taxes and political power to exploit them for centuries. His appeal produced some success; the Reformation flourished on the resentment against foreign papal intervention that had long festered in Germany. In this and other treatises, Luther made it clear that he wanted to present no threat to legitimate political authority, that is, to the power of the German princes.

In 1521, Charles V, the Holy Roman Emperor, who was a devout Catholic, summoned Luther to Worms, giving him a pass of safe conduct. There, Luther was to answer to the charge of heresy, both an ecclesiastical and a civil offense. When asked to recant, Luther replied: "Unless I am convinced of error by the testimony of Scripture or by clear reason . . . I cannot and will not recant anything, for it is neither safe nor honest to act against one's conscience. God help me. Amen." Shortly after this confrontation with the emperor, Luther went into hiding to escape arrest. During that one-year period, he translated the New Testament into German. His followers, or Lutherans, were eventually called *Protestants*—those who protested against the established church—and the term became generic for all followers of the Reformation.

The Appeal and Spread of Lutheranism

Rapidly disseminated by the new printing press, the tenets of Protestantism offered the hope of revitalization and renewal to Protestantism's adherents. Lutheranism appealed to the devout, who resented the worldliness and lack of piety of many clergy. But the movement found its greatest following among German townspeople, who objected to money flowing from their land to Rome in the form of church taxes and payment for church offices. In addition, the Reformation provided the nobility with an unprecedented opportunity to confiscate church lands, eliminate church taxes, and gain the support of their subjects by serving as leaders of a popular and dynamic religious movement. The Reformation also gave the nobles a way of resisting the Catholic Holy Roman Emperor, Charles V, who wanted to extend his authority over the German princes. Resenting the Italian domination of the church, many other Germans who supported Martin Luther believed that they were freeing German Christians from foreign control.

Lutheranism drew support from the peasants as well, for they saw Luther as their champion against their oppressors—both lay and ecclesiastical lords and the townspeople. Indeed, in his writings and sermons, Luther often attacked the greed of the princes and bemoaned the plight of the poor. Undoubtedly, Luther's successful confrontation with the authorities served to inspire the peasants. In 1524, these long-suffering people openly rebelled against their lords. The Peasants' Revolt spread to over one-third of Germany; some 300,000 people took up arms against their masters.

Luther, however, had no wish to associate his movement with a peasant uprising and risk alienating the nobility who supported him. As a political conservative, he hesitated to challenge secular authority; to him, the good Christian was an obedient subject. Therefore, he virulently attacked the rebellious peasants, urging the nobility to become "both judge and executioner" and to "knock down, strangle, and stab" the insurgents. By 1525, the peasants had been put down by the sword. The failure of the Peasants' Revolt meant that the German peasantry remained among the most backward and oppressed until well into the nineteenth century.

Initially, the Holy Roman Emperor, who was at war with France over parts of Italy and whose eastern territories were threatened by the Ottoman Turks, hesitated to intervene militarily in the strife between Lutheran and Catholic princes—a delay that proved crucial. Despite years of warfare, Charles V was unable to subdue the Lutheran princes. The religious conflict was settled by the Peace of Augsburg (1555), which decreed that each territorial prince should determine the religion of his subjects. Broadly speaking, northern Germany became largely Protestant, while Bavaria and other southern territories remained in the Roman Catholic church. The Holy Roman Emperor, who had been successfully challenged by the Lutheran princes, saw his power diminished. The decentralization of the empire and its division into Catholic and Protestant regions would block German unity until the last part of the nineteenth century.

The Spread of the Reformation

Nothing better illustrates the people's dissatisfaction with the church in the early sixteenth century than the rapid spread of Protestantism. There was a pattern to this phenomenon. Protestantism grew strong in Northern Europe—northern Germany, Scandinavia, the Netherlands, and England. It failed in the Latin countries, although not without a struggle in France. In general, Protestantism was an urban phenomenon, and it prospered where local magistrates supported it and where the distance from Rome was greatest.

Calvinism

The success of the Reformation outside Germany and Scandinavia derived largely from the work of John Calvin (1509–1564), a French scholar and theologian. Sometime in 1533 or 1534, Calvin met French followers of Luther and became convinced of the truth of the new theology. He began to spread its beliefs immediately after his conversion, and within a year he and his friends were in trouble with the civil and ecclesiastical authorities.

Calvin soon abandoned his humanistic and literary studies to become a preacher of the Reformation. Even early in his religious experience, he emphasized the power of God over sinful and corrupt humanity. Calvin's God thundered and demanded obedience, and the terrible distance between God and the individual was mediated only by Christ. Calvin embraced a stern theology, holding that God's laws must be rigorously obeyed, that social and moral righteousness must be earnestly pursued, that political life must be carefully regulated, and that human emotions must be strictly controlled.

Even more than Luther, Calvin explained salvation in terms of uncertain predestination: that God, who grants grace for his own inscrutable reasons, knows in advance who will be saved and who will be condemned to hell. Calvin argued that although people are predestined to salvation or damnation, they can never know their fate with certainty in advance. This terrible decree could and did lead some people to despair. To others—in a paradox difficult for the modern mind to grasp—Calvinism gave a sense of self-assurance and righteousness that made the saint—that is, the truly predestined man or woman—into a new kind of European. Most of Calvin's followers seemed to believe that in having understood the fact of predestination, they had received a bold insight into their unique relationship with God.

Calvinists were individuals who assumed that only unfailing dedication to God's law could be seen as a sign of salvation; thus, Calvinism made for stern men and women, active in their congregations and willing to suppress vice in themselves and others. Calvinism could also produce revolutionaries willing to defy any temporal authorities perceived to be in violation of God's laws. For Calvinists, obedience to Christian law became the dominating principle of life. Forced to flee France, Calvin finally sought safety in Geneva, a small, prosperous Swiss city near the French border. There, he eventually established a Protestant church that closely regulated the citizens' personal and social lives. Elders of the Calvinist church governed the city and imposed strict discipline in dress, sexual mores, church attendance, and business affairs; they severely punished irreligious and sinful behavior. Prosperous merchants as well as small shopkeepers saw in Calvinism doctrines that justified the self-discipline they already exercised in their own lives and wished to impose on the unruly masses. They particularly approved of Calvin's economic views, for he saw nothing sinful in commercial activities, unlike many Catholic clergy.

Geneva became the center of international Protestantism. Calvin trained a new generation of Protestant reformers of many nationalities, who carried his message back to their homelands. Calvin's *Institutes of the Christian Religion* (1536), in its many editions, became (after the Bible) the leading textbook of the new theology. In the second half of the sixteenth century, Calvin's theology of predestination spread into France, England, the Netherlands, and parts of the Holy Roman Empire.

Calvin always opposed any recourse to violence and supported the authority of magistrates. Yet when monarchy became their persecutor, his

ST. BARTHOLOMEW'S DAY MASSACRE, 1572, BY FRANÇOIS DUBOIS (1529–1584).

followers felt compelled to resist. Calvinist theologians became the first political theoreticians of modern times to publish cogent arguments for opposition to monarchy and eventually for political revolution. In France and later in the Netherlands, Calvinism became a revolutionary ideology, complete with an underground organization composed of dedicated followers who challenged monarchical authority. In the seventeenth century, the English version of Calvinism—Puritanism—performed the same function. Thus, in certain circumstances, Calvinism possessed the moral force to undermine the claims of the monarchical state on the individual.

France

Although Protestantism was illegal in France after 1534, the Protestant minority, the Huguenots, grew, becoming a well-organized underground movement. Huguenot churches, often under the protection of powerful nobles, assumed an increasingly political character in response to monarch-sponsored persecution. French Protestants became sufficiently organized and militant to challenge their persecutors, King Henry II and the Guise, one of the foremost Catholic families in Europe, and in 1562 civil war erupted between Catholics and Protestants. What followed was one of the most brutal religious wars in the history of Europe. In 1572, on Saint Bartholomew's Day, the gruesome slaughter of thousands of Protestant men, women, and children stained the streets with blood. So intense was the religious hatred at the time that the massacre inspired the pope to have a Mass said in thanksgiving for a Catholic "victory."

After nearly thirty years of brutal fighting throughout France, victory went to the Catholic side—but barely. Henry of Navarre, a Protestant leader, became King Henry IV, though only after he agreed to reconvert to Catholicism. Henry established a tentative peace by granting Protestants limited toleration. In 1598, he issued the Edict of Nantes, the first document in any national state that attempted to institutionalize a degree of religious toleration. In the seventeenth century, the successors of Henry IV (who was assassinated in 1610) gradually weakened and then in 1685 revoked the edict. The theoretical foundations of toleration, as well as its practice, remained tenuous in early modern Europe.

England

The king himself, rather than religious reformers, initiated the Reformation in England. Henry VIII (1509–1547) removed the English church from the jurisdiction of the papacy because the pope refused to grant him an annulment of his marriage to his first wife. The English Reformation thus began as a political act on the part of a self-confident Renaissance monarch. But the Reformation's origins stretched back into the Middle Ages, for England had a long tradition of heresy, as well as anticlericalism, rooted in Wycliffe's actions in the fourteenth century.

When Henry VIII decided that he wanted a divorce from the Spanish princess Catherine of Aragon, in 1527–1528, the pope ignored his request. As the pope stalled, Henry grew more desperate: he needed a male heir and presumed that the failure to produce one lay with his wife. At the same time, he desired the shrewd and tempting Anne Boleyn. Henry VIII arranged to grant himself a divorce by severing England from the church. In 1534, with Parliament's approval, he had himself declared supreme head of the Church of England. In 1536, he dissolved the monasteries and seized their property, which was distributed or sold to his loyal supporters. In most cases, it went to the lesser nobility and landed gentry—large landowners but not nobles. By involving Parliament and the gentry, Henry VIII turned the Reformation into a national movement. Political considerations, not profound theological differences, were at the root of the English Reformation.

Henry VIII was succeeded by his son, Edward VI (1547–1553), a Protestant, who in turn was succeeded by Mary (1553–1558), the daughter of Henry VIII and Catherine of Aragon. A devout Catholic, Mary severely persecuted Protestants. With the succession of Elizabeth I, Henry's second daughter (by Anne Boleyn), in 1558, England again became a Protestant country. Elizabeth's reign, which lasted until 1603, was characterized by a heightened sense of national identity and the persecution of Catholics, who were deemed a threat to national security. Fear of invasion by

Spain, which was bent on returning England to the papacy, contributed to English anti-Catholicism.

In its customs and ceremonies, the English, or Anglican, church as it developed in the sixteenth century differed to only a limited degree from the Roman Catholicism it replaced. The exact nature of England's Protestantism became a subject of growing dispute. Was the Anglican church to be truly Protestant? Were its services and churches to be simple, lacking in "popish" rites and rituals and centered on Scripture and sermon? Obviously, the powerful Anglican bishops would accept no form of Protestantism that might limit their privileges, ceremonial functions, and power. These issues contributed to the English Revolution of the seventeenth century (see Chapter 9).

The Radical Reformation

The leading Protestant reformers generally supported established political authorities, whether they were territorial princes or urban magistrates. For the reformers, human freedom was a spiritual, not a political or social, concept. Yet the Reformation did help trigger revolts among the artisan and peasant classes of Central and then Western Europe. By the 1520s, several radical reformers arose, often from the lower classes of European society. They attempted to channel popular religion and folk beliefs into a new version of reformed Christianity that spoke directly to the temporal and spiritual needs of the oppressed.

Radical reformers proclaimed that God's will was known by his saints—those predestined for salvation. They said that the poor would inherit the earth, which at present was ruled by the Antichrist; the saint's task was to purge this earth of evil and thus make it ready for Christ's Second Coming. For the radicals, the Scriptures, which spoke of God's love for the wretched and lowly, became an inspiration for social revolution. Luther, Calvin, and other reformers vigorously condemned the social doctrines preached by the radical reformers.

The largest group in the Radical Reformation before 1550 has the general name of *Anabaptists*. Having received the inner light—the message of salvation—Anabaptists felt born anew and yearned to be rebaptized. Anabaptists were new Christians, new persons led by the light of conscience to seek reform and renewal of all institutions in preparation for Christ's Second Coming.

In 1534, Anabaptists captured the city of Münster in Westphalia, near the western border of Germany. They seized the property of nonbelievers, burned all books except the Bible, and, in a mood of jubilation and sexual excess, openly practiced polygamy. All the while, the Anabaptists proclaimed that the Day of Judgment was close at hand. Provoked by their actions, Lutheran Prince Philip of Hesse and his army crushed the Anabaptists.

In early modern Europe, *Münster* became a byword for dangerous revolution. Determined to prevent these wild enthusiasts from gaining strength in their own territories, princes attacked them with ferocity. In Münster today, the cages still hang from the church steeple where the Anabaptist leaders were tortured and left to die as a warning to all would-be imitators.

By the late sixteenth century, many radical movements had either gone underground or grown quiet. But a century later, during the English Revolution (1640–1660), the beliefs and political goals of the Radical Reformation surfaced again, threatening to push the revolution in a direction that its gentry leaders desperately feared. Although the radicals failed in England as well, they left a tradition of democratic and antihierarchical thought. The radical assertion that saints, who have received the inner light, are the equal of anyone, regardless of social status, helped shape modern democratic thought.

The Catholic Response

The Protestant threat impelled the Roman Catholic church to institute reforms. At first, the energy for reform came from ordinary clergy, as well as laypeople such as Ignatius Loyola (1491–1556). Trained as a soldier, this pious Spanish reformer sought to create a new religious order, fusing the intellectual excellence of humanism with a reformed Catholicism that would appeal to powerful economic and political groups. Founded in 1534, the Society of Jesus, more commonly

0 200 400 Km.
0 200 400 Mi.
ATLANTIC OCEAN
North Sea
Baltic Sea
Bay of Biscay
Mediterranean Sea
Adriatic Sea
Black Sea
Lutheran
Calvinist (Reformed)
Church of England
Roman Catholic
Huguenot centers
Spread of Calvinism
SCOTLAND
Edinburgh
IRELAND
Dublin
ENGLAND
Oxford
London
NORWAY
DENMARK
LITHUANIA
PRUSSIA
POLAND
Warsaw
Hamburg
BRANDENBURG
Berlin
Wittenberg
Leipzig
Amsterdam
NETHERLANDS
Münster
WESTPHALIA
HOLY
ROMAN
EMPIRE
Brussels
Noyon
Paris
SAXONY
Prague
BOHEMIA
MORAVIA
Worms
Nuremberg
Augsburg
Munich
BAVARIA
Vienna
AUSTRIA
Buda
Pest
TRANSYLVANIA
HUNGARY
Strasbourg
Basel
Zürich
SWITZERLAND
Geneva
Trent
Milan
Venice
Orléans
Nantes
FRANCE
Bordeaux
Toulouse
Avignon
Loyola
SPAIN
Madrid
Lisbon
ITALY
Rome
Naples
Corsica
Sardinia
OTTOMAN EMPIRE

known as the Jesuits, became the backbone of the Catholic Reformation in Southern and Western Europe. The Jesuits combined traditional monastic discipline with a dedication to teaching and an emphasis on the power of preaching. They sought to use both to win converts back to the church.

The Jesuits brought hope: a religious revival based on ceremony, tradition, and the power of the priest to offer forgiveness. In addition, they opened some of the finest schools in Europe. Just as the Lutherans in Germany sought to bring literacy to the masses so that they might read the Bible, the Jesuits sought to bring intellectual enhancement to the laity, especially to the rich and powerful. The Jesuits pursued positions as confessors to princes and urged them to intensify their efforts to strengthen the church in their territories.

By the 1540s, the Counter-Reformation was well under way. The leaders of this Catholic movement attacked many of the same abuses that had impelled Luther to speak out, but they avoided a break with the doctrinal and spiritual authority of the clergy. The Counter-Reformation also took aggressive and hostile measures against Protestantism. The church tried to counter the popular appeal of Protestantism by emphasizing spiritual renewal through faith, prayer, and religious ceremony. It also resorted to sterner means. The Inquisition—the church court dealing with heretics—expanded its activities, and wherever Catholic jurisdiction prevailed, unrepentant Protestant heretics were subject to death or imprisonment. Catholics did not hold a monopoly on persecution: wherever Protestantism obtained official status—in England, Scotland, and Geneva, for instance—Catholics or religious radicals at times faced persecution.

One of the Catholic church's main tools was censorship. By the 1520s, the impulse to censor and burn dangerous books intensified dramatically as the church tried to prevent the spread of Protestant ideas. In the rush to eliminate heretical literature, the church condemned the works of reforming Catholic humanists as well as those of Protestants. The Index of Prohibited Books became an institutional part of the church's life. Over the centuries, the works of many leading thinkers were placed on the Index, which was not abolished until 1966.

The Counter-Reformation policies of education, vigorous preaching, church building, persecution, and censorship did succeed in bringing thousands of people, Germans and Bohemians in particular, back into the church. Furthermore, the church implemented some concrete changes in policy and doctrine. In 1545, the Council of Trent met to reform the church and strengthen it for confronting the Protestant challenge. Over the many years that it was convened (until 1563), the council modified and unified church doctrine; abolished many corrupt practices, such as the selling of indulgences; and vested final authority in the papacy, thereby ending the long and bitter struggle within the church over papal authority. The Council of Trent reaffirmed the church's teaching that both faith and good works were necessary for attaining salvation. It passed a decree that the church would be the final arbiter of the Bible. All compromise with Protestantism was rejected (not that Protestants were eager for it). The Reformation had split Western Christendom irrevocably.

◀ *Map 8.1* The Protestant and Catholic Reformations Europe fractured into competing camps, and religious warfare became a way of life.

The Reformation and the Modern Age

The Renaissance broke with medieval artistic and literary forms and ushered in a vibrant secularism and individualism. Like the Renaissance, the Reformation drew its inspiration from the ancient world. Renaissance humanists and artists sought to imitate and revive classical art and literary forms; Reformation thinkers aspired to restore the spiritual purity of early Christianity, which preceded the growth of a powerful clergy and a dogmatic theology. They used the Gospels in order to undermine the authority of the Church.

At first glance, the Reformation would seem to have renewed the medieval stress on otherworldliness and reversed the direction toward secularism taken by the Renaissance. Attracted to the ancient Stoic doctrine of the autonomous will, Renaissance humanists had broken with Augustine's stern view of original sin, a corrupt human nature, and the individual's inability to achieve salvation through his or her own efforts. Both Luther and Calvin, however, saw human beings as essentially depraved and corrupt and rejected completely the notion that individuals can do something for their own salvation; such an assertion of human will, they held, revealed a dangerous self-confidence in human beings. Whereas the humanists fostered freer discussion and criticism, the Reformation, at times, degenerated into narrow-mindedness and intolerance.

Yet in several important ways, the Reformation contributed to the shaping of modernity. By dividing Christendom into Catholic and Protestant, the Reformation destroyed the religious unity of Europe, the distinguishing feature of the Middle Ages, and weakened the church, the chief institution of medieval society. The Reformation promoted religious pluralism, for in addition to Lutheranism and Calvinism, various other Protestant churches, each with its own distinctive traits, emerged.

During the Middle Ages, popes challenged and at times dominated kings. By strengthening monarchs at the expense of church bodies, the Reformation furthered the growth of the modern secular and centralized state. Protestant rulers repudiated all papal claims to temporal authority and extended their power over the newly established Protestant churches in their lands. In Catholic lands, the weakened church was reluctant to challenge monarchs, whose support it now needed more than ever. This subordination of clerical authority to the throne permitted kings to build strong centralized states, a characteristic of political life of the modern West.

Although absolute monarchy was the immediate beneficiary of the Reformation, indirectly Protestantism contributed to the growth of political liberty—another feature of the modern West. To be sure, neither Luther nor Calvin championed political freedom. For Luther, a good Christian was an obedient subject. Thus, he declared that subjects should obey their rulers' commands: "It is in no wise proper for anyone who would be a Christian to set himself up against his government, whether it act justly or unjustly."[5] And again, "Those who sit in the office of magistrate sit in the place of God, and their judgment is as if God judged from heaven. . . . if the emperor . . . calls me, God calls me."[6] Calvinists created a theocracy in Geneva that closely regulated the citizens' private lives, and Calvin strongly condemned resistance to political authority as wicked. He held that rulers were selected by God and that punishment of bad rulers belonged only to God and not to the ruler's subjects.

Nevertheless, the Reformation also provided a basis for challenging monarchs. Some Protestant theorists, mainly Calvinists, supported resistance to political authorities whose edicts, they believed, contravened God's law as expressed in the Bible. This religious justification for revolution against tyrannical rule helped fuel the resistance of English Calvinists, or Puritans, to the English monarchy in the seventeenth century.

The Reformation advanced the idea of equality. Equality is rooted in the Judeo-Christian belief that all people are the creatures of a single God. In two important ways, however, medieval society contravened the principle of equality. First, feudalism stressed hereditary distinctions between nobles and commoners. Medieval society was hierarchical, arranged in an ascending order of legal ranks, or estates: commoners, nobles, and clergy. Second, the medieval church taught that only the clergy could administer the sacraments, which provided people with the means of attaining salvation; for this reason, they were superior to the laity. Luther, in contrast, held that there was no spiritual distinction between the laity and the clergy. There was a spiritual equality of all believers: all were equally Christian; all were equally priests.

The Reformation also contributed to the creation of an individualistic ethic, which characterizes the modern world. Since Protestants, unlike Catholics, had no official interpreter of Scripture, the individual bore the awesome responsibility of interpreting the Bible according to the dictates of his or her conscience. Protestants confronted the prospect of salvation or damnation entirely on their own. No church provided them with security or certainty, and no priesthood interceded between them and God. Piety was not determined by the church, but by the autonomous individual, whose subjective faith or conscience, illuminated by God, was the source of judgment and authority.

For the Protestant, faith was personal and inward. This new arrangement called for a personal relationship between each individual and God and called attention to the individual's inner religious capacities. Certain that God had chosen them for salvation, many Protestants developed the inner self-assurance and assertiveness that marks the modern individual. Thus, the Protestant emphasis on private judgment in religious matters and on an inner personal conviction accentuated the importance of the individual and helped to mold a new and distinctly modern European.

The Reformation's stress on individual conscience may have contributed to the development of the capitalist spirit, which underlies modern economic life. So argued German sociologist Max Weber in *The Protestant Ethic and the Spirit of Capitalism* (1904). Weber acknowledged that capitalism had existed in Europe before the Reformation; merchant bankers in medieval Italian and German towns, for example, engaged in capitalistic activities. But, he contended, Protestantism (particularly Calvinism) made capitalism more dynamic; it produced a new type of individual who confidently set out to master himself and his environment. Protestant businesspeople believed that they had a religious obligation to prosper, and their faith gave them the self-discipline to do so. Convinced that prosperity was God's blessing and poverty his curse, Calvinists had a spiritual inducement to labor industriously and to avoid laziness.

According to Calvin's doctrine of predestination, God had already determined in advance who would be saved; salvation could not be attained through any worldly actions. Although there was no definite way of discovering who had received God's grace, Calvin's followers came to believe that certain activities were signs that God was working through them, that they had indeed been elected. Thus, Calvinists viewed hard work, diligence, dutifulness, efficiency, frugality, and a disdain for pleasurable pursuits—all virtues that contribute to rational and orderly business procedures and to business success—as signs of election. In effect, Weber argued, Protestantism—unlike Catholicism—gave religious approval to moneymaking and the businesspeople's way of life. Moreover, Calvin's followers seemed to believe that they had attained a special insight into their relationship with God; this conviction fostered a sense of self-assurance and righteousness. Protestantism, therefore, produced a highly individualistic attitude that valued inner strength, self-discipline, and methodical and sober behavior—necessary traits for a middle class seeking business success in a highly competitive world.

❖ ❖ ❖

Notes

1. Giovanni Pico della Mirandola, *Oration on the Dignity of Man,* trans. A. Robert Caponigri (Chicago: Henry Regnery, 1956), p. 7.
2. François Rabelais, *Gargantua and Pantagruel*, trans. Sir Thomas Urquhart (1883), bk. 1, chap. 57.
3. The biblical quotations are from the *Revised Standard Version of the Bible*, copyright © 1946, 1952, and 1971 the National Council of the Churches of Christ in the USA. Used by permission. All rights reserved.
4. John Dillenberger, ed., *Martin Luther: Selections from His Writings* (Garden City, N.Y.: Doubleday, 1961), p. 46, taken from *The Freedom of a Christian* (1520).
5. Quoted in George H. Sabine, *A History of Political Thought* (New York: Holt, Rinehart & Winston, 1961), p. 361.
6. Quoted in Roland Bainton, *Here I Stand* (New York: Abingdon Press, 1950), p. 238.

Suggested Reading

Bartlett, Kenneth, ed., *The Civilization of the Italian Renaissance* (1992). A helpful collection of sources.

Dillenberger, John, ed., *Martin Luther: Selections from His Writings* (1962). Selected for the general reader.

Dixon, C. Scott, ed., *The German Reformation* (1999). A valuable collection of essays on important aspects of the Reformation.

Grimm, Harold J., *The Reformation Era, 1500–1650*, 2nd ed. (1973). A highly regarded narrative.

Hale, John, *The Civilization of Europe in the Renaissance* (1994). An informed and entertaining survey.

Kelley, Donald R., *Renaissance Humanism* (1991). A recent synthesis.

King, Margaret L., *Women of the Renaissance* (1991). A useful survey of a burgeoning field of scholarship.

MacCulloch, D. *Reformation Europe: House Divided* (2003). An excellent general survey.

Marius, Richard, *Martin Luther* (1999). A new biography.

Ozment, Steven E., *Protestants* (1992). The rise of Protestantism.

Pettegree, A. ed., *The Reformation World* (2000). Essays by experts on different countries.

Schiffman, Zachary S., ed., *Humanism and the Renaissance* (2002). Excellent selections of historical interpretation.

Stephens, John, *The Italian Renaissance* (1990). A useful survey.

Thompson, Bard, *Humanists and Reformers: A History of the Renaissance and Reformation* (1996). A well-written, comprehensive study of both movements.

Chapter 9

Political and Economic Transformation: National States, Overseas Expansion, Commercial Revolution

- **Toward the Modern State**
- **Hapsburg Spain**
- **The Growth of French Power**
- **The Growth of Limited Monarchy and Constitutionalism in England**
- **The Holy Roman Empire: The Failure to Unify Germany**
- **European Expansion**
- **Black Slavery and the Slave Trade**
- **The Price Revolution**
- **The Expansion of Agriculture**
- **The Expansion of Trade and Industry**
- **The Fostering of Mercantile Capitalism**
- **Toward a Global Economy**

Focus Questions

1. What are key features of the modern state? In what ways did early modern kings help shape the modern state?
2. Why did England move in the direction of parliamentary government while most countries on the Continent embraced absolutism? Describe the main factors.

3. What were the new forces for expansion operating in early modern Europe?
4. How did European expansion give rise to an emerging world economy?

From the thirteenth to the seventeenth century, a new and unique form of political organization emerged in the West: the dynastic, or national, state. It harnessed the material resources of its territory, directed the energies of the nobility into national service, and increasingly centralized political authority. The national state, a product of dynastic consolidation, is the essential political institution of the modern West.

The disintegration of medieval political forms and the emergence of the modern state coincided with the gradual breakdown of the medieval socioeconomic system, which was based on tradition, hierarchy, and orders or estates. In the medieval system, every group—clergy, lords, serfs, guild members—occupied a particular place and performed a specific function. Society functioned best when each person fulfilled the role allotted to him or her by God and tradition. Early modern times saw the growth of a capitalist market economy whose central focus was the self-sufficient individual, striving, assertive, and motivated by self-interest. This nascent market economy, greatly boosted by the voyages of discovery and the conquest and colonization of other parts of the world, subverted the hierarchically arranged and tradition-bound medieval community. Seeking to enrich their treasuries and extend their power, states promoted commercial growth and overseas expansion. The extension of European hegemony over much of the world was well under way by the eighteenth century. ❖

Toward the Modern State

During the Middle Ages, some kings began to forge national states. However, medieval political forms differed considerably from those that developed later, in the early modern period. In the Middle Ages, kings had to share political power with feudal lords, the clergy, free cities, and representative assemblies. Central authority was tempered by overlapping jurisdictions and numerous and competing allegiances. People saw themselves as members of an estate—clergy, aristocracy, or commoners—rather than as subjects or citizens of a state. Church theorists envisioned Christian Europe as a unitary commonwealth in which spiritual concerns prevailed over secular authority. According to this view, kings, who received their power from God, must never forget their religious obligation to rule in accordance with God's commands as interpreted by the clergy.

In the sixteenth and seventeenth centuries, kings successfully asserted their authority over competing powers, continuing a trend that had begun in the Late Middle Ages. Strong monarchs dominated or crushed the parliaments that had acted as a brake on royal power during the Middle Ages. Increasingly, too, these monarchs subjected lords and ecclesiastical authorities to royal control. They created a bureaucracy to coordinate the activities of the central government. The old medieval political order dissolved. It had been characterized on the one hand by feudal particularism and the strength of local authorities, and on the other by the supranational claims and goals of a universal church. Gradually, the national, territorial state, the hallmark of the modern world, became the essential political unit. Kings were the central figures in the creation of the national state. Strong dynastic states were formed wherever monarchs succeeded in subduing local aristocratic and ecclesiastical power systems. In their struggle to subdue the aristocracy, kings were aided by artillery; the lords' castles quickly became obsolete in the face of royal siege weapons. Where the monarchs failed, as they did in Germany and Italy, no viable states evolved until well into the nineteenth century.

By the early seventeenth century, Europeans had developed the concept of the state: an autonomous political entity to which its subjects owed duties and obligations. The essential prerequisite for the Western concept of the state, as it emerged in the early modern period, was the idea of *sovereignty*. Within its borders, the state was supreme; all other institutions, both secular and religious, had to recognize the state's authority. The art of governing entailed molding the ambitions and strength of the powerful and wealthy so that they could be harnessed to serve the state. Its power growing through war and taxation, the state had become the basic unit of political authority in the West.

Historically, the modern state has been characterized by a devotion to the nation and by feelings of national pride. A national language is used throughout the land, and the people have a sense of sharing a common culture and history, of being distinct from other peoples. There were some signs of growing national feeling during the sixteenth and seventeenth centuries, but this feature of the modern state did not become a major part of European political life until the nineteenth century. During the early modern period, devotion was largely given to a town, a province, a noble, or to the person of the king rather than to the nation, the people as a whole.

In the sixteenth and seventeenth centuries, the idea of liberty, now so basic to Western political life and thought, was only rarely discussed, and then chiefly by Calvinist opponents of absolutism. Not until the mid-seventeenth century in England was there a body of political thought contending that human liberty was compatible with the new modern state. In general, despite the English (and Dutch) developments, absolutism dominated the political structure of early modern Europe. It was not until the late eighteenth and nineteenth centuries that absolutism was widely challenged by advocates of liberty.

The principle of the balance of power, an integral part of modern international relations, also emerged during early modern times. When one state threatened to dominate Europe, as did Spain under Philip II and France under Louis XIV, other states joined forces and resisted. The fear that one state would upset the balance of power and achieve European domination pervaded international relations in later centuries.

Chronology 9.1 ❖ Economic and Political Transformations

1394–1460	Henry the Navigator, prince of Portugal, encourages expansion into Africa for gold and his anti-Muslim crusade
1469	Ferdinand and Isabella begin their rule of Castile and Aragon
1485	Henry VII begins the reign of the Tudor dynasty in England
1488	Bartholomeu Dias reaches the tip of Africa
1492	Christopher Columbus reaches the Caribbean island of Española on his first voyage; the Jews are expelled from Spain; Granada, the last Muslim kingdom in Spain, is conquered, completing the Reconquest
1497	Vasco da Gama sails around the Cape of Good Hope (Africa) to India
1519	Charles V of Spain becomes Hapsburg emperor of the Holy Roman Empire
1519–1521	Hernando Cortés conquers the Aztecs in Mexico
1531–1533	Francisco Pizarro conquers the Incas in Peru
1552	Silver from the New World flows into Europe via Spain, contributing to a price revolution
1556–1598	Philip II of Spain persecutes Jews and Muslims
1562–1598	Religious wars in France
1572	Saint Bartholomew's Day Massacre—Queen Catherine of France orders thousands of Protestants executed
1588	English fleet defeats the Spanish Armada
1598	French Protestants are granted religious toleration by the Edict of Nantes
1624–1642	Cardinal Richelieu, Louis XIII's chief minister, determines royal policies
1640–1660	English Revolution
1648	Treaty of Westphalia ends the Thirty Years' War
1649	Charles I, Stuart king of England, is executed by an act of Parliament
1649–1660	England is co-ruled by Parliament and the army under Oliver Cromwell
1660	Charles II returns from exile and becomes king of England
1685	Louis XIV of France revokes the Edict of Nantes
1688–1689	Revolution in England: end of absolutism
1694	Bank of England is founded
1701	Louis XIV tries to bring Spain under French control

Hapsburg Spain

The Spanish political experience of the sixteenth century was one of the most extraordinary in the history of modern Europe. Spanish kings built a dynastic state that burst through its frontiers and encompassed Portugal, part of Italy, the Netherlands, and enormous areas in the New World. Spain became an intercontinental empire—the first in the West since Roman times.

In the eighth and ninth centuries, the Muslims controlled all of Spain except some tiny Christian kingdoms in the far north. In the ninth century, these Christian states began a five-hundred-year struggle, the Reconquest, to drive the Muslims from the Iberian Peninsula. By the middle of the thirteenth century, Granada in the south was all that remained of Muslim lands in Spain. This long struggle for Christian hegemony in the Iberian Peninsula left the Spanish fiercely religious and strongly suspicious of foreigners. Despite centuries of intermarriage with non-Christians, by the early sixteenth century purity of blood and orthodoxy of faith became necessary for, and synonymous with, Spanish identity.

Ferdinand and Isabella

In 1469, Ferdinand, heir to the throne of Aragon, married Isabella, heir to the throne of Castile. Although Ferdinand and Isabella did not give Spain a single legal and tax system or a common currency, their policies did contribute decisively to Spanish unity and might. They broke the power of aristocrats, who had operated from their fortified castles like kings, waging their private wars at will; they brought the Spanish church into alliance with the state; and in 1492, they drove the Muslims from Granada, the Muslims' last territory in Spain. The crusade against the Muslim infidels accorded with the aims of the militant Spanish church. With a superior army, with the great aristocrats pacified, and with the church and the Inquisition under monarchical control, the Catholic kings expanded their interests and embarked on an imperialist foreign policy that made Spain dominant in the New World.

The Spanish state and church persecuted both Muslims and Jews, who for centuries had contributed substantially to Spanish cultural and economic life. In 1391, thousands of Jews were massacred when anti-Jewish sentiments, fanned by popular preachers, turned to violence in major cities. Under threat of death, many Jews submitted to baptism. In succeeding years, other attacks on Jews led to more conversions. A number of these *conversos*, or New Christians, continued to practice the religion of their fathers in secret, a situation that appalled clerical authorities and the devout Ferdinand and Isabella.

In 1492, in a move to enforce religious uniformity, the crown expelled from Spain Jews who were unwilling to accept baptism. About 150,000 Jews (some estimates are considerably higher) were driven out, including many conversos who opted to stay with their people. The thousands of Jews who underwent conversion and the conversos who remained were watched by the Inquisition—the church tribunal that dealt with insincere converts—for signs of backsliding. Death by fire, sometimes in elaborate public ceremonies, was the ultimate penalty for those of the conversos and their descendants who were suspected of practicing Judaism. Muslims also bore the pain of forced conversions and investigations, torture, and executions conducted by the Inquisition. Finally, in 1609 through 1614, Spain expelled them.

The Reign of Charles V, King of Spain and Holy Roman Emperor

Dynastic marriage constituted another crucial part of Ferdinand and Isabella's foreign policy. They strengthened their ties with the Austrian Hapsburg kings by marrying one of their children, Juana (called "the Mad" for her insanity), to Philip the Fair, son of Maximilian of Austria, the head of the ruling Hapsburg family. Philip and Juana's son Charles inherited the kingdom of Ferdinand and Isabella in 1516 and reigned until 1556. Through his other grandparents, he also inherited the Netherlands, Austria, Sardinia, Sicily, the kingdom of Naples, and Franche Comté in eastern France. In 1519, he was elected Holy Roman Emperor Charles V. Charles became the most powerful ruler in Europe. But his reign saw the emergence of political, economic, and social problems that eventually led to Spain's decline.

Charles's inheritance was simply too vast to be governed effectively, but that was only dimly perceived at the time. The Lutheran Reformation proved to be the first successful challenge to Hapsburg power. It was the first phase of a religious and political struggle between Catholic Spain and Protestant Europe, a struggle that would dominate the last half of the sixteenth century.

The achievements of Charles V's reign rested on the twin instruments of army and bureaucracy. The Hapsburg Empire in the New World was vastly extended but, on the whole, effectively administered and policed. Out of this sprawling empire, with its exploited native populations, came the greatest flow of gold and silver ever witnessed by Europeans. Constant warfare in Europe, coupled with the immensity of the Spanish administrative network, required a steady intake of capital. In the long run, however, this easy access to capital seems to have hurt the Spanish economy. There was no incentive for the development of domestic industry, bourgeois entrepreneurship, or international commerce.

Moreover, constant war engendered and perpetuated a social order geared to the aggrandizement of a military class rather than the development of a commercial class. Although war expanded Spain's power in the sixteenth century, it sowed the seeds for the financial crises of the 1590s and beyond and for the eventual decline of Spain as a world power.

Philip II

Philip II inherited the throne from his father, Charles V, who abdicated in 1556. Charles left his son with a vast empire in both the Old World and the New. Although this empire had been administered competently enough, it was facing the specters of bankruptcy and heresy. A zeal for Catholicism ruled Philip's private conduct and infused his foreign policy. In the 1560s, Philip sent the largest land army ever assembled in Europe into the Netherlands with the intention of crushing Protestant-inspired opposition to Spanish authority. The ensuing revolt of the Netherlands lasted until 1609, and the Spanish lost their industrial heartland as a result of it.

The Dutch established a republic governed by the prosperous and progressive bourgeoisie. Rich from the fruits of manufacture and trade in everything from tulip bulbs to ships and slaves, the Dutch merchants ruled their cities and provinces with fierce pride. In the early seventeenth century, this new nation of only 1.5 million people already practiced the most innovative commercial and financial techniques in Europe.

Philip's disastrous attempt to invade England was also born of religious zeal. Philip regarded an assault on England, the main Protestant power, as a holy crusade against the "heretic and bastard" Queen Elizabeth; he particularly resented English assistance to the Protestant Dutch rebels. Sailing from Lisbon in May 1588, the Spanish Armada, carrying twenty-two thousand seamen and soldiers, met with defeat. More than half of the Spanish ships were destroyed or put out of commission. Many ships were wrecked by storms as they tried to return to Spain by rounding the coasts of Scotland and Ireland. The defeat had an enormous psychological effect on the Spanish, who saw it as divine punishment and openly pondered what they had done to incur God's displeasure.

The End of the Spanish Hapsburgs

After the defeat of the Armada, Spain gradually and reluctantly abandoned its imperial ambitions in Northern Europe. The administrative structure built by Charles V and Philip II remained strong throughout the seventeenth century; nevertheless, by the first quarter of the century, enormous weaknesses in Spanish economic and social life had surfaced. In 1596, Philip II was bankrupt, his vast wealth depleted by the cost of foreign wars. Bankruptcy reappeared at various times in the seventeenth century, while the agricultural economy, at the heart of any early modern nation, stagnated. The Spanish in their golden age had never paid enough heed to increasing domestic production.

Despite these setbacks, Spain was still capable of taking a very aggressive posture during the Thirty Years' War (1618–1648). The Austrian branch of the Hapsburg family joined forces with their Spanish cousins, and neither the Swedes and Germans nor the Dutch could stop them. Only French participation in the Thirty Years' War on the Protestant side tipped the balance decisively against the Hapsburgs. Spanish aggression brought no victories, and with the Peace of Westphalia (1648), Spain officially recognized the independence of the Netherlands and severed its diplomatic ties with the Austrian branch of the family.

By 1660, the imperial age of the Spanish Hapsburgs had ended. The rule of the Protestant princes had been secured in the Holy Roman Empire; the largely Protestant Dutch Republic flourished; Portugal and its colony of Brazil were independent of Spain; and dominance over European affairs had passed to France. The quality of material life in Spain deteriorated rapidly, and the ever-present gap between the rich and the poor widened even more drastically. The traditional aristocracy and the church retained their land and power but failed to produce effective leadership.

The Spanish experience illustrates two aspects of the history of the European state. First, the state as empire could survive and prosper only if the domestic economic base remained sound. The Spanish reliance on bullion from its colonies and the failure to cultivate industry and reform the taxation system spelled disaster. Second, states with a vital and aggressive bourgeoisie, such as England and Holland, flourished at the expense of the regions where the aristocracy and the church dominated and controlled society and its mores—as in Spain's situation. The latter social groups tended to despise manual labor, profit taking, and technological progress. Even though they had been created by kings and dynastic families, after 1700, the major dynastic states were increasingly nurtured by the economic activities of merchants and traders—the bourgeoisie. Yet the bureaucracy of the dynastic states continued to be dominated by men drawn from the lesser aristocracy.

The Growth of French Power

Although both England and France effectively consolidated the power of their central governments, each became a model of a different form of statehood. The English model was a constitutional monarchy in which the king's power was limited by Parliament and the rights of the English people were protected by law and tradition. The French model emphasized at every turn the glory of the king and, by implication, the sovereignty of the state and its right to stand above the interests of its subjects. France's monarchy became absolute, and French kings claimed that they had been selected by God to rule, a theory known as the divine right of kings. This theory gave monarchy a sanctity that various French kings exploited to enforce their commands on the population, including rebellious feudal lords.

The evolution of the French state was a very gradual process, completed only in the late seventeenth century. In the Middle Ages, the French monarchs recognized the rights of representative assemblies—the Estates—and consulted with them. These assemblies (whether regional or national) were composed of deputies drawn from the various elites: the clergy, the nobility, and, significantly, the leaders of cities and towns in a given region. Early modern French kings increasingly wrested power from the nobility, reduced the significance of the Estates, and eliminated interference from the church.

Religion and the French State

In every emergent state, tension existed between the monarch and the papacy. At issue was control over the church within that territory—over its personnel, its wealth, and, of course, its pulpits, from which an illiterate majority learned what their leaders wanted them to know not only about religious issues but also about submission to civil authority. The monarch's power to make church appointments could ensure a complacent church—a church willing to preach obedience to royal authority and to comply on matters of taxes.

For the French monarchs, centuries of tough bargaining with the papacy paid off in 1516, when Francis I (1515–1547) concluded the Concordat of Bologna. Under this agreement, Pope Leo X permitted the French king to nominate, and so in effect appoint, men of his choice to all the highest offices in the French church. The Concordat of Bologna laid the foundation for what became known as the *Gallican church*—a term signifying that the Catholic Church in France was sanctioned and overseen by the French kings. Thus, in the early sixteenth century, the central government had been strengthened at the expense of papal authority and of traditional privileges enjoyed by local aristocracy.

The Protestant Reformation, however, challenged royal authority and threatened the very survival of France as a unified state. Fearful that Protestantism would undermine his power, Francis I declared Protestant beliefs and practices illegal and punishable by fines, imprisonment, and even execution. Nevertheless, the Protestant minority (the Huguenots) grew in strength. From 1562 to 1598, France experienced waves of religious wars, which cost the king control over vast areas of the kingdom. The great aristocratic families, the Guise for the Catholics and the Bourbons for the Protestants, drew up armies that scourged the land, killing and maiming their religious opponents and dismantling the authority of the central government.

In 1579, extreme Huguenot theorists published the *Vindiciae contra Tyrannos (A Defense of Liberty Against Tyrants)*. This statement, combined with a call to action, was the first of its kind in early modern times. It justified rebellion against, and even the execution of, an unjust king. European monarchs might claim power and divinely sanctioned authority, but by the late sixteenth century, their subjects had available the moral and theoretical justification for opposing their monarch's will, by force if necessary, and this justification rested on Scripture and religious conviction. Significantly, this same treatise was translated into English in 1648, a year before Parliament publicly executed Charles I, king of England.

The French monarchy foundered in the face of this kind of political and religious opposition. The era of royal supremacy instituted by Francis I came to an abrupt end during the reign of his successor, Henry II (1547–1559). Wed to Catherine de'Medici, a member of the powerful Italian banking family, Henry occupied himself not with the concerns of government but with the pleasures of the hunt. The sons who succeeded Henry—Francis II (1559–1560), Charles IX (1560–1574), and Henry III (1574–1589)—were uniformly weak. Their mother, Catherine, who was the virtual ruler, ordered the execution of thousands of Protestants by royal troops in Paris—the beginning of the infamous Saint Bartholomew's Day Massacre (1572), which, with the bloodbath that followed, became a symbol of the excesses of religious zeal.

The civil wars begun in 1562 were renewed in the massacre's aftermath. They dragged on until the death of the last Valois king in 1589. The Valois failure to produce a male heir to the throne placed Henry, duke of Bourbon and a Protestant, in line to succeed to the French throne. Realizing that the overwhelmingly Catholic population would not accept a Protestant king, Henry (apparently without much regret) renounced his adopted religion and embraced the church. Henry IV (1589–1610) granted his Protestant subjects and former followers a degree of religious toleration through the Edict of Nantes (1598), but they were never welcomed into the royal bureaucracy in significant numbers. Throughout the seventeenth century, every French king attempted to undermine the Protestants' regional power bases and ultimately to destroy their religious liberties.

The Consolidation of French Monarchical Power

The defeat of Protestantism as a national force set the stage for the final consolidation of the French state in the seventeenth century under the great Bourbon kings, Louis XIII and Louis XIV. Louis XIII (1610–1643) realized that his rule depended on an efficient and trustworthy bureaucracy, a replenishable treasury, and constant vigilance against the localized claims to power by the great aristocracy and Protestant cities and towns. Cardinal Richelieu, who served as Louis XIII's chief minister from 1624 to 1642, became the great architect of French absolutism.

Richelieu's morality rested on one absolute principle, embodied in a phrase he invented: *raison d'état*, reason of state. Richelieu sought to serve the state by bringing under the king's control the disruptive and antimonarchical elements within French society. He increased the power of the central bureaucracy, attacked the power of independent and often Protestant towns and cities, and persecuted the Huguenots. Above all, he humbled the great nobles by limiting their effectiveness as councilors to the king and prohibiting their traditional privileges, such as settling grievances through a duel rather than through court action. Reason of state also guided Richelieu's foreign policy. It required that France turn against Catholic Spain and enter the war that was raging at the time in the Holy Roman Empire on the Protestant—and hence anti-Spanish—side. France's entry into the Thirty Years' War produced a decisive victory for French power on the Continent.

Richelieu died in 1642, and Louis XIII the following year. Cardinal Mazarin, who took charge during the minority of Louis XIV (who was five years old when Louis XIII died), continued Richelieu's policies. Mazarin's heavy-handed actions produced a rebellious reaction, the *Fronde*, a series of street riots that lasted from 1648 to 1653 and that for a time cost the government control over Paris. Centered in Paris and supported by the great aristocracy, the courts, and the city's poorer classes, the Fronde threatened to develop into a full-scale uprising. It might have done so but for one crucial factor: its leadership was divided. Court judges (lesser nobles who had often just risen from the ranks of the bourgeoisie) deeply

The Royal Palace of Versailles. Immense and grand, Versailles was the wonder of the age. Like the person of the king, it said to his subjects: I am grandeur incarnate. Even by today's standards, it is an impressive building, both inside and out.

distrusted the great aristocrats and refused in the end to make common cause with them, and both groups feared disorders among the urban masses.

When Louis XIV finally assumed responsibility for governing in 1661, he vowed that the events he had witnessed as a child during the Fronde would never be repeated. In the course of his reign, he achieved the greatest degree of monarchical power held during the early modern period. No absolute monarch in Western Europe, before or at that time, had so much personal authority or commanded such a vast and effective military and administrative machine. Louis XIV's reign represents the culmination of the process of increasing monarchical authority that had been under way for centuries. Intelligent, cunning, and possessing a unique understanding of the requirements of his office, Louis XIV worked long hours at being king, and he never undertook a venture without an eye to his personal grandeur. The sumptuous royal palace at Versailles was built for that reason; similarly, etiquette and style were cultivated there on a scale never before seen in any European court.

When Mazarin died, Louis XIV did away with the office of first minister; he would rule France alone. The great nobles, "princes of the blood," enjoyed great social prestige but exercised decreasing political influence. Louis XIV treated the aristocrats to elaborate rituals, processions, displays, and banquets; amid all the clamor, however, their political power dwindled.

Louis XIV's domestic policies centered on his incessant search for new revenues. Not only the building of Versailles but also wars cost money, and Louis XIV waged them to excess. To raise capital, he used the services of Jean Baptiste Colbert, a brilliant administrator who improved the methods of tax collecting, promoted new industries, and encouraged international trade. Operating with a total bureaucracy of about a thousand officials and no longer bothering even to consult the parlements or Estates, Louis XIV ruled absolutely in accordance with the principle of divine right—that the monarch is selected to rule by God.

Yet Louis XIV's system was fatally flawed. Without any effective check on his power and on his dreams of international conquest, no limit was imposed on the state's capacity to make war or on the ensuing national debt. Louis XIV coveted vast sections of the Holy Roman Empire; he also sought to curb Dutch commercial prosperity and had designs on the Spanish Netherlands (roughly Belgium and Luxembourg). By the 1680s, his domestic and foreign policies turned violently aggressive. In 1685, he revoked the Edict of Nantes, forcing many of the country's remaining Protestants to flee. In 1689, he embarked on a military campaign to secure territory from the Holy Roman Empire. And in 1701, he tried to bring Spain under the control of the Bourbon dynasty. Louis XIV, however, underestimated the power of his northern rivals, England and the Netherlands. Their combined power, in alliance with the Holy Roman Empire and the Austrians, defeated his ambitions.

Louis XIV's participation in these long wars emptied the royal treasury. By the late seventeenth century, taxes had risen intolerably, and they were levied mostly on those least able to pay—the peasants. Absolutism also meant increased surveillance of the population. Royal authorities censored books; spied on suspected heretics, Protestants, and freethinkers; and tortured and executed opponents of state policy.

In the France of Louis XIV, the dynastic state had reached maturity and had begun to display some of its classic characteristics: centralized bureaucracy, royal patronage to enforce allegiance, a system of taxation universally but inequitably applied, and suppression of political opposition either through the use of patronage or if necessary through force. Another important feature was the state's cultivation of the arts and sciences as a means of increasing national power and prestige. Together, these policies enabled the French monarchy to achieve political stability, enforce a uniform system of law, and channel the country's wealth and resources into the service of the state as a whole.

Yet at his death in 1715, Louis XIV left his successors a system of bureaucracy and taxation that was vastly in need of overhaul but was still locked into the traditional social privileges of the church and nobility to an extent that made reform virtually impossible. The pattern of war, excessive taxation of the lower classes, and expenditures that surpassed revenues had severely damaged French finances. Failure to reform the system led to the French Revolution of 1789.

The Growth of Limited Monarchy and Constitutionalism in England

In 1066, William, duke of Normandy and vassal to the French king, had invaded and conquered England, acquiring at a stroke the entire kingdom. In succeeding centuries, English monarchs continued to strengthen central authority and to tighten the bonds of national unity. At the same time, however, certain institutions and traditions evolved—common law, Magna Carta, and Parliament—that checked royal power and protected the rights of the English people.

Central government in England was threatened after the Hundred Years' War (1337–1453), when English aristocrats brought back from France a taste for warfare. In the ensuing civil war—the War of the Roses (1455–1485)—gangs of noblemen with retainers roamed the English countryside, and lawlessness prevailed for a generation. Only in 1485 did the Tudor family emerge triumphant.

The Tudor Achievement

Victory in the civil war allowed Henry VII (1485–1509) to begin the Tudor dynasty. Henry VII's goal was to check the unruly nobility. To this end, he brought commoners into the government. These commoners, unlike the great magnates, could be channeled into royal service because they craved what the king offered: financial rewards and elevated social status. Although they did not fully displace the aristocracy, commoners were brought into Henry VII's inner circle, into the Privy Council, and into the courts. The strength and efficiency of Tudor government were shown during the Reformation, when Henry VIII (1509–1547) made himself head of the English church.

The Protestant Reformation in England was a revolution in royal, as well as ecclesiastical,

Walker Art Gallery, National Museums Liverpool.

HENRY VIII. Although the ruler of a second-rate power, Henry VIII sought to impress upon his subjects that he was a new and powerful monarch. He sought to compete in style, if not in power, with the French and the Spanish kings.

government. It attacked and defeated the main obstacle to monarchical authority: the power of the papacy. However, no change in religious practice could be instituted by the monarchy alone. Parliament's participation in the Reformation gave it a greater role and sense of importance than it had ever possessed in the past.

At Henry VIII's death, the Tudor bureaucracy and centralized government were strained to the utmost, yet they survived. The government weathered the reign of Henry's sickly son Edward VI (1547–1553) and the extreme Protestantism of some of his advisers; it also survived the brief and deeply troubled reign of Henry's first daughter, Mary (1553–1558), who attempted to return England to Catholicism. At Mary's death, England had come dangerously close to the religious instability and sectarian tension that undermined the French kings during the final decades of the sixteenth century.

Henry's second daughter, Elizabeth I, became queen in 1558 and reigned until her death in 1603. The Elizabethan period was characterized by a heightened sense of national identity. The English Reformation enhanced that sense, as did the increasing fear of foreign invasion by Spain. That fear was abated only by the defeat of the Spanish Armada in 1588. In the seventeenth century, the English would look back on Elizabeth's reign as a golden age. It was the calm before the storm: a time when a new commercial class was formed that, in the seventeenth century, would demand a greater say in government operations.

Religion played a vital role in this realignment of political interests and forces. Much of the old aristocracy clung to the Anglicanism of the Henrican Reformation and in some cases to Catholicism. The newly risen gentry found in the Protestant Reformation of Switzerland and Germany a form of religious worship more suited to their independent and entrepreneurial spirit. Many of them embraced Puritanism, the English version of Calvinism.

The English Revolution, 1640–1660 and 1688–1689

The forces threatening established authority were dealt with ineffectively by the first two Stuart kings, James I (1603–1625) and Charles I (1625–1649). Like their Continental counterparts, both believed in royal absolutism, and both preached, through the established church, the doctrine of the divine right of kings. James I angered Parliament by conducting foreign policy without consulting it. The conflict between Parliament and Charles I centered on taxes and religion.

Badly needing funds in order to wage war, Charles I exacted "forced loans" from subjects and imprisoned without a specific charge those

Elizabeth I, Queen of England. (By kind permission of His Grace the Duke of Bedford and the Trustees of the Bedford Estates. Copyright © His Grace the Duke of Bedford and the Trustees of the Bedford Estates/Woburn Enterprises Ltd.)

who would not pay. Fearing that such arbitrary behavior threatened everyone's property and person, Parliament struck back. In 1628, it refused to grant Charles I tax revenues unless he agreed to the Petition of Right, which stated that the king could not collect taxes without Parliament's consent or imprison people without a specific charge. Thus, the monarch had to acknowledge formally the long-established traditions protecting the rights of the English people.

Nevertheless, tensions between the throne and Parliament persisted, and in 1629 Charles I dissolved Parliament, which would not meet again for eleven years. What forced him to reconvene Parliament in 1640 was his need for funds to defend the realm against an invasion from Scotland. The conflict stemmed from Archbishop William Laud's attempt, approved by Charles I, to impose a common prayer book on Scottish Calvinists, or Presbyterians. Infuriated by this effort to impose Anglican liturgy on them, Scottish Presbyterians took up arms. The Long Parliament—so called because it was not disbanded until 1660—abolished the extralegal courts and commissions that had been used by the king to try opponents, provided for regular meetings of Parliament, and strengthened Parliament's control over taxation. When Puritan members pressed to reduce royal authority even more and to strike at the power of the Anglican Church, a deep split occurred in Parliament's ranks: Puritans and all-out supporters of parliamentary supremacy were opposed by Anglicans and supporters of the king. The ensuing civil war was directed by Parliament, financed by taxes and the merchants, and fought by the New Model Army led by Oliver Cromwell (1599–1658), a Puritan squire who gradually realized his potential for leadership.

Parliament's rich supporters financed the New Model Army, gentlemen farmers led it, and religious zealots filled its ranks, along with the usual cross section of poor artisans and day laborers. This army defeated the king, his aristocratic followers, and the Anglican Church's hierarchy. In January 1649, Charles I was publicly executed by order of Parliament. During the interregnum (time between kings), which lasted eleven years, one Parliament after another joined with the army to govern the country as a republic. In the distribution of power between the army and Parliament, Cromwell proved to be a key element. He had the support of the army's officers and some of its rank and file, and he had been a member of Parliament for many years. His control over the army was secured, however, only after its rank and file was purged of radicals, drawn largely from the poor. Some of these radicals wanted to level society, that is, to redistribute property and to give the vote to all male citizens.

Cromwell's death left the country without effective leadership. Parliament, having secured the interests of its constituency (gentry, merchants, and some small landowners), chose to restore court and crown and invited the exiled son of the executed king to return to the kingship. Having learned the lesson his father had spurned, Charles II (1660–1685) never restored royal absolutism.

But Charles's brother, James II (1685–1688), was a foolishly fearless Catholic and admirer of French absolutism. He gathered at his court a coterie of Catholic advisers and supporters of royal prerogative and attempted to bend Parliament and local government to the royal will. James II's Catholicism was the crucial element in his failure. The Anglican Church would not back him, and political forces similar to those that in 1640 had rallied against his father, Charles I, descended on him. The ruling elites, however, had learned their lesson back in the 1650s: civil war would produce social discontent among the masses. The upper classes wanted to avoid open warfare and preserve the monarchy, but as a constitutional authority, not an absolute one. Puritanism, with its sectarian fervor and its dangerous association with republicanism, was allowed to play no part in this second and last phase of the English Revolution.

In early 1688, Anglicans, some aristocrats, and opponents of royal prerogative formed a conspiracy against James II. Their purpose was to invite his son-in-law, William of Orange, stadholder (head) of the Netherlands and husband of James's Protestant daughter Mary, to invade England and rescue its government from James's control. Having lost the loyalty of key men in the army, powerful gentlemen in the counties, and the Anglican Church, James II fled the country, and William and Mary were declared king and queen by act of Parliament.

This bloodless revolution—sometimes called the Glorious Revolution—created a new political and constitutional reality. Parliament secured its rights to assemble regularly and to vote on all matters of taxation; the rights of habeas corpus and trial by jury (for men of property and social status) were also secured. These rights were in turn legitimated in a constitutionally binding document, the Bill of Rights (1689). All Protestants, regardless of their sectarian bias, were granted toleration.

The English Revolution, in both its 1640 and its 1688 phases, secured English parliamentary government and the rule of law. Eventually, the monarchical element in that system would yield to the power and authority of parliamentary ministers and state officials. The Revolution of 1688–1689 was England's last revolution. In the nineteenth and twentieth centuries, parliamentary institutions would be gradually and peacefully reformed to express a more democratic social reality. The events of 1688–1689 have rightly been described as "the year one," for they fashioned a system of government that operated effectively in Britain and could also be transplanted elsewhere with modification. The British system became a model for other forms of representative government, adopted in France and in the former British colonies, beginning with the United States.

The Holy Roman Empire: The Failure to Unify Germany

In contrast to the experience of the French, English, Spanish, and Dutch in the early modern period, the Germans failed to achieve national unity. This failure is tied to the history of the Holy Roman Empire. That union of various distinct Central European territories was created in the tenth century when Otto I, in a deliberate attempt to revive Charlemagne's empire, was crowned emperor of the Romans. Later, the title was changed to Holy Roman Emperor, with the kingdom consisting mainly of German-speaking principalities.

Most medieval Holy Roman Emperors busied themselves not with administering their territories but with attempting to gain control of the rich Italian peninsula and with challenging the rival authority of various popes. In the meantime, the German nobility extended and consolidated their rule over their peasants and over various towns and cities. The feudal aristocracy's power remained a constant obstacle to German unity.

In the medieval and early modern periods, the Holy Roman Emperors were dependent on their most powerful noble lords—including an archbishop or two—because the office of emperor was elective rather than hereditary. German princes, some of whom were electors—for instance, the archbishops of Cologne and Mainz, the Hohenzollern elector of Brandenburg, the landgrave of Hesse, and the duke of Saxony—were fiercely independent. All belonged to the empire, yet all regarded themselves as autonomous powers. These decentralizing tendencies were highly developed by the fifteenth century.

The Hapsburgs had maneuvered themselves into a position from which they could monopolize the imperial elections. The centralizing efforts of the Hapsburg Holy Roman Emperors Maximilian I (1493–1519) and Charles V (1519–1556) were impeded by the Reformation, which bolstered the Germans' already strong propensity for local independence. The German nobility were

0 200 400 Km.
0 200 400 Mi.
Austrian Hapsburg lands
Spanish Hapsburg lands
Prussian lands
German states
Swedish lands
Boundary of Holy Roman Empire
ATLANTIC OCEAN
North Sea
Baltic Sea
English Channel
Mediterranean Sea
Black Sea
SCOTLAND
Edinburgh
IRELAND
Dublin
Durham
ENGLAND
London
NORWAY
SWEDEN
FINLAND
ESTONIA
LIVONIA
RUSSIA
JUTLAND
DENMARK
Copenhagen
SCHLESWIG
Danzig
PRUSSIA
Vilna
MECKLEN-BURG
Hamburg
POMERANIA
BRANDENBURG
Berlin
Warsaw
POLAND
UNITED NETHERLANDS
Amsterdam
Antwerp
SPANISH NETHERLANDS
Cologne
WEST-PHALIA
HESSE
Mainz
Worms
SAXONY
BOHEMIA
Prague
SILESIA
MORAVIA
BAVARIA
Augsburg
Vienna
AUSTRIA
Paris
Nantes
FRANCE
FRANCHE-COMTÉ
SWITZERLAND
Geneva
SAVOY
PIEDMONT
MILAN
GENOA
FLORENCE
PAPAL STATES
Rome
REPUBLIC OF VENICE
TRANSYLVANIA
MOLDAVIA
WALLACHIA
Belgrade
OTTOMAN EMPIRE
PORTUGAL
Lisbon
CASTILE
Madrid
SPAIN
CATALONIA
ARAGON
VALENCIA
ANDALUSIA
Granada
Corsica (to Genoa)
Sardinia
NAPLES
Naples
Palermo
Sicily
Lepanto
Athens
Crete (To Rep. of Venice)

all too ready to use the Reformation as a vindication of their local power, and indeed, Luther made just such an appeal to their interests. War raged in Germany between the Hapsburgs and the Protestant princes, united for mutual protection in the Schmalkaldic League. The Treaty of Augsburg (1555) conferred on every German prince the right to determine the religion of his subjects. The princes retained their power, and a unified German state was never constructed by the Hapsburgs. Religious disunity and the particularism and provinciality of the German nobility prevented its creation.

When an exhausted Emperor Charles V abdicated in 1556, he gave his kingdom to his son Philip and his brother Ferdinand. Philip inherited Spain and its colonies, as well as the Netherlands, and Ferdinand acquired the Austrian territories; two branches of the Hapsburg family were thus formed. Throughout the sixteenth century, the Austrian Hapsburgs barely managed to control the sprawling and deeply divided German territories. However, they never missed an opportunity to further the cause of Catholicism and to strike at the power of the German nobility.

No Hapsburg was ever more fervid in that regard than the Jesuit-trained Archduke Ferdinand II, who ascended the throne in Vienna in 1619. His policies provoked a war within the empire that engulfed the whole of Europe: the Thirty Years' War. It began when the Bohemians, whose anti-Catholic tendencies could be traced back to Jan Hus, tried to put a Protestant king on their throne. The Austrian and Spanish Hapsburgs reacted by sending an army into the kingdom of Bohemia, and suddenly, the whole empire was forced to take sides along religious lines. Bohemia suffered an almost unimaginable devastation; the ravaging Hapsburg army sacked and burned three-fourths of the kingdom's towns and practically exterminated its aristocracy.

Until the 1630s, it looked as if the Hapsburgs would be able to use the war to enhance their power and promote centralization. But the intervention of Protestant Sweden, led by Gustavus Adolphus and encouraged by France, wrecked Hapsburg ambitions. The ensuing military conflict devastated vast areas of Northern and Central Europe. The civilian population suffered untold hardships. Partly because the French finally intervened directly, the Spanish Hapsburgs emerged from the Thirty Years' War with no benefits. The Treaty of Westphalia gave the Austrian Hapsburgs firm control of the eastern states of the kingdom, with Vienna as their capital. Austria took shape as a dynastic state, while the German territories in the empire remained fragmented by the independent interests of the feudal nobility.

◀ *Map 9.1* Europe, 1648 Europe in 1648, exhausted by war.

European Expansion

The emergence of the modern state paralleled the gradual disintegration of traditional medieval socioeconomic forms. Medieval society was divided into three principal groups—clergy, lords, and peasants. It was believed that this hierarchically arranged social order worked best when each social group performed a specific function ordained by God: the clergy led according to God's commands; the aristocracy, guided by the church, defended Christian interests; and the peasants toiled to provide sustenance for themselves and their superiors. The focus was on a social group performing its proper role, the one assigned to it by God and tradition. In early modern times a capitalist market economy arose whose focus was not on the group but on the individual motivated by self-interest. A new European was emerging, striving, assertive, and willing to break with traditional social forms in order to succeed in the market place. The nascent market economy was greatly aided by the expansion of trade and wealth resulting from the voyages of discovery and the conquest and colonization of the New World.

During the period from 1450 to 1750, Western Europe entered an era of overseas exploration and economic expansion that transformed society. European adventurers discovered a new way to reach the rich trading centers of India by sailing around Africa. They also conquered, colonized, and exploited a new world across the Atlantic. These discoveries and conquests brought about an extraordinary increase in business activity and the supply of money, which stimulated the growth of capitalism. People's values changed in ways that were alien and hostile to the medieval outlook. By 1750, the model Christian in northwestern Europe was no longer the selfless saint but the enterprising businessman. The era of secluded manors and walled towns was drawing to a close. A world economy was emerging in which European economic life depended on the market in Eastern spices, African slaves, and American silver. During this age of exploration and commercial expansion, Europe generated a peculiar dynamism unmatched by any other civilization. A process was initiated that by 1900 would give Europe mastery over most of the globe and wide-ranging influence over other civilizations.

Forces Behind the Expansion

A combination of forces propelled Europeans outward and enabled them to dominate Asians, Africans, and American Indians. European monarchs, merchants, and aristocrats fostered expansion for power and profit. As the numbers of the landed classes exceeded the supply of available land, the sons of the aristocracy looked beyond Europe for the lands and fortunes denied them at home. Nor was it unnatural for them to try to gain these things by plunder and conquest; their ancestors had done the same thing for centuries.

Merchants and shippers also had reason to look abroad. Trade between Europe, Africa, and the Orient had gone on for centuries, but always through intermediaries, who increased the costs and decreased the profits on the European end. Gold from the riverbeds of West Africa had been transported across the Sahara by Arab nomads. Spices had been shipped from India and the East Indies by way of Muslim and Venetian merchants. Western European merchants now sought to break those monopolies by going directly to the source: to West Africa for gold, slaves, and pepper, and to India for pepper, spices, and silks.

The centralizing monarchical state was an important factor in the expansion. Monarchs who had successfully established royal hegemony at home, like Ferdinand and Isabella of Spain, sought opportunities to extend their control overseas. From overseas empires came gold, silver, and commerce, which paid for ever more expensive royal government at home and for war against rival dynasties both at home and abroad.

Religion helped in the expansion because the crusading tradition was well established—especially on the Iberian Peninsula, where a five-hundred-year struggle, known as the Reconquest, to drive out the Muslims had taken place. Cortés, the Spanish conqueror of Mexico, for example, saw himself as following in the footsteps of Paladin Roland, the great medieval military hero who had fought to drive back Muslims and pagans. Prince Henry the Navigator (see the next section) hoped that the Portuguese expansion into Africa would serve two purposes: the discovery of gold and the extension of Christianity at the expense of Islam.

Not only did the West have the will to expand, but it also possessed the technology needed for successful expansion, the armed sailing vessel. This asset distinguished the West from China and the lands of Islam and helps explain why the West, rather than Eastern civilizations, launched an age of conquest resulting in global mastery. Not only were sailing ships more maneuverable and faster in the open seas than galleys (ships propelled by oars), but the addition of guns below deck that could fire on and cripple or sink distant enemy ships gave them another tactical advantage. The galleys of the Arabs in the Indian Ocean and the junks of the Chinese were not armed with such guns. In battle, they relied instead on the ancient tactic of coming up alongside the enemy vessel, shearing off its oars, and boarding to fight on deck.

The gunned ship gave the West naval superiority from the beginning. The Portuguese, for example, made short work of the Muslim fleet sent to drive them out of the Indian Ocean in 1509. That victory at Diu, off the western coast of India, indicated that the West not only had found an all-water route to the Orient, but also was there to stay.

The Portuguese Empire

In the first half of the fifteenth century, a younger son of the king of Portugal, named Prince Henry the Navigator (1394–1460) by English writers,

Biblioteca Casanatense, Rome/Photo: Humberto Nicoletti Serra.

The Portuguese in India. A charming watercolor by a Portuguese traveler in India, this painting mixes what to Western eyes was strange and foreign with the more familiar. The elephant, the clothes, and the elaborate parasols held high by turbaned servants may have seemed exotic, but the hunt, the horse, and the hunting dogs had their counterparts in Western European landed society.

sponsored voyages of exploration and the nautical studies needed to undertake them. The Portuguese first expanded into islands in the Atlantic Ocean. In 1420, they began to settle Madeira and farm there, and in the 1430s, they pushed into the Canaries and the Azores in search of new farmlands and slaves for their colonies. In the middle decades of the century, they moved down the West African coast to the mouth of the Congo River and beyond, establishing trading posts as they went.

By the end of the fifteenth century, the Portuguese had developed a viable imperial economy among the ports of West Africa, their Atlantic islands, and Western Europe—an economy based on sugar, black slaves, and gold. Africans panned gold in the riverbeds of central and western Africa, and the Portuguese purchased it at its source.

The Portuguese did not stop in western Africa. By 1488, Bartholomeu Dias had reached the southern tip of the African continent; a decade later, Vasco da Gama sailed around the Cape of Good Hope and across the Indian Ocean to India. By discovering an all-water route to the Orient, Portugal broke the commercial monopoly on Eastern goods that Genoa and Venice had enjoyed. With this route to India and the islands of the East Indies, the Portuguese found the source of the spices needed to make dried, tough meat palatable. As they had done along the African coast, they established fortified trading posts—most notably at Goa on the western coast of India (Malabar) and at Malacca on the Malay Peninsula.

The Spanish Empire

Spain stumbled onto its overseas empire, and it proved to be the biggest and richest of any until the eighteenth century. Christopher Columbus, who believed that he could reach India by sailing west, won the support of Isabella, queen of Castile. But on his first voyage (1492), he landed on a large Caribbean island, which he named Española (Little Spain). Within decades, two events revealed that Columbus had discovered not a new route to the East, but new continents: Vasco Nuñez de Balboa's discovery of the Pacific Ocean at the Isthmus of Panama in 1513, and the circumnavigation of the globe (1519–1521) by the expedition led by Ferdinand Magellan, which sailed through the strait at the tip of South America that now bears Magellan's name.

Stories of the existence of large quantities of gold and silver to the west lured the Spaniards from their initial settlements in the Caribbean to Mexico. In 1519, Hernando Cortés landed on the Mexican coast with a small army; during two years of campaigning, he managed to defeat the native rulers, the Aztecs, and to conquer Mexico for the Spanish crown. A decade later, Francisco Pizarro achieved a similar victory over the mountain empire of the Incas in Peru.

For good reasons, the Mexican and Peruvian conquests became the centers of the Spanish overseas empire. First, there were the gold hoards accumulated over the centuries by the indigenous rulers for religious and ceremonial purposes. When these supplies were exhausted, the Spanish discovered silver at Potos' in Upper Peru in 1545 and at Zacatecas in Mexico a few years later. From the middle of the century, the annual treasure fleets sailing to Spain became the financial bedrock of Philip II's war against the Muslim Turks and the Protestant Dutch and English.

Not only gold and silver lured Spaniards to the New World. The crusading spirit spurred them on as well. The will to conquer and convert the pagan peoples of the New World stemmed from the crusading tradition developed during the five previous centuries of Spanish history in campaigns against the Muslims. The rewards were what they had always been: the propagation of the true faith, service to the crown, and handsome land grants. The land was especially attractive in the sixteenth century, for the number of *hidalgos* (lesser nobility) was increasing with the general rise in population; as a result, the amount of land available to them at home was shrinking.

In the New World, power and land gradually became concentrated in fewer and fewer hands. In particular, royal officials, their associates, and the church gained substantially in wealth and privilege. As recurrent depressions ruined smaller landowners, they were forced to sell out to their bigger neighbors. Upon their conversion to Christianity, the Indians were persuaded to give more and more land to the church. Thus, Spanish America became permanently divided between the privileged elite and the impoverished masses.

The effects of conquest were severe in other ways. Between 1500 and 1600, the number of Native Americans shrank from about twenty million to little more than two million. The major cause of this catastrophe, however, was not forced labor but the diseases introduced from Europe—dysentery, malaria, hookworm, and smallpox—against which the Indians had little or no natural resistance. Beginning in the 1540s, the position of the natives gradually improved as the crown withdrew grants that gave authority over the native population and took increasing responsibility for controlling the Indians.

Black Slavery and the Slave Trade

European settlers caused great suffering for another group: the black slaves originally brought over from West Africa. During the long period of their dominance in North Africa and the Middle East (from the seventh to the nineteenth century), the Muslim states relied on slave labor and slave soldiers from black Africa south of the Sahara. Blacks were captured by Arab slavers and African chiefs and transported across the Sahara to be sold in the slave markets of North Africa. At its height in the eighteenth century, this trans-Saharan trade may have risen to some ten thousand slaves a year.

But this annual traffic was eventually dwarfed by the slave trade between West Africa and the European colonies in the New World, which began in earnest in the early sixteenth century. As Roland Oliver notes, "By the end of the seventeenth century, stimulated by the growth of plantation agriculture in Brazil and the West Indies, Atlantic shipments had increased to about thirty thousand a year, and by the end of the eighteenth century they were nearly eighty thousand."[1]

Captured in raids by African slavers, the victims—with their hands tied behind their backs and necks connected by wooden yokes or chains—marched to the West African coast where they were herded into specially built prisons. These forced marches from the interior, often covering a distance of hundreds of miles, left the trails littered with dead captives. Probably a greater percentage of Africans perished in this journey than in the ocean crossing.

Those accepted for sale were "marked on the breast with a red-hot iron, imprinting the mark of the French, English or Dutch companies so that each nation may distinguish their own property."[2] Across the centuries, some eleven or twelve million blacks in all were exported to the New World. Of these, some 600,000 ended up in the thirteen colonies of British North America, forming the basis of the slave population of the new United States at the end of the American Revolution.

The conditions of the voyage from Africa, the so-called middle passage, were brutal. Crammed into the holds of ships, some 13 to 30 percent of blacks died on board. Upon arrival in the New World, slaves were greased with palm oil to improve their appearance and paraded naked into the auction hall for the benefit of prospective buyers, who paid top prices for "the strongest, youthfullest, and most beautiful."[3] The standard workload for slaves everywhere was ten or eleven hours a day, six days a week. But some distinction must be made between slavery in the American South and elsewhere in the New World. In Brazil and the West Indies, slaves were worked to exhaustion and death and then replaced. Slaves formed a large majority there and were concentrated on very large plantations. Revolts were frequent but were always crushed and savagely punished. In the American South, by contrast, slaves were a minority dispersed over relatively small holdings; large plantations were few. As a result, revolts and deadly epidemics were rare. After 1808, when the United States abolished the external slave trade, slaveholders could not ruthlessly exploit their slaves if they were to meet the growing need for workers caused by the increasing industrial demand for raw cotton. By 1830, the slave population of the southern states rose through natural increase to more than two million, which represented over one-third of all slaves in the New World.

The Atlantic slave trade had grown to such large volume by the eighteenth century because fields and mines had to be worked, but since the native population had been decimated, an enormous labor shortage existed. Black slaves were imported to satisfy the demand. Not only were they plentiful and cheap to maintain, they were also skilled in farming and mining and could withstand tropical heat, insects, and disease, including the infections brought over from Europe to which the Indians had succumbed.

On the African side, how did suppliers continue to meet this growing New World demand? By 1700, guns imported from Europe were now commonly traded for slaves. With the guns, the West African rulers built armies for capturing other peoples to sell to the Europeans while protecting themselves from being enslaved by rival forces. The desire for profit led to the need for more captives to sell for still more firearms to take still more slaves.

The Price Revolution

Linked to overseas expansion was another phenomenon: an unprecedented inflation during the sixteenth century known as the price revolution. For example, cereal prices multiplied by eight times or more in certain regions in the course of that century, and they continued to rise, although more slowly, during the first half of the seventeenth century. Economic historians have generally assumed that the prices of goods other than cereals increased by half as much as grain prices.

Primary Source

Seventeenth-Century Slave Traders: Buying and Transporting Africans

Dealing in slaves was a profitable business that attracted numerous entrepreneurs. The following account was written by a slave trader in the seventeenth century.

As the slaves came down to Fida from the inland country, they are put into a booth, or prison, built for that purpose, near the beach, all of them together; and when the Europeans are to receive them, they are brought out into a large plain, where the surgeons examine every part of every one of them, to the smallest member, men and women being all stark naked. Such as are allowed good and sound, are set on the one side, and the others by themselves; which slaves so rejected are called Mackrons, being above thirty five years of age, or defective in their limbs, eyes or teeth; or grown grey, or that have venereal disease, or any other imperfection. These being so set aside, each of the others, which have passed as good, is marked on the breast, with a red-hot iron, imprinting the mark of the French, English, or Dutch companies, that so each nation may distinguish their own, and to prevent their being chang'd by the natives for worse, as they are apt enough to do. In this particular, care is taken that the women, as tenderest, be not burnt too hard.

The branded slaves, after this, are returned to their former booth, where the factor [agent] is to subsist them at his own charge, which amounts to about two-pence a day for each of them, with bread and water, which is all their allowance. There they continue sometimes ten or fifteen days, till the sea is still enough to send them aboard; . . . and when it is so, the slaves are carried off by parcels, in bar-canoes, and put aboard the ships in the road. Before they enter the canoes, or come out of the booth, their former Black masters strip them of every rag they have, without distinction of men or women. . . .

The Blacks of Fida are so expeditious at this trade of slaves that they can deliver a thousand every month. . . . If there happens to be no stock of slaves at Fida, the factor must trust the Blacks with his goods, to the value of a hundred and fifty, or two hundred slaves; which goods they carry up into the inland, to buy slaves, at all the markets, for above two hundred leagues up the country, where they are kept like cattle [are kept] in Europe; the slaves sold there being generally prisoners of war, taken from their enemies, like other booty, and perhaps some few sold by their own countrymen, in extreme want, or upon a famine; so also some as a punishment of heinous crimes: tho' many Europeans believe their parent sell their own children, men their wives and relations, which, if it ever happens, is so seldom, that it cannot justly be charged upon a whole nation, as a custom and common practice.

Questions for Analysis

1. How, why, and by whom are the slaves branded?
2. Who are those called "Black masters," and what role do they play in the slave trade?
3. Where do the slaves come from, and how do they initially come to be enslaved?

Elizabeth Donnan, ed., *Documents Illustrative of the Slave Trade*, 293–294.

The main cause of the price revolution was the population growth during the late fifteenth and sixteenth centuries. The population of Europe almost doubled between 1460 and 1620. Until the middle of the seventeenth century, the number of mouths to feed outran the capacity of agriculture to supply basic foodstuffs, causing the vast majority of people to live close to subsistence. Until food production could catch up with the increasing population, prices, especially those of the staple food, bread, continued to rise.

The other principal cause of the price revolution was probably the silver that flowed into Europe from the New World via Spain, beginning in 1552. At some point, the influx of silver may have exceeded the necessary expansion of the money supply and may have begun contributing to the inflation. A key factor in the price revolution, then, was too many people with too much money chasing too few goods. The effects of the price revolution were momentous for the European economy.

The Expansion of Agriculture

The price revolution had its greatest effect on farming. Food prices, which rose roughly twice as much as the prices of other goods, spurred ambitious farmers to take advantage of the situation and to produce for the expanding market. The opportunity for profit drove some farmers to work harder and manage their land better.

All over Europe, landlords held their properties in the form of manors. A particular type of rural society and economy had evolved on these manors in the Late Middle Ages. By the fifteenth century, much manor land was held by peasant tenants according to the terms of a tenure known in England as *copyhold*. The tenants had certain hereditary rights to the land in return for the performance of certain services and the payment of certain fees to the landlord. Principal among these rights was the use of the commons—the pasture, woods, and pond. For the copyholder, access to the commons often made the difference between subsistence and real want because the land tilled on the manor might not produce enough to support a family. Arable land was worked according to ancient custom. The land was divided into strips, and each peasant of the manor was traditionally assigned a certain number of strips. This whole pattern of peasant tillage and rights in the commons was known as the *open-field system*. After changing little for centuries, it was met head-on by the incentives generated by the price revolution.

In England, landlords aggressively pursued the possibilities for profit resulting from the inflation of farm prices. This pursuit required far-reaching changes in ancient manorial agriculture—changes that are called *enclosure*. The open-field system was geared to providing subsistence for the local village and, as such, prevented large-scale farming for a distant market. In the open-field system, the commons could not be diverted to the production of crops for sale. Moreover, the division of the arable land into strips reserved for each peasant made it difficult to engage in profitable commercial agriculture.

English landlords in the sixteenth century launched a two-pronged attack against the open-field system in an effort to transform their holdings into market-oriented, commercial ventures. First they denied their tenant peasantry the use of the commons, depriving poor tenants of critically needed produce; then they changed the conditions of tenure from copyhold to leasehold. Whereas copyhold was heritable and fixed, leasehold was not. When a lease came up for renewal, the landlord could raise the rent beyond the tenant's capacity to pay. Both acts of the landlord forced peasants off the manor or into the landlord's employ as farm laborers. With tenants gone, fields could be incorporated into larger, more productive units. Landlords could hire labor at bargain prices because of the swelling population and the large supply of peasants forced off the land by enclosure. Subsistence farming gave way to commercial agriculture: the growing of a surplus for the marketplace. But rural poverty increased because of the mass evictions of tenant farmers.

In the fifteenth and sixteenth centuries, the Dutch developed a new kind of farming known as *convertible husbandry* that also expanded production. This farming system employed a series of innovations, including the use of soil-restoring legumes, that replaced the old three-field system of crop rotation, which had left one-third of the land unused at any given time. The new techniques used all the land every year and provided a more diversified agriculture.

Indian Workers Mining for Gold, Overseen by Their Spanish Conquerors. The Spanish conquest of the Indians in Latin America filled the coffers of Spain with gold and silver. The native population was decimated, largely by disease, and most native artifacts were destroyed, regarded by the Europeans as heathen work and beneath their consideration. (Gold Mining, from "Santo Domingo Past and Present" by Samuel Hazard, pub. 1873 (engraving), Bry, Theodore de (1528–98) (after)/Private Collection/The Bridgeman Art Library International.)

The Expansion of Trade and Industry

The conditions of the price revolution also caused trade and industry to expand. Population growth that exceeded the capacity of local food supplies stimulated commerce in basic foodstuffs—for example, the Baltic trade with Western Europe. Equally important as a stimulus to trade and industry was the growing income of landlords, merchants, and, in some instances, peasants. This income created a rising demand for consumer goods. Another factor in commercial and industrial expansion was the growth of the state. With increasing amounts of tax revenue to spend, the expanding monarchies of the sixteenth and seventeenth centuries bought more and more supplies—ships, weapons, uniforms, paper—and so spurred economic expansion.

Innovations in Business

Markets tended to shift from local to regional or even to international—a condition that gave rise to the merchant capitalist. The merchant capitalists' operations, unlike those of local producers, extended across local and national boundaries. An essential feature of merchant capitalism was the *putting-out system* of production. The manufacture of woolen textiles is a good example of how the system worked. The merchant capitalist would buy the raw wool from English landlords, who had enclosed their manors to take advantage of the rising price of wool. The merchant's agents collected the wool and took it (put it out) to nearby villages for spinning, dyeing, and weaving. The work was done in the cottages of peasants, many of whom had been evicted from the surrounding manors as a result of enclosure and therefore had to take what work they could get at very low wages. When the wool had been processed into cloth, it was picked up and shipped to market.

A cluster of other innovations in business life accompanied the emergence of the merchant capitalist and the putting-out system. Some of these innovations had roots in the Middle Ages and were important in the evolution of the modern capitalist economy. Banking operations grew more sophisticated, making it possible for depositors to pay their debts by issuing written orders to their banks to make transfers to their creditors' accounts—the origins of the modern check. Accounting methods also improved. The widespread use of double-entry bookkeeping made errors immediately evident and gave a clear picture of the financial position of a commercial enterprise. Very important to overseas expansion was a new form of business enterprise known as the joint-stock company, which allowed small investors to buy shares in a venture. These companies made possible the accumulation of the large amounts of capital needed for large-scale operations, like the building and deployment of merchant fleets, that were quite beyond the resources of one person.

Different Patterns of Commercial Development

England and the Netherlands. In both England and the United Provinces (the Netherlands), the favorable conditions led to large-scale commercial expansion. In the 1590s, the Dutch devised a new ship, the *fluit* or flyboat, to handle bulky grain shipments at the lowest possible cost. This innovation allowed them to capture the Baltic trade, which became a principal source of their phenomenal commercial expansion between 1560 and 1660.

Equally dramatic was their commercial penetration of the Orient. Profits from the European carrying trade built the ships that allowed the Dutch first to challenge and then to displace the Portuguese in the spice trade with the East Indies during the early seventeenth century. The Dutch chartered the United East India Company in 1602 and established trading posts in the islands, which were the beginnings of a Dutch empire that lasted until World War II.

The English traded throughout Europe in the sixteenth and seventeenth centuries, especially with Spain and the Netherlands. The seventeenth century saw the foundation of a British colonial empire along the Atlantic seaboard in North America, from Maine to the Carolinas, and in the West Indies, where the English managed to dislodge the Spanish in some places.

In both England and the Netherlands, government promoted the interests of business. Political power in the Netherlands passed increasingly into the hands of an urban patriciate of merchants and manufacturers, based in cities like Delft, Haarlem, and especially Amsterdam. There, urban interests pursued public policies that served their pocketbooks. In England, because of the revolutionary transfer of power from the king to Parliament, economic policies also reflected the interests of big business, whether agricultural or commercial. Enclosure, for example, was abetted by parliamentary enactment. The Bank of England, founded in 1694, expanded credit and increased business confidence. The Navigation Acts, which proved troublesome to American colonists, placed restrictions on colonial trade and manufacturing in order to prevent competition with English merchants and manufacturers.

France and Spain. France benefited from commercial and industrial expansion, but not to the same degree as England, mainly because of the aristocratic structure of French society. Family

View of a Sixteenth-Century Marketplace. Market towns were growing all over Western Europe after 1500. The increasing population made for brisk business in the marketplace. Note the ships in the harbor, the churches, and the variety of products available to those who could afford them.

ties and social intercourse between the aristocracy and the merchants, like those that developed in England, were much less common in France. Consequently, the French aristocracy remained contemptuous of commerce. Also inhibiting economic expansion were the guilds—remnants of the Middle Ages that restricted competition and production. In France, there was relatively less room than in England for the merchant capitalist operating outside the guild structures.

Spain presents an even clearer example of the failure to grasp the opportunities afforded by the price revolution. By the third quarter of the sixteenth century, Spain possessed the makings of economic expansion: unrivaled amounts of capital in the form of silver, a large and growing population, rising consumer demand, and a vast overseas empire. These factors did not bear fruit because the Spanish value system regarded business as social heresy. The Spanish held in high esteem gentlemen who possessed land gained through military service and crusading ardor, which enabled them to live on rents and privileges. Commerce and industry remained contemptible pursuits.

Numerous wars in the sixteenth century (with France, the Lutheran princes, the Ottoman Turks, the Dutch, and the English) put an increasing strain on the Spanish treasury, despite the annual shipments of silver from the New World. Spain spent its resources on maintaining and extending its imperial power and Catholicism, rather than on investing in economic expansion. In the end, the wars cost more than Spain could handle. The Dutch for a time and the English and the French for a much longer period displaced Spain as the great power. The English and the Dutch had taken advantage of the opportunities presented by the price revolution; the Spanish had not.

akg-images/Joseph Martin.

PEASANT FESTIVAL, **1640, BY DAVID TENIERS THE YOUNGER (1610–1690).** This scene depicts peasant revelry—the rural village at play. The common folk are eating, drinking, and dancing outside what looks like a country tavern. Hardworking farmworkers no doubt deserved their day off. Notice in the lower left of the picture a small group of gentry who owned the land on which the peasants worked. Such landlords indulged the peasants in their merrymaking, but warily and only up to a point because they feared the possibility of a riot and popular rebellion.

THE FOSTERING OF MERCANTILE CAPITALISM

The changes described—especially in England and the Netherlands—represent a crucial stage in the development of the modern economic system known as *capitalism*. This is a system of *private enterprise*: the main economic decisions (what, how much, where, and at what price to produce, buy, and sell) are made by private individuals in their capacity as owners, workers, or consumers.

From 1450 to 1600, several conditions sustained the incentive to invest and reinvest—a basic factor in the emergence of modern capitalism. One was the price revolution stemming from a supply of basic commodities that could not keep pace with rising demand. Prices continued to climb, creating the most powerful incentive of all to invest rather than to consume. Why spend now, those with surplus wealth must have asked, when investment in commercial farming, mining, shipping, and publishing (to name a few important outlets) is almost certain to yield greater wealth in the future?

Additional stimuli for investment came from governments. Governments acted as giant consumers, and throughout the early modern period their appetites were expanding. Merchants who supplied governments with everything from guns to frescoes not only prospered but reinvested as well because of the constancy and growth of government demand. Governments also sponsored new forms of investment, whether to supply the debauched taste for new luxuries at the king's court or to meet the requirements of the military. Moreover, private investors reaped incalculable advantages from overseas empires. Colonies supplied cheap raw materials and cheap (slave) labor and served as markets for exports. They greatly stimulated the construction of both ships and harbor facilities and the sale of insurance.

State policies, known as *mercantilism*, were also aimed at augmenting national wealth and power. According to mercantilist theory, wealth from trade was measured in gold and silver, of which there was believed to be a more or less fixed quantity. The state's goal in international trade became to sell more abroad than it bought, that is, to establish a favorable balance of payments. When the amount received for sales abroad was greater than that spent for purchases, the difference would be an influx of precious metal into the state. By this logic, mercantilists were led to argue for the goal of national sufficiency: a country should try to supply most of its own needs to keep imports to a minimum.

To fuel the national economy, governments subsidized new industries, chartered companies to engage in overseas trade, and broke down local trade barriers, such as guild regulations and internal tariffs. The price revolution, the concentration of wealth in private hands, and government activity combined to provide the foundation for sustained investment and for the emergence of mercantile capitalism. This new force in the world should not be confused with industrial capitalism. The latter evolved with the Industrial Revolution in eighteenth-century England, but mercantile capitalism paved the way for it.

Toward a Global Economy

The transformations considered in this chapter were among the most movements in world history. In an unprecedented development, one small part of the world, Western Europe, had become the lord of the sea-lanes, the master of many lands throughout the globe, and the banker and profit taker in an emerging world economy. Western Europe's global hegemony was to last well into the twentieth century. In conquering and settling new lands, Europeans exported Western culture around the globe, a process that accelerated in the twentieth century.

The effects of overseas expansion were profound. The native populations of the New World were decimated largely because of disease. As a result of the labor shortage, millions of blacks were imported from Africa to work as slaves on plantations and in mines. Black slavery would produce large-scale effects on culture, politics, and society that have lasted to the present day.

The widespread circulation of plant and animal life also had great consequences. Horses and cattle were introduced into the New World. (So amazed were the Aztecs to see men on horseback that at first they thought horse and rider were one demonic creature.) In return, the Old World acquired such novelties as corn, the tomato, and, most important, the potato, which was to become a staple of the Northern European diet. Manioc, from which tapioca is made, was transplanted from the New World to Africa, where it helped sustain the population.

Western Europe was wrenched out of the subsistence economy of the Middle Ages and launched on a course of sustained economic growth. This transformation resulted from the grafting of traditional forms, such as primogeniture—the system of inheritance by the eldest son—and holy war, onto new forces, such as global exploration, price revolution, and convertible husbandry. Out of this change emerged the beginnings of a new economic system, mercantile capitalism. This system, in large measure, paved the way for the Industrial Revolution of the eighteenth and nineteenth centuries and provided the economic thrust for European world predominance.

❖ ❖ ❖

Notes

1. Roland Oliver, *The African Experience* (New York: HarperCollins, 1991), p. 123.
2. Quoted in Basil Davidson, *Africa in History* (New York: Collier Books, 1991), p. 215.
3. Quoted in Richard S. Dunn, *Sugar and Slaves* (Chapel Hill: University of North Carolina Press, 1972), p. 248.

Suggested Reading

Cipolla, Carlo M., *Guns, Sails and Empires* (1965). Connections between technological innovation and overseas expansion, 1400 to 1700.

Davis, David Brion, *The Problem of Slavery in Western Culture* (1966). An authoritative study.

Davis, Ralph, *The Rise of the Atlantic Economies* (1973). A reliable survey of early modern economic history.

Dor Ner, Zvi, *Columbus and the Age of Discovery* (1991). Companion volume to the seven-part PBS series; lavishly illustrated.

Duplessis, Robert S., *Transitions to Capitalism in Early Modern Europe* (1997). A useful overview of a long period, 1450 to 1800.

Elliot, John H., *Empires of the Atlantic World: Britain and Spain in America 1492–1830* (2007). Wide-ranging and well informed.

Horton, James Oliver and Lois E. Horton, *Slavery and the Making of America* (2004). A rich tapestry of incident and insight.

Koenigsberger, H. G., *Monarchies, States, Generals, and Parliaments* (2001). An excellent survey of the various forms of early modern government.

Kolchin, Peter, *American Slavery: 1619–1877* (1993). An informed synthesis.

Parker, Geoffrey, *The Military Revolution: Military Innovation and the Rise of the West* (1988). Sweeping coverage of an important topic.

Parry, J. H., *The Age of Reconnaissance* (1963). A short survey of exploration.

Plumb, J. H., *The Growth of Political Stability in England, 1675–1725* (1967). A basic book, clear and readable.

Sharpe, J. A., *Early Modern England*, 2nd ed., (1997). A readable overview.

Shennan, J. H., *The Origins of the Modern European State* (1974). An excellent brief introduction.

CourseMate

Go to the CourseMate website at **www.cengagebrain.com** for additional study tools and review materials—including audio and video clips—for this chapter.

Chapter 10

Intellectual Transformation: The Scientific Revolution and the Age of Enlightenment

- **The Medieval View of the Universe**
- **A New View of Nature**
- **The Newtonian Synthesis**
- **Prophets of Modern Science**
- **The Meaning of the Scientific Revolution**
- **The Age of Enlightenment: Affirmation of Reason and Freedom**
- **Christianity Assailed: The Search for a Natural Religion**
- **Political Thought**
- **Social and Economic Thought**
- **Conflicts and Politics**
- **The Enlightenment and the Modern Mentality**

Focus Questions

1. How did the Scientific Revolution transform the medieval view of the universe?
2. How did the Scientific Revolution contribute to the shaping of the modern mentality?
3. What were the essential concerns of the philosophes of the Enlightenment?
4. How did the Enlightenment contribute to the shaping of the modern mentality?

The movement toward modernity initiated by the Renaissance was greatly advanced by the Scientific Revolution of the seventeenth century. The Scientific Revolution destroyed the medieval view of the universe and established the scientific method—rigorous and systematic observation and experimentation—as the essential means of unlocking nature's secrets. Increasingly, Western thinkers maintained that nature was a mechanical system governed by laws that could be expressed mathematically. The new discoveries electrified the imagination. Science displaced theology as the queen of knowledge, and reason, which had been subordinate to religion in the Middle Ages, asserted its autonomy. The great confidence in reason inspired by the Scientific Revolution helped give rise to the Enlightenment, which explicitly rejected the ideas and institutions of the medieval past and articulated the essential norms of modernity. ❖

The Medieval View of the Universe

Medieval thinkers had constructed a coherent picture of the universe that blended the theories of two ancient Greeks, Aristotle and Ptolemy of Alexandria, with Christian teachings.* To the medieval mind, the cosmos was a giant ladder, a qualitative order, ascending toward heaven. God was at the summit of this hierarchical universe, and the earth, base and vile, was at the bottom, just above hell. It was also the center of the universe. In the medieval view, the earth's central location meant that the universe centered on human beings, that by God's design, human beings—the only creatures on whom God had bestowed reason and the promise of salvation—were lords of the earth. Around the stationary earth revolved seven transparent spheres, each of which carried one of the "planets"—the moon, Mercury, Venus, the sun, Mars, Jupiter, and Saturn. (Since the earth did not move, it was not considered a planet.) The eighth sphere, in which the stars were embedded, also revolved about the earth. Beyond the stars was a heavenly sphere, the prime mover, that imparted motion to the planets and the stars, so that in one day the entire celestial system turned around the stationary earth. Enclosing the entire system was another heavenly sphere, the Empyrean, where God sat on his throne, attended by angels.

Medieval thinkers inherited Aristotle's view of a qualitative universe. Earthly objects were composed of earth, water, air, and fire, whereas celestial objects, belonging to a higher world, were composed of ether or quintessence—an element too pure and perfect to be found on earth, which consisted of base matter. In contrast to earthly objects, heavenly bodies were incorruptible; that is, they experienced no change. Since the quintessential heavens differed totally from earth, the paths of planets could not follow the same laws that governed the motion of earthly objects. This two-world orientation blended well with the Christian outlook.

Like Aristotle, Ptolemy held that planets moved around the earth in perfect circular orbits and at uniform speeds. However, in reality, the path of planets is not a circle but an ellipse, and planets do not move at uniform speed but accelerate as they approach the sun. Therefore, problems arose that required Ptolemy to incorporate into his system certain ingenious devices that earlier Greek astronomers had employed. For example, to save the appearance of circular orbits, Ptolemy made use of epicycles, small circles attached to the rims of larger circles. A planet revolved uniformly around the small circle, the epicycle, which in turn revolved about the earth in a larger circle. If one ascribed a sufficient number of epicycles to a planet, the planet could seem to move in a perfectly circular orbit.

The Aristotelian–Ptolemaic model of the cosmos did appear to accord with common sense and raw perception: the earth does indeed seem and feel to be at rest. And the validity of this view seemed to be confirmed by evidence, for the model enabled thinkers to predict with considerable accuracy the movement and location of celestial bodies and the passage of time. This geocentric model and the division of the universe into higher and lower worlds also accorded with passages in Scripture. Scholastic philosophers harmonized Aristotelian and Ptolemaic science with Christian theology, producing an intellectually and emotionally

*See also Chapter 7.

Chronology 10.1 ❖ The Scientific Revolution and the Enlightenment

1543	Publication of Copernicus's *On the Revolutions of the Heavenly Spheres* marks the beginning of modern astronomy
1605	Publication of Bacon's *Advancement of Learning*
1610	Publication of Galileo's *The Starry Messenger*, asserting the uniformity of nature
1632	Galileo's teachings are condemned by the church, and he is placed under house arrest
1687	Publication of Newton's *Principia Mathematica*
1690	Publication of Locke's *Two Treatises of Government*
1733	Publication of Voltaire's *Letters Concerning the English Nation*
1751–1765	Publication of the *Encyclopedia*, edited by Diderot
1776	Declaration of Independence
1789	French Revolution begins

satisfying picture of the universe in which everything was arranged according to a divine plan.

A New View of Nature

In several ways, the Renaissance contributed to the Scientific Revolution. The revival of interest in antiquity during the Renaissance led to the rediscovery of some ancient scientific texts, including the works of Archimedes (287–212 B.C.), which fostered new ideas in mechanics, and to improved translations of the medical works of Galen, a contemporary of Ptolemy, which stimulated the study of anatomy. Renaissance art, too, was a factor in the rise of modern science, for it linked an exact representation of the human body to mathematical proportions and demanded accurate observation of natural phenomena. By defining visual space and the relationship between the object and the observer in mathematical terms and by delineating the natural world with unprecedented scientific precision, Renaissance art helped to promote a new view of nature, which later found expression in the astronomy of Copernicus and Kepler and the physics of Galileo.

The Renaissance revival of ancient Pythagorean and Platonic ideas, which stressed mathematics as the key to comprehending reality, also contributed to the Scientific Revolution. Extending the mathematical harmony found in music to the universe at large, Pythagoras (c. 580–507 B.C.) and his followers believed that reality consists fundamentally of numerical relations, which the mind can grasp. Plato maintained that beyond the world of everyday objects made known to us through the senses lies a higher reality, the world of Forms, which contains an inherent mathematical order apprehended only by thought. The great thinkers of the Scientific Revolution were influenced by these ancient ideas of nature as a harmonious mathematical system knowable to the mind.

Nicolaus Copernicus: The Dethronement of the Earth

Modern astronomy begins with Nicolaus Copernicus (1473–1543), a Polish astronomer, mathematician, and church canon. He proclaimed that earth is a planet that orbits a centrally located

TRIAL OF GALILEO. Tried by the Roman Inquisition for ignoring their demand to stop supporting the Copernican Theory, Galileo, fearful of a death sentence, declared that the earth did not circle the sun.

sun together with the other planets. This heliocentric theory served as the kernel of a new world picture that eventually supplanted the medieval view of the universe. Copernicus did not base his heliocentric theory on new observations and new data. What led him to remove the earth from the center of the universe was the complexity and cumbersomeness of the Ptolemaic system, which offended his sense of mathematical order. To Copernicus, the numerous epicycles (the number had been increased since Ptolemy, making the model even more cumbersome) violated the Platonic vision of the mathematical symmetry of the universe.

Concerned that his theories would spark a controversy, Copernicus refused to publish his work, but, persuaded by his friends, he finally relented. His masterpiece, *On the Revolutions of the Heavenly Spheres*, appeared in 1543. As Copernicus had feared, his views did stir up controversy, but the new astronomy did not become a passionate issue until the early seventeenth century, more than fifty years after the publication of *On the Revolutions*. The Copernican theory frightened clerical authorities, who controlled the universities as well as the pulpits, for it seemed to conflict with Scripture. For example, Psalm 93 says: "Yea, the world is established, that it cannot be moved." And Psalm 103 says that God "fixed the earth upon its foundation not to be moved forever." In 1616, the church placed *On the Revolutions* and all other works that ascribed motion to the earth on the Index of Prohibited Books.

Galileo: Uniformity of Nature and Experimental Physics

Galileo Galilei (1564–1642) is the principal reason that the seventeenth century has been called "the century of genius." A Pisan by birth, Galileo was a talented musician and artist and a cultivated humanist; he knew and loved the Latin classics and Italian poetry. He was also an astronomer and physicist who helped shatter the medieval conception of the cosmos and shape the modern scientific outlook. Galileo was indebted to the Platonic tradition, which tried to grasp the mathematical harmony of the universe, and to Archimedes, the Hellenistic mathematician-engineer who had sought a geometric understanding of space and motion.

Galileo rejected the medieval division of the universe into higher and lower realms and proclaimed the modern idea of nature's uniformity. Learning that a telescope had been invented in Holland, Galileo built one for himself and used it to investigate the heavens—the first person to do so. From his observations of the moon, Galileo concluded

> *that the surface of the moon is not smooth, uniform, and precisely spherical as a great number of philosophers believe it (and the other heavenly bodies) to be, but is uneven, rough, and full of cavities and prominences, being not unlike the face of the earth, relieved by chains of mountains and deep valleys.*[1]

This discovery of the moon's craters and mountains and of spots on the supposedly unblemished sun led Galileo to break with the Aristotelian notion that celestial bodies were pure, perfect, and unchangeable. For Galileo, there was no difference in quality between celestial and terrestrial bodies. Nature was not a hierarchical order, in which physical entities were ranked according to their inherent quality; rather, it was a homogeneous system, the same throughout.

With his telescope, Galileo discovered the four moons that orbit Jupiter, an observation that overcame a principal objection to the Copernican system. Galileo showed that a celestial body could indeed move around a center other than the earth, that the earth was not the common center for all celestial bodies, and that a celestial body (the earth's moon or Jupiter's moons) could orbit a planet at the same time that the planet revolved around another body (the sun).

Galileo also pioneered in experimental physics and advanced the modern idea that knowledge of motion should be derived from direct observation and from mathematics. In dealing with problems of motion, he insisted on applying mathematics to the study of moving bodies and did in fact study acceleration by performing experiments, which required careful mathematical measurement. For Aristotelian scholastics, a rock fell because it was striving to reach its proper place in the universe, thereby fulfilling its nature; it was acting in accordance with the purpose God had assigned it. Galileo completely rejected the view that motion is due to a quality inherent in an object. Rather, he said, motion is the relationship of bodies to time and distance. By holding that bodies fall according to uniform and quantifiable laws, Galileo posited an entirely different conceptual system. This system requires that we study angles and distances and search for mathematical ratios but avoid inquiring into an object's quality and purpose—the role God assigned it in a hierarchical universe. Moreover, Galileo's physics implied that celestial objects, which hitherto had belonged to a separate and higher realm, were subject to the same laws that governed terrestrial motion—another sign of nature's uniformity. The traditional belief in a sharp distinction between heavenly and earthly realms was weakened by both Galileo's telescopic observations of the moon and by his mechanistic physics.

For Galileo, the universe was a "grand book which . . . is written in the language of mathematics and its characters are triangles, circles, and other geometric figures without which it is humanly impossible to understand a single word of it."[2] In the tradition of Plato, Galileo sought to grasp the mathematical principles governing reality—reality was physical nature itself, not Plato's higher realm, of which nature was only a poor copy—and ascribed to mathematics absolute authority. Like Copernicus and Kepler (discussed later in this chapter), he believed that mathematics expresses the harmony and beauty of God's creation.

Attack on Authority

Insisting that physical truth is arrived at through observation, experimentation, and reason, Galileo strongly denounced reliance on authority. Scholastic thinkers, who dominated the universities, regarded Aristotle as the supreme authority on questions concerning nature, and university education was based on his works. These doctrinaire Aristotelians angered Galileo, who protested that they sought truth not by opening their eyes to nature and new knowledge but by slavishly relying on ancient texts. In *Dialogue Concerning the Two Chief World Systems—Ptolemaic and Copernican* (1632), Galileo upheld the Copernican view and attacked the unquestioning acceptance of Aristotle's teachings.

Galileo also criticized Roman Catholic authorities for attempting to suppress the Copernican theory. He argued that passages from the Bible had no authority in questions involving nature.

A sincere Christian, Galileo never intended to use the new science to undermine faith. What he desired was to separate science from faith so that reason and experience alone would be the deciding factors on questions involving nature. He could not believe that "God who has endowed us with senses, reason and intellect"[3] did not wish us to use these faculties in order to acquire knowledge. He was certain that science was compatible with Scripture rightly understood, that is, allowing for the metaphorical language of Scripture and its disinterest in conveying scientific knowledge. For Galileo, the aim of Scripture was to teach people the truths necessary for salvation, not to instruct them in the operations of nature, which is the task of science.

Galileo's support of Copernicus aroused the ire of both scholastic philosophers and the clergy, who feared that the brash scientist threatened a world picture that had the support of venerable ancient authorities, Holy Writ, and scholastic tradition. Already traumatized by the Protestant threat, Catholic officials cringed at ideas that might undermine traditional belief and authority.

In 1616, the Congregation of the Index, the church's censorship organ, condemned the teaching of Copernicanism. In 1633, the aging and infirm Galileo was summoned to Rome. Tried and condemned by the Inquisition, he was ordered to abjure the Copernican theory. Not wishing to bring harm to himself and certain that the truth would eventually prevail, Galileo bowed to the Inquisition. He was sentenced to life imprisonment—mostly house arrest at his own villa near Florence—the *Dialogue* was banned, and he was forbidden to write on Copernicanism. Not until 1820 did the church lift the ban on Copernicanism.

Johannes Kepler: Laws of Planetary Motion

Johannes Kepler (1571–1630), a German mathematician and astronomer, combined the Pythagorean-Platonic quest to comprehend the mathematical harmony within nature with a deep commitment to Lutheran Christianity. He contended that God gave human beings the ability to understand the laws of harmony and proportion.

As a true Pythagorean, Kepler yearned to discover the geometric harmony of the planets—what he called the "music of the spheres." Such knowledge, he believed, would provide supreme insight into God's mind. No doubt this mystical quality sparked the creative potential of his imagination, but to be harnessed for science, it had to be disciplined by the rational faculties.

Kepler discovered the three basic laws of planetary motion, which shattered the Ptolemaic cosmology. In doing so, he utilized the data collected by Tycho Brahe, a Danish astronomer, who for twenty years had systematically observed the planets and stars and recorded their positions with far greater accuracy than had ever been done. Kepler sought to fit Tycho's observations into Copernicus's heliocentric model.

Kepler's first law demonstrated that planets move in elliptical orbits—not circular ones, as Aristotle and Ptolemy (and Copernicus) had believed—and that the sun is one focus of the ellipse. This discovery that a planet's path was one simple oval eliminated all the epicycles that had been used to preserve the appearance of circular motion. Kepler's second law showed that planets do not move at uniform speed, as had been believed, but accelerate as they near the sun, and he provided the rule for deciphering a planet's speed at each point in its orbit. His third law

Image Select/Art Resource, N.Y.

Sir Isaac Newton. Newton was a cautious experimentalist, whose discovery of the composition of light laid the foundation of the science of optics.

drew a mathematical relationship between the time it takes a planet to complete its orbit of the sun and its average distance from the sun. On the basis of these laws, one could calculate accurately a planet's position and velocity at a particular time—another indication that the planets were linked together in a unified mathematical system.

Derived from carefully observed facts, Kepler's laws of planetary motion buttressed Copernicanism, for they made sense only in a heliocentric universe. But why did the planets move in elliptical orbits? Why did they not fly off into space or crash into the sun? To these questions Kepler had no satisfactory answers. It was Isaac Newton (1642–1727), the great British mathematician-scientist, who arrived at a celestial mechanics that linked the astronomy of Copernicus and Kepler with the physics of Galileo and accounted for the behavior of planets.

The Newtonian Synthesis

The publication in 1687 of Isaac Newton's *Mathematical Principles of Natural Philosophy* marks the climax of the Scientific Revolution. Newton postulated three laws of motion that joined all celestial and terrestrial objects into a vast mechanical system, whose parts worked in perfect harmony and whose connections could be expressed in mathematical terms, and he invented calculus, which facilitated the expression of physical laws in mathematical equations. Since Copernican astronomy was essential to his all-encompassing theory of the universe, Newton provided mathematical proof for the heliocentric system, and opposition to it dissipated.

Newton's first law is the principle of inertia: that a body at rest remains at rest unless acted on by a force and that a body in rectilinear motion continues to move in a straight line at the same velocity unless a force acts on it. A moving body does not require a force to keep it in motion, as ancient and medieval thinkers had believed. Once started, bodies continue to move; motion is as natural a condition as rest. Newton's second law states that a given force produces a measurable change in a body's velocity; a body's change of velocity is proportional to the force acting on it. Newton's third law holds that for every action or force there is an equal and opposite reaction or force. The sun pulls the earth with the same force that the earth exercises on the sun. An apple falling to the ground is being pulled by the earth, but the apple is also pulling the earth toward it. (However, since the mass of the apple is so small in comparison with that of the earth, the force that the apple exercises on the earth causes no visible change in the earth's motion.)

Newton asserted that the same laws of motion and gravitation that operate in the celestial world also govern the movement of earthly bodies. Ordinary mechanical laws explain both why apples fall to the ground and why planets orbit the sun. Both the planet and the apple are subject to the same force, and the very same mathematical formula describes the sun's action on a planet and the earth's pull on an apple. Newtonian physics ended the medieval division of the cosmos into higher and lower worlds, with different laws operating in each realm. The universe is an integrated, harmonious mechanical system held together by the force of gravity. By demonstrating that the universe contains an inherent mathematical order, Newton realized the Pythagorean and Platonic visions. To his contemporaries, it seemed that Newton had unraveled all of nature's mysteries: the universe was fully explicable. It was as if Newton had penetrated God's mind.

Deeply committed to Anglican Christianity, Newton retained a central place for God in his world system. God for him was the grand architect whose wisdom and skill accounted for nature's magnificent clockwork design. Newton also believed that God periodically intervened in his creation to restore energy to the cosmic system and that there was no conflict between divine miracles and a mechanical universe. However, in future generations, thinkers called deists (see the upcoming section "Christianity Assailed: The Search for a Natural Religion") came to regard miracles as incompatible with a universe governed by impersonal mechanical principles.

With his discovery of the composition of light, Newton also laid the foundation of the science of optics. He was a cautious experimentalist who valued experimental procedures, including drawing appropriate conclusions from accumulated data. Both Newton's mechanical universe and his championing of the experimental method were basic premises of the Age of Enlightenment.

Prophets of Modern Science

The accomplishments of the Scientific Revolution extended beyond the creation of a new model of the universe. They also included the formulation of a new method of inquiry into nature and the recognition that science could serve humanity. Two thinkers instrumental in articulating the implications of the Scientific Revolution were Francis Bacon and René Descartes. Both repudiated the authority of Aristotle and other ancients in scientific matters and urged the adoption of new methods for seeking and evaluating truth.

Francis Bacon: The Inductive Method

Sir Francis Bacon (1561–1626), an English statesman and philosopher, vigorously supported the advancement of science and the scientific method. Although he himself had no laboratory and made no discoveries, his advocacy of the scientific method has earned him renown as a prophet of modern science. Bacon attributed the limited progress of science over the ages to the interference of scholastic philosophers, who sought to bend theories of nature to the requirements of Scripture. Bacon also denounced scholastic thinkers for their slavish attachment to Aristotelian doctrines, which prevented independent thinking and the acquisition of new information about nature. To acquire new knowledge and improve the quality of human life, said Bacon, we should not depend on ancient texts: old authorities must be discarded, and knowledge must be pursued and organized in a new way.

The method that Bacon advocated as the way to truth and useful knowledge was the inductive approach: careful observation of nature and the systematic accumulation of data, drawing general laws from the knowledge of particulars, and testing these laws through constant experimentation. People committed to such a method would never subscribe to inherited fables and myths about nature or invent new ones. Rather, they would investigate nature directly and base their conclusions on observable facts. In his discovery of the circulation of blood, Bacon's contemporary, British physician William Harvey (1578–1657), successfully employed the inductive method championed by Bacon. Grasping the essential approach of modern natural science, Bacon attacked practitioners of astrology, magic, and alchemy for their errors, secretiveness, and enigmatic writings and urged instead the pursuit of cooperative and methodical scientific research that could be publicly criticized.

Bacon was among the first to appreciate the value of the new science for human life. Knowledge, he said, should help us utilize nature for human advantage; it should improve the quality of human life by advancing commerce, industry, and agriculture. Holding that knowledge is power, Bacon urged the state to found scientific institutions and praised progress in technology and the mechanical arts. In Bacon's transvaluation of values, the artisan, mechanic, and engineer advanced knowledge more and contributed more to human betterment than did philosopher-theologians who constructed castles in the air.

René Descartes: The Deductive Method

The scientific method encompasses two approaches to knowledge that usually complement each other: the empirical (inductive) and the rational (deductive). In the inductive approach, which is employed in such descriptive sciences as biology, anatomy, and geology, general principles are derived from the analysis of data collected through observation and experiment. The essential features of the inductive method, as we have seen, were championed by Bacon, who regarded sense data as the foundation of knowledge. In the deductive approach, which is employed in mathematics and theoretical physics, truths are derived in successive steps from first principles, indubitable axioms. In the seventeenth century, the deductive method was formulated by René Descartes (1596–1650), a French mathematician and philosopher, who is also regarded as the founder of modern philosophy.

In the *Discourse on Method* (1637), Descartes expressed his disenchantment with the learning of his day. Since much of what he had believed on the basis of authority had been shown to be untrue, Descartes resolved to seek no knowledge other than that which he might find within himself or within nature. Rejecting as absolutely false anything about which he could have the least doubt, Descartes searched for an incontrovertible truth that could serve as the first principle of knowledge, the basis of an all-encompassing philosophical system.

Descartes found one truth to be certain and unshakable: that it was he who was doing the doubting and thinking. In his dictum "I think, therefore I am," Descartes had his starting point of knowledge. Descartes is viewed as the founder of modern philosophy because he called for the individual to question and if necessary to overthrow all traditional beliefs, and he proclaimed the mind's inviolable autonomy and importance, its ability and right to know truth. His assertions about the power of thought made people aware of their capacity to comprehend the world through their own mental powers.

Descartes saw the method used in mathematics as the most reliable avenue to certain knowledge. By applying mathematical reasoning to philosophical problems, we can achieve the same certainty and clarity evidenced in geometry. Mathematics is the key to understanding both the truths of nature and the moral order underlying human existence. The mathematical, or deductive, approach favored by Descartes consists of finding a self-evident principle, an irrefutable premise, such as a geometric axiom, and then deducing other truths from it through a chain of logical reasoning. The Cartesian deductive method, with its mathematical emphasis, perfectly complements Bacon's inductive approach, which stresses observation and experimentation. The scientific achievements of modern times have stemmed from the skillful synchronization of induction and deduction.

Engraving of René Descartes Tutoring Queen Christina of Sweden. Descartes was rare among major scientists in that he believed passionately in the intelligence of his female followers and correspondents. Rejecting authority, he asserted confidence in the human mind's ability to arrive at truth through its own capacities.

Primary Source

René Descartes, *Discourse on Method*

In this important work in the history of modern philosophy, Descartes describes his search for truth.

I was brought up from childhood on letters, and because I had been led to believe that by this means one could acquire clear and positive knowledge of everything useful in life, I was extremely anxious to learn them. But, as soon as I had completed this whole course of study, at the end of which it is usual to be received into the ranks of the learned, I completely changed my opinion. For I was assailed by so many doubts and errors that the only profit I appeared to have drawn from trying to become educated, was progressively to have discovered my ignorance. And yet I was at one of the most famous schools in Europe, where I thought there must be learned men, if there were any such anywhere on earth. I had learnt there everything the others learned; and further, not contenting myself merely with the subjects taught, I had gone through all the books I could lay my hands on dealing with the occult and rare sciences. . . .

I shall say nothing about philosophy, except that, seeing that it has been cultivated by the very best minds which have ever existed over several centuries and that, nevertheless, not one of its problems is not subject to disagreement, and consequently is uncertain, I was not presumptuous enough to hope to succeed in it any better than others; and seeing how many different opinions are sustained by learned men about one item, without its being possible for more than one ever to be true, I took to be tantamount to false everything which was merely probable. . . .

This is why, as soon as I reached an age which allowed me to emerge from the tutelage of my teachers, I abandoned the study of letters altogether, and resolving to study no other science than that which I could find within myself or else in the great book of the world. . . .

It is true that, while I merely observed the behaviour of others I found little basis in it for certainty, and I noticed almost as much diversity as I had done earlier among the opinions of philosophers. . . . [M]any things which, although they may seem to us very extravagant and ridiculous, are nevertheless commonly accepted and approved by other great peoples. . . .

[On the basis of these experiences with books and people, the first rule Descartes adapted] was never to accept anything as true that I did not know to be evidently so: that is to say, carefully to avoid precipitancy and prejudice, and to include in my judgements nothing more than what presented itself so clearly and so distinctly to my mind that I might have no occasion to place it in doubt. . . .

[A]s I wanted to concentrate solely on the search for truth, I thought I ought to . . . reject as being absolutely false everything in which I could suppose the slightest reason for doubt, in order to see if there did not remain after that anything in my belief which was entirely indubitable. So, because our senses sometimes play us false, I decided to suppose that there was nothing at all which was such as they cause us to imagine it; and because there are men who make mistakes in reasoning, even with the simplest geometrical matters, and make paralogisms, judging that I was as liable to error as anyone else, I rejected as being false all the reasonings I had hitherto accepted as proofs. And finally, considering that all the same thoughts that we have when we are awake can also come to us when we are asleep, without any one of them then being true, I resolved to pretend that nothing which had ever entered my mind was any more true than the illusions of my dreams. But immediately afterwards I became aware that, while I decided thus to think that everything was false, it followed necessarily that I who thought thus must be something; and observing that this truth: *I think, therefore I am,* was so certain and so evident that all the most extravagant suppositions of the sceptics were not capable of shaking it, I judged that I could accept it without scruple as the first principle of the philosophy I was seeking.

Questions for Analysis

1. Why is Descartes so eager to find a new way of knowing?
2. What does the statement "I think, therefore I am" proclaim?

Rene Descartes, *Discourse on Method and The Meditations*, trans. F. E. Sutchliffe, 29, 32–33, 41, 53–54.

The Meaning of the Scientific Revolution

The radical transformation of our conception of the physical universe produced by the Scientific Revolution ultimately transformed our understanding of the individual, society, and the purpose of life. The Scientific Revolution, therefore, was a decisive factor in the shaping of the modern world. It destroyed the medieval worldview, in which the earth occupied the central position, heaven lay just beyond the fixed stars, and every object had its place in a hierarchical and qualitative order. It replaced this view with the modern conception of a homogeneous universe of unbounded space and an infinite number of celestial bodies. Gone were the barriers that separated the heavens and the earth. The glory of the heavens was diminished by the new view that celestial objects were composed of the same stuff and subject to the same laws as all other natural objects. Gone also was the medieval notion that God had assigned an ultimate purpose to all natural objects and to all plant and animal life, that in God's plan everything had an assigned role: we have eyes because God wants us to see and rain because God wants crops to grow. Eschewing ultimate purposes, modern science examines physical nature for mathematical relationships and chemical composition.

In later centuries, further implications of the new cosmology caused great anguish. The conviction that God had created the universe for them, that the earth was fixed beneath their feet, and that God had given the earth the central position in his creation had brought medieval people a profound sense of security. They knew why they were here, and they never doubted that heaven was the final resting place for the faithful. Copernican astronomy dethroned the earth, expelled human beings from their central position, and implied an infinite universe. In the sixteenth and seventeenth centuries, few thinkers grasped the full significance of this displacement. However, in succeeding centuries, this radical cosmological transformation proved as traumatic for the modern mind as did Adam and Eve's expulsion from the Garden of Eden for the medieval mind. Today, we know that the earth is one of billions and billions of celestial bodies, a tiny speck in an endless cosmic ocean, and that the universe is some twelve billion years old. Could such a universe have been created just for human beings? Could it contain a heaven that assures eternal life for the faithful and a hell with eternal fires and torments for sinners?

Few people at the time were aware of the full implications of the new cosmology. One who did understand was Blaise Pascal (1623–1662), a French scientist and mathematician. A devout Catholic, Pascal was frightened by what he called "the eternal silence of these infinite spaces" and realized that the new science could stir doubt, uncertainty, and anxiety, which threatened belief.

The conception of reason advanced by Galileo and other thinkers of the period differed fundamentally from that of medieval scholastics. Scholastic thinkers viewed reason as a useful aid for contemplating divine truth; as such, reason always had to serve theology. Influenced by the new scientific spirit, thinkers now saw the investigation of nature as reason's principal concern. What is more, they viewed this activity as autonomous and not subject to theological authority.

The Scientific Revolution fostered a rational and critical spirit among the intellectual elite. Descartes's methodical doubt, rejection of authority, and insistence on the clarity, precision, and accuracy of an idea and Francis Bacon's insistence on verification pervaded the outlook of the eighteenth-century Enlightenment thinkers; they denounced magic, spells, demons, witchcraft, alchemy, and astrology as vulgar superstitions. Phenomena attributed to occult forces, they argued, could be explained by reference to natural forces. A wide breach opened up between the intellectual elite and the masses, who remained steeped in popular superstitions and committed to traditional Christian dogma.

The creators of modern science had seen no essential conflict between traditional Christianity and the new view of the physical universe and made no war on the churches. Indeed, they believed that they were unveiling the laws of nature instituted by God at the Creation—that at last the human mind could comprehend God's magnificent handiwork. But the new cosmology and new scientific outlook ultimately weakened traditional Christianity, for it dispensed with miracles and the need for God's presence.

The new critical spirit led the thinkers of the Enlightenment to doubt the literal truth of the Bible and to dismiss miracles as incompatible with what science teaches about the regularity of nature. So brilliantly had God crafted the universe, they said, so exquisite a mechanism was nature, that its operations did not require God's intervention. In the generations after the Scientific Revolution, theology, long considered the highest form of contemplation, was denounced as a barrier to understanding or even dismissed as irrelevant, and the clergy rapidly lost their position as the arbiters of knowledge. To many intellectuals, theology seemed sterile and profitless in comparison with the new science. Whereas science promised the certitude of mathematics, theologians seemed to quibble endlessly over unfathomable and, even worse, inconsequential issues. That much blood had been spilled over these questions discredited theology still more. In scientific academies, in salons, and in coffee houses, educated men and some women met to discuss the new ideas, and journals published the new knowledge for eager readers. European culture was undergoing a great transformation, marked by the triumph of a scientific and secular spirit among the intellectual elite.

The Scientific Revolution repudiated reliance on Aristotle, Ptolemy, and other ancient authorities in matters concerning nature and substituted in their place knowledge derived from observation, experimentation, and mathematical thinking. Citing an ancient authority was no longer sufficient to prove a point or win an argument. The new standard of knowledge derived from experience with the world, not from ancient texts or inherited views. This new outlook had far-reaching implications for the Age of Enlightenment. If the authority of ancient thinkers regarding the universe could be challenged, could not inherited political beliefs be challenged as well—for example, the divine right of kings to rule? Impressed with the achievements of science, many intellectuals started to urge the application of the scientific method to all fields of knowledge.

The new outlook generated by the Scientific Revolution served as the foundation of the Enlightenment. The Scientific Revolution gave thinkers great confidence in the power of the mind, which had discovered nature's laws, reinforcing the confidence in human abilities expressed by Renaissance humanists. In time, it was believed, the scientific method would unlock all nature's secrets, and humanity, gaining ever greater knowledge and control of nature, would progress rapidly.

The Age of Enlightenment: Affirmation of Reason and Freedom

The Enlightenment of the eighteenth century was the culmination of the movement toward modernity initiated by the Renaissance. The thinkers of the Enlightenment, called *philosophes*, aspired to create a more rational and humane society. To attain this goal, they attacked medieval otherworldliness, rejected theology as an avenue to truth, denounced the Christian idea of people's inherent depravity, and sought to understand nature and society through reason alone, unaided by revelation or priestly authority. Adopting Descartes's method of systematic doubt, they questioned all inherited opinions and traditions. "We think that the greatest service to be done to men," said Denis Diderot, "is to teach them to use their reason, only to hold for truth what they have verified and proved."[4] The philosophes believed that they were inaugurating an enlightened age. Through the power of reason, humanity was at last liberating itself from the fetters of ignorance, superstition, and despotism with which tyrants and priests had bound it in past ages. Paris was the center of the Enlightenment, but there were philosophes and adherents of their views in virtually every leading city in Western Europe and North America.

In many ways, the Enlightenment grew directly out of the Scientific Revolution. The philosophes sought to expand knowledge of nature and to apply the scientific method to the human world in order to uncover society's defects and to achieve appropriate reforms. Newton had discovered universal laws that explained the physical phenomena. Are there not general rules that also apply to human behavior and social institutions? asked the philosophes. Could a "science of man" be created that would correspond to and complement Newton's science of nature—that would provide clear and certain answers to the problems of the social world in the same way that Newtonian science had solved the mysteries of the physical world?

By relying on the same methodology that Newton had employed to establish certain knowledge of the physical universe, the philosophes hoped to arrive at the irrefutable laws that operated in the realm of human society. They aspired to shape religion, government, law, morality, and economics in accordance with these natural laws. They believed that all things should be reevaluated to see if they accorded with nature and promoted human well-being.

In championing the methodology of science, the philosophes affirmed respect for the mind's capacities and for human autonomy. Individuals are self-governing, they insisted. The mind is self-sufficient; rejecting appeals to clerical or princely authority, it relies on its own ability to think, and it trusts the evidence of its own experience. Rejecting the authority of tradition, the philosophes wanted people to have the courage to break with beliefs and institutions that did not meet the test of reason and common sense and to seek new guideposts derived from experience and reason unhindered by passion, superstition, dogma, and authority. The numerous examples of injustice, inhumanity, and superstition in society outraged the philosophes. Behind their devotion to reason and worldly knowledge lay an impassioned moral indignation against institutions and beliefs that degraded human beings.

Christianity Assailed: The Search for a Natural Religion

The philosophes waged an unremitting assault on traditional Christianity, denouncing it for harboring superstition, promulgating unreason, and fostering fanaticism and persecution. Relying on the facts of experience, as Bacon had taught, the philosophes dismissed miracles, angels, and devils as violations of nature's laws and figments of the imagination that could not be substantiated by the norms of evidence. Applying the Cartesian spirit of careful reasoning to the Bible, they pointed out flagrant discrepancies between various biblical passages and rejected as preposterous the theologians' attempts to resolve these contradictions. David Hume (1711–1776), the Scottish skeptic, wrote in *The Natural History of Religion* (1757):

> *Examine the religious principles, which have, in fact, prevailed in the world. You will scarcely be persuaded, that they are anything but sick men's dreams: Or perhaps will regard them more as the playsome, whimsies of monkies in human shape, than the serious, positive, dogmatical asseverations of a being, who dignifies himself with the name rational.... No theological absurdities so glaring that they have not, sometimes, been embraced by men of the greatest and most cultivated understanding.*[5]

The Inquisition. In one of the first histories of all the world's religions (published in 1723), the engraver Bernard Picart depicted the Inquisition as cold and ruthlessly interrogating (top panel), then as barbarous in its use of torture; at the bottom center is the practice of water-boarding.

With science as an ally, the philosophes challenged Christianity's claim that it possessed infallible truths, and they ridiculed theologians for wrangling over pointless issues and for compelling obedience to doctrines that defied reason. The philosophes arrived at a simple equation: science and its advocates are on the side of good, whereas theology and its priestly exponents promote wickedness. Thus Diderot wrote: "If you want priests you do not need philosophy and if you want philosophers you do not need priests; for the one being by their calling the friends of reason and the promoters of science, the other the enemies of reason and favourers of ignorance, if the first do good, the others do evil."[6]

Moreover, the philosophes assailed Christianity for viewing human nature as evil and human beings as helpless without God's assistance, for focusing on heaven at the expense of human happiness on earth, and for impeding the acquisition of useful knowledge by proclaiming the higher authority of dogma and revelation. Frightened and confused by religion, people have been held in subjection by clergy and tyrants, the philosophes argued. To establish an enlightened society, clerical power must be broken, Christian dogmas repudiated, and the fanaticism that produced tortures, burnings, and massacres purged from the European soul. The philosophes broke with the Christian past, even if they retained the essential elements of Christian morality.

François Marie Arouet (1694–1778), known to the world as Voltaire, was the recognized leader of the French Enlightenment. Few of the philosophes had a better mind, and none had a sharper wit. Living in exile in Britain in the late 1720s, Voltaire acquired a great admiration for English liberty, commerce, science, and religious toleration. Voltaire's angriest words were directed against established Christianity, to which he attributed many of the ills of French society. He regarded Christianity as "the Christ-worshiping superstition," which someday would be destroyed "by the weapons of reason." Many Christian dogmas are incomprehensible, said Voltaire, yet Christians have slaughtered one another to enforce obedience to these doctrines. Voltaire was appalled by all the crimes committed in the name of Christianity.[7]

While some philosophes were atheists, most were deists, including Voltaire and Thomas Paine (1737–1809), the English-American radical. Deists sought to fashion a natural religion that accorded with reason and science, and they tried to adapt the Christian tradition to the requirements of the new science. They denied that the Bible was God's revelation, rejected clerical authority, and dismissed Christian mysteries, prophecies, and miracles—the virgin birth, Jesus walking on water, the Resurrection, and others—as violations of a lawful natural order. They did consider it reasonable that this magnificently structured universe, operating with clockwork precision, was designed and created at a point in time by an all-wise Creator. But in their view, once God had set the universe in motion, he refrained from interfering with its operations. Thus, deists were at odds with Newton, who allowed for divine intervention in the world.

For deists, the essence of religion was morality—a commitment to justice and humanity—and not adherence to rituals, doctrines, or clerical authority. In *The Age of Reason* (1794–1795), Paine declared: "I believe in the equality of man; and I believe that religious duties consist in doing justice, loving mercy, and endeavoring to make our fellow-creatures happy."[8] Deists deemed it entirely reasonable that after death those who had fulfilled God's moral law would be rewarded, while those who had not would be punished.

Political Thought

Besides established religion, the philosophes identified another source of the evil that beset humanity: despotism. If human beings were to achieve happiness, they had to extirpate revealed religion and check the power of their rulers. "Every age has its dominant idea," wrote Diderot; "that of our age seems to be Liberty."[9] Eighteenth-century political thought is characterized by a thoroughgoing secularism; an indictment of despotism, the divine right of kings, and the special privileges of the aristocracy and the clergy; a respect for English constitutionalism because it enshrined the rule of law; and an affirmation of John Locke's theory that government had an obligation to protect the natural rights of its citizens. Central to the political outlook of the philosophes was the conviction that political solutions could be found for the ills that afflicted society.

In general, the philosophes favored constitutional government that protected citizens from the abuse of power. With the notable exception of Rousseau, the philosophes' concern for liberty did not lead them to embrace democracy, for they put little trust in the masses. Several philosophes, notably Voltaire, placed their confidence in reforming despots, like Frederick II of Prussia, who were sympathetic to enlightened ideas. However, the philosophes were less concerned with the form of government—monarchy or republic—than with preventing the authorities from abusing their power.

Seventeenth-Century Antecedents: Hobbes and Locke

The political thought of the Enlightenment was greatly affected by the writings of two seventeenth-century English philosophers: Thomas Hobbes (1588–1679) and John Locke (1632–1704). Hobbes witnessed the agonies of the English civil war, including the execution of Charles I in 1649. These developments fortified his conviction that absolutism was the most desirable and logical form of government. Only the unlimited power of a sovereign, Hobbes wrote in his major work, *Leviathan* (1651), could contain the human passions that disrupt the social order and threaten civilized life; only absolute rule could provide an environment secure enough for people to pursue their individual interests.

Influenced by the new scientific thought that saw mathematical knowledge as the avenue to truth, Hobbes aimed at constructing political philosophy on a scientific foundation and rejected the authority of tradition and religion as inconsistent with a science of politics. Thus, although Hobbes supported absolutism, he dismissed the idea advanced by other theorists of absolutism that the monarch's power derived from God. He also rejected the view of medieval theorists that the state, which belonged to a lower temporal order, was subordinate to the commands of a higher spiritual realm and its corollary that the state should not be obeyed when it violates God's law. Like Machiavelli, Hobbes made no attempt to fashion the earthly city in accordance with Christian teachings. As an astute observer of contemporary affairs, Hobbes, of course, recognized religion's importance in European political life. However, his view of human nature and human life rested on no religious presuppositions. Religious thinkers frequently denounced Hobbes as a heretic, if not an atheist. *Leviathan* is a rational and secular political statement; its significance lies in its modern approach, rather than in Hobbes's justification of absolutism.

Hobbes had a pessimistic view of human nature. Believing that people are innately selfish and grasping, he maintained that competition and dissension, rather than cooperation, characterize human relations. When reason teaches that cooperation is more advantageous than competition, said Hobbes, people are still reluctant to alter their ways, because their behavior is governed more by passion than by reason. Without a stringent authority to make and enforce law, life would be miserable, a war of all against all, he said. Therefore, he prescribed a state with unlimited power, since only in this way could people be protected from one another and civilized life preserved. Although the philosophes generally rejected Hobbes's gloomy view of human nature, they embraced his secular approach to politics, particularly his denunciation of the theory of the divine right of kings. Hobbes's concern with protecting the social order from human antisocial tendencies is still a central consideration of modern political life. His insight that civilization is forever in danger of collapsing into anarchy and savagery is still a poignant message for our times.

In contrast to Hobbes, John Locke maintained that human beings are rational by nature and are moved by a sense of moral obligation; they are capable of transcending a narrow selfishness and of respecting the inherent dignity of others. Viewing people as essentially good and humane, he developed a conception of the state that was fundamentally different from Hobbes's. In the *Two Treatises of Government* (1690), Locke maintained that human beings are born with natural rights to life, liberty, and property, and they establish the state to protect these rights. Consequently, neither executive nor legislature—neither king nor assembly—has the authority to deprive individuals of their natural rights. Whereas Hobbes justified absolute monarchy, Locke explicitly endorsed constitutional government, in which the power to govern derives from the consent of the governed and the state's authority is limited by agreement. Rulers hold their authority under the law; when they act outside the law, they forfeit their right to govern. Thus, if government fails to fulfill the end for which it was established—the preservation of the individual's right to life, liberty, and property—the people have a right to dissolve that government.

Both Hobbes and Locke agreed that the state exists in order to ensure the tranquility, security, and well-being of its citizens. However, they proposed radically different ways of attaining this end. Unlike Hobbes, Locke believed that social well-being encompassed personal freedom. Rejecting Hobbes's view that absolute power can remedy the defects of the state of nature, Locke stated the case for limited government, the rule of law, the protection of fundamental human rights, and the right of resistance to arbitrary power. Underlying Locke's conception of the state is the conviction that people have the capacity for reason and freedom, and that political life can be guided by rational principles: "We are born Free as we are born Rational."[10]

The value that Locke gave to reason and freedom and his theories of natural rights, the rule of law, and the right to resist despotic authority had a profound effect on the Enlightenment and the liberal revolutions of the late eighteenth and early nineteenth centuries. Thus, in the Declaration of Independence, Thomas Jefferson restated Locke's principles to justify the American Revolution. Locke's tenets that property is a natural right and that state interference with personal property leads to the destruction of liberty also became core principles of modern liberalism.

Montesquieu

The contribution of Charles Louis de Secondat, Baron de la Brède et de Montesquieu (1689–1755), to political theory rests essentially on his *Spirit of the Laws* (1748), a work of immense erudition covering many topics. Montesquieu held that the study of political and social behavior is not an exercise in abstract thought but must be undertaken in relation to geographic, economic, and historic conditions. To this end, Montesquieu accumulated and classified a wide diversity of facts, from which he tried to draw general rules governing society. He concluded that different climatic and geographic conditions and different national customs, habits, religions, and institutions give each nation a particular character; each society requires constitutional forms and laws that pay heed to the character of its people. Montesquieu's effort to explain social and political behavior empirically—to found a science of society based on the model of natural science—makes him a forerunner of modern sociology.

Montesquieu regarded despotism as a pernicious form of government, corrupt by its very nature. Ruling as he wishes and unchecked by law, the despot knows nothing of moderation and institutionalizes cruelty and violence. The slave-like subjects, wrote Montesquieu, know only servitude, fear, and misery. Driven by predatory instincts, the despotic ruler involves his state in wars of conquest, caring not at all about the suffering this causes his people. In a despotic society, economic activity stagnates, for merchants, fearful that their goods will be confiscated by the state, lose their initiative. Reformers used Montesquieu's characterization of despotism to show the limitations of absolute monarchy.

To safeguard liberty from despotism, Montesquieu advocated the principle of separation of powers. In every government, said Montesquieu, there are three sorts of powers: legislative, executive, and judiciary. When one person or one body exercises all three powers—if the same body both prosecutes and judges, for example—liberty cannot be preserved. Where sovereignty is monopolized by one person or body, power is abused and political liberty is denied. In a good government, one power balances and checks another power, an argument that impressed the framers of the U.S. Constitution.

Several of Montesquieu's ideals were absorbed into the liberal tradition—constitutional government and the rule of law, separation of powers, freedom of thought, religious toleration, and protection of individual liberty. The conservative tradition drew on Montesquieu's respect for traditional ways of life and his opposition to sudden reforms that ignored a people's history and culture.

Voltaire and King Frederick. The roundtable was beloved by the aristocracy because it claimed every one of them as equals. Here Voltaire visits with Frederick the Great and perhaps imagined himself as an equal.

Voltaire

Unlike Hobbes and Locke, Voltaire was not a systematic political theorist, but a propagandist and polemicist who hurled pointed barbs at all the abuses of the French society. Nevertheless, Voltaire's writings do contain ideas that form a coherent political theory that in many ways expresses the outlook of the Enlightenment.

Voltaire disdained arbitrary power, since it is based on human whim rather than on established law. He described a prince who imprisons or executes his subjects unjustly and without due process as "nothing but a highway robber who is called 'Your Majesty.'" For Voltaire, freedom consisted in being governed by an established and standard code of law that applies equally to all. Without the rule of law, wrote Voltaire, there is no liberty of person, no freedom of thought or of religion, no protection of personal property, no impartial judiciary, and no protection from arbitrary arrest. Underlying Voltaire's commitment to the rule of law was his conviction that power should be used rationally and beneficially.

Voltaire's respect for the rule of law was strengthened by his stay in England between 1726 and 1729, which led to the publication of

The English Letters in 1733. In this work, Voltaire presents an idealized and, at times, inaccurate picture of English politics and society. More important, however, is the fact that his experience with English liberty gave him hope that a just and tolerant society was not a utopian dream, thereby strengthening his resolve to attack the abuses of French society.

As noted earlier, Voltaire was no democrat. He had little confidence in the capacities of the common people, whom he saw as prone to superstition and fanaticism. Nor did he advocate revolution. What he did favor was reforming society through the advancement of reason and the promotion of science and technology. Voltaire himself fought to introduce several reforms into France, including freedom of the press, religious toleration, a fair system of criminal justice, proportional taxation, and curtailment of the privileges of the clergy and nobility.

Rousseau

"Man is born free and everywhere he is in chains."[11] With these stirring words, the Geneva-born French thinker Jean Jacques Rousseau (1712–1778) began *The Social Contract* (1762). Rousseau considered the state as it was then constituted to be unjust and corrupt. It was dominated by the rich and the powerful, who used it to further their interests, whereas the weak knew only oppression and misery. In Rousseau's view, the modern state deprived human beings of their natural freedom and fostered a selfish individualism that undermined feelings of mutuality and concern for the common good.

Rousseau wanted the state to be a genuine democracy, a moral association that bound people together in freedom, equality, and civic devotion. For Rousseau, individuals fulfilled their moral potential not in isolation but as committed members of the community; human character was ennobled when people cooperated with one another and cared for one another. Rousseau admired the ancient Greek city-state, the polis, for it was an organic community in which citizens set aside private interests in order to attain the common good. In *The Social Contract*, he sought to re-create the community spirit and the political freedom that characterized the Greek city-state.

What Rousseau proposed was that each person surrender unconditionally all his rights to the community as a whole and submit to its authority. To prevent the assertion of private interests over the common good, Rousseau wanted the state to be governed in accordance with the general will—an underlying principle that expressed what was best for the community. He did not conceive of the general will as a majority or even a unanimous vote, both of which could be wrong. Rather, it was a plainly visible truth, easily discerned by common sense and by reason and by listening to our hearts. In Rousseau's view, just and enlightened citizens imbued with public spirit would have the good sense and moral awareness to legislate in accordance with the general will.

Like ancient Athens, the state that Rousseau envisioned was a direct democracy, in which the citizens themselves, not their representatives, constituted the lawmaking body. Consequently, the governed and the government were one and the same. Rousseau condemned arbitrary and despotic monarchy, the divine-right theory of kingship, and the traditional view that people should be governed by their betters—lords and clergy—who were entitled to special privileges. He granted sovereignty to the people as a whole and affirmed the principle of equality.

Rousseau remains a leading theorist of democratic thought. His critics assert that his political thought, whose goal is a body of citizens who think alike, buttresses a dangerous collectivism and even totalitarianism. These critics argue that Rousseau did not place constitutional limitations on sovereignty or erect safeguards to protect individual and minority rights from a potentially tyrannical majority. They note, too, that Rousseau rejected entirely the Lockean principle that citizens possess rights independently of the state, as well as the right to act against the state.

Social and Economic Thought

The philosophes rejected the Christian belief that human beings are endowed with a sinful nature, a consequence of Adam and Eve's disobedience of God. They knew from experience, of course, that human beings behave wickedly and seem hopelessly attached to nonrational modes of thinking.

While they retained a certain pessimism about human nature, however, the philosophes generally believed in individuals' essential goodness and in their capacity for moral improvement. "Nature has not made us evil," wrote Diderot, "it is bad education, bad models, bad legislation that corrupt us."[12] And Voltaire declared that a person is "born neither good nor wicked; education, example, the government into which he is thrown—in short, occasion of every kind—determines him to virtue or vice."[13] The philosophes' conception of human nature rested heavily on John Locke's epistemology, or theory of knowledge. To the philosophes, it seemed that Locke had discovered the fundamental principles governing the human mind, an achievement comparable to Newton's discovery of the laws governing physical bodies.

Epistemology, Psychology, and Education

In his *Essay Concerning Human Understanding* (1690), a work of immense significance in the history of philosophy, Locke argued that human beings are not born with innate ideas (the idea of God, principles of good and evil, and rules of logic, for example) divinely implanted in their minds, as Descartes had maintained. Rather, said Locke, the human mind is a blank slate upon which are imprinted sensations derived from contact with the phenomenal world. Knowledge is derived from experience.

Locke's theory of knowledge had profound implications. If there are no innate ideas, said the philosophes, then human beings, contrary to Christian doctrine, are not born with original sin, are not depraved by nature. All that individuals are derives from their particular experiences. If people are provided with a proper environment and education, they will behave morally; they will become intelligent and productive citizens. By the proper use of their reason, people could bring their beliefs, their conduct, and their institutions into harmony with natural law. This was how the reform-minded philosophes interpreted Locke. They preferred to believe that evil stemmed from faulty institutions and poor education, both of which could be remedied, rather than from a defective human nature.

The most important work of Enlightenment educational thought was Rousseau's *Émile* (1762), in which he suggested educational reforms that would instill in children self-confidence, self-reliance, and emotional security—necessary qualities if they were to become productive adults and responsible citizens. If the young are taught to think for themselves, said Rousseau, they will learn to cherish personal freedom. A strong faith in the essential goodness of human nature underlay Rousseau's educational philosophy. He also assumed that youngsters have an equal capacity to learn and that differences in intelligence are due largely to environmental factors.

Rousseau understood that children should not be treated like little adults, for children have their own ways of thinking and feeling. He railed against those who robbed children of the joys and innocence of childhood by chaining them to desks, ordering them about, and filling their heads with rote learning. Instead, he urged that children experience direct contact with the environment to develop their bodies and senses and their curiosity, ingenuity, resourcefulness, and imagination. It is the whole child that concerned Rousseau.

Freedom of Conscience and Thought

The philosophes regarded religious persecution—whose long and bloodstained history included the burning of heretics in the Middle Ages, the slaughter of Jews and Muslims during the First Crusade, and the massacres of the wars of the Reformation—as humanity's most depraved offense against reason. While the worst excesses of religious fanaticism had dissipated by the eighteenth century, examples of religious persecution still abounded, particularly in Catholic lands. In his pleas for tolerance, Voltaire spoke for all the philosophes:

> *I shall never cease . . . to preach tolerance from the housetops . . . until persecution is no more. The progress of reason is slow, the roots of prejudice lie deep. Doubtless, I shall never see the fruits of my efforts, but they are seeds which may one day germinate.*[14]

Censorship was a serious and ever-present problem for the philosophes. After the publication of

Voltaire's *English Letters*, his printer was arrested and the book confiscated and publicly burned as irreligious. On another occasion, when Voltaire was harassed by the authorities, he commented that "it is easier for me to write books than to get them published."[15] Denounced by ecclesiastical and ministerial authorities as a threat to religion and constituted authority, *On the Mind* (1758), by Claude-Adrien Helvetius (1715–1771), was burned by the public executioner. Denis Diderot (1713–1784), the principal editor of the thirty-eight-volume *Encyclopedia,* whose 150 or more contributors included the leading Enlightenment thinkers, had to contend with French authorities, who at times suspended publication. After the first two volumes appeared, the authorities condemned the work for containing "maxims that would tend to destroy royal authority, foment a spirit of independence and revolt . . . and lay the foundations for the corruption of morals and religion."[16] In 1759, Pope Clement XIII condemned the *Encyclopedia* for having "scandalous doctrines [and] inducing scorn for religion."[17] It required careful diplomacy and clever ruses to finish the project and still incorporate ideas considered dangerous by religious and governmental authorities. The *Encyclopedia* had been undertaken in Paris during the 1740s as a monumental effort to bring together all human knowledge and to propagate Enlightenment ideas. Its numerous articles on science and technology and its limited coverage of theological questions attest to the new interests of eighteenth-century intellectuals. With the project's completion in 1772, Diderot and Enlightenment opinion triumphed over clerical, royal, and aristocratic censors.

An article in the *Encyclopedia*, "The Press," conveys the philosophes' yearning for freedom of thought and expression. For them, the term *press* designated more than newspapers and journals; it encompassed everything in print, particularly books.

> *People ask if freedom of the press is advantageous or prejudicial to a state. The answer is not difficult. It is of the greatest importance to conserve this practice in all states founded on liberty. I would even say that the disadvantages of this liberty are so inconsiderable compared to the advantages that this ought to be the common right of the universe, and it is certainly advisable to authorize its practices in all governments.*[18]

Humanitarianism

A humanitarian spirit, which no doubt owed much to Christian compassion, pervaded the outlook of the philosophes. It expressed itself in attacks on torture, which was commonly used to obtain confessions in many European lands; on cruel punishments for criminals; on slavery; and on war. The philosophes' humanitarianism rested on the conviction that human nature was essentially virtuous and that human beings were capable of benevolent feelings toward one another.

In *On Crimes and Punishments* (1764), Cesare Beccaria (1738–1794), an Italian economist and criminologist inspired in part by Montesquieu, condemned torture as inhuman, "a criterion fit for a cannibal."[19] He saw it as an irrational way of determining guilt or innocence, for an innocent person unable to withstand the agonies of torture will confess to anything and a criminal with a high threshold for pain will be exonerated. Influenced by Beccaria's work, reform-minded jurists, legislators, and ministers called for the elimination of torture from codes of criminal justice, and several European lands abolished torture in the eighteenth century.

Though not pacifists, the philosophes denounced war as barbaric and an affront to reason. They deemed it to be a scourge promoted by power-hungry monarchs and supported by fanatical clergy, wicked army leaders, and ignorant commoners. In his literary masterpiece, *Candide* (1759), Voltaire ridiculed the rituals of war.

> *Nothing could be smarter, more splendid, more brilliant, better drawn up than the two armies. Trumpets, fifes, hautboys [oboes], drums, cannons, formed a harmony such as has never been heard even in hell. The cannons first of all laid flat about six thousand men on each side; then the musketry removed from the best of worlds some nine or ten thousand blackguards who infested its surface. The bayonet also was the sufficient reason*

> *for the death of some thousands of men. The whole might amount to thirty thousand souls.*[20]

Voltaire was particularly outraged by the belief that the outcome of this "heroic butchery" was ordained by God. The article "Peace" in the *Encyclopedia* described war as

> *the fruit of man's depravity; it is a convulsive and violent sickness of the body politic. . . . [It] depopulates the nation, causes the reign of disorder . . . makes the freedom and property of citizens uncertain . . . disturbs and causes the neglect of commerce; land becomes uncultivated and abandoned. . . . If reason governed men and had the influence over the heads of nations that it deserves, we would never see them inconsiderately surrender themselves to the fury of war; they would not show that ferocity that characterizes wild beasts.*[21]

Montesquieu, Voltaire, Hume, Benjamin Franklin, Thomas Paine, and other philosophes condemned slavery and the slave trade. In Book 15 of *The Spirit of the Laws*, Montesquieu scornfully refuted all justifications for slavery. Ultimately, he said, slavery, which violates the fundamental principle of justice underlying the universe, derived from base human desires to dominate and exploit other human beings. Adam Smith (see next section), the Enlightenment's leading economic theorist, demonstrated that slave labor was inefficient and wasteful. In 1780, Paine helped draft the act abolishing slavery in Pennsylvania. An article in the *Encyclopedia*, "The Slave Trade," denounced slavery as a violation of the individual's natural rights:

> *If commerce of this kind can be justified by a moral principle, there is no crime, however atrocious it may be, that cannot be made legitimate. . . . Men and their liberty are not objects of commerce; they can be neither sold nor bought. . . . There is not, therefore, a single one of these unfortunate people regarded only as slaves who does not have the right to be declared free.*[22]

The philosophes, although they often enjoyed the company of intelligent and sophisticated women in the famous salons, continued to view women as intellectually and morally inferior to men. Although some philosophes, notably Condorcet (see the upcoming section "The Idea of Progress"), who wrote *Plea for the Citizenship of Women* (1791), did argue for female emancipation, they were the exception. Most retained traditional views, concurring with David Hume, who held that "nature has subjected" women to men and that their "inferiority and infirmities are absolutely incurable."[23] Rousseau, who also believed that nature had granted men power over women, regarded traditional domesticity as a woman's proper role.

> *I would a thousand times rather have a homely girl, simply brought up, than a learned lady and a wit who would make a literary circle of my house and install herself as its president. A female wit is a scourge to her husband, her children, her friends, her servants, to everybody. From the lofty height of her genius, she scorns every womanly duty, and she is always trying to make a man of herself.*[24]

Nevertheless, by clearly articulating the ideals of liberty and equality, the philosophes made a women's movement possible. The growing popularity of these ideals could not escape women, who measured their own position by them. Moreover, by their very nature, these ideals were expansive. Denying them to women would ultimately be seen as an indefensible contradiction.

Thus, Mary Wollstonecraft's *Vindication of the Rights of Woman* (1792), written under the influence of the French Revolution, protested against the prevailing subordination and submissiveness of women and the limited opportunities afforded them to cultivate their minds. If women were also endowed with reason, why should men alone determine the standards and ground rules, she asked pungently. She reminded enlightened thinkers that the same arbitrary power that they objected to when wielded by monarchs and slave owners they condoned when exercised by husbands in domestic life. She considered it an act of tyranny for women "to be excluded from a participation of the natural rights of mankind."[25]

Engraving, Newgate Prison, Eighteenth Century. Prison conditions during the Age of Enlightenment were appalling. Here, a manacled man struggles with a wheelbarrow, and two others are led off to the gallows. Meanwhile, a guard watches over the dungeon filled with bound prisoners, who were as often debtors as criminals.

Laissez-Faire Economics

In *An Inquiry into the Nature and Causes of the Wealth of Nations* (1776), Adam Smith (1732–1790), professor of moral philosophy in Scotland, attacked the theory of mercantilism, which held that a state's wealth was determined by the amount of gold and silver it possessed. According to this theory, to build up its reserves of precious metals, the state should promote domestic industries, encourage exports, and discourage imports. Mercantilist theory called for government regulation of the economy so that the state could compete successfully with other nations for a share of the world's scarce resources. Smith argued that the real basis of a country's wealth was measured by the quantity and quality of its goods and services, not by its storehouse of precious metals. Government intervention, he said, retards economic progress; it reduces the real value of the annual produce of the nation's land and labor. On the other hand, when people pursue their own interests—when they seek to better their condition—they foster economic expansion, which benefits the whole society.

Smith limited the state's authority to maintaining law and order, administering justice, and defending the nation. The concept of *laissez faire*—that government should not interfere with the market—became a core principle of nineteenth-century liberal thought.

The Idea of Progress

"Despite all the efforts of tyranny, despite the violence and trickery of the priesthood, despite the vigilant efforts of all the enemies of mankind," wrote Baron Paul Henri Holbach, "the human race will attain enlightenment."[26] The philosophes were generally optimistic about humanity's future progress. Two main assumptions contributed to this optimism. First, accepting Locke's theory of knowledge, the philosophes attributed evil to a flawed but remediable environment, not to an inherently wicked human nature. Hopeful that a reformed environment would bring out the best in people, they looked forward to a day when reason would prevail over superstition, prejudice, intolerance, and tyranny. Second, the philosophes' veneration of science led them to believe that the progressive advancement of knowledge would promote material and moral progress.

A work written near the end of the century epitomized the philosophes' vision of the future: *Sketch for a Historical Picture of the Progress of the Human Mind* (1794) by Marie Jean Antoine Nicolas Caritat, Marquis de Condorcet (1743–1794). A mathematician and historian of science and a contributor to the *Encyclopedia*, Condorcet campaigned for religious toleration and the abolition of slavery. During the French Revolution, he attracted the enmity of the dominant Jacobin party and in 1793 was forced to go into hiding. Secluded in Paris, he wrote *Sketch*. Arrested in 1794, Condorcet died during his first night in prison, either from exhaustion or from self-administered poison. In *Sketch*, Condorcet lauded recent advances in knowledge that enabled reason to "lift her chains (and) shake herself free"[27] from superstition and tyranny. Passionately affirming the Enlightenment's confidence in reason and science, Condorcet expounded a theory of continuous and indefinite human improvement. He pointed toward a future golden age, characterized by the triumph of reason and freedom.

> *Our hopes for the future condition of the human race can be subsumed under three important heads: the abolition of inequality between nations, the progress of equality within each nation, and the true perfection of mankind. . . .*
>
> *The time will therefore come when the sun will shine only on free men who know no other master but their reason; when tyrants and slaves, priests and their stupid or hypocritical instruments will exist only in works of history and on the stage; and we shall think of them only to pity their victims and their dupes; to maintain ourselves in a state of vigilance by thinking on their excesses; and to learn how to recognize and so to destroy, by force of reason, the first seeds of tyranny and superstition, should they ever dare to reappear amongst us.*[28]

But the philosophes were not starry-eyed dreamers. They knew that progress was painful, slow, and reversible. Voltaire's *Candide* was a protest against a naïve optimism that ignored the granite might of human meanness, ignorance, and irrationality. "Let us weep and wail over the lot of philosophy," wrote Diderot. "We preach wisdom to the deaf and we are still far indeed from the age of reason."[29]

Conflicts and Politics

The major conflicts of the eighteenth century were between Britain and France for control of territory in the New World and between Austria and Prussia for dominance in Central Europe. Then, in the late 1700s, the American and French Revolutions broke out; they helped shape the liberal-democratic tradition.

Warfare and Revolution

In 1740, Prussia, ruled by the aggressive Frederick the Great, launched a successful war against Austria and was rewarded with Silesia, which increased the Prussian population by 50 percent. Maria Theresa, the Austrian queen, never forgave Frederick and in 1756 formed an alliance with France against Prussia. The ensuing Seven Years' War (1756–1763), which involved every major European power, did not significantly change Europe, but it did reveal Prussia's growing might.

At the same time, the French and the English fought over their claims in the New World. England's victory in the conflict (known in American history as the French and Indian War) deprived France of virtually all of its North American possessions and set in motion a train of events that culminated in the American Revolution. The war drained the British treasury, and now Britain had the additional expense of paying for troops to guard the new North American territories that it had gained in the war. As strapped British taxpayers could not shoulder the whole burden, the members of Parliament thought it quite reasonable that the American colonists should help pay the bill; after all, Britain had protected the colonists from the French and was still protecting them in their conflicts with Indians. New colonial taxes and import duties imposed by Parliament produced vigorous protests from the Americans.

The quarrel turned to bloodshed in April and June 1775, and on July 4, 1776, delegates from the various colonies adopted the Declaration of Independence, written mainly by Thomas Jefferson. Applying Locke's theory of natural rights, this document declared that government derives its power from the consent of the governed, that it is the duty of a government to protect the rights of its citizens, and that people have the right to "alter or abolish" a government that deprives them of their "unalienable rights."

Why were the American colonists so ready to throw off British rule? Each of the thirteen colonies had an elected assembly, which acted like a miniature parliament. In these assemblies, Americans gained political experience and quickly learned to be self-governing.

Familiarity with the thought of the Enlightenment and the republican writers of the English Revolution also contributed to the Americans' awareness of liberty. The ideas of the philosophes traversed the Atlantic and influenced educated Americans, particularly Thomas Jefferson and Benjamin Franklin. Like the philosophes, American thinkers expressed a growing confidence in reason, valued freedom of religion and of thought, and championed the principle of natural rights.

American victory came about in 1783 as a result of several factors. George Washington proved to be a superior leader, able to organize and retain the loyalty of his troops. France, seeking to avenge its defeat in the Seven Years' War, helped the Americans with money and provisions and then, in 1778, entered the conflict. Britain had difficulty shipping supplies across three thousand miles of ocean, was fighting the French in the West Indies and elsewhere at the same time, and ultimately lacked commitment to the struggle.

Reformers in other lands quickly interpreted the American victory as a successful struggle of liberty against tyranny. During the Revolution, the various American states drew up constitutions based on the principle of popular sovereignty and included bills of rights that protected individual liberty. They also managed, somewhat reluctantly, to forge a nation. Rejecting both monarchy and hereditary aristocracy, the Constitution of the United States created a republic in which power derived from the people. A system of separation of powers and checks and balances set safeguards against the abuse of power, and the Bill of Rights provided for protection of individual rights. To be sure, the ideals of liberty and equality were not extended to all people—slaves knew nothing of the freedom that white Americans cherished, and women were denied the vote and equal opportunity. But to reform-minded Europeans, it seemed that Americans were fulfilling the promise of the Enlightenment; they were creating a freer and better society.

Enlightened Despotism

The philosophes used the term *enlightened despotism* to refer to an ideal shared by many of them: rule by a strong monarch who would implement rational reforms and remove obstacles to freedom. Some eighteenth-century monarchs and their ministers—Frederick the Great in Prussia, Catherine the Great in Russia, Charles III in Spain, Maria Theresa and, to a greater extent, her son Joseph II in Austria, and Louis XV in France—did institute educational, commercial, and religious reforms.

Behind the reforms of enlightened despots lay the realization that the struggle for power in Europe called for efficient government administration and ample funds. Enlightened despots appointed capable officials to oversee the administration of their kingdoms, eliminate costly corruption, and collect taxes properly. Rulers strengthened the economy by encouraging the expansion of commerce through reduced taxes on goods and through agricultural reforms. In Central and Eastern Europe, some rulers moved toward abolishing serfdom, or at least improving conditions for serfs. (In Western Europe, serfdom had virtually died out.) Provisions were made to care for widows, orphans, and invalids. Censorship was eased, greater religious freedom was granted to minorities, criminal codes were made less harsh, and there were some attempts at prison reform. By these measures, enlightened despots hoped to inspire greater popular support for the state, an important factor in the European power struggle.

The Enlightenment and the Modern Mentality

The philosophes articulated core principles of the modern outlook. Asserting that human beings are capable of thinking independently of authority, they insisted on a thoroughgoing rational and secular interpretation of nature and society. They critically scrutinized authority and tradition and valued science and technology as a means for promoting human betterment. Above all, they sought to emancipate the mind from the bonds of ignorance and superstition and to rescue people from intolerance, cruelty, and oppression. Because of their efforts, torture (which states and Christian churches had endorsed and practiced) was eventually abolished in Western lands, and religious toleration and freedom of speech and of the press became the accepted norms. The arguments that the philosophes marshaled against slavery were utilized by those who fought against the slave trade and called for emancipation. Enlightenment economic thought, particularly Adam Smith's *Wealth of Nations*, gave theoretical support to a market economy based on supply and demand—an outlook that fostered commercial and industrial expansion. The separation of church and state, a basic principle of modern political life, owes much to the philosophes, who frequently cited the dangers of politics inflamed by religious passions. The philosophes' denunciation of despotism and championing of natural rights, equality under the law, and constitutional government are the chief foundations of modern liberal government.

The ideals of the Enlightenment spread from Europe to America and helped shape the political thought of the Founding Fathers. The Declaration of Independence clearly articulated Locke's basic principles: that government derives its authority from the governed; that human beings are born with natural rights, which government has a responsibility to protect; and that citizens have the right to resist a government that deprives them of these rights. The Constitution asserted that the people are sovereign: "We the People of the United States . . . do ordain and establish this Constitution for the United States of America." And it contained several safeguards against despotic power, including Montesquieu's principle of separation of powers, which was also written into several state constitutions. Both the bills of rights drawn up by the various states and the federal Bill of Rights gave recognition to the individual's inherent rights and explicitly barred government from tampering with them—a principal concern of the philosophes.

The *Federalist Papers*, the major American contribution to eighteenth-century political thought, in many ways epitomized Enlightenment thinking. It incorporated specific ideas of Locke, Montesquieu, Hume, and the *Encyclopedia*; analyzed political forms in a rational, secular, and critical spirit; regarded the protection of personal freedom as a principal goal of the state; and expressed a willingness to break with past traditions when they conflicted with good sense. The new American republic, says Peter Gay, was "convincing evidence, to the philosophes . . . that men had some capacity for self-improvement and self-government, that progress might be a reality instead of a fantasy, and that reason and humanity might become governing rather than merely critical principles."[30]

The philosophes broke with the traditional Christian view of human nature and the purpose of life. In that view, men and women were born in sin; suffering and misery were divinely ordained, and relief could come only from God; social inequality was instituted by God; and for many, eternal damnation was a deserved final consequence. In contrast, the philosophes saw injustice and suffering as manmade problems that could be solved through reason; they expressed confidence in people's ability to attain happiness by improving the conditions of their earthly existence and articulated a theory of human progress that did not require divine assistance. Rejecting the idea of a static and immutable order of society instituted by God, the philosophes had confidence that human beings could improve the conditions of their existence, and they pointed to advances in science and technology as evidence of progress.

Thus, the idea of secular progress, another key element of modernity, also grew out of the Enlightenment. After two world wars and countless other conflicts, after Auschwitz and other examples of state-sponsored mass murder, and with the development of weapons of mass destruction, it is difficult to realize that at the beginning of the twentieth century most westerners were committed to a doctrine of perpetual progress that embodied the hopes of the philosophes.

To be sure, the promise of the Enlightenment has not been achieved. More education for more people and the spread of constitutional government have not eliminated fanaticism and superstition, violence and war, or evil and injustice. In the light of twentieth-century and twenty-first century events, it is difficult to subscribe to Condorcet's belief in linear progress, that history is inexorably carrying humanity toward a golden age.

The worldview of the philosophes has come under attack. Building on the critique of early nineteenth-century romantics, critics have accused the philosophes of overvaluing the intellect at the expense of human feelings. According to this view, the philosophes did not recognize the value of the feelings as a source of creativity and did not call for their creative development. Rather, they viewed the emotions as impediments to clear thinking that had to be overcome.

Another failing of the philosophes, critics argue, is that they did seek to understand a past age on its own terms but judged it according to preconceived norms, disdaining and rejecting anything that contradicted their idea of truth and their view of the good society. Such an outlook, say the critics, led the philosophes to underestimate the extent to which the past governs the present. Holding with Hume that human nature remains the same in all nations and ages, the philosophes regarded differences between peoples and civilizations as superficial and inconsequential. Since reason was common to humanity, government, law, morality, education, and all other institutions and systems of thought could be based on universal principles and could apply to all peoples throughout the globe regardless of their cultures and history.

In reality, this meant that the outlook of a small party of thinkers would become normative for all peoples and cultures. Such an undervaluing of the complex relationship between past and present, of human diversity, and of the immense appeal of familiar beliefs, traditions, and institutions—even if they seem so blatantly in opposition to reason—promotes the presumptuous and dangerous belief that society and government can be easily and rapidly molded to fit abstract principles and that reformers need pay only scant attention to historically conditioned cultural forms.

The philosophes' belief in universality, in timeless truths that apply to all peoples at all times, also contains an inherent danger. In politics, it could create true believers totally committed to an abstraction, such as the exploited class or the infallible party. To realize their ideal, these devotees will employ terror and mass murder with a clear conscience. Robespierre and the Reign of Terror during the French Revolution might be viewed as an early manifestation of this attempt to make society adhere to a conceptual grid.

Another criticism is that the philosophes' exuberant view of science and reason prevented them from realizing that reason is a double-edged sword: it could demean as well as ennoble human personality. The philosophes believed that removing thought from the realm of myth and religion and eliminating irrational forms of social organization would foster human emancipation. They could not foresee that modern bureaucracy and technology, both creations of the rational mind, could fashion a social order that devalues and depersonalizes the individual. In its determination to make the social world accord with a theoretical model, rationalism strives for uniformity and efficiency; in the process, it threatens to regulate, organize, and manipulate the individual as it would any material object. Future periods would not only reveal the limitations of reason—its inability to cope with powerful irrational drives and instincts that incite acts of inhumanity—but also the dangers of reason—its capacity to subordinate and sacrifice the individual to theoretical systems, particularly political ideologies.

Nevertheless, despite limitations, the philosophes' achievement should not be diminished. Their ideals became an intrinsic part of the liberal-democratic tradition and inspired nineteenth- and twentieth-century reformers. The spirit of the Enlightenment will always remain indispensable to all those who cherish the traditions of reason and freedom. Isaiah Berlin, the distinguished historian of ideas, eloquently summed up the Enlightenment's importance: "the intellectual power, honesty, lucidity, courage, and disinterested love of the truth of the most gifted thinkers of the eighteenth-century remain to this day without parallel. Their age is one of the best and most hopeful episodes in the life of mankind."[31]

❖ ❖ ❖

Notes

1. Galileo Galilei, *The Starry Messenger, in Discoveries and Opinions of Galileo*, trans. and ed. Stillman Drake (Garden City, N.Y.: Doubleday Anchor Books, 1957), p. 31.
2. Galileo Galilei, *The Assayer*, in *Discoveries and Opinions*, pp. 237–238.
3. Galileo Galilei, "Letter to the Grand Duchess Christina," in *Discoveries and Opinions*, p. 183.
4. Quoted in Frank E. Manuel, *Age of Reason* (Ithaca, N.Y.: Cornell University Press, 1951), p. 28.
5. David Hume, *The Natural History of Religion*, ed. H. E. Root (London: Adam and Charles Black, 1956), p. 75.
6. Denis Diderot, "Discourse of a Philosopher To a King," in *Diderot, Interpreter of Nature: Selected Writings*, ed., Jonathan Kemp, (New York: International Publishers, 1943), 214.
7. Quoted in Ben Ray Redman, ed., *The Portable Voltaire* (New York: Viking Press, 1949), p. 26.
8. Thomas Paine, *The Age of Reason* (New York: Eckler, 1892), p. 5.
9. Quoted in Paul Hazard, *European Thought in the Eighteenth Century* (New Haven, Conn.: Yale University Press, 1954), p. 174.
10. John Locke, *Two Treatises of Government*, ed. Peter Laslett (New York: New American Library, Mentor Books, 1963), *The Second Treatise*, chap. 6, sec. 61, p. 350.
11. Jean Jacques Rousseau, *The Social Contract*, in *The Social Contract and Discourses*, ed. and trans. G. D. H. Cole (New York: Dutton, 1950), bk. 1, chap. 1, p. 3.
12. Quoted in Peter Gay, *The Enlightenment: An Interpretation*, Vol. 2, *The Science of Freedom* (New York: Vintage Books, 1966), p. 170.
13. Quoted in Steven Seidman, *Liberalism and the Origins of European Social Theory* (Berkeley: University of California Press, 1983), p. 30.
14. Voltaire, "Letter to M. Bertrand," in *Candide and Other Writings*, ed. Haskell M. Block (New York: Modern Library, 1956), p. 525.
15. Quoted in Peter Gay, *Voltaire's Politics* (New York: Random House, Vintage Books, 1965), p. 71.
16. Quoted in Stephen J. Gendzier, ed. and trans., *Denis Diderot's The Encyclopedia Selections* (New York: Harper Torchbooks, 1967), p. xxv.
17. Ibid., p. xxvi.
18. Excerpted in Gendzier, *Diderot's Encyclopedia Selections*, p. 199.
19. Cesare Beccaria, *On Crimes and Punishments*, trans. Henry Paolucci (Indianapolis, Ind.: Library of Liberal Arts, 1963), p. 32.
20. Voltaire, *Candide*, in *The Portable Voltaire*, ed. Ben Ray Redman (New York: Viking, 1949), p. 234.
21. Excerpted in Gendzier, *Diderot's Encyclopedia Selections*, pp. 183–184.
22. Excerpted in ibid., pp. 229–230.
23. Quoted in Bonnie S. Anderson and Judith P. Zinsser, *A History of Their Own* (New York: Harper & Row, 1988), Vol. 2, p. 113.
24. Jean Jacques Rousseau, *Emile*, trans. Barbara Foxley (London: Dent, Everyman's Library, 1974), p. 370.
25. Mary Wollstonecraft, *Vindication of the Rights of Woman* (London: Dent, 1929), pp. 11–12.
26. Quoted in Charles Taylor, *Sources of the Self* (Cambridge, Mass.: Harvard University Press, 1989), p. 353.
27. Antoine Nicolas de Condorcet, *Sketch for a Historical Picture of the Progress of the Human*

Mind, trans. June Barraclough (London: Weidenfeld & Nicholas, 1955), p. 124.

28. Ibid., pp. 173–179.
29. Quoted in Gay, *The Enlightenment*, Vol. 1, *The Rise of Modern Paganism*, p. 20.
30. Gay, *The Enlightenment*, Vol. 2, p. 555.
31. Isaiah Berlin, ed., *The Age of Enlightenment* (New York: Mentor Books, 1956), p. 29.

Suggested Reading

Armitage, Angus, *The World of Copernicus* (1951). Good discussion of the old astronomy and the birth of the new.

Cohen, I. B., *The Birth of a New Physics* (1960). A classic study.

Commager, Henry Steele, *The Empire of Reason* (1977). The Enlightenment in the United States.

Drake, Stillman, *Galileo* (1980). By a leading authority.

Gay, Peter, *The Enlightenment: An Interpretation*, 2 vols. (1966). An exhaustive study.

Gleick, James, *Isaac Newton* (2004). A readable biography.

Hampson, Norman, *The Enlightenment* (1968). A useful survey.

Oster, Malcolm, ed., *Science in Europe 1500–1800* (2000). An excellent collection of documents.

Outram, Dorinda, *The Enlightenment* (1995). An accessible synthesis.

Roche, Daniel, *France in the Enlightenment* (1998). A well-regarded overview of the Enlightment.

Rosen, Edward, *Copernicus and the Scientific Revolution* (1984). By a recognized authority.

Shapin, Steven, *The Scientific Revolution* (1996). An up-to-date and readable synthesis.

Yolton, John W., ed., *The Blackwell Companion to the Enlightenment* (1991). An excellent reference work for all phases of the Enlightenment.

Part Four

The Modern West: Progress and Breakdown

1789–1914

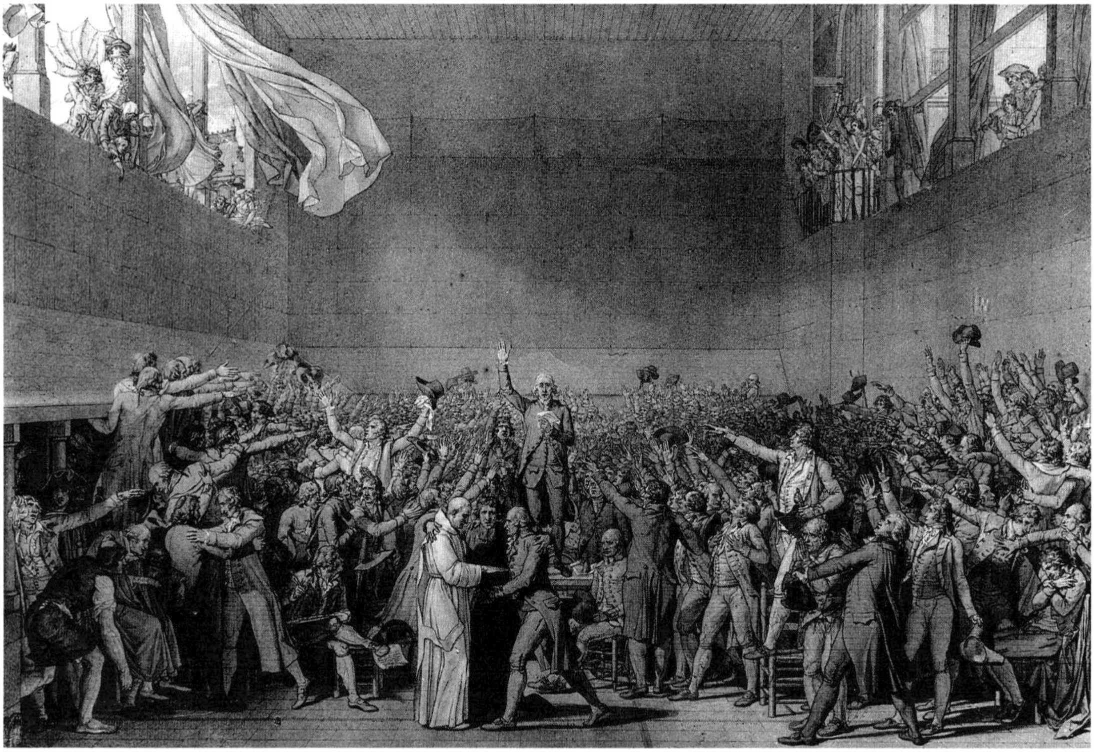

Formation of the National Assembly, *by Jacques Louis David (Detail).*

	Politics and Society	Thought and Culture
1790	French Revolution begins (1789) Declaration of the Rights of Man and of the Citizen (1789) Reign of Terror (1793–1794) Napoleon seizes power (1799)	Kant, *Critique of Pure Reason* (1781) Burke, *Reflections on the Revolution in France* (1790) Wollstonecraft, *Vindication of the Rights of Woman* (1792) Wordsworth, *The Lyrical Ballads* (1798) Beethoven, *Fifth Symphony* (1807–1808) Goya, *The Third of May* (1808) Goethe, *Faust* (1808, 1832)
1810	Napoleon invades Russia (1812) Napoleon defeated at Waterloo (1815) Congress of Vienna (1814–1815) Revolutions in Spain, Italy, Russia, and Greece (1820–1829)	Byron, *Childe Harold's Pilgrimage* (1812) Shelley, *Prometheus Unbound* (1820) Hegel, *The Philosophy of History* (1822–1831)
1830	First railway built in Britain (1830) Revolutions in France, Belgium, Poland, and Italy (1830–1832) Reform Act of 1832 in Britain Irish famine (1845–1849) Revolutions in France, Germany, Austria, and Italy (1848)	Comte, *Course in Positive Philosophy* (1830–1842) De Tocqueville, *Democracy in America* (1835–1840) Marx, *Communist Manifesto* (1848)
1850	Second Empire in France (1852–1870) Commodore Perry opens Japan to trade (1853) Unification of Italy (1859–1870) Civil War in the United States (1861–1865) Unification of Germany (1866–1871) Opening of Suez Canal (1869)	Dickens, *Hard Times* (1854) Flaubert, *Madame Bovary* (1856) Darwin, *Origin of Species* (1859) Mill, *On Liberty* (1859) Impressionism in art: Manet, Monet, Pissarro, Degas, Renoir (1860–1886) Marx, *Capital* (1867) Dostoevsky, *The Idiot* (1868) Mill, *The Subjection of Women* (1869)
1870	Franco-Prussian War (1870–1871) Third Republic in France (1870–1940) Berlin Conference on Africa (1884) Reform Bill of 1884 in Great Britain	Darwin, *Descent of Man* (1871) Nietzsche, *The Birth of Tragedy* (1872) Ibsen, *A Doll's House* (1879) Zola, *The Experimental Novel* (1880) Nietzsche, *The Anti-Christ* (1888)
1890	Dreyfus affair in France (1894–1899) Sino-Japanese War (1894–1895) Boer War in South Africa (1899–1902)	Chamberlain, *The Foundations of the Nineteenth Century* (1899) Durkheim, *Suicide* (1899)
1900	Russo-Japanese War (1904–1905) Anglo-French Entente Cordiale (1904) Anglo-Russian Entente (1907)	Freud, *The Interpretation of Dreams* (1900) Cubism in art: Picasso, Braque (1909–1914) Planck's quantum theory (1900) Lenin, *What Is to Be Done?* (1902) Einstein's theory of relativity (1905,1916) Sorel, *Reflections on Violence* (1908)

Chapter 11

The Era of the French Revolution: Affirmation of Liberty and Equality

- **The Old Regime**
- **The Moderate Stage, 1789–1791**
- **The Radical Stage, 1792–1794**
- **Napoleon and France: Return to Autocratic Rule**
- **Napoleon and Europe: Diffusion of Revolutionary Institutions**
- **The Fall of Napoleon**
- **The Meaning of the French Revolution**

Focus Questions

1. What were the causes of the French Revolution?
2. How did the Enlightenment and American Revolution influence the French Revolution?
3. Why are the reforms of the National Assembly described as the death warrant of the Old Regime?
4. Why and how did the French Revolution move from a moderate to a radical stage?
5. Why does the career of Napoleon Bonaparte continue to fascinate?
6. How did Napoleon both preserve and undermine the ideals of the French Revolution?
7. How did Napoleon speed up the modernization of Europe?
8. Why is the French Revolution a decisive period in the shaping of the modern West?

The outbreak of the French Revolution in 1789 stirred the imagination of Europeans. Both participants and observers sensed that they were living in a pivotal age. On the ruins of the Old Order, founded on privilege and despotism, a new era that promised to realize the ideals of the Enlightenment was forming. These ideals included the emancipation of the human person from superstition and tradition, the triumph of liberty over tyranny, the refashioning of institutions in accordance with reason and justice, and the tearing down of barriers to equality. It seemed that the natural rights of the individual, hitherto a distant ideal, would now reign on earth, ending centuries of oppression and misery. Never before had people shown such confidence in the power of human intelligence to shape the conditions of existence. Never before had the future seemed so full of hope. ❖

The Old Regime

Eighteenth-century French society was divided into three orders, or Estates, which were legally defined groupings. The clergy constituted the First Estate, the nobility the Second Estate, and everyone else the Third Estate. The clergy and nobility, totaling about five hundred thousand out of a population of twenty-six million, enjoyed special privileges, receiving pensions and profitable positions from the king. The social structure of the Old Regime, based on privileges and inequalities sanctioned by law, produced tensions that contributed to the Revolution.

The First Estate

The powers and privileges of the French Catholic church made it a state within a state. As it had done for centuries, the church registered births, marriages, and deaths; collected tithes (a tax on products from the soil); censored books considered dangerous to religion and morals; operated schools; and distributed relief to the poor. Although its land brought in an immense revenue, the church paid no taxes. Instead, it made a "free gift" to the state—the church determined the amount—which was always smaller than direct taxes would have been.

The clergy reflected the social divisions in France. The upper clergy shared the attitudes and way of life of the nobility from which they sprang. The parish priests, commoners by birth, resented the haughtiness and luxurious living of the upper clergy. In 1789, when the Revolution began, many priests sympathized with the reform-minded people of the Third Estate.

The Second Estate

Like the clergy, the nobility was a privileged order. Nobles held the highest positions in the church, the army, and the government. They were exempt from most taxes (or used their influence to evade paying taxes), collected manorial dues from peasants, and owned between one-quarter and one-third of the land. In addition to the income that they drew from their estates, nobles were becoming increasingly involved in such nonaristocratic enterprises as banking and finance. Nobles were the leading patrons of the arts. Many key philosophes—Montesquieu, Condorcet, d'Holbach—were nobles. Most nobles, however, were suspicious and intolerant of the liberal ideas advanced by the philosophes.

All nobles were not equal; there were gradations of dignity among the 350,000 members of the nobility. Enjoying the most prestige were *nobles of the sword*: families that could trace their aristocratic status back several centuries. The highest of the ancient nobles were engaged in the social whirl at Versailles and Paris, receiving pensions and sinecures from the king but performing few useful services for the state. Most nobles of the sword, unable to afford the gilded life at court, remained on their provincial estates, the poorest of them barely distinguishable from prosperous peasants.

Alongside this ancient nobility, a new nobility created by the monarchy had arisen. To obtain money, reward favorites, and weaken the old nobility, French kings had sold titles of nobility to members of the bourgeoisie and had conferred noble status on certain government offices bought by wealthy bourgeois. Particularly significant

Chronology 11.1 ❖ The French Revolution

July 1788	Calling of the Estates General
June 17, 1789	Third Estate declares itself the National Assembly
July 14, 1789	Storming of the Bastille
Late July 1789	The Great Fear
August 4, 1789	Nobles surrender their special privileges
April 20, 1792	Legislative Assembly declares war on Austria
Sept. 21–22, 1792	Abolition of the monarchy
June 1793	Jacobins replace Girondins as the dominant group in the National Convention
July 28, 1794	Robespierre is guillotined

were the *nobles of the robe*, whose ranks included many former bourgeois who had purchased judicial offices in the parlements, or high law courts.

Opinion among the aristocrats was divided. Some nobles, influenced by the liberal ideals of the philosophes, sought to reform France; they wanted to end royal despotism and establish a constitutional government. To this extent, the liberal nobility had a great deal in common with the bourgeoisie. These liberal nobles saw the king's difficulties in 1788 as an opportunity to regenerate the nation under enlightened leadership. When they resisted the king's policies, they claimed that they were opposing royal despotism. But at the same time many nobles remained hostile to liberal ideals and opposed reforms that threatened their privileges and honorific status.

The Third Estate

The Third Estate comprised the bourgeoisie, the peasants, and the urban workers. Although the bourgeoisie provided the leadership for the Revolution, its success depended on the support given by the rest of the Third Estate.

The Bourgeoisie. The bourgeoisie consisted of merchant manufacturers, wholesale merchants, bankers, master craftsmen, doctors, lawyers, intellectuals, and government officials below the top ranks. Although the bourgeoisie had wealth, they lacked social prestige. A merchant, despite his worldly success, felt that his occupation denied him the esteem enjoyed by the nobility.

Influenced by the aristocratic values of the day and envious of the nobility's lifestyle, the bourgeoisie sought to erase the stigma of common birth and to rise socially by becoming landowners. By 1789, the bourgeoisie owned about 20 percent of the land. Traditionally, some of its members had risen socially either by purchasing a judicial or political office that carried with it a title of nobility or by gaining admission to the upper clergy or the officer ranks of the army. Access to the nobility remained open throughout the eighteenth century. Nevertheless, since the highest and most desired positions in the land were reserved for the nobility, able bourgeois were often excluded for a variety of reasons: the high cost of purchasing an office, the limited number of new offices created, the resistance of nobles to their advancement, or the hostility of the older nobility toward those recently ennobled. No doubt these men felt frustrated and came to resent a social system that valued birth more than talent. For most of the century, however, the bourgeoisie did not challenge the existing social structure, including the special privileges of the nobility.

By 1789, the bourgeois had many grievances. They wanted all positions in the church, army, and state to be open to men of talent regardless of birth. They sought a parliament that would make laws for the nation; a constitution that would limit the king's power and guarantee freedom of thought, fair trials, and religious toleration; and administrative reforms that would eliminate waste, inefficiency, and interference with business.

The Peasantry. The condition of the more than twenty-one million French peasants was a paradox. On the one hand, they were better off than peasants in Austria, Prussia, Poland, and Russia, where serfdom still predominated. In France, serfdom had largely disappeared; many peasants owned their land, and some were even prosperous. On the other hand, most French peasants lived in poverty, which worsened in the closing years of the Old Regime.

The typical peasant holding was barely large enough to eke out a living. The rising birthrate (between 1715 and 1789, the population may have increased from eighteen million to twenty-six million) led to the continual subdivision of farms among heirs. Moreover, many peasants did not own land but rented it from a nobleman or a prosperous neighbor. Others worked as sharecroppers, turning over a considerable portion of the harvest to their creditors.

An unjust and corrupt system of taxation weighed heavily on the peasantry. Louis XIV had maintained his grandeur and financed his wars by milking ever more taxes from the peasants, a practice that continued throughout the eighteenth century. An army of tax collectors victimized the peasantry. In addition to royal taxes, peasants paid the tithe to the church and manorial dues to lords.

Although serfdom had ended in most parts of France, lords continued to demand obligations from peasants as they had done in the Middle Ages. Besides performing labor services on the lord's estate, peasants still had to grind their grain in the lord's mill, bake their bread in his oven, press their grapes in his winepress, and give him part of their produce in payment. (These fees were called *banalities.*) In addition, the lord exercised exclusive hunting rights on lands tilled by peasants. Those rights were particularly onerous, for the lord's hunting parties damaged crops. Lords were determined to hold on to these privileges not only because of the income they brought but also because they were symbols of authority and social esteem.

Réunion des Musées Nationaux/Art Resource, N.Y.

"LET'S HOPE THAT THE GAME FINISHES WELL." This political cartoon shows a laboring-class woman carrying smug representatives of the privileged orders on her back.

Urban Laborers. The urban laboring class in this preindustrial age consisted of journeymen working for master craftsmen, factory workers in small-scale industries, and wage earners such as day laborers, gardeners, handymen, and deliverymen, who were paid by those whom they served. Conditions for the urban poor, like those for the peasant wage earners, worsened in the late eighteenth century. From 1785 to 1789, the cost of living increased by 62 percent, while wages rose only by 22 percent. For virtually the entire decade of the Revolution, urban workers struggled to keep body and soul together in the face of food shortages and rising prices, particularly the price of their staple food, bread. Material want drove the urban poor to acts of violence that affected the course of the Revolution.

Inefficient Administration and Financial Disorder

The administration of France was complex, confusing, and ineffective. The practice of buying state offices from the king, introduced as a means of raising money, resulted in many incompetent officeholders. Tariffs on goods shipped from one province to another and differing systems of weights and measures hampered trade. No single law code applied to all the provinces; instead, there were overlapping and conflicting law systems based on old Roman law or customary feudal law, which made the administration of justice slow, arbitrary, and unfair. To admirers of the philosophes, the administrative system was an insult to reason. The Revolution would sweep the system away.

Financial disorders also contributed to the weakness of the Old Regime. In the regime's last years, the government could not raise sufficient funds to cover expenses. By 1787, it still had not paid off the enormous debt incurred during the wars of Louis XIV, let alone the costs of succeeding wars during the eighteenth century, particularly France's aid to the colonists in the American Revolution. The king's gifts and pensions to court nobles and the extravagant court life further drained the treasury.

Finances were in a shambles not because France was impoverished but because of an inefficient and unjust tax system. Although serious, the financial crisis could have been solved if the clergy, nobility, and bourgeoisie had paid their fair share of taxes. With France on the brink of bankruptcy, some of the king's ministers proposed that the nobility and church surrender some of their tax exemptions, but the privileged orders resisted. Some nobles resisted because they were steadfast defenders of noble prerogatives; the more liberal nobles resisted because they saw an opportunity to check absolutism and introduce fundamental reforms that would regenerate the nation.

The resistance of the nobility forced the government, in July 1788, to call for a meeting of the Estates General—a medieval representative assembly that had last met in 1614—to deal with the financial crisis. The body was to convene in May 1789. Certain that they would dominate the Estates General, the nobles intended to weaken the power of the throne. Once in control of the government, they would introduce financial reforms. But the revolt of the nobility against the crown had unexpected consequences. It opened the way for a revolution by the Third Estate that destroyed the Old Regime and with it the aristocracy and its privileges.

The Roles of the Enlightenment and the American Revolution

Revolutions are born in the realm of the spirit. Revolutionary movements, says George Rudé, a historian of the French Revolution, require "some unifying body of ideas, a common vocabulary of hope and protest, something, in short, like a common 'revolutionary psychology.'"[1] For this reason, many historians see a relationship between the Enlightenment and the French Revolution. The philosophes were not revolutionaries themselves, but their attacks on the pillars of the established order and their appeals for a freer, more tolerant society helped to create a revolutionary psychology. As Henri Peyre observes,

> *Eighteenth-century philosophy taught the Frenchman to find his condition wretched, or in any case, unjust and illogical and made him disinclined to the patient resignation to his troubles that had long characterized his ancestors. . . . The propaganda of the "Philosophes" perhaps more than any other factor accounted for the fulfillment of the preliminary condition of the French Revolution, namely discontent with the existing state of things.*[2]

As the Revolution progressed, its leaders utilized the philosophes' ideas and language to attack the foundations of the old order and to justify their own reform program.

The American Revolution, which gave practical expression to the liberal philosophy of the philosophes, also helped to pave the way for the French Revolution. The Declaration of Independence (1776), which proclaimed the natural rights of man and sanctioned resistance against a government that deprived men of these rights, influenced the framers of the Declaration of the Rights of Man and of the Citizen (1789) (see the upcoming section "Reforms of the National Assembly"). The United States showed that a nation could be established on the principle that sovereign power derived from the people. The Americans set an example of social equality unparalleled in Europe. In the United States, there was no hereditary aristocracy, no serfdom, and no state church. Liberal French aristocrats, such as the Marquis de Lafayette, who had fought in the American Revolution, returned to France more optimistic about the possibilities of reforming French society.

A Bourgeois Revolution?

Because the bourgeois were the principal leaders and chief beneficiaries of the French Revolution, many historians have viewed it, along with the English revolutions of the seventeenth century and the growth of capitalism, as "an episode in the general rise of the bourgeoisie."[3] Those who regard the Revolution as a "bourgeois revolution" argue that in the last part of the eighteenth century it became increasingly difficult for the bourgeoisie to gain the most honored offices in the land. According to this view, in the eighteenth century, a decadent and reactionary aristocracy sought to regain the powers that it had lost under Louis XIV. Through parlements, aristocrats blocked reforms proposed by the king that threatened their privileges, and they united to prevent commoners from entering their ranks.

The nobility's determination to safeguard its power and social exclusiveness collided head-on with the aspirations of a wealthy, talented, and progressive bourgeoisie. Finding the path to upward mobility and social dignity barred, the bourgeoisie, imbued with the rational outlook of the Enlightenment, came to perceive nobles as an obstacle to its advancement and the nation's progress. "The essential cause of the Revolution," concludes French historian Albert Soboul, "was the power of a bourgeoisie arrived at its maturity and confronted by a decadent aristocracy holding tenaciously to its privileges."[4] Thus, when the bourgeois found the opportunity during the Revolution, they ended the legal division of France into separate orders.

In recent decades, some historians have challenged this interpretation. These revisionists argue that before 1789 France did not have a self-conscious bourgeois class aspiring to take control of the state in order to promote a capitalist economy—that the nobles and the bourgeoisie did not represent antagonistic classes divided by sharp differences. On the contrary, they were not clearly distinguishable from each other. The bourgeois aspired to noble status, and many nobles were involved in business enterprises—mining, metallurgy, textiles, and overseas trading companies—traditionally considered the province of the bourgeoisie. Abandoning a traditional aristocratic disdain for business, many nobles had acquired the capitalist mentality associated with the middle class. Some nobles also shared with the bourgeois the liberal values of the philosophes and a desire to do away with monarchical despotism and reform France according to rational standards. Thus, French nobles, particularly those who lived in urban centers or had traveled to Britain and the American colonies, were receptive both to new means of livelihood and to progressive ideas.

Moreover, the French nobility was constantly infused with new blood from below. During the eighteenth century, thousands of bourgeois, through marriage, the purchase of an office, or service as local officials—mayors, for example—had some entitlement of nobility. As British historian William Doyle puts it, "the nobility was an open elite, not a hereditary class apart. Nor is it now possible to maintain that this elite grew less open as the eighteenth century went on thanks to some exclusive 'aristocratic reaction.'"[5]

Just prior to 1789, revisionists contend, nobles and prosperous bourgeois were no longer clearly differentiated; the traditional distinctions that had set them apart were now obsolete. France's social elite actually consisted not of a hereditary nobility, but of *notables*—both nobles and bourgeois—distinguished more by wealth than by birth. Bourgeois notables were essentially moderate; they did not seek the destruction of the aristocracy that was accomplished in the opening stage of the Revolution. The elimination of aristocratic privileges was not part of a preconceived bourgeois program, revisionists maintain, but an improvised response to the violent upheavals in the countryside in July and August 1789. Moreover, not until early 1789, when a struggle erupted over the composition of the Estates General (see the next section), did the bourgeoisie start to become conscious of itself as a class with interests that clashed with those of the aristocracy. Until then, both the bourgeoisie and many aristocrats were united around a common and moderate reform program.

Finally, revisionists argue that the feudal nobility was not as decadent or reactionary as traditional accounts would have it. The nobles resisted the king's reforming ministers because they doubted the ability of a despotic and incompetent state to solve the financial crisis. To be sure, there were aristocrats who selfishly wanted to cling to their privileges, but many also aspired to serve the public good by instituting structural changes that would liberate the nation from despotic and inefficient rule and reform its financial and administrative system. It was this desire to institute crucial changes in French political life, say revisionists, that led nobles to press for the convening of the Estates General.

The Moderate Stage, 1789–1791

Since a significant number of nobles were sympathetic to reform, there was no insuperable gulf between the Second and Third Estates as the Estates General prepared to meet. However, it soon became clear that the hopes of reformers clashed with the intentions of many aristocrats.

What had started as a struggle between the crown and the aristocracy was turning into something far more significant: a conflict between the two privileged orders on one side and the Third Estate on the other. One pamphleteer, Abbé Sieyés (1748–1836), expressed the hatred that members of the bourgeoisie felt for the aristocracy. "The privileged order has said to the Third Estate: 'Whatever be your services, whatever be your talents, you shall go thus far and no farther. It is not fitting that you be honored.'" The higher positions in the land, said Sieyés, should be the "reward for talents," not the prerogative of birth. Without the Third Estate, "nothing can progress"; without the nobility, "everything would proceed infinitely better."[6]

Formation of the National Assembly

The Estates General convened at Versailles on May 5, 1789, but was stalemated by the question of procedure. Seeking to control the assembly, the nobility insisted that the three Estates follow the traditional practice of meeting separately and voting as individual bodies. Since the two privileged orders were likely to stand together, the Third Estate would always be outvoted two to one. But the delegates from the Third Estate, unwilling to allow the nobility and the higher clergy to dominate the Estates General, proposed instead that the three Estates meet as one body and vote by head. There were some 610 delegates from the Third Estate; the nobility and clergy together had an equivalent number. Since the Third Estate could rely on the support of sympathetic parish priests and liberal nobles, it would be assured a majority if all the orders met together. As aristocrats and bourgeois became more polarized, antinoble rhetoric gained a growing audience among all segments of the Third Estate. Many commoners now saw the aristocracy as the chief obstacle to reform.

On June 17, the Third Estate made a revolutionary move. It declared itself the National Assembly. On June 20, locked out of their customary meeting hall (apparently by accident), the Third Estate delegates moved to a nearby tennis court and took a solemn oath not to disband until a constitution had been drawn up for France. Louis XVI commanded the National Assembly to separate into orders, but the Third Estate held firm. The steadfastness of the delegates and the menacing actions of Parisians who supported the National Assembly forced Louis XVI to yield. On June 27, he ordered the nobility (some had already done so) and the clergy (a majority had already done so) to join with the Third Estate in the National Assembly.

STORMING OF THE BASTILLE, JULY 14, 1789. A Parisian crowd stormed the dreaded fortress of the Bastille, long identified with the abuses of the Old Regime.

But the victory of the bourgeoisie was not yet secure, for most nobles had not resigned themselves to a bourgeois-dominated National Assembly. It appeared that Louis XVI, influenced by court aristocrats, had resolved to use force against the National Assembly and stop the incipient revolution. At this point, uprisings by the common people of Paris and peasants in the countryside saved the National Assembly, exacerbated hostilities between the Third Estate and the nobility, and ensured the victory of the forces of reform.

Storming of the Bastille

In July 1789, the level of tension in Paris was high for three reasons. First, the calling of the Estates General had aroused hopes for reform. Second, the price of bread was soaring: in August 1788, a Parisian laborer had spent 50 percent of his income on bread; by July 1789, he was spending 80 percent. A third element in the tension was the fear of an aristocratic plot to crush the National Assembly. Afraid that royal troops would bombard and pillage the city, Parisians searched for weapons.

On July 14, eight hundred to nine hundred Parisians gathered in front of the Bastille, a fortress used as a prison and a reviled symbol of royal despotism. They gathered primarily to obtain gunpowder and to remove the cannon that threatened a heavily populated working-class district. As the tension mounted, the Parisians stormed and captured the Bastille. The fall of the Bastille had far-reaching consequences: a symbol of the Old Regime's darkness and despotism had fallen; some court nobles hostile to the Revolution

Women's March to Versailles. A bread shortage and high prices sparked the protest march of thousands of women to Versailles in October 1789. The king was compelled to return to Paris, a sign of his diminishing power, and many aristocrats hostile to the Revolution fled the country.

decided to flee the country; the frightened king told the National Assembly that he would withdraw the troops ringing Paris. The revolutionary act of the Parisians had indirectly saved the National Assembly and its bourgeois leadership.

The Great Fear

Revolution in the countryside also served the interests of the reformers. Inflamed by economic misery and stirred by the uprisings of the Parisians, peasants began to burn manor houses and destroy the registers on which their obligations to the lords were inscribed. The flames of the peasants' insurrection were fanned by rumors that aristocrats were organizing bands of brigands to attack the peasants. The mythical army of brigands never materialized, but the Great Fear, as this episode is called, led more peasants to take up arms. Suspicious of an aristocratic plot to thwart efforts at reform and releasing years of stored-up hatred for the nobles, the peasants attacked the lords' chateaux with great fury.

Like the insurrection in Paris, the peasant upheavals in late July and early August worked to the advantage of the reformers. The attacks provided the National Assembly with an opportunity to strike at noble privileges by putting into law what the peasants had accomplished with the torch—the destruction of feudal remnants. On the night of August 4, 1789, aristocrats seeking to restore calm in the countryside surrendered their special privileges: exclusive hunting rights, tax exemptions, monopoly of highest offices, manorial courts, and the right to demand labor services from peasants.

In the decrees of August 5 and 11, the National Assembly implemented the resolutions of August 4. The Assembly also declared that the planned constitution should be prefaced by a declaration of rights. On August 26, it adopted the Declaration of the Rights of Man and of the Citizen.

October Days

Louis XVI, cool to these reforms, postponed his approval of the August Decrees and the Declaration of Rights. It would require a second uprising by the Parisians to force the king to agree to the reforms and to nail down the victory of the reformers.

On October 5, 1789, Parisian housewives and men marched twelve miles to Versailles to protest the lack of bread to the National Assembly and the king. A few hours later, twenty thousand Paris Guards, a citizen militia sympathetic to the Revolution, also set out for Versailles in support of the protesters. The king had no choice but to promise bread and to return with the demonstrators to Paris. Aware that he had no control over the Parisians and fearful of further violence, Louis XVI approved the August Decrees and the Declaration of Rights. Nobles who had urged the king to use force against the Assembly and had tried to block reforms fled the country in large numbers.

Reforms of the National Assembly

With resistance weakened, the National Assembly continued the work of reform begun in the summer of 1789. Its reforms, which are summarized below, destroyed the Old Regime.

1. *Abolition of special privileges.* By ending the special privileges of the nobility and the clergy in the August Decrees, the National Assembly legalized the equality that the bourgeoisie had demanded. The aristocratic structure of the Old Regime, a remnant of the Middle Ages that had hindered the progressive bourgeoisie, was eliminated.

2. *Statement of human rights.* The Declaration of the Rights of Man and of the Citizen expressed the liberal and universal goals of the philosophes. In proclaiming the inalienable right to liberty of person, freedom of religion and thought, and equal treatment under the law, the declaration affirmed the dignity of the individual. It asserted that government belonged not to any ruler but to the people as a whole, and that its aim was the preservation of the natural rights of the individual. Because the declaration contrasted sharply with the principles espoused by an intolerant clergy, a privileged aristocracy, and a despotic monarch, it has been called the death warrant of the Old Regime. A significant example of the new leadership's commitment to equality and religious toleration was the law passed in 1791 granting civil rights to Jews. Jews were now free to leave the ghettos, to which they had been forcibly confined for centuries to keep them apart from Gentiles, and, in theory, to participate in French society as equal citizens.

3. *Subordination of church to state.* The National Assembly also struck at the privileges of the Roman Catholic Church. The August Decrees declared the end of tithes. To obtain badly needed funds, the Assembly in November 1789 confiscated church lands and put them up for sale. In 1790, the Assembly passed the Civil Constitution of the Clergy, which reduced the number of bishops and priests and transformed the clergy into government officials elected by the people and paid by the state.

Almost all bishops and many priests opposed the Civil Constitution. It divided the French and gave opponents of the Revolution an emotional issue around which to rally supporters. Many devout Catholic peasants, resentful of the Revolution's treatment of the church, would join with aristocrats and clergy in the counterrevolution that would soon emerge.

4. *A constitution for France.* In September 1791, the National Assembly issued a constitution limiting the power of the king and guaranteeing all French citizens equal treatment under the law. Citizens paying less than a specified amount in taxes could not vote. Probably about 30 percent of the males over the age of twenty-five were excluded by this stipulation, and only the more well-to-do citizens were qualified to sit in the Legislative Assembly, a unicameral parliament created to succeed the National Assembly. The drafters of the constitution did not trust illiterate and propertyless men to vote and enact legislation. Nevertheless, the suffrage requirements under the constitution of 1791 were far more generous than those in Britain.

5. *Administrative and judicial reforms.* The National Assembly replaced the patchwork of provincial units with eighty-three new administrative units, or departments, approximately equal in size. Judicial reforms complemented the administrative changes. A standardized system of courts replaced the innumerable jurisdictions of the Old Regime, and the sale of judicial offices was ended. The penal code completed by the National Assembly abolished torture and barbarous punishments.

6. *Aid for business.* The National Assembly abolished all tolls and duties on goods transported within the country, established a uniform system of weights and measures, eliminated the guilds (medieval survivals that blocked business expansion), and forbade workers to form unions or to strike.

By ending absolutism, striking at the privileges of the nobility, and preventing the mass of people from gaining control over the government, the National Assembly consolidated the rule of the bourgeoisie. With one arm, it broke the power of aristocracy and throne; with the other, it held back the common people. Although the reforms benefitted the bourgeoisie, it would be a mistake to view them merely as a selfish expression of bourgeois interests. The Declaration of the Rights of Man and of the Citizen was addressed to all; it proclaimed liberty and equality as the right of all and called on citizens to treat one another with respect.

The Radical Stage, 1792–1794

Pleased with their accomplishments—equality before the law, careers open to talent, a written constitution, parliamentary government—the men of 1789 wished the Revolution to go no further. But revolutionary times are unpredictable. Soon the Revolution moved in a direction neither anticipated nor desired by the reformers. A counterrevolution, led by irreconcilable nobles and alienated churchmen, gained the support of the strongly Catholic peasants. It threatened the Revolution, forcing the revolutionary leadership to resort to extreme measures.

The Sans-Culottes

The discontent of the *sans-culottes**—small shopkeepers, artisans, and wage earners—also propelled the Revolution toward radicalism. Although they had played a significant role in the Revolution, particularly in the storming of the Bastille and in the October Days, they had gained little. The sans-culottes, says French historian Albert Soboul, "began to realize that a privilege of wealth was taking the place of a privilege of birth. They foresaw that the bourgeoisie would succeed the fallen aristocracy as the ruling class."[7] Inflamed by poverty and their hatred of the rich, the sans-culottes insisted that it was the government's duty to guarantee them the "right of existence"—a policy that ran counter to the economic individualism of the bourgeoisie.

The sans-culottes demanded that the government increase wages, set price controls on food supplies, end food shortages, and pass laws to prevent extremes of wealth and poverty. Whereas the men of 1789 sought equality of rights, liberties, and opportunities, the sans-culottes expanded the principle of equality to include narrowing the gap between the rich and the poor. To reduce economic inequality, they called for higher taxes for the wealthy and the redistribution of land. Politically, they favored a democratic republic in which the common man had a voice.

In 1789, the bourgeoisie had demanded equality with the aristocrats: the right to hold the most honored positions in the nation and an end to the special privileges of the nobility. By the close of 1792, the sans-culottes were demanding equality with the bourgeois. They wanted political reforms that would give the poor a voice in the government and social reforms that would improve their lot. The bourgeoisie feared the democratization of the Revolution.

*Literally, *sans-culottes* means "without culottes" and refers to the people who wore the simple trousers of a laborer and not the knee breeches that aristocrats wore before the Revolution.

Foreign Invasion

Despite the pressures exerted by reactionary nobles and clergy on the one hand and discontented sans-culottes on the other, the Revolution might not have taken a radical turn if France had remained at peace. The war that broke out with Austria and Prussia in April 1792 exacerbated internal dissensions, worsened economic conditions, and threatened to undo the reforms of the Revolution. It was in these circumstances that the Revolution moved from its moderate stage to a radical one, which historians refer to as the Second French Revolution.

In June 1791, Louis XVI and the royal family, traveling in disguise, fled Paris for northeastern France to join with *émigrés* (nobles who had left revolutionary France and were organizing a counterrevolutionary army) and to rally foreign support against the Revolution. Discovered at Varennes by a village postmaster, they were brought back to Paris as virtual prisoners. The flight of the king turned many French people against the monarchy, strengthening the position of the radicals who wanted to do away with kingship altogether and establish a republic. But it was foreign invasion that ultimately led to the destruction of the monarchy.

On April 20, 1792, fearful that Austria intended to overthrow the Revolution and eager to spread revolutionary ideals, France declared war on Austria. A combined Austrian and Prussian army commanded by the Duke of Brunswick crossed into France. In an atmosphere already charged with tension, the Duke of Brunswick issued a manifesto declaring that if the royal family were harmed, he would exact a terrible vengeance on the Parisians. On August 10, enraged Parisians and militia from other cities attacked the king's palace, killing several hundred Swiss guards.

In early September, as foreign troops advanced deeper into France, rumors spread that jailed priests and aristocrats were planning to break out of their cells to support the Duke of Brunswick. The Parisians panicked. Driven by fear, patriotism, and murderous impulses, they raided the prisons and massacred eleven hundred to twelve hundred prisoners, including two hundred priests. Most of the victims were not political prisoners but ordinary criminals.

Scala/Art Resource, N.Y.

The Execution of Louis XVI. The king died with dignity. His last words were "I forgive my enemies; I trust that my death will be for the happiness of my people, but I grieve for France, and I fear that she may suffer the anger of the Lord."

On September 21 and 22, the National Convention (the new lawmaking body) abolished the monarchy and established a republic. In December, Louis XVI was placed on trial, and in January 1793 he was executed for conspiring against the liberty of the French people. The uprising of August 10, the September massacres, the creation of a republic, and the execution of Louis XVI all confirmed that the Revolution was taking a radical turn.

Meanwhile, the war continued. Short of supplies, hampered by bad weather, and lacking sufficient manpower, the Duke of Brunswick never did reach Paris. Outmaneuvered at Valmy on September 20, 1792, the foreign forces retreated to the frontier, and the armies of the republic took the offensive. By the beginning of 1793, French forces had overrun Belgium (then a part of the Austrian Empire), the German Rhineland, and the Sardinian provinces of Nice and Savoy. To the peoples of Europe, the National Convention had solemnly announced that it was waging a popular crusade against privilege and tyranny, against aristocrats and princes.

These revolutionary social ideas, the execution of Louis XVI, and, most important, French expansion, which threatened the balance of power, frightened the rulers of Europe. Urged on by Britain, by the spring of 1793 they formed an anti-French alliance. The allies' forces pressed toward the French borders, endangering the republic.

Counterrevolutionary insurrections further undermined the fledgling republic. In the Vendée, in western France, peasants who were protesting against taxation and conscription and were still loyal to their priests and Catholic tradition, which the Revolution had attacked, took up arms against the republic. Led by local nobles, the peasants of the Vendée waged a guerrilla war for religion, royalism, and their traditional way of life. In other quarters, federalists revolted in the provinces, objecting to the power wielded by the centralized government in Paris. The republic was unable to exercise control over much of the country.

The Jacobins

As the republic tottered under the weight of foreign invasion, internal insurrection, and economic crisis, the revolutionary leadership grew still more radical; so too did commoners, the *petit peuple*, who sought vengeance against aristocrats accused of conspiring with foreign states against the Revolution. In June 1793, the Jacobins replaced the Girondins as the dominant group in the National Convention. The Girondins favored a government in which the departments would exercise control over their own affairs. The Jacobins, on the other hand, wanted a strong central government, with Paris as the seat of power. Both Girondins and Jacobins came from the bourgeoisie, but the Girondins opposed government interference in business, whereas the Jacobins supported temporary government controls to deal with the needs of war and economic crisis. This last point was crucial; it won the Jacobins the support of the sans-culottes. On June 2, 1793, some eighty thousand armed sans-culottes surrounded the Convention and demanded the arrest of Girondin delegates—an act that enabled the Jacobins to gain control of the government.

The problems confronting the Jacobins were staggering. They had to cope with civil war, particularly in the Vendée; economic distress; blockaded ports; and foreign invasion. They lived with the terrible dread that if they failed, the Revolution for liberty and equality would perish. Only strong leadership could save the republic. It was provided by the Committee of Public Safety, which organized the nation's defenses, supervised ministers, ordered arrests, and imposed the central government's authority throughout the nation.

The Jacobins continued the work of reform. In 1793, a new constitution expressed Jacobin enthusiasm for political democracy. It contained a new Declaration of Rights, which affirmed and amplified the principles of 1789. By giving all adult males the right to vote, it overcame sans-culotte objections to the constitution of 1791. However, the threat of invasion and the revolts caused the implementation of the new constitution to be postponed, and it was never put into effect. By abolishing both slavery in the French colonies and imprisonment for debt and by making plans for free public education, the Jacobins revealed their humanitarianism and their debt to the philosophes. To halt inflation and gain the support of the poor—both necessary for the war effort—the Jacobins decreed the *law of the maximum*, which fixed prices on bread and other essential goods and raised wages.

The Nation in Arms

To fight the war against foreign invaders, the Jacobins, in an act that anticipated modern conscription, drafted unmarried men between eighteen and twenty-five years of age. They mobilized the country's resources, infused the army with a love for *la patrie* (the nation), and, in a remarkable demonstration of administrative skill, equipped an army of more than 800,000 men. In creating the nation in arms, the Jacobins heralded the emergence of modern warfare. Inspired by the ideals of liberty, equality, and fraternity and commanded by officers who had proved their skill on the battlefield, the citizen soldiers of the republic won decisive victories. In May and June 1794, the French routed the allied forces on the vital northern frontier, and by the end of July, France had become the triumphant master of Belgium.

By demanding complete devotion to the nation, the Jacobin phase of the Revolution also heralded the rise of modern nationalism. In the schools, in newspapers, speeches, and poems, on the stage, and at rallies and meetings of patriotic societies, the French people were told of the glory won by republican soldiers on the battlefield and were reminded of their duties to *la patrie*. "The citizen is born, lives, and dies for the fatherland"—these words were written in public places for all citizens to read and ponder. The soldiers of the Revolution fought not for money or for a king but for the nation. Could this heightened sense of nationality, which concentrated on the special interests of the French people, be reconciled with the Declaration of the Rights of Man, whose principles were addressed to all humanity? The revolutionaries themselves did not understand the implications of the new force that they had unleashed.

The Republic of Virtue and the Reign of Terror

While forging a revolutionary army to deal with external enemies, the Jacobins were also waging war against internal opposition. The pivotal personality in this struggle was Maximilien Robespierre (1758–1794), who had a fervent faith in the rightness of his beliefs and a total commitment to republican democracy. In the early stage of Revolution, Robespierre had strongly supported liberal reforms. He attacked—at times with great fervor—slavery, capital punishment, and censorship; he favored civil rights for Jews; and, in what was considered a radical measure, he supported giving all men the vote regardless of how much property they owned. Robespierre wanted to create a better society founded on reason, good citizenship; and patriotism. In his Republic of Virtue, there would be no kings or nobles; men would be free, equal, and educated; and reason would be glorified and superstition ridiculed. There would be no extremes of wealth or poverty; people's natural goodness would prevail over vice and greed; and laws would preserve, not violate, inalienable rights. In this utopian vision, an individual's duties would be "to detest bad faith and despotism, to punish tyrants and traitors, to assist the unfortunate, to respect the weak, to defend the oppressed, to do all the good one can to one's neighbor, and to behave with justice towards all men."[8] Robespierre pursued his ideal society with religious zeal. Knowing that the Republic of Virtue could not be established while France was threatened by foreign and civil war, and certain that counterrevolutionaries were everywhere, Robespierre urged harsh treatment for enemies of the republic, who "must be prosecuted by all not as ordinary enemies, but as rebels, brigands, and assassins."[9]

With Robespierre playing a key role, the Jacobin leadership executed those they considered enemies of the republic: Girondins who challenged Jacobin authority; federalists who opposed a strong central government emanating from Paris; counterrevolutionary priests and nobles and their peasant supporters; and profiteers who hoarded food. The Jacobins even sought to discipline the ardor of the sans-culottes, who had given them power. Fearful that, uncontrolled, the sans-culottes would undermine central authority and promote anarchy, Robespierrists brought about the dissolution of sans-culotte societies. They also executed sans-culotte leaders known as the *enragés* (literally, madmen), who threatened insurrection against Jacobin rule and pushed for more social reforms than the Jacobins would allow. The enragés wanted to set limits on income and on the size of farms and businesses—policies considered far too extreme by the supporters of Robespierre.

Robespierre and his fellow Jacobins did not make terror a deliberate government policy because they were bloodthirsty or power mad. Instead, they sought to establish a temporary dictatorship in a desperate attempt to save the republic and the Revolution. Deeply devoted to republican democracy, the Jacobins viewed themselves as bearers of a higher faith. Like all other true believers, Robespierre was convinced that he knew the right way and that the new society he envisaged would benefit all humanity. He saw those who impeded its implementation not just as opponents, but as sinners who had to be liquidated for the general good.

Special courts were established in Paris and other cities to try suspects. The proceedings were carried on in haste, and most judgments called for either acquittal or execution. In the Vendée,

Primary Source

Edmund Burke: *Reflections on the Revolution in France*

There were mixed reactions to the French Revolution among thinkers and statesmen in Europe and the United States. In Reflections on the Revolution in France *(1790), Edmund Burke a leading Irish-English statesman and political thinker, attacked the violence and fundamental principles of the Revolution, Burke regarded the revolutionaries as wild-eyed fanatics who had uprooted all established authority, tradition, and institutions, thereby plunging France into anarchy. He wrote Reflections, an excerpt of which follows, before the Terror.*

. . . You [revolutionaries] chose to act as if you had never been moulded into civil society, and had every thing to begin anew. You began ill, because you began by despising every thing that belonged to you. . . . If the last generation of your country appeared without much lustre in your eyes, you might have passed them by, and derived your claims from a more early race of ancestors. . . . Respecting your forefathers, you would. . . . not have chosen to consider the French . . . as a nation of low-born servile wretches until the emancipating year of 1789. . . . By following wise examples you would have. . . . rendered the cause of liberty venerable in the eyes of every worthy mind in the nation. . . . You would have had a free constitution; a potent monarchy; a disciplined army; a reformed and venerable clergy; a mitigated but spirited nobility, to lead your virtue. . . .

Compute your gains: see what is got by those extravagant and presumptuous speculations which have taught your leaders to despise all their predecessors. . . . By following these false lights, France has bought undisguised calamities [to itself]. France, when she let loose the reins of regal authority, doubled the licence, of a ferocious dissoluteness in manners, and of an insolent irreligion in opinions and practices; and has extended through all ranks of life. . . . all the unhappy corruptions that usually were the disease of wealth and power. This is one of the new principles of equality in France. . . .

. . . The science of government . . . requires experience, and even more experience than any person can gain in his whole life, however sagacious and observing he may be. [Therefore] it is with infinite caution that any man ought to venture upon pulling down an edifice which has answered in any tolerable degree for ages the common purposes of society. . . .

where civil war raged, many of the arrested were executed by firing squads without trial. Ironically, most of the executions took place after the frontiers had been secured and the civil war crushed. Of the five hundred thousand people imprisoned for crimes against the republic, some sixteen thousand were sentenced to death by guillotine and another twenty thousand perished in prison before they could be tried. More than two hundred thousand died in the civil war in the provinces, and forty thousand were summarily executed by firing squad, guillotine, and mass drownings ordered by military courts authorized by the Convention.

The Terror was particularly brutal in the Vendée, where the counterrevolution was fought by deeply religious Catholic peasants led by aristocrats who wanted an end to conscription and the mistreatment of their priests. Although untrained and poorly armed, the Vendéans succeeded in capturing a major town in the Loire Valley; in the process they killed some 150 republican soldiers and took 8,000 prisoners. The Republic was imperiled, but in June 1793, seasoned republican forces defeated the Vendéans in the port city of Nantes. This was followed up in October by a crushing defeat in the town of Chalet. Then the mass murders began.

Regarding the Vendéans as superstitious fanatics who fought against the Revolution's ideals and as traitors in league with France's enemies, frenzied republican soldiers, under orders from their superiors, burned villages, slaughtered livestock, and indiscriminately killed tens of thousands of peasants. Some five thousand Vendéans were loaded onto barges that were then sunk in the middle of the Loire River. Perhaps one-quarter of the region's population, women and children included, perished in 1793 and 1794. (To this day, the Vendéans mourn these losses and express contempt for the Revolution.)

When ancient opinions of life are taken away, the loss cannot possibly be estimated. From that moment we have no compass to govern us; nor can we know distinctly to what port we steer. . . .

. . . Nothing is more certain than that our manners, our civilization, and all the good things which are connected with manners and with civilization have in this European world of ours depended for ages upon two principles and were, indeed, the result of both combined: I mean the spirit of a gentleman and the spirit of religion. . . .

Burke next compares the English people with the French revolutionaries.

. . . . Thanks to our sullen resistance to innovation, . . . we still bear the stamp of our forefathers. We are not the converts of Rousseau; we are not the disciples of Voltaire; Helvetius has made no progress amongst us.* Atheists are not our preachers; madmen are not our lawgivers. We know that we have made no discoveries, and we think that no discoveries are to be made, in morality nor many in the great principles of government. . . . We fear God; we look up with awe to kings, with affection to parliaments, with duty to magistrates, with reverence to priests, and with respect to nobility. . . .

. . . We are afraid to put men to live and trade each on his own private stock of reason, because we suspect that this stock in each man is small, and that the individuals would do better to avail themselves of the general bank and capital of nations and of ages.

Questions for Analysis

1. Why is Edmund Burke considered an important theorist in the shaping of conservative thought?
2. What in particular might contemporary conservatives find valuable in Burke's analysis?

---

* Rousseau, Voltaire, and Helvetius were French philosophes of the eighteenth century noted respectively for advocating democracy, attacking the abuses of the Old Regime, and applying scientific reason to human nature and education.

Edmund Burke, *Reflections on the Revolution in France* (London: Printed for J. Dodsley, 1791), pp. 51–55, 90–91, 116–117, 127, 129.

The Jacobins expelled foreign armies, crushed the federalist uprisings, contained the counterrevolutionaries in the Vendée, and prevented anarchy. Without the discipline, order, and unity imposed on France by the Jacobins, it is likely that the republic would have collapsed under the twin blows of foreign invasion and domestic anarchy.

Nonetheless, the Reign of Terror poses fundamental questions about the meaning of the French Revolution and the validity of the Enlightenment conception of the individual. To what extent did the feverish passions and lust for violence demonstrated in the mass executions in the provinces and in the public spectacles in Paris—vast crowds watching and applauding the beheadings—indicate a darker side of human nature beyond the control of reason? Did Robespierre's religion of humanity revive the fanaticism and cruelty of the wars of religion, which had so disgusted the philosophes? Did the Robespierrists, who considered themselves the staunchest defenders of the Revolution's ideals, soil and subvert these ideals by their zeal? The Jacobins mobilized the might of the nation, created the mystique of *la patrie*, imposed dictatorial rule in defense of liberty and equality, and legalized and justified terror committed in the people's name. In so doing, were they unwittingly unleashing new forces—total commitment to a political ideology that promised to regenerate the nation and mass executions carried out in good conscience—that would be harnessed by totalitarian ideologies that were consciously resolved to stamp out the liberal heritage of the Revolution?

The Fall of Robespierre

Feeling the chill of the guillotine blade on their own necks, Robespierre's opponents in the Convention ordered his arrest and the arrest of some of his

Kean Collection/Getty Images.

THE REIGN OF TERROR. During the Terror thousands of men and women were condemned to death by the guillotine, often in front of cheering crowds. In this painting a court official reads the names of those sentenced for execution.

supporters. On July 28, 1794, the tenth of Thermidor according to the new republican calendar, Robespierre was guillotined. After the fall of Robespierre, the machinery of the Jacobin republic was dismantled.

Leadership passed to the property-owning bourgeois who had endorsed the constitutional ideas of 1789 to 1791, the moderate stage of the Revolution. The new leadership, known as Thermidoreans until the end of 1795, wanted no more of the Jacobins or of Robespierre's society. They had viewed Robespierre as a threat to their political power because he would have allowed the common people a considerable voice in the government. They had also deemed him a threat to their property because he would have introduced some state regulation of the economy to aid the poor.

The Thermidorean reaction was a counterrevolution. The new government purged the army of officers who were suspected of Jacobin leanings, abolished the law of the maximum, and declared void the constitution of 1793. A new constitution, approved in 1795, reestablished property requirements for voting. The counterrevolution also produced a counterterror, as royalists and Catholics massacred Jacobins in the provinces.

At the end of 1795, the new republican government, the Directory, was burdened by war, a sagging economy, and internal unrest. The Directory crushed insurrections by Parisian sansculottes, maddened by hunger and hatred of the rich (1795, 1796), and by royalists seeking to restore the monarchy (1797). As military and domestic pressures increased, power began to pass into the hands of generals. One of them, Napoleon Bonaparte, seized control of the government in November 1799, pushing the Revolution into yet another stage.

NAPOLEON AND FRANCE: RETURN TO AUTOCRATIC RULE

Napoleon was born on August 15, 1769, on the island of Corsica, the son of a petty noble. After finishing military school in France, he became an artillery officer. The wars of the French Revolution afforded him an opportunity to advance his career; in 1796, he was given command of the French Army of Italy. In Italy, against the

Chronology 11.2 ❖ Napoleon's Career

1796	Napoleon gets command of the French Army of Italy
November 10, 1799	He helps to overthrow the Directory's rule, establishing a strong executive in France
December 2, 1804	He crowns himself emperor of the French
October 21, 1805	Battle of Trafalgar—French and Spanish fleets are defeated by the British
October 1806	Napoleon defeats the Prussians at Jena, and French forces occupy Berlin
1808–1813	Peninsular War—Spaniards, aided by the British, fight against French occupation
October–December 1812	Grand Army retreats from Russia
October 1813	Allied forces defeat Napoleon at Leipzig
1814	Paris is captured and Napoleon is exiled to Elba
March 20, 1815	Escaping, he enters Paris and begins "hundred days" rule
June 1815	Defeated at Waterloo, Napoleon is exiled to St. Helena

Austrians, Napoleon demonstrated a dazzling talent for military planning and leadership, which earned him an instant reputation. Having tasted glory, he could never do without it. Since he had experienced only success, nothing seemed impossible; he sensed that he was headed for greatness.

In 1799, Napoleon was leading a French army in Egypt when he decided to return to France and make his bid for power. He joined a conspiracy that overthrew the Directory and created an executive office of three consuls. As first consul, Napoleon monopolized power. In 1802, he was made first consul for life, with the right to name his successor. And on December 2, 1804, in a magnificent ceremony at the Cathedral of Notre Dame in Paris, Napoleon crowned himself "Emperor of the French." General, first consul, and then emperor—it was a breathless climb to the heights of power. Napoleon, who once said that he loved "power as a musician loves his violin," was determined never to lose it.

An Enlightened Despot

Napoleon did not identify with the republicanism and democracy of the Jacobins; rather, he belonged to the tradition of eighteenth-century enlightened despotism. Like the reforming despots, he admired administrative uniformity and efficiency; disliked feudalism, religious persecution, and civil inequality; and favored government regulation of trade and industry. He saw in enlightened despotism a means of ensuring political stability and strengthening the state. Napoleon did preserve several gains of the Revolution: equality under the law, careers open to men of talent, promotion of secular education, and the weakening of clerical power. But he suppressed political liberty.

Napoleon succeeded in giving France a strong central government and administrative uniformity. An army of officials subject to the emperor's will reached into every village, linking together the entire nation. This centralized state suited Napoleon's desire for orderly government and rational administration, enabled him to concentrate power in his own hands, and provided him with the taxes and soldiers needed to fight his wars. To suppress irreconcilable opponents, primarily diehard royalists and republicans, Napoleon used the instruments of the police state—secret agents, arbitrary arrest, summary trials, and executions.

Erich Lessing/Art Resource, N.Y.

NAPOLEON ON HIS IMPERIAL THRONE, **BY JEAN-AUGUSTE DOMINIQUE INGRES, 1806.** This portrait captures the character of the self-made emperor, the daring commander, the life dedicated to glory and grandeur.

In still another way he was a precursor of twentieth-century dictators. To prevent hostile criticism of his rule and to promote popular support for his policies and person, Napoleon also shaped public opinion. Liberty of the press came to an end. Printers swore an oath of obedience to the emperor, and newspapers were converted into government mouthpieces.

Napoleon tried to close the breach between the state and the Catholic church that had opened during the Revolution. Such a reconciliation would gain the approval of the mass of the French people, who still remained devoted to their faith, and would also reassure the peasants and bourgeois who had bought confiscated church lands. For these reasons, Napoleon negotiated an agreement with the pope. The Concordat of 1801 recognized Catholicism as the religion of the great majority of the French, rather than as the official state religion (the proposal that the pope desired). Napoleon had achieved his aim. The Concordat made his regime acceptable to Catholics and to owners of former church lands.

Legal, Educational, and Financial Policies

Under the Old Regime, France was plagued by numerous and conflicting law codes. Reflecting local interests and feudal traditions, these codes obstructed national unity and administrative efficiency. Efforts by the revolutionaries to draw up a unified code of laws bogged down. Recognizing the value of such a code in promoting effective administration throughout France, Napoleon pressed for the completion of the project. The Code Napoléon incorporated many principles of the Revolution: equality before the law, the right to choose one's profession, religious freedom, protection of property rights, the abolition of serfdom, and the secular character of the state.

The code also had its less liberal side, denying equal treatment to workers in their dealings with employers, to women in their relations with their husbands, and to children in their relations with their fathers. In making wives inferior to their husbands in matters of property, adultery, and divorce, the code reflected both Napoleon's personal attitude and the general view of the times toward women and family stability. The restoration of slavery in the French colonies—which the Jacobins had abolished—was another violation of equality.

Napoleon's educational policy was in many ways an elaboration of the school reforms initiated during the Revolution. Like the revolutionaries, Napoleon favored a system of public education with a secular curriculum and a minimum of church involvement. For Napoleon, education served a dual purpose: it would provide him with capable officials to administer his laws and trained officers to lead his armies, and it would indoctrinate the young in obedience and loyalty. He established the University of France, a giant board of education that placed education under state control. To this day, the French school system, unlike that in the United States, is strictly centralized, with curriculum and standards set for the entire country.

Napoleon's financial and economic policies were designed to strengthen France and enhance his popularity. To stimulate the economy and to retain the favor of the bourgeois who supported his seizure of power, Napoleon aided industry through tariffs and loans, and he fostered commerce (while also speeding up troop movements) by building or repairing roads, bridges, and canals. To protect the currency from inflation, he established the Bank of France, which was controlled by the nation's leading financiers. By keeping careers open to talent, he endorsed one of the key demands of the bourgeoisie during the Revolution. Fearing a revolution based on lack of bread, he provided food at low prices and stimulated employment for the laboring poor. He endeared himself to the peasants by not restoring feudal privileges and by allowing them to keep the land they had obtained during the Revolution.

Napoleon and Europe: Diffusion of Revolutionary Institutions

Napoleon, the Corsican adventurer, realized Louis XIV's dream of French mastery of Europe. Between 1805 and 1807, he decisively defeated Austria, Prussia, and Russia, becoming the virtual ruler of Europe. In these campaigns, as in his earlier successes in Italy, Napoleon demonstrated his greatness as a military commander.

By 1810, Napoleon dominated the Continent, except for the Balkan Peninsula. The Grand Empire comprised lands annexed to France, vassal states, and cowed allies.

With varying degrees of determination and success, Napoleon extended the reforms of the Revolution to other lands. His officials instituted the Code Napoléon, organized an effective civil service, opened careers to talent, and equalized the tax burden. Besides abolishing serfdom, manorial payments, and the courts of the nobility, they did away with clerical courts, promoted freedom of religion, permitted civil marriage, pressed for civil rights for Jews, and fought clerical interference with secular authority. They also abolished the medieval guilds, introduced a uniform system of weights and measures, eliminated internal tolls, and built roads, bridges, and canals. They promoted secular education and improved public health. Napoleon had launched a Europe-wide social revolution that attacked the privileges of the aristocracy and the clergy—who regarded him as "that crowned Jacobin"—and worked to the advantage of the bourgeoisie. This diffusion of revolutionary institutions weakened the old regime irreparably in much of Europe and speeded up the modernization of nineteenth-century Europe.

Pleased by the overhaul of feudal practices and the reduction of clerical power, many Europeans, particularly the progressive bourgeoisie, welcomed Napoleon as a liberator. But there was another side to Napoleon's rule. Napoleon, the tyrant of Europe, turned conquered lands into satellite kingdoms and exploited them for the benefit of France—a policy that gained him the enmity of many Europeans.

The Fall of Napoleon

In addition to the hostility of subject nationals, Napoleon had to cope with the determined opposition of Great Britain, whose subsidies and encouragements kept resistance to the emperor alive. But perhaps Napoleon's greatest obstacle was his own boundless ambition, which warped his judgment. From its peak, the emperor's career soon slid downhill to defeat, dethronement, and deportation.

Failure to Subdue England

Britain was Napoleon's most resolute opponent. It could not be otherwise, for any power that dominated the Continent could organize sufficient naval might to threaten British commerce, challenge its sea power, and invade the island kingdom. Britain would not make peace with any state that sought European hegemony, and Napoleon's ambition would settle for nothing less.

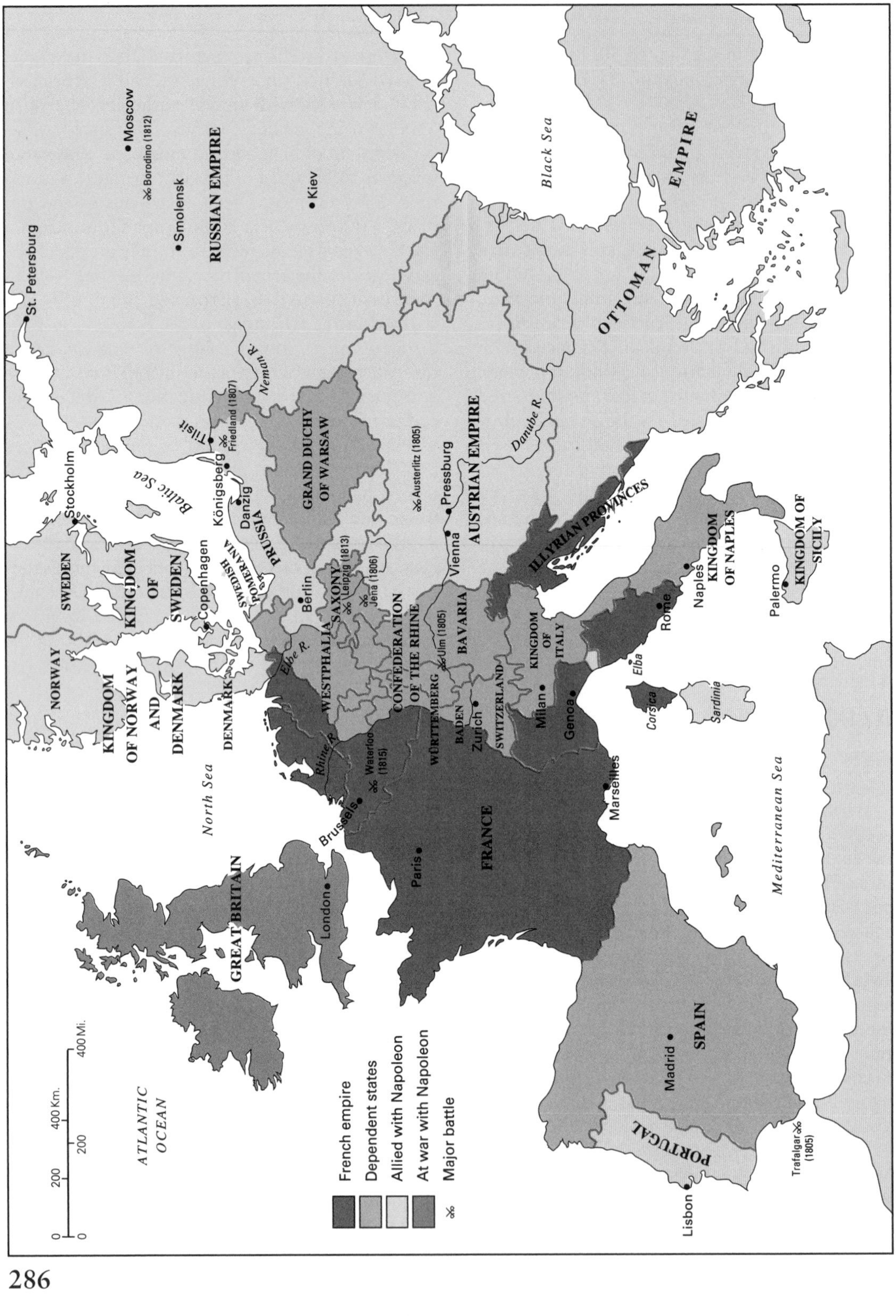
French empire
Dependent states
Allied with Napoleon
At war with Napoleon
Major battle
0 200 400 Km.
0 200 400 Mi.
ATLANTIC OCEAN
GREAT BRITAIN
London
North Sea
KINGDOM OF NORWAY AND DENMARK
NORWAY
DENMARK
KINGDOM OF SWEDEN
SWEDEN
Stockholm
Copenhagen
Baltic Sea
SWEDISH POMERANIA
PRUSSIA
Königsberg
Danzig
Tilsit
Friedland (1807)
Neman R.
St. Petersburg
RUSSIAN EMPIRE
Moscow
Borodino (1812)
Smolensk
Kiev
GRAND DUCHY OF WARSAW
Berlin
SAXONY
Leipzig (1813)
Jena (1806)
WESTPHALIA
Elbe R.
CONFEDERATION OF THE RHINE
Rhine R.
Waterloo (1815)
Brussels
Paris
FRANCE
WÜRTTEMBERG
BADEN
BAVARIA
Ulm (1805)
Zurich
SWITZERLAND
Austerlitz (1805)
Pressburg
Vienna
AUSTRIAN EMPIRE
Danube R.
Black Sea
OTTOMAN EMPIRE
ILLYRIAN PROVINCES
KINGDOM OF ITALY
Milan
Genoa
Marseilles
Corsica
Elba
Sardinia
Rome
Naples
KINGDOM OF NAPLES
Palermo
KINGDOM OF SICILY
Mediterranean Sea
SPAIN
Madrid
PORTUGAL
Lisbon
Trafalgar (1805)

Unable to invade Britain while British warships commanded the English Channel, Napoleon decided to bring what he called "the nation of shopkeepers" to its knees by damaging the British economy. His plan, called the Continental System, was to bar all countries under France's control from buying British goods. However, by smuggling goods onto the Continent and increasing trade with the New World, Britain, although hurt, escaped economic ruin. Besides, the Continental System also punished European lands that were dependent on British imports; the bourgeoisie, generally supportive of Napoleon's social and administrative reforms, turned against him because of the economic distress it caused. Furthermore, Napoleon's efforts to enforce the system enmeshed him in two catastrophic blunders: the occupation of Spain and the invasion of Russia.

The Spanish Ulcer

An ally of France since 1796, Spain proved a disappointment to Napoleon. It failed to prevent the Portuguese from trading with Britain, and it contributed little military or financial aid to France's war effort. Napoleon decided to incorporate Spain into his empire; in 1808, he deposed the Spanish ruler and designated his own brother Joseph as king of Spain.

Napoleon believed that the Spanish would rally round the gentle Joseph and welcome his liberal reforms. This confidence was a fatal illusion. Spanish nobles and clergy feared French liberalism; the overwhelmingly peasant population—illiterate and credulous, intensely proud, fanatically religious, and easily aroused by the clergy—viewed Napoleon as the Devil's agent. Loyal to the Spanish monarchy and faithful to the church, the Spanish fought a "War to the Knife" against the invaders.

Seeking to keep the struggle against Napoleon alive, Britain came to the aid of the Spanish insurgents. The intervention of British troops, commanded by Sir Arthur Wellesley, the future duke of Wellington, led to the ultimate defeat of Joseph in 1813. The "Spanish ulcer" drained Napoleon's treasury, tied down hundreds of thousands of French troops, enabled Britain to gain a foothold on the Continent from which to invade southern France, and inspired patriots in other lands to resist the French emperor.

◀ *Map 11.1* Napoleon's Europe, 1810 By 1810, Napoleon dominated much of the Continent. His Grand Empire comprised lands annexed to France, vassal states, and cowed allies.

Disaster in Russia

Deteriorating relations between Russia and France led Napoleon to his fatal decision to attack the Eastern giant. His creation of the Grand Duchy of Warsaw irritated the tsar, who feared a revival of Polish power and resented French influence on Russia's border. Another source of friction between the tsar and Napoleon was Russia's illicit trade with Britain, in violation of the Continental System. No doubt Napoleon's inexhaustible craving for glory and power also compelled him to strike at Russia.

In June 1812, the Grand Army, 614,000 men strong, crossed the Neman River into Russia. Fighting mainly rearguard battles and retreating according to plan, the tsar's forces lured the invaders into the vastness of Russia, far from their lines of supply. On September 14, the Grand Army, its numbers greatly reduced by disease, hunger, exhaustion, desertion, and battle, entered Moscow, which the Russians had virtually evacuated. To show their contempt for the French conquerors and to deny the French shelter, the Russians set fire to the city, which burned for five days. Taking up headquarters in Moscow, Napoleon waited for Alexander I to admit defeat and come to terms. But the tsar remained intransigent.

Napoleon was in a dilemma: to penetrate deeper into Russia was certain death; to stay in Moscow with winter approaching meant possible starvation. Faced with these alternatives, Napoleon decided to retreat westward. On October 19, 1812, ninety-five thousand troops and thousands of wagons loaded with loot left Moscow for the long trek back. In early November came the first snow and frost. Army stragglers were slaughtered by Russian Cossacks and peasant partisans. In the middle of December, with the Russians in pursuit, the remnants of the Grand Army staggered across the Neman River into East Prussia.

The German War of Liberation

Napoleon's disastrous Russian campaign helped to trigger uprisings in the German states where anti-French feeling was high. Hatred of the French invaders evoked a feeling of national outrage among some Germans, who up to this time had thought only in terms of their own particular state and prince. Some German intellectuals, using the emotional language of nationalism, called for a war of liberation against Napoleon and, in some instances, for the creation of a unified Germany.

Besides kindling a desire for national independence and unity, the disastrous defeat of the Prussians at Jena (1806) and French domination of Germany stimulated a movement for reform among members of the Prussian high bureaucracy and officer corps. To survive in a world altered by the French Revolution, Prussia would have to learn the principal lessons of the Revolution: that aroused citizens fighting for a cause make better soldiers than mercenaries and oppressed serfs, and that officers selected for daring and intelligence command better than nobles possessing only a gilded birthright. The reformers believed that the elimination of social abuses would overcome defeatism and apathy and encourage Prussians to serve the state willingly and to fight bravely for national honor. A revitalized Prussia could then deal with the French.

Among the important reforms introduced in Prussia between 1807 and 1813 were the abolition of serfdom, the granting to towns of a large measure of self-administration, the awarding of army commissions on the basis of merit instead of birth, the elimination of cruel punishment in the ranks, and the establishment of national conscription. In 1813, the reform party forced King Frederick William III to declare war on France. The military reforms did improve the quality of the Prussian army. In the War of Liberation (1813), Prussian soldiers demonstrated far more enthusiasm and patriotism than they had at Jena in 1806, and the French were driven from Germany. The German War of Liberation came on the heels of Napoleon's disastrous Russian campaign.

Final Defeat

After the destruction of the Grand Army, the empire crumbled. Although Napoleon raised a new army, he could not replace the equipment, cavalry horses, and experienced soldiers squandered in Russia. Now he had to rely on schoolboys and overage veterans. Most of Europe joined in a final coalition against France. In October 1813, allied forces from Austria, Prussia, Russia, and Sweden defeated Napoleon at Leipzig; in November, Anglo-Spanish forces crossed the Pyrenees into France. Finally, in the spring of 1814, the allies captured Paris. Napoleon abdicated and was exiled to the tiny island of Elba, off the coast of Italy. The Bourbon dynasty was restored to the throne of France in the person of Louis XVIII, younger brother of the executed Louis XVI and the acknowledged leader of the émigrés.

Only forty-four years of age, Napoleon did not believe that it was his destiny to die on Elba. On March 1, 1815, he landed on the French coast with a thousand soldiers, and three weeks later he entered Paris to a hero's welcome. Raising a new army, Napoleon moved against the allied forces in Belgium. There, the Prussians, led by Field Marshal Gebhard von Blücher, and the British, led by the Duke of Wellington, defeated Napoleon at Waterloo in June 1815. Napoleon's desperate gamble to regain power—the famous "hundred days"—had failed. This time the allies sent Napoleon to Saint Helena, a lonely island in the South Atlantic a thousand miles off the coast of southern Africa. On this gloomy and rugged rock, Napoleon Bonaparte, emperor of France and would-be conqueror of Europe, spent the last six years of his life.

The Meaning of the French Revolution

The French Revolution was a decisive period in the shaping of the modern West. It implemented the thought of the philosophes, destroyed the hierarchical and corporate society of the Old Regime, which was a legacy of the Middle Ages, promoted the interests of the bourgeoisie, and quickened the growth of the modern state.

The French Revolution weakened the aristocracy. With their feudal rights and privileges eliminated, the nobles became simply ordinary citizens. Throughout the nineteenth century, France would be governed by both aristocrats and bourgeoisie; property, not noble birth, determined the composition of the new ruling elite.

The principle of careers being open to talent gave the bourgeois access to the highest positions in the state. Having wealth, talent, ambition, and now opportunity, the bourgeois would play an ever more important role in French political life. Throughout Continental Europe, the reforms of the French Revolution served as a model for progressive bourgeois, who sooner or later would challenge the old regimes in their own lands.

The French Revolution transformed the dynastic state, on which the Old Regime was based, into the modern state: national, liberal, secular, and rational. When the Declaration of the Rights of Man and of the Citizen stated that "the source of all sovereignty resides essentially in the nation," the concept of the state took on a new meaning. The state was no longer merely a territory or a federation of provinces, nor was it the private possession of a king who claimed to be God's lieutenant on earth. In the new conception, the state belonged to the people as a whole. For a government to be legitimate it had to derive its power from the people. And the individual, formerly a subject, was now a citizen with both rights and duties and was governed by laws that permitted no legal distinction between commoners and nobles.

The liberal thought of the Enlightenment found practical expression in the reforms of the Revolution. Absolutism and divine right of monarchy, repudiated in theory by the philosophes, were invalidated by constitutions affirming that sovereignty resides with the people, not with a monarch, and setting limits to the powers of government and by elected parliaments that represented the governed. By providing for equality before the law and the protection of human rights—habeas corpus, trial by jury, civil rights for Protestants and Jews, and freedom of speech and the press—the Revolution struck at the abuses of the Old Regime. Because of violations and interruptions, these gains seemed at times more theoretical than actual. Nevertheless, these liberal ideals reverberated throughout the Continent. In the early nineteenth century, revolutionaries in France and other lands, aspiring for political and social change, took the French Revolution as their inspiration, and the pace of reform quickened.

***And There Is No Remedy*, Etching by Francisco Goya (1746–1828).** Spaniards resisted the installation of Joseph, Napoleon's brother, as king of Spain. Both sides engaged in terrible atrocities in the ensuing Peninsular War. The Spanish painter Francisco Goya captured the war's brutality.

Prior to the Revolution, religion was still closely linked to the state. As a general rule each state had an official religion, a state church that legitimated the ruling power. By disavowing any divine justification for the monarch's power, by depriving the church of its special position, and by no longer limiting citizenship to members of a state church, the Revolution accelerated the secularization of European political life.

Sweeping aside the administrative chaos of the Old Regime, the Revolution attempted to impose rational norms on the state. The sale of public offices, which had produced ineffective and corrupt administrators, was eliminated, and the highest positions in the land were opened to men of talent, regardless of birth. The Revolution abolished the peasantry's manorial obligations, which had hampered agriculture, and swept away barriers to economic expansion. It based taxes on income and streamlined their collection. The destruction of feudal remnants, internal tolls, and the guilds speeded up the expansion of a competitive market economy. In the nineteenth century, reformers in the rest of Europe would follow the lead set by France.

By spreading revolutionary ideals and institutions, Napoleon made it impossible for the traditional rulers to restore the Old Regime intact after the emperor's downfall. He had solidified in France what the Revolution had initiated—the destruction of a society based on orders and legal privileges and the opening of careers to talent regardless of birth. In conquered lands, his administrators undermined the authority of aristocrats and clergy. Napoleon's reforms furthered the rationalization and secularization of society and contributed to the transformation of the dynastic state into the modern national state and to the prominence of the bourgeoisie.

By showing that a decadent old order could be toppled and supplanted by a new one, the French Revolution inspired generations of revolutionaries aspiring to end longstanding abuses and to remodel society. In the process, it unleashed three potentially destructive forces identified with the modern state: total war, nationalism, and a fanatic utopian mentality. All these forces contradicted the rational and universal aims of the reformers as stated in the Declaration of the Rights of Man and of the Citizen. Whereas the restrained wars of the eighteenth century were fought by limited professional soldiers for limited aims, the French Revolution brought conscription and the mobilization of all the state's resources for armed conflict, practices continued by Napoleon. The French emperor raised armies of unprecedented size and sought the complete destruction of the enemy force. The battle of Leipzig, for example, involved 500,000 combatants on both sides, of whom 150,000 were killed or wounded. Almost a million Frenchmen perished in Napoleon's wars. The world wars of the twentieth century were the terrible fulfillment of this new development in warfare.

The French Revolution also gave birth to modern nationalism. During the Revolution, loyalty was directed to the entire nation, not to a village or province or to the person of the king. The whole of France became the fatherland. Under the Jacobins, the French became converts to a secular faith preaching total reverence for the nation. "In 1794 we believed in no supernatural religion; our serious interior sentiments were all summed up in the one idea, how to be useful to the fatherland. Everything else . . . was, in our eyes, only trivial. . . . It was our only religion."[10] Few suspected that the new religion of nationalism was fraught with danger. Louis-Antoine de Saint-Just, a young, ardent Robespierrist, was gazing into the future when he declared: "There is something terrible in the sacred love of the fatherland. This love is so exclusive that it sacrifices everything to the public interest, without pity, without fear, with no respect for the human individual."[11] The philosophes would have deemed nationalism, which demanded total dedication of body and soul to the nation and stifled clear thinking, to be a repudiation of their universalism and hopes for rational solutions to political conflicts. It was a new dogma capable of evoking wild and dangerous passions and a setback for the progress of reason.

The French Revolution gave rise to still another potentially destructive force: a revolutionary mentality that sought to demolish an unjust traditional society and create a new social order that would restore individuals to their natural goodness. The negative side of this lofty vision was its power to whip up an extremism that justified mass murder in the name of a supposedly higher good. Such was the case with Robespierre and other Jacobins. In the twentieth century, Nazis in Germany and radical socialists in Russia, China, and Cambodia, seeing themselves as idealists striving for a social regeneration of humanity, oppressed, terrorized, and murdered with intense dedication—and a clear conscience.

The Revolution attempted to reconstruct society on the basis of Enlightenment thought. The Declaration of the Rights of Man and of the Citizen—whose spirit permeated the reforms of the Revolution—upheld the dignity of the individual, demanded respect for the individual, attributed to each person natural rights, and barred the state from denying these rights. It insisted that society and the state have no higher duty than to promote the freedom and autonomy of the individual. "It is not enough to have overturned the throne," said Robespierre; "our concern is to erect upon its remains holy Equality and the sacred Rights of Man."[12] The tragedy of the

Western experience is that this humanist vision, brilliantly expressed by the Enlightenment and given recognition in the reforms of the French Revolution, would be undermined in later generations. And, ironically, by its fanatical commitment to a seductive ideology that promised worldly salvation—the creation of a republic of virtue and truth—the French Revolution itself contributed to the shattering of this vision. It had spawned total war, aggressive nationalism, terror as government policy, and a revolutionary mentality that sought to change the world through coercion and violence. In the twentieth century, these dangerous forces almost succeeded in crushing the liberty and equality so valued by the French reformers.

❖ ❖ ❖

Notes

1. George Rudé, *Revolutionary Europe, 1783–1815* (New York: Harper Torchbooks, 1966), p. 74.
2. Henri Peyre, "The Influence of Eighteenth-Century Ideas on the French Revolution," *Journal of the History of Ideas,* 10 (1949):73.
3. George Lefebvre, *The French Revolution from 1793 to 1799,* trans. John Hall Stewart and James Friguglietti (New York: Columbia University Press, 1964), Vol. 2, p. 360.
4. Quoted in T. C. W. Blanning, *The French Revolution: Aristocrats Versus Bourgeois?* (Atlantic Highlands, N.J.: Humanities Press, 1987), p. 9. Reprinted with permission from the author.
5. William Doyle, *Origins of the French Revolution* (London: Oxford University Press, 1980), p. 21.
6. Excerpted in John Hall Stewart, ed., *A Documentary Survey of the French Revolution* (New York: Macmillan, 1951), pp. 43–44.
7. Albert Soboul, *The Parisian Sans-Culottes and the French Revolution, 1793–94,* trans. Gwynne Lewis (London: Oxford University Press, 1964), pp. 28–29.
8. Excerpted in George Rudé, ed., *Robespierre* (Englewood Cliffs, N.J.: Prentice-Hall, 1976), p. 72.
9. Ibid., p. 57.
10. Quoted in Carlton J. H. Hayes, *The Historical Evolution of Modern Nationalism* (New York: Richard R. Smith, 1931), p. 55.
11. Quoted in Hans Kohn, *Making of the Modern French Mind* (New York: D. Van Nostrand, 1955), p. 17.
12. Quoted in Christopher Dawson, *The Gods of Revolution* (New York: New York University Press, 1972), p. 83.

Suggested Reading

Andress, David, *The Terror: The Merciless War for Freedom in Revolutionary France* (2005). An admirable synthesis of recent scholarship on the Terror.

Bell, David A., *The First Total War: Napoleon's Europe and the Birth of Warfare as We Know It* (2007). How modern attitudes of warfare emerged in the era of Napoleon.

———, ed., *The Rise and Fall of the French Revolution* (1996). A collection of articles, some by prominent students of the revolution.

Chandler, David, *The Campaigns of Napoleon* (1966). An exhaustive analysis of Napoleon's art of war.

Doyle, William, *The Oxford History of the French Revolution* (1990). Incorporates new thinking on the cause and nature of the Revolution and Gough, Hugh, The Terror in the French Revolution (1998). A brief overview.

Forrest, Alan, *The French Revolution* (1995). Social, political, and ideological changes wrought by the Revolution.

Furet, François, and Mona Ozouf, eds., *A Critical Dictionary of the French Revolution* (1989). Articles on many topics; highly recommended.

Herold, J. Christopher, ed., *The Mind of Napoleon* (1955). A valuable selection from the written and spoken words of Napoleon.

Jones, Peter, ed., *The French Revolution in Social and Political Perspective* (1996). A valuable collection of essays.

Lefebvre, Georges, *The Coming of the French Revolution* (1967). A brilliant analysis of the social structure of the Old Regime and the opening phase of the Revolution.

Markham, Felix, *Napoleon* (1963). A first-rate short biography.

———, *Napoleon and the Awakening of Europe* (1965). An exploration of Napoleon's influence on other lands.

McPhee, Peter, *The French Revolution 1789–1799* (2002). Recent, readable, and reliable.

Sutherland, D. M. G., *France 1789–1815* (1986). Like William Doyle, Sutherland departs from the classic theory of the bourgeois revolution.

Chapter 12

The Industrial Revolution: The Transformation of Society

- **Britain First**
- **Society Transformed**
- **The Rise of Reform in Britain**
- **Responses to Industrialization**
- **Industrialism in Perspective**

Focus Questions

1. What were the causes of the Industrial Revolution? Why did it begin in Britain?
2. How did the Industrial Revolution transform social structure?
3. How did Parliament respond to demands for reform from 1815 to 1848?
4. Why are Saint-Simon, Fourier, and Owen regarded as early socialists?
5. The Industrial Revolution was a principal force in the shaping of the modern world. Discuss this statement.

In the last part of the eighteenth century, as a revolution for liberty and equality swept across France and sent shock waves through Europe, a different kind of revolution—a revolution in industry—was transforming life in Great Britain. In the nineteenth century, the Industrial Revolution spread to the United States and to the

ARPL/Topham/The Image Works.

Woman at Hargreaves's Spinning Jenny. The cotton textile trade was one of the first to be mechanized. In cottage industries, the whole family contributed to the making of thread and cloth. James Hargreaves's spinning jenny, one of the early inventions made by the workers themselves, was an adaptation of his wife's thread-spinning tool.

European continent. Today, it encompasses virtually the entire world; everywhere the drive to substitute machines for human labor continues at a rapid pace.

After 1760, dramatic changes occurred in Britain in the way goods were produced and labor organized. New forms of power, particularly steam, replaced animal strength and human muscle. Better ways of obtaining and using raw materials were discovered, and a new way of organizing production and workers—the factory—came into use. In the nineteenth century, technology moved from triumph to triumph with a momentum unprecedented in human history. The resulting explosion in economic production and productivity transformed society with breathtaking speed.

Industrial development did not proceed at the same pace everywhere. The changes begun in England in the mid 1700s were delayed in France by political and social conflict until after the French Revolution. In the German states, the lack of political unity slowed the growth of industrialization until the 1840s. The sharp economic divisions between north and south, the comparative lack of natural resources, and Italy's slow political unification hampered industrialization. ❖

Britain First

Britain possessed several advantages that enabled it to take the lead in industrialization. Large, easily developed supplies of coal and iron had given the British a long tradition of metallurgy and mining. In the early stages of industrialization, Britain's river transportation system was supplemented by canals and toll roads (turnpikes), which private entrepreneurs financed and built for profit. In addition, the enclosure movement provided factories with a labor pool. During the eighteenth century, great landlords enclosed, or fenced off and claimed as their own, land formerly used in common by villagers for grazing farm animals. Once the peasants were gone, lords could bring this land under cultivation for their own private gain. No longer able to earn a living

© Mary Evans Picture Library/The Image Works.

The Agricultural Revolution: The McCormick Reaper. Harvesting grain with a horse-drawn machine released great numbers of laborers from farms to work in factories or cities. The great demand for labor may explain, in part, the constant search for and investment in mechanical devices for farm and factory in the United States, a major food exporter even today.

from the land, these dispossessed farmers sought work in emerging factories.

Britain also had capital available for investment in new industries. These funds came from wealthy landowners and merchants who had grown rich through commerce, including the slave trade. Interest rates on loans fell in the eighteenth century, stimulating investment. Britain's expanding middle class provided a home market for emerging industries. So, too, did its overseas colonies, which also supplied raw materials—particularly cotton, needed for the developing textile industry. A vigorous spirit of enterprise and the opportunity for men of ability to rise from common origins to riches and fame also help explain the growth of industrialization.

Finally, two European cultural traditions in which Britain shared played crucial roles in the rise of industrialism. One was individualism, which had its roots in both the Renaissance and the Reformation; during the era of the commercial revolution, it manifested itself in hard-driving, ambitious merchants and bankers. This spirit of individualism, combined with the wide latitude states gave to private economic activity, fostered the development of dynamic capitalist entrepreneurs. The second cultural tradition promoting industrialization was the high value Westerners placed on the rational understanding and control of nature. Both individualism and the tradition of reason, concludes historian David S. Landes, "gave Europe a tremendous advantage in the invention and adoption of new technology. The will to mastery, the rational approach to problems that we call scientific method, the competition for wealth and power—together these broke down the resistance of inherited ways and made change a positive good."[1]

Changes in Technology

The Cotton Industry Long the home of an important wool trade, Britain in the eighteenth century jumped ahead in the production of cotton, the industry that first showed the possibility of unprecedented growth rates. British cotton production expanded tenfold between 1760 and 1785, and another tenfold between 1785 and 1825. A

Chronology 12.1 ❖ The Industrial Revolution

1764–1767	Hargreaves invents the spinning jenny
1769	Watt invents the modern steam engine
1785	Cartwright develops the power loom
1825	Workers are allowed to unionize but not to strike
1830	First railway line is built in England
1832	Reform Bill of 1832 expands British voting rights

series of inventions revolutionized the industry and drastically altered the social conditions of the work.

In 1733, long before the expansion started, a simple invention—John Kay's flying shuttle—made it possible for weavers to double their output. The flying shuttle enabled weavers to produce faster than spinners could spin—until James Hargreaves's spinning jenny, perfected by 1768, allowed an operator to work several spindles at once, powered only by human energy. Within five years, Richard Arkwright's water frame spinning machine could be powered by water or animals, and Samuel Crompton's spinning mule (1779) powered many spindles, first by human and later by animal and water energy. These changes improved spinning productivity so much that it caused bottlenecks in weaving until Edmund Cartwright developed a power loom in 1785.* To the end of the century, there was a race to speed up the spinning part of the process and then the weaving part by applying water power to looms or new, larger devices to the spinning jenny.

Arkwright's water frame made it more efficient to bring many workers together, rather than sending work out to individuals in their own homes. This development was the beginning of the factory system, which within a generation would revolutionize the conditions of labor. Because water power drove these early machines, mills were located near rivers and streams. Towns thus grew up where machinery could be powered by water; the factory system concentrated laborers and their families near the factories.

The Steam Engine James Watt, a Scottish engineer, developed the steam engine in the 1760s. Because steam engines ran on coal or wood, not water power, they allowed greater flexibility in locating textile mills. Factories were no longer restricted to the power supplied by a river or a stream or to the space available beside flowing water; they could be built anywhere. With steam, the whole pattern of work changed because weaker, younger, and less skilled workers could be taught the few simple tasks necessary to tend the machine. The shift from male to female and child labor was a major social change.

The Iron Industry Although steam power allowed employers to hire weaker people to operate machinery, it required machines made of stronger metal to withstand the forces generated by the stronger power source. By the 1780s, trial and error had perfected the production of wrought iron, which became the most widely used metal until steel began to be cheaply produced in the 1860s.

The iron industry made great demands on the coal mines to fuel its furnaces. Because steam engines enabled miners to pump water from the mines more efficiently and at a much deeper level, rich veins in existing mines became accessible for the first time. The greater productivity in coal allowed the continued improvement of iron smelting. Then, in 1856, Henry Bessemer developed a process for converting pig iron into steel by speedily removing the impurities in the iron. In the 1860s, William

*Technological developments in America helped to meet the growing demand for raw cotton. Eli Whitney's cotton gin (1793) removed the seeds from raw cotton quickly and cheaply, leading farmers and plantation owners to devote more land to cotton. Within a generation, more laborers were required for the fields and fewer to process the cotton. The increased demand for slave labor had far-reaching repercussions.

Siemens and the brothers Pierre and Émile Martin developed the open-hearth process, which could handle much greater amounts of metal than Bessemer's converter. Steel became so cheap to produce that it quickly replaced iron in industry because of its greater tensile strength and durability.

Transportation The steam engine and iron and steel brought a new era in transport. As machines speeded up factory production, methods of transportation also improved. In 1830, the first railway line was built in England, connecting Manchester and Liverpool; this sparked an age of railway building throughout much of the world. Shipping changed radically with the use of vessels without sails, which had greater tonnage capacity.

Society Transformed

The innovations in agricultural production, business organization, and technology had revolutionary consequences for society, economics, and politics. People were drawn from the countryside into cities, and traditional ways of life changed. Much of the old life persisted, however, particularly during the first half of the nineteenth century. Landed property was still the principal form of wealth, and large landowners continued to exercise political power. From England to Russia, families of landed wealth (often the old noble families) still constituted the social elite. European society remained overwhelmingly rural; as late as the midcentury, only England was half urban. Nevertheless, contemporaries were so overwhelmed by industrialization that they saw it as a sudden and complete break with the past: the shattering of traditional moral and social patterns.

Cities grew in number, size, and population as a result of industrialization. For example, between 1801 and 1851, the population of Birmingham rose from 73,000 to 250,000 and that of Liverpool from 77,000 to 400,000. Industrial cities expanded rapidly, without planning or much regulation by local or national government. So much growth with so little planning

Snark/Art Resource, N.Y.

Railroad Line from Nuremberg to Furth. The spectacle of the arrival and departure of the train attracts townspeople of all classes. Central Europe followed England and France in railroad mania.

Primary Source

James Phillips Kay: Moral and Physical Dissipation

In 1832 James Phillips Kay, a physician, published a pamphlet describing the moral and physical condition of the working class in Manchester. His study, excerpted below, provided additional evidence of the painful effects industrialization had on factory workers and their families.

The township of Manchester chiefly consists of dense masses of houses, inhabited by the population engaged in the great manufactories of the cotton trade. . . . Prolonged and exhausting labour, continued from day to day, and from year to year, is not calculated to develop the intellectual or moral faculties of man. The dull routine of a ceaseless drudgery, in which the same mechanical process is incessantly repeated, resembles the torment of Sisyphus[1]—the toil, like the rock, recoils perpetually on the wearied operative. The mind gathers neither stores nor strength from the constant extension and retraction of the same muscles. The intellect slumbers, in supine inertness; but the grosser parts of our nature attain a rank development.

To condemn man to such severity of toil is, in some measure, to cultivate in him the habits of an animal. He becomes reckless. He disregards the distinguishing appetites and habits of his species. He neglects the comforts and delicacies of life. He lives in squalid wretchedness, on meagre food, and expends his superfluous gains in debauchery. . . .

[T]he population. . . . is crowded into one dense mass, in cottages separated by narrow, unpaved, and almost pestilential streets; in an atmosphere loaded with the smoke and exhalations of a large manufacturing city. The operatives are congregated in rooms and workshops during twelve hours in the day, in an enervating, heated atmosphere, which is frequently loaded with dust or filaments of cotton, or impure from constant respiration, or from other causes. They are engaged in an employment which absorbs their attention, and unremittingly employs their physical energies. They are drudges who watch the movements, and assist the operations, of a mighty material force, which toils with an energy ever unconscious of fatigue. The persevering labour of the operative must rival the mathematical precision, the incessant motion, and the exhaustless power of the machine.

Hence, besides the negative results—the total abstraction of every moral and intellectual stimulus—the absence of variety—banishment from the grateful air and the cheering influences of light, the physical energies are exhausted by incessant toil, and imperfect nutrition. Having been subjected to the prolonged labour of an animal—his physical energy wasted—his mind in supine inaction—the artizan has neither moral dignity nor intellectual nor organic strength to resist the seductions of appetite. His wife and children, too frequently subjected to the same process, are unable to cheer his remaining moments of leisure. Domestic economy is neglected, domestic comforts are unknown. A meal of the coarsest food is prepared with heedless haste, and devoured with equal precipitation. Home has no other relation to him than that of shelter—few pleasures are there—it chiefly presents to him a scene of physical exhaustion, from which he is glad to escape. Himself impotent of all the distinguishing aims of his species, he sinks into sensual sloth, or revels in more degrading licentiousness. His house is ill furnished, uncleanly, often ill ventilated, perhaps damp; his food, from want of forethought and domestic economy, is meagre and innutritious; he is debilitated and hypochondriacal, and falls the victim of dissipation. . . .

The absence of religious feeling, the neglect of all religious ordinances, we conceive to afford substantive evidence of so great a moral degradation of the community, as generally to ensure a concomitant civic debasement. . . .

Questions for Analysis

1. What is Doctor Kay's description of the mental and physical health of a worker in a Manchester cotton mill?
2. Kay does not seem to think the employer, the machines, or the society are responsible for the workers' misery. What do you think?

[1] This refers to the myth of Sisyphus, a cruel king of Corinth, who was condemned in Hades to push a big rock up to the top of a hill, only to have it roll back down again.

James Phillips Kay, M.D., *Moral and Physical Condition of the Working Classes Employed in the Cotton Manufacture in Manchester* (London: James Ridgway, 1832), pp. 6–8, 10–11, 39.

or control led to cities with little sanitation, no lighting, wretched housing, poor transportation, and little security.

Rich and poor alike suffered in this environment of disease, crime, and ugliness, although the poor obviously bore the brunt of these evils. They lived in houses located as close to the factories as possible. The houses were several stories high and built in rows close to each other. Sometimes a whole family huddled together in one room or even shared a room with another family. Open sewers, polluted rivers, factory smoke, and filthy streets allowed disease to spread. In Britain, about twenty-six out of every one hundred children died before the age of five. Almost universally, those who wrote about industrial cities—England's Manchester, Leeds, and Liverpool and France's Lyons—described the stench, the filth, the inhumane crowding, the poverty, and the immorality.

Changes in Social Structure

The Industrial Revolution destroyed forever the old division of society into clergy, nobility, and commoners. The development of industry and commerce caused a corresponding development of the bourgeoisie, a middle class comprising people of common birth who engaged in trade and other capitalist ventures. The wealthiest bourgeois were bankers, factory and mine owners, and merchants, but the middle class also included shopkeepers, managers, lawyers, and doctors. The virtues of work, thrift, ambition, and prudence characterized the middle class as a whole, as did the perversion of these virtues into materialism, selfishness, callousness, and smugness.

From the eighteenth century on, as industry and commerce developed, the middle class grew in size, first in England and then throughout Western Europe. During the eighteenth and nineteenth centuries, the middle class struggled against the entrenched aristocracy to end political, economic, and social discrimination. By the end of the nineteenth century, bourgeois politicians held the highest offices in much of Western Europe and shared authority with aristocrats, whose birth no longer guaranteed them the only political and social power in the nation. As industrial wealth grew more important, the middle class became more influential. Its wealthy members also tended to imitate the aristocracy: it was common throughout Europe for rich bourgeois to spend fortunes buying great estates and emulating aristocratic manners and pleasures.

Industrialization may have reduced some barriers between the landed elites and the middle class, but it sharpened the distinctions between the middle class and the laboring class. Like the middle class, the proletariat encompassed different economic levels: rural laborers, miners, and city workers. Many gradations existed among city workers, from artisans to factory workers and servants. Factory workers were the newest and most rapidly growing social group; at midcentury, however, they did not constitute most of the laboring people in any major city. For example, as late as 1890, they made up only one-sixth of London's population.

The artisans were the largest group of workers in the cities for the first half of the nineteenth century, and in some places for much longer than that. They worked in construction, printing, small tailoring or dressmaking establishments, food preparation and processing, and crafts producing such luxury items as furniture, jewelry, lace, and velvet. Artisans were

LONDON ROW HOUSES. This painting by the French artist Gustave Doré depicts the overcrowded and unsanitary conditions in industrial London. Workers and their families lived in row houses, each just one room wide with a tiny yard in back.

distinct from factory workers; their technical skills were difficult to learn, and traditionally their crafts were acquired in guilds, which still functioned as both social and economic organizations. Artisans were usually educated (they could read and write), lived in one city or village for generations, and maintained stable families, often securing places for their children in their craft. As the Industrial Revolution progressed, however, they found it hard to compete with cheap, factory-produced goods, and their livelihoods were threatened.

Servants were especially numerous in capital cities. In the first half of the nineteenth century in cities like Paris and London, where the number of factories was not great, there were more servants than factory workers. Servants usually had some education. If they married and had a family, they taught their children to read and write and sometimes to observe the manners and values of the household in which the parent had worked.

Working-Class Life

Life was not easy for those whose labor contributed to the industrializing process. Usually, factory workers were recent arrivals from agricultural areas, where they had been driven off the land. They frequently moved to the city without their families, leaving them behind until they could afford to support them in town. These people entered rapidly growing industries, where long hours—sometimes fifteen a day—were not unusual. Farming had meant long hours, too, as had the various forms of labor for piecework rates in the home, but the pace of the machine, the dull routine, and dangerous conditions in factories and mines made work even more oppressive. Miners, for example, labored under the hazards of cave-ins, explosions, and deadly gas fumes. Deep beneath the earth's surface, life was dark, cold, wet, and tenuous. Their bodies stunted and twisted, their

Mansell/Time & Life Pictures/Getty Images.

ENGRAVING FROM THE *ILLUSTRATED TIMES*, 1859. As unemployed workers flooded into the great cities of Europe, homelessness became a pressing social problem. To keep dry and warm, homeless men sometimes slept in coffins made for the living and lined up in a factory or prisonlike building. These facilities were charitable institutions—not the poor-law workhouses—but they too reflected the common belief of the day that poverty was the fault of the poor, who should learn to help themselves.

lungs wrecked, miners toiled their lives away in "the pits."

Sometimes, compared with their lives in the country, the factory workers' standard of living rose, particularly if the whole family found work; the pay for a family might be better than they could have earned for agricultural labor. But working conditions were terrible, as were living conditions. The factories were dirty, hot, unventilated, and frequently dangerous. Workers toiled long hours, were fined for mistakes and even for accidents, were fired at the will of the employer or foreman, and were laid off during slowdowns. They often lived in overcrowded and dirty housing. If they were unmarried or had left their family in the country, they often lived in barracks with other members of their sex. If they lost their jobs, they also lost their shelter.

In the villages they had left, they had been poor, but they were socially connected to family, church, and even local landlords. But in the cities, factory workers labored in plants with twenty to a hundred workers and had little contact with their employers. Instead, they were pushed by foremen to work hard and efficiently to keep up with the machines. Workers had little time on the job to socialize with others; they were fined for talking to one another, for lateness, and for many petty infringements. They often became competitors in order to keep their jobs. Lacking organization, a sense of comradeship, education, and experience of city life, factory workers found little comfort when times were bad.

Workers often developed a life around the pub, the café, or some similar gathering place, where there were drinks and games and the gossip and news of the day. On Sundays, their one day off, workers drank and danced; absenteeism was so great on Monday that the day was called "holy Monday." Gin drinking was denounced on all sides; workers and reformers alike urged temperance. Many workers played sports, and some social organizations grew up around their sporting games. In these and other ways, workers developed a culture of their own—a culture that was misunderstood and often deplored by middle-class reformers.

Many contemporaries felt that the poor—those who were so unfortunate that they needed the assistance of others—were growing in numbers, that their condition was woeful, and that it had actually deteriorated in the midst of increased wealth. If machines could produce so much wealth and so many products, then why, social observers wondered, were there so many poor people? Parliamentary reports and investigations of civic-minded citizens documented the suffering for all to read.

Many reformers believed that the only hope for the workers lay in unified action through trade unions. In England and Western Europe, trade unions grew even when they were illegal. Unions made some headway in protecting their members from unemployment and dangerous working conditions, but strikes were rarely successful. The general public, which was imbued with individualist and laissez-faire principles, saw strikes as an attack on the businessman's right to carry on trade. Not until the 1870s and 1880s was widespread discontent expressed by militant trade unions.

Historians still debate how bad workers' conditions were in the early stages of industrialization. Most workers experienced periods of acute distress, but historians generally conclude that the standard of living slowly improved during the eighteenth and nineteenth centuries. Although historians take an optimistic view of the long-term effects of industrialization, the rapidity of change also wreaked great hardships on the workers of all countries, who endured cruel conditions in factories, mines, and slums.

The Rise of Reform in Britain

Although it was the freest state in Europe in the early decades of the nineteenth century, Britain was far from democratic. A constitutional monarchy, with many limits on the powers of king and state, Britain was nonetheless dominated by aristocrats. Landed aristocrats controlled both the House of Lords and the House of Commons—the House of Lords because they constituted its membership and the House of Commons because they patronized or sponsored men favorable to their interests. The vast majority of people, from the middle class as well as from the working class, could not vote. Many towns continued to be governed by corrupt groups. New industrial towns were not allowed to elect representatives to Parliament; often they lacked a town organization and could not even govern themselves effectively.

The social separation of noble and commoner was not as rigid in Britain as on the Continent. Younger sons of aristocrats did not inherit titles and were therefore obliged to make careers in law, business, the military, and the church. The upper and middle classes mingled much more freely than on the Continent, and the wealthiest merchants tended to buy lands, titles, and husbands for their daughters. However, Parliament, the courts, local government, the established Anglican Church, and the monarchy were all part of a social and political system dominated by aristocratic interests and values. This domination persisted despite the vast changes in social and economic structure that had taken place in the process of industrialization during the second half of the eighteenth century.

Some members of Parliament urged timely reforms. In 1828, Parliament repealed a seventeenth-century act that in effect barred Nonconformists (non-Anglican Protestants) from government positions and from universities; the following year, Catholics gained the right to sit in Parliament. In 1833, slavery was abolished within the British Empire. (The British slave trade had been abolished earlier.) The Municipal Corporations Act (1835) granted towns and cities greater authority over their affairs. This measure created town and city governments that could, if they wished, begin to solve some of the problems of urbanization and industrialization. These municipal corporations could institute reforms such as sanitation, which Parliament encouraged by passing the first Public Health Act in 1848.

Increasingly, reform centered on extending suffrage and enfranchising the new industrial towns. Middle-class men, and even workers, hoped to gain the right to vote. Because of population shifts, some sparsely populated regions—called rotten boroughs—sent representatives to the House of Commons, while many densely populated factory towns had little or no representation. Often a single important landowner controlled many seats in the Commons. Voting was public, which allowed intimidation, and candidates frequently tried to influence voters with drinks, food, and even money.

Intense and bitter feelings built up during the campaign for the Reform Bill of 1832. The House of Commons passed the bill to extend the suffrage by some two hundred thousand, almost double the number who were then entitled to vote. The House of Lords, however, refused to pass the bill. There were riots and strikes in many cities, and mass meetings, both of workers and of middle-class people, took place all over the country. King William IV (1830–1837) became convinced, along with many politicians, that the situation was potentially revolutionary. To defuse it, he threatened to increase the number of the bill's supporters in the House of Lords by creating new peers. This threat brought reluctant peers into line, and the bill was passed. The Reform Act of 1832 extended the suffrage to the middle class and made the House of Commons more representative. The rotten boroughs lost their seats, which were granted to towns. However, because there were high property qualifications, workers did not gain the right to vote.

Workers did obtain some relief when humanitarians pressured Parliament to pass the Factory Act (1833), which legislated that no child under thirteen could work more than nine hours a day and that no one aged thirteen to eighteen could work more than sixty-nine hours a week. The act also provided some inspectors to investigate infractions and punish offenders. That same year, Parliament also banned children under ten from the mines. The Factory Act of 1847 stipulated that boys under eighteen and women could work no more than ten hours a day in factories. At first, workers resented the prohibition of child labor, since their family income would be greatly reduced if their children could not work, but they gradually came to approve of this law. The ten-hour day for adult male workers was not enacted until 1874.

The Chartist reform movement, whose adherents came from the ranks of both intellectual radicals and workers, pressed for political, not economic, reforms. During the 1830s and 1840s, the Chartists agitated for democratic measures such as universal manhood suffrage, the secret ballot, salaries and the abolition of property qualifications for members of Parliament, and annual meetings of Parliament.

The last political effort by the Chartists was led by Feargus O'Connor, a charismatic Irishman who organized a mass demonstration to present a huge petition of demands to Parliament in 1848. The cabinet ignored the great "People's Charter," which had signatures of at least two million names, and the movement died out. But the Chartist platform remained the democratic reform program for the rest of the century, long after the death of Chartism itself at midcentury. All of the Chartists' demands, except for annual elections for members of Parliament, were eventually realized.

At the beginning of the nineteenth century, elementary education in Britain was managed by private individuals and church organizations. Schools were financed by contributions, grants, and fees paid by students. The government neither financed nor promoted education. As a result, very few poor children attended school. Indeed, many government officials feared that educating the poor would incite unrest. If the lower classes read publications attacking Christianity and challenging authority, they would become insolent to their superiors; education would lead them to reject their rank in society. However, many Britons, inheriting the Enlightenment's confidence in education, favored schooling for the poor. In 1833, Parliament began to allocate small sums for elementary education. These funds were inadequate; in 1869, only about half of all children of school age attended school. The Education Act of 1870 gave local governments the power to establish elementary schools. By 1891, these schools were free and attendance was required.

Many workers and radicals believed that the only hope for their class lay in unified action through trade unions. At first, Parliament fought the unions, passing the Combination Acts (1799–1800), which made unions illegal. In 1825, Parliament allowed workers to unionize but forbade them to strike. Unions made some headway in protecting their members from unemployment and dangerous working conditions, but strikes (which remained officially illegal until 1875) were rarely successful and were often suppressed by force.

Unlike the Continental states, England avoided revolution. British politicians thought that it was because they had made timely reforms in the 1830s and 1840s. The political experience of the first half of the nineteenth century laid the foundation for British parliamentary practices, which came to be the model of liberal, progressive, and stable politics. Britain was the symbol for all those who argued for reform rather than revolution.

The Great Exhibition of 1851, by Dickinson. The Crystal Palace exhibition drew enormous crowds from all over Europe to see the products and processes of machine and craft industries. The building itself was a glass structure supported by a cast-iron frame, a construction imitated in many grand railroad terminals, department stores, and auditoriums throughout Europe and the United States.

Responses to Industrialization

The problems created by rapid industrialization profoundly influenced political and social thought. Liberalism, which began as an attempt to safeguard individual rights from oppressive state authority, now had to confront an unanticipated problem: the distress caused by rapid industrialization and urbanization. Also responding to this ordeal was a new group of thinkers, called socialists.

Liberalism

Adopting the laissez-faire theory of Adam Smith, liberals* maintained that a free economy, in which private enterprise would be unimpeded by government regulations, was as important as political freedom to the well-being of the individual and the community. When people acted from self-interest, liberals said, they worked harder and achieved more; self-interest and natural competitive impulses spurred economic activity and ensured the production of more and better goods at the lowest possible price, benefitting the entire nation. For this reason, the government must neither block free competition nor deprive individuals of their property, which was their incentive to work hard and efficiently.

Convinced that individuals were responsible for their own misfortunes, liberals were often unmoved by the misery of the poor. Indeed, they used the principle of laissez faire—that government should not interfere with the natural laws of supply and demand—to justify their opposition to humanitarian legislation intended to alleviate the suffering of the factory workers. Liberals regarded such social reforms as unwarranted and

*See also the following chapter.

dangerous meddling with the natural law of supply and demand.

They drew comfort from the theory advanced by Thomas Malthus (1766–1834) in his *Essay on the Principle of Population* (1798), which supported laissez-faire economics. Malthus asserted that population always grows at a faster rate than the food supply; consequently, government programs to aid the poor and provide higher wages would only encourage larger families and thus perpetuate poverty. Malthus seemed to supply "scientific" justification for opposing state action to help the poor. Poverty, argued Malthusians, was not the fault of factory owners. It was an iron law of nature—the result of population pressure on resources—and could not be eliminated by state policies. According to Malthus, the state could not ameliorate the poor's misery; "the means of redress," he said, "are in their own hands, and in the hands of no other persons whatever."[2] This "means of redress" would be a lowering of the birthrate through late marriages and chastity, but Malthus believed that the poor lacked the self-discipline to refrain from sexual activity. When they received higher wages, they had more children, thereby upsetting the population–resource balance and bringing misery to themselves and others.

A fellow economist, David Ricardo (1772–1823), gave support to Malthus's gloomy outlook. Wages, he said, tended to remain at the minimum needed to maintain workers. Higher wages encouraged workers to have more children, causing an increase in the labor supply, and greater competition for jobs would then force down wages. Ricardo's disciples made his law inflexible. This "iron law of wages" meant bleak prospects for the working poor. Many workers felt that the new science of economics offered them little hope. They argued that the liberals were concerned only with their class and national interests and that they were callous and apathetic toward the sufferings of the poor.

Liberals of the early nineteenth century saw poverty and suffering as part of the natural order and beyond the scope of government. They feared that state intervention in the economy to redress social ills would disrupt the free market, threatening personal liberty and hindering social well-being. In time, however, the liberals modified their position, allowing for government action to protect the poor and the powerless against the economy's ravages.

Early Socialism

Reformers called utopian socialists argued that the liberals' concern for individual freedom and equality had little impact on the poverty, oppression, and gross inequality of wealth that plagued modern society. Liberal ideals, socialists claimed, protected the person and property of the wealthy, while the majority was mired in poverty and helplessness. Asserting that the liberals' doctrine of individualism degenerated into selfish egoism, which harmed community life, socialists demanded the creation of a new society based on cooperation rather than competition. Reflecting the spirit of the Enlightenment and the French Revolution, socialists, like liberals, denounced the status quo for perpetuating injustice and held that people could create a better world. Like liberals, too, they placed the highest value on a rational analysis of society and on transforming society in line with scientifically valid premises whose truth rational people could grasp. Socialists believed that they had discerned a pattern in human society that, if properly understood and acted upon, would lead men and women to an earthly salvation. Thus, utopian socialists were also romantics, for they dreamed of a new social order, a future utopia, where each individual could find happiness and fulfillment. Although they sought to replace the existing social order with a more just arrangement, these early socialists, unlike Karl Marx, did not advocate class warfare. Rather, they aspired to create a new harmonious social order that would reconcile different classes.

Saint-Simon Henri Comte de Saint-Simon (1760–1825) renounced his title during the French Revolution and enthusiastically preached the opportunity to create a new society. His mission, he believed, was to set society right by instilling an understanding of the new age that science and industry were shaping. He argued that just as Christianity had provided social unity and stability during the Middle Ages, so scientific knowledge would bind the society of his time. The scientists, industrialists, bankers, artists, and writers would replace the clergy and the aristocracy as the social elite and would harness technology for the betterment of humanity. Saint-Simon's disciples championed efforts to build great railway and canal systems, including the Suez and Panama Canals. His vision of a scientifically organized society led by trained experts was a powerful force among intellectuals in the nineteenth century.

Fourier Another early French socialist, Charles Fourier (1772–1837), believed that society conflicted with the natural needs of human beings and that this tension was responsible for human misery. Only the reorganization of society so that it would satisfy people's desire for pleasure and contentment would end that misery. Whereas Saint-Simon and his followers had elaborate plans to reorganize society on the grand scale of large industries and giant railway and canal systems, Fourier sought to create small communities that would let men and women enjoy life's simple pleasures.

These communities of about sixteen hundred people, called *phalansteries*, would be organized according to the unchanging needs of human nature. All the people would work at tasks that interested them and would produce things that brought them and others pleasure. Like Adam Smith, Fourier understood that specialization, with its deadening routine, bred boredom and alienation from work and life. Unlike Smith, he did not believe that vastly increased productivity compensated for the evils of specialization. In the phalansteries, money and goods would not be equally distributed; those with special skills and responsibilities would be rewarded accordingly, a system that conformed to nature because people have a natural desire to be rewarded.

Fourier thought that marriage distorted the natures of both men and women, since monogamy restricted their sexual needs and narrowed the scope of their lives to just the family. Instead, people should think of themselves as part of the family of all humanity. Because married women had to devote all their strength and time to household and children, they had no time or energy left to enjoy life's pleasures. Fourier did not call for the abolition of the family, but he did hope that it would disappear of its own accord as society adjusted to his theories. Men and women would find new ways of fulfilling themselves sexually, and the community would be organized so that it could care for the children. Fourier's ideas found some acceptance in the United States, where in the 1840s at least twenty-nine communities were founded on Fourierist principles. None, however, lasted more than five or six years.

Owen In 1799, Robert Owen (1771–1858) became part owner and manager of the New Lanark cotton mills in Scotland. Distressed by the widespread mistreatment of workers, Owen resolved to improve the lives of his employees and show that it was possible to do so without destroying profits. He raised wages, upgraded working conditions, refused to hire children under ten, and provided workers with neat homes, food, and clothing, all at reasonable prices. He set up schools for children and for adults. In every way, he demonstrated his belief that healthier, happier workers produced more than the less fortunate ones. Like Saint-Simon, Owen believed that industry and technology could and would enrich humankind if they were organized according to the proper principles. Visitors came from all over Europe to see Owen's factories.

Just like many philosophes, Owen was convinced that the environment was the principal shaper of character—that the ignorance, alcoholism, and crime of the poor derived from bad living conditions. Public education and factory reform, said Owen, would make better citizens of the poor. Owen came to believe that the entire social and economic order must be replaced by a new system based on harmonious group living rather than on competition. He established a model community at New Harmony, Indiana, but it was short-lived.

Industrialism in Perspective

Like the French Revolution, the Industrial Revolution helped to modernize Europe. Eventually, it transformed every facet of society. In preindustrial society—Europe in the mid-eighteenth century—agriculture was the dominant economic activity and peasants were the most numerous class. Peasant life centered on the family and the village, which country folk rarely left. The new rational and critical spirit associated with the

Enlightenment hardly penetrated rural Europe; there, religious faith, clerical authority, and ancient superstition remained firmly entrenched.

Traditional society was predominantly rural. By the start of the nineteenth century, 20 percent of the population of Britain, France, and Holland lived in cities; in Russia, the figure was only 5 percent. Artisan manufacturing in small shops and trade for local markets were the foundations of the urban economy, although some cities did produce luxury goods for wider markets. Textile manufacturing was conducted through the putting-out system, in which wool was turned into cloth in private dwellings, usually the homes of peasants.

The richest and most powerful class was the aristocracy, whose wealth stemmed from land. Nobles dominated the countryside and enjoyed privileges protected by custom and law. Eighteenth-century aristocrats, like their medieval forebears, viewed society as a hierarchy, in which a person's position in life was determined by his or her inherited status. By championing the ideals of liberty and equality, the French Revolution undermined the traditional power structure of king, aristocracy, and clergy. French reformers further dismantled the religious and political pillars of traditional rural society by advocating the rational and secular outlook of the Enlightenment.

The Industrial Revolution transformed all areas of society. Eventually, agricultural villages and handicraft manufacturing were eclipsed in importance by cities and factories. In the society fashioned by industrialization and urbanization, aristocratic power and values declined; at the same time, the bourgeoisie increased in number, wealth, importance, and power. More and more, a person was judged by talent rather than by birth, and opportunities for upward social mobility expanded. The Industrial Revolution became a great force for democratization: during the nineteenth century, first the middle class and then the working class gained the vote. The Industrial Revolution also hastened the secularization of European life. In the cities, former villagers, separated from traditional communal ties, drifted away from their ancestral religion. In a world being reshaped by technology, industry, and science, Christian mysteries lost their force, and for many salvation became a remote concern. Modernization did not proceed everywhere at the same pace and with the same thoroughness. Generally, premodern social and institutional forms remained deeply entrenched in Eastern and Southern Europe, persisting well into the twentieth century.

Although the Industrial Revolution created many problems, some of which still endure, it was a great triumph. Ultimately, it made possible the highest standard of living in human history and created new opportunities for social advancement, political participation, and educational and cultural development. It also widened the gap between the West and the rest of the world in terms of science and technology. By 1900, Western states, aided by superior technology, extended their power over virtually the entire globe, completing the trend that had begun with the Age of Exploration.

❖ ❖ ❖

Notes

1. David S. Landes, *The Unbound Prometheus: Technological Change and Industrial Development in Western Europe from 1750 to the Present* (Cambridge, Mass.: Harvard University Press, 1969), p. 33.
2. Thomas Robert Malthus, *First Essay on Population,* reprinted for the Royal Economic Society (London: Macmillan, 1926), p. 17.

Suggested Reading

Ashton, T. S., *The Industrial Revolution, 1700–1830* (1962). A still useful account.

Beaudoin, Steven M., ed., *The Industrial Revolution* (2003). A useful collection of essays.

Deane, Phyllis, *The First Industrial Revolution, 1750–1850* (1965). An excellent introduction.

Fisher, Douglas, *Industrial Revolution* (1992). Incorporates the latest scholarship on British industrialization.

Heilbroner, Robert, *The Worldly Philosophers* (1953). Good discussions of early economic thinkers.

Himmelfarb, Gertrude, *The Idea of Poverty: England in the Early Industrial Age* (1983). A brilliant history of English social thought, focused on the condition of the poor.

Jones, E. L., *Growth Recurring* (1988). Concentrates on why industrialization took place in Europe.

Landes, David S., *The Unbound Prometheus: Technological Change and Industrial Development in Western Europe from 1750 to the Present* (1969). A classic treatment of a complex subject.

Laslett, P., *The World We Have Lost* (1984). Classic discussion of the world before industrialization.

Manuel, Frank E., *The Prophets of Paris* (1962). Good discussions of Saint-Simon and Fourier.

Milward, A. S., *Economic Development of Continental Europe, 1780–1870* (1973). A helpful survey.

Stearns, Peter. *The Industrial Revolution in World History* (1993). The spread of industrialization.

CourseMate

Go to the CourseMate website at **www.cengagebrain.com** for additional study tools and review materials—including audio and video clips—for this chapter.

Chapter 13

Thought and Culture in the Early Nineteenth Century

- **Romanticism: A New Cultural Orientation**
- **German Idealism**
- **Conservatism: The Value of Tradition**
- **Liberalism: The Value of the Individual**
- **Nationalism: The Sacredness of the Nation**

Focus Questions

1. How was the Romantic Movement a reaction against the dominant ideas of the Enlightenment?
2. What was the impact of romanticism on European life?
3. What were the attitudes of conservatives and liberals toward the Enlightenment and the French Revolution?
4. What is the relationship between nationalism and liberalism? How do you explain nationalism's great appeal?

After the defeat of Napoleon, the traditional rulers of Europe, some of them just restored to power, were determined to protect themselves and society from future revolutions. As defenders of the status quo, they attacked the reformist spirit of the philosophes, which, they thought, had produced the French Revolution. In conservatism, which championed tradition over reason, hierarchy over equality, and the community over the individual, they found a philosophy to justify their assault on the Enlightenment and the Revolution.

But the forces unleashed by the Revolution had penetrated European consciousness too deeply to be eradicated. One of them was liberalism, which aimed to secure the liberty and equality proclaimed by the Revolution. Another was nationalism, which sought to free subject peoples and unify fragmented nations. Captivated by the dream to redeem humanity, idealistic youth and intellectuals joined in the revolutionary struggle for liberty and nationhood.

The postrevolutionary period also witnessed the flowering of a new cultural orientation. *Romanticism,* with its plea for the liberation of human emotions and the free expression of personality, challenged the Enlightenment stress on rationalism. Although primarily a literary and artistic movement, romanticism also permeated philosophy and political thought, particularly conservatism and nationalism. ❖

***Traveler Looking Over a Sea of Fog,* by Caspar David Friedrich.** A prominent German romantic landscape painter, Friedrich frequently portrayed individuals lost in thought as they confronted fogs, clouds, stars, and other powerful and mysterious natural wonders.

Romanticism: A New Cultural Orientation

The Romantic Movement, which began in the closing decades of the eighteenth century, dominated European cultural life in the first half of the nineteenth century. Most of Europe's leading cultural figures came under its influence. Among the exponents of romanticism were the poets Shelley, Wordsworth, Keats, and Byron in England; the novelist Victor Hugo and the Catholic novelist and essayist Chateaubriand in France; and the writers A. W. and Friedrich Schlegel, the dramatist and poet Schiller, and the philosopher Schelling in Germany. Caspar David Friedrich in Germany and John Constable in England expressed the romantic mood in art, and Beethoven, Schubert, Chopin, and Wagner expressed it in music.

Exalting Imagination and Feelings

Perhaps the central message of the romantics was that the imagination and emotions of the individual should determine the form and content of an artistic creation. This outlook ran counter to the rationalism of the Enlightenment, which itself had been a reaction against the otherworldly Christian orientation of the Middle Ages. The philosophes had attacked religion because it thwarted and distorted reason; romantic poets, philosophers, and artists now denounced the rationalism of the philosophes because it crushed the emotions and impeded creativity.

The philosophes, said the romantics, had turned flesh-and-blood human beings into soulless thinking machines. For human beings to be restored to their true nature, to become whole again, they must be emancipated from the tyranny of excessive intellectualizing; the feelings must be nurtured and expressed. Taking up one of Rousseau's ideas, romantics yearned to rediscover in the human soul the pristine freedom and insight that had been squashed by habits, values, rules, and standards imposed by civilization.

DANTE'S *INFERNO: THE WHIRLWIND OF LOVERS*, BY WILLIAM BLAKE (1757–1827). A radical romantic painter and poet, Blake totally rejected the artistic conventions of the past. His religious and political beliefs were as unique as his art; he spent his life trying to convey tormented inward visions. A prolific illustrator, his imaginative genius was stimulated by great literature such as Dante's *Divine Comedy*. (The Circle of the Lustful: Paolo and Francesca, Gift of W.G. Russell Allen. Image © 2011 Board of Trustees, National Gallery of Art, Washington, DC. Image courtesy Board of Trustees.)

Abstract reason and scientific knowledge, said the romantics, are insufficient guides to knowledge. They provide only general principles about nature and people; they cannot penetrate to what really matters—the uniqueness of each person, of each robin, of each tree, cloud, and lake. The philosophes had concentrated on people in general, focusing on the elements of human nature shared by all people. Romantics, on the other hand, emphasized human diversity and uniqueness—those traits that set one human being apart from others. Discover and express your true self, the romantics urged: play your own music; write your own poetry; paint your own vision of nature; live, love, and suffer in your own way.

Whereas the philosophes had asserted the mind's autonomy—its capacity to think for itself and not depend on authority—romantics gave primary importance to the autonomy of the personality—the individual's need and right to find and fulfill an inner self. To the philosophes, feelings were an obstacle to clear thinking, but to the romantics they were the essence of being human. People could not live by reason alone, said the romantics. They agreed with Rousseau, who wrote: "For us, to exist is to feel and our sensibility is incontestably prior to our reason."[1] For the romantics, reason was cold and dreary, and its understanding of people and life meager and inadequate. Reason could not grasp or express the complexities of human nature or the richness of human experience. By always dissecting and analyzing, by imposing deadening structure and form, and by demanding adherence to strict rules, reason crushed inspiration and creativity and barred true understanding. "The Reasoning Power in

Man," wrote William Blake (1757–1827), the British poet, artist, and mystic, is "an Incrustation [scab] over my Immortal / Spirit."[2]

The romantics saw spontaneous, unbounded feelings, rather than the constricted intellect, as the avenue to truth. By cultivating emotions, intuition, and the imagination, individuals could experience reality and discover their authentic selves. The romantics wanted people to feel and to experience—"To bathe in the Waters of Life," said Blake.[3] Consequently, they insisted that imaginative poets had a greater insight into life than analytical philosophers. "I am certain of nothing but of the holiness of the Heart's affections and the truth of Imagination," wrote John Keats (1795–1821). "O for a Life of Sensations rather than of Thoughts."[4]

The Enlightenment mind had been clear, critical, and controlled. It had adhered to standards of esthetics, thought to be universal, that had dominated European cultural life since the Renaissance. Romantic poets, artists, and musicians broke with these traditional styles and uniform rules—essentially those inherited from the classical tradition—and created new cultural forms and techniques. "We do not want either Greek or Roman Models," Blake declared, "but [should be] just & true to our own Imaginations."[5] Victor Hugo (1802–1885), the dominant figure among French romantics, urged in the Preface to his play *Cromwell:* "Freedom in art! . . . Let us take the hammer to the theories, the poetics [the analysis of poetry] and the systems."[6] The romantics felt deeply that one did not learn how to write poetry or paint pictures by following textbook rules, nor could one grasp the poet's or artist's intent by judging works according to fixed standards.

Only by trusting their own feelings could individuals attain their creative potential and achieve self-realization. Hence, the most beautiful works of art were not photographic imitations of nature but authentic and spontaneous expressions of the artist's feelings, fantasies, and dreams. It was the artist's inner voice that gave a work of art its supreme value. The romantics also explored the inner life of the mind, which Freud would later call the unconscious. It was this layer of the mind—the wellspring of creativity, mysterious, primitive, more elemental and more powerful than reason—that the romantics yearned to revitalize and release. Like Freud, some romantics had an intuitive awareness of the dark side of the unconscious. Buried there, they sensed, were our worst fears and most hideous desires.

Nature, God, History

The philosophes had viewed nature as a lifeless machine: a giant clock, all of whose parts worked together with precision and in perfect harmony. Nature's laws, operating with mathematical certainty, were uncovered by the methodology of science. To the romantics, nature was alive and suffused with God's presence. Nature stimulated the creative energies of the imagination; it taught human beings a higher form of knowledge. As William Wordsworth (1770–1850) wrote in his poem "The Tables Turned,"

> *One impulse from a vernal wood*
> *[spring greenery]*
> *May teach you more of man,*
> *Of moral evil and of good,*
> *Than all the sages can.*[7]

Regarding God as a great watchmaker—a detached observer of a self-operating mechanical universe—the philosophes tried to reduce religion to a series of scientific propositions. Many romantics, on the contrary, viewed God as an inspiring spiritual force and condemned the philosophes for weakening Christianity by submitting its dogmas to the test of reason. For the romantics, religion was not science and syllogism but a passionate and authentic expression of human nature. They called for acknowledgment of the individual as a spiritual being and for cultivation of the religious side of human nature. This appeal accorded with their goal of restoring the whole personality, which, they were convinced, had been fragmented and distorted by the philosophes' excessive emphasis on the intellect.

The philosophes and the romantics viewed the Middle Ages very differently as well. To the former, that period was a time of darkness, superstition, and fanaticism; surviving medieval institutions and traditions only barred progress. The romantics, on the other hand, revered the Middle Ages. To the romantic imagination, the Middle Ages abounded with spiritual sensitivity, Christian mysteries, heroic deeds, and social harmony.

The romantics also disagreed with the philosophes on their conception of history. For the philosophes, history served a didactic purpose by providing examples of human folly. Such knowledge helped people to prepare for a better future, and for that reason alone history was worth studying. To the romantics, a historical period, like an individual, was a unique entity with its own soul. They wanted the historian to portray and analyze the variety of nations, traditions, and institutions that constituted the historical experience, always recognizing what is particular and unique to a given time and place. The romantics' insistence on comprehending the specific details of history and culture within the context of the times is the foundation of modern historical scholarship.

Searching for universal principles, the philosophes had dismissed folk traditions as peasant superstitions and impediments to progress. The romantics, on the other hand, rebelling against the standardization of culture, saw native languages, songs, and legends as the unique creations of a people and the deepest expression of national feeling. The romantics regarded the legends, myths, and folk traditions of a people as the fount of poetry and art and the spiritual source of a people's cultural vitality, creativity, and identity. Consequently, they examined these earliest cultural expressions with awe and reverence. In this way, romanticism played a part in shaping modern nationalism.

The Impact of the Romantic Movement

The romantic revolt against the Enlightenment had an important and enduring impact on European history. By focusing on the creative capacities inherent in the emotions—intuition, instinct, passion, will, empathy—the romantics shed light on a side of human nature that the philosophes had often overlooked or undervalued. By encouraging personal freedom and diversity in art, music, and literature, they greatly enriched European cultural life. Future artists, writers, and musicians would proceed along the path opened by the romantics. Modern art, for example, owes much to the Romantic Movement's emphasis on the legitimacy of human feeling and its exploration of the hidden world of dreams and fantasies. Romantics were among the first to attack the emerging industrial capitalism for subordinating individuals to the requirements of the industrial process and treating them as mere things. By recognizing the distinctive qualities of historical periods, peoples, and cultures, they helped create the modern historical outlook. Because it valued a nation's past, romanticism also contributed to modern nationalism and conservatism.

However, the Romantic Movement had a potentially dangerous side: it served as background to the extreme nationalism of the twentieth century. As Ernst Cassirer has pointed out, the romantics "never meant to politicize but to 'poeticize' the world," and their deep respect for human individuality and national diversity was not compatible with Hitler's racial nationalism. Yet by waging their attack on reason with excessive zeal, the romantics undermined respect for the rational tradition of the Enlightenment and thus set up a precondition for the rise and triumph of Fascist movements. Although their intention was cultural and not political, by idealizing the past and glorifying ancient folkways, legends, native soil, and native language, the romantics introduced a highly charged nonrational component into political life. In later generations, romanticism, particularly in Germany, fused with political nationalism to produce, says Horst von Maltitz, "a general climate of inexact thinking, an intellectual . . . dream world and an emotional approach to problems of political action to which sober reasoning should have been applied."[8]

The romantics' veneration of a people's history and traditions and their search for a nation's soul in an archaic culture would have struck the philosophes as barbarous—a regression to superstition and a triumph of myth over reason. Indeed, when transferred to the realm of politics, the romantics' idealization of the past and fascination with inherited national myths as the source of wisdom did reawaken a way of thinking about the world that rested more on feeling than on reason. In the process, people became committed to nationalist and political ideas that were fraught with danger. The glorification of myth and the folk community constitutes a link, however unintended, between romanticism and extreme nationalism, which culminated in the world wars of the twentieth century.

German Idealism

The romantics' stress on the inner person also found expression in the school of German philosophy called idealism. Idealists held that the world is not something objective that exists independently of individual consciousness. Rather, it is human consciousness, the knowing subject, that builds the world and determines its form. German idealism was partly a response to the challenge posed by David Hume, the great Scottish empiricist and skeptic.

The Challenge Posed by Hume's Empiricism

In his *Treatise of Human Nature* (1739–1740) and *Enquiry Concerning Human Understanding* (1748), Hume cast doubt on the view that scientific certainty was possible. Science rests on the conviction that regularities observed in the past and the present will be repeated in the future: that there does exist an objective reality that rational creatures can comprehend. Hume, however, argued that science cannot demonstrate a *necessary connection* between cause and effect. Because we repeatedly experience a burning sensation when our fingers have contact with a flame, we assume a cause-and-effect relationship. This is unwarranted, said Hume. All we can acknowledge is that there is a constant conjunction between the flame and the burning sensation.

According to Hume, we cannot prove that there is a law at work in nature guaranteeing that a specific cause will produce a specific effect. What we mean by cause and effect is simply something that the mind, through habit, imposes on our sense perceptions. For practical purposes, we can say that two events are in association with each other, but we cannot conclude with certainty that the second was caused by the first—that natural law is operating within the physical universe. Such a radical empiricism undermines the very foundations of science so revered by progressive thinkers.

Immanuel Kant

In the *Critique of Pure Reason* (1781), Immanuel Kant (1724–1804), the great German philosopher and proponent of Newtonianism and the scientific method, undertook the challenge of rescuing reason and science from Hume's empiricism. The mind—the knowing subject—said Kant, is not a *tabula rasa,* a blank slate that passively receives sense impressions, but an active instrument that structures, organizes, and interprets the multiplicity of sensations coming to it. The mind can coordinate a chaotic stream of sensations because it contains its own inherent logic; it is equipped with several categories of understanding, including cause and effect.

Because of the way our mind is constituted, we presuppose a relationship of cause and effect in all our experiences with the objects of this world. The mind imposes structure and order on our sense experiences. Cause and effect and the other categories of the mind permit us to attribute certainty to scientific knowledge. The physical world must possess certain definite characteristics because these characteristics conform to the categories of the mind. The object, said Kant, must "accommodate itself to the subject."

Kant rescued science from Hume's assault: the laws of science are universally valid. But in the process, Kant made scientific law dependent on the mind and its a priori categories. We see nature in a certain way because of the mental apparatus that we bring to it. The mind imposes its own laws on nature—on the raw impressions received by the senses—giving the physical world form, structure, and order. By holding that objects must conform to the rules of the human mind and that it is the knowing subject that creates order within nature, Kant gave primacy to the knower rather than to the objects of knowledge. He saw the mind as an active agent, not a passive recipient of sensations. This "turn in philosophy," which Kant considered as revolutionary as the Copernican theory had been for astronomy, gave unprecedented importance to the power of the mind—to the active and creative knower.

It is a fundamental principle of Kant's thought that we cannot know ultimate reality. Our knowledge is limited to the phenomenal world, the realm of natural occurrences. We can only know things that we experience with our senses and grasp through the active intervention of the mind's categories. We can have no knowledge of a thing-in-itself, that is, of an object's ultimate or real nature—its nature as it is independently of the way we experience it, apart from the way our senses receive it. The human mind can acquire knowledge of only that portion of reality that is revealed through sense experience. We can say nothing about the sun's true nature but only describe the way the sun appears to us—that is, our impression of the sun formed by the mind's ordering of our sense experiences of it. Thus, at the same time that Kant reaffirmed the validity of scientific law, he also limited the range of science and reason to the phenomenal world.

G.W. F. Hegel

Kant had insisted that knowledge of what lies beyond phenomena—knowledge of ultimate or absolute reality itself—is forever denied us. Georg Wilhelm Friedrich Hegel (1770–1831), another German philosopher, could not accept this. He constructed an all-embracing metaphysical system that attempted to explain all reality and uncover the fundamental nature and meaning of the universe and human history—to grasp the wholeness of life.

Adopting Kant's notion that the mind imposes its categories on the world, Hegel emphasized the importance of the thinking subject in the quest for truth. However, Kant held that we can have knowledge only of how a thing appears to us, not of the thing-in-itself. Hegel, in contrast, maintained that ultimate reality, total truth, is knowable to the human mind: the mind can comprehend the truths underlying all existence and can grasp the essential meaning of human experience.

Kant had asserted the essential idealist position that the knowing subject organizes our experiences of the phenomenal world. Hegel took a giant step beyond that view by contending that there exists a universal Mind—Absolute Spirit, the thing-in-itself—whose nature can be apprehended through thought.

Because Hegel viewed Absolute Spirit not as fixed and static, but as evolving and developing, history plays a central role in his philosophical system. History is the development of Spirit in time. In the arena of world history, truth unfolds and makes itself known to the human mind. Like the romantics, Hegel said that each historical period has a distinctive character that separates it from every preceding age. The art, science, philosophy, religion, politics, and leading events are so interconnected that the period may be seen to possess an organic unity, a historical coherence.

Hegel believed that world history reveals a rational process; an internal principle of order underlies historical change. There is a purpose and an end to history: the unfolding of Absolute Spirit. In the course of history, an immanent Spirit manifests itself. Gradually, progressively, and nonrepetitively, it actualizes itself, becoming itself fully. Nations and exceptional human beings, "world-historical" individuals—Alexander the Great, Caesar, Napoleon—are the vehicles through which Spirit realizes its potentialities and achieves self-consciousness. Hegel's philosophy of history gives meaning, purpose, and direction to historical events. Where is history taking us? What is its ultimate meaning? For Hegel, history is humanity's progress from lesser to greater freedom: "The History of the World is none other than the progress of the consciousness of Freedom . . . [It is] the absolute goal of history."[9]

According to Hegel, Spirit manifests itself in history through a dialectical confrontation between opposing ideas or forces; the struggle between one idea (thesis) and its adversary (antithesis) is evident in all spheres of human activity. This clash of opposites gains in intensity, eventually ending in a resolution (synthesis) that unifies and surpasses both opposing views. Thought and history thus enter a new and higher stage, that of synthesis, which, by absorbing the truths within both the thesis and the antithesis, achieves a higher level of truth and a higher stage of history. Soon this synthesis itself becomes a thesis that enters into another conflict with another opposing force; this conflict, too, is resolved by a still higher synthesis. Thus, the dynamic struggle between thesis and antithesis—sometimes expressed in revolutions and war, sometimes in art, religion, and philosophy—and its resolution into a synthesis accounts for movement in history. Or, in Hegelian language, Spirit is closer to realization: its rational essence is progressing from potentiality to actuality. The dialectic is the march of Spirit through human affairs. Historical change is often instituted by world-historical individuals who, unknown to themselves, are agents of Spirit in its progress through history. Since Hegel held that freedom is the essence of Spirit, it is through history that human beings progress toward consciousness of their own freedom. They become self-consciously aware of their own self-determination—their ability to regulate their lives rationally according to their own consciousness.

But for individual freedom to be realized, said Hegel, social and political institutions must be rationally determined and organized: that is, the will of the individual must be harmonized with the needs of the community. For Hegel, freedom is not a matter of securing abstract natural rights for the individual, the goal of the French Revolution. Rather, true freedom is attained only within the social group. Thus, in Hegel's view, human beings discover their essential character—their moral and spiritual potential—only as citizens of a cohesive political community. This view goes back to the city-states of ancient Greece, which Hegel admired. In the state's laws and institutions, which are manifestations of reason and the objectivization of Spirit, individuals find a basis for rationally determining their own lives. In this way, the private interests of citizens become one with the interests of the community.

For Hegel, Absolute Spirit, which is also Ultimate Reason, realizes itself in the state, the highest form of human association. The state joins fragmented individuals together into a community and substitutes a rule of justice for the rule of instincts. It permits individuals to live the ethical life and to develop their human potential. An individual cannot achieve these goals in isolation. Hegel's thought reveals a powerful undercurrent of statism: the exaltation of the state and the subordination of the individual to it. For Hegel, the national state was the embodiment of Universal Reason and the supreme achievement of Absolute Spirit.

German conservatives used Hegel's idea that existing institutions have a rational legitimacy to support their opposition to rapid change. Existing reality, even if it appears cruel and hateful, is the actualization of Absolute Spirit. Therefore, it is inherently necessary and rational and should not be altered.

Some of Hegel's followers, known as Young Hegelians, interpreted Hegel in a radical sense. They rejected his view that the Prussian state, or any German state, was the goal of world history, the realization of freedom. The Germany of their day, held the Young Hegelians, had not attained a harmony between the individual and society; it was not rationally organized and did not foster freedom. These Young Hegelians saw Hegel's philosophy as a means of radically altering the world to make existing society truly rational. The most important of the radical Young Hegelians was Karl Marx. Marx retained Hegel's overarching principle that history contains an inner logic, that it is an intelligible process, and that a dialectical struggle propels history from a lower to a higher stage (see Chapter 15).

Conservatism: The Value of Tradition

To the traditional rulers of Europe—kings, aristocrats, and clergy—the French Revolution was a great evil that had inflicted a near-fatal wound on civilization. Disgusted and frightened by the revolutionary violence, terror, and warfare, the traditional rulers sought to refute the philosophes' worldview, which had spawned the Revolution. To them, natural rights, equality, the goodness of man, and perpetual progress were perverse doctrines that had produced the Jacobin "assassins." In conservatism, they found a political philosophy to counter the Enlightenment ideology.

Edmund Burke's *Reflections on the Revolution in France* (1790) was instrumental in shaping conservative thought. Burke (1729–1797), an Anglo-Irish statesman and political theorist, wanted to warn his countrymen of the dangers inherent in the ideology of the revolutionaries. Although writing in 1790, he astutely predicted that the Revolution would lead to terror and military dictatorship. To Burke, fanatics armed with pernicious principles—abstract ideas divorced from historical experience—had dragged France through the mire of revolution. Burke developed a coherent political philosophy that served as a counterweight to the ideology of the Enlightenment and the Revolution.

Primary Source

Joseph de Maistre, Arch-Conservative

Joseph de Maistre denounced the Enlightenment for spawning the French Revolution, defended the church as a civilizing agent, and affirmed tradition as a model more valuable than instant reforms embodied in "paper constitutions." The following critique of the philosophes, the French Revolution, and manufactured constitutions is taken from de Maistre's Essay on the Generative Principle of Political Constitutions (1808–1809).

One of the major errors of an age that professed them all was to believe that a political constitution could be written and created a priori, whereas reason and experience join in establishing that a constitution is a divine work, and that precisely what is the most basic and the most essentially constitutional in a nation's laws could not possibly be written down. . . .

. . . Didn't people on all sides believe that a constitution was an intellectual creation like an ode or a tragedy? Had not *Thomas Paine* declared, with a profundity that delighted academics, *that a constitution does not exist as long as one can't put it in his pocket?* The eighteenth century, which was aware of nothing [in the supernatural order], had not doubts about anything; that is the rule. I believe that century produced no talented stripling who did not produce three things on graduating from secondary school: a system of education, a constitution, and a utopia. . . .

. . . I do not believe that any doubt remains as to the indisputable truth of the following premises:

The roots of political constitutions preexist any written law *(loi)*.

A constitutional law is not, and cannot be, anything other than the development and the sanction of a pre-existing and unwritten law *(droit)*

. . . He who imagines he can establish a clear, lasting doctrine through writing alone IS A GREAT FOOL. If he truly possessed the authentic seeds of truth, he would be careful not to let himself believe that *with a little black elixir* [ink] *and a pen* he could make them germinate in the universe, defend them against inclement weather, and impart to them the necessary potency. As for he who undertakes to write *laws and civil constitutions*, and who imagines that, because he has written them down he can impart to them appropriate power of conviction and stability, whoever that man may be, either a private individual or a legislator, "this is a source of shame for the author, whether or not anyone has ever said as much to him. For, awake or asleep, ignorance about what activities are right or wrong or good or bad cannot, when seen aright, fail to be a matter for reproach, even if the general mass of people approve of it" (Plato, *Phaedrus*).

. . . No written law could ever found any great, authentic institution. Men themselves, the successive instruments of that establishment's consolidation, do not know what it is destined to become, and imperceptible growth is the true sign of durability, in every possible order of things. . . .

Everything leads us back to the general rule: *Men cannot make constitutions; and no legitimate constitution could ever be written down.* Never has anyone written, and never will anyone write a priori the collection of fundamental laws that are to constitute a civil or religious society. . . .

De Maistre assails the philosophes for attacking religion. Without Christianity, he says, people become brutalized, and civilization degenerates into anarchy.

Nations have never been civilized otherwise than by religion. No other instrument known can exert influence on prehistoric man. . . . What should we think of a generation that has tossed everything, even the very foundations of the social structure, into the air, by making education merely scientific? One could not make a more dreadful mistake; for any educational system that is not based on religion will collapse in a twinkling, or else disseminate nothing but poisons throughout the State. . . . If the control of education is not restored to the priests, and if science is not everywhere relegated to second place, the ills that await us will be incalculable: we shall be brutalized by science, and there is no more degrading brutalization. . . .

So it was only in the first half of the eighteenth century that impiety became a real force. You see it spreading in every direction with incredible energy. From the palace to the hut, it slithers everywhere; it infests everything. . . .

Questions for Analysis

1. Why did Joseph de Maistre believe that man cannot create a constitution?
2. Why did he value Christianity?

The Collected Works of Joseph de Maistre, Essay on the Generative Principle of Political Constitutions, translated by Laurence M. Porter and Richard Lebrun. Used by permission of Laurence M. Porter and Richard Lebrun.

Hostility to the French Revolution

Entranced by the great discoveries in science, the philosophes and French reformers had believed that the human mind could also transform social institutions and ancient traditions according to rational models. Progress through reason became their faith. Dedicated to creating a new future, the revolutionaries abruptly dispensed with old habits, traditional authority, and familiar ways of thought. For them, these traditional ways were a form of bondage that stifled progress.

To the conservatives, who like the romantics venerated the past, this was supreme arrogance and wickedness. They regarded the revolutionaries as presumptuous men who recklessly severed society's links with ancient institutions and traditions and condemned venerable religious and moral beliefs as ignorance. By attacking time-honored ways, the revolutionaries had deprived French society of moral leadership and had opened the door to anarchy and terror. "You began ill," wrote Burke of the revolutionaries, "because you began by despising everything that belonged to you. . . . When ancient opinions and rules of life are taken away, the loss cannot possibly be estimated. From that moment we have no compass to govern us; nor can we know distinctly to what port we steer."[10]

The philosophes and French reformers had expressed unlimited confidence in the power of human reason to understand and to improve society. While appreciating human rational capacities, conservatives also recognized the limitations of reason. They saw the Revolution as a natural outgrowth of an arrogant Enlightenment philosophy that overvalued reason and sought to reshape society according to abstract principles.

Conservatives did not view human beings as good by nature. Human wickedness was not caused by a faulty environment, as the philosophes had proclaimed, but lay at the core of human nature, as Christianity taught. Evil was held in check not by reason, but by tried and tested institutions—monarchy, church, and aristocracy; traditions; and beliefs. Without these habits inherited from ancestors, said conservatives, sinful human nature threatened the social order.

Because monarchy, aristocracy, and the church had endured for centuries, argued the conservatives, they had worth. By despising and uprooting these ancient institutions, revolutionaries had hardened the people's hearts, perverted their morals, and caused them to commit terrible outrages upon one another and upon society. As conservatives saw it, revolutionaries had divorced people and society from their historical settings and reduced them to abstractions; they had drawn up constitutions based on the unacceptable principle that government derives its power from the consent of the governed.

For conservatives, God and history were the only legitimate sources of political authority. States were not made; rather, they were an expression of the nation's moral, religious, and historical experience. No legitimate or sound constitution could be drawn up by a group assembled for that purpose. Scraps of paper with legal terminology and philosophical visions could not produce an effective government. Instead, a sound political system evolved gradually and inexplicably in response to circumstances.

The Quest for Social Stability

The liberal philosophy of the Enlightenment and the French Revolution started with the individual. The philosophes and the revolutionaries envisioned a society in which the individual was free and autonomous. Conservatives, on the other hand, began with the community, which they considered more important than the individual. They believed that society was not a mechanical arrangement of disconnected individuals but a living organism held together by centuries-old bonds. Individualism would imperil social stability, destroy obedience to law, and fragment society into self-seeking, isolated atoms. Whereas the philosophes had attacked Christianity for promoting superstition and fanaticism, conservatives saw religion as the basis of civil society. Catholic conservatives, in particular, held that God had constituted the church and monarchy to check sinful human nature.

Conservatives viewed equality as another pernicious abstraction that contradicted all historical experience. For conservatives, society was naturally hierarchical, and they believed that some men, by virtue of their intelligence, education, wealth, and birth, were best qualified to rule and instruct the less able. They said that by denying the existence of a natural elite and uprooting the long-established and divinely ordained ruling elite, which had learned its art through experience, the revolutionaries had deprived society of effective leaders, brought internal disorder, and prepared the way for Napoleon's dictatorship.

Conservatism pointed to a limitation of the Enlightenment. It showed that human beings and social relationships are far more complex than the philosophes had imagined. People do not always accept the rigorous logic of the philosopher and are not eager to break with ancient ways, however illogical those ways appear. They often find familiar customs and ancestral religions more satisfying guides to life than the blueprints of philosophers. The granite might of tradition remains an obstacle to all the visions of reformers. Conservative theorists warned that revolutionary violence in the pursuit of utopian dreams transforms politics into an ideological crusade that ends in terror and despotism. These warnings bore bitter fruit in the twentieth century.

Liberalism: The Value of the Individual

The decades after 1815 saw a spectacular rise of the bourgeoisie. Talented and ambitious bankers, merchants, manufacturers, professionals, and officeholders wanted to break the stranglehold of the landed nobility—the traditional elite—on political power and social prestige. They also wanted to eliminate restrictions on the free pursuit of profits. The political philosophy of the bourgeoisie was most commonly liberalism. While conservatives sought to strengthen the foundations of traditional society, which had been severely shaken in the period of the French Revolution and Napoleon, liberals strove to alter the status quo and to realize the promise of the Enlightenment and the French Revolution.

The Sources of Liberalism

In the long view of Western civilization, liberalism is an extension and development of the democratic practices and rational outlook that originated in ancient Greece. Also flowing into the liberal tradition is Judeo-Christian respect for the worth and dignity of the individual endowed by God with freedom to make moral choices. But nineteenth-century liberalism had its immediate historical roots in seventeenth-century England. At that time, the struggle for religious toleration by English Protestant dissenters established the principle of freedom of conscience, which is easily translated into freedom of opinion and expression in all matters. The Glorious Revolution of 1688 set limits on the power of the English monarchy. At the same time, John Locke's natural rights philosophy declared that the individual was by nature entitled to freedom, and it justified revolutions against rulers who deprived citizens of their lives, liberty, or property.

The French philosophes helped to shape liberalism. From Montesquieu, liberals derived the theory of the separation of powers and of checks and balances—principles intended to guard against despotic government. The philosophes supported religious toleration and freedom of thought, expressed confidence in the capacity of the human mind to reform society, maintained that human beings are essentially good, and believed in the future progress of humanity—all fundamental principles of liberalism.

The American and French Revolutions were crucial phases in the history of liberalism. The Declaration of Independence gave expression to Locke's theory of natural rights, the Constitution of the United States incorporated Montesquieu's principles and demonstrated that people could create an effective government, and the Bill of Rights protected the person and rights of the individual. In destroying the special privileges of the aristocracy and opening careers to talent, the French National Assembly of 1789 had implemented the liberal ideal of equality under the law. It also drew up the Declaration of the Rights of Man and of the Citizen, which affirmed the dignity and rights of the individual, and a constitution that limited the king's power. Both revolutions explicitly called for the protection of property rights, another basic premise of liberalism.

Individual Liberty

The liberals' primary concern was the enhancement of individual liberty. They agreed with Kant that every person exists as an end in himself and not as an object to be used arbitrarily by others. If uncoerced by government and churches and properly educated, a person can develop into a good, productive, and self-directed human being.

Liberals rejected a legacy of the Middle Ages, the classification of an individual as a commoner or aristocrat on the basis of birth. They held that individuals were not born into a certain station in life but made their way through their own efforts. Taking their cue from the French Revolution, liberals called for an end to all privileges of the aristocracy.

In the tradition of the philosophes, liberals stressed the preeminence of reason as the basis of political life. Unfettered by ignorance and tyranny, the mind could eradicate evils that had burdened people for centuries and begin an age of free institutions and responsible citizens. For this reason, liberals supported the advancement of education.

Liberals attacked the state and other authorities that prevented the individual from exercising the right of free choice, interfered with the right of free expression, and blocked the individual's self-determination and self-development. They agreed with John Stuart Mill (1806–1873), the British philosopher, who declared that "over his own body and mind, the individual is sovereign. . . . that the only purpose for which power can be rightfully exercised over any member of a civilized community, against his will, is to prevent harm to others."[11]

To guard against the absolute and arbitrary authority of kings, liberals demanded written constitutions that granted freedom of speech, the press, and religion; freedom from arbitrary arrest; and the protection of property rights. To prevent the abuse of political authority, they called for a freely elected parliament and the distribution of power among the various branches of government. Liberals held that a government that derived its authority from the consent of the governed, as given in free elections, was least likely to violate individual freedom. A corollary of this principle was that the best government is one that governs least—that is, one that interferes as little as possible with the economic activities of its citizens and does not involve itself in their private lives or their beliefs.

Liberalism and Democracy

Many bourgeois liberals viewed with horror the democratic creed that all people should share in political power. To them, the participation of commoners in politics meant a vulgar form of despotism and the end of individual liberty. They saw the masses—uneducated, unpropertied, inexperienced, and impatient—as lacking both the ability and the temperament to maintain liberty and protect property.

Because bourgeois liberals feared that democracy could crush personal freedom as ruthlessly as any absolute monarch, they called for property requirements for voting and officeholding.

They wanted political power to be concentrated in the hands of a safe and reliable—that is, a propertied and educated—middle class. Such a government would prevent revolution from below, a prospect that caused anxiety among bourgeois liberals.

To be sure, early-nineteenth-century liberals engaged in revolutions, but their aims were always limited. Once they had destroyed absolute monarchy and gained a constitution and a parliament or a change of government, they quickly tried to end the revolution. When the fever of revolution spread to the masses, liberals either withdrew or turned counterrevolutionary, for they feared the stirrings of the multitude.

Although liberalism was the political philosophy of a middle class that was generally hostile to democracy, the essential ideals of democracy flowed logically from liberalism. Eventually, democracy became a later stage in the evolution of liberalism because the masses, their political power enhanced by the Industrial Revolution, pressed for greater social, political, and economic equality. Thus, by the early twentieth century, many European states had introduced universal suffrage, abandoned property requirements for officeholding, and improved conditions for workers.

The confidence of liberal-democrats was shaken in the twentieth century. Growing impatient, in turbulent times, with parliamentary procedures, people in some European countries gave their support to demagogues who promised swift and decisive action. They were willing to trade freedom for economic security, state authority, and national power. Liberalism is based on the assumption that human beings can and do respond to rational argument and that reason will prevail over base human feelings. Recent history shows that this may be an overly optimistic assessment of human nature.

Nationalism: The Sacredness of the Nation

Nationalism is a conscious bond shared by a group of people who feel strongly attached to a particular land and who possess a common language, culture, and history, marked by shared glories and sufferings. Nationalists contend that one's highest loyalty and devotion should be given to the nation. They exhibit great pride in their people's history and traditions and often feel that their nation has been specially chosen by God or history. They assert that the nation—its culture and history—gives meaning to an individual's life and actions. Like a religion, nationalism provides the individual with a sense of community and with a cause worthy of self-sacrifice. Identifying with the nation's collective achievements and its past greatness enhances feelings of self-worth.

In an age when Christianity was in retreat, nationalism became the dominant spiritual force in nineteenth-century European life. Nationalism provided new beliefs, martyrs, and "holy" days that stimulated reverence; it offered membership in a community that satisfied the overwhelming psychological need of human beings for fellowship and identity. And nationalism gave a mission—the advancement of the nation—to which people could dedicate themselves.

The Emergence of Modern Nationalism

The essential components of modern nationalism emerged at the time of the French Revolution. The Revolution asserted the principle that sovereignty derived from the nation, from the people as a whole: the state was not the private possession of the ruler but the embodiment of the people's will. The nation-state was above king, church, estate, guild, or province; it superseded all other loyalties. The French people must view themselves not as subjects of the king, not as Bretons or Normans, not as nobles or bourgeois, but as citizens of a united fatherland, *la patrie*. These two ideas—that the people possess unlimited sovereignty and that they are united in a nation—were crucial in fashioning a nationalist outlook.

As the Revolution moved from the moderate to the radical stage, French nationalism intensified. In 1793 and 1794, when foreign invasion threatened the republic, the Jacobins created a national army, demanded ever greater allegiance to and sacrifice for the nation, and called for the expansion of France's borders to the Alps and the Rhine.

With unprecedented success, the Jacobins used every means—press, schoolroom, and rostrum—to instill a love of country.

The Romantic Movement also awakened nationalist feelings. By examining the language, literature, and folkways of their people, romantic thinkers instilled a sense of national pride in their compatriots. Johann Gottfried Herder (1744–1803), a prominent German writer, conceived the idea of the *Volksgeist*, the soul of the people. For Herder, each people was unique and creative; each expressed its peculiar genius in language, literature, monuments, and folk traditions. Herder did not make the theoretical jump from a spiritual or cultural nationalism to political nationalism; he did not call for the formation of states based on nationality. But his emphasis on the unique culture of a people stimulated a national consciousness among Germans and the various Slavic peoples who lived under foreign rule. Fascination with the Volksgeist prompted intellectuals to investigate the past of their own people, to rediscover their ancient traditions, and to extol their historic language and culture. From this cultural nationalism, it was only a short step to a political nationalism that called for national liberation, unification, and statehood.

The romantics were the earliest apostles of German nationalism. Resisting the French philosophes, who sought to impose universal norms on all peoples, German romantics stressed the uniqueness of the German nation and its history. They restored to consciousness memories of the German past, and they emphasized the peculiar qualities of the German folk and the special destiny of the German nation. The romantics glorified medieval Germany and valued hereditary monarchy and aristocracy as vital links to the nation's past. They saw the existence of each individual as inextricably bound up with folk and fatherland, and they found the self-realization for which they yearned in the uniting of their own egos with the national soul. To these romantics, the national community was the source of artistic and spiritual creativity and the vital force, giving the individual both an identity and a purpose in life. The nation stood above the individual; the national spirit linked isolated souls into a community of brethren.

To the philosophes, the state was a human institution, a rational arrangement between individuals that safeguarded their rights and permitted them to realize their individual goals. To German romantics, such a state was an artificial and lifeless construction. The true German state was something holy, the expression of the divine spirit of the German people; it could not be manufactured to order by the intellect. The state's purpose was neither the protection of natural rights nor the promotion of economic well-being; rather, the state was a living organism that linked each person to a sacred past and reconciled and united heterogeneous wills, imbuing them with a profound sense of community, with which one entered into mystical communion. "This 'Romantic' image of a state founded not on any rational idea of the functions and purposes of a state but on love and perfect communion, is of course a formula for totalitarianism," observes R. J. Hollingdale, "and it was towards a state modeled on this formula that German nationalism continually moved."[12] Building on the romantics' views, radical German nationalists came to propound the dangerous racist idea that national identity was an inherited characteristic—that being and feeling German depended on birth rather than acculturation. Holding this belief, some German nationalists maintained that Jews, no matter how many generations they had resided in Germany, could never be truly German.

Nationalism and Liberalism

In the early 1800s, liberals were the principal leaders and supporters of nationalist movements. They viewed the struggle for national rights—the freedom of a people from foreign rule—as an extension of the struggle for the rights of the individual. There could be no liberty, said liberal nationalists, if people were not free to rule themselves in their own land.

Liberals called for the unification of Germany and Italy, the rebirth of Poland, the liberation of Greece from Turkish rule, and the granting of autonomy to the Hungarians of the Austrian Empire. Liberal nationalists envisioned a Europe of independent states based on nationality and popular sovereignty. Free of foreign domination and tyrant princes, these newly risen states would protect the rights of the individual and strive to create a brotherhood of nationalities in Europe.

In the first half of the nineteenth century, few intellectuals recognized the dangers inherent in nationalism or understood the fundamental contradiction between liberalism and nationalism. For the liberal, the idea of universal natural rights transcended all national boundaries. Inheriting the cosmopolitanism of the Enlightenment, liberalism emphasized what all people had in common, demanded that all individuals be treated equally under the law, and preached toleration. As they grew more extreme, nationalists manifested a narrow, tribal outlook and came to regard the nation as the essential fact of existence. Consequently, they often willingly subverted individual liberty for the sake of national grandeur. Whereas the liberal sought to protect the rights of all within the state, the nationalist often ignored or trampled on the rights of individuals and national minorities.

Liberalism grew out of the rational tradition of the West, but nationalism derived from an emotional attachment to ancient customs and bonds. Because it fulfilled an elemental yearning for community and kinship, nationalism exerted a powerful hold over human hearts, often driving people to political extremism. Liberalism demanded objectivity in analyzing tradition, society, and history; nationalism, however, evoked a mythic and romantic past, frequently a heroic golden age, that often distorted history.

"Nationalism requires . . . much belief in what is patently not so," wryly observes British historian E. J. Hobsbawm.[13] Thus nationalists inflated their people's past achievements and attributed to the nation a peculiar inner spirit that set it apart from others and accounted for its superiority. While constantly declaiming the wrongs that others had inflicted on them, they turned a blind eye to their own mistreatment of other nationalities. Nationalists interpreted history to serve political ends: the unity of their people and the creation of a powerful nation-state.

In the last part of the nineteenth century, the irrational and mythic quality of nationalism intensified. By stressing the unique qualities and history of a particular people, nationalism promoted hatred between nationalities. By kindling deep love for the past, including a longing for ancient borders, glories, and power, nationalism led to wars of expansion. When it roused the emotions to fever pitch, nationalism shattered rational thinking, dragged the mind into a world of fantasy and myth, and introduced extremism into politics. Love of nation became an overriding passion, threatening to extinguish the liberal ideals of reason, freedom, and equality.

❖ ❖ ❖

Notes

1. Quoted in H. G. Schenk, *The Mind of the European Romantics* (Garden City, N.Y.: Doubleday, 1969), p. 4.
2. William Blake, "Milton," in *The Poetry and Prose of William Blake,* ed. David V. Erdman (Garden City, N.Y.: Doubleday, 1965), plate 40, lines 34–36, p. 141.
3. Ibid., plate 41, line 1.
4. Letter of John Keats, November 22, 1817, in *The Letters of John Keats,* ed. Hyder E. Rollins (Cambridge, Mass.: Harvard University Press, 1958), vol. 1, pp. 184–185.
5. Blake, "Milton," Preface, bk. 1, plate 1, p. 95.
6. Quoted in Robert T. Denommé, *Nineteenth-Century French Romantic Poets,* p. 28. Copyright © 1969 by Southern Illinois University Press. All rights reserved. Reprinted with permission.
7. From "The Tables Turned," in *The Complete Poetical Works of Wordsworth,* ed. Andrew J. George (Boston: Houghton Mifflin, 1904, rev. ed., 1982), p. 83.
8. Horst von Maltitz, *The Evolution of Hitler's Germany* (New York: McGraw-Hill, 1973), p. 217.
9. G. W. F. Hegel, *The Philosophy of History,* trans. J. Sibree (New York: Dover, 1956), pp. 19, 23.
10. Edmund Burke, *Reflections on the Revolution in France* (New York: Liberal Arts Press, 1955), pp. 40, 89.
11. John Stuart Mill, *On Liberty,* ed. Currin V. Shields (Indianapolis, Ind.: Bobbs-Merrill, 1956), chap. 1.

12. R. J. Hollingdale, *Nietzsche* (London: Routledge & Kegan Paul, 1973), p. 25.
13. E. J. Hobsbawm, *Nations and Nationalism Since 1780* (Cambridge, Eng.: Cambridge University Press, 1992), p. 12.

Suggested Reading

Arblaster, Anthony, *The Rise and Decline of Western Liberalism* (1984). A critical analysis of liberalism, its evolution and characteristics.

Cranston, Maurice, *The Romantic Movement* (1994). Romanticism as a European phenomenon that crosses national boundaries.

Epstein, Klaus, *The Genesis of German Conservatism* (1966). An analysis of German conservative thought as a response to the Enlightenment and the French Revolution.

Harris, R. W., *Romanticism and the Social Order, 1780–1830* (1969). Involvement of English romantics in social and political questions.

Hobsbawm, E. J., *Nations and Nationalism Since 1780* (1992). Insightful commentary by an always provocative author.

Honour, Hugh, *Romanticism* (1979). A study of the influence of romanticism on the visual arts.

Kohn, Hans, *Prelude to Nation-States* (1967). The emergence of nationalism in France and Germany.

Schapiro, J. S., *Liberalism: Its Meaning and History* (1958). A useful survey with readings.

Schenk, H. G., *The Mind of the European Romantics* (1966). A comprehensive analysis of the Romantic Movement.

Smith, A. D., *Theories of Nationalism* (1972). The relationship between nationalism and modernization.

Weiss, John, *Conservatism in Europe, 1770–1945* (1977). Conservatism as a reaction to social modernization.

Chapter 14

Surge of Liberalism and Nationalism: Revolution, Counterrevolution, and Unification

- **The Congress of Vienna**
- **Revolutions, 1820–1829**
- **Revolutions, 1830–1832**
- **The Revolutions of 1848: France**
- **The Revolutions of 1848: Germany, Austria, and Italy**
- **The Revolutions of 1848: An Assessment**
- **The Unification of Italy**
- **The Unification of Germany**
- **Nationality Problems in the Hapsburg Empire**

Focus Questions

1. Why did Metternich fear liberalism and nationalism?
2. What were the accomplishments and failures of the Congress of Vienna?
3. What were the principal reasons for the revolutions that broke out in Europe in the decades after the Congress of Vienna?
4. Why did the revolutions of 1848 essentially fail?
5. What were the liberal gains in 1848? Why were liberals and nationalists disappointed?
6. How did nationalism promote unity in some lands and division in others?

During the years 1815 through 1848, the forces unleashed by the French Revolution clashed with the traditional outlook of the old regime. The period opened with the Congress of Vienna, which drew up a peace settlement after the defeat of Napoleon, and closed with the revolutions that swept across most of Europe in 1848. Outside France, much of the old regime had survived the stormy decades of the French Revolution and Napoleon. Monarchs still held the reins of political power. Aristocrats, particularly in Central and Eastern Europe, retained their traditional hold on the army and administration, controlled the peasantry and local government, and enjoyed tax exemptions. Determined to enforce respect for traditional authority and to smother liberal ideals, the conservative ruling elites resorted to censorship, secret police, and armed force. But the liberals and nationalists, inspired by the revolutionary principles of liberty, equality, and fraternity, continued to engage in revolutionary action. ❖

The Congress of Vienna

After the defeat of Napoleon, a congress of European powers met at Vienna (1814–1815) to draw up a peace settlement. The delegates wanted to restore stability to a continent torn by revolution and war and to reestablish the balance of power shattered by Napoleonic France.

Statesmen and Issues

The pivotal figure at the Congress of Vienna was Prince Klemens von Metternich (1773–1859) of Austria. A man of the old order, Metternich believed that both domestic and international stability depended on rule by monarchs and respect for the aristocracy. The misguided liberal belief that society could be reshaped according to the ideals of liberty and equality, said Metternich, had led to twenty-five years of revolution, terror, and war. To restore stability and peace, the old Europe must suppress liberal ideas and quash the first signs of revolution.

Metternich also feared the new spirit of nationalism. As a multinational empire, Austria was particularly vulnerable to nationalist unrest. If its ethnic groups—Poles, Czechs, Magyars, Italians, South Slavs, and Romanians—became infected with the nationalist virus, they would destroy the Hapsburg Empire. Moreover, by arousing the masses and setting people against people, nationalism could undermine the foundations of the European civilization that he cherished.

Determined to end the chaos of the Napoleonic period and restore stability to Europe, Metternich wanted to return to power the ruling families deposed by more than two decades of revolutionary warfare. He also sought to reestablish the balance of power in Europe so that no one country could be in a position to dominate the Continent as Napoleon had done. There must be no more Napoleons who obliterate states, topple kings, and dream of European hegemony.

Other nations at the Congress of Vienna included Britain, Russia, France, and Prussia. Representing Britain was Robert Stewart, Viscount Castlereagh (1769–1822), the British foreign secretary, who was realistic and empirically minded. Although an implacable enemy of Napoleon, Castlereagh demonstrated mature statesmanship by not seeking to punish France severely. Tsar Alexander I (1777–1825) attended the congress himself. Steeped in Christian mysticism, the tsar wanted to create a European community based on Christian teachings. Alexander regarded himself as the savior of Europe, an attitude that caused other diplomats to view him with distrust. Representing France was Prince Charles Maurice de Talleyrand-Périgord (1754–1838). A devoted patriot, Talleyrand sought to remove from France the stigma of the Revolution and Napoleon. Prince Karl von Hardenberg (1750–1822) represented Prussia. Like Metternich, Castlereagh, and Talleyrand, the Prussian statesman believed that the various European states, besides pursuing their own national interests, should concern themselves with the well-being of the European community as a whole.

Two interrelated issues threatened to disrupt the conference and enmesh the Great Powers in another war. One was Prussia's intention to annex the German kingdom of Saxony; the other was Russia's demand for Polish territories. The tsar wanted to combine the Polish holdings of Russia, Austria, and Prussia into a new Polish kingdom under Russian control. Both Britain and Austria regarded such an extension of Russian domination into Central Europe as a threat to the balance of power.

Talleyrand suggested that Britain, Austria, and France join in an alliance to oppose Prussia and Russia. This clever move restored France to the family of nations. Now France was no longer the hated enemy but a necessary counterweight to Russia and Prussia. Threatened with war, Russia and Prussia moderated their demands and the crisis ended.

The Settlement

After months of discussion, quarrels, and threats, the delegates to the Congress of Vienna finished their work. Resisting Prussia's demands for a punitive peace, the allies did not punish France severely. They feared that a humiliated France would only prepare for a war of revenge. Besides, Metternich continued to need France to balance the power of both Prussia and Russia. France had to pay a large indemnity over a five-year period and submit to allied occupation until the obligation was met.

Although it lost most of its conquests, France emerged with somewhat more land than it had possessed before the Revolution. To guard against a resurgent France, both Prussia and Holland received territories on the French border. Holland obtained the southern Netherlands (Belgium); Prussia gained the Rhineland and part of Saxony, but not as much as the Prussians had desired. Nevertheless, Prussia emerged from the settlement significantly larger and stronger. Russia obtained Finland and a considerable part of the Polish territories, but not as much as the tsar had anticipated; the congress prevented further Russian expansion into Central Europe. The northern Italian province of Lombardy was restored to Austria, which also received adjacent Venetia. England obtained strategic naval bases: Helgoland in the North Sea, Malta and the Ionian Islands in the Mediterranean, the Cape Colony in South Africa, and Ceylon in the Indian Ocean. Germany was organized into a confederation of thirty-eight (later thirty-nine) states. Norway was given to Sweden. The legitimate rulers, who had been displaced by the Revolution and the wars of Napoleon, were restored to their thrones in France, Spain, Portugal, the Kingdom of the Two Sicilies, the Papal States, and many German states.

The conservative delegates at the Congress of Vienna have often been criticized for ignoring the liberal and nationalist aspirations of the different peoples and turning the clock back to the old regime. Critics have castigated the congress for dealing only with the rights of thrones and not the rights of peoples. But after the experience of two world wars in the twentieth century, some historians today are impressed by the peacemakers' success in restoring a balance of power that effectively stabilized international relations. No one country was strong enough to dominate the Continent, and no Great Power was so unhappy that it resorted to war to undo the settlement. Not until the unification of Germany in 1870–1871 was the balance of power upset; not until World War I in 1914 did Europe have another general war of the magnitude of the Napoleonic wars.

Revolutions, 1820–1829

Russia, Austria, Prussia, and Great Britain agreed to act together to preserve the territorial settlement of the Congress of Vienna and the balance of power. After paying its indemnity, France was admitted into this Quadruple Alliance, also known as the Concert of Europe. Metternich intended to use the Concert of Europe to maintain harmony between nations and internal stability within nations. Toward this end, conservatives in their respective countries censored books and newspapers and imprisoned liberal and nationalist activists.

But repression could not contain the liberal and nationalist ideals unleashed by the French Revolution. The first revolution after the restorations of legitimate rulers occurred in Spain in 1820. Fearing that the Spanish uprising, with its quasi-liberal overtones, would inspire revolutions in other lands, the Concert of Europe empowered France to intervene. In 1823, a hundred thousand French troops crushed the revolution.

Revolutionary activity in Italy also frightened the Concert of Europe. In 1815, Italy consisted of several separate states. In the south, a

Chronology 14.1 ❖ The Surge of Nationalism

1821	Austria crushes revolts in Italy
1823	French troops crush revolt in Spain
1825	Uprising in Russia crushed by Nicholas I
1829	Greece gains its independence from Ottoman Empire
1830	The July Ordinances in France are followed by a revolution, which forces Charles X to abdicate
1831	The Polish revolution fails
1831–1832	Austrian forces crush a revolution in Italy
1848	The Year of Revolution
1862	Bismarck becomes chancellor of Prussia
1864	Austria and Prussia defeat Denmark in a war over Schleswig-Holstein
1866	Seven Weeks' War between Austria and Prussia: Prussia emerges as the dominant power in Germany
1870–1871	Franco-Prussian War: German unification completed
January 18, 1871	William I becomes German kaiser

Bourbon king ruled the Kingdom of the Two Sicilies; the pope governed the Papal States in central Italy; and Hapsburg Austria ruled Lombardy and Venetia in the north. Hapsburg princes subservient to Austria ruled the duchies of Tuscany, Parma, and Modena. Piedmont in the northwest and the island of Sardinia were governed by an Italian dynasty, the House of Savoy.

Besides all these political divisions, Italy was split economically and culturally. Throughout the peninsula, attachment to the local region was stronger than devotion to national unity. Economic ties between north and south were weak; inhabitants of the northern Italian cities felt little closeness to Sicilian peasants. Except for the middle class, most Italians clung to the values of the old regime.

Through novels, poetry, and works of history, an expanding intellectual elite awakened interest in Italy's glorious past. They insisted that a people who had built the Roman Empire and produced the Renaissance must not remain weak and divided, their land occupied by Austrians. These sentiments appealed particularly to university students and the middle class. But the rural masses, illiterate and preoccupied with the hardships of daily life, showed little interest in this struggle for national revival.

Secret societies kept alive the hopes for liberty and independence from foreign rule in the period after 1815. The most important of these societies was the Carbonari, which had clubs in every state in Italy and a membership drawn largely from the middle class and the army. In 1820, the Carbonari enjoyed a few months of triumph in the Kingdom of the Two Sicilies. Supported by the army and militia, they forced King Ferdinand I to grant a constitution and a parliamentary government. But Metternich feared that the germ of revolution would spread to other countries. Supported by Prussia and Russia, Austria suppressed the constitutional government in Naples and another revolution that broke out in Piedmont. In both cases, Austria firmly fixed an absolute ruler on the throne.

A revolution also failed in Russia. During the Napoleonic wars and the occupation of France, Russian officers were introduced to French ideas.

Congress of Vienna, **1815, by Jean Baptiste Isabey (1767–1855).** The delegates to the Congress of Vienna sought to reestablish many features of Europe that had existed before the French Revolution and Napoleon. They can be accused of shortsightedness; nevertheless, the balance of power that they formulated preserved international peace. Metternich is standing before a chair at the left.

Contrasting French liberal attitudes with Russian autocracy, some officers resolved to change conditions in Russia. Like their Western counterparts, they organized secret societies and disseminated liberal ideas within Russia. When Alexander I died, these liberal officers struck. Their uprising in December 1825 was easily smashed by the new tsar, Nicholas I, and the leaders were severely punished.

The revolutions in Spain, Italy, and Russia were suppressed, but the Metternich system also suffered setbacks. Stimulated by the ideals of the French Revolution, the Greeks revolted against their Turkish rulers in 1821. Although the Turkish sultan was the legitimate ruler, Russia, France, and Britain aided the Greek revolutionaries, for they were Christians, whereas the Turks were Muslims; moreover, pro-Greek sentiments were very strong among educated Western Europeans, who had studied the literature and history of ancient Greece. To them, the Greeks were struggling to regain the freedom of their ancient forebears. Not only the pressure of public opinion but also fear of Russian motives led Britain to join in intervention. If Russia carried out its intention of aiding the Greeks on its own, no doubt it would never surrender control. Britain could not permit this extension of Russian power in the eastern Mediterranean. Despite Metternich's objections, Britain, France, and Russia took joint action against the Turks, and in 1829 Greece gained its independence.

Revolutions, 1830–1832

After Napoleon's defeat, a Bourbon king, Louis XVIII (1814–1824), younger brother of the executed Louis XVI, ascended the throne of

France. Recognizing that the French people would not accept a return to the old order, Louis pursued a moderate course. Although his pseudoconstitution, the Charter, declared that the king's power rested on divine right, it acknowledged that citizens possessed fundamental rights: freedom of thought and religion and equal treatment under the law. It also set up a two-house parliament. But peasants, urban workers, and most bourgeois could not meet the property requirements for voting. Louis XVIII was resisted by diehard aristocrats, called *ultras*, who wanted to erase the past twenty-five years of French history and restore the power and privileges of church and aristocracy. It was said of them that "they had forgotten nothing and learnt nothing." Their leader was the king's younger brother, the Comte d'Artois, who after Louis's death in 1824 ascended the throne as Charles X (1824–1830).

The new government aroused the hostility of the bourgeoisie by indemnifying the émigrés for the property they had lost during the Revolution, censoring the press, and giving the church greater control over education. In the election of 1830, the liberal opposition to Charles X won a decisive victory. Charles responded with the July Ordinances, which dissolved the newly elected chamber; the Ordinances also deprived the upper bourgeois of the vote and severely curbed the press.

The bourgeois, students, and workers rebelled. Viewing themselves as heirs of the Jacobins, they hoped to establish a republic, but the wealthy bourgeois who took control of the revolution feared republican radicalism. They offered the throne to the Duc d'Orléans; Charles X abdicated and went into exile in Britain. The new king, Louis Philippe (1830–1848), never forgot that he owed his throne to the rich bourgeois. And the Parisian workers who had fought for a republic and economic reforms to alleviate poverty felt betrayed by the outcome, as did the still disenfranchised petty bourgeois.

The Revolution of 1830 in France set off shock waves in Belgium, Poland, and Italy. The Congress of Vienna had assigned Catholic Belgium to Protestant Holland; from the outset, the Belgians had protested. Stirred by the events in Paris, Belgian patriots proclaimed their independence from Holland and established a liberal government. Inspired by the uprisings in France and Belgium, Polish students, intellectuals, and army officers took up arms against their Russian overlords. The revolutionaries wanted to restore Polish independence, a dream that poets, musicians, and intellectuals had kept alive. Polish courage, however, was no match for Russian might, and Warsaw fell in 1831. The tsar took savage revenge on the revolutionaries. In 1831–1832, the Austrians suppressed another insurrection by the Carbonari in the Papal States. During these uprisings, the peasants gave the Carbonari little support; indeed, they seemed to side with the traditional rulers.

The Revolutions of 1848: France

In 1848, often called the Year of Revolution, uprisings for political liberty and nationhood erupted throughout Europe. The economic crisis of the previous two years had aggravated discontent with the existing regimes, but "it was the absence of liberty," concludes historian Jacques Droz, "which . . . was most deeply resented by the peoples of Europe and led them to take up arms."[1]

The February Revolution

An uprising in Paris set in motion the revolutionary tidal wave that was to engulf much of Europe in 1848. The Revolution of 1830 had broken the back of the ultras in France. There would be no going back to the Old Regime. But King Louis Philippe and his ministers, moderates by temperament and philosophy, had no intention of going forward to democracy.

The government of Louis Philippe was run by a small elite consisting of bourgeois bankers, merchants, and lawyers, as well as aristocrats who had abandoned the hope of restoring the Old Regime. This ruling elite championed the revolutionary ideas of equal treatment under the law and of careers open to talent but feared democracy and blocked efforts to broaden the franchise. (Only about 3 percent of adult French males were qualified to vote.) The opposition—radical republicans, or democrats—wanted to abolish the monarchy and grant all men the vote. The situation

Reunion des Musees Nationaux/Art Resource, N.Y.

***Liberty Leading the People*, 1830, by Eugène Delacroix (1799–1863).** Early-nineteenth-century reformers found their rallying cry in "liberty," a legacy of the French Revolution. In this painting, Delacroix, the leader of the French romantic artists, glorifies liberty.

reached a climax in February 1848, when the bourgeoisie, as well as students and workers, took to the streets to demand reforms; this led to a violent confrontation with soldiers. Unable to pacify the enraged Parisians, Louis Philippe abdicated, and France became a republic.

The June Days: Revolution of the Oppressed

The new bourgeois leaders were committed to political democracy, but only a few favored the social reforms demanded by the laboring poor. A meager harvest in 1846 and an international financial crisis in 1847 that drastically curtailed French factory production aggravated the misery of the working class. Workers who could find jobs labored twelve to fourteen hours a day under brutalizing conditions. In some districts, one out of three children died before the age of five, and everywhere in France, beggars, paupers, prostitutes, and criminals were evidence of the struggle to survive. Prevented by law from striking, unable to meet the financial requirements for voting, and afflicted with massive unemployment, the urban workers wanted relief.

The middle-class leaders of the new republic, however, had little understanding of the workers' plight and little sympathy for it. By reason of occupation and wealth, the middle class saw itself as separate from the working class. To the bourgeoisie, the workers were dangerous creatures, "the wild ones," "the vile mob." But the inhabitants of the urban slums could no longer be ignored. They felt, as Alexis de Tocqueville, the astute statesman and political theorist, stated, "that all that is above them is incapable and unworthy of governing them; that the present distribution of goods [prevalent until now] . . . is unjust; that

Primary Source

Alexis de Tocqueville: The June Days

In his Recollections, *Alexis de Tocqueville described the June Days of 1848.*

I come at last to the insurrection of June, the most extensive and the most singular that has occurred in our history, and perhaps in any other: the most extensive, because, during four days, more than a hundred thousand men were engaged in it; the most singular, because the insurgents fought without a war-cry, without leaders, without flags, and yet with a marvelous harmony and an amount of military experience that astonished the oldest officers.

What distinguished it also, among all the events of this kind which have succeeded one another in France for sixty years, is that it did not aim at changing the form of government, but at altering the order of society. It was not, strictly speaking, a political struggle, in the sense which until then we had given to the word, but a combat of class against class, a sort of Servile War [slave uprising in ancient Rome]. It represented the facts of the Revolution of February in the same manner as the theories of Socialism represented its ideas; or rather it issued naturally from these ideas, as a son does from his mother. We behold in it nothing more than a blind and rude, but powerful, effort on the part of the workmen to escape from the necessities of their condition, which had been depicted to them as one of unlawful oppression, and to open up by main force a road towards that imaginary comfort with which they had been deluded. It was this mixture of greed and false theory which first gave birth to the insurrection and then made it so formidable. These poor people had been told that the wealth of the rich was in some way the produce of a theft practised upon themselves. They had been assured that the inequality of fortunes was as opposed to morality and the welfare of society as it was to nature. Prompted by their needs and their passions, many had believed this obscure and erroneous notion of right, which, mingled with brute force, imparted to the latter an energy, a tenacity and a power which it would never have possessed unaided.

Question for Analysis

1. Alexis de Tocqueville observed that what distinguished the June revolution in Paris was that it aimed to change the order of society, not the form of government. Explain.

The Recollections of Alexis de Tocqueville, trans. Alexander Teixeira de Mattos; ed. J. P. Mayer (New York: Meridian Books, 1947), 150–151.

property rests on a foundation which is not an equitable foundation."[2]

Although the new leaders gave all adult males the vote and abolished censorship, they made only insincere and halfhearted attempts to ease the distress of the urban poor. The government limited the workday to ten hours, legalized labor unions, and established national workshops, which provided food, medical benefits, and employment on public works projects. But to the workers, this was a feeble effort to deal with their monumental hardships. To the property-owning peasantry and bourgeoisie, the national workshops were a hateful concession to socialist radicalism and a waste of government funds. When the government closed the workshops, working-class hostility and despair turned to open rebellion. Again barricades went up in the streets of Paris.

The June revolution in Paris was a revolt against poverty, a cry for the redistribution of property, and a yearning to create a society that would serve the common good. The approximately ten to fifteen thousand insurgents, most from the working class, stood alone. To the rest of the nation, they were barbarians attacking civilized society. Aristocrats, bourgeois, and peasants feared that no one's property would be safe if the revolution succeeded. From hundreds of miles away, Frenchmen flocked to Paris to crush what they considered to be the madness within their midst. After three days of vicious street fighting and atrocities on both sides, the army extinguished the revolt. Some 1,460 lives had been lost, including four generals. The June Days left deep scars on French society. For many years, workers would never forget that the rest of France had united against them; the rest of France would remain terrified of working-class radicalism.

In December 1848, the French people, in overwhelming numbers, elected Louis Napoleon—nephew of the great emperor—president of the Second Republic. They were attracted by the magic of Louis Napoleon's name, and they expected him to safeguard society and property from future working-class disorders. The election, in which all adult males could vote, demonstrated that most Frenchmen were socially conservative; they were unsympathetic to working-class poverty and deeply suspicious of socialist programs.

The Revolutions of 1848: Germany, Austria, and Italy

Like an epidemic, the fever of revolution that broke out in Paris in February raced across the Continent. Liberals, excluded from participation in political life, fought for parliaments and constitutions; many liberals were also nationalists who wanted unity or independence for their nations.

The German States: Liberalism Discredited

After the Congress of Vienna, Germany consisted of a loose confederation of thirty-nine independent states, of which Austria and Prussia were the most powerful. Jealous of their own states' independence and determined to preserve their own absolute authority, the ruling princes detested liberal and nationalist ideals, which, urged on by Metternich, they tried to repress through censorship and the regulation of student associations.

The German nationalism that had emerged during the French occupation intensified during the restoration (the post-Napoleonic period). Inspired in part by the ideas of the romantics, intellectuals insisted that Germans, who shared a common language and culture, should also be united politically. During the restoration, the struggle for German unity and liberal reforms continued to be waged primarily by students, professors, writers, lawyers, and other educated people. The great mass of people, knowing only loyalty to their local prince, remained unmoved by appeals for national unity.

The successful revolt against Louis Philippe, hostility against absolute princes, and the general economic crisis combined to produce uprisings in the capital cities of the German states in March 1848. Throughout Germany, liberals clamored for constitutions, parliamentary government, freedom of thought, and an end to police intimidation. Some called for the creation of a unified Germany governed by a national parliament and headed by a constitutional monarch. The poor of town and countryside, their plight worsened by the great depression of the 1840s, joined the struggle.

Terrified that these disturbances would lead to anarchy, the princes made concessions to the liberals, whom they had previously censored, jailed, and exiled. During March and April 1848, the traditional rulers in Prussia and other German states replaced reactionary ministers with liberals, eased censorship, established jury systems, framed constitutions, formed parliaments, and ended peasant obligations to lords.

Liberals took advantage of their successes to form a national assembly charged with the task of creating a unified and liberal Germany. Representatives from all the German states attended the assembly, which met at Frankfurt. After many long debates, the Frankfurt Assembly approved a federation of German states. The new German union would have a parliament and would be headed by the Prussian king. Austria, with its many non-German nationalities, would be excluded from the federal union. The deputies selected Frederick William IV as emperor of the new Germany, but the Prussian king refused; he would never wear a crown given to him by common

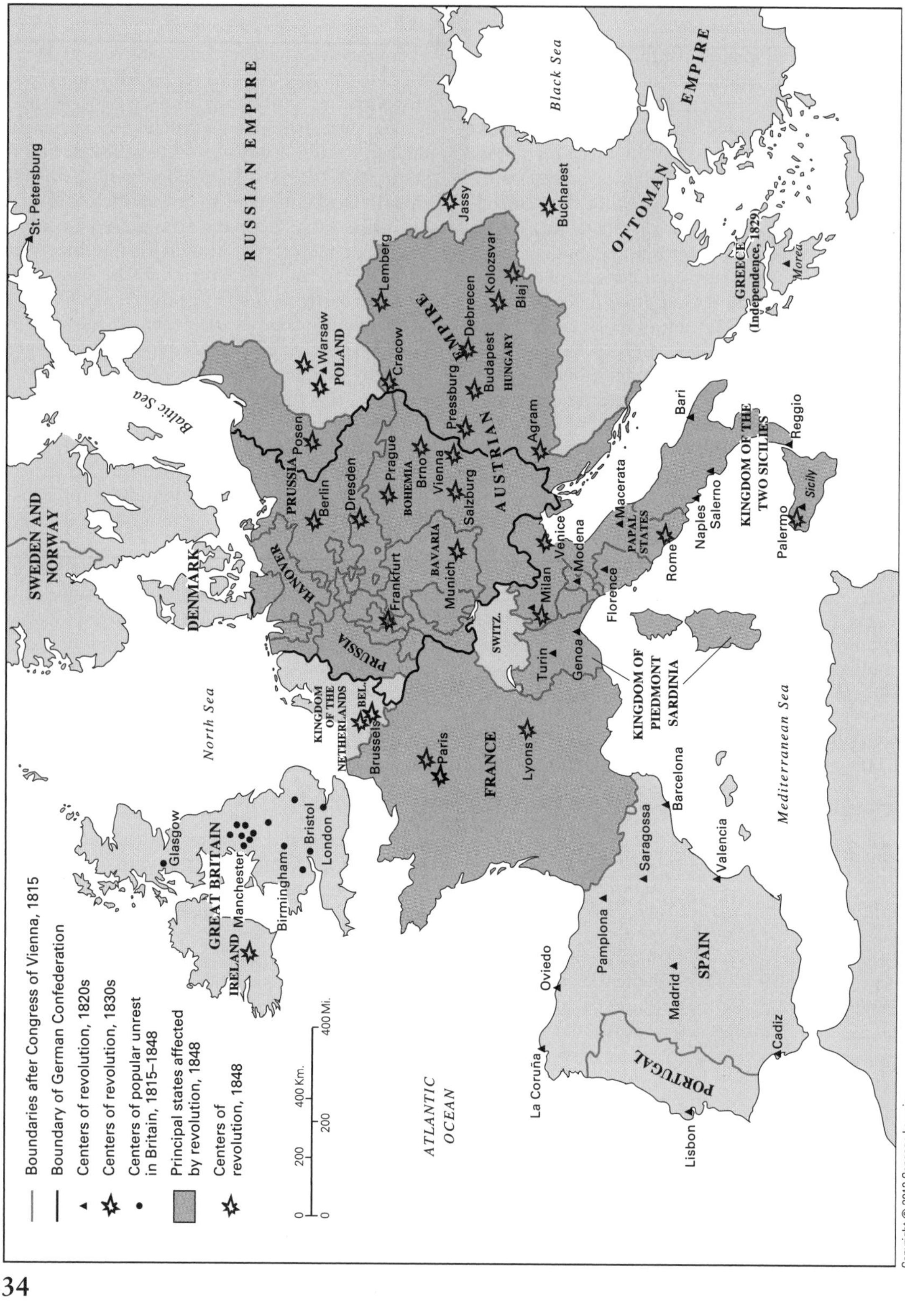
Boundaries after Congress of Vienna, 1815
Boundary of German Confederation
Centers of revolution, 1820s
Centers of revolution, 1830s
Centers of popular unrest in Britain, 1815–1848
Principal states affected by revolution, 1848
Centers of revolution, 1848
0 200 400 Km.
0 200 400 Mi.
RUSSIAN EMPIRE
OTTOMAN EMPIRE
AUSTRIAN EMPIRE
HUNGARY
BOHEMIA
BAVARIA
PRUSSIA
HANOVER
POLAND
DENMARK
SWEDEN AND NORWAY
GREAT BRITAIN
IRELAND
KINGDOM OF THE NETHERLANDS
BEL.
FRANCE
SWITZ.
KINGDOM OF PIEDMONT SARDINIA
PAPAL STATES
KINGDOM OF THE TWO SICILIES
GREECE (Independence, 1829)
SPAIN
PORTUGAL
ATLANTIC OCEAN
North Sea
Baltic Sea
Black Sea
Mediterranean Sea
St. Petersburg
Warsaw
Posen
Berlin
Dresden
Prague
Brno
Vienna
Salzburg
Munich
Frankfurt
Cracow
Lemberg
Jassy
Bucharest
Kolozsvar
Blaj
Debrecen
Budapest
Pressburg
Agram
Venice
Modena
Milan
Turin
Genoa
Florence
Rome
Macerata
Naples
Salerno
Bari
Reggio
Palermo
Sicily
Morea
Glasgow
Manchester
Birmingham
Bristol
London
Brussels
Paris
Lyons
Barcelona
Saragossa
Valencia
Pamplona
Oviedo
Madrid
La Coruña
Cadiz
Lisbon

REVOLUTION IN VIENNA, MAY 1848. A student leads armed railway workers.

people during a period of revolutionary agitation. While the delegates debated, the ruling princes recovered from the first shock of revolution and ordered their armies to crush the revolutionaries. One by one the liberal governments fell.

The rulers of the various German states, supported by the army, the aristocracy, and the bureaucracy, retained their power. German liberalism had failed to unite Germany or to create a constitutional government dominated by the middle class. Liberalism, never securely rooted in Germany, was discredited. In the following decades, many Germans, identifying liberalism with failure, abandoned liberal values and turned to authoritarian Prussia for leadership in the struggle for unification. The fact that authoritarians hostile to the spirit of parliamentary government eventually united Germany had deep implications for future German and European history.

◀ *Map 14.1* Europe's Age of Revolutions
In the decades after the Vienna settlement, Europe experienced a wave of revolution based chiefly on liberalism and nationalism.

In 1848, German political aspirations—the creation of a constitutional government—coincided with the goals of liberals in Western European lands. However, in the late nineteenth century, while Western European states were becoming more liberal, Germany moved in an authoritarian direction. The political systems that prevailed after 1848 stifled the growth of liberal, constitutional government.

Austria: Hapsburg Dominance

The Hapsburg (Austrian) Empire, the product of dynastic marriage and inheritance, had no common nationality or language; it was held together only by the reigning Hapsburg dynasty, its army, and its bureaucracy. The ethnic composition of the empire was enormously complex. The Germans dominated; concentrated principally in Austria, they constituted about 25 percent of the empire's population. The Magyars predominated in the Hungarian lands of the empire. The great bulk of the population consisted of Slavs: Czechs, Poles, Slovaks, Slovenes, Croats, Serbs, and Ruthenians.

In addition, there were Italians in northern Italy and Romanians in Transylvania. The Hapsburg dynasty, aided by the army and the German-dominated civil service, prevented the multinational empire from collapsing into anarchy.

Metternich, it is often said, suffered from a "dissolution complex": he understood that the new forces of nationalism and liberalism could break up the Austrian Empire. Liberal ideas could lead Hapsburg subjects to challenge the authority of the emperor, and nationalist feelings could cause the different peoples of the empire to rebel against German domination and Hapsburg rule. To keep these ideas from infecting Austrian subjects, Metternich's police imposed strict censorship, spied on professors, and expelled from the universities students caught reading forbidden books. Despite Metternich's political police, the universities still remained hotbeds of liberalism.

In 1848, revolutions spread throughout the Austrian Empire, starting in Vienna. Aroused by the abdication of Louis Philippe, Viennese liberals denounced Hapsburg absolutism and demanded a constitution, relaxation of censorship, and restrictions on the police. Intimidated by the revolutionaries, the government allowed freedom of the press, accepted Metternich's resignation, and promised a constitution. The Constitutional Assembly was convened and in August voted the abolition of serfdom. At the same time that the Viennese insurgents were tasting the heady wine of reform, revolts in other parts of the empire—Bohemia, Hungary, and northern Italy—added to the distress of the monarchy.

But the revolutionaries' victory was only temporary, and the defeat of the old order only illusory. The Hapsburg government soon began to recover its balance. The first government victory came with the crushing of the Czechs in Bohemia. In 1848, Czech nationalists wanted the Austrian Empire reconstructed along federal lines that would give the Czechs equal standing with Germans. General Alfred zu Windischgrätz bombarded Prague, the capital of Bohemia, into submission and reestablished Hapsburg control.

In October 1848, the Hapsburg authorities ordered the army to attack Vienna. Against the regular army, the courageous but disorganized and divided students and workers had little hope. In March 1849, the Hapsburg rulers replaced the liberal constitution drafted by the popularly elected Constitutional Assembly with a more conservative one drawn up by their own ministers.

The most serious threat to the Hapsburg realm came from the Magyars in Hungary. Some twelve million people lived in Hungary, five million of whom were Magyars. The other nationalities consisted of South Slavs (Croats and Serbs) and Romanians. Louis Kossuth (1802–1894), a member of the lower nobility, called for both social reform and a deepening of national consciousness in Hungary. Led by Kossuth, the Magyars demanded local autonomy. Hungary would remain within the Hapsburg Empire but have its own constitution and national army and control its own finances. The Hungarian leadership introduced liberal reforms: suffrage for all males who could speak Magyar and owned some property, freedom of religion, freedom of the press, the abolition of serfdom, and the end of the privileges of the nobles and the church. Within a few weeks, the Hungarian parliament changed Hungary from a feudal to a modern liberal state.

But the Hungarian leaders' nationalist dreams towered above their liberal ideals. The Magyars intended to incorporate lands inhabited by Croats, Slovaks, and Romanians into their state (Magyars considered these lands an integral part of historic Hungary) and to transform these peoples into Hungarians. In the spring of 1849, the Hungarians renounced their allegiance to the Hapsburgs and proclaimed Hungary an independent state, with Kossuth as president.

The Hapsburg rulers took advantage of the ethnic animosities inside and outside Hungary. They encouraged Romanians and Croats to resist the new Hungarian government. When Hapsburg forces moved against the Magyars, they were joined by an army of Croats, whose nationalist aspirations had been flouted by the Magyars. The Emperor Francis Joseph, who had recently ascended the Hapsburg throne, also appealed to Tsar Nicholas I for help. The tsar complied, fearing that a successful revolt by the Hungarians might lead the Poles to rise up against their Russian overlords. The Hungarians fought with extraordinary courage but were overcome by superior might.

BARRICADES IN THE STREETS OF FRANKFURT, 1848. In 1848, revolutionary fever spread from France to Germany. In several German states, liberals fought for written constitutions that protected basic rights and parliamentary government that represented the people. At first the ruling princes made concessions, but they quickly regained their nerve and ordered their professional soldiers to crush the revolutionaries.

Italy: Continued Fragmentation

Eager to end the humiliating Hapsburg occupation and domination and to link the disparate states into a unified and liberal nation, Italian nationalists, too, rose in rebellion in 1848. Revolution broke out in Sicily six weeks before the February revolution in Paris. Bowing to the revolutionaries' demands, King Ferdinand II of Naples granted a liberal constitution. The Grand Duke of Tuscany, King Charles Albert of Piedmont-Sardinia, and Pope Pius IX, ruler of the Papal States, also felt compelled to introduce liberal reforms.

Then the revolution spread to the Hapsburg lands in the north. After "Five Glorious Days" (March 18–22) of street fighting, the citizens of Milan forced the Austrians to withdraw. The people had liberated their city. On March 22, the citizens of Venice declared their city free from Austrian rule and set up a republic. King Charles Albert, who hoped to acquire Lombardy and Venetia, declared war on Austria. Intimidated by the insurrections, the ruling princes of the Italian states and Hapsburg Austria had lost the first round.

But soon everywhere in Italy the forces of reaction recovered and reasserted their authority. The Austrians defeated the Sardinians and reoccupied Milan, and Ferdinand II crushed the revolutionaries in the south. Revolutionary disorders in Rome had forced Pope Pius IX to flee in November 1848; in February 1849, the revolutionaries proclaimed Rome "a pure democracy with the glorious title of the Roman Republic." Heeding the pope's call for assistance, Louis Napoleon, the newly elected French president, attacked Rome, destroyed the infant republic, and allowed Pope Pius to return. The last city to fall to the reactionaries was Venice, which the Austrians subjected to a merciless bombardment. Italy was still a fragmented nation.

The Revolutions of 1848: An Assessment

The revolutions of 1848 began with much promise, but they all ended in defeat. "We stood on the threshold of paradise—but the gates slammed in our faces," wrote one dejected intellectual.[3] The revolutionaries' initial success was due less to their strength than to the governments' hesitancy to use their superior force. However, the reactionary leaders of Europe overcame their paralysis and moved decisively to smash the revolutions. The courage of the revolutionaries was no match for the sheer power of regular armies. Thousands were killed and imprisoned; many fled to America.

Class divisions weakened the revolutionaries. The union between middle-class liberals and workers, which brought success in the opening stages of the revolutions, was only temporary. Bourgeois liberals favoring political reforms—constitution, parliament, and protection of basic rights—grew fearful of the laboring poor, who demanded social reforms, that is, jobs and bread. To the bourgeois, the workers were radical Jacobins, a mob driven by dark instincts, and a threat to property. When the working class engaged in revolutionary action, a terrified middle class deserted the cause of revolution or joined the old elites in subduing the workers. These class divisions showed that the liberals' concern for political reforms—the extension of suffrage and parliamentary government—did not satisfy workers who were mired in poverty. The events of 1848 also showed that social issues—the demands of the working class for an alleviation of their misery—would become a prime consideration of European political life in the generations to come.

Intractable nationalist animosities helped to destroy all the revolutionary movements against absolutism in Central Europe. In many cases, the different nationalities hated one another more than they hated the reactionary rulers. Hungarian revolutionaries dismissed the nationalist yearnings of the Croats and Romanians living in Hungary, who in turn helped the Hapsburg dynasty extinguish the nascent Hungarian state. The Germans of Bohemia resisted Czech demands for self-government and the equality of the Czech language with German. When German liberals at the Frankfurt Assembly debated the boundary lines of a united Germany, the problem of Prussia's Polish territories emerged. In 1848, Polish patriots wanted to re-create the Polish nation, but German delegates at the convention, by an overwhelming majority, opposed returning the Polish lands seized by Prussia in the late eighteenth century.

Before 1848, democratic idealists envisioned the birth of a new Europe of free people and liberated nations. The revolutions in Central Europe showed that nationalism and liberalism were not natural allies and that nationalists were often indifferent to the rights of other peoples. Disheartened by these nationalist antagonisms, John Stuart Mill, the English liberal statesman and philosopher, lamented that "the sentiment of nationality so far outweighs the love of liberty that the people are willing to abet their rulers in crushing the liberty and independence of any people not of their race or language."[4] In the revolutions of 1848, concludes the British historian Lewis Namier, "'nationality,' the passionate creed of the intellectuals, invades the politics of central and east-central Europe, and with 1848 starts the Great European War of every nation against its neighbors."[5]

Even though the liberal and nationalist aims of the revolutionaries were not realized, liberal gains were not insignificant. All French men obtained the right to vote; serfdom was abolished in Austria; and parliaments were established in Prussia and other German states.

For German liberalism, however, 1848 was a crucial defeat. Controlled by monarchs and aristocrats hostile to the democratic principles of 1848, the postrevolutionary governments, using the methods of a police state, intimidated and persecuted liberals, large numbers of whom were forced to emigrate. The failure of the revolution and the reactionary policies of the postrevolutionary governments thwarted the growth of a democratic parliamentary system in Germany. Discredited by the failure of 1848, weakened by government intimidation and the loss of many liberals to emigration, and less committed to liberal ideals—which brought no gains in 1848—the German middle class in the period immediately after 1848 became apolitical or willing to sacrifice liberal principles to achieve a united and powerful Germany. Nationalism would supersede liberalism as the principal concern of the German middle class. The failure of liberalism to take strong root in Germany would have dire consequences in the early twentieth century.

In later decades, liberal reforms, including legal guarantees of basic rights, would be introduced peacefully in several European countries—in Germany too, but there power still remained in the hands of preindustrial, semifeudal elites, not with the middle class—for the failure of the revolutions of 1848 convinced many people, including liberals, that popular uprisings were ineffective ways of changing society. The Age of Revolution, initiated by the French Revolution of 1789, had ended.

The Unification of Italy

In 1848, liberals had failed to drive the Austrians out of Italy and unite the Italian nation. By 1870, however, Italian unification had been achieved, mainly through the efforts of three men: Mazzini, Cavour, and Garibaldi.

Mazzini: The Soul of the Risorgimento

Giuseppe Mazzini (1805–1872) dedicated his life to the creation of a united and republican Italy—a goal he pursued with extraordinary moral intensity and determination. Mazzini was both a romantic and a liberal. As a liberal, he fought for republican and constitutional government and held that national unity would enhance individual liberty. As a romantic, he believed that an awakened Italy would lead to the regeneration of humanity. Mazzini was convinced that just as Rome had provided law and unity in the ancient world and the Roman pope had led Latin Christendom during the Middle Ages, so a third Rome, a newly united Italy, would usher in a new age of free nations, personal liberty, and equality.

Mazzini had great charisma, determination, courage, and eloquence; he was also a prolific writer. His idealism attracted the intelligentsia and youth and kept alive the spirit of national unity. He infused the *Risorgimento*, the movement for Italian unity, with spiritual intensity. After his release from prison for participating in the insurrection of 1831, Mazzini went into exile and founded a new organization, Young Italy. Consisting of dedicated revolutionaries, many of them students, Young Italy was intended to serve as the instrument for the awakening of Italy and the transformation of Europe into a brotherhood of free peoples. Mazzini believed that a successful revolution must come from below—from the people, moved by a profound love for their nation. They must overthrow the Hapsburg princes and create a democratic republic.

Cavour and Victory over Austria

The failure of the revolutions of 1848 contained an obvious lesson: that Mazzini's approach, an armed uprising by aroused masses, did not work. The masses were not deeply committed to the nationalist cause, and the revolutionaries were no match for the Austrian army. Italian nationalists now hoped that the kingdom of Piedmont-Sardinia, ruled by an Italian dynasty, would expel the Austrians and lead the drive for unity. Count Camillo Benso di Cavour (1810–1861), the chief minister of Piedmont-Sardinia, became the architect of Italian unity.

Unlike Mazzini, Cavour was neither a dreamer nor a speechmaker but a tough-minded practitioner of *realpolitik*, "the politics of reality." Focusing on the world as it actually was, he dismissed ideals as illusions. A cautious and practical statesman, Cavour realized that mass uprisings could not succeed against Austrian might. Moreover, mistrusting the common people, he did not favor Mazzini's goal of a democratic republic. Cavour

Victor Emmanuel and Garibaldi at the Bridge of Teano (1860). The unification of Italy was the work of the romantic liberal Giuseppe Mazzini, the practical politician Count Cavour, and the seasoned revolutionary Giuseppe Garibaldi. Selflessly, Garibaldi turned over his conquests in the south to Victor Emmanuel in 1861.

had no precise blueprint for unifying Italy. His immediate aim was to increase the territory of Piedmont by driving the Austrians from northern Italy and incorporating Lombardy and Venetia into Piedmont-Sardinia.

To improve Piedmont's image in foreign affairs, Cavour launched a reform program to strengthen the economy. He reorganized the currency, taxes, and the national debt; in addition, he had railways and steamships built, fostered improved agricultural methods, and encouraged new businesses. Within a few years, Piedmont had become a progressive modern state.

In 1855, Piedmont joined England and France in the Crimean War against Russia. Cavour had no quarrel with Russia but sought the friendship of Britain and France and a chance to be heard in world affairs. At the peace conference, Cavour was granted an opportunity to denounce Austria for occupying Italian lands. He soon found a supporter in Napoleon III (the former Louis Napoleon), the French emperor, who hoped that a unified northern Italy would become an ally and client of France.

In 1858, Cavour and Napoleon III reached a secret agreement. If Austria attacked Piedmont, France would aid the Italian state. Piedmont would annex Lombardy and Venetia and parts of the Papal States. For its assistance, France would obtain Nice and Savoy from Piedmont. With this agreement in his pocket, Cavour cleverly maneuvered Austria into declaring war, for it had to appear that Austria was the aggressor. He did so by strengthening Piedmont's army and encouraging volunteers from Austrian-controlled Lombardy to join it.

Supported by French forces and taking advantage of poor Austrian planning, Piedmont conquered Lombardy and occupied Milan. But Napoleon III quickly had second thoughts. If Piedmont took any of the pope's territory, French Catholics would blame their own leader. Even more serious was the fear that Prussia, suspicious of French aims, would aid Austria. For these reasons, Napoleon III, without consulting Cavour, signed an armistice with Austria. Piedmont would acquire Lombardy, but no more. An outraged Cavour demanded that his state continue the war until all northern Italy was liberated, but King Victor Emmanuel of Piedmont accepted the Austrian peace terms. The victory of Piedmont-Sardinia, however, proved greater than Cavour had anticipated. During the conflict, patriots in Parma, Modena, Tuscany, and Romagna (one of the Papal States) had seized power. These new revolutionary governments voted to join with Piedmont.

Garibaldi and Victory in the South

Piedmont's success spurred revolutionary activity in the Kingdom of the Two Sicilies. In the spring of 1860, some one thousand red-shirted adventurers and patriots landed in Sicily. Led by Giuseppe Garibaldi (1807–1882) who, like Mazzini, was a professional revolutionary, they were determined to liberate the land from its Bourbon ruler. Garibaldi held progressive views for his day. He supported the liberation of all subject nationalities, female equality, the right of workers to organize, racial equality, and the abolition of capital punishment. But the cause of Italian national unity was his true religion. After the liberation, Garibaldi that same year invaded the mainland. He occupied Naples without a fight and prepared to advance on Rome.

Cavour, however, feared that an assault on Rome by Garibaldi would lead to French intervention. Napoleon III had pledged to defend the pope's lands, and a French garrison had been stationed in Rome since 1849. Besides, Cavour considered Garibaldi too impulsive and rash, too attracted to republican ideals, and too popular with the masses to lead the struggle for unification.

To head off Garibaldi, Cavour persuaded Napoleon III to approve an invasion of the Papal States by Piedmont. A papal force offered only token opposition, and the Papal States of Umbria and the Marches soon voted for union with Piedmont, as did Naples and Sicily. Refusing to trade on his prestige with the masses to fulfill personal ambition, Garibaldi turned over his conquests to Piedmont's King Victor Emmanuel, who was declared king of Italy in 1861.

Italian Unification Completed

Two regions still remained outside the control of the new Italy: the city of Rome, ruled by the pope and protected by French troops; and Venetia, occupied by Austria. Cavour died in 1861, but the march toward unification continued. During the conflict between Prussia and Austria in 1866, Italy sided with the victorious Prussians and was rewarded with Venetia. During the Franco-Prussian War of 1870, France withdrew its garrisons from Rome; much to the anger of the pope, Italian troops marched in, and Rome was declared the capital of Italy.

The Unification of Germany

In 1848, German liberals and nationalists, believing in the strength of their ideals, had naïvely underestimated the power of the conservative old order. After the failed revolution, some disenchanted revolutionaries retained only a half-hearted commitment to liberalism or embraced conservatism. Others fled the country, weakening the liberal leadership. All liberals came to doubt the effectiveness of revolution as a way to transform Germany into a unified state; all gained a new respect for the realities of power. Abandoning idealism for realism, liberals now thought that German unity would be achieved through Prussian arms, not liberal ideals.

Prussia, Agent of Unification

During the late seventeenth and eighteenth centuries, Prussian kings had fashioned a rigorously trained and disciplined army. The state bureaucracy, often staffed by ex-soldiers, perpetuated the military mentality. As the chief organizations in the state, the army and the bureaucracy drilled into the Prussian people a respect for discipline and authority.

The Prussian throne was supported by the Junkers. These powerful aristocrats, who owned vast estates farmed by serfs, were exempt from most taxes and dominated local government in their territories. The Junkers' commanding position made them officers in the royal army, diplomats, and leading officials in the state bureaucracy. The Junkers knew that a weakening of the king's power would lead to the loss of their own aristocratic prerogatives.

In France in the late 1700s, a powerful and politically conscious middle class had challenged aristocratic privileges. The Prussian monarchy and the Junkers had faced no such challenge, for the Prussian middle class at that time was small and without influence. The idea of the rights of the individual did not deeply penetrate Prussian consciousness or undermine the Prussian tradition of obedience to military and state authority. Liberalism did not take firm root in Germany.

In 1834, under Prussian leadership, the German states, with the notable exception of Austria, established the *Zollverein*, a customs union that abolished tariffs between the states. The customs union stimulated economic activity and promoted a desire for greater unity. The Zollverein led many Germans to view Prussia, not Austria, as the leader of the unification movement.

Bismarck and the Road to Unity

Austria was the chief barrier to the extension of Prussian power in Germany. This was one reason why William I (1861–1888) called for a drastic reorganization of the Prussian army. But the liberals in the lower chamber of the Prussian parliament blocked passage of the army reforms, for they feared that the reforms would greatly increase the power of the monarchy and the military establishment. Unable to secure passage, William withdrew the reform bill and asked the lower chamber for additional funds to cover government expenses. When parliament granted these funds, he used the money to institute the army reforms. Learning from its mistake, the lower chamber would not approve the new budget in 1862 without an itemized breakdown. If the liberals won this conflict between the liberal majority in the lower chamber and the crown, they would, in effect, establish parliamentary control over the king and the army.

At this critical hour, King William asked Otto von Bismarck (1815–1898) to lead the battle against parliament. Descended on his father's side from an old aristocratic family, Bismarck was a staunch supporter of the Prussian monarchy and the Junker class and a devout patriot. He yearned to increase the territory and prestige of his beloved Prussia and to protect the authority of the Prussian king, who, Bismarck believed, ruled by the grace of God. Like Cavour, Bismarck was a shrewd and calculating practitioner of realpolitik.

Liberals were outraged by Bismarck's domineering and authoritarian manner and his determination to preserve monarchical power and the aristocratic order. Set on continuing the reorganization of the army and not bowing to parliamentary pressure, Bismarck ordered the collection of taxes without parliament's approval—an action that would have been unthinkable in Britain or the United States. He dismissed the lower chamber, imposed strict censorship on the press, arrested outspoken liberals, and fired liberals from the civil service. The liberals protested against these arbitrary and unconstitutional moves. What led to a resolution of the conflict was Bismarck's extraordinary success in foreign affairs.

Wars with Denmark and Austria To Bismarck, a war between Austria and Prussia seemed inevitable, for only by removing Austria from German affairs could Prussia extend its dominion over the other German states. Bismarck's first move, however, was not against Austria but against Denmark—in 1864, over the disputed duchies of Schleswig and Holstein. Austria joined as Prussia's ally because it hoped to prevent Prussia from annexing the territories. After Denmark's defeat, Austria and Prussia quarreled over the ultimate disposition of these lands. Bismarck used the dispute to goad Austria into war. The Austrians, on their side, were convinced that Prussia must be defeated if Austria wanted to retain its influence over German affairs.

In the Austro-Prussian war of 1866, Prussia, with astonishing speed, assembled its forces and overran Austrian territory. At the battle of

William I of Prussia. The German emperor in the Hall of Mirrors at Versailles (1871).

Sadowa (or Königgrätz), Prussia decisively defeated the main Austrian forces, and the Seven Weeks' War ended. Prussia took no territory from Austria, but the latter agreed to Prussia's annexation of Schleswig and Holstein and a number of small German states. Prussia, moreover, organized a confederation of North German states, from which Austria was excluded. In effect, Austria was removed from German affairs, and Prussia became the dominant power in Germany.

The Triumph of Nationalism and Conservatism over Liberalism The Prussian victory had a profound impact on political life within Prussia. Bismarck was the man of the hour, the great hero who had extended Prussia's power. Most liberals forgave Bismarck for his authoritarian handling of parliament. The liberal press, which had previously denounced Bismarck for riding roughshod over the constitution, embraced him as a hero. Prussians were urged to concentrate on the glorious tasks ahead and to put aside the constitutional struggle, which seemed petty by contrast.

Bismarck recognized the great appeal of nationalism and used it to expand Prussia's power over other German states and strengthen Prussia's voice in European affairs. By heralding his state as the champion of unification, he gained the support of nationalists throughout Germany. In the past, the nationalist cause had belonged to the liberals, but Bismarck appropriated it to promote Prussian expansion and conservative rule.

Prussia's victory over Austria, therefore, was a triumph for conservatism and nationalism and a defeat for liberalism. The liberal struggle for constitutional government in Prussia collapsed.

The Prussian monarch retained the right to override parliamentary opposition and act on his own initiative. In 1848, Prussian might had suppressed a liberal revolution; in 1866, many liberals, beguiled by Bismarck's military triumphs, gave up the struggle for responsible parliamentary government. They had traded political freedom for Prussian military glory and power.

The capitulation of Prussian liberals demonstrated the essential weakness of the German liberal tradition. German liberals displayed a diminishing commitment to the principles of parliamentary government and a growing fascination with force, military triumph, and territorial expansion. Enthralled by Bismarck's achievement, many liberals abandoned liberalism and threw their support behind the authoritarian Prussian state. Germans of all classes acquired an adoration for Prussian militarism and for the power state, with its Machiavellian guideline that all means are justified if they result in the expansion of German power. In 1848, German liberals had called for "Unity and Freedom." What Bismarck gave them was unity and authoritarianism.

War with France Prussia emerged from the war with Austria as the leading power in the North German Confederation; the Prussian king controlled the armies and foreign affairs of the states within the confederation. To complete the unification of Germany, Bismarck would have to draw the South German states into the new German confederation. But the South German states, Catholic and hostile to Prussian authoritarianism, feared being absorbed by Prussia.

Bismarck hoped that a war between Prussia and France would ignite the nationalist feelings of the South Germans, causing them to overlook the differences that separated them from Prussia. If war with France would serve Bismarck's purpose, it was also not unthinkable to Napoleon III, the emperor of France. The creation of a powerful North German Confederation had frightened the French, and the prospect that the South German states might one day add their strength to the new Germany was terrifying. Both France and Prussia had parties that advocated war.

A cause for war arose over the succession to the vacated Spanish throne. King William of Prussia discussed the issue with the French ambassador and sent Bismarck a telegram informing him of what had ensued. With the support of high military leaders, Bismarck edited the telegram. The revised version gave the impression that the Prussian king and the French ambassador had insulted each other. Bismarck wanted to inflame French feeling against Prussia and arouse German opinion against France. He succeeded. In both Paris and Berlin, crowds of people, gripped by war fever, demanded satisfaction. When France declared a general mobilization, Prussia followed suit; Bismarck had his war.

As Bismarck had anticipated, the South German states came to the aid of Prussia. Quickly and decisively routing the French forces and capturing Napoleon III, the Prussians went on to besiege Paris. Faced with starvation, Paris surrendered in January 1871. France was compelled to pay a large indemnity and to cede to Germany the border provinces of Alsace and Lorraine—a loss that French patriots could never accept.

The Franco-Prussian War completed the unification of Germany. On January 18, 1871, at Versailles, the German princes granted the title of German kaiser (emperor) to William I. A powerful nation had arisen in Central Europe. Its people were educated, disciplined, and efficient; its industries and commerce were rapidly expanding; its army was the finest in Europe. Vigorous, confident, and intensely nationalistic, the new German Empire was eager to play a greater role in world affairs. No nation in Europe was a match for the new Germany. Metternich's fears had been realized: a Germany dominated by Prussia had upset the balance of power. The unification of Germany created fears, tensions, and rivalries that would culminate in world wars.

Nationality Problems in the Hapsburg Empire

In Italy and Germany, nationalism had led to the creation of unified states; in Austria, nationalism eventually caused the destruction of the centuries-old Hapsburg dynasty. A mosaic of different peoples, each with its own history and traditions, the Austrian Empire could not weld together and reconcile antagonistic nationalities when nationalistic consciousness was high. The empire's collapse in the final stages of World War I marked the end of years of hostility among its various subjects.

In the first half of the nineteenth century, the Germans, who constituted less than one-quarter of the population, were the dominant national group in the empire. But Magyars, Poles, Czechs, Slovaks, Croats, Romanians, Ruthenians, and Italians were experiencing national self-awareness. Poets and writers who had been educated in Latin, French, and German began to write in their mother tongue and extol its splendor. By searching their past for glorious ancestors and glorious deeds, writers kindled pride in their native history and folklore and aroused anger against past and present injustices.

In 1848–1849, the Hapsburg monarchy had extinguished the Magyar bid for independence, the Czech revolution in Prague, and the uprisings in the Italian provinces of Lombardy and Venetia. Greatly alarmed by these revolutions, the Austrian power structure resolved to resist pressures for political rights by strengthening autocracy and tightening the central bureaucracy. German and Germanized officials took over administrative and judicial duties formerly handled on a local level. An expanded secret police stifled liberal and nationalist expressions. The various nationalities, of course, resented these efforts at centralization and repression.

The defeats by France and Piedmont in 1859 and by Prussia in 1866 cost Austria its two Italian provinces. The defeat by Prussia also forced the Hapsburg monarchy to make concessions to the Magyars, the strongest of the non-German nationalities: without a loyal Hungary, the Hapsburg monarchy could suffer other humiliations. The Settlement of 1867 split the Hapsburg territories into Austria and Hungary. The two countries retained a common ruler, Francis Joseph (1848–1916), who was emperor of Austria and king of Hungary. Hungary gained complete control over its internal affairs, the administration of justice, and education. A ministry composed of delegates from both lands conducted foreign and military affairs and dealt with common financial concerns.

With the Settlement of 1867, Magyars and Germans became the dominant nationalities in the empire. The other nationalities felt that the German–Magyar political, economic, and cultural domination blocked their own national aspirations. Nationality struggles in the half-century following the Settlement of 1867 consumed the energies of the Austrians and Hungarians. In both lands, however, the leaders failed to solve the problem of minorities—a failure that helped to precipitate World War I and that ultimately led to the dissolution of the empire during the last weeks of the war.

❖ ❖ ❖

Notes

1. Jacques Droz, *Europe Between Revolutions, 1815–1848* (New York: Harper Torchbooks, 1967), p. 248.
2. *The Recollections of Alexis de Tocqueville*, trans. Alexander Teixeira de Mattos (Cleveland, Ohio: Meridian Books, 1969), pp. 11–12.
3. Quoted in Adam Zamoyski, *Holy Madness: Romantics, Patriots and Revolutionaries, 1776–1871* (London: Weidenfeld & Nicolson, 1999), p. 356.
4. Quoted in Hans Kohn, *Nationalism: Its Meaning and History* (Princeton, N.J.: Van Nostrand, 1965), pp. 51–52.
5. Lewis Namier, *1848: The Revolution of the Intellectuals* (Garden City, N.Y.: Doubleday, Anchor, 1964), p. 38.

Suggested Reading

Beales, Derek, *The Risorgimento and the Unification of Italy* (1971). A comprehensive overview, followed by documents.

Crook, Malcolm, ed., *Revolutionary France, 1768–1880* (2001). A series of comprehensive essays by an international team of experts.

Droz, Jacques, *Europe Between Revolutions, 1815– 1848* (1967). A fine survey of the period.

Fasel, George, *Europe in Upheaval: The Revolutions of 1848* (1970). A good introduction.

Fejtö, François, ed., *The Opening of an Era: 1848* (1973). Contributions by nineteen eminent European historians.

Hamerow, T. S., *Restoration, Revolution, Reaction* (1958). An examination of economics and politics in Germany from 1815 through 1871, stressing the problems caused by the transition from agrarianism to industrialism.

———, ed., *Otto von Bismarck* (1962). A collection of readings from leading historians.

Hibbert, Christopher, *Garibaldi and His Enemies* (1965). A vivid portrait of the Italian hero.

Kohn, Hans, *Nationalism: Its Meaning and History* (1965). A concise history of modern nationalism by a leading student of the subject.

Langer, W. L., *Political and Social Upheaval, 1832–1852* (1969). Another volume in The Rise of Modern Europe series, by its editor. Rich in data and interpretation; contains a valuable bibliographical essay.

Robertson, Priscilla, *Revolutions of 1848* (1960). Vividly portrays the events and the personalities involved.

Rodes, John E., *The Quest for Unity: Modern Germany, 1848–1970* (1971). A good survey of German history.

Sigmann, Jean, *1848: The Romantic and Democratic Revolutions in Europe* (1970). A useful survey.

Sperber, Jonathan, *The European Revolution, 1848–1951* (1994). A comprehensive overview.

Steinberg, Jonathan, *Bismarck: A Life* (2011). A recent biography that has received praise.

Chapter 15

Thought and Culture in the Mid-Nineteenth Century: Realism, Positivism, Darwinism, and Social Criticism

- **Realism and Naturalism**
- **Positivism**
- **Darwinism**
- **Marxism**
- **Liberalism in Transition**
- **Feminism: Extending the Principle of Equality**

Focus Questions

1. Why is the mid-nineteenth century described as the Age of Realism? How does realism differ from romanticism?
2. How did Darwin's theory affect conceptions of time, human origins, religious doctrines, and nationalism?
3. What did Marx have in common with the philosophes of the Enlightenment? What relationship did he see between economics and politics? Between economics and thought?
4. How was the evolution of liberalism exemplified in the theories of Mill, Green, and Spencer?
5. How may the feminist movement be regarded as an outgrowth of certain ideals that had emerged during the course of Western history?

The second half of the nineteenth century was marked by great progress in science, a surge in industrialism, and a continuing secularization of life and thought. The main intellectual currents of the century's middle decades reflected these trends. Realism, positivism, Darwinism, Marxism, and liberalism all reacted against romantic, religious, and metaphysical interpretations of nature and society, focusing instead on the empirical world. Adherents of these movements relied on careful observation and strove for scientific accuracy. This emphasis on objective reality helped to stimulate a growing criticism of social ills, for despite unprecedented material progress, reality was often sordid, somber, and dehumanizing. ❖

Realism and Naturalism

Realism, the dominant movement in art and literature in the mid-nineteenth century, opposed the romantic veneration of the inner life and romantic sentimentality. The romantics exalted passion and intuition, let their imaginations transport them to a presumed idyllic medieval past, and sought inner solitude amid nature's wonders. Realists, on the other hand, concentrated on the actual world: social conditions, contemporary manners, and the familiar details of everyday life. With clinical detachment and meticulous care, they analyzed how people looked, worked, and behaved.

Like scientists, realist writers and artists carefully investigated the empirical world. For example, Gustave Courbet (1819–1877), who exemplified realism in painting, sought to practice what he called a "living art." He painted common people and commonplace scenes: laborers breaking stones, peasants tilling the soil or returning from a fair, a country burial, wrestlers, bathers, family groups. In a matter-of-fact style that sought to reproduce the environment just as it is, without any attempt at glorification or deviation, realist artists also depicted floor scrapers, rag pickers, prostitutes, and beggars.

Seeking to portray life as it is, realist writers frequently dealt with social abuses and the sordid aspects of human behavior and social life. In his novels, Honoré de Balzac (1799–1850) described how social and economic forces affected people's behavior. Ivan Turgenev's *Sketches* (1852) portrayed rural conditions in Russia and expressed compassion for the brutally difficult life of serfs. In *War and Peace* (1863–1869), Leo Tolstoy vividly described the manners and outlook of the Russian nobility and the tragedies that attended Napoleon's invasion of Russia. In *Anna Karenina* (1873–1877), he treated the reality of class divisions and the complexities of marital relationships. The novels of Charles Dickens—*Bleak House* (1853), *Hard Times* (1854), and several others—depicted the squalor of life, the hypocrisy of society, and the drudgery of labor in British industrial cities.

Many regard Gustave Flaubert's *Madame Bovary* (1857) as the quintessential realistic novel; it tells the story of a self-centered wife who shows her hatred for her devoted, hardworking, but dull husband by committing adultery. Commenting on the realism of *Madame Bovary,* one critic noted that it "represents an obsession with description. Details are counted one by one, all are given equal value, every street, every house, every book, every blade of grass is described in full."[1]

Literary realism evolved into naturalism when writers tried to demonstrate a causal relationship between human character and the social environment: that certain conditions of life produced predictable character traits in human beings. The belief that the law of cause and effect governed human behavior reflected the immense prestige attached to science in the closing decades of the nineteenth century. The leading naturalist novelist, Émile Zola (1840–1902), probed the slums, brothels, mining villages, and cabarets of France, examining how people were conditioned by the squalor of their environment. Henrik Ibsen (1828–1906), a Norwegian and the leading naturalist playwright, examined with rigorous precision and uncompromising truth the commercial and professional classes, their personal ambitions and family relationships. His *Pillars of Society* (1877) scrutinized bourgeois social pretensions and hypocrisy. In *A Doll's House* (1879), he took up a theme that shocked the late-nineteenth-century bourgeois audience: a woman leaving her husband to seek a more fulfilling life.

In striving for a true-to-life portrayal of human behavior and the social environment, realism and

Burial at Ornans (1849), by Gustave Courbet. All the individuals in this painting were either part of Courbet's family or other local folk, including two veterans of the French Revolution. In contrast to the glamorous settings and brilliant colors of the romantic painters, Courbet portrayed peasants in realistic settings with subdued colors.

naturalism reflected attitudes shaped by science, industrialism, and secularism, which stressed the importance of the external world. The same outlook also gave rise to positivism in philosophy.

Positivism

Positivists viewed science as the highest achievement of the mind and sought to apply a strict empirical approach to the study of society. They believed that the philosopher must proceed like a scientist, carefully assembling and classifying data and formulating general rules that demonstrate regularities in the social experience. Such knowledge, based on concrete facts, would provide the social planner with useful insights. Positivists rejected metaphysics, which, in the tradition of Plato, tried to discover ultimate principles through reason alone, rather than through observation of the empirical world. For positivists, any effort to go beyond the realm of experience to a deeper reality would be a mistaken and fruitless endeavor.

Auguste Comte (1798–1857), the father of positivism, called for a purely scientific approach to history and society: only through a proper understanding of the laws governing human affairs could society, which was in a state of intellectual anarchy, be rationally reorganized. Comte named his system *positivism* because he believed that it rested on sure knowledge derived from observed facts and was therefore empirically verifiable. Like others of his generation, Comte believed that scientific laws underlay human affairs and could be discovered through the methods of the empirical scientist—that is, through recording and systematizing observable data. "I shall bring factual proof," he said, "that there are just as definite laws for the development of the human race as there are for the fall of a stone."[2]

One of the laws that Comte believed he had discovered was the "law of the three stages." The human mind, he asserted, had progressed through three broad historical stages: the theological, the metaphysical, and the scientific. In the theological stage, the most primitive of the three, the mind found a supernatural explanation for the origins and purpose of things, and society was ruled by priests. In the metaphysical stage, which included the Enlightenment, the mind tried to explain things through abstractions—such as "nature," "equality," "natural rights," or "popular sovereignty"—that rested on hope and belief rather than on empirical investigation. The metaphysical stage was a transitional period between the infantile theological stage and the highest stage of society, the scientific, or positive, stage. In this culminating stage, the mind breaks with all illusions inherited from the past, formulates laws based on careful observation of the empirical world, and reconstructs society in accordance with these laws. People remove all mystery from nature and base their social legislation on laws of society similar to the laws of nature discovered by Newton.

Darwinism

In a century distinguished by scientific discoveries, perhaps the most important scientific advance was the theory of evolution formulated by Charles Darwin (1809–1882), an English naturalist. Darwin did for his discipline what Newton had done for physics: he made biology an objective science based on general principles. The Scientific Revolution of the seventeenth century had given people a new conception of space; Darwin radically altered our conception of time and biological life, including human origins.

Natural Selection

During the eighteenth century, almost all people had adhered to the biblical account of creation contained in Genesis: God had instantaneously created every river and mountain and the various species of animal and plant life, giving each species a finished and permanent form distinct from that of every other species. God had designed the bird's wings so that it could fly, the fish's eyes so that it could see under water, and the human being's legs so that people could walk. All this, it was believed, had occurred some five or six thousand years ago.

Gradually, this view was questioned. In 1794, Erasmus Darwin, the grandfather of Charles Darwin, published *Zoonomia, or the Laws of Organic Life,* which offered evidence that the earth had existed for millions of years before the appearance of people and that animals experienced modifications, which they passed on to their offspring. Nearly forty years later, Sir Charles Lyell published his three-volume *Principles of Geology* (1830–1833), which showed that the planet had evolved slowly over many ages.

In December 1831, Charles Darwin sailed as a naturalist on the H.M.S. *Beagle,* which surveyed the shores of South America and some Pacific islands. During the five-year expedition, Darwin collected and examined specimens of plant and animal life; he concluded that many animal species had perished, that new species had emerged, and that there were links between extinct and living species. In *The Origin of Species* (1859) and *The Descent of Man* (1871), Darwin used empirical evidence to show that the wide variety of animal species was due to a process of development over many millennia, and he supplied a convincing theory that explained how evolution operates.

Darwin adopted the Malthusian idea (see Chapter 12) that the population reproduces faster than the food supply, causing a struggle for existence. Not all infant organisms grow to adulthood; not all adult organisms live to old age. The principle of *natural selection* determines which members of the species have a better chance of survival in a world of myriad dangers and limited resources. The offspring of lions, giraffes, or insects are not exact duplicates of their parents. A baby lion might have the potential for being slightly faster or stronger than its parents; a baby giraffe might grow up to have a longer neck than its parents; an insect might have a slightly different color.

These small, random variations give the organism a crucial advantage in the struggle for food and against natural enemies. The organism favored by nature is more likely to reach maturity, to mate, and to pass on its superior qualities to its offspring, some of which will acquire the advantageous trait to an even greater degree than the parent. Over many generations, the favorable characteristic becomes more pronounced and more widespread within the species. Over millennia, natural selection causes the death of old, less adaptable species and the creation of new ones, for genetic changes within a segment of a species can so differentiate its members from the rest of the species that interbreeding is no longer possible. Very few of the

Primary Source

Charles Darwin, *The Descent of Man*

In The Descent of Man *(1871), Charles Darwin argued that human beings have evolved from lower forms of life.*

The main conclusion here arrived at, and now held by many naturalists who are well competent to form a sound judgment, is that man is descended from some less highly organized form. The grounds upon which this conclusion rests will never be shaken, for the close similarity between man and the lower animals in embryonic development, as well as in innumerable points of structure and constitution, both of high and of the most trifling importance . . . are facts which cannot be disputed. They have long been known, but until recently they told us nothing with respect to the origin of man. Now when viewed by the light of our knowledge of the whole organic world, their meaning is unmistakable. The great principle of evolution stands up clear and firm, when these groups of facts are considered in connection with others, such as the mutual affinities of the members of the same group, their geographical distribution in past and present times, and their geological succession. It is incredible that all these facts should speak falsely. He who is not content to look, like a savage, at the phenomena of nature as disconnected, cannot any longer believe that man is the work of a separate act of creation. He will be forced to admit that the close resemblance of the embryo of man to that, for instance, of a dog—the construction of his skull, limbs and whole frame on the same plan with that of other mammals, independently of the uses to which the parts may be put—the occasional reappearance of various structures, for instance of several muscles, which man does not normally possess, but which are common to the Quadrumana*—and a crowd of analogous facts—all point in the plainest manner to the conclusion that man is the co-descendant with other mammals of a common progenitor. . . .

Man may be excused for feeling some pride at having risen, though not through his own exertions, to the very summit of the organic scale; and the fact of his having thus risen, instead of having been aboriginally placed there, may give him hope for a still higher destiny in the distant future. But we are not only here concerned with hopes or fears, only with the truth as far as our reason permits us to discover it; and I have given the evidence to the best of my ability. We must, however, acknowledge, as it seems to me, that man with all his noble qualities, with sympathy which feels for the most debased, with benevolence which extends not only to other men but to the humblest living creature, with his god-like intellect which has penetrated into the movements and constitution of the solar system—with all these exalted powers—Man still bears in his bodily frame the indelible stamp of his lowly origin.

Question for Analysis

1. What did Darwin mean when he said that we "cannot any longer believe that man is the work of a separate act of creation"?

*An order of mammals, Quadrumana includes all primates (monkeys, apes, and baboons) except human beings; the primates' hind feet and forefeet can be used as hands because they have opposable first digits.

Charles Darwin, ***The Descent of Man*** (New York: D. Appleton, 1976), 606–607.

species that dwelt on earth ten million years ago still survive, and many new ones, including human beings, have emerged. People themselves are products of natural selection, evolving from earlier, lower, nonhuman forms of life.

Darwinism and Christianity

Like Newton's law of universal gravitation, Darwin's theory of evolution had revolutionary consequences in areas other than science. Evolution challenged traditional Christian belief. To some, it undermined the infallibility of Scripture and the conviction that the Bible was indeed the Word of God. Natural selection, which Darwin insisted was unplanned and undesigned, could explain the development of the organic world without reference to any divine arrangement or ultimate purpose.

Darwin's theory touched off a great religious controversy between fundamentalists, who defended a literal interpretation of Genesis, and advocates of the new biology. A Methodist publication contended: "We regard this theory, which seeks to eliminate from the universe the immediate, ever-present, all pervasive action of a living and personal God, which excludes the possibility of the supernatural and the miraculous . . . as practically destructive of the authority of divine revelation, and subversive of the foundation of religion and morality."[3] In time, most religious thinkers tried to reconcile evolution with the Christian view that there was a creation and that it had a purpose. These Christian thinkers held that modifications within a species were made by an intelligent creator—that God created and then directed the evolutionary process, that he steered evolution so that it would culminate in the human being.

Darwinism ultimately helped end the practice of relying on the Bible as an authority in questions of science, completing a trend initiated earlier by Galileo. Darwinism contributed to the waning of religious belief and to a growing secular attitude that dismissed or paid scant attention to the Christian view of a universe designed by God and a soul that rises to heaven.

For many, the conclusion seemed inescapable: nature contained no divine design or purpose, and the human species itself, including its vaunted power of the mind, was a chance product of impersonal forces. The core idea of Christianity—that people were children of God participating in a drama of salvation—rested more than ever on faith rather than reason. Some even talked openly about the death of God. The notion that people are sheer accidents of nature was shocking. Copernicanism had deprived people of the comforting belief that the earth had been placed in the center of the universe just for them; Darwinism deprived people of the privilege of being God's special creation, thereby contributing to a feeling of anxiety that persists to the present.

Social Darwinism

Darwin's theories were extended by others beyond the realm in which he had worked. Social thinkers recklessly applied Darwin's conclusions to the social order and produced theories that had dangerous consequences for society. Occasionally, Darwin himself departed from his rigorous empiricism and drew murky conclusions about the mentally and physically handicapped and what he termed the "savage races." But he never intended his discoveries, which applied to the natural world, to serve as a guide for a ruthless social policy that glorified war and justified genocide. Social Darwinists—those who transferred Darwin's scientific theories to social and economic issues—used the terms "struggle for existence" and "survival of the fittest" to buttress an often brutal economic individualism and political conservatism. Successful businessmen, they said, had demonstrated their fitness to prevail in the competitive world of business. Their success accorded with nature's laws and therefore was beneficial to society; those who lost out in the socioeconomic struggle demonstrated their unfitness. Traditionally, failure had been ascribed to human wickedness or to God's plan. Now, it was being attributed to an inferior hereditary endowment.

Using Darwin's model of organisms evolving and changing slowly over tens of thousands of years, conservatives insisted that society, too, should experience change at an unhurried pace. Instant reforms conflicted with nature's laws and wisdom and resulted in a deterioration of the social body.

The loose application of Darwin's biological concepts to the social world also buttressed imperialism,

A CARICATURE OF DARWIN. Darwin's theory of evolution created much controversy and aroused considerable bitterness. In this caricature, the apelike Darwin, holding a mirror, is explaining his theory of evolution to a fellow ape.

racism, nationalism, and militarism—doctrines that preached relentless conflict. Social Darwinists insisted that nations and races were engaged in a struggle for survival in which only the fittest survive and deserve to survive. In their view, war was nature's way of eliminating the unfit. Karl Pearson, a British professor of mathematics, wrote in *National Life from the Standpoint of Science* (1900): "History shows me only one way, and one way only in which a higher state of civilization has been produced, namely the struggle of race with race, and the survival of the physically and mentally fitter race."[4] "We are a conquering race," said U.S. Senator Albert J. Beveridge. "We must obey our blood and occupy new markets, and if necessary, new lands."[5] "War is a biological necessity of the first importance,"[6] asserted the Prussian general Friedrich von Bernhardi in *Germany and the Next War* (1911).

Darwinian biology was used to promote the belief in Anglo-Saxon (British and American) and Teutonic (German) racial superiority. Social Darwinists attributed to racial qualities the growth of the British Empire, the expansion of the United States to the Pacific, and the extension of German power. The domination of other peoples—American Indians, Africans, Asians, Poles—was regarded as the natural right of the superior race.

Social Darwinism also affected racial attitudes in the United States. Too willingly, scholars, joining antiblack polemicists, attributed an inferior biological inheritance to blacks, and some predicted their extinction, seeing them as losers in the Darwinian struggle for existence. Thus, in 1905, William B. Smith, a Tulane University professor, wrote: "The vision . . . of a race vanishing before its superior is not at all dispiriting, but inspiring. . . . The doom that awaits the Negro has been prepared in like measures for all inferior races."[7]

The theory of evolution was a great achievement of the rational mind, but in the hands of the Social Darwinists it served to undermine the Enlightenment tradition. Whereas the philosophes emphasized human equality, Social Darwinists divided humanity into racial superiors and inferiors. The philosophes believed that states would increasingly submit to the rule of law to reduce violent conflicts; Social Darwinists, on the other hand, regarded racial and national conflict as a biological necessity, a law of history, and a means to progress. In propagating a tooth-and-claw version of human and international relations, Social Darwinists dispensed with the humanitarian and cosmopolitan sentiments of the philosophes and distorted the image of progress. Their views promoted territorial aggrandizement and military buildup and led many to welcome World War I. The Social Darwinist notion of the struggle of races for survival became a core doctrine of the Nazi Party after World War I and helped to provide the "scientific" and "ethical" justification for genocide.

Marxism

The failure of the revolutions of 1848 and a growing fear of working-class violence led liberals to abandon revolution and to press for reforms through the political process. In the last part of the nineteenth century, Marxists and anarchists became the chief proponents of revolution. Both liberalism and Marxism shared common principles derived from the Enlightenment. Their adherents believed in the essential goodness and perfectibility of human nature and claimed that their doctrines rested on rational foundations. They wanted to free individuals from the accumulated superstition, ignorance, and prejudices of the past and to fashion a more harmonious and rational society. Both liberals and Marxists believed in social progress and valued the full realization of human talents.

Despite these similarities, liberalism and Marxism differed profoundly. The goal of Marxism—the seizure of power by the working class and the destruction of capitalism—was inimical to bourgeois liberals. So, too, was the Marxist belief that violence and struggle were the essence of history, the instruments of progress, and the vehicle to a higher stage of humanity. Liberals, who placed the highest value on the individual, held that through education and self-discipline people could overcome inequality and poverty. Marxists, however, insisted that without a transformation of the economic system, individual effort by the downtrodden would amount to very little.

Karl Marx (1818–1883) was born of German-Jewish parents (both descendants of prominent rabbis*). To save his job as a lawyer, Marx's father converted to Protestantism. Enrolled at a university to study law, Marx switched to philosophy. In 1842, he was editing a newspaper, which was soon suppressed by the Prussian authorities for its outspoken ideas. Leaving his native Rhineland, Marx went to Paris, where he met another German, Friedrich Engels (1820–1895), who was the son of a prosperous textile manufacturer. Marx and Engels entered into a lifelong collaboration and became members of socialist groups. In February 1848, they published the *Communist Manifesto*, which called for a working-class revolution to overthrow the capitalist system. Forced to leave France in 1849 because of his political views, Marx moved to London, where he remained to the end of his life. There he spent years writing *Capital*—a study and critique of the modern capitalistic economic system, which, he predicted, would be destroyed by a socialist revolution.

*In his writings Marx at times expressed contempt for Jews and Judaism, which he identified with capitalist exploitation.

A Science of History

As did other thinkers influenced by the Enlightenment, Marx believed that human history, like the operations of nature, was governed by scientific law. Marx was a strict materialist: rejecting all religious and metaphysical interpretations of both nature and history, he sought to fashion an empirical science of society. He viewed religion as a human creation—a product of people's imagination and feelings, a consolation for the oppressed—and the happiness it brought as an illusion. Real happiness would come, said Marx, not by transcending the natural world but by improving it. Rather than deluding oneself by seeking refuge from life's misfortunes in an imaginary world, one must confront the ills of society and reform them. This last point was crucial: "The philosophers have only *interpreted* the world in different ways; the point is to *change* it."[8]

The world could be rationally understood and changed, said Marx. People were free to make their own history, but to do so effectively, they must grasp the inner meaning of history: the laws governing human affairs in the past and operating in the present. Marx adopted Hegel's view that history was not an assortment of unrelated and disconnected events, but a progressive development, which, like the growth of a plant, proceeded ineluctably according to its own inner laws (see the section on Hegel in Chapter 13). For both Hegel and Marx, the historical process was governed by objective and rational principles. Marx also adopted Hegel's view that history advanced dialectically—that the clash of opposing forces propelled history into higher stages.

However, Marx also broke with Hegel in crucial ways. For Hegel, it was the dialectical clash of opposing ideas that moved history into the next stage; for Marx, it was the clash of classes representing conflicting economic interests—what is called dialectical materialism—that accounted for historical change and progress. In Hegel's view, history was the unfolding of the metaphysical Spirit, and a higher stage of development was produced by the synthesis of opposing ideas. According to Marx, Hegel's system suffered from mystification. It transcended the realities of the known world; it downgraded the real world, which became a mere attribute of Spirit. Marx saw Hegel's abstract philosophy as diverting attention from the real world and its problems, which cried out for understanding and solution; it was a negation of life.

For Marx, history was explainable solely in terms of natural processes—empirically verifiable developments. Marx valued Hegel's insight that history is a progressive and purposeful process, but he criticized Hegel for embedding his insights in metaphysical, theological fantasy. Hegel, said Marx, had made a mystical principle the real subject of history and thought. But, in truth, it is the real human being, the person living in and conditioned by the objective world—the only true reality—who is the center of history. History is not Spirit aspiring to self-actualization but people becoming fully human, fulfilling their human potential.

For Marx, the moving forces in history were economic and technological factors: the ways in which goods are produced and wealth distributed. They accounted for historical change and were the basis of all culture—politics, law, religion, morals, and philosophy. "The history of humanity," he concluded, "must therefore always be studied and treated in relation to the history of industry and exchange."[9] Marx said that material technology—the methods of cultivating land and the tools for manufacturing goods—determined society's social and political arrangements and its intellectual outlook. For example, the hand mill, the loose yoke, and the wooden plow had given rise to feudal lords, whereas power-driven machines had spawned the industrial capitalists.

Class Conflict

Throughout history, said Marx, there has been a class struggle between those who own the means of production and those whose labor has been exploited to provide wealth for this upper class. The opposing tension between classes has pushed history forward into higher stages. In the ancient world, when wealth was based on land, the struggle was between master and slave, patrician and plebeian; during the Middle Ages, when land was still the predominant mode of production, the struggle was between lord and serf. In the modern industrial world, two sharply opposed classes were confronting each other: the capitalists who owned the factories, mines, banks, and transportation systems, and the exploited wage earners (the proletariat).

According to Marx and Engels, the class with economic power also controlled the state. That class used political power to protect and increase its property and to hold down the laboring class. "Thus the ancient State was above all the slave-owners' state for holding down the slaves," said Engels, "as a feudal State was the organ of the nobles for holding down the . . . serfs, and the modern representative State is the instrument of the exploitation of wage-labor by capital."[10]

Furthermore, Marx and Engels asserted, the class that controlled material production also controlled mental production: that is, the ideas held by the ruling class became the dominant ideas of society. These ideas, presented as laws of nature or moral and religious standards, were regarded as the truth by oppressor and oppressed alike. In reality, however, these ideas merely reflected the special economic interests of the ruling class. Thus, said Marx, bourgeois ideologists would insist that natural rights and laissez-faire economics were laws of nature having universal validity. But these "laws" were born of the needs of the bourgeoisie in its struggle to wrest power from an obsolete feudal regime and to protect its property from the state. Similarly, nineteenth-century slave owners convinced themselves that slavery was morally right—that it had God's approval and was good for the slave. Slave owners and capitalist employers alike may have defended their labor systems by citing universal principles that they thought were true, but in reality their systems rested on a simple economic consideration: slave labor was good for the pocketbook of the slave owner, and laissez faire was good in the same way for the capitalist. They were unaware of the real forces motivating their thinking.

The Destruction of Capitalism

Under capitalism, said Marx, workers knew only poverty. They worked long hours for low wages, suffered from periodic unemployment, and lived in squalid, overcrowded dwellings. Most monstrous of all, they were forced to send their young children into the factories.

Capitalism, as Marx saw it, also produced another kind of poverty: poverty of the human spirit. Under capitalism, the factory worker was reduced to a laboring beast, performing tedious and repetitive tasks in a dark, dreary, dirty cave—an altogether inhuman environment that deprived people of their human sensibilities. Unlike the artisans in their own shops, factory workers found no pleasure and took no pride in their work; they did not have the satisfaction of creating a finished product that expressed their skills. Work, said Marx, should be a source of fulfillment for people. It should enable people to affirm their personalities and develop their potential. By treating people not as human beings but as cogs in the production process, capitalism alienated people from their work, themselves, and one another.

Marx believed that capitalist control of the economy and the government would not endure forever; capitalist society produced its own gravediggers—the working class. The capitalist system would perish just as the feudal society of the Middle Ages and the slave society of the ancient world had perished. From the ruins of a dead capitalist society, a new socioeconomic system, socialism, would emerge.

Marx predicted how capitalism would be destroyed. Periodic unemployment would increase the misery of the workers and intensify their hatred of capitalists. Owners of small businesses and shopkeepers, unable to compete with the great capitalists, would sink into the ranks of the working class, greatly expanding its numbers. Society would become polarized into a small group of immensely wealthy capitalists and a vast proletariat, poor, embittered, and desperate. This monopoly of capital by the few would become a brake on the productive process.

Growing increasingly conscious of their misery, the workers—aroused, educated, and organized by Communist intellectuals—would revolt. "Revolution is necessary," said Marx, "not only because the *ruling class* cannot be overthrown in any other way, but also because only in a revolution *can the class which overthrows it* rid itself of the accumulated rubbish of the past and become capable of reconstructing society."[11] The working-class revolutionaries would smash the government that helped the capitalists maintain their dominance. Then they would confiscate the property of the capitalists, abolish private property, place the means of production in the workers' hands, and organize a new society. The *Communist Manifesto* ends with a ringing call for revolution: "The Communists . . . openly declare that their ends can be attained only by the forcible overthrow of all existing social conditions. Let the ruling classes tremble at a Communist revolution. The proletarians have nothing to lose but their chains. They have a world to win. Workingmen of all countries, unite!"[12]

Marx did not say a great deal about the new society that would be ushered in by the socialist revolution. With the destruction of capitalism, the distinction between capitalist and worker would cease, and with it the class conflict. No longer would society be divided into haves and have-nots, oppressor and oppressed. Since this classless society would contain no exploiters, there would be no need for a state, which was merely an instrument for maintaining and protecting the power of the exploiting class. Thus, the state would eventually wither away. The production and distribution of goods would be carried out through community planning and communal sharing, which would replace the capitalist system of competition. People would work at varied tasks, just as Fourier (see "Responses to Industrialization" in Chapter 12) had advocated, rather than being confined to one form of employment. No longer factory slaves, people would be free to fulfill their human potential, to improve their relationships on a basis of equality with others, and to work together for the common good.

Marxism had immense appeal both for the downtrodden and for intellectuals. It promised to end the injustices of industrial society; it claimed the certainty of science; and it assured adherents that the triumph of their cause was guaranteed by history. In many ways, Marxism was a secular religion: the proletariat became a chosen class, endowed with a mission to achieve worldly salvation for humanity.

Marx's influence grew during the second wave of industrialization, in the closing decades of the nineteenth century, when class bitterness between the proletariat and the bourgeoisie seemed to worsen. Many workers thought that liberals and conservatives had no sympathy for their plight and that the only way to improve their lot was through socialist parties.

Critics of Marx

Critics point out serious weaknesses in Marxism. The rigid Marxist who tries to squeeze all historical events into an economic framework is at a disadvantage. Economic forces alone will not explain the triumph of Christianity in the Roman Empire, the fall of Rome, the Crusades, the French Revolution, modern imperialism, World War I, the rise of Hitler, or the mindset of contemporary Islamic terrorists. Economic explanations fall particularly flat in trying to account for the emergence of modern nationalism, whose appeal, resting on deeply ingrained emotional needs, crosses class lines. The greatest struggles of the twentieth century were not between classes but between nations.

Many of Marx's predictions or expectations failed to materialize. Workers in Western lands did not become the oppressed and impoverished proletariat that Marx had described in the mid-nineteenth century. Because of increased productivity and the efforts of labor unions and reform-minded governments, Western workers improved their lives considerably, so that they now enjoy the highest standard of living in history. The tremendous growth of a middle class of professionals, civil service employees, and small businesspeople belies Marx's prediction that capitalist society would be polarized into a small group of very rich capitalists and a great mass of destitute workers.

Marx believed that socialist revolutions would break out in the advanced industrialized lands. But the socialist revolutions of the twentieth century occurred in underdeveloped, predominantly agricultural countries. The state in Communist lands, far from withering away, grew more centralized, powerful, and oppressive. In no country where Communist revolutionaries seized power did people achieve the liberty that Marx desired. Nor, indeed, have orthodox Communists been able to sustain a viable economic system. The phenomenal collapse of Communist regimes in the former Soviet Union and Eastern Europe in recent years testifies to Marxism's failure. All these failed predictions and expectations seem to contradict Marx's claim that his theories rested on an unassailable scientific foundation.

Liberalism in Transition

In the early part of the nineteenth century, European liberals were preoccupied with protecting the rights of the individual against the demands of the state. They championed laissez faire because they feared that state interference in the economy to redress social evils would threaten property rights and the free market, which they thought were essential to personal liberty. They favored property requirements for voting and officeholding because they were certain that the unpropertied and uneducated masses lacked the wisdom and experience to exercise political responsibility.

In the last part of the century, liberals began to support—though not without reservation and qualification—both extended suffrage and government action to remedy the abuses of unregulated industrialization. This growing concern for the welfare of the laboring poor coincided with and was influenced by an unprecedented proliferation of humanitarian movements on both sides of the Atlantic. Nurtured by both the Enlightenment and Christian teachings, reform movements called for the prohibition of child labor, schooling for the masses, humane treatment for prisoners and the mentally ill, equality for women, the abolition of slavery, and an end to war. By the beginning of the twentieth century, liberalism had evolved into liberal democracy, and laissez faire had been superseded by a reluctant acceptance of some social legislation and government regulation. But from beginning to end, the central concern of liberals remained the protection of individual rights.

John Stuart Mill

The transition from laissez-faire liberalism to a more socially conscious and democratic liberalism

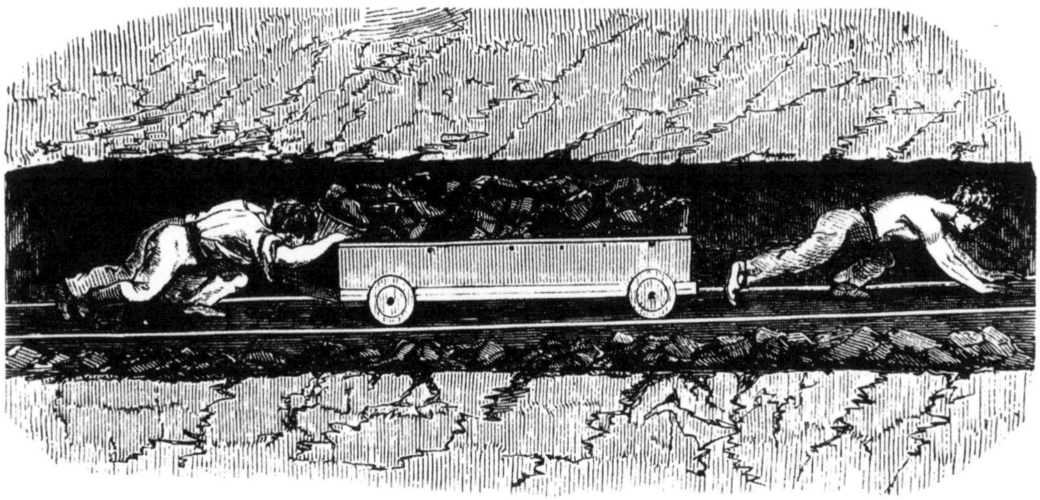

Child Mine Labor, Report of a Parliamentary Commission of Inquiry, 1842. In 1842, the British Parliament passed the Mines Act, prohibiting employment of girls and boys under the age of ten in coal mines. This report, detailing children being forced to drag sledge tubs through narrow tunnels, among other abuses, convinced Parliament to act. Further legislation regulating safety and labor practices in the coal industry followed after 1850.

is seen in the thought of John Stuart Mill (1806–1873), a British philosopher and statesman. Mill's *On Liberty* (1859) is the classic statement of individual freedom and minority rights: that the government and the majority may not interfere with the liberty of another human being whose actions do no injury to others.

Mill regarded freedom of thought and expression and the toleration of opposing and unpopular viewpoints as necessary preconditions for the shaping of a rational, moral, and civilized citizen. Political or social coercion, said Mill, is also a barrier to the full development of the individual. Liberty is a supreme good that benefits both the individual and the community. When we silence an opinion, said Mill, we hurt present and future generations. If the opinion is correct, "we are deprived of the opportunity of exchanging error for truth." If the opinion is wrong—and of this we can never be entirely certain—we "lose the clearer perception and livelier impression of truth produced by its collision with error."[13] Therefore, government has no right to force an individual to hold a view "because it will be better for him to do so, or because it will make him happier, or because in the opinions of others, to do so would be wise, or even right. These are good reasons for remonstrating with him, or reasoning with him, or persuading him, or entreating him, but not for compelling him or visiting him with any evil in case he do otherwise."[14]

Mill would place limits on the power of government, for in an authoritarian state citizens cannot develop their moral and intellectual potential. Although he feared the state as a threat to individual liberty, Mill also recognized the necessity for state intervention to promote individual self-development: the expansion of individual moral, intellectual, and esthetic capacities. For example, he maintained that it was permissible for the state to require children to attend school against the wishes of their parents, to regulate hours of labor, to promote health, and to provide workers' compensation and old-age insurance.

Library of Congress Prints and Photographs Division/LC-USZC4-6888.

Poster Published by the Artists' Suffrage League, Designed by Emily Harding Anderes, c. 1908. This suffragette poster illustrates the fact that British women could not vote in the early twentieth century. The cap and gown of the woman college graduate does not help her find the key that will release her from the imprisoning categorization with felons and the mentally ill, who couldn't vote for Parliament either. Women were leaders in local government—where they were in charge of schools, orphanages, and hospitals—but were unable to vote for members of the House of Commons until after World War I.

Thomas Hill Green

Four thinkers stood out in the late 1800s as the leading figures in the shaping of a new liberal position in Britain: Thomas Hill Green (1836–1882), an Oxford University professor; D. G. Ritchie (1853–1903), who taught philosophy at Oxford and Saint Andrews; J. A. Hobson (1858–1940), a social theorist; and L. T. Hobhouse (1864–1929), an academic who also wrote for the *Manchester Guardian.* In general, they argued that laissez faire protected the interests of the economically powerful class and ignored the welfare of the nation. For example, Green valued private property but could not see how this principle helped the poor. "A man who possesses nothing but his powers of labor and who has to sell these to a capitalist for bare daily maintenance, might as well . . . be denied rights of property altogether."[15]

Green argued that the do-nothing state advocated by traditional laissez-faire liberalism condemned many citizens to destitution, ignorance, and despair. The state must preserve individual liberty and at the same time secure the common good by promoting conditions favorable for the self-development of the majority of the population.

Liberalism, for Green, encompassed more than the protection of individual rights from an oppressive government. A truly liberal society, he said, gives people the opportunity to fulfill their moral potential and human capacities. And social reforms initiated by the state assisted in the realization of this broader conception of liberty. Green and other advocates of state intervention contended that the government has a moral obligation to create social conditions that permit individuals to make the best of themselves. Toward that end, the state should promote public health, ensure decent housing, and provide for education. The uneducated and destitute person cannot be morally self-sufficient or a good citizen, Green and other progressives argued.

Green and his colleagues remained advocates of capitalism but rejected strict laissez faire, which, they said, benefitted only a particular class at the expense of the common good. Overcoming a traditional liberal mistrust of state power, they viewed the state as an ethical institution, assigned it a positive role in improving social conditions, and insisted that state actions need not threaten individual freedom.

In general, by the beginning of the twentieth century, liberals in Britain increasingly acknowledged the need for social legislation; the foundations for the British welfare state were being laid. On the Continent, too, social welfare laws were enacted. To be sure, the motives behind such legislation were quite diverse and often had little to do with liberal sentiments. Nevertheless, in several countries, liberalism was expanding into political and social democracy, a trend that would continue in the twentieth century.

Feminism: Extending the Principle of Equality

Another example of the expansion of liberalism was the emergence of feminist movements in Western Europe and the United States. Feminists insisted that the principles of liberty and equality expressed by the philosophes and embodied in the French Declaration of the Rights of Man and of the Citizen and the American Declaration of Independence be applied to women. Thus, Olympe de Gouges's *Declaration of the Rights of Women* (1791), modeled after the Declaration of the Rights of Man and of the Citizen, the French Revolution's tribute to Enlightenment ideals, stated: "Woman is born free and remains equal to man in rights. . . . The aim of every political association is the preservation of the natural . . . rights of man and woman."[16] And in 1837, English novelist and economist Harriet Martineau observed: "One of the fundamental principles announced in the Declaration of Independence is that governments derive their just power from the consent of the governed. How can the political condition of women be reconciled with this?"[17]

In the United States in the 1830s, Angelina and Sarah Grimké spoke in public—something women rarely did—against slavery and for women's rights. In 1838, Sarah Grimké published *Letters on the Equality of the Sexes and the Condition of Women,* in which she stated emphatically: "Men and women were Created Equal: they are both moral and accountable beings, and whatever is *right* for man to do is *right* for women. . . . How monstrous, how anti-Christian, is the doctrine that woman is to be dependent on man!"[18] The Woman's Suffrage Movement, holding its first convention in 1848 in Seneca Falls, New York, drew up a Declaration of Statements and Principles that broadened the Declaration of Independence: "We hold these truths to be self-evident: that all men and women are created equal." The document protested "that woman has too long rested satisfied in the circumscribed limits which corrupt customs and a perverted application of the Scriptures have marked out for her" and called for the untiring effort of both men and women to secure for women "an equal participation with men in the various trades, professions, and commerce."[19]

In their struggle for equality, feminists had to overcome deeply ingrained premises about female inferiority and deficiencies. Opponents of women's rights argued that feminist demands would threaten society by undermining marriage and the family. An article in the *Saturday Review,* an English periodical, declared that "it is not the interest of States . . . to encourage the existence of women who are other than entirely dependent on man as well for subsistence as for protection and love. . . . Married life is a woman's profession."[20] In 1870, a member of the House of Commons wondered "what would become, not merely of woman's influence, but of her duties at home, her care of the household, her supervision of all those duties and surroundings which make a happy home . . . if we are to see women coming forward and taking part in the government of the country."[21] This concern for the family combined with the traditional, biased view of woman's nature, as one writer for the *Saturday Review* revealed:

> *The power of reasoning is so small in women that they need adventitious help, and if they have not the guidance and check of a religious conscience, it is useless to expect from them self-control on abstract principles. They do not calculate consequences, and they are reckless when they once give way, hence they are to be kept straight only through their affections, the religious sentiment and a well-educated moral sense.*[22]

In contrast to most of their contemporaries, some prominent men did support equal rights for women. "Can man be free if woman be slave?"[23] asked the poet Shelley, who favored female suffrage. So, too, did social theorist Jeremy Bentham and political economist William Thompson, who wrote *Appeal of One Half of the Human Race* (1825). John Stuart Mill thought that differences between the sexes (and between the classes) were due far more to education than to inherited inequalities. Believing that all people—women as well as men—should be able to develop their talents and intellects as fully as possible, Mill was an early champion of female equality, including women's suffrage. In 1867, Mill, as a member of Parliament, proposed that the suffrage be extended to women, but the proposal was rejected by a vote of 194 to 74.

In 1851, Mill had married Harriet Taylor, a longtime friend and a recent widow. An ardent feminist, Harriet Mill influenced her husband's thought. In *The Subjection of Women* (1869), Mill argued that male dominance of women constituted a flagrant abuse of power. He described female inequality as a single relic of an old outlook that had been exploded in everything else. It violated the principle of individual rights and hindered the progress of humanity:

> *. . . the principle which regulates the existing social relations between the two sexes—the legal subordination of one sex to the other—is wrong in itself, and now one of the chief hindrances to human improvement . . . it ought to be replaced by a principle of perfect equality, admitting no power or privilege on the one side, nor disability on the other.*[24]

Mill considered it only just that women be free to take on all the functions and enter all the occupations until then reserved for men. The struggle for female rights became a major issue in several lands at the end of the nineteenth century and the beginning of the twentieth.

❖ ❖ ❖

Notes

1. Quoted in Leonard J. Davis, "Gustave Flaubert," in *The Romantic Century,* Vol. 7 of *European Writers,* ed. Jacques Barzun and George Stade (New York: Charles Scribner's Sons, 1985), p. 1382.
2. Quoted in Ernst Cassirer, *The Problem of Knowledge: Philosophy, Science, and History Since Hegel,* trans. William H. Woglom and Charles W. Hendel (New Haven, Conn.: Yale University Press, 1950), p. 244.
3. Excerpted in Richard Olson, ed., *Science as Metaphor* (Belmont, Calif.: Wadsworth, 1971), p. 124.
4. Karl Pearson, *National Life from the Standpoint of Science* (London: Adam & Charles Black, 1905), p. 21.
5. Quoted in H. W. Koch, "Social Darwinism in the 'New Imperialism,'" in *The Origins of the First World War,* ed. H. W. Koch (New York: Taplinger, 1972), p. 345.
6. Friedrich von Bernhardi, *Germany and the Next War,* trans. Allen H. Powles (New York: Longman, Green, 1914), p. 18.
7. Quoted in George M. Fredrickson, *The Black Image in the White Mind* (New York: Harper Torchbooks, 1972), pp. 26–27.
8. Karl Marx, *Theses on Feuerbach,* excerpted in *Karl Marx: Selected Writings in Sociology and Social Philosophy,* ed. T. B. Bottomore and Maximilien Rubel (London: Watts, 1956), p. 69.
9. Karl Marx, *The German Ideology* (New York: International Publishers, 1939), p. 18.
10. Friedrich Engels, *The Origin of the Family, Private Property & the State,* in *A Handbook of Marxism,* ed. Emile Burns (New York: Random House, 1935), p. 330.
11. Marx, *German Ideology,* p. 69.
12. Karl Marx, *Communist Manifesto,* trans. Samuel Moore (Chicago: Henry Regnery, 1954), pp. 81–82.

13. John Stuart Mill, *On Liberty* (Boston: Ticknor & Fields, 1863), p. 36.
14. Ibid., p. 22.
15. Thomas Hill Green, *Lectures on the Principles of Political Obligation* (Ann Arbor: University of Michigan Press, 1967), p. 219.
16. Excerpted in Eleanor S. Riemer and John C. Fout, eds., *European Women: A Documentary History, 1789–1945* (New York: Schocken Books, 1980), pp. 63–64.
17. Excerpted in Gayle Graham Yates, ed., *Harriet Martineau on Women* (New Brunswick, N.J.: Rutgers University Press, 1985), p. 134.
18. Excerpted in Miriam Schneir, ed., *Feminism: The Essential Historical Writings* (New York: Vintage Books, 1972), pp. 40–41.
19. Ibid., pp. 76, 82.
20. Quoted in J. A. Banks and Olive Banks, *Feminism and Family Planning in Victorian England* (Liverpool: Liverpool University Press, 1965), p. 43.
21. Ibid., p. 46.
22. Ibid., p. 47.
23. Percy Bysshe Shelley, "The Revolt of Islam," canto 2, stanza 43, in *The Complete Poetical Works of Percy Bysshe Shelley,* ed. Thomas Hutchinson (London: Oxford University Press, 1929), p. 63.
24. John Stuart Mill, *The Subjection of Women,* in *On Liberty, Etc.* (London: Oxford University Press, 1924), p. 427.

Suggested Reading

Becker, George J., *Master European Realists of the Nineteenth Century* (1982). Discussions of Flaubert, Zola, Chekhov, and other realists.

Bullock, Alan, and Maurice Shock, eds., *The Liberal Tradition* (1956). Well-chosen selections from the writings of British liberals.

Farrington, Benjamin, *What Darwin Really Said* (1966). A brief study of Darwin's work.

Grant, Damian, *Realism* (1970). A very good short survey.

Hemmings, F. W. J., ed., *The Age of Realism* (1978). A series of essays exploring realism in various countries.

Hofstadter, Richard, *Social Darwinism in American Thought* (1955). A classic treatment of the impact of evolution on American conservatism, imperialism, and racism.

Matthews, Betty, ed., *Marx: A Hundred Years On* (1983). Eleven essays by noted authorities.

McLellan, David, *Karl Marx: His Life and Thought* (1977). A highly regarded biography.

———, ed., *Karl Marx: Selected Writings* (1977). A balanced selection of Marx's writings.

Chapter 16

Europe in the Late Nineteenth Century: Modernization, Nationalism, Imperialism

- **The Advance of Industry**
- **Great Britain: Reform and Unrest**
- **France: A Troubled Nation**
- **Germany: The Power State**
- **Italy: Unfulfilled Expectations**
- **Russia: Tsarist Autocracy**
- **The Rise of Racial Nationalism**
- **The Emergence of the New Imperialism**
- **European Domination of Asia**
- **The Scramble for Africa**
- **The Legacy of Imperialism**

Focus Questions

1. Why is the last part of the nineteenth century called the Second Industrial Revolution?
2. Why is racial nationalism a repudiation of the Enlightenment tradition and a regression to mythical thinking?
3. What is the relationship between medieval and modern anti-Semitism? How does anti-Semitism demonstrate the immense power of mythical thinking?

4. What factors contributed to the rise of the new imperialism in the last part of the nineteenth century?
5. Why and how were Europeans able to dominate African and Asian lands?
6. What is the legacy of imperialism for the contemporary world?

In the last part of the nineteenth century, the accelerated pace of industrialization and urbanization continued the process of modernization that had begun earlier with the Industrial Revolution and had transformed European and American societies. Simultaneously, Western nations built governmental machinery for dealing with great numbers of citizens. This strengthening and centralizing process—*state building*, in modern terminology—became the major activity of Western governments. State building meant not only strengthening central authority but also absorbing previously excluded classes into the nation, primarily through the power of nationalism, which governments fostered. A state's power grew enormously as its government affected the lives of ordinary citizens through military conscription, public education, and broad taxation.

Industrialization facilitated the trends toward centralization by concentrating factory workers in cities and loosening traditional rural ties. It greatly affected international relations as well. The amount of coal and iron produced, the mileage and tonnage of railways and navies, the mechanization of industry, and the skill of the populace became important components of national power.

Nationalism, which intensified during the last part of the nineteenth century, was to turn into the dominant spiritual force of European life.

It grew increasingly belligerent, intolerant, and irrational, threatening both the peace of Europe and the liberal, humanist tradition of the Enlightenment. Nationalism and industrialization were the principal forces behind imperialism, leading European nations and the United States to extend their power over Asian, African, and Latin American lands. ❖

The Advance of Industry

Historians call the second half of the nineteenth century the Second Industrial Revolution because of the great increase in the speed and scale of technological advances and social transformation. It was also characterized by the rise of the middle class to political and social power corresponding to its economic power.

At the midcentury, farming was still the main occupation of people everywhere—even in Britain, where industrialization was most advanced. Even Britain had more domestic servants than factory workers and twice as many agricultural laborers as textile and clothing workers. Large factories were few, and handicrafts still flourished. Sailing ships still outnumbered steamships, and horses carried more freight than trains. This situation, however, changed radically in two spurts: the first between 1850 and 1870, and the second from the 1890s until World War I.

During the first spurt, in Europe and America the shift from hand to machine production accelerated, leading to the concentration of factory workers in industrial cities and the growth of unions. The standard of living for most workers rose. New machines and processes, legislation, and trade union bargaining relieved the worst conditions of early industrialization. At the same time, the first regulations of urban development and sanitation began to improve living conditions. In the more advanced industrial areas, the social organization of the workplace changed: the introduction of heavy equipment resulted in men replacing women and children in the factories. However, women forced out of factories (they would return during World War I) took jobs as domestics, pieceworkers, seamstresses, or laundresses. Children became students as the state and the economy demanded that they acquire at least a minimal education.

The scale of development changed markedly during the second spurt. Giant firms run by boards of directors, including financiers, operated far-flung enterprises of enormous, mechanized factories. These industrial giants were able to control the output, price, and distribution of commodities. They dominated smaller firms, financed and controlled research and development, and expanded far beyond their national frontiers. The "captains of industry"—the owners or managers of these large firms—possessed such extraordinary economic power that they often commanded political power as well. The emergence and concentration of heavy industry in large firms, capitalized by specialist banks, characterized the post-1890 period all over Europe.

Revolutionary technological changes furthered the growth of industry. At the midcentury, all of Europe caught the railroad mania that had seized Britain in the 1840s. This epic expansion of railroads was paralleled in shipping. In 1850, steam-powered ships constituted only 5 percent of the world's tonnage; by 1893, the figure had risen to half of all tonnage. At the turn of the century, two German engineers, Gottlieb Daimler and Karl Benz, joined to perfect the internal combustion engine. Then, an American, Henry Ford, using mass-production assembly-line techniques, brought out his Model T for "the ordinary man," and the automobile age was born. The invention of the diesel engine by another German in 1897 meant that cheaper, more efficient fuel could be used. Diesel engines soon replaced steam engines on giant cargo ships, warships, and luxury liners. In communications, the advent of the telegraph, telephone, and later radio also revolutionized people's lives.

However, economic development was extremely uneven. Central, Southern, and Eastern Europe remained overwhelmingly agricultural and stayed so until World War I and after.

Accelerated Urbanization

More rapid industrialization increased the numbers of northwestern Europeans and Americans who lived in cities, which became more numerous, larger, and more densely populated. Although not an industrial city, London had become a

Chronology 16.1 ❖ Expansion of Western Power

1839–1842	Opium War: the British defeat the Chinese, annexing treaty ports in China and opening them to Western trade
1851–1852	Louis Napoleon Bonaparte overthrows Second Republic, becoming Emperor Napoleon III
1853	Commodore Perry, with U.S. naval forces, opens Japan to trade
1857–1858	Sepoy Mutiny; Britain replaces the East India Company and begins ruling India through a viceroy
1867	Second Reform Bill doubles the English electorate
1869	Opening of the Suez Canal
1870	Third French Republic is established
1870–1871	Franco-Prussian War; Paris Commune; creation of German Empire, with William I as kaiser and Bismarck as chancellor
1876	Stanley sets up posts in the Congo for Leopold II of Belgium
1882	Britain occupies Egypt
1884	Berlin Conference on Africa; Reform Bill grants suffrage to most English men
1894–1906	Dreyfus affair in France
1898	Spanish–American War: United States acquires the Philippines and Puerto Rico and occupies Cuba; battle of Omdurman
1899–1902	Boer War between the British and the Afrikaners
1900	Boxers rebel against foreign presence in China
1904–1905	Russo-Japanese War: the Japanese defeat the Russians
1911	Parliament Act limits power of the House of Lords
1919	Britain grants a legislative assembly in India; Gandhi's passive resistance movement broadens with the Amritsar Massacre

megalopolis of five million people by 1880 and was home to seven million by 1914. Paris increased from two million to three million between 1850 and World War I. Berlin, a city of only half a million in 1866, reached two million by World War I. There were only three German cities of more than a hundred thousand on the eve of unification, but by 1903 there were fifteen.

In the cities, the middle class rose to political, economic, and social prominence, often expressing its newfound importance and prosperity through civic activity. As machinery replaced handicraft, the artisan working class experienced a sharp decline. Factory workers, their ranks swelled by peasants and displaced artisans, emerged as an important social group in cities. Industrialization also created a new, "white-collar" group of clerks, who tried to differentiate themselves from factory workers.

The Rise of Socialist Parties

Between 1850 and 1914, workers' lives improved because of trade union organization and government intervention in the economy. Still, members of the working class faced problems and inequities that drew them to socialist parties, which strove

Hulton Archive/Stringer/Getty Images.

"MATCH GIRLS." The "Match Girls" strike taught the public the human cost of cheap and dangerous products. Here the women pack phosphorus matches in a London factory.

for government control of industry and worker control of government and the workplace. Most workers and their families lived in bleak, overcrowded tenements without central heating or running water. They worked long hours—as many as fifty-five per week in the trades where governments restricted the length of the workweek, and from seventy to seventy-five in unregulated trades. Their jobs were exhausting and monotonous. Workers also suffered from malnutrition. The English men and boys who appeared for medical exams to serve in the Boer War were found to be so physically unfit that their condition prompted reforms to improve the health and education of the laboring class. The working class as a whole suffered from diseases, particularly tuberculosis, and from lack of medical care. Women often died in childbirth owing to inadequate treatment, and men, particularly miners and dockworkers, commonly experienced job accidents that maimed and killed. Socialists argued that these conditions were due to the capitalist profit system, which exploited and impoverished workers and enriched the owners.

Socialist parties grew phenomenally in Germany and rapidly in much of the rest of Europe. Even Russia, which was scarcely industrial, had a Marxist socialist party. The growth of socialism reflected the workers' increased consciousness that they had special needs, which other political parties did not fulfill. However, socialists were divided about tactics. "Orthodox" Marxists believed that socialist-led revolution was the necessary first step for change; this group included Wilhelm Liebknecht and August Bebel of Germany and Jules Guesde of France. Others—"revisionist" Marxists—who were influenced by the German theoretician Eduard Bernstein, urged socialists to forgo revolution and use the existing political and economic systems to build a socialist society.

GREAT BRITAIN: REFORM AND UNREST

The process of reform, begun with the Reform Bill of 1832 and the Factory Acts, continued in the era of the Second Industrial Revolution. The Reform Bill of 1867, skillfully maneuvered through Parliament by Benjamin Disraeli (1804–1881), gave the vote to urban workers, doubling the electorate. Some of Disraeli's fellow members in the Conservative party feared that extending the vote to the largely uneducated masses would ruin the nation, but Disraeli maintained that this democratic advance would strengthen the bonds between the people and the state. Moreover, he believed that the Conservatives' social program and imperialist foreign policy would win the newly enfranchised poor to the party.

The work of electoral reform was continued by the Liberal Party under the leadership of William Gladstone (1809–1898), who served four terms as prime minister. The Ballot Act (1872) provided for the secret ballot, which enabled working-class voters to avoid intimidation by their employers. Next, the Reform Bill of 1884 enfranchised rural laborers; now almost all English males could vote.

Social Reform

Unlike their Continental brothers, British workers on the whole had never been attracted to socialism, and particularly not to Marxism. In the 1880s, however, widespread poverty and new trends in industry—especially monopolies, cartels, and foreign competition—led some labor leaders to urge greater militancy. These conditions brought about the creation of the Labour Party.

The growth of the Labour Party was spurred by the adverse Taff Vale decision (1901), which awarded damages to an employer picketed by a union. If workers could be fined for picketing or other actions restraining trade, their unions could be broken and they would lose the economic gains of half a century. Galvanized by the Taff Vale decision and eager to win reforms for the working class, labor took to politics. In the elections of 1906, the new Labour Party gained twenty-nine members in the House of Commons; it would become an important faction in British politics.

Between 1906 and 1911, the Liberals, led by David Lloyd George (1863–1945) and the then Liberal Winston Churchill (1874–1965), introduced a series of important social measures. Aided by the Labour Party, they enacted a program of old-age pensions, labor exchanges to help the unemployed find work, unemployment and health insurance (a program deeply influenced by Bismarckian social legislation, see the upcoming section "Germany: The Power State"), and minimum wages for certain industries. Parliament also repealed the Taff Vale decision. In the process, however, a constitutional crisis developed between the Liberals, who had Labour support, and the Conservatives, who dominated the House of Lords. The crisis ended with the Parliament Act of 1911, which decreed that the House of Lords could only delay, not prevent, the passage of a bill that the House of Commons had approved.

Feminist Agitation

On the issue of women's suffrage, British democracy was lagging. Influenced by the ideals of the American and French Revolutions, women had begun to protest their unequal status. In 1867, John Stuart Mill proposed extending the vote to women, but his colleagues in Parliament rejected the proposal. The following year, Lydia Becker became the first Englishwoman to speak in public for women's suffrage. Many people, both men and women, viewed female suffrage as too radical a break with tradition. Some asserted that women were represented by their husbands or male relatives and therefore did not need the right to vote. Others protested that women lacked the ability to participate responsibly in political life. Queen Victoria, who supported other reforms, called women's suffrage "that mad, wicked folly."

Although many Liberals and some Labourites favored women's suffrage, women were advised by the leader of the Liberals "to keep on pestering . . . but exercise the virtue of patience." For the women who deemed this advice patronizing and whose patience was running out, a family of feminists advocated a more militant course of action. Emmeline Pankhurst and her daughters Sylvia and Christabel urged demonstrations, invasions of the House of Commons, destruction of property, and hunger strikes. They did not urge these dramatic actions all at once, but when their petitions and demands were ignored, they moved to more and more shocking deeds. Suffragettes began a campaign of breaking windows, starting fires in mailboxes, and chaining themselves to the gates at Parliament. As a gesture of protest, in 1913 one militant threw herself to her death under the king's horse at the races.

When feminists were arrested for violating the law, they staged hunger strikes. Ugly situations resulted, with the police force-feeding the demonstrators and subjecting them to ridicule and rough treatment.

Carson Reviewing Troops of Ulster Volunteers Before World War I. For almost a century the Irish demand for representation, then for home rule (or self-government), had met with political opposition in the British parliament. With Parliament split, Irish nationalists and their opponents, Irish Protestants, armed for civil war. Here a leading member of parliament supports the Irish Protestants who have volunteered for the civil war to keep Ireland in the British empire. The start of the First World War put this treasonous and revolutionary situation out of the public mind only for a couple years.

Feminists continued to press for the right to vote. When women played a major part on the home front in World War I, many of the elite changed their minds, and in 1918, British women over the age of thirty gained the vote. In 1928, Parliament lowered the voting age for women to twenty-one, the same qualifying age as that for male voters.

The Irish Question

Feminist agitation was one explosive issue confronting prewar Britain. Another was the Irish question. While moderate Irish nationalists called for *home rule* (self-government within the British Empire), something favored by many members of Parliament, Irish Catholic militants such as the Irish Republican Brotherhood and the Gaelic League pressed for full independence. Fearing Catholic domination, the Protestant Irish (Ulstermen) in the northern counties of Ulster strongly opposed independence for Ireland. The Ulster Volunteers recruited a large private army and openly trained it for revolution in the event that home rule was enacted. Gangs smuggled guns, soldiers fired on demonstrators, violence bred violence, and civil war seemed close.

In 1916, the Easter Rebellion, an Irish insurrection, was suppressed and its leaders executed. But the English cabinet was moved to proceed with home rule at once. The Irish revolt of 1919–1920 brought matters to a head: Ireland was divided, the overwhelmingly Catholic south gaining independence and the six predominantly Protestant counties of Ulster remaining part of the United Kingdom.

At the beginning of the twentieth century, labor, Irish, and female militancy marred Britain's image of a stable, liberal, constitutional regime. Nevertheless, British parliamentary government survived every crisis and proved itself able to carry the nation successfully through a grueling world war.

France: A Troubled Nation

In 1852, Louis Napoleon Bonaparte (1808–1873), who had been elected president of the Second French Republic in 1848, took the title of emperor in the tradition of his illustrious uncle. Napoleon III ruled in an authoritarian manner, permitting no opposition, censoring the press, and allowing the legislature little power. But in the 1860s, in a drastic shift, he introduced liberal reforms, pardoning political prisoners, removing press censorship, allowing workers the right to form unions, and approving a new constitution with safeguards for individual liberty. His reforms have perplexed historians. Was Napoleon III a sincere believer in liberal ideals who waited until his power was firmly established before implementing these ideals, or did he introduce reforms only because he feared unrest?

Defeat in the Franco-Prussian War (1870–1871) brought down the empire of Napoleon III. Bitter frustration with defeat and hatred of the Prussian invaders led the people of Paris to rise against the armistice signed by the provisional government—the politicians who had replaced Napoleon III. The Paris Commune (1871) began as a patriotic refusal to accept defeat and as a rejection of Napoleon's rule, but it became a rejection of the provisional government as well. Ultimately, the Communards (as those who resisted the Prussians and the provisional government were called) also challenged property owners.

The Communards included followers of the anarchist Joseph Proudhon and groups of republican and socialist veterans of the revolution of 1848, gathered from prisons, from hiding, and from exile. For two months in the spring of 1871, these revolutionaries ruled Paris. Then, Adolphe Thiers, head of the provisional government that still governed the rest of France, ordered an attack on Paris. The fighting was bitter and desperate, with many acts of terrorism and violence. Both sides in this civil war set fires that destroyed large parts of the city they loved. The Communards were defeated and treated as traitors: twenty thousand of them were executed without trial, and those who were tried received harsh sentences—death, life imprisonment, and deportation to prison colonies. Governing classes across Europe viewed the Paris Commune as a sign that the people should be ruled with an iron fist.

At first it seemed that a monarchy would succeed the empire of Napoleon III. But disunity among the monarchists enabled France to become a republic by default. Unlike Britain with its two-party system, the Third French Republic had many political parties, which contributed to instability. No one party had sufficient weight in parliament to provide strong leadership. Prime ministers resigned in rapid succession; cabinets rose and fell frequently, giving the impression of a state without direction. Yet in the process, legislation was enacted that made elementary education free and compulsory and legalized trade unions. The Third Republic survived, though not without major crises; the principal one was the Dreyfus affair, which left France deeply divided.

In 1894, Captain Alfred Dreyfus, an Alsatian-Jewish artillery officer, was wrongly accused of having sold secrets to the Germans. After a court martial, he was condemned to life imprisonment on Devil's Island. Anti-Semitic elements joined with the Republic's opponents—monarchists, army leaders, clerics, and nationalists—to denounce and block every attempt to clear Dreyfus of the charges against him. In the beginning, few people defended Dreyfus; the vast majority felt that the honor of France and the army was at stake. Then individuals, mainly radical republicans, came to his defense, including the writers Anatole France and Émile Zola and the future republican leader Georges Clemenceau, along

After the Fall: LaRoquette Prisoners Before the Firing Squad. The repression of the Paris Commune, which resisted the French provisional government when it tried to make peace with the Prussians, was a brutal bloodbath with atrocities on both sides. When it was over, almost eight thousand were sent into exile, five thousand imprisoned and fined, and many executed. Few could have predicted that the republic established then would survive to World War II.

with university students. They protested and demonstrated, insisting on a retrial and a revision of the verdict. After many humiliations, Dreyfus was finally cleared in 1906.

The result of the victory of the radical republicans, however, was a fierce campaign to root out those opposing the Republic. The radicals expelled Catholic religious orders, confiscated their property, and waged a vigorous campaign to replace the influence of the parish priest with that of the district schoolmaster. Complete separation of church and state was ordered; taxes no longer supported the parishes and religious schools.

Despite progress in the middle of the nineteenth century, French economic development lagged. France had fewer and smaller industries than Britain or Germany, and more French people lived in rural areas and small communities. In the 1880s, both trade unionism and political parties with a socialist program began to make headway and to press for social reform through the democratic parliamentary institutions of the Republic. However, France was very slow to enact social measures such as pensions and regulations governing working conditions, wages, and hours. These measures, which might have improved the lives of ordinary people, were regarded by the ruling elite as hateful socialism; socialists, on the other hand, viewed them as token offerings to buy off workers.

France was a troubled country, and the Third Republic was not a popular regime. The church, the army, socialism, and even memories of the monarchy and the empire inspired deeper passions than did the Republic, which survived only because the dissension among its enemies allowed it to survive. France approached World

War I as a deeply divided country. Yet when World War I broke out, the French people rallied to defend the nation.

GERMANY: THE POWER STATE

Prussia's victory over France in the Franco-Prussian War of 1870–1871 completed the struggle for German unification. The new government, the German Reich (empire), was headed by the king of Prussia. Though the Reichstag (lower house) was elected by universal suffrage, the real power lay in the hands of the emperor and Bismarck, the "Iron Chancellor," who was responsible only to the emperor. The German kaiser (emperor), unlike the British monarch, had considerable control over lawmaking and foreign affairs and commanded the army and navy. The emperor alone could remove the chancellor or the cabinet members from office. The sole control over Bismarck was the Reichstag's refusal to pass the budget, an extreme measure that politicians were usually unwilling to take.

Bismarck's political practices weakened liberal and democratic elements. Nor did German liberals vigorously struggle for basic political and civil liberties; they tolerated evasions of principles and practices that British politicians would never have allowed. While Britain, France, the United States, and other Western states were becoming more democratic, Germany remained a semiautocratic state. The failure of democratic attitudes and procedures to take root in Germany was to have dangerous consequences for the future.

Bismarck regarded parties as incapable of making policy for the country. In Bismarck's mind, the Catholics and the socialists were internationalists who did not place the interests of Germany first. He began to persecute Catholics, who made up about 40 percent of the population. The *Kulturkampf* (struggle for culture) was a series of laws passed in 1873 to subject the church to the state. The laws discriminated against the Jesuits and required state supervision of the church and training of priests in state schools. Catholics had to be married by the state. Churchmen who refused to accept these laws were imprisoned or exiled. German liberals did not defend the civil liberties of the Catholics against these laws. Persecution only strengthened the German Catholics' loyalty to their church, however, and the Catholic Center Party gained support. Prussian conservatives, though Protestant, resented Bismarck's anticlerical policy, which could hurt Lutherans as well as Catholics. With the succession of Leo XIII to the papacy in 1878, Bismarck quietly opened negotiations for peace with the church.

When two attempts were made on William I's life in 1878, Bismarck demanded that the socialists be suppressed. In reality, the socialists, few in number, were not a threat; their immediate practical program was a demand for civil liberties and democracy in Germany. Only the narrowest of conservative views would have labeled the socialists as dangerous, but many in Germany, particularly the aristocratic Junker class, held such a narrow view. The liberals once again did not oppose Bismarck's special legislation—aimed at the socialists—outlawing subversive organizations and authorizing the police to ban meetings and newspapers. The Social Democratic Party, like the Catholic Center Party before, survived the persecution. It grew stronger and better disciplined as the liberals grew weaker, discredited by their unwillingness to act.

Bismarck's policy was not merely repressive. He tried to win the workers by paternalistic social legislation. Like many conservatives, he was disturbed by the effects of industrialization, which had developed at a rapid pace in the 1850s and 1860s. Germany was the first state to enact a program of social legislation for the proletariat; it included insurance against sickness, disability, accidents, and old age. The employer, the state, and the worker each contributed small amounts to an insurance fund.

Despite Bismarck's attempts to woo the workers away from socialism, the German working class continued to support the Social Democratic Party in elections. On the eve of World War I, union membership was roughly three million, and the Social Democratic Party was the largest single party in Germany. The socialists talked revolution, but the unions—the largest and most powerful in Europe—and many party members favored policies of gradual reform. Great numbers of German workers were patriotic, even imperialistic, and thought that their government deserved their loyalty.

By 1900, Germany had caught up with, and in some areas surpassed, Britain in economic growth. Aided by the skill of its scientists and inventors, Germany became a leader in the chemical and electrical industries. It possessed the most extensive sector of large-scale, concentrated industrial and corporate capitalism of any Great Power. Within a short period, Germany had become a strong, industrialized state, ready and eager to play an important role in world affairs. Its growing industrial and military might, linked with an aggressive nationalism, alarmed other countries. This combination of German vitality, aggressiveness, and the fears of its rivals helped lead to World War I.

Italy: Unfulfilled Expectations

Italian nationalists expected greatness from the unification of their country, so long conquered, plundered, divided, and ruled by absolute princes. But the newly unified Italy faced serious problems. An overwhelmingly Roman Catholic country, it was split by religious controversy. Liberals and republicans wanted a secular state, with civil marriage and public education, which was anathema to the church. Furthermore, few Italians could participate in the constitutional monarchy. Of the twenty-seven million citizens, only about two million could vote—even after the reforms of 1881, which tripled the electorate. Liberals could point out that almost every literate male could vote, but this achievement was small consolation to those who had fought for unification but now were denied voting privileges because they did not pass a literacy test.

Among Italian workers, cynicism about the government was so deep that many turned to radical movements, which advocated the rejection of authority and the tactics of terrorism, assassination, and general strikes. Disgust with parliamentary government led the workers to believe that direct action would gain more than elections and parties. Peasants in some rural areas, particularly in the south, were strongly Catholic, loyal to their landlords, and bitterly unhappy with their economic situation; they saw few signs of the new state other than hateful taxation and military conscription.

The ruling elite brushed aside Italy's difficult social and economic problems, concentrating instead on military glory and imperial expansion. The politicians trumpeted Italy's ambitions for Great Power status to justify military expenditures beyond the means of such a poor state. They presented Italy's scramble for African and Mediterranean territories as the solution to all its social ills. The profits from exploiting others would pay for badly needed social reforms, and the raw materials gained would fuel industrialization. None of these promises came true, which deepened the cynicism of a disillusioned people. As a foreign and as a domestic policy, this pursuit of glory was too costly for the fragile nation.

Before World War I, Italy was deeply divided politically. A wave of strikes and rural discontent gave sufficient warning to political leaders so that they declared neutrality, deciding, unlike Russia, not to risk the shaky regime by entering the war. But the appeals of expansionism were too great for them to maintain this policy.

Russia: Tsarist Autocracy

In the middle of the nineteenth century, Russia differed fundamentally from Western Europe. The great movements that had shaped the outlook of the modern West—Renaissance, Reformation, Scientific Revolution, Enlightenment, and Industrial Revolution—had barely penetrated Russia. Autocracy, buttressed by the Orthodox church, reigned supreme; the small and insignificant middle class did not possess the dynamic, critical, and individualistic spirit that characterized the Western bourgeoisie, and the vast majority of the people were illiterate serfs.

After Napoleon's defeat in 1814, some returning Russian officers, asking why Russia could not share the civilized life they had seen in Western Europe, turned revolutionary. The unsuccessful Decembrist uprising in 1825, during the brief interlude between the death of Alexander I (1801–1825) and the accession of Nicholas I (1825–1855), was the effort of a small group of conspirators demanding a constitution. Fear of revolution determined the character of the reign of Nicholas I and of tsarist governments thereafter.

Aware of the subversive influence of foreign ideas, Nicholas decreed an ideology of Russian superiority, called *official nationality*. The Russian people were taught to believe that the Orthodox creed of the Russian church, the autocratic rule of the tsar, and Russia's Slavic culture made the Russian Empire superior to the West. To enforce this contrived invincibility, Nicholas I created the Third Section, a secret agency of police spies, and controlled access to his country from Europe. Indeed, toward the end of his reign, he drew a virtual iron curtain to keep out dangerous influences. His ideal was a monolithic country, run like an army by a vigorous administration centered on the monarch; all Russians were to obey his wise and fatherly commands. Nicholas's successor, Alexander II (1855–1881), was determined to preserve autocratic rule. However, he wanted Russia to achieve what had made Western Europe strong: the energetic support and free enterprise of its citizens. Whether stimulating popular initiative was possible without undermining autocracy was the key puzzle for him and for his successors to the end of the tsarist regime.

Alexander's boldest reforms included the emancipation of the serfs in 1861. They were liberated from bondage to the nobility and given land of their own, but not individual freedom. They remained tied to their villages and to their households, which owned the land collectively. Emancipation did not transform the illiterate peasants into enterprising and loyal citizens. For the nonpeasant minority, a package of other reforms brought new opportunities: limited self-government for selected rural areas and urban settlements, an independent judiciary, trial by jury, and the introduction of a profession novel to Russians: the practice of law.

Meanwhile, Alexander reopened the borders, allowing closer ties with Europe and westernizing Russian society. The rising class of businesspeople and professional experts looked west and conformed to Western middle-class standards. There was some relaxation in the repression of non-Russian minorities. Railroads were constructed, which facilitated agricultural exports and permitted the import of Western goods and capital. For some years, the economy boomed.

More significant in the long run was the flowering of Russian thought and literature among the intelligentsia. These were educated Russians whose minds were shaped by Western schooling and travel, yet who still were prompted by the "Russian soul." They quarreled with fierce sincerity over whether Russia should pursue superiority by imitating the West or by cultivating its own Slavic genius, possibly through a Pan-Slavic movement. Pan-Slavism, which glorified the solidarity of Russians with other Slavic peoples of Eastern Europe, was a popular cause. Even more than the tsars, the intelligentsia hoped for a glorious Russia that would outshine the West.

Yet tsarist autocracy undercut their hopes. The tsar would not permit open discussion likely to provoke rebellion. Liberals advocating gradual change were thwarted by censorship and the police. The 1860s saw the rise of self-righteous fanatics who were ready to match the chicanery of the police and foment social revolution. By the late 1870s, they organized themselves into a secret terrorist organization. In 1881, they assassinated the tsar. The era of reforms ended.

The next tsar, Alexander III (1881–1894), a firm if unimaginative ruler, returned to the repressive policies of Nicholas I. In defense against the revolutionaries, he perfected the police state, even enlisting anti-Semitism in its cause. He updated autocracy and stifled dissent but also promoted economic development. Russia had relied too heavily on foreign loans and goods; it had to build up its own resources. It also needed more railroads to bind its huge empire together. So in 1891 the tsar ordered the construction of the Trans-Siberian Railroad. Soon afterward, Minister of Finance Sergei Witte used railroad expansion to boost heavy industry and industrialization generally.

Yet forced industrialization also brought perils. It propelled the country into alien and often hated ways of life and created a discontented new class of workers. In addition, it promoted literacy and contact with Western Europe and thus helped to increase political agitation. Indispensable for national self-assertion and survival, industrialization strained the country's fragile unity.

The first jolt, the revolution of 1905, followed Russia's defeat by Japan in the Russo-Japanese War. Fortunately for Nicholas II (1894–1917), his soldiers stayed loyal. The autocracy survived, although, as a concession to the revolution, it was now saddled with a parliament, called the Imperial Duma. The new regime, inwardly rejected by Nicholas II, started auspiciously. Under its freedoms, Russian art and literature flourished and the economy progressed. Agrarian reforms introduced the incentives of private property and individual enterprise in the villages. The supporters of the new constitutional experiment hoped for a liberal Russia at last, but in vain.

The Rise of Racial Nationalism

In the first half of the nineteenth century, European nationalism and liberalism went hand in hand. Liberals sought both the rights of the individual and national independence and unification. Liberal nationalists believed that a unified state free of foreign subjugation was in harmony with the principle of natural rights, and they insisted that love of country led to love of humanity. As nationalism grew more extreme, however, its profound difference from liberalism became more apparent. The extreme nationalism of the late nineteenth and early twentieth centuries contributed to World War I and to the rise of Fascism after the war; it was the seedbed of totalitarian nationalism. Nationalism proved more successful than liberalism in attracting allegiance; it was often expressed by a total commitment to the nation and the different classes uniting in a common cause.

Concerned exclusively with the greatness of the nation, extreme nationalists rejected the liberal emphasis on political liberty. Liberals regarded the state as a community of individuals voluntarily bonded by law and citizenship and entitled to the same rights. To extreme nationalists, however, the state was the highest development of a folkish-racial spirit inherited from their ancestors. In their eyes, profound and irreconcilable differences separated "their people" from those who did not share this ancestry. Even if others had dwelled in the land for centuries, such people were seen as unwanted and dangerous aliens. Increasingly, nationalists attacked parliamentary government as an obstacle to national power and greatness and maintained that authoritarian leadership was needed to meet national emergencies. The needs of the nation, they said, transcended the rights of the individual.

Extreme nationalists also rejected the liberal ideal of equality. Placing the nation above everything, nationalists accused national minorities of corrupting the nation's spirit, and they glorified war as a symbol of the nation's resolve and will. In the name of national power and unity, they persecuted minorities at home and stirred up hatred against other nations. Increasingly, they embraced militaristic, imperialistic, and racist doctrines. At the founding of the Nationalist Association in Italy in 1910, one leader declared: "Just as socialism teaches the proletariat the value of class struggle, so we must teach Italy the value of international struggle. But international struggle is war? Well, then, let there be war! And nationalism will arouse the will for a victorious war . . . the only way to national redemption."[1]

Similar sentiments were voiced in 1913 by a German nationalist: "Let us regard war as holy, like the purifying force of fate, for it will awaken in our people all that is great and ready for selfless sacrifice, while it cleanses our soul of the mire of petty egotistical concerns."[2]

Interpreting politics with the logic of emotions, extreme nationalists insisted that they had a sacred mission to regain lands once held in the Middle Ages, to unite with their kinfolk in other lands, or to rule over peoples considered inferior. Loyalty to the nation-state was elevated above all other allegiances. The ethnic state became an object of religious reverence; the spiritual energies that formerly had been dedicated to Christianity were now channeled into the worship of the nation-state, igniting primitive, dark, cruel feelings.

By the beginning of the twentieth century, conservatives had become the staunchest advocates of nationalism, and the nationalism preached by conservative extremists was stripped of Mazzini's humanitarian ideals of liberty, equality, and the fellowship of nations. Particularly in Germany, landholding aristocrats, generals, and clergy, often joined by big industrialists, saw nationalism as a convenient instrument for gaining a mass following in their struggle against democracy, social reform, and socialism. Championing popular nationalist myths and dreams and citing Social Darwinist doctrines, a newly radicalized right, dominated by the elite of German society, hoped to harness the instinctual energies of the masses, particularly the peasants and the lower middle class—shopkeepers, civil servants, and white-collar workers—to conservative causes. Peasants viewed liberalism and a godless Marxism as threats to traditional values, while the lower bourgeoisie feared the power of an organized proletariat. These people were receptive to the rhetoric of ultranationalists, who denounced democracy and Marxism as threats to national unity and Jews as aliens endangering the nation. Nationalism was presented as a victory of idealism over materialism and as the subordination of class and personal interests to the general good of the nation.

Volkish Thought

Extreme nationalism was a general European phenomenon, but it proved especially dangerous in Germany. Bismarck's triumphs lured Germans into a dream world. Many started to yearn for the extension of German power throughout the globe. The past, they said, belonged to France and Britain; the future, to Germany.

The most ominous expression of German nationalism (and a clear example of mythical thinking) was *Volkish* thought. (*Volk* means "folk" or "people"; in this context, "ethnic" might be the best meaning.) German Volkish thinkers sought to bind the German people together through a deep love of their language, traditions, and fatherland. These thinkers felt that Germans were animated by a higher spirit than that found in other peoples. To Volkish thinkers, the Enlightenment and parliamentary democracy were foreign ideas that corrupted the pure German spirit. With fanatical devotion, Volkish thinkers embraced all things German—the medieval past, the German landscape, the simple peasant, the village—and denounced the liberal, humanist tradition of the West as alien to the German soul.

Volkish thought attracted Germans frightened by all the complexities of the modern age—industrialization, urbanization, materialism, class conflicts, and alienation. Seeing their beloved Germany transformed by these forces of modernity, Volkish thinkers yearned to restore the sense of community, the spiritual unity, that they attributed to the preindustrial age. Only by identifying with their sacred soil and sacred traditions could modern Germans escape from the evils of industrial society. Only then could the different classes band together in an organic unity.

The Volkish movement had little support from the working class, which was concerned chiefly with improving its standard of living. The movement appealed mainly to farmers and villagers, who regarded the industrial city as a threat to native values and a vehicle for spreading foreign ideas; to artisans and small shopkeepers, threatened by big business; and to scholars, writers, teachers, and students, who saw in Volkish nationalism a cause worthy of their idealism. The schools were leading agents for the dissemination of Volkish ideas.

Volkish thinkers glorified the ancient Germanic tribes that had overrun the Roman Empire; they contrasted their courageous and vigorous German ancestors with the effete and degenerate Romans. A few tried to harmonize ancient Germanic religious traditions with Christianity. Such attitudes led Germans to see themselves as a heroic people fundamentally different from and better than the English and the French. It also led them to regard German culture as unique—innately superior and opposed to the humanist outlook of the Enlightenment. Like their romantic predecessors, Volkish thinkers held that the German people and culture had a special destiny and a unique mission. They pitted the German soul against the Western intellect—feeling, intuition, spirit, and idealism against a drab rationalism. To be sure, the Western humanist tradition had many supporters in Germany, but the counterideology of Volkish thought was becoming increasingly widespread. This murky, irrational, radically nationalist, and antiliberal outlook shaped by these Volkish thinkers in the late nineteenth century would later undermine support for the democratic Weimar Republic established in Germany after World War I and provide Hitler with receptive listeners. Many of Hitler's supporters hoped that he would transform these Volkish longings into political realities.

The Wiener Library, London.

The Protocols of the Elders of Zion. This infamous forgery, commissioned by the Russian secret police, became an international bestseller and contributed to outrages against Jews. Anti-Semitic organizations continue to publish and circulate it today. The picture is the actual cover of a French edition of the *Protocols*, c. 1934.

Racist doctrines had an especially strong appeal for Volkish thinkers. According to these doctrines, race was the key to history; not only physical features, but also moral, esthetic, and intellectual qualities distinguished one race from another. For racist thinkers, a race demonstrated its vigor and achieved greatness when it preserved its purity; intermarriage between races was contamination that would result in genetic, cultural, and military decline. Unlike liberals, who held that anyone who accepted German law was a member of the German nation, racists argued that a person's nationality was a function of his or her "racial soul" or "blood." Like their Nazi successors, Volkish thinkers claimed that the German race was purer than, and therefore superior to, all other races. Its superiority was revealed in such physical characteristics as blond hair, blue eyes, and fair skin—all signs of inner qualities lacking in other races.

German racial nationalists insisted that Germany had a unique mission; as a superior race, Germans had a national right to dominate other peoples, particularly the "racially inferior" Slavs of the East. The Pan-German Association, whose membership included professors, schoolteachers, journalists, lawyers, and aristocrats, spread racial and nationalist theories and glorified war as an expression of national vitality. A statement from the association's journal sums up its philosophy: "The racial biological ideology tells us that there are races that lead and races that follow. Political history is nothing but the history of struggles among the leading races. Conquests, above all, are always the work of the leading races. Such men can conquer, may conquer, and shall conquer."[3]

Anti-Semitism: The Power and Danger of Mythical Thinking

German racial nationalists singled out Jews as a wicked race and a deadly enemy of the German people. Anti-Semitism, which was widespread in late-nineteenth-century Europe, provides a striking example of the perennial appeal, power, and danger of mythical thinking—of elevating to the level of objective truth ideas that have no basis in fact but provide all-encompassing, emotionally satisfying explanations of life and history. By manufacturing the myth of the wicked Jew, the radical right confirmed the insight reached by the political theorist Georges Sorel (see the section on Sorel under "Irrationalism" in Chapter 17): that people are moved and united by myths that offer simple, clear, and emotionally gratifying resolutions to the complexities of the modern world.

Anti-Semitic organizations and political parties sought to deprive Jews of their civil rights, and anti-Semitic publications proliferated. Edouard

Primary Source

The Pan-German League: Extreme Racial Nationalism

Organized in 1894, the ultranationalist and imperialist Pan-German League called for German expansion both in Europe and overseas. It often expressed blatantly Social Darwinist and racist views, as illustrated in the following article, which appeared in 1913 in the league's principal publication.

The historical view as to the biological evolution of races tells us that there are dominant races and subordinate races. Political history is nothing more than the history of the struggles between the dominant races. Conquest in particular is always a function of the dominant races. . . . Where now in all the world does it stand written that conquering races are under obligations to grant after an interval political rights to the conquered? Is not the practice of political rights an advantage which biologically belongs to the dominant races? . . . What are [these] rights? . . . In my opinion, the rights of men are, first, personal freedom; secondly, the right of free expression of opinion—as well as freedom of the press; . . . and, finally, the right to work, in case one is without means. . . .

. . . The man with political rights sets up schools, and the speech used in the instruction is his speech. . . . The purpose must be to crush the [individuality of the] conquered people and its political and lingual existence. . . .

The conquerors are acting only according to biological principles if they suppress alien languages and undertake to destroy strange popular customs. . . . Only the conquering race must be populous, so that it can overrun territory it has won. Nations that are populous are, moreover, the only nations which have a moral claim to conquest, for it is wrong that in one country there should be overpopulation while close at hand—and at the same time on better soil—a less numerous population stretches its limbs at ease.

[As to the inferior races:] From political life they are to be excluded. They are eligible only to positions of a non-political character, to commercial commissions, chambers of commerce, etc. . . . The principal thing for the conqueror is the outspoken will to rule and the will to destroy the political and national life of the conquered. . . .

Question for Analysis

1. Why is an ideology based on biological racism particularly dangerous?

Conquest and Kultur, compiled by Wallace Notestein and Elmer E. Stoll (Washington, D.C.: Government Printing Office, 1917), 90–91.

Drumont, a French journalist, argued that the Jews, racially inferior and believers in a primitive religion, had gained control of France. Like medieval Christian anti-Semites, Drumont accused Jews of deicide and of using Christian blood for ritual purposes. Drumont's newspaper (established with Jesuit funds) blamed all the ills of France on the Jews, called for their expulsion from the country, and predicted that they would be massacred. French politicians played the anti-Semitic card in order to gain popularity and votes. Fully one-third of the Chamber of Deputies wanted to deprive Jews of the civil rights that they had gained during the French Revolution.

Romania barred most Jews from holding office and from voting, imposed various economic restrictions on them, and limited their admission into secondary schools and universities.

The Romanian government even financed an international congress of anti-Semites, which met in Bucharest in 1886. In German-speaking Austria, Karl Lueger, a leader of the Christian Social Party, founded by conservative German nationalists, exploited anti-Semitism to win elections in overwhelmingly Catholic Vienna. Georg von Schönerer, founder of the German National Party in Austria, wanted to eliminate Jews from all areas of public life.

Russia placed a quota on the number of Jewish students admitted to secondary schools and higher educational institutions, confined Jews to certain regions of the country, and, "to purify the sacred historic capital," expelled about twenty thousand Jews from Moscow. Some government officials encouraged or did nothing to stop *pogroms* (mob violence) against Jews. Between 1903 and 1906, pogroms broke out in 690 towns and villages, most of them in the Ukraine, traditionally a hotbed of anti-Semitism. (Ukrainian folksongs and legends glorified centuries-old massacres of Jews.) The attackers looted, burned, raped, and murdered, generally with impunity. In Russia and several other lands, Jews were put on trial for slaughtering Christian children as part of a Passover ritual—a deranged accusation that survived from the Middle Ages.

Anti-Semitism had a long and bloodstained history in Europe, stemming both from an irrational fear and hatred of outsiders with noticeably different ways and from the commonly accepted myth that the Jews as a people were collectively and eternally cursed for rejecting Christ. Christians saw Jews as the murderers of Christ—an image that promoted terrible anger and hatred. In the Middle Ages, mobs periodically humiliated, tortured, and massacred Jews, and rulers expelled them from their kingdoms. Often barred from owning land and excluded from the craft guilds, medieval Jews concentrated in trade and moneylending—occupations that frequently earned them greater hostility. By the sixteenth century, Jews in a number of lands were forced by law to live in separate quarters of the town, called *ghettos*. Medieval Christian anti-Semitism, which depicted the Jew as vile and Judaism as repulsive, fertilized the soil for modern anti-Semitism.

In the nineteenth century, under the aegis of the liberal ideals of the Enlightenment and the French Revolution, Jews gained legal equality in most European lands. They could leave the ghetto, vote, hold office, and participate in many activities that had been closed to them. Jews took advantage of this new freedom and opportunity.

Motivated by the fierce desire of outsiders to prove their worth and aided by deeply embedded traditions that valued education and family life, many Jews achieved striking success as entrepreneurs, bankers, lawyers, journalists, doctors, scientists, scholars, and performers. For example, in 1880, Jews, who constituted about 10 percent of the Viennese population, accounted for 38.6 percent of the medical students and 23.3 percent of the law students in Vienna. Viennese cultural life before World War I was to a large extent shaped by Jewish writers, artists, musicians, critics, and patrons. All but one of the major banking houses were Jewish. However, most European Jews—peasants, peddlers, and laborers—were quite poor, and many Russian Jews fled to the United States to escape from desperate poverty.

Like other bourgeois, the Jews who were members of the commercial and professional classes gravitated toward liberalism. Moreover, as victims of persecution, they naturally favored societies that were committed to the liberal ideals of legal equality, toleration, the rule of law, and equality of opportunity. Because they strongly supported parliamentary government and the entire system of values associated with the Enlightenment, the Jews became targets for conservatives and Volkish thinkers, who repudiated the humanist and cosmopolitan outlook of liberalism and professed a militant nationalism. To Volkish thinkers, the West represented an alien culture hostile to German racial-national identity—and the Jews, an alien race, symbolized the West.

Anti-Semites invented a mythical evil, the Jew, whom they blamed for all the social and economic ills caused by the rapid growth of industries and cities and for all the new ideas that were undermining the old order. Their anxieties and fears concentrated on the Jews, to whom they attributed everything they considered to be wrong in the modern age, all that threatened the

German Volk. In the mythical world of Volkish thinkers, the Jews were regarded as foreign intruders who could never be loyal to the fatherland; as a lower form of humanity that could infect and weaken the German race; as bearers of a racial soul that precluded them from understanding and contributing to German culture, which they only debased; and as international conspirators who were plotting to dominate Germany and the world. This latter accusation was a secularized and updated version of the medieval myth that Jews were plotting to destroy Christendom. In an extraordinary display of irrationality, Volkish thinkers held that Jews throughout the world were gaining control over political parties, the press, and the economy in order to dominate the planet.

The myth of a Jewish world conspiracy found its culminating expression in a notorious forgery, the *Protocols of the Elders of Zion.* The *Protocols,* written in France by someone in the service of the Russian secret police, sought to justify the tsarist regime's anti-Semitic policies. The forger concocted a tale of a meeting of Jewish elders in the Jewish cemetery of Prague. In these eerie surroundings, the elders plot to take over the world. First published in Russia in 1903, the *Protocols* was widely distributed after World War I and widely believed.

German anti-Semites viewed the *Protocols* as convincing evidence that the Jews were responsible for starting World War I, for Germany's defeat, and for the revolution that toppled the monarchy at the war's end. Nazi propagandists exploited the *Protocols* to justify their quest for power. Even after the *Protocols* was exposed as a blatant forgery, it continued to be translated, believed, and distributed. For anti-Semites, the myth of a Jewish world conspiracy had become an integrating principle; it provided satisfying answers to the crucial questions of existence.

In the Middle Ages, Jews had been persecuted and humiliated primarily for religious reasons. In the nineteenth century, national-racial considerations supplemented the traditional, biased Christian perception of Jews and Judaism. But whereas Christian anti-Semites believed that Jews could escape the curse of their religion through conversion, racial anti-Semites, who used the language of Social Darwinism, said that Germans and Jews belonged to different species of the human race, that Jews were indelibly stained and eternally condemned by their biological makeup. Their evil and worthlessness derived from inherited racial characteristics, which could not be altered by conversion. As one anti-Semitic deputy stated in a speech before the German Reichstag in 1895,

> *If one designates the whole of Jewry, one does so in the knowledge that the racial qualities of this people are such that in the long run they cannot harmonize with the racial qualities of the Germanic peoples and that every Jew who at this moment has not done anything bad may nevertheless under the proper conditions do precisely that, because his racial qualities drive him to do it. . . . [T]he Jews . . . operate like parasites . . . the Jews are cholera germs.*[4]

The Jewish population of Germany was quite small: in 1900, it was only about 497,000, or 0.95 percent, of the total population of 50,626,000. Jews were proud of their many contributions to German economic and cultural life (by the 1930s, 30 percent of the Nobel Prize winners in Germany were Jews). They considered themselves patriotic Germans, relished German literature and music, and regarded Germany as an altogether desirable place to live—a place of refuge and opportunity in comparison to Russia, where Jews lived in terrible poverty and suffered violent attacks.

German anti-Semitic organizations and political parties failed to get the state to pass anti-Semitic laws, and by the early 1900s, these groups had declined in political power and importance. But the mischief had been done. In the minds of many Germans, even in respectable circles, the image of the Jew as an evil and dangerous creature had been firmly planted. It was perpetuated by schools, youth groups, the Pan-German Association, and an array of racist pamphlets and books. Late-nineteenth-century racial anti-Semites had constructed an ideological foundation on which Hitler would later build his movement. In words that foreshadowed Hitler, Paul de Lagarde, professor of oriental languages, said of the Jews: "One does not have dealings with pests and parasites; one does not rear them and cherish them; one destroys them as speedily and thoroughly as possible."[5]

It is, of course, absurd to believe that a nation of fifty million was threatened by half a million citizens of Jewish birth, or that the eleven million Jews of the world (by 1900) had organized to rule the planet. The Jewish birthrate in Germany was low, the rate of intermarriage high, and the desire for complete assimilation into German life great. Within a few generations, the Jewish community in Germany might well have disappeared. Contrary to the paranoid claims of the anti-Semites, the German Jews and the Jews in the rest of Europe were actually quite powerless. There were scarcely any Jews in the ruling circles of governments, armies, civil services, or heavy industries. As events were to prove, the Jews, with no army or state and dwelling in lands where many despised them, were the weakest of peoples. But the race mystics, convinced that they were waging a war of self-defense against a satanic foe, were impervious to rational argument. Anti-Semites, said Theodor Mommsen, the great nineteenth-century German historian, would not listen to "logical and ethical arguments. . . . They listen only to their own envy and hatred, to the meanest instincts. Nothing else counts for them. They are deaf to reason, right, morals. One cannot influence them. . . . [Anti-Semitism] is a horrible epidemic, like cholera—one can neither explain nor cure it."[6]

Racial nationalism, a major element in nineteenth-century intellectual life, attacked and undermined the Enlightenment tradition. Racial nationalists denied equality, scorned toleration, dismissed the idea of the oneness of humanity, and made myth and superstition vital forces in political life. They distorted reason and science to demonize and condemn an entire people and to justify humiliation and persecution. They presented a pathogenic racial ideology, fraught with unreason and hate, as something virtuous and idealistic. That many people, including the educated and the elite, accepted these racial doctrines was an ominous sign for Western civilization. It made plain the tenuousness of the rational tradition of the Enlightenment and showed how receptive the mind is to dangerous myths and how easily human behavior can degenerate into inhumanity.

The Emergence of the New Imperialism

The Second Industrial Revolution coincided with an age of imperialism as European states (and the United States) extended their hegemony over much of the globe. Why did Westerners strive to claim and control most of the world?

Causes

Some historians suggest that the *new imperialism* (to differentiate it from the *colonialism* of settlement and trade that flourished from the sixteenth to the eighteenth century) was a direct result of industrialization. As economic activity and competition intensified, Europeans struggled for raw materials, markets for their manufactured goods, and places to invest their capital. In the late nineteenth century, many politicians and industrialists believed that the only way for their nations to ensure their economic necessities was through the acquisition of overseas territories.

Captains of industry defended the new empires to their sometimes reluctant governments and compatriots, predicting dire consequences if their nation failed to get its share of the world markets and resources. However, their expectations often did not materialize. Historians point to the fact that most areas claimed by Europeans and Americans did not possess profitable sources of raw materials or enough wealth to be good markets. For Europeans and Americans, the primary trading and investment areas were Europe and America rather than Asia or Africa. Some individual businesses made colonial profits, but most colonies proved unprofitable for the Western taxpayer.

The economic motivations for imperialism are inseparable from the intensely nationalistic one: the desire to win glory for the nation. Nationalists in newly unified Germany and Italy demanded colonies as recognition of their countries' Great Power status. Convinced that Britain's standing depended on colonies and naval power, they wanted their nations as well to "have a place in the sun." After its inglorious defeat by Prussia in 1870, France also turned its attention overseas, hoping to recoup some prestige and to add to its manpower (by recruiting colonials) and wealth for future European struggles. For a time, the nationalistic competition among the Europeans led them to extend their power struggles to Africa and Asia.

With its image of national vitality and competition between the fit and the unfit, Social Darwinism was the most extreme ideological expression of nationalism. Social Darwinists vigorously advocated the acquisition of empires as a sign of the nation's strength in the struggle for survival. To them, Europeans—as demonstrated by their advances in science and technology—were more fit than Asians or Africans to prevail in the struggle for dominance. In the popular mind, survival of the fittest justified the exploitation of "lesser breeds" by superior races. This language of race and conflict, of superior and inferior people, was widely used, particularly in Germany, Britain, and the United States.

Not all advocates of empire were Social Darwinists, however. Some believed that the extension of empire, law, order, and industrial civilization would raise "backward peoples" up the ladder of civilization. Many Westerners deemed it their duty as Christians to set an example and to uplift and convert Africans and Asians. Christian missionaries who went to unexplored African regions to preach against slavery, which was still carried on by Arab and African traders, believed that to end slavery, Europeans must provide law, order, and stability.

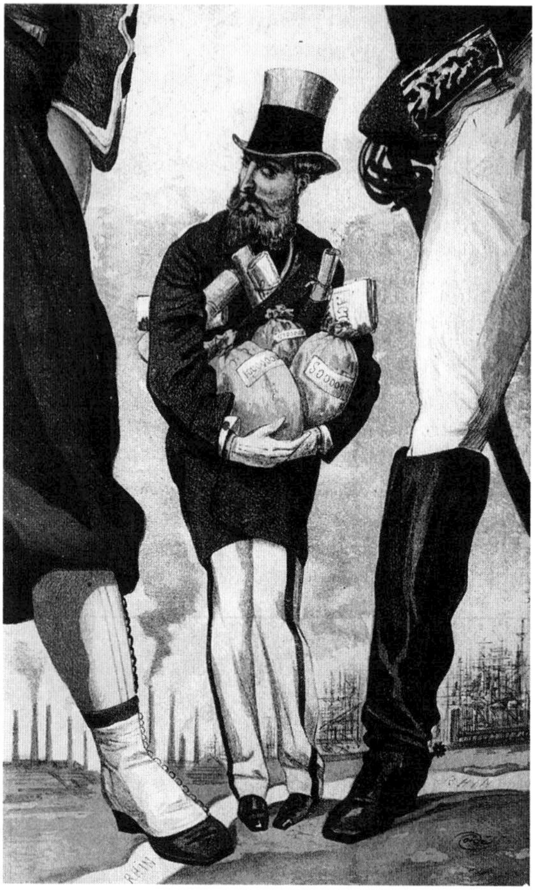

Leopold II of Belgium. The Belgian king had such extravagant tastes and habits that he operated as a private entrepreneur in the Congo, amassing a great fortune. His moneymaking created conditions that were so bad, akin to slavery, that Belgium's parliament took the territory away from him. His claim to the Congo, however, sparked the Great Powers into laying claim to much of Africa.

Control and Resistance

Aided by superior technology and the machinery of the modern state, Europeans established varying degrees of political control over much of the rest of the world. Control could mean outright annexation and the governing of a territory as a colony. In this way, Germany controlled Tanganyika (in east-central Africa) after 1886, and Britain ruled much of India. Control could also mean status as a protectorate, an arrangement whereby the local ruler continued to rule but was directed, or "protected," by a Great Power. That is how the British controlled Egypt after 1882 and maintained authority over their dependent Indian princes, and how France guarded Tunisia. There were also spheres of influence, where, without military or political control, a European nation had special trading and legal privileges that other Europeans did not have. At the turn of the century, the Russians and the British divided Persia (Iran), each recognizing the other's sphere of influence—Russia's in the north and Britain's in the south.

In some non-Western lands, the governing authorities granted Europeans extraterritoriality, or the right of foreigners to a trial by their own laws in other countries. Often, too, Europeans lived a segregated and privileged life in quarters, clubs, and whole sections of foreign lands or cities in which no native was allowed to live.

Many non-Europeans resisted American and European economic penetration and political control in varied ways, and the very process of resistance shaped their history and their self-awareness. Such resistance became a statement of both national and individual identity. It could be violent: the many instances of violent resistance included the Sudanese Muslims' holy war led by the Mahdi Mohammed Ahmed against both Egyptian fellow Muslims, who were regarded as agents of the European nonbelievers, and the Europeans; the Boxer Rebellion in China; and the Sepoy Mutiny in India. Some resisters reacted to Western penetration by arousing nationalist sentiments among their people and by strengthening their nations, sometimes even going to Western universities, military schools, and factories to master the West's modern ways, including advanced technology. Mohandas Gandhi, Jawaharlal Nehru, Sun Zhongshan (Sun Yat-sen), Jiang Jieshi (Chiang Kai-shek), and Mustapha Kemal Atatürk were the most famous leaders of nationalistic resistance to the West.

European Domination of Asia

Western influence in Asia expanded during the middle decades of the nineteenth century. Increased contact with Western ideas and institutions had a profound impact on Asian societies.

India

In the last part of the eighteenth century, the British East India Company became a territorial power in India. It gained the upper hand by making alliances with warring princes, by carrying on trade and collecting taxes, and by commanding armies of *sepoys* (native soldiers). Parliament regulated the chartered monopoly enterprise but in fact did not control it much until the Sepoy Mutiny of 1857–1858. (The Indians call this massive act of resistance the Great Rebellion.) This major popular uprising joined Muslim and Hindu soldiers with some native princes, who finally perceived that the British, rather than neighboring princes, were the true threat to their authority. With the aid of faithful troops from the Punjab, the British repressed the uprising. The rebellion caused Parliament to abolish the East India Company and to make India an integral part of the British Empire. The British ruled some states through dependent Indian princes, but about two-thirds of the subcontinent was ruled directly by about a thousand British officials in the civil service.

At first, the civil service was entirely British, its officials confident of the superiority of their people, law, and society. Later, an elite of Indians, educated in English and trained in administration, became part of it. Indian civil servants, along with soldiers recruited from peoples with military traditions, such as the Gurkhas and the Punjabis, carried out British laws, adding their own interpretations, customs, and traditions. By 1900, a civil service of four thousand Europeans and half a million Indians ruled some three hundred million Indians.

The British built a modern railroad and communications system and developed agriculture and industry to meet the needs of the world market. As a link to areas of food surplus, the railroad reduced the incidence and impact of local famines, which had plagued India's history. British rule also ended internal war and disorder. Population increased as fewer people died of starvation and lives were saved by Western medical practices. But many students of history believe that the Indian masses did not benefit from the economic progress because their landlords now demanded that they pay their debts in money instead of the customary produce. Furthermore, the British flooded the Indian market with cheap, machine-produced English goods, driving native artisans out of business or even deeper into debt.

The racism that excluded the Indian elite from British clubs, hotels, and social gatherings and from top government positions alienated the leaders British rule had created. Many of the older elite of princes and landlords who may have profited from British connections resented the lack of respect for Indian traditions and culture. Educated Indians, demanding equality and self-government, created the Indian National Congress in the

The Sepoy Rebellion: Repelling a Sortie Before Delhi. When Indian troops (Muslims and Hindus) rebelled against foreigners in 1857–1858, the British presence was seriously threatened. Here British rifles defending Delhi sound the retreat. Thinking the troops had withdrawn, the Sepoys were badly defeated when they advanced. "The Mutiny," as the British saw it, or "the Great Rebellion," as the Indians saw it, was short-lived, but relations between Indians and Britons changed forever as the British segregated themselves socially from the people they governed.

1880s. The Congress Party ultimately organized masses of Indians to work toward independence.

In 1919, at Amritsar in Punjab, a British officer commanded his Gurkha troops to fire into a peaceful demonstration until their ammunition was exhausted; 379 Indians died and 1,200 were wounded. Women and children were among the victims. The government punished the officer, but the British community in India gave him a fortune, honoring him for what he had done. The massacre and British behavior stung Indians to action—even those Indians who had supported the British.

Out of this feverish period emerged a gentle but determined revolutionary leader, Mohandas K. Gandhi (1869–1948). He had led the resistance to the vicious system of racial discrimination faced by the Indian community in South Africa and, in the process, developed a doctrine of civil disobedience and nonviolent resistance. He believed that the power of love and spiritual purity would ultimately overthrow British rule in India. His was a spiritually uplifting message and a shrewd political tactic as well. Gandhi called on the Indian elite to give up the privileges allotted by the British and to resign their positions, boycott British schools, and boycott all foreign goods. He dramatically rallied mass support with "the march to the sea": a mass refusal to pay taxes on salt. When imprisoned, Gandhi and his followers fasted for spiritual discipline. But their tactic also threatened the British, for if the confined leaders should starve to death, more civil disturbances might erupt. Gandhi also emphasized the boycott of foreign goods by spinning cotton and wearing

Map 16.1 Asia in 1914 In addition to the lands ▶ depicted in the map under European and American domination, Western states also exercised control over technically sovereign states, particularly China and Siam (Thailand).

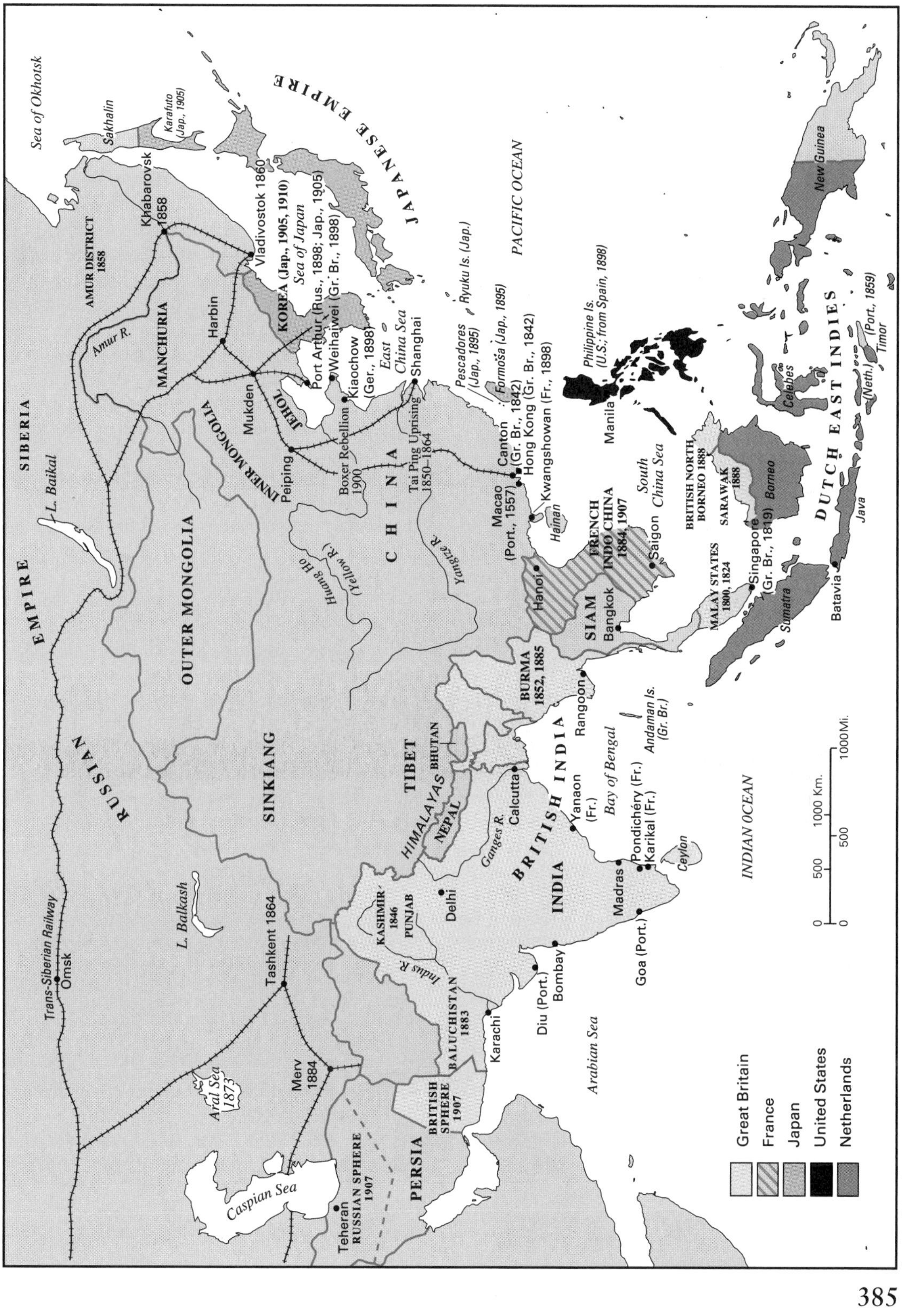
Sea of Okhotsk
Sakhalin
Karafuto (Jap., 1905)
JAPANESE EMPIRE
Khabarovsk 1858
AMUR DISTRICT 1858
Vladivostok 1860
KOREA (Jap., 1905, 1910)
Sea of Japan
Port Arthur (Rus., 1898; Jap., 1905)
Weihaiwei (Gr. Br., 1898)
Kiaochow (Ger., 1898)
East China Sea
Shanghai
Ryuku Is. (Jap.)
PACIFIC OCEAN
Pescadores (Jap., 1895)
Formosa (Jap., 1895)
Canton (Gr. Br., 1842)
Hong Kong (Gr. Br., 1842)
Kwangshowan (Fr., 1898)
Philippine Is. (U.S.; from Spain, 1898)
Manila
SIBERIA
L. Baikal
Amur R.
MANCHURIA
Harbin
Mukden
JEHOL
INNER MONGOLIA
Peiping
Boxer Rebellion 1900
Tai Ping Uprising 1850–1864
CHINA
Macao (Port., 1557)
Hainan
South China Sea
BRITISH NORTH BORNEO 1888
SARAWAK 1888
Borneo
New Guinea
Celebes
DUTCH EAST INDIES
(Port., 1859) Timor
(Neth.)
Java
Batavia
Sumatra
Singapore (Gr. Br., 1819)
MALAY STATES 1800, 1824
FRENCH INDO CHINA 1884, 1907
Saigon
Hanoi
SIAM
Bangkok
Hwang Ho (Yellow R.)
Yangtze R.
RUSSIAN EMPIRE
OUTER MONGOLIA
SINKIANG
TIBET
BHUTAN
NEPAL
HIMALAYAS
BURMA 1852, 1885
Rangoon
Andaman Is. (Gr. Br.)
Bay of Bengal
Calcutta
Yanaon (Fr.)
Ganges R.
BRITISH INDIA
INDIA
Pondichéry (Fr.)
Karikal (Fr.)
Madras
Ceylon
INDIAN OCEAN
Delhi
KASHMIR 1846
PUNJAB
Indus R.
BALUCHISTAN 1883
Karachi
Bombay
Diu (Port.)
Goa (Port.)
Arabian Sea
Trans-Siberian Railway
Omsk
L. Balkash
Tashkent 1864
Merv 1884
Aral Sea 1873
Caspian Sea
Teheran
RUSSIAN SPHERE 1907
PERSIA
BRITISH SPHERE 1907
0 500 1000 Km.
0 500 1000 Mi.
Great Britain
France
Japan
United States
Netherlands

simple native dress. To gain independence, Gandhi was even willing to sacrifice the higher standard of living that an industrial economy could bring to India.

Independence finally came after World War II had exhausted British resources and reduced British power. It was achieved without a war between Britain and India—an accomplishment that many credit to the strength of Gandhi's moral leadership. But even his leadership could not prevent the partition of the country into Muslim Pakistan and predominantly Hindu India. Nor could it prevent conflict between Hindus and Muslims, as bloody massacres following independence clearly revealed.

China

The defeat of the Chinese by the British in the Opium War of 1839–1842 forced the Manchu dynasty to open trade with the West. Before the war, such commerce had been limited, controlled by native monopolists to whom the emperor had granted trading privileges. When the Chinese government destroyed Indian opium being traded by the East India Company, the British aggressively asserted their right to free trade and demanded compensation. In the subsequent war, Britain seized several trading cities along the coast, including Hong Kong, and the Chinese capitulated. In the Treaty of Nanking (1842), the British insisted on determining the tariffs that the Chinese might charge them. Furthermore, British subjects in China would have the right to be tried according to their own law (the right of extraterritoriality). Both provisions undermined the emperor's ability to control the foreigners in his country.

Defeat in the Opium War also forced change on the emperor. He drew on China's mandarins (high officials) to revitalize the Manchu bureaucracy by cleaning out much of the official corruption, which weighed heavily on the poorest taxpayers, and by strengthening China against the Westerners, sometimes by hiring Westerners to train Chinese armies. Nevertheless, widespread economic discontent, hatred of the Manchu (who were regarded by many Chinese as foreign conquerors, even though the conquest had taken place some two hundred years earlier), and religious mysticism led to the Taiping Rebellion of 1850–1864. This uprising seriously threatened the dynasty, which called on Western assistance to suppress the rebels. For this aid, Britain and France extorted additional concessions from the emperor.

For a time, the Europeans seemed content with trading rights in coastal towns and preferential treatment for their subjects. But the Sino-Japanese War of 1894–1895, which Japan won easily because of China's weakness, encouraged the Europeans to mutilate China. Britain, France, Russia, and Germany all scrambled for concessions, protectorates, and spheres of influence. The United States, which insisted that it be given any trading concession that any other state received, proclaimed an "Open Door" policy: that trade should be open to all and that the Great Powers should respect China's territorial integrity. The U.S. action may have restrained the Western powers from partitioning China, but it was also a way to safeguard American interests there.

Chinese traditionalists organized secret societies to expel foreigners and to punish those Chinese who accepted Christianity or any other form of westernization. In 1900, encouraged by Empress Tzu-hsi, the Society of Righteous and Harmonious Fists (called the Boxers by Europeans) attacked foreigners throughout the north of China. An international army of Europeans, Japanese, and Americans suppressed the rebellion, seized Chinese treasures, and forced China to pay an indemnity. They also made China agree to the stationing of foreign troops on its soil.

Chinese discontent with the dynasty deepened, as did unrest and nationalistic opposition to the foreigners. When the Japanese defeated the Russians in 1905, many Chinese argued that the only way to protect their country was to imitate the West, as the Japanese had done. Many signs of growing nationalism appeared. In 1911, nationalist revolutionaries, strongly present among soldiers, workers, and students, overthrew the Manchu and declared a republic. Sun Zhongshan (Sun Yat-sen, 1866–1925), who was in the United States when the revolution broke out, returned to China to become the first president of the republic and the head of the Nationalist Party.

Espousing the Western ideas of democracy, nationalism, and social welfare (the three principles of the people, as Sun called them), the republic struggled to establish its authority over a China torn by civil war and ravaged by foreigners. Russia was claiming Mongolia, and Britain was claiming Tibet. The northern warlords, who were regional leaders with private armies, resisted any attempt to strengthen the republic's army because it might diminish their power. In the south, however, the republic more or less maintained control. After Sun's death, the Guomindong (Kuomintang), under the authoritarian leadership of Jiang Jieshi (Chiang Kai-shek, 1887–1975), tried to westernize by using the military power of the state and introducing segments of a modern economic system. But attacked both from within by the Communists led by Mao Zedong (Mao Tse-tung, 1893–1976), and by the Japanese after 1931, the Guomindong made slow progress. A divided China continued to be at the mercy of outside interests until after World War II.

Japan

Japan, like China, was opened to the West against its will. The Japanese had expelled Europeans in the seventeenth century, remaining isolated for the next two hundred years. By the 1850s, however, as in India and China, social dissension within Japan and foreign pressure combined to force the country to admit outside trade. Americans in particular refused to accept Japanese prohibitions on commercial and religious contacts. Like China, Japan succumbed to superior technological power. In 1853, Commodore Matthew C. Perry sailed into Tokyo Bay, making a show of American strength and forcing the Japanese to sign a number of treaties that granted westerners extraterritoriality and control over tariffs.

A flood of violence surged over Japan. Determined to preserve Japan's independence, a group of *samurai*, the warrior nobility, seized the government. This takeover—the Meiji Restoration of 1867—returned power to the emperor, or Meiji, from the feudal aristocracy, which had ruled in his name for almost seven hundred years. The new government enacted a series of reforms, turning Japan into a powerful, modern, unitary state. Large landowners were persuaded to give their estates to the emperor in exchange for compensation and high-level positions in the government. All classes were made equal before the law. As in France and Germany, universal military service was required, which diminished social privilege and helped to imbue Japanese of all classes with nationalism. The Japanese modeled their constitution on Bismarck's: there was a parliament, but the emperor held the most authority, which he delegated to his ministers to govern in his name without much control from the parliament.

The Meiji regime introduced modern industry and economic competition. Japanese visited factories all over the West and hired Westerners to teach industrial skills. The government built defense industries, backed heavy industry and mining, and developed a modern communications system of railways, roads, and telegraphs. Industry in Japan adopted traditional Japanese values and emphasized cooperation more than competition; relations between employer and employee were paternalistic rather than individualistic and deferential rather than hostile. Within little more than a generation of the Meiji Restoration, Japan moved from economic backwardness to a place among the top ten industrial nations. To underdeveloped countries, Japan became a model of a nation that borrowed from the West yet preserved its traditional values and social structure.

By 1900, Japan had ended the humiliating treaties with the West and become an imperialist power in its own right. It had won Taiwan and Korea in its war with China in 1894–1895, although the Great Powers intervened, forcing the Japanese to return some of the spoils of victory while they themselves grabbed greater spheres of influence from the helpless Chinese. Their self-serving maneuvering infuriated the Japanese. Finally, in 1904, conflict over influence in Manchuria brought Japan and Russia to war, which Japan won. The victory of an Asian power over a Western power had a tremendous impact on Asian nationalists. If Japan could unite its people with nationalism and strong leadership, others should be able to do likewise. Japan's victory inspired anti-Western and nationalist movements throughout China, Indochina, India, and the Middle East.

In the 1930s, extreme militarist and nationalistic groups, which were set on imperial expansion in China, gained the upper hand in Japan. To Asians in the 1930s, Japan seemed to champion Asian racial equality and to oppose Western imperialism. Many leaders of nationalist movements in Burma, India, Indochina, and Indonesia were attracted for a time by Japan's pose. World War II, however, brought Japanese occupation and exploitation, not freedom and equality for Asians.

The Scramble for Africa

The most rapid European expansion took place in Africa. Until the 1870s, Great Power interest in Africa seemed marginal and likely to decline even further. As late as 1880, European nations ruled just a tenth of the continent. Only three decades later, by 1914, Europeans had claimed all of Africa except Liberia (a small territory of freed slaves from the United States) and Ethiopia, which had successfully held off Italian invaders at Adowa in 1896.

The activities of Leopold II, the king of Belgium, spurred expansion. In 1876, as a private entrepreneur, he formed the International Association for the Exploration and Civilization of Central Africa. Leopold sent Henry Stanley (1841–1904) to the Congo River Basin to establish trading posts, sign treaties with the chiefs, and claim the territory for the association. Stanley, an adventurer and a newspaper reporter who had fought on both sides of the American Civil War, had earlier led an expedition to Central Africa in search of David Livingstone, the popular missionary explorer, who was believed to be in danger. For men like Stanley, Leopold's private development efforts promised profit and adventure. For the Africans, they promised brutal exploitation. The French responded to Leopold's actions by immediately establishing a protectorate on the north bank of the Congo. The scramble was on.

The Berlin Conference

Bismarck and Jules Ferry, the premier of France, called an international conference of the Great Powers in Berlin in 1884 to lay some ground rules for the development of Africa south of the Sahara. The Berlin Conference established the rule that a European country had to occupy territory in order to claim it. This led to a mad race to the interior of Africa; it was a field day for explorers and soldiers. As Europeans rushed to claim territory, they ignored both natural and cultural frontiers. Even today, the map of Africa reveals many straight (and thus artificial) boundary lines, rather than the irregular lines of natural boundaries, such as rivers and mountains.

The conference declared that Leopold (as an individual, not as the king of Belgium) was the personal ruler of the Congo Free State. Before long, Leopold's Congo Association was trying to turn a profit with practices as vicious as those of the African slave traders. At the turn of the century, Edward D. Morel, an English humanitarian, produced evidence that slavery, mutilation, brutality, and murder were commonly practiced to force blacks to work for the rubber plantations in the Congo. In response to the outcry of public opinion, in 1908 the Belgian parliament declared the territory a Belgian colony, thus putting an end to Leopold's private enterprise.

The British in Africa

For much of the nineteenth century, British interest in Africa was minimal. The opening in 1869 of the Suez Canal, which Britain viewed as a vital highway to India, greatly increased the strategic value of Egypt. Officially a part of the Ottoman Empire, Egypt had in effect been independent of the Ottoman sultan since the 1830s. When a nearly bankrupt Egypt could not pay its foreign debts and was threatened with internal rebellion, Britain intervened as "protector" in 1882. Prime Minister Gladstone, a "little Englander" (one who opposed empire), promised to withdraw British troops once the situation stabilized.

Not only did the British fail to withdraw from Egypt, they also moved further south into the Sudan to quell a Muslim holy war against Egyptian authority and British influence. In 1885, the Sudanese, led

Map 16.2 Africa in 1914 Africa's rapid ▶ dismemberment is pictured in these two maps. In 1878, there were few enclaves of Europeans along the coasts. By 1914, Africa had been carved up, and all but Ethiopia and Liberia had been claimed.

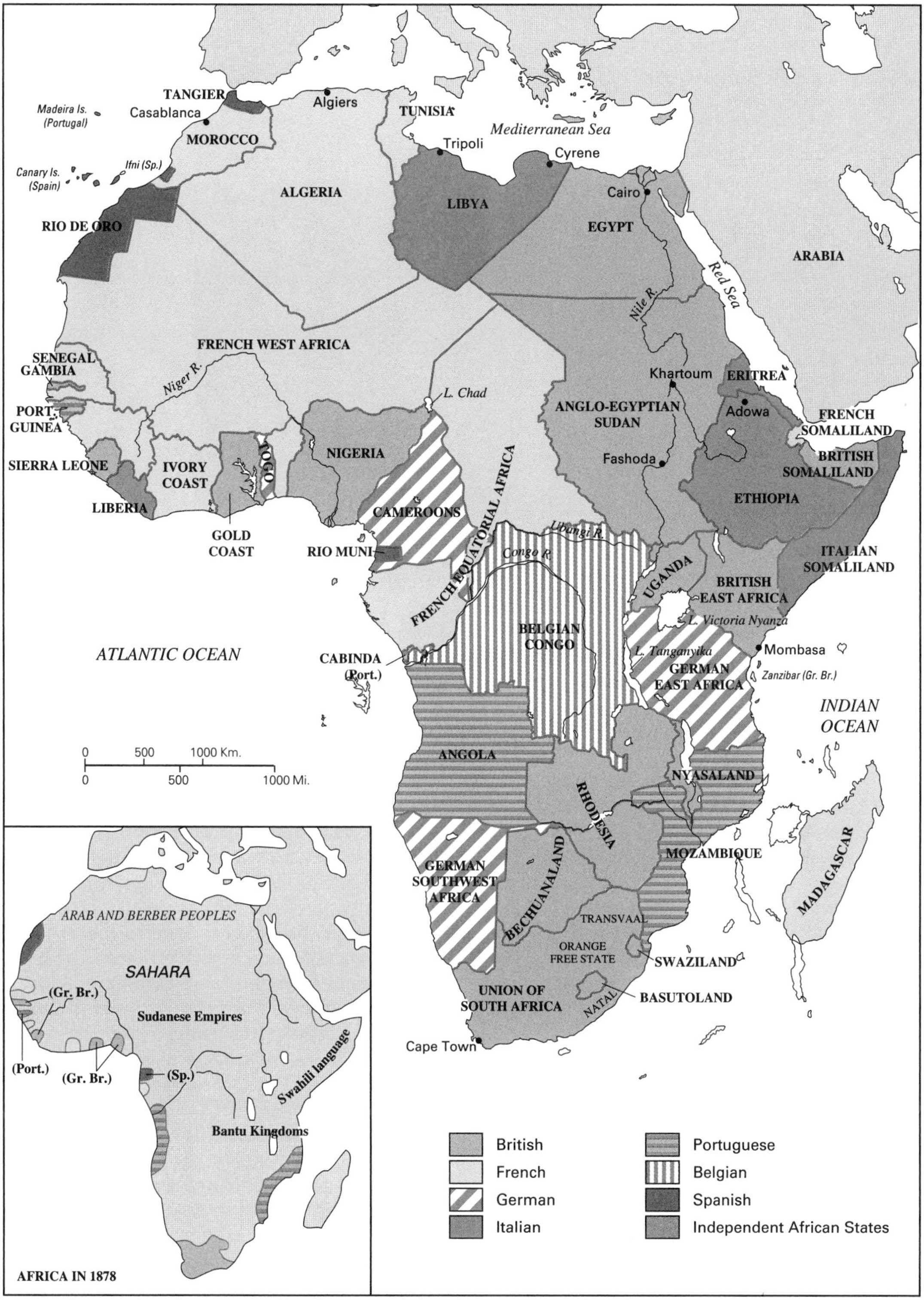
TANGIER
Madeira Is. (Portugal)
Casablanca
Algiers
TUNISIA
Mediterranean Sea
MOROCCO
Tripoli
Cyrene
Canary Is. (Spain)
Ifni (Sp.)
ALGERIA
Cairo
LIBYA
RIO DE ORO
EGYPT
ARABIA
Red Sea
Nile R.
FRENCH WEST AFRICA
SENEGAL
GAMBIA
Niger R.
Khartoum
ERITREA
L. Chad
PORT. GUINEA
ANGLO-EGYPTIAN SUDAN
Adowa
FRENCH SOMALILAND
SIERRA LEONE
IVORY COAST
TOGO
NIGERIA
Fashoda
BRITISH SOMALILAND
LIBERIA
CAMEROONS
FRENCH EQUATORIAL AFRICA
ETHIOPIA
GOLD COAST
RIO MUNI
Ubangi R.
Congo R.
UGANDA
ITALIAN SOMALILAND
BRITISH EAST AFRICA
L. Victoria Nyanza
BELGIAN CONGO
ATLANTIC OCEAN
CABINDA (Port.)
L. Tanganyika
Mombasa
GERMAN EAST AFRICA
Zanzibar (Gr. Br.)
INDIAN OCEAN
0 500 1000 Km.
0 500 1000 Mi.
ANGOLA
NYASALAND
RHODESIA
MOZAMBIQUE
GERMAN SOUTHWEST AFRICA
BECHUANALAND
MADAGASCAR
TRANSVAAL
ORANGE FREE STATE
SWAZILAND
UNION OF SOUTH AFRICA
NATAL
BASUTOLAND
Cape Town
ARAB AND BERBER PEOPLES
SAHARA
(Gr. Br.)
Sudanese Empires
(Port.)
(Gr. Br.)
(Sp.)
Swahili language
Bantu Kingdoms
AFRICA IN 1878
British
French
German
Italian
Portuguese
Belgian
Spanish
Independent African States

Eileen Tweedy/The Art Archive.

THE BATTLE OF OMDURMAN, 1898. A romanticized oil painting depicts the British lancers at the battle of Omdurman in heroic terms. The Muslim fundamentalists who followed the Mahdi in his attempts to expel the Egyptians and British from the Sudan were massacred in 1898 by General Kitchener. As many as 11,000 dervishes were killed, but the British suffered only slight casualties. Paintings such as this fed the public hunger for heroism and thirst for exotic places.

by the Mahdi, who viewed himself as the successor to Muhammad, captured Khartoum and killed the popular General Charles Gordon, the recently appointed governor-general of the Sudan. In 1898, the British, armed with machine guns, mowed down charging Muslims at Omdurman by the thousands, suffering only slight casualties themselves.

Immediately after the battle, British forces confronted the French at Fashoda in the Sudan. In the diplomatic crisis that followed, Britain and France were brought to the brink of war, and public passions were inflamed. However, since France was too divided by the Dreyfus affair at home to risk a showdown with Britain, the French cabinet ordered retreat.

The British also sought territory in South Africa. Cecil Rhodes (1853–1902), who had gone to South Africa for his health in 1870 and made a fortune in diamonds and gold, dreamed of expanding the British Empire. "The British," he declared, "are the finest race in the world and the more of the world we inhabit the better it is for the human race."[7] Rhodes was responsible for acquiring Rhodesia (Zimbabwe), a sizable and wealthy territory, for Britain. He also plotted to involve Britain in a war with the Boers, Dutch farmers and cattlemen who had settled in South Africa in the seventeenth century.

During the Napoleonic wars, the British had gained Cape Town at the southern tip of Africa, a useful provisioning place for trading ships bound for India. Despising British rule and refusing to accept the British abolition of slavery in 1833, the Boers moved northward in a migration called the Great Trek (1835–1837), warring with African tribes along the way. They established two republics, the Transvaal and the Orange Free State, whose independence the British recognized in the 1850s. The republics' democratic practices did not extend to black Africans, who were denied political rights. In 1877, the British annexed the Transvaal, but Boer resistance forced them in 1881 to recognize the Transvaal's independence again.

The discovery of rich deposits of gold and diamonds in the Boer lands reinforced Rhodes's dream of building a great British empire in Africa. In 1895, his close friend Leander Jameson led some six hundred armed men into the Transvaal, hoping to create a pretext for a British invasion. Although the raid failed and both Jameson and Rhodes were disgraced, tensions between Britain and the Boer republics worsened, and in 1899 the Anglo-Boer War broke out.

The Boers were formidable opponents—farmers by day and commandos by night, armed with the latest French and German rifles. To deal with their stubborn foe, the British herded, or "concentrated," thousands of Boers, including women and children, into compounds surrounded by barbed wire, where some twenty-five thousand perished. The nasty war ended in 1902. Hoping to live together in peace with the Boers, the British drew up a conciliatory treaty. In 1910, the former Boer republics were joined with the British territories into the Union of South Africa. Self-government within the British Empire for the British settlers and the Boers did not help the majority black population; it still had to cope with the Boers' deeply entrenched racist attitudes.

Other European Countries in Africa

The cost of imperialism in Africa seemed high not only to the British, but to other imperialists as well. The Italians' defeat at Adowa (1896) by Ethiopians belied Italian dreams of empire and national glory. (Bismarck scoffed that the Italians had enormous appetites but very poor teeth.) Germans could take little heart from their African acquisitions—Southwest Africa (Namibia), East Africa (Tanzania, but not Zanzibar, which was British), the Cameroons, and Togo (part of Ghana today). The German colonies were the most efficiently governed (critics said the most ruthlessly controlled), but they yielded few benefits other than pride of ownership, because they were costly to govern. And the Belgians had obviously gained no prestige from the horrors perpetrated in the Congo. Serious thinkers, contemplating the depths to which Europeans would sink in search of fortune and fame, began to suggest that barbarity characterized the Europeans more than the Africans. The Europeans seemed to be the moral barbarians, as novelist Joseph Conrad and others pointed out. For the most part, honor was fleeting and profits illusory in these new African empires.

The Legacy of Imperialism

World War I was a turning point in the history of imperialism. The principle of self-determination, championed for European nationalities at the peace conference, was seized on by Asian and African intellectuals, who intensified their anti-imperialist efforts. After World War II, the exhausted colonial powers were reluctant to fight rebellious colonies. Moreover, after waging war to destroy Nazi imperialism and racism, European colonial powers had little moral justification to deny other peoples self-determination.

Decades after the decolonization of most of the world, the consequences of imperialism persist. To former colonial peoples, imperialism has been a source of great bitterness, not only because of its economic exploitation but also because of its encouragement of racism and callous disregard of other cultures. Thus, non-Western nationalism has often included anti-Western elements.

Imperialism accelerated the growth of a global market economy, completing the trend that started with the Commercial Revolution of the sixteenth and seventeenth centuries. At the beginning of the twentieth century, in many parts of Europe even the working classes and the peasantry were able to buy goods from faraway places—goods that had previously been available only to the very wealthy. The underdeveloped areas of the world, in turn, found markets for their crops and were able to buy European goods—at least, the wealthy could.

Imperialism has also fostered the spread of Western civilization around the globe. The influence of Western ideas, institutions, techniques, language, and culture is apparent everywhere. English and, to some extent, French are international languages. African and Asian lands have adopted, often with limited success, democracy and parliamentary government from the West. Socialism, a Western ideology, has been transplanted in some Third World countries. Industrialism and modern science, both achievements of the West, have become globalized. So, too, have Western agricultural techniques, business practices, medicine, legal procedures, school curricula, architecture, music, and dress. That Turkish women are no longer required to wear the veil, that Chinese women no longer have their feet bound, that Indians have outlawed untouchability, that (with exceptions) Arabs, Africans, and Indians no longer practice slavery—all these changes have occurred under the influence of Western ideas. (To be sure, cultural forms have not moved in only one direction: African and Asian ways have also influenced Western lands.) The impact of Western ways on Asian and African lands is one of the most crucial developments of our time.

❖ ❖ ❖

Notes

1. Cited in Edward R. Tannenbaum, *1900: The Generation Before the Great War* (Garden City, N.Y.: Doubleday, 1976), p. 337.
2. Quoted in Roger Chicklering, *Imperial Germany and the Great War, 1914–1918* (Cambridge: Cambridge University Press, 1998) p. 9.
3. Cited in Horst von Maltitz, *The Evolution of Hitler's Germany* (New York: McGraw-Hill, 1973), p. 33.
4. Quoted in Raul Hilberg, *The Destruction of the European Jews* (Chicago: Quadrangle, 1967), pp. 10–11.
5. Quoted in Helmut Krausnick, Hans Buchheim, Martin Broszat, and Hans-Adolf Jacobsen, *Anatomy of the SS State*, trans. Richard Barry et al. (London: William Collins Sons, 1968), p. 9.
6. Quoted in Peter G. J. Pulzer, *The Rise of Political Anti-Semitism in Germany and Austria* (New York: Wiley, 1964), p. 299.
7. Joseph E. Flint, *Cecil Rhodes* (Boston: Little, Brown, 1974), p. 248.

Suggested Reading

Blackburn, David, *History of Germany, 1780–1918: The Long Nineteenth Century* (2002). German cultural and national history.

Brunschwig, Henri, *French Colonialism: 1871–1914. Myths and Realities* (trans. 1964). An excellent study of French imperialism.

Fischer, Klaus P., *The History of an Obsession* (1998). A superb study of German–Jewish relations, particularly the delusionary character of anti-Jewish thinking.

Ford, Colin, and Brian Harrison, *A Hundred Years Ago* (1983). An excellent social history of Britain, with fine photographs.

Hochschild, Adam, *King Leopold's Ghost: A Story of Greed, Terror, and Heroism in Colonial Africa* (1998). A vivid account of Leopold's Congo Association's vicious exploitation of Africans.

Joll, James, *Europe Since 1870* (1973). A valuable general survey, particularly good on socialism in the individual nations.

Kemp, Tom, *Industrialization in Nineteenth-Century Europe* (1985). Readable general survey incorporating recent scholarship.

Mack Smith, Denis, *Italy: A Modern History, rev. ed.* (1969). An excellent survey, emphasizing the theme of the failure of Italy to develop viable liberal institutions or economic solutions.

———, *The Crisis of German Ideology* (1964). Explores the dark side of German nationalism; an excellent study of Volkish thought.

Packenham, Thomas, *The Scramble for Africa* (1991). A superb narrative.

——— , *Antisemitic Myths: A Historical and Contemporary Anthology* (2008). Documents illustrating the history and pathology of anti-Semitism.

Robinson, R. E., John Gallagher, and Alice Denny, *Africa and the Victorians: The Official Mind of Imperialism* (1961). An essential book for this fascinating subject; well written and controversial.

Rose, J. H., *Development of the European Nations, 1870–1914* (2005). Details European Politics and International Relations.

Thornton, A. P., *The Imperial Idea and Its Enemies: A Study in British Power, 2nd ed.* (1985). An interesting study of the ideas and policies of British imperialism.

Webb, R. K., *Modern England from the Eighteenth Century to the Present* (1968). A well-informed, readable book that is balanced on controversial issues.

CourseMate

Go to the CourseMate website at **www.cengagebrain.com** for additional study tools and review materials—including audio and video clips—for this chapter.

Chapter 17

Modern Consciousness: New Views of Nature, Human Nature, and the Arts

- **Irrationalism**
- **Freud: A New View of Human Nature**
- **Social Thought: Confronting the Irrational and the Complexities of Modern Society**
- **The Modernist Movement**
- **Modern Physics**
- **The Enlightenment Tradition in Disarray**

Focus Questions

1. In what ways did late modern thought and the arts break with the Enlightenment tradition?
2. How did the thought of Nietzsche, Bergson, and Sorel exemplify the growing power and appeal of irrationalism?
3. What did Freud contribute to an understanding of irrationalism? What is his relationship to the Enlightenment tradition?
4. How did the modernist movement in the arts break with the standards of esthetics that had governed European culture since the Renaissance?
5. How did modern physics alter the Newtonian conception of the universe?
6. In what ways was the Enlightenment tradition in disarray by the early twentieth century?

The modern mentality may be said to have passed through two broad phases: early modernity and late modernity. Formulated during the era of the Scientific Revolution and the Enlightenment, early modernity stressed confidence in reason, science, human goodness, and humanity's capacity to improve society. Then, in the late nineteenth and early twentieth centuries, a new outlook took shape. Late modern thinkers and scientists achieved revolutionary insights into human nature, the social world, and the physical universe; writers and artists opened up hitherto unimagined possibilities for artistic expression.

These developments produced a shift in European consciousness. The mechanical model of the universe, which had dominated the Western outlook since Newton, was fundamentally altered. The Enlightenment view of human rationality and goodness was questioned, and the belief in natural rights and objective standards governing morality came under attack. Rules of esthetics that had governed the arts since the Renaissance were discarded. Shattering old beliefs, late modernity left Europeans without landmarks—without generally accepted cultural standards or agreed-upon conceptions about human nature and the meaning of life.

The late modern period was marked by extraordinary creativity in thought and the arts. Yet imaginative and fruitful as these changes were for Western intellectual and cultural life, they also helped to create the disoriented, fragmented, and troubled era that characterized the twentieth century. ❖

IRRATIONALISM

While many intellectuals continued to adhere to the outlook identified with the Enlightenment, some thinkers in the late nineteenth century challenged the basic premises of the philosophes and their nineteenth-century heirs. In particular, they repudiated the Enlightenment conception of human rationality, stressing instead the irrational side of human nature. Regarding reason as sovereign, the philosophes had defined human beings by their capacity to think critically; now thinkers saw blind strivings and animal instincts as the primary fact of human existence. It seemed that reason exercised a very limited influence over human conduct, and that impulses, drives, and instincts—all forces below the surface—determined behavior much more than did logical consciousness. Carrying this view further, intellectuals argued that the universal principles advanced by rational thought often expressed self-interest, not truth.

The problem of irrationalism is manifold. Some thinkers, while recognizing the weakness of reason, continued to value it and sought to preserve it as an essential ingredient of civilized life. Some studied manifestations of the irrational in myth, religion, the arts, and politics in a logical and systematic way in order to gain a more complete understanding of human nature and human behavior. Others, concentrating on the creative potential of the irrational, urged nourishing the feelings, which they considered vital to artistic creativity and a richer existence. Still others celebrated violence as a healthy expression of the irrational.

The new insights into the irrational side of human nature and the growing assault on reason had immense implications for political life. In succeeding decades, these currents of irrationalism would become ideologized and politicized by unscrupulous demagogues, who sought to mobilize and manipulate the masses. The popularity of Fascist movements, which openly denigrated reason and exalted race, blood, action, and will, demonstrated the naïveté of nineteenth-century liberals, who believed that reason had triumphed in human affairs.

Nietzsche

The principal figure in the "dethronement of reason" and the glorification of the irrational was the German philosopher Friedrich Nietzsche (1844–1900). Nietzsche's writings are not systematic treatises but collections of aphorisms, often containing internal contradictions. Consequently, his philosophy lends itself to misinterpretation and misapplication. For example, Nazi theorists distorted Nietzsche to justify their notions of the German master race.

akg-images.

FRIEDRICH NIETZSCHE WITH HIS MOTHER. Possessing the intuitive genius of a great poet, Nietzsche grasped the crucial problem afflicting the modern European soul: what path should the individual take in a world where God is dead? Nietzsche's answer to this question—the overman who creates his own values—lent itself to considerable misinterpretation and distortion and had little constructive social value.

Nietzsche attacked the accepted views and convictions of his day as a hindrance to a fuller and richer existence. He denounced social reform, parliamentary government, and universal suffrage; ridiculed the vision of progress through science; condemned Christian morality; and mocked the liberal belief in human beings' essential goodness and rationality. We must understand, he said, that life, which is replete with cruelty, injustice, uncertainty, and absurdity, is not governed by rational principles. There exist no absolute standards of good and evil whose truth can be demonstrated by reflective reason. Nothing is true; there is no higher purpose or sense to the universe or human existence. There is only the naked individual living in a godless and absurd world.

Modern bourgeois society, said Nietzsche, was decadent and enfeebled—a victim of the excessive development of the rational faculties at the expense of will and instinct. Against the liberal-rationalist stress on the intellect, Nietzsche urged recognition of the dark, mysterious world of instinctual desires—the true forces of life. Smother the will with excessive intellectualizing, and you snuff out the spontaneity that sparks cultural creativity and ignites a zest for living. The critical and theoretical outlook destroys the creative instincts. To realize his multifaceted potential, man must stop relying on the intellect and nurture again the instinctual roots of human existence.

Christianity, with all its prohibitions, restrictions, and demands to conform, also stifles the human impulse for life, said Nietzsche, the son of a Lutheran pastor. Christian morality must be obliterated, for it is fit only for the weak, the slave. According to Nietzsche, the triumph of Christianity in the ancient world was an attempt of the resentful slave and the slavelike plebeian to prevent their aristocratic superiors from expressing their heroic natures and to strike back at those noble spirits, whom they envied. Their way of striking back was to condemn as evil the very traits that they themselves lacked—strength, power, assertiveness, and a zest for life—and to make their own base, wretched, and life-negating values the standard of all things. Then they saddled people with guilt if they deviated from these contemptible values. This transvaluation of values engineered by Christianity, said Nietzsche, led to a deterioration of life and culture.

Although the philosophes had rejected Christian doctrines, they had largely retained Christian ethics. Unlike the philosophes, however, Nietzsche did not attack Christianity because it was contrary to reason. He attacked it because, he said, it gave man a sick soul. It was life-denying. Blocking the free and spontaneous exercise of human instincts, it made humility, weakness, and self-abnegation virtues and pride a vice. In short, Christianity extinguished the spark of life in man. This spark of life, this inner yearning that fosters self-creation, must again burn.

"God is dead," proclaimed Nietzsche. God is man's own creation. Dead also are all the inherited truths based on nature and reason. There are no higher worlds, no transcendent or metaphysical truths, no morality derived from God or nature, and no natural rights, scientific socialism, or inevitable progress. We wander through an eternal nothing in which all the old values and truths have lost their intelligibility. This *nihilism*—the belief that moral and social values have no validity—had caused a crisis in European life. But the death of God and of all transcendental truths could mean the liberation of man, insisted Nietzsche. Man can surmount nihilism by adopting a new orientation that gives primacy to the superior man—the *overman* or *superman* who asserts his will, gives order to chaotic passions, makes great demands on himself, and lives life with a fierce joy. The overman aspires to self-perfection; without fear or guilt he rejects traditional religion and morality and creates his own values and defines his own self, his own life. Such a man could overcome the deadening uniformity and mediocrity of modern civilization. He could undo democracy and socialism, which have made masters out of cattlelike masses, and surmount the shopkeeper's spirit, which had made man soft and degenerate.

European society, as Nietzsche saw it, lacked heroic figures; everyone belonged to a vast herd, but there were no shepherds. Europe could be saved only by the emergence of such a higher type of man—one who would not be held back by the egalitarian rubbish preached by Christians, democrats, and socialists. "A declaration of war on the masses by *higher* man is needed," said Nietzsche, to end "the dominion of *inferior* men." Europe required "the annihilation of *suffrage universal,* i.e., the system through which the lowest natures prescribe themselves as laws for the higher."[1] Europe needed a new breed of rulers, a true aristocracy of masterful men.

Nietzsche conceived of the overman as a new kind of man who breaks with accepted morality and sets his own standards. He does not repress his instincts but asserts them. He destroys old values and asserts his prerogative as master. Free of Christian guilt, he proudly affirms his own being; dispensing with Christian "thou shalt not," he instinctively says, "I will." He dares to be himself. Because he is not like other people, traditional definitions of good and evil have no meaning for him. He does not allow his individuality to be stifled. He makes his own values, those that flow from his very being. He knows that life is meaningless but lives it laughingly, instinctively, fully.

The overman understands and exemplifies the ultimate fact of life: that "the most fearful and fundamental desire in man [is] his drive for power,"[2] that human beings crave and strive for power ceaselessly and uncompromisingly. It is perfectly natural for human beings to want to dominate nature and other human beings; inherent in human nature is the desire "to overpower . . . to overthrow . . . to become master, [to] thirst for enemies and antagonisms and triumphs."[3] This will to power is not a product of rational reflection but flows from the very essence of human existence. As the motivating force in human behavior, it governs everyday life and is the determining factor in political life. The enhancement of power brings supreme enjoyment: "The love of power is the demon of men. Let them have everything—health, food, a place to live, entertainment—they are and remain unhappy and low-spirited; for the demon waits and waits and will be satisfied. Take everything from them and satisfy this and they are almost happy—as happy as men and demons can be."[4] The masses, cowardly and envious, will condemn the higher man as evil; this has always been their way. Thus, Nietzsche castigates democracy because it "represents the disbelief in great human beings and an elite society,"[5] and Christianity because it imposes an unnatural morality, one that affirms meekness, humility, and compassion.

The influence of Nietzsche's philosophy is still a matter of controversy and conjecture. Perhaps better than anyone else, Nietzsche grasped the crucial problem of modern society and culture: that with the "death of God," traditional moral values had lost their authority and binding power. In a world where nothing is true, all is permitted. Nietzsche foresaw that the future, an age without values, would be violent and sordid, and he urged individuals to face themselves and life free of illusions, pretense, and hypocrisy. Nietzsche is also part of the general nineteenth-century trend that sought to affirm the human being and earthly aspirations rather than God or salvation. Furthermore, Nietzsche's rejection of God and metaphysics, as well as of all-embracing theories of history (Hegelianism and Marxism, for example) that attempt to impose rational patterns on the past and the present, is crucial to the development of existentialism (see "Existentialism" in Chapter 19) and the movement in contemporary thought called postmodernism (see Epilogue).

However, no social policy could be derived from Nietzsche's heroic individualism, which taught that "there are higher and lower men and that a single individual can . . . justify the existence of whole millennia."[6] Nietzsche thought only of great individuals, humanity's noblest specimens, who overcome mediocrity and the artificiality of all inherited values; the social community and social injustice did not concern him. "The weak and ill-constituted shall perish: first principle of our philanthropy. And one shall help them to do so."[7] Surely, these words offer no constructive guidelines for dealing with the problems of modern industrial civilization.

Likewise, Nietzsche had no constructive proposals for dealing with the disintegration of rational and Christian certainties. Instead, his vitriolic attack on European institutions and values helped erode the rational foundations of Western civilization. This assault appealed immensely to intellectuals in Central Europe, who saw Nietzsche's philosophy as liberating an inner energy. Thus, many young people, attracted to Nietzsche, welcomed World War I; they viewed it as an esthetic experience and thought that it would clear a path to a new heroic age. They took Nietzsche's words literally: "A society that definitely and *instinctively* gives up war and conquest is in decline."[8]

Nazi theorists tried to make Nietzsche a forerunner of their movement. They sought from him a philosophical sanction for their own thirst for power, contempt for the weak, ruthlessness, and glorification of action. They also wanted this sanction for their cult of the heroic and their Social Darwinist revulsion for human equality. Recasting Nietzsche in their own image, the Nazis viewed themselves as Nietzsche's supermen: members of a master race who, by force of will, would conquer all obstacles and reshape the world according to their self-created values. Some German intellectuals were drawn to Nazism because it seemed a healthy affirmation of life, the life with a new purpose for which Nietzsche called.

Detesting German nationalism and militarism, Nietzsche himself scoffed at the notion of German racial superiority, disdained (despite some unfortunate remarks) anti-Semitism, and denounced state worship. He would have abhorred Hitler and would have been dismayed at the twisting of his idea of the will to power into a prototype Fascist principle. The men that he admired were passionate but self-possessed individuals who, by mastering their own chaotic passions, would face life and death courageously, affirmatively, and creatively. Such men make great demands on themselves. Nevertheless, as Janko Lavrin points out, "Practically all the fascist and Nazi theories can find some support in Nietzsche's texts, provided one gives them the required twist."[9]

Nietzsche's extreme and violent denunciation of Western democratic principles, including equality, his praise of power, his call for the liberation of the instincts, his elitism, which denigrates and devalues all human life that is not strong and noble, and his spurning of humane values provided a breeding ground for violent, antirational, antiliberal, and inhumane movements. His philosophy, which included loose talk about the virtues of pitiless warriors, the breeding of a master race, and the annihilation of the weak and the ill constituted, is conducive to a politics of extremes that knows no moral limits.

Bergson

Another thinker who reflected the growing irrationalism of the age was Henri Bergson (1859–1941), a French philosopher of Jewish background. Originally attracted to positivism, Bergson turned away from the positivistic claim that science could explain everything and fulfill all human needs. Such an emphasis on the intellect, said Bergson, sacrifices spiritual impulses, imagination, and intuition and reduces the soul to a mere mechanism.

The methods of science cannot reveal ultimate reality, Bergson insisted. European civilization must recognize the limitations of scientific rationalism. Our capacity for intuition, whereby the mind achieves an immanent relationship with the object—participates in it—tells us more about reality than the method of analysis employed by science. The intuitive experience—something like the artist's instant comprehension of a natural scene—is a direct avenue to truth that is closed to the calculations and measurements of science. Bergson's philosophy pointed away from science toward religious mysticism.

Primary Source

Friedrich Nietzsche: *The Will to Power*

First published in 1901, one year after Nietzsche's death, The Will to Power *consists of the author's notes written in the years 1883 to 1888. The following passages from this work show Nietzsche's contempt for democracy and socialism and proclaim the will to power.*

728 (March–June 1888)

. . . A society that definitely and *instinctively* gives up war and conquest is in decline: it is ripe for democracy and the rule of shopkeepers. . . .

752 (1884)

. . . Democracy represents the disbelief in great human beings and an elite society: "Everyone is equal to everyone else." "At bottom we are one and all self-seeking cattle and mob."

753 (1885)

I am opposed to 1. socialism, because it dreams quite naively of "the good, true, and beautiful" and of "equal rights"—(anarchism also desires the same ideal, but in a more brutal fashion); 2. parliamentary government and the press, because these are the means by which the herd animal becomes master.

765 (Jan–Fall 1888)

. . . Another Christian concept, no less crazy, has passed even more deeply into the tissue of modernity: the concept of the "equality of souls before God." This concept furnishes the prototype of all theories of equal rights: mankind was first taught to stammer the proposition of equality in a religious context, and only later was it made into morality: no wonder that man ended by taking it seriously, taking it practically!—that is to say, politically, democratically, socialistically. . . .

854 (1884)

In the age of *suffrage universel,* i.e., when everyone may sit in judgment on everyone and everything, I feel impelled to reestablish *order of rank.*

861 (1884)

A declaration of war on the masses by *higher men* is needed! Everywhere the mediocre are combining in order to make themselves master! Everything that makes soft and effeminate, that serves the ends of the "people" or the "feminine," works in *favor* of *suffrage universel,* i.e., the dominion of *inferior* men. But we should take reprisal and bring this whole affair (which in Europe commenced with Christianity) to light and to the bar of judgment.

862 (1884)

A doctrine is needed powerful enough to work as a breeding agent: strengthening the strong, paralyzing and destructive for the world-weary.

The annihilation of the decaying races. Decay of Europe.—The annihilation of slavish evaluations.—Dominion over the earth as a means of producing a higher type.—The annihilation of the tartuffery [hypocrisy] called "morality." . . . The annihilation of *suffrage universel*; i.e., the system through which the lowest natures prescribe themselves as laws for the higher.—The annihilation of mediocrity and its acceptance. . . .

870 (1884)

The root of all evil: that the slavish morality of meekness, chastity, selflessness, absolute obedience, has triumphed. . . .

874 (1884)

The degeneration of the rulers and the ruling classes has been the cause of the greatest mischief in history! Without the Roman Caesars and Roman society, the insanity of Christianity would never have come to power.

997 (1884)

I teach: that there are higher and lower men, and that a single individual can under certain circumstances justify the existence of whole millennia—that is, a full, rich, great, whole human being in relation to countless incomplete fragmentary men.

Question for Analysis

1. Why did Friedrich Nietzsche attack democracy and socialism? How do you respond to his attack?

To his admirers, Bergson's philosophy liberated the person from the constraints of positivism, mechanism, and materialism. It extolled the creative potential of intuition, the mystical experience, and the poetic imagination—those forces of life that resist categorization by the scientific mind. A protest against modern technology and bureaucracy and against all the features of mass society that seemed to stifle individual uniqueness and spontaneity, it sought to reaffirm the primacy of the individual in an increasingly mechanized and bureaucratic world. The popularity of Bergson's intuitionism and vitalism, with their depreciation of reason, symptomized the unsuspected strength and appeal of the nonrational—another sign that people were searching for new alternatives to the Enlightenment worldview.

Sorel

Nietzsche proclaimed that irrational forces constitute the essence of human nature, and Bergson held that a nonrational intuition brought insights unattainable by scientific thinking. Georges Sorel (1847–1922), a French social theorist, recognized the political potential of the nonrational. Like Nietzsche, Sorel was disillusioned with contemporary bourgeois society, which he considered decadent, soft, and unheroic. Whereas Nietzsche called for the higher man to rescue society from decadence and mediocrity, Sorel placed his hopes in the proletariat, whose position made them courageous, virile, and determined. Sorel wanted the proletariat to destroy the existing order. This overthrow, said Sorel, would be accomplished through a general strike: a universal work stoppage that would bring down the government and give power to the workers.

Sorel saw the general strike as having the appeal of a great mobilizing myth. What was important was not that the general strike actually take place, but that its image stir all the anticapitalist resentments of the workers and inspire them to carry out their revolutionary responsibilities. Sorel understood the extraordinary potency of myth for eliciting total commitment and inciting heroic action. Because it appeals to the imagination and feelings, myth is an effective way of moving the masses to revolt. By believing in the myth of the general strike, workers would soar above the moral decadence of bourgeois society and bear the immense sacrifices that their struggle called for. Sorel thought that the only recourse for workers was direct action and violence, which he regarded as ennobling, heroic, and sublime—a means of restoring grandeur to a flabby world.

Sorel's pseudoreligious exaltation of violence and mass action, his condemnation of liberal democracy and rationalism, and his recognition of the power and political utility of fabricated myths would find concrete expression in the Fascist movements after World War I. Sorel heralded the age of mass political movements committed to revolutionary violence and of myths manufactured by propaganda experts determined to destroy democracy.

Freud: A New View of Human Nature

In many ways, Sigmund Freud (1856–1939), an Austrian-Jewish physician who spent most of his adult life in Vienna, was a child of the Enlightenment. Like the philosophes, Freud identified civilization with reason and regarded science as the avenue to knowledge. But in contrast to the philosophes, Freud focused on the massive power and influence of nonrational drives. Whereas Nietzsche glorified the irrational and approached it with a poet's temperament, Freud recognized its potential danger. He sought to comprehend it scientifically and wanted to regulate it in the interests of civilization. Unlike Nietzsche, Freud did not belittle the rational but always strove to salvage respect for reason. Better than anyone, Freud recognized reason's limitations and the power of the nonrational, but he never wavered in his support of reason.

Freud's explorations of the world of the unconscious had a profoundly upsetting impact on our conception of the self. Freud himself viewed his theories as a great blow to human pride, to "man's craving for grandiosity."

> *Humanity has, in the course of time, had to endure from the hands of science two great outrages upon its naive self-love. The first was when it realized that our earth was not the center of the universe, but only a tiny speck in a world-system of a magnitude hardly conceivable; this is associated in our minds with the name of Copernicus. . . . The second was when biological research robbed man of his peculiar privilege of having been specially created, and relegated him to a descent from the animal world, implying an ineradicable animal nature in him: this transvaluation has been accomplished in our own time upon the investigations of Charles Darwin. . . . But man's craving for grandiosity is now suffering the third and most bitter blow from present-day psychological research which is endeavoring to show the "ego" of each of us that he is not even master in his own house, but that he must remain content with the veriest scrap of information about what is going on unconsciously in his own mind.*[10]

Freud held that people are not fundamentally rational; human behavior is governed primarily by powerful inner forces, which are hidden from consciousness. These instinctual strivings, rather than rational faculties, constitute the greater part of the mind. Freud's great achievement was his exploring of the world of the unconscious with the tools and temperament of a scientist. He showed that the irrational contained a structure that could be empirically explained and rationally explored.

After graduating from medical school, Freud specialized in the treatment of nervous disorders. His investigations led him to conclude that childhood fears and experiences, often sexual in nature, accounted for neuroses: disorders in thinking, feeling, and behavior that interfere with everyday acts of personal and social life. Neuroses can take several forms, including hysteria, anxiety, depression, and obsessions. So painful and threatening were these childhood emotions and experiences that his patients banished them from conscious memory to the realm of the unconscious.

To understand and treat neurotic behavior, Freud said, it was necessary to look behind overt symptoms and bring to the surface emotionally charged experiences and fears—childhood traumas—that lie buried in the unconscious, along with primitive impulses. The key to the unconscious, in Freud's view, was the interpretation of dreams. An individual's dreams, said Freud, reveal his or her secret wishes—often socially unacceptable desires and frightening memories. Too painful to bear, they get locked up in the deepest dungeons of our unconscious. But even in their cages, the demons remain active, continuing to haunt us and to generate conflicts. Our distress is

© Mary Evans/SIGMUND FREUD COPYRIGHTS/The Image Works.

Freud and His Daughter Anna (1912). Sigmund Freud, the father of psychoanalysis, penetrated the world of the unconscious in a scientific way. He concluded that powerful drives govern human behavior more than reason does. His explorations of the unconscious produced an image of the human being that broke with the Enlightenment's view of the individual's essential goodness and rationality.

real and even excruciating, but we do not know its source.

The *id,* the subconscious seat of the instincts, said Freud, is a "cauldron full of seething excitations," which constantly demand gratification. The id is primitive and irrational. It knows no values and has no awareness of good and evil. Unable to endure tension, it demands sexual release, the termination of pain, the cessation of hunger. When the id is denied an outlet for its instinctual energy, we become frustrated, angry, and unhappy. Gratifying the id is our highest pleasure. But the full gratification of instinctual demands is detrimental to civilized life. That is why the *ego*, which stands for reason, seeks to hold the id in check, to bring it in line with reality.

Freud postulated a harrowing conflict between the relentless strivings of our instinctual nature and the requirements of civilization. Civilization, for Freud, required the renunciation of instinctual gratification and the mastery of animal instincts, a thesis he developed in *Civilization and Its Discontents* (1930). Although Freud's thoughts in this work were no doubt influenced by the great tragedy of World War I and the rise of Fascist movements in several European lands, the main theme could be traced back to his earlier writings. Human beings derive their highest pleasure from sexual fulfillment, said Freud, but unrestrained sexuality drains off psychic energy needed for creative artistic and intellectual life; it also directs energies away from work needed to preserve communal life. Hence society, through the family, the priest, the teacher, and the police, imposes rules and restrictions on our animal nature. In effect, it implants a conscience in human beings that serves to check antisocial drives.

But this is immensely painful. The human being is caught in a tragic bind. Society's demand for repression of instincts in the interest of civilization causes terrible frustration. Equally distressing, the violation of society's rules under the pressure of instinctual needs evokes terrible feelings of guilt. Either way, people suffer; civilized life simply entails too much pain for people. It seems that the price we pay for civilization is neurosis. Most people cannot endure the amount of instinctual renunciation that civilization requires. There are times when our elemental human nature rebels against all the restrictions and "thou shalt nots" demanded by society, against all the misery and torment imposed by civilization.

"Civilization imposes great sacrifices not only on man's sexuality but also on his aggressivity,"[11] said Freud. People are not good by nature, as the philosophes had taught, but are predisposed to behave cruelly and brutally. They are "creatures among whose instinctual endowments is to be reckoned a powerful share of aggressiveness." Their first inclination is not to love their neighbor, but to "satisfy their aggressiveness on him, to exploit his capacity for work without compensation, to use him sexually without his consent, to seize

THE SCREAM, **1893, BY EDVARD MUNCH (1863–1944).** The dark forces of emotional torment and sexual aberration fill the canvases of the Norwegian postimpressionist Edvard Munch. (© The Museum of Modern Art/Licensed by Scala/Art Resource, N.Y., © 2011 The Munch Museum/The Munch-Ellingsen Group/Artists Rights Society [ARS], New York.)

his possessions, to humiliate him, to cause him pain, to torture and to kill him."[12]

Man is wolf to man, Freud concluded. "Who has the courage to dispute it in the face of all the evidence in his own life and in history?"[13] Civilization "has to use its utmost efforts in order to set limits to man's aggressive instincts," but "in spite of every effort these endeavors of civilization have not so far achieved very much."[14] People find it difficult to do without "the satisfaction of this inclination to aggression."[15] When circumstances are favorable, this primitive aggressiveness breaks loose and "reveals man as a savage beast to whom consideration towards his own kind is something alien."[16] For Freud, "the inclination to aggression is an original self-subsisting disposition in man" and it "constitutes the greatest impediment to civilization."[17] Aggressive impulses drive people apart, threatening society with disintegration. Freud believed that an unalterable core of human nature is ineluctably in opposition to civilized life. To this extent, everyone is potentially an enemy of civilization.

Freud's awareness of the irrational and his general pessimism regarding people's ability to regulate it in the interests of civilization did not lead him to break faith with the Enlightenment tradition, for Freud did not celebrate the irrational. He was too cognizant of its self-destructive nature for that. Civilization is indeed a burden, but people must bear it because the alternative is far worse. In the tradition of the philosophes, Freud sought truth based on a scientific analysis of human nature and believed that reason was the best road to social improvement. Like the philosophes, he was critical of religion, regarding it as a pious illusion—a fairy tale in conflict with reason. Freud wanted people to throw away what he believed was the crutch of religion, to break away from childlike dependence and become self-sufficient.

A humanitarian like the philosophes, Freud sought to relieve human misery by making people aware of their true nature, particularly their sexuality. He wanted society to soften its overly restrictive sexual standards because they were injurious to mental health. One enduring consequence of the Freudian revolution is the recognition of the enormous importance played by childhood in the shaping of the adult's personality. The neurotic disorders that burden adults begin in early childhood. Freud urged that we show greater concern for the emotional needs of children.

Although Freud was undoubtedly a child of the Enlightenment, in crucial ways he differed from the philosophes. Regarding the Christian doctrine of original sin as myth, the philosophes had believed that people's nature was essentially good. If people took reason as their guide, evil could be eliminated. Freud, on the other hand, asserted, in secular and scientific terms, a pessimistic view of human nature. He saw evil as rooted in human nature rather than as a product of a faulty environment. Education and better living conditions would not eliminate evil, as the philosophes had expected, nor would abolition of private property, as Marx had declared. The philosophes venerated reason; it had enabled Newton to unravel nature's mysteries and would permit people to achieve virtue and reform society. Freud, who wanted reason to prevail, understood that its soft voice had to compete with the thunderous roars of the id. Freud broke with the optimism of the philosophes. His awareness of the immense pressures that civilization places on our fragile egos led him to be generally pessimistic about the future.

Unlike Marx, Freud had no vision of utopia. He saw the crude, destructive tendencies of human nature as an ever-present obstacle to harmonious social relations. That Freud was hounded out of Vienna by the Nazis and his four sisters were murdered by them simply for being Jewish is a telling footnote to his view of human nature, the power of the irrational, and the fragility of civilization.

Social Thought: Confronting the Irrational and the Complexities of Modern Society

The end of the nineteenth century and the beginning of the twentieth mark the great age of sociological thought. The leading sociological thinkers of the period all regarded science as the only valid model for arriving at knowledge, and all claimed that their thought rested on a scientific foundation. They struggled with some of the crucial problems of modern society. How can society achieve coherence and stability when the customary associations and attachments that had characterized village life have been ruthlessly dissolved by the rapidly developing industrial-urban-capitalist order—which elevates often selfish individualism over symbiotic communal ties that had characterized preindustrial society—and when religion no longer unites people? What are the implications of the nonrational for political life? How can people preserve their individuality in a society that is becoming increasingly regimented? In many ways, twentieth-century dictatorships were responses to the dilemmas of modern society analyzed by these social theorists. And twentieth-century dictators would employ these social theorists' insights into group and mass psychology for the purpose of gaining and maintaining power.

Durkheim

Émile Durkheim (1858–1917), a French scholar of Jewish background and heir to Comte's positivism, was an important founder of modern sociology. Like Comte, he brought the scientific method to the study of society. Durkheim tried to show that the essential elements of modern times—secularism, rationalism, and individualism—put society at risk of breaking apart into a disconnected mass of self-seeking, antagonistic individuals. In traditional society, the social order was derived from God; he determined a person's place and function, which was confirmed by birth and custom. However, modern people, skeptical and individualistic, would not accept such restraints.

The weakening of the traditional ties that bind the individual to society constituted, for Durkheim, the crisis of modern urban, industrial society. Without collective values and common beliefs, society is threatened with disintegration and the individual with disorientation. Modern people, said Durkheim, suffer from *anomie*—a condition of anxiety caused by the collapse of values. They do not feel integrated into a collective community and find no purpose in life. In *Suicide* (1897), Durkheim maintained that "the exceptionally high number of voluntary deaths manifests the state of deep disturbances from which civilized societies are suffering and bears witness to its gravity."[18] The pathology of modern society is also demonstrated by a high level of boredom, anxiety, and pessimism. Modern people are driven to suicide by intense competition, the disappointment and frustration resulting from unfulfilled expectations, and a lack of commitment to moral principles. People must limit their aspirations and exercise discipline over their desires and passions, said Durkheim. They must stop wanting more. Religion once spurred people to view restraint and the renunciation of desires as virtues, but it can no longer do so.

Although Durkheim approved of modernity, he noted that modern ways have not brought happiness or satisfaction to the individual. Modern scientific and industrial society requires a new set of principles that would bind the various classes into a cohesive social order and help to overcome the feelings of restlessness and dissatisfaction that torment people. Durkheim called for a secular and rational system of morality to replace Christian dogma and fulfill this need.

Durkheim focused on a crucial dilemma of modern life. On the one hand, modern urban civilization has provided the individual with unparalleled opportunities for self-development and material improvement. On the other, the breakdown of traditional communal bonds stemming from the spread of rationalism and individualism has produced a sense of isolation and alienation. Twentieth-century totalitarian movements sought to integrate these uprooted and alienated souls into new collectivities: a proletarian state based on workers' solidarity or a racial state based on ethnic "purity" and nationalism.

Pareto

Like Comte, Vilfredo Pareto (1848–1923), an Italian economist and sociologist, aimed to construct a system of sociology on the model of the physical sciences. His studies led him to conclude that social behavior does not rest primarily on reason but rather on nonrational instincts and sentiments. These deeply rooted and essentially changeless feelings are the fundamental elements in human behavior. Although society may change, human nature remains essentially the same. Whoever seeks to lead and to influence people must appeal not to logic but to elemental feelings. Most human behavior is nonrational; nonlogical considerations also determine people's beliefs. Like Marx and Freud, Pareto was convinced that we cannot accept a person's word at face value. Instead, we find the real cause of human behavior in human instincts and sentiments. People do not act according to carefully thought-out theories; they act first from nonlogical motivations and then construct a rationalization to justify their behavior. Much of Pareto's work focused on the nonrational elements of human conduct and the various beliefs invented to give the appearance of rationality to behavior that derives from feeling and instinct.

Pareto divided society into two strata: the elite and the masses. Elites have always existed, said Pareto, because human beings are unequal by nature and because the goods that all people seek cannot be shared equally. Because struggle is a general law of life, elites and masses will exist in all societies. The belief that a democracy constitutes rule by a people is a myth, said Pareto. In actuality, a small group of party leaders controls the political system. Pareto also rejected as naïve Marx's vision of the end of the class struggle.

In the tradition of Machiavelli, Pareto held that a successful ruling elite must—with cunning and if necessary with violence—exploit the feelings and impulses of the masses to its own advantage. Democratic states, he said, delude themselves in thinking that the masses are really influenced by rational argument. Pareto predicted the emergence of new political leaders who would master the people through propaganda and force, always appealing to sentiment rather than to reason. To this extent, Pareto was an intellectual forerunner of Fascism, which preached an authoritarian elitism. Mussolini praised Pareto and proudly claimed him as a source of inspiration.

Weber

Probably the most prominent social thinker of the age, the German academic Max Weber (1864–1920) was a leading shaper of modern sociology. Weber believed that Western civilization, unlike the other civilizations of the globe, had virtually eliminated myth, mystery, and magic from its conception of nature and society. This process of rationalization—the "disenchantment of the world," as Weber called it—was most conspicuous in Western science, but it was also evident in politics and economics. Weber considered Western science an attempt to understand and master nature through reason, and Western capitalism an attempt to organize work and production in a rational manner. The Western state has a rational, written constitution, rationally formulated law, and a bureaucracy of trained government officials that administers the affairs of state according to rational rules and regulations.

Weber understood the terrible paradox of reason. Reason accounts for brilliant achievements in science and economic life, but it also despiritualizes life by ruthlessly eliminating centuries-old traditions, denouncing deeply felt religious beliefs as superstition, and regarding human feelings and passions as impediments to clear thinking. The process of disenchantment shattered the basis for belief in transcendental values; in a thoroughly disenchanted world, life is without ultimate purpose or intrinsic meaning and the individual is soulless. This is the dilemma of modern individuals, said Weber. Secular rationality is shaping a world in which standards cannot claim ultimate sanction. A disenchanted world contains no inherited truths, no God-given answers to the human being's desperate need for meaning. We are now confronted with an immense and unprecedented burden: how to create for ourselves values that give meaning to life in a world deprived of certainty.

Secular rationality has produced still another awesome problem, said Weber. It has fostered self-liberation, for it enables human beings to overcome illusions and take control of the environment and of themselves, but it is also a means of self-enslavement, for it produces institutions, giant public and corporate bureaucracies, that depersonalize life. Modern officials, said Weber, are emotionally detached. Concerned only with the efficient execution of tasks, they employ reason in a cold and calculating way; such human feelings as compassion and affection are ruled out as hindrances to effectiveness. In the name of efficiency, people are placed in "steel cages"—that is, treated impersonally as mere objects—and thus are deprived of their autonomy. The prospect existed that people would refuse to endure this violation of their spiritual needs and would reverse the process of disenchantment by seeking redemption in the irrational. Weber himself, however, was committed to the ideals of the Enlightenment and to perpetuating the rational scientific tradition.

Like Freud, Weber was aware of the power of the irrational in social life. One expression of the irrational that he analyzed in considerable depth was the charismatic leader who attracts people by force of personality. Charismatic leaders may be religious prophets, war heroes, demagogues, or others who possess this extraordinary personality that attracts and dominates others. People yearn for charismatic leadership, particularly during times of crisis. The leader claims a mission—a sacred duty—to lead the people during the crisis; the leader's authority rests on the people's belief in the mission and their faith in the leader's extraordinary abilities. A common allegiance to the charismatic leader unites the community. In an age that has seen its share of dictators and demagogues, the question of why people are drawn to the charismatic savior—why they succumb to his authority, and why they alter their lives in order to implement his vision—is of crucial concern to historians and social theorists.

The Modernist Movement

At the same time that Freud and the social theorists were breaking with the Enlightenment view of human nature and society, artists and writers sought to liberate the imagination from traditional forms of artistic and literary expression that had governed European cultural life since the Renaissance. They adhered to Nietzsche's dictum: "What is needed above all is an absolute scepticism toward all inherited concepts."[19] Rejecting both classical and realist models, they subordinated form and objective reality to the inner life—to feelings, imagination, and the creative process. These avant-garde writers and artists found new and creative ways to express the explosive primitive forces within the human psyche that increasingly had become the subject of contemporary thinkers. Their experimentations produced a great cultural revolution called *modernism* that still profoundly influences the arts. In some ways, modernism was a continuation of the Romantic Movement, which had dominated European culture in the early nineteenth century. Both movements subjected to searching criticism cultural styles that had been formulated during the Renaissance and that had roots in ancient Greece.

Breaking with Conventional Modes of Esthetics

Even more than romanticism, modernism aspired to an intense introspection—a heightened awareness of self—and saw the intellect as a barrier to the free expression of elemental human emotions. Modernist artists and writers abandoned conventional literary and artistic models and experimented with new modes of expression. They liberated the imagination from the restrictions of conventional forms and enabled their audience, readers and viewers alike, to share in the process of creation, often unconscious, and to discover fresh insights into objects, sounds, people, and social conditions. They believed that there were further discoveries to be made in the arts, further possibilities of expression, that past masters had not realized. The consequence of their bold venture, wrote the literary critic and historian Irving Howe, was nothing less than the "breakup of the traditional unity and continuity of Western culture."[20]

Like Freud, modernist artists and writers probed beyond surface appearances for a more profound reality hidden in the human psyche. Writers such as Thomas Mann, Marcel Proust, James Joyce, August Strindberg, D. H. Lawrence, and Franz Kafka explored the inner life of the individual and the psychopathology of human relations in order to lay bare the self. They dealt with the predicament of alienated and estranged men and women who rejected the values and customs of their day, and they depicted the anguish of people burdened by guilt, torn by internal conflicts, and driven by an inner self-destructiveness. Besides showing the overwhelming might of the irrational and the seductive power of the primitive and the instinctual, they also broke the silence about sex that had prevailed in Victorian literature.

From the Renaissance through the Enlightenment and into the nineteenth century, Western esthetic standards had been shaped by the conviction that the universe embodied an inherent mathematical order. A corollary of this conception of the outer world as orderly and intelligible was the view that art should imitate reality, that it should mirror nature. Since the Renaissance, artists had deliberately made use of laws of perspective and proportion; musicians had used harmonic chords, which brought rhythm and melody into a unified whole; writers had produced works according to a definite pattern, which included a beginning, middle, and end.

Modernist culture, however, acknowledged no objective reality of space, motion, and time that has the same meaning to all observers. Rather, reality can be grasped in many ways; a multiplicity of frames of reference apply to nature and human experience. Consequently, reality is what the viewer perceives it to be through the prism of the imagination. "There is no outer reality," said the modernist German poet Gottfried Benn, "there is only human consciousness, constantly building, modifying, rebuilding new worlds out of its own creativity."[21] Modernism is concerned less with the object itself than with how the artist experiences it—with the sensations that an object evokes in the artist's very being and with the meaning the artist's imagination imposes on reality. Sociologist Daniel Bell makes this point in reference to painting:

> *Modernism . . . denies the primacy of an outside reality, as given. It seeks either to rearrange that reality, or to retreat to the self's interior, to private experience as the source of its concerns and aesthetic preoccupations. . . . There is an emphasis on the self as the touchstone of understanding and on the activity of the knower rather than the character of the object as the source of knowledge. . . . Thus one discerns the intentions of modern painting . . . to break up ordered space.*[22]

Dispensing with conventional forms of esthetics, which stressed structure and coherence, modernism propelled the arts onto uncharted seas. Modernists abandoned the efforts of realists and naturalists to produce a clinical and objective description of the external world; instead, they probed subjective views and visions and the inner world of the unconscious, searching within its primitive layer for an authentic inner self. Recoiling from a middle-class, industrial civilization, which prized rationalism, organization, clarity, stability, and definite norms and values, modernist writers and artists were fascinated by the bizarre, the mysterious, the unpredictable, the primitive, the irrational, and the formless. Writers, for example, experimented with new techniques to convey the intense struggle between the conscious and the unconscious and to explore the aberrations and complexities of human personality and the irrationality and absurdity of human behavior. In particular, they devised a new way, the stream of consciousness, to exhibit the mind's every level—both conscious reflection and unconscious strivings—and to capture how thought is punctuated by spontaneous outbursts, disconnected assertions, random memories, hidden desires, and persistent fantasies. The stream of consciousness is not narrated memory but a flow of feelings and thoughts in which the boundary between consciousness and unconsciousness is blurred. It attempts to reveal the mystery and complexity of the inner person, the hidden drives, desires, torments, and obsessions that intrigued Freud.

Modern artists deliberately plunged into the world of the unconscious in search of the instinctual, the fantastic, the primitive, and the mysterious, which they believed yielded a truth higher than that given by analytical thought. They embarked on a voyage into the mind's interior in the hopes of finding fantastic stimulants that would spark the creative imagination. Composers engaged in open revolt against the conventional rules and standards of musical composition. For example, the Austrian composer Arnold Schöenberg (1874–1951) purposefully abandoned traditional scales and harmonic chords to produce atonal music that "seeks to express all that swells in us subconsciously like a dream."[23] The Russian composer Igor Stravinsky (1882–1971) experimented with both atonality and primitive rhythms. When Stravinsky's ballet *The Rite of Spring* was performed in Paris in 1913, the theater audience rioted to protest the composition's break with tonality, its use of primitive, jazzlike rhythms, and its theme of ritual sacrifice.

Modern Art

The modernist movement, which began near the end of the nineteenth century, was in full bloom before World War I and would continue to flower in the postwar world. Probably the clearest expression of the modernist viewpoint is found in art. In the late nineteenth century, artists began to turn away from the standards that had characterized art since the Renaissance. No longer committed to depicting how an object appears to the eye or to organizing space mathematically, they searched for new forms of representation. Increasingly, artists sought to penetrate the deepest recesses of the unconscious, which they saw as the wellspring of creativity and the dwelling place of a higher truth. Inspired by dreams, nightmares, and powerful emotions, they often represented the world in a startling manner that deviated from the Renaissance's search for form and the ideal. Paul Klee (1879–1940), a prominent Swiss painter, described modern art in these words: "Each [artist] should follow where the pulse of his own heart leads. . . . Our pounding heart drives us down, deep down to the source of all. What springs from this source, whether it may be called dream, idea or phantasy—must be taken seriously."[24]

Between 1909 and 1914, a new style, *cubism*, was developed by Pablo Picasso (1881–1973) and Georges Braque (1882–1963). Exploring the interplay between the flat world of the canvas and the three-dimensional world of visual perception, they sought to paint a reality deeper than what the eye sees at first glance. One art historian describes cubism as follows: "The cubist is not interested in usual representational standards. It is as if he were walking around the object he is analyzing, as one is free to walk around a piece of sculpture for successive views. But he must represent all these views at once."[25] The cubists' effort to depict something from multiple perspectives rather than from a single point in space and their need to deliberately deform objects in order to achieve this effect mark a radical break with artistic conventions.

Throughout the period from 1890 to 1914, artists were deemphasizing subject matter and stressing the expressive power of such formal qualities as line, color, and space. It is not surprising that some artists, such as Piet Mondrian (1872–1944), a Dutch painter, and Wassily Kandinsky (1866–1944), a Russian residing in Germany, finally created abstract art, a nonobjective art totally devoid of reference to the visible world. In breaking with the Renaissance view of the world as inherently orderly and rational and stressing the power of the imagination, modern artists opened up new possibilities for artistic expression. They also exemplified the growing appeal and force of the nonrational in European life.

Modern Physics

Until the closing years of the nineteenth century, the view of the universe held by the Western mind was based on the classical physics of Newton. It included the following principles: (1) time, space, and matter were objective realities that existed

LES DEMOISELLES D'AVIGNON **(1907), BY PABLO PICASSO.** Picasso's painting exemplified new trends in art. Rather than conforming with classical and Renaissance conventions of representation, Picasso aimed to interpret visual reality in accord with his own sensibilities. (Digital Image © The Museum of Modern Art/Licensed by SCALA/ Art Resource, N.Y./© 2011 Estate of Pablo Picasso/Artists Rights Society (ARS), New York.)

independently of the observer; (2) the universe was a giant machine, whose parts obeyed strict laws of cause and effect; (3) the atom, indivisible and solid, was the basic unit of matter; (4) heated bodies emitted radiation in continuous waves; and (5) through further investigation it would be possible to gain complete knowledge of the physical universe.

Between the 1890s and the 1920s, this view of the universe was shattered by a second Scientific Revolution. The discovery of x rays by William Konrad Roentgen in 1895, of radioactivity by Henri Bequerel in 1896, and of the electron by J. J. Thomson in 1897 led scientists to abandon the conception of the atom as a solid and indivisible particle. Rather than resembling a billiard ball, the atom consisted of a nucleus of tightly packed protons separated from orbiting electrons by empty space.

In 1900, Max Planck (1858–1947), a German physicist, proposed the quantum theory, which holds that a heated body radiates energy not in a continuous, unbroken stream, as had been believed, but in intermittent spurts, or jumps, called quanta. Planck's theory of discontinuity in energy radiation challenged a cardinal principle of classical physics: that action in nature was strictly continuous. In 1913, Niels Bohr, a Danish scientist, applied Planck's theory of energy quanta to the interior of the atom and discovered that the

Black Weft, by Wassily Kandinsky. Kandinsky was a leader of a group of avant-garde painters in Munich, called Der Blaue Reiter (The Blue Rider), whose goal was to challenge the limits of artistic expression. In this painting, he has removed virtually all traces of the physical world, thereby creating a nonobjective artwork that bears little to no resemblance to the natural world. (Réunion des Musées Nationaux/Art Resource, N.Y.; © 2011 Artists Rights Society (ARS), New York/ADAGP, Paris.)

Newtonian laws of motion could not fully explain what happened to electrons orbiting an atomic nucleus. As physicists explored the behavior of the atom further, it became apparent that its nature was fundamentally elusive and unpredictable.

Newtonian physics says that, given certain conditions, we can predict what will follow. For example, if an airplane is flying north at four hundred miles per hour, we can predict its exact position two hours from now, assuming that the plane does not alter its course or speed. Quantum mechanics teaches that in the subatomic realm we cannot predict with certainty what will take place; we can only say that, given certain conditions, it is *probable* that a certain event will follow. This principle of uncertainty was developed in 1927 by the German scientist Werner Heisenberg, who showed that it is impossible to determine at one and the same time both an electron's precise speed and its position. In the small-scale world of the electron, we enter a universe of uncertainty, probability, and statistical relationships. No improvement in measurement techniques will dispel this element of chance and provide us with complete knowledge of the universe.

The theory of relativity, developed by Albert Einstein (1879–1955), a German-Swiss physicist of Jewish lineage, was instrumental in shaping modern physics; it altered classical conceptions of space and time. Newtonian physics had viewed space as a distinct physical reality, a stationary medium through which light traveled and matter moved. Time was deemed a fixed and rigid framework that was the same for all observers and existed independently of human experience. For Einstein, however, neither space nor time had an independent existence; neither could be divorced from human experience. Once asked to explain briefly the essentials of relativity, Einstein replied: "It was formerly believed that if all material things disappeared out of the universe, time and space would be left. According to the relativity theory, however, time and space disappear together with the things."[26]

Contrary to all previous thinking, the relativity theory holds that time differs for two observers traveling at different speeds. Imagine twin brothers involved in space exploration, one as an astronaut and the other as a rocket designer who never leaves earth. The astronaut takes off in the most advanced spaceship yet constructed, one that achieves a speed close to the maximum attainable in our universe—the speed of light. After traveling several trillion miles, the spaceship turns around and returns to earth. According to the experience of the ship's occupant, the whole trip took about two years. But when the astronaut lands on earth, he finds totally changed conditions. His brother has long since died, for according to earth's calendars some two hundred years have elapsed since the rocket ship set out on its journey. Such an occurrence seemed to defy all commonsense experience, yet experiments supported Einstein's claims.

Einstein's work encompassed motion, matter, and energy as well. Motion, too, is relative: the

AP Photo.

Albert Einstein (1879–1955), a Principal Architect of Modern Physics. Forced to flee Nazi Germany, Einstein became a U.S. citizen. He was appointed to the Institute for Advanced Study at Princeton, New Jersey.

only way we can describe the motion of one body is to compare it with another moving body. This means that there is no motionless, absolute, fixed frame of reference anywhere in the universe. In his famous equation, $E = mc^2$, Einstein showed that matter and energy are not separate categories, but rather two different expressions of the same physical entity. The source of energy is matter, and the source of matter is energy. Tiny quantities of matter could be converted into staggering amounts of energy. The atomic age was dawning.

The discoveries of modern physics transformed the world of classical physics. Whereas nature had been regarded as something outside the individual—an objective reality existing independently of ourselves—modern physics teaches that our position in space and time determines what we mean by reality and that our very presence affects reality itself. When we observe a particle with our measuring instruments, we are interfering with it, knocking it off its course; we are participating in reality. Nor is nature fully knowable, as the classical physics of Newton had presumed; uncertainty, probability, and even mystery are inherent in the universe.

We have not yet felt the full impact of modern physics, but there is no doubt that it has been part of a revolution in human perceptions. Jacob Bronowski, a student of science and culture, concludes:

> *One aim of the physical sciences has been to give an exact picture of the material world. One achievement of physics in the twentieth century has been to prove that that aim is unattainable. . . . There is no absolute knowledge. . . . All information is imperfect. We have to treat it with humility. That is the human condition; and that is what quantum physics says. . . . The Principle of Uncertainty . . . fixed once and for all the realization that all knowledge is limited.*[27]

Like Darwin's theory of human origins, Freud's theory of human nature, and the transformation of classical space by modern artists, the modifications of the Newtonian picture by modern physicists have enlarged our understanding. At the same time, they have contributed to the sense of uncertainty and disorientation that characterized the twentieth century.

The Enlightenment Tradition in Disarray

Most nineteenth-century thinkers carried forward the spirit of the Enlightenment, particularly in its emphasis on science and its concern for individual liberty and social reform. In the tradition of the philosophes, nineteenth-century thinkers regarded science as humanity's greatest achievement and believed that through reason society could be reformed. The spread of parliamentary government and the extension of education, along with the many advances in science and technology, seemed to confirm the hopes of the philosophes for humanity's future progress.

But at the same time, the Enlightenment tradition was being undermined. In the early nineteenth century, the romantics revolted against the

Enlightenment's rational-scientific spirit in favor of human will and feeling. Romantic nationalists valued the collective soul of the nation—ancient traditions rooted in a hoary and dateless past—over reason and individual freedom. Conservatives emphasized the limitations of reason and attacked the political agenda of the Enlightenment and the French Revolution. In the closing decades of the nineteenth century, the Enlightenment tradition was challenged by Social Darwinists, who glorified violence and saw conflict between individuals and between nations as a law of nature. They considered the right of the powerful to predominate to be a right of nature, beyond good and evil, and they castigated humanitarianism as weakness. Echoing Sorel, several thinkers trumpeted the use of force in social and political controversies.

Furthermore, a number of thinkers, rejecting the Enlightenment view of people as fundamentally rational, held that subconscious drives and impulses govern human behavior more than reason does. If this is so, then individuals are not essentially autonomous, masters of their own selves. Several of these thinkers urged celebrating and extolling the irrational, which they regarded as the true essence of human beings and of life. They glorified an irrational vitality, or Nietzsche's will to power, which transcended considerations of good and evil. "I have always considered myself a voice of what I believe to be a greater renaissance—the revolt of the soul against the intellect—now beginning in the world," wrote the Irish poet William Butler Yeats.[28] German advocates of "life philosophy" explicitly called the mind "the enemy of the soul."

Even the theorists who studied the individual and society in a scientific way pointed out that below a surface of rationality lies a substratum of irrationality, which constitutes a deeper reality. The conviction was growing that reason was a puny instrument when compared with the volcanic strength of nonrational impulses, that these impulses pushed people toward destructive behavior and made political life precarious, and that the nonrational did not bend very much to education. The Enlightenment's image of the autonomous individual who makes rational decisions after weighing the choices (a fundamental premise of liberalism and democracy) no longer seemed tenable. Often the individual is not the master of his or her own person; human freedom is limited by human nature.

Liberalism, which owed much to the Enlightenment, was also undermined by theorists who rejected the idea of natural rights. The view that all individuals are born with inalienable rights had provided the philosophical basis of classical liberalism. It was now argued, however, that natural rights were not a law of nature or a higher truth; rather, they were simply a human creation, a product of a specific set of circumstances at a particular stage in history, notably the emergence of the bourgeoisie. Could commitment to parliamentary government, the rule of law, and other liberal-democratic institutions and practices survive this assault on the core principle of liberalism?

Other theorists argued that the ideas of right, truth, and justice do not have an independent value; rather, they are merely tools used by elites in their struggle to gain and maintain power. Opponents of liberalism and democracy utilized the theory of elites advanced by Pareto, as well as the new stress on human irrationality, as proof that the masses were incapable of self-government and that they had to be led by their betters. Many intellectuals of the right employed the new social theories to devalue the individualist and rational bases of liberal democracy bequeathed by the Enlightenment.

At the beginning of the twentieth century, the dominant mood remained that of confidence in Europe's future progress and in the values of European civilization. However, certain disquieting trends were already evident; they would grow to crisis proportions in succeeding decades. Although few people may have realized it, the Enlightenment tradition was in disarray.

The thinkers of the Enlightenment believed in an orderly, machinelike universe; natural law and natural rights operating in the social world; objective rules that gave form and structure to artistic productions; the essential rationality and goodness of the individual; and science and technology as instruments of progress. This coherent worldview, which had produced an attitude of certainty, security, and optimism, was in the process of dissolution by the early twentieth century. The commonsense Newtonian picture of the physical universe, with its inexorable laws of cause and effect, was fundamentally altered; the belief in natural rights and objective standards governing morality was undermined; rules and modes of expression that were at the very heart of Western esthetics were abandoned; and confidence in human rationality and goodness weakened. Furthermore, science and technology were accused of forging a mechanical, bureaucratic, and materialistic world that stifled intuition and feelings, thereby diminishing the self. To redeem the self, some thinkers urged a heroic struggle, which easily was channeled into primitive nationalism and martial crusades.

This radical attack on the moral and intellectual values of the Enlightenment, as well as on liberalism and democracy, included the denunciation of reason, exaltation of force, quest for the heroic, and yearning for a new authority; it constitutes the intellectual background of the Fascist movements that emerged after World War I. Holding the Enlightenment tradition in contempt and fascinated by power and violence, many people, including intellectuals, would exalt Fascist ideas and lionize Fascist leaders.

When the new century began, most Europeans were optimistic about the future, some even holding that European civilization was on the threshold of a golden age. Few suspected that European civilization would soon be gripped by a crisis that threatened its very survival. The powerful forces of irrationalism that had been hailed by Nietzsche, analyzed by Freud, and creatively expressed in modernist culture would erupt with devastating fury in twentieth-century political life, particularly in the form of extreme nationalism and racism that extolled violence. Confused and disillusioned people searching for new certainties and values would turn to political ideologies that openly rejected reason, lauded war, and scorned the inviolability of the human person. Dictators, utilizing the insights into the unconscious and the nonrational advanced by Freud and the social theorists, succeeded in manipulating the minds of the masses to an unprecedented degree.

These currents began to form at the end of the nineteenth century, but World War I brought them together in a tidal wave. World War I accentuated the questioning of established norms and the dissolution of Enlightenment certainties. It caused many people to see Western civilization as dying and beyond redemption. Exacerbating the spiritual crisis of the preceding generation, the war shattered Europe's political and social order. It also gave birth to totalitarian ideologies that nearly obliterated the legacy of the Enlightenment. The world wars of the twentieth century, with their millions of dead and mutilated, and the totalitarian experiments, which trampled on human dignity, bore out Nietzsche's warning that in a nihilistic world all is permitted.

❖ ❖ ❖

Notes

1. Friedrich Nietzsche, *The Will to Power,* trans. Walter Kaufmann and R. J. Hollingdale, ed. Walter Kaufmann (New York: Vintage Books, 1968), pp. 458–459.
2. Ibid., pp. 383–384.
3. Friedrich Nietzsche, *The Genealogy of Morals,* Essay 1, sec. 13 (New York: The Modern Library, 1954), p. 656.
4. Quoted in R. J. Hollingdale, *Nietzsche* (London: Routledge & Kegan Paul, 1973), p. 82.
5. Nietzsche, *Will to Power,* p. 397.
6. Ibid., p. 518.
7. Friedrich Nietzsche, *Twilight of the Idols and The Anti-Christ,* trans. R. J. Hollingdale (New York: Penguin, 1972), p. 116.
8. Nietzsche, *Will to Power,* p. 386.
9. Janko Lavrin, *Nietzsche* (New York: Charles Scribner's Sons, 1971), p. 113.
10. Sigmund Freud, *A General Introduction to Psychoanalysis,* trans. Joan Riviere (Garden City, N.Y.: Garden City Publishing Co., 1943), p. 252.

11. Sigmund Freud, *Civilization and Its Discontents* (New York: Norton, 1961), p. 62.
12. Ibid., p. 58.
13. Ibid.
14. Ibid., p. 59.
15. Ibid., p. 61.
16. Ibid., p. 59.
17. Ibid., p. 69.
18. Émile Durkheim, *Suicide: A Study in Sociology,* trans. John Spaulding and George Simpson (New York: The Free Press, 1951), p. 391.
19. Quoted in Christopher Butler, *Early Modernism: Literature, Music, and Painting in Europe, 1900–1916* (New York: Oxford University Press), p. 2.
20. Irving Howe, ed., *The Idea of the Modern in Literature and the Arts* (New York: Horizon Press, 1967), p. 16.
21. Ibid., p. 15.
22. From *The Cultural Contradictions of Capitalism* by Daniel Bel, pp. 110, 112. Copyright © 1976 by Basic Books. Reprinted by permission of Basic Books, a member of Perseus Books Group.
23. Excerpted in Piero Weiss and Richard Taruskin, eds., *Music in the Western World: A History in Documents* (New York: Schirmen Books, 1984), p. 428.
24. Paul Klee, *On Modern Art,* trans. Paul Findlay (London: Faber & Faber, 1948), p. 51.
25. John Canaday, *Mainstreams of Modern Art* (New York: Holt, 1961), p. 458.
26. Quoted in A. E. E. McKenzie, *The Major Achievements of Science* (New York: Cambridge University Press, 1960), vol. 1, 310.
27. Jacob Bronowski, *The Ascent of Man* (Boston: Little, Brown, 1973), p. 353.
28. Quoted in Roland N. Stromberg, *Redemption by War,* p. 65. University Press of Kansas, 1982. Copyright © 1982 by University Press of Kansas. All rights reserved. Reprinted with permission.

Suggested Reading

Aschheim, Steven E., *The Nietzsche Legacy in Germany, 1890–1990* (1992). How Germans, including Nazis, interpreted Nietzsche.

Baumer, Franklin, *Modern European Thought* (1977). A well-informed study of modern thought.

Bradbury, Malcolm, and James McFarlane, eds., *Modernism, 1890–1930* (1974). Essays on various phases of modernism; valuable bibliography.

Gay, Peter, *Freud: A Life for Our Times* (1988). A highly recommended study.

Hamilton, G. H., *Painting and Sculpture in Europe, 1880–1940* (1967). An authoritative work.

Hollingdale, R. J., *Nietzsche* (1973). Lucid and insightful.

Hughes, H. Stuart, *Consciousness and Society* (1958). Good on social thinkers.

Kolocotroni, Vassiliki, Jane Goldman, and Olga Taxidou, eds., *Modernism: An Anthology of Sources and Documents* (1998). An array of selections covering the breadth and variety of modernism.

Masur, Gerhard, *Prophets of Yesterday* (1961). Studies in European culture from 1890 to 1914.

Nelson, Benjamin, ed., *Freud and the Twentieth Century* (1957). A valuable collection of essays.

Panek, Richard, *The Invisible Century: Einstein, Freud and the Search for Hidden Universes* (2009). A talented science writer explores the journey of discovery of these great thinkers.

Stromberg, Roland N., *European Intellectual History Since 1789* (1986). A helpful text.

Zeitlin, I. M., *Ideology and the Development of Sociological Theory* (1968). Examines in detail the thought of major shapers of sociological theory.

Part Five

Western Civilization in Crisis: World Wars and Totalitarianism

1914–1945

When the war in Europe ended in May 1945, many areas lay devastated, none more so than the once picturesque German city of Dresden, in which some 35,000 people had perished in a terror bombing by Allied planes in February 1945. Europe was faced with the awesome task of reconstructing a continent in ruins.

	Politics and Society	*Thought and Culture*
1910	World War I (1914–1918) United States declares war on Germany (1917) Bolshevik Revolution in Russia (1917) Wilson announces his Fourteen Points (1918) Treaty of Versailles (1919)	Bohr: Quantum theory of atomic structure (1912) Stravinsky, *The Rite of Spring* (1913) Pareto, *Treatise on General Sociology* (1916) Spengler, *The Decline of the West* (1918, 1922) Dadaism in art (1915–1924) Barth, *The Epistle to the Romans* (1919)
1920	Mussolini seizes power in Italy (1922) First Five-Year Plan starts rapid industrialization in the Soviet Union (1928) Forced collectivization of agriculture in the Soviet Union (1929) Start of the Great Depression (1929)	Wittgenstein, *Tractatus Logico-Philosophicus* (1921–1922) Eliot, *The Waste Land* (1922) Mann, *Magic Mountain* (1924) Cassirer, *The Philosophy of Symbolic Forms* (1923–1929) Surrealism in art (c. 1925) Hitler, *Mein Kampf* (1925–1926) Kafka, *The Trial* (1925) Heidegger, *Being and Time* (1927) Lawrence, *Lady Chatterley's Lover* (1928) Remarque, *All Quiet on the Western Front* (1929)
1930	Hitler becomes chancellor of Germany (1933) Stalin orders mass purges in the Soviet Union (1936–1938) Hitler sends troops into the Rhineland (1936) Rome–Berlin Axis (1936) Spanish Civil War (1936–1939) Franco establishes a dictatorship in Spain (1939) Nazi-Soviet Nonaggression Pact (1939) German troops invade Poland: World War II begins (1939)	Freud, *Civilization and Its Discontents* (1930) Ortega y Gasset, *The Revolt of the Masses* (1930) Jaspers, *Man in the Modern Age* (1930) Jung, *Modern Man in Search of a Soul* (1933) Toynbee, *A Study of History* (1934–1961) Keynes, *The General Theory of Employment, Interest, and Money* (1936) Picasso, *Guernica* (1937) Steinbeck, *The Grapes of Wrath* (1939)
1940	Germany invades Belgium, Holland, Luxembourg, and France (1940) Japan attacks Pearl Harbor: United States enters war against Japan and Germany (1941) War in Europe ends (1945) United States drops atomic bombs on Japan; Japan surrenders (1945)	Hemingway, *For Whom the Bell Tolls* (1940) Koestler, *Darkness at Noon* (1941) Fromm, *Escape from Freedom* (1941) Camus, *The Stranger* (1942) Sartre, *Being and Nothingness* (1943) Orwell, *1984* (1949)

Chapter 18

World War I: The West in Despair

- Aggravated Nationalist Tensions in Austria-Hungary
- The German System of Alliances
- The Triple Entente
- The Drift Toward War
- War as Celebration
- Stalemate in the West
- Other Fronts
- The Collapse of the Central Powers
- The Peace Conference
- The Russian Revolution of 1917
- The War and European Consciousness

Focus Questions

1. How did the nationality problem in Austria-Hungary contribute to the outbreak of World War I?
2. In assessing responsibility for the war, what arguments have been advanced by historians for each of the major countries involved?
3. Why did many Europeans celebrate the coming of war?
4. Why was trench warfare so deadly?
5. What was Germany's reaction to the Treaty of Versailles?
6. What was Wilson's peace program? What obstacles did he face?
7. Why did the Provisional Government and liberal democracy fail in Russia in 1917?
8. How did World War I transform the consciousness of Europeans?

Prior to 1914, the dominant mood in Europe was one of pride in the accomplishments of Western civilization and confidence in its future progress. Advances in science and technology, the rising standard of living, the spread of democratic institutions, and Europe's position of power in the world all contributed to a sense of optimism, as did the expansion of social reform and the increase in literacy for the masses. Furthermore, since the defeat of Napoleon, Europe had avoided a general war, and since the Franco-Prussian War (1870–1871), the Great Powers had not fought each other. Few people recognized that the West's outward achievements masked an inner turbulence that was propelling Western civilization toward a cataclysm. The European state system was failing.

By 1914, national states, answering to no higher power, were fueled by an explosive nationalism and were grouped into alliances that faced each other with ever-mounting hostility. Nationalist passions, overheated by the popular press and expansionist societies, poisoned international relations. Nationalist thinkers propagated pseudoscientific racial and Social Darwinist doctrines that glorified conflict and justified the subjugation of other peoples. Committed to enhancing national power, statesmen lost sight of Europe as a community of nations sharing a common civilization. Caution and restraint gave way to belligerency in foreign relations.

The failure of the European state system was paralleled by a cultural crisis. Some European intellectuals attacked the rational tradition of the Enlightenment and celebrated the primitive, the instinctual, and the irrational. Increasingly, young people were drawn to philosophies of action that ridiculed liberal, bourgeois values and viewed war as a purifying and ennobling experience. Colonial wars, colorfully portrayed in the popular press, ignited the imagination of bored factory workers and daydreaming students and reinforced a sense of duty and an urge for gallantry among soldiers and aristocrats. These "splendid" little colonial wars helped fashion an attitude that made war acceptable, if not laudable. Yearning to break loose from their ordinary lives and to embrace heroic values, many Europeans regarded violent conflict as the highest expression of individual and national life. "If only there were a war, even an unjust one," wrote George Heym, a young German writer, in 1912. "This peace is so rotten."[1] The popular historian Heinrich von Treitschke (1834–1896), whose lectures influenced many students who were to rise to positions of importance in the German army and administration, expressed the prevailing mood: "Those who preach the nonsense about everlasting peace do not understand the life of the [German] race. . . . [T]o banish war from history would be to banish all progress."[2] Although technology was making warfare more brutal and dangerous, Europe retained a romantic illusion about combat.

While Europe was seemingly progressing in the art of civilization, the mythic power of nationalism and the primitive appeal of conflict were driving European civilization to the abyss. Few people recognized the potential crisis—certainly not the statesmen whose reckless blundering allowed the Continent to stumble into war. ❖

Aggravated Nationalist Tensions in Austria-Hungary

On June 28, 1914, a young terrorist, with the support of a secret Serbian nationalist society called Union or Death (more popularly known as the Black Hand), murdered Archduke Francis Ferdinand, heir to the throne of Austria-Hungary. Six weeks later, the armies of Europe were on the march; an incident in the Balkans had sparked a world war. An analysis of why Austria-Hungary felt compelled to attack Serbia and why the other powers became enmeshed in the conflict shows how explosive Europe was in 1914. And nowhere were conditions more volatile than in Austria-Hungary, the scene of the assassination.

With its several nationalities, each with its own history and traditions and often conflicting aspirations, Austria-Hungary stood in opposition to nationalism, the most powerful spiritual force of the age. Perhaps the supranational Austro-Hungarian Empire was obsolete in a world of states based on the principle of nationality. Dominated by Germans and Hungarians, the empire remained unable either to satisfy the grievances or to contain the nationalist aims of its minorities, particularly

Primary Source

Friedrich von Bernhardi: *Germany and the Next War*

A militaristic attitude that glorified war was widespread in Germany prior to World War I. The following excerpt comes from Friedrich von Bernhardi's work Germany and the Next War *(1911), which was immensely popular in his country.*

. . . War is a biological necessity of the first importance, a regulative element in the life of mankind which cannot be dispensed with, since without it an unhealthy development will follow, which excludes every advancement of the race, and therefore all real civilization. "War is the father of all things." The sages of antiquity long before Darwin recognized this.

The struggle for existence is, in the life of Nature, the basis of all healthy development. . . . The law of the stronger holds good everywhere. Those forms survive which are able to procure themselves the most favourable conditions of life, and to assert themselves in the universal economy of Nature. The weaker succumb. . . .

Struggle is, therefore, a universal law of Nature, and the instinct of self-preservation which leads to struggle is acknowledged to be a natural condition of existence.

Strong, healthy, and flourishing nations increase in numbers. From a given moment they require a continual expansion of their frontiers, they require new territory for the accommodation of their surplus population. Since almost every part of the globe is inhabited, new territory must, as a rule, be obtained at the cost of its possessors—that is to say, by conquest, which thus becomes a law of necessity.

The right of conquest is universally acknowledged.

. . . Vast territories inhabited by uncivilized masses are occupied by more highly civilized States, and made subject to their rule. Higher civilization and the correspondingly greater power are the foundations of the right to annexation. . . .

Lastly, in all times the right of conquest by war has been admitted. It may be that a growing people cannot win colonies from civilized races, and yet the State wishes to retain the surplus population which the mother-country can no longer feed. Then the only course left is to acquire the necessary territory by war. Thus the instinct of self-preservation leads inevitably to war, and the conquest of foreign soil. It is not the possessor, but the victor, who then has the right. . . .

In such cases might gives the right to occupy or to conquer. Might is at once the supreme right, and the dispute as to what is left is decided by the arbitrament of war. War gives a biologically just decision, since its decisions rest on the very nature of things. . . .

The knowledge, therefore, that war depends on biological laws leads to the conclusion that every attempt to exclude it from international relations must be demonstrably untenable.

Question for Analysis

1. What conclusions did Friedrich von Bernhardi draw from his premise that war was a biological necessity?

Friedrich von Bernhardi, *Germany and the Next War*, trans. Allan H. Fowles (New York: Longmans, Greens, 1914), 18, 21–24.

Chronology 18.1 ❖ World War I

1882	Formation of the Triple Alliance of Germany, Austria-Hungary, and Italy
1894	Alliance between Russia and France
1904	Anglo-French Entente
1907	Anglo-Russian Entente
1908	Bosnian crisis
June 28, 1914	Archduke Francis Ferdinand of Austria is assassinated at Sarajevo
August 4, 1914	Germans invade Belgium
September 1914	First Battle of the Marne saves Paris
May 1915	Italy enters the war on the Allies' side
Spring 1915	Germany launches offensive that forces Russia to abandon Galicia and most of Poland
February 1916	General Pétain leads French forces at Verdun; Germans fail to capture the fortress town
July–November 1916	Battle of the Somme: the Allies suffer 600,000 casualties
January 1917	Germany launches unrestricted submarine warfare
April 6, 1917	United States declares war on Germany
November 1917	Bolsheviks take power in Russia
March 1918	Russia signs the Treaty of Brest-Litovsk, losing territory to Germany and withdrawing from the war
March 21, 1918	Germans launch a great offensive to end the war
June 3, 1918	Germans advance to within fifty-six miles of Paris
August 8, 1918	British victory at Amiens
October 1918	Turkey is forced to withdraw from the war after several British successes
November 3, 1918	Austria-Hungary signs armistice with the Allies
November 11, 1918	Germany signs armistice with the Allies, ending World War I
January 1919	Paris Peace Conference
June 28, 1919	Germany signs the Treaty of Versailles

the Czechs and South Slavs (Croats, Slovenes, and Serbs).

Heightened agitation among the several nationalities, which worsened in the decade before 1914, created terrible anxieties among Austrian leaders. The fear that the empire would be torn apart by rebellion caused Austria to pursue a forceful policy against any nation that fanned the nationalist feelings of its Slavic minorities. In particular, this policy meant worsening tensions between Austria and small Serbia, which had been independent of the Ottoman Empire since 1878.

Captivated by Western ideas of nationalism, the Serbs sought to create a Greater Serbia by

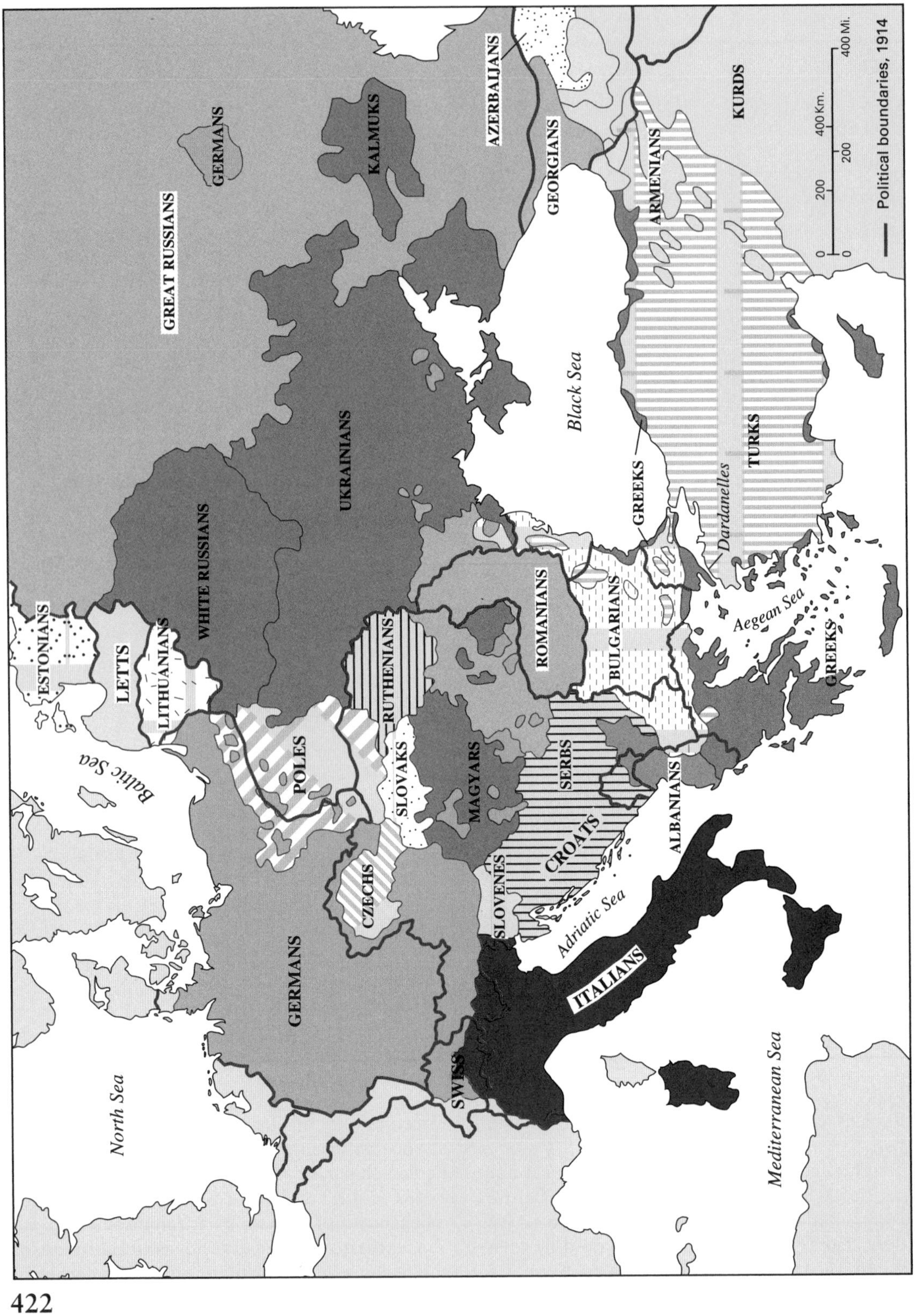

GREAT RUSSIANS
GERMANS
KALMUKS
AZERBAIJANS
GEORGIANS
ARMENIANS
KURDS
0 200 400 Km.
0 200 400 Mi.
Political boundaries, 1914
ESTONIANS
LETTS
LITHUANIANS
WHITE RUSSIANS
UKRAINIANS
Black Sea
GREEKS
TURKS
Dardanelles
RUTHENIANS
ROMANIANS
BULGARIANS
Aegean Sea
GREEKS
Baltic Sea
POLES
SLOVAKS
MAGYARS
SERBS
ALBANIANS
CROATS
CZECHS
SLOVENES
Adriatic Sea
GERMANS
ITALIANS
SWISS
North Sea
Mediterranean Sea

uniting with their racial kin, the South Slavs who dwelled in Austria-Hungary. Since some seven million South Slavs lived in the Hapsburg Empire, the dream of a Greater Serbia, shrilly expressed by Serbian nationalists, caused nightmares in Austria. Fearing that continued Serbian agitation would encourage the South Slavs to press for secession, some Austrian leaders urged the destruction of the Serbian menace.

The tensions arising from the multinational character of the Austro-Hungarian Empire in an age of heightened nationalist feeling set off the explosion in 1914. Unable to solve its minority problems and fearful of Pan-Serbism, Austria-Hungary felt itself in a life-or-death situation. This sense of desperation led it to lash out at Serbia after the assassination of Archduke Francis Ferdinand.

The German System of Alliances

The war might have been avoided, or might have remained limited to Austria and Serbia, had Europe in 1914 not been divided into two hostile alliance systems. Such a situation contains inherent dangers. For example, knowing that it has the support of allies, a country might pursue a more provocative and reckless course and be less conciliatory during a crisis. Furthermore, a conflict between two states might spark a chain reaction, drawing in the other powers and transforming a limited war into a general war. That is what happened after the assassination. This dangerous alliance system originated with Bismarck and the Franco-Prussian War.

The New German Empire

The unification of Germany in 1870 and 1871 turned the new state into an international power of the first rank, upsetting the balance of power in Europe. For the first time since the wars of the French Revolution, a nation was in a position to dominate the European continent. To German nationalists, the unification of Germany was both the fulfillment of a national dream and the starting point for an even more ambitious goal: extending German power in Europe and the world.

As the nineteenth century drew to a close, German nationalism became more extreme. Believing that Germany must either grow or die, nationalists pressed the government to build a powerful navy, acquire colonies, gain a much greater share of the world's markets, and expand German interests and influence in Europe. Sometimes these goals were expressed in the language of Social Darwinism: that nations are engaged in an eternal struggle for survival and domination. Decisive victories against Austria (1866) and France (1871), the formation of the German Reich, rapid industrialization, and the impressive achievements of German science and scholarship had molded a powerful and dynamic nation. Imbued with great expectations for the future, Germans became increasingly impatient to see the fatherland gain its "rightful" place in world affairs—an attitude that alarmed non-Germans.

Bismarck's Goals

Under Bismarck, who did not seek additional territory but wanted only to preserve the recently achieved unification, Germany pursued a moderate and cautious foreign policy. One of Bismarck's principal goals was to keep France isolated and friendless. Deeply humiliated by its defeat in the Franco-Prussian War and the loss of Alsace and Lorraine, France found its nationalists yearning for a war of revenge against Germany. Even though the French government, aware of Germany's strength, was unlikely to initiate such a conflict, the issue of Alsace-Lorraine increased tensions between the two countries.

Bismarck also hoped to prevent a war between Russia and Austria-Hungary, for such a conflict could lead to German involvement, the breakup of Austria-Hungary, and Russian expansion in Eastern Europe. To maintain peace and Germany's existing borders, Bismarck forged complex alliances. In the 1880s, he created the Triple Alliance, consisting of Germany, Austria-Hungary, and Italy, as well as an alliance with Russia.

◀ *Map* 18.1 Various Ethnic Groups in Europe Before World War.

Bismarck conducted foreign policy with restraint, forming alliances not to conquer new lands but to protect Germany from aggression by either France or Russia. His aim was to preserve order and stability in Europe, not to launch war. But in 1888, a new emperor ascended the German throne. When the young Kaiser William II (1888–1918) clashed with his aging prime minister, Bismarck was forced to resign (1890). Lacking Bismarck's diplomatic skills, his cool restraint, and his determination to keep peace in Europe, the new German leaders pursued a belligerent and imperialistic foreign policy in the ensuing years—a policy that frightened other states, particularly Britain. Whereas Bismarck considered Germany a satiated power, these men insisted that Germany must have its place in the sun.

The first act of the new leadership was to permit the treaty with Russia to lapse, allowing Germany to give full support to Austria, which was considered a more reliable ally. Whereas Bismarck had warned Austria to act with moderation and caution in the Balkans, his successors not only failed to hold Austria in check but also actually encouraged Austrian aggression. This proved fatal to the peace of Europe.

The Triple Entente

Fear of Germany

When Germany broke with Russia in 1890, France was quick to take advantage of the situation. Worried by Germany's increasing military strength, expanding industries, growing population, and alliance with Austria and Italy, France coveted Russia as an ally. In 1894, France and Russia entered into an alliance; the isolation forced on France by Bismarck had ended. France hoped that the alliance would deter German aggression, for Germany was now threatened with a two-front war.

Germany's growing military and industrial might also alarmed Great Britain. In addition, its spectacular industrial growth had made Germany a potent trade rival of England. Britain was distressed, too, by Germany's increased efforts to become a great colonial power—a goal demanded by German nationalists. But most troubling was Germany's decision to build a great navy. Germany was already the strongest land power on the Continent. Achieving naval parity with England would give Germany the potential to threaten Britain's overseas empire and to blockade the British Isles, depriving Britain of food and supplies. Germany's naval program was the single most important reason that Britain moved closer first to France and then to Russia. Germany's naval construction, designed to increase its stature as a Great Power but not really necessary for its security, was one indication that German leaders had abandoned Bismarck's policy of good sense. Eager to add the British as an ally and demonstrating superb diplomatic skill, France moved to end longstanding colonial disputes with Britain. The Entente Cordiale of 1904 accomplished this conciliation. England had emerged from its self-imposed isolation.

Wishing to counter Germany's Triple Alliance with a strong alliance of their own, French diplomats now sought to ease tensions between their Russian ally and their new British friend. Two events convinced Russia to adopt a more conciliatory attitude toward Britain: a humiliating and unexpected defeat in the Russo-Japanese War of 1904–1905 and a working-class revolution in 1905. Shocked by defeat, its army bordering on disintegration, and its workers restive, Russia was now receptive to settling its imperial disputes with Britain over Persia, Tibet, and Afghanistan—a decision encouraged by France. In the Anglo-Russian Entente of 1907, as in the Anglo-French Entente Cordiale of 1904, the former rivals conducted themselves in a conciliatory, if not friendly, manner. In both instances, what engendered this spirit of cooperation was fear of Germany.

Europe was now broken into two hostile camps: the Triple Entente of France, Russia, and Britain and the Triple Alliance of Germany, Austria-Hungary, and Italy. The costly arms race and the maintenance of large standing armies by all the states except Britain increased fear and suspicion between the alliances.

German Reactions

Germany denounced the Triple Entente as a hostile anti-German coalition designed to encircle and crush Germany; to survive, Germany must break this ring. Considering Austria-Hungary to be its only reliable ally, Germany resolved to preserve the power and dignity of the Hapsburg Empire. If Austria-Hungary fell from the ranks of Great Powers, Germany would have to stand alone against its enemies. At all costs, Austria-Hungary must not be weakened.

But this assessment suffered from dangerous miscalculations. First, Germany overstressed the hostile nature of the Triple Entente. In reality, France, Russia, and Britain had drawn closer together not to wage aggressive war against Germany but to protect themselves against burgeoning German military, industrial, and diplomatic power. Second, by linking German security to Austria, Germany greatly increased the chances of war. Growing more and more apprehensive of Pan-Serbism, Austria might well decide that only a war could prevent its empire from disintegrating. Confident of German support, Austria would be more likely to resort to force; fearing any diminution of Austrian power, Germany would be more likely to give Austria that support.

The Drift Toward War

Starting in 1908, several crises tested the competing alliances, pushing Europe closer to war. Particularly significant was the Bosnian affair, which involved Russia, Austria-Hungary, and Serbia. This incident contained many of the ingredients that eventually ignited the war in 1914.

The Bosnian Crisis

Russia's humiliating defeat by Japan in 1905 had diminished its stature as a Great Power. The new Russian foreign minister, Alexander Izvolsky, hoped to gain a diplomatic triumph by compelling Ottoman Turkey to allow Russian warships to pass through the Dardanelles, fulfilling a centuries-old dream of extending Russian power into the Mediterranean.

Russia made a deal with Austria: if Austria would support Russia's move to open the Dardanelles, Russia would permit Austrian annexation of the provinces of Bosnia and Herzegovina. Officially a part of the Ottoman Empire, these provinces had been administered by Austria-Hungary since 1878. The population consisted mainly of ethnic cousins of the Serbs. A formal annexation would certainly infuriate the Serbs, who hoped one day to make the region part of a Greater Serbia.

In 1908, Austria proceeded to annex the provinces, but Russia met stiff resistance from England and France when it presented its case for opening the straits to Russian warships. Austria had gained a diplomatic victory, while Russia suffered another humiliation. Even more enraged than Russia was Serbia, which threatened to invade Bosnia to liberate its cousins from Austrian oppression. The Serbian press openly declared that Austria-Hungary must perish if the South Slavs were to achieve liberty and unity. A fiery attitude also prevailed in Vienna: Austria-Hungary could not survive unless Serbia was destroyed.

During this period of intense hostility between Austria-Hungary and Serbia, Germany supported its Austrian ally. To keep Austria strong, Germany would even agree to the dismemberment of Serbia and its incorporation into the Hapsburg Empire. Unlike Bismarck, who tried to hold Austria in check, German leadership now coolly envisioned an Austrian attack on Serbia, and just as coolly offered German support if Russia intervened.

Balkan Wars

The Bosnian crisis pushed Germany and Austria closer together, brought relations between Austria and Serbia to the breaking point, and inflicted another humiliation on Russia. The first Balkan War (1912) continued these trends. The Balkan states of Montenegro, Serbia, Bulgaria, and Greece attacked the dying Ottoman Empire. In a brief campaign, the Balkan armies captured the Turkish empire's European territory, with the exception of Constantinople. Because it was on the victorious side, landlocked Serbia gained the Albanian coast and thus a long-desired outlet to the sea. Austria was determined to keep its enemy from reaping this reward, and Germany, as in the Bosnian crisis, supported its ally. Unable to secure Russian support, Serbia was forced to surrender the territory, which became the state of Albania.

Incensed Serbian nationalists accelerated their campaign of propaganda and terrorism against

Bettmann/Corbis.

The Assassination of Archduke Francis Ferdinand. Immediately after the assassination, Austrian authorities arrest one of the assassins.

Austria. Believing that another humiliation would irreparably damage its prestige, Russia vowed to back Serbia in its next confrontation with Austria. And Austria had exhausted its patience with Serbia. Emboldened by German encouragement, Austria wanted to end the Serbian threat once and for all. Thus, the ingredients for war between Austria and Serbia, a war that might easily draw in Russia and Germany, were present. Another incident might well start a war. It came in 1914.

Assassination of Francis Ferdinand

On June 28, 1914, Francis Ferdinand was assassinated while making a state visit to Sarajevo, the capital of Bosnia. Young Gavrilo Princip, who was part of a team of Bosnian terrorists linked to the Black Hand, fired two shots at close range into the archduke's car. Francis Ferdinand and his wife died within fifteen minutes. By killing the archduke, the terrorists hoped to bring tensions in the Hapsburg Empire to a boiling point and to prepare the way for revolution.

For many years, leaders of Austria had yearned for war with Serbia in order to end the agitation for the union of the South Slavs. Now, they reasoned, the hour had struck. But war with Serbia would require the approval of Germany. Believing that Austria was Germany's only reliable ally and that a diminution of Austrian power and prestige threatened German security, German statesmen encouraged their ally to take up arms against Serbia. Germany and Austria wanted a quick strike to overwhelm Serbia before other countries were drawn into the conflict.

Germany Encourages Austria

Confident of German backing, on July 23 Austria presented Serbia with an ultimatum and demanded a response within forty-eight hours. The terms of the ultimatum were so harsh that it was next to impossible for Serbia to accept them. This reaction was the one that Austria intended, as it sought a military solution to the crisis rather than a diplomatic one. But Russia would not remain indifferent to an Austro-German effort to liquidate Serbia. Russia feared that an Austrian conquest of Serbia was just the first step in an Austro-German plan to dominate the Balkans. Such an extension of German and Austrian power in a region bordering Russia was unthinkable to the tsar's government. Moreover, after suffering repeated reverses in foreign affairs, Russia would not tolerate another humiliation. As Germany had decided to back its Austrian ally, Russia resolved not to abandon Serbia.

Serbia responded to Austria's ultimatum in a conciliatory manner, agreeing to virtually all Austrian demands. But it refused to let Austrian officials enter Serbia to investigate the assassination. Having already discarded the idea of a peaceful settlement, Austria insisted that Serbia's failure to accept one provision meant that the entire ultimatum had been rejected. It ordered the mobilization of the Austrian army.

This was a crucial moment for Germany. Would it continue to support Austria, knowing that an Austrian attack on Serbia would probably bring Russia into the conflict? Determined not to desert Austria and believing that a showdown with Russia was inevitable anyway, the German war party, with the military cajoling and persuading the civilian authorities, continued to urge Austrian action against Serbia. They argued that it was better to fight Russia in 1914 than a few years later, when the tsar's empire, which already had a huge reserve of manpower and was rapidly building strategic railroads and expanding its Baltic fleet, would be stronger. Confident of the superiority of the German army, the war party claimed that Germany could defeat both Russia and France and that Britain's army was too weak to make a difference.

On July 28, 1914, Austria declared war on Serbia. Russia, with the assurance of French support, proclaimed partial mobilization aimed at Austria alone. But the military warned that partial mobilization would throw the slow-moving Russian war machine into total confusion if the order had to be changed suddenly to full mobilization. Moreover, the only plans the Russian general staff had drawn up called for full mobilization, that is, for war against both Austria and Germany. Pressured by his generals, the tsar gave the order for full mobilization on July 30. Russian forces would be arrayed against Germany as well as Austria.

Because the country that struck first gained the advantage of fighting according to its own plans rather than having to improvise in response to the enemy's attack, generals tended to regard mobilization by the enemy as an act of war. Therefore, when Russia refused a German warning to halt mobilization, Germany, on August 1, ordered a general mobilization and declared war on Russia. Two days later, Germany also declared war on France, believing that France would support its Russian ally. Besides, German battle plans were based on a war with both Russia and France. Thus, a war between Germany and Russia automatically meant a German attack on France.

When Belgium refused to allow German troops to march through Belgian territory into France, Germany invaded the small nation, which brought Britain, pledged to guarantee Belgian neutrality, into the war. Britain could never tolerate German troops directly across the English Channel in any case, nor could it brook German mastery of Western Europe.

The Question of Responsibility

The question of whether any one power was mainly responsible for the war has intrigued historians. In assessing blame, historians have focused on Germany's role. German historian Fritz Fischer argues that Germany's ambition to dominate Europe was the underlying cause of the war. Germany encouraged Austria to strike at Serbia, knowing that an attack on Serbia could mean war with Russia and its French ally. Believing that it

© Archives Larousse, Paris, France/Giraudon/The Bridgeman Art Library International.

For many people, the declaration of war was a cause for celebration. Few Europeans realized what a horror the war would turn out to be.

had the military advantage, Germany was willing to risk such a war. Hence, "her leaders must bear a substantial share of the historical responsibility for the outbreak of general war in 1914."[3]

Attracted by Social Darwinist ideas that foresaw an inevitable racial struggle between Germans and Slavs, by militarist doctrines that glorified war, and by a nationalist drive for *Lebensraum* (more living space), continues Fischer, Germany sought to become the foremost economic and political power in Europe and to play a far greater role in world politics; to achieve this goal, it was willing to go to war. Fischer supports his position by pointing to Germany's war aims, drawn up immediately after the outbreak of war, which called for the annexation of neighboring territories and the creation of satellite states, that is, imposing German hegemony over Europe. Fischer's thesis had distressed Germans for it implies that there is continuity between Germany's territorial ambitions at the time of World War I and Hitler's territorial goals—that Nazi imperialism was not an aberration in German history but coincided with the wishes of Germany's traditional ruling elite. Fischer's critics stress, however, that Social Darwinism and militarism enthralled other nations besides Germany and that this was not peculiarly German, but rather part of a general European sickness. They argue further that Germany would have preferred a limited war between Austria and Serbia and before the war had no plans to annex and dominate neighboring lands.

Historians also attribute blame to the other powers. Austria bears responsibility for its determination to crush Serbia and for its insistent avoidance of a negotiated settlement. Serbia's responsibility stems from its pursuing an aggressive Pan-Serbian policy, which set it on a collision course with Austria-Hungary. In 1913, Sir Fairfax Cartwright, the British ambassador to Vienna, warned: "Serbia will some day set Europe by the ears, and bring about a universal war on the Continent. I cannot tell you how exasperated people are getting here at the continual worry which that little country causes to Austria."[4] Russia bears responsibility for instituting general mobilization, thereby turning a limited war between Austria-Hungary and Serbia into a European war; France, for failing to restrain Russia and indeed for encouraging its ally to mobilize; and England, for failing to make clear that it would support its allies. Had Germany seen plainly that Britain would intervene, it might have been more cautious. Finally blame falls on diplomats and statesmen for their ineptness and their lack of imagination in dealing with a crisis that could have been resolved without war.

Some historians, dismissing the question of responsibility, regard the war as an obvious sign that European civilization was in deep trouble. Viewed in the broad perspective of European history, the war marked a culmination of dangerous forces in European life: the belief expressed by some theorists that violent conflict was a natural, inevitable, and worthy feature of human relations and a belligerent nationalism that pitted nation against nation in a struggle for survival. It also pointed to the flaws and perils of the alliance system, which set off a chain reaction, and the failure of the European state system that glorified national power at the expense of a common European civilization. Nor do European leaders and statesmen escape blame. Had Austro-Hungarian and Russian policymakers been more willing to compromise and less willing to risk war and had German and French officialdom tried to restrain their allies, the tragedy could have been averted.

War as Celebration

When war was certain, an extraordinary phenomenon occurred. Crowds gathered in capital cities and expressed their loyalty to the fatherland and their readiness to fight. It seemed as if people wanted violence for its own sake. War seemed to offer an escape from the dull routine of classroom, job, and home and from the emptiness, drabness, mediocrity, and pettiness of bourgeois society—from "a world grown old and cold and weary," as Rupert Brooke, a young British poet, put it.[5] To some, war was a "beautiful . . . sacred moment" that satisfied an "ethical yearning."[6] To many people, especially youth and intellectuals, war seemed a healthy and heroic antidote to what was regarded as an unbearably decadent and soul-destroying machine age and to the bourgeois preoccupation with work, profits, and possessions. But more significantly, the outpouring of patriotic sentiments demonstrated the immense power that nationalism exercised over the European mind. With extraordinary success, nationalism welded millions of people into a collectivity ready to devote body and soul to the nation, especially during its hour of need. All believed that their country was a victim of aggression.

In Paris, men marched down the boulevards singing the stirring words of the French national anthem, the "Marseillaise," while women showered young soldiers with flowers. A participant in these days recalls: "Young and old, civilians and military men burned with the same excitement. . . . [T]housands of men eager to fight would jostle one another outside recruiting offices, waiting to join up. . . . The word 'duty' had a meaning for them, and the word 'country' had regained its splendor."[7] The term *union sacrée* (sacred union) was coined to express the sense of oneness, inclusiveness, and devotion to the nation that gripped French men and women at the time.

Similarly, in Germany, "flowers were thrown at us from every window; everyone wanted to shake hands with the departing soldiers. . . . Musicians played. . . . People cried and sang at the same time. . . . Nobody could resist the ebullient feeling."[8] "It is a joy to be alive," editorialized one newspaper. "We wished so much for this hour. . . . The sword which has been forced into our hand will not be sheathed until our aims are won and our territory extended as far as necessity demands."[9] Writing about those momentous days, the British mathematician-philosopher Bertrand Russell recalled his horror and "amazement that average men and women were delighted at the prospect of war. . . . [T]he anticipation of carnage was delightful to something like ninety percent of the population. I had to revise my views on human nature."[10]

Soldiers bound for battle and wives and sweethearts seeing them off at train stations were in a holiday mood. "My dear ones, be proud that you live in such a time and in such a nation and that you . . . have the privilege of sending those you love into so glorious a battle," wrote a young German law student to his family.[11] The young warriors yearned to do something noble and altruistic, to win glory, and to experience life at its most intense.

The martial mood also captivated many of Europe's most distinguished intellectuals. They shared Rupert Brooke's sentiments: "Now God be thanked Who has matched us with His hour, / And caught our youth, and wakened us from sleeping."[12] To the prominent German historian Friedrich Meinecke, August 1914 was "one of the great moments of my life which suddenly filled my soul with the deepest confidence in our people and the profoundest joy."[13] In November 1914, Thomas Mann (see "Intellectuals and Artists in Troubled Times" in Chapter 19), the distinguished German writer, saw the war as "purification, liberation . . . an enormous hope; [it] set the hearts of poets aflame. . . . How could the artist, the soldier in the artist," he asked, "not praise God for the collapse of a peaceful world with which he was fed up, so exceedingly fed up?"[14] Besides being gripped by a thirst for excitement and a quest for the heroic, some intellectuals welcomed the war because it unified the nation in a spirit of fraternity and altruism. It was a return, some felt, to the organic roots of human existence, a way of overcoming a sense of individual isolation. War, in the view of some intellectuals, would spiritually regenerate the nation. It would resurrect glory, honor, and heroism; it would awaken a spirit of self-sacrifice and dedication and give life an overriding purpose in a world suffocating from bourgeois materialism and drabness.

Thus, a generation of European youth marched off to war joyously, urged on by their teachers and cheered by their delirious nations. It must be emphasized, however, that the soldiers who went off to war singing and the statesmen and generals who welcomed war or did not try hard enough to prevent it expected a short, decisive, gallant conflict. Few envisioned what World War I turned out to be: four years of barbaric, senseless slaughter. The cheers of deluded chauvinists, naïve idealists, and fools drowned out the words of those—principally socialists, labor leaders, pacifists, and left-leaning liberals—who realized that Europe was stumbling into darkness. "The lamps are going out all over Europe," said British Foreign Secretary Edward Grey. "We shall not see them lit again in our lifetime."

Stalemate in the West

On August 4, 1914, the German army invaded Belgium. German war plans, drawn up years earlier, chiefly by General Alfred von Schlieffen, called for the army to swing through Belgium to outflank French border defenses, envelop the French forces, and destroy the enemy by attacking its rear. With the French army smashed and Paris isolated, German railroads—an extensive system of tracks, carefully planned by the general staff, had been constructed in the previous decade—would rush the victorious troops to the Eastern front to bolster the small force that had been assigned to hold off the Russians. Everything depended on speed. France must be taken before the Russians could mobilize sufficient numbers to invade Germany. The Germans were confident that they would defeat France in two months or less.

But things did not turn out the way the German military had anticipated. Moving faster than the Germans expected, the Russians invaded East Prussia, which led General Helmuth von Moltke to transfer troops from the French front, hampering the German advance. By early September, the Germans had reached the Marne River, forty miles from Paris. With their capital at their backs, the regrouped French forces, aided by the British, fought with astounding courage. Moreover, in their rush toward Paris, the Germans had unknowingly exposed their flank, which the French attacked. The British then penetrated a gap that opened up between the German armies, forcing the Germans to retreat. The First Battle of the Marne had saved Paris. With no side achieving a decisive victory, the war entered a new and unexpected phase: the deadlock of trench warfare.

For over four hundred miles across northern France, from the Alps to the North Sea, the op-

Map 18.2 World War I, 1914–1918 This map ▶ shows Europe divided into competing alliances and German advances into France and Eastern Europe once war broke out.

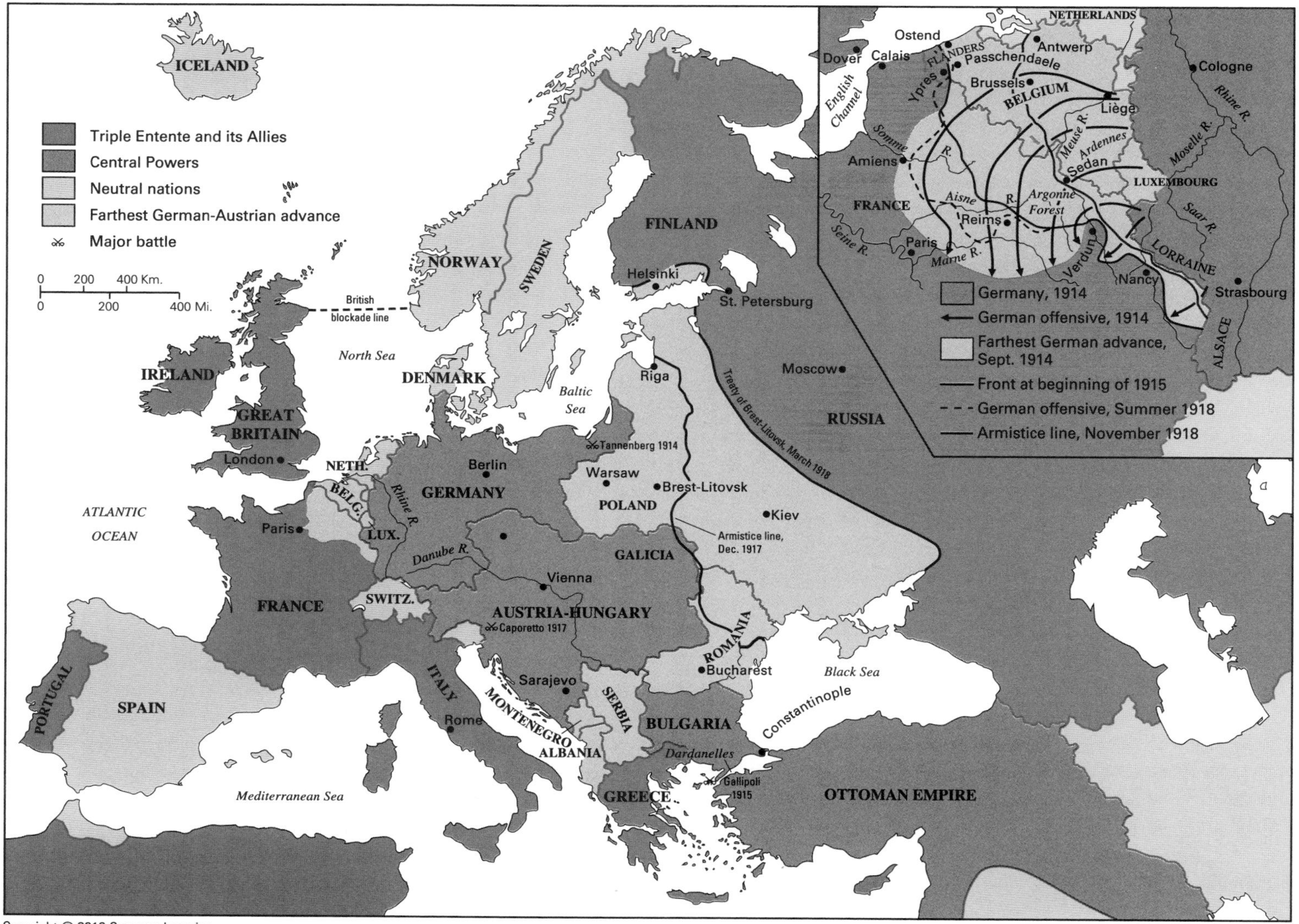

Triple Entente and its Allies
Central Powers
Neutral nations
Farthest German-Austrian advance
Major battle
0 200 400 Km.
0 200 400 Mi.
ICELAND
NORWAY
SWEDEN
FINLAND
Helsinki
St. Petersburg
Moscow
RUSSIA
IRELAND
GREAT BRITAIN
London
British blockade line
North Sea
DENMARK
Baltic Sea
Riga
Treaty of Brest-Litovsk, March 1918
Tannenberg 1914
NETH.
BELG.
LUX.
Rhine R.
Berlin
GERMANY
Warsaw
Brest-Litovsk
POLAND
Kiev
Armistice line, Dec. 1917
ATLANTIC OCEAN
Paris
Danube R.
GALICIA
Vienna
SWITZ.
FRANCE
AUSTRIA-HUNGARY
Caporetto 1917
ROMANIA
Bucharest
Black Sea
PORTUGAL
SPAIN
ITALY
Rome
Sarajevo
MONTENEGRO
SERBIA
BULGARIA
Constantinople
ALBANIA
Dardanelles
Gallipoli 1915
GREECE
Mediterranean Sea
OTTOMAN EMPIRE
NETHERLANDS
Ostend
Dover
Calais
FLANDERS
Passchendaele
Antwerp
Cologne
English Channel
Ypres
Brussels
BELGIUM
Liège
Rhine R.
Somme
Meuse R.
Ardennes
Moselle R.
Amiens
Sedan
LUXEMBOURG
FRANCE
Aisne R.
Argonne Forest
Saar R.
Reims
Seine R.
Paris
Marne R.
Verdun
LORRAINE
Nancy
Strasbourg
ALSACE
Germany, 1914
German offensive, 1914
Farthest German advance, Sept. 1914
Front at beginning of 1915
German offensive, Summer 1918
Armistice line, November 1918

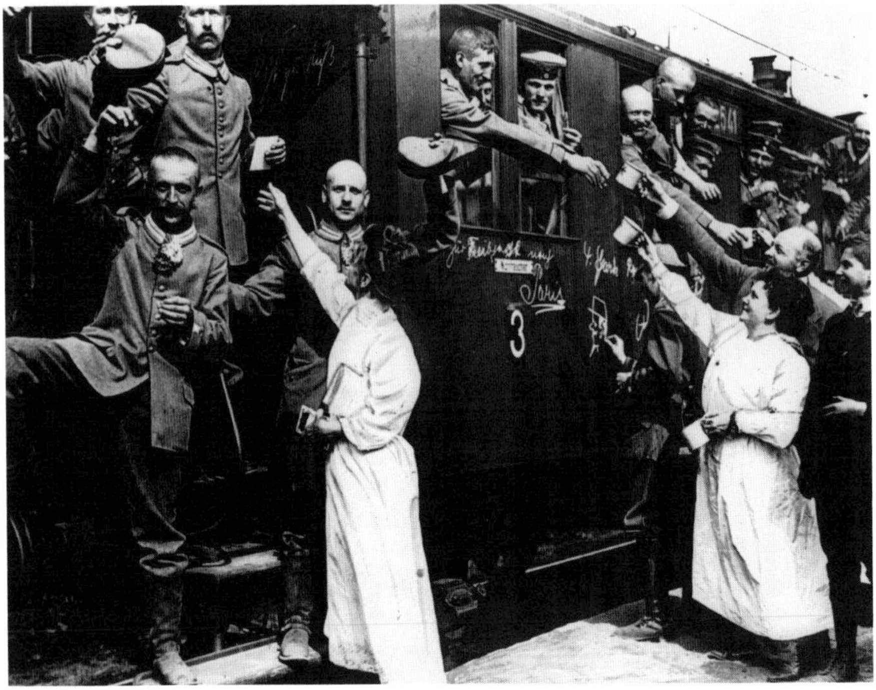

Troops Leaving Berlin, 1914. "The sword has been forced into our hand," said Germans at the outbreak of war. German troops mobilized eagerly and efficiently; here a trainload is leaving for the Western front. (Haeckel, Georg (1873–1942) and Haeckel, Otto (1872–1945)/© SZ Photo/Scherl/The Bridgeman Art Library International.)

posing sides both constructed a vast network of trenches. These trenches had underground dugouts, and barbed wire stretched for yards before the front trenches as a barrier to attack. Behind the front trenches were other lines to which soldiers could retreat and from which support could be sent. Between the opposing armies lay "no man's land," a wasteland of mud, shattered trees, torn earth, and broken bodies. In the trenches, soldiers were reduced to a primitive existence. Sometimes they stood knee-deep in freezing water or slimy mud; the stench from human waste, rotting corpses, and unwashed bodies overwhelmed the senses; rats, made more fecund and larger by easy access to food, including decaying flesh, swarmed over the dead and scampered across the wounded and the sleeping; and ubiquitous lice caused intense discomfort and disease, which frequently required hospitalization for several weeks. After days of uninterrupted, fearsome, earsplitting bombardment by artillery, even the most stouthearted were reduced to shivering, whimpering creatures. Unless the dugouts were fortified with concrete, soldiers rarely survived a direct hit; sometimes they were simply burned alive. The agonizing cries and pleas of the wounded, left to die on the battlefield because it was too dangerous to attempt a rescue, shattered the nerves of the men in the trenches. Trench warfare was a futile battle of nerves, endurance, and courage, waged to the constant thunder of heavy artillery, which pulverized both ramparts and men. And in April 1915, the Germans introduced poison gas, which added to the war's horror. It was also butchery. As attacking troops climbed over their trenches and advanced bravely across no man's land, they were decimated by heavy artillery and chewed up by rapid machine-gun fire from weapons which could fire 500 or more rounds a minute. If they did penetrate the frontline trenches of the enemy, they would soon be thrown back by a counterattack.

Corbis.

Women in the Factories During World War I. Women found employment in the war industry. Their patriotism and productive labor caused opposition to women's suffrage to dissipate.

Despite a frightful loss of life, little land changed hands. The Allied generals in particular, unfeeling and totally lacking in imagination, persisted in ordering greater but still ineffective frontal attacks by masses of infantry, hoping to wear down German manpower, which was inferior to their own. Once German reserves could not replenish losses, they reasoned, a breakthrough would be possible. But this strategy achieved nothing. The generals ordered still greater attacks to end the stalemate; this only increased the death toll, for the advantage was always with the defense, which possessed machine guns, magazine rifles, and barbed wire. Tanks could redress the balance, but the generals, committed to old concepts, did not make effective use of them. And whereas the technology of the machine gun had been perfected, the motorized tanks, a newly developed weapon, often broke down. Gains and losses of land were measured in yards, but the lives of Europe's youth were squandered by the hundreds of thousands. Against artillery, barbed wire, and machine guns, human courage had no chance, but the generals—uncomprehending, unfeeling, and incompetent—persisted in their mass attacks. This futile effort at a breakthrough wasted untold lives to absolutely no purpose.

In 1915, neither side could break the deadlock. Hoping to bleed the French army dry and force its surrender, the Germans, in February 1916, attacked the town of Verdun. Knowing that the French could never permit a retreat from this ancient fortress, they hoped that France would suffer such a loss of men that it would be unable to continue the war. France and Germany suffered more than a million casualties at Verdun—including some 300,000 dead—which one military historian calls "the greatest battle in world history."[15] When the British opened a major offensive on July 1, however, the Germans had to channel their reserves to the new front, relieving the pressure on Verdun.

At the end of June 1916, the British, assisted by the French, attempted a breakthrough at the

Somme River. On July 1, after seven days of intense, unprecedented bombardment intended to destroy German defenses, the British climbed out of their trenches and ventured into no man's land. But German positions had not been destroyed. Emerging from their deep dugouts, German machine gunners fired repeatedly at the British, who had been ordered to advance in rows. Marching into concentrated machine-gun fire and desperately searching for a way through the still-intact German wire, few British troops ever made it across no man's land. Out of the 110,000 who attacked, some 57,000 fell dead or wounded—most in the first hour of the assault—"the heaviest loss ever suffered in a single day by a British army or by any army in the First World War."[16] When the battle of the Somme ended in mid-November, Britain and France had lost more than 600,000 men, and the military situation remained essentially unchanged. The only victor was the war itself, which was devouring Europe's youth at an incredible rate.

In December 1916, General Robert Nivelle was appointed commander in chief of the French forces. Having learned little from past French failures to achieve a breakthrough, Nivelle ordered another mass attack for April 1917. The Germans discovered the battle plans on the body of a French officer and withdrew to a shorter line on high ground, constructing the strongest defense network of the war. Knowing that the French had lost the element of surprise and pushing aside the warnings of leading statesmen and military men, Nivelle went ahead with the attack. "The offensive alone gives victory; the defensive gives only defeat and shame," he told the president and the minister of war.[17]

The Nivelle offensive, which began on April 16, was another bloodbath. Sometimes the fire was so intense that the French could not make it out of their own trenches. Although French soldiers fought with courage, the situation was hopeless. Still, Nivelle persisted with the attack; after ten days, French casualties numbered 187,000. The disgraced Nivelle was soon relieved of his command.

Other Fronts

While the Western front hardened into a stalemate, events moved more decisively on the Eastern front. In August 1914, the Russians, with insufficient preparation, invaded East Prussia. After some initial successes, which sent a scare into the German general staff, the Russians were soundly defeated at the battle of Tannenberg (August 26–30, 1914) and forced to withdraw from German territory, which remained inviolate for the rest of the war.

Meanwhile, Germany's ally Austria was having no success against Serbia and Russia. An invasion of Serbia was thrown back, and an ill-conceived offensive against Russia cost Austria its Galician provinces. Germany had to come to Austria's rescue. In the spring of 1915, the Germans made a breakthrough that forced the Russians to abandon Galicia and most of Poland. In June 1916, the Russians launched an offensive that opened a wide breach in the Austrian lines, but they could not maintain it. A German counteroffensive forced a retreat and cost the Russians more than a million casualties.

In March 1917, food shortages and disgust with the great loss of life exploded into a spontaneous revolution in Russia, and the tsar was forced to abdicate. The new government, dominated by liberals, opted to continue the war despite the weariness of the Russian masses. In November 1917, a second revolution brought to power the Bolsheviks, or Communists, who promised "Peace, Land, Bread." In March 1918, the Bolsheviks, to end the war, signed the punitive Treaty of Brest-Litovsk, in which Russia surrendered Poland, the Ukraine, Finland, and the Baltic provinces to Germany.

Several countries that were not belligerents in August 1914—among them the Ottoman Empire and Italy—joined the war later. That autumn, the Ottoman Turks entered the conflict as allies of Germany. Before the war, Germany had cultivated the Ottoman Empire's friendship by training the Turkish army; for their part, the Turks wanted German help in case Russia attempted to seize the Dardanelles. Hoping to supply Russia and, in turn, obtain badly needed Russian grain, the Allies did decide to capture the Dardanelles. In April 1915, a combined force of British, French, Australian, and New Zealander troops stormed the Gallipoli Peninsula on the European side of the Dardanelles. Ignorance of amphibious warfare, poor intelligence, and the fierce resistance of the Turks prevented the Allies from getting off the beaches and taking the heights. The Gallipoli campaign cost the Allies 252,000 casualties, and they had gained nothing.

Although a member of the Triple Alliance, Italy remained neutral when war broke out. In May 1915, on the promise of receiving Austrian territory, Italy entered the war on the side of the Allies. The Austrians repulsed a number of Italian offensives along the frontier and in 1916 took the offensive against Italy. A combined German and Austrian force finally broke through the Italian lines in the fall of 1917 at Caporetto, and the Italians retreated in disorder, leaving behind huge quantities of weapons. Germany and Austria took some 275,000 prisoners.

The Collapse of the Central Powers

The year 1917 seemed disastrous for the Allies. The Nivelle offensive had failed, the French army had mutinied, a British attack at Passchendaele did not bring the expected breakthrough and added some three hundred thousand casualties to the list of butchery, and the Russians, torn by revolution and gripped by war weariness, were close to making a separate peace. But there was one encouraging development for the Allies. In April 1917, the United States declared war on Germany.

American Entry

From the outset, America's sympathies lay with the Allies. To most Americans, Britain and France were democracies, threatened by an autocratic and militaristic Germany. These sentiments were reinforced by British propaganda, which depicted the Germans as cruel "Huns." Since most war news came to the United States from Britain, anti-German feeling gained momentum. What precipitated American entry was the German decision of January 1917 to launch a campaign of unrestricted submarine warfare. The Germans were determined to deprive Britain of war supplies and to starve it into submission. Their resolve meant that German U-boats would torpedo both enemy and neutral ships in the war zone around the British Isles. Since the United States was Britain's principal supplier, American ships became a target of German submarines.

Angered by American loss of life and materiel, as well as by the violation of the doctrine of freedom of the seas, and fearing a diminution of prestige if the United States took no action, President Woodrow Wilson (1856–1924) pressed for American entry. Also at stake was American security, which would be jeopardized by German domination of Western Europe. Leading American statesmen and diplomats worried that such a radical change in the balance of power would threaten American national interests. As German submarines continued to attack neutral shipping, President Wilson, on April 2, 1917, urged Congress to declare war on Germany. It did so on April 6.

Germany's Last Offensive

With Russia out of the war, General Erich Ludendorff prepared for a decisive offensive before the Americans could land sufficient troops in France to help the Allies. A war of attrition now favored the Allies, who could count on American supplies and manpower. Without an immediate and decisive victory, Germany could not win the war. On March 21, 1918, the Germans launched an offensive that was intended to bring victory in the west.

Suddenly, the deadlock was broken; it was now a war of movement. Within two weeks, the Germans had taken some 1,250 square miles. But British resistance was astonishing, and the Germans, exhausted and short of ammunition and food, called off the drive. A second offensive against the British, in April, also had to be called off, as the British contested every foot of ground. Both campaigns depleted German manpower, while the Americans were arriving in great numbers to strengthen Allied lines and uplift morale. At the end of May, Ludendorff resumed his offensive against the French. Attacking unexpectedly, the Germans broke through and advanced to within fifty-six miles of Paris by June 3. However, reserves braced the French lines, and in the battle of Belleau Wood (June 6–25, 1918), the Americans checked the Germans.

Hulton Archive/Getty Images.

Wilson and Clemenceau Arrive at Versailles, June 18, 1919. The idealism of President Wilson (center) clashed with Premier Clemenceau's (left) determination to enhance France's security.

In mid-July, the Germans tried again, crossing the Marne River in small boats. Although in one area they advanced nine miles, the offensive failed against determined American and French opposition. By August 3, the Second Battle of the Marne had ended. The Germans had thrown everything they had into their spring and summer offensives, but it was not enough. The Allies had bent, but, reinforced and encouraged by American arms, they did not break. Now they began to counterattack, with great success.

Meanwhile, German allies, deprived of support from a hard-pressed Germany, were unable to cope. An Allied army of Frenchmen, Britons, Serbs, and Italians compelled Bulgaria to sign an armistice on September 29. Shortly afterward, British successes in the Middle East forced the Turks to withdraw from the war. In the streets of Vienna, people were shouting "Long live peace! Down with the monarchy!" The Austro-Hungarian Empire was rapidly disintegrating into separate states based on nationality.

By early October, the last defensive position of the Germans had crumbled. The army's spirit collapsed as well; war-weary soldiers, sensing that the war was lost, surrendered in large numbers and refused orders to return to the front. Fearing that the Allies would invade the fatherland and shatter the reputation of the German army, Ludendorff wanted an immediate armistice. However, he needed to find a way to obtain favorable armistice terms from President Wilson and to shift the blame for the lost war from the military and the kaiser to civilian leadership. Cynically, he urged the creation of a popular parliamentary government in Germany. But events in Germany went further than the general had anticipated. Whereas Ludendorff sought a limited monarchy, the shock of defeat and widespread hunger sparked a revolution that forced the kaiser to abdicate. On November 11, the new German Republic signed an armistice ending the hostilities.

The Peace Conference

In January 1919, representatives of the Allied Powers assembled in Paris to draw up peace terms; President Wilson was also there. The war-weary masses turned to Wilson as the prophet who would have the nations beat their swords into plowshares.

Wilson's Hope for a New World

For Wilson, the war had been fought against autocracy. He hoped that a peace settlement based on liberal-democratic ideals would sweep away the foundations of war, and he expressed these hopes in several speeches, including the famous Fourteen Points of January 1918. None of Wilson's principles seemed more just than the idea of self-determination: the right of a people to have its own state, free of foreign domination. In particular, this goal meant (or was interpreted to mean) the return of Alsace and Lorraine to France, the creation of an independent Poland, a readjustment of the frontiers of Italy to incorporate Austrian lands inhabited by Italians, and an opportunity for Slavs of the Austro-Hungarian Empire to form their own states.

Aware that a harshly treated Germany might well seek revenge, engulfing the world in another cataclysm, Wilson insisted that there should be a "peace without victory." A just settlement would encourage a defeated Germany to work with the victorious Allies in building a new Europe. To preserve peace and help remake the world, Wilson urged the formation of the League of Nations, an international parliament to settle disputes and discourage aggression. Wilson wanted a peace of justice to preserve Western civilization in its democratic and Christian form.

Problems of Peacemaking

Wilson's negotiating position was undermined by the Republican Party's victory in the congressional elections of November 1918. Before the election, Wilson had appealed to the American people to cast their ballots for Democrats as a vote of confidence in his diplomacy. But instead, Americans sent twenty-five Republicans and only fifteen Democrats to the Senate. Whatever the motives of the American people in voting Republican—apparently their decision rested on local and national, not international, issues—the outcome diminished Wilson's prestige at the conference table. To his fellow negotiators, Wilson was trying to preach to Europe when he could not command the support of his own country. Since the Senate must ratify any American treaty, European diplomats worried that what Wilson agreed to the Senate might reject, which is precisely what happened.

Another obstacle to Wilson's peace program was France's demand for security and revenge. Nearly the entire war on the Western front had been fought on French territory. Many French industries and farms had been ruined; the country mourned the loss of half its young men. Representing France at the conference table was Georges Clemenceau (1841–1929), nicknamed "the Tiger." Nobody loved France or hated Germany more. Cynical, suspicious of idealism, and not sharing Wilson's hope for a new world or his confidence in the future League of Nations, Clemenceau demanded that Germany be severely punished and its capacity to wage war destroyed.

Seeing Germany's greater population and superior industrial strength as a long-term threat and doubting that its military tradition would let it resign itself to defeat, Clemenceau wanted guarantees that the wars of 1870–1871 and 1914–1918 would not be repeated. The latter war had shown that without the help of Britain and the United States, France would have again been at the mercy of Germany. Since there was no certainty that these states would again aid France, Clemenceau wanted to use his country's present advantage to cripple Germany.

The intermingling of European nationalities was another barrier to Wilson's program. Because in so many regions of Central Europe there was a mixture of nationalities, no one could create a Europe completely free of minority problems; some nationalities would always feel that they had been treated shabbily. And the various nationalities were not willing to moderate their demands or lower their aspirations. For example, Wilson's Fourteen Points called for the creation of an independent Poland with secure access to the sea. But between Poland and the sea lay territory populated by Germans. Giving this land to Poland would violate German self-determination; denying it to Poland would mean that the new country had little chance of developing a sound economy. No matter what the decision, one people would regard it as unjust. Similarly, to provide the new Czechoslovakia with defensible borders, it would be necessary to give it territory inhabited mostly by Germans. This, too, could be viewed as a denial of German self-determination, but not granting the territory to Czechoslovakia would mean that the new state would not be able to defend itself against Germany.

Secret treaties drawn up by the Allies during the war also interfered with Wilson's program. These agreements dividing up German, Austrian, and Ottoman territory did not square with the principle of self-determination. For example, to entice Italy into entering the war, the Allies had promised it Austrian lands that were inhabited predominantly by Germans and Slavs. Italy was not about to repudiate its prize because of Wilson's principles.

Finally, the war had generated great bitterness, which persisted after the guns had been silenced. Both the masses and their leaders demanded retribution and held exaggerated hopes for territory and reparations. In such an atmosphere of postwar enmity, the spirit of compromise and moderation could not overcome the desire for spoils and punishment.

The Settlement

After months of negotiations, often punctuated by acrimony, the peacemakers hammered out a settlement. Five treaties made up the Peace of Paris: one each with Germany, Austria, Hungary, Bulgaria, and Turkey. Of the five, the Treaty of Versailles, which Germany signed on June 28, 1919, was the most significant.

France regained Alsace and Lorraine, lost to Germany in the Franco-Prussian War of 1870–1871. The treaty also barred Germany from placing fortifications in the Rhineland. The French military had wanted to take the Rhineland from Germany and break it up into one or more republics under French suzerainty. Under this arrangement, French control would extend to the Rhine River, which was a natural defensive border; one had only to destroy the bridges to prevent a German invasion of France. With Germany deprived of this springboard for invasion, French security would be immensely improved. Recognizing that the German people would never permanently submit to the amputation of the Rhineland, which was inhabited by more than five million Germans and contained key industries, Wilson and British Prime Minister David Lloyd George (1863–1945) resisted these French demands.

Faced with the opposition of Wilson and Lloyd George, Clemenceau backed down and agreed instead to Allied occupation of the Rhineland for fifteen years, the demilitarization of the region, and an Anglo-American promise of assistance if Germany attacked France in the future. This last point, considered vital by France, proved useless. The alliance went into effect only if both the United States and Britain ratified it. Since the Security Treaty did not get past the U.S. Senate, Britain also refused to sign it. The French people felt that they had been duped and wronged.

A related issue concerned French demands for annexation of the coal-rich Saar Basin, which adjoined Lorraine. By obtaining this region, France would weaken Germany's military potential and strengthen its own. France argued that this would be just compensation for the deliberate destruction of the French coal mines by the retreating German army at the end of the war. But here, too, France was disappointed. The final compromise called for a League of Nations commission to govern the Saar Basin for fifteen years, after which the inhabitants would decide whether their territory would be ceded to France or returned to Germany.

In eastern Germany, in certain districts of Silesia that had a large Polish population, a plebiscite determined the future of the region. Part of Upper Silesia was ceded to Poland. The settlement also gave Poland a corridor cut through West Prussia and terminating in the Baltic port of Danzig; Danzig itself was declared an international city, to be administered by a League of Nations commission. The Germans would never resign themselves to this loss of territory that separated East Prussia from the rest of Germany.

The victorious nations were awarded control of German colonies and Ottoman lands. However, these nations held colonies not outright but as mandates under the supervision of the League, which would protect the interests of the native peoples. The mandate system implied the ultimate end of colonialism, for it clearly opposed the exploitation of colonial peoples and asserted independence as the rightful goal for subject nations.

Other issues revolved around the German military forces and reparations. To prevent a resurgence of militarism, the German army was limited to one hundred thousand volunteers and deprived of heavy artillery, tanks, and warplanes. The German navy was limited to a token force, which did not include submarines. The issue of war reparations caused great bitterness between Wilson and his French and British adversaries. The American delegation wanted the treaty to fix a reasonable sum that Germany would have to pay and specify the period of years allotted for payment. But no such items were included; they were left for future consideration. The Treaty of Versailles presented Germany with an open-ended bill that would probably take generations to pay. Moreover, Article 231, which preceded the reparation clauses, placed sole responsibility for the war on Germany and its allies. The Germans responded to this accusation with contempt.

In separate treaties, the conference dealt with the dissolution of the Hapsburg Empire. During the final weeks of the war, the Austro-Hungarian Empire had crumbled as the various nationalities proclaimed their independence from Hapsburg rule. In most cases, the peacemakers ratified with treaties what the nationalities had already accomplished in fact. Serbia joined with Austrian lands inhabited by Croats and Slovenes to become Yugoslavia. Czechoslovakia arose from the predominantly Czech and Slovak regions of Austria. Hungary, which broke away from Austria to become a separate country, had to cede considerable land to Romania and Yugoslavia. Austria turned over to Italy the South Tyrol, inhabited by two hundred thousand Austrian Germans. This clear violation of the principle of self-determination greatly offended liberal opinion. Deprived of its vast territories and prohibited from union with Germany, the new Austria was a third-rate power.

Assessment and Problems

The Germans unanimously denounced the Treaty of Versailles, for in their minds the war had ended not in German defeat but in a stalemate. They regarded the armistice as the prelude to a negotiated settlement among equals, based on Wilson's call for a peace of justice. Instead, the Germans were barred from participating in the negotiations. And they viewed the terms of the treaty as humiliating and vindictive—designed to keep Germany militarily and economically weak.

When the United States had entered the war, the Germans protested, Wilson had stated that the enemy was not the German people but their government. Surely, the Germans now argued, the new German democracy should not be punished for the sins of the monarchy and the military. To the Germans, the Treaty of Versailles was not the dawning of the new world that Wilson had promised, but an abomination—a vile crime.

Critics in other lands also condemned the treaty as a punitive settlement in flagrant violation of Wilsonian idealism. The peacemakers, they argued, should have set aside past hatreds and, in cooperation with the new democratic German Republic, forged a just settlement to serve as the foundation of a new world. Instead, they burdened the fledgling German democracy with reparations that were impossible to pay, insulted it with the accusation of war guilt, and deprived it of territory in violation of the principle of self-determination. All these provisions, said the critics, would only exacerbate old hatreds and fan the flames of German nationalism. This was a poor beginning for democracy in Germany and for Wilson's new world.

The treaty's defenders, however, insisted that if Germany had won the war, it would have imposed a far harsher settlement on the Allies. They pointed to German war aims, which called for the annexation of parts of France and Poland, the reduction of Belgium and Romania to satellites, and German expansion in central Africa. They pointed also to the treaty of Brest-Litovsk, which Germany had compelled Russia to sign in 1918, as an example of Germany's ruthless appetite. An insatiable Germany gained 34 percent of Russia's population, 32 percent of its farmland, 54 percent of its industrial enterprises, and 89 percent of its coal mines. Moreover, they maintained that the peace settlement did not repudiate Wilson's principles. The new map of Europe was the closest approximation of the ethnic distribution of its peoples that Europe had ever known.

What is most significant about the Treaty of Versailles is that it did not solve the German problem. Germany was left weakened but unbroken—its industrial and military power only temporarily contained, and its nationalist fervor not only undiminished but stoked higher by a peace treaty that all political parties viewed as unjust, dictated, and offensive to national pride. The real danger in Europe was German unwillingness to accept defeat or surrender the dream of expansion.

Would France, Britain, and the United States enforce the treaty against a resurgent Germany? The war had demonstrated that an Allied victory depended on American intervention. But in 1920, the U.S. Senate, angry that Wilson had not taken Republicans with him to Paris and fearing that membership in the League of Nations would involve America in future wars, refused to ratify the Treaty of Versailles. Britain, feeling guilty over the treatment of Germany, lacked the will for enforcement and even came to favor revising the treaty. Therefore, the responsibility for preserving the settlement rested primarily with France, which was not encouraging. Germany had greater industrial potential than France and, with Russia now Communist, France could not count on Russian manpower to balance Germany's much larger population. The Paris peace settlement left Germany resentful but potentially powerful, and to the east lay small and weak states—some of them with sizable German minorities—that could not check a rearmed Germany.

The Russian Revolution of 1917

One consequence of the war that influenced the course of European and world history in momentous ways was the Russian Revolution of 1917 and the resultant triumph of the Bolsheviks. The people of Russia had initially responded to the war with a show of patriotic fervor. But the realities of war quickly dimmed this ardor. The ill-equipped and poorly led Russian armies suffered huge losses. In July 1915, the minister of war wrote this dismal report:

> *The soldiers are without doubt exhausted by the continued defeats and retreats. Their confidence in final victory and in their leaders is undermined. Ever more threatening signs of impending demoralization are evident. Cases of desertion and voluntary surrender to the enemy are becoming more frequent. It is difficult to expect enthusiasm and selflessness from men sent into battle unarmed and ordered to pick up the rifles of their dead comrades.*[18]

By 1916 the home front began to fall apart. Shops were empty, money had no value, and hunger and cold stalked the working quarters of cities and towns. Factory workers, many of them women replacing husbands, brothers, and sons who were at the front, toiled long hours for wages that could not keep up with the accelerating inflation. When they protested, the government resorted to heavy-handed repression. By January 1917, nearly all Russians, soldiers and civilians alike, had lost trust in their autocratic government. But Tsar Nicholas II, determined to preserve autocracy, resisted any suggestion that he liberalize the regime for the sake of the war effort.

Autocracy was ready to collapse at the slightest blow. In early March (February 23 by the calendar then in use*), a strike, riots in the food lines, and street demonstrations in Petrograd (formerly Saint Petersburg) flared into sudden, unpremeditated revolution. The soldiers, who in 1905 had massacred peaceful protesters, now rushed to support the striking workers. The Romanov dynasty, after three hundred years of rule (1613–1917), came to an end. The Provisional Government was set up—provisional until a representative Constituent Assembly, to be elected as soon as possible, could establish a permanent regime.

The Problems of the Provisional Government

The collapse of autocracy was followed by what supporters in Russia and the West hoped would be a liberal-democratic regime pledged to give Russia a constitution. In reality, however, the course of events from March to November 1917 resembled a free-for-all—a no-holds-barred fight for the succession to autocracy, with only the fittest surviving. Events demonstrated the desperate state of the Russian Empire. Its vast size promoted internal disunity; increasing hardships raised the fury of the accumulated resentments to raw brutality among the masses. National minorities took advantage of the anarchy to dismember the country.

Among the potential successors to the tsars, the liberals of various shades seemed at first to enjoy the best chances. They represented the educated and forward-looking elements in Russian society that had arisen after the reforms of the 1860s: lawyers, doctors, professional people of all kinds, intellectuals, businesspeople and industrialists, many landowners, and even some bureaucrats. Liberals had opposed autocracy and earned a reputation for leadership.

The liberals had joined the March revolution only reluctantly, for they were afraid of the masses and the violence of the streets. They dreaded social revolution that could result in the seizure of factories, dispossession of landowners, and tampering with property rights. Although most leaders of the Provisional Government had only modest means, they were capitalists, believing in private enterprise as the means of promoting economic progress. Their ideal was a constitutional monarchy, its leadership entrusted to the educated and propertied elite familiar with the essentials of statecraft.

Unfortunately, the liberals misunderstood the mood of the people. Looking to the Western

*Until March 1918, events in Russia were dated by the Julian calendar, thirteen days behind the Gregorian calendar used in the West. By the Julian calendar, the first revolution occurred in February and the second in October.

Sovfoto/Eastfoto.

Women Demonstrate in Petrograd, 1917. The collapse of the tsarist regime was followed by a period of political fermentation, meetings, and concern about food shortages. Women demonstrated for increased bread supplies. The poster reads, "Comrades, workers, and soldiers, support our demands!"

democracies—including, after April 1917, the United States—for political and financial support, the liberals decided to continue the war on the side of the Allies. The decision antagonized the war-weary masses, along with the Russian soldiers, almost two million of whom had deserted. The liberals also antagonized the Russian peasants by not confiscating and redistributing the landlords' lands free of charge. As Russian nationalists who wanted their country to remain undivided, the liberals opposed national minorities—Finns, Ukrainians, Georgians, and others—who sought self-determination; hence, they lost the minorities' support.

Frustrated by the Provisional Government's inaction on the land question, peasants began taking matters into their own hands. They seized the nobles' land and torched their estates, sometimes putting them to death. The peasants began to divide the landlords' land among themselves, which encouraged more soldiers to desert in order to claim a share of the land. The breakdown of the railways stopped factory production; enraged workers ousted factory managers and owners. Consumer goods grew scarce and prices soared, and the peasants could see no reason to sell their crops if they could buy nothing in return. Thus, the specter of famine in the cities arose. Hardships and anger mounted. Adding to the disorder were the demands of the non-Russian nationalities for self-determination and even secession.

Freedom in Russia was leading to dissolution and chaos. The largely illiterate peasant masses had no experience with or understanding of the institutions, habits, and attitudes of a free society. Without their cooperation, Russian liberalism collapsed. This outcome demonstrated the difficulty of establishing Western liberal-democratic forms of government in countries lacking a sense of unity, a strong middle class, and a tradition of responsible participation in public affairs.

By July 1917, when Aleksandr Kerensky (1881–1970), a radical lawyer of great eloquence, took over the leadership of the Provisional Government, it had become clear that law and order could be upheld only by brute force. In late August and early September, a conspiracy led by a right-wing general, Lavr Kornilov, sought to establish a military dictatorship. Kornilov had the support not only of the officer corps and the tsarist officials, but also of many liberals who were fed up with anarchy. What stopped the general was not Kerensky's government (which had no troops), but the workers of Petrograd. Their agitators demoralized Kornilov's soldiers, proving that a dictatorship of the right had no mass support. The workers also repudiated Kerensky and the Provisional Government, as well as their own moderate leaders; henceforth, they supported the Bolsheviks.

Lenin and the Rise of Bolshevism

Revolutionary movements had a long history in Russia, going back to the early nineteenth century, when educated Russians began to compare their country unfavorably with Western Europe. They, too, wanted constitutional liberty and free speech in order to make their country modern. Prohibited from speaking out in public, they went underground, giving up their liberalism as ineffective. They saw revolutionary socialism, with its idealistic vision and compassion for the multitude, as a better ideology in the harsh struggle with the tsar's police. By the 1870s, many socialists had evolved into austere and self-denying professional revolutionaries who, in the service of the cause, had no moral scruples, just as the police had no scruples in the defense of the tsars. Bank robbery, murder, assassination, treachery, and terror were not seen as immoral if they served the revolutionary cause.

In the 1880s and 1890s, revolutionaries had learned industrial economics and sociology from Marx; from Marxism they had also acquired a vision of a universal and inevitable progression toward socialism and Communism that satisfied their semireligious craving for salvation in this world, not the next. Marxism also allied them with socialist movements in other lands, giving them an internationalist outlook. History, they believed, was on their side, as it was for all the proletarians and oppressed peoples in the world.

By 1900, a number of able young Russians had rallied to revolutionary Marxism; almost all of them were educated or came from privileged families. The most promising was Vladimir Ilyich Ulyanov, known as Lenin (1870–1924), the son of a teacher and school administrator who had attained the rank of a nobleman. Lenin had studied law but practiced revolution instead. His first contribution lay in adapting Marxism to Russian conditions; to do so, he took considerable liberties with Marx's teaching. His second contribution followed from the first: outlining the organization of an underground party capable of surviving against the tsarist police. It was to be a tightly knit conspiratorial elite of professional revolutionaries. Its headquarters would be safely located abroad, and it would have close ties to the masses, that is, to the workers and other potentially revolutionary elements.

Two other prominent Marxists close to Lenin were Leon Trotsky (1879–1940) and Joseph Stalin (1879–1953). Trotsky, whose original name was Lev Bronstein, was the son of a prosperous Jewish farmer from southern Russia and was soon known for his brilliant pen. Less prominent until after the Revolution, Stalin (the man of steel) was originally named Iosif Dzhugashvili; he was from Georgia, beyond the Caucasus Mountains. Bright enough to be sent to the best school in the area, he dropped out for a revolutionary career. While they were still young, Lenin, Trotsky, and Stalin were all hardened by arrest, imprisonments, and exile to Siberia. Lenin and Trotsky later lived abroad, while Stalin, following a harsher course, stayed in Russia; for four years before 1917, he was banished to bleakest northern Siberia and conditioned to ruthlessness for life.

In 1903, the Russian Marxists split into two factions, the moderate Mensheviks, so named after finding themselves in a minority (*menshinstvo*) at a rather unrepresentative vote at the Second Party Congress, and the extremist Bolsheviks, who at that moment were in the majority (*bolshinstvo*). They might more accurately have been called the "softs" and the "hards." The "softs" (Mensheviks) preserved basic moral scruples; they would not stoop to crime or undemocratic methods for the sake of political success. For that the "hards" (Bolsheviks) ridiculed them, noting that a dead, imprisoned, or unsuccessful revolutionary was of little use.

Meanwhile, Lenin perfected Bolshevik revolutionary theory. He violated Marxist tradition

V. I. Lenin. Red Army soldiers leaving for battle in the civil war are addressed by Lenin in Moscow in May 1920.

by paying close attention to the revolutionary potential of peasants (thereby anticipating Mao Zedong). Lenin also looked closely at the numerous peoples in Asia who had recently fallen under Western imperialist domination. These people, he sensed, constituted a potential revolutionary force. In alliance with the Western—and Russian—proletariat, they might overthrow the worldwide capitalist order. The Bolsheviks, the most militant of all revolutionary socialists, were ready to assist in that gigantic struggle.

Lenin was a Russian nationalist as well as a socialist internationalist; he had a vision of a modern and powerful Russian state destined to be a model in world affairs. Russian Communism was thus nationalist Communism. The Bolsheviks saw the abolition of income-producing property by the dictatorship of the proletariat as the most effective way of mobilizing the country's resources. Yet the Bolshevik mission was also internationalist. The Russian Revolution was intended to set off a world revolution, liberating all oppressed classes and peoples around the world and achieving a higher stage of civilization.

Lenin's Opportunity

On April 16, 1917, Lenin, with German help, arrived in Petrograd from exile in Switzerland. (The Germans provided Lenin with a secret train to take him to Petrograd; they hoped that the Bolshevik leader, who wanted Russia to withdraw from the "capitalist" war, would initiate a revolution and gain power.) The Provisional Government, he said, could not possibly preserve Russia from disintegration. Most of the soldiers, workers, and peasants would repudiate the Provisional Government's cautious liberalism in favor of a regime expressing their demand for peace and land. Nothing would stop them from avenging themselves for centuries of oppression. Lenin also felt that only complete state control of the economy could rescue the country from disaster. The sole way out, he insisted, was the dictatorship of the proletariat backed by *soviets* (councils) of soldiers, workers, and peasants, particularly the poorer peasants.

Lenin prepared his party for the second stage of the Revolution of 1917: the seizure of power by the Bolsheviks. His slogan, "Peace, Land, and Bread," held a magnetic attraction for the desperate Russian masses. The Bolsheviks' determined effort to win over the disheartened soldiers proved particularly effective. Many of the people who supported the Bolsheviks interpreted Lenin's other powerful slogan—"All Power to the Soviets"—to mean that the Bolsheviks aimed to create a democratic socialist state that would institute needed social reforms. They did not anticipate the creation of Bolshevik dictatorship.

Conditions favored the Bolsheviks, as Lenin had predicted. The Bolsheviks obtained majorities in the soviets. The peasants were in active revolt, seizing the land themselves. The Provisional Government lost all control over the course of events.

On November 6 (October 24 by the old calendar), Lenin urged immediate action: "The government is tottering. It must be *given the death blow* at all costs. To delay action is fatal." [19] On the following day, the Bolsheviks, meeting little resistance, seized power. Lenin permitted the elections for the Constituent Assembly that had been scheduled by the Provisional Government. In a free election, the Bolsheviks received only 24 percent of the vote. After meeting once in January 1918, however, the Constituent Assembly was disbanded by the Bolsheviks.

The Bolsheviks Survive

Lenin contended that he was guiding the Russian proletariat and all humanity toward a higher social order, symbolizing—in Russia and much of the world—the rebellion of the disadvantaged against Western (or "capitalist") dominance. That is why in 1918 he changed the name of his party from Bolshevik to Communist, which implied a concern for the human community. For Lenin, as for Marx, a world without exploitation was humanity's noblest ideal.

But staggering adversity confronted Lenin after his seizure of power. In the prevailing anarchy, Russia lay open to the German armies. Under the Treaty of Brest-Litovsk, signed in March 1918—the lowest point in Russian history for over two hundred years—Russia lost Finland, Poland, and the Baltic provinces, all regions inhabited largely by non-Russians. It also lost the rebellious Ukraine, its chief industrial base and breadbasket. Yet Lenin had no choice but to accept the humiliating terms.

The War and European Consciousness

"There will be wars as never before on earth," Nietzsche had predicted. World War I bore him out. Modern technology enabled the combatants to kill with unprecedented efficiency; modern nationalism infused both civilians and soldiers with the determination to fight until the enemy was totally beaten. Exercising wide control over its citizens, the modern state mobilized its human, material, and spiritual resources to wage total war. As the war hardened into a savage and grueling fight, the statesmen did not press for a compromise peace; instead, they demanded ever more mobilization, ever more escalation, and ever more sacrifices.

The Great War profoundly altered the course of Western civilization, deepening the spiritual crisis that had helped to produce it. How could one speak of the inviolability of the individual when Europe had become a slaughterhouse, or of the primacy of reason when nations permitted slaughter to go unabated for four years? How could the mind cope with this spectacle of a civilization turning against itself, destroying itself in an orgy of organized violence? A young French soldier, shortly before he was killed at Verdun, expressed the disillusionment that gripped the soldiers in the trenches: "Humanity is mad! It must be mad to do what it is doing. What a massacre! What scenes of horror and carnage, I cannot find words to translate my impressions. Hell cannot be so terrible. Men are mad!" [20] The war, said British poet Robert Graves, provoked an "inward scream" that still reverberates. The agony caused by the astronomical casualty figures—some 9.4 million dead and 21 million wounded, many of them pathetically mutilated and disfigured or mentally deranged—touched millions of homes. For a generation, millions of grieving widows and orphaned children were a tragic reminder of Europe's descent into savagery. Now only the naïve could believe in continuous progress. Western civilization had entered an age of violence, anxiety, and doubt.

The war left many with the gnawing feeling that Western civilization had lost its vitality and was caught in a rhythm of breakdown and disintegration. It seemed that Western civilization was fragile and perishable, that Western people, despite their extraordinary accomplishments, were never more than a step or two away from barbarism. Surely, any civilization that could allow such senseless slaughter to last had entered its decline and could look forward to only the darkest of futures.

European intellectuals were demoralized and disillusioned. The orderly, peaceful, rational world of their youth had been wrecked. The Enlightenment worldview, weakened in the nineteenth century by the assault of romantics, Social Darwinists, extreme nationalists, race mystics, and glorifiers of the irrational, was now disintegrating. The enormity of the war had destroyed faith in the capacity of reason to deal with crucial social and political questions. Civilization seemed to be

The Survivors **(1922), by Käthe Kollwitz.** With an estimated 9.4 million dead and 21 million wounded, World War I shattered the hope that Western Europe had been making continuous progress toward a rational and enlightened civilization.

fighting an unending and hopeless battle against the irrational elements in human nature. It appeared that war would be a recurring phenomenon in the twentieth century.

Scientific research had produced more efficient weapons to kill and maim Europe's youth. The achievements of Western science and technology, which had been viewed as a boon for humanity and the clearest testament to the superiority of European civilization, were called into question. Confidence in the future gave way to doubt. The old beliefs in the perfectibility of humanity, the blessings of science, and ongoing progress now seemed an expression of naïve optimism and post-Christian myths; the war had exposed them as fraudulent. As A. J. P. Taylor concludes,

> *The First World War was difficult to fit into the picture of a rational civilization advancing by ordered stages. The civilized men of the twentieth century had outdone in savagery the barbarians of all preceding ages, and their civilized virtues—organization, mechanical skill, self-sacrifice—had made war's savagery all the more terrible. Modern man had developed powers which he was not fit to use. European civilization had been weighed in the balance and found wanting.*[21]

This disillusionment heralded a loss of faith in liberal-democratic values—a loss of faith that contributed to the widespread popularity of Fascist ideologies in the postwar world. Having lost confidence in the power of reason to solve the problems of the human community, in liberal doctrines of individual freedom, and in the institutions of parliamentary democracy, many people turned to Fascism as a simple saving faith. Far from making the world safe for democracy, as Wilson and other liberals had hoped, World War I gave rise to totalitarian movements that would nearly destroy democracy.

The war produced a generation of young people who had reached their maturity in combat. Violence had become a way of life for millions of soldiers hardened by battle and for millions of civilians aroused by four years of propaganda. The relentless massacre of Europe's young men had a brutalizing effect. Violence, cruelty, suffering, and even wholesale death seemed to be natural and acceptable components of human existence. The sanctity of the individual seemed to be liberal and Christian claptrap.

The fascination with violence and contempt for life persisted in the postwar world. Many returned veterans yearned for the excitement of battle and the fellowship of the trenches—what one French soldier called "the most tender human experience." After the war, a young English officer reminisced: "There was an exaltation, in those days of comradeship and dedication, that would have come in few other ways."[22] A fraternal bond united the men of the trenches. But many veterans also shared a primitive attraction to war's fury. A Belgian veteran expressed it this way:

> *The plain truth is that if I were to obey my native animal instincts—and there was little hope for anything else while I was in the trenches—I should enlist again in any future war, or take part in any sort of fighting, merely to experience again that voluptuous thrill of the human brute who realizes his power to take away life from other human beings who try to do the same to him. What was first accepted as a moral duty became a habit . . . had become a need.*[23]

The British novelist D. H. Lawrence (1885–1930) understood that the brutality and hate unleashed by the war ruined old Europe and would give rise to even greater evils. On the day the armistice was signed, he warned prophetically:

> *I suppose you think the war is over and that we shall go back to the kind of world you lived in before it. But the war isn't over. The hate and evil is greater now than ever. Very soon war will break out again and overwhelm you. . . . The crowd outside thinks that Germany is crushed forever. But the Germans will soon rise again. Europe is done for. . . . The war isn't over. Even if the fighting should stop, the evil will be worse because the hate will be damned up in men's hearts and will show itself in all sorts of ways.*[24]

Particularly in Germany, the veterans who aspired to recapture the exhilaration experienced in combat made ideal recruits for extremist political movements that glorified action and brutality and promised to rescue society from a decadent liberalism. Both Hitler and Mussolini, themselves ex-soldiers imbued with the ferocity of the front, knew how to appeal to veterans. The lovers of violence and the harbingers of hate who became the leaders of Fascist parties would come within a hairsbreadth of destroying Western civilization. The intensified nationalist hatreds following World War I also helped fuel the fires of World War II. The Germans swore to regain lands lost to the Poles. Many Germans, like the embittered Hitler, were consumed by anguish over a defeat that they believed never should have happened and over the humiliating Treaty of Versailles; a desire for revenge festered in their souls. Italy, too, felt aggrieved because it had not received more territory from the dismembered Austro-Hungarian Empire.

Yet, while some veterans clung to an aggressive militarism, others aspired to build a more humane world. Such veterans embraced democratic and socialist ideals and resolved that the horror should never be repeated. Tortured by the memory of the Great War, European intellectuals wrote pacifist plays and novels and signed pacifist declarations. In the 1930s, an attitude of "peace at any price" discouraged resistance to Nazi Germany in its bid to dominate Europe.

During World War I, new weapons were introduced, particularly the tank and the fighter plane, which revolutionized the future of warfare. Prior to World War II, imaginative military planners recognized that planes and tanks, properly deployed, could penetrate and smash the enemy's defenses, circumventing the stalemate of trench warfare. Planes also meant terror from the skies, for bombs could pulverize a city, killing and maiming tens of thousands of civilians.

World War I was total war; it encompassed the entire nation and was without limits. States demanded total victory and total commitment from their citizens. They regulated industrial production, developed sophisticated propaganda techniques to strengthen morale, and exercised ever-greater control over the lives of their people, organizing and disciplining them like soldiers. This total mobilization of nations' human and material resources provided a model for future dictators. With ever-greater effectiveness and ruthlessness, dictators would centralize power and manipulate thinking. The ruthless dictatorships that emerged in Russia, Germany, and Italy were products of the war. The war gave Communists the opportunity to seize power in Russia, and the mentality of the front helped to mold the Fascist movements that emerged in Italy and Germany. And both Hitler and Stalin drew a moral lesson from the immense loss of life in the trenches: a desired political end justifies vast human sacrifice. The barbarism of the trenches would be eclipsed by the horrors inflicted on people by totalitarian regimes and a second world war begot by World War I. The noble sentiment, widely publicized during the war that this was to be "the war to end all wars," proved to be still another naïve fantasy.

❖ ❖ ❖

Notes

1. Quoted in Roland N. Stromberg, *Redemption by War,* p. 24. University Press of Kansas, 1982. Copyright © 1982 by University Press of Kansas. All rights reserved. Reprinted with permission.
2. Heinrich von Treitschke, *Politics,* excerpted in *Germany's War Mania* (New York: Dodd, Mead, 1915), pp. 222–223.
3. Fritz Fischer, *Germany's Aims in the First World War* (New York: Norton, 1967), p. 88.
4. Quoted in Joachim Remak, *The Origins of World War I* (New York: Holt, 1967), p. 135.
5. Rupert Brooke, "Peace," in *Collected Poems of Rupert Brooke* (New York: Dodd, Mead, 1941), p. 111.
6. Quoted in Joachim C. Fest, *Hitler* (New York: Harcourt Brace Jovanovich, 1973), p. 66.
7. Roland Dorgelès, "After Fifty Years," excerpted in *Promise of Greatness*, ed. George A. Panichas (New York: John Day, 1968), pp. 14–15.
8. Quoted in Joseph E. Persico, *Eleventh Month, Eleventh Day, Eleventh Hour: Armistice Day, 1918* (New York: Random House, 2004), 27.
9. Quoted in Barbara Tuchman, *The Guns of August* (New York: Macmillan, 1962), p. 145.
10. Bertrand Russell, *The Autobiography of Bertrand Russell, 1914–1944* (Boston: Little, Brown, 1951, 1956), Vol. 2, 4–6.
11. Quoted in Robert G. L. Waite, *Vanguard of Nazism* (New York: Norton, 1969), p. 22.
12. Brooke, "Peace," p. 111.
13. Quoted in James Joll, "The Unspoken Assumptions," in *The Origins of the First World War*, ed. H. W. Koch (New York: Taplinger, 1972), p. 318.
14. Quoted in Peter Gay, *Freud: A Life for Our Time* (New York: Norton), p. 348.
15. S. L. A. Marshall, *The American Heritage History of World War I* (New York: Dell, 1966), p. 215.
16. A. J. P. Taylor, *A History of the First World War* (New York: Berkeley, 1966), p. 84.

17. Quoted in Richard M. Watt, *Dare Call It Treason* (New York: Simon & Schuster, 1963), p. 169.
18. Excerpted in Ronald Kowalski, ed., *The Russian Revolution, 1917–1921* (New York: Routledge, 1997), p. 20.
19. V. I. Lenin, "Letter to the Central Committee," reproduced in Saul N. Silverman, ed., *Lenin* (Englewood Cliffs, NJ, Prentice-Hall, 1972), 74.
20. Quoted in Alistair Horne, *The Price of Glory* (New York: Harper, 1967), p. 240.
21. A. J. P. Taylor, *From Sarajevo to Potsdam* (New York: Harcourt, Brace & World), 1966, pp. 55–56.
22. Quoted in Modris Eksteins, *Rites of Spring: The Great War and the Birth of the Modern Age* (New York: Doubleday Anchor Books, 1989), p. 232.
23. Quoted in Eric J. Leed, *No Man's Land: Combat and Identity in World War I* (New York: Cambridge University Press, 1979), p. 201.
24. Quoted in Samuel Hynes, *A War Imagined* (New York: Atheneum, 1991), p. 266.

Suggested Reading

Figues, Orlando, *A People's Tragedy* (1996). A recent study of the Russian Revolution; thorough, detailed, anecdotal, and comprehensive.

Gilbert, Martin, *The First World War* (1994). A recent survey; contains illuminating anecdotal material.

Joll, James, *The Origins of the First World War* (1984). Excellent work of synthesis.

Keegan, John. *The First World War* (1999). A superb military historian at his best.

Koch, H. W., ed. *The Origins of the First World War* (1972). Useful essays, particularly those dealing with the glorification of war before 1914.

Lafore, Laurence, *The Long Fuse* (1971). A beautifully written study of the causes of the conflict.

Leed, Eric J., *No Man's Land: Combat and Identity in World War I* (1979). The impact of the war on the men who participated in it.

MacMillan, Margaret, *Paris 1919: Six Months That Changed the World* (2001). An instructive study of the Paris Conference.

Panichas, George A., ed., *Promise of Greatness* (1968). Recollections of the war by people of prominence.

Persico, Joseph E., *Eleventh Month, Eleventh Day, Eleventh Hour: Armistice Day 1918* (2004). A compelling account of the war's climax.

Service, Robert, *The Russian Revolution, 1900–1927* (1990). A brief overview.

Stone, Norman, *World War I: A Short History (2009)*. A stimulating study by a distinguished scholar.

Strachan, Hew, ed., *The Oxford Illustrated History of the First World War* (1998). Essays by an international team of specialists on many phases of the war, including causes, battles, and consequences.

Stromberg, Roland N., *Redemption by War: The Intellectuals and 1914* (1982). A superb analysis of the reasons that so many intellectuals welcomed the war.

Tuchman, Barbara, *The Guns of August* (1962). A beautifully written account of the opening weeks of World War I.

Winter, J. M., *The Experience of World War I* (1995). Excellent illustrations and eye-witness accounts are integrated into a gripping narrative.

——— et. al., eds., *The Great War and the Twentieth Century* (2000). Essays by accomplished scholars on the war and its enduring impact.

Art as History: The Renaissance to the Present

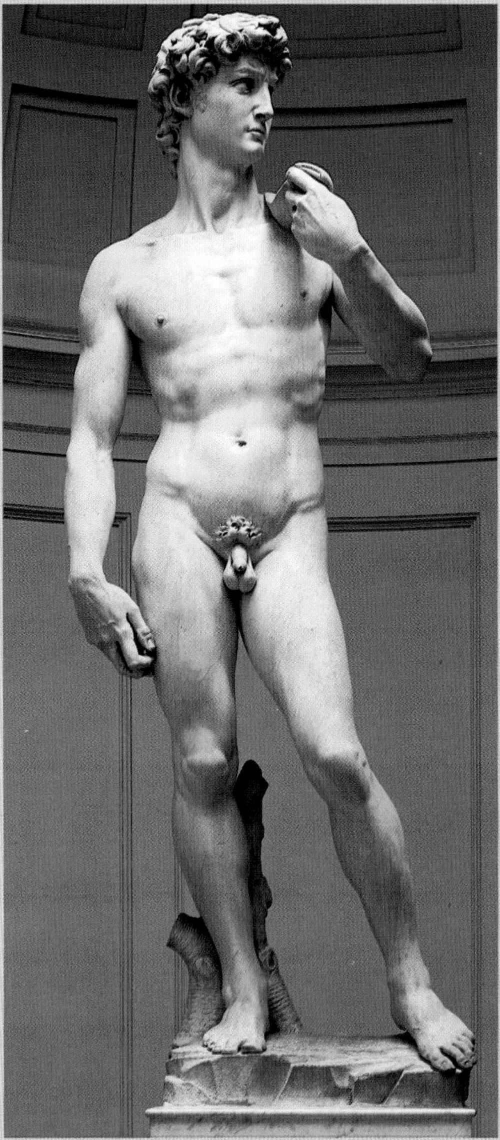

Michelangelo Buonarotti: *David*, 1504 A towering marble sculpture, Michelangelo's David is one of the crowning masterpieces of the High Renaissance. During the Middle Ages, artists depicted the nude figure for specific, often moral, reasons: tormented sinners at the Last Judgment, for example. Michelangelo's use of nudity breaks with this tradition. What does his heroic, idealized portrayal of the biblical David reveal about the secular spirit of the Renaissance? (Scala/Art Resource, N.Y.)

The visual arts are a particularly rich source of information for historians of the modern West. Revolutionary changes in art styles reflect the stages and complexities of the modern age. What insights into modern history can be derived from examining these works of art?

Pieter Brueghel the Elder: *Hunters in the Snow*, 1565. Brueghel's treatment of landscape art resulted from the technique he acquired when he studied in Italy during the Renaissance. His depiction of objects in three-dimensional space achieves a depth of perspective that is entirely new, virtually ushering in a new age in art, and superseding the "flat" two-dimensional space of medieval art. Compare Brueghel's painting with the manuscript illustration "April" from Les Très Riches Heures of Jean, Duke of Berry (see the art essay in Chapter 7). How does it differ? What makes it "modern"? (Erich Lessing/Kunsthistoriches, Vienna/Art Resource, N.Y.)

Rembrandt van Rijn (1606–1669): ***Self-Portrait at Old Age*****, 1669.** Rembrandt was influenced in his early years by Italian painters' use of light. He also was highly introspective and produced a series of sixty-two self-portraits during his lifetime. The portraits revealed a variety of attitudes and poses, ranging from youthful and flamboyant to aging and distraught. In this painting, the fifty-fifth of the self-portraits, Rembrandt stares back at us with the calm assurance of a man who has mastered his art and life. What words would you use to describe the emotions conveyed in this self-portrait? How does Rembrandt use light and darkness in this painting? (Erich Lessing/National Gallery, London/Art Resource, N.Y.)

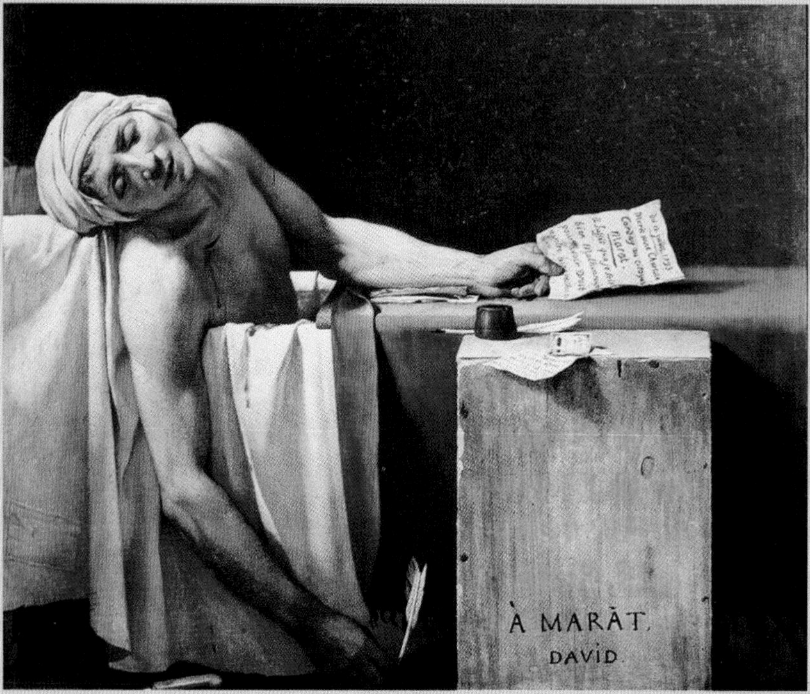

Jacques Louis David: *The Death of Marat*, 1793. This painting was done during the French Revolution by David, a foremost exponent of the neo-classical style and an ardent revolutionary. It shows Marat, a revolutionary leader, after he had been stabbed to death by a crazed woman who had handed him a personal petition to read. What does this stark depiction of the death scene reveal about David's perception of the episode and his indebtedness to the classical style of antiquity? How does his treatment of the moment of death differ from a work such as the Laocoön group's treatment of the same theme? (Bridgeman-Giraudon/Art Resource, N.Y.)

J. M. W. Turner (1775–1851): ***Burning of the Houses of Parliament*****, c. 1835.** Turner was preoccupied with shimmering light. Although he often used literary themes for his paintings, in accordance with romantic taste the people, buildings, and ships were often obscured. What does this painting reveal about his temperament and perception of the world? (Oil on canvas. H. 36¼" W. 48½". Philadelphia Museum of Art: The John H. McFadden Collection.)

Georges Seurat: Sunday ***Afternoon on the Island of La Grande Jatte*****, 1884–1886.** Seurat belonged to a late-nineteenth-century artistic movement called impressionism, which wanted to depict objects in the instant they impress themselves on the passive human eye. This position was opposed to the early-nineteenth-century movement of romanticism, which wanted to reveal how the act of seeing an object expresses a mood or feeling. Describe what Seurat's painting contains. How does it compare to a romantic work, such as Turner's *Burning of the Houses of Parliament*? (Georges Seurat French, 1859–1891, A Sunday on La Grande Jatte—1884, 1884–86, Oil on canvas, 81 3/4 × 121 1/4 in. (207.5 × 308.1 cm), Helen Birch Bartlett Memorial Collection, 1926.224, The Art Institute of Chicago.)

Pablo Picasso (1881–1973): ***Les Demoiselles d'Avignon,*** **1907** The cubists distorted perspective to give viewers the feeling of seeing objects and people "in the round" and over time. In this picture, Picasso painted the female nude in the strong cubist style to express the forces of nature: he goes beyond the conscious level. Can a correlation be made between some twentieth-century art and the scientific examination of the unconscious?

Edward Hopper (1882–1967): *Nighthawks*, 1942. American painter Edward Hopper is one of the most notable American realist artists of the twentieth century. Set in 1942 in an all-night diner, *Nighthawks* depicts loneliness and alienation. The couple seems disconnected as the man converses with the waiter and the fourth figure sits alone at the counter. Exposed and vulnerable in the bright light, these people suffer from existential loneliness. What details does Hopper use to convey this sense of loneliness? What historical events in 1942 might Hopper have been responding to in this painting? (Edward Hopper American, 1882–1967, Nighthawks, 1942, Oil on canvas, 84.1 × 152.4 cm (33 1/8 × 60 in.), Friends of American Art Collection, 1942.51, The Art Institute of Chicago.)

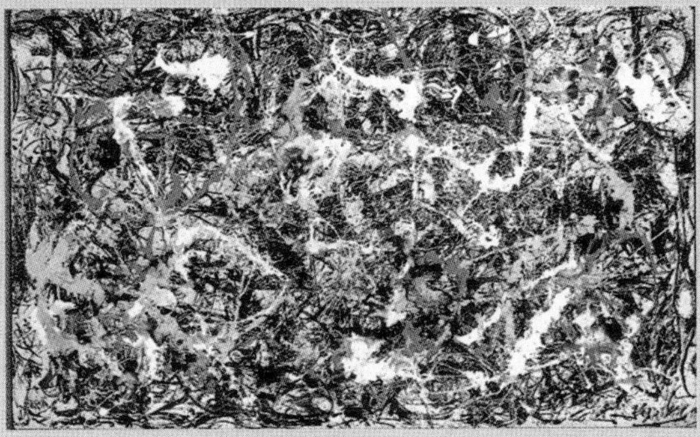

Jackson Pollock (1912–1956): *Convergence*, 1952. American artist Jackson Pollock poured and splattered his colors on the canvas instead of applying them with a brush or palette knife. This style of painting, known as action painting, allowed Pollock to walk around the canvas and work on it from all sides and angles. His *Convergence* may at first seem to be a canvas used as a drop cloth, but each application of color was made in a controlled and studied manner. Pollock was part of the abstract-expressionist movement, in which artists strived to express their emotions through color and abstract, nonrepresentational forms. What emotions does this painting convey to you? Why might it have been important for an abstract-expressionist like Pollock to move around the canvas instead of painting in a more traditional manner? (© 2011 The Pollock-Krasner Foundation/ Artists Rights Society (ARS), New York.)

Frank O. Gehry (1929–): Guggenheim Museum at Bilbao, Spain, 1997. American architect Frank Gehry is famous for his innovative use of materials—twisting, bending, and turning metal into shapes that affect the emotions. Gehry views architecture as an art form, like painting and sculpture, that is expressive of human feeling and emotion. His Guggenheim Museum in Bilbao, Spain consists of organically interrelated, contrasting shapes composed of a multiplicity of materials, ranging from limestone and glass to titanium. It provides the city of Bilbao with a dramatic architectural centerpiece that attracts thousands of visitors each year. In what ways does this museum prove Gehry's assertion that architecture is an art form capable of stirring human emotion? (© Steve Vidler/SuperStock.)

Chapter 19

An Era of Totalitarianism

- **The Nature of Totalitarianism**
- **Communist Russia**
- **The Stalin Revolution**
- **The Nature and Appeal of Fascism**
- **The Rise of Fascism in Italy**
- **The New German Republic**
- **The Rise of Hitler**
- **Nazi Germany**
- **Liberalism and Authoritarianism in Other Lands**
- **Intellectuals and Artists in Troubled Times**
- **Existentialism**
- **The Modern Predicament**

Focus Questions

1. What are the distinctive features of a totalitarian state?
2. What motivated Stalin to make terror a government policy? What motivated Communist bureaucrats to participate in Stalin's inhumanities?
3. What were the essential features of the Fascist movements that arose in Europe after World War I?
4. What were Hitler's attitudes toward liberalism, war, race, the Jews, and propaganda?
5. In what ways did Nazism conflict with the core values of both the Enlightenment and Christianity? Why did the Nazi regime attract so many supporters?

6. What lessons might democratic societies draw from the Nazi experience?
7. Why and how did European intellectual and cultural life convey a mood of pessimism and disillusionment after World War I?
8. How did art and literature express a social conscience during the 1920s and 1930s?
9. What were the different ways that intellectuals struggled with the crisis of European society in an era of world wars and totalitarianism?
10. What were some of the conditions that gave rise to existentialism? What are the basic principles of existentialism?

In the 1930s, the term *totalitarianism* was used to describe the Fascist regime in Italy, the National Socialist regime in Germany, and the Communist regime in the Soviet Union. To a degree that far exceeds the ancient tyrannies and early modern autocratic states, these dictatorships aspired to and, with varying degrees of success, attained control over the individual's consciousness and behavior and all phases of political, social, and cultural life. To many people, it seemed that a crisis-riddled democracy was dying and that the future belonged to these dynamic totalitarian movements.

Totalitarianism was a twentieth-century phenomenon, for such all-embracing control over the individual and society could be achieved only in an age of modern ideology, technology, and bureaucracy. The totalitarian state was more completely established in Germany and the Soviet Union than in Italy, where cultural and historic conditions impeded the realization of the totalitarian goal of monolithic unity and total control.

The ideological aims and social and economic policies of Hitler and Stalin differed fundamentally. However, both Soviet Russia and

Nazi Germany shared the totalitarian goal of total domination of both the individual and institutions, and both employed similar methods to achieve it. Mussolini's Italy is more accurately called authoritarian, for the party-state either did not intend to control all phases of life or lacked the means to do so. Moreover, Mussolini hesitated to use the ruthless methods that Hitler and Stalin employed so readily. ❖

The Nature of Totalitarianism

Striving for total unity, control, and obedience, the totalitarian dictatorship is the antithesis of liberal democracy. It abolishes all competing political parties, suppresses individual liberty, eliminates or regulates private institutions, and utilizes the modern state's bureaucracy and technology to impose its ideology and enforce its commands. The party-state determines what people should believe—what values they should hold. There is no room for individual thinking, private moral judgment, or individual conscience. The individual possesses no natural rights that the state must respect. The state regards individuals merely as building blocks, the human material to be hammered and hewed into a new social order. It seeks to create an efficiently organized and stable society—one whose members do not raise troublesome questions or hold unorthodox opinions.

Nevertheless, the totalitarian dictatorship is also an unintended consequence of liberal democracy. It emerged in an age in which, because of the French and Industrial Revolutions, the masses had become a force in political life. The totalitarian leader seeks to gain and preserve power by harnessing mass support. Hitler, in particular, built a party within the existing constitutional system and exploited the electoral process in order to overthrow the democratic government.

Unlike previous dictatorial regimes, the dictatorships of both the left and the right sought to legitimatize their rule by gaining the masses' approval. They claimed that their governments were higher and truer expressions of the people's will. The Soviet and Nazi dictatorships established their rule in the name of the people—the German Volk or the Soviet proletariat.

A distinctive feature of totalitarianism is the overriding importance of the leader, who is seen as infallible and invincible. The masses' slavish adulation of the leader and their uncritical acceptance of the dogma that the leader or the party is always right promote loyalty, dedication, and obedience and distort rational thinking.

Totalitarian leaders want more than power for its own sake; in the last analysis, they seek to transform the world according to an all-embracing ideology, a set of convictions and beliefs, which, says Hannah Arendt, "pretend[s] to know the mysteries of the whole historical process—the secrets of the past, the intricacies of the present, the uncertainties of the future."[1] The ideology constitutes a higher and exclusive truth based on a law of history or social development that, says Karl Dietrich Bracher, "reduce[s] the past and the future to a single historical principle of struggle, no matter whether by state, nation, people, race, or class."[2] The ideology contains a dazzling vision of the future—a secular New Jerusalem—that strengthens the will of the faithful and attracts converts. Like a religion, the totalitarian ideology provides its adherents with beliefs that make society and history intelligible, that explain all of existence in an emotionally gratifying way.

The ideology satisfies a human yearning for complete certitude. Like a religion, it creates true believers, who feel that they are participating in a great cause—a heroic fight against evil—that gives meaning to their lives. During World War II, a German soldier fighting on the Eastern front wrote to his brother that the battle "is for a new ideology, a new belief, a new life! I am glad that I can participate . . . in this war of light and darkness."[3] Also like a religion, the totalitarian party gives isolated and alienated individuals a sense of belonging, a feeling of camaraderie; it enables a person to lose himself or herself in the comforting and exhilarating embrace of a mass movement.

Not only did the totalitarian religion-ideology supply followers with a cause that claimed absolute goodness, it also provided a Devil. For the Soviets, the source of evil and the cause of all the people's hardships were the degenerate capitalists, reactionary peasants who resisted collectivization, the traitorous Trotskyites, or the saboteurs and foreign agents who impeded the realization of the socialist society. For the Nazis, the Devil was the conspirator Jew. These "evil" ones must be eliminated in order to realize the totalitarian movement's vision of the future.

Thus, totalitarian regimes liquidate large segments of the population designated as "enemies of the people." Historical necessity or a higher purpose demands and justifies their liquidation. The appeal to historical necessity has all the power of a great myth. Presented as a world-historical struggle between the forces of good and the forces of evil, the myth incites fanaticism and numbs the conscience. Traditional rules of morality have no meaning; seemingly decent people engage in terrible acts of brutality with no remorse, convinced that they are waging a righteous war.

Totalitarians are utopians inspired by idealism; they seek the salvation of their nation, their race, or humanity. They believe that the victory of their cause will usher in the millennium, a state of harmony and bliss. Such a vision is attractive to people burdened by economic insecurity or spiritual disorientation. The history of the twentieth century demonstrates how easily utopian beliefs can be twisted into paranoid fantasies, idealistic sentiments transformed into murderous fanaticism, and destructive components of human nature mobilized and directed by demagogues.

Unlike earlier autocratic regimes, the totalitarian dictatorship is not satisfied with its subjects' outward obedience; it demands the masses' unconditional loyalty and enthusiastic support. It strives to control the inner person—to shape thoughts, feelings, and attitudes in accordance with the party ideology, which becomes an official creed. It does not rule by brute force alone but seeks to create a "new man," one who dedicates himself body and soul to the party and its ideology. Such unquestioning, faithful subjects can be manipulated by the party. The disinterested search for truth, justice, and goodness—the exploration of those fundamental moral, political, and religious questions that have characterized the Western intellectual tradition for centuries—is abandoned. Truth, justice, and goodness are what the party deems them to be, and ideological deviation is forbidden.

The totalitarian dictatorship deliberately politicizes all areas of human activity. Ideology pervades works of literature, history, philosophy, art, and even science. It dominates the school curriculum and influences everyday speech and social relations. The state is concerned with everything its citizens do; there is no distinction between public and private life, and every institution comes under the party-state's authority. If voluntary support for the regime cannot be generated by indoctrination, then the state unhesitatingly resorts to terror and violence to compel obedience. People live under a constant strain. Fear of the secret police is ever present; it produces a permanent state of insecurity, which induces people to do everything that the regime asks of them and to watch what they say and do.

Communist Russia

In 1918, the infant Soviet government was threatened with civil war. Tsarist officers had gathered troops in the south; other anti-Communist centers rose in Siberia, and still others in the extreme north and along the Baltic coast. The political orientation of these anti-Communist groups, generally called Whites in contrast to the Communist Reds, combined all shades of opinion, from moderate socialist to reactionary, the latter usually predominating. Generally the Whites were monarchists who identified with the old tsarist regime. The Whites received support from foreign governments, which freely intervened. Until their own revolution in November 1918, the Germans occupied much of southern Russia. England, France, and the United States sent troops to points in northern and southern European Russia; England, Japan, and the United States also sent troops to Siberia. At first, they wanted to offset German expansion, but later they hoped to overthrow the Communist regime. In May and June 1918, Czech prisoners of war, about to be evacuated, precipitated anti-Communist uprisings along the Trans-Siberian Railroad, bringing the civil war to fever pitch. In July 1918, the Communists murdered Nicholas II and his entire family.

The Communists speeded the buildup of their own Red Army. Recruited from the remnants of the tsarist army and its officer corps, the Red Army was reinforced by compulsory military service and strict discipline; including the execution of deserters. Trotsky reintroduced the death penalty, which had been outlawed by the Provisional

Government. Threatened with death if they refused, many tsarist officers served in the Red Army. They were closely watched by Trotsky's ruthless political commissars, who were also responsible for the political reliability and morale of the troops. Trotsky ordered the formation of "blocking units" to machine-gun retreating soldiers. The civil war was brutal; both sides butchered civilians and their own comrades.

Hard-pressed as Lenin's party was, by the autumn of 1920 it had prevailed over its enemies. The Whites were divided among themselves and discredited by their association with the tsarist regime; the Communists had greater popular support, the advantage of interior communications, and superior political skills. The war-weary foreign interventionists called off their efforts to overthrow the Bolshevik regime by force.

The Communist victory in the civil war exacted a staggering price. Reds and Whites alike carried the tsarist tradition of political violence to a new pitch of horror. Some 1.2 million combatants on both sides perished. In addition, the Communists killed some 250,000 peasants who resisted grain requisitions and executed tens of thousands of political opponents. Adding to the death toll were some 100,000 Jews, victims of pogroms perpetrated largely by Whites and Ukrainian nationalists. Compounding the nation's anguish was the famine of 1921–1922, which claimed some five million victims.

War Communism and the New Economic Policy

Besides the extreme misery brought on by the world war and civil war, the Russian people had to endure the rigors of the policy known as War Communism. It was introduced in 1918 to deal with plummeting agricultural and economic production, rampant inflation, and desperate hunger in the cities. Under War Communism, the state took over the means of production and greatly limited the sphere of private ownership; it conscripted labor and, in effect, confiscated grain from the peasants in order to feed workers in the cities. War Communism devastated the economy even further and alienated workers and peasants. The state-run factories were mismanaged, workers stayed away from their jobs or performed poorly, and peasants resisted the food requisition detachments that the government sent to seize their grain.

There was even open rebellion. In March 1921, sailors at the Kronstadt naval base and workers in nearby Petrograd—people who in 1917 had been ready to give their lives for the Revolution—rose against the repression that had been introduced during the civil war; they called for the establishment of socialist democracy. Trotsky ruthlessly suppressed that uprising, but the lesson was clear: the Communist regime had to implement a strategic retreat from War Communism and to restore a measure of stability to the country.

In 1921, the Communist Party adopted the New Economic Policy, called NEP, which lasted until 1928. Under a system that Lenin characterized as "state socialism," the government retained control of finance, industry, and transportation—"the commanding heights" of the economy—but allowed the rest of the economy to return to private enterprise. The peasants, after giving part of their crops to the government, were free to sell the rest in the open market; traders could buy and sell as they pleased. With the resumption of small-scale capitalism, an air of normal life returned.

One-Party Dictatorship

While the Communists were waging a fierce struggle against the Whites, they instituted a militant dictatorship run by their party. Numbering about five hundred thousand members in 1921, the Communist Party was controlled by a small, tight core of professional political leaders, the best of them unusually disciplined in personal dedication to the Revolution.

Under its constitution, the Russian Communist Party, as its formal title read, was a democratic body. Its members elected delegates to periodic party congresses; these in turn elected the membership of the central committee, which originally held the reins of leadership. However, power soon shifted to a smaller and more intimate group, the *politburo* (political bureau), which assumed a dictatorial role. The key leaders—Lenin, Trotsky, Stalin, and a few others—determined policy, assigned tasks, and appointed important officials. The party dominated all public agencies; its leaders held the chief positions in government. No other political parties were tolerated, and trade unions became agents of the regime. Never before had the people of Russia been forced into such abject dependence on their government.

Impatient with the endless disputes among righteous and strong-willed old revolutionaries, Lenin, in agreement with other top leaders, demanded unconditional submission to his decisions. He even ordered that dissidents be disciplined and political enemies be terrorized. No price was too high to achieve monolithic party unity. Believing that they were creating a new and better society that would serve as a model for the rest of humanity, the Communists felt no moral objection to the use of force or even terror, including executions and forced-labor camps. The dreaded Cheka, a ruthless secret police organization, executed some two hundred thousand people from 1919 to 1925. The means Lenin employed for ruling his backward country denied the human values that Marx had taken from the Enlightenment and put into his vision of a socialist society. Lenin was perfectly willing to use state terror to promote the class struggle.

The Communists abolished the power of the Orthodox church, which was the traditional ally of tsarism and the enemy of innovation. They were militant atheists, believing with Marx that religion was the "opium of the people"; God had no place in their vision of a better society.

The Communists also simplified the alphabet, changed the calendar to the Gregorian system prevailing in the capitalist West, and brought theater and all arts, until then reserved for the elite, to the masses. Above all, they wiped out—by expropriation, discrimination, expulsion, and execution—the educated upper class of bureaucrats, landowners, professional people, and industrialists.

In the spring of 1918, Lenin argued that the Russian workers had not yet matched capitalist performance: "The Russian worker is a bad worker compared with the workers of the advanced, i.e., western countries." To overcome this fatal handicap, Lenin relentlessly hammered home the need for "iron discipline at work" and "unquestioning obedience" to a single will,

Forging Socialism. Men and women work equally in this socialist realist propaganda poster from 1921.

that of the Communist Party. There was no alternative: "Large-scale machinery calls for absolute and strict unity of will, which directs the joint labors of hundreds and thousands and tens of thousands of people. A thousand wills are subordinated to one will."[4] In these words lay the essence of subsequent Soviet industrialization. The entire economy was to be monolithic, rationally planned in its complex interdependence, and pursuing a single goal: overcoming the weaknesses of Russia, so disastrously demonstrated in the war.

In attempting to transform their Soviet Russia into a modern, industrialized, socialist state that would serve as a model for the world, the Communists imposed a new autocracy even more authoritarian than tsarism. The minds of the people came under unprecedented government control. In education, from kindergarten through university, in press and radio, and in literature and the arts, the Communist Party tried to fashion people's thoughts to create the proper "consciousness." The party made Marxism-Leninism the sole source of truth, eliminating as best it could all rival creeds, whether religious, political, or philosophical. Minds were to be as reliably uniform as machine processes and totally committed to the party, and they were to be protected against all subversive capitalist influences.

Lenin molded the Soviet Union into an international revolutionary force, the champion of anticapitalism and of the liberation of colonial peoples. The Russian Revolution inspired nationalistic ambitions for political self-determination and cultural self-assertion among a growing number of peoples around the world, especially in Asia. It appealed particularly to intellectuals educated in the West (or in westernized schools) yet identifying themselves with their downtrodden compatriots.

To have a political tool for world revolution Lenin created the Communist—or Third—International (Comintern). The most radical successor to earlier socialist international associations, it helped organize small Communist parties in Western Europe, which in time became dependable, although rather powerless, agents of Soviet Russia. In Asia, where no proletariat existed, Lenin tried to work closely with incipient nationalist movements. Lenin and the Bolshevik Revolution gained the admiration and instinctive loyalty of colonial and semicolonial peoples in what would come to be called the Third World. Soviet Russia now stood out as the Communist alternative to the capitalist West.

The Stalin Revolution

Lenin died in 1924, and the task of achieving the goal that he had set was taken up by Stalin. The "man of steel" was crude and vulgar, toughened by the revolutionary underground and tsarist prisons and by the roughest aspects of Russian life. Relentlessly energetic but relatively inconspicuous among key Communists, Stalin had been given, in 1922, the unwanted and seemingly routine task of general secretary of the party. Shrewd and methodical, he used this position to his own advantage, building up a reliable party cadre—apparatus men, or *apparatchiki,* as they came to be called—and dominating the party as not even Lenin had done. When he was challenged, particularly by Trotsky and his associates, in the protracted struggles for the succession to Lenin, it was too late to unseat him. None of Stalin's rivals could rally the necessary majorities at the party congresses; none could match Stalin's skill in party infighting or in making rough and anarchic people into docile members of the Communist Party apparatus.

Modernizing Russia: Industrialization and Collectivization

To Stalin, Russia's most pressing need was not world revolution, but the fastest possible buildup of Soviet power through industrialization. The country could not afford to risk near-annihilation again, as it had done in the world war and then in the civil war. Communist pride dictated that the country be made as strong as possible. Stalin set forth the stark reckoning of Russian history in a speech delivered in 1931, three years after launching a program of massive industrialization.

> *Those who fall behind get beaten. But we do not want to be beaten. No, we refuse to be beaten. One feature of the history of old Russia was the continual beatings she suffered for falling behind, for her backwardness. All beat her—for her backwardness, for military backwardness, cultural backwardness, political backwardness, for industrial backwardness, for agricultural backwardness. She was beaten because to do so was profitable and could be done with impunity. . . . You are backward, you are weak—therefore you are wrong, hence you can be beaten and enslaved. You are mighty, therefore you are right, hence we must be wary of you. Such is the law of the exploiters. . . . That is why we must no longer lag behind.*[5]

Stalin decided on all-out industrialization at the expense of the toiling masses. Peasants and workers, already poor, would be required to make tremendous sacrifices of body and spirit to overcome the nation's weaknesses. Abandoning the NEP, Stalin decreed a series of Five-Year Plans, the first and most experimental one commencing in 1928. The industrialization drive was heralded as a vast economic and social revolution, undertaken by the state according to a rational plan. The emphasis lay on heavy industry: the construction of railroads, power plants, steel mills, and military hardware such as tanks and warplanes. Production of consumer goods was cut to the minimum, and all small-scale private trading, revived under the NEP, came to an end—with disastrous results for the standard of living. Having just come within sight of their pre-1914 standard of living, Russians now found their expectations dashed for decades.

Thus, a new, grim age began, with drastic material hardships and profound anguish. Harsh punishments, including denial of food cards and imprisonment, were meted out for lateness, slowness, or incompetence. But many people, particularly the young, were fired to heroic exertions. They were proud to sacrifice themselves for the building of a superior society. And many common factory workers had the opportunity to attend school and become engineers and administrators, which tied them to the regime. When the Great Depression in the capitalist countries put millions out of work, no Soviet citizen suffered from unemployment; gloom pervaded the West, but confidence and hope, artificially fostered by the party, buoyed up many people in Soviet Russia. The first two Five-Year Plans dramatically and rapidly increased Russia's industrial infrastructure as factories, mines, dams, and railroads were feverishly constructed. At no time, though, did the planning produce Western-style efficiency, and workers, who labored in a herculean way, actually suffered a decline in real wages. The regime concentrated on heavy industry, not consumer goods or improving the standard of living.

Meanwhile, a second and far more brutal revolution overtook Soviet agriculture, for the peasants had to be forcibly integrated into the planned economy through collectivization. Agriculture—the peasants, their animals, and their fields—had to submit to the same rational control as industry. Collectivization meant the pooling of farmlands, animals, and equipment for the sake of more efficient, large-scale production. The Bolshevik solution for the backwardness of Russian agriculture was for the peasants to be organized like factory workers. But knowing the peasants' distaste for the factory, their attachment to their own land, and their stubbornness, the party had hesitated to carry out its ambitious scheme. In 1929, however, Stalin believed that, for the sake of industrialization, he had no choice. If the Five-Year Plan was to succeed, the government had to receive planned crops of planned amounts and quality at planned times. This could only be accomplished, Stalin thought, by destroying the independent peasantry and creating huge agricultural factories. With collectivization, the ascendancy of the party over the people of Russia became almost complete.

The peasants paid a ghastly price. Stalin declared war on the Russian countryside. He ordered that the *kulaks,* the most enterprising and well-to-do peasants, be "liquidated as a class." Many were killed outright, and millions were deported to forced-labor camps in the far north, where many ultimately perished from hunger or abuse. Their poorer and less efficient neighbors were herded onto collective farms at the point of a bayonet.

The peasants struck back, sometimes in pitched battles. The horror of forced collectivization broke the spirit even of hardened officials. "I am an old Bolshevik," sobbed a secret police colonel to a fellow passenger on a train; "I worked in the underground against the Tsar and then I fought in the civil war. Did I do all that in order that I should now surround villages with machine guns and order my men to fire indiscriminately into crowds of peasants? Oh, no, no!"[6] Typically, however, the local officials and activists who stripped the peasants of their possessions and searched for hidden grain viewed themselves as idealists building a new society that was in the best interests of a suffering humanity, an outlook that justified ruthlessness. Their dedication to the triumph of Communism overcame all doubts caused by the sight of starving people and the sounds of wailing women and children.

Defeated but unwilling to surrender their livestock, the peasants slaughtered their animals, gorging themselves in drunken orgies against the days of inevitable famine. The country's cattle herds declined by one-half, inflicting irreparable secondary losses as well. The number of horses, crucial for rural transport and farm work, fell by one-third. Crops were not planted or not harvested, the Five-Year Plan was disrupted, and from 1931 to 1933 millions starved to death.

FORCED LABOR IN THE GULAG. All those accused of disloyalty to the party and not killed outright ended up in one of the gulags, or forced-labor camps. Forced labor was designed as a punishment and also as a means of obtaining raw materials from inhospitable regions in the far north. In this photo, deported peasants and political prisoners using primitive technology are engaged in constructing the canal linking Leningrad with the White Sea. Millions perished in the gulags.

The suffering was most cruel in the Ukraine, where famine killed three million people—the earlier figure of six million is now rejected—many after extreme abuse and persecution. In order to buy industrial equipment abroad so that industrialization could proceed on target, the Soviet Union had to export food, as much of it as possible and for prices disastrously lowered by the Great Depression. Let the peasants in the Ukrainian breadbasket starve so that the country could grow strong! Moreover, Stalin relished the opportunity to punish the Ukrainians for their disloyalty during the civil war and their resistance to collectivization.

By 1935, practically all farming in Russia was collectivized. The kulaks had been wiped out as a class, and the peasants grumbled about the rise of a new serfdom.

Stalin had hoped to create technically efficient "factory farms" that would provide inexpensive food for the massive industrial labor force. But in reality, collectivization stifled agricultural production. Enraged peasants had slaughtered livestock rather than turn it over to the state; mismanagement and unenthusiastic collective farmers resulted in a precipitous decline in agricultural production. For decades collective farming failed to achieve the levels of production previously reached in the 1920s.

Total Control

To quash resistance and mold a new type of suitably motivated and disciplined citizen, Stalin unleashed a third revolution, the revolution of totalitarianism. Only Communist regimentation and monolithic control by the party over state and society, he believed, could liberate Russia from its historic inferiority. Moreover, the totalitarian state accorded with his desire to exercise total control over the party and the nation. Stalin's totalitarianism aimed at a complete reconstruction of state and society, down to the innermost recesses of human consciousness. It called for a "new man" suited to the needs of Soviet industrialism.

The revolution of totalitarianism encompassed all cultural activity. Religion, which offered an alternative worldview, came under attack. Priests were jailed, organized worship discouraged, and churches converted into barns. All media of communication—literature, the arts, music, the stage—were forced into subservience to the Five-Year Plan and Soviet ideology. In literature, as in all other art, an official style was promulgated. Called *socialist realism,* it was expected to describe the world as the party saw it or hoped to shape it. Novels in the social realist manner told how the romances of tractor drivers and milkmaids or of lathe operators and office secretaries led to new victories of production under the Five-Year Plan. Composers found their music examined for remnants of bourgeois spirit; they were to write simple tunes suitable for heroic times. Everywhere huge, high-color posters showed men and women hard at work with radiant faces, calling others to join them; often Stalin, the wise father and leader, was shown among them. In this way, artistic creativity was locked into a dull, utilitarian straitjacket of official cheerfulness; creativity was allowed only to boost industrial productivity. Behind the scenes, all artists were disciplined to conform to the will of the party or be crushed.

Education, from nursery school to university, was likewise harnessed to train dutiful and loyal citizens, and Soviet propaganda made a cult of Stalin that bordered on deification. Thus, a writer declared in 1935:

> *Centuries will pass and the generations still to come will regard us as the happiest of mortals, as the most fortunate of men, because we . . . were privileged to see Stalin, our inspired leader. Yes, and we regard ourselves as the happiest of mortals because we are the contemporaries of a man who never had an equal in world history. The men of all ages will call on thy name, which is strong, beautiful, wise, and marvellous. Thy name is engraven on every factory, every machine, every place on the earth, and in the hearts of all men.*[7]

Stalin unleashed raw terror to break stubborn wills and compel conformity. Terror had been used as a tool of government ever since the Bolshevik Revolution (and the tsars had also used it, intermittently). After the start of the first Five-Year Plan, show trials were staged that denounced as saboteurs the engineers who disagreed with Stalin's production timetable. The terror used to herd the peasants onto collective farms was even greater. Stalin also used terror to crush opposition and to instill an abject fear both in the ranks of the party and in Russian society at large.

Purges had long been used to rid the party of weaklings. After 1934, however, they became an instrument of Stalin's drive for unchallenged personal power. Stalin's paranoia led him to see enemies and threats to his rule everywhere. In 1936, his vindictive terror broke into the open. The first batch of victims, including many founders of the Communist Party, were accused of conspiring with the exiled Trotsky to set up a "terrorist center" and of scheming to terrorize the party. After being sentenced to death, they were immediately executed. In 1937, the next group, including prominent Communists of Lenin's day, were charged with cooperating with foreign intelligence agencies and wrecking "socialist reconstruction," the term for Stalin's revolution; they too were executed. Shortly afterward, a secret purge decimated the military high command—for which the country paid a heavy price when Germany attacked in 1941. Almost half the country's seventy thousand officers were either shot or sent to the camps—after the Nazi invasion many of these prisoners were rehabilitated and restored to active duty.

In 1938, the last and biggest show trial advanced the most bizarre accusation of all: sabotage, espionage, and attempting to dismember the Soviet Union and kill all its leaders (including Lenin in 1918). In the public hearings, some defendants refuted the public prosecutor, but in the end all confessed, usually after torture and threats to their family, before being executed. Western observers were aghast at the cynical charges and at the physical and mental tortures used to obtain the confessions. Under Stalin, the revolution was devouring its own children at a rate that far surpassed earlier revolutions.

The great trials, however, involved only a small minority of Stalin's victims; many more perished in silence without the benefit of legal proceedings. The terror first hit members of the party, especially the Old Bolsheviks, who had joined before the Revolution; they were the most independent-minded members and therefore the most dangerous to Stalin. But Stalin also diminished the cultural elite that had survived the Lenin revolution. Thousands of engineers, scientists, industrial managers, scholars, and artists disappeared; accused of counterrevolutionary crimes, they were shot or sent to forced-labor camps, where many perished. No one was safe. To frighten the common people in all walks of life, men, women, and even children were dragged into the net of Stalin's secret police, leaving the survivors with a soul-killing reminder: submit or else. "In the years of the terror," recalled one victim, "there was not a house in the country where people did not sit trembling at night."[8]

The forced-labor camps to which Stalin's victims were deported played an important role in the Soviet economy. Slave labor constructed the White Sea–Baltic Canal, which the regime held up as a monument of Communist achievement. Mining, logging, and construction enterprises in remote parts of the country also depended on forced labor. It is estimated that from 1929 to the death of Stalin in 1953, some 18 million people were confined to the Gulag, as Stalin's system of concentration camps came to be known. Many perished from abuse, starvation, and bone-crushing labor in freezing weather. As in Nazi concentration camps, administrators and guards deliberately dehumanized and brutalized the prisoners, whom the regime designated as "filth" and "enemies of the people."

Stalin may have orchestrated the terror, but large numbers of party members believed that terror, which was decimating their own ranks, was necessary. The memory of the vicious civil war, when domestic and foreign enemies sought to overthrow the new Bolshevik regime, and the resistance of the kulaks to collectivization created a siege mentality among the Communist leadership. Everywhere they saw anti-Soviets plotting against the party; they defined these enemies as Trotskyites, former kulaks, Whites who had fought in the civil war, members of outlawed anti-Soviet political parties, foreign agents, criminals, cattle and horse thieves, contraband smugglers, bandits, and so on. Party officials saw terror as a legitimate way both of protecting the party—to which they were ideologically committed and from which they derived prestige, power, and material benefits—and of protecting the Soviet experiment, which they viewed as humanity's best hope.

The toll of the purges is reckoned in many millions; it included Trotsky, who in 1940 was murdered in Mexico. The bloodletting was ghastly, as Stalin's purge officials themselves followed each other into death and ignominy.

Stalin was untroubled by the waste of life. He believed that without the total obedience of the Russian people, the Soviet economy could not be effectively and quickly mobilized, and that terror was necessary to compel compliance. In Stalin's mind, totalitarianism was necessary to save Russia from foreign enemies that would devour it. No doubt, the terror was also an expression of his craving for personal power and his vengeful and suspicious, some say clinically paranoid, nature. He saw enemies everywhere, took pleasure in selecting victims, and reveled in his omnipotence. By showing party officials and the Russian masses how vulnerable they were, how dependent they were on his will, Stalin frightened them into servility. For good reason, Stalin has been called a twentieth-century Ivan the Terrible. Like the sixteenth-century tsar, for whom he expressed admiration, Stalin stopped at no brutality to establish personal autocracy.

But more than a craving for personal power motivated Stalin. He regarded himself as Lenin's heir, responsible for securing and expanding the Revolution and defending it against foreign and domestic enemies. The only way to do this was to create a powerful Soviet Union through rapid modernization.

The Nature and Appeal of Fascism

Liberals viewed the Great War as a conflict between freedom and autocracy and expected an Allied victory to accelerate the spread of democracy throughout Europe. Right after the war, it seemed that liberalism would continue to advance as it had in the nineteenth century. The collapse of the autocratic German and Austrian Empires had led to the formation of parliamentary governments throughout Eastern and Central Europe. Yet within two decades, in an extraordinary turn of events, democracy seemed in its death throes. In Spain, Portugal, Italy, and Germany, and in all the newly created states of Central and Eastern Europe except Czechoslovakia, democracy collapsed, and various forms of authoritarian government emerged. The defeat of democracy and the surge of authoritarianism was best exemplified by the triumph of Fascist movements in Italy and Germany.

The emergence of Fascist movements in more than twenty European lands after World War I was a sign that liberal society was in a state of disorientation and dissolution. The cultural pessimism, disdain for reason, elitism, romantic glorification of action and heroism, and contempt for liberal values voiced by many intellectuals and nationalists before the war found expression after the war in the antidemocratic and irrational Fascist ideologies which altered European political life. Fascism marked the culmination of the dangerous trends inherent in the extreme nationalism and radical conservatism of the late nineteenth century and in the repudiation of modern Western civilization by disenchanted intellectuals.

As a Europe-wide phenomenon, Fascism was a response to a postwar society afflicted with spiritual disintegration, economic dislocation, political instability, and thwarted nationalist hopes. A general breakdown of meaning and values led people to search for new beliefs and new political arrangements. Fascism was an expression of fear that the Bolshevik Revolution would spread westward. It was also an expression of hostility to democratic values and a reaction to the failure of liberal institutions to solve the problems of modern industrial society; with brutal frankness, Fascist leaders proclaimed that individual freedom, a relic of a dying liberal age and a barrier to national greatness, would be dispensed with. Anything seemed better than the ineffectual parliaments that appeared helpless in the face of mounting misery. Moreover, in many European lands, democracy had shallow roots. Having little familiarity with or appreciation of the procedures and values of constitutional government, people were susceptible to antidemocratic ideologies and demagogues.

Fascist movements were marked by a determination to eradicate liberalism and Marxism—to undo the legacy of the French Revolution of 1789 and the Bolshevik Revolution of 1917. Fascists believed that theirs was a spiritual revolution, that they were initiating a new era in history and building a new civilization on the ruins of liberal democracy. "We stand for a new principle in the world," said Mussolini. "We stand for the sheer, categorical, definitive antithesis to the world of democracy . . . to the world which still abides by the fundamental principles laid down in 1789."[9] The chief principle of Nazism, said Hitler, "is to abolish the liberal concept of the individual and the Marxist concept of humanity, and to substitute for them the Volk community, rooted in the soil and united by the bond of its common blood."[10] The Fascists' uniforms, songs, flags, parades, mass rallies, and cult of physical strength and violence all symbolized this call for a reawakened and reunited people.

Fascists accused liberal society of despiritualizing human beings and transforming them into materialistic creatures whose highest ideal was moneymaking. Regarding liberalism as bankrupt and parliamentary government as futile, many people yearned for an authoritarian government led by military men and nationalists. To Fascists and their sympathizers, democracy seemed an ineffective and enfeebled old order ready to be overthrown. Idealistic youth and intellectuals rejoiced in Fascist activism. They saw Fascism as a revolt against the mediocrity of the liberal state and modern mass society and a reaffirmation of the noblest human qualities: heroism and dedication to one's people. Fascists saw themselves as participants in a dynamic mass movement that would rectify the weaknesses and irresolution of parliamentary government and rid the nation of corrosive foreign influences. For them, the triumph of Fascism would mark a new beginning for their nation and a new era in world history.

The Fascist vision of a regenerated nation—a new order led by a determined and heroic elite—arising from the ruins of a decadent old order had the appeal of great myth; it evoked belief, commitment, and loyalty. The myth of rebirth—a nation cured of evil and building a new and vigorous society—had a profound impact on people dissatisfied with liberal society and searching for new beliefs. The myth of the nation reborn answered a metaphysical yearning to give meaning to life and history. It provided an emotionally gratifying worldview at a time when many people had lost their confidence in liberal-democratic ideals and institutions.

Fascists regarded Marxism as another enemy, for class conflict divided and weakened the state. To Fascists, the Marxist call for workers of the world to unite meant the death of the national community. Fascism, in contrast, would reintegrate the proletariat into the nation and end class hostilities by making people at all levels feel that they were a needed part of the nation. Fascism thus offered a solution to the problem of insecurity and isolation in modern industrial society.

Attacking the rational tradition of the Enlightenment, Fascism exalted will, blood, feeling, and instinct. Intellectual discussion and critical analysis, said Fascists, cause national divisiveness; reason promotes doubt, enfeebles the will, and hinders instinctive, aggressive action. Fascism made a continual appeal to the emotions as a means of integrating the national community. This flow of emotion fueled irrational and dangerous desires, beliefs, and expectations that blocked critical judgment and responsible action. Glorifying action for its own sake, Fascists aroused and manipulated brutal and primitive impulses and carried into politics the combative spirit of the trenches. They formed private armies, which attracted veterans—many of them rootless, brutal, and maladjusted men who sought to preserve the loyalty, camaraderie, and violence of the front.

Fascists exalted the leader—who, according to the Fascist view, intuitively grasped what was best for the nation—and called for rule by an elite of dedicated party members. The leader and the party would relieve the individual of the need to make decisions. Convinced that the liberal stress on individual freedom promoted national divisiveness, Fascists pressed for monolithic unity: one leader, one party, one ideology, and one national will.

Fascism drew its mass support from the lower middle class: small merchants, artisans, white-collar workers, civil servants, and peasants of moderate means, all of whom were frightened both by big capitalism and by Marxism. They hoped that Fascism would protect them from the competition of big business and prevent the hated working class from establishing a Marxist state, which would threaten their property. The lower middle class saw in Fascism a non-Communist way of overcoming economic crises and restoring traditional respect for family, native soil, and nation. Furthermore, many of these people saw Fascism as a way of attacking the existing social order, which denied them opportunities for economic advancement and social prestige.

Although a radicalized middle class gave Fascist movements their mass support, the Fascists could not have captured the state without the aid of existing ruling elites: landed aristocrats, industrialists, and army leaders. In Russia, the Bolsheviks had to fight their way to power; in Italy and Germany, the old ruling order virtually handed power to the Fascists. In both countries, Fascist leaders succeeded in reassuring the conservative elite that they would not institute widespread social reforms or interfere with private property and would protect the nation from Communism. Even though the old elite abhorred Fascist violence and demagoguery, it entered into an alliance with the Fascists to protect its interests.

In their struggle to bring down the liberal state, Fascist leaders aroused primitive impulses and tribal loyalties; they made use of myths and rituals to mobilize and manipulate the masses. Organizing their propaganda campaigns with the rigor of a military operation, Fascists stirred and dominated the masses and confused and undermined their democratic opposition, breaking its will to resist. Fascists were most successful in countries with weak democratic traditions. When parliamentary government faltered, it had few staunch defenders, and many people were drawn to charismatic demagogues who promised direct action.

The proliferation of Fascist movements demonstrated that the habits of democracy are not quickly learned, easily retained, or even desired. Particularly during times of crisis, people lose patience with parliamentary discussion and constitutional procedures, sink into nonrational modes of thought and behavior, and are easily manipulated by unscrupulous politicians. For the sake of economic or emotional security and national grandeur, they will often willingly sacrifice political freedom. Fascism starkly manifested the immense power of the irrational; it humbled liberals, making them permanently aware of the limitations of reason and the fragility of freedom.

The Fascist goal of maximum centralization of power was furthered by developments during World War I: the expansion of bureaucracy, the concentration of industry into giant monopolies, and the close cooperation between industry and the state. The instruments of modern technology—radio, motion pictures, public address systems, telephone, and teletype—made it possible for the state to indoctrinate, manipulate, and dominate its subjects.

The Rise of Fascism in Italy

Postwar Unrest

Although Italy had been on the winning side in World War I, the country resembled a defeated nation. Food shortages, rising prices, massive unemployment, violent strikes, workers occupying factories, and peasants squatting on the uncultivated periphery of large estates created a climate of crisis. Italy required effective leadership and a reform program, but party disputes paralyzed the liberal government. With several competing parties, the liberals could not organize a solid majority that could cope with the domestic crisis.

The middle class was severely stressed. To meet its accelerating expenses, the government had increased taxes, but the burden fell unevenly on small landowners, owners of small businesses, civil service workers, and professionals. Large landowners and industrialists feared that their nation was on the verge of a Bolshevik-style revolution. In truth, Italian socialists had no master plan to seize power. Peasant squatters and urban strikers were responding to the distress in their own regions and did not significantly coordinate their efforts with those in other localities. Besides, when workers realized that they could not keep the factories operating, their revolutionary zeal waned and they started to abandon the plants. The workers' and peasants' poorly led and futile struggles did not portend a Red revolution. Nevertheless, the industrialists and landlords, with the Bolshevik Revolution still vivid in their minds, were taking no chances.

Adding to the unrest was national outrage at the terms of the World War I peace settlement. Italians felt that despite their sacrifices—five hundred thousand dead and one million wounded—they had been robbed of the fruits of victory. Italy had been denied the Dalmatian coast, the Adriatic port of Fiume, and territory in Africa and the Middle East. Nationalists blamed the liberal government for what they called a "mutilated victory." In 1919, a force of war veterans, led by the poet and adventurer Gabriele D'Annunzio (1863–1938), seized Fiume, to the delirious joy of Italian nationalists and the embarrassment of the government. D'Annunzio's occupation of the port lasted more than a year, adding fuel to the flames of Italian nationalism and demonstrating the weakness of the liberal regime in imposing its authority on rightist opponents.

Mussolini's Seizure of Power

Benito Mussolini (1883–1945), a former socialist and World War I veteran, exploited the unrest in postwar Italy in order to capture control of the state. In 1919, he organized the Fascist Party, which attracted converts from among the discontented, the disillusioned, and the uprooted. Many Italians viewed Mussolini as the leader who would gain Fiume, Dalmatia, and colonies and win for Italy its rightful place of honor in international affairs. Hardened battle veterans joined the Fascist movement to escape the boredom and idleness of civilian life. They welcomed the opportunity to wear the uniforms of the Fascist militia (called the Black Shirts), parade in the streets, and fight socialist and labor union opponents. Squads of the Black Shirts *(squadristi)* raided socialist and trade union offices, destroying property and beating the occupants. As socialist Red Shirts responded in kind, Italy soon appeared to be drifting toward civil war.

MUSSOLINI WITH HIS TROOPS. The Italian dictator deliberately tried to sustain an image of a virile warrior. Although Mussolini established a one-party state, he was less successful than Hitler or Stalin in creating a totalitarian regime.

Hoping that Mussolini would rescue Italy from Bolshevism, industrialists and landowners contributed large sums to the Fascist Party. The lower middle class, fearful that the growing power of labor unions and the Socialist Party threatened their property and social prestige, viewed Mussolini as a protector. Middle-class university students, searching for adventure and an ideal, and army officers, dreaming of an Italian empire and hostile to parliamentary government, were also attracted to Mussolini's party. Mussolini's philosophy of action intrigued intellectuals disenchanted with liberal politics and parliamentary democracy. His nationalism, activism, and anti-Communism gradually seduced elements of the power structure: capitalists, aristocrats, army officers, the royal family, and the church. Regarding liberalism as bankrupt and parliamentary government as futile, many of these people yearned for a military dictatorship.

In 1922, Mussolini made his bid for power. Speaking at a giant rally of his followers in late October, he declared: "Either they will give us the government or we shall take it by descending on Rome. It is now a matter of days, perhaps hours." A few days later, the Fascists began their march on Rome. It would have been a relatively simple matter to crush the twenty thousand Fascist marchers, who were armed with little more than pistols and rifles, but King Victor Emmanuel III (1869–1947) refused to act. The king's advisers, some of them sympathetic to Mussolini, exaggerated the strength of the Fascists. Believing that he was rescuing Italy from terrible violence, the king appointed Mussolini prime minister.

Mussolini had bluffed his way to power. Fascism had triumphed not because of its own strength—the Fascist Party had only 35 of 535 seats in parliament—but because the liberal government, indecisive and fearful of violence, did not counter force with force. In the past, the liberal state had not challenged Fascist acts of terror; now it feebly surrendered to Fascist blustering and threats. No doubt liberals hoped that, once in power, the Fascists would forsake terror, pursue moderate aims, and act within the constitution. But the liberals were wrong; they had completely misjudged Fascism's antidemocratic character.

The Fascist State in Italy

Gradually, Mussolini moved toward establishing a dictatorship. In 1925 and 1926 he eliminated non-Fascists from his cabinet, dissolved opposition parties, smashed the independent trade unions, suppressed opposition newspapers, replaced local mayors with Fascist officials, and organized a secret police to round up troublemakers. Many anti-Fascists fled the country or were deported.

Mussolini was less successful than Hitler and Stalin in fashioning a totalitarian state. The industrialists, the large landowners, the church, and to some extent even the army never fell under the complete domination of the party. Nor did the regime possess the mind of its subjects with the same thoroughness as the Nazis did in Germany. Life in Italy was less regimented and the individual less fearful than in Nazi Germany or Communist Russia.

Like Communist Russia and Nazi Germany, however, Fascist Italy used mass organizations and mass media to control minds and regulate behavior. As in the Soviet Union and the Third Reich, the regime created a cult of the leader. "Mussolini goes forward with confidence, in a halo of myth, almost chosen by God, indefatigable and infallible, the instrument employed by Providence for the creation of a new civilization," wrote the philosopher Giovanni Gentile.[11] To convey the image of a virile leader, Mussolini had himself photographed bare-chested or in a uniform and a steel helmet. Elementary school textbooks depicted him as the savior of the nation, a modern-day Julius Caesar.

Fascist propaganda urged that the grandeur of the Roman Empire be restored through conquest. It also inculcated habits of discipline and obedience: "Mussolini is always right." "Believe! Obey! Fight!" Propaganda also glorified war: "A minute on the battlefield is worth a lifetime of peace." The press, radio, and cinema idealized life under Fascism, implying that Fascism had eradicated crime, poverty, and social tensions. Schoolteachers and university professors were compelled to swear allegiance to the Fascist government and to propagate Fascist ideals, while students were urged to criticize instructors who harbored liberal attitudes. Millions of youths belonged to Fascist organizations, in which they participated in patriotic ceremonies and social functions, sang Fascist hymns, and wore Fascist uniforms. They submerged their own identities in the group.

Denouncing economic liberalism for promoting individual self-interest, Fascists also attacked socialism for instigating conflicts between workers and capitalists, which divided and weakened the nation. The Fascist way of resolving tensions between workers and employers was to abolish independent labor unions, prohibit strikes, and establish associations or corporations that included both workers and employers within a given industry. In theory, representatives of labor and capital would cooperatively solve their particular industry's labor problems; in practice, however, the representatives of labor turned out to be Fascists who protected the interests of the industrialists. Although the Fascists lauded the cooperative system as a creative approach to modern economic problems, in reality it played a minor role in Italian economic life. Big business continued to make its own decisions, paying scant attention to the corporations.

Nor did the Fascist government solve Italy's longstanding economic problems. To curtail the export of capital and to reduce the nation's dependence on imports in case of war, Mussolini sought to make Italy self-sufficient. To win the "battle of grain," the Fascist regime brought marginal lands under cultivation and urged farmers to concentrate on wheat rather than other crops. While wheat production increased substantially, total agricultural output fell because wheat had been planted on land more suited to animal husbandry and fruit cultivation. To make Italy industrially self-sufficient, the regime limited imports of foreign goods, with the result that Italian consumers paid higher prices for goods manufactured in Italy. Mussolini posed as the protector of the little people, but under his regime the power and profits of big business grew and the standard of living of small farmers and urban workers slipped.

Although anticlerical since his youth, Mussolini was also expedient. He recognized that coming to terms with the church would improve his image with Catholic public opinion. The Vatican regarded Mussolini's regime as a barrier against atheistic Communism and as less hostile to church interests and more amenable to church direction than a liberal government. Pope Pius XI (1922–1939) was an ultraconservative whose hatred of liberalism and secularism led him to believe that the Fascists would increase the influence of the church in the nation.

In 1929, the Lateran Accords recognized the independence of Vatican City, repealed many of the anticlerical laws passed under the liberal government, and made religious instruction compulsory in all secondary schools. Relations between the Vatican and the Fascist government remained fairly good throughout the decade of the 1930s. When Mussolini invaded Ethiopia and intervened in the Spanish Civil War, the church supported him. Although the papacy criticized Mussolini for drawing closer to Hitler and introducing anti-Jewish legislation, it never broke with the Fascist regime.

The New German Republic

In the last days of World War I, a revolution brought down the German government, a semi-authoritarian monarchy, and led to the creation of a democratic republic. The new government,

THE SPELLBINDER. Hitler was a superb orator who knew how to reach the hearts of his listeners. The masses, he said, are aroused by the spoken, not the written, word.

headed by Chancellor Friedrich Ebert (1871–1925), a Social Democrat, signed the armistice agreement ending the war. Many Germans blamed the creators of the new democratic leadership for the defeat—a baseless accusation, for the German generals, knowing that the war was lost, had sought an armistice. In February 1919, the recently elected National Assembly met at Weimar and proceeded to draw up a constitution for the new state. The Weimar Republic—born in revolution, which most Germans detested, and military defeat, which many attributed to the new government—faced an uncertain future. The legend that traitors, principally Jews and Social Democrats, cheated Germany of victory was created and propagated by the conservative right—generals, high-ranking bureaucrats, university professors, and nationalists, who wanted to preserve the army's reputation and bring down the new and hated democratic Weimar Republic.

Threats from Left and Right

Dominated by moderate socialists, the infant republic faced internal threats from both the radical left and the radical right. In January 1919, the newly established German Communist party, or Spartacists, disregarding the advice of their leaders Rosa Luxemburg and Karl Liebknecht, took to the streets of Berlin and declared Ebert's government deposed. To crush the revolution, Ebert turned to the Free Corps: volunteer brigades of ex-soldiers and adventurers led by officers loyal to the emperor, who had been fighting to protect the eastern borders from encroachments by the new states of Poland, Estonia, and Latvia. The men of the Free Corps relished action and despised Bolshevism and many of them would later become prominent in Hitler's party. They suppressed the revolution and murdered Luxemburg and Liebknecht on January 15.

The Spartacist revolt and the short-lived "soviet" republic in Munich (and others in Baden and Brunswick) had a profound effect on the German psyche. The Communists had been easily subdued, but fear of a Communist insurrection remained deeply embedded in the middle and upper classes—a fear that drove many of their members into the ranks of the Weimar Republic's right-wing opponents.

Refusing to disband as the government ordered, in March 1920 the right-wing Free Corps marched into Berlin and declared a new government, headed by Wolfgang Kapp, a staunch German nationalist. Insisting that it could not fire on fellow soldiers, the German army, the *Reichswehr*, made no move to defend the republic. A general strike called by the labor unions prevented Kapp from governing, and the coup collapsed. However, the Kapp Putsch demonstrated that the loyalty of the army to the republic was doubtful and that important segments of German society supported the overthrow, by violence if necessary, of the Weimar Republic and its replacement by an authoritarian government driven by a nationalist credo.

Economic Crisis

In addition to uprisings by the left and right, the republic was burdened by economic crisis. Unable to meet the deficit in the national budget, the government simply printed more money, causing the value of the German mark to decline precipitously. In 1919, the mark stood at 8.9 to the dollar; in November 1923, a dollar could be exchanged for 4 billion marks. Bank savings, war bonds, and pensions, representing years of toil and thrift, became worthless. Blaming the government for this disaster, the ruined middle class became more receptive to ultrarightist movements that aimed to bring down the republic.

A critical factor in the collapse of the German economy was the French occupation of the Ruhr in January 1923. With the economy in shambles, the republic had defaulted on reparation payments. The French premier, Raymond Poincaré (1860–1934), ordered French troops into the Ruhr—the nerve center of German industry. Responding to the republic's call for passive resistance, factory workers, miners, and railway workers in the Ruhr refused to work for the French. Paying salaries to striking workers and officials contributed to the mark's free fall.

Gustav Stresemann, who became chancellor in August 1923, skillfully placed the republic on the path to recovery. He declared Germany's willingness to make reparation payments and issued a new currency, backed by a mortgage on German real estate. To protect the value of the new currency, the government did not print another issue. Inflation receded, and confidence was restored.

A new arrangement regarding reparations also contributed to the economic recovery. In 1924, the parties accepted the Dawes Plan, which reduced reparations and based them on Germany's economic capacity. During the negotiations, France agreed to withdraw its troops from the Ruhr—another step toward easing tensions for the republic.

From 1924 to 1929, economic conditions improved. Foreign capitalists, particularly Americans, were attracted by high interest rates and the low cost of labor. Their investments in German businesses stimulated the economy. By 1929, iron, steel, coal, and chemical production exceeded prewar levels. The value of German exports also surpassed that of 1913. Real wages were higher than before the war, and improved unemployment benefits also made life better for the workers. It appeared that Germany had achieved political stability, as threats from the extremist parties of the left and the right subsided. Given time and continued economic stability, democracy might have taken firmer root in Germany. But then came the Great Depression. The global economic crisis that began in October 1929 starkly revealed how weak the Weimar Republic was.

Fundamental Weaknesses of the Weimar Republic

German political experience provided poor soil for transplanting an English democratic parliamentary system. Before World War I, Germany had been a semiautocratic state, ruled by an emperor who commanded the armed forces, controlled foreign policy, appointed the chancellor, and called and dismissed parliament. This authoritarian system blocked the German people from acquiring democratic habits and attitudes; still accustomed to rule from above, still adoring the power-state, many Germans sought to destroy the democratic Weimar Republic.

Traditional conservatives—the upper echelons of the civil service, judges, industrialists, large landowners, and army leaders—scorned democracy and hated the republic. They regarded the revolution against the monarchy in the last weeks of the war as a treacherous act and the establishment of a democratic republic as a violation of Germany's revered tradition of hierarchical leadership. Nor did the middle class feel a commitment to the liberal-democratic principles on which the republic rested. The traditionally nationalistic middle class identified the republic with the defeat in war and the humiliation of the Versailles treaty. Rabidly antisocialist, this class saw the leaders of the republic as Marxists who would impose on Germany a working-class state. Right-wing intellectuals often attacked democracy as a barrier to the true unity of the German nation. In the tradition of nineteenth-century Volkish thinkers, they disdained reason and political freedom, glorifying instead race, instincts, and action. By doing so, they turned many Germans against the republic, eroding the popular support on which democracy depends.

The Weimar Republic also showed the weaknesses of the multiparty system. With the vote spread over a number of parties, no one party held a majority of seats in the parliament (Reichstag), so the republic was governed by a coalition of several parties. But because of ideological differences, the coalition was always unstable and in danger of failing to function. This is precisely what happened during the Great Depression. When effective leadership was imperative, the government could not act. Political deadlock caused Germans to lose what little confidence they had in the democratic system. Support for the parties that wanted to preserve democracy dwindled, and extremist parties that aimed to topple the republic gained strength. Seeking to bring down the republic were the Communists on the left and two rightist parties—the Nationalists and the National Socialist German Workers' Party, led by Adolf Hitler.

The Rise of Hitler

Adolf Hitler (1889–1945) was born in Austria on April 20, 1889, the fourth child of a minor civil servant. A poor student in secondary school, although by no means unintelligent, Hitler left high school and lived idly for more than two years. In 1907 and again in 1908, the Vienna Academy of Fine Arts rejected his application for admission. Hitler did not try to learn a trade or to work steadily but earned some money by painting picture postcards. He read a lot, especially in art, history, and military affairs. He also read the racist, nationalist, anti-Semitic, and Pan-German literature that abounded in multinational Vienna. The racist treatises preached the danger posed by mixing races, called for the liquidation of racial inferiors, and marked the Jew as the embodiment of evil and the source of all misfortune.

In Vienna, Hitler came into contact with Georg von Schönerer's Pan-German movement. For Schönerer, the Jews were evil not because of their religion or because they rejected Christ but because they possessed evil racial qualities. Schönerer's followers wore watch chains with pictures of hanged Jews attached. Hitler was particularly impressed with Karl Lueger, the mayor of Vienna, a clever demagogue who skillfully manipulated the anti-Semitic feelings of the Catholic Viennese for his own political advantage. In Vienna, Hitler also acquired a hatred for Marxism and democracy and grew convinced that the struggle for existence and the survival of the fittest were the essential facts of the social world.

When World War I began, Hitler was in Munich. He welcomed the war as a relief from his daily life, which lacked purpose and excitement. "Overpowered by stormy enthusiasm," he later declared, "I fell down on my knees and thanked Heaven from an overflowing heart for granting me the good fortune of being permitted to live at this time."[12] Volunteering for the German army, Hitler found battle exhilarating and twice received the Iron Cross for serving as a runner. The experience of battle taught Hitler to prize discipline, regimentation, leadership, authority, struggle, and ruthlessness—values that he carried with him into the politics of the postwar world.

The shock of Germany's defeat and revolution intensified Hitler's commitment to racial nationalism. To lead Germany to total victory over its racial enemies became his obsession. Germany's defeat and shame, he said, were due to the creators of the republic, the "November criminals," and behind them was a Jewish-Bolshevik world conspiracy.

The Nazi Party

In 1919, Hitler joined a small right-wing extremist group. Displaying fantastic energy and extraordinary ability as a demagogic orator, propagandist, and organizer, Hitler quickly became the leader of the party, whose name was changed to National Socialist German Workers' Party (commonly called the Nazi Party). As leader, Hitler insisted on absolute authority and total allegiance—a demand that coincided with the postwar longing for a strong leader who would set right a shattered nation.

Like Mussolini, Hitler incorporated military attitudes and techniques into politics. Uniforms, salutes, emblems, flags, and other symbols imbued party members with a sense of solidarity and camaraderie. At mass meetings, Hitler was a spellbinder who gave stunning performances. His pounding fists, throbbing body, wild gesticulations, hypnotic eyes, rage-swollen face, and repeated, frenzied denunciations of the Versailles treaty, Marxism, the republic, and Jews inflamed and mesmerized the audience. Hitler instinctively grasped the innermost feelings of his audience, their resentments and longings. "The intense will of the man, the passion of his sincerity seemed to flow from him into me. I experienced an exaltation that could be likened only to religious conversion," said one early admirer.[13]

In November 1923, Hitler tried to seize power in Munich, in the state of Bavaria, as a prelude to toppling the republic. The attempt, which came to be known as the Beer Hall Putsch, failed miserably. Ironically, however, Hitler's prestige increased, for when he was put on trial he used it as an opportunity to denounce the republic and the Versailles treaty and to proclaim his philosophy of racial nationalism. His impassioned speeches, publicized by the press and received favorably by a judge sympathetic to right-wing nationalism, earned Hitler a nationwide reputation and a light sentence: five years' imprisonment with the promise of quick parole. While in prison, Hitler dictated *Mein Kampf,* a rambling and turgid work that contained the essence of his worldview. The unsuccessful Munich Putsch taught Hitler a valuable lesson: armed insurrection against superior might fails. He would gain power not by force but by exploiting the instruments of democracy—elections and party politics. He would use apparently legal means to destroy the Weimar Republic and impose a dictatorship.

Hitler's Worldview

Racial Nationalism Hitler's thought comprised a patchwork of nineteenth-century anti-Semitic, Volkish, Social Darwinist, antidemocratic, and anti-Marxist ideas. From these ideas, many of which enjoyed wide popularity, Hitler constructed a worldview rooted in racial myths and fantasies. Nazism rejected both the Judeo-Christian and the Enlightenment traditions and sought to found a new world order based on racial nationalism. For Hitler, race was the key to understanding world history. He believed that a reawakened, racially united Germany led by men of iron will would carve out a vast European empire and would deal a decadent liberal civilization its deathblow. It would conquer Russia, eradicate Communism, and reduce to serfdom the subhuman Slavs, "a mass of born slaves who feel the need of a master."[14]

In the tradition of crude Volkish nationalists and Social Darwinists, Hitler divided the world into superior and inferior races and pitted them against each other in a struggle for survival. For him, this fight for life was a law of nature and of history.

The Jew as Devil An obsessive and virulent hatred of Jews dominated Hitler's mental outlook. In waging war against the Jews, Hitler believed that he was defending Germany from its worst enemy, a sinister force that stood in total opposition to the new world he envisioned. In his mythical interpretation of the world, the Aryan was the originator and carrier of civilization. As descendants of the Aryans, the German race embodied creativity, bravery, and loyalty. As the opposite of the Aryan, the Jews, who belonged to a separate biological race, personified the vilest qualities. "Two worlds face one another," said Hitler, "the men of God and the men of Satan! The Jew is the anti-man, the creature of another god. He must have come from another root of the human race. I set the Aryan and the Jew over and against each other."[15] Everything Hitler despised—liberalism, intellectualism, pacifism, parliamentarianism, internationalism, Marxism, modern art, and individualism—he attributed to Jews.

Hitler's anti-Semitism served a functional purpose as well. By concentrating all evil in one enemy, "the conspirator and demonic" Jew, Hitler provided true believers with a simple, all-embracing, and emotionally satisfying explanation for their misery. By defining themselves as the racial and spiritual opposites of Jews, Germans of all classes felt joined together in a Volkish union.

The surrender to myth served to disorient the German intellect and to unify the nation. When the mind accepts an image such as Hitler's image of Jews as vermin, germs, and satanic conspirators, it has lost all sense of balance and objectivity. Such a disoriented mind is ready to believe and to obey, to be manipulated and led, to brutalize and to tolerate brutality. It is ready to be absorbed into the will of the collective community. That many people, including intellectuals and members of the elite, accepted these racial ideas shows the enduring power of mythical thinking and the vulnerability of reason. In 1933, the year Hitler took power, Felix Goldmann, a German-Jewish writer, commented astutely on the irrational character of Nazi anti-Semitism: "The present-day politicized racial anti-Semitism is the embodiment of myth, . . . nothing is discussed . . . only felt, . . . nothing is pondered critically, logically or reasonably, . . . only inwardly perceived, surmised. . . . We are apparently the last [heirs] of the Enlightenment."[16]

The Importance of Propaganda Hitler understood that in an age of political parties, universal suffrage, and a popular press—the legacies of the French and Industrial Revolutions—the successful leader must win the support of the masses. This could be achieved best with propaganda. To be effective, said Hitler, propaganda must be aimed principally at the emotions. The masses are not moved by scientific ideas or by objective and abstract knowledge but by primitive feelings, terror, force, and discipline. Propaganda must reduce everything to simple slogans incessantly repeated and must concentrate on one enemy. The masses are aroused by the spoken, not the written, word—by a storm of hot passion erupting from the speaker "which like hammer blows can open the gates to the heart of the people."[17]

The most effective means of stirring the masses and strengthening them for the struggle ahead, Hitler had written in *Mein Kampf,* is the mass meeting. Surrounded by tens of thousands of people, individuals lose their sense of individuality and no longer see themselves as isolated. They become members of a community bound together by an esprit de corps reminiscent of the trenches during the Great War. Bombarded by the cheers of thousands of voices, by marching units, by banners, by explosive oratory, individuals become convinced of the truth of the party's message and the irresistibility of the movement. Their intellects overwhelmed, their resistance lowered, they lose their previous beliefs and are carried along on a wave of enthusiasm. Their despair over the condition of their nation turns to hope, and they derive a sense of belonging and mission. They feel that they are participants in a mighty movement that is destined to regenerate the German nation and initiate a new historical age. "The man who enters such a meeting doubting and wavering leaves it inwardly reinforced; he has become a link to the community."[18]

Hitler Gains Power

After serving only nine months of his sentence, Hitler left prison in December 1924. He continued to build his party and waited for a crisis that would rock the republic and make his movement a force in national politics. The Great Depression, which began in the United States at the end of 1929, provided that crisis. Desperate and demoralized people lined up in front of government unemployment offices. Street peddlers, beggars, and youth gangs proliferated; suicides increased, particularly among middle-class people shamed by their descent into poverty, idleness, and uselessness. As Germany's economic plight worsened, the German people became more amenable to Hitler's radicalism. His propaganda techniques worked. The Nazi Party went from 810,000 votes in 1928 to 6,400,000 in 1930, and its representation in the Reichstag soared from 12 to 107.

To the lower middle class, the Nazis promised effective leadership and a solution to the economic crisis. But Nazism was more than a class movement. It appealed to the discontented and disillusioned from all segments of the population: embittered veterans, romantic nationalists, idealistic intellectuals, industrialists and large landowners frightened by Communism and social democracy, rootless and resentful people who felt they had no place in the existing society, the unemployed, lovers of violence, and newly enfranchised youth yearning for a cause. And always there was the immense attraction of Hitler, who tirelessly worked his oratorical magic on increasingly enthusiastic crowds, confidently promising leadership and national rebirth. Many Germans were won over by his fanatical sincerity, his iron will, and his conviction that he was chosen by fate to rescue Germany.

In the election of July 31, 1932, the Nazis received 37.3 percent of the vote and won 230 seats—far more than any other party, but still not a majority. Franz von Papen, who had resigned from the chancellorship, persuaded the aging president, Paul von Hindenburg (1847–1934), to appoint Hitler as chancellor. In this decision, Papen had the support of German industrialists and aristocratic landowners, who regarded Hitler as a useful instrument to fight Communism, block social reform, break the backs of organized labor, and rebuild the armament industry.

Never intending to rule within the spirit of the constitution, Hitler, who took office on January 30, 1933, quickly moved to assume dictatorial powers. In February 1933, a Dutch drifter with Communist leanings set a fire in the Reichstag. Hitler persuaded Hindenburg to sign an emergency decree suspending civil rights on the pretext that the state was threatened by internal subversion. The chancellor then used these emergency powers to arrest, without due process, Communist and Social Democratic deputies.

In the elections of March 1933, the German people elected 288 Nazi deputies in a Reichstag of 647 seats. With the support of 52 deputies of the Nationalist Party and in the absence of Communist deputies, who were under arrest, the Nazis now had a secure majority. Later that month, Hitler bullied the Reichstag into passing the Enabling Act, which permitted the chancellor to enact legislation independently of the Reichstag. With astonishing passivity, the political parties had allowed the Nazis to dismantle the government and make Hitler a dictator with unlimited power. Hitler had used the instruments of democracy to destroy the republic and create a totalitarian state.

Nazi Germany

The Nazis moved to subjugate all political and economic institutions and all culture to the will of the party. The party became the state and its teachings the soul of the German nation. There could be no separation between private life and politics and no rights of the individual that the state must respect. Ideology must pervade every phase of daily life, and all organizations must come under party control. For both Communists and Nazis, ideology was "a grand transcendent fiction [or] metamyth" that provided adherents with answers to the crucial questions of life and history.[19] Joseph Goebbels (see the upcoming section "Shaping the 'New Man'") summed up this totalitarian goal as follows: "It is not enough to reconcile people more or less to our regime, to move them towards a position of neutrality towards us, we want rather to work on people until they are addicted to us."[20] An anonymous Nazi poet expressed the totalitarian credo in these words:

> *We have captured all the positions*
> *And on the heights we have planted*
> *The banners of our revolution.*
> *You had imagined that that was all that we wanted*
> *We want more*
> *We want all*
> *Your hearts are our goal*
> *It is your souls we want.*[21]

The Leader-State

The Third Reich was organized as a leader-state, in which Hitler, the *führer* (leader), embodied and expressed the real will of the German people, commanded the supreme loyalty of the nation, and held omnipotent power. As a Nazi political theorist stated, "The authority of the Fuehrer is total and all embracing . . . it is subject to no checks or controls; it is circumscribed by no . . . individual rights; it is . . . overriding and unfettered."[22]

In June 1933, the Social Democratic Party was outlawed, and within a few weeks the other political parties simply disbanded on their own. In May 1933, the Nazis had seized the property of the trade unions, arrested the leaders, and ended collective bargaining and strikes. The newly established German Labor Front, an instrument of the party, became the official organization of the working class.

Unlike the Bolsheviks, the Nazis did not destroy the upper classes of the old regime. Hitler made no war against the industrialists. He wanted from them loyalty, obedience, and a war machine. German businessmen prospered but exercised no influence on political decisions. The profits of industry rose, and workers lauded the regime for ending the unemployment crisis through an extensive program of public works, the restoration of conscription, and rearmament.

Nazism conflicted with the core values of Christianity. "The heaviest blow that ever struck humanity was the coming of Christianity," said Hitler to intimates during World War II.[23] Because Nazism could tolerate no other faith alongside itself, the Nazis, recognizing that Christianity was a

Primary Source

Ernst Huber: "The Authority of the Führer Is . . . All-Inclusive and Unlimited"

In Verfassüngsrecht des grossdeutschen Reiches *(Constitutional Law of the Greater German Reich), legal scholar Ernst Rudolf Huber (1903–1990) offered a classic explication of the basic principles of National Socialism. The following excerpts from that work describe the nature of Hitler's political authority.*

The Führer-Reich of the [German] people is founded on the recognition that the true will of the people cannot be disclosed through parliamentary votes and plebiscites but that the will of the people in its pure and uncorrupted form can only be expressed through the Führer. Thus a distinction must be drawn between the supposed will of the people in a parliamentary democracy, which merely reflects the conflict of the various social interests, and the true will of the people in the Führer-state, in which the collective will of the real political unit is manifested. . . .

It would be impossible for a law to be introduced and acted upon in the Reichstag which had not originated with the Führer or, at least, received his approval. The procedure is similar to that of the plebiscite: The lawgiving power does not rest in the Reichstag; it merely proclaims through its decision its agreement with the will of the Führer, who is the lawgiver of the German people.

The Führer unites in himself all the sovereign authority of the Reich; all public authority in the state as well as in the movement is derived from the authority of the Führer. We must speak not of the state's authority but of the Führer's authority if we wish to designate the character of the political authority within the Reich correctly. The state does not hold political authority as an impersonal unit but receives it from the Führer as the executor of the national will. The authority of the Führer is complete and all-embracing; it unites in itself all the means of political direction; it extends into all fields of national life; it embraces the entire people, which is bound to the Führer in loyalty and obedience. The authority of the Führer is not limited by checks and controls, by special autonomous bodies or individual rights, but it is free and independent, all-inclusive and unlimited. It is not, however, self-seeking or arbitrary and its ties are within itself. It is derived from the people; that is, it is entrusted to the Führer by the people. It exists for the people and has its justification in the people; it is free of all outward ties because it is in its innermost nature firmly bound up with the fate, the welfare, the mission, and the honor of the people.

The following passage is from another Nazi theorist.

The people cannot as a rule announce its will by means of majority vote but only through its embodiment in one man, or in a few men. The principle of the *identity* of the ruler and those who are ruled, of the government and those who are governed has been very forcibly represented as the principle of democracy. But this identity. . . . becomes mechanistic and superficial if one seeks to establish it in the theory that the people are at once the governors and the governed. . . . A true organic identity is only possible when the great mass of the people recognizes its embodiment in one man and feels itself to be one nature with him.

Question for Analysis

1. Point out several ways that Ernst Huber's views represent a rejection of Western liberalism.

Readings on Fascism and National Socialism, selected by members of the Department of Philosophy at the University of Colorado (Denver: Alan Swallow, n.d.), 74, 76–77.

rival claimant for the German soul, moved to repress the Protestant and Catholic churches. In the public schools, religious instruction was cut back and the syllabus was changed to omit the Jewish origins of Christianity. Christ was depicted not as a Jew, heir to the prophetic tradition of Hebrew monotheism, but as an Aryan hero. The Gestapo (secret state police) censored church newspapers, scrutinized sermons and church activities, forbade some clergymen to preach, dismissed the opponents of Nazism from theological schools, and arrested some clerical critics of the regime.

The clergy were well represented among the Germans who resisted Nazism; some were sent to concentration camps or were executed. But these courageous clergy were not representative of the German churches, which, as organized institutions, capitulated to and cooperated with the Nazi regime. Both the German Evangelical (Lutheran) and German Catholic churches demanded that their faithful render loyalty to Hitler; both turned a blind eye to Nazi persecution of Jews. Even before World War II and the implementation of genocide, many Evangelical churches banned baptized Jews from entering their temples and dismissed pastors with Jewish ancestry. Some clergy, reared in a traditional anti-Semitic theological environment, regarded Nazi measures as just punishment for those who had rejected Christ. During the war, both Catholic and Evangelical churches condemned resistance and found much in the Third Reich to admire, and both supported Hitler's war. The prominent Lutheran theologian who "welcomed that change that came to Germany in 1933 as a divine gift and miracle" voiced the sentiments of many members of the clergy.[24]

The Nazis instituted many anti-Jewish measures designed to make outcasts of the Jews. Thousands of Jewish doctors, lawyers, musicians, artists, and professors were barred from practicing their professions, and Jewish members of the civil service were dismissed. A series of laws tightened the screws of humiliation and persecution. Marriage or sexual encounters between Germans and Jews were forbidden. Universities, schools, restaurants, pharmacies, hospitals, theaters, museums, and athletic fields were gradually closed to Jews. The propaganda machine, including the schools and media, conditioned Germans to see the Jew as an evil, alien, and dangerous parasite. The Nazis also expropriated Jewish property, an act of thievery that benefited numerous individual Germans and business firms.

In November 1938, using as a pretext the assassination of a German official in Paris by a seventeen-year-old Jewish youth whose family the Nazis had mistreated, the Nazis organized an extensive pogrom. Nazi gangs murdered scores of Jews, destroyed 267 synagogues, and burned and vandalized 7,500 Jewish-owned businesses all over Germany—an event that became known as Night of the Broken Glass *(Kristallnacht)*. Some thirty thousand Jews were thrown into concentration camps. The Reich then imposed on the Jewish community a fine of one billion marks. These measures were a mere prelude, however. During World War II, the genocidal murder of European Jewry became a cardinal Nazi objective. As a rule, German academic and clerical elites did not protest; indeed, many agreed with the National Socialists' edicts. The Jews were simply abandoned.

Shaping the "New Man"

The Ministry of Popular Enlightenment, headed by Joseph Goebbels (1897–1945), controlled the press, book publishing, the radio, the theater, and the cinema. Nazi propaganda sought to condition the mind to revere the führer and to obey the new regime. Its intent was to deprive individuals of their capacity for independent thought. By concentrating on the myth of race and the cult of the infallible führer—the German messiah sent by destiny to redeem the fatherland—Nazi propaganda tried to disorient the rational mind and to give the individual new standards to believe in and obey. Propaganda aimed to mold the entire nation to think and respond as the leader-state directed.

The regime made a special effort to reach young people. All youths between the ages of ten and eighteen were urged and then required to join the Hitler Youth, and all other youth organizations were dissolved. At camps and rallies, young people paraded, sang, saluted, and chanted: "We were slaves; we were outsiders in our own country. So were we before Hitler united us. Now we would fight against Hell itself for our leader."[25] The schools, long breeding grounds of nationalism, militarism, antiliberalism, and anti-Semitism, now indoctrinated the young in Nazi ideology.

© Bettmann/Corbis.

ADOLF HITLER BEFORE HIS LABOR ARMY AT NUREMBERG, GERMANY, SEPTEMBER 1938.

The Nazis instructed teachers how certain subjects were to be taught, and to ensure obedience members of the Hitler Youth were asked to report teachers who did not conform.

In May 1933, professors and students proudly burned books, many of them written by Jews, considered a threat to Nazi ideology, in a display of cultural barbarism that gave prophetic meaning to the famous words of Heinrich Heine, the great nineteenth-century German-Jewish poet: "Wherever they burn books they will also, in the end, burn people." As books removed from public and private libraries were hurled into the flames, students danced.

Many academics praised Hitler and the new regime. Some 10 percent of the university faculty, principally Jews, Social Democrats, and liberals, were dismissed, and their colleagues often approved. "From now on it will not be your job to determine whether something is true but whether it is in the spirit of the National Socialist revolution," the new minister of culture told university professors.[26] Numerous courses on "racial science" and Nazi ideology were introduced into the curriculum. Many German academics, some of them noted scholars, willingly, if not enthusiastically, loaned their talents and learning to the new regime.

Symbolic of the Nazi regime were the monster rallies staged at Nuremberg. Scores of thousands roared, marched, and worshiped at their leader's feet. These true believers, the end product of Nazi indoctrination, celebrated Hitler's achievements and demonstrated their loyalty to their savior. Everything was brilliantly orchestrated to impress Germans and the world with the irresistible power,

Bildarchiv Preussischer Kulturbesitz/Art Resource, N.Y.

Nazi Culture. The Nazis considered jazz to be racially degenerate Jewish and black music.

determination, and unity of the Nazi movement and the greatness of the führer. Armies of youths waving flags, storm troopers bearing weapons, and workers shouldering long-handled spades paraded past Hitler, who stood at attention, his arm extended in the Nazi salute. The endless columns of marchers, the stirring martial music played by huge bands, the forest of flags, the chanting and cheering of spectators, and the burning torches and beaming spotlights united the participants into a racial community. "Wherever Hitler leads we follow," thundered thousands of Germans in a giant chorus.

Terror was another means of ensuring compliance and obedience. The instruments of terror were the Gestapo and the *Schutzstaffel* (SS), which was organized in 1925 to protect Hitler and other party leaders and to stand guard at party meetings. Under the leadership of Heinrich Himmler (1900–1945), a fanatical believer in Hitler's racial theories, the SS was molded into an elite force of disciplined, dedicated, and utterly ruthless men. Many Germans, seduced by Nazi propaganda, accepted terror as a legitimate weapon against subversives and racial defilers who threatened the new Germany. Informers often denounced to the security forces fellow Germans suspected of Communist leanings, having business or sexual relations with Jews, or criticizing Hitler. Recent research shows the Gestapo, relatively few in number, could not function effectively without the assistance of civilians willing to inform on their neighbors and even family members.

Mass Support

The Nazi regime became a police state characterized by mass arrests, the persecution of Jews, and concentration camps that institutionalized terror. Yet fewer heads had rolled than people expected, and in many ways life seemed normal. The Nazis skillfully established the totalitarian state without upsetting the daily life of the great majority of the population. Moreover, Hitler, like Mussolini, was careful to maintain the appearance of legality. By not abolishing parliament or repealing the constitution, he could claim that his was a legitimate government.

To people concerned with little except family, job, and friends—and this includes most people in any country—life in the first few years of the Third Reich seemed quite satisfying. Most Germans believed that the new government was trying to solve Germany's problems in a vigorous and sensible manner, in contrast to the ineffective Weimar leadership. By 1936, the invigoration of the economy, stimulated in part by rearmament, had virtually eliminated unemployment, which had stood at six million jobless when Hitler took power. An equally astounding achievement in the eyes of the German people was Hitler's bold termination of the humiliating Versailles treaty, the rebuilding of the German war machine, and the restoration of German power in international affairs. It seemed to most Germans that Hitler had awakened a sense of self-sacrifice and national dedication among

© Topham/The Image Works.

Young Nazis Burning Books in Salzburg, Austria, 1938. Heinrich Heine, the great nineteenth-century German-Jewish poet, once said that people who burn books end up burning people.

a people dispirited by defeat and economic depression.

The frenzied adoration shown by the German people for Hitler both in peacetime and in war and their faith in his mission to regenerate the German nation is an extraordinary phenomenon that continues to intrigue historians and social psychologists and to astonish new generations of Europeans, including Germans. It was considerably different for other dictators of Hitler's generation. Whatever devotion the Italians felt for Mussolini quickly faded once he brought the country into war. And the Soviet people's bonds to Stalin, particularly for non-Russian ethnic groups, were often based more on fear than genuine adulation. The German people's hero worship of Hitler and their positive view of his dictatorship were not driven by terror and for many endured for the duration of the war. Nor did ordinary Germans have to be coerced to support and serve the Nazi state. Rarely in history has a nation been so spellbound by a leader.

There was some opposition to the Hitler regime. Social Democrats and Communists in particular organized small cells. Some conservatives, who considered Hitler a threat to traditional German values, and some clergy, who saw Nazism as a pagan religion in conflict with Christian morality, also formed small opposition groups. But only the army could have toppled Hitler. Some generals, even before World War II, urged resistance, but the overwhelming majority of German officers either preferred the new regime—which had smashed Marxism within Germany, destroyed an ineffective democracy, and restored Germany's military might and pride—or considered it dishonorable to break their oath of loyalty to Hitler. Most of these officers would remain loyal until the bitter end. Very few Germans realized that their country was passing through a long night of barbarism, and still fewer considered resistance. The great majority of Germans would remain loyal to their führer and would serve the Nazi regime until its collapse.

Liberalism and Authoritarianism in Other Lands

After World War I, in country after country, parliamentary democracy collapsed and authoritarian leaders came to power. In most of these countries, liberal ideals had not penetrated deeply. Proponents of liberalism met resistance from conservative elites.

The Spread of Authoritarianism

Spain and Portugal In both Spain and Portugal, parliamentary regimes faced strong opposition from the church, the army, and large landowners. In 1926, army officers overthrew the Portuguese republic that had been created in 1910, and gradually Antonio de Oliveira Salazar (1889–1970), a professor of economics, emerged as dictator. In Spain, after antimonarchist forces won the election of 1931, King Alfonso XIII (1902–1931) left the country, and Spain was proclaimed a republic. But the new government, led by socialists and liberals, faced the determined opposition of the traditional ruling elite. The reforms introduced by the republic—expropriation of large estates, reduction of the number of army officers, dissolution of the Jesuit order, and the closing of church schools—only intensified the old order's hatred.

The difficulties of the Spanish republic mounted: workers, near starvation, rioted and engaged in violent strikes; the military attempted a coup; and Catalonia, with its long tradition of separatism, tried to establish its autonomy. Imitating France (see the upcoming section on France), the parties of the left, including the Communists, united in the Popular Front, which came to power in February 1936. In July 1936, General Francisco Franco (1892–1975), stationed in Spanish Morocco, led a revolt against the republic. He was supported by army leaders, the church, monarchists, landlords, industrialists, and the Falange, a newly formed Fascist party. Spain was torn by a bloody civil war. Aided by Fascist Italy and Nazi Germany, Franco won in 1939 and established a dictatorship.

Eastern and Central Europe Parliamentary government in Eastern Europe rested on weak foundations. Predominantly rural, these countries lacked the sizable professional and commercial classes that had promoted liberalism in Western Europe. Only Czechoslovakia had a substantial native middle class with a strong liberal tradition. The rural masses of Eastern Europe, traditionally subjected to monarchical and aristocratic authority, were not used to political thinking or civic responsibility. Students and intellectuals, often gripped by a romantic nationalism, were drawn to antidemocratic movements. Right-wing leaders also played on the fear of Communism. When parliamentary government failed to solve internal problems, the opponents of the liberal state seized the helm. Fascist movements, however, had little success in Eastern Europe. Rather, authoritarian regimes headed by traditional ruling elites—army leaders or kings—extinguished democracy there.

The Western Democracies

While liberal governments were everywhere failing, the great Western democracies—the United States, Britain, and France—continued to preserve democratic institutions. In Britain and the United States, Fascist movements were merely a nuisance. In France, however, Fascism was more of a threat because it exploited a deeply ingrained hostility in some quarters to the liberal ideals of the French Revolution.

The United States The central problem faced by the Western democracies was the Great Depression, which started in the United States. In the 1920s, hundreds of thousands of Americans had bought stock on credit; this buying spree sent stock prices soaring well beyond what the stocks were actually worth. In late October 1929, the stock market was hit by a wave of panic selling, causing prices to plummet. Within a few weeks, the value of stocks listed on the New York Stock Exchange fell by some $26 billion. A ruinous chain reaction followed over the next few years. Businesses cut production and unemployment soared; farmers who were unable to meet mortgage payments lost their land; banks that had made poor investments closed down. American investors withdrew the capital they had invested in Europe, causing European banks and businesses to fail. Throughout the world, trade declined and unemployment rose.

When President Franklin Delano Roosevelt (1882–1945) took office in 1933, more than thirteen million Americans—one-quarter of the labor force—were out of work. Hunger and despair showed on the faces of the American people. Moving away from laissez faire, Roosevelt instituted a comprehensive program of national planning, economic experimentation, and reform known as the New Deal. Although the American political and economic system faced a severe test, few Americans turned to Fascism or Communism; the government engaged in national planning but did not break with democratic values and procedures.

Britain Even before the Great Depression, Britain faced severe economic problems. Loss of markets to foreign competitors hurt British manufacturing, mining, and shipbuilding; rapid development of water and oil power reduced the demand for British coal, and outdated mining equipment put Britain in a poor competitive position. To decrease costs, mine owners in 1926 called for salary cuts; the coal miners countered with a strike and were joined by workers in other industries. To many Britons, the workers were leftist radicals trying to overthrow the government. Many wanted the state to break the strike. After nine days, industrial workers called it off, but the miners held out for another six months; they returned to work with longer hours and lower pay. The general strike had failed. However, because the workers had not called for revolution and had refrained from violence, the fear that British workers would follow the Bolshevik path abated.

The Great Depression cast a pall over Britain. The Conservative Party leadership tried to stimulate exports by devaluing the pound and to encourage industry by providing loans at lower interest rates, but in the main it left the task of recovery to industry itself. Not until Britain began to rearm did unemployment decline significantly. Despite the economic slump of the 1920s and the Great Depression, Britain remained politically stable, a testament to the strength of its parliamentary tradition. Neither the Communists nor the newly formed British Union of Fascists gained mass support.

France In the early 1920s, France was concerned with restoring villages, railroads, mines, and forests that had been ruined by the war. From 1926 to 1929, France was relatively prosperous; industrial and agricultural production expanded, tourism increased, and the currency was stable. Although France did not feel the Great Depression as painfully as the United States and Germany, the nation was hurt by the decline in trade and production and the rise in unemployment. The political instability that had beset the Third Republic virtually since its inception continued, and hostility to the republic mounted. The rift between liberals and conservatives, which had divided the country since the Revolution and had grown worse with the Dreyfus affair (see "France: A Troubled Nation" in Chapter 16), continued to plague France during the Depression. As the leading parties failed to solve the nation's problems, a number of Fascist groups gained strength.

Fear of growing Fascist strength at home and in Italy and Germany led the parties of the left to form the Popular Front. In 1936, Léon Blum (1872–1950), a socialist and a Jew, became premier. Blum's Popular Front government instituted more reforms than any other ministry in the history of the Third Republic. To end a wave of strikes that tied up production, Blum gave workers a forty-hour week and holidays with pay and guaranteed them the right to collective bargaining. He took steps to nationalize the armaments and aircraft industries. To reduce the influence of the wealthiest families, he put the Bank of France under government control. By raising prices and buying wheat, he aided farmers. Conservatives and Fascists denounced Blum as a Jewish socialist who was converting the fatherland into a Communist state. "Better Hitler than Blum," grumbled French rightists.

Despite significant reforms, the Popular Front could not revitalize the economy. His political support eroding, Blum resigned in 1937, and the Popular Front, always a tenuous alliance, soon fell apart. Through democratic means, the Blum government had tried to give France its own New Deal, but the social reforms passed by the Popular Front only intensified hatred between the working classes and the rest of the nation. France had preserved democracy against the onslaught of domestic Fascists, but it was a demoralized and divided nation that confronted a united and dynamic Nazi Germany.

Intellectuals and Artists in Troubled Times

The presuppositions of the Enlightenment, already eroding in the decades before World War I, seemed near collapse after 1918—another casualty of trench warfare. Economic distress, particularly during the Great Depression, also profoundly disoriented the European mind. Westerners no longer possessed a frame of reference, a common outlook for understanding themselves, their times, or the past. The core values of Western civilization—the self-sufficiency of reason, the inviolability of the individual, and the existence of objective norms—no longer seemed inspiring or binding.

The crisis of consciousness evoked a variety of responses. Some intellectuals, having lost faith in the essential meaning of Western civilization, turned their backs on it or found escape in their art. Others sought a new hope in the Soviet experiment or in Fascism. Still others reaffirmed the rational humanist tradition of the Enlightenment. Repelled by the secularism, materialism, and rootlessness of the modern age, Christian thinkers urged Westerners to find renewed meaning and purpose in their ancestral religion. A philosophical movement called existentialism, which rose to prominence after World War II, aspired to make life authentic in a world stripped of universal values.

Postwar Pessimism

After World War I, Europeans looked at themselves and their civilization differently. It seemed that in science and technology they had unleashed powers that they could not control, and belief in the stability and security of European civilization appeared to be an illusion. Also illusory was the expectation that reason would banish surviving signs of darkness, ignorance, and injustice and usher in an age of continual progress. European intellectuals felt that they were living in a "broken world." In an age of heightened brutality and mobilized irrationality, the values of old Europe seemed beyond recovery. "All the great words," wrote D. H. Lawrence "were cancelled out for that generation."[27] The fissures discernible in European civilization before 1914 had grown wider and deeper. To be sure, Europe also had its optimists—those who found reason for hope in the League of Nations and in the easing of international tensions and improved economic conditions in the mid-1920s. However, the Great Depression and the triumph of totalitarianism intensified feelings of doubt and disillusionment.

Expressions of pessimism abounded after World War I. In 1919, Paul Valéry stated: "We modern civilizations have learned to recognize that we are mortal like the others. We feel that a civilization is as fragile as life."[28] "We are living today under the sign of the collapse of civilization,"[29] declared humanitarian Albert Schweitzer in 1923. German philosopher Karl Jaspers noted in 1932 that "there is a growing awareness of imminent ruin tantamount to a dread of the approaching end of all that makes life worthwhile."[30]

T. S. Eliot's *The Waste Land* (1922) also conveys a sense of foreboding. In his image of a collapsing European civilization, Eliot creates a macabre scenario. Hooded hordes, modern-day barbarians, swarm over plains and lay waste to cities. Jerusalem, Athens, Alexandria, Vienna, and London—each once a great spiritual or cultural center—are now "falling towers." Amid this destruction, one hears "high in the air / Murmur of maternal lamentation."[31]

Carl Gustav Jung, a Swiss psychologist, stated in *Modern Man in Search of a Soul* (1933):

> *I believe I am not exaggerating when I say that modern man has suffered an almost fatal shock, psychologically speaking, and as a result has fallen into profound uncertainty. . . . The revolution in our conscious outlook, brought about by the catastrophic results of the World War, shows itself in our inner life by the shattering of our faith in ourselves and our own worth. . . . I realize only too well that I am losing my faith in the possibility of a rational organization of the world, the old dream of the millennium, in which peace and harmony should rule, has grown pale.*[32]

In 1936, Dutch historian Johan Huizinga wrote in a chapter entitled "Apprehension of Doom":

> *We are living in a demented world. And we know it. . . . Everywhere there are doubts as to the solidity of our social structure, vague*

> *fears of the imminent future, a feeling that our civilization is on the way to ruin. . . . almost all things which once seemed sacred and immutable have now become unsettled, truth and humanity, justice and reason. . . . The sense of living in the midst of a violent crisis of civilization, threatening complete collapse, has spread far and wide.*[33]

The most influential expression of pessimism was Oswald Spengler's *The Decline of the West.* The first volume was published in July 1918, as the Great War was drawing to a close, and the second volume in 1922. The work achieved instant notoriety, particularly in Spengler's native Germany, shattered by defeat. Spengler viewed history as an assemblage of many different cultures, which, like living organisms, experience birth, youth, maturity, and death. What contemporaries pondered most was Spengler's insistence that Western civilization had entered its final stage and that its death could not be averted.

To an already troubled Western world, Spengler offered no solace. The West, like other cultures and like any living organism, was destined to die; its decline was irreversible and its death inevitable, and the symptoms of degeneration were already evident. Spengler's gloomy prognostication buttressed the Fascists, who claimed that they were creating a new civilization on the ruins of the dying European civilization.

Literature and Art: Innovation, Disillusionment, and Social Commentary

Postwar pessimism did not prevent writers and artists from continuing the cultural innovations begun before the war. In the works of D. H. Lawrence, Marcel Proust, André Gide, James Joyce, Franz Kafka, T. S. Eliot, and Thomas Mann, the modernist movement achieved a brilliant flowering. Often these writers gave expression to the troubles and uncertainties of the postwar period.

Franz Kafka (1883–1924), a Czech Jew, grasped the dilemma of the modern age perhaps better than any other novelist of his generation. In Kafka's world, human beings are caught in a bureaucratic web that they cannot control. They live in a nightmare society dominated by oppressive, cruel, and corrupt officials and amoral torturers: a world where cruelty and injustice are accepted facts of existence, power is exercised without limits, and victims cooperate in their own destruction. Traditional values and ordinary logic do not operate in such a world. In *The Trial* (1925), for example, the hero is arrested without knowing why, and he is eventually executed, a victim of institutional evil that breaks and destroys him "like a dog." In these observations, Kafka proved to be a prophet of the emerging totalitarian state. (Kafka's three sisters perished in the Holocaust.)

Kafka expressed the feelings of alienation and isolation that characterize the modern individual; he explored life's dreads and absurdities, offering no solutions or consolation. In Kafka's works, people are defeated and unable to comprehend the irrational forces that contribute to their destruction. The mind yearns for coherence, but, Kafka tells us, uncertainty, if not chaos, governs human relationships. We can be sure neither of our own identities nor of the world we encounter, for human beings are the playthings of unfathomable forces, too irrational to master.

Before World War I, German writer Thomas Mann (1875–1955) had earned a reputation for his short stories and novels, particularly *Buddenbrooks* (1901), which portrays the decline of a prosperous bourgeois family. In *The Magic Mountain* (1924), Mann reflected on the decomposition of bourgeois European civilization. The setting for the story is a Swiss sanitarium whose patients, drawn from several European lands, suffer from tuberculosis. The sanitarium symbolizes Europe, and it is the European psyche that is diseased. *The Magic Mountain* raised, but did not resolve, crucial questions. Was the epoch of rational humanist culture drawing to a close? Did Europeans welcome their spiritual illness in the same way that some of the patients in the sanitarium had a will to illness? How could Europe rescue itself from decadence?

In 1931, two years before Hitler took power, Mann, in an article entitled "An Appeal to Reason," described National Socialism and the extreme nationalism it espoused as a rejection of the Western rational tradition and a regression to primitive and barbaric modes of behavior. Nazism, he wrote, "is distinguished by . . . its absolute unrestraint, its orgiastic, radically antihumane, frenziedly dynamic character. . . . Everything is possible, everything is permitted as a weapon against human decency. . . . Fanaticism turns into a means of salvation . . . politics becomes an opiate for the masses . . . and reason veils her face."[34]

Shattered by World War I, disgusted by Fascism's growing strength, and moved by the suffering caused by the Depression, many writers became committed to social and political causes. Erich Maria Remarque's *All Quiet on the Western Front* (1929) was one of many antiwar novels. George Orwell's *The Road to Wigan Pier* (1937) recorded the bleak lives of English workers. In *The Grapes of Wrath* (1939), John Steinbeck captured the anguish of American farmers driven from their land by the Dust Bowl and foreclosure during the Depression. Few issues stirred the conscience of intellectuals as did the Spanish Civil War, and many of them volunteered to fight with the Spanish republicans against the Fascists. Ernest Hemingway's *For Whom the Bell Tolls* (1940) expressed the sentiments of these idealists.

The new directions taken in art before World War I—abstractionism and expressionism—continued in the postwar decades. Picasso, Mondrian, Kandinsky, Matisse, Rouault, Braque, Modigliani, and other masters continued to refine their styles. In addition, new art trends emerged, mirroring the trauma of a generation that had experienced the war and lost its faith in Europe's moral and intellectual values.

In 1915 in Zurich, artists and writers founded a movement, called Dada, to express their revulsion against the war and the civilization that spawned it. From neutral Switzerland, the movement spread to Germany and Paris. Dada shared in the postwar mood of disorientation and despair. Dadaists viewed life as essentially absurd (*Dada* is a nonsense term) and cultivated indifference. "The acts of life have no beginning or end. Everything happens in a completely idiotic way,"[35] declared the poet Tristan Tzara, one of Dada's founders and its chief spokesman. Dadaists expressed contempt for artistic and literary standards and rejected both God and reason. "Through reason man becomes a tragic and ugly figure," said one Dadaist; "beauty is dead," said another. Tzara declared:

> *What good did the theories of the philosophers do us? Did they help us to take a single step forward or backward? . . . We have had enough of the intelligent movements that have stretched beyond measure our credulity in the benefits of science. What we want now is spontaneity. . . . because everything that issues freely from ourselves, without the intervention of speculative ideas, represents us.*[36]

For Dadaists, the world was nonsensical and reality disordered; hence, they offered no solutions to anything. "Like everything in life, Dada is useless,"[37] said Tzara. Despite their nihilistic aims and "calculated irrationality," however, Dadaist artists, such as Marcel Duchamp, were innovative and creative.

Dada ended as a formal movement in 1924 and was succeeded by surrealism. Surrealists inherited from Dada a contempt for reason; they stressed fantasy and made use of Freudian insights and symbols in their art to reproduce the raw state of the unconscious and to arrive at truths beyond reason's grasp. In their attempt to break through the constraints of rationality to reach a higher reality—that is, a "surreality"—leading surrealists such as Max Ernst (1891–1976), Salvador Dali (1904–1989), and Joan Miro (1893–1983) used unconventional techniques to depict an external world devoid of logic and normal appearances.

Like writers, artists expressed a social conscience. George Grosz combined a Dadaist sense of life's meaninglessness with a new realism to depict the moral degeneration of middle-class German society. In *After the Questioning* (1935), Grosz, then living in the United States, dramatized Nazi brutality; in *The End of the World* (1936), he expressed his fear of another impending world war. Käthe Kollwitz, also a German artist, showed a deep compassion for the sufferer: the unemployed, the hungry, the ill, and the politically oppressed. William Gropper's *Migration* (1932) dramatized the suffering of the same dispossessed farmers described in Steinbeck's novel *The Grapes of Wrath*. Philip Evergood, in *Don't Cry Mother* (1938–1944), portrayed the apathy of starving children and their mother's terrible helplessness.

***The Night* (1918–1919), by Max Beckmann (1884–1950).** Max Beckmann's paintings gave expression to the disillusionment and spiritual unease that afflicted postwar Germany. When the Nazis included his works in the Degenerate Art Exhibition (1937), he left the country. In *The Night,* Beckmann, himself a veteran of the front, depicts brutal men engaging in terrible violence. (Erich Lessing/Art Resource, N.Y./© 2011 Artists Rights Society (ARS), New York/VG Bild-Kunst, Bonn.)

In his etchings of maimed, dying, and dead soldiers, German artist Otto Dix produced a powerful visual indictment of the Great War's cruelty and suffering. Max Beckmann's service in the German army during World War I made him acutely aware of violence and brutality, which he expressed in *The Night* (1918–1919) and other paintings. Designated a "degenerate artist" by the Nazis, Beckmann went into exile. In *Guernica* (1937), Picasso memorialized the Spanish village decimated by saturation bombing during the Spanish Civil War. In the *White Crucifixion* (1938), Marc Chagall, a Russian-born Jew who had settled in Paris, depicted the terror and flight of Jews in Nazi Germany.

Communism: "The God That Failed"

The economic misery of the Depression and the rise of Fascist barbarism led many intellectuals to find a new hope, even a secular faith, in Communism. They considered the Soviet experiment a new beginning that promised a better future for all humanity. These intellectuals praised the Soviet Union—a "workers' paradise"—for supplanting capitalist greed with socialist cooperation, for replacing a haphazard economic system marred by repeated depressions with one based on planned production, and for providing employment for everyone when joblessness was endemic in capitalist lands. American literary critic Edmund Wilson said that in the Soviet Union one felt at the "moral top of the world where the light never really goes out."[38] To these intellectuals, it seemed that in the Soviet Union a vigorous and healthy civilization was emerging and that only Communism could stem the tide of Fascism. For many, however, the attraction was short lived. Sickened by Stalin's purges and terror, the denial of individual freedom, and the suppression of truth, they came to view the Soviet Union as another totalitarian state and Communism as another "god that failed."

One such intellectual was Arthur Koestler (1905–1983). Born in Budapest of Jewish ancestry and educated in Vienna, Koestler worked as a correspondent for a leading Berlin newspaper chain. He joined the Communist Party at the very end of 1931 because he "lived in a disintegrating society thirsting for faith," was moved by the misery caused by the Depression, and saw Communism as the "only force capable of resisting the onrush of the primitive [Nazi] horde."[39] Koestler visited the Soviet Union in 1933, experiencing firsthand both the starvation brought on by forced collectivization and the propaganda that grotesquely misrepresented life in Western lands. While his faith was shaken, he did not break with the party until 1938, in response to Stalin's liquidations.

In *Darkness at Noon* (1941), Koestler explored the attitudes of the Old Bolsheviks who were imprisoned, tortured, and executed by Stalin. These dedicated Communists had served the party faithfully, but Stalin, fearing opposition, hating intellectuals, and driven by megalomania, denounced them as enemies of the people. In *Darkness at Noon,* the leading character, the imprisoned Rubashov, is a composite of the Old Bolsheviks. Although innocent, Rubashov, without being physically tortured, publicly confesses to political crimes that he never committed.

Rubashov is aware of the suffering that the party has brought to the Russian people:

> *[I]n the interests of a just distribution of land we deliberately let die of starvation about five million farmers and their families in one year. . . . [To liberate] human beings from the shackles of industrial exploitation . . . we sent about ten million people to do forced labour in the Arctic regions . . . under conditions similar to those of antique galley slaves.*[40]

Pained by his own complicity in the party's crimes, including the betrayal of friends, Rubashov questions the party's philosophy that the individual should be subordinated and, if necessary, sacrificed to the regime. Nevertheless, Rubashov remains the party's faithful servant; true believers do not easily break with their faith. By confessing, Rubashov performs his last service for the revolution. For the true believer, everything—truth, justice, and the sanctity of the individual—is properly sacrificed to the party.

Reaffirming the Christian Worldview

By calling into question core liberal beliefs—the essential goodness of human nature, the primacy of reason, the efficacy of science, and the inevitability of progress—World War I led thinkers to find in Christianity an alternative view of the human experience and the crisis of the twentieth century. Christian thinkers, including Karl Barth, Paul Tillich, Reinhold Niebuhr, Christopher Dawson, Jacques Maritain, and T. S. Eliot, affirmed the reality of evil in human nature. They assailed liberals and Marxists for holding too optimistic a view of human nature and human reason and for postulating a purely rational and secular philosophy of history. For these thinkers, the Christian conception of history as a clash between human will and God's commands provided an intelligible explanation of the tragedies of the twentieth century. They agreed with the leading French Catholic thinker Jacques Maritain (1882–1973), who argued that "anthropomorphic humanism," which held that human beings by themselves alone can define life's purpose and create their own values, had utterly failed. Without guidance from a transcendental source, Maritain insisted, reason is powerless to control irrational drives, which threaten to degrade human existence. Without commitment to God's values, we find substitute faiths in fanatic and belligerent ideologies and unscrupulous leaders. For democracy to survive, he said, it must be infused with Christian love and compassion.

Reaffirming the Ideals of Reason and Freedom

Several thinkers tried to reaffirm the ideals of rationality and freedom that had been trampled by totalitarian movements. In *The Treason of the Intellectuals* (1927), Julien Benda (1867–1956), a French cultural critic of Jewish background, castigated intellectuals for intensifying hatred between nations, classes, and political factions. "Our age is indeed the age of the *intellectual organization of political hatreds*," he wrote. These intellectuals, said Benda, do not pursue justice or truth but proclaim that "even if our country is wrong, we must think of it in the right." They scorn outsiders, extol harshness and action, and proclaim the superiority of instinct and will to intelligence; or they "assert that the intelligence to be venerated is that which limits its activities within the bounds of national interest." The logical end of this xenophobia, said Benda, "is the organized slaughter of nations and classes."[41]

José Ortega y Gasset (1883–1955), descendant of a noble Spanish family and a professor of philosophy, gained international recognition with the publication of *The Revolt of the Masses* (1930). According to Ortega, European civilization, the product of a creative elite, was degenerating into barbarism because of the growing power of the masses, for the masses lacked the mental discipline and commitment to reason needed to preserve Europe's intellectual and cultural traditions. Ortega did not equate the masses with the working class and the elite with the nobility; it was an attitude of mind, not a class affiliation, that distinguished the "mass-man" from the elite.

The mass-man, said Ortega, has a commonplace mind and does not set high standards for himself. Faced with a problem, he "is satisfied with thinking the first thing he finds in his head," and "crushes . . . everything that is different, everything that is excellent, individual, qualified, and select. Anybody who is not like everybody, who does not think like everybody, runs the risk of being eliminated."[42] Such intellectually vulgar people, declared Ortega, cannot understand or preserve the processes of civilization. The Fascists, for him, exemplified this revolt of the masses:

> *Under Fascism there appears for the first time in Europe a type of man who does not want to give reasons or to be right, but simply shows himself resolved to impose his opinions. This is the new thing: the right not to be reasonable, the "reason of unreason." Hence I see the most palpable manifestation of the new mentality of the masses, due to their having decided to rule society without the capacity for doing so.*[43]

Since the mass-man does not respect the tradition of reason, he does not enter into rational dialogue with others or defend his opinions logically, said Ortega. Rejecting reason, the mass-man glorifies violence—the ultimate expression of barbarism. As Ortega saw it, if European civilization was to be rescued from Fascism and Communism, the elite must sustain civilized values and provide leadership for the masses.

A staunch defender of the Enlightenment tradition, Ernst Cassirer (1874–1945), a German philosopher of Jewish lineage, emigrated after Hitler came to power, eventually settling in the United States. Just prior to Hitler's triumph, in 1932, Cassirer wrote about the need to uphold and reenergize that tradition: "More than ever before, it seems to me, the time is again ripe for applying . . . self-criticism to the present age, for holding up to it that bright clear mirror fashioned by the Enlightenment. . . . The age which venerated reason and science as man's highest faculty cannot and must not be lost even for us."[44]

In his last work, *The Myth of the State* (1946), Cassirer described Nazism as the triumph of mythical thinking over reason. The Nazis, he wrote, cleverly manufactured myths—of the race, the leader, the party, the state—that disoriented the intellect. The Germans who embraced these myths surrendered their capacity for independent judgment, leaving themselves vulnerable to manipulation by the Nazi leadership. To contain the destructive powers of political myths, Cassirer urged strengthening the rational humanist tradition and called for the critical study of political myths, for "in order to fight an enemy you must know him. . . . We should carefully study the origin, the structure, the methods, and the technique of the political myths. We should see the adversary face to face in order to know how to combat him."[45]

George Orwell (1903–1950), a British novelist and political journalist, wrote two powerful indictments of totalitarianism: *Animal Farm* (1945) and *1984* (1949). In *Animal Farm*, based in part on his experiences with Communists during the Spanish Civil War, Orwell satirized the totalitarian regime built by Lenin and Stalin in Russia. In *1984*, Orwell, who was deeply committed to human dignity and freedom, warned that these great principles were now permanently menaced by the concentration and abuse of political power. "If you want a picture of the future, imagine a boot

JEAN PAUL SARTRE AND SIMONE DE BEAUVOIR. Existentialism was a major philosophical movement of the twentieth century. Sartre and de Beauvoir were two of its principle exponents.

stamping on a human face forever," says a member of the ruling elite as he tortures a victim in the dungeons of the Thought Police.[46]

The society of *1984* is ruled by the Inner Party, which constitutes some 2 percent of the population. Heading the Party is Big Brother—most likely a mythical figure created by the ruling elite to satisfy people's yearning for a leader. The Party indoctrinates people to love Big Brother, whose picture is everywhere. The Ministry of Truth resorts to thought control to dominate and manipulate the masses and to keep Party members loyal and subservient. Independent thinking is destroyed. Objective truth no longer exists. Truth is whatever the Party decrees at the moment. If the Party were to proclaim that two plus two equals five, it would have to be believed. In this totalitarian society of the future, all human rights are abolished, people are arrested merely for their thoughts, and children spy on their parents.

EXISTENTIALISM

The philosophical movement that best exemplified the anxiety and uncertainty of Europe in an era of world wars was existentialism. Like writers and artists, existentialist philosophers were responding to a European civilization that seemed to be in the throes of dissolution. Although existentialism was most popular after World War II, expressing the anxiety and despair of many intellectuals who had lost confidence in reason and progress, several of its key works were written prior to or during the war.

What route should people take in a world where old values and certainties had dissolved, where universal truth was rejected and God's existence denied? How could people cope in a society where they were menaced by technology, manipulated by impersonal bureaucracies, and overwhelmed by feelings of anxiety? If the universe lacks any overarching meaning, what meaning could one give to one's own life? These questions were at the crux of existentialist philosophy.

Existentialism does not lend itself to a single definition, for its principal theorists did not adhere to a common body of doctrines. For example, some existentialists were atheists, like Jean Paul Sartre, or omitted God from their thought, like Martin Heidegger; others, like Karl Jaspers, believed in God but not in Christian doctrines; still others, like Gabriel Marcel and Nikolai Berdyaev, were Christians; and Martin Buber was a believing Jew.

That there are no timeless truths that exist independently of and prior to the individual human being and that serve as ultimate standards of virtue is a core principle of existentialism. Existence—our presence in the here-and-now—precedes and takes precedence over any presumed absolute values. The moral and spiritual values that society tries to impose cannot define the individual person's existence. Our traditional morality rests on no foundation whose certainty can be either demonstrated by reason or guaranteed by God. There are simply no transcendent absolutes; to think otherwise is to surrender to illusion. It is the first principle of existentialism, said Jean Paul Sartre (1905–1980), the prominent French existentialist, that we must choose our own ethics, define ourselves, and give our own meaning to our life.

For existentialists, human nature is not fixed or constant; each person is like no other. Self-realization comes when one affirms one's own uniqueness. One becomes less than human when one permits one's life to be determined by a mental outlook—a set of rules and values—imposed by others.

Existentialists maintained that we are alone in a universe that is indifferent to our expectations and needs, and death is ever stalking us. Awareness of this elementary fact of existence evokes a sense of overwhelming anxiety and depression. Existence is essentially absurd. There is no purpose to our presence in the universe. We simply find ourselves here; we do not know and will never find out why. Compared with the eternity of time that preceded our birth and will follow our death, the short duration of our existence seems trivial and inexplicable. And death, which irrevocably terminates our existence, testifies to the ultimate absurdity of life. We are free. We must face squarely the fact that existence is purposeless and absurd. In doing so, we can give our life meaning. It is in the act of choosing freely from among different possibilities that the individual shapes an authentic existence. There is a dynamic quality to human existence; the individual has the potential to become more than he or she is.

The Modern Predicament

The process of fragmentation in European thought and arts, which had begun at the end of the nineteenth century, accelerated after World War I. Increasingly, philosophers, writers, and artists expressed disillusionment with the rational humanist tradition of the Enlightenment. They no longer shared the Enlightenment's confidence in either reason's capabilities or human goodness, and they viewed perpetual progress as an illusion.

For some thinkers, the crucial problem was the great change in the European understanding of truth. Since the rise of philosophy in ancient Greece, Western thinkers had believed in the existence of objective, universal truths: truths that were inherent in nature and applied to all peoples at all times. (Christianity, of course, also taught the reality of truth as revealed by God.) It was held that such truths—the natural rights of the individual, for example—could be apprehended by the intellect and could serve as a standard for individual aspirations and social life. The recognition of these universal principles, it was believed, compelled people to measure the world of the here-and-now in the light of rational and universal norms and to institute appropriate reforms. It was the task of philosophy to reconcile human existence with the objective order.

During the nineteenth century, the existence of universal truth came into doubt. A growing historical consciousness led some thinkers to maintain that what people considered truth was merely a reflection of their culture at a given stage in history—their perception of things at a specific point in the evolution of human consciousness. These thinkers held that universal truths were not woven into the fabric of nature. There were no natural rights of life, liberty, and property that constituted the individual's birthright; there were no standards of justice or equality inherent in nature and ascertainable by reason. Rather, people themselves elevated the beliefs and values of an age to the status of objective truth. The normative principles—the self-evident truths proclaimed by Jefferson—which for the philosophes constituted a standard for political and social reform and a guarantee of human rights, were no longer linked to the natural order, to an objective reality that could be confirmed by reason. As Hannah Arendt noted, "We certainly no longer believe, as the men of the French Revolution did, in a universal cosmos of which man was a part and whose natural laws he had to imitate and conform to."[47]

This radical break with the traditional attitude toward truth contributed substantially to the crisis of European consciousness that marked the first half of the twentieth century. Traditional values and beliefs, whether those inherited from the Enlightenment or those taught by Christianity, no longer gave Europeans a sense of certainty and security. People were left without a normative order to serve as a guide to living—and without such a guide might be open to nihilism. For if nothing is fundamentally true—if there are no principles of morality and justice that emanate from God or can be derived from reason—then it can be concluded, as Nietzsche understood, that everything is permitted. Some scholars interpreted Nazism as the culminating expression of a nihilistic attitude grown ever more brutal.

By the early twentieth century, the attitude of Westerners toward reason had undergone a radical transformation. Some thinkers, who had placed their hopes in the rational tradition of the Enlightenment, were distressed by reason's inability to resolve the tensions and conflicts of modern industrial society. Moreover, the growing recognition of the nonrational—of human actions determined by hidden impulses—led people to doubt that reason played the dominant role in human behavior. Other thinkers viewed the problem of reason differently. They assailed the attitude of mind that found no room for Christianity because its teachings did not pass the test of reason and science. Or they attacked reason for fashioning a technological and bureaucratic society that devalued and crushed human passions and stifled individuality. These thinkers insisted that human beings cannot fulfill their potential, cannot live wholly, if their feelings are denied. They agreed with D. H. Lawrence's critique of rationalism: "The attribution of rationality to human nature, instead of enriching it, now seems to me to have impoverished it. It ignored certain powerful and valuable springs of feeling. Some of the spontaneous, irrational outbursts of human nature can have a sort of value from which our schematism was cut off."[48]

While many thinkers focused on reason's limitations, others, particularly existentialists, pointed out that reason was a double-edged sword: it could demean, as well as ennoble and liberate, the individual. These thinkers attacked all theories that subordinated the individual to a rigid ideological or political system.

Responding to the critics of reason, its defenders insisted that it was necessary to reaffirm the rational tradition first proclaimed by the Greeks and given its modern expression by the Enlightenment. Reason, they maintained, was indispensable to civilization. What these thinkers advocated was broadening the scope of reason to accommodate the insights into human nature advanced by the romantics, Nietzsche, Freud, modernist writers and artists, and others who explored the world of feelings, will, and the subconscious. They also stressed the need to humanize reason so that it could never threaten to reduce a human being to a thing—a mere instrument used to realize some socioeconomic blueprint.

In the decades shaped by world wars and totalitarianism, intellectuals raised questions that went to the heart of the dilemma of modern life. How can civilized life be safeguarded against human irrationality, particularly when it is channeled into political ideologies that idolize the state, the leader, the party, or the race? How can individual human personality be rescued from a relentless rationalism that organizes the individual as it would any material object? Do the values associated with the Enlightenment provide a sound basis on which to integrate society? Can the individual find meaning in what many now regarded as a meaningless universe? World War II and the Holocaust gave these questions a special poignancy.

❖ ❖ ❖

Notes

1. Hannah Arendt, *The Origins of Totalitarianism* (New York: World, Meridian Books, 1958), p. 469.
2. Karl Dietrich Bracher, *The Age of Ideologies*, trans. Erwald Osers (New York: St. Martin's Press, 1984), p. 83.
3. Quoted in Omer Bartov, *Hitler's Army: Soldiers, Nazis, and War in the Third Reich* (New York: Oxford University Press, 1992), p. 166.
4. V. I. Lenin, "The Immediate Tasks of the Soviet Government," in *The Lenin Anthology*, ed. Robert C. Tucker (New York: Norton, 1975), pp. 448 ff.

5. J. V. Stalin, "Speech to Business Executives" (1931), in *A Documentary History of Communism from Lenin to Mao*, ed. Robert V. Daniels (New York: Random House, 1960), Vol. 2, p. 22.
6. Quoted in Isaac Deutscher, *Stalin: A Political Biography* (New York: Oxford University Press, 1966), p. 325.
7. Excerpted in T. H. Rigby, ed., *Stalin* (Englewood Cliffs, N.J.: Prentice-Hall, 1966), p. 111.
8. Quoted in Jonathan Glover, *Humanity: A Moral History of the Twentieth Century* (New Haven, Conn.: Yale University Press, 1999), p. 241.
9. Quoted in Zeev Sternhill, "Fascist Ideology," in *Fascism: A Reader's Guide*, ed. Walter Laqueur (Berkeley: University of California Press, 1976), p. 338.
10. Quoted in John Weiss, *The Fascist Tradition* (New York: Harper & Row, 1967), p. 9.
11. Quoted in Max Gallo, *Mussolini's Italy* (New York: Macmillan, 1973), p. 218.
12. Adolf Hitler, *Mein Kampf*, trans. Ralph Manheim (Boston: Houghton Mifflin, 1962), p. 161.
13. Quoted in Joachim C. Fest, *Hitler*, trans. Richard and Clara Winston (New York: Harcourt Brace Jovanovich, 1974), p. 162.
14. *Hitler's Secret Conversations, 1941–1944*, with an introductory essay by H. R. Trevor Roper (New York: Farrar, Straus & Young, 1953), p. 28.
15. Quoted in Lucy S. Dawidowicz, *The War Against the Jews, 1933–1945* (New York: Holt, Rinehart & Winston, 1975), p. 21.
16. Quoted in Uri Tal, "Consecration of Politics in the Nazi Era," in *Judaism and Christianity Under the Impact of National Socialism*, ed. Otto Dov Kulka and Paul R. Mendes Flohr (Jerusalem: Historical Society of Israel, 1987), p. 70.
17. Adolf Hitler, *Mein Kampf* (Boston: Houghton Mifflin, 1962), p. 107.
18. Ibid., p. 479.
19. Quoted in Zbigniew Brzezinski, *Out of Control* (New York: Charles Scribner's Sons, 1993) p. 19.
20. Quoted in David Welch, ed., *Nazi Propaganda* (Totowa, N.J.: Barnes & Noble, 1983), p. 5.
21. Quoted in J. S. Conway, *The Nazi Persecution of the Churches* (New York: Basic Books, 1968), p. 202.
22. Quoted in Helmut Krausnick, Hans Buchheim, Martin Broszart, and Hans-Adolf Jacobsen, *Anatomy of the SS State* (London: Collins, 1968), p. 128.
23. *Hitler's Secret Conversations*, p. 6.
24. Quoted in Hermann Graml et al., *The German Resistance to Hitler* (Berkeley: University of California Press, 1970), p. 206.
25. Quoted in T. L. Jarman, *The Rise and Fall of Nazi Germany* (New York: New York University Press, 1956), p. 182.
26. Quoted in Karl Dietrich Bracher, *The German Dictatorship*, trans. Jean Steinberg (New York: Praeger, 1970), p. 268.
27. Quoted in Barbara Tuchman, *The Guns of August* (New York: Macmillan, 1962), p. 489.
28. Quoted in Hans Kohn, "The Crisis in European Thought and Culture," in *World War I: A Turning Point in Modern History*, ed. Jack J. Roth (New York: Alfred A. Knopf, 1967), p. 28.
29. Quoted in Franklin L. Baumer, "Twentieth-Century Version of the Apocalypse," *Cahiers d'Histoire Mondiale (Journal of World History)*, 1 (January 1954), p. 624.
30. Ibid.
31. T. S. Eliot, "The Waste Land," in *Collected Poems*, 1909–1962 (New York: Harcourt, Brace, 1970), p. 67.
32. Carl Gustav Jung, *Modern Man in Search of a Soul*, trans. W. S. Dell and Cary F. Baynes (New York: Harcourt, Brace, 1933), pp. 231, 234–235.
33. Johan Huizinga, *In the Shadow of Tomorrow* (London: Heinemann, 1936), pp. 1–3.
34. Thomas Mann, "An Appeal to Reason," excerpted in *Sources of the Western Tradition*, 8th ed. Marvin Perry ed., (Boston: Wadsworth, Cengage Learning, 2012), Vol. 2, pp. 349–350.
35. Tristan Tzara, "Lecture on Dada (1922)," trans. Ralph Mannheim, in *The Dada Painters and Poets*, ed. Robert Motherwell (New York: Witterborn, Schultz, 1951), p. 250.
36. Ibid., p. 248.
37. Ibid., p. 251.
38. Quoted in David Caute, *The Fellow Travellers* (New York: Macmillan, 1973), p. 64.
39. Richard Crossman, ed., *The God That Failed* (New York: Bantam Books, 1951), pp. 15, 21.
40. Arthur Koestler, *Darkness at Noon* (New York: Macmillan, 1941), pp. 158–159.
41. Julien Benda, *The Betrayal of the Intellectuals*, trans. Richard Aldington (Boston: Beacon,

1955), pp. 21, 38, 122, 162. The book is commonly known by its first translation, *The Treason of the Intellectuals.*

42. José Ortega y Gasset, *The Revolt of the Masses* (New York: Norton, 1957), pp. 63, 18.
43. Ibid., p. 73.
44. Ernst Cassirer, *The Philosophy of the Enlightenment*, trans. Fritz C. A. Koelln and James P. Pettegrove (Boston: Beacon, 1955), pp. xi–xii.
45. Ernst Cassirer, *The Myth of the State* (New Haven, Conn.: Yale University Press, 1946), p. 296.
46. George Orwell, *1984* (New York: Harcourt, Brace, 1949; paperback, The New American Library, 1961), p. 220.
47. Cited in Harry S. Kariel, *In Search of Authority* (Glencoe, Ill.: The Free Press, 1964), p. 246.
48. Quoted in Anthony Arblaster, *The Rise and Decline of Western Liberalism* (Oxford: Basil Blackwell, 1984), p. 81.

Suggested Reading

Bracher, Karl Dietrich, *The German Dictatorship* (1970). A highly regarded analysis of all phases of the Nazi state.

Burleigh, Michael, and Wolfgang Wippermann, *The Racial State: Germany 1933–1945* (1991). Persecution of Jews, Gypsies, mentally handicapped, and homosexuals; analysis.

Conquest, Robert, *The Harvest of Sorrow: Soviet Collectivization and the Terror-Famine* (1986). The human consequences of collectivization.

Fischer, Klaus, *Nazi Germany: A New History* (1995). An excellent synthesis.

Fitzpatrick, Sheila, *Stalinism* (1999). Ordinary life in Stalin's Russia in the 1930s.

Fritzsche, Peter, *Germans into Nazis* (1998). Explains why Germans were attracted to the Nazi movement.

Gregor, Neil, ed., *Nazism* (2000) A collection of essays on many phases of National Socialism.

Jackel, Eberhard, *Weltanschauung* (1972). A perceptive analysis of Hitler's worldview.

Kershaw, Ian, *The Nazi Dictatorship: Problems of Interpretation* (2000). A masterful work of synthesis.

Mack Smith, Denis, *Mussolini* (1982). By a leading historian of modern Italy.

Medvedev, Roy, *Let History Judge: The Origins and Consequences of Stalinism,* rev. ed. (1990). Includes newly available material on Stalin's crimes of the 1930s.

Montefiore, Simon Sebag, *Stalin: The Court of the Red Tsar* (2004). A close-up portrait of Stalin and his circle, drawing on new archival material.

Overy, Richard, *The Dictators: Hitler's Germany and Stalin's Russia* (2004). An excellent comparative study.

Razgon, Lev, *True Stories* (1997). A survivor's account of Stalin's camps.

Rosenbaum, Ron, *Explaining Hitler* (1998). Interviews with leading historians about Hitler's life and career. The author knows how to ask questions and interpret answers.

Rousso, Henry, ed., *Stalinism and Nazism: History and Memory Compared* (1999). Valuable essays on these totalitarian movements.

Volkogonov, Dmitri, *Stalin: Triumph and Tragedy* (1991). The first Soviet biography based on hitherto unavailable archive material.

Von Laue, Theodore H., *Why Lenin? Why Stalin? Why Gorbachev?* 3rd ed. (1993). A brief survey of the rise and fall of the Soviet Union.

Chapter 20

World War II: Western Civilization in the Balance

- **The Road to War**
- **The Nazi Blitzkrieg**
- **The New Order**
- **The Turn of the Tide**
- **The Legacy of World War II**

Focus Questions

1. What were Hitler's foreign policy aims?
2. Why did Britain and France pursue a policy of appeasement, and with what effect?
3. What was the nature of the new order that the Nazis established in conquered Europe?
4. What factors led to the defeat of the Nazis?
5. In your opinion, what is the meaning of the Holocaust for Western civilization? For Jews? For Christians? For Germans?
6. What is the legacy of World War II?

From the early days of his political career, Hitler dreamed of forging a vast German empire in Central and Eastern Europe. He believed that only by waging a war of conquest against Russia could the German nation gain the living space and security it required and, as a superior race, deserved. War was an essential component of National Socialism's racist ideology, which postulated an eternal struggle between races and the shaping of a new order in Europe based on race; war also accorded with Hitler's temperament. For the former corporal from the trenches, the Great War had never ended. Hitler aspired to political power because he wanted to mobilize the material and human resources of the German nation for war and conquest.

Although historians may debate the question of responsibility for World War I, few would deny that World War II was Hitler's war. Most would concur with the assessment of French historian Pierre Renouvin: "It appears to be an almost incontrovertible fact that the Second World War was brought on by the actions of the Hitler government, that these actions were the expression of a policy laid down well in advance in *Mein Kampf,* and that this war could have been averted up until the last moment if the German government had so wished."[1] Western statesmen had sufficient warning that Hitler was a threat to peace and to the essential values of Western civilization. In the 1920s, Hitler had openly proclaimed his commitment to a war of revenge and expansion, and in the 1930s he scrapped the Versailles Treaty and openly prepared for such a conflict. But Western statesmen, not fully grasping Hitler's ruthlessness and ideological obsession with creating a German racial empire and underestimating his Machiavellian cunning in foreign policy, failed to rally their people and take a stand until Germany had greatly increased its capacity to wage aggressive war. ❖

The Road to War

After consolidating his power and mobilizing the nation, Hitler moved to implement his foreign policy objectives: the destruction of the Versailles treaty, the conquest and colonization of Eastern Europe, and the domination and exploitation of racial inferiors. In foreign affairs, Hitler demonstrated the same blend of opportunism and singleness of purpose that had brought him to power. Here, too, he displayed an uncanny understanding of his opponents' weaknesses; and here, too, his opponents underestimated his skills and intent. As in his climb to power, he made use of propaganda to undermine his opponents' will to resist. The Nazi propaganda machine, which had effectively won the minds of the German people, became an instrument of foreign policy. To promote social and political disorientation in other lands, the Nazis propagated anti-Semitism worldwide. Nazi propagandists also tried to draw international support for Hitler as Europe's best defense against the Soviet Union and Bolshevism.

British and French Foreign Policies

As Hitler had anticipated, the British and the French backed down when faced with his violations of the Versailles treaty and threats of war. Haunted by the memory of World War I, Britain and France went to great lengths to avoid another catastrophe—a policy that had the overwhelming support of public opinion. Because Britain believed that Germany had been treated too severely by the Versailles treaty and knew that its own military forces were woefully unprepared for war, from 1933 to 1938 the British were amenable to making concessions to Hitler. Although France had the strongest army on the Continent, it was prepared to fight only a defensive war—the reverse of its World War I strategy. France built immense fortifications, called the Maginot Line, to protect its borders from a German invasion, but it lacked a mobile striking force that could punish an aggressive Germany. The United States, concerned with the problems of the Great Depression and standing aloof from Europe's troubles, did nothing to strengthen the resolve of France and Britain. Since both France and Britain feared and mistrusted the Soviet Union, the grand alliance of World War I was not renewed. There was an added factor: suffering from a failure of leadership and political and economic unrest that eroded national unity, France was experiencing a decline in morale and a loss of nerve. It consistently turned to Britain for direction.

British statesmen championed a policy of appeasement: giving in to Germany in the hope that a satisfied Hitler would not drag Europe through another world war. British policy rested on the disastrous illusion that Hitler, like his Weimar predecessors, sought peaceful revision of the Versailles treaty and that he could be contained through concessions. Accepting the view that Nazi propaganda cleverly propagated and exploited, some British appeasers also regarded Hitler as a

HITLER AND HIS AIDES IN FRONT OF THE EIFFEL TOWER. In 1940, after military successes in Belgium and Holland, the German forces overcame France. Hitler (center, right) saw the fall of France as a proof of the invincibility of the Reich and a predestined reversal of the humiliation felt by Germans at their defeat in World War I.

defender of European civilization and the capitalist economic order against Soviet Communism. Appeasement, which in the end was capitulation to blackmail, failed. Germany grew stronger and the German people more devoted to the führer. Hitler did not moderate his ambitions, and the appeasers did not avert war.

Breakdown of Peace

To realize his foreign policy aims, Hitler required a formidable military machine. Germany must rearm. The Treaty of Versailles had limited the size of the German army to a hundred thousand volunteers; restricted the navy's size; forbidden the production of military aircraft, heavy artillery, and tanks; and disbanded the general staff. In March 1935, Hitler declared that Germany was no longer bound by the Versailles treaty. Germany would restore conscription, build an air force (which it had been doing secretly), and strengthen its navy. France and Britain offered no resistance.

A decisive event in the breakdown of peace was Italy's invasion of Ethiopia in October 1935. The League of Nations called for economic sanctions against Italy, and most League members restricted trade with the aggressor. But Italy continued to receive oil, particularly from American suppliers, and neither Britain nor France sought to restrain Italy. Mussolini's subjugation of Ethiopia discredited the League of Nations, which had already been weakened by its failure to deal effectively with Japan's invasion of the mineral-rich Chinese province of Manchuria in 1931. The fall of Ethiopia, like that of Manchuria, evidenced the League's reluctance to check aggression with force.

Remilitarization of the Rhineland On March 7, 1936, Hitler marched troops into the Rhineland, violating the Versailles treaty, which called for the demilitarization of these German border lands. German generals had cautioned Hitler that such a move would provoke a French invasion of Germany, which the German army could not repulse. But Hitler gambled that France and Britain, lacking the will to fight, would take no action.

Hitler had assessed the Anglo-French mood correctly. The remilitarization of the Rhineland did not greatly alarm Britain. After all, Hitler was not expanding Germany's borders but only sending soldiers to its frontier. Such a move, reasoned British officials, did not warrant risking a war, and France would not act alone. Moreover, the French general staff overestimated German military strength and thought only of defending French soil from a German attack, not of initiating a strike against Germany.

Spanish Civil War The Spanish Civil War of 1936–1939 was another victory for Fascism. Nazi Germany and Fascist Italy aided Franco (see "Liberalism and Authoritarianism in Other Lands" in Chapter 19); the Soviet Union supplied

David Low/London Evening Standard/Solo Syndication.

APPEASEMENT. Haunted by the memory of World War I, many French and British officials and ordinary citizens would go to great lengths to appease Germany in order to avoid a second world war. Soon after Hitler's remilitarization of the Rhineland, cartoonist David Lowe called the leaders of England and France spineless.

the Spanish republic. By October 1937, some sixty thousand Italian "volunteers" were fighting in Spain. Hitler sent between five thousand and six thousand men and hundreds of planes, which proved decisive in winning the war. By comparison, the Soviet Union's aid was meager. Viewing the conflict as a struggle between democracy and Fascism, thousands of Europeans and Americans volunteered to fight for the republic.

Without considerable help from France, the Spanish republic was doomed, but Prime Minister Léon Blum feared that French intervention might lead to war with Germany. Moreover, supplying the republic would have dangerous consequences at home because French rightists were sympathetic to Franco's conservative-clerical authoritarianism. In 1939, the republic fell, and Franco established a dictatorship, imprisoning or banishing to labor camps more than one million Spaniards and executing another two hundred thousand. The Spanish Civil War provided Germany with an opportunity to test weapons and pilots and demonstrated again that France and Britain lacked the determination to fight Fascism.

Anschluss with Austria One of Hitler's aims was incorporation of Austria into the Third Reich, but the Treaty of Versailles had expressly prohibited the union (Anschluss) of the two German-speaking countries. In March 1938, under the pretext of preventing violence, Hitler ordered his troops into Austria, which was made a province of the German Reich.

Many Austrians welcomed the Anschluss. The idea of a Greater Germany appealed to their Pan-German sentiments, and they hoped that Hitler's magic would produce economic recovery. Moreover, depriving Jews of their rights, property, and occupations had widespread appeal among traditionally anti-Semitic Austrians. The Viennese celebrated by ringing church bells, waving swastika banners, and spontaneously beating, robbing, and humiliating Jews, including tearing Torah scrolls, shearing the beards of rabbis, and forcing whole families to scrub sidewalks. The Austrians' euphoria over the Anschluss and their treatment of Jews astonished many observers, including the German occupiers.

Sudetenland, Munich, Prague Hitler obtained Austria merely by threatening to use force. Another threat would give him the Sudetenland of Czechoslovakia. Of the 3.5 million people living in the Sudetenland, some 2.8 million were ethnic Germans. Encouraged and instructed by Germany, the Sudeten Germans, led by Konrad Henlein, shrilly denounced the Czech government for "persecuting" its German minority and depriving it of its right to self-determination. The Sudeten Germans agitated for local autonomy and the right to profess the National Socialist ideology. Behind this demand was the goal of German annexation of the Sudetenland and the destruction of Czechoslovakia.

While negotiations between the Sudeten Germans and the Czech government proceeded, Hitler's propaganda machine accused the Czechs of hideous crimes against the German minority and warned of retribution. Hitler also ordered his generals to prepare for an invasion of Czechoslovakia. Fighting between Czechs and Sudeten Germans heightened the tensions. Seeking to preserve peace, Prime Minister Neville Chamberlain (1869–1940) of Britain offered to confer with Hitler, who then extended an invitation.

Britain's position regarding Czechoslovakia—the only democracy in Eastern Europe—was somewhat different from that of France. In 1924, France and Czechoslovakia had concluded an agreement of mutual assistance in the event that either was attacked by Germany. Czechoslovakia had a similar agreement with Russia, but with the provision that Russian assistance depended on France first fulfilling the terms of its agreement. Britain had no commitment to Czechoslovakia. Swallowing Hitler's propaganda, some British officials believed that the Sudeten Germans were indeed a suppressed minority entitled to self-determination and that the Sudetenland, like Austria, was not worth a war that could destroy Western civilization. Hitler, they said, only wanted to incorporate Germans living outside Germany; he was only carrying the noble principle of self-determination to its logical conclusion. Once these Germans lived under the German flag, argued these British officials, Hitler would be satisfied. In any case, Britain's failure to rearm between 1933 and 1938 weakened its position. The British chiefs of staff believed that the nation was not prepared to fight and that it was necessary to sacrifice Czechoslovakia to buy time.

Czechoslovakia's fate was decided at the Munich Conference (September 1938), attended by Chamberlain, Hitler, Mussolini, and Prime Minister Édouard Daladier (1884–1970) of France. The Munich Pact gave the Sudetenland to Germany. Both Chamberlain and Daladier were showered with praise by the people of Britain and France for keeping the peace. Hitler regarded these Western leaders as "little worms."

Chamberlain's critics have insisted that the Munich agreement was an enormous blunder and tragedy. Chamberlain, they say, was a fool to believe that Hitler, who sought domination over Europe, could be bought off with the Sudetenland. Hitler regarded concessions by Britain and France as signs of weakness; they only increased his appetite for more territory. Furthermore, argue the critics, it would have been better to fight Hitler in 1938 than a year later, when war actually did break out. To be sure, in the year following the Munich agreement, Britain increased its military arsenal, but so did Germany, which built submarines, planes, and heavy tanks; strengthened western border defenses; and trained more pilots. The Czechs had a sizable number of good tanks, and the Czech people were willing to fight to preserve their nation's territorial integrity. While the main elements of the German army were battling the Czechs, the French, who could mobilize a hundred divisions, could have broken through the German West Wall, which was defended by only five regular and four reserve divisions; then they could have invaded the Rhineland and devastated German industrial centers in the Ruhr. (Such a scenario, of course, depended on the French overcoming their psychological reluctance to take the offensive, which was doubtful given the attitude of the French general staff.)

After the annexation of the Sudetenland, Hitler plotted to crush Czechoslovakia out of existence. He encouraged the Slovak minority in Czechoslovakia, led by a Fascist priest, Josef Tiso, to demand complete separation. On the pretext of protecting the Slovak people's right of self-determination, Hitler ordered his troops to enter Prague. In March 1939, Czech independence ended.

The destruction of Czechoslovakia was a different matter from the remilitarization of the Rhineland, the Anschluss with Austria, and the annexation of the Sudetenland. In all these previous cases, Hitler could claim the right of self-determination, Woodrow Wilson's grand principle. However, the occupation of Prague and the end of Czech independence showed that Hitler really sought European hegemony. Outraged statesmen now demanded that the führer be deterred from further aggression.

Poland After Czechoslovakia, Hitler turned to Poland and demanded, among other things, that Danzig be returned to Germany. Poland refused to restore the port, which was vital to its economy. On May 22, 1939, Hitler and Mussolini entered into the Pact of Steel, promising mutual aid in the event of war. The following day, Hitler told his officers that Germany's real goal was the destruction of Poland. "Danzig is not the objective. It is a matter of expanding our living space in the East, of making our food supplies secure. . . . There is therefore no question of sparing Poland, and the decision remains to attack Poland at the first suitable opportunity."[2]

Britain, France, and the Soviet Union had been engaged in negotiations since April. The Soviet Union wanted a mutual assistance pact, including joint military planning, and demanded bases in Poland and Romania in preparation for a German attack. Britain was reluctant to endorse these demands, fearing that a mutual assistance pact with Russia might cause Hitler to embark on a mad adventure that would drag Britain into war. Moreover, Poland would not allow Russian troops on its soil, fearing Russian expansion.

At the same time, Russia was conducting secret talks with Nazi Germany. Unlike the Allies, Germany could tempt Stalin with territory that would serve as a buffer between Germany and Russia. Besides, a treaty with Germany would give Russia time to strengthen its armed forces. On August 23, 1939, the two totalitarian states signed a nonaggression pact, stunning the world. A secret section of the pact called for the partition of Poland between Russia and Germany and Russian control over Lithuania, Latvia, and Estonia. By signing such an agreement with his enemy, Hitler had pulled off an extraordinary diplomatic coup: he blocked the Soviet Union, Britain, and France from duplicating their World War I alliance against Germany. The Nazi–Soviet Pact was the green light for an invasion of Poland, and at dawn on September 1, 1939, German troops crossed the frontier. When Germany did not respond to their demand for a halt to the invasion, Britain and France declared war.

THE NAZI BLITZKRIEG

The Conquest of Poland

Germany struck at Poland with speed and power. The German air force, the *Luftwaffe,* destroyed obsolete Polish planes, struck railways, hampering Polish mobilization; attacked tanks; pounded defense networks; and bombed Warsaw, terrorizing the population. Tanks opened up breaches in the Polish defenses, and mechanized columns overran the foot-marching Polish army, trapping large numbers of soldiers. The Polish high command could not cope with the incredible speed and coordination of German air and ground attacks. By September 8, the Germans had advanced to the outskirts of Warsaw. On September 17, Soviet troops invaded Poland from the east. On September 27, Poland surrendered. In less than a month, the Nazi *blitzkrieg* (lightning war) had vanquished Poland.

The Fall of France

For Hitler, the conquest of Poland was only the prelude to a German empire stretching from the Atlantic to the Urals. When weather conditions were right, he would unleash a great offensive in the west. In early April 1940, the Germans struck at Denmark and Norway. Denmark surrendered within hours. A British and French force tried to assist the Norwegians, but the landings, badly coordinated and lacking in air support, failed.

On May 10, 1940, Hitler launched his offensive in the west with an invasion of neutral Belgium, Holland, and Luxembourg. On May 14, after the Luftwaffe had bombed Rotterdam, destroying the center of the city and killing many people, the Dutch surrendered. Meeting almost no resistance, German panzer (tank) divisions had moved through the narrow mountain passes of Luxembourg and the dense forest of Ardennes in southern Belgium. Thinking that the forest of Ardennes could not be penetrated by a major German force, the French had only lightly fortified the western extension of the Maginot Line. But on May 12, German units were on French soil near Sedan. Then the Germans raced across northern France to the sea, which they reached on May 20, cutting the Anglo-French forces in two.

The Germans now sought to surround and annihilate the Allied forces converging on the French seaport of Dunkirk, the last port of escape. But probably fearing that German tanks would lose mobility in the rivers and canals around Dunkirk, Hitler called them off just as they prepared to take the port. Instead, he ordered the Luftwaffe to wipe out the Allied troops, but fog and rain prevented German planes from operating at full strength, and British pilots inflicted heavy losses on the attackers. While the Luftwaffe bombed the beaches, some 338,000 British and French troops were ferried across the English Channel by destroyers, merchant ships, motorboats, fishing boats, tugboats, and private yachts. Hitler's personal decision to hold back his tanks made "the miracle of Dunkirk" possible.

Meanwhile, the battle for France was turning into a rout. With authority breaking down, demoralization spreading, and resistance dying, the French cabinet appealed for an armistice. It was signed on June 22 in the same railway car in which Germany had agreed to the armistice ending World War I.

How can the collapse of France be explained? France had somewhat fewer pilots and planes, particularly bombers, than Germany, but many French planes never left the airfields. France had planes, but the High Command either did not use them—which is still a cause of astonishment—or did not deploy them properly. In contrast, the German air force was an integral part of an offensive operation, providing support for advancing tanks and infantry and bombing behind enemy lines. As for tanks, the French had as many as the Germans, and some were superior, but they were spread among the infantry divisions, unlike the Germans, who organized their tanks in large formations in order to drive through enemy lines. Nor was German manpower overwhelming. France met disaster largely because its military leaders, unlike the German command, had not mastered the psychology and technology of motorized warfare. Put succinctly, the French were badly outgeneraled. One senses also that there was a loss of will among the French people—the result of internal political disputes, poor leadership, the years of appeasement and lost opportunities, and German propaganda, which depicted Nazism as irresistible and the führer as a man of destiny. It was France's darkest hour.

According to the terms of the armistice, Germany occupied northern France and the coast. The French military was demobilized, and the French government, now located at Vichy in the south, would collaborate with the German authorities in occupied France, even to the point of passing racial laws and assisting the Germans in deporting 75,000 Jews, including 8,000 children under the age of thirteen, to the Nazi murder factory at Auschwitz. The leaders of Vichy and their supporters, many of them prominent intellectuals and anti-Dreyfusards in their youth, shared in the antidemocratic, anti-Marxist, and anti-Semitic tradition of the radical right that had arrayed itself against the Third French Republic since the late nineteenth century. Refusing to recognize defeat, General Charles de Gaulle (1890–1970) escaped to London and organized the Free French forces. The Germans gloried in their revenge; the French wept in their humiliation; and the British gathered their courage, for they now stood alone.

German Atrocities. The invading Germans treated the Russian people, whom they regarded as racial inferiors, in a savage manner. They deliberately starved to death Russian prisoners of war and engaged in atrocities against civilians. Here Russians are looking for relatives and friends among seven thousand Crimean villagers slaughtered by the Germans.

The Battle of Britain

Hitler expected that, after his stunning victories in the West, Britain would make peace. The British, however, continued to reject Hitler's peace overtures, for they envisioned only a bleak future if Hitler dominated the Continent. After the German victory in Norway, Chamberlain's support in the House of Commons had eroded, and he had been replaced by Winston Churchill, who had opposed appeasement. Dynamic, courageous, and eloquent, Churchill had the capacity to stir and lead his people in the struggle against Nazism. "The Battle of Britain is about to begin," Churchill told them. "Upon this battle depends the survival of Christian civilization. . . . [I]f we fail, then . . . all we have known and cared for will sink into the abyss of a new Dark Age."[3]

Finding Britain unwilling to come to terms, Hitler proceeded in earnest with invasion plans. But a successful crossing of the English Channel and the establishment of beachheads on the English coast depended on control of the skies. Marshal Hermann Goering assured Hitler that his Luftwaffe could destroy the British Royal Air Force (RAF), and in early August 1940, the Luftwaffe began massive attacks on British air and naval installations. Virtually every day during the battle of Britain, weather permitting, hundreds of planes fought in the sky above Britain. Convinced that Goering could not fulfill his promise to destroy British air defenses and unwilling to absorb more losses in planes and trained pilots, Hitler called off the invasion. The development of radar by British scientists, the skill and courage of British fighter pilots, and the unwillingness of Germany to absorb more losses in planes and pilots saved Britain in its struggle for survival. With the invasion of Britain called off, the Luftwaffe concentrated on bombing English cities, industrial centers, and ports in the hopes of eroding Britain's military potential and undermining civilian morale. Every night for months, the inhabitants of London sought shelter in subways and cellars to escape

Stalingrad, February 1943. In this photograph, the Russians are rescuing the bombed-out city of Stalingrad from the Nazi invaders.

German bombs, while British planes rose time after time to make the Luftwaffe pay the price. British morale never broke during the "Blitz."

Britain, by itself, had no hope of defeating the Third Reich. What ultimately changed the course of the war were Germany's invasion of the Soviet Union in June 1941 and Japan's attack on the United States on December 7, 1941. With the entry of these two powers, a coalition was created that had the human and material resources to reverse the tide of battle.

The Invasion of Russia

The obliteration of Bolshevism and the conquest, exploitation, and colonization of Russia by the German master race were cardinal elements of Hitler's ideology. To prevent any interference with the forthcoming invasion of Russia, the Balkan flank had to be secured. On April 6, 1941, the Germans struck at both Greece, where an Italian attack had failed, and Yugoslavia. Yugoslavia was quickly overrun, and Greece, although aided by fifty thousand British, New Zealander, and Australian troops, fell at the end of April.

For the war against Russia, Hitler had assembled a massive force: some four million men, 3,300 tanks, and 2,000 planes. Evidence of the German buildup abounded, but a stubborn Stalin ignored these warnings. Desperate to avoid war with Nazi Germany, Stalin would take no action that he feared might provoke Hitler. Consequently, the Red Army was vulnerable to the German blitzkrieg. In the early hours of June 22, 1941, the Germans launched their offensive over a wide front. Raiding Russian airfields, the Luftwaffe destroyed 1,200 aircraft on the first day. The Germans drove deeply into Russia, cutting up and surrounding the disorganized and unprepared Russian forces. The Russians suffered horrendous losses. In a little more than three months, 2.5 million Russian soldiers had been killed, wounded, or captured and 14,000 tanks destroyed. Describing the war as a crusade to save Europe from "Jewish Bolshevik subhumans," German propaganda claimed that victory was assured.

But there were also disquieting signs for the Nazi invaders. The Russians, who had a proven capacity to endure hardships, fought doggedly and courageously for the motherland, and the government would not consider capitulation.

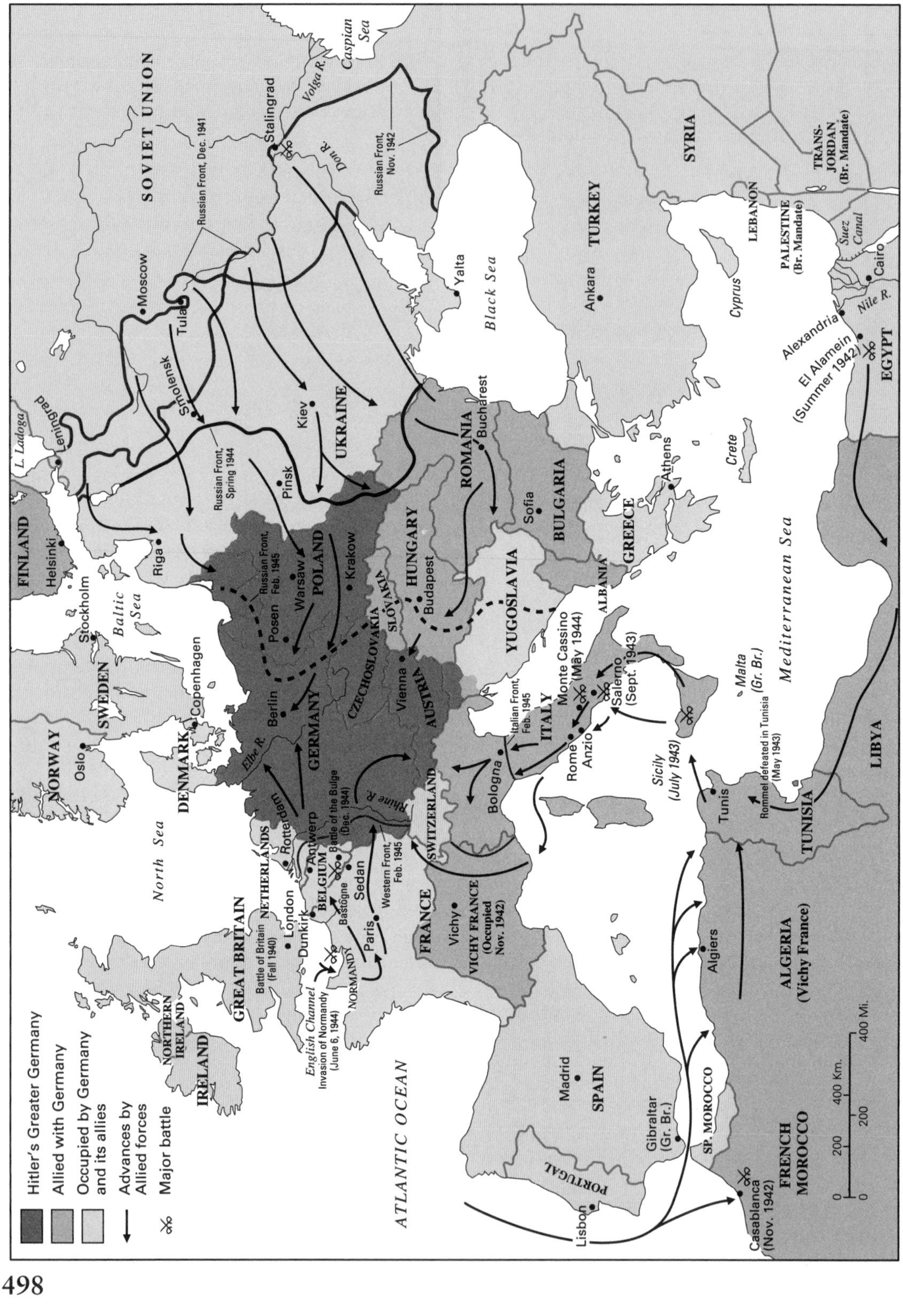
Hitler's Greater Germany
Allied with Germany
Occupied by Germany and its allies
Advances by Allied forces
Major battle
SOVIET UNION
Moscow
Leningrad
L. Ladoga
Tula
Smolensk
Kiev
UKRAINE
Pinsk
Stalingrad
Volga R.
Don R.
Caspian Sea
Russian Front, Dec. 1941
Russian Front, Nov. 1942
Russian Front, Spring 1944
Russian Front, Feb. 1945
Yalta
Black Sea
TURKEY
Ankara
SYRIA
LEBANON
PALESTINE (Br. Mandate)
TRANS-JORDAN (Br. Mandate)
Suez Canal
Cairo
Nile R.
Alexandria
El Alamein (Summer 1942)
EGYPT
Cyprus
Crete
Athens
GREECE
BULGARIA
Sofia
ROMANIA
Bucharest
YUGOSLAVIA
ALBANIA
HUNGARY
Budapest
SLOVAKIA
CZECHOSLOVAKIA
AUSTRIA
Vienna
POLAND
Warsaw
Krakow
Posen
Riga
FINLAND
Helsinki
Stockholm
Baltic Sea
SWEDEN
NORWAY
Oslo
DENMARK
Copenhagen
GERMANY
Berlin
Elbe R.
Rhine R.
NETHERLANDS
Rotterdam
Antwerp
BELGIUM
Battle of the Bulge (Dec. 1944)
Bastogne
Sedan
Western Front, Feb. 1945
SWITZERLAND
North Sea
GREAT BRITAIN
London
Dunkirk
Battle of Britain (Fall 1940)
NORTHERN IRELAND
IRELAND
English Channel
Invasion of Normandy (June 6, 1944)
NORMANDY
Paris
FRANCE
Vichy
VICHY FRANCE (Occupied Nov. 1942)
ITALY
Italian Front, Feb. 1945
Bologna
Rome
Anzio
Monte Cassino (May 1944)
Salerno (Sept. 1943)
Sicily (July 1943)
Malta (Gr. Br.)
Mediterranean Sea
Tunis
Rommel defeated in Tunisia (May 1943)
TUNISIA
LIBYA
ALGERIA (Vichy France)
Algiers
FRENCH MOROCCO
Casablanca (Nov. 1942)
SP. MOROCCO
Gibraltar (Gr. Br.)
SPAIN
Madrid
PORTUGAL
Lisbon
ATLANTIC OCEAN
0 200 400 Km.
0 200 400 Mi.

Russian reserve strength was far greater than the Germans had estimated. Far from its supply lines, the Wehrmacht (German army) was running short of fuel, and trucks and cars had to contend with primitive roads that turned into seas of mud when the autumn rains came. Compounding the supply problem were attacks behind German lines by Russian partisans determined to inflict pain on the hated invaders. Early and bitter cold weather hampered the German attempt to capture Moscow. The Germans advanced to within twenty miles of Moscow, but on December 6, a Red Army counterattack forced them to postpone the assault on the Russian capital.

By the end of 1941, Germany had conquered vast regions of Russia but had failed to bring the country to its knees. There would be no repetition of the collapse of France. Moreover, by moving machinery and workers east far beyond the German reach, the Soviets were able to replenish their military hardware, which was almost totally destroyed during the first six months of the war. Driven by patriotic fervor—and by fear of the omnipresent NKVD agents searching for malingerers—Russian factory workers toiled relentlessly, heroically. Soon many of them, the wives and daughters of soldiers at the front, were producing more planes and tanks than Germany. The Russian campaign demonstrated that the Russian people would make incredible sacrifices for their land and that the Nazis were not invincible.

The New Order

By 1942, Germany ruled virtually all of Europe, from the Atlantic to deep into Russia. Some conquered territory was annexed outright; other lands were administered by German officials; in still other countries, the Germans ruled through local officials sympathetic to Nazism or willing to collaborate with the Germans. On this vast empire, Hitler and his henchmen imposed a new order designed to serve the interests of the master race.

◀ *Map 20.1* **World War II: The European Theater** By 1942, Germany ruled virtually all of Europe from the Atlantic to deep into Russia. Germany's defeat at Stalingrad in Russia and El Alamein in North Africa were decisive turning points.

Exploitation and Terror

The Germans systematically looted the countries they conquered, taking gold, art treasures, machinery, and food supplies back to Germany and exploiting the industrial and agricultural potential of non-German lands to aid the German war economy. The Nazis also made slave laborers of conquered peoples. Some seven million people from all over Europe were wrested from their homes and transported to Germany. These forced laborers, particularly the Russians and Poles, whom Nazi ideology classified as a lower form of humanity, lived in wretched, unheated barracks and were poorly fed and overworked; many died of disease, hunger, and exhaustion. Many of Germany's most prominent firms collaborated in the enslavement and brutalization of foreign workers. The ransacking of occupied lands, the seizure of Jewish property throughout Europe, and the exploitation of foreign forced labor kept Germans largely prosperous and content until the last year of the war.

The Nazis ruled by force and terror. The prison cell, the torture chamber, the firing squad, and the concentration camp symbolized the new order. In the Polish province annexed to Germany, the Nazis jailed and executed intellectuals and priests, closed all schools and most churches, and forbade Poles to hold professional positions. In the region of Poland administered by German officials, most schools above the fourth grade were shut down. The Germans were especially ruthless toward the Russians. Soviet political officials were immediately executed; many prisoners of war were herded into camps and deliberately starved to death. In all, the Germans took some 5.5 million Russian prisoners, of whom about 3.5 million perished, primarily from starvation.

German soldiers routinely abused innocents: they stripped Russian peasants of their winter clothing and boots before driving them into the freezing outdoors to die of cold and starvation, slaughtered large numbers of hostages, burned whole villages to the ground in reprisal for partisan attacks, and deported massive numbers of people for slave labor. To the German invaders drenched in Nazi ideology, the Russians were "Asiatic bestial hordes" led by sinister "subhuman" Jews who aimed to destroy Germany. Recent studies, largely by German historians, demonstrate how committed the Wehrmacht command—and not just the SS who committed genocide and other atrocities—was to Nazi ideological aims, how willingly senior and junior officers propagated Nazi ideology among the troops. Letters and diaries reveal how ideologically devoted average soldiers were to Nazism. Both the high command and common soldiers were implicated in war crimes, including the extermination of the Jews.

The Holocaust

Against the Jews of Europe, the Germans waged a war of extermination. The task of imposing the "Final Solution of the Jewish Problem" was given to Himmler's SS. Himmler fulfilled his grisly duties with fanaticism and bureaucratic efficiency. He and the SS believed that they had a holy mission to rid the world of worthless life—a satanic foe that was plotting to destroy Germany. Regarding themselves as righteous and courageous idealists who were writing a glorious chapter in the history of Germany, the SS tortured and murdered with immense dedication.

Special squads of the SS—the *Einsatzgruppen*, trained for mass murder—followed on the heels of the German army into Russia. Entering captured villages and cities, they rounded up Jewish men, women, and children, herded them to execution grounds, and slaughtered them with machine-gun and rifle fire at the edge of open trenches, which sometimes were piled high with thousands of victims, including severely wounded people who would suffocate to death when the pit was filled with earth. Aided by Ukrainian, Lithuanian, and Latvian auxiliaries, the Einsatzgruppen massacred some 1.3 million Russian Jews—the commanders kept meticulous records of each *Aktion*. Not just the SS, but units of the regular German army, the Wehrmacht, actively participated in the rounding up of Jews and sometimes in the shootings. Despite the denials of staff officers after the war, evidence from their own files reveals that they knew full well that the extermination of the Jews was state policy that their soldiers were helping to implement. To speed up the Final Solution, extermination camps were built in Poland. Jews from all over Europe were rounded up, jammed into sealed cattle cars, and shipped to Treblinka, Auschwitz, and other death camps, where they entered another world:

> *Corpses were strewn all over the road; bodies were hanging from the barbed wire fence; the sound of shots rang in the air continuously. Blazing flames shot into the sky; a giant smoke cloud ascended about them. Starving, emaciated human skeletons stumbled forward toward us, uttering incoherent sounds. They fell down right in front of our eyes gasping out their last breath.*
>
> *Here and there a hand tried to reach up, but when this happened an SS man came right away and stepped on it. Those who were merely exhausted were simply thrown on the dead pile. . . . Every night a truck came by, and all of them, dead or not, were thrown on it and taken to the crematory.*[4]

SS doctors quickly inspected the new arrivals—"the freight," as they referred to them. Those unfit for work, including children, were immediately exterminated in gas chambers. Those not gassed faced a living death in the camp, which also included non-Jewish inmates. The SS relished their absolute power over the inmates and took sadistic pleasure in humiliating and brutalizing their Jewish victims. When exhausted, starved, diseased, and beaten prisoners became unfit for work, generally within a few months, they were sent to the gas chambers.

Many of the SS were true believers, committed to racist and Social Darwinist fantasies. To realize their mythic vision of ultimate good, they had to destroy the Jews, whom Nazi ideology designated as less-than-human but also immensely evil, powerful, and dangerous enemies of Germany and Aryan civilization. For these racist ideologues, Jews were unworthy of life. A Jewish physician-inmate at Auschwitz asked one of the Nazi doctors who selected Jews for the gas chamber how he could reconcile extermination with the Hippocratic oath he took to preserve life. The Nazi replied:

> *Of course I am a doctor and I want to preserve life. And out of respect for human life I would remove a gangrenous appendix from a diseased body. The Jew is the gangrenous appendix in the body of mankind.*[5]

Assisting the SS was an army of bureaucrats, transportation employees, town officials, local police, and other involved in rounding up and deporting Jews to the death camps. Many Germans and their collaborators in occupied lands were ordinary people doing their duty as they had been trained to do, following orders the best way they knew how. They were morally indifferent bureaucrats, concerned with techniques and effectiveness, and careerists and functionaries seeking to impress superiors with their ability to get the job done. These people quickly adjusted to the routine of mass murder. Thus, as Konnilyn G. Feig notes, thousands of German railway workers "treated the Jewish cattle-car transports as a special business problem that they took pride in solving so well."[6] German physicians who selected Jews for the gas chambers were concerned only with technical problems and efficiency, and those doctors who performed unspeakable medical experiments on Jews viewed their subjects as laboratory animals. German industrialists who worked Jewish slave laborers to death considered only cost-effectiveness in their operations. So, too, did the firms that built the gas chambers and the furnaces, whose durability and performance they guaranteed.

An eyewitness reports that engineers from Topf and Sons experimented with different combinations of corpses, deciding that "the most economical and fuel-saving procedure would be to burn the bodies of a well-nourished man and an emaciated woman or vice versa together with that of a child, because, as the experiments had established, in this combination, once they had caught fire, the dead would continue to burn without any further coke being required."[7] Rudolf Hoess, the commandant of Auschwitz, who exemplified the bureaucratic mentality, noted that his gas chambers were more efficient than those used at Treblinka because they could accommodate far more people. The Germans were so concerned with efficiency and cost that—to conserve ammunition or gas and not slow down the pace from the time victims were ordered to undress until they were hurried into the gas chambers—toddlers were taken from their mothers and thrown live into burning pits or mass graves.

When the war ended, the SS murderers and those who had assisted them returned to families and jobs, resuming a normal life, free of remorse and untroubled by guilt. "The human ability to normalize the abnormal is frightening indeed," observes sociologist Rainer C. Baum.[8] Mass murderers need not be psychopaths. It is a "disturbing psychological truth," states Robert Jay Lifton, that "ordinary people can commit demonic acts."[9]

There have been many massacres during the course of world history. And the Nazis murdered many non-Jews in concentration camps and in reprisal for acts of resistance. What is unique about the Holocaust—the systematic extermination of European Jewry—was the Nazis' determination to murder, without exception, every single Jew who came within their grasp, and the fanaticism, ingenuity, cruelty, and systematic way (industrialized murder) with which they pursued this goal. Despite the protests of the army, the SS murdered Jews whose labor was needed for the war effort, and when Germany's military position was desperate, the SS still diverted military personnel and railway cars to deport Jews to the death camps.

The Holocaust was the grisly fulfillment of Nazi racial theories. Believing that they were cleansing Europe of a lower and dangerous race that threatened the German people, Nazi executioners performed their evil work with dedication and resourcefulness, with precision and moral indifference—a gruesome testament to human irrationality and wickedness. Using the technology and bureaucracy of a modern state, the Germans killed approximately six million Jews—*two-thirds* of the Jewish population of Europe. Some 1.5 million of the murdered were children; almost 90 percent of Jewish children in German-occupied lands perished. Tens of thousands of entire families were wiped out without a trace. Centuries-old Jewish community life vanished, never to be restored. Burned into the soul of the Jewish people was a wound that could never entirely heal. For generations to come Germans would be compelled to reflect on this most shameful period in their history.

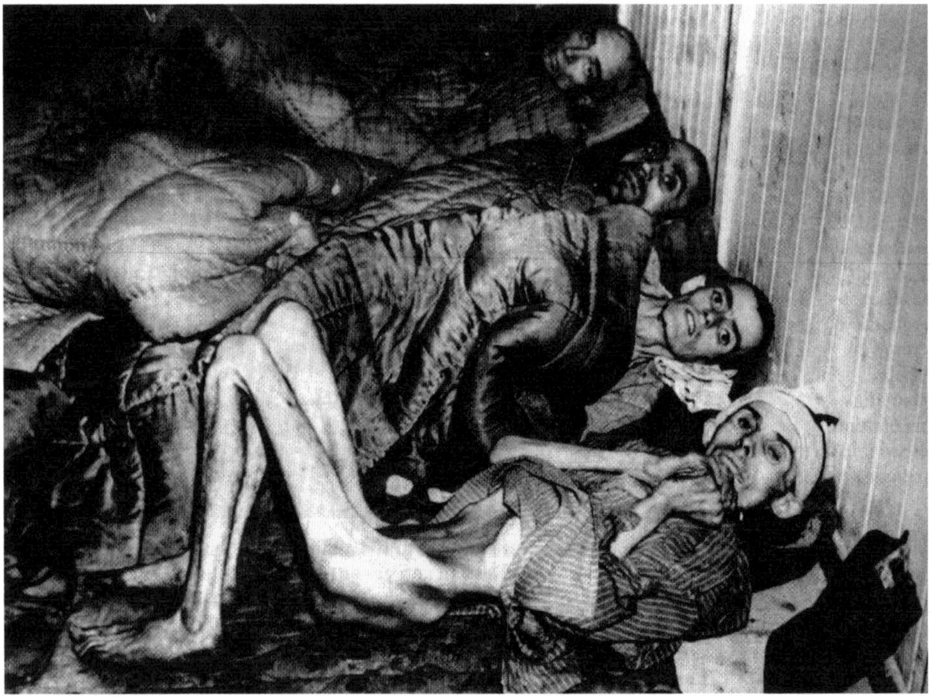

CONCENTRATION CAMP SURVIVORS. Thousands of emaciated and diseased inmates of German concentration camps died in the weeks after liberation by the Allies. These camps will forever remain a monument to the capacity of human beings for inhumanity.

Written into the history of Western civilization was an episode that would forever cast doubt on the Enlightenment conception of human goodness, rationality, and the progress of civilization.

Resistance

Each occupied country had its collaborators, including government officials, business elites, and right-wing intellectuals, who welcomed the demise of democracy, saw Hitler as Europe's best defense against Communism, and profited from the sale of war materiel. Each country also produced a resistance movement that grew stronger as Nazi barbarism became more visible and the prospects of a German defeat more likely. The Nazis retaliated by torturing and executing captured resistance fighters and killing hostages—generally fifty for every German killed.

In Western Europe, the resistance rescued downed Allied airmen, radioed military intelligence to Britain, and sabotaged German installations. Norwegians blew up the German stock of heavy water needed for atomic research. The Danish underground sabotaged railways and smuggled into neutral Sweden almost all of Denmark's eight thousand Jews just before they were to be deported to the death camps. After the Allies landed on the coast of France in June 1944, the French resistance delayed the movement of German reinforcements and liberated sections of the country.

In Eastern Europe, resistance took the form of guerrilla warfare and sabotage. In August 1944, with Soviet forces approaching Warsaw, the Poles staged a full-scale revolt against the German occupiers. The Poles appealed to the Soviets, camped ten miles away, for help. Thinking about a future Russian-dominated Poland, the Soviets did not move. After sixty-three days of street fighting and the massacre of Polish hostages, remnants of the Polish underground surrendered, and the Germans methodically destroyed what was left of Warsaw. In the Soviet Union, Russian partisans numbered several hundred thousand men and women. Operating behind the German lines, they sabotaged railways, destroyed trucks, and killed thousands of German soldiers in hit-and-run attacks. In Yugoslavia, the mountains and forests provided excellent terrain for guerrilla warfare. The leading Yugoslav resistance army was headed by Josip Broz (1892–1980), better known as Tito. Moscow-trained, intelligent, and courageous, Tito organized his partisans into a disciplined fighting force that tied down a huge German army and ultimately liberated the country from German rule. Jews participated in the resistance in all countries and were particularly prominent in the French resistance. Specifically Jewish resistance organizations emerged in Eastern Europe, and revolts took place in the ghettos and concentration camps. In the spring of 1943, the surviving Jews of the Warsaw ghetto, armed with only a few guns and homemade bombs, fought the Germans for several weeks.

Italy and Germany also had resistance movements. After the Allies landed in Italy in 1943, bands of Italian partisans helped to liberate Italy from Fascism and the German occupation. In Germany, army officers plotted to assassinate the führer. On July 20, 1944, Colonel Claus von Stauffenberg planted a bomb at a staff conference attended by Hitler, but the führer escaped serious injury. In retaliation, some five thousand suspected anti-Nazis were imprisoned, two hundred of whom were immediately tortured and executed in barbarous fashion. More would be executed in succeeding months.

The Turn of the Tide

While Germany was subduing Europe, its ally, Japan, was extending its dominion over much of Asia. Seeking raw materials and secure markets for Japanese goods and driven by a xenophobic nationalism, Japan in 1931 had attacked Manchuria in northern China. Quickly overrunning the province, the Japanese established the puppet state of Manchukuo in 1932. After a period of truce, the war against China was renewed in July 1937. Japan captured leading cities, including China's principal seaports, and inflicted heavy casualties on the poorly organized Chinese forces, obliging the government of Jiang Jieshi (Chiang Kai-shek) to withdraw to Chungking in the interior.

The Japanese Offensive

In 1940, after the defeat of France and with Britain standing alone against Nazi Germany, Japan eyed Southeast Asia—French Indochina, British Burma and Malaya, and the Dutch East Indies. From these lands, Japan planned to obtain the oil, rubber, and tin vitally needed by Japanese industry and enough rice to feed the nation. Japan hoped that a quick strike against the American fleet in the Pacific would give it time to enlarge and consolidate its empire. On December 7, 1941, the Japanese struck with carrier-based planes at Pearl Harbor in Hawaii. Taken by surprise—despite warning signs—the Americans suffered a total defeat: the attackers sank 17 ships, including 7 of the 8 battleships; destroyed 188 airplanes and damaged 159 others; and killed 2,403 men. The Japanese lost only 29 planes. After the attack on Pearl Harbor, Germany declared war on the United States. Now the immense American industrial capacity could be put to work against the Axis powers—Germany, Italy, and Japan. American factories produced planes, tanks, and ships at a pace and scale that astonished both friend and foe. The American arsenal supplied Britain and the Soviet Union with badly needed equipment.

Defeat of the Axis Powers

By the spring of 1942, the Axis powers held the upper hand. The Japanese empire included the coast of China, Indochina (Vietnam), Thailand, Burma, Malaya, the Dutch East Indies (Indonesia), the Philippines, and other islands in the Pacific. Germany controlled Europe almost to Moscow. When the year ended, however, the Allies seemed assured of victory. Three decisive battles—Midway, Stalingrad, and El Alamein—reversed the tide of war.

Japanese Empire, 1931
Japanese Empire, 1942
Extent of Japanese expansion
Allied advances
SOVIET UNION
ASIA
MONGOLIA
MANCHURIA
Peiping (Peking)
KOREA
JAPAN
Tokyo
Hiroshima
Nagasaki
CHINA
Shanghai
Taiwan
Okinawa 1945
Iwo Jima 1945
BURMA
Hong Kong
THAILAND
FRENCH INDOCHINA
Manila
Philippine Is.
Leyte 1944
Guam 1944
Saipan
Mariana Is.
MALAYA
Singapore
Borneo
Sumatra
Dutch East Indies
Java
New Guinea
Caroline Is.
Wake
Marshall Is.
Tawara 1943
Gilbert Is.
Solomon Is.
Guadalcanal 1942
PACIFIC OCEAN
Midway 1942
Hawaiian Is.
Pearl Harbor
Attu
Kiska 1943
Aleutian Is.
INDIAN OCEAN
AUSTRALIA
Brisbane
0 500 1000 Km.
0 500 1000 Mi.

In June 1942, the main body of the Japanese fleet headed for Midway, eleven hundred miles northwest of Pearl Harbor; another section sailed toward the Aleutian Islands, in an attempt to divide the American fleet. But the Americans had broken the Japanese naval code and were aware of the Japanese plan. On June 4, 1942, the two navies fought a strange naval battle; it was waged entirely by carrier-based planes, for the fleets were too far from each other to use their big guns. American pilots destroyed four Japanese aircraft carriers stacked with planes. The battle of Midway cost Japan the initiative. With American industrial production accelerating, the opportunity for a Japanese victory had passed.

After being stymied at the outskirts of Moscow in December 1941, the Germans renewed their offensive in the spring and summer of 1942. Hitler's goal was Stalingrad, the great industrial center located on the Volga River; control of Stalingrad would give Germany command of vital rail transportation and access to the oil fields of the Caucasus. The battle of Stalingrad was an epic struggle in which Russian soldiers and civilians fought for every building and street of their city. In this urban battlefield, scarred by mile after mile of destroyed buildings and mountains of rubble, the combatants were separated by mere yards; snipers, some of them Russian women, lurked in the maze of ruins; and tough Russian soldiers stealthily and ceaselessly attacked at night with bayonets and daggers; here the blitzkrieg, which had brought the Germans immense success in their earlier offensives, did not apply. So brutal was the fighting that at night half-crazed dogs sought to escape the city by swimming across the river. One German soldier wrote in his diary at the end of December: "The horses have already been eaten . . . the soldiers look like corpses or lunatics looking for something to put in their mouths. They no longer take cover from Russian shells; they haven't the strength to walk, run away and hide."[10]

◀ *Map 20.2* **World War II: The Pacific Theater** The battle of Midway was a major turning point in the Pacific theater. The map also shows the island-hopping of the Americans that brought them closer to Japan. The battles of Iwo Jima and Okinawa were particularly brutal.

A Russian counterattack in November, planned by General (later Marshal) Georgi Zhukov, caught the Germans in a trap. With his soldiers exhausted and desperately short of food, medical supplies, weapons, and ammunition, Friedrich Paulus, commander of the Sixth Army, urged Hitler to order a withdrawal before the Russians closed the ring. The führer refused. After suffering tens of thousands of additional casualties, their position hopeless, the remnants of the Sixth Army surrendered on February 2, 1943. Some 260,000 German soldiers had perished in the battle of Stalingrad, and another 110,000 were taken prisoner.

The Soviet High Command, which had performed terribly in the early days of the German offensive, distinguished itself at Stalingrad. At the battle of Kursk in July 1943, Russian military leaders again demonstrated an increasing ability to master the technique of modern warfare. Analyzing correctly that the Germans would attack the Kursk salient, Marshal Georgi Zhukov turned the area into a fortress. Although Soviet casualties were greater than the Germans, the Red Army had beaten back the best combat units of the Wehrmacht, inflicting heavy losses of men and materiel in the process. The operation, which included an epic tank battle, had depleted the German military of almost all its reserves on the Eastern Front. The momentum had turned. The Wehrmacht and its panzer armies were now on the defensive. The initiative had passed to the Red Army.

In January 1941, the British were routing the Italians in northern Africa. Hitler assigned General Erwin Rommel (1891–1944) to halt the British advance. Rommel drove the British out of Libya and, with strong reinforcements, might have taken Egypt and the Suez Canal. But Hitler's concern was with seizing Yugoslavia and Greece and preparing for the invasion of Russia. Early in 1942, Rommel resumed his advance, intending to conquer Egypt. The British Eighth Army, commanded by General Bernard L. Montgomery, stopped him at the battle of El Alamein in October 1942. The victory of El Alamein was followed by an Anglo-American invasion of northwest Africa in November 1942. By May 1943, the Germans and Italians were defeated in northern Africa.

After securing northern Africa, the Allies, seeking complete control of the Mediterranean, invaded Sicily in July 1943 and quickly conquered

Primary Source

Historical Division, War Department: *Omaha Beachhead*

Ultimately the success of the Allied invasion of France, D-day, depended on what happened during the first few hours. If the Allies had failed to secure beachheads, the operation would have ended in disaster. As the following reading illustrates, some of the hardest fighting took place on Omaha Beach, which was attacked by the Americans. This extract, published in 1945, comes from a study prepared in the field by the Second Information and Historical Service attached to the First Army and by the Historical Section, European Theater of Operations.

The outstanding fact about these first two hours of action is that despite heavy casualties, loss of equipment, disorganization, and all the other discouraging features of the landings, the assault troops did not stay pinned down behind the sea wall and embankment. At half-a-dozen or more points on the long stretch, they found the necessary drive to leave their cover and move out over the open beach flat toward the bluffs. Prevented by circumstance of mislandings from using carefully rehearsed tactics, they improvised assault methods to deal with what defenses they found before them. In nearly every case where advance was attempted, it carried through the enemy beach defenses. . . .

Various factors, some of them difficult to evaluate, played a part in the success of these advances. . . . But the decisive factor was leadership. Wherever an advance was made, it depended on the presence of some few individuals, officers and noncommissioned officers, who inspired, encouraged, or bullied their men forward, often by making the first forward moves. On Easy Red a lieutenant and a wounded sergeant of divisional engineers stood up under fire and walked over to inspect the wire obstacles just beyond the embankment. The lieutenant came back and, hands on hips, looked down disgustedly at the men lying behind the shingle bank. "Are you going to lay there and get killed, or get up and do something about it?" Nobody stirred, so the sergeant and the officer got the materials and blew the wire. On the same sector, where a group advancing across the flat was held up by a marshy area suspected of being mined, it was a lieutenant of engineers who crawled ahead through the mud on his belly, probing for mines with a hunting knife in the absence of other equipment. When remnants of an isolated boat section of Company B, 116th Infantry, were stopped by fire from a well-concealed emplacement, the lieutenant in charge went after it single-handed. In trying to grenade the rifle pit he was hit by three rifle bullets and eight grenade fragments, including some from his own grenade. He turned his map and compass over to a sergeant and ordered his group to press on inland. . . .

. . . Col. George A. Taylor arrived in the second section at 0815 and found plenty to do on the beach. Men were still hugging the embankment, disorganized, and suffering casualties from mortar and artillery fire. Colonel Taylor summed up the situation in terse phrase: "Two kinds of people are staying on this beach, the dead and those who are going to die—now let's get the hell out of here." Small groups of men were collected without regard to units, put under charge of the nearest noncommissioned officer, and sent on through the wire and across the flat, while engineers worked hard to widen gaps in the wire and to mark lanes through the minefields.

Question for Analysis

1. What drove the almost paralyzed American soldiers to move across the open beaches and attack German positions?

Omaha Beachhead, prepared by the Historical Division, War Department (Washington D.C.: U.S. Government Printing Office, 1945), 58–59, 71.

the island. Mussolini's fellow Fascist leaders turned against him, and the king dismissed him as prime minister. In September, the new government surrendered to the Allies, and in the following month, Italy declared war on Germany. Italian partisans—their number would grow to three hundred thousand—resisted the occupying German troops, who were determined to hold on to central and northern Italy. At the same time, the Allies fought their way up the peninsula. Captured by partisans, Mussolini was executed on April 28, 1945, and his dead body, hanging upside down, was publicly displayed.

On June 6, 1944, D-day, the Allies landed on the beaches of Normandy in France. They had assembled a massive force for the liberation of Europe: two million men and over seven thousand vessels. The success of D-day depended on securing the beaches, which the Allies did despite stubborn German resistance. On some beaches the soldiers struggled ashore in the face of intense enemy fire. At Omaha Beach, the Americans almost did not make it. Landing craft packed with soldiers were destroyed by German mines. Weighed down by heavy equipment, men drowned as they were tossed by high waves; others were killed or wounded by machine-gun fire before reaching the beach. Much of the heavy armor was lost. Those who stumbled ashore hugged the embankment and sheltered themselves behind whatever barrier they could find to escape the German guns firing from the cliffs. Traumatized by ferocious German fire and the wounded and dead surrounding them, and often leaderless, the soldiers, many of them facing combat for the first time, seemed paralyzed. But amid the chaos, men began to advance and overwhelm the German positions.

By the end of July, the Allies had built up their strength in France to a million men, and after much hard fighting, by the end of August drove the Germans out of most of France.

After their heady victories in France, Allied commanders thought that Germany was virtually finished, that the war would be over before the end of the year. But Germany mobilized its remaining manpower and regrouped divisions that had been shattered in France. And through a herculean effort, the German armaments industry continued to function at a high level, despite massive Allied bombardments. In the autumn, the Allied advance was halted as the revamped German forces inflicted heavy casualties on the Allies in southern Holland, the German border city of Aachen, and the Huertgen Forest on the border of Belgium and Germany. Nevertheless, as winter approached the situation looked hopeless for Germany. Brussels and the vital port of Antwerp fell to the Allies; Allied planes mass bombed German cites in terror raids that took a horrendous toll of life, creating a morale problem. Although German civilians continued to perform their duties in the workplace, many had lost hope in a German victory and only wanted the war to end. By destroying fuel depots and the transportation network, the air bombardments helped erode Germany's industrial potential.

Desperate, Hitler made one last gamble. In mid-December 1944, he launched an offensive to split the Allied forces and regain the vital port of Antwerp. The Allies were taken by surprise in the Battle of the Bulge, but a heroic defense by the Americans at Bastogne—an important road junction—helped stop the German offensive. German losses in Hitler's failed gamble proved insurmountable. With its reserve strength now depleted beyond restitution and its industrial capacity eroded by Allied bombings, Germany lacked the manpower, tanks, planes, and fuel to forestall an Allied assault into its heartland from the west or to turn back the Red Army.

In June 1944, the Russians launched a major offensive advancing into the Baltic states, Poland, and Hungary. By February 1945, they stood within one hundred miles of Berlin. Yet German soldiers continued to fight with remarkable skill, inflicting proportionately greater casualties than they suffered. They were driven by a fanatic devotion to Hitler and Nazi racial ideology, loyalty to their comrades and the endangered fatherland, and fear of both vengeful Russians and the SS and other special units charged with executing "defeatists."

By April 1945, British, American, and Russian troops were penetrating deeper into Germany from east and west. From his underground bunker near the chancellery in Berlin, Hitler, physically exhausted and emotionally unhinged, engaged in wild fantasies about new German victories. On April 30, 1945, with the Russians only blocks away, the führer took his own life.

Hiroshima After the Atomic Bomb. The mass destruction of Hiroshima ushered in a new age. Nuclear weapons gave humanity the capacity to destroy civilization.

On May 7, 1945, a demoralized and devastated Germany surrendered unconditionally.

In the Pacific war, after the victory at Midway in June 1942, American forces attacked strategic islands held by Japan. American troops had to battle their way up beaches and through jungles tenaciously defended by Japanese soldiers, who believed that death was preferable to the disgrace of surrender. In March 1945, twenty-one thousand Japanese perished on Iwo Jima; another hundred thousand died on Okinawa in April 1945 as they contested for every inch of the island.

On August 6, 1945, the United States dropped an atomic bomb on Hiroshima, killing more than seventy-eight thousand people and demolishing 60 percent of the city. President Harry S Truman said that he ordered the atomic attack to avoid an American invasion of the Japanese homeland, which would have cost hundreds of thousands of lives. Truman's decision has aroused considerable debate. Some analysts maintain that dropping the bomb was unnecessary. They say that Japan, deprived of oil, rice, and other essentials by an American naval blockade and defenseless against unrelenting aerial bombardments, was close to surrender and had indicated as much. It has been suggested that because the Soviet Union was about to enter the conflict against Japan, Truman wanted to end the war immediately, thus depriving the U.S.S.R. of an opportunity to extend its influence in East Asia. On August 8, Russia did enter the war against Japan, invading Manchuria. After a second atomic bomb was dropped on Nagasaki on August 9, the Japanese asked for peace.

The Legacy of World War II

World War II was the most destructive war in history. The total war waged by the combatants also enveloped civilians, who were victims of reprisals, genocide, slave labor, and aerial bombardment of cities. Estimates of the number of dead range as high as fifty million, including some twenty-five million Russians (one in three Russians lost a father) who sacrificed more than the other participants in both population and material resources.

(In comparison the United States suffered 400,000 battle deaths.) The war produced a vast migration of peoples unparalleled in modern European history. The Soviet Union annexed the Baltic lands of Latvia, Lithuania, and Estonia, forcibly deporting many of the native inhabitants into central Russia. The bulk of East Prussia was taken over by Poland, and Russia annexed the northeastern portion. Millions of Germans fled the invading Russians, who, bent on revenge for the misery the Nazis had inflicted on their kin and country, committed numerous atrocities, including indiscriminate killing and mass rape, before Soviet authorities ended the mayhem. Millions more Germans were driven out of Poland, Czechoslovakia, Yugoslavia, Romania, and Hungary—places where their ancestors had lived for centuries—by vengeful Eastern Europeans. Moreover, leaders in these countries, driven by nationalist aspirations, welcomed an opportunity to rid their nations of an ethnic minority, particularly since so many of these Germans had aided the Nazi occupiers. In 1945 and 1946, some twelve million to thirteen million Germans were driven westward. Expelled from their homes, often with only a few minutes' warning, they had to leave almost everything behind. Those herded into internment camps were brutalized by Polish and Czech guards who relished the opportunity to torment Germans. Tens of thousands died from malnutrition, disease, exposure, and mistreatment; thousands more committed suicide.

Material costs were staggering. Everywhere cities were in rubble; bridges, railway systems, waterways, and harbors destroyed; farmlands laid waste; livestock killed; coal mines wrecked. Homeless and hungry people wandered the streets and roads. Europe faced the gigantic task of rebuilding. Yet Europe did recover from this material blight, and with astonishing speed.

Women in the belligerent countries served in the armed forces, and in the Soviet Union they were actively involved in combat. Some 2,000 Soviet women fought as snipers, some with great effectiveness. Soviet women also flew fighter planes and drove tanks and some 200,000 fought with partisans. Women were active in the resistance movements in occupied Europe, and some were captured, tortured, and killed by the Nazis. Britain also planted female spies in occupied France, some of whom fell victim to the Nazis.

In the United States and Britain, women volunteers performed such noncombat duties as flight testing, ferrying planes to different bases, driving ambulances, serving as telegraphers and mechanics, and caring for the wounded in hospitals. Thousands of nurses served in the different branches of service. The role of British women in the tracking incoming German planes proved invaluable in the Battle of Britain.

In both the United States and Britain, with men going off to war, large numbers of women, many of them housewives, worked in factories producing armaments needed for the war effort. While some 70 to 75 percent of American women chose to remain at home, that same percentage of British women were employed. When the war ended, many American women were forced to give up their jobs to provide work for the returning soldiers and resumed being housewives, a role that they and their husbands often preferred. Nevertheless, the new possibilities created by the war gave women more confidence in their abilities and in time helped spark a woman's movement that pressed for equal opportunity in employment and education.

The war produced a shift in power arrangements. The United States and the Soviet Union emerged as the two most powerful states in the world. The traditional Great Powers—Britain, France, and Germany—were now dwarfed by these *superpowers*. The United States had the atomic bomb and immense industrial might; the Soviet Union had the largest army in the world and was extending its dominion over Eastern Europe. With Germany defeated, the principal incentive for Soviet–American cooperation had evaporated.

After World War I, nationalist passions had intensified. After World War II, Western Europeans progressed toward unity. The Hitler years had convinced many Europeans of the dangers inherent in extreme nationalism, and fear of the Soviet Union prodded them toward greater cooperation.

World War II accelerated the disintegration of Europe's overseas empires. The European states could hardly justify ruling over Africans and Asians after they had fought to liberate European lands from German imperialism. Nor could they ask their people, exhausted by the Hitler years and concentrating all their energies on reconstruction, to fight new wars against Africans and Asians pressing for independence. In the years just after the war, Great Britain surrendered India, France lost Lebanon and Syria, and the Dutch departed from Indonesia. In the 1950s and 1960s, virtually every colonial territory gained independence. Where a colonial power resisted granting the colony independence, the price was bloodshed.

The consciousness of Europe, already profoundly damaged by World War I, was again grievously wounded. Nazi racial theories showed that even in an age of advanced science, the mind remains attracted to irrational beliefs and mythical imagery; Nazi atrocities proved that people will torture and kill with religious zeal and machinelike indifference. This regression to mythical thinking and savagery bears out Walter Lippmann's contention that "men have been barbarians much longer than they have been civilized. They are only precariously civilized, and within us there is the propensity, persistent as the force of gravity, to revert under stress and strain, or under temptation, to our first natures."[11] And the behavior of German intellectuals also contained a painful lesson, says German historian Karl Dietrich Bracher: "The intellectuals who supported the Nazis in one way or another all document that the mind can be temporarily seduced, that people can be bribed with careers and fame, that thinking people, especially, are tempted by an irrational cult of action and are peculiarly susceptible to ('one-dimensional') answers and promises of salvation."[12]

The Nazi assault on reason and freedom demonstrated anew the fragility of Western civilization. This assault would forever cast doubt on the Enlightenment conception of human goodness, secular rationality, and the progress of civilization through advances in science and technology.

The Holocaust was heightened irrationality and organized evil on an unprecedented scale. Auschwitz, Treblinka, Sobibor, and the other death factories represent the triumph of human irrationality over reason—the surrender of the mind to a bizarre racial mythology that provided a metaphysical and pseudoscientific justification for mass murder. They also represent the ultimate perversion of reason. A calculating reason manufactured and organized lies and demented beliefs into a structured system with its own inner logic and employed sophisticated technology and administrative techniques to destroy human beings spiritually and physically. Science and technology, venerated as the great achievement of the Western mind, had made mass extermination possible. The philosophes had not foreseen the destructive power inherent in reason. Historian Omer Bartov poses this disturbing question about the failure of reason and the Western humanist tradition:

> *What was it that induced Nobel Prize–winning scientists, internationally respected legal scholars, physicians known throughout the world for their research into the human body and their desire to ameliorate the lot of humanity, to become not merely opportunist accomplices, but in many ways the initiators and promoters of this attempt to subject the human race to a vast surgical operation by means of mass extermination of whole categories of human beings? What was there (or is there) in our culture that made the concept of transforming humanity by means of eugenic and racial cleansing seem so practical and rational?*[13]

Both the Christian and the Enlightenment traditions had failed the Germans and many other Europeans. Conversely, Hitler's supporters had betrayed civilization, as Joachim Wieder, a German officer and veteran of Stalingrad, concluded after the war:

> *By means of a destructive battle against universal educational and cultural powers of classic antiquity, humanism, and Christianity, an anti-intellectual political religion of power had successively extracted the German people from the best of the commonly-held European body of human thought and thereby also out of the commitment to the objective concepts of truth, compassion, and justice.*[14]

And "what is both historically unique and persistently disturbing about the Holocaust," notes Bernhard Schlink, a prominent German novelist, "is that Germany, with its cultural heritage and place among civilised nations, was capable of those kinds of atrocities. It elicits troubling questions: if the ice of culturally-advanced civilisation upon which one fancied oneself safely standing, was in fact so thin at that time, then how safe is the ice we live upon today?"[15]

Auschwitz marked a rupture in the progressive development of European civilization. It demonstrated that against the forces of mythical thinking, fanaticism, and human beings' propensity for evil, our rational faculties, so admired by the philosophes of the Enlightenment and their liberal heirs, have limited power. Some intellectuals, shocked by the irrationality and horrors of the Hitler era, drifted into despair. To these thinkers, life was absurd, without meaning; human beings could neither comprehend nor control it. In 1945, only the naïve could have faith in continuous progress or believe in the essential goodness of the individual. The future envisioned by the philosophes seemed more distant than ever. Nevertheless, this profound disillusionment was tempered by hope. Democracy had, in fact, prevailed over Nazi totalitarianism and terror. Perhaps, then, democratic institutions and values would spread throughout the globe, and the newly established United Nations would promote world peace.

Finally, World War II saw major advances in weaponry, none more significant than the atomic bomb, that made war more lethal. That states now possess nuclear weapons capable of destroying one another, and even civilization and the planet, is another ever- present, ever- terrifying legacy of World War II.

❖ ❖ ❖

Notes

1. Pierre Renouvin, *World War II and Its Origins* (New York: Harper & Row, 1969), p. 167.
2. *Documents on German Foreign Policy, 1918–1945* (London: Her Majesty's Stationery Office, 1956), Vol. 6, series D, no. 433.
3. Winston S. Churchill, *The Second World War: Their Finest Hour* (Boston: Houghton Mifflin, 1949), Vol. 2, pp. 225–226.
4. Judith Sternberg Newman, *In the Hell of Auschwitz* (New York: Exposition, 1964), p. 18.
5. Quoted in Robert Jay Lifton, *The Nazi Doctors* (New York: Basic Books, 1986), p. 16.
6. Konnilyn G. Feig, *Hitler's Death Camps* (New York: Holmes & Meier, 1979), p. 37.
7. Quoted in Steven T. Katz, "Technology and Genocide: Technology as a 'Form of Life,'" in *Echoes from the Holocaust*, ed. Alan Rosenberg and Gerald E. Meyers (Philadelphia: Temple University Press, 1988), p. 281.
8. Rainer C. Baum, "Holocaust: Moral Indifference as the Form of Modern Evil," in *Echoes from the Holocaust*, ed. Rosenberg and Meyers, p. 83.
9. Robert Jay Lifton, *The Nazi Doctors* (New York: Basic Books, 1968), p. 5.
10. Richard Overy, *Why the Allies Won* (New York: W. W. Norton, 1955), p. 82.
11. Walter Lippmann, *The Public Philosophy* (Boston: Little, Brown, 1955), p. 86.
12. Karl Dietrich Bracher, *Turning Points in Modern Times*, trans. Thomas Dunlap (Cambridge, Mass.: Harvard University Press, 1995), p. 198.
13. Omer Bartov, *Germany's War and the Holocaust: Disputed Histories* (Ithaca, N.Y.: Cornell University Press, 2003), p. 136.
14. Joachim Wieder, *Stalingrad: Memories and Assessments*, trans. Helmut Bogler (London: Arms and Armor, 1993), 87.
15. Bernhard Schlink, *Guilt About the Past* (Toronto: House of Anansi, 2009), 29.

Suggested Reading

Aly, Götz, *Hitler's Beneficiaries: Plunder, Racial War, and the Nazi Welfare State* (2007). The systematic plundering of Europe by the Nazi regime worked to the great material benefit of the German people and was a principle reason why they enthusiastically supported the Nazi regime during the war.

Ambrose, Stephen E., *D-Day* (1994). Based on oral histories from people who were there.

Bartov, Omer, *Hitler's Army* (1992). Excellent material on the indoctrination of the German soldier.

Bauer, Yehuda, *A History of the Holocaust* (1982). An authoritative study.

Bell, P. M. H., *The Origins of the Second World War in Europe* (1986). An intelligent survey.

Calvocoressi, Peter, and Guy Wint, *Total War* (1972). A good account of World War II.

Dear, I. C. B., *The Oxford Companion to World War II* (1995). A superb reference work.

Des Pres, Terrence, *The Survivors* (1976). A sensitive analysis of life in the death camps.

Evans, Richard J., *The Third Reich at War* (2008). A recent study by a highly respected historian.

Hastings, Max, *Armageddon: The Battle for Germany, 1944–1945* (2004). A gripping account of the final months of the war.

Keegan, John, *The Second World War* (1989). A survey by a leading military historian.

Klee, Ernst, Willi Dressen, and Volker Riess, eds., *The Good Old Days* (1988). Documents show perpetrators and bystanders not only as indifferent to the suffering of Jews, but also deriving pleasure from it.

Murray, Williamson, and Allen R. Miller, *A War to Be Won* (2000). An analysis of the operations and tactics employed by the belligerents.

Overy, Richard, *Why the Allies Won* (1995). A brilliant analysis.

Snyder, Timothy, *Bloodlands: Europe Between Hitler and Stalin* (2010). An original analysis of the place where millions of Europeans were murdered by the two dictators.

Weinberg, Gerhard L., *A World at Arms* (1994). A study based on extraordinary knowledge of the sources.

Wette, Wolfram, *The Wehrmacht: History, Myth, Reality* (2006). Shows the involvement of the German army in war crimes.

Wiesel, Elie, *Night* (1960). A moving personal record of the Holocaust.

Part Six

The Contemporary World

AP Photo/Carmen Taylor.

The Destruction of the World Trade Center's Twin Towers

	Politics and Society	Thought and Culture
1940	Yalta agreement (1945) United Nations established (1945) Marshall Plan for recovery of Europe (1947) Cold War starts (1947) State of Israel established (1948) North Atlantic Treaty Organization (NATO) established (1949) Division of Germany (1949) Triumph of Communism in China (1949)	Wiener, *Cybernetics* (1948) Orwell, *1984* (1949) de Beauvoir, *The Second Sex* (1949)
1950	Korean War (1950–1953) European Economic Community (EEC) established (1957) *Sputnik* launched: space age begins (1957)	Camus, *The Rebel* (1951) Discovery of DNA by Crick and Watson (1951–1953) Djilas, *The New Class* (1957) Chomsky, *Syntactic Structures* (1957) Grass, *The Tin Drum* (1959) Snow, *The Two Cultures and the Scientific Revolution* (1959)
1960	Berlin Wall built (1961) Cuban missile crisis (1962) Vietnam War (1963–1973)	Carson, *Silent Spring* (1962) Pope John XXIII, *Pacem in Terris* (Peace on Earth) (1963) McLuhan, *Understanding Media* (1964) Levi-Strauss, *The Savage Mind* (1966)
1970	Détente in East–West relations (1970s)	Solzhenitsyn, *The Gulag Archipelago* (1974–1978) Wilson, *Sociobiology* (1975) Lyotard, *The Postmodern Condition* (1979)
1980	Gorbachev becomes leader of Soviet Union (1985) Explosion at Chernobyl nuclear power plant (1986) Peaceful overthrow of Communist governments in Eastern Europe (1989) Berlin Wall demolished (1989)	Creation of the Internet (1983) Gorbachev, *Perestroika* (1987)
1990	Reunification of Germany (1990) Charter of Paris for a New Europe (1990) Official end of Cold War (1990) Persian Gulf War (1991) Yugoslav federation breaks up and civil war begins (1991) Collapse of the Soviet Union (1991) European Union ratifies the Maastricht Treaty (1993) Dayton Agreement ends civil war in former Yugoslavia (1995)	Fukuyama, *The End of History and the Last Man* (1992) Huntington, *The Clash of Civilizations and the Remaking of the World Order* (1998)
2000	Terrorist attack on World Trade Center (2001) U.S.-led war in Iraq; fall of Saddam Hussein (2003)	

Chapter 21

Europe After World War II: Recovery and Realignment, 1945–1989

- **The Cold War**
- **Decolonization**
- **Building a New Europe: Unity and Recovery**
- **The Soviet Bloc**

Focus Questions

1. What were the origins of and key developments in the Cold War?
2. What conditions made possible the "revolution" of 1989 in Eastern Europe?
3. What are the main problems confronting the European Union?
4. What factors led to the collapse of Communism and the end of the Cold War?
5. What is the historical significance of Communism's collapse?

At the end of World War II, Winston Churchill described Europe as "a rubble heap, a charnel house, a breeding ground for pestilence and hate."[1] Millions had perished. Industry, transportation, and communication had come to a virtual standstill; bridges, canals, dikes, and farmlands were ruined. Ragged, worn people picked among the rubble and bartered their valuables for food.

Europe was politically cut in half, for in pursuing Hitler's armies, Soviet troops had overrun Eastern Europe and penetrated into the heart of Germany. Europe's future now depended on two countries, the United States and the Soviet Union, which soon became embroiled in a bitter Cold War. The Soviet Union, exhausted by World War II and anxious about security, imposed its grim tradition of dictatorship on Eastern Europe, while the United States, virtually unharmed by the war, brought the boon of its wealth and power to help rebuild Western Europe. Henceforth, the United States stood out as the heir to and guardian of the Western tradition, a political giant come into its own. ❖

The Cold War

Origins

The Cold War (the American financier Bernard Baruch coined the phrase in 1947) stemmed from the divergent historical experiences and the incompatible political ambitions of the United States and the Soviet Union. The wartime coalition of the United States, Britain, and the Soviet Union was based solely on temporary political expediency—the need to defeat the common enemy. Both the United States and Britain had long disdained the Communist system and feared its spread to Western Europe, and the Soviet Union had a profound distrust for Western capitalist states, particularly Germany, which in both world wars had invaded Russia, leaving behind death and destruction. Fearing a revival of German power, Stalin was determined to protect Soviet security by annexing border regions and establishing subservient Communist governments throughout Eastern Europe.

Protecting the Soviet Union from its capitalist enemies was one major concern for Stalin. The other was to retain his absolute personal rule. The epic struggle against the Nazi invaders had further hardened Stalin. Sixty-six years old in 1945, Stalin displayed in his last years an unrelenting ruthlessness and paranoid suspiciousness. And as leader in the victorious war against Nazi Germany, his authority was unquestioned and his stature had grown immensely. The cult of the great leader was shaped and propagated by a vast propaganda machine that included the state-controlled media and educational institutions.

As the Red Army fought its way west in 1944 and 1945, Eastern European Communists, trained in the Soviet Union, followed. The Baltic states (Lithuania, Latvia, and Estonia), seized after the Nazi–Soviet Pact of 1939 and then lost to Hitler, were reincorporated into the Soviet Union. The Soviet Union also annexed part of East Prussia; Ruthenia in eastern Czechoslovakia, whose population was predominantly Ukrainian; parts of Romania; and eastern Poland; for which the Poles were compensated with German territory, including much of East Prussia. Elsewhere, Stalin respected, at least outwardly, the national sovereignty of the occupied countries by ruling through returning native Communists and whatever sympathizers he could find. In the Soviet-occupied zone of Germany, Stalin arranged for the establishment of Communist rule. Stalin knew that in free elections Communists had little chance of winning and that left to their own devices these countries would return to their traditional anti-Russian orientation. In these new Soviet client states, Stalin retained a morbid fear of nationalist and anti-Communist insurgencies backed by the capitalist West. Poles, for example, had bitter historical memories of being under Russian rule until after World War I. Strongly Catholic, they also hated the atheistic Communist ideology and resented the Soviet Union for invading eastern Poland in 1939 and deporting hundreds of thousands of Poles to desolate regions of the Soviet Union, for massacring thousands of Polish officers during the war, and for not helping the Polish insurrection against the Nazis in 1944. And it would be extremely difficult to win the hearts of Czechs and Hungarians, who were extremely patriotic and identified with Western Europe, and of the Baltic nations, who hated Russian domination. Successfully defying Stalin was Yugoslavia under the leadership of the pugnacious Marshal Tito, who had led the Yugoslav resistance movement against Nazi occupation. A hardened Communist, Tito was also a Yugoslav patriot who resisted Soviet occupation of his country. Backed by his people, Tito pursued an independent course.

The Communist regimes in the satellite countries could only be maintained by force and terror. And as President Ronald Reagan declared in 1982, "the regimes planted by totalitarianism have had more than

Primary Source

Milovan Djilvas: *The New Class*

In 1956, Milovan Djilas (1911–1995), a Yugoslav Communist and political commentator, wrote The New Class, *an early and devastating critique of the Communist system. Under Communism, he said, government bureaucrats, all members of the Communist Party, constitute a privileged "exploiting and governing class."*

Earlier revolutions, particularly the so-called bourgeois ones, attached considerable significance to the establishment of individual freedoms immediately following cessation of the revolutionary terror. Even the revolutionaries considered it important to assure the legal status of the citizenry. Independent administration of justice was an inevitable final result of all these revolutions. The Communist regime in the U.S.S.R. is still remote from independent administration of justice after forty years of tenure. The final results of earlier revolutions were often greater legal security and greater civil rights. This cannot be said of the Communist revolution. . . .

In contrast to earlier revolutions, the Communist revolution, conducted in the name of doing away with classes, has resulted in the most complete authority of any single new class. Everything else is sham and an illusion. . . .

This new class, the bureaucracy, or more accurately the political bureaucracy, has all the characteristics of earlier ones as well as some new characteristics of it own. Its origin had its special characteristics also, even though in essence it was similar to the beginnings of other classes. . . . The new class may be said to be made up of those who have special privileges and economic preference because of the administrative monopoly they hold. . . .

The mechanism of Communist power is perhaps the simplest which can be conceived, although it leads to the most refined tyranny and the most brutal exploitation. The simplicity of this mechanism originates from the fact that one party alone, the Communist Party, is the backbone of the entire political, economic, and ideological activity. The entire public life is at a standstill or moves ahead, falls behind or turns around according to what happens in the party forums. . . .

. . . Communist control of the social machine . . . restricts certain government posts to party members. These jobs, which are essential in any government but especially in a Communist one, include assignments with police, especially the secret police; and the diplomatic and officers corps, especially positions in the information and political services. In the judiciary only top positions have until now been in the hands of Communists. . . .

Only in a Communist state are a number of both specified and unspecified positions reserved for members of the party. The Communist government, although a class structure, is a party government; the Communist army is a party army; and the state is a party state. More precisely, Communists tend to treat the army and the state as their exclusive weapons.

The exclusive, if unwritten, law that only party members can become policemen, officers, diplomats, and hold similar positions, or that only they can exercise actual authority, creates a special privileged group of bureaucrats. . . .

A citizen in the Communist system lives oppressed by the constant pangs of his conscience, and the fear that he has transgressed. He is always fearful that he will have to demonstrate that he is not an enemy of socialism, just as in the Middle Ages a man constantly had to show his devotion to the Church. . . .

. . . Tyranny over the mind is the most complete and most brutal type of tyranny; every other tyranny begins and ends with it. . . .

History will pardon Communists for much, establishing that they were forced into many brutal acts because of circumstances and the need to defend their existence. But the stifling of every divergent thought, the exclusive monopoly over thinking for the purpose of defending their personal interests, will nail the Communists to a cross of shame in history. . . .

Question for Analysis

1. How did Milovan Djilas characterize the "new class"? What were its qualities? How did it wield its power?

Milovan Djilas, *The New Class* (New York: Frederick A. Praeger, 1957), 27, 36, 70, 72, 132, 144, 146.

30 years to establish their legitimacy. But none—not one regime—has yet been able to risk free elections. Regimes planted by bayonets do not take root."[2]

Local populations, and their supporters in Western European lands, viewed the Soviet occupation of Eastern Europe as a calamity. But unwilling to risk another war, Western countries were powerless to intervene. By the end of 1948, the lands of Eastern Europe had become Soviet satellites. Wartime cooperation between the former allies, admittedly tenuous and forced, was replaced by suspicion and hostility, initiating the era of the Cold War. For the next forty-five years, the two parts of the Continent would be known as East Europe and West Europe: two camps of opposing ideologies. In Churchill's famous words, "From Stettin in the Baltic to Trieste in the Adriatic, an iron curtain has descended across the Continent."[3]

American leaders were profoundly concerned: they had the responsibility of rallying Western Europe, and possibly the world, against universal Communism, another form of totalitarianism that threatened both freedom and the free market. And, in what was a significant consequence of the war, the three Axis powers—(West) Germany, Italy, and Japan—embraced democratic principles and sided with the United States and its allies in their hostility to Communism and Soviet expansion. At the same times, the United States was concerned about the rapid growth of Communist parties throughout non–Soviet occupied Europe. The specter of these countries ruled by Communist parties with allegiance to the Soviet Union was a gnawing worry.

Cold War Mobilization

In March 1947, fearing Soviet penetration in the eastern Mediterranean, President Truman proclaimed the Truman Doctrine: "It must be the policy of the United States to support free peoples who are resisting attempted subjugation by armed minorities or by outside pressures."[4] The Truman Doctrine was the centerpiece of the new policy of *containment,* of holding Soviet power within its then-current boundaries. U.S. military and economic support soon went to Greece and Turkey. Thus, a sharp reversal took place in American foreign policy; prewar American isolation gave way to worldwide vigilance against any Soviet effort at expansion.

Later that year, the United States took a major step toward strengthening the West. In June 1947, Secretary of State George C. Marshall announced an impressive program of economic aid, formally called the European Recovery Program but widely known as the Marshall Plan. By 1952, when the plan terminated, it had supplied Europe with a total of $13.15 billion in aid—a modest pump-priming for the subsequent record upswing in U.S., Western European, and even global prosperity. Western Europe recovered, and the United States gained economically strong allies and trading partners.

In 1948, Stalin, seeking greater control in East Germany, cut off access to West Berlin. In response, the United States and Britain organized a massive airlift of supplies to the city, preserving the western outpost in East Germany.

The United States strove to contain Soviet power by establishing in 1949 the North Atlantic Treaty Organization. NATO linked the armed forces of the United States, Canada, Portugal, Norway, Iceland, Denmark, Italy, Britain, France, and the Benelux countries (an acronym for Belgium, the Netherlands, and Luxembourg). Greece and Turkey soon joined; West Germany was included in 1956, and Spain in 1982. In response to NATO, the Soviet Union formed the Warsaw Pact, consisting of the armed forces of the Soviet Union and its European satellites.

Chronology 21.1 ❖ Europe After 1945

1945	United Nations founded; Eastern Europe occupied by Red Army
1947	Cold War starts; Marshall Plan inaugurated
1948	Stalinization of Eastern Europe; Tito's Yugoslavia breaks with the Soviet Union
1949	NATO formed
1953	Stalin dies
1956	Khrushchev's secret speech on Stalin's crimes; the Polish October; the Hungarian uprising crushed
1957	*Sputnik* launched: space age begins; EEC established
1961	Berlin Wall built, dividing the city of Berlin
1962	Cuban missile crisis
1963–1973	Vietnam War
1964	Khrushchev ousted; Brezhnev and Kosygin installed as leaders in U.S.S.R.
1968	Czechoslovakia's "Prague Spring": Dubček's "socialism with a human face"
1971	Détente in East–West relations
1979	Soviet Union invades Afghanistan
1980	Solidarity trade union formed in Poland
1982	Brezhnev dies, succeeded by Andropov (d. 1984) and Chernenko (d. 1985)
1985	Gorbachev becomes U.S.S.R. leader
1988	Soviet Union withdraws from Afghanistan
1989	Year of liberation in Eastern Europe
1990	Reunification of Germany; Charter of Paris for a New Europe: official end of the Cold War
1991	Persian Gulf War; Yeltsin elected Russian president; collapse of Soviet Union; Yugoslav federation breaks up and civil war begins
1993	Czechoslovakia splits into Czech Republic and Slovakia; elections for new Russian constitution and parliament; European Union ratifies Maastricht Treaty
1994	South Africa elects multiracial government; war breaks out between Russia and Chechnya
1995	Dayton Agreement ends civil war in Bosnia
1996	Yeltsin reelected president of Russia; truce ends hostilities in Chechnya
1999	NATO invades Kosovo; Russia again attacks Chechnya
2001	Terrorist attack on World Trade Center; War on Terrorism in Afghanistan
2003	United States and Britain crush regime of Saddam Hussein

Military alliances and forces were backed up by ever more powerful armaments. Sooner than expected, in 1949, the Soviet Union exploded its own atomic device. Thereafter, the arms race escalated to hydrogen bombs and intercontinental ballistic missiles (ICBMs). Threatened by Soviet ICBMs, the United States lost its territorial invulnerability, which its geography had guaranteed until then.

The U.S.–Soviet rivalry extended into outer space. In 1957, the Soviet government sent the first *sputnik* (satellite) into orbit around the earth, shocking complacent Americans into a keen awareness of their vulnerability. For some years, the Soviet Union remained ahead in the prestigious field of space exploration, sending the first astronaut, Yuri Gagarin, into orbit in 1961. The United States caught up in 1969 by landing a man on the moon.

All along, science and technology contributed to the escalation of the ominous arms race. Determined to gain the advantage in order to discourage an enemy attack, each side developed ever more sophisticated weapons and long-range delivery systems that, if used, could have destroyed all civilized life.

Confrontations

Korean War In June 1950, war broke out in Korea, a country divided in 1945 between a pro-Soviet Communist regime in the north and a pro-American regime in the south. Eager to restore Korean national unity and mistakenly assuming U.S. nonintervention, the North Korean army invaded South Korea, possibly with Stalin's approval. Immediately, the United States took countermeasures, gaining U.N. backing for a war against North Korea. Under the command of General Douglas MacArthur, South Korean and U.S. troops, assisted by a token force from other U.N. members, fought their way north toward the Chinese border. Fearing for his own security, Mao Zedong, head of Communist China, dispatched "volunteers" to drive back the approaching enemy in a surprise attack. Forced to retreat, General MacArthur's troops eventually withdrew from North Korea. Peace was restored in 1953, with the division of Korea reaffirmed. South Korea became an outpost of U.S. power.

Cuban Missile Crisis Confrontation between the superpowers rose to a terrifying climax in 1962 during the Cuban missile crisis. In 1959, the infamous dictatorship of Fulgencio Batista had been toppled by Fidel Castro (b. 1927), a left-wing revolutionary who turned Cuba into a Communist-style dictatorship. After an American attempt to overthrow him—the bungled Bay of Pigs operation—Castro was ready to turn his country into an outpost of Soviet power. Nikita Khrushchev (discussed later in the chapter) planned to exploit this foothold in the Western Hemisphere by installing Soviet nuclear missiles in Cuba. Although the United States had for some time stationed nuclear weapons in Turkey, within easy reach of Soviet targets, the reverse situation—allowing a major Soviet threat close to home—alarmed the country. President John F. Kennedy demanded that Khrushchev withdraw the Soviet missiles from Cuba. The Cold War confrontation threatened to turn into a very hot nuclear war. However, Khrushchev backed down—a move that contributed to his fall from power two years later. No Soviet missiles were stationed in Cuba.

Vietnam War The new countries emerging from colonial rule in Asia and Africa offered seductive opportunities for Communist expansion. From the U.S. perspective, the biggest challenge arose in Vietnam, where the Communist regime in the north threatened to take over South Vietnam as well. The threat had started with the partition of the country in 1954. From the north, the authoritarian regime of Ho Chi Minh (1890–1969), backed by indigenous nationalism and Soviet aid, cast its shadow over a disorganized south. Providing South Vietnam with the stability and strength needed to resist Communist infiltration required increasing U.S. aid—including troops to fight off the Communist guerrillas, the Vietcong. If the Communists prevailed, the argument ran, all the other countries in East and Southeast Asia emerging from colonial rule would fall like dominoes to Communist rule. Under President Lyndon B. Johnson, who assumed office in 1963, U.S. intervention in South Vietnam became the undeclared Vietnam War.

The U.S. government shipped to Vietnam nearly half a million soldiers equipped with the most advanced chemical weapons and electronic equipment available. Yet victory eluded the American forces. The North Vietnamese government and its people withstood the cruelest punishment of bombs and chemical weapons ever inflicted on

Bogged Down in Vietnam. Americans defended South Vietnam against a threatened takeover by Communist North Vietnam. Between 1964 and 1973, U.S. involvement in the unsuccessful Vietnam War cost tens of thousands of Vietnamese and American lives, ruined South Vietnam, and polarized U.S. public opinion over the morality of the war.

human beings. Nor was South Vietnam spared; virtually every South Vietnamese family saw relatives killed or maimed and their farms and livelihoods ruined.

As domestic opposition to the war increased and Vietcong resistance could not be broken, President Richard M. Nixon, elected in 1968, realized that the war had to be ended by "peace with honor." While he initiated negotiations with North Vietnam, U.S. forces put pressure on the enemy by attacking Communist bases and supply routes in neighboring Cambodia and Laos. Civilians were bombed more fiercely than in World War II. In 1973, by agreement with North Vietnam, the United States withdrew its forces from the area. In 1975, the North Vietnamese swept aside the inept South Vietnamese army and unified the country under a Communist dictatorship. Ho Chi Minh had triumphed against the mightiest nation in the world.

In the wake of the American withdrawal, Cambodian Communists—the Khmer Rouge—seized power under their leader, Pol Pot. He drove more than two million people from the capital city of Phnom Penh and tried to establish a new order based on ideologically regimented rural communes. The result was genocide in which hundreds of thousands of people perished.

Decolonization

World War II, in which many colonial soldiers loyally fought for their masters, stirred up demands among non-Western peoples for an end to Western colonial rule and for political independence. After all, freedom and self-determination were prominent Allied war slogans. Exhausted by the war, European colonial powers had little strength left for colonial rule. In this setting, a mighty groundswell of decolonization, supported by the ideals of the United Nations, eventually propelled African and Asian lands into independent statehood.

Decolonization often sparked brutal struggles of building modern states among peoples who were utterly unprepared for this effort. For example, in 1960 the Belgians pulled out of the Congo,

Map 21.1 Western Europe After 1945 To counter the Communist threat from the Soviet Union, Western European countries, formerly enemies, cooperated for their mutual protection. The majority of countries joined NATO for security against Communist attack, and six countries within Europe formed the Common Market (the forerunner of the European Union) to facilitate trade and economic integration.

leaving behind some thirty Congolese university graduates to fill four thousand administrative posts. Moreover, divided by historic, ethnic, and tribal animosities, newly independent states were often torn by civil war. In many African lands, army officers seized power; these ruthless rulers treated the countries as their private fiefs. Thus, Mobutu Sese Seko, who ruled mineral-rich Zaire for thirty-two years, amassed one of the world's largest fortunes and purchased luxurious mansions abroad while poverty raged among his people. Nor did peoples with different traditions adjust

Berlin Wall. The Berlin Wall, swiftly erected by the East German Communist regime in 1961, divided the city of Berlin for twenty-eight years.

to the institutions and procedures of Western democracy. Even today in some parts of Africa, one-party dictatorships remain in power, often dressed up as democracies; corrupt officials use their offices to acquire personal fortunes; and tribal and ethnic conflicts decimate the population.

Building a New Europe: Unity and Recovery

Although Europeans share a common cultural heritage, the diversity of their history and national temperaments has burdened them in the past with incessant warfare. After two ruinous world wars, many people at last began to feel that the price of violent conflict had become excessive; war no longer served any national interest. And the extension of Soviet power made some form of Western European unity attractive, if not imperative.

In 1951, the chief Continental consumers and producers of coal and steel, the two items most essential for the rebuilding of Western Europe, created the European Coal and Steel Community (ECSC). Its six members, France, West Germany, the Netherlands, Belgium, Luxembourg, and Italy, intended to put the Ruhr industrial complex, the heart of German industrial power, under international control, thereby promoting cooperation and reconciliation, as well as economic strength.

Emboldened by the success of the ECSC, in 1957 the six countries established the European Economic Community (EEC), also known as the Common Market, a customs union that created a free market among the member states and sought to improve living conditions in them. In 1973, Great Britain, Ireland, and Denmark joined the original members in what was now called the European Community (EC); in 1981 Greece and in 1986 Spain and Portugal became members. The EC constituted the world's largest single trading bloc, conducting more than one-fifth of the world's commerce. In this framework of growing cooperation, the major countries of Western Europe experienced a political and economic revival, which contributed to Western superiority in the Cold War.

A most striking fact of recent history in the West has been the unprecedented economic advance. Between the early 1950s and the late 1970s, production in Western Europe and the United States surpassed all previous records. The rapid postwar economic boom suffered a setback in the 1970s, due in part to the drastic increase in oil prices imposed by the Organization of Petroleum Exporting Countries (OPEC). Recovery revived and prosperity continued throughout the 1980s. However, unemployment in Western Europe remained high, even in West Germany, the strongest country economically.

Stimulated by the expansion of U.S. multinational corporations into Western Europe and by the opportunities offered by the European Community, many European companies have turned multinational and grown larger than any nationalized industry. The Western European economy came to be dominated by gigantic private and public enterprises tied to other parts of the world.

Boosted by rising standards of living and by U.S. power, the overall trend of political life in the West since World War II has been toward constitutional democracy. Although Spain and Portugal retained their prewar dictatorships until the mid-1970s and Greece for a time wavered between democracy and dictatorship, by the late 1970s even these countries had conformed to the common pattern.

Great Britain and France

Impoverished by the war and vulnerable in its dependence on imported food and raw material, Great Britain lost its leading role in world politics after World War II. It peacefully dismantled its colonial empire, and British seapower was replaced by the American navy and air force. The postwar Labour government, allied with powerful trade unions, provided Britons with a measure of economic security through social programs and extensive government control over important branches of the economy. Such controls, however, placed Britain at a disadvantage vis-à-vis its European competitors.

In 1979, at a low point in the economy, the voters elected a Conservative government led by Margaret Thatcher, the "Iron Lady" and the first woman prime minister. She dominated English politics for the next decade, fighting inflation and rigorously encouraging individual initiative and free enterprise. During the Thatcher years, the British economy improved, and London regained its former luster as a financial center. Still, industries were declining, causing a rise in unemployment. Civic tensions—terrorism by the Irish Republican Army, which sought to drive Britain from Northern Ireland, and resentment at the influx of Indians, Pakistanis, West Indians, and other people from former colonies—also took their toll. In addition, despite their EC membership, the English clung to their traditional insular detachment from their neighbors on the Continent.

Across the English Channel, France, liberated from German occupation, was reorganized democratically under the Fourth Republic and soon achieved respectable economic growth, despite frequent changes of government (twenty-six in twelve years). A major problem that France faced in these years was decolonization. In Indochina (now Vietnam), the colonial liberation movement inflicted a resounding defeat on the French army in 1954. In Algeria, French settlers and soldiers were determined to thwart independence. The long and bloody Algerian conflict had serious repercussions.

In 1958, the agitation to keep Algeria under French control, supported by certain army circles, reached a dangerous point. To prevent a right-wing coup aided by the army, General Charles de Gaulle stepped forward. He had been the leader of the Free French forces in World War II and president for a brief period after the war ended. De Gaulle established the Fifth Republic, with a strong executive authority, and sought to raise the country again to prominence by building its nuclear strength, making France independent of NATO, and renewing French influence in Africa. In 1962, he arranged a cease-fire in Algeria, allowing it to achieve independence. In 1968, demonstrations by students and workers demanding educational reform and social justice, which were supported by the Communist Party, greatly alarmed de Gaulle. He quickly called a general election, in which a frightened electorate gave him a landslide victory. However, unable to revise the constitution in his favor, he resigned in 1969.

The Fifth Republic continued under a government firmly based on a stable centrist majority, flanked by two radical parties. On the left, the Communist Party gradually lost credibility because of its loyalty to Moscow. On the extreme right, the ultranationalist *Front National* took hold, stirring up hatred against the increasing number of Muslim immigrants from North Africa. Under the pressure of the newcomers, the French, even more than the English, feared for their national identity.

Amid the economic and political uncertainties of the times, François Mitterand, a moderate socialist who became president in 1981, maintained the Gaullist tradition. His country was the third largest nuclear power and the fourth largest economy in the world, deriving 70 percent of its energy from nuclear power plants. All along, France was a leading architect of European unity without surrendering its French character.

Italy and Germany

Italy, half the size of France yet larger in population by a few million, became a democratic republic in 1946. Its government, however, has been weak and unstable. The life span of an Italian cabinet to the present has often been less than a year. A lengthy peninsula stretching out into the Mediterranean, the country offered a sharp contrast between north and south. The north was efficient and prosperous, whereas the south was backward and infiltrated by the Mafia. Centered in Sicily, the Mafia was a source of political corruption and even occasional terror against the government.

Division also characterized the political parties, from Communists to Christian Democrats. The Italian Communists, relatively free from corruption, well organized, and oriented toward Europe rather than Moscow, usually gained a quarter of the vote. On the other hand, the Christian Democrats—allied with the Vatican and constituting the majority party—were poorly disciplined, like the other non-Communist parties, and riven by corruption.

Yet the Italian economy proved to be a surprising success, despite the fact that the government was perennially in debt and unemployment ran high, especially in the south. Even more than France, Italy has been overrun by legal and illegal immigrants from Asia and Africa, straining the country's resources. It has been the most unruly of the major European countries, but no troublemaker for its neighbors.

In 1945, its cities in ruins, Germany had been defeated, occupied, and branded as a moral outcast. Divided among the four occupying powers—the United States, Britain, France, and the Soviet Union—the German nation was politically extinct. Extensive eastern lands were lost to Poland and the Soviet Union; some territory was returned to France. By 1949, two new and chastened Germanys had emerged. West Germany (the Federal Republic of Germany), formed from the three western zones of occupation, faced the hostile, Soviet-dominated East Germany (the German Democratic Republic). The former capital city of Berlin, inside East Germany, was similarly divided into western and eastern zones of occupation. The partition of Germany signified the destruction of Germany's traditional identity and ambition. The national trauma reached a climax in August 1961, when the East German government suddenly threw up a wall between East and West Berlin and tightly sealed off East from West Germany. West Germany thus became the crucial frontier of the Cold War, radiating Western superiority into the Soviet bloc.

The Cold War proved a boon to the West Germans; it contributed to their integration into the emerging new Europe and to the reduction of old hatreds. Located next door to the Red Army, the West Germans, along with the Western armed forces stationed on their soil, were in a strategic position for defending Western Europe. Moreover, German industrial expertise was indispensable for rebuilding the Western European economy. On this basis, West Germany (far larger than its Communist counterpart to the east and the most populous of all Western European countries) began to build a new political identity.

The architect of the new West Germany was Konrad Adenauer, its chancellor from 1949 to 1963. He sought to restore respect for Germany in cooperation with the leading states of Western Europe and the United States. As a patriot, he reestablished a cautious continuity with the German past. He also had Germany shoulder responsibility for the crimes of the Nazi regime and assume the payment of indemnifications and pensions to the Jewish victims and survivors of the Nazi era, as well as the payment of reparations to the state of Israel, which had been established in May 1948 and where many survivors were building a new life. Under Adenauer's guidance, the West Germans also threw themselves into rebuilding their economy; the whole world soon admired the German "economic miracle." As a result, democracy put down roots among the West German people, strengthening their solidarity with their former European enemies. West Germany was admitted to NATO in 1957 and, together with East Germany, to the United Nations in 1972. It joined France in promoting the European Community.

During these years, West German prosperity and a generous admission policy attracted ambitious immigrants, many from Turkey, for the booming economy needed additional workers. Political extremists did not endanger political stability, except for one party, the Greens, which called attention to the destruction of the environment, industrial pollution, and the dangers of nuclear power. Loosely organized, the Greens expressed a romantic alienation from contemporary society and politics but achieved no lasting success. In 1982, the voters turned conservative, electing the leader of the Christian Democratic Union, Helmut Kohl, chancellor. Kohl continued Adenauer's policy of integrating West Germany, now the most prominent country in Western Europe, into the Cold War alliance against Soviet Communism.

The Soviet Bloc

Stalin's Last Years

For the Soviet Union, World War II was another cruel landmark in the long succession of wars, revolutions, and crises that had afflicted the country since 1914. Nothing basically changed after the war. The liberation from terror and dictatorship that many soldiers had hoped for as a reward for their heroism never occurred.

Corrupted by unlimited power and unrestrained adulation, Stalin displayed in his last years an unrelenting ruthlessness and a suspiciousness that turned into paranoia. He found no reason to relax control. The country still had immense problems: the large anti-Soviet populations in Eastern Europe; the destruction wreaked by the war; the political unreliability of returning soldiers and prisoners of war; and the overwhelming strength of the United States. Stalin's indomitable ambition, undiminished by age (he was sixty-six years old in 1945), was to build up Soviet power in his lifetime, whatever the human cost. More Five-Year Plans and more terror were needed.

On this familiar note, the Soviet Union slid from war into peace, staggering through the hardships and hunger of the war's aftermath, mourning its dead, and desperately short of men. Planning, much selfless hard work, manpower released from the army, and resources requisitioned from all occupied territories brought industrial production back to prewar levels within three years—no mean achievement.

In his last years, Stalin withdrew into virtual isolation, surrounded by a few fawning and fearful subordinates, and his paranoia worsened. Before he died, he "recognized" a plot among the doctors, most of them Jews, who treated him and personally issued orders for their torture (which killed one of them), and the press circulated vicious anti-Semitic propaganda. Had Stalin not died it is likely that he would have launched a murderous campaign against Soviet Jews. When on March 5, 1953, the failing dictator died of a stroke, his advisers sighed with relief, but many people wept. To them, Stalin was the godlike leader and savior of the nation. The human costs of his regime were immense, but of his achievements in raising Soviet power there can be no doubt. By 1949, Soviet Russia possessed the atomic bomb. By 1953, at the same time as the United States, it had the hydrogen bomb as well.

Khrushchev

After Stalin's death, leadership was assumed by a team headed by Nikita Khrushchev (1954–1964), who breathed fresh air into Soviet life. Khrushchev was the driving force behind the "thaw" that emptied the forced-labor camps and allowed most of the nationalities forcibly resettled during the war to return to their native regions. In a speech at the Twentieth Party Congress in February 1956, Khrushchev even dared to attack Stalin himself. His audience gasped with horror as he recited the facts: "Of the 139 members and candidates of the Party Central Committee who were elected at the 17th Congress (1934), 98 persons, i.e., 70 percent, were arrested and shot."[5] In this vein, Khrushchev cited example after example of Stalin's terror. Without criticizing the Soviet system, Khrushchev acknowledged and rejected the excesses of Stalinism.

Khrushchev's revelations created a profound stir around the world and prompted defection from Communist ranks everywhere. Among the Soviet satellite countries, Poland was on the brink of rebellion by 1956; a workers' uprising forced a change of leadership. In Hungary in 1956, the entire Communist regime was overthrown, but the Soviet army reoccupied the country and crushed the uprising.

In foreign policy, Khrushchev professed to promote peace. But while trying to reduce the role of the army, he also made some provocative moves by threatening Western access to West Berlin and placing missiles in Cuba; U.S. pressure forced him to withdraw in both cases. In 1960, not wishing to help Communist China build atomic weapons, he withdrew, after mutual recrimination, all Soviet advisers, causing a break between the two Communist nations. Mao then charged him with "revisionism" as well as imperialism.

Eager to prod his country toward a higher level of Marxist-Leninist ideology, Khrushchev presented a new party program and impatiently pressed for reforms in industry, agriculture, and party organization. His ceaseless reorganizations, impatient manner, and extravagant promises antagonized wide sections of state and party administration. In October 1964, while he was on vacation, his comrades in the Politburo unceremoniously ousted him for "ill health" or, as they later added, his "hare-brained schemes." He was retired and allowed to live out his years in peace.

Khrushchev was succeeded by a group of leaders acting in common. Among these men, Leonid Brezhnev (1906–1982) gradually rose to the fore. Under his leadership, the government of the U.S.S.R. turned from a personal dictatorship into an oligarchy: the collective rule of a privileged minority. Brezhnev's style stressed reasoned agreement rather than command. Soviet officials breathed more easily, and Soviet society in turn grew less authoritarian.

Never before in Soviet history had the country enjoyed such external security. As a result, the rigors of totalitarian rule could be relaxed and the country could be opened, cautiously, to the outside world. For instance, young people were allowed access to Western styles of music and dress. More issues of state policy were opened to public debate, and more latitude was granted to artistic expression. Interest in religion revived.

Changes in Eastern Europe

Realizing that continued repression of the satellite countries would provoke trouble, Stalin's successors began to relax their controls. A new era dawned for Eastern Europe. The Soviet satellites began to move toward greater national self-determination, searching for their own forms of industrialization, collectivization of agriculture, and Communist dictatorship. The history of the region after 1953 was thus a series of experiments to determine what deviations from Soviet practice in domestic politics and what measure of self-assertion in foreign policy the Kremlin would tolerate.

No event proved more crucial than Khrushchev's attack on Stalin in 1956. It set off a political earthquake throughout the bloc, discrediting Stalinists and encouraging moderates in the parties, reviving cautious discussions among intellectuals, and even arousing visions of national self-determination.

The first rumbles of protest were heard in June 1956 in Poland—the largest and most troublesome of the satellite countries. The crisis came to a head in October: would Poland revolt, inviting invasion by the Red Army, or would Khrushchev ease Soviet control? The Soviet boss yielded in return for a Polish pledge of continued loyalty to the Soviet Union. Thereafter, Poland breathed more freely, clinging to its Catholicism as a cornerstone of its national identity.

Although the "Polish October" ended peacefully, events moved to a brutal showdown in Hungary. The Stalinists had suppressed national pride in Hungary for too long. On October 20, 1956, anti-Soviet feeling boiled over in an uprising in Budapest, forcing Soviet troops to withdraw from the country. A moderate Communist

AP Photo/Peter Winterbach.

Soviet Tanks in Prague, Czechoslovakia, August 1968. The Warsaw Pact invasion, led by the Soviet Union, crushed Dubček's liberalization of Communist rule.

government took over the reins. Eager to capture popular sentiment, it called for Western-style political democracy and Hungary's withdrawal from the Warsaw Pact. Thoroughly alarmed and supported by Mao and even Tito, the Soviet leaders struck back. On November 4, 1956, Soviet troops reentered Hungary and crushed all opposition.

But the bold uprising left its mark. The new Communist leader of Hungary, János Kádar, was a moderate. With Khrushchev's approval, he built a pragmatic regime of consumer-oriented "goulash Communism" that granted considerable opportunity to private enterprise. Kádar's regime also allowed non-Communists to participate extensively in public affairs. Relaxation and decentralization of planning made possible in the 1970s a remarkable increase in popular prosperity and individual freedom. The Hungarian experiment became the envy of all other Soviet-bloc countries.

After 1956, Soviet leaders grew more circumspect in their approach to the satellite countries' internal affairs, allowing increasing diversity of political development. The post-Stalin permissiveness was never without risks, however, even under the milder regime of Brezhnev, as was shown in Czechoslovakia in 1968. A new group of Czech Communists, led by Alexander Dubček, sought to liberalize their regime to include non-Communists, permit greater freedom of speech, and rid the economy of the rigidities that for so long had prevented prosperity. Their goal was a "humanist democratic socialism," or "socialism with a human face": a Communist Party supported by public goodwill rather than by the secret police.

This program panicked the governments of East Germany, Poland, and the Soviet Union. On August 21, East German, Polish, Hungarian, and Soviet troops, under the provisions of the Warsaw Pact, carried out a swift and well-prepared occupation of Czechoslovakia but failed to break the rebellious will of its reformers. While Soviet tanks rumbled through Prague, an extraordinary Czechoslovak party congress met secretly in choked fury. Never had the Soviet leaders encountered such united resistance by a Communist Party. Nonetheless, the revolt ended in failure. The party was purged, all reforms were canceled, and the country was reduced to abject hopelessness. But the Soviet Union paid a high price. A cry of moral outrage resounded around the world; protests were heard even in Moscow.

Extraordinary events occurred in Poland. Industrial workers, theoretically the real masters in Communist regimes, embarrassed their government by taking the lead in pressing for freedom and a better standard of living. When a Polish cardinal became Pope John Paul II in 1978, patriotism surged. In 1980, workers under the leadership of an electrician named Lech Walesa succeeded, with the blessing of the church, in forming an independent labor union. Called Solidarity, the union engaged in numerous strikes. In 1981, matters came to a head: some of Solidarity's more radical members spoke of bringing free elections to Poland. In December, a military dictatorship, formed suddenly under General Wojciech Jaruzelski, imposed martial law. Walesa and other leaders of Solidarity were arrested, and protesting workers were dispersed by force.

The German Democratic Republic (East Germany) at first shared the fate of all Soviet satellites. Under the leadership of German Communists who had spent the Nazi years in the Soviet Union, industry was nationalized, agriculture collectivized, and the people regimented under the Communist Party (here called the Socialist Unity Party). But protests against Stalinism appeared earlier here than elsewhere. In June 1953, the workers of Berlin staged an uprising, gaining some concessions. Then followed a steady exodus of skilled manpower to West Germany, mostly through West Berlin. More than three million people escaped before the East German government, in August 1961, suddenly constructed the infamous "Berlin Wall" and built equally deadly barriers along the entire border with West Germany. For a time, all contact between East and West Germany ceased.

With renewed control over their people, the Communist leaders—first Walter Ulbricht and then, starting in the early 1970s, Erich Honecker—successfully advanced the economy. The East Germans enjoyed the highest standard of living in the Soviet bloc. In 1972, détente opened diplomatic relations with West Germany and promoted closer economic ties. After 1985, East Germans cheered the progress of reform in the Soviet Union—their leader, Honecker, denounced it as "a march to anarchy"—and hoped for similar benefits at home.

The Gorbachev Years

Brezhnev died in 1982; his immediate successors, chosen by agreement among top party officials, were old men who survived in office only for a short time. Former KGB chief Yuri Andropov (aged sixty-eight), in poor health from the start, died in early 1984. He was replaced by Konstantin Chernenko, a man of Brezhnev's generation, likewise in poor health, who lasted until early 1985. In that year, Mikhail Gorbachev (b. 1931) took over, representing a younger and more sophisticated age group, whose members had started their careers in the calmer times after Stalin's death.

Self-confident, energetic, and articulate, Gorbachev was keenly aware of his country's problems and eager to confront them. He knew that the Soviet Union had to update its industrial and agricultural productivity to compete with Japan, South Korea, Taiwan, the countries of Western Europe, and the United States; in particular, the Soviet Union lagged in the design and production of computers. A sobering demonstration of inefficiency and mismanagement occurred in late April 1986 when, because of staff misjudgment, a reactor at the nuclear power plant at Chernobyl exploded, spewing dangerous radiation high into the atmosphere; poisonous fallout covered much of Europe. Wherever Gorbachev looked, the mismanagement caused by rigid, centralized planning stifled innovation.

Gorbachev demanded no less than a fundamental reorganization—*perestroika*—of the Soviet system, with the party in charge but responding more readily to the plans and hopes of Soviet citizens. Even more than his predecessors,

Map 21.2 Eastern Europe After 1945 During ▶ and after World War II the Soviet Union extended its rule halfway across Europe. Repressive Communist governments in Eastern Europe were controlled by Moscow. Yugoslavia, under President Tito, defied Moscow and became a Communist state with links to Western Europe and the United States.

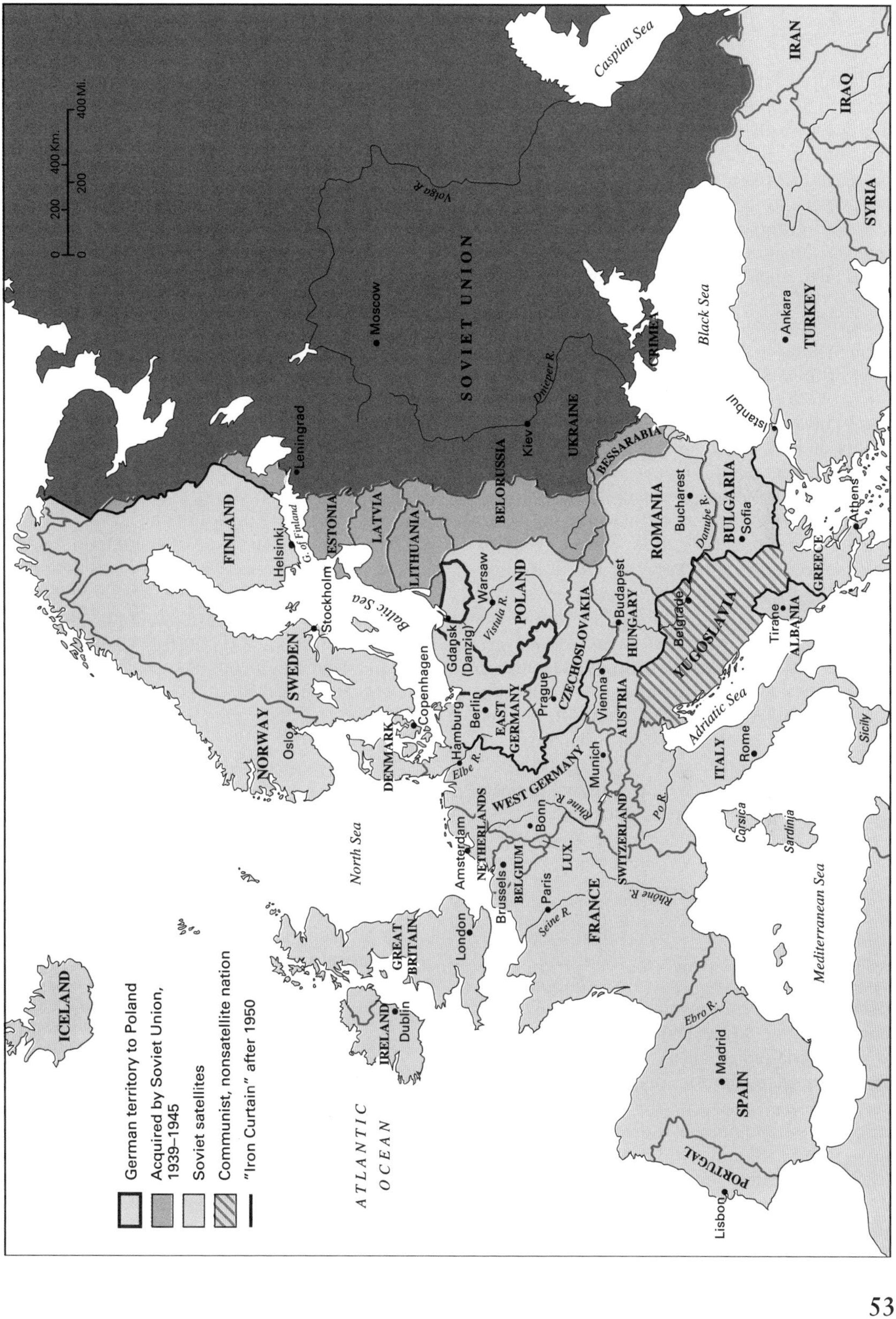
German territory to Poland
Acquired by Soviet Union, 1939–1945
Soviet satellites
Communist, nonsatellite nation
"Iron Curtain" after 1950
0 200 400 Km.
0 200 400 Mi.
ICELAND
IRELAND
Dublin
GREAT BRITAIN
London
ATLANTIC OCEAN
North Sea
NORWAY
Oslo
SWEDEN
Stockholm
FINLAND
Helsinki
G. of Finland
DENMARK
Copenhagen
Baltic Sea
NETHERLANDS
Amsterdam
BELGIUM
Brussels
LUX.
FRANCE
Paris
Seine R.
Rhône R.
WEST GERMANY
Bonn
Rhine R.
Munich
Hamburg
Elbe R.
EAST GERMANY
Berlin
Gdansk (Danzig)
POLAND
Warsaw
Vistula R.
CZECHOSLOVAKIA
Prague
AUSTRIA
Vienna
SWITZERLAND
HUNGARY
Budapest
YUGOSLAVIA
Belgrade
ALBANIA
Tirane
GREECE
Athens
ROMANIA
Bucharest
Danube R.
BULGARIA
Sofia
ITALY
Rome
Po R.
Corsica
Sardinia
Sicily
Adriatic Sea
Mediterranean Sea
SPAIN
Madrid
Ebro R.
PORTUGAL
Lisbon
ESTONIA
LATVIA
LITHUANIA
BELORUSSIA
BESSARABIA
UKRAINE
Kiev
Dnieper R.
CRIMEA
SOVIET UNION
Leningrad
Moscow
Volga R.
Caspian Sea
Black Sea
Istanbul
TURKEY
Ankara
SYRIA
IRAQ
IRAN

he advocated "the democratization of society," hoping to stimulate participation by ordinary citizens, especially at their places of work and in local administration. He called for multiple candidates for elected posts, a novel experience for Soviet voters. To loosen up administrative rigidity, he also granted greater freedom to local entrepreneurs in agriculture, industry, and consumer services, demanding that supply and demand be closely coordinated, as in a free market.

Gorbachev promoted a new policy, *glasnost* (openness), in the discussion of public affairs. Let all the problems of Soviet society, hitherto kept under cover, be openly discussed: corruption, abuse of power, disregard for legality, and stifling of criticism. Domestic news began to depict Soviet reality more accurately. There was also a new candor about the Soviet past. During the seventieth anniversary of the Bolshevik Revolution, Gorbachev asserted that "the guilt of Stalin . . . for the wholesale repressive measures and acts of lawlessness is enormous and unforgivable."[6] Gorbachev then assured Soviet citizens that they should not hesitate to speak out freely. Academics, writers, and artists responded enthusiastically. As contacts with the outside world increased, Western ideals, culture, and respect for human rights entered Soviet minds as never before. Far-reaching economic changes designed to loosen the restraints of central planning and to promote a market economy accompanied the political reforms.

The End of the Cold War

Gorbachev also sought to ease international tensions. National security in the nuclear age, he stressed, called for superpower cooperation for the sake of common survival. Moreover, he thought that the Soviet Union was more imperiled by internal rot than by foreign aggression. Plagued by incompetent managers, lethargic and alcoholic workers, corruption, and a loss of confidence in Communist leadership, the Soviet Union lagged far behind the capitalist West, particularly the United States. And the high cost of the Cold War impeded the reforms that his socialist country so urgently needed. In the spirit of glasnost, Gorbachev frankly admitted that the adverse prospects of his country's economy forced him to advocate not only "normal international relations," but also an end to the arms race. Setting an example, with a touch of Western sartorial elegance, he traveled abroad and cautiously lifted the restrictions barring access to the outside world. Jewish emigration was eased; foreign firms were invited to help stimulate the Soviet economy; and high-level discussions between Russians and Americans became commonplace.

By the end of 1988, Gorbachev withdrew the Soviet army from Afghanistan, admitting that the 1979 invasion had been a mistake. He liberated Eastern Europe from Soviet domination, permitting the dissolution of the Warsaw Pact, the Soviet military alliance in the area, and gave approval to German reunification. He surrendered the Leninist claim to the superiority of Soviet Communism and stopped support for Marxist regimes in the Third World. Unilaterally demobilizing sizable units of the Red Army in 1988, he also stopped nuclear testing. At summit meetings—with President Reagan and later with President George H. W. Bush—Gorbachev successfully pressed for strategic arms reduction. In late 1991, both the United States and the Soviet Union agreed to scrap a significant part of their nuclear arsenals.

The Collapse of Communism

1989: The Year of Liberation Perestroika and glasnost spread among the peoples of Eastern Europe, resentful of Soviet domination and worried by growing economic hardships. During 1989 and 1990, Eastern Europeans showed their distaste for Communist leadership and demanded democratic reforms. Faced with a rising tide of popular discontent, Communist leaders resigned or agreed

Map 21.3 Post–Cold War Europe and the Former Soviet Union ▶ Instead of the stark postwar division of Europe into three blocs—Western Europe, Eastern Europe, and the Soviet Union—the continent is now a patchwork of independent countries, some with new names. Russia remains the largest country, but the former Soviet Republics have claimed their territory on Russia's eastern and southern borders. Within Europe, East and West Germany have reunited, while Yugoslavia has split up.

RUSSIA
0 200 400 Km.
0 200 400 Mi.
KAZAKHSTAN
Caspian Sea
Baku
AZERBAIJAN
IRAN
IRAQ
SYRIA
GEORGIA
Tbilisi
Yerevan
ARMENIA
Volga R.
Don R.
Moscow
Black Sea
CRIMEA
Ankara
TURKEY
Istanbul
Dnieper R.
Kiev
UKRAINE
MOLDOVA
Chisinau
St. Petersburg
FINLAND
Helsinki
Tallinn
ESTONIA
Riga
LATVIA
LITHUANIA
Vilnius
Minsk
BELARUS
ROMANIA
Bucharest
Danube R.
BULGARIA
Sofia
Athens
GREECE
Skopje
MACEDONIA
Belgrade
SERBIA
Sarajevo
BOSNIA AND HERZEGOVINA
MONTENEGRO
Tirana
ALBANIA
Adriatic Sea
Zagreb
CROATIA
Ljubljana
SLOVENIA
Budapest
HUNGARY
Bratislava
SLOVAKIA
Vienna
AUSTRIA
Prague
CZECH REPUBLIC
Warsaw
POLAND
Vistula R.
Baltic Sea
Stockholm
SWEDEN
Oslo
NORWAY
Copenhagen
DENMARK
Gdansk (Danzig)
Berlin
GERMANY
Hamburg
Elbe R.
Amsterdam
NETHERLANDS
Luxembourg
LUX.
Brussels
BELGIUM
Paris
Seine R.
FRANCE
Rhine R.
Danube R.
Bern
SWITZERLAND
Po R.
ITALY
Rome
Sicily
Corsica
Sardinia
Mediterranean Sea
Rhône R.
North Sea
London
GREAT BRITAIN
Dublin
IRELAND
ICELAND
ATLANTIC OCEAN
Ebro R.
Madrid
SPAIN
Lisbon
PORTUGAL

© Regis Bossu/Sygma/Corbis.

The Wall Came Tumbling Down. The Berlin Wall, symbol of the division of Germany, was breached in November 1989. Young people excitedly clambered onto the partially demolished wall while East and West Berliners thronged the streets.

to reforms. People around the world cheered the opening of a new era in Eastern Europe.

In Poland, public pressure had forced General Jaruzelski to end his dictatorship and appoint a civilian government. Struggling with a deteriorating economy, Jaruzelski legalized the highly popular Solidarity union in 1989. Permitted to run against Communist Party candidates in a free election, Solidarity won an overwhelming victory. The once jailed Solidarity members now sat in the Polish parliament next to their former jailers. In December 1990, Lech Walesa, who was instrumental in forming Solidarity, was elected president.

Encouraged by events in Poland, Hungary abolished its Communist bureaucracy in May 1989. By the end of the year, a multiparty system was in place, with two non-Communist parties, the Democratic Forum and the Alliance of Free Democrats, competing for leadership. Hungary had shaken off Soviet domination and embraced the ideals of democracy and free enterprise.

An even more momentous upheaval occurred in 1989 in East Germany. More than 340,000 people voted for freedom and prosperity with their feet, escaping to West Germany across the recently opened borders of Hungary and Czechoslovakia. Far larger numbers took to the streets in protest against the regime. Hoping to restore calm, Honecker's colleagues deposed their sickly, old, hard-line boss, but antigovernment demonstrations continued. On November 6, when almost a million demonstrators crammed the streets of East Berlin, the Communist government resigned. On November 9, in an explosion of patriotic fervor, the Berlin Wall was breached; tens of thousands of East Germans flocked into West Berlin, where they were welcomed with flowers and champagne. Liberated East Germany was soon reunited with West Germany, with Gorbachev's ultimate approval.

In Bulgaria, the dramatic events in Berlin led to the resignation of Tedor Zhivkov, the longest-serving Communist dictator in the Soviet bloc and an opponent of reform. Bulgaria had joined the quest for democratic government and private enterprise.

While democratic reforms triumphed elsewhere, Romania's Nicholae Ceausescu, long bent on pursuing his own dictatorial course and hostile to Gorbachev's reforms, ruthlessly enforced his own rule, ordering his soldiers to shoot into a crowd of antigovernment demonstrators. But popular resentment was too powerful to contain, and even the army turned against the dictator. On December 25, 1989, Ceausescu and his wife were tried and executed. The most hardened symbol of Communist rule, defying to the last the common trend toward democratic freedom, had ignominiously fallen.

Faced with massive demonstrations in Prague and urged by Gorbachev himself to institute democratic reform, Czechoslovakia's Communist leaders resigned on November 24, 1989. Václav Havel, a leading dissident writer and outspoken advocate of democracy who had been jailed for his views, was chosen president on December 25.

Shocked by the news of Ceausescu's execution and Havel's election, the Yugoslav Communist Party caved in. Its central committee suggested the formation of a multiparty system, which was fully adopted in January 1990.

Except for Albania, where the Communist Party held on until free elections in February 1991, all of Eastern Europe had liberated itself from Soviet domination—a breathtaking change, accomplished unexpectedly within a single year. Viewed as a whole, events in Eastern Europe had taken a surprisingly peaceful course, prompted by a number of favorable factors. First, Gorbachev had been willing to let the satellite peoples go their own way. Second, led by intellectuals and clergy, the people united against repression, foreign domination, and economic misery, which so vividly contrasted with the prosperity of Western Europe. Third, like Gorbachev, the Communist rulers had lost confidence in their Marxist-Leninist ideology; they knew that they had forfeited their legitimacy. Finally, the evidence of progress under freedom and democracy in the West had penetrated deep into East Europe and had heightened popular expectations. The revolutionary changes of 1989 constituted an overwhelming victory for Western forms of government and ways of life.

The Disintegration of the Soviet Union The transformation and spiritual rebirth that Gorbachev hoped for the Soviet Union did not occur. In October 1990, Gorbachev conceded that "unfortunately, our society is not ready for the procedures of a law-based state. We don't have that level of political culture, those traditions. All that will come in the future."[7] Meanwhile, the Soviet Union was experiencing a breakdown of effective government, economic collapse, corruption, and spiraling crime. In response to the mounting crisis, the liberals, most strongly represented in Moscow and Leningrad among the young generation open to Western ways, pressed, under Boris Yeltsin's guidance, for speedy westernization, including a multiparty system and a market economy. On the opposite side, the Communist hard-liners prepared to revive the old system, relying on the army and the security forces to restore order and hold the country together. In August 1991, they staged a coup, imprisoning Gorbachev and deposing him as president of the Soviet Union. Their aim was to establish a new Communist dictatorship.

However, the conspirators, all of them high officials appointed by Gorbachev, grossly misjudged the people's revulsion against the Communist Party. The KGB's vanguard forces defected to Yeltsin, who led a fervent popular protest at a risk to his life. The emotional outburst in favor of democracy quickly spread from Moscow to other cities, and the coup collapsed within three days. The chief victim of the coup, apart from its leaders, was the Communist Party, now repudiated by Gorbachev himself and swept aside by public fury. Racked by the deteriorating economy and the growing nationalist sentiments among the various ethnic groups, the Soviet Union fell to pieces. The Baltic nations—Lithuania, Latvia, and Estonia—established their independence shortly after the coup, and a new Commonwealth of Independent

States, consisting of eleven former republics of the collapsed Soviet Union, was proclaimed in December 1991. At the end of the month, Gorbachev, the last leader of the Soviet Union, resigned as president of a now-defunct country. Boris Yeltsin, president of Russia, the most powerful of the new independent states, became the informal leader of the commonwealth. Its ideology discredited, its economy shattered, and its government transformed into a confederation of sovereign states, the Soviet Union had collapsed as a major force in world affairs. Only one superpower remained.

The Death of an Ideal?

The sudden and unexpected collapse of Communism in Eastern Europe in 1989 seemed to discredit Marxism irrevocably. Reformers in Eastern European lands liberated from Communist oppression expressed revulsion for the socialist past and a desire to regenerate their countries with an infusion of Western liberal ideals and institutions. Havel, the newly elected president of a free Czechoslovakia, expressed this disillusionment with the past and hope for a new democratic future:

> *The worst of it is that we live in a spoiled moral environment. We have become morally ill because we are used to saying one thing and thinking another. We have learned not to believe in anything, not to care about each other, to worry only about ourselves. . . . The previous regime, armed with a proud and intolerant ideology, reduced people into the means of production. . . . Many of our citizens died in prison in the 1950's. Many were executed. Thousands of human lives were destroyed.*
>
> *Perhaps you are asking what kind of republic I am dreaming about. I will answer you: a republic that is independent, free, democratic, a republic with economic prosperity and also social justice.*[8]

Marxism had become a failed ideology propped up only by force in the few surviving Communist regimes: For many intellectuals, including once ardent Communists, "scientific socialism," which claimed to have deciphered the essential meaning and direction of history, no longer seems scientific nor relevant to current needs. It is merely another idea that was given too much credence and is now ready to be swept into the dustbin of history. Political theorist Francis Fukuyama suggests that the decline of Communism and the end of the Cold War reveal a larger process at work, "the ultimate triumph of Western liberal democracy":

> *The twentieth century saw the developed world descend into a paroxysm of ideological violence, as liberalism contended first with the remnants of absolutism, then bolshevism and Fascism, and finally an updated Marxism that threatened to lead to the ultimate apocalypse of nuclear war. But the century that began full of self-confidence in the ultimate triumph of Western liberal democracy seems at its close to be returning full circle to where it started . . . to an unabashed victory of economic and political liberalism. The triumph of the West, of the Western idea, is evident first of all in the total exhaustion of viable systematic alternatives to Western liberalism. . . . What we may be witnessing . . . is the end point of mankind's ideological evolution and the universalization of Western liberal democracy as the final form of government.*[9]

❖ ❖ ❖

Notes

1. Quoted in Walter Laqueur, *Europe Since Hitler* (Baltimore: Penguin Books, 1970), p. 118.
2. Quoted in Melvyn P. Lefler, *For the Soul of Mankind: The United States, the Soviet Union, and the Cold War* (New York: Hill and Wang, 2007), p. 340.
3. Winston S. Churchill, "Sinews of Peace: Address, March 5, 1946," *Vital Speeches of the Day,* March 15, 1946, p. 3.

4. "The Truman Doctrine," in *Major Problems in American Foreign Policy: Documents and Essays,* ed. Thomas G. Paterson (Lexington, Mass.: Heath, 1978), Vol. 2, p. 290.
5. Nikita S. Khrushchev in *The Crimes of the Stalin Era: Special Report to the 20th Congress of the Communist Party of the Soviet Union,* annotated by Boris I. Nicolaevsky (New York: The New Leader, 1956), p. 20.
6. Gorbachev's speech at the seventieth anniversary of the Bolshevik Revolution, quoted in *The New York Times,* November 3, 1987, p. A3.
7. Quoted in Anthony Lewis, "Et Tu Eduard," *The New York Times,* December 21, 1990, p. A39.
8. *The New York Times,* January 2, 1990, p. A13.
9. Francis Fukuyama, "The End of History," *The National Interest* (Summer 1989), pp. 3–4.

Suggested Reading

Fursenko, Aleksandr, and Timothy Naftali, *"One Hell of a Gamble": Khrushchev, Castro, and Kennedy, 1958–1964* (1997). An excellent account of the Cuban missile crisis.

Garton-Ash, Timothy, *The Magic Lantern: The Revolution of '89 Witnessed in Warsaw, Budapest, Berlin, and Prague* (1990). A lively account of the death of Communism in Eastern Europe, conveying the exhilaration of the time.

Gorbachev, Mikhail S., *Memoirs* (1996). The tumultuous years of reform in the Soviet Union.

Havel, Václav, *Summer Meditations* (1992). An excellent selection of essays by the president of the Czech Republic.

Leffler, Melvyn P., *For the Soul of Mankind: The United States, the Soviet Union, and the Cold War* (2007). A study of the fears, threats, and ideological clashes between the two superpowers throughout four decades.

Chapter 22

The Troubled Present

- **The Post–Cold War World**
- **New and Old Threats: Muslim Immigration and the Resurgence of Anti-Semitism**
- **Our Global Age: Cultural Clashes and Terrorism**

Focus Questions

1. What effect did the collapse of Communism have on the political situation in Eastern Europe and the new Russia?
2. What problems are faced by the European Union?
3. Why are Europeans concerned about Muslim immigrants?
4. What are the reasons for the surge of anti-Semitism in contemporary Europe?
5. Why has terrorism been described as the "dark side of globalization"?
6. What are the motivations and goals of radical Muslims?
7. How would you characterize Taliban leaders and their followers?
8. Why have some analysts questioned the war in Afghanistan and Iraq?

Since 1989, momentous events have utterly changed the world. The superpower polarization of world politics ended, and a new, multicentered, unstable world order has emerged. Western civilization and its ideals have been transformed into a transcultural worldwide modernity. At the same time, however, traditional cultural diversity still simmers. The end of the Cold War introduced a new uncertainty into human affairs. On the one hand, global interdependence promotes peaceful cooperation; on the other, it causes a clash of cultural traditions, giving rise to contagious violence and extremism. ❖

The Post-Cold War World

Post-Communist Russia and the Former Soviet Republics

Throughout the 1990s and into the twenty-first century, the Russian Federal Republic has been struggling to bring its political and economic systems into conformity with the Western model while coping with its loss of territory and superpower status. The collapse of the Soviet Union revealed Russia to be a weak, poorly developed society beset by profound problems.

Yeltsin's "Shock Therapy." Marred by mismanagement, waste, and lack of incentives, the Soviet economic system had failed miserably in comparison with Western capitalism. In order to reform the economy and improve the standard of living of the Russian people, which lagged far behind living standards in Western lands, President Yeltsin, emerging in 1990 as the leader of the new Russia, made a sudden switch in 1992 from a state-run economy to private ownership and a capitalist market system. This precipitous transfer of state firms to private ownership—"shock therapy"—in many ways proved a disaster. The chief beneficiaries of privatization were often the same inefficient managers who had controlled the economy during the Soviet era and amassed wealth by unscrupulous means. Industrial decline, the withdrawal of government subsidies, and ruinous inflation reduced millions of people dependent on pensions to hand-to-mouth subsistence. Many working Russians also sank into poverty as real wages plummeted some 40 percent from 1992 to 1998. Workers often had to wait two to six months for their paychecks, and unemployment soared.

With popular unrest mounting and facing opposition from Communist hard-liners, Yeltsin was forced to slow his liberalization of the economy; the social costs—public confusion over bewildering changes, a sharp decline in the standard of living, and the loss of productivity leading to shortages—were too high. "No more experiments," advised slogans spray-painted on walls.

Adding to the intractable problems of the new Russia were soaring crime and corruption. Yeltsin consolidated his power by making alliances with a small group of businessmen, the "oligarchs," who had grown wealthy by acquiring former state-owned enterprises at extremely low prices. They plundered the firms for assets, concentrating Russia's wealth in their own hands, and they gained control of banks "that operate in a pathological fashion." As law enforcement deteriorated, organized crime became a major force in Russian life.

The oligarchs financed Yeltsin's bid for reelection as president, which he won with an astonishing 65 percent of the vote in 1996 despite suffering a heart attack during the election campaign. At age sixty-six and in frail health, Yeltsin could no longer provide effective leadership for his vast, fragmented country, and in 1997, he frankly acknowledged the difficulties that he and his country faced: "After creating a new political system, we failed to outfit it with new tools of government, and we ourselves did not learn to govern in a new way."[1]

Nevertheless, by winning reelection with the support of the oligarchs, Yeltsin vanquished the Communists in the Duma, the new legislature. In addition, by permitting the oligarchs to buy up the major state enterprises, he smashed Soviet central planning. It would be impossible in these circumstances to reinstate Communism in Russia. But the situation was dangerous because many key enterprises, including banks and the media, were now controlled by unscrupulous oligarchs. In return for their support of Yeltsin, they became an inner political circle in the Kremlin, controlling the country's policies. No wonder Russians began to feel that the government itself had been "privatized."

In August 1998 everything changed. The dysfunctional banking system precipitated a second currency collapse, wiping out Russians' savings and livelihoods. Among the casualties were many of the oligarchs. Some were ruined by the collapse of their banks, others went abroad, and the remainder backed out of public life. Suddenly their political influence, which had been paramount since 1995, diminished dramatically, and a new generation of businessmen began to emerge.

Yeltsin resigned on New Year's Eve 1999. His grasp of events had become increasingly uncertain, and he was obviously incapable of ruling. He thus became the first Russian leader to give up power voluntarily. In his demoralized, bankrupt, and corrupt post-Communist country, Yeltsin contended with problems beyond the capacity of the most astute politician. He made appalling mistakes, but he was determined to go down in history as the man who made the restoration of Communism in Russia impossible. It was no mean achievement.

Putin: Clamping Down. Yeltsin's chosen successor, Vladimir Putin, was determined to make his mark as a strongman during his short term as Yeltsin's prime minister by reopening the war in Chechnya, a small Islamic enclave in the Caucasus, at war for centuries with the conquering Russians. After two years of ruthless fighting, at great political damage to Yeltsin, the defeated Russian armies withdrew in 1996, leaving the burden of the final settlement of Chechnya's independence to the future. The war resumed in 1999 when Chechen rebels invaded neighboring Dagestan in an effort to establish a united, independent, Islamic state in the Caucasus. At the same time, a terrorist attack on apartment blocks in Russian cities killed more than three hundred people and maimed many more. Putin put the blame for the attack on Chechens and stormed into the Caucasus to force the invaders out of Dagestan. The Chechen capital, Grozny, was razed; the main victims were elderly Russian residents, the rebels having already escaped to the mountains. Russian troops took control of the war-devastated Caucasus region, but the Chechen leaders remained at large and continued guerrilla attacks on Russian soldiers.

Vladimir Putin became president of Russia at a time when modest economic stability was beginning to emerge. His objective was to establish a strong centralized state. To this end, he struck at the power of troublesome oligarchs, dismembering an oil group and absorbing their property into the state-controlled oil and gas company. This spectacular government takeover sent a chill through the energy sector of the economy and alarmed foreign investors, who worried that property rights might exist only at the whim of the Russian government. But Putin's popularity increased among people resentful of the oligarchs' wealth.

More alarmingly, President Putin steadily increased government control of the media (previously owned by two of the oligarchs) and completely eroded freedom of the press. These actions drew immediate criticism from Western countries, which had hoped that Russia would follow a democratic path in allowing a free media and encouraging discussion and criticism of political issues.

The Chechen conflict continued in the background, springing dramatically onto the front pages in October 2002 when pro-Chechen terrorists seized a theater in Moscow in the middle of a performance. In the resulting counterattack, all the hostage takers and 129 hostages were killed by an inept gas attack on the theater by Russian authorities. The worst terrorist attack in Russia took place on the first day of the new school year in 2004. Chechen fighters seized a school in Beslan in the Caucasus and held hundreds of children, parents, and teachers hostage. More than three hundred hostages died, many of them children. The massacre led to worldwide revulsion, and Putin denounced it as part of global Islamic terrorism.

The principal motive of the Chechen fighters is independence from Russia. This is unacceptable to the Russian government; Putin has claimed that there are two thousand potential ethnic conflicts in multiethnic Russia and that granting independence to any region or nationality would weaken the fabric of the fragile country. His tough, efficient image shaken by the well-planned Chechen attack, Putin moved to reassert his authority: "[Terrorists] strive for the breakup of the state, for the ruin of Russia[.] I am sure that the unity of the country is the main prerequisite for victory over terror,"[2] he declared, making it clear that unity meant control from the top.

Exhausted by years of turmoil, many Russians supported Putin; they appreciated his strong leadership and welcomed his imposed order. Others saw it as authoritarianism triumphing over Russia's nascent democracy. Putin was taking his country back to one-party rule. His immediate associates in the Kremlin were drawn from the *siloviki*, former security officials who shared his hard-line law-and-order orientation and had no patience for the checks, balances, and uncertainties of democracy.

The Russian constitution limits the president to two consecutive terms in office. Long before Putin's term was up in March 2008, Western Kremlin-watchers began to speculate about his successor. In the fall of 2007, he moved dramatically to continue his power by appointing obscure minister Dmitry Medvedev as his prime minister and grooming him as his successor as president. Putin further announced that he would lead his party, United Russia, in the December 2007 election; its victory gave him a seat in the lower house of Parliament, from which he then became prime minister. Though well within the terms of the democratic constitution, it was a cynical maneuver. The small opposition parties were furious but powerless to intervene.

Putin has sought to restore Russia's power and influence lost in the decades after the breakup of the Soviet Union. He has deliberately stirred nationalist sentiments among the Russian people, crushed the revolt in Chechnya, and invaded neighboring Georgia. Putin ordered the invasion when Georgia tried to retake South Ossetia, one of two regions that had broken away from Georgian control in the 1990s and achieved de facto independence. Both of these break-away regions are close to Russia, and Mikhail Saakashvili, the pro-Western president of Georgia, is close to the United States and wants his country to join NATO. In preventing Georgia from reasserting its authority over the two break-away regions, Moscow was also displaying its power to Washington.

The gap between Russia and the West remains enormous. Russia is still a huge, poor country riddled with crime and corruption; it is burdened with a crumbling infrastructure, high inflation, and desperate rural poverty. Its health and social services are in crisis due to increasing heart attacks, strokes, and illnesses caused by excessive smoking, drug addiction, alcoholism, drug-resistant tuberculosis, and AIDS. Life expectancy has declined. There are 160 deaths for every 100 births, and the United Nations projects an astounding population decline from about 146 million in the year 2000 to about 104 million by 2050. It is feared that a physically weakened and diminished workforce may undermine Russia's economic recovery.

Unrealistic optimism at the time of the Soviet collapse that Russia would emerge as a free, democratic, and market-oriented state has changed to pessimism. Building a democratic civic society took centuries in the West; Russia cannot achieve that in one generation.

Central and Eastern Europe After 1989

After a century of war, occupation, and dictatorship, hopes ran high in the former Soviet satellite countries of Central and Eastern Europe. Western ideals of freedom and democracy had penetrated deep into the eastern lands and had heightened popular expectations. By 1990, however, the euphoria of the previous year began to vanish. How could democratic government and market economies be adapted to the tension-ridden traditions of that troubled area now suspended between the remnants of Communist rule and the glittering promise of Western life?

The countries that were closest to Western Europe geographically—Poland, Hungary, and the Czech Republic—were also closest to Western political and economic systems and eager to move toward full democracy and market economies. The economic prospects began to improve with the help of Western aid. Poland, Hungary, and the Czech Republic shifted their economic emphasis from east to west, increasing trade and economic integration with Western Europe. The three countries achieved political stability and security through their membership in NATO in 1999 and, together with seven other countries, opened negotiations to join the European Union (discussed later in the chapter).

In the 1990s, the former Yugoslavia became the most troubled region of Europe. Cobbled together after World War I as an artificial state composed of sharply different ethnic groups dominated by Serbians, Yugoslavia was torn apart by the nationalist ambitions set off by the collapse of the Soviet Union. In July 1991, Slovenia seceded; Croatia and Bosnia attempted to follow in 1992, ending Serbian domination. Because there were large Serbian populations in both Croatia and Bosnia, Yugoslav president Slobodan Milosevic, a Serb nationalist, refused to give up control and unleashed the Serb army, augmented by Bosnian Serbs, on the two countries. Ethnic hatred exploded, centered on Bosnia, a splintered mountainous region. Its major ethnic groups—43 percent Muslim, 17 percent Catholic Croat, and 31 percent Orthodox Serb—were scattered in multiethnic communities; there were few ethnically consolidated areas.

Muslims, Croats, and Serbs ruthlessly fought each other. The Bosnian Serbs, hoping to join with Serbia in a Greater Serbia, conquered 70 percent of Bosnia, conducting a brutal "ethnic cleansing" of Muslims while submitting Sarajevo, Bosnia's capital, to bloody bombardment. All sides, but most of all the Serbs, committed heinous atrocities, provoking moral outrage. A U.N. force of sixty thousand peacekeepers vainly tried to halt ethnic cleansing by Serbs. NATO used its air force for the first time in its fifty-year history, against the Bosnian Serbs. In November 1995, the United States stepped forward, in negotiations held in Dayton, Ohio, to promote peace. The Dayton Agreement proposed a Bosnian government equally shared by Muslims, Croats, and Serbs. But the outrageous inhumanities of the Bosnian civil war posed troubling questions. Why were Western European countries and the United States so reluctant to intervene? Why did the United States enter so late? Can a foreign military presence soften deeply entrenched local hatreds?

New violence erupted between Serbs and ethnic Albanians in the Yugoslav province of Kosovo. This is a sacred place for Serbs, the site of Orthodox shrines and of the battle of Kosovo in 1389, in which the Ottoman Turks defeated the Serbs, ruling Kosovo until 1912. The Serbs regard the battle as the birth of the Serb nation. Ethnic antagonism has persisted between Serbs and the predominantly Muslim Albanians who form 90 percent of the population of two million. In 1998, President Milosevic, seeking to shore up his power by manipulating Serbian nationalist feelings, sent Serbian forces to crush Albanian separatists fighting for an independent Kosovo.

Repelled by the forced expulsions and massacres of innocent villagers, NATO felt compelled to intervene. Despite a threat of NATO air strikes, Milosevic, a dictator whose hands already were stained with the blood of thousands of victims in Bosnia, refused to allow a NATO peacekeeping force into Kosovo. NATO launched air strikes on

© Anthony Suau/Gallery Stock.

Funeral in Bosnia. A funeral of one of tens of thousands of Muslim victims of the civil war in the former Yugoslavia, which raged from 1992 to 1995. The principal aggressor was Serbia, intent on seizing territory in Bosnia and Croatia in order to create a "greater Serbia."

Serbia in March 1999. At the same time special Serbian forces, determined to drive Albanians out of Kosovo, stormed into the region. Carrying the practice of ethnic cleansing in the region to a new level of brutality, they terrorized and murdered Albanians, systematically burned villages, confiscated valuables, and compelled their victims to flee the province. Hundreds of thousands of Albanian refugees streamed out of the country into neighboring lands, creating a massive humanitarian crisis.

The unrelenting NATO bombardment of Serbia, expected to be brief and decisive, continued for eleven weeks—so too did the ethnic cleansing of Kosovo—until Milosevic capitulated. Eventually the Kosovo Albanians were allowed to return to their ravaged country. A force of forty thousand NATO and U.N. troops remained in Kosovo to assist with relief efforts, prevent revenge attacks on the remaining Serb population, and enable an administration to be put in place to guarantee Kosovo's autonomy.

The U.N. International Criminal Tribunal for the former Yugoslavia indicted President Milosevic and Bosnian Serb and Croatian leaders and military commanders on charges of genocide and crimes against humanity. Milosevic went on trial in 2002 but died in 2006 before sentencing.

After the war, the former Yugoslavia, mired in poverty and dependent on foreign aid, consisted only of a dysfunctional federation of Serbia, Montenegro, and Kosovo. Tiny Montenegro declared its independence in June 2006, while Kosovo remained part of Serbia and an international protectorate of the United Nations. Its Albanian leadership, eager for a future apart from Serbia, declared independence in February 2008. America and most European countries recognized Kosovo's independence, but Serbia, bitterly opposed to the loss of sacred historical territory in Kosovo and backed by its ally, Russia, denounced Kosovo's independence as illegal.

The European Union

After the end of World War II, six Western European nations began a slow process of economic, political, and cultural integration. The collapse of Soviet power supplied a sudden jolt for accelerating this trend. In 1991, in the Dutch city of Maastricht, the members of the European Community, now twelve in number, negotiated the Maastricht Treaty, designed to shape Europe into a unified economic and political force. By 1993, the member states had ratified the treaty and, in recognition of its aims, the European Community became the European Union. The common monetary unit, the euro, now outpaces the dollar as a currency for worldwide use. The new Europe, whose goal is the free movement of goods, labor, capital, and services between countries, has become a powerful presence in world affairs.

On May 1, 2004, the European Union accepted ten new members, eight of which had been former Communist countries—the Czech Republic, Estonia, Hungary, Latvia, Lithuania, Poland, Slovakia, and Slovenia—together with Cyprus and Malta. They were followed in 2007 by Romania and Bulgaria. This ambitious enlargement of the EU marked the historic reintegration of a continent that had been divided for forty-five years by the iron curtain. The original club of six members has now grown to a political entity of twenty-seven members and five hundred million inhabitants and is the world's biggest economic and trading bloc. All the new members had made progress toward a market economy and had demonstrated acceptable standards of democracy and human rights. However, the new countries are much poorer than previous entrants to the EU and naturally hope to increase their prosperity and employment. Many Europeans are reluctant to surrender national interests to a European-wide organization.

The three largest countries in the European Union are France, Germany, and the United Kingdom. France and Germany are the largest countries in terms of area, with populations of sixty-two million and eighty-three million, respectively; they have traditionally set the agenda for the EU. France and the United Kingdom are nuclear powers. The United Kingdom, with a population of sixty million crammed into its small islands, maintains a special relationship with the United States.

In the United Kingdom, Prime Minister Margaret Thatcher resigned in 1990 in the face of conservative criticism. Her successor, John Major, maintained an uncertain majority in Parliament, increasingly troubled by political scandals and the rising popularity of the Labour party. In the election of 1997, that party, revitalized by Tony Blair, its young and lively leader in close touch with the people, scored an impressive victory.

Under his leadership, the Labour party moved to the political center. It endorsed a pro-business, pro-enterprise policy which limited benefits for the poor, and jettisoned the old working-class/state-ownership image. This policy gave the country an unusually strong economy, and London became a vibrant worldwide financial center.

In Northern Ireland, where Protestant and Catholics had long been at war with each other, Blair helped to end the conflict and create an elected assembly. Although at times threatening to breakdown, the experiment in power sharing continues to function. In bringing the two sides together, Blair had succeeded where every previous prime minister had failed. Prime Minister Blair, despite strong opposition in Britain, supported the United States–led invasion of Iraq in 2003 and committed forces to the coalition. He saw his country as an important bridge between the EU and America—a stance that became increasingly unpopular both in his own country and within the EU. All the promise of Blair's early years and his extraordinary popularity were eroded by his unwavering support of the detested war in Iraq. He resigned in mid 2007 and was succeeded by Gordon Brown, who had been Blair's impressive chancellor of the Exchequer and his rival for the past decade. Brown was also less supportive of the Iraq War and announced troop withdrawals to be completed by the end of 2008. With his support waning, Brown resigned in 2010 and was replaced by David Cameron, a Conservative who entered into a coalition with left-leaning Liberal Democrats.

France, including the Mediterranean island of Corsica, has the largest territorial state in Europe. Proud of their historical tradition, the French cherish their past and are uneasy about the intrusion of alien ways, especially from the United States. Despite high unemployment and productivity harmed by a thirty-five-hour workweek and job protection, the French are hostile to reforms that threaten their entitlements.

At home, the Socialist François Mitterrand, president until 1995, named a moderate conservative, Jacques Chirac, as his prime minister in 1986. Succeeding Mitterrand as president, Chirac remained in power for the next twelve years, continuing the tradition of a strong, centralized state with generous welfare benefits. Chirac had no viable opposition, apart from a perennial gadfly, Jean Marie Le Pen, an anti-immigration, anti-EU, antiglobalization, anti-Semitic, racist candidate of the far right, who qualified, astonishingly, for a presidential runoff election against Chirac in 2002. He lost resoundingly, but the affair revealed a troubling undercurrent in French society.

In 2004, President Chirac was at the center of a storm that divided the six million Muslims living in France. A law banned the wearing of symbols of religion in France's traditionally secular schools; it was aimed primarily at the headscarves worn by Muslim girls. This reaffirmation of the secular nature of the French state and its insistence on cultural uniformity was at odds with the policies of other EU countries, which have accepted multiculturalism and tolerate headscarves in schools.

Following the policies of de Gaulle, the French government still wants to play its part in world affairs, for instance, opposing U.S. policies in the Middle East. President Chirac's stand against participation in the Iraq War in 2003 brought him renewed popularity in France. At the same time, however, France worked closely with NATO to preserve peace in the Balkans. Its chief concern is cooperation with Germany in creating an effective European Union that balances French and German aspirations. Chirac was identified with a vision of a powerful, politically integrated Europe, serving as a French-led counterweight to the United States.

In 2007, Nicolas Sarkozy succeeded the aging Chirac. He came to office claiming a mandate for change that included domestic reforms, a new relationship with the United States, and an active role in the European Union, as well as fighting global poverty and global warming.

Sarkozy's plans to reform rules on labor, tighten welfare rules, and review public health insurance schemes started with abolishing the "special regimes" that allowed utilities and transport workers to retire at fifty on a full pension. It led to a one-day strike, but the public backed Sarkozy, not the strikers. It was a crucial change and hinted at success for future reforms.

Germany has the largest population in Europe and is proud of the peaceful reunification of its western and eastern parts in 1990 and the relocation of its capital from Bonn to Berlin. Helmut Kohl, as chancellor of West Germany, was the architect of the reunited Germany; he poured huge amounts of West German money into what had been the Communist German Democratic Republic, hoping for quick integration. However, attitudes and habits developed under Communism have persisted; having no experience with democracy, the seventeen million former East Germans were somewhat disillusioned with unification. Unemployment was as high as 25 percent because Communist-era factories closed and no new industries were established. The rise in right-wing violence since reunification is particularly severe in the old East Germany, where neo-Nazis and skinheads, usually underemployed and alienated youth, have been responsible for outbreaks of lawlessness and brutality against "outsiders"—immigrants and Jews—whom they regard as parasites draining away the country's resources and diluting its national character.

Kohl's conservative chancellorship ended after sixteen eventful years. In 1998, Germans elected Gerhard Schröder, leader of the Social Democrats, as his successor. Schröder's party formed a coalition with the Greens, who scaled down their environmental and pacifist radicalism.

The costs of German reunification are still considerable; they have had a dampening effect on Germany's economy. The German government's vision for the future, called Agenda 2010, advocates much-needed labor-market reform and tax cuts in order to stimulate demand and cut unemployment which hit a postwar record in 2005. Gradually, Agenda 2010 started to make a difference under Angela Merkel, Germany's first woman chancellor, who took office in 2005.

In the last few years several countries in the European Union have been burdened with severe economic problems. The current crisis is somewhat related to the global financial meltdown in 2008 precipitated by American banks lowering standards for granting mortgages and Wall Street's reckless speculation in these mortgages. But the European economy also had its own deficiencies particularly states borrowing excessive sums beyond their capacity to pay back and a collapsing real estate bubble that caused unemployment to soar in several countries. In the hardest hit countries—Portugal, Ireland, Greece, and Spain—investor confidence fell markedly, increasing borrowing costs that accentuated an alarming budget deficit. To deal with the crisis, several countries have slashed or plan to slash civil service salaries and staff and raise the retirement age, moves that anger a large segment of the population. Because of the Euro Monetary Union's (EMU) collective support, and with Germany paying the lion's share, a major default on bonds by a member country has so far been averted. Nevertheless, economists continue to warn that if European countries do not tighten the reins on spending, their deficits will soar increasing the danger of defaulting.

But will Europeans accept cutting government entitlements which provide cradle to grave social welfare, including national health care, early retirement with substantial pensions, and generous unemployment benefits? Imposing heavy demands on national budgets, generosity on this scale is unsustainable, a problem made more severe as the European population ages. This means that fewer taxpaying workers will be required to support growing numbers of retirees. Raising money for these programs differs considerably across the Continent. For example, Germans pay heavily—in addition to regular income tax assessments, mandatory social security and health insurance charges are deducted from their paychecks. On the other hand, for Greeks, direct contributions for these benefits are minimal. Regarding these entitlements as their due, many Europeans will resist government attempts to limit them in order to cope with escalating deficits.

New and Old Threats: Muslim Immigration and the Resurgence of Anti-Semitism

Among the problems that have burdened Europe in the first decade of the twenty-first century are the threat of terrorism by radical Islamists; the failure of millions of Muslim immigrants to integrate into European society; and a resurgence of anti-Semitism. The issue of terrorism is discussed in the next section.

Muslim Immigration

In the 1950s and 1960s, Western Europe's booming economy created a demand for cheap labor that was met by an influx of millions of Muslims from Turkey, Pakistan, and North Africa.

In succeeding decades, additional millions of Muslim immigrants from the Middle East and sub-Saharan Africa, many of them illegal, settled in various European lands. Like other immigrants, they sought to join relatives, find economic opportunities, or escape from oppressive regimes. Several of these countries, including France, Germany, Britain, Belgium, Holland, Spain, and Denmark, now have substantial Muslim populations. The problem is that many Muslims remain profoundly alienated from European society and at odds with its values. European liberal democracy, which espouses religious freedom, equal rights for women, separation of church and state, and freedom of expression, noticeably conflicts with many facets of Islamic society.

In describing the failure of Muslim integration, analysts refer to the demands of some Muslim groups that they be governed by their own religious law rather than the law of the land. They also cite the perpetuation in Europe by some Muslims of cultural mores that sanction polygamy, forced marriages between young girls and much older men, wife-beating, and so-called honor killings of "wayward" females, and require women to keep their bodies and faces hidden from view; the high crime rate among Muslims—in Britain Muslims are 2 percent of the population, but more than 8 percent of the prison population; and the emergence of extremist Islamist cells in European lands that have participated in several terrorist acts—much of the planning for the 9/11 attacks took place in Hamburg, Germany. British commentators have raised a difficult question. In the past, they say, immigrant Jews and recently Sikhs and Hindus have thrived in Britain, even when confronted with prejudice. Why, they ask, is the integration of Muslim immigrants in Western society so fraught with problems?

In the fall of 2005, the suburbs of Paris and scores of other French cities were convulsed by two weeks of rioting—nearly 9,000 cars were set afire and schools, shops, and churches burned to the ground—by young Muslim males from the bleak housing projects inhabited principally by North African immigrants. That the great majority of rioters were not recent immigrants but had been born in France was particularly distressing to officials, for the French government prided itself on creating a uniform French identity that superseded ethnic and religious origins. Whatever the aspirations of the government, many French citizens remain resentful of North African immigrants, whom they view as an alien minority that, unlike other immigrants, has failed to integrate into French society. They point to the immigrants' preference for native cultural traditions, the high cost of welfare payments they receive, and the high crime rate among them—Muslims, about 10 percent of the nation, constitute more than 50 percent of France's prison population. Numerous commentators, however, interpreted the riots as a rebellion by a resentful underclass protesting discrimination, segregation, poverty, and a staggering unemployment rate—as much as 40 percent—for young Muslim males.

Faced with what is perceived as a rapidly growing, unassimilable Muslim minority that is hostile to Western values, lives in isolated communities, often does not speak the host nation's language, and recruits and finances terrorists, Europe is experiencing a backlash against Muslim immigrants and multiculturalism. An increasing number of Europeans now say that the premise of multiculturalism—assigning equal value to and tolerating Islamic traditions—was a mistake, for several of these traditions undermine democracy and fragment the nation. As the Indian-born Salman Rushdie observed: "No society, no matter how tolerant, can expect to thrive if its citizens don't prize what citizenship means."[3] The sentiments of Jan Wolter, a Dutch judge, are shared by many native Europeans: "We demand a new social contract. We no longer accept that people don't learn our language, we require that they send their daughters to school, and we demand they stop bringing in young brides from the desert and locking them up in third floor apartments."[4] In February 2011, Prime Minister David Cameron attacked Britain's policy of multiculturalism, maintaining that it fostered segregated communities where Islamic terrorism thrived. There is the fear that extremist right-wing political parties, ultrantionalistic, racist, and intolerant, will capitalize on this wave of anti-immigrant sentiment that is sweeping across Europe.

Increasingly governments are introducing tighter immigration laws and are deporting Muslim radicals. They are also trying to work with moderate Muslims who support integration into European society and value Europe's liberal-democratic tradition. However, successful integration, say some commentators, is a two-way street. It is necessary that

European society also address the socioeconomic problems burdening Muslims, overcome racist attitudes toward immigrants, and recognize the fact that numerous Muslims do work and pay taxes, respect the laws of their adopted country, and reject extremism; most importantly, Muslims must be made to feel that their religion is not being attacked and insulted. For many years to come, Europeans will be confronted with—or tormented by—the question of Islam's place in their countries. And there is the fear that extreme rightists, obsessed with Muslim immigration and muticulturalism, might turn violent as in the case of a Norwegian self-described Christian crusader who killed more than 75 people in a car bomb attack in a busy government plaza and in a shooting spree at a youth camp.

Resurgence of Anti-Semitism

In the decades following the Holocaust, overt anti-Semitism appeared to have receded in Western Europe. The outbursts of the traditionally anti-Semitic far right did not greatly affect the surviving Jews and their descendants, who represented a model of successful integration. In recent years, however, there has been a significant upsurge of anti-Semitic incidents in European lands, including physical assaults; the firebombing of Jewish synagogues, schools, and homes; and the desecration of Jewish cemeteries with Nazi symbols—much of it, but not all, initiated by the growing number of Muslims residing in Western Europe. Denis MacShane, a Labour member of Parliament who in 2007 chaired a committee of British parliamentarians that studied anti-Semitism in Britain, concluded that "hatred of Jews has reached new heights in Europe."[5] Similar conclusions were reached by the United States State Department and the Parliamentary Assembly of the Council of Europe.

"It is Islamism [Muslim extremism] that has unleashed new twenty-first century anti-Semitism," observes MacShane, "and it is impossible to discuss the problem without dealing with Islamism."[6] The creation of Israel on what is perceived as inviolable Muslim land and the Jewish state's ongoing conflict with the Palestinians have stirred the cauldron of Jew-hatred in the Arab and Muslim world. Now reaching epidemic proportions, anti-Semitism has become a principal theme in the Middle Eastern media and a motivation for attacks on Jews by Muslims living in Europe. As Cardinal Tucci, the director of Vatican Radio, stated in November 2003: "Now in the whole Muslim world, in the media, the radio, television, in schools, a whole system inciting to anti-Semitism exists. It is the worst anti-Semitism that can be imagined after Nazi anti-Semitism, if not its equal."[7]

Contemporary Muslim anti-Semitism borrows considerably from traditional European anti-Semitism—Christian, nationalist, and Nazi. Like the Nazis, much of the Muslim world perceives Jews as a criminal people that threatens all humanity, blames the Jews for their misfortunes, and holds out the image of a utopian future once Israel is eradicated and the Jews eliminated. As in Nazi Germany, the media in the Arab and Muslim world are often filled with repulsive caricatures of Jews—dark, stooped, sinister, hook-nosed, devil-like creatures—many of them taken from Nazi works. In Arab sermons, classrooms school books, and on the Internet, Jews are often referred to as "accursed," "descendants of apes and pigs," "the scum of the human race," "the rats of the world," "bacteria," "vampires," "usurers," and "whoremongers."

Reminiscent of Nazi propaganda, no accusation against Jews is too absurd not to be included in the litany of Jewish evil propagated in the Muslim media, and not just by extremists. Hamas, the radical Palestinian organization that rules Gaza, maintains that Jews were responsible for the French Revolution, the Russian Revolution, both world wars, and the atomic bombing of Hiroshima and Nagasaki. Osama bin Laden maintained that Jews "in accordance with their religion, believe that human beings are their slaves and that those who refuse [to recognize this] should be put to death."[8] The Arab media have even revived the outrageous medieval blood libel that Jews are required to murder non-Jewish children in order to obtain their blood for making unleavened bread for Passover. Holocaust denial is widespread in the Middle East; so too is celebrating Hitler's mass murder of Jews. A columnist for *Al-Akhbar*, considered a moderate newspaper sponsored by the Egyptian government, gives "thanks to Hitler of blessed memory," for taking revenge against Jews—although Muslims "do have a complaint against him for his revenge on them was not enough."[9] And Dr. Ahmed Abu Halabiyah, rector of advanced studies at the Islamic University of

Gaza, is more representative than unique; similar sentiments are frequently voiced in the Arab media: "The Jews . . . must be butchered and must be killed. . . . It is forbidden to have mercy in your hearts for the Jews in any place and in any land, make war on them anywhere that you find yourself. Any place that you meet them, kill them."[10]

Propagated over the Internet and by radical imams in mosques throughout Europe, this demonization of the Jew—together with scenes of violent conflict between Israelis and Palestinians and Hezbollah frequently depicted on television—has incited Muslim youth in Europe to acts of intimidation, physical assault, and vandalism against Jews; it has also led to organized campaigns of vilification of Jews on college campuses. On a positive note, in some European lands, Muslim and Jewish organizations are engaged in interfaith dialogue, and some Muslim intellectuals and religious leaders have condemned anti-Semitic outbursts.

In addition to the anti-Semitic incidents initiated by Muslims residing in various European lands, analysts have pointed to the ongoing Jew-hatred of the far right, and a rather new phenomenon, a growing and insidious anti-Semitism afflicting the left.

As in the past, European anti-Semitism remains a bulwark of the far right, traditionally hostile to the Enlightenment's legacy of reason, political freedom, and tolerance. Principally extreme nationalists, racists, Fascists, and neo-Nazis, they propagate Holocaust denial and Jewish conspiracy theories—Jews invented a "Holocaust hoax" in order to extract compensation from Germany; Jews control the world's media and finances and are conspiring to dominate the planet; Jews are the real power behind the U.S. government; Jews are a threat to the nation.

During the Nazi era and for decades before, the left—liberals, socialists, trade unionists, and intellectuals, including many academics—had been the strongest defenders of Jews against their detractors and oppressors. But now the distinguishing feature of the "new anti-Semitism" is its adoption by a New Left that employs anti-Semitic language and imagery—linking the Star of David with the swastika—to express its support of the Palestinians and to delegitimize Israel; for them, Israelis are today's Nazis and Israel is a criminal state that should disappear. Analysts point out that this goes beyond criticism of Israeli policies, which is, of course, legitimate. Nazism is a recognized symbol of evil. When New Left intellectuals draw parallels between the Jewish state and the Third Reich, they intend to say that Israelis—and by extension Jews everywhere, the vast majority of whom support Israel—are morally equivalent to Nazis, that is, they are irredeemably evil. Such demonization of Jews is a revival of traditional anti-Semitism in a new garb. And its message is widely propagated in European universities by Islamic organizations and their New Left allies.

Many Europeans are concerned about the revival of anti-Semitism. They recognize that Jew-hatred and the irrational myths associated with it, which undermine rational thinking and incite barbaric violence, transcend a purely Jewish concern. They threaten the core values of Western civilization, as Nazism so painfully demonstrated.

Our Global Age: Cultural Clashes and Terrorism

In the twenty-first century, globalization continues relentlessly; the world is being knit ever closer together by the spread of Western ideals, popular culture (particularly American), free-market capitalism, and technology. Government officials and business and professional people all over the world dress in Western clothes. Women follow Western fashions in dress and makeup. People line up to eat at McDonald's, see a Hollywood movie, or attend a rock concert. Everywhere people are eager to adopt the latest technology that originated in the West but is now also manufactured in other, particularly Asian, lands. Advanced technology intensifies the means of communication, not only through television and radio but also with faxes, e-mail, cellular phones, and the Internet.

These developments promote shared interests among individuals and businesses, some of them multinational corporations, throughout the globe, reducing the importance of national frontiers. "Globalization," in the words of one commentator, "is about the disappearance of boundaries—cultural and economic boundaries, physical boundaries, linguistic boundaries—and the challenge of organizing our world in their absence."[11] All these factors combined are reshaping Western and non-Western societies in a relentless adjustment that causes both deep hardships and possibilities for a better life.

The ideals of freedom and democracy, historical accomplishments of Western civilization, exert a powerful influence worldwide; they are also part of the process of westernization. Unlike technology, they cannot be easily put into practice outside the countries of their origin. However, they inspire human ambitions everywhere. They have even become part of the rhetoric of dictatorships.

At the same time, strong cultural traditions still divide the world. Traditional ways of life, often at odds with the demands of modernization and democratization, remain deeply engrained in many lands. Among people deeply committed to their own cultural traditions or feeling left behind by modernization, the process of globalization has provoked a powerful backlash, nowhere more so than in the Muslim world. The hatred of radical Muslims for the West, which they see as a threat to traditional Islam, is a striking example of the clash of cultures in a world being increasingly connected.

On September 11, 2001, nineteen Muslim Arabs, most of them from Saudi Arabia, hijacked four planes: two of them they crashed into the World Trade Center in New York, bringing down both towers; a third plane rammed into the Pentagon in Washington, D.C., causing severe damage; the fourth plane, apparently headed for the White House, crashed in a field in Pennsylvania when passengers heroically attacked the hijackers. In all, almost three thousand people perished in the worst terrorist attack in history. The meticulously planned operation was the work of Al Qaeda, an international terrorist network of militant Muslims, or Islamists, as they call themselves. In 1998, it was responsible for the deadly bombings of the American embassies in Kenya and Tanzania, which killed hundreds, and in 2000, it detonated a bomb next to the U.S. destroyer *Cole* in the harbor of Aden, costing the lives of seventeen American sailors.

The leader of Al Qaeda, Osama bin Laden, scion of an immensely wealthy Saudi family, operated from Afghanistan with the protection of the radical fundamentalist Taliban, who ruled the country, transforming it into a repressive regime based on a rigid interpretation of Islamic law. In particular, the Taliban imposed oppressive rules for women, permitting beatings by male relatives, prohibiting females from working, barring them from schools, and demanding that they wear a garment—the burka—that covered them from head to foot. Violators could be severely beaten, imprisoned, or executed.

When Taliban leaders refused to turn bin Laden over to the United States, President George W. Bush, supported by an international coalition, launched a military campaign whose ultimate goal was the destruction of international terrorism. Local Afghan forces opposed to the Taliban, assisted by American airpower—which proved decisive—defeated the Taliban in a few weeks. But the new democratically elected government, backed by American and NATO troops, faces immense problems: local warlords who defy central authority, a resurgence of Taliban fighters—many of them coming from the lawless tribal regions of neighboring Pakistan—and a country impoverished by years of warfare and misrule. Compounding the problems faced by the struggling new government is the tremendous increase in opium traffic—in 2006, it was estimated that Afghanistan provided 92 percent of the world's illegal opium crop. Drug trafficking has fostered armed militias, corrupted local officials who impede the progress toward democracy, and provided a resurgent Taliban with funds to continue the struggle against the new Afghan government backed by American and NATO troops.

Afghan officials, many of them corrupt and inefficient, generally owe their prime loyalties to family and tribe and not to the nation. Unable to provide security in large areas of the country or improve the standard of living, the government is unpopular with the Afghan people. American and coalition forces have succeeded in killing and capturing numerous midlevel Taliban leaders, but they have been less successful in providing security and essential services for the Afghan people. To promote instability, the Taliban deliberately targets for assassination local Afghan officials and virtually anyone cooperating with the Americans. Suicide bombings and homemade explosives placed at roadsides and in cars have caused civilian casualties to climb. The Taliban also threatens working women and has forced the closing of girls' schools.

Primary Source

United Nations Secretary-General, Ending Violence Against Women, "the Systematic Domination of Women by Men"

In October 2006 the United Nations released the Secretary-General's in-depth study of violence against women, which concluded that "the pervasiveness of violence against women across the boundaries of nation, culture, race, class and religion points to its roots in patriarchy—the systematic domination of women by men." Excerpts from the study follow.

A number of key means through which male dominance and women's subordination are maintained are common to many settings. These include: . . . control over women's sexuality and reproductive capacity; cultural norms and practices that entrench women's unequal status; State structures and processes that legitimize and institutionalize gender inequalities; and violence against women. Violence against women is both a means by which women's subordination is perpetuated and a consequence of their subordination.

Violence against women serves as a mechanism for maintaining male authority. When a woman is subjected to violence for transgressing social norms governing female sexuality and family roles, for example, the violence is not only individual but, through its punitive and controlling functions, also reinforces prevailing gender norms. . . .

When the State fails to hold the perpetrators accountable, . . . [it] sends a message to society that male violence against women is both acceptable and inevitable. As a result, patterns of violent behaviour are normalized. . . .

Cultural justifications for restricting women's human rights have been asserted by some States and by social groups within many countries claiming to defend cultural tradition. . . . [R]eligious "fundamentalisms" in diverse geographic and religious contexts has become a serious challenge to efforts to secure women's human rights. . . .

Femicide [the murder of women] takes place in many contexts . . . [including] the protection of family "honour". For example, crimes committed in the name of "honour", usually by a brother, father, husband or other male family member, are a means of controlling women's choices, not only in the area of sexuality but also in other aspects of behaviour, such as freedom of movement. . . .

Crimes against women committed in the name of "honour" may occur within the family or within the community. . . . UNFPA estimated that 5,000 women are murdered by family members each year in "honour killings" around the world. . . .

Trafficking is a form of violence against women that takes place in multiple settings and usually involves many different actors including families, local brokers, international criminal networks and immigration authorities. Trafficking in human beings takes place both between and within countries. The majority of the victims of human trafficking are women and children, and many are trafficked for purposes of sexual exploitation.

Question for Analysis

1. According to the UN study, what means are used to maintain male dominance and female subordination?

Ending Violence Against Women: From Words to Action, Study of the Secretary-General, October 9, 2006.

A Culture Clash. The Niqab worn by this Muslim woman on a street in Brussels covers the body from head to toe, leaving only a slit for the eyes. Maintaining that such dress demeans women, Europeans are increasingly urging banning it outside the home.

After almost ten years of conflict—the longest war in American history—Americans have grown increasingly disenchanted with the war, and President Barack Obama has planned to start pulling out troops in 2011. Worsening the Taliban threat exponentially is the movement's spread to Pakistan, where armed Taliban insurgents, drawing recruits from the masses of poor and committed Muslims, have challenged the central government's authority. Although not a very likely prospect, there could be no more frightening development than the Taliban and other Muslim extremists gaining power in Pakistan, which possesses a nuclear arsenal.

On numerous occasions President Bush and his chief advisers declared that the attack on Afghanistan was directed against "evil doers" and not against Muslims in general or their faith. However, bin Laden and his followers viewed their struggle against the United States as a jihad or holy war against the infidel. Bin Laden and other Arabs from Morocco to Yemen, devoted to a militant Islam, had fought in Afghanistan to drive out the Soviets. During that conflict, bin Laden and his cohorts drew up plans for the creation of an Islamic world-state governed by Islamic law, a revival of the medieval caliphate. In 1998, bin Laden told his followers that the stationing of American troops, an army of "Crusaders," in Saudi Arabia, "the land of the two holy mosques," demonstrated that America was waging war against God, Muhammad, and Muslims. Bin Laden wanted to drive Westerners and Western values out of Islamic lands and impose a narrow, intolerant version of Islam on the Muslim world. His followers are zealots who are convinced that they are doing God's will. Recruits for suicide missions are equally convinced that they are waging holy war against the enemies of God and their centers of evil, for which they will be richly rewarded in Paradise. In 1998, bin Laden called "on every Muslim who believed in Allah and wishes to be rewarded to comply with Allah's order to kill the Americans and plunder their money wherever and whenever they find it. . . . to launch the raid on Satan's U.S troops and the devil's supporters allying with them."[12]

To be sure, the actions of bin Laden and his followers violated core Islamic teachings against killing civilians. At the same time, however, terrorists find religious justification for their actions in Islamic tradition. The early followers of Muhammad, says Bernard Lewis, divided the world

> *into two houses: the House of Islam, in which a Muslim government ruled and Muslim law prevailed, and the House of War, the rest of the world . . . ruled by infidels. Between the two, there was to be a perpetual state of war until the entire world either embraced Islam or submitted to the rule of the Muslim state. . . . For Osama bin Laden, 2001 marks the resumption of the war for the religious dominance of the world that began in the seventh*

> *century. For him and his followers, this is the moment of opportunity. Today America exemplifies the civilization that embodies the leadership of the House of War, and it . . . has become degenerate and demoralized, ready to be overthrown.*[13]

The hatred of radical Muslims for the West shows that in an age of globalism the world is still divided by strong cultural traditions. It also reveals how the problems confronting the Middle East—authoritarian governments, the suppression of human rights, rampant corruption, mushrooming populations, high unemployment, and the ongoing Arab–Israeli conflict—have a global impact. All these factors have led many disillusioned Muslims to place their hopes for a better life in a radical Islam that promises to restore a glorious past and guarantee entrance to Paradise. Fostering religious fanaticism and intolerance are the numerous religious schools financed by Saudi Arabia that have been established in many parts of the Muslim world. In these schools youngsters are given little or no secular education and from an early age are indoctrinated in the tenets of radical Islamism: hatred of the West, holy war against the infidel, the Jew as Devil, and the virtue of martyrdom for the faith.

After September 11, several terrorist operations in Europe and the United States were thwarted, including attempts to explode an airplane headed for Detroit and planting an explosive device in Times Square. But terrorists, either loosely or directly affiliated with Al Qaeda, succeeded in other operations, most of them suicide bombings that killed and wounded thousands of innocents. In July 2005, Muslim suicide bombers killed more than fifty people and injured seven hundred in a terrorist attack on London's transit system. In a second attack two weeks later, the bombs failed to detonate and the suspected suicide bombers were arrested. A year later British security forces foiled a terrorist plot to blow up several transatlantic flights departing from Heathrow airport that would have killed more people than had perished on September 11. That the planners and perpetrators of these attacks were British citizens terrorizing their fellow citizens discomforted analysts; they feared that the millions of Muslims dwelling in Europe were potential recruits for extremist Islamic groups, including Al Qaeda, engaged in holy war against the West and that European cities would become targets of fanatical suicide bombers. Likewise, U.S. officials are disconcerted by the rising number of terrorist attempts on American soil by Islamic radicals who are American citizens. (To be sure, the overwhelming number of American Muslims are loyal citizens and do not support terrorism.)

A tenacious United States, and other countries with varying degrees of determination and effectiveness, have combated militant Islam. The tracking down, capture, and killing of Al Qaeda leaders and rigorous international efforts to destabilize Al Qaeda's vast financial network had weakened the terrorist organization. Then on May 1, 2011 President Barak Obama announced that a superbly orchestrated operation by the CIA and Navy Seals killed bin Laden—not in a cave in Pakistan's remote tribal lands, where it was generally thought he was hiding, but in a large, specially built compound with tall security fences in an upscale section of a town only 70 miles from the capital.

But the death of bin Laden does not mean the end of Al Qaeda or Islamist terrorism. With Al Qaeda located in numerous countries, international terrorism remains a threat to world stability. Moreover, throughout the globe there are many affiliated, but independent, Islamist groups and freelancers that are inspired by bin Laden's ideology. Like bin Laden, these offshoots regard Muslims as victims of Western exploitation and believe that their faith demands that they fight and conquer nonbelievers. The seething discontent in the Muslim world, particularly among Arabs, continues to provide Al Qaeda with zealous recruits—although the death of Al Qaeda's inspirational leader may impede recruitment—willing to inflict maximum casualties on civilians, even if doing so means blowing themselves up in the process. And Al Qaeda can rely on trained operatives who have served the organization for years. The West takes seriously Al Qaeda's vow to avenge the killing of their leader. And it is likely that affiliated jihadists groups have made a similar vow. Moreover, despite the seizure of Al Qaeda's assets, local cells continue to receive substantial funds from wealthy Arab donors, from money collected from the faithful purportedly for charitable causes, and from criminal activities. It is hoped that the death of bin Laden, Al Qaeda's principal fund raiser, particularly from fellow wealthy Saudi Arabians, will diminish Al Qaeda's cash supply. But terrorist undertakings do not require great sums of money. The bombings of a night club in Bali that killed 202 people, including 82 Australians, cost less than $35,000, the London subway bombings less than $500, and the September 11 attacks under $500,000. And Al Qaeda, with local support, has set up training camps in the remote tribal areas of Pakistan and the mountains and deserts of Yemen, which analysts fear is becoming a new Afghanistan. Employing robotic drones, commando teams, and trained local operatives, the United States is engaged in a shadow war against terrorists in these and other countries.

AP Photo/Laurent Rebours.

DOWNFALL OF A TYRANT. After Baghdad, the capital of Iraq, had been taken by American forces in April 2003, the twenty-foot stature of Saddam Hussein was pulled down by Iraqis with the assistance of a U.S. vehicle.

The events of September 11 may have signaled a new type of warfare for a new century. Free and open societies like the United States are vulnerable to attack, less from states that are deterred by America's might—as in the Cold War—than by stateless conspiratorial groups employing modern computers, communications, and difficult-to-trace financial operations to organize and finance terrorism. Such groups are not deterred by America's arsenal. And there is the fearful prospect that a rogue state will supply these groups with biological, chemical, and eventually nuclear weapons to wage war by proxy.

It was just such a fear that led President Bush in March 2003 to order an invasion of Iraq. The war was supported by Great Britain, which provided military assistance, but France, Germany, and Russia strongly opposed the decision. In about three weeks, U.S. and British forces, in an awesome display of operational planning and precision weaponry suffering minimal casualties, destroyed Iraq's military hardware and decimated its armies. The victorious coalition forces uncovered torture chambers, where "enemies" of Hussein's regime were brutalized, and mass graves, where thousands were slaughtered at the tyrant's command.

But vexing problems remained. Could the United States install a democratic regime in a country torn by ethnic, religious, and tribal hatreds; where some Iraqis regarded the Americans as hated occupiers; and where democratic traditions and attitudes were largely lacking?

The United States declared that it had invaded Iraq to overthrow a ruthless dictator who had used poison gas against Iranian forces and Kurdish rebels in the 1980s and was now feverishly amassing an arsenal of biological and chemical weapons and was also seeking a nuclear capability. Now, warned the United States, there was a danger that Hussein would supply these weapons of mass destruction (WMD) to be used against Americans. However, American intelligence was faulty. When no such weapons were found in the months after Iraq's defeat, critics in several lands accused the United States of pursuing a reckless foreign policy.

After crushing the Iraqi army, coalition forces still faced guerrilla warfare from hard-liners loyal to Hussein and his Baath party and from militant Islamists, or jihadists—many of them Arabs from other lands, particularly Saudi Arabia—who saw themselves engaged in a holy war against hated Americans. American soldiers were confronted with numerous daily attacks, but they did succeed in killing and capturing many of the top leadership of the Baath party, including Hussein's two notorious sons, Uday and Qusay, who had routinely imprisoned, tortured, and murdered many Iraqis. And in December 2003, Saddam Hussein was captured. Put on trial by Iraqi authorities and found guilty of crimes against humanity, Saddam was executed by hanging at the end of December 2006.

The insurgents, predominantly Sunni Muslims who had received favored treatment under Saddam—the ruling elite were virtually all Sunnis—also targeted Shi'ite Muslims, who constitute the majority of the population and had been cruelly oppressed by Saddam. By murdering Shi'ite clerics, pilgrims, and worshipers and bombing their mosques, the insurgents hoped to trigger a sectarian conflict that would make the new Iraq ungovernable. Their frequent suicide car bombings, often in crowded sections, made daily life extremely insecure in Baghdad and in other parts of the country. Shi'ite militia and death squads responded in kind, kidnapping, torturing, and executing Sunnis.

The continued loss of American lives, the spiraling cost of pacifying and reconstructing Iraq, and the failure to find weapons of mass destruction led more Americans to question President Bush's policies. In February 2007, President Bush announced a new security operation, the "surge," which called for sending more American troops to Iraq and greater American involvement in curtailing sectarian violence, particularly in Baghdad. By early 2008, the surge seemed to be working. Suicide bombings, sectarian violence, civilian deaths, and American casualties were down considerably. Another encouraging sign was the growing split between Iraqi Sunni insurgents and foreign jihadists. Repelled by the jihadists' brutality, religious extremism, and domineering ways, some Sunni insurgents, including Baathists who had been loyal to Hussein and Sunni tribesmen, joined with the American forces in the fight against Al Qaeda in Iraq.

President Barack Obama, who took office in January 2009, was committed to withdrawing American forces from Iraq. At the end of August 2010, all American combat troops left the country. Still remaining were some fifty thousand troops assigned to assist and advise Iraqi security forces, who now have total responsibility for securing the country. By the end of 2011, virtually all American troops will be out of Iraq. More than 4,450 American soldiers died in the seven-and-a-half year conflict; there were more than one hundred thousand Iraqi fatalities. Although deaths caused by insurgents are down considerably, continued horrific suicide bombings, directed largely against Shi'ites, the army, and the police, intensified concerns that Iraqi security forces may not be able to protect life and property after the Americans depart. Religious and ethnic conflicts continue to block the establishment of a stable, democratic government.

The United States had hoped that the toppling of Saddam's murderous rule and the construction of a free, democratic, and viable Iraq would foster the spread of democracy in other parts of the Middle East, defusing radicalism and anti-American sentiments. Although this still remains a possibility, many analysts conclude that the Iraqi imbroglio demonstrates once more the immense difficulty of transplanting Western democratic values and institutions to regions whose history, cultural traditions, and religious, ethnic, and tribal rivalries, do not easily mesh with democracy. Analysts also argue that the war in Iraq diverted military resources away from Afghanistan, enabling the Taliban to reconstitute its forces. And they point to a larger concern: the increasingly costly and unpopular wars in Iraq and Afghanistan (along with the failure to get Iran to halt its nuclear enrichment program) illustrate the limitations of American power. The American military has demonstrated the ability to wage successful counterterrorism campaigns, but, say some analysts, it should not be entrapped into nation-building, an amorphous objective fraught with uncertainty that is beyond the capacity of the military, or, indeed, of the U.S. government.

In early 2011, a wave of popular protest against autocratic rulers—what has been called the "Arab Spring" swept across—the Arab world, a region where democracy has been dismissed as an impossible dream. Many of the participants were alienated and educated youth clamoring for jobs and political freedom. Long ruling strongmen were forced out in Tunisia and Egypt and protests resounded in Algeria, Yemen, Bahrain, Jordan, Syria, and Libya. In Syria, President Bashar-al Assad's police and army used lethal force against protesters, killing thousands. In Libya, there was open rebellion against Muammar el-Qaddafi's forty year tyranny. To protect civilians, NATO, including the United States, provided air support for the rebels. While Western policy makers welcome this democratic thrust in the Arab world, they are concerned about the outcome. Will the secular and democratic movement be usurped by well-organized radical Islamists who are poised and eager to exploit any instability and breakdown of authority? Will embryonic democracies and established secular autocracies be replaced by anti-Western theocratic regimes that foster a fanatic fundamentalism and terrorism. For example, Egyptian Coptic Christians, who have faced violent attacks and church burnings, are fearful of emboldened Islamists.

International terrorism is a major source of concern in today's interconnected world. However, there are others. Western science, medicine, humanitarianism, and economic progress have produced an unprecedented population explosion in Asia, Africa, the Middle East, and Latin America. For countless millennia the world's population remained almost stationary, slowly beginning to grow in the eighteenth century. At the height of Western imperialism, in 1900, the world's population reached 1.6 billion. Fifty years later, it reached 2.5 billion, and by the year 2000, it skyrocketed to 6.1 billion. Despite immense losses of life in two world wars, totalitarian terror, local famines, and other calamities, the world's population nearly quadrupled within a century. And in 2011, the world's population will pass seven billion. A spiraling population places immense pressure on the earth's resources and exacerbates both national and international problems.

The economic disparity between the rich and the poor, which sharply separates the industrialized from the developing countries, is further cause for concern. According to the World Bank, some 1.1 billion people live in *extreme* poverty—defined as struggling to survive on less than one dollar a day. (Another 1.6 billion people in poverty live on less than two dollars a day.) Each year eight million poverty-stricken people—some twenty thousand a day—perish because they lack safe drinking water, proper nutrition, bed nets to protect them from malaria-carrying mosquitoes, adequate hospitals, and life-saving drugs. In 2010, United Nations officials reported that 925 million people are undernourished, including 30 percent of the population of sub-Saharan Africa. In many regions of sub-Saharan Africa, the cycle of poverty and death, exacerbated by calamitous civil wars and the ravages of AIDS, has grown more vicious and tragic.

Destructive civil conflicts continue to rage. Strife in the Congo left some 3.8 million people dead between 1998 and 2003. More than two decades of warfare in southern Sudan cost two million lives before a peace treaty was signed between the government and the rebels in 2005. The actions of Arab militias against blacks in Sudan's Darfur region has been called genocidal. Most frightening for the future is the development of weapons of mass destruction by states that do not share Western democratic values. North Korea, a ruthless Communist dictatorship, possesses nuclear weapons. So too does Pakistan, which is afflicted with political instability and Taliban insurgents. Iran, headed by Islamic fundamentalists who have financed and provided military assistance to terrorist organizations, is moving ahead with plans to develop nuclear energy that, despite denials, will no doubt include nuclear weapons.

But there are also encouraging signs, even if mixed with misgivings. The Cold War, despite some recent friction, has ended, and NATO, the United Nations, and the African Union have provided security forces to quell violent conflicts in several regions. Impressive economic growth in many lands, including South and East Asia, has significantly broadened the middle class and reduced poverty, a testament to the effectiveness of the free market, although worldwide repercussions are still felt from the financial crisis of 2008 caused by wild speculation in the American mortgage market. And several other conditions could stifle economic growth: soaring oil prices, the threat of run away inflation, and the debt crisis burdening Europe.

Another hopeful sign is the spread of democracy in various parts of the world. Democracy has replaced repressive Communist regimes in Central and Eastern Europe, and American intervention and pressure have produced some democratic gains—even if fragile and limited—in the Middle East. Democratic institutions and values continue to attract activists throughout the globe, but promising democratic experiments have also been thwarted by the resurgence of authoritarian forces, notably in the new Russia and several countries in sub-Saharan Africa.

How can peaceful global interdependence be advanced, given the persistent cultural and political differences that divide the world, promoting hatred and inciting violence? Can the present generation of Western peoples, above all, Americans, help shape the development of the global community in accordance with the highest ideals of Western civilization: reason, freedom, and respect for human dignity?

❖ ❖ ❖

Notes

1. Boris Yeltsin, "Yeltsin Addresses Parliament on the State of the Nation," *Current Digest of the Post-Soviet Press,* April 9, 1997, p. 1.
2. Quoted in Steven Lee Myers, "Opponents Call Putin's Overhaul Plan a Step Back," *The New York Times,* September 14, 2004, p. 1A.
3. Quoted in *The Economist,* October 21, 2006, p. 68.
4. Quoted in "The End of Tolerance," *Newsweek International,* March 6, 2006.
5. Denis MacShane, "The New Anti-Semitism," *The Washington Post,* September 4, 2007, p. A17.
6. Denis MacShane, *Globalising Hatred: The New Antisemitism* (London: Weidenfeld & Nicolson, 2008), p. xi.
7. Quoted in Bat Ye'or, *Eurabia: The Euro-Arab Axis* (Madison, N.J.: Fairleigh Dickinson University Press, 2005, 2006), pp. 240–241.
8. Quoted in Raymond Ibrahim, ed. and trans., *The Al Qaeda Reader* (New York: Broadway Books, 2007), p. 277.
9. Quoted in Gabriel Schoenfeld, *The Return of Anti-Semitism* (San Francisco: Encounter Books, 2004), p. 13.
10. Quoted in Itamar Marcus and Barbara Crook, "Kill a Jew—Go to Heaven: The Perception of the Jew in Palestinian Society," *Jewish Political Studies Review,* Vol. 17, Nos. 3-4 (Fall 2005), p. 127. Copyright © 2005 Jerusalem Center for Public Affairs. Reprinted with permission.
11. Tony Judt, "Europe vs. America," *New York Review of Books,* February 10, 2005, p. 41.
12. From www.fas.org/irp/world/para/docs/980223-Fatwa.htm.
13. Bernard Lewis, "Revolt of Islam," *The New Yorker*, November 19, 2001, pp. 52, 62.

Suggested Reading

Bhagwati, Jagdish, *In Defense of Globalism* (2004). How globalism works, and how it can work better.

Caldwell, Christopher, *Reflections on the Revolution in Europe: Immigration, Islam, and the West* (2009). European culture challenged by Muslim immigrants.

Freeland, Chrystia, *Sale of the Century: Russia's Wild Ride from Communism to Capitalism* (2000). A colorful account of the takeover of state-owned firms by Russian oligarchs.

Habeck, Mary R. *Knowing the Enemy: Jihadist Ideology and the War on Terror* (2006). A clear analysis of the ideology of jihadism.

Hodge, James F., and Gideon Rose, eds., *How Did This Happen: Terrorism and the New War* (2001). Wide-ranging essays on the attack of September 11, 2001.

Hoffman, Bruce, *Inside Terrorism* (rev. ed., 2006). Insight into the historical evolution of terrorism and the terrorist mindset.

Jack, Andrew, *Inside Putin's Russia* (2004). Increasing stability and increasing authoritarianism under Putin.

Perry, Marvin, and Howard E. Negrin, eds., *The Theory and Practice of Islamic Terrorism: An Anthology* (2008). A useful collection of readings on an increasingly important topic.

Phares, Wallace, *Future Jihad* (2005). Strong on the historical roots of jihad and the strategies of contemporary jihadists.

Rieff, David, *Slaughterhouse: Bosnia and the Failure of the West* (1995). The responsibility of the Western nations for the Bosnian genocide.

Schoenfeld, Gabriel, *The Return of Anti-Semitism* (2004). An analysis of a disturbing trend in both the Islamic world and Europe.

Epilogue

Reaffirming the Core Values of the Western Tradition

In recent years, modern Western civilization, whose core values were articulated during the Enlightenment, has come under severe attack from several quarters, including religious thinkers, intellectuals loosely called postmodernists, advocates of the poor and oppressed, and militant Muslims. Some religious thinkers deplore the modern age for its espousal of secular rationality, the central legacy of the Enlightenment. These thinkers argue that reason without God degenerates into an overriding concern for technical efficiency—an attitude of mind that produces Auschwitz, Stalin's labor camps, weapons of mass destruction, and the plundering and polluting of the environment. The self without God degenerates into selfish competition, domination, exploitation, and unrestrained hedonism. Human dignity conceived purely in secular terms does not permit us to recognize the *thou* of another human being, to see our neighbor as someone who has been dignified by God; and removing God from life ends in spiritual emptiness and gnawing emotional distress. These critics of the Enlightenment tradition urge the reorientation of thinking around God and transcendent moral absolutes. Without such a reorientation, they argue, liberal democracy cannot resist the totalitarian temptation or overcome human wickedness.

Postmodernists argue that modernity founded on the Enlightenment legacy, which once was viewed as a progressive force emancipating the individual from unreasonable dogmas, traditions, and authority, has itself become a source of repression through its own creations: technology, bureaucracy, consumerism, materialism, the nation-state, ideologies, and a host of other institutions, procedures, and norms. Aversion to a technoscientific culture and to its methodology leads postmodernists to devalue the principle of objectivity in the social sciences and to give greater weight to the subjective, to feelings, intuition, and fantasy, to the poetry of life. Postmodernists contend that the evaluation of data and reasoned arguments, no matter how logical they seem, reveal only personal preferences and biases. In their view, science has no greater claim to truth than does religion, myth, or witchcraft. In a world marked by cultural diversity and individual idiosyncrasies, there are no correct answers, no rules that apply everywhere and to everyone. Moreover, like those who point out the dangers of reason not directed by spiritual values, postmodernists argue that reason fosters oppressive governments, military complexes, and stifling bureaucracies. Nor has it solved our problems.

Expressing disdain for Western humanism, which ascribes an inherent dignity to human beings, urges the full development of the individual's potential, and regards the rational, self-determining human being as the center of existence, postmodernists claim that humanism has failed. The humanist vision of socialist society ended in Stalinism, and liberal humanism proved no more effective a barrier to Nazism than did Christianity. In our own day, they ask, has the rational humanist tradition been able to solve the problems of overpopulation, worldwide pollution, world hunger, poverty, and war that ravage our planet? Closer to home, has reason coped successfully with urban blight, homelessness, violence, racial tensions, or drug addiction? Moreover, postmodernists contend that the Western tradition, which has been valued as a great and creative human achievement, is fraught with gender, class, and racial bias. In their view, it is merely a male, white, Eurocentric interpretation of things, and the West's vaunted ideals are really a cloak of hypocrisy intended to conceal, rationalize, and legitimate the power, privileges, and preferences of white, European, male elites.

People who identify with victims of exploitation, discrimination, and persecution throughout the globe also attack the Western tradition. They point to the modern West's historic abuses: slavery, imperialism, racism, ethnocentrism, sexism, class exploitation, and the ravaging of the environment. They accuse Westerners of marginalizing the poor, women, and people of color by viewing them as the "other." Furthermore, they condemn the West for arrogantly exalting Western values and achievements and belittling, or even destroying, indigenous peoples and cultures. Finding Western civilization intrinsically flawed, some critics seek a higher wisdom in non-Western traditions—African, Asian, or Native American.

Radical Muslims, who were responsible for or applaud September 11, view Western civilization as a threat to traditional Islam and plot its destruction. Their vision of an Islamic society based on a strict interpretation of the Koran clashes head-on with core principles of Western democracy—separation of church and state, religious toleration, protection of basic rights, and female equality.

Defenders of the Enlightenment heritage argue that this heritage, despite its flaws, still has a powerful message for us. They caution against devaluing and undermining the modern West's unique achievements: the tradition of *rationality,* which makes possible a scientific understanding of the physical universe and human nature, the utilization of nature for human betterment, and the identification and reformation of irrational and abusive institutions and beliefs; the tradition of *political freedom,* which is the foundation of democratic institutions; the tradition of *inner freedom,* which asserts the individual's capacity for ethical autonomy, the ability and duty to make moral choices; the tradition of *humanism,* which regards individuals as active subjects, with both the right and the capacity to realize their full human potential; the tradition of *equality,* which demands equal treatment under the law; and the tradition of *human dignity,* which affirms the inviolable integrity and worth of the human personality and is the driving force behind what is now a global quest for social justice and human rights.

The modern struggle for human rights—initiated during the Enlightenment, advanced by the French Revolution, and embodied in liberalism—continues in the contemporary age. Two crucial developments in this struggle are the civil rights movement in the United States and the feminist movement. Spokespersons for these movements have used ideas formulated by Western thinkers in earlier struggles for liberty and equality. Thus, one reason for the success of Martin Luther King's policy of direct action was that he both inspired and shamed white America to live up to its Judeo-Christian and democratic principles. Though written more than thirty years ago, the insights of the French social theorist Jacques Ellul still apply.

> *The essential, central, undeniable fact is that the West was the first civilization in history to focus attention on the individual and on freedom. . . . The West, and the West alone, is responsible for the movement that has led to the desire for freedom. . . . Today men point the finger of outrage at slavery and torture. Where did that kind of indignation originate? What civilization or culture cried out that slavery was unacceptable and torture scandalous? Not Islam, or Buddhism, or Confucius, or Zen, or the religions and moral codes of Africa and India! The West alone has defended the inalienable rights of the human person, the dignity of the individual. . . . The West attempted to apply in a conscious, methodical way the implications of freedom. . . . The West discovered what no one else had discovered: freedom and the individual. . . . I see no other satisfactory model that can replace what the West has produced.**

The roots of these ideals are ultimately found in the West's Greek and Judeo-Christian heritage, but it was the philosophers of the Enlightenment who clearly articulated them for the modern age. To be sure, these ideals are a goal, not a finished achievement, and nothing should make Westerners more appreciative of the preciousness of these ideals and more alert to their precariousness than examining the ways they have been violated and distorted over the course of centuries. It is equally true that every age has to rethink and revitalize this tradition in order to adapt it to the needs of its own time.

Therefore, it is crucial in this age of globalism, with its heightened sense of ethnic and cultural diversity, that Westerners become sensitized to the histories and traditions of all cultures. But it is equally crucial in an era of global interdependence and tension that Westerners continuously affirm and reaffirm the core values of their heritage and not permit this priceless legacy to be dismissed or negated. As the history of the twentieth century demonstrates, when we lose confidence in this heritage, we risk losing our humanity, and civilized life is threatened by organized barbarism.

*Jacques Ellul, *The Betrayal of the West,* trans. J. O'Connell (New York: Seabury, 1978), 17–19, 29.

Index

Note: Page numbers followed by *ph* refer to photographs. Page numbers followed by *m* refer to maps.

Western Tradition

FROM ANCIENT TIMES TO PRESENT

Accompanied by

READINGS IN LITERATURE AND THOUGHT

CODE OF HAMMURABI

Two distinct approaches to choice of punishment for crime are found in Hammurabi's code with its numerous laws. In some instances, the guilty party is required to pay a monetary compensation to the victim, a tradition traceable to the earliest known Sumerian laws. Another approach, also found in the later Hebrew codes of law, is the principle of exact retaliation: "an eye for an eye, a tooth for a tooth."

Another feature of Hammurabi's code is that the penalties vary according to the social status of the victim. Three classes are represented: free men and women (called patricians in the reading here); commoners (or *plebeians*), not wholly free, but dependents of the state or perhaps serfs on landed estates; and slaves. The patricians are protected by the law of retaliation. People of the lower classes receive only monetary compensation if they are victims of a crime.

196. If a man has knocked out the eye of a patrician, his eye shall be knocked out.

197. If he has broken the limb of a patrician, his limb shall be broken.

198. If he has knocked out the eye of a plebeian or has broken the limb of a plebeian, he shall pay one mina[1] of silver.

199. If he has knocked out the eye of a patrician's servant, or broken the limb of a patrician's servant, he shall pay half his value.

200. If a patrician has knocked out the tooth of a man that is his equal, his tooth shall be knocked out.

201. If he has knocked out the tooth of a plebeian, he shall pay one-third of a mina of silver. . . .

209. If a man has struck a free woman with child, and has caused her to miscarry, he shall pay ten shekels[2] for her miscarriage.

210. If that woman die, his daughter shall be killed.

211. If it be the daughter of a plebeian, that has miscarried through his blows, he shall pay five shekels of silver.

212. If that woman die, he shall pay half a mina of silver.

213. If he has struck a man's maid and caused her to miscarry, he shall pay two shekels of silver.

214. If that woman die, he shall pay one-third of a mina of silver.

Many laws relating to business transactions show the importance of trade in Mesopotamian society and the willingness of the government to intervene in order to regulate the practices of the marketplace.

---

218. If a surgeon has operated with the bronze lancet on a patrician for a serious injury, and has caused his death, or has removed a cataract for a patrician, with the bronze lancet, and has made him lose his eye, his hands shall be cut off.

219. If the surgeon has treated a serious injury of a plebeian's slave, with the bronze lancet, and has caused his death, he shall render slave for slave.

220. If he has removed a cataract with the bronze lancet, and made the slave lose his eye, he shall pay half his value.

221. If a surgeon has cured the limb of a patrician, or has doctored a diseased bowel, the patient shall pay five shekels of silver to the surgeon.

222. If he be a plebeian, he shall pay three shekels of silver.

223. If he be a man's slave, the owner of the slave shall give two shekels of silver to the doctor. . . .

228. If a builder has built a house for a man, and finished it, he shall pay him a fee of two shekels of silver, for each SAR[3] built on.

229. If a builder has built a house for a man, and has not made his work sound, and the house he built has fallen, and caused the death of its owner, that builder shall be put to death.

[1]The mina was a weight of silver used to express monetary value.
[2]The shekel, also a weight of monetary value, was worth far less than the mina.
[3]SAR was a measure of land.

230. If it is the owner's son that is killed, the builder's son shall be put to death.

231. If it is the slave of the owner that is killed, the builder shall give slave for slave to the owner of the house.

232. If he has caused the loss of goods, he shall render back whatever he has destroyed. Moreover, because he did not make sound the house he built, and it fell, at his own cost he shall rebuild the house that fell. . . .

271. If a man has hired oxen, a wagon, and its driver, he shall pay one hundred and sixty KA[4] of corn daily. . . .

275. If a man has hired a boat, its hire is three ŠE[5] of silver daily.

The outcome of some procedures depended upon the will of the gods: for example, an accused woman could place her fate in the hands of a god by plunging into a river, canal, or reservoir; if she did not drown, she was declared innocent. In other cases, legal culpability could be removed by invoking a god to bear witness to the truth of one's testimony. The law was particularly harsh on perjurers and those who made grave charges that they could not prove in court.

---

1. If a man has accused another of laying a nêrtu (death spell?) upon him, but has not proved it, he shall be put to death.

2. If a man has accused another of laying a kiˇspu (spell) upon him, but has not proved it, the accused shall go to the sacred river, he shall plunge into the sacred river, and if the sacred river shall conquer him, he that accused him shall take possession of his house. If the sacred river shall show his innocence and he is saved, his accuser shall be put to death. He that plunged into the sacred river shall appropriate the house of him that accused him.

3. If a man has borne false witness in a trial, or has not established the statement that he has made, if that case be a capital trial, that man shall be put to death.

4. If he has borne false witness in a civil law case, he shall pay the damages in that suit. . . .

9. If a man has lost property and some of it be detected in the possession of another, and the holder has said, "A man sold it to me, I bought it in the presence of witnesses"; and if the claimant has said, "I can bring witnesses who know it to be property lost by me"; then the alleged buyer on his part shall produce the man who sold it to him and the witnesses before whom he bought it; the claimant shall on his part produce the witnesses who know it to be his lost property. The judge shall examine their pleas. The witnesses to the sale and the witnesses who identify the lost property shall state on oath what they know. Such a seller is the thief and shall be put to death. The owner of the lost property shall recover his lost property. The buyer shall recoup himself from the seller's estate.

The laws concerned with family relationships placed great power in the hands of husbands and fathers, yet the code tried to protect women and children from neglect and mistreatment. Divorce initiated by either husband or wife was permitted under specific circumstances.

---

141. If a man's wife, living in her husband's house, has persisted in going out, has acted the fool, has wasted her house, has belittled her husband, he shall prosecute her. If her husband has said, "I divorce her," she shall go her way; he shall give her nothing as her price of divorce. If her husband has said, "I will not divorce her," he may take another woman to wife; the wife shall live as a slave in her husband's house.

142. If a woman has hated her husband and has said, "You shall not possess me," her past shall be inquired into, as to what she lacks. If she has been discreet, and has no vice, and her husband has gone out, and has greatly belittled her, that woman has no blame, she shall take her marriage-portion and go off to her father's house.

143. If she has not been discreet, has gone out, ruined her house, belittled her husband, she shall be drowned. . . .

[4]KA stood for a bulk measure.

[5]ŠE was another monetary weight of silver.

148. If a man has married a wife and a disease has seized her, if he is determined to marry a second wife, he shall marry her. He shall not divorce the wife whom the disease has seized. In the home they made together she shall dwell, and he shall maintain her as long as she lives. . . .

168. If a man has determined to disinherit his son and has declared before the judge, "I cut off my son," the judge shall inquire into the son's past, and, if the son has not committed a grave misdemeanor such as should cut him off from sonship, the father shall (not) disinherit his son.

169. If he has committed a grave crime against his father, which cuts him off from sonship, for the first offence he shall pardon him. If he has committed a grave crime a second time, the father shall cut off his son from sonship. . . .

195. If a son has struck his father, his hands shall be cut off.

One of the most unusual features of the law dealt with the failure of the government officials of a city or a district to prevent banditry. The code held the governor re-sponsible for the breach of the peace and required him to compensate the bandit's victim. Government officials found guilty of extortion, bribery, or use of public employees for private purposes were severely punished.

---

23. If the highwayman has not been caught, the man that has been robbed shall state on oath what he has lost and the city or district governor in whose territory or district the robbery took place shall restore to him what he has lost.

24. If a life (has been lost), the city or district governor shall pay one mina of silver to the deceased's relatives. . . .

34. If either a governor, or a prefect, has appropriated the property of a levymaster,[6] has hired him out, has robbed him by high-handedness at a trial, has taken the salary which the king gave to him, that governor, or prefect, shall be put to death. . . .

[6]A levymaster was a military official.

HYMNS TO THE PHARAOHS

The first reading is a hymn to the new god-king Ramesses IV (c. 1166 B.C.). The second reading is a hymn to a deceased pharaoh, perhaps Unnos (c. 2600 B.C.).

TO RAMESSES IV

What a happy day! Heaven and earth rejoice, (for) thou art the great lord of Egypt.
They that had fled have come again to their towns, and they that were hidden have again come forth.
They that hungered are satisfied and happy, and they that thirsted are drunken.
They that were naked are clad in fine linen, and they that were dirty have white garments.
They that were in prison are set free, and he that was in bonds is full of joy.
They that were at strife in this land are reconciled. High Niles [beneficial floods] have come from their sources, that they may refresh the hearts of others.
Widows, their houses stand open, and they suffer travellers to enter.
Maidens rejoice and repeat their songs of gladness (?). They are arrayed in ornaments and say (?):
"——— he createth generation on generation. Thou ruler, thou wilt endure for ever."
The ships rejoice on the deep ———.
They come to land with wind or oars,
They are satisfied . . . when it is said:
"King Hekmaatrē-Beloved-of-Amūn[1] again weareth the crown.
The son of [the sun-god] Rē, Ramesses, hath received the office of his father."
All lands say unto him:
"Beautiful is Horus on the throne of Amu¯n who sendeth him forth,
(Amu¯n) the protector of the Prince, who bringeth every land."

TO A DECEASED PHARAOH

The King has not died the death: he has become one who rises (like the morning sun) from the horizon. He rests from life (like the setting sun) in the West, but he dawns anew in the East. O King, you have not departed dead: you have departed living! Have you said that he would die?—nay, he dies not: this king lives for ever. He has escaped his day of death. O lofty one among the imperishable stars!—you shall not ever perish. Loose the embalming bandages!—they are not bandages (at all): they are the tresses of the goddess Nephthys (as she leans down over you). Men fall, and their name ceases to be: therefore God takes hold of this king by his arm, and leads him to the sky, that he may not die upon earth amongst men. This king flies away from you, you mortals. He is not of the earth, he is of the sky. He flies as a cloud to the sky, he who was like a bird at the masthead. He goes up to heaven like the hawks, and his feathers are like those of the wild geese; he rushes at heaven like a crane, he kisses heaven like the falcon, he leaps to heaven like the locust. He ascends to the sky! He ascends to the sky on the wind, on the wind! The stairs of the sky are let down for him that he may ascend thereon to heaven. O gods, put your arms under the king: raise him, lift him to the sky. To the sky! To the sky! To the great throne amongst the gods!

[1] Hekmaatrē was another name of this pharaoh.

GUIDELINES FOR THE RULER

Generally, pharaohs were mindful of their responsibilities. To prepare his son to rule, a pharaoh or his vizier (a high executive officer) might compile a list of instructions, like the ones that follow. These instructions were most likely composed by a vizier of King Issi (c. 2400 B.C.).

If thou art a leader and givest command to the multitude, strive after every excellence, until there be no fault in thy nature. Truth is good and its worth is lasting, and it hath not been disturbed since the day of its creator,[1] whereas he that transgresseth its ordinances is punished. It lieth as a (right) path in front of him that knoweth nothing. Wrong-doing (?) hath never yet brought its venture to port. Evil indeed winneth wealth, but the strength of truth is that it endureth, and the (upright) man saith: "It is the property of my father.". . .[2]

The following excerpts come from the instructions of Amenemhet I (1991–1962 B.C.), who prepared them for his son.

I gave to the poor and nourished the orphan, I caused him that was nothing to reach the goal, even as him that was of account. . . .

None hungered in my years, none thirsted in them. Men dwelt in (peace) through that which I wrought; . . . all that I commanded was as it should be. . . .

These instructions were prepared for King Merikare (c. 2050 B.C.) by his father.

Be not evil, it is good to be kindly. Cause thy monument[3] to endure through the love of thee. . . . Then men thank God on thine account, men praise thy goodness and pray for thine health. . . . But keep thine eyes open, one that is trusting will become one that is afflicted. . . .

Do right so long as thou abidest on the earth. Calm the weeper, oppress no widow, expel no man from the possessions of his father. . . . Take heed lest thou punish wrongfully.

Exalt not the son of one of high degree more than him that is of lowly birth, but take to thyself a man because of his actions.

[1] Rē [the sun god], who brought truth into the world.

[2] That my father brought me up in the ways of truth is the best thing that he has bequeathed me.

[3] The remembrance of thee.

HYMN TO ATON

Akhenaten's religious outlook inspired remarkable works of art and literature. In the following hymn, Akhenaten glorifies Aton in words that are reminiscent of Psalm 104 (see page 31).

Thou appearest beautifully on the horizon of heaven,
Thou living Aton, the beginning of life!
When thou art risen on the eastern horizon,
Thou hast filled every land with thy beauty.
Thou art gracious, great, glistening, and high over every land;
Thy rays encompass the lands to the limit of all that thou hast made. . . .
At daybreak, when thou arisest on the horizon,
When thou shinest as the Aton by day,
Thou drivest away the darkness and givest thy rays.
The Two Lands[1] are in festivity *every day,*
Awake and standing upon (their) feet,
For thou hast raised them up.
Washing their bodies, taking (their) clothing,
Their arms are (raised) in praise at thy appearance.
All the world, they do their work.

All beasts are content with their pasturage;
Trees and plants are flourishing.
The birds which fly from their nests,
Their wings are (stretched out) in praise to thy *ka.*[2]
All beasts spring upon (their) feet.
Whatever flies and alights,
They live when thou hast risen (for) them.
The ships are sailing north and south as well,
For every way is open at thy appearance.
The fish in the river dart before thy face;
Thy rays are in the midst of the great green sea.

Creator of seed in women,
Thou who makest fluid into man,
Who maintainest the son in the womb of his mother,
Who soothest him with that which stills his weeping,
Thou nurse (even) in the womb,
Who givest breath to sustain all that he had made!
When he descends from the womb to breathe
On the day when he is born,
Thou openest his mouth completely,
Thou suppliest his necessities.
When the chick in the egg speaks within the shell,
Thou givest him breath within it to maintain him.
When thou hast made him his fulfillment within the egg, to break it,
He comes forth from the egg to speak at his completed (time);
He walks upon his legs when he comes forth from it.

[1]The Two Lands were the two political divisions of Egypt, Upper and Lower Egypt. They were usually governed by the same king.
[2]The *ka* was a protective and guiding spirit, which each person was thought to have.

How manifold it is, what thou hast made!
They are hidden from the face (of man).
O sole god, like whom there is no other!
Thou didst create the world according to thy desire,
Whilst thou wert alone:
All men, cattle, and wild beasts,
Whatever is on earth, going upon (its) feet,
And what is on high, flying with its wings.
The countries of Syria and Nubia,[3] the *land* of Egypt,
Thou settest every man in his place,
Thou suppliest their necessities:
Everyone has his food, and his time of life is reckoned.
Their tongues are separate in speech,
And their natures as well;
Their skins are distinguished,
As thou distinguishest the foreign peoples.
Thou makest a Nile in the underworld,[4]
Thou bringest it forth as thou desirest
To maintain the people (of Egypt)
According as thou madest them for thyself,
The lord of all of them, wearying (himself) with them,
The lord of every land, rising for them,
The Aton of the day, great of majesty.

[3]Syria was an ancient country, larger than modern Syria, north of modern Israel and Jordan; Nubia was a kingdom located south of the first cataract of the Nile. It is now in Sudan.
[4]The Egyptians believed that the source of their Nile was in a huge body of water, which they called Nun, under the earth.

ENUMA ELISH

THE BABYLONIAN GENESIS

The Mesopotamian creation epic *Enuma Elish* (Poem of Creation) is another example of mythical thinking. Marduk, the chief god of Babylon, slays Tiamat, a primal mother identified with the salt sea, and then proceeds to construct the cosmos from her carcass.

"Stand thou up, that I and thou meet in single combat!"
When Tiamat heard this,
She was like one possessed; she took leave of her senses.
In fury Tiamat cried out aloud.
To the roots her legs shook both together.
She recites a charm, keeps casting her spell,
While the gods of battle sharpen their weapons.
Then joined issue Tiamat and Marduk, wisest of gods.
They strove in single combat, locked in battle.
The lord spread out his net to enfold her,
The Evil Wind, which followed behind, he let loose in her face.
When Tiamat opened her mouth to consume him,
He drove in the Evil Wind that she close not her lips.
As the fierce winds charged her belly,
Her body was distended and her mouth was wide open.
He released the arrow, it tore her belly,
It cut through her insides, splitting the heart.
Having thus subdued her, he extinguished her life.
He cast down her carcass to stand upon it.
After he had slain Tiamat, the leader,
Her band was shattered, her troupe broken up;
And the gods, her helpers who marched at her side,
Trembling with terror, turned their backs about,
In order to save and preserve their lives.
Tightly encircled, they could not escape.
He made them captives and he smashed their weapons.
Thrown into the net, they found themselves ensnared;
Placed in cells, they were filled with wailing;
Bearing his wrath, they were held imprisoned.

When he had vanquished and subdued his adversaries,

[Marduk] turned back to Tiamat whom he had bound.
The lord trod on the legs of Tiamat,
With his unsparing mace he crushed her skull.
When the arteries of her blood he had severed,
The North Wind bore (it) to places undisclosed.
On seeing this, his fathers were joyful and jubilant,
They brought gifts of homage, they to him.
Then the lord paused to view her dead body,

That he might divide the monster and do artful works.
He split her like a shellfish into two parts:
Half of her he set up and ceiled it as sky,
Pulled down the bar and posted guards.
He bade them to allow not her waters to escape.
He crossed the heavens and surveyed the regions.

[There] He constructed stations for the great gods.
Fixing their astral likenesses as constellations.
He determined the year by designating the zones:
He set up three constellations for each of the twelve months.

In her [Tiamat's] belly he established the zenith.
The Moon he caused to shine, the night (to him) entrusting.
He appointed him a creature of the night to signify the days....
When Marduk hears the words of the gods.
His heart prompts (him) to fashion artful works.
Opening his mouth, he addressed [the god] Ea
To impart the plan he had conceived in his heart:
"Blood I will mass and cause bones to be.
I will establish a savage, 'man' shall be his name.
Verily, savage-man I will create.
He shall be charged with the service of the gods
  That they might be at ease!"

LAMENT FOR UR

THE GODS AND HUMAN DESTINY

Mesopotamians and Egyptians believed that their destinies were determined by the gods. Drought, hurricanes, sickness, law, and foreign invasion were all attributed to divine intervention. In the "Lament for Ur," the assembly of the gods decides to punish the Sumerian city-state of Ur.

Enlil called the storm.
    The people mourn.
Winds of abundance he took from the land.
    The people mourn.
Good winds he took away from Sumer.
    The people mourn.
Deputed [assigned] evil winds.
    The people mourn.
Entrusted them to Kingaluda, tender of storms.
He called the storm that annihilates the land.
    The people mourn.
He called disastrous winds.
    The people mourn.
Enlil—choosing Gibil (fire god) as his helper—
called the (great) hurricane of heaven.
    The people mourn.
The (blinding) hurricane howling across the skies—
    the people mourn—
the storm that annihilates the land roaring over the earth—
    the people mourn—
the tempest unsubduable like breaks through levees,
beats down upon, devours the city's ships,
(all these) he gathered at the base of heaven.
    The people mourn.
(Great) fires he lit that heralded the storm.
    The people mourn.
And lit on either flank of furious winds the searing heat of desert.
Like flaming heat of noon this firescorched....
The storm ordered by Enlil in hate, the storm which wears away the country,
covered Ur like a cloth,
    veiled it like a linen sheet....
On that day did the storm leave the city; that city was a ruin.
O father Nanna (the moon god), that town was left a ruin.
    The people mourn.
On that day did the storm leave the country.
    The people mourn.
Its people ('s corpses), not potsherds, littered the approaches.
The walls were gaping;
the high gates, the roads, were piled with dead.
In the wide streets,
    where feasting crowds (once) gathered,
jumbled they lay.

In all the streets and roadways bodies lay.
In open fields that used to fill with dancers, the people lay in heaps.
The country's blood now filled its holes.
   like metal in a mold;
bodies dissolved—like butter left in the sun.

GENESIS

The first two chapters from the book of Genesis follow. The first chapter presents the *cosmogony* and *anthropology* of the Jews. Hebrew cosmogony—that is, their view of the generation of the universe and all that is in it—exemplifies God's majesty and power. Although Genesis is similar to other Near Eastern creation myths, it also sharply breaks with the essential outlook of the time. In Genesis, nature is no longer inhabited by mythical gods, and inanimate objects are not suffused with life. The Hebrews did not worship the moon and stars and mountains and rivers, but they regarded nature as the orderly creation of one supreme and eternal being.

How the Hebrews conceived of the creation of men and women and their position in the universe—the anthropology of the Jews—is dealt with in verses 26–31. The Hebrews' conception of the individual created in God's image and subordinate to nothing except God is as revolutionary as their idea of God, for this conception confers great value and dignity upon human beings.

1 In the beginning God created the heavens and the earth. 2 The earth was without form and void, and
darkness was upon the face of the deep; and the Spirit of God was moving over the face of the waters.
3 And God said, "Let there be light"; and there was light. 4 And God saw that the light was good; and
God separated the light from the darkness. 5 God called the light Day, and the darkness he called Night.
And there was evening and there was morning, one day.
6 And God said, "Let there be a firmament in the midst of the waters, and let it separate the waters
from the waters." 7 And God made the firmament and separated the waters which were under the firma-
ment from the waters which were above the firmament. And it was so. 8 And God called the firmament
Heaven. And there was evening and there was morning, a second day.
9 And God said, "Let the waters under the heavens be gathered together into one place, and let the
dry land appear." And it was so. 10 God called the dry land Earth, and the waters that were gathered
together he called Seas. And God saw that it was good. 11 And God said, "Let the earth put forth vegeta-
tion, plants yielding seed, and fruit trees bearing fruit in which is their seed, each according to its kind,
upon the earth." And it was so. 12 The earth brought forth vegetation, plants yielding seed according to
their own kinds, and trees bearing fruit in which is their seed, each according to its kind. And God saw
that it was good. 13 And there was evening and there was morning, a third day.
14 And God said, "Let there be lights in the firmament of the heavens to separate the day from the
night; and let them be for signs and for seasons and for days and years, 15 and let them be lights in the
firmament of the heavens to give light upon the earth." And it was so. 16 And God made the two great
lights, the greater light to rule the day, and the lesser light to rule the night; he made the stars also. 17 And
God set them in the firmament of the heavens to give light upon the earth, 18 to rule over the day and
over the night, and to separate the light from the darkness. And God saw that it was good. 19 And there
was evening and there was morning, a fourth day.
20 And God said, "Let the waters bring forth swarms of living creatures, and let birds fly above the
earth across the firmament of the heavens." 21 So God created the great sea monsters and every living
creature that moves, with which the waters swarm, according to their kinds, and every winged bird ac-
cording to its kind. And God saw that it was good. 22 And God blessed them, saying, "Be fruitful and
multiply and fill the waters in the seas, and let birds multiply on the earth." 23 And there was evening
and there was morning, a fifth day.
24 And God said, "Let the earth bring forth living creatures according to their kinds: cattle and creep-
ing things and beasts of the earth according to their kinds." And it was so. 25 And God made the beasts
of the earth according to their kinds and the cattle according to their kinds, and everything that creeps
upon the ground according to its kind. And God saw that it was good.
26 Then God said, "Let us make man in our image, after our likeness; and let them have dominion
over the fish of the sea, and over the birds of the air, and over the cattle, and over all the earth, and over

every creeping thing that creeps upon the earth." 27 So God created man in his own image, in the image
of God he created him; male and female he created them. 28 And God blessed them, and God said to
them, "Be fruitful and multiply, and fill the earth and subdue it; and have dominion over the fish of
the sea and over the birds of the air and over every living thing that moves upon the earth." 29 And God
said, "Behold, I have given you every plant yielding seed which is upon the face of all the earth, and
every tree with seed in its fruit; you shall have them for food. 30 And to every beast of the earth, and to
every bird of the air, and to everything that creeps on the earth, everything that has the breath of life, I
have given every green plant for food." And it was so. 31 And God saw everything that he had made, and
behold, it was very good. And there was evening and there was morning, a sixth day. (Genesis 1)

The second chapter of Genesis contains a retrospective view of the creation of the universe; a second account of man's creation from "the dust of the ground," a description of the Garden of Eden, into which man was placed, with the injunction that he may eat freely of every tree in the garden, except the tree of the knowledge of good and evil, and an account of God's creation of woman from the rib of man as a companion for him. In Genesis, Eden was an idyllic garden, a paradise, in which the first human beings lived. It has been compared to the mythic land of the blessed, Dilmun, described in the Babylonian epic *Gilgamesh*. In Eden, human beings were free of death, illness, pain, and a consciousness of evil, or sin.

---

1 Thus the heavens and the earth were finished, and all the host of them. 2 And on the seventh day
God finished his work which he had done, and he rested on the seventh day from all his work which he
had done. 3 So God blessed the seventh day and hallowed it, because on it God rested from all his work
which he had done in creation.

4 These are the generations of the heavens and the earth when they were created.
In the day that the Lord God made the earth and the heavens, 5 when no plant of the field was yet in
the earth and no herb of the field had yet sprung up—for the Lord God had not caused it to rain upon
the earth, and there was no man to till the ground; 6 but a mist went up from the earth and watered the
whole face of the ground 7 then the Lord God formed man of dust from the ground, and breathed into
his nostrils the breath of life; and man became a living being. 8 And the Lord God planted a garden in
Eden, in the east; and there he put the man whom he had formed. 9 And out of the ground the Lord
God made to grow every tree that is pleasant to the sight and good for food, the tree of life also in the
midst of the garden, and the tree of the knowledge of good and evil. . . .

15 The Lord God took the man and put him in the garden of Eden to till it and keep it. 16 And the
Lord God commanded the man, saying, "You may freely eat of every tree of the garden; 17 but of the tree
of the knowledge of good and evil you shall not eat, for in the day that you eat of it you shall die."

18 Then the Lord God said, "It is not good that the man should be alone; I will make him a helper fit
for him." 19 So out of the ground the Lord God formed every beast of the field and every bird of the air,
and brought them to the man to see what he would call them; and whatever the man called every living
creature, that was its name. 20 The man gave names to all cattle, and to the birds of the air, and to every
beast of the field; but for the man there was not found a helper fit for him. 21 So the Lord God caused
a deep sleep to fall upon the man, and while he slept took one of his ribs and closed up its place with
flesh; 22 and the rib which the Lord God had taken from the man he made into a woman and brought
her to the man.

23 Then the man said,
"This at last is bone of my bones
  and flesh of my flesh;
she shall be called Woman,
  because she was taken out of Man."

24 Therefore a man leaves his father and his mother and cleaves to his wife, and they become one flesh.
25 And the man and his wife were both naked, and were not ashamed. (Genesis 2)

GENESIS

THE ORIGINS OF SIN

The third chapter of Genesis deals with the origin of evil. When Adam and Eve disobeyed God by eating from the tree of knowledge, they were driven from the Garden of Eden. For the Hebrews the expulsion from paradise marks the beginning of human history, suffering, and death. This passage provides one of the fundamental explanations of evil in the Western tradition, the Judaic conception, later to be refashioned by Saint Paul into the Christian notion of original sin. The language of the biblical narrative is seemingly naive and framed in mythic imagery, but the ideas that it presents are profound and timeless.

1Now the serpent was more subtle than any other wild creature that the LORD God had made. He
said to the woman, "Did God say, 'You shall not eat of any tree of the garden'?" 2And the woman said
to the serpent, "We may eat of the fruit of the trees of the garden; 3but God said, 'You shall not eat of
the fruit of the tree which is in the midst of the garden, neither shall you touch it, lest you die.'" 4But
the serpent said to the woman, "You will not die. 5For God knows that when you eat of it your eyes will
be opened, and you will be like God, knowing good and evil." 6So when the woman saw that the tree
was good for food, and that it was a delight to the eyes, and that the tree was to be desired to make one
wise, she took of its fruit and ate; and she also gave some to her husband, and he ate. 7Then the eyes of
both were opened, and they knew that they were naked; and they sewed fig leaves together and made
themselves aprons.

8 And they heard the sound of the LORD God walking in the garden in the cool of the day, and the
man and his wife hid themselves from the presence of the LORD God among the trees of the garden.
9But the LORD God called to the man, and said to him, "Where are you?" 10And he said, "I heard the
sound of thee in the garden, and I was afraid, because I was naked; and I hid myself." 11He said, "Who
told you that you were naked? Have you eaten of the tree of which I commanded you not to eat?"
12The man said, "The woman whom thou gavest to be with me, she gave me fruit of the tree, and I ate."
13Then the LORD God said to the woman, "What is this that you have done?" The woman said, "The
serpent beguiled me, and I ate."

14 The LORD God said to the serpent, "Because you have done this, cursed are you above all cattle, and above all wild animals; upon your belly you shall go, and dust you shall eat all the days of your life.

15I will put enmity between you and the woman, and between your seed and her seed; he shall bruise your head, and you shall bruise his heel."

16To the woman he said, "I will greatly multiply your pain in childbearing; in pain you shall bring forth children, yet your desire shall be for your husband, and he shall rule over you."

17And to Adam he said, "Because you have listened to the voice of your wife, and have eaten of the tree of which I commanded you, 'You shall not eat of it,' cursed is the ground because of you; in toil you shall eat of it all the days of your life;

18thorns and thistles it shall bring forth to you; and you shall eat the plants of the field.

19In the sweat of your face you shall eat bread till you return to the ground, for out of it you were taken; you are dust, and to dust you shall return."

20The man called his wife's name Eve, because she was the mother of all living. 21And the LORD God
made for Adam and for his wife garments of skins, and clothed them. 22 Then the LORD God said,
"Behold, the man has become like one of us, knowing good and evil; and now, lest he put forth his
hand and take also of the tree of life, and eat, and live for ever"—23therefore the LORD God sent him
forth from the garden of Eden, to till the ground from which he was taken. 24He drove out the man; and
at the east of the garden of Eden he placed the cherubim [winged angels], and a flaming sword which
turned every way, to guard the way to the tree of life. (Genesis 3)

PSALM 8

In the following song, the psalmist rejoices in the greatness of God. He marvels in the Lord's love for human beings, expressed in their having been given dominion over the earth and its creatures.

O Lord, our Lord,
how majestic is thy name in all the earth!

Thou whose glory above the heavens is chanted
2 by the mouth of babes and infants,
thou hast founded a bulwark because of thy foes,
to still the enemy and the avenger.

3 When I look at thy heavens, the work of thy fingers,
the moon and the stars which thou hast established;
4 what is man that thou art mindful of him,
and the son of man that thou dost care for him?
5 Yet thou hast made him little less than God,
and dost crown him with glory and honor.
6 Thou hast given him dominion over the works of thy hands;
thou hast put all things under his feet,
7 all sheep and oxen,
and also the beasts of the field,
8 the birds of the air, and the fish of the sea,
whatever passes along the paths of the sea.

9 O Lord, our Lord,
how majestic is thy name in all the earth!

PSALM 104

Psalm 104 praises God's majesty and lauds him for the wonders of his creation—the earth and all its creatures.
Bless, the Lord, O my soul!

O Lord my God, thou art very great!
Thou art clothed with honor and majesty,
2 who coverest thyself with light as with a garment,
who hast stretched out the heavens like a tent,
3 who hast laid the beams of thy chambers on the waters,
who makest the clouds thy chariot,
who ridest on the wings of the wind,
4 who makest the winds thy messengers, fire and flame thy ministers.
5 Thou didst set the earth on its foundations, so that it should never be shaken.
6 Thou didst cover it with the deep as with a garment;
the waters stood above the mountains.
7 At thy rebuke they fled;
at the sound of thy thunder they took to flight.
8 The mountains rose, the valleys sank down
to the place which thou didst appoint for them.
9 Thou didst set a bound which they should not pass,
so that they might not again cover the earth.
10 Thou makest springs gush forth in the valleys; they flow between the hills,
11 they give drink to every beast of the field; the wild asses quench their thirst.
12 By them the birds of the air have their habitation;
they sing among the branches.
13 From thy lofty abode thou waterest the mountains;
the earth is satisfied with the fruit of thy work.
14 Thou dost cause the grass to grow for the cattle,
and plants for man to cultivate,
that he may bring forth food from the earth,
15 and wine to gladden the heart of man,
oil to make his face shine,
and bread to strengthen man's heart.
16 The trees of the Lord are watered abundantly,
the cedars of Lebanon which he planted.
17 In them the birds build their nests;
the stork has her home in the fir trees.
18 The high mountains are for the wild goats;
the rocks are a refuge for the badgers.
19 Thou hast made the moon to mark the seasons;
the sun knows its time for setting.
20 Thou makest darkness, and it is night,
when all the beasts of the forest creep forth,
21 The young lions roar for their prey,
seeking their food from God.
22 When the sun rises, they get them away
and lie down in their dens.
23 Man goes forth to his work
and to his labor until the evening.

24 O LORD, how manifold are thy works!
In wisdom hast thou made them all;
the earth is full of thy creatures.
25 Yonder is the sea, great and wide,
which teems with things innumerable,
living things both small and great.
26 There go the ships,
and Leviathan [a sea monster] which thou didst form to sport in it.
27 These all look to thee,
to give them their food in due season.
28 When thou givest to them, they gather it up;
when thou openest thy hand, they are
filled with good things.
29 When thou hidest thy face, they are dismayed;
when thou takest away their breath, they die
and return to their dust.
30 When thou sendest forth thy Spirit, they are created;
and thou renewest the face of the ground.
31 May the glory of the LORD endure for ever,
may the LORD rejoice in his works,
32 who looks on the earth and it trembles,
who touches the mountains and they smoke!
33 I will sing to the LORD as long as I live;
I will sing praise to my God while I have being.
34 May my meditation be pleasing to him,
for I rejoice in the LORD.
35 Let sinners be consumed from the earth,
and let the wicked be no more!
Bless the LORD, O my soul!
Praise the LORD!

THUCYDIDES

THE MELIAN DIALOGUE AND THE REVOLUTION AT CORCYRA

The Athenians, who saw no conflict between imperialism and democracy, considered it natural for strong states to dominate weaker ones. This view coincided with the position of those Sophists (see page 54) who argued that might makes right. The classic expression of this view is found in Thucydides' history.

During the war, Athens decided to invade the island of Melos, which resisted this unprovoked act of aggression. Thucydides reconstructed a dialogue based on a meeting between Athenian envoys and Melian officials, who tried unsuccessfully to persuade the Athenians not to launch an unjust war. Subsequently, Athens attacked. After capturing the town, the Athenians slaughtered the men, enslaved the women and children, and colonized the territory. The first selection is the famous Melian Dialogue. In the second selection, Thucydides describes the revolution in Corcyra, one of several conflicts that broke out within the city-states during the Peloponnesian War.

MELIANS No one can object to each of us putting forward our own views in a calm atmosphere. That is perfectly reasonable. What is scarcely consistent with such a proposal is the present threat, indeed the certainty, of your making war on us. We see that you have come prepared to judge the argument yourselves, and that the likely end of it all will be either war, if we prove that we are in the right, and so refuse to surrender, or else slavery.

ATHENIANS If you are going to spend the time in enumerating your suspicions about the future, or if you have met here for any other reason except to look the facts in the face and on the basis of these facts to consider how you can save your city from destruction, there is no point in our going on with this discussion. If, however, you will do as we suggest, then we will speak on.

MELIANS It is natural and understandable that people who are placed as we are should have recourse to all kinds of arguments and different points of view. However, you are right in saying that we are met together here to discuss the safety of our country and, if you will have it so, the discussion shall proceed on the lines that you have laid down.

ATHENIANS Then we on our side will use no fine phrases saying, for example, that we have a right to our empire because we defeated the Persians, or that we have come against you now because of the injuries you have done us—a great mass of words that nobody would believe. And we ask you on your side not to imagine that you will influence us by saying that you, though a colony of Sparta, have not joined Sparta in the war, or that you have never done us any harm. Instead we recommend that you should try to get what it is possible for you to get, taking into consideration what we both really do think; since you know as well as we do that when these matters are discussed by practical people, the standard of justice depends on the equality of power to compel and that in fact the strong do what they have the power to do and the weak accept what they have to accept.

MELIANS Then in our view (since you force us to leave justice out of account and to confine ourselves to self-interest)—in our view it is at any rate useful that you should not destroy a principle that is to the general good of all men—namely, that in the case of all who fall into danger there should be such a thing as fair play and just dealing, and that such people should be allowed to use and to profit by arguments that fall short of a mathematical accuracy. And this is a principle which affects you as much as anybody, since your own fall would be visited by the most terrible vengeance and would be an example to the world.

ATHENIANS ...What we shall do now is to show you that it is for the good of our own empire that we are here and that it is for the preservation of your city that we shall say what we are going to say. We do not want any trouble in bringing you into our empire, and we want you to be spared for the good both of yourselves and of ourselves.

MELIANS And how could it be just as good for us to be the slaves as for you to be the masters?

ATHENIANS You, by giving in, would save yourselves from disaster; we, by not destroying you, would be able to profit from you.

MELIANS So you would not agree to our being neutral, friends instead of enemies, but allies of neither side?

ATHENIANS No, because it is not so much your hostility that injures us; it is rather the case that, if we were on friendly terms with you, our subjects would regard that as a sign of weakness in us, whereas your hatred is evidence of our power....[Our subjects think] that those who still preserve their independence do so because they are strong, and that if we fail to attack them it is because we are afraid. So that by conquering you we shall increase not only the size but the security of our empire. We rule the sea and you are islanders, and weaker islanders too than the others; it is therefore particularly important that you should not escape....

MELIANS Then surely, if such hazards are taken by you to keep your empire...we who are still free would show ourselves great cowards and weaklings if we failed to face everything that comes rather than submit to slavery.

ATHENIANS No, not if you are sensible. This is no fair fight, with honour on one side and shame on the other. It is rather a question of saving your lives and not resisting those who are far too strong for you.

MELIANS Yet we know that in war fortune sometimes makes the odds more level than could be expected from the difference in numbers of the two sides. And if we surrender, then all our hope is lost at once, whereas, so long as we remain in action, there is still a hope that we may yet stand upright.

ATHENIANS Hope, that comforter in danger! If one already has solid advantages to fall back upon, one can indulge in hope....[D]o not be like those people who, as so commonly happens, miss the chance of saving themselves in a human and practical way, and, when every clear and distinct hope has left them in their adversity, turn to what is blind and vague, to prophecies and oracles and such things which by encouraging hope lead men to ruin.

MELIANS It is difficult, and you may be sure that we know it, for us to oppose your power.... Nevertheless we trust that the gods will give us fortune as good as yours, because we are standing for what is right against what is wrong; and as for what we lack in power, we trust that it will be made up for by our alliance with the Spartans, who are bound, if for no other reason, then for honour's sake, and because we are their kinsmen, to come to our help. Our confidence, therefore, is not so entirely irrational as you think.

ATHENIANS ...Our opinion of the gods and our knowledge of men lead us to conclude that it is a general and necessary law of nature to rule wherever one can....[W]ith regard to your views about Sparta and your confidence that she, out of a sense of honour, will come to your aid, we must say that we congratulate you on your simplicity but do not envy you your folly....

...You, if you take the right view...will see that there is nothing disgraceful in giving way to the greatest city in Hellas when she is offering you such reasonable terms—alliance on a tribute-paying basis and liberty to enjoy your own property. And, when you are allowed to choose between war and safety, you will not be so insensitively arrogant as to make the wrong choice. This is the safe rule—to stand up to one's equals, to behave with deference towards one's superiors, and to treat one's inferiors with moderation. Think it over again, then, when we have withdrawn from the meeting, and let this be a point that constantly recurs to your minds— that you are discussing the fate of your country, that you have only one country, and that its future for good or ill depends on this one single decision which you are going to make.

The Athenians then withdrew from the discussion. The Melians, left to themselves, reached a conclusion which was much the same as they had indicated in their previous replies. Their answer was as follows:

MELIANS Our decision, Athenians, is just the same as it was at first. We are not prepared to give up in a short moment the liberty which our city has enjoyed from its foundation for 700 years. We put our trust in the fortune that the gods will send and which has saved us up to now, and in the help of men—that is, of the Spartans; and so we shall try to save ourselves. But we invite you to allow us to be friends of yours and enemies to neither side, to make a treaty which shall be agreeable to both you and us, and so to leave our country.

During the war, revolutions broke out in several city-states as democrats, those who believed in decision making by citizen participation, and oligarchs, those who wanted the rule of a select few, competed for power. In these conflicts, traditional standards of morality were set aside and dangerous passions were unleashed. Thucydides' account of the revolution at Corcyra shows how the stresses of war precipitated a moral collapse and a deterioration in the quality of political life.

...The Corcyraeans continued to massacre those of their own citizens whom they considered to be their enemies. Their victims were accused of conspiring to overthrow the democracy, but in fact men were often killed on grounds of personal hatred or else by their debtors because of the money that they owed. There was death in every shape and form. And, as usually happens in such situations, people went to every extreme and beyond it. There were fathers who killed their sons; men were dragged from the temples or butchered on the very altars; some were actually walled up in the temple of Dionysus [a god of drunken revelry] and died there.

So savage was the progress of this revolution, and it seemed all the more so because it was one of the first which had broken out. Later, of course, practically the whole of the Hellenic world was convulsed, with rival parties in every state—democratic leaders trying to bring in the Athenians, and oligarchs trying to bring in the Spartans. In peacetime there would have been no excuse and no desire for calling them in, but in time of war, when each party could always count upon an alliance which would do harm to its opponents and at the same time strengthen its own position, it became a natural thing for anyone who wanted a change of government to call in help from outside. In the various cities these revolutions were the cause of many calamities—as happens and always will happen while human nature is what it is, though there may be different degrees of savagery, and, as different circumstances arise, the general rules will admit of some variety. In times of peace and prosperity cities and individuals alike follow higher standards, because they are not forced into a situation where they have to do what they do not want to do. But war is a stern teacher; in depriving them of the power of easily satisfying their daily wants, it brings most people's minds down to the level of their actual circumstances.

So revolutions broke out in city after city, and in places where the revolutions occurred late the knowledge of what had happened previously in other places caused still new extravagances of revolutionary zeal, expressed by an elaboration in the methods of seizing power and by unheard-of atrocities in revenge. To fit in with the change of events, words, too, had to change their usual meanings. What used to be described as a thoughtless act of aggression was now regarded as the courage one would expect to find in a party member; to think of the future and wait was merely another way of saying one was a coward; any idea of moderation was just an attempt to disguise one's unmanly character; ability to understand a question from all sides meant that one was totally unfitted for action. Fanatical enthusiasm was the mark of a real man, and to plot against an enemy behind his back was perfectly legitimate self-defence. Anyone who held violent opinions could always be trusted, and anyone who objected to them became a suspect. To plot successfully was a sign of intelligence, but it was still cleverer to see that a plot was hatching. If one attempted to provide against having to do either, one was disrupting the unity of the party and acting out of fear of the opposition. In short, it was equally praiseworthy to get one's blow in first against someone who was going to do wrong, and to denounce someone who had no intention of doing any wrong at all. Family relations were a weaker tie than party membership, since party members were more ready to go to any extreme for any reason whatever. These parties were not formed to enjoy the benefits of the established laws, but to acquire power by overthrowing the existing regime and the members of these parties felt confidence in each other not because of any fellowship in a religious communion, but because they were partners in crime. If an opponent made a reasonable speech, the party in power, so far from giving it a generous reception, took every precaution to see that it had no practical effect....

Love of power, operating through greed and through personal ambition, was the cause of all these evils. To this must be added the violent fanaticism which came into play once the struggle had broken out. Leaders of parties in the cities had programmes which appeared admirable—on one side political equality for the masses, on the other the safe and sound government of the aristocracy—but in professing to serve the public interest they were seeking to win the prizes for themselves. In their struggles for ascendancy nothing was barred; terrible indeed were the actions to which they committed themselves, and in taking revenge they went farther still. Here they were deterred neither by the claims of justice nor by the interests of the state; their one standard was the pleasure of their own party at that particular moment, and so, either by means of condemning their enemies on an illegal vote or by violently usurping power over them, they were always ready to satisfy the hatreds of the hour. Thus neither side had any use for conscientious motives; more interest was shown in those who could produce attractive arguments to justify some disgraceful action. As for the citizens who held moderate views, they were destroyed by both the extreme parties, either for not taking part in the struggle or in envy at the possibility that they might survive.

As the result of these revolutions, there was a general deterioration of character throughout the Greek world. The simple way of looking at things, which is so much the mark of a noble nature, was regarded as a ridiculous quality and soon ceased to exist. Society had become divided into two ideologically hostile camps, and each side viewed the other with suspicion. As for ending this state of affairs, no guarantee could be given that would be trusted, no oath sworn that people would fear to break; everyone had come to the conclusion that it was hopeless to expect a permanent settlement and so, instead of being able to feel confident in others, they devoted their energies to providing against being injured themselves. As a rule those who were least remarkable for intelligence showed the greater powers of survival. Such people recognized their own deficiencies and the superior intelligence of their opponents; fearing that they might lose a debate or find themselves outmanoeuvred in intrigue by their quick-witted enemies, they boldly launched straight into action; while their opponents, over-confident in the belief that they would see what was happening in advance, and not thinking it necessary to seize by force what they could secure by policy, were the more easily destroyed because they were off their guard.

Certainly it was in Corcyra that there occurred the first examples of the breakdown of law and order. There was the revenge taken in their hour of triumph by those who had in the past been arrogantly oppressed instead of wisely governed; there were the wicked resolutions taken by those who, particularly under the pressure of misfortune, wished to escape from their usual poverty and coveted the property of their neighbours; there were the savage and pitiless actions into which men were carried not so much for the sake of gain as because they were swept away into an internecine struggle by their ungovernable passions. Then, with the ordinary conventions of civilized life thrown into confusion, human nature, always ready to offend even where laws exist, showed itself proudly in its true colours, as something incapable of controlling passion, insubordinate to the idea of justice, the enemy to anything superior to itself; for, if it had not been for the pernicious power of envy, men would not so have exalted vengeance above innocence and profit above justice. Indeed, it is true that in these acts of revenge on others men take it upon themselves to begin the process of repealing those general laws of humanity which are there to give a hope of salvation to all who are in distress, instead of leaving those laws in existence, remembering that there may come a time when they, too, will be in danger and will need their protection.

ARISTOTLE

HISTORY OF ANIMALS, POLITICS, AND *NICOMACHEAN ETHICS*

Scientific thinking encompasses both rationalism and empiricism. Rationalism—pursuit of truth through thought alone, independent of experience with the natural world—was advocated by Plato. This approach points in the direction of theoretical mathematics. Like Plato, Aristotle valued reason, but unlike his teacher he also had great respect for the concrete details of nature obtained through sense experience. In *History of Animals*, Aristotle demonstrated his empirical approach: observing nature and collecting, classifying, and analyzing data. Aristotle's empiricism is the foundation of such sciences as geology, botany, and biology. The first excerpt, a careful observation of the development of a chick embryo, illustrates Aristotle's empiricism.

When he turned to the study of politics, Aristotle also followed an empirical methodology. He undertook a series of historical studies of the constitutions of 158 Greek states. The most significant and complete study that has survived describes the constitution of Athens. On the basis of these extensive surveys, Aristotle proceeded to write *Politics*, his masterwork of political philosophy, excerpted in the second reading.

Like Socrates and Plato, Aristotle based his ethics on reason. People could achieve moral well-being, said Aristotle, when they avoided extremes of behavior and rationally chose the way of moderation. In his *Nicomachean Ethics*, dedicated to his son Nicomachus, Aristotle described the "proud man." This passage, excerpted in the third reading, sketches characteristics that make up the Greek ideal of excellence.

HISTORY OF ANIMALS

. . . With the common hen after three days and three nights there is the first indication of the embryo; with larger birds the interval being longer, with smaller birds shorter. Meanwhile the yolk comes into being, rising towards the sharp end, where the primal element of the egg is situated, and where the egg gets hatched; and the heart appears, like a speck of blood, in the white of the egg. This point beats and moves as though endowed with life, . . . and a membrane carrying bloody fibres now envelops the yolk. . . . A little afterwards the body is differentiated, at first very small and white. The head is clearly distinguished, and in it the eyes, swollen out to a great extent. This condition of the eyes lasts on for a good while, as it is only by degrees that they diminish in size and collapse. At the outset the under portion of the body appears insignificant in comparison with the upper portion. . . . The life-element of the chick is in the white of the egg, and the nutriment comes through the navel-string out of the yolk.

When the egg is now ten days old the chick and all its parts are distinctly visible. The head is still larger than the rest of its body, and the eyes larger than the head, but still devoid of vision. The eyes, if removed about this time, are found to be larger than beans, and black; if the cuticle be peeled off them there is a white and cold liquid inside, quite glittering in the sunlight, but there is no hard substance whatsoever. Such is the condition of the head and eyes. At this time also the larger internal organs are visible. . . .

About the twentieth day, if you open the egg and touch the chick, it moves inside and chirps; and it is already coming to be covered with down, when, after the twentieth day is past, the chick begins to break the shell. The head is situated over the right leg close to the flank, and the wing is placed over the head. . . .

In the following selection from *Politics*, Aristotle begins by defining the nature of a state and its purpose.

POLITICS

It is clear therefore that the state cannot be defined merely as a community dwelling in the same place and preventing its members from wrong-doing and promoting the exchange of goods and services.

Certainly all these must be present if there is to be a state, but even the presence of every one of them does not *ipso facto* [by that fact] make a state. The state is intended to enable all, in their households and their kinships, to live well, meaning by that a full and satisfying life. . . .

He then addresses the problem of where the sovereign power of the state ought to reside.

. . . "Where ought the sovereign power of the state to reside?" With the people? With the propertied classes? With the good? With one man, the best of all the good? With one man, the tyrant? There are objections to all these. Thus suppose we say the people is the supreme authority, then if they use their numerical superiority to make a distribution of the property of the rich, is not that unjust? It has been done by a valid decision of the sovereign power, yet what can we call it save the very height of injustice? Again, if the majority, having laid their hands on everything, distribute the possessions of the few, they are obviously destroying the state. But that cannot be goodness which destroys its possessor and justice cannot be destructive of the state. So it is clear that this process, though it may be the law, cannot be just. Or, if that is just, the actions taken by a tyrant must be just; his superior power enables him to use force, just as the masses force their will on the rich. Thirdly, if it is just for the few and wealthy to rule, and if they too rob and plunder and help themselves to the goods of the many, is that just? If it is, then it is just in the former case also. The answer clearly is that all these three are bad and unjust. The fourth alternative, that the good should rule and have the supreme authority, is also not free from objection; it means that all the rest must be without official standing, debarred from holding office under the constitution. The fifth alternative, that one man, the best, should rule, is no better; by making the number of rulers fewer we leave still larger numbers without official standing. It might be objected too that it is a bad thing for any human being, subject to all possible disorders and affections of the human mind, to be the sovereign authority, which ought to be reserved for the law itself. . . .

. . . [A]t the moment it would seem that the most defensible, perhaps even the truest, answer to the question would be to say that the majority ought to be sovereign. . . . For where there are many people, each has some share of goodness and intelligence, and when these are brought together, they become as it were one multiple man with many pairs of feet and hands and many minds. So too in regard to character and powers of perception. That is why the general public is a better judge of works of music and poetry; some judge some parts, some others, but their joint pronouncement is a verdict upon the whole. . . .

Aristotle seeks to determine what is the best constitution. His conclusion reflects the premise developed in his *Ethics* that moderation, or the middle way, is the path to virtue in all things. So, Aristotle says that in forming a constitution for the state, power should reside in the hands of the middle class rather than the aristocracy or the poor.

If we were right when in our *Ethics* we stated that Virtue is a Mean and that the happy life is life free and unhindered and according to virtue, then the best life must be the middle way, [or the mean] . . . between two extremes which it is open to those at either end to attain. And the same principle must be applicable to the goodness or badness of cities and states. For the constitution of a city is really the way it lives.

In all states there are three sections of the community—the very well-off, the very badly-off, and those in between. Seeing therefore that it is agreed that moderation and a middle position are best, it is clear that in the matter of possessions to own a middling amount is best of all. This condition is most obedient to reason, and following reason is just what is difficult both for the exceedingly rich, handsome, strong, and well-born, and for the opposite, the extremely poor, the weak, and the downtrodden. The former commit deeds of violence on a large scale, the latter are delinquent and wicked in petty ways. The misdeeds of the one class are due to *hubris* [overweening pride, arrogance], the misdeeds of the other to rascality. . . . There are other drawbacks about the two extremes. Those who have a superabundance of all that makes for success, strength, riches, friends, and so forth, neither wish to hold office nor understand the work; and this is ingrained in them from childhood on; even at school they are so full of their superiority that they have never learned to do what they are told. Those on the other hand who are greatly deficient in these qualities are too subservient. So they cannot command and can only obey in a servile régime, while the others cannot obey in any régime and can command only in a master-slave relationship. The result is a state not of free men but of slaves and masters, the one full of envy, the other of contempt. Nothing could be farther removed from friendship or from the whole idea of a shared partnership in a state. . . . The state aims to consist as far as possible of those who are like and equal, a condition found chiefly among the middle section. . . . The middle class is also the steadiest element, the least eager for change. They neither covet, like the poor, the possessions of others, nor do others covet theirs, as the poor covet those of the rich. . . .

It is clear then both that the political partnership which operates through the middle class is best, and also that those cities have every chance of being well-governed in which the middle class is large, stronger if possible than the other two together, or at any rate stronger than one of them. . . . For this reason it is a happy state of affairs when those who take part in the life of the state have a moderate but adequate amount of property. . . . Tyranny often emerges from an over-enthusiastic democracy or from an oligarchy, but much more rarely from middle-class constitutions or from those very near to them.

The superiority of the middle type of constitution is clear also from the fact that it alone is free from fighting among factions. Where the middle element is large, there least of all arise faction and counter-faction among citizens. . . .

The following selection from *Ethics* shows how Aristotle's ethical theory rests on the principles of moderation and balance. Aristotle notes that some people become "angry at the wrong things, more than is right, and longer, and cannot be appeased until they inflict vengeance or punishment." On the other extreme, foolish and slavish people endure every insult without defending themselves. Between these extremes is the proud man, "who is angry at the right thing and with the right people, and, further, as he ought, when he ought, and as long as he ought." Even-tempered and moderate in all things, such a man "tends to be unperturbed and not to be led by passion."

ETHICS

. . . In the first place, then, as has been said, the proud man is concerned with honours; yet he will also bear himself with moderation towards wealth and power and all good or evil fortune, whatever may befall him, and will be neither over-joyed by good fortune nor over-pained by evil. For not even towards honour does he bear himself as if it were a very great thing. . . .

He does not run into trifling dangers, nor is he fond of danger, because he honours few things; but he will face great dangers, and when he is in danger he is unsparing of his life, knowing that there are conditions on which life is not worth having. And he is the sort of man to confer benefits, but he is ashamed of receiving them; for the one is the mark of a superior, the other of an inferior. And he is apt to confer greater benefits in return; for thus the original benefactor besides being paid will incur a debt to him, and will be the gainer by the transaction. They seem also to remember any service they have done, but not those they have received (for he who receives a service is inferior to him who has done it, but the proud man wishes to be superior), and to hear of the former with pleasure, of the latter with displeasure. . . . It is a mark of the proud man also to ask for nothing or scarcely anything, but to give help readily, and to be dignified towards people who enjoy high position and good fortune, but unassuming towards those of the middle class; for it is a difficult and lofty thing to be superior to the former, but easy to be so to the latter, and a lofty bearing over the former is no mark of ill-breeding, but among humble people it is as vulgar as a display of strength against the weak. Again, it is characteristic of the proud man not to aim at the things commonly held in honour, or the things in which others excel; to be sluggish and to hold back except where great honour or a great work is at stake, and to be a man of few deeds, but of great and notable ones. He must also be open in his hate and in his love (for to conceal one's feelings, i.e. to care less for truth than for what people will think, is a coward's part), and must speak and act openly; for he is free of speech because he is contemptuous, and he is given to telling the truth, except when he speaks in irony to the vulgar. He must be unable to make his life revolve round another, unless it be a friend; for this is slavish, and for this reason all flatterers are servile and people lacking in self-respect are flatterers. Nor is he given to admiration; for nothing to him is great. Nor is he mindful of wrongs; for it is not the part of a proud man to have a long memory, especially for wrongs, but rather to overlook them. Nor is he a gossip; for he will speak neither about himself nor about another, since he cares not to be praised nor for others to be blamed; nor again is he given to praise; and for the same reason he is not an evil-speaker, even about his enemies, except from haughtiness. With regard to necessary or small matters he is least of all men given to lamentation or the asking of favours; for it is the part of one who takes such matters seriously to behave so with respect to them. He is one who will possess beautiful and profitless things rather than profitable and useful ones; for this is more proper to a character that suffices to itself.

Further, a slow step is thought proper to the proud man, a deep voice, and a level utterance; for the man who takes few things seriously is not likely to be hurried, nor the man who thinks nothing great to be excited, while a shrill voice and a rapid gait are the results of hurry and excitement.

Such, then, is the proud man; the man who falls short of him is unduly humble, and the man who goes beyond him is vain.

CATO THE ELDER: HOSTILITY TO GREEK PHILOSOPHY

Some conservative Romans were hostile to the Greek influence, which they felt threatened traditional Roman values. Cato the Elder (also the Censor; 234–149 b.c.) denounced Socrates for undermining respect for Athenian law and warned that Greek philosophy might lure Roman youth into similar subversive behavior. The following passage from Plutarch's *Lives* shows Cato's hostility to Greek philosophy.

He was now grown old, when Carneades the Academic, and Diogenes the Stoic, came as deputies from Athens to Rome, praying for release from a penalty of five hundred talents laid on the Athenians, in a suit, to which they did not appear, in which the Oropians were plaintiffs and Sicyonians[1] judges. All the most studious youth immediately waited on these philosophers, and frequently, with admiration, heard them speak. But the gracefulness of Carneades's oratory, whose ability was really greatest, and his reputation equal to it, gathered large and favourable audiences, and ere long filled, like a wind, all the city with the sound of it. So that it soon began to be told that a Greek, famous even to admiration, winning and carrying all before him, had impressed so strange a love upon the young men, that quitting all their pleasures and pastimes, they ran mad, as it were, after philosophy; which indeed much pleased the Romans in general; nor could they but with much pleasure see the youth receive so welcomely the Greek literature, and frequent the company of learned men. But Cato, on the other side, seeing the passion for words flowing into the city, from the beginning took it ill, fearing lest the youth should be diverted that way, and so should prefer the glory of speaking well before that of arms and doing well. And when the fame of the philosophers increased in the city, and Caius Acilius, a person of distinction, at his own request, became their interpreter to the senate at their first audience, Cato resolved, under some specious pretence, to have all philosophers cleared out of the city; and, coming into the senate, blamed the magistrates for letting these deputies stay so long a time without being despatched, though they were persons that could easily persuade the people to what they pleased; that therefore in all haste something should be determined about their petition, that so they might go home again to their own schools, and declaim to the Greek children, and leave the Roman youth to be obedient, as hitherto, to their own laws and governors.

Yet he did this not out of any anger, as some think, to Carneades; but because he wholly despised philosophy, and out of a kind of pride scoffed at the Greek studies and literature; as, for example, he would say, that Socrates was a prating, seditious fellow, who did his best to tyrannise over his country, to undermine the ancient customs, and to entice and withdraw the citizens to opinions contrary to the laws. Ridiculing the school of Isocrates,[2] he would add, that his scholars grew old men before they had done learning with him, as if they were to use their art and plead causes in the court of Minos in the next world. And to frighten his son from anything that was Greek, in a more vehement tone than became one of his age, he pronounced, as it were, with the voice of an oracle, that the Romans would certainly be destroyed when they began once to be infected with Greek literature; though time indeed has shown the vanity of this his prophecy; as, in truth, the city of Rome has risen to its highest fortune while entertaining Grecian learning. Nor had he an aversion only against the Greek philosophers, but the physicians also; for having, it seems, heard how Hippocrates, when the king of Persia sent for him, with offers of a fee of several talents, said, that he would never assist barbarians who were enemies of the Greeks; he affirmed, that this was now become a common oath taken by all physicians, and enjoined his son to have a care and avoid them.

[1]The Oropians came from the town of Oropus in east central Greece. Sicyonians came from the city of Sicyon in southern Greece.
[2]Isocrates (436–338 B.C.) was an Athenian orator whose students distinguished themselves as orators, historians, and statesmen.

QUINTUS LUCRETIUS VESPILLO

A FUNERAL EULOGY FOR A ROMAN WIFE

Documenting intimate relationships between Roman men and women is difficult because ordinary people were unlikely to write about such things. Although personal records are scant or now lost, glimpses have survived in the writings of historians and poets or as inscriptions on tombstones.

In the late Republic, it became more common for distinguished men to pronounce funeral eulogies for distinguished female as well as male members of their families. One such eulogy was composed by the ex-Consul Quintus Lucretius Vespillo for his wife Turia, who died about 8 B.C. Though marriages among persons of the higher social ranks were usually undertaken for political and economic considerations, clearly this couple had gone beyond such a formal alliance to achieve a most touching love.

Before the day fixed for our marriage, you were suddenly left an orphan, by the murder of your parents in the solitude of the country. . . .

Through your efforts chiefly, their death did not remain unavenged. . . .

In our day, marriages of such long duration, not dissolved by divorce, but terminated by death alone, are indeed rare. For our union was prolonged in unclouded happiness for forty-one years. Would that it had been my lot to put an end to this our good fortune and that I as the older—which was more just—had yielded to fate.

Why recall your inestimable qualities, your modesty, deference, affability, your amiable disposition, your faithful attendance to the household duties, your enlightened religion, your unassuming elegance, the modest simplicity and refinement of your manners? Need I speak of your attachment to your kindred, your affection for your family—when you respected my mother as you did your own parents and cared for her tomb as you did for that of your own mother and father,—you who share countless other virtues with Roman ladies most jealous of their fair name? These qualities which I claim for you are your own, equalled or excelled by but few; for the experience of men teaches us how rare they are.

With common prudence we have preserved all the patrimony which you received from your parents. Intrusting it all to me, you were not troubled with the care of increasing it; thus did we share the task of administering it, that I undertook to protect your fortune, and you to guard mine. . . .

You gave proof of your generosity not only towards several of your kin, but especially in your filial devotion. . . . You brought up in your own home, in the enjoyment of mutual benefits, some young girls of your kinship. And that these might attain to a station in life worthy of our family, you provided them with dowries. . . .

I owe you no less a debt than Cæsar Augustus [27 B.C.–A.D. 14, emperor of Rome] himself, for this my return from exile to my native land. For unless you had prepared the way for my safety, even Cæsar's promises of assistance had been of no avail. So I owe no less a debt to your loyal devotion than to the clemency of Cæsar.

Why shall I now conjure up the memory of our domestic counsels and plans stored away in the hidden recesses of the heart?—That, aroused by the sudden arrival of messages from you to a realization of the present and imminent perils, I was saved by your counsel? That you suffered me not to be recklessly carried away by a foolish rashness, or that, when bent on more temperate plans, you provided for me a safe retreat, having as sharers in your plans for my safety, when an exile,—fraught with danger as they were for you all,—your sister and her husband. . . .

Vespillo then relates what happened to his wife when she begged his enemy M. Lepidus to honor her husband's writ of pardon from Octavian Caesar.

. . . Then prostrating yourself at his feet, he not only did not raise you up,—but, dragged along and abused as though a common slave, your body all covered with bruises, yet with unflinching steadfastness of purpose, you recalled to him Cæsar's edict (of pardon) and the letter of felicitation on my return, that accompanied it. Braving his taunts and suffering the most brutal treatment, you denounced these cruelties publicly so that he (Lepidus) was branded as the author of all my perils and misfortunes. And his punishment was not long delayed.

Could such courage remain without effect? Your unexampled patience furnished the occasion for Cæsar's clemency, and, by guarding my life, he branded the infamous and savage cruelty (of the tyrant Lepidus). . . .

When all the world was again at peace and the Republic reestablished, peaceful and happy days followed. We longed for children, which an envious fate denied us. Had Fortune smiled on us in this, what had been lacking to complete our happiness? But an adverse destiny put an end to our hopes. . . . Disconsolate to see me without children . . . you wished to put an end to my chagrin by proposing to me a divorce, offering to yield the place to another spouse more fertile, with the only intention of searching for and providing for me a spouse worthy of our mutual affection, whose children you assured me you would have treated as your own. . . .

I will admit that I was so irritated and shocked by such a proposition that I had difficulty in restraining my anger and remaining master of myself. You spoke of divorce before the decree of fate [death] had forced us to separate, and I could not comprehend how you could conceive of any reason why you, still living, should not be my wife, you who during my exile had always remained most faithful and loyal. . . .

Would that our time of life had permitted our union to have endured until I, the older, had passed away—which was more just—and that you might perform for me the last sad rites and that I might have departed, leaving you behind, with a daughter to replace me at your side.

By fate's decree your course was run before mine. You left me the grief, the heart-ache, the longing for you, the sad fate to live alone. . . .

The conclusion of this discourse will be that you have deserved all, and that I remain with the chagrin of not being able to give you all. Your wishes have always been my supreme law; and whatever it will be permitted me to accord them still, in this I shall not fail.

May the gods, the Manes [spirits of dead ancestors, considered godlike], assure and protect your repose!

SALLUST

MORAL DETERIORATION

In the dark days of the Republic after the assassination of Julius Caesar in 44 b.c., the Roman politician and historian Sallust (Gaius Sallustius Crispus, 86–35 b.c.) reflected on the causes of the Republic's collapse. In his account of a failed coup d'état that occurred in 63 b.c., Sallust contrasted the virtues of the early Republic with the moral decline that set in after the destruction of Carthage. Having failed to be elected consul in 63 b.c., Catiline, a Roman noble, organized a conspiracy to seize the state. The coup d'état was thwarted by the vigorous action of the consul Cicero, who arrested the known conspirators and had them executed. Catiline, who led an army against the forces loyal to the government, was defeated and killed.

In peace and war [in the early Republic], as I have said, virtue was held in high esteem. The closest unity prevailed, and avarice was a thing almost unknown. Justice and righteousness were upheld not so much by law as by natural instinct. They quarrelled and fought with their country's foes; between themselves the citizens contended only for honour. In making offerings to the gods they spared no expense; at home they lived frugally and never betrayed a friend. By combining boldness in war with fair dealing when peace was restored, they protected themselves and the state. There are convincing proofs of this. In time of war, soldiers were often punished for attacking against orders or for being slow to obey a signal of recall from battle, whereas few ever ventured to desert their standards or to give ground when hard pressed. In peace, they governed by conferring benefits on their subjects, not by intimidation; and when wronged they would rather pardon than seek vengeance.

Thus by hard work and just dealing the power of the state increased. Mighty kings were vanquished, savage tribes and huge nations were brought to their knees; and when Carthage, Rome's rival in her quest for empire, had been annihilated [in 146 b.c.], every land and sea lay open to her. It was then that fortune turned unkind and confounded all her enterprises. To the men who had so easily endured toil and peril, anxiety and adversity, the leisure and riches which are generally regarded as so desirable proved a burden and a curse. Growing love of money, and the lust for power which followed it, engendered every kind of evil. Avarice destroyed honour, integrity, and every other virtue, and instead taught men to be proud and cruel, to neglect religion, and to hold nothing too sacred to sell. Ambition tempted many to be false, to have one thought hidden in their hearts, another ready on their tongues, to become a man's friend or enemy not because they judged him worthy or unworthy but because they thought it would pay them, and to put on the semblance of virtues that they had not. At first these vices grew slowly and sometimes met with punishment; later on, when the disease had spread like a plague, Rome changed: her government, once so just and admirable, became harsh and unendurable.

Reflecting on the last stages of the Republic's decline, Sallust believed that men had learned a most dangerous lesson: that they could gain power and wealth through violence and corruption rather than through virtue and self-restraint.

Never in its history—it seems to me—had the empire of Rome been in such a miserable plight. From east to west all the world had been vanquished by her armies and obeyed her will; at home there was profound peace and abundance of wealth, which mortal men esteem the chiefest of blessings. Yet there were Roman citizens obstinately determined to destroy both themselves and their country. In spite of two senatorial decrees, not one man among all the conspirators was induced by the promise of reward to betray their plans, and not one deserted from Catiline's camp. A deadly moral contagion had infected all their minds. And this madness was not confined to those actually implicated in the plot. The whole of the lower orders, impatient for a new régime, looked with favour on Catiline's enterprise.[1] In this they only did what might have been expected of them. In every country paupers envy respectable

[1]This surely cannot have been true. Sallust must be exaggerating the popular support for the conspiracy.

citizens and make heroes of unprincipled characters, hating the established order of things and hankering after innovation; discontented with their own lot, they are bent on general upheaval. Turmoil and rebellion bring them carefree profit, since poverty has nothing to lose.

The city populace were especially eager to fling themselves into a revolutionary adventure. There were several reasons for this. To begin with, those who had made themselves conspicuous anywhere by vice and shameless audacity, those who had wasted their substance by disgraceful excesses, and those whom scandalous or criminal conduct had exiled from their homes—all these had poured into Rome till it was like a sewer. Many, remembering Sulla's victory,[2] and seeing men who had served under him as common soldiers now risen to be senators, or so rich that they lived as luxuriously as kings, began to hope that they too, if they took up arms, might find victory a source of profit. Young men from the country, whose labour on the farms had barely kept them from starvation, had been attracted by the private and public doles available at Rome, and preferred an idle city life to such thankless toil. These, like all the rest, stood to gain by public calamities. It is no wonder, therefore, that these paupers, devoid of moral scruple and incited by ambitious hopes, should have held their country as cheap as they held themselves. Those also to whom Sulla's victory had brought disaster by the proscription of their parents, the confiscation of their property, and the curtailment of their civil rights, looked forward with no less sanguine expectations to what might result from the coming struggle. Moreover, all the factions opposed to the Senate would rather see the state embroiled than accept their own exclusion from political power.

Such was the evil condition by which, after an interval of some years, Rome was once more afflicted. After the restoration of the power of the tribunes in the consulship of Pompey and Crassus,[3,4] this very important office was obtained by certain men whose youth intensified their natural aggressiveness. These tribunes began to rouse the mob by inveighing against the Senate, and then inflamed popular passion still further by handing out bribes and promises, whereby they won renown and influence for themselves. They were strenuously opposed by most of the nobility, who posed as defenders of the Senate but were really concerned to maintain their own privileged position. The whole truth—to put it in a word—is that although all disturbers of the peace in this period put forward specious pretexts, claiming either to be protecting the rights of the people or to be strengthening the authority of the Senate, this was mere pretence: in reality, every one of them was fighting for his personal aggrandizement. Lacking all self-restraint, they [stopped] at nothing to gain their ends, and both sides made ruthless use of any successes they won.

[2] 1Lucius Cornelius Sulla (c. 138–78 B.C.) was a successful politician and general, whose rivalry with another politician and general, Gaius Marius (c. 155–86 B.C.), led to civil war. After seizing Rome and massacring his opponents, Sulla made himself dictator and increased the power of the aristocratic senate, suppressing the office of tribune of the people. The latter had been used by Tiberius and Gaius Gracchus, among others, to better the condition of the poorer classes.

[3] In 70 B.C.

[4]Pompey (Gnaeus Pompeius, 106–48 B.C.) and Crassus (Marcus Licinius Crassus, c. 115–53 B.C.) held the office of consul in 55 B.C. In 59 B.C., together with Julius Caesar, they had formed a political alliance called a triumvirate (meaning "group of three men"), which dominated Roman government for the next decade.

DIO CASSIUS

CARACALLA'S EXTORTIONS

The reign (a.d. 211–217) of Caracalla provides an early example of the crushing demands imposed by the state on its citizenry. The following account comes from the *Roman History* of Dio Cassius.

[Caracalla] was fond of spending money upon the soldiers, great numbers of whom he kept in attendance upon him, alleging one excuse after another and one war after another; but he made it his business to strip, despoil, and grind down all the rest of mankind, and the senators by no means least. In the first place, there were the gold crowns that he was repeatedly demanding, on the constant pretext that he had conquered some enemy or other; and I am not referring, either, to the actual manufacture of the crowns—for what does that amount to?—but to the vast amount of money constantly being given under that name by the cities for the customary "crowning," as it is called, of the emperors. Then there were the provisions that we were required to furnish in great quantities on all occasions, and this without receiving any remuneration and sometimes actually at additional cost to ourselves—all of which supplies he either bestowed upon the soldiers or else peddled out; and there were the gifts which he demanded from the wealthy citizens and from the various communities; and the taxes, both the new ones which he promulgated and the ten per cent. tax that he instituted in place of the five per cent. tax applying to the emancipation of slaves, to bequests, and to all legacies. . . . But apart from all these burdens, we were also compelled to build at our own expense all sorts of houses for him whenever he set out from Rome, and costly lodgings in the middle of even the very shortest journeys; yet he not only never lived in them, but in some cases was not destined even to see them. Moreover, we constructed amphitheatres and race-courses wherever he spent the winter or expected to spend it, all without receiving any contribution from him; and they were all promptly demolished, the sole reason for their being built in the first place being, apparently, that we might become impoverished.

The emperor himself kept spending the money upon the soldiers, as we have said, and upon wild beasts and horses; for he was for ever killing vast numbers of animals, both wild and domesticated, forcing us to furnish most of them, though he did buy a few. One day he slew a hundred boars at one time with his own hands. . . . In everything he was very hot-headed and very fickle, and he furthermore possessed the craftiness of his mother and the Syrians, to which race she belonged. He would appoint some freedman or other wealthy person to be director of the games in order that the man might spend money in this way also; and he would salute the spectators with his whip from the arena below and beg for gold pieces like a performer of the lowest class. . . . To such an extent was the entire world, so far as it owned his sway, devastated throughout his whole reign, that on one occasion the Romans at a horse-race shouted in unison this, among other things: "We shall do the living to death,[1] that we may bury the dead." Indeed, he often used to say: "Nobody in the world should have money but me; and I want it to bestow upon the soldiers." Once when Julia [Domna, his mother] chided him for spending vast sums upon them and said, "There is no longer any source of revenue, either just or unjust, left to us," he replied, exhibiting his sword, "Be of good cheer, mother: for as long as we have this, we shall not run short of money."

Moreover to those who flattered him he distributed both money and goods.

[1]Or . . . "We are stripping the living."

SALVIAN

POLITICAL AND SOCIAL INJUSTICE

The growing hatred of citizens for the Roman state is well delineated in a book called *The Governance of God*, by Salvian (Salvianus) of Marseilles (c. a.d. 400–470). A Christian priest, Salvian was an eyewitness to the end of Roman rule in Gaul. He describes the political and moral causes of the collapse of the Roman state in the west in the following reading.

What towns, as well as what municipalities and villages are there in which there are not as many tyrants as *curiales*.[1] Perhaps they glory in this name of tyrant because it seems to be considered powerful and honored. For, almost all robbers rejoice and boast, if they are said to be more fierce than they really are. What place is there, as I have said, where the bowels of widows and orphans are not devoured by the leading men of the cities, and with them those of almost all holy men? . . . Not one of them [widows and orphans], therefore, is safe. In a manner, except for the very powerful, neither is anyone safe from the devastation of general brigandage, unless they are like the robbers themselves. To this state of affairs, indeed, to this crime has the world come that, unless one is bad, he cannot be safe. . . .

All the while, the poor are despoiled, the widows groan, the orphans are tread underfoot, so much so that many of them, and they are not of obscure birth and have received a liberal education, flee to the enemy lest they die from the pain of public persecution. They seek among the barbarians the dignity of the Roman because they cannot bear barbarous indignity among the Romans. Although these Romans differ in religion and language from the barbarians to whom they flee, and differ from them in respect to filthiness of body and clothing, nevertheless, as I have said, they prefer to bear among the barbarians a worship unlike their own rather than rampant injustice among the Romans.

Salvian tells how Roman citizens are deserting Rome to live under the rule of the Goths and other barbarian invaders. Moreover, in many parts of Spain and Gaul (France), peasants called *Bagaudae* have rebelled and established zones free from Roman authority.

Thus, far and wide, they migrate either to the Goths[2] or to the Bagaudae, or to other barbarians everywhere in power; yet they do not repent having migrated. They prefer to live as freemen under an outward form of captivity than as captives under an appearance of liberty. Therefore, the name of Roman citizens, at one time not only greatly valued but dearly bought, is now repudiated and fled from, and it is almost considered not only base but even deserving of abhorrence.

And what can be a greater testimony of Roman wickedness than that many men, upright and noble and to whom the position of being a Roman citizen should be considered as of the highest splendor and dignity, have been driven by the cruelty of Roman wickedness to such a state of mind that they do not wish to be Romans? . . .

I am now about to speak of the Bagaudae who were despoiled, oppressed and murdered by evil and cruel judges. After they had lost the right of Roman citizenship, they also lost the honor of bearing the Roman name. We blame their misfortunes on themselves. We ascribe to them a name which signifies their downfall. We give to them a name of which we ourselves are the cause. We call them rebels. We call those outlaws whom we compelled to be criminal.

For, by what other ways did they become Bagaudae, except by our wickedness, except by the wicked ways of judges, except by the proscription and pillage of those who have turned the assessments of

[1]The *curiales* were members of the municipal councils. In the late years of the Roman Empire, they were forced to act as tax collectors for the central government and to pay from their own pockets whatever sums they could not collect from the overtaxed inhabitants.

[2]The Goths were Germanic tribes that invaded Rome. The Visigoths invaded Italy in the early fifth century and seized Rome for a few days. This was the first time in eight centuries that a foreign enemy had entered the capital. Later the Visigoths occupied large areas of Spain and Gaul. In the late fifth century, the Ostrogoths invaded and conquered Italy, establishing a kingdom there.

public taxes into the benefit of their own gain and have made the tax levies their own booty? Like wild beasts, they did not rule but devoured their subjects, and feasted not only on the spoils of men, as most robbers are wont to do, but even on their torn flesh and, as I may say, on their blood.

Thus it happened that men, strangled and killed by the robberies of judges, began to live as barbarians because they were not permitted to be Romans. They became satisfied to be what they were not, because they were not permitted to be what they were. They were compelled to defend their lives at least, because they saw that they had already completely lost their liberty. . . .

But what else can these wretched people wish for, they who suffer the incessant and even continuous destruction of public tax levies. To them there is always imminent a heavy and relentless proscription. They desert their homes, lest they be tortured in their very homes. They seek exile, lest they suffer torture. The enemy is more lenient to them than the tax collectors. This is proved by this very fact, that they flee to the enemy in order to avoid the full force of the heavy tax levy. This very tax levying, although hard and inhuman, would nevertheless be less heavy and harsh if all would bear it equally and in common. Taxation is made more shameful and burdensome because all do not bear the burden of all. They extort tribute from the poor man for the taxes of the rich, and the weaker carry the load for the stronger. There is no other reason that they cannot bear all the taxation except that the burden imposed on the wretched is greater than their resources. . . .

Therefore, in the districts taken over by the barbarians, there is one desire among all the Romans, that they should never again find it necessary to pass under Roman jurisdiction. In those regions, it is the one and general prayer of the Roman people that they be allowed to carry on the life they lead with the barbarians. And we wonder why the Goths are not conquered by our portion of the population, when the Romans prefer to live among them rather than with us. Our brothers, therefore, are not only altogether unwilling to flee to us from them, but they even cast us aside in order to flee to them.

THE GOSPEL ACCORDING TO SAINT MATTHEW

In the gospel of Saint Matthew, Jesus outlined to his disciples the attitudes pleasing to God; this is the famous Sermon on the Mount.

1 Seeing the crowds, he went up on the mountain, and when he sat down his disciples came to him.
2 And he opened his mouth and taught them, saying:
3 "Blessed are the poor in spirit, for theirs is the kingdom of heaven.
4 "Blessed are those who mourn, for they shall be comforted.
5 "Blessed are the meek, for they shall inherit the earth.
6 "Blessed are those who hunger and thirst for righteousness, for they shall be satisfied.
7 "Blessed are the merciful, for they shall obtain mercy.
8 "Blessed are the pure in heart, for they shall see God.
9 "Blessed are the peacemakers, for they shall be called sons of God.
10 "Blessed are those who are persecuted for righteousness' sake, for theirs is the kingdom of heaven.
11 "Blessed are you when men revile you and persecute you and utter all kinds of evil against you
falsely on my account. 12 Rejoice and be glad, for your reward is great in heaven, for so men perse-
cuted the prophets who were be-fore you. . . ."

A characteristic feature of Jesus' teaching—one that angered the Jewish leaders—was a demand that his followers go beyond the letter of the Jewish law. In the tradition of the Hebrew prophets, Jesus stressed the ethical demands that underlie this law and urged a moral transformation of human character, based on a love of God and neighbor. In the next reading from Saint Matthew, Jesus reinterpreted the Hebrew commandments on killing, adultery, divorce, vengeance, the definition of a neighbor, and almsgiving.

---

17 "Think not that I have come to abolish the law and the prophets; I have come not to abolish them
but to fulfil them....
21 "You have heard that it was said to the men of old, 'You shall not kill; and whoever kills shall be
liable to judgment.' 22 But I say to you that every one who is angry with his brother shall be liable to
judgment; whoever insults his brother shall be liable to the council, and whoever says, 'You fool!' shall
be liable to the hell of fire. 23 So if you are offering your gift at the altar, and there remember that your
brother has something against you, 24 leave your gift there before the altar and go; first be reconciled to
your brother, and then come and offer your gift. 25 Make friends quickly with your accuser....
27 "You have heard that it was said, 'You shall not commit adultery.' 28 But I say to you that every one
who looks at a woman lustfully has already committed adultery with her in his heart. 29 If your right eye
causes you to sin, pluck it out and throw it away; it is better that you lose one of your members than
that your whole body be thrown into hell. 30 And if your right hand causes you to sin, cut it off and
throw it away; it is better that you lose one of your members than that your whole body go into hell.
31 "It was also said, 'Whoever divorces his wife, let him give her a certificate of divorce.' 32 But I say to
you that every one who divorces his wife, except on the ground of unchastity, makes her an adulteress;
and whoever marries a divorced woman commits adultery....
38 "You have heard that it was said, 'An eye for an eye and a tooth for a tooth.' 39 But I say to you, Do
not resist one who is evil. But if any one strikes you on the right cheek, turn to him the other also; 40 and
if any one would sue you and take your coat, let him have your cloak as well; 41 and if any one forces
you to go one mile, go with him two miles. 42 Give to him who begs from you, and do not refuse him
who would borrow from you.
43 "You have heard that it was said, 'You shall love your neighbor and hate your enemy.' 44 But I say to
you, Love your enemies and pray for those who persecute you, 45 so that you may be sons of your Father
who is in heaven.... (Matthew 5)

1 "Beware of practicing your piety before men in order to be seen by them; for then you will have no
reward from your Father who is in heaven.
2 "Thus, when you give alms, sound no trumpet before you, as the hypocrites do in the synagogues‡
and in the streets, that they may be praised by men. Truly, I say to you, they have their reward. 3 But
when you give alms, do not let your left hand know what your right hand is doing, 4 so that your alms
may be in secret; and your Father who sees in secret will reward you. . . ." (Matthew 6)

‡Synagogues, originally a name given to substitutes outside Judea for the Temple in Jerusalem, coexisted with the Temple; they were places for public prayer and study of the Hebrew Scriptures.—Eds.

SAINT JEROME

THE AGONY OF SOLITUDE IN THE DESERT

The Christian's vision of the world was honed in the isolation of the desert. The price of such insight was the agony that came with self-denial and solitude. Saint Jerome (A.D. 374–419), who lived in the desert during the fourth century, vividly described this suffering in a letter written to his female pupil Eustochium. He recounts the effects of the desert's austerity, which debilitated his body and disoriented his mind with delirious memories of earlier years and "enchantments" in Rome.

"Oh, how many times did I, set in the desert, in that vast solitude parched with the fires of the sun that offers a dread abiding to the monk, how often did I think myself back in the old Roman enchantments. There I sat solitary, full of bitterness; my disfigured limbs shuddered away from the sackcloth, my dirty skin was taking on the hue of the Ethiopian's flesh: every day tears, every day sighing: and if in spite of my struggles sleep would tower over and sink upon me, my battered body ached on the naked earth. Of food and drink I say nothing, since even a sick monk uses only cold water, and to take anything cooked is wanton luxury. Yet that same I, who for fear of hell condemned myself to such a prison, I, the comrade of scorpions and wild beasts, was there, watching the maidens in their dances: my face haggard with fasting, my mind burnt with desire in my frigid body, and the fires of lust alone leaped before a man prematurely dead. So, destitute of all aid, I used to lie at the feet of Christ, watering them with my tears, wiping them with my hair, struggling to subdue my rebellious flesh with seven days' fasting. I do not blush to confess the misery of my hapless days: rather could I weep that I am not what I was once. I remember crying out till day became one with night, nor ceasing to beat my breast until my Lord would chide and tranquillity return. I grew to dread even my cell, with its knowledge of my imaginings; and grim and angry with myself, would set out solitary to explore the desert: and wherever I would spy the depth of a valley or a mountainside or a precipitous rock, there was my place of prayer, there the torture-house of my unhappy flesh: and, the Lord Himself is witness, after many tears, and eyes that clung to heaven, I would sometimes seem to myself to be one with the angelic hosts."

SAINT BENEDICT OF NURSIA

THE BENEDICTINE RULE

The monastic way of life soon spread from Egypt to Palestine and Syria and eventually throughout the Christian Roman Empire. In Italy, Benedict of Nursia (c. 480–547), scion of a wealthy Roman family, founded twelve monasteries, the best known being at Monte Cassino in the mountains of southern Italy. Benedict wrote a set of rules for the governance of his monks; the Benedictine Rule became the model for many monasteries throughout Latin Christendom. In the following extract, Benedict summarizes the purpose and principles of monastic life.

. . . Therefore we are constrained to found a school for the service of the Lord. In its organization we hope we shall ordain nothing severe, nothing burdensome; but if there should result anything a little irksome by the demands of justice for the correction of vices and the persevering of charity, do not therefore, through fear, avoid the way of salvation, which cannot be entered upon save through a narrow entrance, but in which, as life progresses and the heart becomes filled with faith, one walks in the unspeakable sweetness of love; but never departing from His control, and persevering in His doctrine in the monastery until death, let us with patience share in the sufferings of Christ, that we may be worthy to be partakers in His kingdom. . . .

WHAT THE ABBOT SHOULD BE LIKE

The abbot who is worthy to rule a monastery ought to remember by what name they are called, and to justify by their deeds the name of a superior. For he is believed to take the place of Christ in the monastery, since he is called by his name, as the apostle says: "Ye have received the spirit of adoption of sons, whereby we call, Abba, Father."

And so the abbot ought not (God forbid) to teach or decree or order anything apart from the precept of the Lord; but his rules and his teaching ought always to be leavened with the leaven of divine justice in the minds of his disciples; and let the abbot be always mindful that in the great judgment of God, both his teaching and the obedience of his disciples will be weighed in the balance. And let the abbot know that whatever the master finds lacking in the sheep will be charged to the fault of the shepherd. Only in case the pastor has shown the greatest diligence in his management of an unruly and disobedient flock, and has given his whole care to the correction of their evil doings, will that pastor be cleared at the judgment of God and be able to say with the prophet, "I have not hid thy righteousness within my heart, I have declared thy faithfulness and thy salvation, but they despising have scorned me"; then let the punishment of eternal death itself fall upon the disobedient sheep of his care.

Therefore when anyone takes on himself the name of abbot, he should govern his disciples by a twofold teaching, that is, let him show forth all the good and holy things by his deeds rather than by his words; to ready disciples he ought to set forth the commands of God in words, but to the hard of heart, and to the simple-minded he ought to illustrate the divine precepts in his deeds. And all things which he has taught his disciples to be wrong, let him demonstrate in his action that they should not be done, lest sometime God should say to him, a sinner: "Why dost thou declare my statutes or take my testimony in thy mouth? Thou hast hated instruction and cast My word behind thee"; and again: "Thou who hast seen the mote in thy brother's eyes, hast not seen the beam in thine own eye."

Let him not be a respecter of persons in the monastery. Let not one be loved more than another, unless he shall have found someone to be better than another in good deeds and in obedience; let not a freeman be preferred to one coming from servitude, unless there be some good and reasonable cause; but if according to the dictates of justice it shall have seemed best to the abbot, let him do this with anyone of any rank whatsoever; otherwise let each keep his own place, since, whether bound or free, we are all one in Christ, and under one God we bear the same burden of service, for there is no respect of persons with God; only in this regard are we distinguished with him if we are found better and more humble than others in our good deeds. Therefore let his love for all be the same, and let one discipline be put upon all according to merit. . . .

ABOUT CALLING THE BROTHERS TO COUNCIL

Whenever anything especial is to be done in the monastery, the abbot shall convoke the whole body and himself set forth the matter at issue. And after listening to the advice of the brothers, he shall consider it by himself, and shall do what he shall have judged most useful. Now we say all should be called to the council, because the Lord often reveals to the younger brother what is best to be done.

But let the brothers give advice with all subjection of humility and not presume to defend boldly what seemed good to them, but rather rely on the judgment of the abbot, and all obey him in what he has judged to be for their welfare. But just as it is fitting that the disciples obey the master, so is it incumbent on him to dispose everything wisely and justly.

Therefore, let all follow the rule of the master in all things, and let no one depart from it rashly; let no one in the monastery follow the desire of his own heart. And let no one strive with his abbot shamelessly either within or without the monastery; and if he shall have presumed to do so, let him be subjected to the regular discipline. And let the abbot himself do all things in the fear of God and in the observance of the rule, knowing that he must without doubt render account unto God, the most just judge, for all his judgments.

If there are any matters of minor importance to be done for the welfare of the monastery, let the abbot take the advice only of the elders, as it is written: "Do all things with counsel, and after it is done thou wilt not repent."

CONCERNING THOSE WHO, BEING OFTEN REBUKED, DO NOT AMEND

If any brother, having frequently been rebuked for any fault, do not amend even after he has been excommunicated, a more severe rebuke shall fall upon him;—that is, the punishment of the lash shall be inflicted upon him. But if he do not even then amend; or, if perchance—which God forbid,—swelled with pride he try even to defend his works: then the abbot shall act as a wise physician. If he have applied . . . the ointments of exhortation, the medicaments [medicines] of the Divine Scriptures; if he have proceeded to the last blasting of excommunication, or to blows with rods, and if he sees that his efforts avail nothing: let him also—what is greater—call in the prayer of himself and all the brothers for him: that God who can do all things may work a cure upon an infirm brother. But if he be not healed even in this way, then at last the abbot may use the pruning knife, as the apostle says: "Remove evil from you," etc.: lest one diseased sheep contaminate the whole flock.

WHETHER BROTHERS WHO LEAVE THE MONASTERY OUGHT AGAIN TO BE RECEIVED

A brother who goes out, or is cast out, of the monastery for his own fault, if he wish to return, shall first promise every amends for the fault on account of which he departed; and thus he shall be received into the lowest degree—so that thereby his humility may be proved. But if he again depart, up to the third time he shall be received. Knowing that after this every opportunity of return is denied to him.

CONCERNING BOYS UNDER AGE, HOW THEY SHALL BE CORRECTED

Every age or intelligence ought to have its proper bounds. Therefore as often as boys or youths, or those who are less able to understand how great is the punishment of excommunication: as often as such persons offend, they shall either be afflicted with excessive fasts, or coerced with severe blows, that they may be healed.

CONCERNING THE RECEPTION OF GUESTS

All guests who come shall be received as though they were Christ; for He Himself said: "I was a stranger and ye took Me in." And to all, fitting honour shall be shown; but, most of all, to servants of the faith and to pilgrims. When, therefore, a guest is announced, the prior or the brothers shall run to meet him, with every office of love. And first they shall pray together; and thus they shall be joined together in peace. Which kiss of peace shall not first be offered, unless a prayer have preceded; on account of the wiles of the devil. In the salutation itself, moreover, all humility shall be exhibited. In the case of all guests arriving or departing: with inclined head, or with prostrating of the whole body upon the ground, Christ, who is also received in them, shall be adored.

The monks gathered together for prayer seven times in the course of the day. Prayers were chanted from set texts.

CONCERNING THE ART OF SINGING

Whereas we believe that there is a divine presence, and that the eyes of the Lord look down everywhere upon the good and the evil: chiefly then, without any doubt, we may believe that this is the case when we are assisting at divine service. Therefore let us always be mindful of what the prophets say: "Serve the Lord in all fear"; and before the face of the Divinity and His angels; and let us so stand and again, "Sing wisely"; and "in the sight of the angels I will sing unto thee." Therefore let us consider how we ought to conduct ourselves and sing that our voice may accord with our intention.

CONCERNING REVERENCE FOR PRAYER

If when to powerful men we wish to suggest anything, we do not presume to do it unless with reverence and humility: how much more should we supplicate with all humility, and devotion of purity, God who is the Lord of all. And let us know that we are heard, not for much speaking, but for purity of heart and compunction of tears. And, therefore, prayer ought to be brief and pure; unless perchance it be prolonged by the influence of the inspiration of the divine grace. When assembled together, then, let the prayer be altogether brief; and, the sign being given by the prior, let us rise together.

CONCERNING THE DAILY MANUAL LABOR

Idleness is the enemy of the soul. And therefore, at fixed times, the brothers ought to be occupied in manual labour; and again, at fixed times, in sacred reading.

CONCERNING HUMILITY

. . . If we wish to attain to the height of the greatest humility, and to that divine exaltation which is attained by the humility of this present life, we must mount by our own acts that ladder which appeared in a dream to Jacob,[1] upon which angels appeared unto him ascending and descending. For that ascent and descent can only be understood by us to be this: to ascend by humility, to descend through pride. . . .

Now the first grade of humility is this: keeping the fear of God before his eyes, let him avoid forgetfulness and ever remember all the precepts of the Lord; and continually consider in his heart that eternal life which is prepared for those who fear God, just as the mockers of God fall into hell. . . .

[1]Jacob, a patriarch of ancient Israel, had a dream about angels ascending and descending a ladder between heaven and earth; the dream is recounted in the Old Testament.

The fifth grade of humility is this, if one reveals to the abbot in humble confession all the vain imaginings that come into his heart, and all the evil he has done in secret. . . .

This is the eighth grade of humility; if a monk do nothing except what the common rule of the monastery or the examples of his superior urges him to do.

The ninth grade of humility is this: if a monk keep his tongue from speaking and keeping silence speaks only in answer to questions, since the Scripture says that "sin is not escaped by much speaking," and "a talkative man is not established in the earth."

The tenth grade of humility is this, that he be not easily moved nor prompt to laughter, since it is written: "The fool raiseth his voice in laughter."

The eleventh grade of humility is this: if, when the monk speaks, he says few words and those to the point, slowly and without laughter, humbly and gravely; and be not loud of voice, as it is written: "A wise man is known by his few words."

The twelfth grade of humility is this: that a monk conduct himself with humility not only in his heart but also in his bearing, in the sight of all; that is, in the service of God, in the oratory [chapel], in the monastery, in the garden, on the road, in the field; and everywhere, sitting or walking or standing, let him always have his head bowed, and his eyes fixed on the ground. Always mindful of his sins, let him think of himself as being already tried in the great judgment, saying in his heart what that publican, spoken of in the gospel, said with his eyes fixed on the earth: "Lord, I a sinner am not worthy to lift mine eyes to the heavens;" and again with the prophet: "I am bowed down and humbled wheresoever I go." . . .

SAINT BENEDICT OF NURSIA

THE CHRISTIAN WAY OF LIFE

In the following selection from his monastic book of rules, Saint Benedict of Nursia (see page 174) advises his monks on the attitudes and conduct necessary to live a virtuous Christian life.

WHAT ARE THE INSTRUMENTS OF GOOD WORKS?

In the first place, to love the Lord God with the whole heart, whole soul, whole strength, then his neighbor as himself.

Then not to kill, not to commit adultery, not to steal, not to covet, not to bear false witness, to honor all men, and what anyone would not have done to him, let him not do to another. To deny himself, that he may follow Christ, to chasten the body, to renounce luxuries, to love fasting. To relieve the poor, to clothe the naked, to visit the sick, to bury the dead, to help in tribulation, to console the afflicted.

To make himself a stranger to the affairs of the world, to prefer nothing before the love of Christ, not to give way to anger, not to bear any grudge, not to harbour deceit in the heart, not to forsake charity. Not to swear, lest haply he perjure himself, to utter truth from his heart and his mouth. Not to return evil for evil, not to do injuries, but rather to bear them patiently, to love his enemies, not to curse again those who curse him, but rather to bless them, to endure persecution for righteousness' sake. Not to be proud, not given to wine, not gluttonous, not addicted to sleep, not slothful, not given to murmur, not a slanderer. To commit his hope to God; when he sees anything good in himself to attribute it to God, and not to himself, but let him always know that which is evil is his own doing, and impute it to himself. To fear the day of judgment, to dread hell, to desire eternal life with all spiritual longing, to have the expectation of death every day before his eyes. To watch over his actions at all times, to know certainly that in all places the eye of God is upon him; those evil thoughts which come into his heart to dash to pieces on Christ, and to make them known to his spiritual senior. To keep his lips from evil and wicked discourse, not to be fond of much talking, not to speak vain words or such as provoke laughter, not to love much or violent laughter. To give willing attention to the sacred readings, to pray frequently every day, to confess his past sins to God, in prayer, with tears and groanings; from thence forward to reform as to those sins.

Not to fulfill the desires of the flesh, to hate his own will, in all things to obey the commands of the abbot, even though he himself (which God forbid) should do otherwise, remembering our Lord's commands: "What they say, do; but what they do, do ye not." Not to desire to be called a saint before he is one, but first to be one that he may be truly called one; every day to fulfill the commands of God in his deeds, to love chastity, to hate no one, not to have jealousy or envy, not to love contention, to avoid self-conceit; to reverence seniors, to love juniors, to pray for enemies in the love of Christ, to be reconciled with his adversary, before the going down of the sun, and never to despair of the mercy of God. . . .

SAINT JOHN CHRYSOSTOM

DISCOURSES AGAINST JUDAIZING CHRISTIANS

A particularly fierce attack on Jews was made by John Chrysostom (347–407), a prominent church father. John sought to discourage Christians from participating in Jewish festivals, which still maintained their attraction for converts. In a series of sermons, he repeatedly castigated the Jews as demons and deicides. Since Jews are hated by God, he told the congregation, it is also a Christian's duty to hate these pitiable and miserable people.

What is this disease? The festivals of the pitiful and miserable Jews are soon to march upon us one after the other and in quick succession: the feast of Trumpets,[1] the feast of Tabernacles,[2] the fasts.[3] There are many in our ranks who say they think as we do. Yet some of these are going to watch the festivals and others will join the Jews in keeping their feasts and observing their fasts. I wish to drive this perverse custom from the Church right now. . . . But now that the Jewish festivals are close by and at the very door, if I should fail to cure those who are sick with the Judaizing disease, I am afraid that, because of their ill-suited association and deep ignorance, some Christians may partake in the Jews' transgressions; once they have done so, I fear my discourses on these transgressions will be in vain. For if they hear no word from me today, they will then join the Jews in their fasts; once they have committed this sin, it will be useless for me to apply the remedy.

And so it is that I hasten to anticipate this danger and prevent it. . . .

But do not be surprised that I called the Jews pitiable. They really are pitiable and miserable. When so many blessings from heaven came into their hands, they thrust them aside and were at great pains to reject them. . . . From their childhood they read the prophets, but they crucified him whom the prophets had foretold. We did not hear the divine prophecies but we did worship him of whom they prophesied. And so they are pitiful because they rejected the blessings which were sent to them, while others seized hold of these blessings and drew them to themselves. . . .

Many, I know, respect the Jews and think that their present way of life is a venerable one. This is why I hasten to uproot and tear out this deadly opinion. . . . [T]he synagogue is not only a brothel and a theater; it also is a den of robbers and a lodging for wild beasts. . . . [W]hen God forsakes a people, what hope of salvation is left? When God forsakes a place, that place becomes the dwelling of demons.

But at any rate the Jews say that they, too, adore God. God forbid that I say that. No Jew adores God! Who says so? The Son of God says so. For he said: "If you were to know my Father, you would also know me. But you neither know me nor do you know my Father."[4] Could I produce a witness more trustworthy than the Son of God?

If, then, the Jews fail to know the Father, if they crucified the Son, if they thrust off the help of the Spirit, who should not make bold to declare plainly that the synagogue is a dwelling of demons? God is not worshipped there. Heaven forbid! From now on it remains a place of idolatry. But still some people pay it honor as a holy place. . . .

. . . In our churches we hear countless discourses on eternal punishments, on rivers of fire, on the venomous worm, on bonds that cannot be burst, on exterior darkness. But the Jews neither know nor dream of these things. They live for their bellies, they gape for the things of this world, their condition is no better than that of pigs or goats because of their wanton ways and excessive gluttony. They know but one thing: to fill their bellies and be drunk, to get all cut and bruised, to be hurt and wounded while fighting for their favorite charioteers. . . .

[1] This is the New Year or Rosh Ha-Shanah, which falls on the first of Tishri (Sept.–Oct.).

[2] This falls on the fifteenth of Tishri and lasts a week, during which the Jews danced and "made merry before the Lord" (cf. Lv 23.33–43).

[3] The fasts here referred to would seem to be the Ten Days of Penitence between Rosh Ha-Shanah and Yom Kippur (the Day of Atonement).

[4] John 8:19.

. . . Indeed the synagogue is less deserving of honor than any inn. It is not merely a lodging place for robbers and cheats but also for demons. This is true not only of the synagogues but also of the souls of the Jews, as I shall try to prove at the end of my discourse. . . .

But I must get back again to those who are sick. Consider, then, with whom they are sharing their fasts. It is with those who shouted: "Crucify him, Crucify him,"[5] with those who said: "His blood be upon us and upon our children."[6] . . . Is it not strange that those who worship the Crucified keep common festival with those who crucified him? Is it not a sign of folly and the worst madness?

Since there are some who think of the synagogue as a holy place, I must say a few words to them. Why do you reverence that place? Must you not despise it, hold it in abomination, run away from it? They answer that the Law and the books of the prophets are kept there. What is this? Will any place where these books are be a holy place? By no means! This is the reason above all others why I hate the synagogue and abhor it. They have the prophets but do not believe them; they read the sacred writings but reject their witness—and this is a mark of men guilty of the greatest outrage.

Tell me this. If you were to see a venerable man, illustrious and renowned, dragged off into a tavern or den of robbers: if you were to see him outraged, beaten, and subjected there to the worst violence, would you have held that tavern or den in high esteem because that great and esteemed man had been inside it while undergoing that violent treatment? I think not. Rather, for this very reason you would have hated and abhorred the place.

Let that be your judgment about the synagogue, too. For they brought the books of Moses and the prophets along with them into the synagogue, not to honor them but to outrage them with dishonor. When they say that Moses and the prophets knew not Christ and said nothing about his coming, what greater outrage could they do to those holy men than to accuse them of failing to recognize their Master, than to say that those saintly prophets are partners of their impiety? And so it is that we must hate both them and their synagogue all the more because of their offensive treatment of those holy men. . . .

Therefore, flee the gatherings and holy places of the Jews. Let no man venerate the synagogue because of the holy books; let him hate and avoid it because the Jews outrage and maltreat the holy ones, because they refuse to believe their words, because they accuse them of the ultimate impiety. . . .

Certainly it is the time for me to show that demons dwell in the synagogue, not only in the place itself but also in the souls of the Jews. . . . Do you see that demons dwell in their souls and that these demons are more dangerous than the ones of old? And this is very reasonable. In the old days the Jews acted impiously toward the prophets; now they outrage the Master of the prophets. Tell me this. Do you not shudder to come into the same place with men possessed, who have so many unclean spirits, who have been reared amid slaughter and bloodshed? Must you share a greeting with them and exchange a bare word? Must you not turn away from them since they are the common disgrace and infection of the whole world? Have they not come to every form of wickedness? Have not all the prophets spent themselves making many and long speeches of accusation against them?[7]. . .

Tell me this. If a man were to have slain your son, would you endure to look upon him, or to accept his greeting? Would you not shun him as a wicked demon, as the devil himself? They slew the Son of your Lord; do you have the boldness to enter with them under the same roof? After he was slain he heaped such honor upon you that he made you his brother and coheir. But you dishonor him so much that you pay honor to those who slew him on the cross, that you observe with them the fellowship of the festivals, that you go to their profane places, enter their unclean doors, and share in the tables of

[5]Lk 23.21.

[6]Mt 27.25. Chrysostom obviously holds the position, which was common for centuries, that all Jews are responsible for Christ's passion and death. Vatican II's "Declaration on the Relationship of the Church to Non-Christian Religions" states that these "cannot be blamed on all the Jews then living, without distinction, nor upon the Jews of today. Although the Church is the new people of God, the Jews should not be presented as repudiated or cursed by God, as if such views followed from the holy Scriptures." A footnote at this point says that Cardinal Bea and others explained Mt 27.25 as the cry of a Jerusalem crowd that had no right to speak for the whole Jewish people.

[7] Chrysostom argues from the guilt of their forebears to the guilt of contemporary Jews.

demons. For I am persuaded to call the fasting of the Jews a table of demons because they slew God. If the Jews are acting against God, must they not be serving the demons? . . .

Meanwhile, I ask you to rescue your brothers, to set them free from their error, and to bring them back to the truth. . . . I want them to learn these facts from you and to free themselves from their wicked association with the Jews. I want them then to show themselves sincere and genuine Christians. I want them to shun the evil gatherings of the Jews and their synagogues, both in the city and in the suburbs, because these are robbers' dens and dwellings of demons.

BEDE

HISTORY OF THE ENGLISH CHURCH AND PEOPLE

The English monk called the Venerable Bede (673–735), in his *History of the English Church and People*, cites a letter from Pope Gregory I (the Great) written in 601. In the letter, the pope forwarded instructions for Augustine of Canterbury, whom he had appointed leader of a mission to convert the English to Christianity. He wrote his emissary to tell Augustine to win the favor of the pagan English by accommodating the requirements of Christian beliefs to the existing non-Christian cultural practices, as the excerpt shows.

When these [missionaries] had left, the holy father Gregory sent after them letters worthy of our notice, which show most clearly his unwearying interest in the salvation of our nation. The letter runs as follows:

"To our well loved son Abbot[1] Mellitus: Gregory, servant of the servants of God.

"Since the departure of yourself and your companions, we have been somewhat anxious, because we have received no news of the success of your journey. Therefore, when by God's help you reach our most reverend brother, Bishop Augustine,[2] we wish you to inform him that we have been giving careful thought to the affairs of the English, and have come to the conclusion that the temples of the idols in that country should on no account be destroyed. He is to destroy the idols, but the temples themselves are to be aspersed [sprinkled] with holy water, altars set up, and relics enclosed in them. For if these temples are well built, they are to be purified from devil-worship,[3] and dedicated to the service of the true God. In this way, we hope that the people, seeing that its temples are not destroyed, may abandon idolatry and resort to these places as before, and may come to know and adore the true God. And since they have a custom of sacrificing many oxen to devils, let some other solemnity be substituted in its place, such as a day of Dedication[4] or the Festivals of the holy martyrs [saints' days] whose relics are enshrined there. On such occasions they might well construct shelters of boughs for themselves around the churches that were once temples, and celebrate the solemnity with devout feasting. They are no longer to sacrifice beasts to the Devil, but they may kill them for food to the praise of God, and give thanks to the Giver of all gifts for His bounty. If the people are allowed some worldly pleasures in this way, they will more readily come to desire the joys of the spirit. For it is certainly impossible to eradicate all errors from obstinate minds at one stroke, and whoever wishes to climb to a mountain top climbs gradually step by step, and not in one leap. It was in this way that God revealed Himself to the Israelite people in Egypt, permitting the sacrifices formerly offered to the Devil to be offered thenceforward to Himself instead. So He bade them sacrifice beasts to Him, so that, once they became enlightened, they might abandon a wrong conception of sacrifice, and adopt the right. For, while they were to continue to offer beasts as before, they were to offer them to God instead of to idols, thus transforming the idea of sacrifice. Of your kindness, you are to inform our brother Augustine of this policy, so that he may consider how he may best implement it on the spot. God keep you safe, my very dear son." . . .

---

[1]The elected head of a monastic community, the abbot was supposed to rule justly and paternally following the constitution (rule) of the community.

[2]Augustine (not to be confused with Augustine of Hippo) was an Italian monk who was sent in 597 to convert the English to Christianity. He established his see (bishopric) at Canterbury and founded others at Rochester and London, successfully directing missionary activity in the southern part of what is now England.

[3]As Christianity was monotheistic, it denied the validity of any other gods. Therefore, Christians customarily designated the pagan deities as "devils," or evil spirits.

[4]The anniversary of the dedication or consecration of a church was celebrated as a holiday.

ROBERT THE MONK

APPEAL OF URBAN II TO THE FRANKS

Pope Urban's speech, as reported by Robert the Monk, shows how skillfully the pope appealed to the Frankish lords.

"O race of the Franks, O people who live beyond the mountains, O people loved and chosen of God, as is clear from your many deeds, distinguished over all other nations by the situation of your land, your catholic faith, and your regard for the holy church, we have a special message and exhortation for you. For we wish you to know what a grave matter has brought us to your country. The sad news has come from Jerusalem and Constantinople that the people of Persia, an accursed and foreign race [the Turks], enemies of God, 'a generation that set not their heart aright, and whose spirit was not steadfast with God' (Ps. 78:8), have invaded the lands of those Christians and devastated them with the sword, rapine, and fire. Some of the Christians they have carried away as slaves, others they have put to death. The churches they have either destroyed or turned into mosques. They desecrate and overthrow the altars. . . . They have taken from the Greek empire a tract of land so large that it takes more than two months to walk through it. Whose duty is it to avenge this and recover that land, if not yours? For to you more than to other nations the Lord has given the military spirit, courage, agile bodies, and the bravery to strike down those who resist you. Let your minds be stirred to bravery by the deeds of your forefathers, and by the efficiency and greatness of...[Charlemagne], and of . . . his son [Louis the Pious], and of the other kings who have destroyed [Muslim] kingdoms, and established Christianity in their lands. You should be moved especially by the holy grave of our Lord and Saviour which is now held by unclean peoples, and by the holy places which are treated with dishonor and irreverently befouled with their uncleanness.

"O bravest of knights, descendants of unconquered ancestors, do not be weaker than they, but remember their courage. . . . Let no possessions keep you back, no solicitude for your property. Your land [France] is shut in on all sides by the sea and mountains, and is too thickly populated. There is not much wealth here, and the soil scarcely yields enough to support you. On this account you kill and devour each other, and carry on war and mutually destroy each other. Let your hatred and quarrels cease, your civil wars come to an end, and all your dissensions stop. Set out on the road to the holy sepulchre [site of Jesus' burial], take the land from that wicked people, and make it your own. That land which, as the Scripture says, is flowing with milk and honey, God gave to the children of Israel. Jerusalem is the best of all lands, more fruitful than all others, as it were a second Paradise of delights. This land our Saviour [Jesus] made illustrious by his birth, beautiful with his life, and sacred with his suffering; he redeemed it with his death and glorified it with his tomb. This royal city is now held captive by her enemies, and made pagan by those who know not God. She asks and longs to be liberated and does not cease to beg you to come to her aid. She asks aid especially from you because, as I have said, God has given more of the military spirit to you than to other nations. Set out on this journey and you will obtain the remission of your sins and be sure of the incorruptible glory of the kingdom of heaven."

When Pope Urban had said this and much more of the same sort, all who were present were moved to cry out with one accord, "It is the will of God, it is the will of God." When the pope heard this he raised his eyes to heaven and gave thanks to God, and, commanding silence with a gesture of his hand, he said: "My dear brethren. . . . [L]et these words be your battle cry, because God caused you to speak them. Whenever you meet the enemy in battle, you shall all cry out, 'It is the will of God, it is the will of God.' . . . Whoever therefore shall determine to make this journey and shall make a vow to God and shall offer himself as a living sacrifice, holy, acceptable to God (Rom. 12:1), shall wear a cross on his brow or on his breast. And when he returns after having fulfilled his vow he shall wear the cross on his back. In this way he will obey the command of the Lord, 'Whosoever doth not bear his cross and come after me is not worthy of me'" (Luke 14:27).

BERNARD GUI

THE WALDENSIAN TEACHINGS

One major heretical movement was that of the Waldensians, or Poor Men of Lyons, founded about 1173 by Peter Waldo (d. 1217), a rich merchant of Lyons, France, who gave away his wealth to the poor and began to preach in villages in southeastern France. Neither a priest nor a theologian, Waldo had the Bible translated from Latin into the common language of the people and preached the gospel message without the consent of church authorities. Small groups of Waldo's converts soon were found in towns and villages throughout southeastern France, northern Italy, and Switzerland. Within less than a decade, the Waldensians had aroused the clergy's hostility and were condemned as heretics by Pope Lucius III at a council in Verona in 1184. Gradually, influenced by other heretical groups, the Waldensians adopted a more radical stance toward the medieval church. In the following reading from *Manual of an Inquisitor*, a fourteenth-century Dominican friar, Bernard Gui, describes the origin and the teachings of the Waldensians. The Waldensian criticisms of the church would be echoed in the writings of the leading Protestant reformers of the sixteenth century.

The sect and heresy of the Waldenses or Poor of Lyons began about the year of our Lord 1170. Its moving spirit and founder was a certain citizen of Lyons named Waldes, or Waldens, from whom his followers received their name. He was a rich man who, having given up all his property, resolved to devote himself to poverty and to evangelical perfection, just as the apostles had done. He had procured for himself translations of the Gospels and some other books of the Bible in vernacular French, also some texts from St. Augustine, St. Jerome, St. Ambrose, and St. Gregory, arranged topically, which he and his adherents called "sentences." On frequently reading these over among themselves, although very seldom understanding them aright, they were carried away by their emotions and, although they had but little learning, they usurped the function of the apostles by daring to preach "in the streets and the broad ways."

This man Waldes, or Waldens, won over to a like presumption many people of both sexes, made men and women his accomplices, and sent them out to preach as his disciples. They, men and women alike, although they were stupid and uneducated, wandered through villages, entered homes, preached in the squares and even in churches, the men especially, and spread many errors everywhere. Moreover, when they were summoned by the archbishop of Lyons, John of the Fair Hands, and by him forbidden such audacity, they were not at all willing to obey, alleging as excuse for their madness that "we ought to obey God rather than men," Who had commanded His apostles to "preach the gospel to every creature." By virtue of a false profession of poverty and a feigned appearance of sanctity, they arrogated to themselves what had been said to the apostles. Boldly declaring that they were imitators and successors of these apostles, they cast aspersions upon prelates and clergy for abundant wealth and lives of luxury.

Thus, through presumptuously usurping the office of preaching, they became teachers of error. After they had been warned to desist, they rendered themselves disobedient and contumacious, for which they were excommunicated and driven from that city and their native land. Finally, indeed, because they remained obdurate, they were pronounced schismatics [rebels] at a certain council which was held at Rome...and were then condemned as heretics. And so, as they had grown in number on the earth, they scattered throughout that province and neighboring areas and into the region of Lombardy [northern Italy]. Separated and cut off from the Church, when they mingled with other heretics and imbibed their errors, they combined with their own fantasies the errors and heresies of heretics of earlier days....

...Now, the principal heresy of the aforesaid Waldenses was and still continues to be contempt of ecclesiastical authority. Then, having been excommunicated for this and given over to Satan, they were plunged by him into countless errors, and they combined with their own fantasies the errors of heretics of an earlier day.

The foolish followers and impious teachers of this sect hold and teach that they are not subject to our lord pope, the Roman pontiff, or to other prelates of the Roman Church, for they declare that the Roman Church persecutes and censures them unjustly and unduly. Also, they declare positively that they cannot be excommunicated by the said Roman pontiff and prelates, to none of whom ought obedience be given should he enjoin or command the members and teachers of this sect to desert and abjure it—this despite the fact that it has been condemned as heretical by the Roman Church.

Also, they hold and teach that every oath, in or out of court, without exception or qualification, has been forbidden by God as unlawful and sinful....

Also, out of the same font of error, the aforesaid sect and heresy declares that any judicial process is forbidden by God and is, consequently, a sin and that it is contrary to God's command for any judge, in any case or for any reason, to sentence a man to corporal punishment involving bloodshed, or to death. They seize on the words of the Holy Gospels—"Judge not that ye be not judged"; "Thou shalt not kill"'; and other similar passages—without the proper explanation essential to their interpretation. This they do without understanding the sense or accepting the signification or explanation which the Holy Roman Church wisely perceives and transmits to the faithful in accordance with the teaching of the Fathers [early Christian theologians], the doctors, and the canonical decrees.

Also, as it strays from the way and the right path, this sect does not accept or consider valid, but despises, rejects, and damns the canonical decrees, the decretals [judgments] of the supreme pontiffs, the rules concerning observance of fasts and holy days, and the precepts of the Fathers.

Also, in a more pernicious error in respect of the sacrament of penance and the keys [papal powers to legislate] of the Church, these [Waldensians] hold, and teach that, just as the apostles had it from Christ, they have from God alone and from no other the power to hear confessions from men and women who wish to confess to them, to give absolution, and to impose penance. And they do hear the confessions of such persons, they do give absolution [forgiveness] and impose penance, although they are not priests or clerics ordained by any bishop of the Roman Church but are laymen and nothing more. They do not claim to have any such power from the Roman Church, but rather disclaim it....

Also, this sect and heresy ridicules the indulgences [remissions of punishments due to sin] which are published and granted by prelates of the Church, asserting that they are of no value whatever.

In regard to the sacrament of the Eucharist [communion, celebration of the Last Supper] they err, saying, not publicly but in private among themselves, that if the priest who celebrates or consecrates the Mass is a sinner, the bread and wine do not change into the body and blood of Christ in the sacrament of the altar; and in their view anyone is a sinner who is not a member of their sect. Also, they say that any righteous person, even though he be a layman and not a cleric ordained by a Catholic bishop, can perform the consecration of the body and blood of Christ, provided only that he be a member of their sect. This they apply even to women, with the same proviso that they belong to their sect. Thus they teach that every holy person is a priest.

LOVE AS JOYOUS, PAINFUL, AND HUMOROUS

The following poems were all composed by southern French troubadours. In the first selection a poet sings the praises of his beloved.

I wandered through a garden, 'twas filled with flowers the rarest,
And of all these brilliant blossoms I culled the very fairest;
So fine its shape, so sweet its scent, its hues so richly blent,
That heaven, I'm sure, created it itself to represent.
My lady is so charming, my lady is so meek,
Such tenderness is in her smile, such beauty in her cheek;
Such kisses blossom on her lip, such love illumines her eye—
Oh, never was there neath the stars a man so blest as I!
I gaze, I thrill with joy, I weep, in song my feelings flow—
A song of hope, delight, desire, with passion all aglow—
A fervent song, a pleading song, a song in every line—
Of thanks and praise to her who lists no other songs but mine.
Oh, hear me sweet! Oh, kiss me sweet! Oh, clasp me tenderly!
Thy beauties many, many touch, but none that love like me.

The following two poems tell of a lover's failure to win the affections of his beloved.

Now that the air is fresher
and the world turned green,
I shall sing once more
of the one I love and desire,
but we are so far apart
that I cannot go and witness
how my words might please her.
And nothing can console me
but death, for evil tongues
(may God curse them)
have made us part.
And alas, I so desired her
that now I moan and cry
half mad with grief.
I sing of her, yet her beauty
is greater than I can tell,
with her fresh color, lovely eyes,
and white skin, untanned
and untainted by rouge.
She is so pure and noble
that no one can speak ill of her.
But above all, one must praise,
it seems to me, her truthfulness,
her manners and her gracious speech,
for she never would betray a friend;
and I was mad to believe
what I heard tell of her
and thus cause her to be angry.
I never intended to complain;

and even now, if she so desires,
she could bring me happiness
by granting what I seek.
I cannot go on like this much longer,
for since she's been so far away
I've scarcely slept or eaten.
Love is sweet to look upon
but bitter upon parting;
one day it makes you weep
and another skip and dance,
for now I know that the more
one enters love's service,
the more fickle it becomes.
Messenger, go with Godspeed
and bring this to my lady,
for I cannot stay here much longer
and live, or be cured elsewhere,
unless I have her next to me,
naked, to kiss and embrace
within a curtained room.

I said my heart was like to break,
   And that my soul was cast,
By passion's tide, just like a wreck
Disabled by the blast.
I swore an oath that what I felt
Was like to turn my head;
I sighed—such sighs!—and then I knelt,
But not a word she said!
I preached of Grace in moving strain;
I told her she was fair;
I whispered what renown she'd gain,
By listening to my prayer.
I spoke of needle and of pole,
And other things I'd read;
But unto all my rigmarole—
Why not a word she said!
I prayed her then my love to test,
To send me near or far—
I'd squelch the dragon in his den,
I'd yoke him to my car.
I'd risk for her, as faithful knight,
My eyes, or limbs, or head,
Being quite prepared to fool or fight—
But not a word she said!
I argued that, if poor in cash,
Yet I was rich in mind;
Of rivals vowed to make a hash,
When such I chanced to find.
I knit my brows, I clenched my hand,

I tried to wake her dread;
In quiet wise, you'll understand—
But not a word she said!

Troubadours could also be playful. Sometimes they mocked women who labored too hard to preserve a youthful beauty.

That creature so splendid is but an old jade;
Of ointment and padding her beauty is made;
Unpainted if you had the hap to behold her,
You'd find her all wrinkles from forehead to shoulder.
What a shame for a woman who has lost all her grace
To waste thus her time in bedaubing her face!
To neglect her poor soul I am sure is not right of her,
For a body that's going to corruption in spite of her.

Sometimes they even mocked this obsession with romance.

You say the moon is all aglow,
  The nightingale a-singing—
I'd rather watch the red wine flow,
  And hear the goblets ringing.
You say 'tis sweet to hear the gale
  Creep sighing through the willows—
I'd rather hear a merry tale,
  'Mid a group of jolly fellows!
You say 'tis sweet the stars to view
  Upon the waters gleaming—
I'd rather see, 'twixt me and you
  And the post, my supper steaming.

MAGNA CARTA

Feudal nobles sought to limit the arbitrary powers of kings by compelling them to issue written charters of liberties. These earliest constitutions spelled out the rights of subjects and the obligations of rulers. In 1215 King John of England (1199–1216) was compelled to recognize the liberties of his vassals, the clergy, and the towns in the Great Charter (*Magna Carta*). The king and his agents were forbidden to act arbitrarily, and the king swore to govern by due process of law. Similar written constitutions checking the powers of kings and princes were achieved in other parts of Europe.

The Magna Carta asserted the feudal rights of the subjects of a monarch who allegedly tried to rule by personal will rather than by law. Though many of its detailed clauses subsequently lost their significance, three notions embedded in the Magna Carta became rooted in English constitutional tradition: that the king cannot levy a tax without the consent of his feudal council (later Parliament); that no one may be imprisoned or otherwise damaged except through due process of law and trial by jury of his (or her) peers; and that the king himself is subject to the law, and if he violates the rights of his subjects, he may be legally disobeyed and deposed. Significant portions of the document follow.

1. In the first place [I, John,] have granted to God and by this our present Charter have confirmed, for us and our heirs in perpetuity, that the English church shall be free, and shall have its rights undiminished and its liberties unimpaired. . . . We have also granted to all the free men of our realm for ourselves and our heirs for ever, all the liberties written below, to have and hold, them and their heirs from us and our heirs. . . .

12. No scutage[1] or aid[2] is to be levied in our realm except by the common counsel of our realm, unless it is for the ransom of our person, the knighting of our eldest son or the first marriage of our eldest daughter; and for these only a reasonable aid is to be levied. Aids from the city of London are to be treated likewise.

13. And the city of London is to have all its ancient liberties and free customs both by land and water. Furthermore, we will and grant that all other cities, boroughs, towns and ports shall have all their liberties and free customs.

14. And to obtain the common counsel of the realm for the assessment of an aid (except in the three cases aforesaid) or a scutage, we will have archbishops, bishops, abbots, earls and greater barons[3] summoned individually by our letters; and we shall also have summoned generally through our sheriffs and bailiffs[4] all those who hold of us in chief [hold a fief from the king], with at least forty days' notice, and at a fixed place; and in all letters of summons we will state the reason for the summons. And when the summons has thus been made, the business shall go forward on the day arranged according to the counsel of those present, even if not all those summoned have come. . . .

20. A free man shall not be amerced [fined] for a trivial offence, except in accordance with the degree of the offence; and for a serious offence he shall be amerced according to its gravity, saving his livelihood; and a merchant likewise, saving his merchandise; in the same way a villein [serf] shall be amerced saving his wainage;[5] if they fall into our mercy. And none of the aforesaid amercements shall be imposed except by the testimony of reputable men of the neighbourhood.

21. Earls and barons shall not be amerced except by their peers and only in accordance with the nature of the offence. . . .

[1]Scutage was a tax paid by knights to the king of England, their feudal overlord, in place of performing actual military service. In the absence of danger of war, the levying of scutage was considered an abuse of the king's authority.

[2]Aid, in this sense, was any obligation, usually financial, due from a vassal to his lord. The word was later used to indicate a tax on income or property paid by his subjects to the English king.

[3]Barons were vassals holding fiefs directly from the king; earls ("counts" in other lands) were nobles who managed counties or shires.

[4]The sheriff was a royal official responsible for the carrying out of laws in a shire or county; bailiffs were his assistants.

[5]Wainage (or gainage) is a collective term meaning farming tools and implements, including such things as wagons (wains).

38. Henceforth no bailiff shall put anyone on trial by his own unsupported allegation, without bringing credible witnesses to the charge.

39. No free man shall be taken or imprisoned or disseised [dispossessed] or outlawed or exiled or in any way ruined, nor will we go or send against him, except by the lawful judgement of his peers or by the law of the land.

40. To no one will we sell, to no one will we deny or delay right or justice.

41. All merchants are to be safe and secure in leaving and entering England, and in staying and travelling in England, both by land and by water, to buy and sell free from all maletotes [unjust taxes] by the ancient and rightful customs, except, in time of war, such as come from an enemy country. And if such are found in our land at the outbreak of war they shall be detained without damage to their persons or goods, until we or our chief justiciar [legal official] know how the merchants of our land are treated in the enemy country; and if ours are safe there, the others shall be safe in our land.

42. Henceforth anyone, saving his allegiance due to us, may leave our realm and return safe and secure by land and water, save for a short period in time of war on account of the general interest of the realm and excepting those imprisoned and outlawed according to the law of the land, and natives of an enemy country, and merchants, who shall be treated as aforesaid. . . .

JEAN DE VENETTE

THE BLACK DEATH

Until the fourteenth century, the population of Europe had increased steadily from its low point in the centuries immediately following the fall of the Roman Empire in the West. Particularly from the eleventh century on, landlords tried to raise their income by bringing new land into cultivation. By improving farming technology, building dikes, draining marshland, and clearing forests, European peasants produced much more food, which permitted more people to survive and multiply. That advance in population tapered off by the early fourteenth century due to many crop failures and wars, which wasted the countryside and led to economic stagnation. But the greatest catastrophe began in the fall of 1347, when sailors returning to Sicily from eastern Mediterranean ports brought with them a new disease, bubonic plague. Within the next three years, from one-quarter to one-third of the population of Europe died from what became known, because of some of its symptoms, as the Black Death. Most who caught the plague died, though some survived. No one knew its cause or cure. We now know that the bacteria were transmitted by fleas from infected rats. The unsanitary living conditions of medieval towns and low standards of personal cleanliness helped to spread the disease. The people were so terrified by the incomprehensible pattern of the disease's progress that superstition, hysteria, and breakdown of civility were common.

The progress of the plague as it made its way through Europe and speculation on its causes, the terrible toll of victims, and various moral responses to the crisis are described in the following reading from the chronicle of Jean de Venette (c. 1308–c. 1368), a French friar who lived through the events described.

In a.d. 1348, the people of France and of almost the whole world were struck by a blow other than war. For in addition to the famine which I described in the beginning and to the wars which I described in the course of this narrative, pestilence and its attendant tribulations appeared again in various parts of the world. . . . All this year and the next, the mortality of men and women, of the young even more than of the old, in Paris and in the kingdom of France, and also, it is said, in other parts of the world, was so great that it was almost impossible to bury the dead. People lay ill little more than two or three days and died suddenly, as it were in full health. He who was well one day was dead the next and being carried to his grave. Swellings appeared suddenly in the armpit or in the groin—in many cases both—and they were infallible signs of death. This sickness or pestilence was called an epidemic by the doctors. Nothing like the great numbers who died in the years 1348 and 1349 has been heard of or seen or read of in times past. This plague and disease came from *ymaginatione* or association and contagion, for if a well man visited the sick he only rarely evaded the risk of death. Wherefore in many towns timid priests withdrew, leaving the exercise of their ministry to such of the religious as were more daring. In many places not two out of twenty remained alive. So high was the mortality at the Hôtel-Dieu [an early hospital] in Paris that for a long time, more than five hundred dead were carried daily with great devotion in carts to the cemetery of the Holy Innocents in Paris for burial. A very great number of the saintly sisters of the Hôtel-Dieu who, not fearing to die, nursed the sick in all sweetness and humility, with no thought of honor, a number too often renewed by death, rest in peace with Christ, as we may piously believe.

This plague, it is said, began among the unbelievers [Muslims], came to Italy, and then crossing the Alps reached Avignon [site of the papacy in that period], where it attacked several cardinals and took from them their whole household. Then it spread, unforeseen, to France, through Gascony [now part of the south of France] and Spain, little by little, from town to town, from village to village, from house to house, and finally from person to person. It even crossed over to Germany, though it was not so bad there as with us. During the epidemic, God of His accustomed goodness deigned to grant this grace, that however suddenly men died, almost all awaited death joyfully. Nor was there anyone who died without confessing his sins and receiving the holy viaticum [the Eucharistic bread given to the sick or dying]. . . .

Some said that this pestilence was caused by infection of the air and waters, since there was at this time no famine nor lack of food supplies, but on the contrary great abundance. As a result of this theory of infected water and air as the source of the plague the Jews were suddenly and violently charged with infecting wells and water and corrupting the air. The whole world rose up against them cruelly on this account. In Germany and other parts of the world where Jews lived, they were massacred and slaughtered by Christians, and many thousands were burned everywhere, indiscriminately. The unshaken, if fatuous, constancy of the [Jewish] men and their wives was remarkable. For mothers hurled their children first into the fire that they might not be baptized and then leaped in after them to burn with their husbands and children. It is said that many bad Christians were found who in a like manner put poison into wells. But in truth, such poisonings, granted that they actually were perpetrated, could not have caused so great a plague nor have infected so many people. There were other causes; for example, the will of God and the corrupt humors and evil inherent in air and earth. Perhaps the poisonings, if they actually took place in some localities, reenforced these causes. The plague lasted in France for the greater part of the years 1348 and 1349 and then ceased. Many country villages and many houses in good towns remained empty and deserted. Many houses, including some splendid dwellings, very soon fell into ruins. Even in Paris several houses were thus ruined, though fewer here than elsewhere.

After the cessation of the epidemic, pestilence, or plague, the men and women who survived married each other. There was no sterility among the women, but on the contrary fertility beyond the ordinary. Pregnant women were seen on every side. . . . But woe is me! the world was not changed for the better but for the worse by this renewal of population. For men were more avaricious and grasping than before, even though they had far greater possessions. They were more covetous and disturbed each other more frequently with suits, brawls, disputes, and pleas. Nor by the mortality resulting from this terrible plague inflicted by God was peace between kings and lords established. On the contrary, the enemies of the king of France and of the Church were stronger and wickeder than before and stirred up wars on sea and on land. Greater evils than before [swarmed] everywhere in the world. And this fact was very remarkable. Although there was an abundance of all goods, yet everything was twice as dear, whether it were utensils, victuals, or merchandise, hired helpers or peasants and serfs, except for some hereditary domains which remained abundantly stocked with everything. Charity began to cool, and iniquity with ignorance and sin to abound, for few could be found in the good towns and castles who knew how or were willing to instruct children in the rudiments of grammar.

Jean de Venette vividly describes one of the more bizarre reactions to the terrible plague, the sudden appearance of the Flagellants. Marching like pilgrims across the countryside, the Flagellants were a group of laymen and laywomen who sought divine pardon for their sins by preaching repentance to others and scourging themselves in a quasi-liturgical ceremony in local churches or marketplaces. The movement foreshadowed events in which moral, social, and economic discontent would increasingly manifest itself in the form of religiously justified popular uprisings against civil and clerical authorities.

In the year 1349, while the plague was still active and spreading from town to town, men in Germany, Flanders, Hainaut [east of Flanders], and Lorraine uprose and began a new sect on their own authority. Stripped to the waist, they gathered in large groups and bands and marched in procession through the crossroads and squares of cities and good towns. There they formed circles and beat upon their backs with weighted scourges, rejoicing as they did so in loud voices and singing hymns suitable to their rite and newly composed for it. Thus for thirty-three days they marched through many towns doing their penance and affording a great spectacle to the wondering people. They flogged their shoulders and arms with scourges tipped with iron points so zealously as to draw blood. But they did not come to Paris nor to any part of France, for they were forbidden to do so by the king of France, who did not want them. He acted on the advice of the masters of theology of the University of Paris, who said that this new sect had been formed contrary to the will of God, to the rites of Holy Mother Church, and to the salvation of all their souls. That indeed this was and is true appeared shortly. For Pope Clement VI was fully informed concerning this fatuous new rite by the masters of Paris through emissaries reverently sent to him and, on the grounds that it had been damnably formed, contrary to law, he forbade the Flagellants under threat of anathema [excommunication] to practise in the future the public penance which they had so presumptuously undertaken. His prohibition was just, for the Flagellants, supported by certain fatuous priests and monks, were enunciating doctrines and opinions which were beyond measure evil, erroneous, and fallacious. For example, they said that their blood thus drawn by the scourge and poured out was mingled with the blood of Christ. Their many errors showed how little they knew of the Catholic faith. Wherefore, as they had begun fatuously of themselves and not of God, so in a short time they were reduced to nothing. On being warned, they desisted and humbly received absolution and penance at the hands of their prelates as the pope's representatives. Many honorable women and devout matrons, it must be added, had done this penance with scourges, marching and singing through towns and churches like the men, but after a little like the others they desisted.

SIR JOHN FROISSART

THE PEASANT REVOLT OF 1381

In 1381, a rebellion of peasants and poor artisans in England threatened the political power of the ruling class. The rebellion, which was crushed and whose leaders were betrayed and executed, revealed the massive discontent of the lower classes and the specter of social upheaval that hovered over late medieval society. The following account of the rebellion is by Sir John Froissart (c. 1337–c. 1410), a French historian and poet who chronicled the Hundred Years' War between France and England, which wreaked havoc in the countries concerned.

While these conferences [of English nobles] were going forward there happened great commotions among the lower orders in England, by which that country was nearly ruined. In order that this disastrous rebellion may serve as an example to mankind, I will speak of all that was done from the information I had at the time. It is customary in England, as well as in several other countries, for the nobility to have great privileges over the commonality; that is to say, the lower orders are bound by law to plough the lands of the gentry, to harvest their grain, to carry it home to the barn, to thrash and winnow it; they are also bound to harvest and carry home the hay. All these services the prelates and gentlemen exact of their inferiors; and in the counties of Kent, Essex, Sussex, and Bedford, these services are more oppressive than in other parts of the kingdom. In consequence of this the evil[ly] disposed in these districts began to murmur, saying, that in the beginning of the world there were no slaves, and that no one ought to be treated as such, unless he had committed treason against his lord, as Lucifer had done against God; but they had done no such thing, for they were neither angels nor spirits, but men formed after the same likeness as these lords who treated them as beasts. This they would bear no longer; they were determined to be free, and if they laboured or did any work, they would be paid for it. A crazy priest in the county of Kent, called John Ball, who for his absurd preaching had thrice been confined in prison by the Archbishop of Canterbury, was greatly instrumental in exciting these rebellious ideas. Every Sunday after mass, as the people were coming out of church, this John Ball was accustomed to assemble a crowd around him in the marketplace and preach to them. On such occasions he would say, "My good friends, matters cannot go on well in England until all things shall be in common; when there shall be neither vassals nor lords; when the lords shall be no more masters than ourselves. How ill they behave to us! for what reason do they thus hold us in bondage? Are we not all descended from the same parents, Adam and Eve? And what can they show, or what reason can they give, why they should be more masters than ourselves? They are clothed in velvet and rich stuffs, ornamented with ermine and other furs, while we are forced to wear poor clothing. They have wines, spices, and fine bread, while we have only rye and the refuse of the straw; and when we drink, it must be water. They have handsome seats and manors, while we must brave the wind and rain in our labours in the field; and it is by our labour they have wherewith to support their pomp. We are called slaves, and if we do not perform our service we are beaten, and we have no sovereign to whom we can complain or who would be willing to hear us. Let us go to the king and remonstrate with him; he is young, and from him we may obtain a favourable answer, and if not we must ourselves seek to amend our condition." With such language as this did John Ball harangue the people of his village every Sunday after mass. The archbishop, on being informed of it, had him arrested and imprisoned for two or three months by way of punishment; but the moment he was out of prison, he returned to his former course. Many in the city of London envious of the rich and noble, having heard of John Ball's preaching, said among themselves that the country was badly governed, and that the nobility had seized upon all the gold and silver. These wicked Londoners, therefore, began to assemble in parties, and to show signs of rebellion; they also invited all those who held like opinions in the adjoining counties to come to London; telling them that they would find the town open to them and the commonalty of the same way of thinking as themselves, and that they would so press the king, that there should no longer be a slave in England.

By this means the men of Kent, Essex, Sussex, Bedford, and the adjoining counties, in number about 60,000, were brought to London, under command of Wat Tyler, Jack Straw, and John Ball. This Wat Tyler, who was chief of the three, had been a tiler of houses—a bad man and a great enemy to the nobility. . . .

With regard to the common people of London, numbers entertained these rebellious opinions, and on assembling at the bridge asked of the guards, "Why will you refuse admittance to these honest men? they are our friends, and what they are doing is for our good." So urgent were they, that it was found necessary to open the gates, when crowds rushed in and took possession of those shops which seemed best stocked with provisions; indeed, wherever they went, meat and drink were placed before them, and nothing was refused in the hope of appeasing them. Their leaders, John Ball, Jack Straw, and Wat Tyler, then marched through London, attended by more than 20,000 men, to the palace of the Savoy, which is a handsome building belonging to the Duke of Lancaster [the king's uncle], situated on the banks of the Thames on the road to Westminster: here they immediately killed the porters, pushed into the house, and set it on fire. Not content with this outrage, they went to the house of the Knight-hospitalers of Rhodes, dedicated to St. John of Mount Carmel, which they burnt together with their church and hospital.

After this they paraded the streets, and killed every Fleming [citizen of Flanders] they could find, whether in house, church, or hospital: they broke open several houses of the Lombards [Italian bankers], taking whatever money they could lay their hands upon. They murdered a rich citizen, by name Richard Lyon, to whom Wat Tyler had formerly been servant in France, but having once beaten him, the [scoundrel] had never forgotten it; and when he had carried his men to his house, he ordered his head to be cut off, placed upon a pike, and carried through the streets of London. Thus did these wicked people act, and on this Thursday they did much damage to the city of London. Towards evening they fixed their quarters in a square, called St. Catherine's, before the Tower, declaring that they would not depart until they had obtained from the king every thing they wanted—until the Chancellor [chief financial officer] of England had accounted to them, and shown how the great sums which were raised had been expended. Considering the mischief which the mob had already done, you may easily imagine how miserable, at this time, was the situation of the king and those who were with him. . . .

. . . Now observe how fortunately matters turned out, for had these scoundrels succeeded in their intentions, all the nobility of England would have been destroyed; and after such success as this the people of other nations would have rebelled also, taking example from those of Ghent and Flanders, who at the time were in actual rebellion against their lord; the Parisians indeed the same year acted in a somewhat similar manner; upwards of 20,000 of them armed themselves with leaden maces and caused a rebellion. . . .

JOHN WYCLIFFE

CONCERNING THE POPE'S POWER

A threat to papal power and to the medieval ideal of a universal Christian community guided by the church came from radical reformers, who questioned the function and authority of the entire church hierarchy. These heretics in the Late Middle Ages were forerunners of the Protestant Reformation.

A principal dissenter was the Englishman John Wycliffe (c. 1320–1384). By stressing a personal relationship between the individual and God and by claiming that the Bible itself, rather than church teachings, is the ultimate Christian authority, Wycliffe challenged the fundamental position of the medieval church: that the avenue to salvation passed through the church alone. He denounced the wealth of the higher clergy and sought a return to the spiritual purity and material poverty of the early church. To Wycliffe, the wealthy, elaborately organized hierarchy of the church was unnecessary and wrong. The splendidly dressed and propertied bishops had no resemblance to the simple people who first followed Christ. Indeed, these worldly bishops, headed by a princely and tyrannical pope, were really anti-Christians, the "fiends of Hell." Wycliffe wanted the state to confiscate church property and the clergy to embrace poverty. By denying that priests changed the bread and wine of communion into the substance of the body and blood of Christ, Wycliffe rejected the special powers of the clergy.

The church deprived the Lollards—an order of poor priests that spread Wycliffe's teachings—of their priestly functions. In the early fifteenth century, some of Wycliffe's followers were burned at the stake.

In the following selection from a pamphlet concerning the pope, Wycliffe contrasts the pope unfavorably with Jesus. The text, originally written in Middle English, was rendered into Modern English by Alfred J. Andrea. The explanatory notes are Andrea's.

Christ was a very poor man from His birth to His death and forswore worldly riches and begging,[1] in accord with the state of primal innocence,[2] but Antichrist, in contrast to this, from the time that he is made pope to the time of his death, covets worldly wealth and tries in many shrewd ways to gain riches. Christ was a most meek man and urged that we learn from Him, but people say that the pope is the proudest man on earth, and he makes lords kiss his feet,[3] whereas Christ washed His apostles' feet. Christ was a most unpretentious man in life, deeds, and words. People say that this pope is not like Christ in this way, for whereas Christ went on foot to cities and little towns alike, they say this pope desires to live in a castle in a grand manner. Whereas Christ came to John the Baptist to be baptized by him, the pope summons people to come to him wherever he might be, yea, as though Christ Himself, and not the pope, had summoned them to Him. Christ embraced young and poor in token of his humility; people say that the pope desires to embrace worldly prestige and not good people for the sake of God, lest he dishonor himself. Christ was busy preaching the Gospel, and not for worldly prestige or for profit; people say that the pope allows this, but he would gladly make laws to which he gives more prestige and sanction than Christ's law. Christ so loved His flock that He laid down his life for them and suffered sharp pain and death in order to bring them to bliss. People say that the pope so loves the prestige of this world that he grants people absolution that guarantees a straight path to Heaven[4] so that they might perform acts that redound to his honor. And so this foolishiness could be the cause of the death, in body and soul, of many thousands of people. And how does he follow Christ in this way? Christ was so patient and suffered wrongs so well that He prayed for His enemies and taught His

[1]Apparently, an oblique attack on the mendicant friars, who claimed to follow a life of Apostolic Poverty in imitation of Jesus and his apostles. Wycliffe despised the friars.

[2]The presumed innocence of Adam and Eve before the Fall.

[3]A long-standing tradition.

[4]A reference to the Roman Church's indulgences, which had become increasingly systemized and popular during the twelfth and thirteenth centuries.

apostles not to take vengeance. People say that the pope of Rome wishes to be avenged in every way, by killing and by damning and by other painful means that he devises. Christ taught people to live well by the example of His own life and by His words, for He did what He taught and taught in a manner that was consonant with His actions. People say that the pope acts contrary to this. His life is not an example of how other people should live, for no one should live like him, inasmuch as he acts in a manner that accords to his high state. In every deed and word, Christ sought the glory of God and suffered many assaults on His manhood for this goal; people say that the pope, to the contrary, seeks his own glory in every way, yea, even if it means the loss of the worship of God. And so he manufactures many groundless gabblings.

If these and similar accusations are true of the pope of Rome, he is the very Antichrist and not Christ's vicar on earth.

CANONS AND DECREES OF THE COUNCIL OF TRENT

On doctrinal matters, the council gave an authoritative Catholic response to Protestant teachings on a host of issues. In the following excerpt from the decrees of the Council of Trent (1545–1563), the council condemned the Protestant view that faith alone was necessary for salvation and insisted on the integration of both faith and good works in the process of salvation. This position allowed the council to defend such traditional Catholic practices as monasticism, indulgences, masses for the dead, almsgiving, pilgrimages, veneration of saints, and other pious works.

THE NECESSITY OF PREPARATION FOR JUSTIFICATION [SALVATION] IN ADULTS, AND WHENCE IT PROCEEDS

It is furthermore declared that in adults the beginning of that justification must proceed from the predisposing grace of God through Jesus Christ, that is, from His vocation, whereby, without any merits on their part, they are called; that they who by sin had been cut off from God, may be disposed through His quickening and helping grace to convert themselves to their own justification by freely assenting to and cooperating with that grace; so that, while God touches the heart of man through the illumination of the Holy Ghost, man himself neither does absolutely nothing while receiving that inspiration, since he can also reject it, nor yet is he able by his own free will and without the grace of God to move himself to justice in His sight. Hence, when it is said in the sacred writings: *Turn ye to me, and I will turn to you* [Zach. 1:3], we are reminded of our liberty; and when we reply: *Convert us, O Lord, to thee, and we shall be converted* [Lam. 5:21], we confess that we need the grace of God. . . .

HOW THE GRATUITOUS JUSTIFICATION OF THE SINNER BY FAITH IS TO BE UNDERSTOOD

But when the Apostle [Paul] says that man is justified by faith and freely, these words are to be understood in that sense in which the uninterrupted unanimity of the Catholic Church has held and expressed them, namely, that we are therefore said to be justified by faith, because faith is the beginning of human salvation, the foundation and root of all justification, *without which it is impossible to please God* [Heb. 11:6] and to come to the fellowship of His sons; and we are therefore said to be justified gratuitously [unearned, as a freely given gift], because none of those things that precede justification, whether faith or works, merit the grace of justification. For, *if by grace, it is not now by works, otherwise,* as the Apostle says, *grace is no more grace* [Rom. 11:6]. . . .

IN WHAT THE JUSTIFICATION OF THE SINNER CONSISTS, AND WHAT ARE ITS CAUSES

. . . For though no one can be just except he to whom the merits of the passion of our Lord Jesus Christ are communicated, yet this takes place in that justification of the sinner, when by the merit of the most holy passion, *the charity of God is poured forth by the Holy Ghost in the hearts* [Rom. 5:5] of those who are justified and inheres in them; whence man through Jesus Christ, [with] whom he is [now one], receives in that justification, together with the remission of sins, all these infused at the same time, namely, faith, hope and charity. For faith, unless hope and charity be added to it, neither unites man perfectly with Christ nor makes him a living member of His body. For which reason it is most truly said that *faith without works is dead* [James 2:17, 20] and of no profit, and *in Christ Jesus neither circumcision availeth anything nor uncircumcision, but faith that worketh by charity* [Gal. 5:6, 6:15]. This faith, conformably to Apostolic tradition, catechumens [candidates for baptism] ask of the Church before the sacrament of baptism, when they ask for the faith that gives eternal life, which without hope and charity faith cannot give. Whence also they hear immediately the word of Christ: *If thou wilt enter into life, keep the commandments* [Matt. 19:17]. . . .

The council also condemned individual interpretation of the Bible and set up controls over the publication and sale of unauthorized religious books. It approved the cult of the saints and the use of images, practices condemned by Calvin and the Anabaptists.

Furthermore, to check unbridled spirits, it [the council] decrees that no one relying on his own judgment shall, in matters of faith and morals pertaining to the edification of Christian doctrine, distorting the Holy Scriptures in accordance with his own conceptions, presume to interpret them contrary to that sense which holy mother Church, to whom it belongs to judge of their true sense and interpretation, has held and holds, or even contrary to the unanimous teaching of the [church] Fathers, even though such interpretations should never at any time be published. Those who act contrary to this shall be made known by the ordinaries [bishops] and punished in accordance with the penalties prescribed by the law.

And wishing, as is proper, to impose a restraint in this matter on printers also, who, now without restraint, thinking what pleases them is permitted them, print without the permission of ecclesiastical superiors the books of the Holy Scriptures and the notes and commentaries thereon of all persons indiscriminately, often with the name of the press omitted, often also under a fictitious press-name, and what is worse, without the name of the author, and also indiscreetly have for sale such books printed elsewhere, (this council) decrees and ordains that in the future the Holy Scriptures, especially the old Vulgate [Latin] Edition, be printed in the most correct manner possible, and that it shall not be lawful for anyone to print or to have printed any books whatsoever dealing with sacred doctrinal matters without the name of the author, or in the future to sell them, or even to have them in possession, unless they have first been examined and approved by the ordinary [the local bishop], under penalty of anathema [condemnation and excommunication] and fine. . . .

ON THE INVOCATION, VENERATION, AND RELICS OF SAINTS, AND ON SACRED IMAGES

The holy council commands all bishops and others who hold the office of teaching and have charge of the *cura animarum* [care of souls], that in accordance with the usage of the Catholic and Apostolic Church, received from the primitive times of the Christian religion, and with the unanimous teaching of the holy Fathers and the decrees of sacred councils, they above all instruct the faithful diligently in matters relating to intercession and invocation of the saints, the veneration of relics, and the legitimate use of images, teaching them that the saints who reign together with Christ offer up their prayers to God for men, that it is good and beneficial suppliantly to invoke them and to have recourse to their prayers, assistance and support in order to obtain favors from God through His Son, Jesus Christ our Lord, who alone is our redeemer and savior. . . . Also, that the holy bodies of the holy martyrs and of others living with Christ, which were the living members of Christ and the temple of the Holy Ghost, to be awakened by Him to eternal life and to be glorified, are to be venerated by the faithful, through which many benefits are bestowed by God on men. . . . Moreover, that the images of Christ, of the Virgin Mother of God, and of the other saints are to be placed and retained especially in the churches, and that due honor and veneration is to be given them. . . .

The Council of Trent condemned the Protestant view that clergy were no different than lay people and reaffirmed the Catholic belief that the clergy, for their administration of the church's sacraments, are specially ordained intermediaries between God and human beings. Whereas Luther admitted only three sacraments—baptism, the Eucharist, and penance or confession—and Calvin only two—baptism and the Eucharist—the Council of Trent decreed that there were seven sacraments in the Catholic Church, including ordination of the clergy.

CANONS ON THE SACRAMENTS IN GENERAL

Canon 1. If anyone says that the sacraments of the New Law were not all instituted by our Lord Jesus Christ, or that there are more or less than seven, namely, baptism, confirmation, Eucharist, penance, extreme unction, order and matrimony, or that any one of these seven is not truly and intrinsically a sacrament, let him be anathema [cursed]. . . .

Can. 10. If anyone says that all Christians have the power to administer the word and all the sacraments, let him be anathema. . . .

CANONS ON THE SACRAMENT OF ORDER

Canon 1. If anyone says that there is not in the New Testament a visible and external priesthood, or that there is no power of consecrating and offering the true body and blood of the Lord and of forgiving . . . sins, but only the office and bare ministry of preaching the Gospel; or that those who do not preach are not priests at all, let him be anathema. . . .

Can. 4. If anyone says that by sacred ordination the Holy [Spirit] is not imparted and that therefore the bishops say in vain: *Receive ye the Holy [Spirit]*, or that by it a character is not imprinted, or that he who has once been a priest can again become a layman, let him be anathema.

Can. 5. If anyone says that the holy unction which the Church uses in ordination is not only not required but is detestable and pernicious, as also are the other ceremonies of order, let him be anathema.

Can. 6. If anyone says that in the Catholic Church there is not instituted a hierarchy by divine ordinance, which consists of bishops, priests and ministers, let him be anathema.

Can. 7. If anyone says that bishops are not superior to priests, or that they have not the power to confirm and ordain, or that the power which they have is common to them and to priests, or that orders conferred by them without the consent or call of the people or of the secular power are invalid, or that those who have been neither rightly ordained nor sent by ecclesiastical and canonical authority, but come from elsewhere, are lawful ministers of the word and of the sacraments, let him be anathema.

The passions aroused by the Reformation culminated in vicious religious persecution. Regarding Protestants as dangerous heretics who had affronted God and threatened his church, Catholic clergy and rulers tried to eliminate them, often by fire and sword. Protestants also engaged in persecution, principally against the Anabaptists, a Protestant sect that deviated from the teachings of the main Protestant reformers.

EPIC OF GILGAMESH[1]

The *Epic of Gilgamesh* involves the gods in human activities. Because King Gilgamesh, son of a human father and the goddess Ninsun, drives his subjects too hard, they appeal to the gods for help. The gods decide that a man of Gilgamesh's immense vigor and strength requires a rival with similar attributes with whom he can contend. The creation goddess, Aruru, is instructed to create a man worthy of Gilgamesh. From clay she fashions Enkidu in the image of Anu, the god of the heavens and father of all the gods. Enkidu is a powerful man who roams with the animals and destroys traps set by hunters, one of whom appeals to King Gilgamesh. The two of them, accompanied by a harlot, find Enkidu at a watering place frequented by animals. The harlot removes her clothes and seduces Enkidu, who spends a week with her, oblivious to everything else. After this encounter, the bond between Enkidu and the animals is broken. He now enters civilization and is befriended by Gilgamesh, with whom he slays the terrible monster Humbaba. Returning to Uruk after the encounter with Humbaba, Gilgamesh washes away the grime of battle and dons his royal clothes; thus arrayed he attracts the goddess of love, Ishtar, patroness of Uruk, who proposes marriage, but because of Ishtar's previous marriages and infidelities, Gilgamesh refuses. Ishtar falls into a bitter rage and appeals to her father, the god Anu, to unleash the fearful Bull of Heaven on Gilgamesh. However, Gilgamesh and Enkidu together slay the beast. To avenge the deaths of Humbaba and the Bull of Heaven, the gods decide that Enkidu shall die. In the following passage, Enkidu dreams of his impending death and the House of Darkness, from which no one returns.

When the daylight came Enkidu got up and cried to Gilgamesh, "O my brother, such a dream I had last night. Anu, Enlil, Ea and heavenly Shamash took counsel together, and Anu said to Enlil, 'Because they have killed the Bull of Heaven, and because they have killed Humbaba who guarded the Cedar Mountain one of the two must die.' ..."

So Enkidu lay stretched out before Gilgamesh: his tears ran down in streams and he said to Gilgamesh, "O my brother, so dear as you are to me, brother, yet they will take me from you." Again he said, "I must sit down on the threshold of the dead and never again will I see my dear brother with my eyes."

... In bitterness of spirit he poured out his heart to his friend. "It was I who cut down the cedar, I who levelled the forest, I who slew Humbaba and now see what has become of me. Listen, my friend, this is the dream I dreamed last night. The heavens roared, and earth rumbled back an answer; between them stood I before an awful being, the sombre-faced man-bird; he had directed on me his purpose. His was a vampire face, his foot was a lion's foot, his hand was an eagle's talon. He fell on me and his claws were in my hair, he held me fast and I smothered; then he transformed me so that my arms became wings covered with feathers. He turned his stare towards me, and he led me away to the palace of Irkalla, the Queen of Darkness, to the house from which none who enters ever returns, down the road from which there is no coming back.

"There is the house whose people sit in darkness; dust is their food and clay their meat. They are clothed like birds with wings for covering, they see no light, they sit in darkness. I entered the house of dust and I saw the kings of the earth, their crowns put away for ever; rulers and princes, all those who once wore kingly crowns and ruled the world in the days of old. They who had stood in the place of the gods like Anu and Enlil, stood now like servants to fetch baked meats in the house of dust, to carry cooked meat and cold water from the water-skin. In the house of dust which I entered were high priests and acolytes, priests of the incantation and of ecstasy; there were servers of the temple, and there was

Etana, that king of Kish whom the eagle carried to heaven in the days of old. I saw also Samuqan, god of cattle, and there was Ereshkigal the Queen of the Underworld; and Belit-Sheri squatted in front of her, she who is recorder of the gods and keeps the book of death. She held a tablet from which she read. She raised her head, she saw me and spoke: 'Who has brought this one here?' Then I awoke like a

[1] Throughout the text, titles original to the source appear in italics. Titles added by the editors are not italicized.

man drained of blood who wanders alone in a waste of rushes; like one whom the bailiff has seized and his heart pounds with terror."

Gilgamesh had peeled off his clothes, he listened to his words and wept quick tears, Gilgamesh listened and his tears flowed. . . .

This day on which Enkidu dreamed came to an end and he lay stricken with sickness. One whole day he lay on his bed and his suffering increased. He said to Gilgamesh, the friend on whose account he had left the wilderness, "Once I ran for you, for the water of life, and I now have nothing." A second day he lay on his bed and Gilgamesh watched over him but the sickness increased. A third day he lay on his bed, he called out to Gilgamesh, rousing him up. Now he was weak and his eyes were blind with weeping. Ten days he lay and his suffering increased, eleven and twelve days he lay on his bed of pain. Then he called to Gilgamesh, "My friend, the great goddess cursed me and I must die in shame. I shall not die like a man fallen in battle; I feared to fall, but happy is the man who falls in the battle, for I must die in shame." And Gilgamesh wept over Enkidu. With the first light of dawn he raised his voice and said to the counsellors of Uruk:

"Hear me, great ones of Uruk,
I weep for Enkidu, my friend,
Bitterly moaning like a woman mourning
I weep for my brother.
O Enkidu, my brother,
You were the axe at my side,
My hand's strength, the sword in my belt,
The shield before me,
A glorious robe, my fairest ornament;
An evil Fate has robbed me.
All the people of Eridu
Weep for you Enkidu.
***
What is this sleep which holds you now?
You are lost in the dark and cannot hear me."

He touched his heart but it did not beat, nor did he lift his eyes again. When Gilgamesh touched his heart it did not beat. So Gilgamesh laid a veil, as one veils the bride, over his friend. He began to rage like a lion, like a lioness robbed of her whelps. This way and that he paced round the bed, he tore out his hair and strewed it around. He dragged off his splendid robes and flung them down as though they were abominations.

In the first light of dawn Gilgamesh cried out, "I made you rest on a royal bed, you reclined on a couch at my left hand, the princes of the earth kissed your feet. I will cause all the people of Uruk to weep over you and raise the dirge of the dead. The joyful people will stoop with sorrow; and when you have gone to the earth I will let my hair grow long for your sake, I will wander through the wilderness in the skin of a lion." The next day also, in the first light, Gilgamesh lamented; seven days and seven nights he wept for Enkidu, until the worm fastened on him. Only then he gave him up to the earth, for the Anunnaki, the judges [of the dead],[2] had seized him. . . .

In his despair, Gilgamesh is confronted with the reality of his own death. Yearning for eternal life, he seeks Utnapishtim, legendary king of the city of Shur- rupak, a man to whom the gods had granted everlasting life.

Bitterly Gilgamesh wept for his friend Enkidu; he wandered over the wilderness as a hunter, he roamed over the plains; in his bitterness he cried, "How can I rest, how can I be at peace? Despair is in my heart. What my brother is now, that shall I be when I am dead. Because I am afraid of death I will

[2] Throughout the text, words in brackets have been added as glosses by the editors. Brackets around glosses from the original sources have been changed to parentheses to distinguish them.

go as best I can to find Utnapishtim whom they call the Faraway, for he has entered the assembly of the gods." So Gilgamesh travelled over the wilderness, he wandered over the grasslands, a long journey, in search of Utnapishtim, whom the gods took after the deluge; and they set him to live in the land of Dilmun, in the garden of the sun; and to him alone of men they gave everlasting life. . . .

In the garden of the gods, Gilgamesh speaks with Siduri, the divine winemaker, who tells him that his search for eternal life is hopeless.

"... My friend who was very dear to me and who endured dangers beside me, Enkidu my brother, whom I loved, the end of mortality has overtaken him. I wept for him seven days and nights till the worm fastened on him. Because of my brother I am afraid of death, because of my brother I stray through the wilderness and cannot rest. But now, young woman, maker of wine, since I have seen your face do not let me see the face of death which I dread so much."

She answered, "Gilgamesh, where are you hurrying to? You will never find that life for which you are looking. When the gods created man they allotted to him death, but life they retained in their own keeping. As for you, Gilgamesh, fill your belly with good things; day and night, night and day, dance and be merry, feast and rejoice. Let your clothes be fresh, bathe yourself in water, cherish the little child that holds your hand, and make your wife happy in your embrace; for this too is the lot of man."

But Gilgamesh said to Siduri, the young woman, "How can I be silent, how can I rest, when Enkidu whom I love is dust, and I too shall die and be laid in the earth. You live by the sea-shore and look into the heart of it; young woman, tell me now, which is the way to Utnapishtim, the son of Ubara- Tutu? What directions are there for the passage; give me, oh, give me directions, I will cross the Ocean if it is possible; if it is not I will wander still farther in the wilderness." . . .

Siduri instructs Gilgamesh how to reach Utnapishtim. Ferried across the "waters of death" by a boatman, Gilgamesh meets Utnapishtim. But he, too, cannot give Gilgamesh the eternal life for which he yearns.

. . . "Oh father Utnapishtim, you who have entered the assembly of the gods, I wish to question you concerning the living and the dead, how shall I find the life for which I am searching?"

Utnapishtim said, "There is no permanence. Do we build a house to stand for ever, do we seal a contract to hold for all time? Do brothers divide an inheritance to keep for ever, does the flood-time of rivers endure? It is only the nymph of the dragon-fly who sheds her larva and sees the sun in his glory. From the days of old there is no permanence. The sleeping and the dead, how alike they are, they are like a painted death. What is there between the master and the servant when both have fulfilled their doom? When the Anun- naki, the judges, come together, and Mammetun the mother of destinies, together they decree the fates of men. Life and death they allot but the day of death they do not disclose." . . .

The tale concludes with one of the many ancient stories of a great flood. In the West, the best known of these stories is the Hebrew account of Noah and his ark in Genesis (chapters 6-9). However, the *Epic of Gilgamesh* contains quite possibly an older version of the story—one that is quite similar to the Genesis account. The two accounts have several similarities: Both were worldwide floods that destroyed all the animals and humans except those who were saved in a huge boat built by a single righteous man,

Noah in Genesis and Utnapishtim in *Gilgamesh;* both boats landed on a mountaintop; and both men sent out birds to find out whether the waters had subsided. There are also differences: in the Genesis account, God sent the forty-day flood as a punishment for human sinfulness, whereas in *Gilgamesh,* a council of the gods decided to destroy humanity with a six-day flood because humans had become too numerous and noisy. In the Gilgamesh account, it was Enlil, the god of the earth, who proposed the idea of the flood, and his plan was approved by the other gods, even by his father, Anu, the chief of the Sumer- ian gods. The only opposition came from Enlil's brother Ea, the god of fresh water and the creator of humans. Ea warned Utnapishtim of the impending flood and told him to build a boat. Enlil's flood was made even more destructive by the Annunaki, the gods of the underworld, and by Niurta, the god of war. After the flood, Ishtar, goddess of love and the daughter of Anu, placated the gods and made possible the reconciliation between Enlil and Utnapishtim.

. . . "You know the city Shurrupak, it stands on the banks of Euphrates? That city grew old and the gods that were in it were old. There was Anu, lord of the firmament, their father, and warrior Enlil their counsellor, Ninurta the helper, and Ennugi watcher over canals; and with them also was Ea. In those days the world teemed, the people multiplied, the world bellowed like a wild bull, and the great god was aroused by the clamour. Enlil heard the clamour and he said to the gods in council, 'The uproar of mankind is intolerable and sleep is no longer possible by reason of the babel.' So the gods agreed to exterminate mankind. Enlil did this, but Ea because of his oath warned me in a dream. He whispered their words to my house of reeds, 'Reed-house, reed- house! Wall, O wall, hearken reed-house, wall reflect; O man of Shurrupak, son of Ubara-Tutu; tear down your house and build a boat, abandon possessions and look for life, despise worldly goods and save your soul alive. Tear down your house, I say, and build a boat. These are the measurements of the barque as you shall build her: let her beam equal her length, let her deck be roofed like the vault that covers the abyss; then take up into the boat the seed of all living creatures.'

"When I had understood I said to my lord, 'Behold, what you have commanded I will honour and perform, but how shall I answer the people, the city, the elders?' Then Ea opened his mouth and said to me, his servant, 'Tell them this: I have learnt that Enlil is wrathful against me, I dare no longer walk in his land nor live in his city; I will go down to the Gulf to dwell with Ea my lord. But on you he will rain down abundance, rare fish and shy wild-fowl, a rich harvest- tide. In the evening the rider of the storm will bring you wheat in torrents.

"In the first light of dawn all my household gathered round me, the children brought pitch and the men whatever was necessary. On the fifth day I laid the keel and the ribs, then I made fast the planking. The ground-space was one acre, each side of the deck measured one hundred and twenty cubits, making a square. I built six decks below, seven in all, I divided them into nine sections with bulkheads between. I drove in wedges where needed, I saw to the punt-poles, and laid in supplies. The carriers brought oil in baskets, I poured pitch into the furnace and asphalt and oil; more oil was consumed in caulking, and more again the master of the boat took into his stores. I slaughtered bullocks for the people and every day I killed sheep. I gave the shipwrights wine to drink as though it were river water, raw wine and red wine and oil and white wine. There was feasting then as there is at the time of the New Year's festival; I myself anointed my head. On the seventh day the boat was complete.

"Then was the launching full of difficulty; there was shifting of ballast above and below till two thirds was submerged. I loaded into her all that I had of gold and of living things, my family, my kin, the beast of the field both wild and tame, and all the craftsmen. I sent them on board, for the time that Shamash had ordained was already fulfilled when he said, 'In the evening, when the rider of the storm sends down the destroying rain, enter the boat and batten her down.' The time was fulfilled, the evening came, the rider of the storm sent down the rain. I looked out at the weather and it was terrible, so I too boarded the boat and battened her down. All was now complete, the battening and the caulking; so I handed the tiller to Puzur-Amurri the steersman, with the navigation and the care of the whole boat.

"With the first light of dawn a black cloud came from the horizon; it thundered within where Adad, lord of the storm was riding. In front over hill and plain Shullat and Hanish, heralds of the storm, led on. Then the gods of the abyss rose up; Nergal pulled out the dams of the nether waters, Ninurta the war-lord threw down the dykes, and the seven judges of hell, the Annunaki, raised their torches, lighting the land with their livid flame. A stupor of despair went up to heaven when the god of the storm turned daylight to darkness, when he smashed the land like a cup. One whole day the tempest raged, gathering fury as it went, it poured over the people like the tides of battle; a man could not see his brother nor the people be seen from heaven. Even the gods were terrified at the flood, they fled to the highest heaven, the firmament of Anu; they crouched against the walls, cowering like curs. Then Ishtar the sweet-voiced Queen of Heaven cried out like a woman in travail: 'Alas the days of old are turned to dust because I commanded evil; why did I command this evil in the council of all the gods? I commanded wars to destroy the people, but are they not my people, for I brought them forth? Now like the spawn of fish they float in the ocean.' The great gods of heaven and of hell wept, they covered their mouths.

"For six days and six nights the winds blew, torrent and tempest and flood overwhelmed the world, tempest and flood raged together like warring hosts. When the seventh day dawned the storm from the south subsided, the sea grew calm, the flood was stilled; I looked at the face of the world and there was silence, all mankind was turned to clay. The surface of the sea stretched as flat as a roof-top; I opened a hatch and the light fell on my face. Then I bowed low, I sat down and I wept, the tears streamed down my face, for on every side was the waste of water. I looked for land in vain, but fourteen leagues distant there appeared a mountain, and there the boat grounded; on the mountain of Nisir the boat held fast, she held fast and did not budge. One day she held, and a second day on the mountain of Nisir she held fast and did not budge. A third day, and a fourth day she held fast on the mountain and did not budge; a fifth day and a sixth day she held fast on the mountain. When the seventh day dawned I loosed a dove and let her go. She flew away, but finding no resting-place she returned. Then I loosed a swallow, and she flew away but finding no resting-place she returned. I loosed a raven, she saw that the waters had retreated, she ate, she flew around, she cawed, and she did not come back. Then I threw everything open to the four winds, I made a sacrifice and poured out a libation on the mountain top. Seven and again seven cauldrons I set up on their stands, I heaped up wood and cane and cedar and myrtle. When the gods smelled the sweet savour, they gathered like flies over the sacrifice. Then, at last, Ishtar also came, she lifted her necklace with the jewels of heaven that once Anu had made to please her. 'O you gods here present, by the lapis lazuli round my neck I shall remember these days as I remember the jewels of my throat; these last days I shall not forget. Let all the gods gather round the sacrifice, except Enlil. He shall not approach this offering, for without reflection he brought the flood; he consigned my people to destruction.'

"When Enlil had come, when he saw the boat, he was wrath and swelled with anger at the gods, the host of heaven, 'Has any of these mortals escaped? Not one was to have survived the destruction.' Then the god of the wells and canals Ninurta opened his mouth and said to the warrior Enlil, 'Who is there of the gods that can devise without Ea? It is Ea alone who knows all things.' Then Ea opened his mouth and spoke to warrior Enlil, 'Wisest of gods, hero Enlil, how could you so senselessly bring down the flood?

Lay upon the sinner his sin,
Lay upon the transgressor his transgression,
Punish him a little when he breaks loose,
Do not drive him too hard or he perishes;
Would that a lion had ravaged mankind
Rather than the flood,
Would that a wolf had ravaged mankind
Rather than the flood,
Would that famine had wasted the world
Rather than the flood,
Would that pestilence had wasted mankind
Rather than the flood.

It was not I that revealed the secret of the gods; the wise man learned it in a dream. Now take your counsel what shall be done with him.

"Then Enlil went up into the boat, he took me by the hand and my wife and made us enter the boat and kneel down on either side, he standing between us. He touched our foreheads to bless us saying, 'In time past Utnapishtim was a mortal man; henceforth he and his wife shall live in the distance at the mouth of the rivers.' Thus it was that the gods took me and placed me here to live in the distance, at the mouth of the rivers."

MESOPOTAMIAN WISDOM LITERATURE

The following selection reveals the pessimism that pervaded Mesopotamian life. The sufferer tries to do everything that he believes the gods want of him but cannot escape misfortune.

I survived to the next year; the appointed time passed.
I turn around, but it is bad, very bad;
My ill luck increases and I cannot find what is right.
I called to my god, but he did not show his face,
I prayed to my goddess, but she did not raise her head.
Even the diviner with his divination could not make a prediction,
And the interpreter of dreams with his libation could not elucidate my case.
I sought the favor of the . . . spirit, but he would not enlighten me;
The exorcist with his ritual could not appease the divine wrath against me.
What strange conditions everywhere!
When I look behind (me), there is persecution, trouble.
Like one who has not made libations to his god,
Nor invoked his goddess when he ate,
Does not make prostrations nor recognize (the necessity of) bowing down,
In whose mouth supplication and prayer are lacking,
Who has even neglected holy days, and ignored festivals,
Who was negligent and did not observe the gods' rites,
Did not teach his people reverence and worship,
But has eaten his food without invoking his god,
And abandoned his goddess by not bringing a flour offering,
Like one who has gone crazy and forgotten his lord,
Has frivolously sworn a solemn oath by his god, (like such a one) do I appear.
For myself, I gave attention to supplication and prayer:
My prayer was discretion, sacrifice my rule.
The day for worshipping the god was a joy to my heart;
The day of the goddess's procession was profit and gain to me.
The king's blessing—that was my joy,
And the accompanying music became a delight for me.
I had my land keep the god's rites,
And brought my people to value the goddess's name.
I made the praise for the king like a god's,
And taught the people respect for the palace.
I wish I knew that these things would be pleasing to one's god!
What is good for oneself may be offense to one's god,
What in one's own heart seems despicable may be proper to one's god.
Who can know the will of the gods in heaven?
Who can understand the plans of the underworld gods?
Where have humans learned the way of a god?
He who was alive yesterday is dead today.
One moment he is worried, the next he is boisterous.
One moment he is singing a joyful song,
A moment later he wails like a professional mourner.
Their condition changes (as quickly as) opening and shutting (the *eyes).*
When starving they become like corpses,

When full they oppose their god.
In good times they speak of scaling heaven,
When they are troubled they talk of going down to hell.
I am *perplexed* at these things; I have not been able to understand their significance.
As for me, exhausted, a windstorm is driving me on!
Debilitating Disease is let loose upon me:
An Evil Wind has blown (from the) horizon,
Headache has sprung up from the surface of the underworld. . . .
(They all joined in) and came on me together.
(They *struck)* my head, they enveloped my skull;
(My) face is gloomy, my eyes flow.
They have wrenched my neck muscles and made (my) neck limp.
They struck (my chest,) beat my breast.
They affected my flesh and made me shake,
(In) my epigastrium [abdomen] they kindled a fire.
They churned up my bowels, . . . (they) . . . my . . .
Causing the discharge of phlegm, they tired out my (lungs).
They tired out my limbs and made my *fat* quake.
My upright stance they knocked down like a wall,
My robust figure they laid down like a rush [a grasslike plant]. . . .
My eyes stare straight ahead, but cannot see,
My ears are open, but cannot hear.
Feebleness has overcome my whole body,
An attack of illness has fallen upon my flesh.
Stiffness has taken over my arms,
Weakness has come upon my knees,
My feet forget their motion.
(A stroke) has got me; I choke like someone prostrate.
Death has *(approached*) and has covered my face.
If someone is concerned about me, I am not even able to answer the one who inquires.
(My . . .) weep, but I cannot control myself.
A snare is laid on my mouth,
And a bolt keeps my lips barred. . . .
My malady is indeed protracted.
Through not eating, my looks have become strange,
My flesh is flaccid, and my blood has ebbed away.
My bones look separated, and are covered (only) with my skin.
My flesh is inflamed, and the . . . -disease has afflicted me.
I have taken to a bed of *bondage;* going out is a pain;
My house has become my prison. . . .
I spent the night in my dung like an ox,
And wallowed in my excrement like a sheep.
My symptoms are beyond the exorcist,
And my omens have confused the diviner.
The exorcist could not diagnose the nature of my sickness,
Nor could the diviner set a time limit on my illness.
My god has not come to the rescue nor taken me by the hand;
My goddess has not shown pity on me nor gone by my side.

JOB

THE PROBLEM OF UNDESERVED SUFFERING

Written sometime between the seventh and the fourth centuries b.c., the Book of Job is one of the best examples of Hebrew wisdom literature. It is concerned with profound questions. Why do the righteous often suffer and the wicked prosper? And why does God permit such injustice? The Book of Job does not provide conclusive answers to these questions, but it does impel us to ponder them and to think about our relationship to God.

In the prologue, the first two chapters of the book, God tells Satan[1] that there is none like his servant Job, "a wholehearted and an upright man that feareth God and shunneth evil." Satan replies that Job is loyal only because God has protected him from misfortune. Put an end to his good fortune, says Satan, and Job "will blaspheme Thee to Thy face." Accepting the challenge, God permits Satan to destroy Job's children, take away his possessions, and afflict him with painful boils all over his body. Still Job does not curse God.

So far Job has accepted his fate uncomplainingly. But then in the company of three friends, Eliphaz, Bildad, and Zophar, he laments his misfortune and protests that God has treated him unjustly. Why is this happening, he asks, since he has not knowingly sinned? And why does a merciful God continue to make him suffer?

3 [1]After this opened Job his mouth, and cursed his day.
[2]And Job spoke and said:
[3]Let the day perish wherein I was born,
And the night wherein it was said: "A man-child is brought forth."
[4]Let that day be darkness. . . .
[11]Why died I not from the womb?
Why did I not perish at birth? . . .

7 [11]Therefore I will not refrain my mouth;
I will speak in the anguish of my spirit;
I will complain in the bitterness of my soul.
[12]Am I a sea, or a sea-monster,
That Thou settest a watch over me?
[13]When I say: "My bed shall comfort me,
My couch shall ease my complaint";
[14]Then Thou scarest me with dreams,
And terrifest me through visions;
[15]So that my soul chooseth strangling,
And death rather than these my bones.
[16]I loathe it; I shall not live alway;
Let me alone; for my days are vanity.
[17]What is man, that Thou shouldest magnify him,
And that thou shouldst set thy heart upon him,
[18]And that Thou shouldest remember him every morning,
And try him every moment?
[19]How long wilt Thou not look away from me,
Nor let me alone till I swallow down my spittle?
[20]If I have sinned, what do I unto Thee, O Thou watcher of men?

---

[1]At this stage in Jewish thought, Satan is simply a member of God's court; he is not the enemy of God and the leader of the forces of evil as he is later depicted, particularly at the time of Jesus and in early Christian writings.

Why hast Thou set me as a mark for Thee,
So that I am a burden to myself?
21 And why dost Thou not pardon my transgression,
And take away mine iniquity?
For now shall I lie down in the dust;
And Thou wilt seek me, but I shall not be. . . .

9 22 It is all one—therefore I say:
He destroyeth the innocent and the wicked.
23 If the scourge slay suddenly,
He will mock at the calamity of the guiltless.
24 The earth is given into the hand of the wicked;
He coverth the faces of the judges thereof;
If it be not He, who then is it?
25 Now my days are swifter than a runner;
They flee away, they see no good.

Job's friends take the orthodox position that "God will not cast away an innocent man,/Neither will he uphold the evil-doers. . . ." But Job replies that God is destroying an innocent man.

16 22 God delivereth me to the ungodly,
And casteth me into the hands of the wicked.
12 I was at ease, and He broke me asunder;
Yea, He hath taken me by the neck, and dashed me to pieces;
He hath also set me up for His mark.
13 His archers compass me round about,
He cleaveth my reins asunder, and doth not spare;
He poureth out my gall upon the ground.
14 He breaketh me with breach upon breach;
He runneth upon me like a giant.
15 I have sewed sackcloth upon my skin,
And have laid my horn in the dust.
16 My face is reddened with weeping,
And on my eyelids is the shadow of death;
17 Although there is no violence in my hands,
And my prayer is pure. . . .

19 6 Know now that God hath subverted my cause,
And hath compared me with His net.
7 Behold, I cry out: "Violence!" but I am not heard;
I cry aloud, but there is no justice.
8 He hath fenced up my way that I cannot pass,
And hath set darkness in my paths.
9 He hath stripped me of my glory,
And taken the crown from my head.
And my hope hath He plucked up like a tree.
11 He hath also kindled His wrath against me,

And He counteth me unto Him as one of His adversaries. . . .

Job protests that the wicked often go unpunished, while he who aspired to righteousness is made to suffer.

21 7Wherefore do the wicked live,
Become old, yea, wax mighty in power?
8Their seed is established in their sight with them,
And their offspring before their eyes.
9Their houses are safe, without fear,
Neither is the rod of God upon them.
10Their bull gendereth, and faileth not;
Their cow calveth, and casteth not her calf.
11They send forth their little ones like a flock,
And their children dance.
12They sing to the timbrel and harp,
And rejoice at the sound of the pipe.
13They spend their days in prosperity,
And peacefully they go down to the grave.
14Yet they said unto God: "Depart from us;
For we desire not the knowledge of Thy ways.
15What is the Almighty, that we should serve Him?
And what profit should we have, if we pray unto Him?" . . .

29 12Because I delivered the poor that cried,
The fatherless also, that had none to help him.
13The blessing of him that was ready to perish came upon me;
And I caused the widow's heart to sing for joy.
14I put on righteousness, and it clothed itself with me;
My justice was as a robe and a diadem.
15I was eyes to the blind,
And feet was I to the lame.
16I was a father to the needy;
And the cause of him that I knew not I searched out.
17And I broke the jaws of the unrighteous,
And plucked the prey out of his teeth.

Elihu, a young man, joins the symposium. He is angry with Job for his self-righteousness, for trying to justify himself rather than God, and with Job's friends, for having found no answer to Job's dilemma. But in proclaiming God's justice, Elihu essentially repeats the friends' arguments.

30 16And now my soul is poured out within me;
Days of affliction have taken hold upon me.
17In the night my bones are pierced, and fall from me,
And my sinews take no rest.
18By the great force [of my disease] is my garment disfigured;
It bindeth me about as the collar of my coat.
19He hath cast me into the mire,

And I am become like dust and ashes.
[20]I cry onto Thee, and Thou dost not answer me;
I stand up, And Thou lookest at me.
[21]Thou art turned to be cruel to me;
With the might of Thy hand Thou hatest me.
[22]Thou liftest me up to the wind,
Thou causest me to ride upon it;
And Thou dissolvest my substance.
[23]For I know that Thou wilt bring me to death,
And to the house appointed for all living.

34 [10]Therefore hearken unto me, ye men of understandin
Far be it from God, that He should do wickedness;
And from the Almighty, that He should commit iniquity.
For the work of a man will He requite unto him,
And cause every man to find according to his ways.
[12]Yea, of a surety, God will not do wickedly,
Neither will the Almighty pervert justice.
[13]Who gave Him a charge over the earth?
Or who hath disposed the whole world?
[14]If He set His heart upon man,
If He gather unto Himself his spirit and his breath;
[15]All flesh shall perish together,
And man shall return unto dust.
[16]If now thou hast understanding, hear this;
Hearken to the voice of my words. . . .
[31]For hath any said unto God:
"I have borne chastisement, though I offend not;
[32]That which I see not teach Thou me;
If I have done iniquity, I will do it no more"?
[33]Shall His recompense be as thou wilt? For thou loathest it,
So that thou must choose, and not I;
Therefore speak what thou knowest.
[34]Men of understanding will say unto me,
Yea, every wise man that heareth me:
[35]"Job speaketh without knowledge,
And his words are without discernment."
[36]Would that Job were tried unto the end,
Because of his answering like wicked men.
[37]For he addeth rebellion unto his sin,
He clappeth his hands among us,
And multiplieth his words against God.

36 [5]Behold, God is mighty, yet He despiseth not any;
He is mighty in strength of understanding.
[6]He preserveth not the life of the wicked;
But giveth to the poor their right.
[7]He withdraweth not His eyes from the righteous;

But with kings upon the throne
He setteth them for ever, and they are exalted.
8 And if they be bound in fetters,
And be holden in cords of affliction;
9 Then He declareth unto them their work,
And their transgressions, that they have behaved themselves proudly.
10 He openeth also their ear to discipline,
And commandeth that they return from iniquity.
11 If they hearken and save Him,
They shall spend their days in prosperity,
And their years in pleasures.
12 But if they hearken not, they shall perish by the sword,
And they shall die without knowledge.

Then God, "out of the whirlwind," replies to Job. But in God's response, we do not find a clear answer to the problem of undeserved suffering. Instead, God, in a series of rhetorical questions, reminds Job that he alone is the creator and sustainer of the universe and that it is the obligation of Job, a mere mortal, to honor his creator and not find fault with him. Awed by God's majesty and power, a humbled Job declares, "I abhor my words and repent." In an epilogue, God responds by restoring Job's good fortune.

AMOS AND ISAIAH

SOCIAL JUSTICE

By the eighth century b.c. a significant disparity existed between the wealthy and the poor. Small farmers in debt to moneylenders faced the loss of their land or even bondage. Amos, a mid-eighth-century prophet, felt a tremendous compulsion to speak out in the name of God against these injustices.

AMOS

5 [21]I hate, I despise your feasts,
And I will take no delight in your solemn assemblies.
[22]Yea, though ye offer me burnt-offerings and your meal-offerings, I will not accept them;
Neither will I regard the peace-offerings of your fat beasts.
[23]Take thou away from Me the noise of thy songs;
And let Me not hear the melody of thy psalteries.
[24]But let justice well up as waters,
And righteousness as a mighty stream.

The prophets' insistence that rituals were not the essence of the law and their passion for righteousness are voiced in the Scriptures by Isaiah of Jerusalem, who lived in the mid-eighth century B.C. Scholars agree that Isaiah of Jerusalem did not write all sixty-six chapters that make up the Book of Isaiah. Some material appears to have been written by his disciples and interpreters, and Chapters 40 to 55, composed two centuries later, are attributed to a person given the name Second Isaiah. The following verses come from Isaiah of Jerusalem.

ISAIAH

1 [11]To what purpose is the multitude of your sacrifices unto Me?
Saith the Lord;
I am full of the burnt-offerings of rams,
And the fat of fed beasts;
And I delight not in the blood
Of bullocks, or of lambs, or of he-goats.
[12]When ye come to appear before Me,
Who hath required this at your hand,
To trample My courts?
[13]Bring no more vain oblations;
It is an offering of abomination unto Me;
New moon and sabbath, the holding of convocations—
I cannot endure iniquity along with the solemn assembly.
[14]Your new moons and your appointed seasons
My soul hateth;
They are a burden unto Me;
I am weary to bear them.
[15]And when ye spread forth your hands,
I will hide Mine eyes from you;

Yea, when ye make many prayers,
I will not hear;
Your hands are full of blood.
16Wash you, make you clean,
Put away the evil of your doings
From before Mine eyes,
Cease to do evil;
17Learn to do well;
Seek justice, relieve the oppressed,
Judge the fatherless, plead for the widow.

Isaiah denounced the rich and the powerful for exploiting the poor.

3 13The LORD standeth up to plead,
And standeth to judge the peoples.
14The LORD will enter into judgment
With the elders of His people, and the princes thereof.
"It is ye that have eaten up the vineyard;
The spoil of the poor is in your houses;
15What mean ye that ye crush My people,
And grind the face of the poor?"
Saith the Lord, the GOD of hosts.

HOMER

ILIAD

The following passages from the *Iliad* illustrate the Homeric ideal of excellence. In the first, Hector of Troy, son of King Priam, prepares for battle. Hector's wife Andromache pleads with him to stay within the city walls, but Hector, in the tradition of the Homeric hero, feels compelled to engage in combat to show his worth and gain honor.

Hector looked at his son and smiled, but said nothing. Andromache, bursting into tears, went up to him and put her hand in his. "Hector," she said, "you are possessed. This bravery of yours will be your end. You do not think of your little boy or your unhappy wife, whom you will make a widow soon. Some day the Achaeans [Greeks] are bound to kill you in a massed attack. And when I lose you I might as well be dead. There will be no comfort left, when you have met your doom—nothing but grief. I have no father, no mother, now. My father fell to the great Achilles when he sacked our lovely town, Cilician Thebe[1] of the High Gates. ... I had seven brothers too at home. In one day all of them went down to Hades' House.[2] The great Achilles of the swift feet killed them all. . . ."

"So you, Hector, are father and mother and brother to me, as well as my beloved husband. Have pity on me now; stay here on the tower; and do not make your boy an orphan and your wife a widow. ..."

"All that, my dear," said the great Hector of the glittering helmet, "is surely my concern. But if I hid myself like a coward and refused to fight, I could never face the Trojans and the Trojan ladies in their trailing gowns. Besides, it would go against the grain, for I have trained myself always, like a good soldier, to take my place in the front line and win glory for my father and myself. ..."

As he finished, glorious Hector held out his arms to take his boy. But the child shrank back with a cry to the bosom of his girdled nurse, alarmed by his father's appearance. He was frightened by the bronze of the helmet and the horsehair plume that he saw nodding grimly down at him. His father and his lady mother had to laugh. But noble Hector quickly took his helmet off and put the dazzling thing on the ground. Then he kissed his son, dandled him in his arms, and prayed to Zeus [the chief god] and the other gods: "Zeus, and you other gods, grant that this boy of mine may be, like me, pre-eminent in Troy; as strong and brave as I; a mighty king of Ilium [Troy]. May people say, when he comes back from battle, 'Here is a better man than his father.' Let him bring home the bloodstained armour of the enemy he has killed, and make his mother happy."

Hector handed the boy to his wife, who took him to her fragrant breast. She was smiling through her tears, and when her husband saw this he was moved. He stroked her with his hand and said: "My dear, I beg you not to be too much distressed. No one is going to send me down to Hades before my proper time. But Fate is a thing that no man born of woman, coward or hero, can escape. Go home now, and attend to your own work, the loom and the spindle, and see that the maidservants get on with theirs. War is men's business; and this war is the business of every man in Ilium, myself above all."

Many brave Greek warriors die in battle, including Achilles' best friend Patroclus, slain by the Trojan Hector. Torn by grief and rage, Achilles now sets aside his quarrel with Agamemnon (who has appealed to Achilles) and joins the battle.

Nestor's son halted before him with the hot tears pouring down his checks and gave him the lamentable news: "Alas, my royal lord Achilles! I have a dreadful thing to tell you—I would to God it were not true. Patroclus has been killed. They are fighting round his naked corpse and Hector of the flashing helmet has your arms."

When Achilles heard this he sank into the black depths of despair. He picked up the dark dust in both his hands and poured it on his head. He soiled his comely face with it, and filthy ashes settled on

[1] In the Iliad the Cilices lived in southern Asia Minor.

[2] Hades refers both to the god of the underworld and to the underworld itself.

his scented tunic. He cast himself down on the earth and lay there like a fallen giant, fouling his hair and tearing it out with his own hands. The maidservants whom he and Patroclus had captured caught the alarm and all ran screaming out of doors. They beat their breasts with their hands and sank to the ground beside their royal master. On the other side, Antilochus shedding tears of misery held the hands of Achilles as he sobbed out his noble heart, for fear that he might take a knife and cut his throat.

Suddenly Achilles gave a loud and dreadful cry, and his lady Mother heard him where she sat in the depths of the sea beside her ancient Father. Then she herself took up the cry of grief, and there gathered round her every goddess, every Nereid that was in the deep salt sea. . . . "Ah misery me, the unhappy mother of the best of men! I brought into the world a flawless child to be a mighty hero and eclipse his peers. I nursed him as one tends a little plant in a garden bed, and he shot up like a sapling. I sent him to Ilium with his beaked ships to fight against the Trojans; and never again now shall I welcome him to Peleus' house. And yet he has to suffer, every day he lives and sees the sun; and I can do no good by going to his side. But I *will* go, none the less, to see my darling child and hear what grief has come to him, although he has abstained from fighting."

With that she left the cave. The rest went with her, weeping, and on either side of them the surging sea fell back. When they reached the deep-soiled land of Troy, they came up one by one onto the beach, where the Myrmidon ships were clustered round the swift Achilles. His lady Mother went up to him as he lay groaning there, and with a piercing cry took her son's head in her hands and spoke to him in her compassion. "My child," she asked him, "why these tears? What is it that has grieved you? Tell me and do not keep your sorrow to yourself. Some part, at any rate, of what you prayed for when you lifted up your hands to Zeus has been fulfilled by him. The Achaeans have been penned in at the ships for want of you, and have suffered horribly."

Achilles of the nimble feet gave a great sigh. "Mother," he said, "it is true that the Olympian has done that much in my behalf. But what satisfaction can I get from that, now that my dearest friend is dead, Patroclus, who was more to me than any other of my men, whom I loved as much as my own life? I have lost Patroclus. And Hector, who killed him, has stripped him of my splendid armour, the huge and wonderful arms that the gods gave Peleus as a wedding-present on the day when they married you off to a mortal man. Ah, how I wish that you had stayed there with the deathless salt-sea Nymphs and that Peleus had taken home a mortal wife! But you became my mother; and now, to multiply *your* sorrows too, you are going to lose your son and never welcome him at home again. For I have no wish to live and linger in the world of men, unless, before all else, Hector is felled by my spear and dies, paying the price for slaughtering Menoetius' son."

Thetis wept. She said: "If that is so, my child, you surely have not long to live; for after Hector's death you are doomed forthwith to die."

"Then *let* me die forthwith," Achilles said with passion, "since I have failed to save my friend from death. He has fallen, far from his motherland, wanting my help in his extremity. So now, since I shall never see my home again, since I have proved a broken reed to Patroclus and all my other comrades whom Prince Hector killed, and have sat here by my ships, an idle burden on the earth, I, the best man in all the Achaean force, the best in battle, defeated only in the war of words . . . Ah, how I wish that discord could be banished from the world of gods and men, and with it anger, insidious as trickling honey, anger that makes the wisest man flare up and spreads like smoke through his whole being, anger such as King Agamemnon roused in me that day! However, what is done is better left alone, though we resent it still, and we must curb our hearts perforce. I will go now and seek out Hector, the destroyer of my dearest friend. As for my death, when Zeus and the other deathless gods appoint it, let it come. . . . But for the moment, glory is my aim. I will make these Trojan women and deep-bosomed daughters of Dardanus wipe the tears from their tender checks with both their hands as they raise the dirge, to teach them just how long I have been absent from the war. And you, Mother, as you love me, do not try to keep me from the field. You will never hold me now."

"Indeed, my child," said Thetis of the Silver Feet, "it could not be an evil thing for you to rescue your exhausted comrades from destruction. But your beautiful burnished armour is in Trojan hands. Hector of the flashing helmet is swaggering about in it himself—not that he will enjoy it long, for he is very near to death. So do not think of throwing yourself into the fight before you see me here again. I will come back at sunrise to-morrow with a splendid set of armour from the Lord Hephaestus." . . .

All night long the Achaeans wept and wailed for Patro- clus. The son of Peleus was their leader in the melancholy dirge. He laid his man-killing hands on his comrade's breast and uttered piteous groans, like a bearded lion when a huntsman has stolen his cubs from a thicket and he comes back too late, discovers his loss and follows the man's trail through glade after glade, hoping in his misery to track him down. Thus Achilles groaned among his Myrmidons. He thought with a pang of the idle words he had let fall one day at home in his attempts to reassure Patroclus' noble father. "I told Menoetius," he said, "that I would bring him back his son to Opus from the sack of Ilium, covered with glory and laden with his share of plunder. But Zeus makes havoc of the schemes of men; and now the pair of us are doomed to redden with our blood one patch of earth, here in the land of Troy. For I shall never see my home again, nor be welcomed there by Peleus the old charioteer and my Mother Thetis, but shall be swallowed by the earth I stand on. So then, Patroclus, since I too am going below, but after you, I shall not hold your funeral till I have brought back here the armour and the head of Hector, who slaughtered you, my noble-hearted friend. And at your pyre I will cut the throats of a dozen of the highborn youths of Troy, to vent my wrath on them for killing you. Till then, you shall lie as you are by my beaked ships, wailed and wept for day and night by the Trojan women and the deep-bosomed daughters of Dardanus whom we captured after much toil, with our own hands and our long spears, when we sacked rich cities full of men."

Prince Achilles then told his followers to put a big three-legged cauldron on the fire and make haste to wash the clotted gore from Patroclus' body. They put a large cauldron on the glowing fire, filled it with water, and brought faggots, which they kindled beneath it. The flames began to lick the belly of the cauldron and the water grew warm. When it came to the boil in the burnished copper, they washed the corpse, anointed it with olive oil and filled the wounds with an unguent nine years old. Then they laid it on a bier and covered it from head to foot with a soft sheet, over which they spread a white cloak. And for the rest of the night the Myrmidons with the great runner Achilles wept and wailed for Patroclus.

King Priam urges his son not to fight the mighty Achilles, but Hector, despite his fears, resolves to face Achilles.

"Hector!" the old man called, stretching out his arms to him in piteous appeal. "I beg you, my dear son, not to stand up to that man alone and unsupported. You are courting defeat and death at his hands. He is far stronger than you, and he is savage. The dogs and vultures would soon be feeding on his corpse (and what a load would be lifted from my heart!) if the gods loved him as little as I do—the man who has robbed me of so many splendid sons, killed them or sold them off as slaves to the distant isles. Even to-day there are two of them I cannot find among the troops that have taken refuge in the town, Lycaon and Polydorus, children of mine by the Princess Laothoe. If the enemy have taken them alive, we will ransom them presently with bronze and gold, of which she has plenty, for Altes, the honourable old man, gave his daughter a fortune. But if they are dead by now and in the Halls of Hades, there will be one more sorrow for me and their mother who brought them into the world, even though the rest of Ilium will not mourn for them so long—unless you join them and also fall to Achilles. So come inside the walls, my child, to be the saviour of Troy and the Trojans; and do not throw away your own dear life to give a triumph to the son of Peleus. Have pity too on me, your poor father, who is still able to feel. Think of the hideous fate that Father Zeus has kept in store for my old age, the horrors I shall have to see before I die, the massacre of my sons, my daughters mauled, their bedrooms pillaged, their babies dashed on the ground by the brutal enemy, and my sons' wives hauled away by foul Achaean hands. Last of all my turn will come to fall to the sharp bronze, and when someone's javelin or sword has laid me dead, I shall be torn to pieces by ravening dogs at my own street door. The very dogs I have fed at table and trained to watch my gate will loll about in front of it, maddened by their master's blood. Ah, it looks well enough for a young man killed in battle to lie there with his wounds upon him: death can find nothing to expose in him that is not beautiful. But when an old man is killed and dogs defile his grey head, his grey beard and his privy parts, we plumb the depths of human degradation."

As he came to an end, Priam plucked at his grey locks and tore the hair from his head; but he failed to shake Hector's resolution. And now his mother in her turn began to wail and weep. Thrusting her dress aside, she exposed one of her breasts in her other hand and implored him, with the tears running down her checks. "Hector, my child," she cried, "have some regard for this, and pity me. How often have I given you this breast and soothed you with its milk! Bear in mind those days, dear child. Deal with your enemy from within the walls, and do not go out to meet that man in single combat. He is a savage; and you need not think that, if he kills you, I shall lay you on a bier and weep for you, my own, my darling boy; nor will your richly dowered wife; but far away from both of us, beside the Argive ships, you will be eaten by the nimble dogs."

Thus they appealed in tears to their dear son. But all their entreaties were wasted on Hector, who stuck to his post and let the monstrous Achilles approach him. As a mountain snake, who is maddened by the poisonous herbs he has swallowed, allows a man to come up to the lair where he lies coiled, and watches him with a baleful glitter in his eye, Hector stood firm and unflinching, with his glittering shield supported by an outwork of the wall. But he was none the less appalled, and groaning at his plight he took counsel with his indomitable soul. He thought: "If I retire behind the gate and wall, Polydamas will be the first to cast it in my teeth that, in this last night of disaster when the great Achilles came to life, I did not take his advice and order a withdrawal into the city, as I certainly ought to have done. As it is, having sacrificed the army to my own perversity, I could not face my countrymen and the Trojan ladies in their trailing gowns. I could not bear to hear some commoner say: 'Hector trusted his own right arm and lost an army.' But it *will* be said, and then I shall know that it would have been a far better thing for me to stand up to Achilles, and either kill him and come home alive or myself die gloriously in front of Troy."

When Achilles approaches Hector brandishing a "formidable . . . spear . . . and the bronze on his body glowed like a blazing fire, . . . Hector looked up, saw him, and began to tremble. He no longer had the heart to stand his ground . . . and ran away in terror." Achilles relentlessly pursues the fleeing Hector. But then Hector stops and addresses Achilles.

"My lord Achilles, I have been chased by you three times round the great city of Priam without daring to stop and let you come near. But now I am going to run away no longer. I have made up my mind to fight you man to man and kill you or be killed. But first let us make a bargain, you with your gods for witness, I with mine—no compact could have better guarantors. If Zeus allows me to endure, and I kill you, I undertake to do no outrage to your body that custom does not sanction. All I shall do, Achilles, is to strip you of your splendid armour. Then I will give up your corpse to the Achaeans. Will you do that same for me?"

Achilles of the nimble feet looked at him grimly and replied: "Hector, you must be mad to talk to me about a pact. Lions do not come to terms with men nor does the wolf see eye to eye with the lamb—they are enemies to the end. It is the same with you and me. Friendship between us is impossible, and there will be no truce of any kind till one of us has fallen and glutted the stubborn god of battles with his blood. So summon any courage you may have. This is the time to show your spearmanship and daring. Not that anything is going to save you now, when Pallas Athene is waiting to fell you with my spear. This moment you are going to pay the full price for all you made me suffer when your lance mowed down my friends."

With this Achilles poised and hurled his long-shadowed spear. But illustrious Hector was looking out and managed to avoid it. He crouched, with his eye on the weapon; and it flew over his head and stuck in the ground. But Pallas Athene snatched it up and brought it back to Achilles.

Hector the great captain, who had not seen this move, called across to the peerless son of Peleus: "A miss for the godlike Achilles! It seems that Zeus gave you the wrong date for my death! You were too cocksure. But then you're so glib, so clever with your tongue—trying to frighten me and drain me of my strength. Nevertheless, you will not make me run, or catch me in the back with your spear. Drive it through my breast as I charge—if you get the chance. But first you will have to dodge this one of mine. And Heaven grant that all its bronze may be buried in your flesh! This war would be an easier business for the Trojans, if you, their greatest scourge, were dead."

With that he swung up his long-shadowed spear and cast. And sure enough he hit the centre of Achilles' shield, but his spear rebounded from it. Hector was angry at having made so fine a throw for nothing, and he stood there discomfited, for he had no second lance. He shouted aloud to Dei- phobus of the white shield, asking him for a long spear. But Deiphobus was nowhere near him; and Hector, realizing what had happened, cried: "Alas! So the gods did beckon me to my death! I thought the good Deiphobus was at my side; but he is in the town, and Athene has fooled me. Death is no longer far away; he is staring me in the face and there is no escaping him. Zeus and his Archer Son must long have been resolved on this, for all their goodwill and the help they gave me. So now I meet my doom. Let me at least sell my life dearly and have a not inglorious end, after some feat of arms that shall come to the ears of generations still unborn."

Hanging down at his side, Hector had a sharp, long and weighty sword. He drew this now, braced himself, and swooped like a high-flying eagle that drops to earth through the black clouds to pounce on a tender lamb or a crouching hare. Thus Hector charged, brandishing his sharp sword. Achilles sprang to meet him, inflamed with savage passion. He kept his front covered with his decorated shield; his glittering helmet with its four plates swayed as he moved his head and made the splendid golden plumes that Hephaestus had lavished on the crest dance round the top; and bright as the loveliest jewel in the sky, the Evening Star when he comes out at nightfall with the rest, the sharp point scintillated on the spear he balanced in his right hand, intent on killing Hector, and searching him for the likeliest place to reach his flesh.

Achilles saw that Hector's body was completely covered by the fine bronze armour he had taken from the great Patroclus when he killed him, except for an opening at the gullet where the collar bones lead over from the shoulders to the neck, the easiest place to kill a man. As Hector charged him, Prince Achilles drove at this spot with his lance; and the point went right through the tender flesh of Hector's neck, though the heavy bronze head did not cut his windpipe, and left him able to address his conqueror. Hector came down in the dust and the great Achilles triumphed over him. "Hector," he said, "no doubt you fancied as you stripped Patroclus that you would be safe. You never thought of me: I was too far away. You were a fool. Down by the hollow ships there was a man far better than Patroclus in reserve, the man who has brought you low. So now the dogs and birds of prey are going to maul and mangle you, while we Achaeans hold Patroclus' funeral."

"I beseech you," said Hector of the glittering helmet in a failing voice, "by your knees, by your own life and by your parents, not to throw my body to the dogs at the Achaean ships, but to take a ransom for me. My father and my lady mother will pay you bronze and gold in plenty. Give up my body to be taken home, so that the Trojans and their wives may honour me in death with the ritual of fire."

The swift Achilles scowled at him. "You cur," he said, "don't talk to me of knees or name my parents in your prayers. I only wish that I could summon up the appetite to carve and eat you raw myself, for what you have done to me. But this at least is certain, that nobody is going to keep the dogs from you, not even if the Trojans bring here and weigh out a ransom ten or twenty times your worth, and promise more besides; not if Dardanian Priam tells them to pay your weight in gold—not even so shall your lady mother lay you on a bier to mourn the son she bore, but the dogs and birds of prey shall eat you up."

Hector of the flashing helmet spoke to him once more at the point of death. "How well I know you and can read your mind!" he said. "Your heart is hard as iron—I have been wasting my breath. Nevertheless, pause before you act, in case the angry gods remember how you treated me, when your turn comes and you are brought down at the Scaean Gate in all your glory by Paris and Apollo."

Death cut Hector short and his disembodied soul took wing for the House of Hades, bewailing its lot and the youth and manhood that it left. But Prince Achilles spoke to him again though he was gone. "Die!" he said. "As for my own death, let it come when Zeus and the other deathless gods decide."

Then he withdrew his bronze spear from the corpse and laid it down. As he removed the bloodstained arms from Hector's shoulders, other Achaean warriors came running up and gathered round. They gazed in wonder at the size and marvellous good looks of Hector. And not a man of all who had collected there left him without a wound. As each went in and struck the corpse, he looked at his friends, and the jest went round: "Hector is easier to handle now than when he set the ships on fire."

After stripping Hector, the swift and excellent Achilles stood up and made a speech to the Achaeans. "My friends," he said, "Captains and Counsellors of the Argives; now that the gods have let us get the better of this man, who did more damage than all the rest together, let us make an armed reconnaissance round the city and find out what the Trojans mean to do next, whether they will abandon their fortress now that their champion has fallen, or make up their minds to hold it without Hector's help. But what am I saying? How can I think of anything but the dead man who is lying by my ships unburied and unwept—Patroclus, whom I shall never forget as long as I am still among the living and can walk the earth, my own dear comrade, whom I shall remember even though the dead forget their dead, even in Hades' Halls? So come now, soldiers of Achaea, let us go back to the hollow ships carrying this corpse and singing a song of triumph: 'We have won great glory. We have killed the noble Hector, who was treated like a god in Troy.'"

The next thing that Achilles did was to subject the fallen prince to shameful outrage. He slit the tendons at the back of both his feet from heel to ankle, inserted leather straps, and made them fast to his chariot, leaving the head to drag. Then he lifted the famous armour into his car, got in himself, and with a touch of his whip started the horses, who flew off with a will. Dragged behind him, Hector raised a cloud of dust, his black locks streamed on either side, and dust fell thick upon his head, so comely once, which Zeus now let his enemies defile on his own native soil.

Thus Hector's head was tumbled in the dust. When his mother saw what they were doing to her son, she tore her hair, and plucking the bright veil from her head cast it away with a loud and bitter cry. His father groaned in anguish, the people round them took up the cry of grief, and the whole city gave itself up to despair. They could not have lamented louder if Ilium had been going up in flames, from its frowning citadel to its lowest street. In his horror the old king made for the Dardanian Gate, bent on going out, and when his people had with difficulty stopped him, he grovelled in the dung and implored them all, calling on each man by his name. "Friends, let me be," he said. "You overdo your care for me. Let me go out of the town alone to the Achaean ships. I want to plead with this inhuman monster, who may perhaps be put to shame by Hector's youth and pity my old age. After all he too has a father of the same age as myself, Peleus, who gave him life and brought him up to be a curse to all the Trojans, though none of them has suffered at his hands so much as I, the father of so many sons butchered by him in the heyday of their youth. And yet, though I bewail them all, there is one for whom I mourn still more, with a bitter sorrow that will bring me to the grave; and that is Hector. Ah, if he could only have died in my arms! Then we could have wept and wailed for him to our hearts' content, I and the mother who brought him, to her sorrow, into the world."

Thus Priam, through his tears. The citizens of Troy added their moans to his; and now Hecabe led the Trojan women in a poignant lament. "My child!" she cried. "Ah, misery me! Why should I live and suffer now that you are dead? Night and day in Troy you were my pride, and to every man and woman in the town a saviour whom they greeted as a god. Indeed you were their greatest glory while you lived. Now, Death and Destiny have taken you away."

Thus Hecabe wailed and wept. But Hector's wife had not yet heard the news. No one in fact had even gone to tell her that her husband had remained outside the gates. She was at work, in a corner of her lofty house, on a purple web of double width, which she was decorating with a floral pattern. In her innocence, she had just called to the ladies-in-waiting in her house to put a big cauldron on the fire so that Hector could have a hot bath when he came home from the battle— never dreaming that far away from all baths he lay dead at the hands of Achilles and bright-eyed Athene. But now the keening and moaning at the battlements reached her ears. She trembled all over and dropped her shuttle on the floor. She called again to her ladies-in-waiting: "Come with me, two of you: I must see what has happened. That was my husband's noble mother that I heard; and as for me, my heart is in my mouth and I cannot move my legs. Some dreadful thing is threatening the House of Priam. Heaven defend me from such news, but I am terribly afraid that the great Achilles has caught my gallant husband by himself outside the town and chased him into the open; indeed that he may have put an end already to the headstrong pride that was Hector's passion. For Hector would never hang back with the crowd; he always sallied out in front of all the rest and let no one be as daring as himself."

As she finished, Andromache, with palpitating heart, rushed out of the house like a mad woman, and her maidservants went with her. When they came to the wall, where the men had gathered in a crowd, she climbed up on the battlements, searched the plain, and saw them dragging her husband in front of the town—the powerful horses were hauling him along at an easy canter towards the Achaean ships. The world went black as night before Andromache's eyes. She lost her senses and fell backward to the ground, dropping the whole of her gay headdress from her head, the coronet, the cap, the plaited snood and the veil that golden Aphrodite gave her on the day when Hector of the flashing helmet, having paid a princely dowry for his bride, came to fetch her from Eetion's house. As she lay there in a dead faint, her husband's sisters and his brothers' wives crowded around her and supported her between them. When at length she recovered and came to herself, she burst out sobbing and made her lament to the ladies of Troy.

"Alas, Hector; alas for me!" she cried. "So you and I were born under the same unhappy star, you here in Priam's house and I in Thebe under wooded Placus in the house of Eetion, who brought me up from babyhood, the unlucky father of a more unlucky child, who wishes now that she had never seen the light of day. For you are on your way to Hades and the unknown world below, leaving me behind in misery, a widow in your house. And your son is no more than a baby, the son we got between us, we unhappy parents. You, Hector, now that you are dead, will be no joy to him, nor he to you. Even if he escapes the horrors of the Achaen war, nothing lies ahead of him but hardship and trouble, with strangers eating into his estate. An orphaned child is cut off from his playmates. He goes about with downcast looks and tear-stained cheeks. In his necessity he looks in at some gathering of his father's friends and plucks a cloak here and a tunic there, till someone out of charity holds up a wine-cup to his mouth, but only for a moment, just enough to wet his lips and leave his palate dry. Then comes another boy, with both his parents living, who beats him with his fists and drives him from the feast and jeers at him. 'Out you go!' he shouts 'You have no father dining here.' So the child runs off in tears to his widowed mother—little Astyanax, who used to sit on his father's knees and eat nothing but marrow and mutton fat, and when he was sleepy and tired of play, slept in a bed, softly cradled in his nurse's arms, full of good cheer. But now, with his father gone, evils will crowd in on Astyanax, Protector of Troy, as the Trojans called him, seeing in you the one defence of their long walls and gates. And you, by the beaked ships, far from your parents, will be eaten by the wriggling worms when the dogs have had their fill, lying naked, for all the delicate and lovely clothing made by women's hands that you possess at home. All of which I am going to burn to ashes. It is of no use to you: you will never lie in it. But the men and women of Troy shall accord you that last mark of honour."

Thus Andromache lamented through her tears, and the women joined in her lament.

In this passage, the grief-stricken Priam goes to Achilles and requests Hector's body. Achilles responds with compassion. This scene shows that although Homer sees the essence of life as the pursuit of glory, he is also sensitive to life's brevity and to the suffering that pervades human existence.

. . . Big though Priam was, he came in unobserved, went up to Achilles, grasped his knees and kissed his hands, the terrible, man-killing hands that had slaughtered many of his sons. Achilles was astounded when he saw King Priam, and so were all his men. . . .

But Priam was already praying to Achilles. "Most worshipful Achilles," he said, "think of your own father, who is the same age as I, and so has nothing but miserable old age ahead of him. No doubt his neighbours are oppressing him and there is nobody to save him from their depredations. Yet he at least has one consolation. While he knows that you are still alive, he can look forward day by day to seeing his beloved son come back from Troy; whereas my fortunes are completely broken. I had the best sons in the whole of this broad realm, and now not one, not one I say, is left. There were fifty when the Achaean expedition came. Nineteen of them were borne by one mother and the rest by other ladies in my palace. Most of them have fallen in action, and Hector, the only one I still could count on, the bulwark of Troy and the Trojans, has now been killed by you, fighting for his native land. It is to get him back from you that I have come to the Achaean ships, bringing this princely ransom with me. Achilles, fear the gods, and be merciful to me, remembering your own father, though I am even more entitled to compassion, since I have brought myself to do a thing that no one else on earth has done—I have raised to my lips the hand of the man who killed my son."

Priam had set Achilles thinking of his own father and brought him to the verge of tears. Taking the old man's hand, he gently put him from him; and overcome by their memories they both broke down. Priam, crouching at Achilles' feet, wept bitterly for man-slaying Hector, and Achilles wept for his father, and then again for Patroclus. The house was filled with the sounds of their lamentation. But presently, when he had had enough of tears and recovered his composure, the excellent Achilles leapt from his chair, and in compassion for the old man's grey head and grey beard, took him by the arm and raised him. Then he spoke to him from his heart: "You are indeed a man of sorrows and have suffered much. How could you dare to come by yourself to the Achaean ships into the presence of a man who has killed so many of your gallant sons? You have a heart of iron. But pray be seated now, here on this chair, and let us leave our sorrows, bitter though they are, locked up in our own hearts, for weeping is cold comfort and does little good. We men are wretched things, and the gods, who have no cares themselves, have woven sorrow into the very pattern of our lives."

HESIOD

WORKS AND DAYS

While Homer's epics concentrate on heroes striving to win honor as defined by a chivalric aristocratic ideal, Hesiod's later poem, *Works and Days,* excerpted below, describes the daily ordeal of common folk struggling to feed their families.

A man of the soil, Hesiod also maintains that honest labor promotes the good life. For Hesiod, the farmer who perseveres in his daily labor demonstrates *arete* (excellence); heroes are not only made on the battlefield, but also on the farm in the farmer's confrontation with the land and nature.

But it is Hesiod's concern with justice that gives the poem stature. Cheated by his brother, Perses, out of part of their father's estate, Hesiod feels compelled to instruct Perses and others about the virtues of justice. He attributes the wretched condition of social life, including civil war and slaughter, to a breakdown of moral standards. Hesiod believed that human beings could improve their lot if they embraced justice which is the best thing they have. An awareness of justice is what distinguishes human beings from other creatures. Human beings are faced with the choice between *Dike* (straight judgment and justice) which safeguards society and *Hybris* (best defined here as insolence that is prone to violence) which destroys it. Honoring justice is what distinguishes a civilized society from a state of savagery.

Hesiod used the language and imagery of myth to express a concern for justice and an awareness of a universal moral order. In succeeding centuries, Greek thinkers would discuss these issues using the language and categories of philosophy.

But you, Perses, hearken to justice and don't honor Hybris.
Hybris is a bad thing for the poor man, for not even the rich man
easily bears it but staggers under its burdensome weight and
meets with calamity. Better it is to go on the road in
the other direction to Justice. Justice wins over Hybris,
finally coming in victor. The fool by suffering learns this.
For the oath-god Horkos runs after crooked injustice,
and there's an uproar when justice is dragged off, when she is seized by
gift-eating men who interpret the laws with crooked decisions.
Justice departs deploring the city, its people and ways,
being hidden in air and bringing evil to men
who would make her an exile and do not apportion her straightly.
But for those who give justice to stranger and native alike,
straight pronouncements of justice, and stray not at all from her path,
theirs is a flourishing city, a people who prosper and grow.
Peace, the nurse of the young, is over their land, and they are
never afflicted with anguishing war by far-seeing Zeus.
Never do famine and ruin accompany men of straight justice,
but they enjoy in bountiful feasts the fruits of their labors.
Earth produces her plenty for them. The trees in the mountains
bear for them nuts on their outsides, swarms of bees in their centers.
Thick and soft is the wool which heavily covers their sheep.
And their wives are bearers of children resembling their fathers.
They abound in continuous plenty and have no need to
travel in ships, for the grain-giving earth provides them with food.
But upon those who are lovers of hybris and hard-hearted deeds

far-seeing Zeus, son of Kronos, dispenses his punishing justice.
Often even a whole city pays for the wrong of one person
who is a doer of evil and worker of ruinous folly.
Zeus, son of Kronos, sends terrible suffering from heaven upon them,
famine together with plague, and makes the people to perish.
Nor do their women bear children, but they have withering homes,
as the Olympian Zeus devises. And sometimes he makes them
pay by giving their broad army defeat or bringing their wall down,
or he, Zeus, son of Kronos, destroys their ships on the sea.
Kings, I beg you to take careful note of this punishing justice,
for there are here nearby among men immortal spirits
who take note of all who with crooked injustice trample
each other down, having no thought of divine retribution.
There are thirty thousand spirits on the bountiful earth,
immortal sentinels of Zeus, strict guardians of mortal men,
who keep a watch on cases at law and hard-hearted deeds,
being hidden in air and going all over the earth.
And there is also the virgin Justice, the daughter of Zeus,
who is honored and held in respect by the gods of Olympos.
When she is harmed by anyone scorning her, crookedly speaking,
she immediately goes to her seat by Zeus, son of Kronos, her father,
and informs on the unjust judge, so that the people
pay for the crimes of their kings who making baneful decisions
twist what is right into wrong with crooked pronouncements of justice.
Beware of these things, O Kings, and see that you straighten your verdicts,
eaters of gifts, and no longer think of crooked decisions.
He who devises harm for another is harming himself,
and from the plan that is harmful most harm comes to the planner.
The eye of Zeus that sees all things and observes all things
now, if only it so wills, sees this state of affairs, and
this sort of justice that our city harbors does not escape it.
Now neither would I myself be just in my dealings with men nor
hope that my son be, since it will be a bad thing to be just,
if the deviser of greater injustice will have greater justice.
But I hope Zeus of the Counsels will not yet bring this to pass.
Perses, I beg you carefully to ponder these things in your heart and
hearken to Justice and think not at all of insolent might.
For this law is allotted to men by Zeus, son of Kronos:
fish and beasts of the wild and birds that fly in the air
eat one another, since Justice has no dwelling among them;
but to men he gives Justice, which is the greatest of blessings.
If one is willing to speak what he sees to be justice, what he
knows is the right thing, far-seeing Zeus grants him a blessed life.
But if he witnesses falsely and willfully perjures himself,
being a liar, a harmer of Justice, incurably blind,
he is leaving his family a gloomier future existence.
He who swears truly creates for his family future prosperity.

SOPHOCLES

OEDIPUS THE KING

The major characters of the play are Oedipus, king of Thebes; Jokasta, queen of Thebes, mother and wife of Oedipus; and Kreon, brother of Jokasta. The plot of the play revolves around two prophecies made by the oracle at Delphi. The first one is made to his parents, Jokasta and Laios, before Oedipus was born: it predicted that their son would grow up to kill his father. The second prophecy, made to Oedipus himself as an adult, foretold that he would kill his father and marry his mother. Oedipus, in his futile attempt to avoid this fate, ended up fulfilling both prophecies.

The play begins with a plague decimating Thebes. Oedipus agrees to send Kreon to consult the oracle at Delphi about how to gain relief from the plague. The oracle tells Kreon that the killer of Laios is alive and living in Thebes, and that he must be found and punished to end the plague. Oedipus vows to punish the killer, but the blind prophet Teiresias tells him that he, Oedipus, had unknowingly killed Laios; Oedipus accuses Kreon of plotting with Teiresias to steal the throne. When Oedipus informs Jokasta about the prophet's words, she assures him that it cannot be true, for long ago when another prophet had made the prediction that the son of Laios would grow up to kill his father, she and Laios had exposed their son to the elements when he was three days old to make sure that the prophet's words could not become true.

Events do not turn out, as Oedipus discovers, the way a person thinks and desires that they should: the individual is impotent before a relentless fate, which governs human existence. It seems beyond imagining that Oedipus, whom all envied for his intelligence, courage, and good works, would suffer such dreadful misfortune.

But tragedy also gives Oedipus the strength to assert his moral independence. Although struck down by fate, Oedipus remains an impressive figure. In choosing his own punishment, self-inflicted blindness, Oedipus demonstrates that he still possesses the distinctly human qualities of choosing and acting, that he still remains a free man responsible for his actions. Despite his misery, Oedipus is able to confront a brutal fate with courage and to demonstrate nobility of character.

Thebes. Open space outside the palace.
A group of Citizens is waiting. Enter Oedipus.

OEDIPUS

Thebans. My people. Children.
What is it? Garlands, branches,
Cries, prayers, incense on every altar—
What d'you want of me? I'm here,
In person: here, children, here,
Your father, your saviour, your Oedipus.
You, sir. Speak for them. What is it?
Why are they here? Are they afraid?
In need? I'll help them, do what I can.
To ignore such a gathering, I'd be made of stone.

PRIEST

Majesty. Oedipus. Ruler of Thebes.
We're at your feet. Old, young, fledglings.
Priests—I of Zeus. Young men: warriors.
Others kneel in the marketplace,
In Athene's temple, in the fire-shrine.
We're drowning, Majesty. Storm, blood, death.
We're choking. Crops, parched.
Animals, dead in the fields. Women, barren.
Plague howls through the city, scours us.
The Underworld grows fat on us.
We're here, lord, not praying, you're not a god,
Begging: your children, our father, you'll help us,
We trust you, the storm of fate,
We trust you. You helped us before:
When the Sphinx was here,
Gulping our blood, you came,
You rescued us. A man, a mortal,
No different from the rest of us,
You knew what to do;
With God's help, you saved us.
Majesty, we're on our knees.
Help us, find a way now.
Ask the gods, ask mortals, act.
Your city, lord, save it, save it.
You helped us before, made us glad before,
Don't leave us now. "He saved them once.

Then stood and watched them die"—
Don't let that be your story.
Don't rule a desert.
Your kingdom, Majesty, your people:
Steer us full sail, full cargo, not a ship of ghosts.

OEDIPUS
Dear children, little ones,
I knew you'd come. You're sick, in pain—
And none of you feels pain like mine,
Your king. You weep individual tears,
Each for yourself; I weep for all—
For you, for Thebes, for me.
I wasn't asleep: this isn't new to us.
For weeks we've wept,
Cudgelled our brains, thought what to do.
There was one way, only one. We did it.
His Honour, her Majesty's own brother—
We sent him to Delphi, Apollo's oracle,
To ask what I must do or say to save us.
He should be here. I'm surprised.
He's been away for days. I swear to you,
Whatever the advice he brings, God's word,
I'll do it. I'll obey it. I'll never flinch.

PRIEST
Your words give us hope.
And look: he's here. His Honour: here.

OEDIPUS
Apollo! He's smiling.
God grant good news.

PRIEST
A laurel-crown, full berried.
That means—

OEDIPUS
We'll ask him.
As Kreon enters.
Your Honour. Brother-in-law. Good news?

KREON
None better. If we obey,
If we do as Apollo says, we're saved.

OEDIPUS
If, lord? There's doubt?
What does he say?

KREON
Shall I tell your Majesty inside,
In private, or here, where everyone—

OEDIPUS
Let everyone hear.
Their pain's my pain. Their burden's mine.

KREON
God's words, then, Majesty.
Apollo's words. There's cancer in the city.
Malignant. Diagnosed.
We must root it out, or die.

OEDIPUS
How root it out? What cancer?

KREON
Death. Majesty. A man's death.
We must find the killer, and banish him
Or give death for death.

OEDIPUS
Whose death?

KREON
Laios, Majesty. Before you came,
Our lord before you came.

OEDIPUS
We know the name. Never knew the man.

KREON
We must find his killers and punish them. God's words.

OEDIPUS
Where, find? It's years ago.

KREON
Here, Majesty.
"Look carefully, you'll find": Apollo's words.

OEDIPUS
This Laios—where was he killed?
In Thebes? In the fields? Away?

KREON
He visited the oracle, they say,
And never came back.

OEDIPUS
No witnesses? Fellow-travellers?

KREON
One, Majesty. The rest are dead.
A poor witness, terrified.
Only one small clue.

OEDIPUS
What clue?

KREON
A band of men, he said.
Outlaws. Many hands. That's all.

OEDIPUS
Outlaws. The King?
They wouldn't dare. Unless—
Hired killers? Was this a plot?

KREON
We didn't pursue it.
Laios was dead. We'd problems.

Oedipus

Your king was murdered
And you did nothing. What problems?

Kreon

The Sphinx, Majesty.
More urgent than Laios.
The riddle of the Sphinx.

Oedipus

I'll settle this. I'll find the truth.
God's orders, Apollo's words, I'll do it.
For Thebes, for Apollo. I'll hunt this down.
I must. This touches us ourselves.
The old king dead—we could be next.
By helping Laios, we help ourselves
Up, children.
Your garlands, your branches.
You: fetch the people. I'll do it.
With God's help, win or lose, I'll do it.

Exit.

Priest

We have what we asked.
He's promised. Apollo, fulfil your words.
Come down to us. Save us. Heal us.

Music. Enter Chorus.

Chorus

Sweet voice of God,
From Apollo's golden shrine,
What word for Thebes?
I shake, I cry.
Ee-AY-ee-e, DAH-lee-e, pe-AHN!
What's happening?
New pain? Old agony reborn?
Speak, child of golden Hope,
Immortal, speak!
Come down to us,
Athene, child of Zeus;
Bright Artemis,
Come down to us.
Apollo, archer, yoh! Come down,
Help us, save us now.
In the whirlwind of fate, of death,
You rescued us before—
Come, save us now.
Disaster, pain.
What's left for us?
No life, no green,
Dead children.
Our loved ones slip from us,
Shadows, smoke,
Ghosts in the dark of death.
Countless they lie,
Our city lies.
Dead corpses, weep for them
Wives, mothers.
Cry to the gods, cry, cry,
Help us, help,
Sweet gods, come help us now.
No clash of swords,
No hiss of spears—
Death, silent, stealthy,
He's here, he's here!
What darkness spares
Bright daylight snatches.
Zeus, father, strike him,
End him, the lightning-flash.
Apollo, come.
Bow springing,
Arrows dancing, dancing.
Artemis,
Bacchos lord of Thebes,
Dance him down,
Bright torches bring
And dance him, dance him down.

Dance. Music ends. Enter Oedipus.

Oedipus

Your prayers are answered.
If you hear my words, hear and obey,
Your prayers are answered.
I know nothing of this murder. It's news to me.
I came to Thebes afterwards. How could I know?
But now, concerning Laios son of Labdakos,
I make this proclamation: if anyone knows
How he met his death, who murdered him—
That person must speak, tell all.
No need for fear: no punishment,
Safe conduct from the city.
Was it a stranger, a foreigner?
Tell me the name, you'll be rewarded.
But if you say nothing—
To protect yourself perhaps,
Or one of your friends—be warned.
No one in Thebes, in all my lands,
Will speak to you, or shelter you,
Give water, food, a place at God's altar
On pain of death. Banishment.
You caused this plague.
God speaks; I speak God's words.
Hear and obey.

As for the murderer—
One man or a member of a gang
I curse him. Misery, life no-life.
And if he's mine,
If all unknowing I harbour him at home,
May all I pray for him be done to me.
Your task: obey. For me, for God, for Thebes.
Our country, torn, abandoned, cries out for this.
That such a man should die—your king—
And you do nothing! God orders it: find them.
I give my word, your king. I hold his throne,
His power, his wife (the mother of my heirs,
His own being dead, himself being . . . gone)
I'll fight for him as they would, as if he were
My own dead father. Laios, son of Labdakos,
Descendant of Kadmos, Agenor, Polydoros,
I'll find your murderer. I'll make him pay.
Solemn words. Heed them, or suffer.
Those who turn away: parched crops,
Dead children, barrenness—
All they suffer now, and more.
Those who help, good people of Thebes,
May Justice and all the gods be with you now.

CHORUS
Majesty, your curse . . . I'll say what I can.
I didn't kill him. I've no idea who did.
Apollo ordered this. Perhaps the oracle—

OEDIPUS
If it chooses.
Who can force a god to speak?

CHORUS
Unless—

OEDIPUS
Say it.

CHORUS
Teiresias, Majesty.
God's voice on earth.
Perhaps he knows.

OEDIPUS
His Honour suggested that.
I sent for the man. Urgent messengers.
Twice. He's still not here.

CHORUS
There's nothing else.
Rumours . . . guesses.

OEDIPUS
What rumours? Even they might help.

CHORUS
Some said he was killed by passers-by.

OEDIPUS
Said, yes. No witnesses.

CHORUS
They'll come forward.
They'll hear your curse, and speak.

OEDIPUS
But not the murderer. He'll not fear words.

CHORUS
If anything's known, Teiresias knows it.
He's here, Majesty. They're bringing him:
God's voice, the voice of truth.

Enter Teiresias, led by a Servant.

OEDIPUS
Teiresias,
You know every secret, on earth, in heaven.
You're blind, but you see, you understand.
Our city's tottering; only you can save it.
Apollo's words—those, too, you'll know:
We'll die unless we find who murdered Laios,
And punish them. Speak, Eminence.
What secrets have you heard,
From birds or other messengers?
Tell us. Save yourself, your city, me.
Put an end to it, the pollution
We suffer for Laios' death.
You have us in your hands.
No finer work for a mortal than helping others.
Speak, Eminence.

TEIRESIAS
Feoo, feoo.
What use is knowledge,
When it makes bad worse?
I should have remembered.
I should have stayed away.

OEDIPUS
What's the matter?

TEIRESIAS
Send me home, before it's too late
For you, for me. Don't make me speak.

OEDIPUS
You know, and refuse to tell? You must.
Your own city, Eminence: your Thebes.

TEIRESIAS
You've spoken, Majesty.
Words of ill-omen.
I won't add to them.

OEDIPUS
We're on our knees, Eminence.

TEIRESIAS
Don't ask me to speak. I won't.
OEDIPUS
So Thebes must die. Your fault.
TEIRESIAS
My pain if I speak. Your pain. I won't.
OEDIPUS
Coward! Traitor!
You'd infuriate a stone!
What kind of man are you?
TEIRESIAS
What kind of man are you, my lord?
Your fury.
OEDIPUS
You spurn your own city, and I'm not to feel fury?
TEIRESIAS
It's coming; it'll happen;
My speaking won't stop it.
OEDIPUS
So, tell me. What difference does it make?
TEIRESIAS
Rage all you like, I'm dumb.
OEDIPUS
You go too far with me. I'll say what I think.
I think your Eminence, you had a hand in this.
You planned it, you set it up,
You'd have killed him yourself,
If you'd not been blind.
TEIRESIAS
Is that what you think?
You made a decree just now. Obey it.
Not another word, to me, to them.
The plague-bringer, polluter of Thebes,
Is you.
OEDIPUS
You'll suffer for this.
TEIRESIAS
I speak what I know.
OEDIPUS
Who told you? Birds?
TEIRESIAS
You forced me to speak.
OEDIPUS
Again. Say it again.
TEIRESIAS
You want it clearer still?
OEDIPUS
I want no doubt.
TEIRESIAS
You're hunting a murderer.
You've found him. You.
OEDIPUS
You'll feel pain for this.
TEIRESIAS
More fury, Majesty? Shall I say still more?
OEDIPUS
Say what you like. You're raving.
TEIRESIAS
Intimacy, hideous intimacy with her you love.
You're floundering, Majesty, you're drowning—
OEDIPUS
And you, your Eminence: you're dead.
TEIRESIAS
The power of truth.
OEDIPUS
You're blind.
TEIRESIAS
You'll remember that word, Majesty.
You'll hear it again. Then you, too, will see.
OEDIPUS
Night's all you know. Darkness.
You can't hurt me, hurt those with eyes.
TEIRESIAS
God hurts, Majesty. Not prophets.
OEDIPUS
His Honour. He planned this.
This work is his.
TEIRESIAS
Your work, Majesty.
Your own unaided work.
OEDIPUS
Money! Power! Fame!
How hobbled you are
With other people's envy!
They gave it me, this power I hold,
Gave it me freely, unasked, my city—
And now his Honour plots to steal it.
I trusted him, and he bribes this conjurer
To spirit it away, whose skill is blind,
Whose purse alone has eyes. You, tell me:
Who says you see so clearly?
Where were you then,
When the riddling Sphinx entwined our Thebes?
Your birds, your heavenly voices,
Where were they then?
When they needed a prophet,

A professional, I solved it.
Oedipus. I answered the riddle.
I alone. Native wit.
No birds, no magic. Brains.
And now you try to topple me.
You want to make his Honour king—
And bask in him.
You'll end this pollution? The pair of you?
If I didn't think you senile,
I'd teach you sense.

CHORUS
Your Eminence, he spoke out of turn.
You too, Majesty, your temper.
We need coolness, not fury,
To do what God commands.

TEIRESIAS
King you may be. But still I'll answer.
Point by point. I demand it
I serve Apollo, I'm not your slave,
And I owe his Honour no favours.
You taunt me with blindness. But what of you?
Where are your eyes, Majesty?
You did what should not be done,
You live where you should not live,
You're married where you should not be married.
You're drowning, Majesty.
Don't you understand? You cancer them all,
Your flesh and blood, the dead, the living.
Your father, your mother:
Their curse will bring you darkness
Where now there's light,
Will send you hurtling from Thebes,
Headlong from Thebes.
Where will they end,
What hills won't echo them,
Your shrieks, howls,
When you know at last
What parentage brought you here,
What harbour of pain after such fair sailing?
Agonies crowding, crowding,
Yourself and your children,
All one, all one.
Shout how you like, accuse his Honour, me—
No human being on Earth will match your fall.

OEDIPUS
Be quiet! Crawl home! Get out!

TEIRESIAS
You sent for me.

OEDIPUS
I sent for a prophet, not a madman.

TEIRESIAS
They'd not call me mad, your parents.

OEDIPUS
Now what does that mean? My parents?

TEIRESIAS
Today you were born, and today you die.

OEDIPUS
Another riddle.

TEIRESIAS
You boast you're good at them.

OEDIPUS
I earned this throne by them.

TEIRESIAS
And now you'll earn this pain.

OEDIPUS
I saved this city. You call that pain?

TEIRESIAS
I've no more to say. Boy, take me home.

OEDIPUS
Yes, take him. He scalds our ears.
Take him; dump him; make us clean of him.

TEIRESIAS
I'm not afraid. I'm safe from you.
I'll say it again, what I came to say.
The murderer, the man you're hunting
With all these oaths and threats,
The killer of Laios, is here in Thebes.
He thinks he's a foreigner. He's not.
He's a Theban, a native, and doesn't know.
He's drowning. He sees, and he'll be blind.
He's rich, he'll be poor. A proud man, a beggar.
He'll tap his way with a blind man's stick
In a foreign country. His children with him.
His sons his brothers,
His daughters his sisters,
His wife his mother,
His father his victim.
You asked for riddles. Solve these—
And then, if you can, say my prophecies are lies.

Exit. Exit Oedipus. Music.

CHORUS
God's word in sacred cave
Denounces him, criminal,
Crime of crimes, blood-hands,
Unspeakable. Who? Who?
Run, escape,
Galloping, galloping.

God's son pelts after him
In thunder, with lightning;
The Furies, untiring, hunt him down.
White snow on mountain peak—
A beacon, God's orders:
Track him down. Where? Where?
Bull, wild-eyed,
Snorting, high hills, forests,
Earth's deeps, far underground,
Cowering from heaven's eye
That hunts him, unsleeping, hunts him down.
Words of fear, fear them,
The prophet spoke:
How can we trust him?
We must, we must.
Hearts pound. We're blind.
Unheard-of—a quarrel? When?
Our Oedipus came from Corinth,
Rules Thebes, our Thebes.
We honour him. What does it mean?
Zeus knows, Apollo:
They understand.
Teiresias is mortal—
How can he know?
Proof, wait for proof,
Then believe it. The Sphinx,
When the Sphinx was here,
I saw it, he answered,
He knew. I won't condemn him now.

Music ends. Enter Kreon.

KREON
People of Thebes, they say his Majesty
Is accusing me. I'm here, I'll answer.
If he thinks, as things now are in Thebes,
I've undermined him with words, or deeds,
If he offers proof, I'd rather die than live.
To be branded traitor—by his Majesty, by you,
By my own dear citizens! I'd rather die.

CHORUS
Wait, your Honour. Wait and see.
He was hot with fury.

KREON
I bribed that prophet to lie to him?
Is that what he said? And did he say why?

CHORUS
Your Honour, he gave no reasons.

KREON
But he meant it? He was ... in control?

CHORUS
Your Honour: his Majesty. Ours not to
question.
He's coming. Now.

Enter Oedipus.

OEDIPUS
You! Impudence!
You plot to kill me, steal
My throne from under me—and visit me?
Zeus above! D'you think I'm a fool?
Afraid? Did you think I wouldn't notice?
You dig a pit for me,
Under my nose, and think I'll fall?
That's not how kings are toppled, fool.
You need brains, money, accomplices,
To catch a king.

KREON
That's enough. Majesty.
You've made your charges.
Listen, now.
My turn to speak, to answer.

OEDIPUS
Speak, answer. You're good at that.
But I'm not good at listening—to traitors.

KREON
I said, listen.

OEDIPUS
I said, traitor.

KREON
You think no one's right but you,
No one else deserves hearing. You're mad.

OEDIPUS
You think you can undermine your king
And escape with your life. You're mad.

KREON
If that was true, I'd agree with you.
But what is it you say I've done?

OEDIPUS
You advised me, did you or didn't you,
To send for that. . . astrologer?

KREON
I'd do the same again.

OEDIPUS
How long ago did Laios . . . ?

KREON
What?

OEDIPUS
Meet his end?

KREON
Years ago.

OEDIPUS
And was that bird-interpreter in business then?
KREON
Highly respected, just as now.
OEDIPUS
So. That was when he mentioned me.
KREON
I never heard him.
OEDIPUS
This murder: you did enquire?
KREON
Of course we enquired.
OEDIPUS
So why did our learned friend say nothing?
KREON
I don't know. I can't explain.
OEDIPUS
You can. You know exactly.
KREON
What d'you mean?
OEDIPUS
He plotted this with you: to make this charge.
KREON
Is that what he says? Now, Majesty, you answer.
OEDIPUS
Your Honour, certainly. I didn't kill the king.
KREON
You married my sister?
OEDIPUS
Of course I did.
KREON
You share royal power with her?
OEDIPUS
Whatever she asks, is hers.
KREON
And I share that power, third among equals?
OEDIPUS
And first among traitors.
KREON
You don't know what you're saying.
I want to be king, you say? I want to exchange
A quiet life, easy sleep at night, royal rank,
For the panic and turbulence of being king?
Now, thanks to you, I've all I need.
His Honour, revered, respected, safe—
They smile to see me, they shake my hand,
If they want your favour, they come to me,
I bestow your bounty. All that you say I'd give
For a crown, for the hedged-in life of being a king?
A traitor? Ambitious? I'd not be such a fool.
It's easily proved.
Apollo, Delphi: go there, ask him.
Was the oracle I brought the one he gave me?
And as for Teiresias, that "astrologer"—
If you find any plot between his Eminence and me,
Kill me. Put me to death. I'll guide your hand.
But not on blind suspicion, Majesty. To know
Our friends is as vital as knowing our enemies.
When we drive out friends, we shrink our lives,
our own dear lives. To know an enemy,
One day's enough; to know a friend takes time.
CHORUS
Fair words, Majesty. Take time to ponder—
OEDIPUS
He's poised to strike, and you say take time?
KREON
You want me out of Thebes?
OEDIPUS
I want you dead.
KREON
For nothing?
OEDIPUS
For ambition.
KREON
You're mad.
OEDIPUS
For justice.
KREON
Except for me.
OEDIPUS
A traitor.
KREON
You've heard nothing.
OEDIPUS
I've heard enough.
KREON
Dictator.
OEDIPUS
Thebes is mine.
KREON
Yours alone? Not mine?
CHORUS
Lords. Someone's coming.
Her Majesty, Jokasta.
Let her help you. Settle this.

Enter Jokasta.

JOKASTA

Fools!
The city's dying.
Aren't you ashamed?
Brawling like children.
Majesty, go in. Your Honour, home.
Have done with it.

KREON

Sister.
His Majesty, your husband,
Is trying to make up his royal mind:
Is he to banish me, or kill me?

OEDIPUS

Exactly.
His Honour, your brother
The schemer, the traitor. Trapped.

KREON

If this is true, if any of it's true,
Kill me. As God's my witness, kill me.

JOKASTA

Hear what he says, my lord.
For your sake, mine, the city's sake.
Music.

CHORUS

In God's name. Majesty—

OEDIPUS

What?

CHORUS

Respect his oath.
He called God's name.

OEDIPUS

You know what you ask?

CHORUS

I know what I ask.

OEDIPUS

Ask again.

CHORUS

An innocent man, a friend,
He swore in God's name.
Spare him.

OEDIPUS

And condemn myself?
To death? To exile?

CHORUS

No, Majesty.
By the Sun who sees all, knows all,
I don't mean that.
Our city's dying, tormented—
And now our princes quarrel, pain on pain.

Music ends.

OEDIPUS

So, spare him. And if I die of it,
If I'm driven out of the land I love,
On your head be it. Because you ask,
I do it. Not for him. Oh, not for him.

KREON

So merciful, so gracious!
You'll regret this. When your fury cools,
You'll regret it. You scald yourself.

OEDIPUS

In God's name, get out!

KREON

As you wish. They know I'm innocent.

Exit. Music.

CHORUS

Lady, go in.
Take his Majesty. Go in.

JOKASTA

First tell me what's happened.

CHORUS

Suspicion . . . accusation . . . unjust.

JOKASTA

From both?

CHORUS

From both.

JOKASTA

What words?

CHORUS

Lady, they're said.
As things now are,
They're best forgotten.

OEDIPUS

So old you are, so wise—
And all you do is blunt me.

CHORUS

Majesty, again I say it:
Fools only, madmen,
Would try to drag you down.
We were sinking before; you saved us,
You set us on course, you brought us home.
Now a second storm: we need you, need you.
Music ends.

JOKASTA

Husband,
Tell me. What is it?
This fury—why?

OEDIPUS

Wife,
I'll tell you.

His Honour's accusation.

JOKASTA

What accusation, to cause such rage?

OEDIPUS

Laios' murder. His Honour accuses me.

JOKASTA

There's evidence?

OEDIPUS

He spoke with another's mouth. A prophet.

JOKASTA

A prophet!
Husband, listen to me.
No human being on Earth
Need fear what prophets say.
I'll prove it.
A prophet came to Laios—
Not God, a prophet only—
And told him that one day his son,
His son and mine, would kill him.
But Laios was killed,
The whole world knows,
By strangers, at a crossroads,
Where three roads meet.
His son was exposed to die, at three days old:
We pegged his ankles and left him to die
Where no one ever went.
The prophecy was wrong.
The son never killed the father.
The father was not killed
By his own son's hand.
Ignore what prophets say!
What God wants us to know,
In his own good time, he'll tell us.

OEDIPUS

Wife.
What you said. I'm frightened.

JOKASTA

Husband.
What is it?

OEDIPUS

Where three roads meet, you said.
Laios was killed at a crossroads,
Where three roads meet.

JOKASTA

They said so at the time.
They'll say so still.

OEDIPUS

Where?
This crossroads, where?

JOKASTA

In Phokis.
Where the road from Daulia joins
The road from Delphi—

OEDIPUS

When?
When was he killed?

JOKASTA

A day or two before you came to Thebes.

OEDIPUS

O Zeus!
What will you do to me?

JOKASTA

Oedipus, what is it?

OEDIPUS

Laios. Tell me.
What did he look like?

JOKASTA

Tall. Greying hair. Like you.

OEDIPUS

Oee moee.
Myself. I cursed myself.

JOKASTA

What is it?
Husband. I'm frightened.

OEDIPUS

Not blind, the prophet.
He saw, he saw.
One more thing. Answer.

JOKASTA

If I can, I will.

OEDIPUS

Was he alone?
Or was there a bodyguard,
A royal bodyguard?

JOKASTA

Five men. One officer. The royal carriage.

OEDIPUS

Aee aee.
I knew it. Jokasta, who told you?
Who brought back news?

JOKASTA

The man who escaped. The only one.

OEDIPUS

He's here? Still in palace service?

JOKASTA

When he found you here,
On his master's throne,
He begged me on his knees
To send him away,

Up-country, mountain pastures,
As far as possible.
A good man, loyal—I did as he asked.

OEDIPUS
Can they find him?
Find him and bring him?

JOKASTA
Of course. But husband, why?

OEDIPUS
Jokasta,
I said . . . what I should not have said.
Too much. I have to see this man.

JOKASTA
They'll fetch him.
But what's the matter?
Husband. Majesty.
Who else should you tell but me?

OEDIPUS
As you say.
If what I fear is true,
Who else should I tell but you?
Listen, then.
My father was Polybos of Corinth,
My mother Merope.
I was high-born, well-regarded.
One day ... a strange thing . . . nothing . . .
A drunk at dinner said I wasn't my father's son.
I was angry, but did nothing then.
Next day I asked them,
My father and mother. They dismissed it.
A drunken insult, no more. I believed them.
But it lay there, the accusation.
Nagged my mind. In the end,
Without a word to my parents,
I left for Delphi, consulted the oracle.
The god made no straight answer,
Told me instead a prophecy beyond belief. . .
I was to murder my father,
Mate with my mother
And sire a brood that would sicken all who
saw it.
I never went home.
Between me and Corinth,
I put the stars.
To prevent the oracle, the foulness.
I wandered . . . anywhere.
I came to the place
Where that king of yours, you say,
Was killed. Listen, Jokasta.
I'll tell you exactly what happened.
There was a crossroads. Three roads.
Servants, an outrider, a carriage.
Exactly as you describe.
They ordered me out of the way.
The lord, the officer. The coachman jostled me.
I lost my temper, hit him—
And the lord in the carriage
Lashed out at me, whip in the face.
I dragged him out, killed him.
Left him lying, and dealt with the rest of them.
If that was Laios, if that old man was Laios,
There's no one on Earth more cursed than I.
They must turn me away, no words, no shelter,
The whole of Thebes. My own decree. I killed,
And I sleep in the bed of the man I killed.
God's curse is mine. I cancer all I touch.
Exile. How can I go home, to Corinth,
To kill my father Polybos and mate with
Merope
My mother? God's curse. Fate treads me down.
Zeus, light of day, let me not live to see it.
Let me slip away, vanish, wiped from the earth,
And never see that day, that cancer.

CHORUS
Wait, Majesty.
Wait till you hear the witness.

OEDIPUS
The shepherd. My only hope.

JOKASTA
How, hope, my lord?

OEDIPUS
His story. If what he says
Is the same as yours. I'm safe.

JOKASTA
What was it I said?

OEDIPUS
A gang. Passers-by.
Not one man, many.
If he says "men", I'm safe. If not. . .

JOKASTA
He'll not change what he said.
He can't. I heard him, all Thebes heard him.
In any case, Majesty, even if Lord Laios
Was killed by a single man,
The prophecy still was wrong.
"His own son will kill him",
Apollo said. Laios' son, my son—
The baby we left to die.
Prophets, Majesty!
Don't give them the time of day!

OEDIPUS
I hear you.
But still, the shepherd,
Send someone to fetch the shepherd.
JOKASTA
As your Majesty pleases.
Now, husband, come inside.
Exeunt. Music.
CHORUS
God give us reverence,
In word and deed.
There are laws, enthroned,
High in Olympos,
God's laws, born of no mortal,
Unaging, eternal.
Pride breeds the tyrant.
Bloated, distended,
Climbing the high peaks,
Then falling, falling.
No cure. God send us honour,
For Thebes, protect us.
Those who march in pride,
Who fear no justice,
Laugh at gods—
Greed rules them,
Dishonour—
God's arrows, how will they dodge them?
And if they do, if they slip free of fate,
What use are these prayers, these dances?
If oracles lie
Why should we fear them?
Not Delphi,
Shrine of shrines,
Olympia—
Zeus, god of gods, do you hear us?
Your power, Apollo's ancient power, denied.
The age of the gods is over.
Music ends. Enter Jokasta, with offerings.
JOKASTA
My lords, these garlands, these offerings:
We go to pray. His Majesty's mind
Is distracted, ragged with terror:
His judgement's gone, he ignores what's past.
Refuses to listen to common sense.
Hears only what feeds his fear.
Apollo, lord, come down,
Be near. Accept these offerings,
Give us peace, calm our fear,
Our helmsman's distracted,
Oh help us, lord.
Enter Corinthian.
Corinthian
Friends.
I'm a stranger here.
His Majesty's palace?
Please tell me.
Or better than that,
Lord Oedipus himself.
CHORUS
It's here. He's here, inside.
And this is her Majesty, the queen.
Corinthian
Lady, all happiness,
Yours and his Majesty's, forever.
JOKASTA
We return your greeting.
You bring us news?
Corinthian
I bring his Majesty good news.
JOKASTA
Where from, sir?
Corinthian
Corinth. Joy mixed with tears.
JOKASTA
Explain.
Corinthian
Your husband, Lord Oedipus:
They want to make him king.
JOKASTA
In Corinth? But Polybos—
Corinthian
Dead, lady. He lies in his grave.
JOKASTA
Oedipus' father, dead?
Corinthian
As I stand before you.
JOKASTA
Slave, fetch his Majesty. Now.
Oracles, prophecies, where are you now?
This king my lord shunned all these years,
For fear of killing him—he's dead. By Fate,
Not by his Majesty's hand at all, by Fate.
Enter Oedipus.
OEDIPUS
I grant your request, Jokasta.
As you ask, I'm here. What is it?
JOKASTA
Hear this man,
And then see what you think of oracles.

OEDIPUS
Who is he?

JOKASTA
He's from Corinth. Your father,
Lord Polybos, his Majesty—is dead.

OEDIPUS
Sir, is this true?
Corinthian.
True, Majesty. Lord Polybos is dead.

OEDIPUS
Assassination? Sickness?

CORINTHIAN
It doesn't take much to end an old man's life.

OEDIPUS
Sickness, then.

CORINTHIAN
Old age, my lord.

OEDIPUS
Feoo, feoo.
Jokasta, so much for birds and omens.
I was to kill my father. They said so.
And now he's dead, buried,
And I was here all the time,
My sword undrawn—unless
My absence killed him, makes me a murderer.
All those oracles, they're dead,
He's bundled them up
And taken them to Hades. Worthless.

JOKASTA
I said exactly so.

OEDIPUS
Fear blocked my ears.

JOKASTA
There's nothing left to fear.

OEDIPUS
My mother . . . mating with my mother . . .

JOKASTA
You're still afraid of that?
Fate rules our lives, not prophecy.
Live each day as it comes.
You're afraid of mating with your mother
As thousands of men have done before you,
But in their dreams. Put it out of your mind,
Be easy.

OEDIPUS
Yes, if she'd died,
The mother who bore me.
But so long as she lives,
Whatever you say, I'll be afraid.

JOKASTA
Your father's dead.

OEDIPUS
It's her I fear.

CORINTHIAN
Excuse me, Majesty. Who is it you fear?

OEDIPUS
Merope, sir, the queen.

CORINTHIAN
Why, lord?

OEDIPUS
A fearful oracle.

CORINTHIAN
Can you tell a stranger?

OEDIPUS
"You'll kill your father
And mate with your mother"—
Apollo's words. Ever since
I heard them, I've kept from Corinth.
Years. I've kept from my parents;
I've prospered.

CORINTHIAN
That fear kept you away?

OEDIPUS
That and killing my father.

CORINTHIAN
Majesty,
If I ended these fears forever . . . ?

OEDIPUS
Undying gratitude.

CORINTHIAN
It was for that I came—
And to bring you home, my lord.

OEDIPUS
I won't go back to them, my parents.

CORINTHIAN
You still don't understand.

OEDIPUS
In God's name, tell me.

CORINTHIAN
You're afraid of them?

OEDIPUS
Because of the oracle.

CORINTHIAN
Afraid of double guilt?

OEDIPUS
The stain of it.

CORINTHIAN
Be easy, then.
Lord Polybos was no relation.

OEDIPUS
Not my father?
CORINTHIAN
No more than I am.
OEDIPUS
You? How?
CORINTHIAN
Neither of us.
OEDIPUS
I was his son.
CORINTHIAN
You were a gift to him. From me.
OEDIPUS
He loved me.
CORINTHIAN
Before you came, he was childless.
OEDIPUS
A "gift." You . . . gave me.
Did you buy me, or find me?
CORINTHIAN
I found you.
In the woods. On Mount Kithairon.
OEDIPUS
You were travelling there?
CORINTHIAN
Tending sheep, my lord.
OEDIPUS
A shepherd.
CORINTHIAN
—who rescued you.
OEDIPUS
From what?
What was wrong with me?
CORINTHIAN
Your ankles, Majesty—
OEDIPUS
They've been weak from birth.
CORINTHIAN
They were pinned together. I freed them.
OEDIPUS
I still have the scars.
CORINTHIAN
You were named for them, Majesty.
Oedipus: Swell-foot.
OEDIPUS
Who pinned them?
My father, my mother?
CORINTHIAN
The other man, perhaps.
OEDIPUS
What other man?
CORINTHIAN
The one who found you, gave you to me.
OEDIPUS
Who was it?
CORINTHIAN
He came from Thebes, he said.
One of Laios' men.
OEDIPUS
Laios!
CORINTHIAN
This man managed the royal flocks.
OEDIPUS
Can I speak to him? Is he still alive?
CORINTHIAN
Your people know that, not I.
OEDIPUS
You, sir. You . . . you.
Do any of you know
The man he means, the shepherd?
Is he here, still working?
This whole thing hangs on him.
CHORUS
Majesty, you sent for him just now.
It's the same man.
Her Majesty will tell you.
She knew him.
OEDIPUS
Jokasta?
This is the same man?
JOKASTA
Don't ask.
It's gossip. Not important.
Leave it.
OEDIPUS
It could tell me who I am.
JOKASTA
In God's name, stop.
For your own sake, stop now.
You'll kill us both.
OEDIPUS
She may have been a slave, my mother—
But why should that touch you?
JOKASTA
Majesty, on my knees, I beg you—
OEDIPUS
I'll know who I am.
JOKASTA
For your own sake, husband—

Oedipus
That's enough.
Jokasta
Don't ask whose son you are.
Oedipus
Someone bring that shepherd.
Let her go in and enjoy her snobbery.
Jokasta
Eeoo, eeoo,
THEES-teen-e
No more words.
No more. No more.
Exit
Chorus
She's gone, Oedipus
Her Majesty. Storms of grief.
Silence. What's happening?
Oedipus
Storms, silence, I'll know who I am.
She's highborn, ashamed of me, a slave.
But I call myself Fate's child.
The son of Fate
Who gives all good to mortals.
I'm not ashamed.
My sisters are the seasons,
My life in step with theirs.
I am what I am,
And I will know what I am.
Music.
Chorus
If I'm a prophet,
See what's to come,
Skilled in the ways of God,
Tomorrow Kithairon will fill our song.
Lord Oedipus is no one's son but yours:
You're his father, mother, nurse,
We'll dance for you, dance
Who gave us our our king.
Apollo ee-EH-i-e, hear us.
Who was your mother?
A mountain-nymph,
Immortal bride of Pan
Who walks the hills? Apollo loves our fields,
Our meadowland—was it he who fathered you?
Was it Hermes, who rules Kisthene,
Did Dionysos welcome you
From your mother's arms,
A nymph who dances on the hills?
Dance. Music ends. Enter Shepherd, guarded.

Oedipus
My lords,
I never saw the shepherd,
The man we sent for.
But this must be him. He's old;
My guards are bringing him.
You've seen him before.
Look, and say: is this the man?
Chorus
One of Laios' most trusted slaves.
Oedipus
You: Corinthian.
Is this the same man?
Corinthian
Yes, Majesty.
Oedipus
Old man, come here.
Answer directly.
Were you once Laios' slave?
Shepherd
Yes, Majesty.
Born in the palace.
Oedipus
What were your duties?
Shepherd
I was a shepherd, Majesty.
Oedipus
On the plain, or far away?
Shepherd
Kithairon, sometimes.
Other places.
Oedipus
And this man here—
Shepherd
What man, Majesty?
Oedipus
D'you recognise him?
Shepherd
I ... can't remember.
Corinthian
It's hardly surprising, Majesty.
I'll remind him. Three summers
We spent together on Kithairon.
He had two flocks of sheep, I had one.
When winter came, we separated:
I drove my animals back to Corinth.
He brought his home, here,
To Laios' folds. Is this not true?
Shepherd
Years ago. I think so.

CORINTHIAN
And d'you remember the child,
The child you gave me,
To bring up as my own?
SHEPHERD
What child?
What d'you mean?
CORINTHIAN
He's grown up now.
This man: his Majesty.
SHEPHERD
You're lying.
Go to Hell. You're lying.
OEDIPUS
Control yourself.
You're lying.
SHEPHERD
Master, my dear, I'm not.
OEDIPUS
You deny what he says about the child?
SHEPHERD
It's nonsense.
OEDIPUS
Tell the truth, willingly, or—
SHEPHERD
Majesty
OEDIPUS
Take him.
SHEPHERD
Majesty, I'll tell you.
OEDIPUS
You gave him the child he speaks of?
SHEPHERD
Yes, Majesty.
I should have hanged myself.
OEDIPUS
Tell the truth, or you'll still be hanged.
SHEPHERD
Majesty,
If I tell what I know, I'm dead.
OEDIPUS
Take him away.
SHEPHERD
No, Majesty.
I told you: I gave him the child.
OEDIPUS
Where did you get it?
Was it your own? Someone else's?
SHEPHERD
Someone else's.
OEDIPUS
Whose?
Tell me.
SHEPHERD
Majesty, don't ask me.
OEDIPUS
Tell me. Whose child was it?
SHEPHERD
They say it was a child . . . of Laios' house.
OEDIPUS
A slave's? Someone else's? Answer!
SHEPHERD
Majesty, I daren't.
OEDIPUS
You must.
SHEPHERD
If I speak, I'll die.
OEDIPUS
And I if I hear. But hear I must.
SHEPHERD
They said it was . . .
His own son. His Majesty's son.
She'll tell you, her Majesty, inside.
She'll tell you.
OEDIPUS
She gave you the child?
SHEPHERD
Yes, Majesty.
OEDIPUS
With what orders?
SHEPHERD
Majesty, to kill.
OEDIPUS
His own mother?
SHEPHERD
There was an oracle.
OEDIPUS
Oracle?
SHEPHERD
That he would kill his parents.
OEDIPUS
You gave him to this old man?
SHEPHERD
I pitied him, Majesty.
I thought,
"I'll send him away, far away."
This man took him, saved him—
Doomed him.
If you're who he says you are,
Majesty, you're doomed.

Oedipus
Eeoo, eeoo.
Now I see, I know.
Born where I should not have been born,
Killing where I should not have killed,
Mating where I should not have mated:
Now at last, I see.
Exeunt all but Chorus. Music.
Chorus
Who lays true claim to happiness?
In the grey dawn we wake, we know
How all our joy was smoke, was dream.
Look now at Oedipus, at mortal fate.
How proud he stood, how high! He broke
The subtle Sphinx, he was a tower,
A lighthouse, in the agony of Thebes:
He was Majesty, master, lord of lords.
He strode the peaks, he fell.
Disaster, pain,
His mother's husband,
His children's brother—
Hidden, hidden in the dark.
Time found him out. Time saw.
Time brought him down.
Weep for his honour lost.
Who dazzled us, destroyed us.
The Majesty of Thebes.
Music ends. Enter Servant.
Servant
Lords, great ones,
It's happened, such things, such foulness,
The palace, inside, it's happened.
Rivers, washing, foulness,
It's there, it's there. They're hiding.
They're coming, we'll see them.
We'll shut our eyes, we'll see them.
They did it.
They hurt themselves,
They did it, they did it.
Chorus
We know what we know.
What could be worse than that?
Servant
I'll tell you. Tell you.
Her Majesty, Jokasta, her Majesty,
Is dead.
Chorus
Poor lady. How?
Servant
Her own hand.
She did it. You haven't seen,
Don't know . . . I'll tell it,
Her agony, every detail.
She ran like a wild woman.
Hooks of hands, tearing at her hair.
Across the courtyard. Inside.
She barred the door.
She screamed at Laios.
His Majesty long dead.
His child, his son
Who was to kill the father
And mate with the mother,
Man-child, child-man, brother-father . . .
Silence.
Nothing else.
She died.
We didn't see.
His Majesty burst in, our eyes were on him,
Watching him, we didn't see her die.
He was shouting, running, room after room.
"A sword! Where is she?
Wife no-wife. Mother-mistress.
Seedbed."
None of us moved.
Some god showed him the way.
He was howling, a hunting dog.
He smashed down the door,
Burst the bolt from the socket—
And there she was, dangling,
A pendulum.
He bellowed like a bull.
Unfastened her, laid her on the ground.
Then . . . There were pins,
Gold pins, fastening her dress.
He snatched them, stabbed his eyes,
Shouting "See nothing now. Not see
What I did, what they do to me,
Not see, not see.
Darkness. See dead. Not living see."
Each word, he stabbed and stabbed.
Blood spurted, poured,
White cheeks, black beard, red matted, red.
That's how it is with them:
His Majesty, her Majesty.
How blessed they were, how happy—
Now death, tears, pain, all's theirs.
Chorus
Where is he now?
Servant
Inside. Shouting.

"Open the door. Show them.
The people, show them.
His father's murderer.
His mother's—I won't say it.
Banish me, drive me away,
My judgement, the curse I spoke.
I'll not stay here."
His strength has gone.
He's blind. Crushed.
They're opening the doors.
See for yourself.
A sight to turn all loathing into tears.

Music. Oedipus is revealed.

CHORUS
All human pain is here.
Why, lord, why? Such madness,
Such pouncing on disaster.
Which god bears down on you?
Feoo, feoo.
I can't bear it. Can't bear to look.
So much to ask, to say to you
And I shudder, I turn away.

OEDIPUS
Aee aee. Aee aee.
Feoo feoo.
THEEStanoss eYOH.
Where now? Where go now?
I hear my own voice, fading.
God, where are you taking me?

CHORUS
To a place
None may speak of, none may see.

OEDIPUS
Yoh.
Darkness.
It billows,
If fills, it chokes.
Oee moee.
Stabbing, pins,
Pain,
What I did to them.

CHORUS
Pain on pain, your agony,
The torment of those you loved.

OEDIPUS
Yoh.
You're here,
My friend, still my friend.
Feoo feoo.
Stayed by me.
It's dark.
I recognise your voice.

CHORUS
How could you bear it?
Your eyes, your own eyes?
What god was this?

OEDIPUS
Apollo's words, his oracle,
My hands, no one else, these hands.
Why should I see?
Ugliness. I need no eyes.

CHORUS
It's as you say.

OEDIPUS
What have I left to see,
To hear, to love?
Take me away. Please,
Take me, I'm dead,
God's cursed me, dead.

CHORUS
What you did,
What's happened here—
Why did you solve this riddle?

OEDIPUS
Damn him, damn him who found me,
Unpinned my ankles, saved me.
I should have died then, not lived
To savage those I love.

CHORUS
What you say is true.

OEDIPUS
No father-killer then,
Mother-husband.
God's enemy, their son,
The cursed ones,
Their brother, my children.
Evil outrunning evil.
All foulness, its name is Oedipus.
Music ends.

CHORUS
Even so, Majesty—
To blind yourself! Does any crime
Deserve such punishment?

OEDIPUS
Enough!
Enough wise counsel!
What I did was right.
Was I to use these eyes to look on him,
There in the Underworld, the father I killed,
Or on her, my mother? For what I did to them

I should be ripped apart.
My children, was I to smile at them,
Sown where I sowed them? What eyes have I
For Thebes, my Thebes, its towers, its temples?
Its king! I tore myself from Thebes:
I cursed myself, decreed my own exile,
Unclean, unclean,
Laios' son who fouled the gods.
Eyes, ears—
I should dam up my ears,
Seal myself, silence, darkness.
No more hurting.
Why, Kithairon, yoh?
Why shelter me, not kill me,
Why let me come to Thebes?
Corinth, Polybos I called my father,
Why didn't you see, destroy,
The festering soul, your princeling?
Crossroads, three roads,
A stand of trees, you drank his blood,
My father's blood, my own heart's blood,
I poured it,
You drank and drank, remember?
I came to Thebes, I married.
Married! Seed, blood-seeding seed,
The father, mother, wife,
The husband-son,
The children-brothers-sisters,
All one, all evil.
I did it, won't speak of it.
Foulness. In the name of God,
Hide me, kill me, drown me,
The sea, all gone, away.
Over here.
Touch me. It's all right.
You're frightened. Don't be.
My sin, my guilt, it's not contagious.
Enter Kreon, with Servants bringing
two small children, Antigone and Ismene.

CHORUS
His Honour's here.
He'll hear your prayers, decide what to do.
His Honour: as things now are,
He holds all power in Thebes.

OEDIPUS
Oee moee.
How can I ask him?
After all I did, I said,
What can I say to him?

KREON
Oedipus, I won't laugh at you,
Throw back in your face
What you said before.
You men: respect your fellow-citizens,
Respect the Sun above, lord of all life.
Neither he, nor the cleansing rain,
Nor Mother Earth, should see
This foulness. Take it inside.
Let those it most concerns,
Its own relatives, ourselves, take care of it.

OEDIPUS
Wait. Such kindness,
So unexpected, so undeserved.
One favour. For your own sake, Majesty, not mine.

KREON
What is it you ask so humbly?

OEDIPUS
Banish me. Now.
Where no one in Thebes will see me.

KREON
We await Apollo's orders.

OEDIPUS
It was clear enough.
The oracle. The father-killer must die.

KREON
Things are different now.
We must ask again.

OEDIPUS
About. . . this?
The gods' plaything? Ask what?

KREON
They decide, and we obey.
You know that now.

OEDIPUS
I order you, then ... I beg you . . .
Her Majesty, inside,
Bury her, funeral rites.
Your sister, Majesty.
As for me, send me away,
Send me far from Thebes.
Kithairon, there let me live, there die.
They chose it, my father, my mother.
They wanted me dead: I'll die.
How, I don't know.
No sickness will end my life, nothing ordinary.
Something strange, terrible—I've been saved for that.
Well, let it come.

Your Honour, one more thing: the children.
Not the boys, they're grown.
They can look after each other.
My daughters. My poor little girls.
They sat beside me,
Never ate a meal
Without their father, shared all I had
Take care of them.
Let me hold them, stroke them.
Your Honour, Majesty,
They're here. It's as if I saw them.
They're crying. I hear them.
You did it. You pitied me.
You did it. My darlings.
Let me touch them, speak to them.

KREON
I know what they mean to you.

OEDIPUS
God reward you, a better fate than mine.
Darlings, where are you? Come here.
Let me hold you, your brother's hands.
They stole your father's eyes, his bright eyes,
Your father knew nothing, saw nothing,
Sowed you where he himself was sown.
I'm crying for you: look.
I can't see you. I see your future.
Bitterness, unhappiness.
On the city's feast-days, what will you do?
Shouting, dancing. You'll sit at home in tears
When you're old enough to marry,
Who'll have you? Who'll take you
For what you are, forget your father
Who killed where he should not have killed,
Married where he should not have married,
Made children where he was made?
That's what they'll say.
You'll die unmarried, dry old maids.
Majesty, Menoikeus' son, we're dead,
Their parents. You're all they have.
Be kind to them. Don't make them
Outcasts, beggars, wanderers.
Don't make them me.
They're little girls. Your sister's children.
Be kind to them. Say yes, Majesty.
Touch my hand.
Antigone, Ismene, I won't say more.
When you're older, you'll understand.
Be happy. Be happier than me.

KREON
Enough now. Go in.
Music.

OEDIPUS
No choice.

KREON
It's time.

OEDIPUS
You know what I ask?

KREON
Ask again, as we go inside.

OEDIPUS
Send me far from Thebes.

KREON
God's choice, not mine.

OEDIPUS
Cursed by God, I go.

KREON
They'll give what you ask.

OEDIPUS
You know this?

KREON
I promise nothing.

OEDIPUS
Take me inside.

KREON
Leave the children.

OEDIPUS
No! No!

KREON
Give no more orders.
You were powerful once; no more.

CHORUS
People of Thebes, see: Oedipus.
He solved the riddle. He ruled this land.
All envied him. His power, his wealth.
Now the storms of life have swamped him.
Look at him now, and learn:
We're mortal. Count none of us happy
Till we come, untroubled, to the day we die.

Exeunt.

ARISTOPHANES

LYSISTRATA POLITICAL SATIRE

Aristophanes (c. 448—c. 380 b.c.), the greatest Athenian comic playwright, wrote *Lysistrata* in 412 b.c. to convey his revulsion for the Peloponnesian War that was destroying Greece. In the play, the women of Athens, led by Lysistrata, resolve to refrain from sexual relations with their husbands until the men make peace. When the women seize the Acropolis—the rocky hill in the center of Athens— the men resort to force but are doused with water. At this point a commissioner, accompanied by four constables, enters and complains about the disturbance; Koryphaios, one of the doused men, vents his anger. The ensuing dialogue between the commissioner and Lysistrata reflects some attitudes of Greek men and women toward each other.

COMMISSIONER . . . That's what women are good for: a complete disaster.

MAN 1 Save your breath for actual crimes, Commissioner. Look what's happened to us. Insolence, insults, insuffer- able effrontery, and apart from that, they've soaked us. It looks as though we pissed in our tunics.

COMMISSIONER By Poseidon, that liquid deity, you got what you deserved. It's all our own fault. We taught them all they know. We are the forgers of fornication. We sowed in them sexual license and now we reap rebellion . . . (shrugs) What do you expect? This is what happens. . . . (indicates doors of Acropolis) Take my own case.

I'm the Commissioner for Public Safety. I've got men to pay. I need the money and look what happens. The women have shut me out of the public treasury. (taking command) All right, men. On your feet. Take up that log over there. Form a line. Get a move on. You can get drunk later. I'll give you a hand. (They ram the gates without success. After three tries, as they are stepping back, Lysistrata opens the door. Calonike and Myrrhine accompany her.)

LYSISTRATA Put that thing down! I'm coming out of my own free will. What we want here is not bolts and bars and locks, but common sense.

COMMISSIONER Sense? Common sense? You . . . you . . . you. . . . Where's a policeman? Arrest her! Tie her hands behind her back.

LYSISTRATA (who is carrying wool on a spindle or a knitting nee- dle) By Artemis, goddess of the hunt, if he touches me, you'll be dropping one man from your payroll. (Lysistrata jabs him)

COMMISSIONER What's this? Retreat? Get back in there. Grab her, the two of you.

MYRRHINE (holding a large chamber pot) By Artemis, goddess of the dew, if you lay a hand on her, I'll kick the shit out of you.

COMMISSIONER Shit? Disgusting. Arrest her for using ob- scene language.

CALONIKE (carrying a lamp) By Artemis, goddess of light, if you lay a finger on her, you'll need a doctor.

COMMISSIONER Apprehend that woman. Get her, NOW!

BOEOTIAN (from the roof, with a broom) By Artemis, goddess of witchcraft, if you go near her, I'll break your head open.

COMMISSIONER Good God, what a mess. Athens' finest dis- graced! Defeated by a gaggle of girls. Close ranks, men! On your marks, get set, CHARGE!

LYSISTRATA (holds her hands up and they stop) Hold it! We've got four battalions of fully equipped infantry women back there.

COMMISSIONER Go inside and disarm them.

LYSISTRATA (gives a loud whistle and women crowd the bottlenecks and the doorway with brooms, pots and pans, etc.) Attack! De- stroy them, you sifters of flour and beaters of eggs, you pressers of garlic, you dough girls, you bar maids, you market militia. Scratch them and tear them, bite and kick. Fall back, don't strip the enemy—the day is ours. (the policemen are overpowered)

COMMISSIONER (in tears) Another glorious military victory for Athens!

LYSISTRATA What did you think we were? There's not an ounce of servility in us. A woman scorned is something to be reckoned with. You underestimated the capacity of freeborn women.

COMMISSIONER Capacity? I sure as hell did. You'd cause a drought in the saloons if they let you in.

MAN 1 Your honor, there's no use talking to animals. I know you're a civil servant, but don't overdo it.

MAN 2 Didn't we tell you? They gave us a public bath, fully dressed, without any soap.

WOMAN 2 What did you expect, sonny? You made the first move—we made the second. Try it again and you'll get an- other black eye. (flute) We are really sweet little stay-at- homes by nature, all sweetness and light, good little virgins, perfect dolls (they all rock to and fro coyly). But if you stick your finger in a hornet's nest, you're going to get stung.

MEN All (and drums—they beat their feet rhythmically on the ground)

Oh Zeus, Oh Zeus.
Of all the beasts that thou has wrought,
What monster's worse than woman?
Who shall encompass with his thought
Their endless crimes? Let me tell you ... no man!
They've seized the heights, the rock, the shrine.
But to what end I know not.
There must be reasons for the crime (to audience)
Do you know why? (pause) I thought not.

MAN 1 Scrutinize those women. Assess their rebuttals.

MAN 2 'Twould be culpable negligence not to probe this af- fair to the bottom.

COMMISSIONER (as if before a jury) My first question is this, gentlemen of the . . . What possible motive could you have had in seizing the Treasury?

LYSISTRATA We wanted to keep the money. No money, no war.

COMMISSIONER You think that money is the cause of the war?

LYSISTRATA Money is the cause of all our problems. . . . They'll not get another penny.

COMMISSIONER Then what do you propose to do?

LYSISTRATA Control the Treasury.

COMMISSIONER Control the Treasury?

LYSISTRATA Control the Treasury. National economics and home economics—they're one and the same.

COMMISSIONER No, they're not.

LYSISTRATA Why do you say so?

COMMISSIONER The national economy is for the war effort.

LYSISTRATA Who needs the war effort?

COMMISSIONER How can we protect the city?

LYSISTRATA Leave that to us.

ALL MEN You?

ALL WOMEN Us.

COMMISSIONER God save us.

LYSISTRATA Leave that to us.

COMMISSIONER Subversive nonsense!

LYSISTRATA Why get so upset? There's no stopping us now.

COMMISSIONER It's a downright crime.

LYSISTRATA We must save you.

COMMISSIONER (pouting) What if I don't want to be saved?

LYSISTRATA All the more reason to.

COMMISSIONER Might I ask where you got these ideas of war and peace?

LYSISTRATA If you'll allow me, I'll tell you.

COMMISSIONER Out with it then, or I'll . . .
LYSISTRATA Relax and put your hands down.
COMMISSIONER I can't help myself. You make me so damned angry.
CALONIKE Watch it.
COMMISSIONER Watch it yourself, you old wind bag.
LYSISTRATA Because of our natural self-restraint, we women have tolerated you men ever since this war began. We tol- erated you and kept our thoughts to ourselves. (You never let us utter a peep, anyway.) But that does not mean that we were happy with you. We knew you all too well. Very often, in the evening, at suppertime, we would listen to you talk of some enormously important decision you had made. Deep down inside all we felt was pain, but we would force a smile and ask, "How was the assembly today, dear? Did you get to talk about peace?" And my husband would answer, "None of your business. Shut up!" And I would shut up.
CALONIKE I wouldn't have.
COMMISSIONER I'd have shut your mouth for you.
LYSISTRATA But then we would find out that you had passed a more disgusting resolution, and I would ask you, "Dar- ling, how did you manage to do something so absolutely stupid?" And my husband would glare at me and threaten to slap my face if I did not attend to the distaff side of things. And then he'd always quote Homer: "The men must see to the fighting."
COMMISSIONER Well done. Well done.
LYSISTRATA What do you mean? Not to let us advise against your idiocy was bad enough, but then again we'd actually hear you out in public saying things like, "Who can we draft? There's not a man left in the country." Someone else would say, "Quite right, not a man left. Pity." And so we women got together and decided to save Greece. There was no time to lose. Therefore, you keep quiet for a change and listen to us. For we have valuable advice to give this country. If you'll listen, we'll put you back on your feet again.
COMMISSIONER You'll do what? I'm not going to put up with this. I'm not going . . .
LYSISTRATA SILENCE!
COMMISSIONER I categorically decline to be silent for a woman. Women wear hats.
LYSISTRATA If that's what is bothering you, try one on and shut up! (puts one on him)
CALONIKE Here's a spindle.
MYRRHINE And a basket of wool.
CALONIKE Go on home. There's a sweetheart. Put on your girdle, wind your wool, and mind the beans don't boil over.
LYSISTRATA "THE WOMEN MUST SEE TO THE FIGHTING."
COMMISSIONER Beside the point, beside the point. Things are in a tangle. How can you set them straight?
LYSISTRATA Simple.
COMMISSIONER Explain.
LYSISTRATA Do you know anything about weaving? Say the wool gets tangled. We lift it up, like this, and work out the knots by winding it this way and that, up and down, on the spindles. That's how we'll unravel the war. We'll send our envoys this way and that, up and down, all over Greece.
COMMISSIONER Wool? Spindles? Are you out of your mind? War is a serious business.
LYSISTRATA If you had any sense, you'd learn a lesson from women's work.
COMMISSIONER Prove it.
LYSISTRATA The first thing we have to do is give the wool a good wash, get the dirt out of the fleece. We beat out the musk and pick out the hickies. Do the same for the city. Lambast the loafers and discard the dodgers. Then our spoiled wool—that's like your job-hunting sycophants— sack the spongers, decapitate the dabblers. But toss to- gether into the wool basket the good [resident] aliens, the allies, the strangers, and begin spinning them into a ball. The colonies are loose threads;

pick up the ends and gather them in. Wind them all into one, make a great bobbin of yarn, and weave, without bias or seam, a garment of gov- ernment fit for the people.

COMMISSIONER It's all very well this weaving and bob- bing—when you have absolutely no earthly idea what a war means.

LYSISTRATA You disgusting excuse for a man! The pain of giving birth was only our first pain. You took our boys and sent them to their deaths in Sicily.

COMMISSIONER Quiet! I beg you, let that memory lie still.

LYSISTRATA And now, when youth and beauty are still with us and our blood is hot, you take our husbands away, and we sleep alone. That's bad enough for us married women. But I pity the virgins growing old, alone in their beds.

COMMISSIONER Well, men grow old too, you know.

LYSISTRATA But it's not the same. A soldier's discharged, bald as a coot he may be, and . . . zap! he marries a nymphette. But a woman only has one summer, and when that has slipped by, she can spend her days and her years consulting oracles and fortune tellers, but they'll never send her a husband.

MEN ALL There's something rotten in the state of Athens. An ominous aroma of constitutional rot. My nose can smell a radical dissenter, An anarchist, tyrannous, feminist plot.

The Spartans are behind it.
They must have masterminded
This anarchist, tyrannous, feminist plot.

PLATO

THE APOLOGY

Knowledge of Socrates' trial comes principally from *The Apology* written by Plato, Socrates' most illustrious student. (The original meaning of *apology* was a defense or explanation.) In the first passage from *The Apology,* Socrates tells the court that the Delphic Oracle, the prophetess of Apollo at Delphi, had said that there was no one wiser than Socrates. Not considering himself wise, Socrates resolved to discover what the oracle meant, by conversing with people reputed to be wise.

I went to a man who seemed wise: thinking that there, if anywhere, I should prove the answer wrong, and be able to say to the oracle, "You said that I am the wisest of men; but this man is wiser than I am." So I examined him—I need not tell you his name, he was a public man, but this was the result, Athenians. When I conversed with him, I came to see that, though many persons, and chiefly he himself, thought that he was wise, yet he was not wise. And then I tried to show him that he was not wise, though he fancied that he was; and by that I gained his hatred, and the hatred of many of the bystanders. So when I went away, I thought to myself, "I am wiser than this man: neither of us probably knows anything that is really good, but he thinks that he has knowledge, when he has it not, while I, seeing that I have no knowledge, do not think that I have." In this point, at least, I seem to be a little wiser than he is; I do not think that I know what I do not know. Next I went to another man, who seemed to be still wiser, with just the same result. And there again I gained his hatred. . . . After the public men I went to the poets, tragic, dithyrambic [frenzied], and others, thinking there to find myself manifestly more ignorant than they. So I took up the poems on which I thought that they had spent most pains, and asked them what they meant wishing also for instruction. I am ashamed to tell you the truth, my friends, but I must say it. In short, almost any of the bystanders would have spoken better about the works of these poets than the poets themselves. So I soon found that it is not by wisdom that the poets create their works, but by a certain natural power, and by inspiration, like soothsayers and prophets: for though such persons say many fine things, they know nothing of what they say. And the poets seemed to me to be in a like case. And at the same time I perceived that, because of their poetry, they thought that they were the wisest of men in other matters too, which they were not. So I went away again, thinking that I had the same advantage over them as over the public men.

Finally I went to the artisans: for I was conscious, in a word, that I had no knowledge at all, and I was sure that I should find that they knew many fine things. And in that I was not mistaken. They knew what I did not know, and so far they were wiser than I. But, Athenians, it seemed to me that the skilled craftsmen made the same mistake as the poets. Each of them claimed to have great wisdom in the highest matters because he was skilful in his own art; and this fault of theirs threw their real wisdom into the shade. So I asked myself on behalf of the oracle whether I would choose to remain as I was, neither wise in their wisdom nor ignorant in their ignorance, or to have both, as they had them. And I made answer to myself and to the oracle that it were better for me to remain as I was.

This search, Athenians, has gained me much hatred of a very fierce and bitter kind, which has caused many false accusations against me; and I am called by the name of wise. For the bystanders always think that I am wise myself in any matter wherein I convict another man of ignorance. But in truth, my friends, perhaps it is God who is wise: and by this oracle he may have meant that man's wisdom is worth little or nothing. He did not mean, I think, that Socrates is wise: he only took me as an example, and made use of my name, as though he would say to men: "He among you is wisest, who, like Socrates, is convinced that for wisdom he is verily worthless." And therefore I still go about searching and testing every man whom I think wise, whether he be a citizen or a stranger, according to the word of the God [Apollo]; and whenever I find that he is not wise, I point that out to him in the service of the God. And

I am so busy in this pursuit that I have never had leisure to take any part worth mentioning in public matters, or to look after my private affairs. I am in very great poverty by my service to the God.

And besides this, the young men who follow me about, who are the sons of wealthy persons and with much leisure, by nature delight in hearing men cross-questioned: and they often imitate me among themselves: then they try their hand at cross-questioning other people. And, I imagine, they find a great abundance of men who think that they know a great deal, when in truth they know little or nothing. And then the persons who are cross-questioned are angry with me instead of with themselves: and say that Socrates is an abominable fellow who corrupts the young. And when they are asked, Why, what does he do? what does he teach? they have nothing to say; but, not to seem at a loss, they repeat the stock charges against all philosophers, and say that he investigates things in the air and under the earth, and that he teaches people to disbelieve in the gods, and "to make the worst appear the better reason." For I fancy they would not like to confess the truth, that they are shown up as mere ignorant pretenders to knowledge. And so they have filled your ears with their fierce slanders for a long time, for they are zealous and fierce, and numerous: they are well-disciplined too, and plausible in speech. . . .

Had Socrates been willing to compromise and to stop teaching his philosophy, it is likely that he would not have received the death penalty. However, for Socrates the pursuit of truth was the highest human activity; it involved the person's whole being. It transformed the individual, enabling him to live in accordance with moral values that had been arrived at through thought and that could be defended rationally.

. . . But I know well that it is evil and base to do wrong and to disobey my better, whether he be man or god. And I will never choose what I know to be evil, and fear and fly from what may possibly be a good. And so, even if you acquit me now, and do not listen to Anytus' [his prosecutor's] argument that I ought never to have been brought to trial, if I was to be acquitted; and that as it is, you are bound to put me to death, because if I were to escape, all your children would forthwith be utterly corrupted by practising what Socrates teaches: if you were therefore to say to me, "Socrates, this time we will not listen to Anytus: we will let you go: but on this condition, that you cease from carrying on this search, and from philosophy: if you are found doing that again, you shall die:" I say, if you offered to let me go on these terms, I should reply:—"Athenians, I hold you in the highest regard and love; but I will obey the God rather than you: and as long as I have breath and power I will not cease from philosophy, and from exhorting you and setting forth the truth to any of you whom I meet, saying as I am wont, 'My excellent friend, you are a citizen of Athens, a city very great and very famous for wisdom and power of mind: are you not ashamed of caring so much for the making of money, and for reputation and honour? Will you not spend thought or care on wisdom and truth and the perfecting of your soul?'" And if he dispute my words, and say that he does care for these things, I shall not forthwith release him and go away: I shall question him and cross-examine him: and if I think that he has not virtue, though he says that he has, I shall reproach him for setting the least value on the most important things; and the greater value on the more worthless. This shall I do to every one whom I meet, old or young, citizen or stranger; but especially to the citizens, for they are more nearly akin to me. For know well, the God commands me so to do. And I think that nothing better has ever happened to you in your city than my service to the God. For I spend my whole life in going about persuading you all, both young and old, to give your first and chiefest care to the perfection of your souls: and not till you have done that to care for your bodies or your wealth. I tell you, that virtue does not come from wealth, but that wealth and every other good, whether public or private, which men have, come from virtue. If then I corrupt the youth by this teaching, the mischief is great; but if any man says that I teach anything else, he speaks falsely. And therefore, Athenians, I say, either listen to Anytus, or do not listen to him: either acquit me, or do not acquit me: but be sure that I shall not alter my life; no, not if I have to die for it many times.

Do not interrupt me, Athenians. Remember the request which I made to you, and listen to my words. I think that it will do you good to hear them. I have something more to say to you, at which perhaps you will cry out: but do not do that. Be sure that if you kill me, a man such as I say I am, you will harm yourselves more than you will harm me. Meletus [another prosecutor] and Anytus can do me no harm; that is impossible, for I do not think that God will allow a good man to be harmed by a bad one. They may indeed kill me, or drive me into exile, or deprive me of my civil rights; and perhaps Meletus and others think these things great evils. But I do not think so: I think that to do as he is doing, and to try to kill a man unjustly, is a much greater evil. And now, Athenians, I am not going to argue for my own sake at all, as you might think, but for yours, that you may not sin against the God and reject his gift to you, by condemning me. If you put me to death, you will hardly find another man to fill my place. The God has sent me to attack the city, if I may use a ludicrous simile, just as if it were a great and noble horse, which was rather sluggish from its size and needed a gadfly to rouse it: and I think that I am the gadfly that the God has set upon the city: for I never cease settling on you as it were at every point, and rousing, and exhorting, and reproaching each man of you all day long. You will hardly find any one else, my friends, to fill my place: and, if you take my advice, you will spare my life. You are indignant, as drowsy persons are when they are awakened, and, of course, if you are persuaded by Anytus, you could easily kill me with a single blow, and then sleep on undisturbed for the rest of your lives. . . .

Perhaps someone will say, "Why cannot you withdraw from Athens, Socrates, and hold your peace?" It is the most difficult thing in the world to make you understand why I cannot do that. If I say that I cannot hold my peace because that would be to disobey the God, you will think that I am not in earnest and will not believe me. And if I tell you that no greater good can happen to a man than to discuss human excellence every day and the other matters about which you have heard me arguing and examining myself and others, and that an unexamined life is not worth living, then you will believe me still less. But that is so, my friends, though it is not easy to persuade you. . . .

Socrates is convicted and sentenced to death.

. . . Perhaps, my friends, you think that I have been convicted because I was wanting in the arguments by which

I could have persuaded you to acquit me, if I had thought it right to do or to say anything to escape punishment. It is not so. I have been convicted because I was wanting, not in arguments, but in impudence and shamelessness—because I would not plead before you as you would have liked to hear me plead, or appeal to you with weeping and wailing, or say and do many other things which I maintain are unworthy of me, but which you have been accustomed to from other men. But when I was defending myself, I thought that I ought not to do anything unworthy of a free man because of the danger which I ran, and I have not changed my mind now. I would very much rather defend myself as I did, and die, than as you would have had me do, and live. . . .

And now I wish to prophesy to you, Athenians, who have condemned me. For I am going to die, and that is the time when men have most prophetic power. And I prophesy to you who have sentenced me to death that a far more severe punishment than you have inflicted on me will surely over- take you as soon as I am dead. You have done this thing, thinking that you will be relieved from having to give an ac- count of your lives. But I say that the result will be very dif- ferent. There will be more men who will call you to account, whom I have held back, though you did not recognize it. And they will be harsher toward you than I have been, for they will be younger, and you will be more indignant with them. For if you think that you will restrain men from reproaching you for not living as you should, by putting them to death, you are very much mistaken. That way of escape is neither possible nor honorable. It is much more honorable and much easier not to suppress others, but to make yourselves as good as you can. This is my parting prophecy to you who have condemned me.

PLATO

THE REPUBLIC

In *The Republic,* Plato proposed organizing government in harmony with the needs of human nature. Those people who are driven by a desire for food, possessions, and sexual gratification, Plato said, should be farmers, tradesmen, or artisans. Those who are naturally courageous and assertive should be soldiers. And the few who have the capacity for wisdom—the philosophers—should be entrusted with political power.

In the ideal state, Plato asserted, the many would be ruled by the few who have a natural endowment for leadership. These philosopher-kings, the finest product of the state's carefully designed educational program, would wield absolute power: the people would lose their right to participate in political affairs, and the state would manufacture propaganda and strictly control education in order to keep the masses obedient. In exchange, the citizens would gain leaders distinguished by their rationality, wisdom, and virtue. In the form of a dialogue between Socrates and a man called Glaucon, Plato in the following reading presented his views on the character of the philosopher.

[SOCRATES] Unless either philosophers become kings in their countries or those who are now called kings and rulers come to be sufficiently inspired with a genuine desire for wisdom; unless that is to say, political power and philosophy meet together . . . there can be no rest from troubles, my dear Glaucon, for states, nor yet, as I believe, for all mankind. . . . There is no other way of happiness either for the state or for the individual. . . .

Now ... we must, I think, define . . . whom we mean by these lovers of wisdom who, we have dared to assert, ought to be our rulers. Once we have a clear view of their character, we shall be able to defend our position by pointing to some who are naturally fitted to combine philosophic study with political leadership, while the rest of the world should accept their guidance and let philosophy alone.

[GLAUCON] Yes, this is the moment for a definition. . . .

[S] ... One trait of the philosophic nature we may take as already granted: a constant passion for any knowledge that will reveal to them something of that reality which endures for ever and is not always passing into and out of existence. And, we may add, their desire is to know the whole of that reality; they will not willingly renounce any part of it as relatively small and insignificant, as we said before when we compared them to the lover and to the man who covets honour.

[G] True.

[S] Is there not another trait which the nature we are seeking cannot fail to possess—truthfulness, a love of truth and a hatred for falsehood that will not tolerate untruth in any form?

[G] Yes, it is natural to expect that.

[S] It is not merely natural, but entirely necessary that an instinctive passion for any object should extend to all that is closely akin to it; and there is nothing more closely akin to wisdom than truth. So the same nature cannot love wisdom and falsehood; the genuine lover of knowledge cannot fail, from his youth up, to strive after the whole of truth.

[G] I perfectly agree.

[S] Now we surely know that when a man's desires set strongly in one direction, in every other channel they flow more feebly, like a stream diverted into another bed. So when the current has set towards knowledge and all that goes with it, desire will abandon those pleasures of which the body is the instrument and be concerned only with the pleasure which the soul enjoys independently—if, that is to say, the love of wisdom is more than a mere pretence. Accordingly, such a one will be temperate and no lover of money; for he will be the last person to care about the things for the sake of which money is eagerly sought and lavishly spent.

[G] That is true.

[S] Again, in seeking to distinguish the philosophic nature, you must not overlook the least touch of meanness. Nothing could be more contrary than pettiness to a mind constantly bent on grasping the whole of things, both divine and human.

[G] Quite true.

[S] And do you suppose that one who is so high-minded and whose thought can contemplate all time and all existence will count this life of man a matter of much concern?

[G] No, he could not.

[S] So for such a man death will have no terrors.

[G] None.

[S] A mean and cowardly nature, then, can have no part in the genuine pursuit of wisdom.

[G] I think not.

[S] And if a man is temperate and free from the love of money, meanness, pretentiousness, and cowardice, he will not be hard to deal with or dishonest. So, as another indication of the philosophic temper, you will observe whether, from youth up, he is fair-minded, gentle, and sociable.

[G] Certainly.

[S] Also you will not fail to notice whether he is quick or slow to learn. No one can be expected to take a reasonable delight in a task in which much painful effort makes little headway. And if he cannot retain what he learns, his for- getfulness will leave no room in his head for knowledge; and so, having all his toil for nothing, he can only end by hating himself as well as his fruitless occupation. We must not, then, count a forgetful mind as competent to pursue wisdom; we must require a good memory.

[G] By all means.

[S] Further, there is in some natures a crudity and awkwardness that can only tend to a lack of measure and proportion; and there is a close affinity between proportion and truth. Hence, besides our other requirements, we shall look for a mind endowed with measure and grace, which will be instinctively drawn to see every reality in its true light.

[G] Yes.

[S] Well then, now that we have enumerated the qualities of a mind destined to take its full part in the apprehension of reality, have you any doubt about their being indispensable and all necessarily going together?

[G] None whatever.

[S] Then have you any fault to find with a pursuit which none can worthily follow who is not by nature quick to learn and to remember, magnanimous and gracious, the friend and kinsman of truth, justice, courage, temperance?

Plato said that genuine philosophers are "those whose passion it is to see the truth." For Plato, unlike the Sophists, standards of beauty, justice, and goodness exist that are universally valid—that apply to all peoples at all times. Plato held that these standards are in a higher world, the realm of Forms or Ideas. This world of Forms is known only through the mind, not the senses. For example, a sculptor observes many bodies but they all possess flaws; in his mind's eye he perceives the world of Ideas and tries to reproduce with his art the perfect human form. Plato says that the ordinary person, basing opinion on everyday experience, has an imperfect understanding of beauty, goodness, and justice, whereas the philosopher, through reason, reaches beyond sense perception to the realm of Forms and discovers truth. Such people are the natural rulers of the state; only they are capable of a correct understanding of justice; only they have the wisdom to reform the state in the best interests of all its citizens.

The distinction between a higher world of truth and a lower world of imperfection, deception, and illusion is illustrated in Plato's famous "Allegory of the Cave." Plato, through the dialogue of Socrates and Glaucon, compares those persons without a knowledge of the Forms to prisoners in a dark cave.

[S] Next, said I, here is a parable to illustrate the degrees in which our nature may be enlightened or unenlightened. Imagine the condition of men living in a sort of cavernous chamber underground, with an entrance open to the light and a long passage all down the cave. Here they have been from childhood, chained by the leg and also by the neck, so that they cannot move and can see only what is in front of them, because the chains will not let them turn their heads. At some distance higher up is the light of a fire burning behind them; and between the prisoners and the fire is a track with a parapet built along it, like the screen at a puppet-show, which hides the performers while they show their puppets over the top.

[G] I see, said he.

[S] Now behind this parapet imagine persons carrying along various artificial objects, including figures of men and animals in wood or stone or other materials, which project above the parapet. Naturally, some of these persons will be talking, others silent.

[G] It is a strange picture, he said, and a strange sort of prisoners.

[S] Like ourselves, I replied; for in the first place prisoners so confined would have seen nothing of themselves or of one another, except the shadows thrown by the fire-light on the wall of the Cave facing them, would they?

[G] Not if all their lives they had been prevented from moving their heads.

[S] And they would have seen as little of the objects carried past.

[G] Of course.

[S] Now, if they could talk to one another, would they not suppose that their words referred only to those passing shadows which they saw?

[G] Necessarily.

[S] And suppose their prison had an echo from the wall facing them? When one of the people crossing behind them spoke, they could only suppose that the sound came from the shadow passing before their eyes.

[G] No doubt.

[S] In every way, then, such prisoners would recognize as reality nothing but the shadows of those artificial objects.

[G] Inevitably. . . .

To the prisoners chained in the cave, the shadows of the artificial objects constitute reality. When a freed prisoner ascends from the cave to the sunlight, he sees a totally different world. Returning to the cave, he tries to tell the prisoners that the shadows are only poor imitations of reality, but they laugh at him, for their opinions have been shaped by the only world they know. The meaning of the parable is clear: the philosophers who ascend to the higher world of Forms possess true knowledge; everyone else possesses mere opinions, deceptive beliefs, and illusions. The philosophers have a duty to guide the ignorant.

[S] Now consider what would happen if their release from the chains and the healing of their unwisdom should come about in this way. Suppose one of them were set free and forced suddenly to stand up, turn his head, and walk with eyes lifted to the light; all these movements would be painful, and he would be too dazzled to make out the objects whose shadows he had been used to see. What do you think he would say, if someone told him that what he had formerly seen was meaningless illusion, but now, being somewhat nearer to reality and turned towards more real objects, he was getting a truer view? Suppose further that he were shown the various objects being carried by and were made to say, in reply to questions, what each of them was. Would he not be perplexed and believe the objects now shown him to be not so real as what he formerly saw?

[G] Yes, not nearly so real.

[S] And if he were forced to look at the fire-light itself, would not his eyes ache, so that he would try to escape and turn back to the things which he could see distinctly, convinced that they really were clearer than these other objects now being shown to him?

[G] Yes.

[S] And suppose someone were to drag him away forcibly up the steep and rugged ascent and not let him go until he had hauled him out into the sunlight, would he not suffer pain and vexation at such treatment, and, when he had come out into the light, find his eyes so full of its radiance that he could not see a single one of the things that he was now told were real?

[G] Certainly he would not see them all at once.

[S] He would need, then, to grow accustomed before he could see things in that upper world. At first it would be easiest to make out shadows, and then the images of men and things reflected in water, and later on the things themselves. After that, it would be easier to watch the heavenly bodies and the sky itself by night, looking at the light of the moon and stars rather than the Sun and the Sun's light in the day-time.

[G] Yes, surely.

[S] Last of all, he would be able to look at the Sun and contemplate its nature, not as it appears when reflected in water or any alien medium, but as it is in itself in its own domain.

[G] No doubt.

[S] And now he would begin to draw the conclusion that it is the Sun that produces the seasons and the course of the year and controls everything in the visible world, and moreover is in a way the cause of all that he and his companions used to see.

[G] Clearly he would come at last to that conclusion.

[S] Then if he called to mind his fellow prisoners and what passed for wisdom in his former dwelling place, he would surely think himself happy in the change and be sorry for them. They may have had a practice of honouring and commending one another, with prizes for the man who had the keenest eye for the passing shadows and the best memory for the order in which they followed or accompanied one another, so that he could make a good guess as to which was going to come next. Would our released prisoner be likely to covet those prizes or to envy the men exalted to honour and power in the Cave? Would he not feel like Homer's Achilles, that he would far sooner "be on earth as a hired servant in the house of a landless man" or endure anything rather than go back to his old beliefs and live in the old way?

[G] Yes, he would prefer any fate to such a life.

[S] Now imagine what would happen if he went down again to take his former seat in the Cave. Coming suddenly out of the sunlight, his eyes would be filled with darkness. He might be required once more to deliver his opinion on those shadows, in competition with the prisoners who had never been released, while his eyesight was still dim and unsteady; and it might take some time to become used to the darkness. They would laugh at him and say that he had gone up only to come back with his sight ruined; it was worth no one's while even to attempt the ascent. If they could lay hands on the man who was trying to set them free and lead them up, they would kill him.

[G] Yes, they would.

[S] Every feature in this parable, my dear Glaucon, is meant to fit our earlier analysis. The prison dwelling corresponds to the region revealed to us through the sense of sight, and the fire-light within it to the power of the Sun. The ascent to see the things in the upper world you may take as standing for the upward journey of the soul into the region of the intelligible; then you will be in possession of what I surmise, since that is what you wish to be told. Heaven knows whether it is true; but this, at any rate, is how it appears to me. In the world of knowledge, the last thing to be perceived and only with great difficulty is the essential Form of Goodness. Once it is perceived, the conclusion must follow that, for all things, this is the cause of whatever is right and good; in the visible world it gives birth to light and to the lord of light, while it is itself sovereign in the intelligible world and the parent of intelligence and truth. Without having had a vision of this Form no one can act with wisdom, either in his own life or in matters of state. . . .

For Plato, the perfect state, like the well-formed soul, is one governed by reason. By contrast, in the imperfect state, as in the imperfect soul, greed, selfishness, desire, and disorder predominate. Democracy is flawed, said Plato, because most people lack the ability to deal intelligently with matters of state. In the end, the democratic state degenerates into anarchy, and the way is prepared for a tyrant. Plato viewed the tyrant as the most despicable of persons. A slave to his own passions, said Plato, the tyrant is like a lunatic who "dreams that he can lord it over all mankind and heaven besides." The character of the philosopher is the very opposite of the sick soul of the tyrant. In the following passage, Plato discusses what he regards as democracy's weaknesses.

[S] And when the poor win, the result is a democracy. They kill some of the opposite party, banish others, and grant the rest an equal share in civil rights and government, officials being usually appointed by lot.

[G] Yes, that is how a democracy comes to be established, whether by force of arms or because the other party is terrorized into giving way.

[S] Now what is the character of this new régime? Obviously the way they govern themselves will throw light on the democratic type of man.

[G] No doubt.

[S] First of all, they are free. Liberty and free speech are rife everywhere; anyone is allowed to do what he likes.

[G] Yes, so we are told.

[S] That being so, every man will arrange his own manner of life to suit his pleasure. The result will be a greater variety of individuals than under any other constitution. So it may be the finest of all, with its variegated pattern of all sorts of characters. Many people may think it the best, just as women and children might admire a mixture of colours of every shade in the pattern of a dress. At any rate if we are in search of a constitution, here is a good place to look for one. A democracy is so free that it contains a sample of every kind; and perhaps anyone who intends to found a state, as we have been doing, ought first to visit this emporium of constitutions and choose the model he likes best.

[G] He will find plenty to choose from.

[S] Here, too, you are not obliged to be in authority, however competent you may be, or to submit to authority, if you do not like it; you need not fight when your fellow citizens are at war, nor remain at peace when they do, unless you want peace; and though you may have no legal right to hold office or sit on juries, you will do so all the same if the fancy takes you. . . .

. . . When he [the democrat] is told that some pleasures should be sought and valued as arising from desires of a higher order, others chastised and enslaved because the desires are base, he will shut the gates of the citadel against the messengers of truth, shaking his head and declaring that one appetite is as good as another and all must have their equal rights. So he spends his days indulging the pleasure of the moment, now intoxicated with wine and music, and then taking to a spare diet and drinking nothing but water; one day in hard training, the next doing nothing at all, the third apparently immersed in study. Every now and then he takes a part in politics, leaping to his feet to say or do whatever comes into his head. . . . His life is subject to no order or restraint, and he has no wish to change an existence which he calls pleasant, free, and happy.

That well describes the life of one whose motto is liberty and equality. . . .

In a democratic country you will be told that liberty is its noblest possession, which makes it the only fit place for a free spirit to live in.

[G] True; that is often said.

[S] Well then, as I was saying, perhaps the insatiable desire for this good to the neglect of everything else may transform a democracy and lead to a demand for despotism. A democratic state may fall under the influence of unprincipled leaders, ready to minister to its thirst for liberty with too deep draughts of this heady wine; and then, if its rulers are not complaisant enough to give it unstinted freedom, they will be arraigned as accursed oligarchs and punished. Law-abiding citizens will be insulted as nonentities who hug their chains; and all praise and honour will be bestowed, both publicly and in private, on rulers who behave like subjects and subjects who behave like rulers. In such a state the spirit of liberty is bound to go to all lengths. . . .

. . . The parent falls into the habit of behaving like the child, and the child like the parent: the father is afraid of his sons, and they show no fear or respect for their parents, in order to assert their freedom. ... To descend to smaller matters, the schoolmaster timidly flatters his pupils, and the pupils make light of their masters as well as of their attendants. Generally speaking, the young copy their elders, argue with them, and will not do as they are told; while the old, anxious not to be thought disagreeable tyrants, imitate the young and condescend to enter into their jokes and amusements. . . .

Putting all these items together, you can see the result: the citizens become so sensitive that they resent the slightest application of control as intolerable tyranny, and in their resolve to have no master they end by disregarding even the law, written or unwritten.

[G] Yes, I know that only too well.

[S] Such then, I should say, is the seed, so full of fair promise, from which springs despotism.

LUCRETIUS
DENUNCIATION OF RELIGION

The writings of the Greek philosopher Epicurus (see page 91) soon won admirers in Rome. Lucretius (c. 96—c. 55 b.c.), the leading Roman Epicurean philosopher, lived in a time of civil war, which was fostered by two generals, Marius and Sulla. Distraught by the seemingly endless strife, Lucretius yearned for philosophical tranquillity. Like Epicurus, he believed that religion prompted people to perform evil deeds and caused them to experience terrible anxiety about death and eternal punishment. Like his mentor, Lucretius advanced a materialistic conception of nature, one that left no room for the activity of gods— mechanical laws, not the gods, governed all physical happenings. To dispel the fear of punishment after death, Lucretius marshaled arguments to prove that the soul perishes with the body. He proposed that the simple life, devoid of political involvement and excessive passion, was the highest good. Epicurus' disparagement of politics and public service and rejection of the goals of power and glory ran counter to the accepted Roman ideal of virtue. On the other hand, his praise of the quiet life amid a community of friends and his advice on how to deal with life's misfortunes with serenity had great appeal to first-century Romans who were disgusted with civil strife.

In the following selection from *On the Nature of Things,* Lucretius expresses his hostility to religion and his admiration for Epicurus, "the first to stand firm in defiance" of the fables about the gods.

When before our eyes man's life lay groveling, prostrate,
Crushed to the dust under the burden of Religion
(Which thrust its head from heaven, its horrible face
Glowering over mankind born to die),
One man, a Greek [Epicurus], was the first mortal who dared
Oppose his eyes, the first to stand firm in defiance.
Not the fables of gods, nor lightning, nor the menacing
Rumble of heaven could daunt him, but all the more
They whetted his keen mind with longing to be
First to smash open the tight-barred gates of Nature.
His vigor of mind prevailed, and he strode far
Beyond the fiery battlements of the world,
Raiding the fields of the unmeasured All.
Our victor returns with knowledge of what can arise,
What cannot, what law grants each thing its own
Deep-driven boundary stone and finite scope.
Religion now lies trampled beneath our feet,
And we are made gods by the victory.

In Greek mythology, Agamemnon was compelled to sacrifice his daughter Iphigenia. A seer had declared that the goddess Artemis demanded the sacrifice. For Lucretius, this event illustrates how religion "gives birth to evil and blasphemous deeds."

You hear these things, and I fear you'll think yourself
On the road to evil, learning the fundamentals
Of blasphemy. Not so! Too often Religion
Herself gives birth to evil and blasphemous deeds.
At Aulis, for instance: the pride of the Greek people,
The chosen peers, defiled Diana's[3] altar

[3] Diana was the Roman goddess of nature and protector of women.

With the shameful blood of the virgin Iphigenia.
As soon as they tressed her hair with the ritual fillet [headband],
The tassels spilling neatly upon each cheek,
And she sensed her grieving father beside the altar
With the acolytes nearby, hiding the knife,
And countrymen weeping to look upon her—mute
With fear, she fell to her knees, she groped for the earth.
Poor girl, what good did it do her then, that she
Was the first to give the king the name of "father"?
Up to the altar the men escorted her, trembling:
Not so that when her solemn rites were finished
She might be cheered in the ringing wedding-hymn,
But filthily, at the marrying age, unblemished
Victim, she fell by her father's slaughter-stroke. . . .

Lucretius attempts to explain why people came to believe in powerful gods.

How the idea of gods spread to all nations,
Stocking their cities with altars and making men tremble
To undertake the solemn rites, which flourish
With all our luxury and magnificence
(Even now sowing in us the seeds of horror,
Urging us on to rear across the world
New shrines to the gods to crowd on festival days),
Is not hard to explain in a few words.
In those days mortal men saw while awake
The excellent countenances of the gods,
Or rather in dreams they gasped at their vast size.
Men lent sensation to these giant forms
For they moved their limbs, it seemed, and spoke proud words
As arrogant as their beauty and great strength.
Eternal life they gave them, for their faces
And their physiques persisted ever-present,
And they thought that beings endowed with such great power
Could never be put to rout by any force.
They thought the gods preeminently blest,
For the fear of death could hardly trouble them;
Also because in dreams they saw them do
Miraculous things, and many, without an effort.
Then too they saw the systems of the sky
Turn in sure order, and the changing seasons,
But could not understand why this occurred.
Their refuge, then: assign to the gods all things,
Have them steer all things with a single nod.
In the heavens they placed the holy haunts of the gods
For through the heavens wheeled the night and the moon,
The moon and the day, the night and night's stark signs,
And night-roaming torches of heaven and gliding flames,
Clouds, sun, storms, snow, high winds and hail and lightning
And the sudden growl and great and menacing rumble.
Unhappy human race—to grant such feats

To gods, and then to add vindictiveness!
What wailing did they bring forth for themselves,
What wounds for us, what tears for our descendants!
It's no piety to be seen at every altar,
To cover your head and turn to the stone idol,
Or to flatten yourself on the ground and lift your palms
To the shrines, or to spray altars with the blood
Of cattle—so much!—or to string vow on vow.
To observe all things with a mind at peace
Is piety. For when we look up to the heavenly
Shrines of this great world, the stars that glitter, the sky
Studded, when we think of the journeying sun and moon,
Then in hearts heavy-laden with other cares
That Trouble is roused to boot, and rears its head—
That the limitless power of gods, the power that wheels
The stars and planets, may be aimed at us.
Then ignorance assails the mind in doubt
About the universe's origin,
About the end, how long the walls of the world
Can suffer the straining of such stir and motion,
Or whether, granted everlasting health
By the gods, they can in endless course disdain
The turning age and the vast strength of time.
And worse, whose soul does not contract in fear
Of the gods, whose limbs don't crawl with terror when
The scorched earth under the terrible lightning bolt
Quakes, and a grumbling rolls through the great sky?
Don't people and nations tremble, and arrogant kings
Cringe, stricken into shock by fear of the gods,
Lest for some foul deed done or proud word said
The heavy time has come to pay the price?
When a high hard gale across the plains of the sea
Rakes a commander and his fleet along
With all his mighty elephants and legions,
Won't he beseech the "Peace of the Gods" in terror
And pray for peaceful breezes and fair winds?
In vain, for the whirlpool's got him anyway
And borne him down unto the shoals of Death.
So thoroughly is human grandeur crushed
By a hidden force; the glorious rods and axes,
Those splendid mockeries, are trampled under.
Well, when the whole earth staggers underfoot
And cities are battered and fall, or threaten to fall,
What wonder if self-loathing seizes men
And they grant wondrous power over all affairs
To gods, to steer and rule the universe?

CICERO
ADVOCATE OF STOICISM

Marcus Tullius Cicero (106—43 b.c.), a leading Roman statesman, was also a distinguished orator, an unsurpassed Latin stylist, and a student of Greek philosophy. His letters, more than eight hundred of which have survived, provide modern historians with valuable insights into late republican politics. His orations before the Senate and law courts have been models of eloquence and rhetorical technique for students of Latin and later European languages.

Like many other Romans, Cicero was influenced by Stoicism. Cicero adopted the Stoic belief that natural law governs the universe and applies to all and that all belong to a common humanity. The gift of reason, which is common to all people, enables us to comprehend this natural law and to order our lives in accordance with its principles, which are unchangeable and eternal. Natural law as understood by right reason commands people to do what is right and deters them from doing what is wrong. Thus there is a unity of knowledge and virtue. For Cicero, the laws of the state should accord with the natural law underlying the universe. Adherence to such rationally formulated laws creates a moral bond among citizens and the peoples of all nations and states. In the following passage from his philosophic treatise, *The Laws,* Cicero explored the implications of the Stoic concept of natural law.

. . . Now let us investigate the origins of Justice.

Well then, the most learned men have determined to begin with Law, and it would seem that they are right, if, according to their definition, Law is the highest reason, implanted in Nature, which commands what ought to be done and forbids the opposite. This reason, when firmly fixed and fully developed in the human mind, is Law. And so they believe that Law is intelligence whose natural function it is to command right conduct and forbid wrongdoing. They think that this quality has derived its name in Greek from the idea of granting to every man his own, and in our language I believe it has been named from the idea of choosing. For as they have attributed the idea of fairness to the word law, so we have given it that of selection, though both ideas properly belong to Law. Now if this is correct, as I think it to be in general, then the origin ofJustice is to be found in Law, for Law is a natural force; it is the mind and reason of the intelligent man, the standard by which Justice and Injustice are measured. But since our whole discussion has to do with the reasoning of the populace, it will sometimes be necessary to speak in the popular manner, and give the name of law to that which in written form decrees whatever it wishes, either by command or prohibition. For such is the crowd's definition of law. But in determining what Justice is, let us begin with that supreme Law which had its origin ages before any written law existed or any State had been established.

... I shall seek the root of Justice in Nature, under whose guidance our whole discussion must be conducted.

. . . [T]hat animal which we call man, endowed with foresight and quick intelligence, complex, keen, possessing memory, full of reason and prudence, has been given a certain distinguished status by the supreme God who created him; for he is the only one among so many different kinds and varieties of living beings who has a share in reason and thought, while all the rest are deprived of it. But what is more divine, I will not say in man only, but in all heaven and earth, than reason? And reason, when it is full grown and perfected, is rightly called wisdom. Therefore, since there is nothing better than reason, and since it exists both in man and God, the first common possession of man and God is reason. But those who have reason in common must also have right reason in common. And since right reason is Law, we must believe that men have Law also in common with the gods. Further, those who share Law must also share Justice; and those who share these are to be regarded as members of the same commonwealth. If indeed they obey the same authorities and powers, this is true in a far greater degree; but as a matter of fact they do obey this celestial system, the divine mind, and the God of transcendent power.

Hence we must now conceive of this whole universe as one commonwealth of which both gods and men are members.

Moreover, virtue exists in man and God alike, but in no other creature besides; virtue, however, is nothing else than Nature perfected and developed to its highest point; therefore there is a likeness between man and God. As this is true, what relationship could be closer or clearer than this one? For this reason, Nature has lavishly yielded such a wealth of things adapted to man's convenience and use that what she produces seems intended as a gift to us, and not brought forth by chance; and this is true, not only of what the fertile earth bountifully bestows in the form of grain and fruit, but also of the animals; for it is clear that some of them have been created to be man's slaves, some to supply him with their products, and others to serve as his food. Moreover innumerable arts have been discovered through the teachings of Nature; for it is by a skilful imitation of her that reason has acquired the necessities of life. . . .

. . . [O]ut of all the material of the philosophers' discussions, surely there comes nothing more valuable than the full realization that we are born for Justice, and that right is based, not upon men's opinions, but upon Nature. This fact will immediately be plain if you once get a clear conception of man's fellowship and union with his fellow-men. For no single thing is so like another, so exactly its counterpart, as all of us are to one another. Nay, if bad habits and false beliefs did not twist the weaker minds and turn them in whatever direction they are inclined, no one would be so like his own self as all men would be like all others. And so, however we may define man, a single definition will apply to all. This is a sufficient proof that there is no difference in kind between man and man; for if there were, one definition could not be applicable to all men; and indeed reason, which alone raises us above the level of the beasts and enables us to draw inferences, to prove and disprove, to discuss and solve problems, and to come to conclusions, is certainly common to us all, and, though varying in what it learns, at least in the capacity to learn it is invariable. For the same things are invariably perceived by the senses, and those things which stimulate the senses, stimulate them in the same way in all men; and those rudimentary beginnings of intelligence to which I have referred, which are imprinted on our minds, are imprinted on all minds alike; and speech, the mind's interpreter, though differing in the choice of words, agrees in the sentiments expressed. In fact, there is no human being of any race who, if he finds a guide, cannot attain to virtue.

MARCUS AURELIUS

MEDITATIONS

Emperor Marcus Aurelius Antoninus (a.d. 161—180) was the last of the great Roman Stoics and the last of the so-called Five Good Emperors. His death brought an end to the Pax Romana. A gentle and peace-loving man, Marcus Aurelius was not spared violence and personal misfortune during his reign. Troops returning from Syria brought back a plague, which spread throughout the Empire. Marcus hurried to the east to quell an uprising by the commander of the forces in Asia, who declared himself emperor. Although the mutiny quickly died out, Marcus Aurelius' wife perished on the journey. Four of his five sons died young, and his fifth son, Commodus, who succeeded to the throne, was a tyrant.

For the last fourteen years of his life, Marcus Aurelius had to deal with tribesmen from north of the Danube who broke through the defenses and plundered what is now the Balkan peninsula. Marcus took personal command of the hard-pressed legions on the frontier. During this period he wrote the *Meditations,* twelve books containing his reflections on duty, human dignity, the self- sufficiency of reason, and other themes traditionally discussed by Stoic thinkers. Written in Greek, this deeply personal expression of Stoic philosophy has been called "the highest ethical product of the ancient mind." Excerpts from the *Meditations* follow.

BOOK TWO

Begin each day by telling yourself: Today I shall be meeting with interference, ingratitude, insolence, disloyalty, ill-will, and selfishness—all of them due to the offenders' ignorance of what is good or evil. But for my part I have long perceived the nature of good and its nobility, the nature of evil and its meanness, and also the nature of the [evildoer] himself, who is my brother (not in the physical sense, but as a fellow- creature similarly endowed with reason and a share of the divine); therefore none of those things can injure me, for nobody can implicate me in what is degrading. Neither can I be angry with my brother or fall foul of him; for he and I were born to work together, like a man's two hands, feet, or eyelids, or like the upper and lower rows of his teeth. To obstruct each other is against Nature's law—and what is irritation or aversion but a form of obstruction?

A little flesh, a little breath, and a Reason to rule all— that is myself. ... As one already on the threshold of death, think nothing of the first—of its viscid [thick] blood, its bones, its web of nerves and veins and arteries. The breath, too; what is that? A whiff of wind; and not even the same wind, but every moment puffed out and drawn in anew. But the third, the Reason, the master—on this you must concentrate. Now that your hairs are grey, let it play the part of a slave no more, twitching puppetwise at every pull of self- interest; and cease to fume at destiny by ever grumbling at today or lamenting over tomorrow. . . .

Hour by hour resolve firmly, like a Roman and a man, to do what comes to hand with correct and natural dignity, and with humanity, independence, and justice. Allow your mind freedom from all other considerations. This you can do, if you will approach each action as though it were your last, dismissing the wayward thought, the emotional recoil from the commands of reason, the desire to create an impression, the admiration of self, the discontent with your lot. See how little a man needs to master, for his days to flow on in quietness and piety: he has but to observe these few counsels, and the gods will ask nothing more.

BOOK THREE

If mortal life can offer you anything better than justice and truth, self-control and courage—that is, peace of mind in the evident conformity of your actions to the laws of reason, and peace of mind under the visitations of a destiny you cannot control—if, I say, you can discern any higher ideal, why, turn to it with your whole soul, and rejoice in the prize you have found. . . .

Never value the advantages derived from anything involving breach of faith, loss of self-respect, hatred, suspicion, or execration of others, insincerity, or the desire for something which has to be veiled and curtained. One whose chief regard is for his own mind, and for the divinity within him and the service of its goodness, will strike no poses, utter no complaints, and crave neither for solitude nor yet for a crowd. . . . No other care has he in life but to keep his mind from straying into paths incompatible with those of an intelligent and social being. . . .

BOOK FOUR

Men seek for seclusion in the wilderness, by the seashore, or in the mountains—a dream you have cherished only too fondly yourself. But such fancies are wholly unworthy of a philosopher, since at any moment you choose you can retire within yourself. Nowhere can man find a quieter or more untroubled retreat than in his own soul; above all, he who possesses resources in himself, which he need only contemplate to secure immediate ease of mind—the ease that is but another word for a well-ordered spirit. Avail yourself often, then, of this retirement, and so continually renew yourself. Make your rules of life brief, yet so as to embrace the fundamentals; recurrence to them will then suffice to remove all vexation, and send you back without fretting to the duties to which you must return. . . .

If the power of thought is universal among mankind, so likewise is the possession of reason, making us rational creatures. It follows, therefore, that this reason speaks no less universally to us all with its "thou shalt" or "thou shalt not." So then there is a world-law; which in turn means that we are all fellow-citizens and share a common citizenship, and that the world is a single city. Is there any other common citizenship that can be claimed by all humanity? And it is from this world-polity that mind, reason, and law themselves derive. If not, whence else? As the earthy portion of me has its origin from earth, the watery from a different element, my breath from one source and my hot and fiery parts from another of their own elsewhere (for nothing comes from nothing, or can return to nothing), so too there must be an origin for the mind. . . .

BOOK FIVE

At day's first light have in readiness, against disinclination to leave your bed, the thought that "I am rising for the work of man." Must I grumble at setting out to do what I was born for, and for the sake of which I have been brought into the world? Is this the purpose of my creation, to lie here under the blankets and keep myself warm? "Ah, but it is a great deal more pleasant!" Was it for pleasure, then, that you were born, and not for work, not for effort? Look at the plants, the sparrows, ants, spiders, bees, all busy at their own tasks, each doing his part towards a coherent world-order; and will you refuse man's share of the work, instead of being prompt to carry out Nature's bidding? "Yes, but one must have some repose as well." Granted; but repose has its limits set by nature, in the same way as food and drink have; and you overstep these limits, you go beyond the point of sufficiency; while on the other hand, when action is in question, you stop short of what you could well achieve.

VIRGIL

THE AENEID

Publius Vergilius Maro or Virgil (70—19 b.c.), the first important poet of the Augustan Age, was born of humble stock and educated in rhetoric and literature, as well as philosophy, particularly Epicureanism. He admired Augustus, his patron, for ending the civil wars and bringing order to the Roman world. Augustus urged Virgil to compose a grand opus that would glorify Rome's imperial achievement. Virgil began his task in 29 b.c., but it took him ten years to produce the *Aeneid,* which became a masterpiece in world literature, and made Virgil the "Homer of the Romans." The *Aeneid* is a long poem that recounts the tale of Aeneas and the founding of Rome. In the *Iliad,* Homer dealt with the conflict between the early Greeks and the Trojans. Roman legend held that a Trojan remnant led by Prince Aeneas, son of Venus (the goddess of love), and a mortal father, Anchises, escaped the sacking of Troy. The first six books of the *Aeneid* describe the wanderings of Aeneas and demonstrated the influence of Homer's *Odyssey;* the last six books detail wars in Italy and show the *Iliad's* imprint.

In Book Six, Aeneas and the Trojans arrive at Cumae, an ancient city in Campania, near present-day Naples, Italy. There, Aeneas consults with the Sybil, prophetess and priestess of Apollo, about how to descend into the underworld. In the following passage, the Sibyl interrupts Aeneas' prayers to tell him about the difficulty of the journey he is about to undertake. She tells him that to gain admittance to the underworld, he must acquire a golden bough, but before embarking on such a mission, he must first bury the body of his friend.

Breaking in, the Sibyl said:
"Offspring
Of gods by blood, Trojan Anchises' son,
The way downward is easy from Avernus.[1]
Black Dis's[2] door stands open night and day.
But to retrace your steps to heaven's air,
There is the trouble, there is the toil. A few
Whom a benign Jupiter[3] has loved or whom
Fiery heroism has borne to heaven,
Sons of gods, could do it. All midway
Are forests, then Cocytus,[4] thick and black,
Winds through the gloom. But if you feel such love,
And such desire to cross the Stygian[5] water
Twice, to view the night of Tartarus[6] twice—
If this mad effort's to your liking, then
Consider what you must accomplish first.
A tree's deep shade conceals a bough whose leaves
And pliant twigs are all of gold, a thing
Sacred to Juno[7] of the lower world.
The whole grove shelters it, and thickest shade
In dusky valleys shuts it in. And yet
No one may enter hidden depths

---

[1] Avernus is the site of an extinct volcano in southern Italy where a lake formed.

[2] Dis refers to the Underworld itself but it can also mean the Roman god of the Underworld, commonly identified as Pluto.

[3] Jupiter is the chief Roman god who commands the sky, light, and weather.

[4] Cocytus (wailing) is a river in the Underworld that flows into the Acheron River.

[5] Stygian water is a reference to the Styx River in the Underworld.

[6] Tartarus is the lowest region of the Underworld where wicked people are punished.

[7] Juno is the wife of Jupiter who is jealous of her husband's many affairs with both goddesses and mortal women.

Below the earth unless he picks this bough,
The tree's fruit, with its foliage of gold.
Proserpina[8] decreed this bough, as due her,
Should be given into her own fair hands
When torn away. In place of it a second
Grows up without fail, all gold as well,
Flowering with metallic leaves again.
So lift your eyes and search, and once you find it
Pull away the bough. It will come willingly,
Easily, if you are called by fate.
If not, with all your strength you cannot conquer it,

Cannot lop it off with a sword's edge.
A further thing is this: your friend's dead body—
Ah, but you *don't* know!—lies out there unburied,
Polluting all your fleet with death
While you are lingering, waiting on my counsel
Here at my door. First give the man his rest,
Entomb him; lead black beasts to sacrifice;
Begin with these amends. Then in due course
You'll see the Stygian forest rise before you,
Regions not for the living." . . .

Before descending further, Aeneas and the Sibyl make sacrifices to the gods and goddesses of the underworld. Sibyl banishes the "unblest" before allowing Aeneas to go deeper into the cave mouth. Once he is inside the Underworld, Aeneas encounters Cares, Disease, Dread, Hunger, and Discord, as well as a plethora of hellish monsters. He finally looks upon "the souls of the unburied."

The cavern was profound, wide-mouthed, and huge,
Rough underfoot, defended by dark pool
And gloomy forest. Overhead, flying things
Could never safely take their way, such deathly
Exhalations rose from the black gorge
Into the dome of heaven. The priestess here
Placed four black bullocks, wet their brows with wine,
Plucked bristles from between the horns and laid them
As her first offerings on the holy fire,
Caging aloud to Hecatë[9] supreme
In heaven and Erebus.[10] Others drew knives
Across beneath and caught warm blood in bowls.
Aeneas by the sword's edge offered up
To Night, the mother of the Eumenidë[11]s,
And her great sister, Earth, a black-fleeced lamb,
A sterile cow to thee, Proserpina.
Then for the Stygian king he lit at night
New altars where he placed over the flames
Entire carcasses of bulls, and poured

[8] *Proserpina* is the wife of Pluto, god of the Underworld.
[9] *Hecatë* is a divinity of the Underworld.
[10] Erebus is the lower region of the Undreworld—a place of shadows and mystery
[11] Eumenidës are the Furies, who came to be known as "The Benevolent Ones," relating to the kind way they treated Orestes after he sought refuge in Athens, following the murder of his mother.

Rich oil on blazing viscera. Only see:
Just at the light's edge, just before sunrise,
Earth rumbled underfoot, forested ridges
Broke into movement, and far howls of dogs
Were heard across the twilight as the goddess
Nearer and nearer came.
"Away, away,"
The Sibyl cried, "all those unblest, away!
Depart from all the grove! But you, Aeneas,
Enter the path here, and unsheathe your sword.
There's need of gall and resolution now."
She flung herself wildly into the cave-mouth,
Leading, and he strode boldly at her heels.
Gods who rule the ghosts; all silent shades;
And Chaos[1] and infernal Fiery Stream,
And regions of wide night without a sound,
May it be right to tell what I have heard,
May it be right, and fitting, by your will,
That I describe the deep world sunk in darkness
Under the earth.
Now dim to one another
In desolate night they walked on through the gloom,
Through Dis's homes all void, and empty realms,
As one goes through a wood by a faint moon's
Treacherous light, when Jupiter veils the sky
And black night blots the colors of the world.
Before the entrance, in the jaws of Orcus,[2]
Grief and avenging Cares have made their beds,
And pale Diseases and sad Age are there,
And Dread, and Hunger that sways men to crime,
And sordid Want—in shapes to affright the eyes—
And Death and Toil and Death's own brother, Sleep,
And the mind's evil joys; on the door sill
Death-bringing War, and iron cubicles
Of the Eumenides, and raving Discord,
Viperish hair bound up in gory bands.
In the courtyard a shadowy giant elm
Spreads ancient boughs, her ancient arms where dreams,
False dreams, the old tale goes, beneath each leaf
Cling and are numberless. There, too,
About the doorway forms of monsters crowd—
Centaurs,[3] twiformed Scyllas,[4] hundred-armed
Briareus,[5] and the Lernaean hydra[6]

[1] Chaos was, prior to creation, a vast darkness from which everything else was created.
[2] *Orcus* represents Death and was often confused with Pluto. His name is also associated with the Underworld, the place to which he carried people away by force.
[3] Centaurs are mythical creatures with the body and legs of a horse and the head, arms and torso of a man.
[4] *Sycllas* was a sea nymph who became a sea monster.
[5] *Briareus* is one of three mythical giants, called Hecatonchires, with fifty heads and 100 arms who assisted the gods in their battle with the Titans.
[6] *Lernaean Hydra* is a nine-headed monster.

Hissing horribly, and the Chimaera[7]
Breathing dangerous flames, and Gorgons,[8] Harpies,[9]

Huge Geryon,[10] triple-bodied ghost.
Here, swept by sudden fear, drawing his sword,
Aeneas stood on guard with naked edge
Against them as they came. If his companion,
Knowing the truth, had not admonished him
How faint these lives were—empty images
Hovering bodiless—he had attacked
And cut his way through phantoms, empty air.

The path goes on from that place to the waves
Of Tartarus's Acheron.[11] Thick with mud,
A whirlpool out of a vast abyss
Boils up and belches all the silt it carries
Into Cocytus. Here the ferryman,
A figure of fright, keeper of waters and streams,
Is Charon,[12] foul and terrible, his beard
His sordid cloak hung from a shoulder knot.
Alone he poles his craft and trims the sails
And in his rusty hull ferries the dead,
Old now—but old age in the gods is green.

Here a whole crowd came streaming to the banks,
Mothers and men, the forms with all life spent
Of heroes great in valor, boys and girls
Unmarried, and young sons laid on the pyre
Before their parents' eyes—as many souls
As leaves that yield their hold on boughs and fall
Through forests in the early frost of autumn,
Or as migrating birds from the open sea
That darken heaven when the cold season comes
And drives them overseas to sunlit lands.
There all stood begging to be first across
And reached out longing hands to the far shore.

But the grim boatman now took these aboard,
Now those, waving the rest back from the strand.
In wonder at this and touched by the commotion,
Aeneas said:
"Tell me, Sister, what this means,
The crowd at the stream. Where are the souls bound?
How are they tested, so that these turn back,

[7] Chimaera is a three-headed monster, with the front quarters of a lion, the hind quarters of a goat, and the tail of a serpent that breathes fire.
[8] *Gorgon* is one of the three sister monsters with snakes for hair, who turned anyone who looked at them to stone.
[9] *Harpies* are monsters that have the body of a bird and the head of a woman.
[10] *Geryon* is a monster who a a large herd of red cattle.
[11] *Acheron* (woe) is a river in the Underworld.
[12] *Charon* is the Ferryman on the Styx River.

While those take oars to cross the dead-black water?"

Briefly the ancient priestess answered him:

"Cocytus is the dear pool that you see,
The swamp of Styx[13] beyond, infernal power
By which the gods take oath and fear to break it.
All in the nearby crowd you notice here
Are pauper souls, the souls of the unburied.
Charon's the boatman. Those the water bears
Are souls of buried men. He may not take them
Shore to dread shore on the hoarse currents there
Until their bones rest in the grave, or till
They flutter and roam this side a hundred years;
They may have passage then, and may return,
To cross the deeps they long for." . . .

Aeneas finally encounters the sad ghost of his father Anchises—the goal of his mission. Anchises points out to his son those souls destined for reincarnation in another body.

"Tell us, happy souls,
And you, great seer, what region holds Anchises,
Where is his resting place? For him we came
By ferry across the rivers of Erebus."
And the great soul answered briefly:
"None of us
Has one fixed home. We walk in shady groves
And bed on riverbanks and occupy
Green meadows fresh with streams. But if your hearts
Are set on it, first cross this ridge; and soon
I shall point out an easy path."
So saying,
He walked ahead and showed them from the height
The sweep of shining plain. Then down they went
And left the hilltops.
Now Aeneas' father
Anchises, deep in the lush green of a valley,
Had given all his mind to a survey
Of souls, till then confined there, who were bound
For daylight in the upper world. By chance
His own were those he scanned now, all his own
Descendants, with their futures and their fates,
Their characters and acts. But when he saw
Aeneas advancing toward him on the grass,
He stretched out both his hands in eagerness
As tears wetted his cheeks. He said in welcome:

"Have you at last come, has that loyalty
Your father counted on conquered the journey?
Am I to see your face, my son, and hear

[13] *Styx* (hateful) is the nine-looped river surrounding the underworld.

Our voices in communion as before?
I thought so, surely; counting the months I thought
The time would come. My longing has not tricked me.
I greet you now, how many lands behind you,
How many seas, what blows and dangers, son!
How much I feared the land of Libya
Might do you harm."
Aeneas said;
"Your ghost,
Your sad ghost, father, often before my mind,
Impelled me to the threshold of this place.
My ships ride anchored in the Tuscan sea.
But let me have your hand, let me embrace you,
Do not draw back."
At this his tears brimmed over
And down his cheeks. And there he tried three times
To throw his arms around his father's neck,
Three times the shade untouched slipped through his hands
Weightless as wind and fugitive as dream.
Aeneas now saw at the valley's end
A grove standing apart, with stems and boughs
Of woodland rustling, and the stream of Lethe[14]
Running past those peaceful glades. Around it
Souls of a thousand nations filled the air,
As bees in meadows at the height of summer
Hover and home on flowers and thickly swarm
On snow-white lilies, and the countryside
Is loud with humming. At the sudden vision
Shivering, at a loss, Aeneas asked
What river flowed there and what men were those
In such a throng along the riverside.
His father Anchises told him:
"Souls for whom
A second body is in store: their drink
Is water of Lethe, and it frees from care
In long forgetfulness. For all this time
I have so much desired to show you these
And tell you of them face to face—to take
The roster of my children's children here,
So you may feel with me more happiness
At finding Italy."
"Must we imagine,
Father, there are souls that go from here
Aloft to upper heaven, and once more
Return to bodies' dead weight? The poor souls,
How can they crave our daylight so?"
"My son,
I'll tell you, not to leave you mystified,"
Anchises said, and took each point in order: . . .

[14] *Lethe* is the rive of forgetfulness.

Later, Anchises describes the illustrious future that will be Rome's. Then, as Aeneas watches a procession of figures from the great Roman past, Augustus appears "beautifully formed" and "in shining armor." An- chises then relates to Aeneas the burdens a ruler must bear as he carries the weight of his people's concerns, knowing he can only correct a limited number of problems before his finite time on earth comes to an end. Anchises also weeps because he knows that the Augustan Golden Age will never again be repeated in the history of Rome. The in- tensely patriotic Virgil thus ascribed to Rome a divine mission to bring peace and civilized life to the world, and he praised Augustus as a divinely appointed ruler who had fulfilled Rome's mission.

. . . Turn your two eyes
This way and see this people, your own Romans.
Here is Caesar, and all the line of Julius
[founder of the Julian family],
All who shall one day pass under the dome
Of the great sky: this is the man, this one,
Of whom so often you have heard the promise,
Caesar Augustus, son of the deified [Julius Caesar],
Who shall bring once again an Age of Gold
To Latium,[15] to the land where Saturn [Roman god] reigned
In early times. He will extend his power
Beyond the Garamants[16] and Indians,
Over far territories north and south
Others will cast more tenderly in bronze
Their breathing figures, I can well believe,
And bring more lifelike portraits out of marble;
Argue more eloquently, use the pointer
To trace the paths of heaven accurately
And accurately foretell the rising stars.
Roman, remember by your strength to rule
Earth's peoples—for your arts are to be these:
To pacify, to impose the rule of law,
To spare the conquered, battle down the proud.

"See there, how Marcellus[17] comes
With spoils of the commander that he killed:
How the man towers over everyone.
Cavalry leader, he'll sustain the realm
Of Rome in hours of tumult, bringing to heel
The Carthaginians and rebellious Gaul,
And for the third time in our history
He'll dedicate an enemy general's arms
To Father Romulus."[18]
But here Aeneas
Broke in, seeing at Marcellus' side
A young man beautifully formed and tall
In shining armor, but with clouded brow
And downcast eyes:
"And who is that one, Father,

[15] *Latium* was the ancient country in which stood the towns of Lavinium

[16] *Garamants* (Garamantes) were a warlike nomadic people living in the northwestern Sahara.

[17] *Marcellus* was the son of Octavia, Augustus' sister, who was adopted by Augustus, but who died at the age of nineteen. Virgil reputedly attended the funeral.

[18] *Romulus*, along with his twin brother, Remus, are considered to be the legendary founders of Rome. They were suckled by a she-wolf and raised by a shepherd. Romulus also served as Rome's first king.

Walking beside the captain as he comes:
A son, or grandchild from the same great stock?
The others murmur, all astir. How strong
His presence is! But night like a black cloud
About his head whirls down in awful gloom."
His father Anchises answered, and the tears
Welled up as be began:
"Oh, do not ask
About this huge grief of your people, son.
Fate will give earth only a glimpse of him,
Not let the boy live on. Lords of the sky,
You thought the majesty of Rome too great
If it had kept these gifts. How many groans
Will be sent up from that great Field of Mars[19]
To Mars' proud city, and what sad rites you'll see,
Tiber, as you flow past the new-built tomb.
Never will any boy of Ilian race
Exalt his Latin forefathers with promise
Equal to his; never will Romulus' land
Take pride like this in any of her sons.
Weep for his faithful heart, his old-world honor,
His sword arm never beaten down! No enemy
Could have come through a clash with him unhurt,
Whether this soldier went on foot or rode,
Digging his spurs into a lathered mount.
Child of our mourning, if only in some way
You could break through your bitter fate. For you
Will be Marcellus. Let me scatter lilies,
All I can hold, and scarlet flowers as well,
To heap these for my grandson's shade at least,
Frail gifts and ritual of no avail."

So raptly, everywhere, father and son
Wandered the airy plain and viewed it all.
After Anchises had conducted him
To every region and had fired his love
Of glory in the years to come, he spoke
Of wars that he must fight, of Laurenitines,
And of Latinus' city, then of how
He might avoid or bear each toil to come.

There are two gates of Sleep, one said to be
Of horn, whereby the true shades pass with ease,
The other all white ivory agleam
Without a flaw, and yet false dreams are sent
Through this one by the ghosts to the upper world.
Anchises now, his last instructions given,
Took son and Sibyl there and let them go
By the Ivory Gate.

[19] *Mars* was the father of Romulus and the Roman god of war.

Aeneas made his way
Straight to the ships to see his crews again,
Then sailed directly to Caieta's[20] port.
Bow anchors out, the sterns rest on the beach.

[20] *Caieta* is the place where Aeneas' nurse was buried.

OVID

THE ART OF LOVE

The greatest of the Latin elegists during the Golden Age was Publius Ovidius Naso or Ovid (43 b.c.—a.d. 17). Unlike Horace and Virgil, Ovid did not experience the civil wars during his adult years. Consequently, he was less inclined To praise the Augustan peace. He was married three times and supposedly had a mistress, Corinna, to whom he wrote Amores (love letters). As a result of his marriages and affairs, Ovid's poetry reveals a preference for romance and humor and a fondness for love and sensual themes.

Ovid is best remembered for his advice to lovers contained in his most famous work—*Ars Amatoria* (Art of Love). Written when Ovid was fifty years old, the poem concerns itself with the art of seduction and is divided into three books. Book I deals with how to attract a woman who is the object of a man's desire.

Few indeed
Will turn you down—and (willing or not) a male proposition
Is something they all enjoy. Draw a blank,
Rejection brings no danger. But why should you be rejected
When new thrills delight, when what's not ours
Has more allure than what is? The harvest's always richer
In another man's fields, the herd
Of our neighbour has fuller udders.
But first you must get acquainted
With your quarry's maid—she can help
In the early stages. Make sure she enjoys the full confidence
Of her mistress: make sure you can trust
Her with your secret liaison. Corrupt her with promises,
Corrupt her with prayers. If
She's willing, you'll get what you want. She'll await the propitious
Time (like a doctor) when her mistress is in
A receptive, seducible mood, when she's bursting out all over
With cheerfulness, like a wheat-crop in rich soil.
When hearts are rejoicing, and have no sorrow to constrict them,
They're wide open. Venus[1] can steal
In by persuasive guile. Grim Troy long faced her besiegers,
But a light-hearted change of mood
Fell for that troop-gravid horse.
Another time to try her
Is when she's been miffed by a rival. Make it your job
To ensure she gets her revenge. Prime her maid to egg her on while
Combing her hair each morning, put an oar in
To boost Ma'am's plain sailing, sigh to herself, and murmur:
"What a pity it is you can't just pay him out
With a tit-for-tat, then talk about *you* in persuasive
Language, swear you're dying of mad
Passion. But lose no time, don't let the wind subside or
The sails drop slack. Fury, like brittle ice,
Melts with delay. . . .

[1] Venus (Greek, Aphrodite) was the Roman goddess of love.

This selection from Book II tells a man how he can retain a woman once he has acquired her.

Don't give your mistress costly
Presents: let them be small, but chosen with skill
And discretion. At harvest-time, when fields are full, boughs heavy,
Send round a basket of fruit—
Say it came from your country estate (though you really bought it
At some smart city shop). Give her grapes,
Or the chestnuts to which Amaryllis[2] was so devoted—
No, not chestnuts, she's off them these days:
Much too cheap. Why not try a poulterer's hoop of thrushes
By way of remembrance? (It's shameful to use such gifts
In the hope of a death, to bribe the elderly or barren:
I've no time for those who give presents a bad name.)
Would you be well advised to send her love-poems?
Poetry, I fear, is held in small esteem.
Girls praise a poem, but go for expensive presents.
Any illiterate oaf can catch their eye
Provided he's rich. Today is truly the Golden
Age: gold buys honours, gold
Procures love. If Homer dropped by—with all the Muses,[3]
But empty-handed—he'd be shown the door.
There *are* a few cultured girls (not many, it's true), and others
Who'd like to be cultured, but aren't;
Flatter any of these with poems: a bravura declamation
Even of trash—this will suffice to win
Their approval. Clever or stupid, they'll take a poem fashioned
In the small hours, for *them* as a cute little gift.
Make your mistress ask as a favour for what you intended,
All along, to do yourself
In the way of self-interest. You've promised manumission
To one slave? See that he begs it, first, from her.
You plan to spare another his flogging, or the chain-gang?
Then put her in your debt for a "change of heart"
That never existed. The benefit's yours, give her the credit,
Waste not want not, while she
Plays the Lady Bountiful. You're anxious to keep your mistress?
Convince her she's knocked you all of a heap
With her stunning looks. If it's purple she's wearing, praise purple;
When she's in a silk dress, say silk
Suits her best of all; if her mantle's gold-embroidered
Say she's dearer than gold to you; if tweeds
Take her fancy, back tweeds. She's in her slip? She inflames you
(Tell her) with passion—but ask, at the same time,
Very, shyly, "Aren't you cold?" Compliment the way she's parted
Or curled her hair, Admire
Her singing voice, her gestures as she dances,
Cry "Encore!" when she stops. You can even praise

[2] Amaryllis in classical poetry—the general name for a shepherdess.
[3] Muses were the nine daughters of Zeus and Mnemosyne, each of whom presided over a different science or art.

Her performance in bed, her talent for love-making—
Spell out what turned you on.
Though she may show fiercer in action than any Medusa,
Her lover will always describe her as kind
And gentle. But take care not to give yourself away while
Making such tongue-in-cheek compliments, don't allow
Your expression to ruin the message. Art's most effective
When concealed. Detection discredits you for good. . . .
Take care not to criticize girls for their shortcomings: many
Have found it advantageous to pretend
Such things didn't exist. Andromeda's[4] dusky complexion
Left wing-footed Perseus[5] silent. Although
Everyone else thought Andromache[6] too large a woman,
To Hector[7] alone she looked
Just the right size. Habit breeds tolerance: a long-established
Love will condone much, whereas
At first it's all-sensitive. While a new graft's growing
In the green cortex, a light
Breeze can detach it; but soon time-strengthened, the tree will
Outface all winds, hold firm,
Bear adopted fruit. Time heals each physical blemish,
The erstwhile flaw will fade:
Young nostrils cannot abide the stink of tanning leather,
But age inures them to it, after a while
They don't even notice the smell. Labels minimize feelings—
She's blacker than pitch? Try "brunette".
If she squints, compare her to Venus. She croaks? She's Minerva![8]
A living skeleton? "Svelte" is the word. Call her "trim"
When she's minuscule, or "plumpish" when she's a Fat Lady—
Use proximate virtues to camouflage each fault.
Don't ask her age, don't inquire under just which consul
She was born—leave that kind of chore
To the Censor's[9] office, especially if she's past her girlish
Prime, and already plucking those first
White hairs. Such ladies, in this (or even a higher) age-group
Are good value, a field worth sowing, ready to bear.
Besides, they possess a wider range of knowledge
And experience, the sole source
Of true skill: they make up for their years with sophistication,
Camouflaging their age through art; they know
A thousand postures—name yours—for making love in,
More ways than any pillow-book could reveal,
They need no stimuli to warm up their passions—
Men and women should share the same

[4]*Andromeda*, wife of Perseus, whom he rescued from a sea serpent.
[5]*Perseus*, a son of Zeus, who killed the Gorgon Medusa.
[6]*Andromache*, Trojan wife of Hector, who was captured by the Greeks during the fall of Troy.
[7]According to Homer's Iliad, Hector was the Trojan prince who was killed by the Greek war hero Achilles.
[8]*Minerva* was the Roman goddess of wisdom.
[9]A censor was one of two men in ancient Rome charged with watching over public morality and behavior, and who was responsible for taking the public census.

Pleasures. I hate it unless both lovers reach a climax:
That's why I don't much go for boys.
I can't stand a woman who puts out because she has to,
Who lies there dry as a bone
With her mind on her knitting. Pleasure by way of duty
Holds no charms for me, I don't want
Any dutiful martyrs. I love the sights that betray their rapture,
That beg me to go slow, to keep it up
Just a little longer. It's great when my mistress comes, eyes swooning,
Then collapses, can't take any more
For a long while. Such joys attend you in your thirties:
Nature does not bestow them on green youth.
For the hasty, new-bottled wine; for me, a vintage
Laid down long years before.

Book III is reserved for Ovid's advice to women, such as this selection that details how a woman can best hide her physical flaws and charm her love, but he warns that as a women she should do everything without appearing to be artificial.

But don't let your lover find all those jars and bottles
On your dressing-table: the best
Make-up remains unobtrusive. A face so thickly plastered
With pancake it runs down your sweaty neck
Is bound to create repulsion. And that goo from unwashed fleeces—
Athenian maybe, but my dear, the *smell!*—
That's used for face-cream: avoid it. When you have company
Don't dab stuff on your pimples, don't start cleaning your teeth:
The result may be attractive but the *process* is sickening—
Much that is vile in the doing gives pleasure when done.
A statue—signed, let's say, by that industrious sculptor
Myron[10]—began as a mere lump
Of deadweight marble; the gold for your ring must first be
Worked and shaped, your woollen dress was made
From greasy yarn; that splendid representation of Venus
Posed naked, wringing out her seawet hair,
Was a rough and uncut stone once. So leave us to imagine
You're asleep while you're at your toilet: only emerge
When the public picture's complete. I don't want to know how
That complexion's built up. Shut your door,
Don't reveal the half-finished process. Most of your actions
Would offend if you didn't conceal them: there's a lot
Men are better not knowing. Look closely at those splendid
Gold statues adorning the theatre—thin gilded foil
On a wooden frame! That's why the public can't come near them
Till they're finished—and that's why you
Should keep men out while you're making up. Still, I don't forbid you
To let them watch you comb your rippling hair
Out down your back—but mind you don't lose your temper
As you tear at those tangled knots! . . .
A flawless face is a rarity: mask each blemish,
Hide your physical faults—as far as you can.

[10] Myron was a Greek sculptor who lived during the fifth century b.c.; his most famous work is the *Discus Thrower.*

Sit, if you're short, lest standing you seem to be sitting;
Stretch out that pint-sized form,
Recline on a couch (but discourage rude measurement by spreading
A wrap or blanket across your legs).
The over-lean girl should wear more amply textured
Dresses, a robe that's draped
Loose from her shoulders. Puce [purplish brown] stripes offset a pallid
Complexion, while Nilotic [Egyptian or from the Nile re-
gion of Egypt] linen transforms
The swarthy. Got ugly feet? Just keep them hidden
In smart white bootees. Scrawny calves? Don't raise
Your skirt above the ankle. Protruding collar-bones?
Mask them with pads.
Is your trouble a flat bust?
Wear a good bra. If you have rough nails, coarse fingers,
Don't gesture too much while you talk.
Bad breath? You should never converse on an empty stomach
And keep your mouth well back from your lover's face!
If your teeth are decayed, or horsy, or protruding,
A guffaw can cost you dear. Believe it or not,
Girls even learn how to laugh: in their quest for decorum
This is one more skill they must acquire.
Don't open the mouth too wide, control those dimples, keep your
Teeth concealed behind your lips,
Don't split your sides with endless hilarity, but rather
Laugh in a restrained, a ladylike way—
Some women distort their features with lop-sided guffaws, some
Get so cross-eyed with mirth
You'd swear they were weeping. Others utter a harsh unlovely
Braying noise, like a she-ass hitched to the mill.
Where does art not enter ? Girls learn to make even tears attractive,
To cry when and how they please.
Indeed, some mispronounce words with deliberate affectation,
Bring them lispingly off the tongue:
Charm lurks in such errors of consciously faulty diction—
What grace of speech they had they soon unlearn.
These hints are useful, so pay them proper attention—
And mind you learn to walk in a feminine way!
No mean part of elegance derives from gait and carriage:
These can attract or repel
Admiring strangers. One girl sways her hips artfully, catches
The breeze with her flowing mantle, points her feet
In short dainty steps; another—like some red-cheeked peasant housewife—
Clumps and waddles along, with hearty strides.
Moderation's best, as so often: don't play the country bumpkin,
But equally, don't lay your affectations on
Too thick. No harm, though, in baring your left-hand shoulder
And upper arm: for those
With a milk-white skin this works wonders—just let me see it,
And I'm mad to press kisses on the naked flesh!

JUVENAL

THE SATIRES

In the following passage from his *Satires,* Juvenal focuses on the underside of life in Rome: crowded, noisy, and unsafe streets; bullies itching to fight; criminals who steal and murder; and the suffering poor.

... A man's word
Is believed just to the extent of the
wealth in his coffers stored.
Though he swear on all the altars from
here to Samothrace,[1]
A poor man isn't believed. . . .
Anyway, a poor man's the butt of jokes if
his cloak has a rip
Or is dirty, if his toga is slightly soiled, if
a strip
Of leather is split in his shoes and gapes,
if coarse thread shows
New stitches patching not one but many
holes. Of the woes
Of unhappy poverty, none is more
difficult to bear
Than that it heaps men with ridicule.
Says an usher, "How dare
You sit there? Get out of the rows
reserved for knights to share. . . ."
. . . What poor man ever inherits
A fortune or gets appointed as clerk to a
magistrate?
Long ago the penniless Romans ought to
have staged a great
Mass walkout. It's no easy job for a man
to advance
When his talents are balked by his
impoverished circumstance,
But in Rome it's harder than
elsewhere. . . .
Here most of the sick die off because
they get no sleep
(But the sickness is brought on by the
undigested heap
Of sour food in their burning stomachs),
for what rented flat
Allows you to sleep? Only rich men in
this city have that.
There lies the root of the illness—carts

[1]Samothrace, an island in the northern Aegean Sea, is best known today as the place where the famous statue of the Winged Victory (Nike) was found.

rumbling in narrow streets
And cursing drivers stalled in a traffic
jam—it defeats
All hope of rest. . . .
. . . Though we hurry, we merely crawl;
We're blocked by a surging mass ahead,
a pushing wall
Of people behind. A man jabs me,
elbowing through, one socks
A chair pole against me, one cracks my
skull with a beam, one knocks
A wine cask against my ear. My legs are
caked with splashing
Mud, from all sides the weight of
enormous feet comes smashing
On mine, and a soldier stamps his
hobnails through to my sole. . . .
... a piece of a pot
Falls down on my head, how often a
broken vessel is shot
From the upper windows, with what a
force it strikes and dints
The cobblestones! . . .
The besotted bully, denied his chance in
the shabby bars
Of killing somebody, suffers torments,
itching to fight.
Like Achilles[2] bemoaning his friend, he
tosses about all night,
Now flat on his face, now on his back—
there's no way at all
He can rest, for some men can't sleep till
after a bloody brawl.
But however rash and hot with youth
and flushed with wine,
He avoids the noble whose crimson cloak
and long double line
Of guards with brass lamps and torches
show they're too much to handle.
But for me, whom the moon escorts, or
the feeble light of a candle
Whose wick I husband and trim—he
has no respect for me.
Now hear how the pitiful fight begins—
if a fight it be,
When he delivers the punches and I am
beaten to pulp.
He blocks my way and tells me to stop. I
stop, with a gulp—

[2]Achilles, the Greeks' most formidable warrior in Homer's Iliad, was torn by grief when his best friend Patroclus was killed by the Trojans.

What else can you do when a madman
  stronger than you attacks? . . .
This is the poor man's freedom: having
  been soundly mauled
And cut to pieces by fists, he begs and
  prays, half dead,
To be allowed to go home with a few
  teeth still in his head.
But these aren't your only terrors. For
  you can never restrain
The criminal element. Lock up your
  house, put bolt and chain
On your shop, but when all's quiet,
  someone will rob you or he'll
Be a cutthroat perhaps and do you in
  quickly with cold steel. . . .

Juvenal also gives us an unflattering picture of women and marriage.

You once had your wits about you,
Postumus; but now you think
Of taking a wife? What Fury, what
  serpents, are driving you mad?
Can you let a termagant [shrewish woman]
  boss you when rope is so easily had
And so many windows open on dizzy
  leaps and the height
Of the Aemilian bridge so handy?
If none of these modes of flight
Is to your taste, don't you think it
  might be better to take
Some boy as bedmate, who'd never
  quarrel all night, or make
You promise gifts as you twine, or
  complain if you resist
His pleas and sleep, instead of panting,
  and leave him unkissed? . . .
And who is so deeply in love he never
  shrinks at all
From the very woman he praises to the
  skies—what's more,
Hates her at least sixteen hours out
  of the twenty-four? . . .
If you don't intend to love the woman
  you embrace
And marry in legal form, there seems
  no reason for you
To marry, no reason why you should
  waste the supper and new
Wedding cakes that must be given to
  well-stuffed guests who leave

When the party's over, or waste the
gift of the bridal eve,
The rich tray gleaming with coins
engraved with victories
In Dacia and Germany. If you simply
must appease
Yourself with a wife and are devoted
to one, incline
Your head, submit your neck to the
marriage yoke. You'll find
No woman who spares the man who loves
her. Though she glow
With passion, she loves to torment
and plunder her lover. So,
The more he's good and desirable as
a husband, the less
Beneficial by far will be his wife.
You'll never address
A gift if she says no, never sell
things if she objects,
Never buy anything unless she consents.
And she will select
Your friends for you and turn your now
aged friend from the door. . . .
You'll have to despair of knowing
any peace at home
If your mother-in-law's alive. She
teaches your wife to delight
In stripping you of wealth. . . .
There's hardly a case in court that
a woman's fuss didn't start.
The bed where a wife lies never is free
of complaints and a host
Of quarrels back and forth. There'll
be little sleep in that bed.
There she assails her husband, worse
than a tigress is said
To be at the loss of her cubs. Aware
of her own secret deeds,
She pretends to grieve, denounces
the boys he's known, and weeps
At some feigned mistress, always with
floods of tears at hand
Ever ready at their station, waiting
for her command
On how they should flow. You think,
poor worm, it's love they show. . . .

THE GOSPEL ACCORDING TO JOHN

CREATION FROM "THE WORD"

The primary meaning of the Greek term *logos* is "word," and that is the way it is translated in the first fourteen verses of the first chapter of the Gospel According to John. John, however, uses the term somewhat like Philo, asserting that the Logos was God, that he preexisted from eternity, and that he was active in the creation. Then John introduces John the Baptist who baptized Jesus and bore witness to him (cf. Matthew 3:1-17, Mark 1:1—11, and Luke 3:1-23). Finally, John announces that Jesus was the incarnation of the Logos, that he was the Son of God in the flesh sent from God the Father and that those who believe in him will also become children of God.

PROLOGUE

In the beginning was the Word:
the Word was with God.
and the Word was God.
He was with God in the beginning.
Through him all things came into being,
not one thing came into being except through him.
What has come into being in him was life,
life that was the light of men;
and light shines in darkness,
and darkness could not overpower it.
A man came, sent by God.
His name was John.
He came as a witness,
to bear witness to the light,
so that everyone might believe through him.
He was not the light,
he was to bear witness to the light.
The Word was the real light
that gives light to everyone;
he was coming into the world.
He was in the world
that had come into being through him,
and the world did not recognise him.
He came to his own
and his own people did not accept him.
But to those who did accept him
he gave power to become children of God,
to those who believed in his name
who were born not from human stock
or human desire
or human will
but from God himself.
The Word became flesh,
he lived among us,
and we saw his glory,
the glory that he has from the Father as only Son of the Father,
full of grace and truth.

TERTULLIAN

WHAT HAS JERUSALEM TO DO WITH ATHENS?

A native of Carthage, Tertullian (Quintus Septimus Florens Tertullianus, c. a.d. 160-c. 240) became a Christian about a.d. 190 and thereafter was a defender of Christian morals against both pagans and less rigorous Christians. He emphasized the sacredness of life and the Christian abhorrence of violence. His *Prescriptions Against Heretics* reveals hostility toward Greco-Roman learning, an attitude shared by some other early Christian thinkers.

. . . Worldly wisdom culminates in philosophy with its rash interpretation of God's nature and purpose. It is philosophy that supplies the heresies[1] with their equipment. . . . The idea of a mortal soul was picked up from the Epicureans,[2] and the denial of the restitution of the flesh was taken from the common tradition of the philosophical schools. . . . Heretics and philosophers [ponder] the same themes and are caught up in the same discussions. What is the origin of evil and why? The origin of man, and how? ... A plague on Aristotle, who taught them dialectic [logical argumentation], the art which destroys as much as it builds, which changes its opinions like a coat, forces its conjectures, is stubborn in argument, works hard at being contentious and is a burden even to itself. For it reconsiders every point to make sure it never finishes a discussion.

From philosophy come those fables and . . . fruitless questionings, those "words that creep like as doth a canker." To hold us back from such things, the Apostle [Paul] testifies expressly in his letter to the Colossians [Colossians 2:8] that we should beware of philosophy. "Take heed lest any man [beguile] you through philosophy or vain deceit, after the tradition of men," against the providence of the Holy Ghost. He had been at Athens where he had come to grips with the human wisdom which attacks and perverts truth, being itself divided up into its own swarm of heresies by the variety of its mutually antagonistic sects. What has Jerusalem to do with Athens, the Church with [Plato's] Academy, the Christian with the heretic? Our principles come from the Porch of Solomon,[3] who had himself taught that the Lord is to be sought in simplicity of heart. I have no use for a Stoic or a Platonic or a dialectic Christianity. After Jesus Christ we have no need of speculation, after the Gospel no need of research. When we come to believe, we have no desire to believe anything else; for we begin by believing that there is nothing else which we have to believe.

---

[1]A heresy is any belief that differs from official or standard doctrine.

[2]Chapter 4, page 88.

[3]The Stoic philosophers took their name from the Greek word *stoa*, covered walk, the place where Zeno, their founder, used to teach. *Porch of Solomon* is used to designate the teachings of King Solomon, who built the great Temple in Jerusalem. Tertullian makes it clear he follows Solomon's wisdom.

CLEMENT OF ALEXANDRIA

IN DEFENSE OF GREEK LEARNING

In the following passage, Clement of Alexandria (c. a.d. 150—c. 220) expresses his admiration for Greek learning. A Greek Christian theologian, Clement combined Christianity with Platonism.

The Greeks should not be condemned by those who have merely glanced at their writings, for comprehension of these works requires careful investigation. Philosophy is not the originator of false practices and base deeds as some have calumniated it; nor does it beguile us and lead us away from faith.

Rather philosophy is a clear image of truth, a divine gift to the Greeks. Before the advent of the Lord, philosophy helped the Greeks to attain righteousness, and it is now conducive to piety; it supplies a preparatory teaching for those who will later embrace the faith. God is the cause of all good things: some given primarily in the form of the Old and the New Testament; others are the consequence of philosophy. Perchance too philosophy was given to the Greeks primarily till the Lord should call the Greeks to serve him. Thus philosophy acted as a schoolmaster to the Greeks, preparing them for Christ, as the laws of the Jews prepared them for Christ.

The way of truth is one. But into it, as into a perennial river, streams flow from all sides. We assert that philosophy, which is characterized by investigation into the form and nature of things, is the truth of which the Lord Himself said, "I am the truth." Thus Greek preparatory culture, including philosophy itself, is shown to have come down from God to men.

Some do not wish to touch either philosophy or logic or to learn natural science. They demand bare faith alone, as if they wished, without bestowing any care on the vine, straightway to gather clusters from the first. I call him truly learned who brings everything to bear on the truth; so that from geometry, music, grammar, and philosophy itself, he culls what is useful and guards the faith against assault. And he who brings everything to bear on a right life, learning from Greeks and non-Greeks, this man is an experienced searcher after truth. And how necessary it is for him who desires to be partaker of the power of God to treat of intellectual subjects by philosophising.

According to some, Greek philosophy apprehended the truth accidentally, dimly, partially. Others will have it that Greek philosophy was instituted by the devil. Several hold that certain powers descending from heaven inspired the whole of philosophy. But if Greek philosophy does not comprehend the whole of truth and does not encompass God's commandments, yet it prepares the way for God's teachings; training in some way or other, molding character, and fitting him who believes in Providence for the reception of truth.

THE APOSTLE PAUL

THE SUBMISSIVE ROLE OF WOMEN

Passages in the New Testament concerning the role of women in Christian society have greatly affected the Western view of the relationship between the sexes. Paul's letter to the Ephesians and his first letter to Timothy contain passages emphasizing the traditional, submissive role of women in the Christian Church.

Although conservative theologians accept the Pauline authorship of these letters, liberal scholars date Ephesians about a.d. 95, thirty years after Paul's death, and 1 Timothy about a.d. 130. If the later dates are correct, the following passages reflect the attitude of the developing Christian Church rather than Paul's own opinion. Nonetheless, these passages, and others like them, have had an enormous influence on Christian attitudes toward women.

EPHESIANS 6

The morals of the home

Be subject to one another out of reverence for Christ. Wives should be subject to their husbands as to the Lord, since, as Christ is head of the Church and saves the whole body, so is a husband the head of his wife; and as the Church is subject to Christ, so should wives be to their husbands, in everything. Husbands should love their wives, just as Christ loved the Church and sacrificed himself for her to make her holy by washing her in cleansing water with a form of words, so that when he took the Church to himself she would be glorious, with no speck or wrinkle or anything like that, but holy and faultless. In the same way, husbands must love their wives as they love their own bodies; for a man to love his wife is for him to love himself. A man never hates his own body, but he feeds it and looks after it; and that is the way Christ treats the Church, because we are parts of his Body. *This is why a man leaves his father and mother and becomes attached to his wife, and the two become one flesh.* This mystery has great significance, but

I am applying it to Christ and the Church. To sum up: you also, each one of you, must love his wife as he loves himself; and let every wife respect her husband.

TIMOTHY 2

Women in the assembly

Similarly, women are to wear suitable clothes and to be dressed quietly and modestly, without braided hair or gold and jewellery or expensive clothes; their adornment is to do the good works that are proper for women who claim to be religious. During instruction, a woman should be quiet and respectful. I give no permission for a woman to teach or to have authority over a man. A woman ought to be quiet, because Adam was formed first and Eve afterwards, and it was not Adam who was led astray but the woman who was led astray and fell into sin. Nevertheless, she will be saved by child-bearing, provided she lives a sensible life and is constant in faith and love and holiness.

AUGUSTINE OF HIPPO

WOMEN, SEX, AND MARRIAGE

Augustine (Aurelius Augustinus, a.d. 354—430), bishop of Hippo (now Souk- Ahras in modern Algeria), was one of the great intellects of the early Christian Church. He is best known as a theologian, but his ideas about women, sex, and marriage had a crucial influence on Western attitudes about these subjects during medieval and modern times. Augustine's belief that women ought to be subject to their husbands is evident in a passage from his *Confessions* where he describes the relationship that his mother Monica had with his father Patricius.

When she reached a marriageable age, she was given to a husband whom she served as lord. . . . She also endured his infidelities, never quarreling with her husband about them. . . . Though he had an excellent, friendly disposition, he also had a terrible temper. She learned not to oppose, either with actions or words, an angry husband. . . . Many wives, whose husbands were more gentle than hers, carried marks of blows on their dishonored faces, and talking among themselves they would complain about the behavior of their husbands. But my mother, speaking in jest but with serious intent, would blame their tongues, saying to them that they had heard the marriage contract read and they were bound to regard it as an instrument by which they were made servants; accordingly, they should bear in mind their agreement and they ought not to oppose their lords. They, knowing that she endured such a wild husband, were amazed that it had never been rumored, nor was there any clear sign, that Patricius had beaten his wife or that there had been any domestic strife between them, even for one day. When they asked her in confidence why this was so, she taught them her rule which I have mentioned above. Those who followed it, thanked her for it; those who did not follow it, were still molested and subjected.

For Augustine, there is a hierarchy of piety when it comes to the sexual life of the Christian. The highest moral stance is virginity, but failing that, marriage without sex is better than marriage with sex. Thus, the ideal marriage is a "spiritual" marriage with complete sexual abstinence. But because such a condition is beyond most people, sexual intercourse and procreation in marriage is good and guiltless if there is no sexual pleasure involved. Augustine's view of women and marriage was based in his firm belief that any sexual pleasure is sinful and evil, whether in or out of marriage. He believed that before the fall of Adam and Eve, when God originally instituted marriage, sex and procreation could have occurred without lust. But lust resulted from their disobedience, and because of lust, their original sin is passed on from parents to children. In the following selection, Augustine contrasts the good of marriage with the evil lust that is responsible for sin being passed from parents to children.

It is then manifest that that [lust] must not be laid to the account of marriage, in spite of which, even if it had not come into being, marriage would have existed. The good of marriage is not taken away by the evil, although the evil is by marriage turned to a good use. Such, however, is the present condition of mortal men, that the connubial intercourse and lust are simultaneous in action; and on this account it happens, that as the lust is blamed, so also the nuptial commerce, however lawful and honourable, is thought to be reprehensible by those persons who either are unwilling or unable to draw the distinction between them. . . .

The evil, however, at which even marriage blushes for shame is not the fault of marriage, but of the lust of the flesh. Yet because without this evil it is impossible to effect the good purpose of marriage, even the procreation of children, whenever this process is approached, secrecy is sought, witnesses are removed, and even the presence of the very children which happen to be born of the process is avoided as soon as they reach the age of observation. Thus it comes to pass that marriage is permitted to effect all that is lawful in its state, only it must not forget to conceal all that is improper. Hence it follows that infants, although incapable of sinning, are yet not born without the contagion of sin,—not, indeed, because of what is lawful in matrimony, but of its improper element: for from the lawful a natural creature is born; from the improper, sin. Of the natural creature so born, God is the Maker, who created man, and who united male and female under the law of the nuptial union; but of the sin the origin lies in the subtlety of the devil who deceives, and in the will of the man who yields to the deception.

In the following selection, Augustine blames the wife for the evil lust associated with sexual intercourse, thus further revealing his attitude about women and marriage.

Therefore, if I were to ask any good Christian who has a wife, and even though he may still be having children by her, whether he would like to have his wife in that kingdom; mindful in my case of the promises of God, and of that life where this incorruptible shall put on incorruption, and this mortal shall put on immortality; [though] at present hesitating from the greatness, or at least from a certain degree of love, he would reply with execration that he is strongly averse to it. Were I to ask him again, whether he would like his wife to live with him there, after the resurrection, when she had undergone that angelic change which is promised to the saints, he would reply that he desires this as strongly as he dislikes the other. Thus a good Christian is found in one and the same woman to love the creature of God, whom he desires to be transformed and renewed; but to hate the corruptible and mortal conjugal connection and sexual intercourse: *i.e.* to love in her what is characteristic of a human being, to hate what belongs to her as a wife.

Finally, in a treatise on the subject of marriage, Augustine concludes that it is better not to marry, but those who cannot restrain themselves should follow the advice of the Apostle Paul in 1 Corinthians 7:9.

[I]t is a good to marry, since it is a good to beget children, to be the mother of a family; but it is better not to marry, since it is better for human society itself not to have need of marriage. For, such is the present state of the human race that not only some who do not check themselves are taken up with marriage, but many are wanton and given over to illicit intercourse. Since the good Creator draws good out of their evils, there is no lack of numerous progeny and an abundance of generation whence holy friendships might be sought out.

In this regard it is gathered that in the earliest times of the human race, especially to propagate the people of God, through whom the Prince and Saviour of all peoples might both be prophesied and be born, the saints were obliged to make use of this good of marriage, to be sought not for its own sake but as necessary for something else. But now, since the opportunity for spiritual relationship abounds on all sides and for all peoples for entering into a holy and pure association, even they who wish to contract marriage only to have children are to be admonished that they practice the greater good of continence.

And so it seems to me that at this time only those who do not restrain themselves ought to be married in accord with this saying of the same Apostle: "But if they do not have self- control, let them marry, for it is better to marry than to burn."

AUGUSTINE OF HIPPO

THE CITY OF GOD

Augustine of Hippo was one of the great theologians of the early Christian church. He formulated a view of life and of the individual that became definitive for Western Christians until it was partially superseded by the writings of Thomas Aquinas in the thirteenth century. Although Augustine admired the achievements of Socrates and Plato, he could not accept their central premise: that in the search for truth the individual relied on reason alone.

The sacking of Rome by the Visigoths in a.d. 410 shocked the entire Roman world. Pagans blamed the catastrophe on the Christians; by abandoning the old gods, said pagans, Christians had brought down the wrath of heaven on Rome. In reply to these charges, Saint Augustine wrote the *City of God,* setting forth the Christian view of the world and humanity.

The theme of the first group of passages from Augustine's *City of God* is a crucial element in the Christian outlook: that when human beings turn away from God to follow their own desires as Adam and Eve did, they fall into evil and become afflicted with many miseries, which can only be relieved through God's grace.

I have already said, in previous Books, that God had two purposes in deriving all men from one man. His first purpose was to give unity to the human race by the likeness of nature. His second purpose was to bind mankind by the bond of peace, through blood relationship, into one harmonious whole. I have said further that no member of this race would ever have died had not the first two [Adam and Eve]—one created from nothing and the second from the first—merited this death by disobedience. The sin which they committed was so great that it impaired all human nature—in this sense, that the nature has been transmitted to posterity with a propensity to sin and a necessity to die. . . .

When a man lives "according to man" and not "according to God" he is like the Devil. . . .

When man lives according to himself, that is to say, according to human ways and not according to God's will, then surely he lives according to falsehood. Man himself, of course, is not a lie, since God who is his Author and Creator could not be the Author and Creator of a lie. Rather, man has been so constituted in truth that he was meant to live not according to himself but to Him who made him—that is, he was meant to do the will of God rather than his own. It is a lie not to live as a man was created to live.

Man indeed desires happiness even when he does so live as to make happiness impossible. . . . The happiness of man can come not from himself but only from God, and that to live according to oneself is to sin, and to sin is to lose God. . . .

Moreover, our first parents [Adam and Eve] only fell openly into the sin of disobedience because, secretly, they had begun to be guilty. Actually, their bad deed could not have been done had not bad will preceded it; what is more, the root of their bad will was nothing else than pride. For, "pride is the beginning of all sin." And what is pride but an appetite for inordinate exaltation? Now, exaltation is inordinate when the soul cuts itself off from the very Source [God] to which it should keep close and somehow makes itself and becomes an end to itself. This takes place when the soul becomes inordinately pleased with itself, and such self-pleasing occurs when the soul falls away from the unchangeable Good which ought to please the soul far more than the soul can please itself. Now, this falling away is the soul's own doing, for, if the will had merely remained firm in the love of that higher immutable Good which lighted its mind into knowledge and warmed its will into love, it would not have turned away in search of satisfaction in itself and, by so doing, have lost that light and warmth. And thus Eve would not have believed that the serpent's lie was true, nor would Adam have preferred the will of his wife to the will of God. . . .

This life of ours—if a life so full of such great ills can properly be called a life—bears witness to the fact that, from its very start, the race of mortal men has been a race condemned. Think, first, of that dreadful abyss of ignorance from which all error flows and so engulfs the sons of Adam in a darksome pool that no one can escape without the toll of toils and tears and fears. Then, take our very love for all those things that prove so vain and poisonous and breed so many heartaches, troubles, griefs, and fears; such insane joys in discord, strife, and war; such wrath and plots of enemies, deceivers, sycophants; such fraud and theft and robbery; such perfidy and pride, envy and ambition, homicide and murder, cruelty and savagery, lawlessness and lust; all the shameless passions of the impure—fornication and adultery, incest and unnatural sins, rape and countless other uncleannesses too nasty to be mentioned; the sins against religion—sacrilege and heresy, blasphemy and perjury; the iniquities against our neighbors—calumnies and cheating, lies and false witness, violence to persons and property; the injustices of the courts and the innumerable other miseries and maladies that fill the world, yet escape attention.

It is true that it is wicked men who do such things, but the source of all such sins is that radical canker [sinfulness] in the mind and will that is innate in every son of Adam. . . .

Yet, for all this blight of ignorance and folly, fallen man has not been left without some ministries of Providence, nor has God, in His anger, shut up His mercies. There are still within the reach of man himself, if only he will pay the price of toil and trouble, the twin resources of law and education. With the one, he can make war on human passion; with the other, he can keep the light of learning lit even in the darkness of our native ignorance. . . .

From this all but hell of unhappiness here on earth, nothing can save us but the grace of Jesus Christ, who is our Saviour, Lord and God. In fact, the very meaning of the name, Jesus, is Saviour, and when we say "save" we mean, especially, that He saves us from passing from the misery of this mortal life to a still more miserable condition, which is not so much a life as death. . . .

Augustine saw a conflict between the earthly city, visible, temporal, and corrupt, and the City of God, invisible, eternal, and perfect. Those Christians favored with God's grace lived in this earthly city as strangers and pilgrims passing through on their journey to their true homeland, the heavenly kingdom. The fate of the earthly city was of no ultimate concern to these Christians. For Augustine, this earthly world represented the forces of evil that would finally be destroyed at the end of time, when Christ would come again.

What we see, then, is that two societies have issued from two kinds of love. Worldly society has flowered from a selfish love which dared to despise even God, whereas the communion of saints is rooted in a love of God that is ready to trample on self. In a word, this latter relies on the Lord, whereas the other boasts that it can get along by itself. The city of man seeks the praise of men, whereas the height of glory for the other is to hear God in the witness of conscience. The one lifts up its head in its own boasting; the other says to God: "Thou art my glory, thou liftest up my head."

In the city of the world both the rulers themselves and the people they dominate are dominated by the lust for domination; whereas in the City of God all citizens serve one another in charity, whether they serve by the responsibilities of office or by the duties of obedience. The one city loves its leaders as symbols of its own strength; the other says to its God: "I love thee, O Lord, my strength." Hence, even the wise men in the city of man live according to man, and their only goal has been the goods of their bodies or of the mind or of both; though some of them have reached a knowledge of God, "they did not glorify him as God or give thanks but became vain in their reasonings, and their senseless minds have been darkened. For while professing to be wise" (that is to say, while glorying in their own wisdom, under the domination of pride), "they have become fools, and they have changed the glory of the incorruptible God for an image made like to corruptible man and to birds and four-footed beasts and creeping things" (meaning that they either led their people, or imitated them, in adoring idols shaped like these things), "and they worshiped and served the creature rather than the Creator who is blessed forever." In the City of God, on the contrary, there is no merely human wisdom, but there is a piety which worships the true God as He should be worshiped and has as its goal that reward of all holiness whether in the society of saints on earth or in that of angels of heaven, which is "that God may be all in all." . . .

Augustine says that history reveals the intermingling of the City of God and the City of Man in time and space, and the incessant combat between the partisans of these two cities. This struggle will continue until time itself is annulled by God when Christ returns—and the saints are separated from sinners at the Last Judgment. Then the saints will join Jesus and be with him for eternity, and the sinners will be separated from God and confined to hell, also for eternity.

... In the eternal City of God, each and all of the citizens are personally immortal with an immortality which the holy angels never lost and which even human beings can come to share. This is to be achieved by the supreme omnipotence of the Creator, the Founder of the City. . . .

Who can measure the happiness of heaven, where no evil at all can touch us, no good will be out of reach; where life is to be one long laud extolling God, who will be all in all; where there will be no weariness to call for rest, no need to call for toil, no place for any energy but praise. . . .

. . . There will be such poise, such grace, such beauty as become a place where nothing unbecoming can be found. Wherever the spirit wills, there, in a flash, will the body be. Nor will the spirit ever will anything unbecoming either to itself or to the body.

In heaven, all glory will be true glory, since no one could ever err in praising too little or too much. True honor will never be denied where due, never be given where undeserved, and, since none but the worthy are permitted there, no one will unworthily [pursue] glory. Perfect peace will reign, since nothing in ourselves or in any others could disturb this peace.

MUHAMMAD

THE KORAN

Islamic standards of morality and rules governing daily life are set by the Koran, the book that Muslims believe contains the words of Allah as revealed to Muhammad. Muslims see their religion as the completion and perfection of Judaism and Christianity. They regard the ancient Hebrew prophets as sent from God and value their messages about compassion and the oneness of humanity. Muslims also regard Jesus as a great prophet but do not consider him divine. They see Muhammad as the last and greatest of the prophets and believe that he was entirely human, not divine. Muslims worship only Allah, the creator and ruler of heaven and earth, a single, all-powerful God who is merciful, compassionate, and just. Following are excerpts from the Koran.

GOD

God: there is no god but Him, the Living, the Eternal One. Neither slumber nor sleep overtakes Him. His is what the heavens and the earth contain. Who can intercede with Him except by His permission? He knows what is before and behind men. They can grasp only that part of His knowledge which He wills. His throne is as vast as the heavens and the earth, and the preservation of both does not weary Him. He is the Exalted, the Immense One. (2:255—257)

In the Name of God, the Compassionate, the Merciful

It is the Merciful who has taught the Koran.

He created man and taught him articulate speech. The sun and the moon pursue their ordered course. The plants and the trees bow down in adoration.

He raised the heaven on high and set the balance of all things, that you might not transgress that balance. Give just weight and full measure.

He laid the earth for His creatures, with all its fruits and blossom-bearing palm, chaff-covered grain and scented herbs. Which of your Lord's blessings would you deny?

He created man from potter's clay, and the jinn [spirits] from smokeless fire. Which of your Lord's blessings would you deny? (55:1-18)

All that is in the heavens and the earth gives glory to God. He is the Mighty, the Wise One.

It is He that has sovereignty over the heavens and the earth. He ordains life and death, and has power over all things.

He is the First and the Last, the Visible and the Unseen. He has knowledge of all things.

It was He who created the heavens and the earth in six days, and then mounted the throne. He knows all that goes into the earth and all that emerges from it, all that comes down from heaven and all that ascends to it. He is with you wherever you are. God is cognizant of all your actions.

He has sovereignty over the heavens and the earth. To God shall all things return. He causes the night to pass into the day, and causes the day to pass into the night. He has knowledge of the inmost thoughts of men. (57:1-7)

RIGHTEOUSNESS AND MERCY

Righteousness does not consist in whether you face towards the East or the West. The righteous man is he who believes in God and the Last Day, in the angels and the Book and the prophets; who, though he loves it dearly, gives away his wealth to kinsfolk, to orphans, to the destitute, to the traveller in need and to beggars, and for the redemption of captives; who attends to his prayers and renders the alms levy; who is true to his promises and steadfast in trial and adversity and in times of war. Such are the true believers; such are the God-fearing. (2:176-178)

Serve God and associate none with Him. Show kindness to parents and kindred, to orphans and to the destitute, to near and distant neighbours, to those that keep company with you, to the traveller in need, and to the slaves you own. God does not love arrogant and boastful men, who are themselves niggardly and enjoin others to be niggardly; who conceal the riches which God of His bounty has bestowed upon them (We have prepared a shameful punishment for the unbelievers); and who spend their wealth for the sake of ostentation, believing neither in God nor in the Last Day. He that chooses Satan for his friend, an evil friend has he. (4:36-39)

CHRISTIANITY

And remember the angels' words to Mary. They said:[4] "God has chosen you. He has made you pure and exalted you above womankind. Mary, be obedient to your Lord; bow down and worship with the worshippers."

This is an account of a divine secret. We reveal it to you.[5] You were not present when they cast lots to see which of them should have charge of Mary; nor were you present when they argued about her.

The angels said to Mary: "God bids you rejoice in a word from Him. His name is the Messiah, Jesus the son of Mary. He shall be noble in this world and in the hereafter, and shall be one of those who are favoured. He shall preach to men in his cradle and in the prime of manhood, and shall lead a righteous life."

"Lord" she said, "how can I bear a child when no man has touched me?"

He replied: "Even thus. God creates whom He will. When He decrees a thing He need only say: 'Be,' and it is. He will instruct him in the Scriptures and in wisdom, in the Torah and in the Gospel, and send him forth as an apostle to the Israelites. He will say: 'I bring you a sign from your Lord. From clay I will make for you the likeness of a bird. I shall breathe into it and, by God's leave, it shall become a living bird. By God's leave I shall heal the blind man and the leper, and raise the dead to life. I shall tell you what to eat and what to store up in your houses. Surely that will be a sign for you, if you are true believers. I come to confirm the Torah which preceded me and to make lawful to you some of the things you are forbidden. I bring you a sign from your Lord: therefore fear God and obey me. God is my Lord and your Lord: therefore serve Him. That is a straight path.'" (3:42-51)

People of the Book,[6] do not transgress the bounds of your religion. Speak nothing but the truth about God. The Messiah, Jesus the son of Mary, was no more than God's apostle and His Word which He cast to Mary: a spirit from Him. So believe in God and His apostles and do not say: "Three." Forbear, and it shall be better for you. God is but one God. God forbid that He should have a son! His is all that the heavens and the earth contain. God is the all-sufficient protector. The Messiah does not disdain to be a servant of God, nor do the angels who are nearest to Him. Those who through arrogance disdain His service shall all be brought before Him. (4:171-172)

HEAVEN AND HELL

THAT WHICH IS COMING

In the Name of God, the Compassionate, the Merciful

When that which is coming comes—and no soul shall then deny its coming—some shall be abased and others exalted.

---

[4] Cf. Luke i, 26-38

[5] Muhammad.

[6] Christians

When the earth shakes and quivers, and the mountains crumble away and scatter abroad into fine dust, you shall be divided into three multitudes: those on the right (blessed shall be those on the right); those on the left (damned shall be those on the left); and those to the fore (foremost shall be those). Such are they that shall be brought near to their Lord in the gardens of delight: a whole multitude from the men of old, but only a few from the latter generations.

They shall recline on jewelled couches face to face, and there shall wait on them immortal youths with bowls and ewers and a cup of purest wine (that will neither pain their heads nor take away their reason); with fruits of their own choice and flesh of fowls that they relish. And theirs shall be the dark-eyed houris [beautiful virgins], chaste as hidden pearls: a guerdon [reward] for their deeds.

There they shall hear no idle talk, no sinful speech, but only the greeting, "Peace! Peace!"

Those on the right hand—happy shall be those on the right hand! They shall recline on couches raised on high in the shade of thornless sidrs and clusters of talh;[7] amidst gushing waters and abundant fruits, unforbidden, neverending.

We created the houris and made them virgins, loving companions for those on the right hand: a multitude from the men of old, and a multitude from the latter generations.

As for those on the left hand (wretched shall be those on the left hand!) they shall dwell amidst scorching winds and seething water: in the shade of pitch-black smoke, neither cool nor refreshing. For they have lived in comfort and persisted in the heinous sin,[8] saying: "When we are once dead and turned to dust and bones, shall we be raised to life? And our forefathers, too?"

Say: "Those of old, and those of the present age, shall be brought together on an appointed day. As for you sinners who deny the truth, you shall eat the fruit of the Zaqqum tree and fill your bellies with it. You shall drink scalding water: yet you shall drink it as the thirsty camel drinks."

Such shall be their fare on the Day of Reckoning. (56: 1-56)

WOMEN

Men have authority over women because God has made the one superior to the other, and because they spend their wealth to maintain them. Good women are obedient. They guard their unseen parts because God has guarded them. As for those from whom you fear disobedience, admonish them and send them to beds apart and beat them. Then if they obey you, take no further action against them. Surely God is high, supreme.

If you fear a breach between a man and his wife, appoint an arbiter from his people and another from hers. If they wish to be reconciled God will bring them together again. Surely God is all-knowing and wise. (4:34-35)

[7] Probably the banana fruit.
[8] Idolatry.

THOUSAND AND ONE ARABIAN NIGHTS

Each individual tale exists within a larger framework story, which takes place in the islands off India and China. Shahryar accedes to the empire of his father, while his younger brother, Shah Zaman, becomes "King of Samarkand in Barbarian land." At his brother's court, Shah Zaman witnesses Shahryar's wife committing adultery and other illicit acts, and he tells his brother of his wife's betrayal. Shahryar, vowing revenge, commands that his wife be put to death along with all of her attendants and their companions. He then swears an oath— to marry a maiden every night, to violate her virginity, and to slay her the next morning. Eventually, there are virtually no virgins left in the realm, except for the two daughters of Shahryar's Chief Wazir, the elder of whom is Scheherazade.

Trusting in her own intelligence and wit, Scheherazade asks to marry King Shahryar, because she believes she can offer herself as a ransom for other women. Her father objects, but Scheherazade remains intransigent and prepares for her night with Shahryar by concocting a plan with her sister, Dunyazade. After Scheherazade is ravished by Shahryar, she signals for Dunyazade, who then begs Shahryar to allow Scheherazade to tell her a story. The trick, however, is that Scheherazade never finishes the tale, thereby prolonging her life.

The following tale deals with a *jinni* (better known by its Anglicized name "genie"). In Islamic folklore, jinn (the plural of jinni) are mythical demons or spirits (some good, many evil) who are considered to be lower than the angels. Since they were created from a smokeless fire, they can conceivably assume any form. King Sulayman (Solomon) confined many of them using magic, but the rest of them were destined to wander in solitary, obscure places around the world. In a multitude of ways, jinn are very much like human beings, including their need to eat, to reproduce, and to die. Jinn also savor punishing human beings for their errors, but they can be controlled by those who possess the correct knowledge of their behavior. Of special importance is the value the fisherman of this tale places on the role of Allah (God) in his life.

THE FISHERMAN AND THE JINNI

It is Related, O auspicious King, that there was once a fisherman, very old and poor, who was married and had three children.

He used to cast his net four times a day, never more often. Now once, when he had gone to the shore at noon, he set down his basket and, casting his net, waited for it to sink to the bottom. When it had done so he twitched the cords and found it so heavy that he could not pull it in. So, bringing the ends to shore, he made them fast to a wooden stake. Then he undressed and, diving into the sea, laboured till he had hauled the net ashore. Dressing himself again in high good humour he examined the net and found that it contained a dead ass. Disgusted at this sight, he exclaimed: "Be it as Allah wills!" and added: "Yet it is a strange gift that Allah has seen good to send me." Then he recited this verse:

Blind diver in the dark
Of night and loss,
Luck delights not in energy;
Cease, and be still.

After he had freed the net and squeezed the water out of it, he waded into the sea and cast it again, invoking the name of Allah. When the net had sunk to the bottom, he again tried to pull it ashore but this time it was even heavier and harder to shift. Thinking that he had caught some great fish, he fastened the ends to the stake and, undressing again, dived in and carried the net to shore. This time he found a great earthen jar full of mud and sand. In his disappointment at this sight, he proclaimed these verses:

I said I wished that fortune would die or fly away,
Who lets a man be virtuous and then keeps back his pay.
I left my house to look for luck
(A search I now abandon);

She dropped the wise men in the muck
For all the fools to stand on,
And, having fixed this state of things,
She either died or sprouted wings.

Then he threw away the jar and cleaned his net, asking pardon from Allah the while for his lack of submission to the divine will. And finally, coming down to the sea, he cast for the third time and waited for the net to sink. When he hauled in this time, the net was full of broken pots and pieces of glass. Seeing this, he recited the stanza of a certain poet.

Be not astonished that the golden wind
Blow the world forward, leaving you behind.
There are no dinars[9] in a rose-wood pen
For any but a merchant's hand to find.

Then lifting his face to the sky, he cried: "Allah, Allah! Thou knowest that I cast my net but four times in the day; and see! I have already cast it thrice." After this, he once more cast his net into the sea, again invoking the name of Allah, and waited for it to sink. This time, in spite of all his efforts, he could not move the net an inch, so hard was it held against the rocks below the water. Again he undressed crying: "Be it as Allah wills!" and diving for the fourth time, began to work the net until he had freed it and brought it to shore. This time he found in it a great jar of yellow copper, heavy and unhurt, its mouth stopped with lead and sealed with the seal of the lord Sulayman, son of David. Seeing this, the fisherman was delighted and said: "Here is something that I can sell at the market of the coppersmiths. It must be worth at least ten dinars of gold." Then, after trying to shake the jar and finding it too heavy he continued: "First I had better open the jar and hide whatever it contains in my basket; then I shall be able to sell the thing itself to the coppersmiths." So he took his knife and began to work the lead until he had removed it.

Then he turned the jar over and shook it, but nothing came out except a cloud of smoke which rose to the blue sky and also spread along the earth. Finally the smoke, to the utter amazement of the fisherman, came clear of the vase and shaking and thickening, turned to an *Ifrit*[10] whose head reached to the clouds while his feet were on the ground. The head of this Ifrit was like a dome, his hands like pitchforks, his legs like the masts of a ship, and his mouth like a cave in which the teeth had the appearance of great stones. His nostrils were like jugs, his eyes like torches, and his hair was dusty and matted. At the appearance of this being the fisherman was so frightened that his muscles quivered, his teeth chattered together, and he stood with burning mouth, and eyes that could not see the light.

When the Jinni, in his turn, saw the fisherman, he cried: "There is no other God but Allah, and Sulayman is Allah's prophet!" Then, speaking directly to the fisherman, he said: "O great Sulayman, O thou prophet of Allah, slay me not. Never again will I be disobedient or mutiny against thy just decrees." Then said the fisherman: "Darest thou, O blasphemous giant, to call Sulayman the prophet of Allah? Sulayman has been dead for eighteen hundred years and we have come to the end of the world's time. What tale is this? How did you come to be in this jar?" At these words the Jinni altered his tone and said: "There is no other God but Allah. I bring good news, O fisherman!" "What news is that?" asked the poor man. And the Jinni answered: "News of your death, instant and most horrible." "Let Allah be far from rewarding you for such news, prince of the Afarit! Why do you wish my death and how have I deserved it? I delivered you out of your jar, breaking your long imprisonment in the sea." But the Ifrit only answered: "Consider and choose the manner of death you would prefer and the way that I shall kill you." "But what is my fault? What is my fault?" repeated the wretched fisherman. "Listen to my story and you shall know," said the Ifrit. "Speak then, and make your tale a short one," said the fisherman, "for my soul is ready to run out of my feet for very fear." So the Ifrit began:

Know that I am Sakhr El-Jinni, one of the rebel Afarit who mutinied against Sulayman, son of David. There was a time when Sulayman sent his wazir Assef, son of Barkhia, against me, who overpow-

[9] The Islamic dinar is 4.3 grams of gold.
[10] Ifrit (plural Afarit) is a diabolic, evil spirit.

ered me in spite of all my strength and led me into the presence of Sulayman. You may believe that at that moment I humbled myself very low. Sulayman, seeing me, prayed to Allah and conjured me both to take that faith and to promise him obedience. When I refused, he had this jar brought before him and imprisoned me within it. Then he sealed it with lead and impressed thereon the Most High Name. Lastly, certain faithful Jinn took me upon their shoulders at his order and cast me into the middle of the sea. I stayed in the water for a hundred years and kept on saying: "I shall give eternal riches to him who sets me free!" But the hundred years passed and no one set me free. So, when I was entering on the second hundred years, I swore: "To him who sets me free will I both show and give all the treasures upon earth!" But no one freed me, and four hundred years passed away, and I said: "To him who frees me I will give the three wishes of his heart!" But still no one set me free. So I flew into a heat of passion in my jar and swore: "Now I will kill the man who frees me, my only gift being the choice of the death!" And it is you, O fisherman, who have set me free; therefore I let you choose the death you die.

Hearing the Ifrit speak in this way, the fisherman could not help exclaiming: "O Allah, the bad luck of it! It *would* have been left for me to do this freeing! Spare me, O Jinni, and Allah will spare you; kill me, and be very sure that He will raise up one to slay you also." Then said the Ifrit: "I shall kill you because you freed me. There is no help for it." On this the fisherman exclaimed: "Prince of the Afarit, indeed! Is this how you repay good with evil? The proverb does not lie which says:

If you would know the taste of bitterness
Seek sorrow out and comfort her distress;
You need not feed a jackal cub to see
Just how ungrateful gratitude can be."

But the Ifrit said: "You have used words enough. Prepare to meet your end." Then the fisherman reasoned with himself in this way: "Though I am a man and he is a Jinni, yet Allah has given me my share of brains. I think I see a trick, a stroke of subtlety, which may undo him yet." Then aloud to the Ifrit he said: "You are determined that I should die?" And when the other said: "No doubt of that!" the fisherman solemnly addressed him thus: "I conjure you by the Most High Name graved on the seal of Sulayman to answer me one question truthfully!" And when the Ifrit, dashed by hearing the Most High Name, promised that he would answer truthfully, the fisherman asked: "How could this jar which, as it is, scarcely could hold a foot or hand of yours, have ever held the whole of you?" "Can it be that you doubt this thing?" asked the Ifrit. And the other answered: "Never would I believe it unless I saw you with my own eyes entering the jar!"

But at this point Shahrazade saw the coming of morning and fell silent.

BOETHIUS

THE CONSOLATION OF PHILOSOPHY

Boethius (480-c. 525), a descendant of a noble family, was an important figure in the intellectual life of this transitional period. He was the last Latin-speaking scholar of the Roman world to have mastered the Greek language and to have an intimate knowledge of Greek philosophy. He translated some of Aristotle's treatises on logic into Latin and wrote commentaries on Aristotle, Cicero, and Porphyry, a Neoplatonist philosopher. Boethius served the Ostrogoth Theodoric I, who ruled Italy. A sudden turn of fortune deprived him of power and prestige when Theodoric ordered him executed for allegedly participating in a plot against the throne. While in prison awaiting execution, Boethius wrote *The Consolation of Philosohy* in which he sought comfort from Lady Philosophy.

In Book 1 of *The Consolation of Philosophy.* Boethius despairs of his recent change in fortune when Lady Philosophy, the personification of highest capabilities of human reason, appears. He tells her that he had become a public servant because of Plato's judgment that wise men ought to be rulers. Despite his innocence he has been condemned to death. How is it possible, he wonders, that the wicked should prevail over virtue; how can God permit such injustice? Lady Philosophy begins by reminding him that the world is governed by divine reason. Then she tells him that there are two basic causes for his sickness—he no longer understands that God rules the world, and he has forgotten his own human identity, that is, he no longer knows that he possesses an immortal soul. Book 2 features a discussion about the fickle nature of the goddess Fortune, who no longer favors Boethius. Lady Philosophy reminds Boethius of the bountiful blessings that Fortune had previously bestowed on him. Then, in the tradition of Plato and the Stoics, she tells him that Fortune can never take away the happiness that resides within a person. Happiness is the highest good of a rational person. She goes on to inform him that Fortune will have no power over him after this life is over, when his mind, the higher aspect of the soul, will continue to live, free from the prison of this world. Finally, she reminds him that even a tyrant cannot control a free mind.

"So why, mortal men, do you pursue happiness outside yourselves, when it lies within?" Error and ignorance derange you. I shall briefly outline for you the hinge on which the greatest happiness turns. Is there anything more precious to you than yourself? Nothing, you will reply. Well then, as long as you are in command of yourself, you will possess what you would never wish to lose, and what Fortune can never withdraw from you. So that you may acknowledge that true happiness cannot reside in this realm of chance, you must grasp this argument: If happiness is the highest good of a rational nature, and if what can be taken from you in any way cannot be the highest (for what cannot be taken away ranks higher than what can), it is obvious that the fluidity of Fortune cannot hope to win happiness. . . .

"Now you are that same person who I know held the rooted conviction, instilled by numerous proofs, that the minds of men are in no wise mortal, and since it is obvious that the happiness which chance brings ends with the body's death, there can be no doubt, assuming that such happiness can confer well-being, that when death signals the end the whole human race is plunged into misery. Yet we know that many have come to enjoy such well-being not only in death, but even in pain and torture. So how can that happiness whose cessation does not make us wretched induce well- being in us by its presence? . . . How can a person exercise rights over any other, except over his body and that which ranks below his body, namely his fortune? You can exercise no dominion whatever, can you, over a free mind? Or disturb from its natural serenity a mind at one with itself through the steadying influence of reason? When the tyrant thought that by a torture he would force a free man to betray his associates in the conspiracy against him, the free man bit through his tongue, and threw it in the face of the storming tyrant. In this way that sage made a virtue out of the tortures which the tyrant believed were instruments of cruelty. ..."

The theme of Book 3 is the essence of true happiness and how to achieve it. Lady Philosophy points out that there are five false paths to happiness: the ambition for wealth, high position, power, fame, and physical pleasures. Then, in the form of a Platonic dialogue in the following passage, she points Boethius to the true Good, which resides in God, who is true happiness. Humans can attain goodness and happiness by becoming as godlike as possible.

CHAPTER 10

"So now that you have seen what is the shape of the imperfect good, and also that of the perfect good, I think that I must now show you the region in which the perfection of happiness is set.

"Any consideration of this must, I think, first investigate whether any good of this kind, as defined by you a little earlier, can exist in this world. We shall thus ensure that we are not beguiled by some vacuous mental image which is remote from the true reality lying before us. Now it cannot be denied that the perfect good exists, and that it is, so to say, the source of all goods, for everything said to be imperfect is so described because it is less than perfect. The logical conclusion is that if in any class of objects something imperfect appears, that class must also contain something perfect; for if such perfection is removed, one cannot even imagine how that which is called imperfect has come into existence. The universe does not take its rise from things which were curtailed or incomplete; rather, it issues from things which are intact and fully developed, and it disintegrates into this parlous and sterile world of ours. Now if, as we demonstrated a little earlier, there is what we may call imperfect happiness in a good that is brittle, there can be no doubt of the existence of some unalloyed and perfect happiness."

"That conclusion," I said, "is as solid and as true as it can possibly be."

"Now as for the abode of that happiness," she went on, "ponder it in this way. The belief which human minds share demonstrates that God, the source of all things, is good; for since nothing better than God can be imagined, who can doubt that if something has no better, it is good? Reason in fact establishes that God's goodness is such as to demonstrate further that perfect good resides within him. Were this not the case, he could not be the source of all things, for there would be something more preeminent, which would be in possession of perfect good, and would be seen to take precedence ahead of him, since all perfect things clearly take precedence over things less complete. So to prevent the argument advancing into infinity, we must allow that the highest God is totally full of the highest and perfect good. Now we have established that the perfect good is true happiness, so true happiness must reside in the highest God."

"I grant that," I said. "No possible counter-argument can be raised against it."

"But we have already conceded that the highest good is happiness."

"Indeed we have," I replied.

"And so," she said, "we must acknowledge that God is happiness itself."

"I cannot refute your earlier assertions", I said, "and I do see that this rider necessarily follows."

"Now consider," she added, "whether the same conclusion is also reached even more demonstrably from this: there cannot be two highest goods which differ from each other. Indeed, it is clear that if two goods differ, the one is not the other, and accordingly neither can possibly be perfect, since each lacks the other. Now clearly if something is not perfect, it is not the highest. So it is totally impossible for highest goods to differ from each other. But we have concluded that both happiness and God are the highest good, so the highest divinity must itself be the highest happiness."

"No possible conclusion", I said, "could be truer in fact, surer in logic, or worthier of God."

"But we have shown that God and true happiness are one and the same."

"We have indeed," I said.

"Therefore we can safely conclude that God's substance too lies in the good itself, and nowhere else. …"

Book 4 addresses a second theme: Why is there so much evil and suffering in the world? Why is vice so dominant while virtue struggles to survive? In response, Lady Philosophy maintains that evil does not prevail. Evil people will never escape punishment; they are weak. Good people become divine by attaining the good, and they are powerful. Boethius then brings up another, closely related issue—the seemingly irrational operation of chance in the world that appears to be antithetical to the governance of Providence. Lady Philosophy explains that Fate operates in this world according to the plan of Providence, divine reason. This leads into the topic of Book 5, where Boethius wonders whether there is such a thing as chance. Lady Philosophy answers that chance cannot exist because Providence rules the universe. Boethius then asks the inevitable question: How can humans have free will if all is governed by divine Providence?

CHAPTER 3

At this I said: "I fear that I am further disconcerted by a still more difficult doubt."

"What is it?" she asked. "Mind you, I can guess what is worrying you."

"There seems to be a considerable contradiction and inconsistency", I said, "between God's foreknowing all things and the existence of any free will. If God foresees all things and cannot be in any way mistaken, then what Providence has foreseen will happen must inevitably come to pass. So if God has prior knowledge from eternity not only of men's actions but also of their plans and wishes, there will be no freedom of will; for the only action and any sort of intention which can possibly exist in the future will be foreknown by divine Providence, which cannot be misled. If such actions and aspirations can be forcibly diverted in some direction other than was foreseen, certain foreknowledge of the future will no longer exist, but instead there will be vacillating opinion; and I regard it is sacrilege to believe this of God.

"I do not subscribe to the argument by which some believe that they can disentangle this knotty problem. What they suggest is that Providence's foreknowledge of a future event is not the cause of its happening, but that it is the other way round. Since something is about to happen, this cannot be hidden from divine Providence, and in this sense, they claim, the element of necessity is reversed Their argument is that things foreseen do not therefore happen by necessity, but that things which will happen are necessarily foreseen. The assumption here is that we are toiling over the problem of which is the cause of which: is foreknowledge the cause of the necessity of future events, or is the necessity of future events the cause of Providence? In fact, however, we are struggling to show that whatever the sequence of causes, the outcome of things foreknown is necessary, even if such foreknowledge does not appear to impose an inevitable outcome upon future events. ..."

If God foresees everything and if what God foresees must happen, how can humans be free to choose what they wish to choose? Indeed, if what God knows will happen must happen, then God must be responsible for everything that happens; he must even be responsible for evil. In that case, rewarding the good and punishing evil would be meaningless.

"Once this is admitted, the extent of the decline in human fortunes becomes evident. Rewards or punishments offered to good or wicked men are pointless, for they have not been won by any free, and voluntary impulse of their minds. What is now considered utterly just—punishments for the wicked and rewards for the good—will be seen to be the greatest injustice imaginable, because they have been impelled to commit good or evil not by their own will, but, by the unchanging necessity of what will be. So neither vices nor virtues will exist at all; instead all the deserts of people are mingled and undifferentiated in the melting pot. More- over—and nothing more heinous than this can be imagined—since the entire ordering of human affairs derives from Providence, and no discretion is granted to our human intentions, our vices as well are to be ascribed to the author of all things good. ..."

Lady Philosophy's answer concludes the *Consolation*. Human reason is not able to know the way that God knows. Limited human reason sees all things as past, present, and future, but the infinite divine intelligence sees all things as eternally present. In his eternal present, God sees things that will happen in what humans consider to be the future. Nonetheless, humans have a free will. An event is necessary because of God's knowledge of it, but things happen as a result of the free will of humans. Moreover, every time humans change their minds, Providence has already anticipated these future actions. The human will is free. Therefore, humans must act virtuously, because God will punish the evil actions that he has foreseen in his perfect knowledge.

EINHARD

CHARLEMAGNE'S APPRECIATION OF LEARNING

The revival of classical learning and the visual arts under Charlemagne is called the Carolingian Renaissance, a cultural awakening that helped shape medieval civilization. One of Charlemagne's most significant decisions was ordering the making of copies of old manuscripts dating back to Roman times. Much of today's knowledge of Roman learning and literature comes from surviving Carolingian copies of older Latin texts that no longer exist. In the first reading, Charlemagne's biographer Einhard describes western Europe's greatest royal patron of the liberal arts since the fall of the western Roman Empire.

Charles [Charlemagne] had the gift of ready and fluent speech, and could express whatever he had to say with the utmost clearness. He was not satisfied with command of his native language merely, but gave attention to the study of foreign ones, and in particular was such a master of Latin that he could speak it as well as his native tongue; but he could understand Greek better than he could speak it. He was so eloquent, indeed, that he might have passed for a teacher of eloquence. He most zealously cultivated the liberal arts, held those who taught them in great esteem, and conferred great honors upon them. He took lessons in grammar of the deacon Peter of Pisa,[1] at that time an aged man. Another deacon, Albin of Britain, surnamed Alcuin, a man of Saxon extraction, who was the greatest scholar of the day, was his teacher in other branches of learning. The King spent much time and labor with him studying rhetoric, dialectics, and especially astronomy; he learned to reckon, and used to investigate the motions of the heavenly bodies most curiously, with an intelligent scrutiny. He also tried to write, and used to keep tablets and blanks in bed under his pillow, that at leisure hours he might accustom his hand to form the letters; however, as he did not begin his efforts in due season, but late in life, they met with ill success.

He cherished with the greatest fervor and devotion the principles of the Christian religion, which had been instilled into him from infancy. Hence it was that he built the beautiful basilica[2] at Aix-la-Chapelle,[3] which he adorned with gold and silver and lamps, and with rails and doors of solid brass. He had the columns and marbles for this structure brought from Rome and Ravenna,[4] for he could not find such as were suitable elsewhere. He was a constant worshipper at this church as long as his health permitted, going morning and evening, even after nightfall, besides attending mass; and he took care that all the services there conducted should be administered with the utmost possible propriety, very often warning the sextons not to let any improper or unclean thing be brought into the building or remain in it. He provided it with a great number of sacred vessels of gold and silver and with such a quantity of clerical robes that not even the doorkeepers who fill the humblest office in the church were obliged to wear their everyday clothes when in the exercise of their duties. He was at great pains to improve the church reading and psalmody [singing], for he was well skilled in both, although he neither read in public nor sang, except in a low tone and with others.

He was very forward in succoring the poor, and in that gratuitous generosity which the Greeks call alms, so much so that he not only made a point of giving in his own country and his own kingdom, but when he discovered that there were Christians living in poverty in Syria, Egypt, and Africa, at Jerusalem, Alexandria, and Carthage, he had compassion on their wants, and used to send money over the seas to them. . . .

---

[1]Peter of Pisa, a famous grammarian (in Latin, the international language of the Middle Ages), was brought from Italy to teach at the school in Charlemagne's palace. He encouraged interest in pre-Christian classical writing, which influenced the court poets of that era.

[2]A basilica is usually a rectangular-shaped church, whose main chamber is divided by columns into a central nave and side aisles. There was usually a semicircular apse at the narrow end facing the east, which was the visual focal point and the location of the main altar.

[3]Aix-la-Chapelle, now Aachen, was Charlemagne's capital. It was located in what is now western Germany, near the Netherlands-Belgium frontier.

[4] Ravenna, in northeastern Italy, was the final capital of the western Roman Empire, in the fifth century; in the sixth and seventh centuries it was the capital of the Byzantine governors of Italy. Ravenna is famous for its magnificent sixth-century churches and mosaic art.

BEOWULF

As the poem opens, the reader is introduced to *Evil* in the guise of the monster, Grendel, who each evening terrorizes the court of Hrothgar, the Danish king, by devouring a number of his warriors. *Good* is presented in the form of Beowulf, a prince of the Geats,[1] who seeks to gain a name for himself by slaying Grendel. During his first encounter with Grendel at Hrothgar's court, Beowulf tears the monster's arm off at the shoulder. Later that night, Beowulf confronts Grendel's mother who seeks vengeance upon Hrothgar's court by carrying off his chief advisor. Beowulf becomes a hero in the eyes of the Danes when he follows Gren- del's mother to a haunted lake and slays her with a magical sword under the water. The Danes give Beowulf treasure and lands as a reward for helping them rid their territory of the race of evil monsters. The long, first part of the poem concludes with Beowulf returning to the Geats, telling his uncle, King Hygelac, of his deeds, and honoring his liege lord by giving him his reward.

The second section of the poem, excerpted below, opens with Beowulf ascending the throne of the Geats after his uncle and his cousin are killed on the battlefield. He rules the kingdom peacefully for fifty years, "until a certain one, a dragon, began to rule in the dark nights." Knowing that if he is successful in slaying the dragon he will gain the dragon's treasure, Beowulf, even though he is an old man, challenges the dragon to single combat. During the dragon's first attack, Beowulf is engulfed in flames and his terrified men betray him by fleeing.

Then he addressed each dear companion
one final time, those fighters in their helmets,
resolute and high-born: "I would rather not
use a weapon if I knew another way
to grapple with the dragon and make good my boast
as I did against Grendel in days gone by.
But I shall be meeting molten venom
in the fire he breathes, so I go forth
in mail-shirt and shield. I won't shift a foot
when I meet the cave-guard: what occurs on the wall
between the two of us will turn out as fate,
overseer of men, decides. I am resolved.
I scorn further words against this sky-borne foe.
"Men at arms, remain here on the barrow [a mound of earth],
safe in your armour, to see which one of us
is better in the end at bearing wounds
in a deadly fray. This fight is not yours,
nor is it up to any man except me
to measure his strength against the monster
or to prove his worth. I shall win the gold
by my courage, or else mortal combat,
doom of battle, will bear your lord away."
Then he drew himself up beside his shield.
The fabled warrior in his warshirt and helmet
trusted in his own strength entirely
and went under the crag. No coward path.
Hard by the rock-face that hale veteran,
a good man who had gone repeatedly
into combat and danger and come through,
saw a stone arch and a gushing stream

[1] 'The poet presents the Geats as a tribe situated in the southeastern part of Sweden.

that burst from the barrow, blazing and wafting
a deadly heat. It would be hard to survive
unscathed near the hoard, to hold firm
against the dragon in those flaming depths.
Then he gave a shout. The lord of the Geats
unburdened his breast and broke out
in a storm of anger. Under grey stone
his voice challenged and resounded clearly.
Hate was ignited. The hoard-guard recognized
a human voice, the time was over
for peace and parleying. Pouring forth
in a hot battle-fume, the breath of the monster
burst from the rock. There was a rumble under ground.
Down there in the barrow, Beowulf the warrior
lifted his shield: the outlandish thing
writhed and convulsed and vehemently
turned on the king, whose keen-edged sword,
an heirloom inherited by ancient right,
was already in his hand. Roused to a fury,
each antagonist struck terror in the other.
Unyielding, the lord of his people loomed
by his tall shield, sure of his ground,
while the serpent looped and unleashed itself.
Swaddled in flames, it came gliding and flexing
and racing towards its fate. Yet his shield defended
the renowned leader's life and limb
for a shorter time than he meant it to:
that final day was the first time
when Beowulf fought and fate denied him
glory in battle. So the king of the Geats
raised his hand and struck hard
at the enamelled scales, but scarcely cut through:
the blade flashed and slashed yet the blow
was far less powerful than the hard-pressed king
had need of at that moment. The mound-keeper
went into a spasm and spouted deadly flames:
when he felt the stroke, battle-fire
billowed and spewed. Beowulf was foiled
of a glorious victory. The glittering sword,
infallible before that day,
failed when he unsheathed it, as it never should have.
For the son of Ecgtheow, it was no easy thing
to have to give ground like that and go
unwillingly to inhabit another home
in a place beyond; so every man must yield
the leasehold of his days.
It was not long
until the fierce contenders clashed again.
The hoard-guard took heart, inhaled and swelled up
and got a new wind; he who had once ruled

was furled in fire and had to face the worst.
No help or backing was to be had then
from his high-born comrades; that hand-picked troop
broke ranks and ran for their lives
to the safety of the wood. But within one heart
sorrow welled up: in a man of worth
the claims of kinship cannot be denied. . . .

When the dragon attacks a second time, Beowulf stabs it in the neck and breaks his magical sword. It is Beowulf, however, who is mortally wounded in the third attack when the dragon bites him in the neck. Finally, Beowulf's loyal retainer Wiglaf, his only defender, attempts to avenge his lord's mortal wound by driving his sword into the dragon's stomach, but it is Beowulf who wields the fatal blow.

"As God is my witness,
I would rather my body were robed in the same
burning blaze as my gold-giver's body
than go back home bearing arms.
That is unthinkable, unless we have first
slain the foe and defended the life
of the prince of the Weather-Geats. I well know
the things he has done for us deserve better.
Should he alone be left exposed
to fall in battle? We must bond together,
shield and helmet, mail-shirt and sword."
Then he waded the dangerous reek and went
under arms to his lord, saying only:
"Go on, dear Beowulf, do everything
you said you would when you were still young
and vowed you would never let your name and fame
be dimmed while you lived. Your deeds are famous,
so stay resolute, my lord, defend your life now
with the whole of your strength. I shall stand by you."
After those words, a wildness rose
in the dragon again and drove it to attack,
heaving up fire, hunting for enemies,
the humans it loathed. Flames lapped the shield,
charred it to the boss, and the body armour
on the young warrior was useless to him.
But Wiglaf did well under the wide rim
Beowulf shared with him once his own had shattered
in sparks and ashes.
Inspired again
by the thought of glory, the war-king threw
his whole strength behind a sword-stroke
and connected with the skull. And Naegling snapped.
Beowulf's ancient iron-grey sword
let him down in the fight. It was never his fortune
to be helped in combat by the cutting edge
of weapons made of iron. When he wielded a sword,
no matter how blooded and hard-edged the blade
his hand was too strong, the stroke he dealt

(I have heard) would ruin it. He could reap no advantage.
Then the bane of that people, the fire-breathing dragon,
was mad to attack for a third time.
When a chance came, he caught the hero
in a rush of flame and clamped sharp fangs
into his neck. Beowulf's body
ran wet with his life-blood: it came welling out.
Next thing, they say, the noble son of Weohstan
saw the king in danger at his side
and displayed his inborn bravery and strength.
He left the head alone, but his fighting hand
was burned when he came to his kinsman's aid.
He lunged at the enemy lower down
so that his decorated sword sank into its belly
and the flames grew weaker.
Once again the king
gathered his strength and drew a stabbing knife
he carried on his belt, sharpened for battle.
He stuck it deep into the dragon's flank.
Beowulf dealt it a deadly wound.
They had killed the enemy, courage quelled his life;
that pair of kinsmen, partners in nobility,
had destroyed the foe. So every man should act,
be at hand when needed; but now, for the king,
this would be the last of his many labours
and triumphs in the world.
Then the wound
dealt by the ground-burner earlier began
to scald and swell; Beowulf discovered
deadly poison suppurating inside him,
surges of nausea, and so, in his wisdom,
the prince realized his state and struggled
towards a seat on the rampart. He steadied his gaze
on those gigantic stones, saw how the earthwork
was braced with arches built over columns.
And now that thane unequalled for goodness
with his own hands washed his lord's wounds,
swabbed the weary prince with water,
bathed him clean, unbuckled his helmet.
Beowulf spoke: in spite of his wounds,
mortal wounds, he still spoke
for he well knew his days in the world
had been lived out to the end: his allotted time
was drawing to a close, death was very near.
"Now is the time when I would have wanted
to bestow this armour on my own son,
had it been my fortune to have fathered an heir
and live on in his flesh. For fifty years
I ruled this nation. No king
of any neighbouring clan would dare

face me with troops, none had the power
to intimidate me. I took what came,
cared for and stood by things in my keeping,
never fomented quarrels, never
swore to a lie. All this consoles me,
doomed as I am and sickening for death;
because of my right ways, the Ruler of mankind
need never blame me when the breath leaves my body
for murder of kinsmen. Go now quickly,
dearest Wiglaf, under the grey stone
where the dragon is laid out, lost to his treasure;
hurry to feast your eyes on the hoard.
Away you go: I want to examine
that ancient gold, gaze my fill
on those garnered jewels; my going will be easier
for having seen the treasure, a less troubled letting-go
of the life and lordship I have long maintained."

THOMAS AQUINAS

SUMMA THEOLOGICA

An alternative approach to that of Augustine and Anselm was provided by Thomas Aquinas (1225—1274), a friar of the Order of Preachers (Dominicans), who taught theology in Paris and later in Italy. Along with Augustine and Anselm, Aquinas believed that God was the source of all truth, that human nature was corrupted by the imprint of the original sin of Adam and Eve, and that God revealed himself through the Bible and in the person of Jesus Christ. But, in contrast to Augustine and Anselm, Aquinas expressed great confidence in the power of reason to investigate the natural world.

Aquinas held that as both faith and reason came from God, they were not in opposition to each other; properly understood, they supported each other. Because reason was no enemy of faith, it should not be feared. In addition to showing renewed respect for reason, Aquinas—influenced by Aristotelian empiricism (the acquisition of knowledge of nature through experience)—valued knowledge of the natural world. He saw the natural and supernatural worlds not as irreconcilable and hostile to each other, but as a continuous ascending hierarchy of divinely created orders of being moving progressively toward the Supreme Being. In constructing a synthesis of Christianity and Aristotelianism, Aquinas gave renewed importance to the natural world, human reason, and the creative human spirit. Nevertheless, by holding that reason was subordinate to faith, he remained a typically medieval thinker.

In his most ambitious work, the *Summa Theologica,* Aquinas specifically rejects Anselm's ontological argument. Nonetheless, Aquinas argues that God's existence, even though it is a matter of faith, can be proven by natural reason, drawing on experience and evidence from nature. In the following selection, Aquinas argues for God's existence, building his argument on the categories of Aristotelian philosophy.

WHETHER GOD EXISTS?

The existence of God can be proved in five ways.

The first and more manifest way is the argument from motion. It is certain, and evident to our senses, that in the world some things are in motion. Now whatever is moved is moved by another, for nothing can be moved except it is in potentiality to that towards which it is moved; whereas a thing moves inasmuch as it is in act. For motion is nothing else than the reduction of something from potentiality to actuality. But nothing can be reduced from potentiality to actuality, except by something in a state of actuality. Thus that which is actually hot, as fire, makes wood, which is potentially hot, to be actually hot, and thereby moves and changes it. Now it is not possible that the same thing should be at once in actuality and potentiality in the same respect, but only in different respects. For what is actually hot cannot simultaneously be potentially hot; but it is simultaneously potentially cold. It is therefore impossible that in the same respect and in the same way a thing should be both mover and moved, *i.e.,* that it should move itself. Therefore, whatever is moved must be moved by another. If that by which it is moved be itself moved, then this also must needs be moved by another, and that by another again. But this cannot go on to infinity, because then there would be no first mover, and, consequently, no other mover, seeing that subsequent movers move only inasmuch as they are moved by the first mover; as the staff moves only because it is moved by the hand. Therefore it is necessary to arrive at a first mover, moved by no other; and this everyone understands to be God.

The second way is from the nature of efficient cause. In the world of sensible things we find there is an order of efficient causes. There is no case known (neither is it, indeed, possible) in which a thing is found to be the efficient cause of itself; for so it would be prior to itself, which is impossible. Now in efficient causes it is not possible to go on to infinity, because in all efficient causes following in order, the first is the cause of the intermediate cause, and the intermediate is the cause of the ultimate cause, whether the intermediate cause be several, or one only. Now to take away the cause is to take away the effect. Therefore, if there be no first cause among efficient causes, there will be no ultimate, nor any intermediate, cause. But if in efficient causes it is possible to go on to infinity, there will be no first efficient cause, neither will there be an ultimate effect, nor any intermediate efficient causes; all of which is plainly false. Therefore it is necessary to admit a first efficient cause, to which everyone gives the name of God.

The third way is taken from possibility and necessity, and runs thus. We find in nature things that are possible to be and not to be, since they are found to be generated, and to be corrupted, and consequently, it is possible for them to be and not to be. But it is impossible for these always to exist, for that which can not-be at some time is not. Therefore, if everything can not-be, then at one time there was nothing in existence. Now if this were true, even now there would be nothing in existence, because that which does not exist begins to exist only through something already existing. Therefore, if at one time nothing was in existence, it would have been impossible for anything to have begun to exist; and thus even now nothing would be in existence—which is absurd. Therefore, not all beings are merely possible, but there must exist something the existence of which is necessary. But every necessary thing either has its necessity caused by another, or not. Now it is impossible to go on to infinity in necessary things which have their necessity caused by another, as has been already proved in regard to efficient causes. Therefore we cannot but admit the existence of some being having of itself its own necessity, and not receiving it from another, but rather causing in others their necessity. This all men speak of as God.

The fourth way is taken from the graduation to be found in things. Among beings there are some more and some less good, true, noble, and the like. But *more* and *less* are predicated of different things according as they resemble in their different ways something which is the maximum, as a thing is said to be hotter according as it more nearly resembles that which is hottest; so that there is something which is truest, something best, something noblest, and, consequently, something which is most being, for those things that are greatest in truth are greatest in being. . . . Now the maximum in any genus is the cause of all in that genus, as fire, which is the maximum of heat, is the cause of all hot things. . . . Therefore there must also be something which is to all beings the cause of their being, goodness, and every other perfection; and this we call God.

The fifth way is taken from the governance of the world. We see that things which lack knowledge, such as natural bodies, act for an end, and this is evident from their acting always, or nearly always, in the same way, so as to obtain the best result. Hence it is plain that they achieve their end, not fortuitously, but designedly. Now whatever lacks knowledge cannot move towards an end, unless it be directed by some being endowed with knowledge and intelligence; as the arrow is directed by the archer. Therefore some intelligent being exists by whom all natural things are directed to their end; and this being we call God.

THE SONG OF ROLAND

CONFLICT BETWEEN CHRISTIANITY AND ISLAM

The Song of Roland presents these historical events as a classic confrontation between good and evil, between the Christian king, Charlemagne, and the Saracen king of Spain, Marsile. The poem begins with Charlemagne having conquered all of Spain except for Zaragoza, which Marsile still controls. As a peace overture, Marsile offers to convert to Christianity and to become Charlemagne's vassal if he will return with his army to Aachen. Roland counsels Charlemagne to reject the offer, but Roland's stepfather, Ganelon, argues that it would be wrong to continue to fight against a foe who seeks clemency. Roland then nominates Ganelon for the treacherous task of negotiating with Marsile. Angry at Roland, Ganelon conspires with Marsile to bring about Roland's death in battle. Ganelon manipulates the situation so that Roland is in command of the rear guard, and, as Charlemagne's army withdraws from Spain through the pass, Roland's troops are overwhelmed by the Saracens. In the following passage, the battle tide turns against Roland, his friend Count Oliver, and Archbishop Turpin.

127

Count Roland calls to Oliver:
"Comrade, sir, you will grant, I'm sure,
That the Archbishop is a very good knight.
There is no finer one on the face of the earth,
He is formidable with lance and spear."
The Count replies: "Come on, let's go help him!"
When they heard this, the Franks began striking anew.
The blows are hard and the fighting is heavy,
The Christians suffer very heavy losses.
One could see then Roland and Oliver
Striking and slashing with their swords!
The Archbishop strikes with his spear.
We have a good idea of the number they killed:
It is written in the documents and records,
The Chronicle says that there were more than four thousand.
It went well with them during four assaults,
But afterward the fifth brought them to ruin and grief.
The French knights are now all dead,
Except for sixty whom God has spared.
Before they die, they will sell their lives dearly.

128

Count Roland sees the great slaughter of his men.
He calls his companion Oliver:
"Dear sir, dear comrade, in God's name, what do you make of this?
You see so many good knights lying on the ground!
Sweet France, the fair, is to be pitied,
How impoverished she is now of such knights!
O dear King, what a shame you're not here!
Dear Oliver, how shall we do it,
How shall we break the news to him?"

Oliver said: "I don't know how to reach him.
I'd rather die than have something to blame ourselves for."

129.

Roland said: "I shall sound the oliphant.
Charles, who is going through the pass, will hear it.
I give you my word that the Franks will return now."
Oliver said: "That would be dishonorable
And a reproach to all your relatives,
The shame of it would last the rest of their lives!
When I told you to, you did nothing at all,
Don't expect my consent to do it now.
If you sound the horn, it will not be a brave act.
See how bloody both your arms are!"
The Count replies: "I have struck mighty fine blows!"

130.

Roland says: "Our battle is hard,
I shall sound the horn and Charles will hear it."
Oliver said: "That would not be a heroic deed!
When I told you to, comrade, you did not deign to.
If the King had been here, we would have suffered no harm.
Those who are with him over there are not to be blamed."
Oliver said: "By this beard of mine,
If I manage to see my fair sister Aida again,
You shall never lie in her arms!"

131.

Roland said: "Why are you angry with me?"
The other replies: "Comrade, you brought it on yourself,
For heroism tempered with common sense is a far cry from madness;
Reasonableness is to be preferred to recklessness.
Frenchmen have died because of your senselessness.
We shall never again be of service to Charles.
If you had believed me, my lord would have come,
We would have fought or won (?) this battle,
King Marsile would be captured or slain.
We have come to rue your prowess, Roland!
Charlemagne will not have any help from us.
There shall never be such a man again until Judgment Day.
You will die here and France will be dishonored.
Today our loyal companionage comes to an end,
Before nightfall, our parting will be very sad."

132.

The Archbishop hears them quarreling.
He urges on his horse with his pure gold spurs.

He comes up to them, he began to reprove them:
"Sir Roland and you, Sir Oliver,
In God's name I beg you, don't argue!
Sounding the horn would be of no use to us now,
Nevertheless it is best:
Let the King come and he will be able to avenge us,
The men of Spain must not return home joyful.
Our Frenchmen will dismount,
They will find us dead and cut to pieces.
They will raise us in coffins on sumpters,
They will shed tears of sorrow and pity for us.
They will bury us in hallowed ground within church walls,
Neither wolves, nor pigs, nor dogs will devour us."
Roland replies: "Well said, sir."

At this Point Roland blows the oliphant, a natural horn made from ivory, to signal the emperor that he and his troops need help. Charlemagne hears the horn and, despite Ganelon's assurance that there is no battle, he prepares to go to Roland's defense. Oliver dies first, and then, the Archbishop. Finally, Roland dies, just before Charlemagne arrives. When Charlemagne finds Roland's body, he vows vengeance. Back in Aachen, Ganelon is put on trial for treason, found guilty, and executed by being pulled apart by four horses. The following passage tells of Roland's death.

135.

Count Roland's mouth is bleeding,
The temple of his brain has burst.
He sounds the oliphant in agony and in pain,
Charles heard it, and his Frenchmen too.
The King said: "That horn has been blowing a long time!"
Duke Naimes replies: "A worthy knight is pouring out his suffering!
There is a battle, so help me.
The one who begs you to pretend you have heard nothing has betrayed him.
To arms, shout your battle cry,
Save your noble household:
You hear as plain as can be Roland signaling his distress!"

136.

The Emperor has ordered his trumpets to be sounded.
The French dismount, they arm themselves
With hauberks, helmets, and gilded swords.
They have fine shields and long and sturdy spears,
And white, red, and blue ensigns.
All the knights of the army mount their war-horses,
They spur furiously until they are out of the pass.
They say to one another:
"If only we could see Roland before he's killed,
We would strike mighty blows with him!"
But what is the use? They have tarried too long. . . .

139.

King Charles rides like fury,
His white beard is spread over his hauberk.
The knights from France all spur furiously,
They are all in a state of blind anger
For not being with Roland, the captain,
Who is fighting the Saracens of Spain.
He is so badly hurt I do not think his soul can remain in him.
God! what men, the sixty who are in his company!
No king or captain ever had finer.

140.

Roland gazes at the mountains and hills.
He sees so many men from France lying dead,
He weeps over them like a noble knight:
"My lord barons, God have mercy on you!
May He grant Paradise to all your souls,
May He cause them to lie among the holy flowers!
I have never seen worthier knights than you,
You have served me constantly and for so long!
You have conquered such great nations for Charles!
The Emperor raised you, but how unfortunate the outcome!
Land of France, you are a very sweet realm,
Today made desolate by such a cruel disaster!
French knights, I see you dying for my sake:
I cannot protect or save you.
May God, who never did lie, help you!
Oliver, my friend, I must not fail you,
I shall die of sorrow if nothing else kills me.
Comrade, sir, let's go strike again!"

156

Count Roland is fighting nobly,
But his body is covered with sweat and is very hot.
He has an ache and a great pain in his head,
His temple is burst because he sounded the horn.
But he wants to know if Charles will come,
He draws the oliphant, he sounded it feebly.
The Emperor halted and listened to it.

164.

Count Roland sees his peers dead
And Oliver, whom he loved so well,
He was moved with pity, he begins to weep.
His face lost all its color.
He suffered such pain that he could no longer stand,
Willy-nilly, he falls to the ground.

The Archbishop said: "You are to be pitied. worthy knight!"

165.

When the Archbishop saw Roland faint,
He suffered greater anguish than ever before.
He stretched out his hand and took the oliphant.
At Roncevaux there is a running stream,
He wants to go there, he will give some water to Roland.
He turns and goes away with short, faltering steps.
He is so weak that he cannot go any farther,
He has not the strength to, he has lost too much blood.
In less time than it would take a man to cover a single acre,
His heart fails him and he falls forward.
His death is gripping him hard.

166.

Count Roland recovers from his swoon,
He rises to his feet, but he is suffering great pain.
He gazes uphill and he gazes downhill:
On the green grass, beyond his companions,
He sees the noble warrior lying,
It is the Archbishop, whom God sent in his name.
The Archbishop says his confession, he gazes upward,
He has joined and raised both hands toward heaven,
And he prays God to grant him Paradise.
Charles's warrior Turpin is dead.
By fighting great battles and preaching many fine sermons,
He was always a relentless fighter against the pagans.
May God grant him his holy blessing!

167.

Count Roland sees the Archbishop on the ground:
He sees his entrails spilled outside his body,
His brain is oozing out beneath his forehead.
Over his breast, on the sternum,
He has crossed his beautiful white hands.
Roland laments over him in a loud voice, as is customary in his land:
"Ah, noble man, high-born knight,
I commend you this day to God in His celestial Glory!
No man shall ever serve Him more willingly.
There never was such a prophet since the Apostles
To keep the Faith and to win men over.
May your soul not endure any suffering!
May it find the gate of Paradise open!"

168.

Roland feels that death is near,

His brain is coming out through his ears.
He prays God to call his Peers,
And then, for his own sake, he prays the angel Gabriel.
He took the oliphant so as not to incur any blame,
And his sword Durendal with his other hand.
Where no crossbow can shoot a bolt,
He goes in the direction of Spain to a fallow field.
He climbs a hill and halts beneath two beautiful trees.
There are four blocks made of marble there.
He fell backward on the green grass,
He fainted there, for death is near.

169.

The mountains are high and the trees are very high,
There are four shiny marble blocks there.
Count Roland faints on the green grass.
A Saracen is watching him all the while,
He feigns death and lies amid the others.
He smeared his body and his face with blood,
He rises to his feet and makes a dash forward.
He was well proportioned, strong, and very brave,
Through pride he embarks upon an act of fatal folly.
He seized Roland's body and his weapons,
And he said these words: "Charles's nephew is vanquished!
I shall carry this sword to Arabia."
But as the Saracen was pulling, the Count came round a bit.

170.

Roland feels the Saracen stealing his sword from him,
He opened his eyes and said these words to him:
"I don't believe you're one of our men!"
He holds on to the oliphant, he does not want to part with it for a single moment,
And he strikes him on the helmet, whose gold is wrought with gems.
He smashes the steel, the head, the bones,
He knocked both his eyes out of his head,
He tumbled him over dead at his feet.
Afterward he says: "Dirty pagan, whatever possessed you
To seize me rightly or wrongly?
No one will hear of this without thinking you were mad.
My oliphant is split at the wide end now,
The crystal and the gold ornaments have fallen off."

171

Roland notices that his sight is failing him,
He rises to his feet and exerts himself to the utmost,
All color has faded from his face.
There is a dark stone in front of him,

He strikes it ten blows in bitterness and frustration.
The steel grates, but it is not smashed or nicked.
"Oh," said the Count, "Holy Mary, help me!
Oh, Durendal, noble one, you are to be pitied!
Since I am finished, I no longer have you in my care.
I have won so many battles in the field with you
And conquered so many vast lands
Over which white-bearded Charles rules!
May no turn-tail ever possess you!
A very good knight has owned you for a long time,
Never again shall there be such a sword in blessed France."

172.

Roland struck the sardonyx stone,
The steel grates, but it does not break or nick.
Seeing that he cannot smash it,
He begins to lament over it to himself:
"Oh, Durendal, how beautiful you are, how clear, how bright!
How you shine and flash against the sun!
Charles was in the valleys of Maurienne
When God instructed him from heaven on high by His angel
To give you to a captain count:
So the great, noble king girded me with it.
With it I conquered Anjou and Brittany,
With it I conquered Poitou and Maine,
With it I conquered Normandy the free,
With it I conquered Provence and Aquitaine,
Lombardy and all Romagna;
With it I conquered Bavaria and all Flanders,
Burgundy, all Poland,
And Constantinople, which rendered homage to him,
And he does as he wishes in Saxony;
With it I conquered Scotland, . . .
And England, which he held under his jurisdiction;
With it I conquered so many countries and lands
Over which white-bearded Charles rules.
I feel sad and heavy-hearted for this sword,
I would rather die than have it remain with the pagans.
God, our Father, do not let France be dishonored in this way!"

173.

Roland struck a dark stone,
He whacks off more than I can say.
The sword grates, but neither shatters nor breaks,
It rebounds upward toward heaven.
The Count, seeing that he cannot smash it,
Laments over it softly to himself:
"Oh, Durendal, how beautiful you are and how very holy!

There are many relics in the golden hilt:
Saint Peter's tooth, some of Saint Basil's blood,
Some of my lord Saint Denis's hair,
Some of Saint Mary's clothing.
It is not right for the pagans to own you,
You must be served by Christians.
May no coward ever possess you!
With you I conquered many vast lands
Over which white-bearded Charles rules,
And the Emperor is powerful and mighty as a consequence."

174.

Roland feels that death is overcoming him, It descends from his head to his heart.
He ran beneath a pine tree,
He lay down prone on the green grass.
He places his sword and (also?) his oliphant beneath him.
He turned his head toward the pagan army:
He did this because he earnestly desires
That Charles and all his men say
That the noble Count died as a conqueror.
He beats his breast in rapid succession over and over again,
He proffered his gauntlet to God for his sins.

175

Roland feels that his time is up,
He is on a steep hill, his face turned toward Spain.
He beat his breast with one hand:
"Mea culpa, Almighty God,
For my sins, great and small,
Which I committed from the time I was born
To this day when I am overtaken here!"
He offered his right gauntlet to God,
Angels from heaven descend toward him.

EVERYMAN

In the manner of the chorus of a Greek tragedy, the play opens with a prologue, spoken by the Messenger, who explains the plot to the audience.

PROLOGUE

MESSENGER

I pray you all give your audience,
And hear this matter with reverence,
By figure a moral play—
The *Summoming of Everyman* called it is,
That of our lives and ending shows
How transitory we be all our day.
This matter is wondrous precious,
But the intent of it is more gracious,
And sweet to bear away.
The story saith,—Man, in the beginning,
Look well, and take good heed to the ending,
Be you never so gay!
Ye think sin in the beginning full sweet,
Which in the end causeth the soul to weep,
When the body lieth in clay.
Here shall you see how Fellowship and Jollity,
And Strength, Pleasure, and Beauty,
Will fade from thee as flower in May.
For ye shall hear how our heaven's king
Calleth Everyman to a general reckoning.
Give audience, and hear what he doth say.

The audience immediately becomes aware that Everyman is nearing the end of his life and is about to be held accountable for having been enamored of the "seven deadly sins." (The seven deadly sins are pride, greed, lust, envy, gluttony, anger, and sloth.) Subsequently, Everyman is approached by Death and is amazed to discover the meaning of such phrases as "Death giveth no warning" and the "Tide abideth no man." Death's greater function, however, is to educate Everyman into the larger issues of life and death, and at times, Death is almost sympathetic to Everyman's struggle against sin.

DEATH

I am Death, that no man dreadeth.
That every man arrests and no man spareth;
For it is God's commandment
That all to me should be obedient.

EVERYMAN

O Death, thou comest when I had thee least in mind;
In thy power it lieth me to save,
Yet of my goods will I give thee, if ye will be kind,
Yea, a thousand pound shalt thou have,
But defer this matter till another day!

DEATH

Everyman, it may not be by no way;
set not by gold, silver, nor riches,
Nor by pope, emperor, king, duke, nor princes,

For if I would receive gifts great,
All the world I might get;
But my custom is clean contrary.
I give thee no respite. Come, do not tarry!

EVERYMAN

Alas, shall I have no longer respite?
I may say Death giveth no warning.
To think on thee it maketh my heart sick,
For all unready is my book of reckoning.
But twelve year if I might have abiding,
My counting book I would make so clear
That thy reckoning I should not need to fear.
Wherefore, Death, I pray thee, for God's mercy,
Spare me till I be provided of remedy.

DEATH

Thee availeth not to cry, weep, and pray,
But haste thee lightly that thou go the journey,
And prove thy friends if thou can.
For, know thou well, the tide abideth no man,
And in the world each living creature
For Adam's sin must die by nature.

EVERYMAN

Death, if I should this pilgrimage take,
And my reckoning surely make,
Show me, for Saint Charity,
Should I not come again shortly?

DEATH

No, Everyman. If thou be once there
Thou mayst nevermore come here,
Trust me verily.

EVERYMAN

Gracious God, in the high seat celestial,
Have mercy on me in this my need;
Shall I have no company from this vale terrestrial
Of mine acquaintance the way to lead?

DEATH

Yea, if any be so hardy
That would go with thee and bear thee company.
Hasten to be gone to God's magnificence,
Thy reckoning to give before his presence.
What, thinkest thou thy life is given thee,
And thy worldly goods also?

EVERYMAN

had thought so, verily.

DEATH

Nay, nay, it was but lent thee!
For as soon as thou dost go,
Another awhile shall have it and then go therefro
Even as thou hast done.
Everyman, thou art mad. Thou hast thy wits five,

And here on earth will not amend thy life,
For suddenly do I come.

Everyman

wretched caitiff,[2] whither shall I flee,
That I might escape this endless sorrow!
Now, gentle Death, spare me till to-morrow,
That I may amend me
With good advisement.

Death

Nay, thereto I will not consent,
Nor no man will I respite,
But to the heart suddenly I shall smite
Without any advisement.
And now out of thy sight I will me hie.
See thou make thee ready shortly,
For thou mayst say this is the day
That no man living may escape away.

Death withdraws.

Characters representing his friends and family—Fellowship, Kindred, Cousin, and Goods—then relate incidents of Everyman's earlier lifestyle in a universal way, carefully avoiding any indication that such behavior is unique to Everyman. Recognizing that none of these brings hope of salvation, Everyman, in despair, asks: "My Good-Deeds, where be you?" and implores her to help him. In her reply, Good-Deeds offers the assistance of her sister, Knowledge, because she is too weak to help him alone, due to Everyman's neglect of her.

Everyman

O, to whom shall I make my moan
For to go with me in that heavy journey?
First Fellowship said he would with me be gone;
His words were very pleasant and gay,
But afterward he left me alone.
Then spake I to my kinsmen all in despair,
And they also gave me words fair.
They lacked no fair speaking,
But they forsook me in the ending.
Then went I to my Goods that I loved best,
In hope to have comfort, but there had I least.
For my Goods sharply did me tell
That he bringeth many into Hell.
Then of myself I was ashamed,
And so I am worthy to be blamed,
Thus may I well myself hate.
Of whom shall I now counsel take?
think that I shall never speed
Till that I go to my Good-Deed,
But, alas, she is so weak,
That she can neither go nor speak.
Yet will I venture on her now.—
My Good-Deeds, where be you?

Enter Good-Deeds.

---

[2]A caitiff is a base, despicable person.

GOOD-DEEDS
Here I lie cold in the ground.
Thy sins have me sore-bound
That I cannot stir.
EVERYMAN
O, Good-Deeds, I stand in fear;
I must pray you for counsel,
For help now would come right well.
GOOD-DEEDS
Everyman, I have understanding
That you be summoned account to make
Before Messias, of Jerusalem the King.
If you walk by me that journey I would take.
EVERYMAN
Therefore I come to you, my moan to make—
I pray you, that ye will go with me.
GOOD-DEEDS
I would full fain, but I cannot stand, verily.
EVERYMAN
Why, is there anything did you befall?
GOOD-DEEDS
Yea, sir, and I may thank you of all;
If ye had perfectly cheered me,
Your book of account now full ready would be.
Look on the books of your works and deeds—
Oh, see how they under your feet lie,
Unto your soul's heaviness.
EVERYMAN
Our Lord Jesus, help me!
For one letter here I cannot see.
GOOD-DEEDS
There is a blind reckoning in time of distress!
EVERYMAN
Good-Deeds, I pray you, help me in this need.
Or else I am for ever damned indeed.
Therefore help me to a reckoning
Before the Redeemer of all thing,
That king is, and was, and ever shall.
GOOD-DEEDS
Everyman, I am sorry for your fall,
And fain would I help you, if I were able.
EVERYMAN
Good-Deeds, your counsel I pray you give me.
GOOD-DEEDS
That shall I do verily.
Though that on my feet I may not go,
I have a sister that shall with you also,
Called Knowledge, which shall with you abide,
To help you to make that dreadful reckoning.
Enter Knowledge.

KNOWLEDGE
Everyman, I will go with thee, and be thy guide,
In utmost need to go by thy side.

For the remainder of the play, Knowledge (recognition of one's sins) is Everyman's guide. With her help, Everyman acquires new "friends"—Discretion, Strength, Five-Wits, and Beauty. Knowledge then counsels him to go to a priest and receive the sacraments. Content to stand before God on his own diminutive merits, Everyman questions Knowledge's advice, but Five-Wits admonishes him and reminds him that salvation from sin only comes from the administration of the sacraments by the priesthood of the church.

EVERYMAN
My friends, come hither and be present,
Discretion, Strength, my Five-Wits, and Beauty.
Discretion, Strength, Five-Wits and Beauty enter.
BEAUTY
Here at your will we be all ready.
What will ye that we should do?
GOOD-DEEDS
That ye would with Everyman go,
And help him in his pilgrimage.
Advise me, will ye with him or not in that voyage?
STRENGTH
We will bring him all thither,
To his help and comfort, ye may believe me.
DISCRETION
So will we go with him all together.
EVERYMAN
Almighty God, loved mayest thou be,
I give thee laud that I have hither brought
Strength, Discretion, Beauty, and Five-Wits; I lack nought!
And my Good-Deeds, with Knowledge clear,
All stay in my company at my will here;
I desire no more to my business.
STRENGTH
And I, Strength, will stand by you in distress,
Though thou wouldest in battle fight on the ground.
FIVE-WITS
And though it were through the world round,
We will not depart for sweet nor sour.
BEAUTY
No more will I unto death's hour,
Whatsoever thereof befall.
DISCRETION
Everyman, advise you first of all,
Go with a good advisement and deliberation.
We all give you virtuous monition
That all shall be well.
EVERYMAN
My friends, hearken what I will tell.
I pray God reward you in his heavenly sphere.
Now hearken, all that be here,

For I will make my testament
Here before every one present.
In alms half my good I will give with my hands twain
In the way of charity, with good intent,
And the other half shall remain
In quiet to be returned where it ought to be.
This I do in despite of the fiend of hell,
To go quit of his peril
Ever after and this day.

KNOWLEDGE

Everyman, hearken what I say.
Go to priesthood, I advise,
And receive of him in any wise
The holy sacrament and ointment together,
Then shortly see ye turn again hither.
We will all await you here.

FIVE-WITS

Yea, Everyman, haste you that ye ready be.
There is no emperor, king, duke, nor baron,
That of God hath commission,
As hath the least priest in the world's design.
For of the blessed sacraments pure and benign,
He beareth the keys and thereof hath the cure
For man's redemption, that is ever sure;
Which God for our soul's medicine
Gave us out of his heart with great pine.
Here in this transitory life, for thee and me,
The blessed sacraments seven there be,[3]Baptism, confirmation, with priesthood good,
And the sacrament of God's precious flesh and blood,
Marriage, the holy extreme unction, and penance;
These seven be good to have in remembrance,
Gracious sacraments of high divinity.

EVERYMAN

Fain would I receive that holy body
And meekly to my spiritual father I will go.

FIVE-WITS

Everyman, that is the best that ye can do.
God will you to salvation bring,
For priesthood exceedeth all other thing.
To us Holy Scripture they do teach,
And convert man from his sin heaven to reach;
God hath to them more power given
Than to any angel that is in heaven.
With five words he may consecrate
God's body in flesh and blood to make,
And holdeth his maker between his hands,
The priest bindeth and unbindeth all bands,
Both in earth and in heaven,

[3]The seven sacraments to which Five-Wits refers are more commonly known as follows: Baptism, Confirmation, Ordination ("priesthood good"), Eucharist ("God's precious flesh and blood"), Marriage, Last Rites ("holy the extreme unction"), and Penance.

He ministers all the sacraments seven.—
Though we kissed thy feet thou wert worthy,
Thou art surgeon that cureth sin deadly.
No remedy we find that is good
But only under priesthood.
Everyman, God gave priests that dignity,
And setteth them in his stead among us to be—
Thus be they above angels in degree.

Everyman departs.

As his strength wanes, Everyman asks his new friends to accompany him to the grave, but for their own reasons, each must refuse. Good-Deeds, however, offers to go with him and speaks to him about the vanity of human existence. Everyman and Good-Deeds then descend into the grave, the Angel speaks, and the drama concludes with an epilogue, spoken by the Doctor who relates the moral of the play.

Everyman

I had thought surer I should have you found.

Exit Strength.

He that trusteth in his Strength

She deceiveth him at the length.
Both Strength and Beauty forsaking me,
Yet they promised me fair and lovingly.

Discretion

Everyman, I will after Strength be gone,
As for me I will leave you alone.

Everyman

Why, Discretion, will ye forsake me?

Discretion

Yea, in faith, I will go from thee,
For when Strength goeth before
I follow after evermore.

Everyman

Yet, I pray thee, for the love of Trinity,
Look in my grave once piteously.

Discretion

Nay, so nigh will I not come.
Farewell, every one!

Exit Discretion.

Everyman

all thing faileth, save God alone;
Beauty, Strength, and Discretion;
For when Death bloweth his blast
They all run from me full fast.

Five-Wits

Everyman, my leave now of thee I take;
will follow the other, for here I thee forsake.

Everyman

Alas! then my I wail and weep,
For I took you for my best friend.

Five-Wits

I will not longer thee keep.

Now farewell, and there an end.
Exit Five-Wits.
EVERYMAN
Jesu, have forsaken me!
GOOD-DEEDS
Nay, Everyman, I will bide with thee,
will not forsake thee indeed,
Thou shalt find me a good friend at need.
EVERYMAN
Gramercy, Good-Deeds, now, may I true friends see.
They have forsaken me every one.
I loved them better than my Good-Deeds alone.
Knowledge, will ye forsake me also?
KNOWLEDGE
Yea, Everyman, when ye to death do go,
But not yet for no manner of danger.
EVERYMAN
Gramercy, Knowledge, with all my heart.
KNOWLEDGE
Nay, yet I will not from hence depart,
Till I be sure where ye shall come.
EVERYMAN
Methinketh, alas, that I must be on,
To make my reckoning and debts to pay,
For I see my time is nigh spent away.
Take example, all ye that this do hear or see,
How they that I loved best do forsake me,
Except my Good-Deeds that bideth truly.
GOOD-DEEDS
All earthly things are but vanity:
Beauty, Strength, and Discretion, do man forsake,
Foolish friends and kinsmen, that fair spake,
All flee save Good-Deeds, and he am I.
EVERYMAN
Have mercy on me, God most mighty;
And stand by me, thou Mother and Maid, holy Mary.
GOOD-DEEDS
Fear not, I will speak for thee.
EVERYMAN
Here I cry God mercy.
GOOD-DEEDS
Shorten our end, and diminish our pain.
Let us go and never come again.
EVERYMAN
Into Thy hands, Lord, my soul I commend.
Receive it, Lord, that it be not lost!
As thou boughtest me, me so defend,
And rescue from the fiend's boast,
That I may appear with that blessed host
That shall be saved at the day of doom.

in *manus tuas* [into your hands]—of might's utmost
Forever—*commendo spiritum meum* [I command my spirit].
Everyman and Good-Deeds enter the grave.

KNOWLEDGE

Now hath he suffered what we all shall endure,
But Good-Deeds shall make all sure.
Now hath he made ending—
Methinketh I hear angels sing
And make great joy and melody,
Where Everyman's soul received shall be.

An Angel appears.

ANGEL

Come, excellent elect spouse to Jesu!
Hereabove thou shalt go
Because of thy singular virtue.
Now the soul is taken from the body so,
Thy reckoning is crystal-clear.
Now shalt thou into the heavenly sphere,
Unto which all ye shall come
That live well before the day of doom.

EPILOGUE

DOCTOR

This moral men may have in mind:
Ye hearers, take it of worth, old and young,
And forsake pride, for he deceiveth you in the end,
And remember Beauty, Five-Wits, Strength, and
Discretion,
They all at the last do Everyman forsake,
Alone his Good-Deeds there doth he take.
But beware, if they be small
Before God, man hath no help at all.
No excuse may there be for Everyman—
Alas, what shall he do then?
For after death amends may no man make,
For then mercy and pity him forsake.
If his reckoning be not clear when he come,
God will say—*ite maledicti in ignem xternum.*[4]
And he that hath his account whole and sound,
High in heaven he shall be crowned,
Unto which place God bring us all thither
That we may live body and soul together.
Thereto help blessed Trinity.
Amen, say ye, for Saint Charity.
Thus endeth this moral play of Everyman.

[4]Go into the eternal fire, ye cursed ones.

GIOVANNI BOCCACCIO

THE DECAMERON

***The Decameron* opens in Florence just after the bubonic plague ravaged Europe in 1348—1349. In the opening pages, Boccaccio, in striking detail, describes the effects of the disease and the fanatical fear people had of being infected.**

In the year 1348 after the fruitful incarnation of the Son of God, that most beautiful of Italian cities, noble Florence, was attacked by deadly plague. It started in the East either through the influence of the heavenly bodies or because God's just anger with our wicked deeds sent it as a punishment to mortal men; and in a few years killed an innumerable quantity of people. Ceaselessly passing from place to place, it extended its miserable length over the West. Against this plague all human wisdom and foresight were vain. Orders had been given to cleanse the city of filth, the entry of any sick person was forbidden, much advice was given for keeping healthy; at the same time humble supplications were made to God by pious persons in procession, and otherwise. And yet, in the beginning of the spring of the year mentioned, its horrible results began to appear, and in a miraculous manner. The symptoms were not the same as in the East, where a gush of blood from the nose was the plain sign of inevitable death; but it began both in men and women with certain swellings in the groin or under the armpit. They grew to the size of a small apple or an egg, more or less, and were vulgarly called tumours. In a short space of time these tumours spread from the two parts named all over the body. Soon after this the symptoms changed and black or purple spots appeared on the arms or thighs or any other part of the body, sometimes a few large ones, sometimes many little ones. These spots were a certain sign of death, just as the original tumour had been and still remained.

No doctor's advice, no medicine could overcome or alleviate this disease. An enormous number of ignorant men and women set up as doctors in addition to those who were trained. Either the disease was such that no treatment was possible or the doctors were so ignorant that they did not know what caused it, and consequently could not administer the proper remedy. In any case very few recovered; most people died within about three days of the appearance of the tumours described above, most of them without any fever or other symptoms.

The violence of this disease was such that the sick communicated it to the healthy who came near them, just as a fire catches anything dry or oily near it. And it even went further. To speak to or go near the sick brought infection and a common death to the living; and moreover, to touch the clothes or anything else the sick had touched or worn gave the disease to the person touching.

What I am about to tell now is a marvellous thing to hear; and if I and others had not seen it with our own eyes I would not dare to write it, however much I was willing to believe and whatever the good faith of the person from whom I heard it. So violent was the malignancy of this plague that it was communicated, not only from one man to another, but from the garments of a sick or dead man to animals of another species, which caught the disease in that way and very quickly died of it. One day among other occasions I saw with my own eyes (as I said just now) the rags left lying in the street of a poor man who had died of the plague; two pigs came along and, as their habit is, turned the clothes over with their snouts and then munched at them with the result that they both fell dead almost at once on the rags, as if they had been poisoned.

From these and similar or greater occurrences, such fear and fanciful notions took possession of the living that almost all of them adopted the same cruel policy, which was entirely to avoid the sick and everything belonging to them. By so doing, each one thought he would secure his own safety.

Some thought that moderate living and the avoidance of all superfluity would preserve them from the epidemic. They formed small communities, living entirely separate from everybody else. They shut themselves up in houses where there were no sick, eating the finest food and drinking the best wine very temperately, avoiding all excess, allowing no news or discussion of death and sickness, and passing the time in music and suchlike pleasures. Others thought just the opposite. They thought the sure cure for the plague was to drink and be merry, to go about singing and amusing themselves, satisfying every appetite they could, laughing and jesting at what happened. They put their words into practice, spent day and night going from tavern to tavern, drinking immoderately, or went into other people's houses, doing only those things which pleased them. This they could easily do because everyone felt doomed and had abandoned his property, so that most houses became common property and any stranger who went in made use of them as if he had owned them. And with all this bestial behaviour, they avoided the sick as much as possible.

In this suffering and misery of our city, the authority of human and divine laws almost disappeared, for, like other men, the ministers and the executors of the laws were all dead or sick or shut up with their families, so that no duties were carried out. Every man was therefore able to do as he pleased.

Many others adopted a course of life midway between the two just described. They did not restrict their victuals so much as the former, nor allow themselves to be drunken and dissolute like the latter, but satisfied their appetites moderately. They did not shut themselves up, but went about, carrying flowers or scented herbs or perfumes in their hands, in the belief that it was an excellent thing to comfort the brain with such odours; for the whole air was infected with the smell of dead bodies, of sick persons and medicines.

Others again held a still more cruel opinion, which they thought would keep them safe. They said that the only medicine against the plaguestricken was to go right away from them. Men and women, convinced of this and caring about nothing but themselves, abandoned their own city, their own houses, their dwellings, their relatives, their property, and went abroad or at least to the country round Florence, as if God's wrath in punishing men's wickedness with this plague would not follow them but strike only those who remained within the walls of the city, or as if they thought nobody in the city would remain alive and that its last hour had come.

Not everyone who adopted any of these various opinions died, nor did all escape. Some when they were still healthy had set the example of avoiding the sick and, falling ill themselves, died untended.

One citizen avoided another, hardly any neighbour troubled about others, relatives never or hardly ever visited each other. Moreover, such terror was struck into the hearts of men and women by this calamity, that brother abandoned brother, and the uncle his nephew, and the sister her brother, and very often the wife her husband. What is even worse and nearly incredible is that fathers and mothers refused to see and tend their children, as if they had not been theirs.

Thus, a multitude of sick men and women were left without any care except from the charity of friends (but these were few), or the greed of servants, though not many of these could be had even for high wages. Moreover, most of them were coarse-minded men and women, who did little more than bring the sick what they asked for or watch over them when they were dying. And very often these servants lost their lives and their earnings. Since the sick were thus abandoned by neighbours, relatives and friends, while servants were scarce, a habit sprang up which had never been heard of before. Beautiful and noble women, when they fell sick, did not scruple to take a young or old manservant, whoever he might be, and with no sort of shame, expose every part of their bodies to these men as if they had been women, for they were compelled by the necessity of their sickness to do so. This, perhaps, was a cause of looser morals in those women who survived.

In this way many people died who might have been saved if they had been looked after. Owing to the lack of attendants for the sick and the violence of the plague, such a multitude of people in the city died day and night that it was stupefying to hear of, let alone to see. From sheer necessity, then, several ancient customs were quite altered among the survivors.

The custom had been (as we still see it today), that women relatives and neighbours should gather at the house of the deceased, and there lament with the family. At the same time the men would gather at the door with the male neighbours and other citizens. Then came the clergy, few or many according to the dead person's rank; the coffin was placed on the shoulders of his friends and carried with funeral pomp of lighted candles and dirges to the church which the deceased had chosen before dying. But as the fury of the plague increased, this custom wholly or nearly disappeared, and new customs arose. Thus, people died, not only without having a number of women near them, but without a single witness. Very few indeed were honoured with the piteous laments and bitter tears of their relatives, who, on the contrary, spent their time in mirth, feasting and jesting. Even the women abandoned womanly pity and adopted this custom for their own safety. Few were they whose bodies were accompanied to church by more than ten or a dozen neighbours. Nor were these grave and honourable citizens but grave-diggers from the lowest of the people who got themselves called sextons, and performed the task for money. They took up the bier and hurried it off, not to the church chosen by the deceased but to the church nearest, preceded by four or six of the clergy with few candles and often none at all. With the aid of the grave-diggers, the clergy huddled the bodies away in any grave they could find, without giving themselves the trouble of a long or solemn burial service.

The plight of the lower and most of the middle classes was even more pitiful to behold. Most of them remained in their houses, either through poverty or in hopes of safety, and fell sick by thousands. Since they received no care and attention, almost all of them died. Many ended their lives in the streets both at night and during the day; and many others who died in their houses were only known to be dead because the neighbours smelled their decaying bodies. Dead bodies filled every corner. Most of them were treated in the same manner by the survivors, who were more concerned to get rid of their rotting bodies than moved by charity towards the dead. With the aid of porters, if they could get them, they carried the bodies out of the houses and laid them at the doors, where every morning quantities of the dead might be seen. They then were laid on biers, or as these were often lacking, on tables.

Often a single bier carried two or three bodies, and it frequently happened that a husband and wife, two or three brothers, or father and son were taken off on the same bier. It frequently happened that two priests, each carrying a cross, would go out followed by three or four biers carried by porters; and where the priests thought there was one person to bury, there would be six or eight, and often, even more. Nor were these dead honoured by tears and lighted candles and mourners, for things had reached such a pass that people cared no more for dead men than we care for dead goats. Thus it plainly appeared that what the wise had not learned to endure with patience through the few calamities of ordinary life, became a matter of indifference even to the most ignorant people through the greatness of this misfortune.

Such was the multitude of corpses brought to the churches every day and almost every hour that there was not enough consecrated ground to give them burial, especially since they wanted to bury each person in the family grave, according to the old custom. Although the cemeteries were full they were forced to dig huge trenches, where they buried the bodies by hundreds. Here they stowed them away like bales in the hold of a ship and covered them with a little earth, until the whole trench was full.

Not to pry any further into all the details of the miseries which afflicted our city, I shall add that the surrounding country was spared nothing of what befell Florence. The villages on a smaller scale, were like the city; in the fields and isolated farms the poor wretched peasants and their families were without doctors and any assistance, and perished in the highways, in their fields and houses, night and day, more like beasts than men. Just as the townsmen became dissolute and indifferent to their work and property, so the peasants, when they saw that death was upon them, entirely neglected the future fruits of their past labours both from the earth and from cattle, and thought only of enjoying what they had. Thus it happened that crows, asses, sheep, goats, pigs, fowls and even dogs, those faithful companions of man, left the farms and wandered at their will through the fields, where the wheat crops stood abandoned, unreaped and ungarnered. Many of these animals seemed endowed with reason, for, after they had pastured all day, they returned to the farms for the night of their own free will, without being driven.

Returning from the country to the city, it may be said such was the cruelty of Heaven, and perhaps in part of men, that between March and July more than one hundred thousand persons died within the walls of Florence, what between the violence of the plague and the abandonment in which the sick were left by the cowardice of the healthy. And before the plague it was not thought that the whole city held so many people.

Oh, what great palaces, how many fair houses and noble dwellings, once filled with attendants and nobles and ladies, were emptied to the meanest servant! How many famous names and vast possessions and renowned estates were left without an heir! How many gallant men and fair ladies and handsome youths, whom Galen, Hippocrates and ^esculapius themselves would have said were in perfect health, at noon dined with their relatives and friends, and at night supped with their ancestors in the next world!

After describing the effects of the disease, Boccaccio allows the plot to commence. Seven ladies and three young men, fearful of the plague, decide to flee into the country. Once there, they agree to tell stories to pass the time—each person is to tell ten tales over a ten-day period, for a total of one hundred stories. Boccaccio's stories frequently feature sensual love between men and women, and the tone is quite secular. Often the theme of love is coupled with criticism of licentious clergymen as is evident in the second tale of the eighth day, which relates how a priest arranges to have sex with a woman on a day when her husband goes into town on business.

Fair ladies, I mean to tell you a little tale about those who are constantly injuring us without our being able to injure them in the same way—I mean the priests, who have declared a Crusade against our wives, and seem to think that when they can get on one of them they have obtained forgiveness of their sins as much as if they had brought the Sultan captive from Alexandria to Avignon. We poor men of the world cannot do the like to them, although we should avenge ourselves by attacking no less eagerly the mothers, sisters, female friends and daughters of priests. So I mean to tell you about a pleasant love affair, which is not long but amusing from its conclusion; and you may at least learn from it that priests are not to be believed in everything.

In Varlungo, a village which is not far from here (as each of you knows or has heard) there was a worthy priest, most valiant of person in the service of ladies. Although he could not read much, every Sunday at the foot of an elm he comforted his parishioners with good and holy discourses. And when the male parishioners were absent, there never was a priest who more willingly visited their wives, taking them fairings and holy water and a few candle-ends, and giving them his blessing.

Now, among all his female parishioners one especially charmed him. This was one Monna Belcolore, the wife of a labourer, who went by the name of Bentivegna del Mazzo. She was a pleasant, fresh, brown-skinned, buxom peasant- girl, who knew how to grind the mill better than anyone. Moreover, she was a skilled performer on the cymbals and could sing: "The water flows in the cleft," and, waving a pocket handkerchief in her hand, dance Sellinger's Round better than any of her neighbours. All these things so charmed our priest that he was frantic about her, and rambled about all day trying to catch a glimpse of her. When he knew she was in church on Sunday morning, he lifted up his voice with a *Kyrie* or a *Sanctus* to show her what a fine singing voice he had, and brayed like an ass; whereas, if she were not there, he passed over them very hurriedly. But yet he acted in such a way that neither Bentivegna del Mazzo nor any other man observed him.

In order to become more familiar with Monna Belcolore, he was continually sending her gifts. At one time he sent her a bunch of fresh garlic bulbs, for he grew the best of anyone in the district in his garden, which he dug with his own hands; then a little basket of peas in their pods or a bunch of fresh onions or shallots. Choosing his time, he would gaze at her in a gloomy way and heap amorous reproaches on her, while she with rustic awkwardness pretended not to notice and went her way disdainfully; so that messer priest could not come to the point.

One afternoon when the priest was sauntering along he met Bentivegna del Mazzo with a laden ass; and after joking with him, asked him where he was going. Bentivegna replied:

"Why, father, I'm going into the city on business and I'm taking these things to Ser Bonacorri da Ginestreto, who is helping me about some lawsuit where I've got to appear before the clerk to the justice of the 'Sizes."

Said the priest:

"Well done, my son, go, with my blessing, and come back soon. And if you see Lapuccio or Naldino don't forget to tell them to bring the straps for my harness."

Bentivegna said it should be done, and as he went off in the direction of Florence the priest thought that now was the time to go to Belcolore and try his luck. So, putting his best foot forward, he made no pause until he reached her cottage, which he entered, saying:

"God bless this house—who is within?"

Belcolore, who was in the hay shed, heard him and said:

"O father, you're kindly welcome. But what are you doing out in this heat?"

"So God be good to me," replied the priest. "I came to spend a little time with you, for I met your good man going into the town."

Belcolore came down and took a seat and began to sift some cabbage seed which her husband had gathered.

"Ah, Belcolore," said the priest, "must you always make me die in this way?"

Belcolore giggled, and said:

"Why, what do I do?"

"You don't do anything," said the priest, "but you won't let me do to you what I want to do and what God commands."

"Get away with you!" said Belcolore. "Priests don't do such things."

"Yes, we do," said the priest, "and better than other men. Why not? And we are better workers than other men. Do you know why? Because we only grind at harvest time. But you'll find it out for yourself if you'll only lie still and let me go."

"What good would it do me," said Belcolore, "when all you priests are as mean as you can be?"

"I don't know," said the priest. "Ask what you want. Do you want a pair of shoes or some ribbons or a piece of fine cloth, or what do you want?"

"Right you are, brother!" said Belcolore. "I don't want any of those things, but if you are so fond of me will you do me a service, and I'll do what you want?"

"Say what you want," said the priest, "and I'll gladly do it."

Then said Belcolore:

"On Saturday I have to go to Florence, to hand in the wool I have spun and to have my spinning-wheel mended. If you'll lend me five lire, which I know you have, I can take out of pawn my dark petticoat and my best girdle which I had to take to uncle, and you know that without them I can't go to church or anywhere else; and then I'll always do what you want."

"So help me God," said the priest. "I haven't them with me; but trust me, and you shall have them gladly before Saturday."

"Yes," said Belcolore, "you're all great promisers, and keep your word not at all. Do you think you can treat me like Biliuzza, who went away with nothing but promises? God's Faith, it was that sent her on the streets. If you haven't got them, go and get them."

"Ah!" said the priest, "don't make me go back home now. I see that my luck has been so good that no one else is here, and perhaps when I came back someone would be here and interrupt us. I don't know when there will be such a good chance as now."

"Ah, well!" said she. "If you want to go, go; if not, stay as you are."

The priest saw that she would not do what he wanted unless she were *salvum me fac,* and would do nothing *sine custodia;* so he said:

"I see you don't believe I would get them; to convince you I'll leave with you my cloak of Turkish cloth."

Belcolore lifted her head, and said:

"Yes? And what is your cloak worth?"

"What's it worth?" said the priest. "Why, it comes from Douai in Touai and some of our people would call it Fourai. Not a fortnight ago I paid seven lire for it to Lotto the old clothes man and made five soldi on the bargain, according to what Buglietto told me, and you know he's an expert in all such cloths."

"Oh, is it?" said Belcolore. "God help me, I should never have thought so; but give it me first."

Messer priest, who had shot his bolt, took off his cloak and gave it to her. And when she had put it away, she said:

"Father, come along to the hayloft. Nobody ever goes there."

There the priest gave her the sweetest flopping kisses and enjoyed her for a long space of time, making her a relative of the Lord God. He then departed in his cassock, as if he had been to a wedding; and returned to his church.

But when he reflected that all the candle-ends he collected in a whole year were not worth one half of five lire, he felt he had made a mistake, regretted having left his cloak behind, and began to think of some means of getting his cloak back for nothing. And since he was a very cunning fellow, he thought of a way of getting it back, which succeeded. The next day was a festival, and he sent a little boy to Monna Belcolore's house to ask her to lend him her stone mortar, because that morning Binguccio dal Poggio and Nuto Bugli- etti were going to dine with him and he wanted to make sauce. Belcolore sent him the mortar. And at dinner time when the priest knew Bentivegna del Mazzo and Belcolore would be eating, he sent for the parish clerk, and said:

"Take this mortar to Belcolore and say: 'The parson thanks you and will you send him back the cloak which the little boy left as a pledge?'"

The clerk went off to Belcolore's cottage with the mortar and found her at table with Bentivegna. He laid down the mortar and delivered his message. When Belcolore heard him ask for the cloak she tried to speak, but Bentivegna interrupted her angrily.

"So you take pledges from the parson, do you? By Christ, I'd like to give you a good wipe in the nose. Give it back at once, and a pox on you. And henceforth if he wants anything of ours, even the ass, don't you say 'No' to him!"

Belcolore got up grumbling and went to the chest under the bed, took out the cloak, and as she gave it to the clerk, she said:

"Say to the priest: 'Belcolore says that she prays God you may never again grind sauce in her mortar, not having done her any honour in this.'"

The clerk went off with the cloak and delivered the message to the priest, who said, laughing:

"When you see her, tell her that if she won't lend the mortar, I won't lend the pestle—tit for tat."

Bentivegna supposed his wife said these words because he had scolded her, and thought no more about them. But Belcolore was furious with the parson, and would not speak to him until vintage time. Then, after threatening to send the priest into the biggest devil's mouth, she made it up with him over new wine and hot chestnuts, and thereafter they often gorged together. Instead of the five lire the priest mended her cymbals and hung her up a large bell; and she was well satisfied.

GEOFFREY CHAUCER

THE CANTERBURY TALES

The following passages are taken from Chaucer's *General Prologue* in which he creates vignettes of his pilgrims, including their occupation and appearance, as they assemble at the Tabard Inn in Southwark, not far from where Chaucer lived.

[O]ne day
In Southwark, at *The Tabard,* as I lay
Ready to go on pilgrimage and start
For Canterbury, most devout at heart,
At night there came into that hostelry
Some nine and twenty in a company
Of sundry folk happening then to fall
In fellowship, and they were pilgrims all
That towards Canterbury meant to ride.
The rooms and stables of the inn were wide;
They made us easy, all was of the best.
And shortly, when the sun had gone to rest,
By speaking to them all upon the trip
I soon was one of them in fellowship
And promised to rise early and take the way
To Canterbury, as you heard me say.
But none the less, while I have time and space,
Before my story takes a further pace,
It seems a reasonable thing to say
What their condition was, the full array
Of each of them, as it appeared to me
According to profession and degree,
And what apparel they were riding in;
And at a Knight I therefore will begin.
There was a *Knight,* a most distinguished man,
Who from the day on which he first began
To ride abroad had followed chivalry,
Truth, honour, generousness and courtesy.
He had done nobly in his sovereign's war
And ridden into battle, no man more,
As well in christian as in heathen places,
And ever honoured for his noble graces. . . .
He was of sovereign value in all eyes.
And though so much distinguished, he was wise
And in his bearing modest as a maid.
He never yet a boorish thing had said
In all his life to any, come what might;
He was a true, a perfect gentle-knight. . . .
He had his son with him, a fine young *Squire,*
A lover and cadet, a lad of fire

With locks as curly as if they had been pressed.
He was some twenty years of age, I guessed.
In stature he was of a moderate length,
With wonderful agility and strength. . . .
He was embroidered like a meadow bright
And full of freshest flowers, red and white.
Singing he was, or fluting all the day;
He was as fresh as is the month of May.
Short was his gown, the sleeves were long and wide;
He knew the way to sit a horse and ride.
He could make songs and poems and recite,
Knew how to joust and dance, to draw and write.
He loved so hotly that till dawn grew pale
He slept as little as a nightingale.
Courteous he was, lowly and serviceable,
And carved to serve his father at the table. . . .
There also was a *Nun,* a Prioress.[1]
Her way of smiling very simple and coy. . . .
Her greatest oath was only 'By St Loy!'
And she was known as Madam Eglantyne.
And well she sang a service, with a fine
Intoning through her nose, as was most seemly,
And she spoke daintily in French. . . .
She certainly was very entertaining,
Pleasant and friendly in her ways, and straining
To counterfeit a courtly kind of grace,
A stately bearing fitting to her place,
And to seem dignified in all her dealings.
As for her sympathies and tender feelings,
She was so charitably solicitous
She used to weep if she but saw a mouse
Caught in a trap, if it were dead or bleeding. . . .
She was all sentiment and tender heart.
Her veil was gathered in a seemly way,
Her nose was elegant, her eyes glass-grey;
Her mouth was very small, but soft and red,
Her forehead, certainly, was fair of spread,
Almost a span across the brows, I own;
She was indeed by no means undergrown. . . .
A *Monk* there was, one of the finest sort
Who rode the country; hunting was his sport.
A manly man, to be an Abbot able;
Many a dainty horse he had in stable.
His bridle, when he rode, a man might hear
Jingling in a whistling wind as clear,
Aye, and as loud as does the chapel bell
Where my lord Monk was Prior of the cell. . . .
He let go by the things of yesterday
And took the modern world's more spacious way. . . .

[1] A Prioress is the woman in charge of an abbey of nuns.

Hunting a hare or riding at a fence
Was all his fun, he spared for no expense.
I saw his sleeves were garnished at the hand
With fine grey fur, the finest in the land,
And on his hood, to fasten it at his chin
He had a wrought-gold cunningly fashioned pin;
Into a lover's knot it seemed to pass.
His head was bald and shone like looking-glass;
So did his face, as if it had been greased.
He was a fat and personable priest;
His prominent eyeballs never seemed to settle.
They glittered like the flames beneath a kettle;
Supple his boots, his horse in fine condition.
He was a prelate fit for exhibition,
He was not pale like a tormented soul.
He liked a fat swan best, and roasted whole. . . .
There was a *Friar,* a wanton one and merry,
A Limiter,[2] a very festive fellow.
In all Four Orders[3] there was none so mellow
So glib with gallant phrase and well-turned speech.
He'd fixed up many a marriage, giving each
Of his young women what he could afford her.
He was a noble pillar to his Order.
Highly beloved and intimate was he
With County folk within his boundary,
And city dames of honour and possessions;
For he was qualified to hear confessions,
Or so he said, with more than priestly scope;
He had a special license from the Pope.
Sweetly he heard his penitents at shrift
With pleasant abolution, for a gift.
He was an easy man in penance-giving
Where he could hope to make a decent living. . . .
There was a *Merchant* with a forking beard
And motley dress; high on his horse he sat,
Upon his head a Flemish beaver hat
And on his feet daintily buckled boots.
He told of his opinions and pursuits
In solemn tones, and how he never lost. . . .
This estimable Merchant so had set
His wits to work, none knew he was in debt,
He was so stately in negotiation,
Loan, bargain and commercial obligation.
He was an excellent fellow all the same;
To tell the truth I do not know his name.
An *Oxford Cleric,* still a student though,
One who had taken logic long ago,

[2] A Limiter is a begging friar, granted a specific district in which to beg in, thus limiting his activities.
[3] The Four Orders refers to the Dominican Order, the Franciscan Order, the Carmelite Order, and the Austin Friars—all of which are mendicant friars.

Was there. . . . By his bed
He preferred having twenty books in red
And black, of Aristotle's philosophy,
To having fine clothes, fiddle or psaltery. . . .
Whatever money from his friends he took
He spent on learning or another book
And prayed for them most earnestly, returning
Thanks to them thus for paying for his learning.
His only care was study, and indeed
He never spoke a word more than was need,
Formal at that, respectful in the extreme,
Short, to the point, and lofty in his theme.
The thought of moral virtue filled his speech
And he would gladly learn, and gladly teach. . . .
There was a *Franklin*[4] with him, it appeared;
White as a daisy-petal was his beard.
A sanguine man, high-coloured and benign,
He loved a morning sop of cake in wine. . . .
His bread, his ale were finest of the fine
And no one had a better stock of wine.
His house was never short of bake-meat pies,
Of fish and flesh, and these in such supplies
It positively snowed with meat and drink
And all the dainties that a man could think.
According to the seasons of the year
Changes of dish were ordered to appear. . . .
As Sheriff he checked audit, every entry.
He was a model among landed gentry. . . .
A worthy *woman* from beside *Bath* city
Was with us, somewhat deaf, which was a pity. . . .
In all the parish not a dame dared stir
Towards the altar steps in front of her,
And if indeed they did, so wrath was she
As to be quite put out of charity. . . .
Bold was her face, handsome, and red in hue.
A worthy woman all her life, what's more
She'd had five husbands, all at the church door,
Apart from other company in youth;
No need just now to speak of that, forsooth.[5] . . .
A holy-minded man of good renown
There was, and poor, the *Parson* to a town,
Yet he was rich in holy thought and work.
He also was a learned man, a clerk,
Who truly knew Christ's gospel and would preach it
Devoutly to parishioners, and teach it. . . .
He stayed at home and watched over his fold
So that no wolf should make the sheep miscarry.
He was a shepherd and no mercenary.

[4] A Franklin is a class of landowner who is not a noble but is, nonetheless, free by virtue of his birth.
[5] Forsooth means certainly.

Holy and virtuous he was, but then
Never contemptuous of sinful men,
Never disdainful, never too proud or fine,
But was discreet in teaching and benign. . . .
The *Miller* was a chap of sixteen stone,[6]
A great stout fellow big in brawn and bone.
He did well out of them, for he could go
And win the ram at any wrestling show.
His mighty mouth was like a furnace door.
A wrangler and buffoon, he had a store
Of tavern stories, filthy in the main.
His was a master-hand at stealing grain.
He felt it with his thumb and thus he knew
Its quality and took three times his due. . . .
There was a *Summoner*[7] with us in the place
Who had a fire-red cherubinnish face,[8]
For he had carbuncles. His eyes were narrow,
He was as hot and lecherous as a sparrow.
Black, scabby brows he had, and a thin beard.
Children were afraid when he appeared. . . .
Garlic he loved, and onions too, and leeks,
And drinking strong wine till all was hazy.
Then he would shout and jabber as if crazy,
And wouldn't speak a word except in Latin. . . .
Now I have told you shortly, in a clause,
The rank, the array, the number and the cause
Of our assembly in this company. . . .
And now the time has come for me to tell
How we behaved that evening; I'll begin
After we had alighted at the Inn,
Then I'll report our journey, stage by stage,
All the remainder of our pilgrimage.
But first I beg of you, in courtesy,
Not to condemn me as unmannerly
If I speak plainly and with no concealings
And give account of all their words and dealings,
Using their very phrases as they fell.
Our *Host* gave us great welcome; everyone
Was given a place and supper was begun.
He served the finest victuals you could think,
The wine was strong and we were glad to drink.
A very striking man our Host withal,
And fit to be a marshal in a hall. . . .
"My lords," he said, "now listen for your good,
And please don't treat my notion with disdain.
This is the point. I'll make it short and plain.
Each one of you shall help to make things slip

[6] Sixteen stone is approximately 224 pounds
[7] A Summoner is someone paid to "summon" a sinner to trial in a church court.
[8] Cherubinnish face refers to the cherubs of medieval art, who are generally portrayed as having faces the color of fire.

By telling two stories on the outward trip
To Canterbury, that's what I intend,
And, on the homeward way to journey's end
Another two, tales from the days of old;
And then the man whose story is best told,
That is to say who gives the fullest measure
Of good morality and general pleasure,
He shall be given a supper, paid by all,
Here in this tavern, in this very hall,
When we come back again from Canterbury.
And in the hope to keep you bright and merry
I'll go along with you myself and ride
All at my own expense and serve as guide.
I'll be the judge, and those who won't obey
Shall pay for what we spend upon the way.
Now if you all agree to what you've heard
Tell me at once without another word,
And I will make arrangements early for it." . . .

THE NUN'S PRIEST'S TALE

During the pilgrimage, the Knight interrupts the Monk's dull recital of a series of brief tragedies, and the Host calls upon him to tell another type of tale, but he refuses to do so. The Host then turns to the Nun's Priest for a new story. "The Nun's Priest's Tale," patterned after a fable by Marie de France (see page 188), is one of the most popular, captivating, and worldly beast fables ever written. The cock (Chantecleer), his hens, and the nefarious fox behave has if they were part of Homer's *Iliad* and *Odyssey,* or Virgil's *Aeneid.* Part of the joke comes from our awareness of the wide discrepancy between the description and the reality, as, for example, when the Priest tells us that the cock, walking on tiptoe, is regal or kinglike; another part comes from the shifting back and forth in tone between the seemingly serious and the plainly ridiculous, as when the hen cites a "learned authority" at one point and then recommends that the cock take a digestive of worms.

Once upon a time there was a poor old widow who lived in a small cottage beside a grove standing in a dale. This widow, since the day that she was last a wife, lived patiently a very simple life because her goods and her income were small. By handling thriftily what God sent her she supported herself and also her two daughters. She had three large sows, no more, three cows, and a sheep called Malle. Her "bower" and her "hall" in which she ate many a scanty meal were very sooty. [The words "bower" and "hall" are appropriate to the mansion or palace of a nobleman. We learn that the widow's hovel was a single room which also included the roosting place for the chickens.] She didn't need a spicy sauce; no dainty morsel passed through her throat. Her meals were appropriate to her clothing. Over-eating never made her sick. An abstemious diet was her medicine—that, and exercise and contentment at heart. Gout didn't keep her from dancing. Apoplexy didn't hurt her head. She drank no wine, neither red or white. Her table was served mostly with white and black—milk and black bread with which she found no fault, broiled bacon and, sometimes, an egg or two, for she was a sort of dairy woman.

She had a yard enclosed with dry sticks outside of which was a dry ditch. In the yard she had a cock named Chantecleer [clear singer]. No one in all the land was his equal in crowing. His voice was merrier than the merry organ played in the church on mass-days. His crowing in his "lodge" [again, upperclass] was more exact than any clock or any abbey's horologe. By nature he knew the ascension of the equinoctial [celestial equator] in that town; for each time it ascended 15 degrees he crowed; no one could indicate the hour more correctly.

His comb was redder than fine coral and battlemented like a castle wall. His bill was as black and shiny as jet. His legs and his toes were like azure; his nails whiter than the lily-flower. His feathers were colored like burnished gold.

This noble cock had in his governance seven hens to do what gave him pleasure. They were his sisters and his paramours.[1] They were wonderously like him in color. The one of them who had the most beautifully colored throat was named lovely Demoiselle Pertelote. She was courteous, discreet, meek, and companionable [words appropriate in praise of a noblewoman]. Since the day when she was seven nights old, she behaved so beautifully that she had Chantecleer's heart completely in her power. He loved her so much that all went well with him. When the bright sun arose, what a joy it was to hear them sing in sweet accord, "My beloved has gone to the country!" For in that time, as I understand it, birds and beasts knew how to talk and sing.

One dawn it happened that, as Chantecleer among all his wives sat on the porch, which was in the hall (and lovely Pertelote sat closest to him), he began to groan in his throat like a man who is sorely troubled in a dream. When Pertelote heard him roar in this way, she was aghast and said, "Dear heart, what is wrong with you that you groan like that. You are usually a good sleeper. Shame on you."

And he answered, "Madame, I pray you, don't take it amiss. By God, I dreamed right now that I was in such trouble that even now my heart is badly frightened. Now, for God's sake, interpret my dream fa-

[1]A paramour is an illicit lover.

vorably and keep my body out of a foul prison. I dreamed that I roamed up and down in our yard, and there I saw a beast, rather like a dog, who wanted to seize me and kill me. His color was between yellow and red, and his tail and both ears were tipped with black. His snout was small, and his two eyes were glowing. I still almost die from fear when I think of his looks. No doubt, this caused my groaning."

"For shame, coward," she said, "for shame. Alas, by God above, how you have lost my heart and all my love. I cannot love a coward, by my faith. For certainly, whatever any woman may say, we all desire, if it is possible, to have husbands who are brave, wise, generous, and discreet, and not a stingy man, nor a fool, nor one who is aghast at every weapon, nor a braggart, by God above! How dare you say—for shame—to your beloved that anything could make you afraid? You don't have a man's heart even though you have a beard. Alas, can you be aghast of dreams? God knows, a dream is nothing but empty illusions. Dreams are caused by over-eating, and by fumes and mixtures when bodily fluids [humors] are too abundant in a person. Certainly, the dream you dreamed last night comes from a superfuity of red bile [choler]. It causes people in their dreams to dread arrows, and fires with red flames, red beasts and to fear that they will bite, also conflict and big and little whelps. In the same way the fluid melancholy [the humor black bile] causes many a man to cry out in his sleep for fear of black bears and black bulls or else black devils which want to seize them. I could tell about other humors, too, which cause distress to many a man in his sleep. But I'll pass over all that as lightly as possible."

"Consider Cato, who was so wise a man, didn't he say this: 'Pay no attention to dreams'? [Cato was the author of a Latin primer or first reading book.]

"Now, sire, when you fly down from the beams, for the love of God, take a laxative. May my soul and life be in peril if I am not giving you the best possible advice. I wouldn't lie to you in saying that on should purge yourself both of choler and melancholy. And so that you won't delay, though there is no pharmacist in this town, I myself will teach you what will be best for your health and benefit, and I will find in our yard those herbs which by nature have the power to purge you below and also above. For love of God, don't forget this: You are very choleric in your mixture of humors. Beware lest the sun in rising should find you filled with hot humors. Because, if you do, I would dare to bet a penny that you will have a ter- tain fever or an ague that may cause your death. For a day or two you will take digestives of worms before you take your laxatives of spurge-laurel, centaury, and fumitory, or else of hellebore, which grows there, or caper berry or gaiter berry, or pleasant herb-ivy growing in our yard. Peck them right up where they grow and eat them. Be merry, husband; dread no dream. I call tell you no more."

"Madame," he said, "Many thanks for your learned advice. But, nevertheless, concerning Lord Cato, who has such great renown for wisdom, though he told us not to dread dreams, by God, men may read in old books about many a man of more authority than Cato ever had, so help me, who say the very reverse of this advice, and who have well found by experience that dreams are significations both of joy and of tribulations which people endure in this present life. There is no need to devise arguments about this; the real proof is revealed in the event."

"One of the greatest authorities whom men read says this: Once upon a time two men, with very good intentions, went on a pilgrimage, and it so happened that they came to a town where there was such a congregation of people and so few rooms for sleeping that they couldn't find so much as a cottage in which they might both be lodged for the night. For that night they must necessarily separate. Each went to his hostelry and took such lodging as befell him. One of them was lodged far away in a yard with plow-oxen; the other was lodged well enough as was his chance or fortune which commonly governs all of us."

"It so happened that, long before day, the second man dreamed where he lay in his bed that his fellow pilgrim called to him and said, 'Alas, tonight I shall be murdered where I lie in an ox's stall. Help me, dear brother, or I'll die. In all haste, come to me'. Because of fear the man roused abruptly from his sleep, but when he was wholly awake, he turned over and took no heed. It seemed to him that his dream was only foolishness. He had the same dream a second time. In his third dream, it seemed to him that his companion came to him and said, 'I have now been slain. Look at my bloody wounds, deep and wide. Get up early in the morning, and at the west gate of the town you will see a cart load of dung in which my corpse is secretly hidden. Have that cart stopped by the authorities. To tell the truth, my gold caused me to be murdered'. And with a pitiful, pale face he told him every detail of how he had been killed. Now believe me, the man who dreamed found that his dream was entirely true, for in the morning, at daybreak, he took his way to his companion's inn, and when he came to the ox's stall, he begun to call his companion."

"The innkeeper answered him right away saying, 'Sire, your companion has gone. As soon as it was day, he went out of town'. The traveler, remembering his dream, became suspicious and went without hesitation to the town's west gate and found there a dung-cart going out as if to manure the land—a cart just like the one the dead man had described. He began boldly to cry for vengeance and justice on this felony. 'My companion was murdered during the night and lies dead in this cart. I call upon the authorities who rule this city, Harrow! [This cry—a legal one—announced to all who heard it that a crime was being committed. Everyone who heard the cry was duty bound to help capture the felon.] Here my companion lies slain.'"

"What more should I say. The people came out, overturned the cart, and found the newly murdered man in the middle of the dung."

"O blessed God, who art so just and true, thou revealest murder always. Murder will out, we see that day after day. Murder is so loathsome and abominable to God, who is so just and reasonable, that He will not suffer it to remain concealed though it may remain unknown for a year or two. Murder will out; this is my conclusion."

"And immediately the officers of the town seized the carter and the hosteler and put them to torture so that they confessed their wicked deed and were hanged by the neck."

"Thus may men see that dreams are to be feared. And indeed, in the next chapter of the same book I read—I'm not lying, so help me—that two men wanted for a certain purpose, to cross the sea to a far country. But the wind was contrary and made them stay in the city which stood on the side of a harbor. Then a few days later toward evening the wind changed and blew in exactly the way they wanted. Cheerful and glad they went to bed, determined to sail early next morning. But a great marvel happened to one of them. As he lay sleeping, he dreamed, near dawn, a wondrous dream. It seemed to him that a man stood beside his bed and commanded him to remain in the city and said to him, 'If you sail tomorrow, you will be drowned'. The traveler awoke and told his dream to his companion and begged him to give up his voyage, for that day at least. His companion, who lay by his bed side, laughed and made fun of him. 'No dream', he said, 'can so frighten me as to cause me to give up my plans. I wouldn't give a straw for your dream. Dreams are only illusions and deceits. Men dream constantly of owls and apes and many other illusions. Men dream of things that never have been nor ever will be. But since I see that you are determined to remain here and wilfully miss your tide, God knows, it makes me sorry, but still goodbye'. And thus he took his leave and went away. But before he had sailed fully half his course—I don't know why or what bad luck fell upon it, but by chance the ship's bottom split open, and man and ship sank in the sight of nearby ships which had sailed with it on the same tide."

"And, therefore, dear lovely Pertelote, from such examples you may learn that no man should be too careless about dreams, for I tell you certainly that many a dream is greatly to be feared."

"Consider the 'Life of St. Kenelm', the son of Kenulfus, the noble king of Mercia. In Kenelm's 'Life' I read that a little before he was murdered he saw his own murder in a dream. His nurse expounded to him every detail of his dream and told him to take great care against treason; but he was only seven years old and, therefore gave little importance to any dream; he was so holy at heart. By God, I'd give my shirt for you to have read this legend as I have."

"Madame Pertelote, truly, Macrobius who wrote about the 'Dream of Scipio'[2] asserts the validity of dreams and says that they are warnings of things which will be seen in the future. And, furthermore, I beg you to consider Daniel, in the Old Testament, whether he believed that dreams were illusions. Read there about Joseph, too, and you will see that dreams are sometimes—I don't say all dreams—warnings

[2]Scipio was a Roman commander who conquered Carthage in North Africa. Cicero wrote "Scipio's Dream" in which he asserted the former greatness of the Roman Republic.

of future events. Consider Lord Pharaoh, the king of Egypt, and his baker and his butler, too, whether they didn't experience the effects of dreams. Whoever studies the histories of various kingdoms will read many wondrous things about dreams. For example, Croesus, king of Lydia, didn't he have a dream that he sat in a tree which signified that he would be hanged? Another example, Andromache, Hector's wife: The night before the day when Hector was to lose his life, she dreamed that he would be killed if he went into battle that day. She warned him but could not prevail upon him to stay. He went out to fight and was at once slain by Achilles. But that is too long a story to tell. Besides it is nearly day, and I must not remain here. But briefly, in conclusion, I say that I will have some misfortune from my dream. And furthermore, I say that I don't put any trust in laxatives because I know very well that they are poisonous. I repudiate them. I don't like them at all."

"But let's speak of pleasant things and stop all this. Madame Pertelote, by heaven, God has shown me much favor in one thing: When I see the beauty of your face, you are so scarlet red around your eyes that it makes me dread to die. It is certainly true, *In principio, mulier est hominis confusio.* [In the beginning, woman is the ruination of man]. Madame, the meaning of this Latin is: Woman is man's joy and all his happiness. For when at night I feel your soft side—even though I cannot tread you because, alas, our perch is to, narrow—I am so full of comfort and joy that I defy both dream and vision."

And with that word, they—and all his other hens—flew down from the beam because it was day. And with a cluck he began to call them because he had found a kernel of wheat which lay in the yard. He was very regal; he was no longer afraid. He feathered and trod Pertelote twenty times before it was fully daylight. He looked as if he were a grim lion as he roamed up and down on his toes: he didn't deign to set his foot to the ground. He clucks every time he finds a kernel, and all his wives run to him. Thus as royal as a prince in his great hall, I leave Chantecleer in his pasture, and later I will tell his adventure.

When March—the month the world began and in which God made man—when March was over and one day more, it happened that Chantecleer, in all his pride, his seven hens walking beside him, cast up his eyes to the bright sun which had passed through 21° and a little more in the sign of Taurus, and Chantecleer knew by nature, not by any learning, that it was the third hour of the day, he crowed with a cheerful sound and said, "The sun has climbed 21° and more in the heavens. Madame Pertelote, joy of my world, listen to the happy birds—how they sing! And look at the fresh flowers—how they bloom! My heart is full of merriment and comfort."

But suddenly a terrible thing happened to him: for happiness always turns into grief. Worldly happiness, God knows, is soon gone. And if a rhetorician really knew how to write well, he could write it in a chronicle as a most noteworthy truth. Now let everyone listen to me because this story is as true as *The Book of Lancelot de Lac,* which women admire so greatly. Now I will return to my theme.

A fox, full of crafty wickedness, who had lived in that grove for three years, on that very night (as the great vision had foretold) broke through the hedge into the yard where handsome Chantecleer and his wives were accustomed to walk. The fox lay still in a bed of cabbages, waiting for a time to fall upon Chantecleer, as eagerly as do all murderers who lie in wait to murder men.

O false murderer, lurking in your den! O, new Judas Iscariot, new Ganelon [who betrayed Charlemagne and Roland], false dissembler! O, Greek Sinon who brought Troy to utter ruin!

O, Chantecleer! May the morning be accursed on which you flew from the beam into the yard! You had been warned by your dreams that this day would be perilous for you. But what God foreknows must be—according to the opinion of certain learned men. Any great scholar will tell you that in the universities there has been great altercation and great disputation on this subject, and it has involved a hundred thousand men. But I am not able to sift it to the bran [get down to the bare truth] as the holy doctor Augustine is able to, or Boethius, or Bishop Bradwardine—whether God's foreknowledge forces men of necessity to do a thing. By "necessity" I mean *simple necessity;* or whether I have been given free choice to do that thing or not do it, even though God foreknew it before it was done. Or whether his foreknowledge does not force it at all except by *conditional necessity.*

I don't want to have anything to do with that question. My story is about a cock, as you are about to hear, who, to his sorrow, took his wife's advice to walk in the yard on the morning when he had dreamed that dream I told you of. Women's advice is very often harmful; a woman's advice first brought mankind to woe, and made Adam leave Paradise where he had been happy and wholly at ease. But because I don't know whom I might displease if I blame the advice of women, forget it; I said it as a joke. Read the authorities where they deal with this subject, and you will learn what they say about women. These are the cock's words, not mine. I can't discern any harm in any woman.

Lovely Pertelote lies in the sun pleasantly bathing herself in the sand, and all her sisters near her. And Chantecleer freely sings more merrily than the mermaids in the sea; for *Physiologos [The Beastiary]* says that they sing very well and merrily. And it so happened that as Chantecleer glanced at a butterfly among the cabbages, he became aware of the fox who lay very close to the ground. He didn't in the least wish to crow then, but immediately cried out, "Cock, cock!" and startled like a man frightened to the heart; because an animal by nature desires to flee from his natural enemy if he should see him. Chantecleer, the moment he spied the fox, wanted to flee, but quickly the fox said, "Noble sire, alas, where do you want to go? Are you afraid of me? I am your friend. Indeed, I would be worse than a friend if I wanted to do any harm or injury to you. I haven't come to spy out your private affairs. But truly the only cause of my coming was to listen to you sing. My lord, your father—God bless his soul—and also your mother (bless her for her gentility) have both been in my house to my great pleasure. And certainly, sire, I would gladly please you. For when people talk about singing, I always say—may I lose my eyes if I'm lying—that, except for you, I never heard any man sing the way your father used to in the morning. Surely, all he sang was from the heart. And to make his voice stronger he would shut both his eyes very tightly, and stand on his tiptoes, and stretch his neck out until it was long and small around. And also he was so perceptive that no man anywhere could surpass him in singing or in wisdom. I have read among the verses of the book *Lord*

Burnel the Ass,[3] that there was a cock who, when he was young and ignorant, was injured in the leg by a priest's son. In revenge, the cock made the priest's son lose his benefice [appointment to a church office]. [The cock didn't wake him on the day he was to receive the office.] But certainly there is no comparison between the subtlety of this cock and the wisdom and discretion of your father. Now sing, sire, for the love of heaven, and let's see if you are able to imitate your father."

Chantecleer began to beat his wings like a man who cannot espy treachery; he was too carried away by the flattery.

Alas, O noble lords, how many false flatterers and liars are in your courts who please you much more, believe me, than any man who tells you the truth. Read *Ecclesiastes*[4] on flatterers, and beware, lords, of their treachery.

Chantecleer stood high on his toes, stretched out his neck, kept his eyes tightly closed and began to crow his very loudest crow. Lord Russell the fox immediately leapt up, grabbed Chantecleer by the neck, threw him over his back, and started to carry him off toward the woods because, as yet, no one, pursued him.

O destiny which no one can escape! Alas that Chante- cleer flew down from the roost. Alas that his wife denied the significance of dreams. And all this misfortune happened on a Friday.

O Venus, goddess of pleasure, since Chantecleer was your devout worshiper and did all in his power to serve you (more for sensual delight than for procreation), how could you let him die on your day?

O Godfrey,[5] dear sovereign master [of rhetoric], when your worthy King Richard[6] was slain, how exquisitely you lamented his death. Why don't I have your skill and learning so that I could reproach

[3]Lord Burnel the Ass is a medieval satire by Nigel Wireker (in the twelfth century) that refers to a priest who broke a cock's leg by throwing a rock at him. Consequently, the cock refused to crow on the day of the priest's ordination, thus making him late.

[4]Ecclesiastes is a book in the Old Testament.

[5]Godrey was an English duke who became the ruler of Jerusalem and the Christian territories following the First Crusade.

[6]King Richard, who ruled England from 1189—1199, was best known as Richard, the Lion-Heart.

Friday, as you did because your king was killed on a Friday? Then I would show you how ably I would lament for Chantecleer's fear and pain.

When Troy was captured and Pyrrhus[7] seized Priam[8] by the beard and killed him, as the *Aeneid* says, the ladies of the city never made half such a cry and lamentation as the hens of the yard made when they saw what was happening to Chantecleer. But Madame Pertelote shrieked most sovereignly, much louder than Hasdrubal's[9] wife shrieked when the Romans killed her husband and burned Carthage. She was so full of grief and despair that she rushed into the fire and burned herself with a steadfast heart. O woeful hens, you cried out exactly as, when Nero[10] burned Rome, the wives of the senators cried out because their husbands had lost their lives, for Nero, though they were guiltless, had them slain.

Now, I'll return to my story.

The simple widow and her two daughters at once rushed outdoors when they heard the hens cry out in their grief. The women saw the fox going toward the grove carrying the cock away on his back; they cried, "Out! Harrow!" and "Weilawey! Look! Look! the fox," and they ran after him. Many men with staves ran with them. The dogs took up the chase—Colle, Talbot, and Garland, and also Malkyn with a distaff in her hand. There ran also the cow, the calf, and even the hogs— they were so frightened by the barking of the dogs and the shouting of the men and women that the hogs ran as if to break their hearts. They yowled like fiends in hell. The ducks cried out as if they were being killed; out of fear the geese flew over the trees; out of the hive came a swarm of bees. The noise was so hideous—surely Jack Straw [leader of the great Peasant Revolt, 1381] and all his followers never made shouts so shrill, when they were killing a Fleming as that day were made against the fox. Men brought trumpets of brass, wood, horn, and bone upon which they blew and tooted; the others shrieked and whooped. It seemed as if the heavens might fall.

Now, good men, I pray you all, listen. Behold how Fortune reverses suddenly the hope and pride of her enemy! The cock, lying upon the fox's back, though deeply frightened, spoke to the fox and said, "Sire, God help me, if I were you,

I'd say, 'Turn back, all you proud louts! May a pestilence fall upon you! Now that I have reached the edge of the woods, the cock will stay here, and indeed I will eat him right away.'"

The fox answered, "That's just what I'll do." And as he spoke those words, the cock quickly escaped from the fox's mouth and flew immediately up to the branch of a tree.

When the fox realized that the cock was gone, he said, "Alas Chantecleer, I did you a wrong by making you afraid when I seized you and carried you out of the yard. But, sire, I didn't do it with any wicked intention. Come down, and I will tell you what I meant to do. I'll tell you the truth, God help me."

"No," said the cock, "then I would say, 'A curse on both of us', but first a curse on me, my blood, and my bones, if I let you trick me more than once. Never again with your flattery will you cause me to sing and close my eyes, for the man who wilfully closes his eyes when he should keep them open—may God never let him prosper."

"No," the fox said, "may God give great misfortune to the man who controls himself so badly that he yaks when he should shut up."

Notice well what happens when one is reckless and careless and puts his trust in flattery.

But you who think this tale is some foolishness—all about a cock and a hen, consider instead the moral lesson in the story, for St. Paul says that every thing that is written is indeed written for our instruction. Take the wheat and throw away the chaff.

And now, O God, if it be thy will, as Our Lord says, make us all good men and bring us into the bliss of heaven. Amen.

[7]Pyrrhus was the son of Greek warrior, Achilles, hero of the Trojan War.

[8]Priam was King of Troy.

[9]Hasdrubal was a Roman conqueror during the Punic Wars.

[10]Nero was the Roman Emperor from A.D. 54—68, who was blamed for the great fire that destroyed much of Rome in 64.

CHRISTINE DE PIZAN

THE BOOK OF THE CITY OF LADIES AND JOAN OF ARC

In an age when most females were under the authority of men and received, at best, only an elementary education, Christine de Pizan (c. 1364—c. 1430) was an exceptional woman. She was born in Venice, and when she was five years old, her father, Tomasso de Pizzano, an astrologer, natural philosopher, and mathematician, accepted a position at the court of Charles V in France. Charles was interested in learning and education—founding the royal library, commissioning translations of scientific and classical works (including Aristotle), and redecorating the Louvre to house an eminent library.

In 1380, when Christine was fifteen years old, she was married to Etienne de Castel, the husband her father had chosen for her. Through Etienne's position as a court secretary, Christine came into contact with educated men who introduced her to Latin prose and the works of Petrarch and Boccaccio. Charles V's untimely death in 1380 was followed by the death of her father in 1387, and, three years later, of her beloved husband. Suddenly, at the age of twenty-five, Christine found herself a widow with a daughter, two sons, a niece, and her mother to support. Seeking consolation for her grief, she began to write poetry. Learning that her poetry was well received, Christine proceeded to write courtly love poetry, as well as poems about the French court, and mythology; later, she turned her interest toward the writers of antiquity. The success of her works accorded her the patronage of such distinguished people as Philip the Bold, the Duke of Burgundy, Queen Isabella of Bavaria, the English Earl of Salisbury, and Jean, Duke of Berry.

Christine is best remembered for her extended work on the role of women in society in which she addresses such weighty issues as the ability of women to govern, their aptitude for learning, and the criminality of rape. In 1405, she authored *Cité de dames* (The Book of the City of Ladies). The structure of the book is patterned after Augustine's *City of God,* and the thematic material depends heavily on the works of Boccaccio. *The Book of the City of Ladies* is divided into three parts and describes Christine's vision of a city—founded by the goddesses Reason, Discretion, and Justice—reserved for women who have made significant contributions to society. In the following selection, Christine explains how she came to write the book as a rejoinder to those who "write such awful, damning things about women and their ways."

THE BOOK OF THE CITY OF LADIES

1. Here begins the Book of the City of Ladies, the first chapter of which explains why and for what purpose the book was written.

One day, I was sitting in my study surrounded by many books of different kinds, for it has long been my habit to engage in the pursuit of knowledge. My mind had grown weary as I had spent the day struggling with the weighty tomes of various authors whom I had been studying for some time. I looked up from my book and decided that, for once, I would put aside these difficult texts and find instead something amusing and easy to read from the works of the poets. As I searched around for some little book, I happened to chance upon a work which did not belong to me but was amongst a pile of others that had been placed in my safekeeping. I opened it up and saw from the title that it was by Matheolus.[1] With a smile, I made my choice. Although I had never read it, I knew that, unlike many other works, this one was said to be written in praise of women. Yet I had scarcely begun to read it when my dear mother called me down to supper, for it was time to eat. I put the book to one side, resolving to go back to it the following day.

The next morning, seated once more in my study as is my usual custom, I remembered my previous desire to have a look at this book by Matheolus. I picked it up again and read on a little. But, seeing the kind of immoral language and ideas it contained, the content seemed to me likely to appeal only to those who enjoy reading works of slander and to be of no use whatsoever to anyone who wished to pursue virtue or to improve their moral standards. I therefore leafed through it, read the ending, and

[1] Matheolus refers to a poem, "The Lamentations of Matheolus" (c. 1295) by Mathieu of Boulogne, that disparages women.

decided to switch to some more worthy and profitable work. Yet, having looked at this book, which I considered to be of no authority, an extraordinary thought became planted in my mind which made me wonder why on earth it was that so many men, both clerks and others, have said and continue to say and write such awful, damning things about women and their ways. I was at a loss as to how to explain it. It is not just a handful of writers who do this, nor only this Matheolus whose book is neither regarded as authoritative nor intended to be taken seriously. It is all manner of philosophers, poets and orators too numerous to mention, who all seem to speak with one voice and are unanimous in their view that female nature is wholly given up to vice.

As I mulled these ideas over in my mind again and again, I began to examine myself and my own behaviour as an example of womankind. In order to judge in all fairness and without prejudice whether what so many famous men have said about us is true, I also thought about other women I know, the many princesses and countless ladies of all different social ranks who have shared their private and personal thoughts with me. No matter which way I looked at it and no matter how much I turned the question over in my mind, I could find no evidence from my own experience to bear out such a negative view of female nature and habits. Even so, given that I could scarcely find a moral work by any author which didn't devote some chapter or paragraph to attacking the female sex, I had to accept their unfavourable opinion of women since it was unlikely that so many learned men, who seemed to be endowed with such great intelligence and insight into all things, could possibly have lied on so many different occasions. It was on the basis of this one simple argument that I was forced to conclude that, although my understanding was too crude and ill-informed to recognize the great flaws in myself and other women, these men had to be in the right. Thus I preferred to give more weight to what others said than to trust my own judgement and experience.

I dwelt on these thoughts at such length that it was as if I had sunk into a deep trance. My mind became flooded with an endless stream of names as I recalled all the authors who had written on this subject. I came to the conclusion that God had surely created a vile thing when He created woman. Indeed, I was astounded that such a fine craftsman could have wished to make such an appalling object which, as these writers would have it, is like a vessel in which all the sin and evil of the world has been collected and preserved. This thought inspired such a great sense of disgust and sadness in me that I began to despise myself and the whole of my sex as an aberration in nature.

With a deep sigh, I called out to God: "Oh Lord, how can this be? Unless I commit an error of faith, I cannot doubt that you, in your infinite wisdom and perfect goodness, could make anything that wasn't good. Didn't you yourself create woman especially and then endow her with all the qualities that you wished her to have? How could you possibly have made a mistake in anything? Yet here stand women not simply accused, but already judged, sentenced and condemned! I just cannot understand this contradiction. If it is true, dear Lord God, that women are guilty of such horrors as so many men seem to say, and as you yourself have said that the testimony of two or more witnesses is conclusive, how can I doubt their word? Oh God, why wasn't I born a male so that my every desire would be to serve you, to do right in all things, and to be as perfect a creature as man claims to be? Since you chose not to show such grace to me, please pardon and forgive me, dear Lord, if I fail to serve you as well as I should, for the servant who receives fewer rewards from his lord is less obligated to him in his service."

Sick at heart, in my lament to God I uttered these and many other foolish words since I thought myself very unfortunate that He had given me a female form.

Using examples from classical antiquity, biblical history, and French history, Christine, with the help of Lady Reason and "three ladies" (symbolizing virtue), lay the foundation of the City of Ladies by figuratively "digging up" the misogynistic, disparaging, and critical remarks made about women by past writers. Reason challenges the writers, arguing that women possess the same moral and intellectual qualities as men.

---

8. Christine explains how Reason instructed her and helped her to begin digging up the ground in order to lay the foundations.

Lady Reason replied to my words, saying: "Stand up now, daughter, and without further delay let us make our way to the Field of Letters. There we will build the City of Ladies on flat, fertile ground, where fruits of all kinds flourish and fresh streams flow, a place where every good thing grows in abundance. Take the spade of your intelligence and dig deep to make a great trench all around where you see the line I have traced. I'll help to carry away the hods of earth on my shoulders."

Obeying her instructions, I jumped to my feet: thanks to the three ladies, my body felt much stronger and lighter than before. She took the lead and I followed on behind. When we came to the spot she had described, I began to excavate and dig out the earth with the spade of my intelligence, just as she had directed me to do. The first fruit of my labours was this: "My lady, I'm remembering that image of gold being refined in the furnace that you used before to symbolize the way many male writers have launched a full-scale attack on the ways of women. I take this image to mean that the more women are criticized, the more it redounds to their glory. But please tell me exactly what it is that makes so many different authors slander women in their writings because, if I understand you correctly, they are wrong to do so. Is it Nature that makes them do this? Or, if it is out of hatred, how can you explain it?"

Reason answered my questions, saying: "My dear daughter, in order to help you see more clearly how things stand, let me carry away this first load of earth. I can tell you that, far from making them slander women, Nature does the complete opposite. There is no stronger or closer bond in the world than that which Nature, in accordance with God's wishes, creates between man and woman. Rather, there are many other different reasons which explain why men have attacked women in the past and continue to do so, including those authors whose works you have already mentioned. Some of those who criticized women did so with good intentions: they wanted to rescue men who had already fallen into the clutches of depraved and corrupt women or to prevent others from suffering the same fate, and to encourage men generally to avoid leading a lustful and sinful existence. They therefore attacked all women in order to persuade men to regard the entire sex as an abomination."

"My lady," I said, "forgive me for interrupting you. Were they right to do so, since they were acting with good intentions? Isn't it true that one's actions are judged by one's intentions?"

"You're wrong, my dear girl," she replied, "because there is no excuse for plain ignorance. If I killed you with good intentions and out of stupidity, would I be in the right? Those who have acted in this way, whoever they may be, have abused their power. Attacking one party in the belief that you are benefiting a third party is unfair. So is criticizing the nature of all women, which is completely unjustified, as I will prove to you by analogy. Condemning all women in order to help some misguided men get over their foolish behaviour is tantamount to denouncing fire, which is a vital and beneficial element, just because some people are burnt by it, or to cursing water just because some people are drowned in it. You could apply the same reasoning to all manner of things which can be put to either good or bad use. In none of these cases should you blame the thing in itself if foolish people use it unwisely. You yourself have made these points elsewhere in your writings. Those who subscribe to these opinions, whether in good or bad faith, have overstepped the mark in order to make their point. It's like somebody cutting up the whole piece of cloth in order to make himself a huge coat simply because it's not going to cost him anything and no one is going to object. It thus stops anyone else from using the material. If instead, as you yourself have rightly remarked, these writers had tried to find ways to save men from indulging in vice and from frequenting debauched women by attacking only the morals and the habits of those who were evidently guilty of such behaviour, I freely admit that they would have produced texts which were extremely useful. It's true that there's nothing worse than a woman who is dissolute and depraved: she's like a monster, a creature going against its own nature, which is to be timid, meek and pure. I can assure you that those writers who condemn the entire female sex for being sinful, when in fact there are so many women who are extremely virtuous, are not acting with my approval. They've committed a grave error, as do all those who subscribe to their views. So let us throw out these horrible, ugly, misshapen stones from your work as they have no place in your beautiful city.

"Other men have criticized women for different reasons: some because they are themselves steeped in sin, some because of a bodily impediment, some out of sheer envy, and some quite simply because they naturally take delight in slandering others. There are also some who do so because they like to flaunt their erudition: they have come across these views in books and so like to quote the authors whom they have read.

"Those who criticize the female sex because they are inherently sinful are men who have wasted their youth on dissolute behaviour and who have had affairs with many different women. These men have therefore acquired cunning through their many experiences and have grown old without repenting of their sins. Indeed, they look back with nostalgia on the appalling way they used to carry on when they were younger. Now that old age has finally caught up with them and the spirit is still willing but the flesh has grown weak, they are full of regret when they see that, for them, the 'good old days' are over and they can merely watch as younger men take over from where they have had to leave off. The only way they can release their frustration is to attack women and to try to stop others from enjoying the pleasures that they themselves used to take. You very often see old men such as these going around saying vile and disgusting things, as in the case of your Matheolus, who freely admits that he is just an impotent old man who would still like to satisfy his desires. He's an excellent example to illustrate my point as he's typical of many other similar cases.

"Yet, thank goodness, not all old men are full of depravity and rotten to the core like a leper. There are many other fine, decent ones whose wisdom and virtue have been nourished by me and whose words reflect their good character, since they speak in an honourable and sober fashion. Such men detest all kinds of wrongdoing and slander. Thus, rather than attacking and defaming individual sinners, male or female, they condemn all sins in general. Their advice to others is to avoid vice, pursue virtue and stick to the straight and narrow.

"Those men who have attacked women because of their own bodily impediments, such as impotence or a deformed limb, are all bitter and twisted in the mind. The only pleasure they have to compensate for their incapacity is to slander the female sex since it is women who bring such joy to other men. That way they are convinced that they can put others off enjoying what they themselves have never had.

"Those men who have slandered the opposite sex out of envy have usually known women who were cleverer and more virtuous than they are. Out of bitterness and spite, envious men such as these are driven to attack all women, thinking that they can thereby undermine these individuals' good reputation and excellent character, as in the case of the author of *On Philosophy* whose name I've forgotten. In this book, he goes to great lengths to argue that men should on no account praise women and that those who do so are betraying the title of his book: their doctrine is no longer 'philosophy' but 'philofolly'. However, I can assure you that it is definitely he who is the arch-exponent of 'philofolly' because of all the false reasoning and erroneous conclusions he comes out with in his book.

"As for those men who are slanderous by nature, it's not surprising if they criticize women, given that they attack everyone indiscriminately. You can take it from me that any man who wilfully slanders the female sex does so because he has an evil mind, since he's going against both reason and nature. Against reason, because he is lacking in gratitude and failing to acknowledge all the good and indispensable things that woman has done for him both in the past and still today, much more than he can ever repay her for. Against nature, in that even the birds and the beasts naturally love their mate, the female of the species. So man acts in a most unnatural way when he, a rational being, fails to love woman.

"Finally, there are those who dabble in literature and delight in mimicking even the very finest works written by authors who are greatly superior to them. They think themselves to be beyond reproach since they are merely repeating what others have already said. Believe me, this is how they set about making their defamatory remarks. Some of them scribble down any old nonsense, verse without rhyme or reason, in which they discuss the ways of women, or princes, or whoever it might be, when it is they themselves, whose habits leave much to be desired, who are most in need of moral self-improvement. Yet the common folk, who are as ignorant as they are, think that it's the best thing they've ever read."

JOAN OF ARC

Christine's final work, dated July 31, 1429, is a joyous poem about Joan of Arc's victory at Orléans and the coronation of Charles VII (1422-1461) at Rheims. Christine lauds "the Maid of Orléans" who delivered France from England, and she views Joan of Arc's triumph as a victory for womanhood.

DANTE ALIGHIERI

THE DIVINE COMEDY

Dante Alighieri was a poet, political philosopher, soldier, and politician. Born in 1265 in Florence, Italy, he died in exile in 1321. His greatest work, *The Divine Comedy,* was composed of one hundred cantos (individual poems) and written not in Latin, the language of learning, but in the Tuscan Italian dialect of the common people. The poem is an elaborate allegory in which each character and event can be understood on two or more levels—for example, a literal description of the levels of hell and Dante's (and every Christian's) struggle to overcome a flawed human nature and to ward off worldly sin. Dante, representing all human beings, is guided through the afterworlds: hell (inferno), purgatory (purgatorio), and heaven (paradiso). The Roman poet Virgil conducts him through hell and purgatory; Beatrice, his long-dead beloved, leads him through heaven to the point where he sees God in all his glory.

Dante synthesized the various elements of the medieval outlook, and he summed up, with immense feeling, the medieval understanding of the purpose of life. The *Inferno* relates the power of God, the Father; the *Purgatorio* depicts the wisdom of Jesus as God's son; and the *Paradiso* portrays the love of the Holy Spirit. Furthermore, to illustrate the importance of the Trinity, Dante designed the *Comedy* with a strict numerological plan—each part contains 33 cantos. He chose 33 cantos for each part to correspond with the traditional belief that Jesus lived 33 years. By multiplying 33 x 3 = 99 and adding 1 canto for the introduction, the total is 100 cantos. One hundred is the square of 10, and for Dante, 10 was a perfect number because it consisted of the square of the Trinity (3), plus 1, symbolizing the triune God—God the "Three-In-One." Because the *Comedy* symbolizes the spiritual journey of every Christian who yearns for salvation but fears it will be denied because of human sinfulness, the *Comedy* later came to be better known as the "Divine Comedy."

The first canto of the *Inferno* opens on Good Friday (the day Christians traditionally associate with the crucifixion of Jesus) as Dante—the symbol for every Christian—wanders from "the True Way" and finds himself "alone in a dark wood" of error and despair. He then meets the Latin poet Virgil. In the descent through the nine concentric circles of hell, Virgil describes the nature and significance of each region through which they pass. In each section of hell, sinners are punished in proportion to their earthly sins. Over the entrance gate to hell, Dante reads these words:

I AM THE WAY INTO THE CITY OF WOE.
I AM THE WAY TO A FORSAKEN PEOPLE.
I AM THE WAY INTO ETERNAL SORROW,
SACRED JUSTICE MOVED MY ARCHITECT.
I WAS RAISED HERE BY DIVINE OMNIPOTENCE,
PRIMORDIAL LOVE AND ULTIMATE INTELLECT.
ONLY THOSE ELEMENTS TIME CANNOT WEAR
WERE MADE BEFORE ME, AND BEYOND TIME I STAND
ABANDON ALL HOPE YE WHO ENTER HERE.

In the following selection from Canto IV, Limbo, Dante describes the first circle of hell. Dante and Virgil meet the virtuous pagans and unbaptized children who, because "they lacked Baptism's grace, which is the door of the true faith," are permitted neither to enter heaven nor to suffer in hell proper. Here they encounter the classical authors of antiquity—Homer, Horace, Ovid, and Lucan—and they pass into "a great Citadel" of reason where they meet celebrated heroes, including Hector, Aeneas, and Caesar. Finally, they are greeted by Aristotle, "the master of those who know," who is surrounded by "the great souls of philosophy," such as Thales, Heraclitus, Anaxagoras, Socrates, Hippocrates, Democritus, Plato, Diogenes, Zeno, Ptolemy, and Galen.

CIRCLE ONE: LIMBO

The Virtuous Pagans

Dante wakes to find himself across Acheron. The Poets are now on the brink of Hell itself, which Dante conceives as a great funnel-shaped cave lying below the northern hemisphere with its bottom point at the earth's center. Around this great circular depression runs a series of ledges, each of which Dante calls a *Circle.* Each circle is assigned to the punishment of one category of sin.

As soon as Dante's strength returns, the Poets begin to cross the *First Circle.* Here they find the *Virtuous Pagans.* They were born without the light of Christ's revelation and, therefore, they cannot come into the light of God, but they are not tormented. Their only pain is that they have no hope.

Ahead of them Dante sights a great dome of light, and a voice trumpets through the darkness welcoming Virgil back, for this is his eternal place in Hell. Immediately the great Poets of all time appear—*Homer, Horace, Ovid,* and *Lucan.* They greet Virgil, and they make Dante a sixth in their company.

With them Dante enters the Citadel of Human Reason and sees before his eyes the Master Souls of Pagan Antiquity gathered on a green, and illuminated by the radiance of Human Reason. This is the highest state man can achieve without God, and the glory of it dazzles Dante, but he knows also that it is nothing compared to the glory of God.

A monstrous clap of thunder broke apart
the swoon that stuffed my head; like one awakened
by violent hands, I leaped up with a start.
And having risen; rested and renewed,
I studied out the landmarks of the gloom
to find my bearings there as best I could.
And I found I stood on the very brink of the valley
called the Dolorous Abyss, the desolate chasm
where rolls the thunder of Hell's eternal cry,
so depthless-deep and nebulous and dim
that stare as I might into its frightful pit
it gave me back no feature and no bottom.
Death-pale,[1] the Poet spoke: "Now let us go
into the blind world waiting here below us.
I will lead the way and you will follow."
And I, sick with alarm at his new pallor,
cried out, "How can I go this way when you
who are my strength in doubt turn pale with terror?"
And he: "The pain of these below us here,
drains the color from my face for pity,
and leaves this pallor you mistake for fear.
Now let us go, for a long road awaits us."
So he entered and so he led me in
to the first circle and ledge of the abyss.
No tortured wailing rose to greet us here
but sounds of sighing rose from every side,
sending a tremor through the timeless air,
a grief breathed out of untormented sadness,
the passive state of those who dwelled apart,
men, women, children—a dim and endless congress.

[1] death pale: Virgil is most likely affected here by the return to his own place in Hell. "The pain of these below," then (line 19), would be the pain of his own group in Limbo (the Virtuous Pagans) rather than the total of Hell's suffering.

And the Master said to me: "You do not question[2]
what souls these are that suffer here before you?
I wish you to know before you travel on
that these were sinless. And still their merits fail,
for they lacked Baptism's grace, which is the door
of the true faith you were born to. Their birth fell
before the age of the Christian mysteries,
and so they did not worship God's Trinity
in fullest duty. I am one of these.
For such defects are we lost, though spared the fire
and suffering Hell in one affliction only:
that without hope we live on in desire."
I thought how many worthy souls there were
suspended in that Limbo, and a weight
closed on my heart for what the noblest suffer.
"Instruct me, Master and most noble Sir,"
I prayed him then, "better to understand
the perfect creed that conquers every error:
has any, by his own or another's merit,
gone ever from this place to blessedness?"
He sensed my inner question and answered it:
"I was still new to this estate of tears
when a Mighty One[3] descended here[4] among us,
crowned with the sign of His victorious years.
He took from us the shade of our first parent,
of Abel, his pure son, of ancient Noah,
of Moses, the bringer of law, the obedient.
Father Abraham, David the King,
Israel with his father and his children,
Rachel, the holy vessel of His blessing,
and many more He chose for elevation
among the elect. And before these, you must know,
no human soul had ever won salvation."
We had not paused as he spoke, but held our road
and passed meanwhile beyond a press of souls
crowded about like trees in a thick wood.
And we had not traveled far from where I woke
when I made out a radiance before us
that struck away a hemisphere of dark.
We were still some distance back in the long night,
yet near enough that I half-saw, half-sensed,
what quality of souls lived in that light.
"O ornament of wisdom and of art,

---

[2] You do not question: A master touch of characterization. Virgil's amour propre is a bit piqued at Dante's lack of curiosity about the position in Hell of Virgil's own kind. And it may possibly be, by allegorical extension, that Human Reason must urge the soul to question the place of reason. The allegorical point is conjectural, but such conjecture is certainly one of the effects inherent in the use of allegory; when well used, the central symbols of the allegory continue indefinitely to suggest new interpretations and shades of meaning.

[3] a Mighty One: Christ. His name is never directly uttered in Hell.

[4] descended here: The legend of the Harrowing of Hell is Apocryphal. It is based on I Peter iii, 19: "He went and preached unto the spirits in prison." The legend is that Christ in the glory of His resurrection descended into Limbo and took with Him to Heaven the first human souls to be saved. The event would, accordingly, have occurred in 33 or 34 A.D. Virgil died in 19 B.C.

what souls are these whose merit lights their way
even in Hell. What joy sets them apart?"
And he to me: "The signature of honor
they left on earth is recognized in Heaven
and wins them ease in Hell out of God's favor."
And as he spoke a voice rang on the air:
"Honor the Prince of Poets; the soul and glory
that went from us returns. He is here! He is here!"
The cry ceased and the echo passed from hearing;
I saw four mighty presences come toward us
with neither joy nor sorrow in their bearing.
"Note well," my Master said as they came on,
"that soul that leads the rest with sword in hand
as if he were their captain and champion.
It is Homer, singing master of the earth.
Next after him is Horace, the satirist,
Ovid is third, and Lucan is the fourth.
Since all of these have part in the high name
the voice proclaimed, calling me Prince of Poets,
the honor that they do me honors them."
So I saw gathered at the edge of light
the masters of that highest school whose song
outsoars all others like an eagle's flight.
And after they had talked together a while,
they turned and welcomed me most graciously,
at which I saw my approving Master smile.
And they honored me far beyond courtesy,
for they included me in their own number,
making me sixth in that high company.[5]
So we moved[6] toward the light, and as we passed
we spoke of things as well omitted here
as it was sweet to touch on there. At last
we reached the base of a great Citadel[7]
circled by seven towering battlements
and by a sweet brook flowing round them all.
This we passed over as if it were firm ground.[8]

---

[5] making me sixth in that high company: Merit and self-awareness of merit may well be a higher thing than modesty. An additional point Dante may well have had in mind, however, is the fact that he saw himself as one pledged to continue in his own times the classic tradition represented by these poets.

[6] 103—105. These lines amount to a stylistic note. It is good style ('l tacere e bello where bello equals "good style") to omit this discussion, since it would digress from the subject and, moreover, his point is already made. Every great narrator tends to tell his story from climax to climax. There are times on the other hand when Dante delights in digression. (See General Note to Canto XX.)

[7] A GREAT CITADEL. The most likely allegory is that the Citadel represents philosophy (that is, human reason without the light of God) surrounded by seven walls which represent the seven liberal arts, or the seven sciences, or the seven virtues. Note that Human Reason makes a light of its own, but that it is a light in darkness and forever separated from the glory of God's light. The sweet brook flowing round them all has been interpreted in many ways. Clearly fundamental, however, is the fact that it divides those in the Citadel (those who wish to know) from those in the outer darkness.

[8] as if it were firm ground: Since Dante still has his body, and since all others in Hell are incorporeal shades, there is a recurring narrative problem in the Inferno (and through the rest of the Commedia): how does flesh act in contact with spirit? In the Purgatorio Dante attempts to embrace the spirit of Casella and his arms pass through him as if he were empty air. In the Third Circle, below (Canto VI, 34—36), Dante steps on some of the spirits lying in the slush and his foot passes right through them. (The original lines offer several possible readings of which I have preferred this one.) And at other times Virgil, also a spirit, picks Dante up and carries him bodily. It is clear, too, that Dante means the spirits of Hell to be weightless. When Virgil steps into Phlegyas' bark (Canto VIII) it does not settle into the water, but it does when Dante's living body steps aboard. There is no narrative reason why Dante should not sink into the waters of this stream and Dante

Through seven gates I entered with those sages
and came to a green meadow blooming round.
There with a solemn and majestic poise
stood many people gathered in the light,
speaking infrequently and with muted voice.
Past that enameled green we six withdrew
into a luminous and open height
from which each soul among them stood in view.
And there directly before me on the green
the master souls of time were shown to me.
I glory in the glory I have seen!
Electra stood in a great company
among whom I saw Hector and Aeneas
and Caesar in armor with his falcon's eye.
I saw Camilla, and the Queen Amazon
across the field. I saw the Latin King
seated there with his daughter by his throne.
And the good Brutus who overthrew the Tarquin:
Lucrezia, Julia, Marcia, and Cornelia;
and, by himself apart, the Saladin.
And raising my eyes a little I saw on high
Aristotle, the master of those who know,
ringed by the great souls of philosophy.
All wait upon him for their honor and his.
I saw Socrates and Plato at his side
before all others there. Democritus
who ascribes the world to chance, Diogenes,
and with him there Thales, Anaxagoras,
Zeno, Heraclitus, Empedocles.
And I saw the wise collector and analyst—
Dioscorides I mean. I saw Orpheus there,
Tully, Linus, Seneca the moralist,
Eculid the geometer, and Ptolemy,
Hippocrates, Galen, Avicenna,
and Averrhoes of the Great Commentary.
I cannot count so much nobility;
my longer theme pursues me so that often
the word falls short of the reality.
The company of six is reduced by four.
My Master leads me by another road
away from that serenity to the roar
and trembling air of Hell. I pass from light
into the kingdom of eternal night.

In the lower circles of hell, Dante and Virgil experience all of hell's torments—burning sand, violent storms, darkness, and fearful monsters that whip, claw, bite, and tear sinners apart. The ninth circle, the lowest, is reserved for Lucifer and traitors. Lucifer has three faces, each a different color, and two batlike wings. In each mouth he gnaws on the greatest traitors in history: Judas

---

follows no fixed rule in dealing with such phenomena, often suiting the physical action to the allegorical need. Here, the moat probably symbolizes some requirement (The Will to Know) which he and the other poets meet without difficulty.

Iscariot, who betrayed Jesus, and Brutus and Cassius, who assassinated Caesar. Dante and Virgil climb over the body of Lucifer, and Dante describes how they emerge from hell after three days—symbolizing Christ's "harrowing of hell."

CANTO XXXIV

ninth circle: cocytus *Compound Fraud*

round four: *judecca The Treacherous to Their Masters*

the center *Satan*

"On march the banners of the King," Virgil begins as the Poets face the last depth. He is quoting a medieval hymn, and to it he adds the distortion and perversion of all that lies about him. "On march the banners of the King—of Hell." And there before them, in an infernal parody of Godhead they see Satan in the distance, his great wings beating like a windmill. It is their beating that is the source of the icy wind of Cocytus, the exhalation of all evil.

All about him in the ice are strewn the sinners of the last round,Judecca, named for Judas Iscariot. These are the Treacherous to Their Masters. They lie completely sealed in the ice, twisted and distorted into every conceivable posture. It is impossible to speak to them, and the Poets move on to observe Satan.

He is fixed into the ice at the center to which flow all the rivers of guilt; and as he beats his great wings as if to escape, their icy wind only freezes him more surely into the polluted ice. In a grotesque parody of the Trinity, he has three faces, each a different color, and in each mouth he clamps a sinner whom he rips eternally with his teeth. Judas Iscariot is in the central mouth: Brutus and Cassius in the mouths on either side.

Having seen all, the Poets now climb through the center, grappling hand over hand down the hairy flank of Satan himself—a last supremely symbolic action—and at last, when they have passed the center of all gravity, they emerge from Hell. A long climb from the earth's center to the Mount of Purgatory awaits them, and they push on without rest, ascending along the sides of the river Lethe, till they emerge once more to see the stars of Heaven, just before dawn on Easter Sunday.

"On march the banners of the King[9] of Hell,"
my Master said. "Toward us. Look straight ahead:
can you make him out at the core of the frozen shell?"
Like a whirling windmill seen afar at twilight,
or when a mist has risen from the ground—
just such an engine rose upon my sight
stirring up such a wild and bitter wind
I cowered for shelter at my Master's back,
there being no other windbreak I could find.
I stood now where the souls of the last class
(with fear my verses tell it) were covered wholly;
they shone below the ice like straws in glass.
Some lie stretched out; others are fixed in place
upright, some on their heads some on their soles;
another, like a bow, bends foot to face.
When we had gone so far across the ice

[9] On march the banners of the King: The hymn (Vexilla regis prodeunt) was written in the sixth century by Venantius Fortunatus, Bishop of Poitiers. The original celebrates the Holy Cross, and is part of the service for Good Friday to be sung at the moment of uncovering the cross.

that it pleased my Guide to show me the foul creature[1]
that once had worn the grace of Paradise,
he made me stop, and, stepping aside, he said:
"Now see the face of Dis! This is the place
where you must arm your soul against all dread."
Do not ask, Reader, how my blood ran cold
and my voice choked up with fear. I cannot write it:
this is a terror that cannot be told.
I did not die, and yet I lost life's breath:
imagine for yourself what I became,
deprived at once of both my life and death.
The Emperor of the Universe of Pain
jutted his upper chest above the ice;
and I am closer in size to the great mountain
the Titans make around the central pit,
than they to his arms. Now, starting from this part,
imagine the whole that corresponds to it!
If he was once as beautiful as now
he is hideous, and still turned on his Maker,
well may he be the source of every woe!
With what a sense of awe I saw his head
towering above me! for it had three faces:[2]
one was in front, and it was fiery red;
the other two, as weirdly wonderful,
merged with it from the middle of each shoulder
to the point where all converged at the top of the skull;
the right was something between white and bile;
the left was about the color one observes
on those who live along the banks of the Nile.
Under each head two wings rose terribly,
their span proportioned to so gross a bird:
I never saw such sails upon the sea.
They were not feathers—their texture and their form
were like a bat's wings—and he beat them so
that three winds blew from him in one great storm:
it is these winds that freeze all Cocytus.
He wept from his six eyes, and down three chins
the tears ran mixed with bloody froth and pus.[3]
In every mouth he worked a broken sinner
between his rake-like teeth. Thus he kept three
in eternal pain at his eternal dinner.
For the one in front the biting seemed to play
no part at all compared to the ripping: at times
the whole skin of his back was flayed away.
"That soul that suffers most," explained my Guide,
"is Judas[4] Iscariot, he who kicks his legs

[1] *the fowl creature: Satan.*
[2] three faces: Numerous interpretations of these three faces exist. What is essential to all explanation is that they be seen as perversions of the qualities of the Trinity.
[3] bloody froth and pus: The gore of the sinners he chews which is mixed with his slaver.
[4] Judas: Note how closely his punishment is patterned on that of the Simoniacs (Canto XIX).

on the fiery chin and has his head inside.
Of the other two, who have their heads thrust forward,
the one who dangles down from the black face
is Brutus: note how he writhes without a word.
And there, with the huge and sinewy arms,[5] is the soul
of Cassius.—But the night is coming on[6]
and we must go, for we have seen the whole."
Then, as he bade, I clasped his neck, and he,
watching for a moment when the wings
were opened wide, reached over dexterously
and seized the shaggy coat of the king demon;
then grappling matted hair and frozen crusts
from one tuft to another, clambered down.
When we had reached the joint where the great thigh
merges into the swelling of the haunch,
my Guide and Master, straining terribly,
turned his head to where his feet had been
and began to grip the hair as if he were climbing;
so that I thought we moved toward Hell again.
"Hold fast!" my Guide said, and his breath came shrill[7]
with labor and exhaustion. "There is no way
but by such stairs to rise above such evil."
At last he climbed out through an opening
in the central rock, and he seated me on the rim;
then joined me with a nimble backward spring.
I looked up, thinking to see Lucifer
as I had left him, and I saw instead
his legs projecting high into the air.
Now let all those whose dull minds are still vexed
by failure to understand what point it was
I had passed through, judge if I was perplexed.
"Get up. Up on your feet," my Master said.
"The sun already mounts to middle tierce,[8]
and a long road and hard climbing lie ahead."
It was no hall of state we had found there,
but a natural animal pit hollowed from rock
with a broken floor and a close and sunless air.
"Before I tear myself from the Abyss,"
I said when I had risen, "O my Master,
explain to me my error in all this:
where is the ice? and Lucifer—how has he
been turned from top to bottom: and how can the sun
have gone from night to day so suddenly?"
And he to me: "You imagine you are still

---

[5] huge and sinewy arms: The Cassius who betrayed Caesar was more generally described in terms of Shakespeare's "lean and hungry look." Another Cassius is described by Cicero (Catiline III) as huge and sinewy. Dante probably confused the two.

[6] the night is coming on: It is now Saturday evening.

[7] his breath came shrill: Cf. Canto XXIII, 85, where the fact that Dante breathes indicates to the Hypocrites that he is alive. Virgil's breathing is certainly a contradiction.

[8] middle tierce: In the canonical day tierce is the period from about six to nine A.M. Middle tierce, therefore, is seven-thirty. In going through the center point, they have gone from night to day. They have moved ahead twelve hours.

on the other side of the center where I grasped
the shaggy flank of the Great Worm of Evil
which bores through the world—you were while I climbed
down,
but when I turned myself about, you passed
the point to which all gravities are drawn.
You are under the other hemisphere where you stand;
the sky above us is the half opposed
to that which canopies the great dry land.
Under the midpoint of that other sky
the Man who was born sinless and who lived
beyond all blemish, came to suffer and die.
You have your feet upon a little sphere
which forms the other face of the Judecca.
There it is evening when it is morning here.
And this gross Fiend and Image of all Evil
who made a stairway for us with his hide
is pinched and prisoned in the ice-pack still.
On this side he plunged down from heaven's height,
and the land that spread here once hid in the sea
and fled North to our hemisphere for fright;
and it may be that moved by that same fear,
the one peak[9] that still rises on this side
fled upward leaving this great cavern[10] here."
Down there, beginning at the further bound
of Beelzebub's dim tomb, there is a space
not known by sight, but only by the sound
of a little stream[11] descending through the hollow
it has eroded from the massive stone
in its endlessly entwining lazy flow."
My Guide and I crossed over and began
to mount that little known and lightless road
to ascend into the shining world again.
He first, I second, without thought of rest
we climbed the dark until we reached the point
where a round opening brought in sight the blest
and beauteous shining of the Heavenly cars.
And we walked out once more beneath the Stars.[12]

As Dante and Virgil are about to reach the summit of Mount Purgatory, Beatrice replaces Virgil as Dante's guide. In the final canto of the Paradiso, Dante and Beatrice ascend to the highest heaven, the Empyrean, which is located beyond Saturn, the last of the seven planets, beyond the circle of stars that encloses the planets and above the Primum Mobile—the outermost sphere revolving around the Earth. Here at the summit of the universe is a realm of pure light that radiates truth, goodness, and happiness, where God is found. Dante glimpses the vision of God—a mystical experience in which the aim of his life is realized.

[9] the one peak: The Mount of Purgatory.
[10] this great cavern: The natural animal pit of line 98. It is also "Beelzebub's dim tomb," line 131.
[11] a little stream: Lethe. In classical mythology, the river of forgetfulness, from which souls drank before being born. In Dante's symbolism it flows down from the top of Purgatory, where it washes away the memory of sin from the souls that have achieved purity. That memory it delivers to Hell, which drawn all sin to itself.
[12] *Stars*: As part of his total symbolism Dante ends each of the three divisions of the *Commedia* with this word. Every conclusion of the upward soul is toward the stars. God's shining symbols of hope and virtue. It is just before dawn of Easter Sunday that the Poets emerge—a further symbolism.

Little by little as my vision grew
it penetrated further through the aura
54 of the high lamp which in Itself is true.
What then I saw is more than tongue can say.
Our human speech is dark before the vision.
57 The ravished memory swoons and falls away.
As one who sees in dreams and wakes to find
the emotional impression of his vision
60 still powerful while its parts fade from his mind—
just such am I, having lost nearly all
the vision itself, while in my heart I feel
63 the sweetness of it yet distill and fall.
So, in the sun, the footprints face from snow.
On the wild wind that bore the tumbling leaves
66 the Sybil's oracles were scattered so.
Light Supreme who doth Thyself withdraw
so far above man's mortal understanding,
69 lend me again some glimpse of what I saw;
make Thou my tongue so eloquent it may
of all Thy glory speak a single clue
72 to those who follow me in the world's day;
for by returning to my memory
somewhat, and somewhat sounding in these verses,
75 Thou shalt show man more of Thy victory.
So dazzling was the splendor of that Ray,
that I must certainly have lost my senses
78 had I, but for an instant, turned away.
And so it was, as I recall, I could
the better bear to look, until at last
81 my vision made one with the Eternal Good.
Oh grace abounding that had made me fit
to fix my eyes on the eternal light
84 until my vision was consumed in it!
saw within Its depth how It conceives
all things in a single volume bound by Love,
87 of which the universe is the scattered leaves;
substance, accident, and their relation
so fused that all I say could do no more
90 than yield a glimpse of that bright revelation.
I think I saw the universal form
that binds these things, for as I speak these words
93 I feel my joy swell and my spirits warm.
Twenty-five centuries since Neptune saw
the Argo's keel have not moved all mankind,
96 recalling that adventure, to such awe
as I felt in an instant. My tranced being
stored fixed and motionless upon that vision,
99 ever more fervent to see in the act of seeing.
Experiencing that Radiance, the spirit
is so indrawn it is impossible

BISHOP JACQUES-BENIGNE BOSSUET

POLITICS DRAWN FROM THE VERY WORDS OF HOLY SCRIPTURE

Louis XIV was the symbol of absolutism, a term applied to those early modern states where monarchs exercised power free of constitutional restraints. Theorists of absolutism like Bishop Jacques-Benigne Bossuet (1627–1704) argued that monarchs received their authority directly from God. Following are excerpts from Bossuet's *Politics Drawn from the Very Words of Holy Scripture* (1707).

THIRD BOOK, IN WHICH ONE BEGINS TO EXPLAIN THE NATURE AND THE PROPERTIES OF ROYAL AUTHORITY

Article II, Royal Authority is Sacred

1st Proposition, God establishes kings as his ministers, and reigns through them over the peoples We have already seen that all power comes from God.

"The prince, St. Paul adds, is God's minister to thee for good. But if thou do that which is evil, fear: for he beareth not the sword in vain. For he is God's minister: an avenger to execute wrath upon him that doth evil."

Thus princes act as ministers of God, and his lieutenants on earth. It is through them that he exercises his Empire. . . .

It is in this way that we have seen that the royal throne is not the throne of a man, but the throne of God himself. "God hath chosen Solomon my son, to sit upon the throne of the kingdom of the Lord over Israel." And again: "Solomon sat on the throne of the Lord."

And in order that no one believe that it was peculiar to the Israelites to have kings established by God, here is what Ecclesiasticus says: "Over every nation he set a ruler." . . .

Thus he governs all peoples, and gives them, all of them, their kings; though he governs Israel in a more particular and announced fashion.

2nd Proposition, The person of kings is sacred It appears from all this that the person of kings is sacred, and that to attempt anything against them is a sacrilege. . . . [T]hey are sacred through their charge, as being the representatives of divine majesty, deputized by his providence for the execution of his plans. It is thus that God calls Cyrus his anointed. . . .

One must protect kings as sacred things; and whoever neglects to guard them is worthy of death. . . .

3rd Proposition, One must obey the prince by reason of religion and conscience . . . Even if rulers do not acquit themselves of this duty [punishment of evildoers and praise of the good], one must respect in them their charge and their ministry. "Servants, be subject to your masters with all fear, not only to the good and gentle, but also to the angry and unjust."

There is thus something religious in the respect one gives to the prince. The service of God and respect for kings are inseparable things, and St. Peter places these two duties together: "Fear God, Honor the King."

God, moreover, has put something divine into kings. "I have said: You are Gods, and all of you the sons of the most High." It is God himself whom David makes speak in this way. . . .

4th Proposition, Kings should respect their own power, and use it only for the public good Their power coming from on high, as has been said, they must not believe that they are the owners of it, to use it as they please; rather must they use it with fear and restraint, as something which comes to them from God, and for which God will ask an accounting of them.

FOURTH BOOK, ON THE CHARACTERISTICS OF ROYALTY (CONTINUATION)

First Article, Royal Authority is Absolute

1st Proposition, The prince need account to no one for what he ordains . . . Without this absolute authority, he can neither do good nor suppress evil: his power must be such that no one can hope to escape him; and, in fine, the sole defense of individuals against the public power, must be their innocence. . . .

2nd Proposition, When the prince has decided, there can be no other decision The judgments of sovereigns are attributed to God himself. . . .

[N]o one has the right to judge or to review after him.

One must, then, obey princes as if they were justice itself, without which there is neither order nor justice in affairs.

They are gods, and share in some way in divine independence. "I have said: You are gods, and all of you the sons of the most High."

Only God can judge their judgments and their persons. . . .

It follows from this that he who does not want to obey the prince, is . . . condemned irremissibly to death as an enemy of public peace and of human society. . . .

The prince can correct himself when he knows that he has done badly; but against his authority there can be no remedy except his authority.

3rd Proposition, There is no co-active force against the prince One calls co-active [coercive] force a power to constrain and to execute what is legitimately ordained. To the prince alone belongs legitimate command; to him alone belongs co-active force as well.

It is for that reason also that St. Paul gives the sword to him alone. "If thou do that which is evil, fear; for he beareth not the sword in vain."

In the state only the prince should be armed: otherwise everything is in confusion, and the state falls back into anarchy.

He who creates a sovereign prince puts everything together into his hands, both the sovereign authority to judge and all the power of the state.

JAMES I

TRUE LAW OF FREE MONARCHIES AND A SPEECH TO PARLIAMENT

An articulate defense of the divine right of monarchy was composed by James VI, who was king of Scotland (1567–1625) and as James I (1603–1625) also was king of England. A scholar as well as a king, James in 1598 anonymously published a widely read book called the *True Law of Free Monarchies.* He claimed that the king alone was the true legislator. James's notions of the royal prerogative and of the role of Parliament are detailed in the following passages from the *True Law* and a speech to Parliament.

TRUE LAW

Prerogative and Parliament

According to these fundamental laws already alleged, we daily see that in the parliament (which is nothing else but the head court of the king and his vassals) the laws are but craved by his subjects, and only made by him at their [proposal] and with their advice: for albeit the king make daily statutes and ordinances, [imposing] such pains thereto as he thinks [fit], without any advice of parliament or estates, yet it lies in the power of no parliament to make any kind of law or statute, without his sceptre [that is, authority] be to it, for giving it the force of a law. . . . And as ye see it manifest that the king is over-lord of the whole land, so is he master over every person that inhabiteth the same, having power over the life and death of every one of them: for although a just prince will not take the life of any of his subjects without a clear law, yet the same laws whereby he taketh them are made by himself or his predecessors; and so the power flows always from himself. . . . Where he sees the law doubtsome or rigorous, he may interpret or mitigate the same, lest otherwise *summum jus* be *summa injuria* [the greatest right be the greatest wrong]: and therefore general laws made publicly in parliament may upon . . . [the king's] authority be mitigated and suspended upon causes only known to him.

As likewise, although I have said a good king will frame all his actions to be according to the law, yet is he not bound thereto but of his good will, and for good example-giving to his subjects. . . . So as I have already said, a good king, though he be above the law, will subject and frame his actions thereto, for example's sake to his subjects, and of his own free will, but not as subject or bound thereto. . . .

In a speech before the English Parliament in March 1610, James elaborated on his exalted theory of the monarch's absolute power.

A SPEECH TO PARLIAMENT

. . . The state of monarchy is the supremest thing upon earth: for kings are not only God's lieutenants upon earth and sit upon God's throne, but even by God himself they are called gods. There be three principal [comparisons] that illustrate the state of monarchy: one taken out of the word of God, and the two other out of the grounds of policy and philosophy. In the Scriptures kings are called gods, and so their power after a certain relation compared to the Divine power. Kings are also compared to fathers of families: for a king is truly *parens patriae* [parent of the country], the politic father of his people. And lastly, kings are compared to the head of this microcosm of the body of man. . . .

I conclude then this point touching the power of kings with this axiom of divinity, That as to dispute what God may do is blasphemy, . . . so is it sedition in subjects to dispute what a king may do in the height of his power. But just kings will ever be willing to declare what they will do, if they will not incur the curse of God. I will not be content that my power be disputed upon; but I shall ever be willing to make the reason appear of all my doings, and rule my actions according to my laws. . . .

Now the second general ground whereof I am to speak concerns the matter of grievances. . . . First then, I am not to find fault that you inform yourselves of the particular just grievances of the people; nay I must tell you, ye can neither be just nor faithful to me or to your countries that trust and employ you, if you do it not. . . . But I would wish you to be careful to avoid [these] things in the matter of grievances.

First, that you do not meddle with the main points of government: that is my craft . . . to meddle with that, were to lessen me. I am now an old king . . . ; I must not be taught my office.

Secondly, I would not have you meddle with such ancient rights of mine as I have received from my predecessors, possessing them *more majorum* [as ancestral customs]: such things I would be sorry should be accounted for grievances. All novelties are dangerous as well in a politic as in a natural body: and therefore I would be loath to be quarrelled in my ancient rights and possessions: for that were to judge me unworthy of that which my predecessors had and left me.

THOMAS HOBBES

LEVIATHAN

Hobbes was influenced by the new scientific thought that saw mathematical knowledge as the avenue to truth. Using geometry as a model, Hobbes began with what he believed were self-evident axioms regarding human nature, from which he deduced other truths. He aimed at constructing political philosophy on a scientific foundation and rejected the authority of tradition and religion as inconsistent with a science of politics. Thus, although Hobbes supported absolutism, he dismissed the idea advanced by other theorists of absolutism that the monarch's power derived from God. He also rejected the idea that the state should not be obeyed when it violated God's law. *Leviathan* is a rational and secular political statement. In this modern approach, rather than in Hobbes's justification of absolutism, lies the work's significance.

Hobbes had a pessimistic view of human nature. Believing that people are innately selfish and grasping, he maintained that competition and dissension, rather than cooperation, characterize human relations. Even when reason teaches that cooperation is more advantageous than competition, Hobbes observed that people are reluctant to alter their ways, because passion, not reason, governs their behavior. In the following passages from *Leviathan*, Hobbes describes the causes of human conflicts.

Nature hath made men so equall, in the faculties of body, and mind; as that though there bee found one man sometimes manifestly stronger in body, or of quicker mind than another; yet when all is reckoned together, the difference between man, and man, is not so considerable, as that one man can thereupon claim to himselfe any benefit, to which another may not pretend, as well as he. For as to the strength of body, the weakest has strength enough to kill the strongest, either by secret machination, or by confederacy with others, that are in the same danger with himselfe. . . .

And as to the faculties of the mind . . . men are . . . [more] equall than unequall. . . .

From this equality of ability, ariseth equality of hope in the attaining of our Ends. And therefore if any two men desire the same thing, which neverthelesse they cannot both enjoy, they become enemies; and in the way to their End, . . . endeavour to destroy, or subdue one another. . . . If one plant, sow, build, or possesse a convenient Seat, others may probably be expected to come prepared with forces united, to dispossesse, and deprive him, not only of the fruit of his labour, but also of his life, or liberty. . . .

So that in the nature of man, we find three principall causes of quarrell. First, Competition; Secondly, Diffidence; Thirdly, Glory.

The first, maketh men invade for Gain; the second, for Safety; and the third, for Reputation. The first use Violence, to make themselves Masters of other men's persons, wives, children, and cattell; the second, to defend them; the third, for trifles, as a word, a smile, a different opinion, and any other signe of undervalue, either direct in their Persons, or by reflexion in their Kindred, their Friends, their Nation, their Profession, or their Name.

Hereby it is manifest, that during the time men live without a common Power to keep them all in awe, they are in that condition which is called Warre; and such a warre, as is of every man, against every man. . . .

Hobbes then describes a state of nature—the hypothetical condition of humanity prior to the formation of the state—as a war of all against all. For Hobbes, the state of nature is a logical abstraction, a device employed to make his point. Only a strong ruling entity—the state—will end the perpetual strife and provide security. For Hobbes, the state is merely a useful arrangement that permits individuals to exchange goods and services in a secure environment. The ruling authority in the state, the sovereign, must have supreme power, or society will collapse and the anarchy of the state of nature will return.

Whatsoever therefore is consequent to a time of Warre, where every man is Enemy to every man; the same is consequent to the time, wherein men live without other security, than what their own strength, and their own invention shall furnish them withall. In such condition, there is no place for Industry; because the fruit thereof is uncertain: and consequently no Culture of the Earth; no Navigation, nor use of the commodities that may be imported by Sea; no commodious Building; no Instruments of moving, and removing such things as require much force; no Knowledge of the face of the Earth; no account of Time; no Arts; no Letters; no Society; and which is worst of all, continuall feare, and danger of violent death; And the life of man, solitary, poore, nasty, brutish, and short. . . .

The Passions that encline men to Peace, are Feare of Death; Desire of such things as are necessary to commodious living; and a Hope by their Industry to obtain them. And Reason suggesteth convenient Articles of Peace, upon which men may be drawn to agreement. . . .

And because the condition of Man, (as hath been declared in the precedent Chapter) is a condition of Warre of every one against every one; in which case every one is governed by his own Reason; and there is nothing he can make use of, that may not be a help unto him, in preserving his life against his enemyes; It followeth, that in such a condition, every man has a Right to every thing; even to one another's body. And therefore, as long as this naturall Right of every man to every thing endureth, there can be no security to any man, (how strong or wise soever he be,) of living out the time, which Nature ordinarily alloweth men to live. . . .

. . . If there be no Power erected, or not great enough for our security; every man will and may lawfully rely on his own strength and art, for caution against all other men. . . .

The only way to erect . . . a Common Power, as may be able to defend them from the invasion of [foreigners] and the injuries of one another, and thereby to secure them in such sort, as that by their owne industrie, and by the fruites of the Earth, they may nourish themselves and live contentedly; is, to conferre all their power and strength upon one Man, or upon one Assembly of men, that may reduce all their Wills, by plurality of voices, unto one Will . . . and therein to submit their Wills, every one to his Will, and their Judgements, to his Judgment. This is more than Consent, or Concord; it is a reall Unitie of them all, in one and the same Person, made by Covenant of every man with every man, in such manner, as if every man should say to every man, *I Authorise and give up my Right of Governing my selfe, to this Man, or to this Assembly of men, on this condition, that thou give up thy Right to him, and Authorise all his Actions in like manner.* This done, the Multitude so united in one Person, is called a Common-wealth. . . . For by this Authorite, given him by every particular man in the Common-wealth, he hath the use of so much Power and Strength . . . conferred on him, that by terror thereof, he is inabled to forme the wills of them all, to Peace at home, and mutuall [aid] against their enemies abroad. And in him consisteth the Essence of the Common-wealth; which (to define it,) is *One Person, of whose Acts a great Multitude, by mutuall Covenants one with another, have made themselves every one the Author, to the end he may use the strength and means of them all, as he shall think expedient, for their Peace and Common Defence.*

And he that carryeth this Person, is called Soveraigne, and said to have *Soveraigne Power*; and every one besides, his Subject. . . .

. . . They that have already Instituted a Common-wealth, being thereby bound by Covenant . . . cannot lawfully make a new Covenant, amongst themselves, to be obedient to any other, in any thing whatsoever, without his permission. And therefore, they that are subjects to a Monarch, cannot without his leave cast off Monarchy, and return to the confusion of a disunited Multitude; nor transferre their Person from him that beareth it, to another Man, or other Assembly of men: for they . . . are bound, every man to every man, to [acknowledge] . . . that he that already is their Soveraigne, shall do, and judge fit to be done; so that [those who do not obey] break their Covenant made to that man, which is injustice: and they have also every man given the Soveraignty to him that beareth their Person; and therefore if they depose him, they take from him that which is his own, and so again it is injustice. . . . And whereas some men have pretended for their disobedience to their Soveraign, a new Covenant, made, not with men, but with God; this also is unjust: for there is no Covenant with God, but by mediation of some body that representeth God's Person; which none doth but God's Lieutenant, who hath the Soveraignty under God. But this pretence of Covenant with God, is so evident a [lie], even in the pretenders own consciences, that it is not onely an act of an unjust, but also of a vile, and unmanly disposition. . . .

. . . Consequently none of [the sovereign's] Subjects, by any pretence of forfeiture, can be freed from his Subjection.

GALILEO GALILEI

THE STARRY MESSENGER

In the following reading from *The Starry Messenger* (1610), Galileo reported the findings observed through his telescope, which led him to proclaim the uniformity of nature, a key principle of modern science.

About ten months ago a report reached my ears that a certain Fleming [a native of Flanders][1] had constructed a spyglass by means of which visible objects, though very distant from the eye of the observer, were distinctly seen as if nearby. Of this truly remarkable effect several experiences were related, to which some persons gave credence while others denied them. A few days later the report was confirmed to me in a letter from a noble Frenchman at Paris, Jacques Badovere,[2] which caused me to apply myself wholeheartedly to inquire into the means by which I might arrive at the invention of a similar instrument. This I did shortly afterwards, my basis being the theory of refraction. First I prepared a tube of lead, at the ends of which I fitted two glass lenses, both plane on one side while on the other side one was spherically convex and the other concave. Then placing my eye near the concave lens I perceived objects satisfactorily large and near, for they appeared three times closer and nine times larger than when seen with the naked eye alone. Next I constructed another one, more accurate, which represented objects as enlarged more than sixty times. Finally, sparing neither labor nor expense, I succeeded in constructing for myself so excellent an instrument that objects seen by means of it appeared nearly one thousand times larger and over thirty times closer than when regarded with our natural vision.

It would be superfluous to enumerate the number and importance of the advantages of such an instrument at sea as well as on land. But forsaking terrestrial observations, I turned to celestial ones, and first I saw the moon from as near at hand as if it were scarcely two terrestrial radii [a measure of distance, obscure today] away. After that I observed often with wondering delight both the planets and the fixed stars, and since I saw these latter to be very crowded, I began to seek (and eventually found) a method by which I might measure their distances apart. . . .

Now let us review the observations made during the past two months, once more inviting the attention of all who are eager for true philosophy to the first steps of such important contemplations. Let us speak first of that surface of the moon which faces us. For greater clarity I distinguish two parts of this surface, a lighter and a darker; the lighter part seems to surround and to pervade the whole hemisphere, while the darker part discolors the moon's surface like a kind of cloud, and makes it appear covered with spots. Now those spots which are fairly dark and rather large are plain to everyone and have been seen throughout the ages; these I shall call the "large" or "ancient" spots, distinguishing them from others that are smaller in size but so numerous as to occur all over the lunar surface, and especially the lighter part. The latter spots had never been seen by anyone before me. From observations of these spots repeated many times I have been led to the opinion and conviction that the surface of the moon is not smooth, uniform, and precisely spherical as a great number of philosophers believe it (and the other heavenly bodies) to be, but is uneven, rough, and full of cavities and prominences, being not unlike the face of the earth, relieved by chains of mountains and deep valleys. . . .

With his telescope, Galileo discovered four moons orbiting Jupiter, an observation that overcame a principal objection to the Copernican system. Galileo showed that a celestial body could indeed move around a center other than the earth; that earth was not the common center for all celestial bodies; that a celestial body (earth's moon or Jupiter's moons) could orbit a planet at the same time that the planet revolved around another body (namely, the sun).

[1]Credit for the original invention is generally assigned to Hans Lipperhey, a lens grinder in Holland who chanced upon this property of combined lenses and applied for a patent on it in 1608.

[2]Badovere studied in Italy toward the close of the sixteenth century and is said to have been a pupil of Galileo's in about 1598. When he wrote concerning the new instrument in 1609, he was in the French diplomatic service at Paris, where he died in 1620.

On the seventh day of January in this present year 1610, at the first hour of night, when I was viewing the heavenly bodies with a telescope, Jupiter presented itself to me; and because I had prepared a very excellent instrument for myself, I perceived (as I had not before, on account of the weakness of my previous instrument) that beside the planet there were three starlets, small indeed, but very bright. Though I believed them to be among the host of fixed stars, they aroused my curiosity somewhat by appearing to lie in an exact straight line parallel to the ecliptic, and by their being more splendid than others of their size. Their arrangement with respect to Jupiter and each other was the following:

East * * o * *West*

that is, there were two stars on the eastern side and one to the west. The most easterly star and the western one appeared larger than the other. I paid no attention to the distances between them and Jupiter, for at the outset I thought them to be fixed stars, as I have said.[3] But returning to the same investigation on January eighth—led by what, I do not know—I found a very different arrangement. The three starlets were now all to the west of Jupiter, closer together, and at equal intervals from one another as shown in the following sketch:

East o * * * *West*

On the tenth of January, however, the stars appeared in this position with respect to Jupiter:

East * * o *West*

that is, there were but two of them, both easterly, the third (as I supposed) being hidden behind Jupiter. . . . There was no way in which such alterations could be attributed to Jupiter's motion, yet being certain that these were still the same stars I had observed . . . my perplexity was now transformed into amazement. I was sure that the apparent changes belonged not to Jupiter but to the observed stars, and I resolved to pursue this investigation with greater care and attention. . . .

I had now decided beyond all question that there existed in the heavens three stars wandering about Jupiter as do Venus and Mercury about the sun, and this became plainer than daylight from observations on similar occasions which followed. Nor were there just three such stars; four wanderers complete their revolutions about Jupiter. . . .

Here we have a fine and elegant argument for quieting the doubts of those who, while accepting with tranquil mind the revolutions of the planets about the sun in the Copernican system, are mightily disturbed to have the moon alone revolve about the earth and accompany it in an annual rotation about the sun. Some have believed that this structure of the universe should be rejected as impossible. But now we have not just one planet rotating about another while both run through a great orbit around the sun; our own eyes show us four stars which wander around Jupiter as does the moon around the earth, while all together trace out a grand revolution about the sun in the space of twelve years.

[3]The reader should remember that the telescope was nightly revealing to Galileo hundreds of fixed stars never previously observed. His unusual gifts for astronomical observation are illustrated by his having noticed and remembered these three merely by reason of their alignment, and recalling them so well that when by chance he happened to see them the following night he was certain that they had changed their positions.

GALILEO GALILEI

LETTER TO THE GRAND DUCHESS CHRISTINA AND DIALOGUE CONCERNING THE TWO CHIEF WORLD SYSTEMS—PTOLEMAIC AND COPERNICAN

The first reading illustrates Galileo's active involvement in a struggle for freedom of inquiry many years before the *Dialogue* was published. In 1615, in a letter addressed to Grand Duchess Christina of Tuscany, Galileo argued that passages from the Bible had no authority in scientific disputes.

The second reading (from the *Dialogue*) reveals Galileo's views on Aristotle. Medieval scholastics regarded Aristotle as the supreme authority on questions concerning nature, an attitude that was perpetuated by early modern scholastics. Galileo insisted that such reliance on authority was a hindrance to scientific investigation, that it is through observation, experiment, and reason that one arrives at physical truth.

BIBLICAL AUTHORITY

Some years ago, as Your Serene Highness well knows, I discovered in the heavens many things that had not been seen before our own age. The novelty of these things, as well as some consequences which followed from them in contradiction to the physical notions commonly held among academic philosophers, stirred up against me no small number of professors—as if I had placed these things in the sky with my own hands in order to upset nature and overturn the sciences. They seemed to forget that the increase of known truths stimulates the investigation, establishment, and growth of the arts; not their diminution or destruction.

Showing a greater fondness for their own opinions than for truth, they sought to deny and disprove the new things which, if they had cared to look for themselves, their own senses would have demonstrated to them. To this end they hurled various charges and published numerous writings filled with vain arguments, and they made the grave mistake of sprinkling these with passages taken from places in the Bible which they had failed to understand properly, and which were ill suited to their purposes. . . .

. . . Men who were well grounded in astronomical and physical science were persuaded as soon as they received my first message. There were others who denied them or remained in doubt only because of their novel and unexpected character, and because they had not yet had the opportunity to see for themselves. These men have by degrees come to be satisfied. But some, besides allegiance to their original error, possess I know not what fanciful interest in remaining hostile not so much toward the things in question as toward their discoverer. No longer being able to deny them, these men now take refuge in obstinate silence, but being more than ever exasperated by that which has pacified and quieted other men, they divert their thoughts to other fancies and seek new ways to damage me. . . .

. . . Possibly because they are disturbed by the known truth of other propositions of mine which differ from those commonly held, and therefore mistrusting their defense so long as they confine themselves to the field of philosophy, these men have resolved to fabricate a shield for their fallacies out of the mantle of pretended religion and the authority of the Bible. These they apply, with little judgment, to the refutation of arguments that they do not understand and have not even listened to.

First they have endeavored to spread the opinion that such propositions in general are contrary to the Bible and are consequently damnable and heretical. . . . Hence they have had no trouble in finding men who would preach the damnability and heresy of the new doctrine from their very pulpits with unwonted confidence, thus doing impious and inconsiderate injury not only to that doctrine and its followers but to all mathematics and mathematicians in general. . . .

. . . They go about invoking the Bible, which they would have minister to their deceitful purposes. Contrary to the sense of the Bible and the intention of the holy [Church] Fathers, if I am not mistaken, they would extend such authorities until even in purely physical matters—where faith is not involved—they would have us altogether abandon reason and the evidence of our senses in favor of some biblical passage, though under the surface meaning of its words this passage may contain a different sense.

I hope to show that I proceed with much greater piety than they do, when I argue not against condemning [Copernicus'] book, but against condemning it in the way they suggest—that is, without understanding it, weighing it, or so much as reading it. For Copernicus never discusses matters of religion or faith, nor does he use arguments that depend in any way upon the authority of sacred writings which he might have interpreted erroneously. He stands always upon physical conclusions pertaining to the celestial motions, and deals with them by astronomical and geometrical demonstrations, founded primarily upon sense experiences and very exact observations. He did not ignore the Bible, but he knew very well that if his doctrine were proved, then it could not contradict the Scriptures when they were rightly understood. . . .

The reason produced for condemning the opinion that the earth moves and the sun stands still is that in many places in the Bible one may read that the sun moves and the earth stands still. Since the Bible cannot err, it follows as a necessary consequence that anyone takes an erroneous and heretical position who maintains that the sun is inherently motionless and the earth movable.

With regard to this argument, I think in the first place that it is very pious to say and prudent to affirm that the holy Bible can never speak untruth—whenever its true meaning is understood. But I believe nobody will deny that it is often very abstruse, and may say things which are quite different from what its bare words signify. Hence in expounding the Bible if one were always to confine oneself to the unadorned grammatical meaning, one might fall into error. . . .

. . . Now the Bible, merely to condescend to popular capacity, has not hesitated to obscure some very important pronouncements, attributing to God himself some qualities extremely remote from (and even contrary to) His essence. Who, then, would positively declare that this principle has been set aside, and the Bible has confined itself rigorously to the bare and restricted sense of its words, when speaking but casually of the earth, of water, of the sun, or of any other created thing? Especially in view of the fact that these things in no way concern the primary purpose of the sacred writings, which is the service of God and the salvation of souls—matters infinitely beyond the comprehension of the common people.

This being granted, I think that in discussions of physical problems we ought to begin not from the authority of scriptural passages, but from sense-experiences and necessary demonstrations. . . . Nothing physical which sense-experience sets before our eyes, or which necessary demonstrations prove to us, ought to be called in question (much less condemned) upon the testimony of biblical passages which may have some different meaning beneath their words. . . .

. . . I do not feel obliged to believe that that same God who has endowed us with senses, reason, and intellect has intended to forgo their use and by some other means to give us knowledge which we can attain by them. He would not require us to deny sense and reason in physical matters which are set before our eyes and minds by direct experience or necessary demonstrations. . . .

It is obvious that such [anti-Copernican] authors, not having penetrated the true senses of Scripture, would impose upon others an obligation to subscribe to conclusions that are repugnant to manifest reason and sense, if they had any authority to do so. God forbid that this sort of abuse should gain countenance and authority, for then in a short time it would be necessary to proscribe all the contemplative sciences. People who are unable to understand perfectly both the Bible and the sciences far outnumber those who do understand. The former, glancing superficially through the Bible, would arrogate to themselves the authority to decree upon every question of physics on the strength of some word which they have misunderstood, and which was employed by the sacred authors for some different purpose. And the smaller number of understanding men could not dam up the furious torrent of such people, who would gain the majority of followers simply because it is much more pleasant to gain a reputation for wisdom without effort or study than to consume oneself tirelessly in the most laborious disciplines.

Galileo attacked the unquestioning acceptance of Aristotle's teachings in his *Dialogue Concerning the Two Chief World Systems—Ptolemaic and Copernican.* In the *Dialogue,* Simplicio is an Aristotelian and Salviati is a spokesman for Galileo; Sagredo, a third participant, introduces the problem of relying on the authority of Aristotle.

ARISTOTELIAN AUTHORITY

Sagredo One day I was at the home of a very famous doctor in Venice, where many persons came on account of their studies, and others occasionally came out of curiosity to see some anatomical dissection performed by a man who was truly no less learned than he was a careful and expert anatomist. It happened on this day that he was investigating the source and origin of the nerves, about which there exists a notorious controversy between the Galenist and Peripatetic doctors.1 The anatomist showed that the great trunk of nerves, leaving the brain and passing through the nape, extended on down the spine and then branched out through the whole body, and that only a single strand as fine as a thread arrived at the heart. Turning to a gentleman whom we knew to be a Peripatetic philosopher, and on whose account he had been exhibiting and demonstrating everything with unusual care, he asked this man whether he was at last satisfied and convinced that the nerves originated in the brain and not in the heart. The philosopher, after considering for awhile, answered: "You have made me see this matter so plainly and palpably that if Aristotle's text were not contrary to it, stating clearly that the nerves originate in the heart, I should be forced to admit it to be true." . . .

Simplicio But if Aristotle is to be abandoned, whom shall we have for a guide in philosophy? Suppose you name some author.

Salviati We need guides in forests and in unknown lands, but on plains and in open places only the blind need guides. It is better for such people to stay at home, but anyone with eyes in his head and his wits about him could serve as a guide for them. In saying this, I do not mean that a person should not listen to Aristotle; indeed, I applaud the reading and careful study of his works, and I reproach only those who give themselves up as slaves to him in such a way as to subscribe blindly to everything he says and take it as an inviolable decree without looking for any other reasons. This abuse carries with it another profound disorder, that other people do not try harder to comprehend the strength of his demonstrations. And what is more revolting in a public dispute, when someone is dealing with demonstrable conclusions, than to hear him interrupted by a text (often written to some quite different purpose) thrown into his teeth by an opponent? If, indeed, you wish to continue in this method of studying, then put aside the name of philosophers and call yourselves historians, or memory experts; for it is not proper that those who never philosophize should usurp the honorable title of philosopher.

GALILEO GALILEI

GALILEO BEFORE THE INQUISITION

The following selection is drawn from the records of the Inquisition, which found Galileo guilty of teaching Copernicanism.

Whereas you, Galileo, son of the late Vincenzo Galilei, Florentine, aged seventy years, were in the year 1615 denounced to this Holy Office for holding as true the false doctrine taught by some that the Sun is the center of the world and immovable and that the Earth moves, and also with a diurnal motion; for having disciples to whom you taught the same doctrine; for holding correspondence with certain mathematicians of Germany concerning the same; for having printed certain letters, entitled "On the Sunspots," wherein you developed the same doctrine as true; and for replying to the objections from the Holy Scriptures, which from time to time were urged against it, by glossing the said Scriptures according to your own meaning: and whereas there was thereupon produced the copy of a document in the form of a letter, purporting to be written by you to one formerly your disciple, and in this divers propositions are set forth, following the position of Copernicus, which are contrary to the true sense and authority of Holy Scripture:

This Holy Tribunal being therefore of intention to proceed against the disorder and mischief thence resulting, which went on increasing to the prejudice of the Holy Faith, by command of His Holiness and of the Most Eminent Lords Cardinals of this supreme and universal Inquisition, the two propositions of the stability of the Sun and the motion of the Earth were by the theological Qualifiers qualified as follows:

The proposition that the Sun is the center of the world and does not move from its place is absurd and false philosophically and formally heretical, because it is expressly contrary to the Holy Scripture.

The proposition that the Earth is not the center of the world and immovable but that it moves, and also with a diurnal motion, is equally absurd and false philosophically and theologically considered at least erroneous in faith.

But whereas it was desired at that time to deal leniently with you, it was decreed at the Holy Congregation held before His Holiness on the twenty-fifth of February, 1616, that his Eminence the Lord Cardinal Bellarmine should order you to abandon altogether the said false doctrine and, in the event of your refusal, that an injunction should be imposed upon you by the Commissary of the Holy Office to give up the said doctrine and not to teach it to others, not to defend it, nor even discuss it; and failing your acquiescence in this injunction, that you should be imprisoned.

And, in order that a doctrine so pernicious might be wholly rooted out and not insinuate itself further to the grave prejudice of Catholic truth, a decree was issued by the Holy Congregation of the Index prohibiting the books which treat of this doctrine and declaring the doctrine itself to be false and wholly contrary to the sacred and divine Scripture.

And whereas a book appeared here recently, printed last year at Florence, the title of which shows that you were the author, this title being: "Dialogue of Galileo Galilei on the Great World Systems"; and whereas the Holy Congregation was afterward informed that through the publication of the said book the false opinion of the motion of the Earth and the stability of the Sun was daily gaining ground, the said book was taken into careful consideration, and in it there was discovered a patent violation of the aforesaid injunction that had been imposed upon you, for in this book you have defended the said opinion previously condemned and to your face declared to be so, although in the said book you strive by various devices to produce the impression that you leave it undecided, and in express terms as probable: which, however, is a most grievous error, as an opinion can in no wise be probable which has been declared and defined to be contrary to divine Scripture.

Therefore by our order you were cited before this Holy Office, where, being examined upon your oath, you acknowledged the book to be written and published by you. You confessed that you began to write the said book about ten or twelve years ago, after the command had been imposed upon you as above; that you requested license to print it without, however, intimating to those who granted you this license that you had been commanded not to hold, defend, or teach the doctrine in question in any way whatever.

We say, pronounce, sentence, and declare that you, the said Galileo, by reason of the matters adduced in trial, and by you confessed as above, have rendered yourself in the judgment of this Holy Office vehemently suspected of heresy, namely, of having believed and held the doctrine—which is false and contrary to the sacred and divine Scriptures—that the Sun is the center of the world and does not move from east to west and that the Earth moves and is not the center of the world; and that an opinion may be held and defended as probable after it has been declared and defined to be contrary to the Holy Scripture; and that consequently you have incurred all the censures and penalties imposed and promulgated in the sacred canons and other constitutions, general and particular, against such delinquents. From which we are content that you be absolved, provided that, first, with a sincere heart and unfeigned faith, you abjure, curse, and detest before us the aforesaid errors and heresies and every other error and heresy contrary to the Catholic and Apostolic Roman Church in the form to be prescribed by us for you.

And, in order that this your grave and pernicious error and transgression may not remain altogether unpunished and that you may be more cautious in the future and an example to others that they may abstain from similar delinquencies, we ordain that the book of the "Dialogue of Galileo Galilei" be prohibited by public edict. . . .

RENÉ DESCARTES

DISCOURSE ON METHOD

In the *Discourse on Method* (1637), Descartes proclaimed the mind's autonomy and importance, and its ability and right to comprehend truth. In this work he offered a method whereby one could achieve certainty and thereby produce a comprehensive understanding of nature and human culture. In the following passage from the *Discourse on Method*, he explained the purpose of his inquiry. How he did so is almost as revolutionary as the ideas he wished to express. He spoke in the first person, autobiographically, as an individual employing his own reason, and he addressed himself to other individuals, inviting them to use their reason. He brought to his narrative an unprecedented confidence in the power of his own judgment and a deep disenchantment with the learning of his times.

PART ONE

From my childhood I lived in a world of books, and since I was taught that by their help I could gain a clear and assured knowledge of everything useful in life, I was eager to learn from them. But as soon as I had finished the course of studies which usually admits one to the ranks of the learned, I changed my opinion completely. For I found myself saddled with so many doubts and errors that I seemed to have gained nothing in trying to educate myself unless it was to discover more and more fully how ignorant I was.

Nevertheless I had been in one of the most celebrated schools in Europe, where I thought there should be wise men if wise men existed anywhere on earth. I had learned there everything that others learned, and, not satisfied with merely the knowledge that was taught, I had perused as many books as I could find which contained more unusual and recondite knowledge. . . . And finally, it did not seem to me that our times were less flourishing and fertile than were any of the earlier periods. All this led me to conclude that I could judge others by myself, and to decide that there was no such wisdom in the world as I had previously hoped to find. . . .

I revered our theology, and hoped as much as anyone else to get to heaven, but having learned on great authority that the road was just as open to the most ignorant as to the most learned, and that the truths of revelation which lead thereto are beyond our understanding, I would not have dared to submit them to the weakness of my reasonings. I thought that to succeed in their examination it would be necessary to have some extraordinary assistance from heaven, and to be more than a man.

I will say nothing of philosophy except that it has been studied for many centuries by the most outstanding minds without having produced anything which is not in dispute and consequently doubtful. I did not have enough presumption to hope to succeed better than the others; and when I noticed how many different opinions learned men may hold on the same subject, despite the fact that no more than one of them can ever be right, I resolved to consider almost as false any opinion which was merely plausible. . . .

This is why I gave up my studies entirely as soon as I reached the age when I was no longer under the control of my teachers. I resolved to seek no other knowledge than that which I might find within myself, or perhaps in the great book of nature. I spent a few years of my adolescence traveling, seeing courts and armies, living with people of diverse types and stations of life, acquiring varied experience, testing myself in the episodes which fortune sent me, and, above all, thinking about the things around me so that I could derive some profit from them. For it seemed to me that I might find much more of the truth in the cogitations [reflections] which each man made on things which were important to him, and where he would be the loser if he judged badly, than in the cogitations of a man of letters in his study, concerned with speculations which produce no effect, and which have no consequences to him. . . .

. . . After spending several years in thus studying the book of nature and acquiring experience, I eventually reached the decision to study my own self, and to employ all my abilities to try to choose the right path. This produced much better results in my case, I think, than would have been produced if I had never left my books and my country. . . .

PART TWO

. . . As far as the opinions which I had been receiving since my birth were concerned, I could not do better than to reject them completely for once in my lifetime, and to resume them afterwards, or perhaps accept better ones in their place, when I had determined how they fitted into a rational scheme. And I firmly believed that by this means I would succeed in conducting my life much better than if I built only upon the old foundations and gave credence to the principles which I had acquired in my childhood without ever having examined them to see whether they were true or not. . . .

. . . Never has my intention been more than to try to reform my own ideas, and rebuild them on foundations that would be wholly mine. . . . The decision to abandon all one's preconceived notions is not an example for all to follow. . . .

As for myself, I should no doubt have . . . [never attempted it] if I had had but a single teacher or if I had not known the differences which have always existed among the most learned. I had discovered in college that one cannot imagine anything so strange and unbelievable but that it has been upheld by some philosopher; and in my travels I had found that those who held opinions contrary to ours were neither barbarians nor savages, but that many of them were at least as reasonable as ourselves. I had considered how the same man, with the same capacity for reason, becomes different as a result of being brought up among Frenchmen or Germans than he would be if he had been brought up among Chinese or cannibals; and how, in our fashions, the thing which pleased us ten years ago and perhaps will please us again ten years in the future, now seems extravagant and ridiculous; and I felt that in all these ways we are much more greatly influenced by custom and example than by any certain knowledge. Faced with this divergence of opinion, I could not accept the testimony of the majority, for I thought it worthless as a proof of anything somewhat difficult to discover, since it is much more likely that a single man will have discovered it than a whole people. Nor, on the other hand, could I select anyone whose opinions seemed to me to be preferable to those of others, and I was thus constrained to embark on the investigation for myself.

Nevertheless, like a man who walks alone in the darkness, I resolved to go so slowly and circumspectly that if I did not get ahead very rapidly I was at least safe from falling. Also, I did not want to reject all the opinions which had slipped irrationally into my consciousness since birth, until I had first spent enough time planning how to accomplish the task which I was then undertaking, and seeking the true method of obtaining knowledge of everything which my mind was capable of understanding. . . .

Descartes' method consists of four principles that place the capacity to arrive at truth entirely within the province of the human mind. First one finds a self-evident principle, such as a geometric axiom. From this general principle, other truths are deduced through logical reasoning. This is accomplished by breaking a problem down into its elementary components and then, step by step, moving toward more complex knowledge.

. . . I thought that some other method [besides that of logic, algebra, and geometry] must be found to combine the advantages of these three and to escape their faults. Finally, just as the multitude of laws frequently furnishes an excuse for vice, and a state is much better governed with a few laws which are strictly adhered to, so I thought that instead of the great number of precepts of which logic is composed, I would have enough with the four following ones, provided that I made a firm and unalterable resolution not to violate them even in a single instance.

The first rule was never to accept anything as true unless I recognized it to be evidently such: that is, carefully to avoid precipitation and prejudgment, and to include nothing in my conclusions unless it presented itself so clearly and distinctly to my mind that there was no occasion to doubt it.

The second was to divide each of the difficulties which I encountered into as many parts as possible, and as might be required for an easier solution.

The third was to think in an orderly fashion, beginning with the things which were simplest and easiest to understand, and gradually and by degrees reaching toward more complex knowledge, even treating as though ordered materials which were not necessarily so.

The last was always to make enumerations so complete, and reviews so general, that I would be certain that nothing was omitted. . . .

What pleased me most about this method was that it enabled me to reason in all things, if not perfectly, at least as well as was in my power. In addition, I felt that in practicing it my mind was gradually becoming accustomed to conceive its objects more clearly and distinctly. . . .

Descartes was searching for an incontrovertible truth that could serve as the first principle of philosophy. His arrival at the famous dictum "I think, therefore I am" marks the beginning of modern philosophy.

PART FOUR

. . . As I desired to devote myself wholly to the search for truth, I thought that I should . . . reject as absolutely false anything of which I could have the least doubt, in order to see whether anything would be left after this procedure which could be called wholly certain. Thus, as our senses deceive us at times, I was ready to suppose that nothing was at all the way our senses represented them to be. As there are men who make mistakes in reasoning even on the simplest topics in geometry, I judged that I was as liable to error as any other, and rejected as false all the reasoning which I had previously accepted as valid demonstration. Finally, as the same precepts which we have when awake may come to us when asleep without their being true, I decided to suppose that nothing that had ever entered my mind was more real than the illusions of my dreams. But I soon noticed that while I thus wished to think everything false, it was necessarily true that I who thought so was something. Since this truth, *I think, therefore I am*, was so firm and assured that all the most extravagant suppositions of the sceptics[1] were unable to shake it, I judged that I could safely accept it as the first principle of the philosophy I was seeking.

[1]The skeptics belonged to the ancient Greek philosophic school that held true knowledge to be beyond human grasp and treated all knowledge as uncertain.

JOHN LOCKE
SECOND TREATISE ON GOVERNMENT

Locke said that originally, in establishing a government, human beings had never agreed to surrender their natural rights to any state authority. The state's founders intended the new polity to preserve these natural rights and to implement the people's will. Therefore, as the following passage from Locke's *Second Treatise on Government* illustrates, the power exercised by magistrates cannot be absolute or arbitrary.

. . . *Political power* is that power, which every man having in the state of nature, has given up into the hands of the society, and therein to the governors, whom the society hath set over itself, with this express or tacit trust, that it shall be employed for their good, and the preservation of their property: now this *power*, which every man has *in the state of nature*, and which he parts with to the society in all such cases where the society can secure him, is to use such means, for the preserving of his own property, as he thinks good, and nature allows him; and to punish the breach of the law of nature in others, so as (according to the best of his reason) may most conduce to the preservation of himself, and the rest of mankind. So that the *end and measure of this power*, when in every man's hands in the state of nature, being the preservation of all of his society, that is, all mankind in general, it can have no other *end or measure*, when in the hands of the magistrate, but to preserve the members of that society in their lives, liberties, and possessions; and so cannot be an absolute, arbitrary power over their lives and fortunes, which are as much as possible to be preserved; but a *power to make laws*, and annex such *penalties* to them, as may tend to the preservation of the whole, by cutting off those parts, and those only, which are so corrupt, that they threaten the sound and healthy, without which no severity is lawful. And this *power has its original only from compact*, and agreement, and the mutual consent of those who make up the community. . . .

These are the *bounds*, which the trust, that is put in them by the society, and the law of God and nature, have *set to the legislative* power of every common-wealth, in all forms of government.

First, They are to govern by *promulgated established laws*, not to be varied in particular cases, but to have one rule for rich and poor, for the favourite at court, and the country man at plough.

Secondly, These *laws* also ought to be designed *for* no other end ultimately, but *the good of the people*.

Thirdly, They must *not raise taxes* on the *property of the people, without the consent of the people*, given by themselves, or their deputies. And this properly concerns only such governments, where the *legislative* is always in being, or at least where the people have not reserved any part of the legislative to deputies, to be from time to time chosen by themselves.

Fourthly, The *legislative* neither must *nor can transfer the power of making laws* to any body else, or place it any where, but where the people have. . . .

If government fails to fulfill the end for which it was established—the preservation of the individual's right to life, liberty, and property—the people have a right to dissolve that government.

. . . The *legislative acts against the trust* reposed in them, when they endeavour to invade the property of the subject, and to make themselves, or any part of the community, masters, or arbitrary disposers of the lives, liberties, or fortunes of the people.

The reason why men enter into society, is the preservation of their property; and the end why they chuse and authorize a legislative, is, that there may be laws made, and rules set, as guards and fences to the properties of all the members of the society, to limit the power, and moderate the dominion of every part and member of the society: for since it can never be supposed to be the will of the society, that the legislative should have a power to destroy that which every one designs to secure, by entering into society, and for which the people submitted themselves to legislators of their own making; whenever the *legislators endeavour to take away, and destroy the property of the people*, or to reduce them to slavery under arbitrary power, they put themselves into a state of war with the people, who are thereupon absolved from any farther obedience, and are left to the common refuge, which God hath provided for all men, against force and violence. Whensoever therefore the *legislative* shall transgress this fundamental rule of society; and either by ambition, fear, folly or corruption, *endeavour to grasp* themselves, *or put into the hands of any other, an absolute power* over the lives, liberties, and estates of the people; by this breach of trust they *forfeit the power* the people had put into their hands for quite contrary ends, and it devolves to the people, who have a right to resume their original liberty, and, by the establishment of a new legislative, (such as they shall think fit) provide for their own safety and security, which is the end for which they are in society. What I have said here, concerning the legislative in general, holds true also concerning the supreme executor, who having a double trust put in him, both to have a part in the legislative, and the supreme execution of the law, acts against both, when he goes about to set up his own arbitrary will as the law of the society. He *acts* also *contrary to his trust*, when he either employs the force, treasure, and offices of the society, to corrupt the *representatives*, and gain them to his purposes; or openly pre-engages the *electors*, and prescribes to their choice, such, whom he has, by sollicitations, threats, promises, or otherwise, won to his designs; and employs them to bring in such, who have promised beforehand what to vote, and what to enact. . . .

Locke responds to the charge that his theory will produce "frequent rebellion." Indeed, says Locke, the true rebels are the magistrates who, acting contrary to the trust granted them, violate the people's rights.

. . . Such *revolutions happen* not upon every little mismanagement in public affairs. *Great mistakes* in the ruling part, many wrong and inconvenient laws, and all the *slips* of human frailty, will be *borne by the people* without mutiny or murmur. But if a long train of abuses, prevarications and artifices, all tending the same way, make the design visible to the people, and they cannot but feel what they lie under, and see whither they are going; it is not to be wondered at, that they should then rouze themselves, and endeavour to put the rule into such hands which may secure to them the ends for which government was at first erected. . . .

. . . I answer, that *this doctrine* of a power in the people of providing for their safety a-new, by a new legislative, when their legislators have acted contrary to their trust, by invading their property, is *the best defence against rebellion*, and the probablest means to hinder it: for *rebellion* being an opposition, not to persons, but authority, which is founded only in the constitutions and laws of the government; those, whoever they be, who by force break through, and by force justify their violation of them, are truly and properly *rebels*: for when men, by entering into society and civil government, have excluded force, and introduced laws for the preservation of property, peace, and unity amongst themselves, those who set up force again in opposition to the laws, do [rebel], that is, bring back again the state of war, and are properly rebels: which they who are in power, (by the pretence they have to authority, the temptation of force they have in their hands, and the flattery of those about them) being likeliest to do; the properest way to prevent the evil, is to shew them the danger and injustice of it, who are under the greatest temptation to run into it.

The end of government is the good of mankind; and which is *best for mankind*, that the people should always be exposed to the boundless will of tyranny, or that the rulers should be sometimes liable to be opposed, when they grow exorbitant in the use of their power, and employ it for the destruction, and not the preservation of the properties of their people?

THOMAS JEFFERSON

DECLARATION OF INDEPENDENCE

Written in 1776 by Thomas Jefferson (1743–1826) to justify the American colonists' break with Britain, the Declaration of Independence enumerated principles that were quite familiar to English statesmen and intellectuals. The preamble to the Declaration, excerpted below, articulated clearly Locke's philosophy of natural rights. Locke had viewed life, liberty, and property as the individual's essential natural rights; Jefferson substituted the "pursuit of happiness" for property.

A DECLARATION BY THE REPRESENTATIVES OF THEUNITED STATES OF AMERICA, INGENERAL CONGRESS ASSEMBLED.

When in the Course of human Events, it becomes necessary for one People to dissolve the Political Bands which have connected them with another, and to assume among the Powers of the Earth, the separate and equal Station to which the Laws of Nature and of Nature's God entitle them, a decent Respect to the Opinions of Mankind requires that they should declare the causes which impel them to the Separation.

We hold these Truths to be self-evident, that all Men are created equal, that they are endowed by their Creator with certain unalienable Rights, that among these are Life, Liberty, and the Pursuit of Happiness—That to secure these Rights, Governments are instituted among Men, deriving their just Powers from the Consent of the Governed, That whenever any Form of Government becomes destructive of these Ends, it is the Right of the People to alter or to abolish it, and to institute new Government, laying its Foundation on such Principles, and organizing its Powers in such Form, as to them shall seem most likely to effect their Safety and Happiness. Prudence, indeed, will dictate that Governments long established should not be changed for light and transient Causes; and accordingly all Experience hath shewn, that Mankind are more disposed to suffer, while Evils are sufferable, than to right themselves by abolishing the Forms to which they are accustomed. But when a long Train of Abuses and Usurpations, pursuing invariably the same Object, evinces a Design to reduce them under absolute Despotism, it is their right, it is their duty, to throw off such Government, and to provide new Guards for their future Security. Such has been the patient Sufferance of these Colonies; and such is now the Necessity which constrains them to alter their former Systems of Government. The History of the present King of Great-Britain is a History of repeated Injuries and Usurpations, all having in direct Object the Establishment of an absolute Tyranny over these States. . . .

THOMAS PAINE

THE AGE OF REASON

Exemplifying the deist outlook was Thomas Paine (1737–1809), an Englishman who moved to America in 1774. Paine's *Common Sense* (1776) was an eloquent appeal for American independence. Paine is also famous for *The Rights of Man* (1791–1792), in which he defended the French Revolution. In *The Age of Reason* (1794–1796), he denounced Christian mysteries, miracles, and prophecies as superstition and called for a natural religion that accorded with reason and science.

I believe in one God, and no more; and I hope for happiness beyond this life.

I believe in the equality of man; and I believe that religious duties consist in doing justice, loving mercy, and endeavoring to make our fellow-creatures happy.

But, lest it should be supposed that I believe many other things in addition to these, I shall, in the progress of this work, declare the things I do not believe, and my reasons for not believing them.

I do not believe in the creed professed by the Jewish church, by the Roman church, by the Greek church, by the Turkish church, by the Protestant church, nor by any church that I know of. My own mind is my own church. . . .

When Moses told the children of Israel that he received the two tablets of the [Ten] commandments from the hands of God, they were not obliged to believe him, because they had no other authority for it than his telling them so; and I have no other authority for it than some historian telling me so. The commandments carry no internal evidence of divinity with them; they contain some good moral precepts, such as any man qualified to be a lawgiver, or a legislator, could produce himself, without having recourse to supernatural intervention. . . .

When also I am told that a woman called the Virgin Mary, said, or gave out, that she was with child without any cohabitation with a man, and that her betrothed husband, Joseph, said that an angel told him so, I have a right to believe them or not; such a circumstance required a much stronger evidence than their bare word for it; but we have not even this—for neither Joseph nor Mary wrote any such matter themselves; it is only reported by others that *they said so*—it is hearsay upon hearsay, and I do not choose to rest my belief upon such evidence.

It is, however, not difficult to account for the credit that was given to the story of Jesus Christ being the son of God. He was born when the heathen mythology had still some fashion and repute in the world, and that mythology had prepared the people for the belief of such a story. Almost all the extraordinary men that lived under the heathen mythology were reputed to be the sons of some of their gods. It was not a new thing, at that time, to believe a man to have been celestially begotten; the intercourse of gods with women was then a matter of familiar opinion. Their Jupiter [chief Roman god], according to their accounts, had cohabited with hundreds: the story, therefore, had nothing in it either new, wonderful, or obscene; it was conformable to the opinions that then prevailed among the people called Gentiles, or Mythologists, and it was those people only that believed it. The Jews who had kept strictly to the belief of one God, and no more, and who had always rejected the heathen mythology, never credited the story. . . .

Nothing that is here said can apply, even with the most distant disrespect, to the real character of Jesus Christ. He was a virtuous and an amiable man. The morality that he preached and practised was of the most benevolent kind; and though similar systems of morality had been preached by Confucius [Chinese philosopher], and by some of the Greek philosophers, many years before; by the Quakers [members of the Society of Friends] since; and by many good men in all ages, it has not been exceeded by any. . . .

. . . The resurrection and ascension [of Jesus Christ], supposing them to have taken place, admitted of public and ocular demonstration, like that of the ascension of a balloon, or the sun at noon-day, to all Jerusalem at least. A thing which everybody is required to believe, requires that the proof and evidence of it should be equal to all, and universal; and as the public visibility of this last related act was the only evidence that could give sanction to the former part, the whole of it falls to the ground, because that evidence never was given. Instead of this, a small number of persons, not more than eight or nine, are introduced as proxies for the whole world, to say they saw it, and all the rest of the world are called upon to believe it. But it appears that Thomas [one of Jesus' disciples] did not believe the resurrection, and, as they say, would not believe without having ocular and manual demonstration himself. *So neither will I*, and the reason is equally as good for me, and for every other person, as for Thomas.

It is in vain to attempt to palliate or disguise this matter. The story, so far as relates to the supernatural part, has every mark of fraud and imposition stamped upon the face of it. Who were the authors of it is as impossible for us now to know, as it is for us to be assured that the books in which the account is related were written by the persons whose names they bear; the best surviving evidence we now have respecting this affair is the Jews. They are regularly descended from the people who lived in the times this resurrection and ascension is said to have happened, and they say, *it is not true.*

JEAN JACQUES ROUSSEAU

THE SOCIAL CONTRACT

In the opening chapters of *The Social Contract*, Rousseau rejected the principle that one person has a natural authority over others. All legitimate authority, he said, stemmed from human traditions, not from nature. Rousseau had only contempt for absolute monarchy and in *The Social Contract* sought to provide a theoretical foundation for political liberty.

[To rulers who argued that they provided security for their subjects, Rousseau responded as follows:]

It will be said that the despot assures his subjects civil tranquillity. Granted; but what do they gain, if the wars his ambition brings down upon them, his insatiable avidity, and the vexatious conduct of his ministers press harder on them than their own dissensions would have done? What do they gain, if the very tranquillity they enjoy is one of their miseries? Tranquillity is found also in dungeons; but is that enough to make them desirable places to live in? The Greeks imprisoned in the cave of the Cyclops lived there very tranquilly, while they were awaiting their turn to be devoured. . . .

Even if each man could alienate himself, he could not alienate his children: they are born men and free; their liberty belongs to them, and no one but they has the right to dispose of it. Before they come to years of discretion, the father can, in their name, lay down conditions for their preservation and well-being, but he cannot give them irrevocably and without conditions: such a gift is contrary to the ends of nature, and exceeds the rights of paternity. It would therefore be necessary, in order to legitimize an arbitrary government, that in every generation the people should be in a position to accept or reject it; but, were this so, the government would be no longer arbitrary.

To renounce liberty is to renounce being a man, to surrender the rights of humanity and even its duties. For him who renounces everything no indemnity is possible. Such a renunciation is incompatible with man's nature; to remove all liberty from his will is to remove all morality from his acts.

Like Hobbes and Locke, Rousseau refers to an original social contract that terminates the state of nature and establishes the civil state. The clash of particular interests in the state of nature necessitates the creation of civil authority.

I suppose men to have reached the point at which the obstacles in the way of their preservation in the state of nature [are] greater than the resources at the disposal of each individual for his maintenance in that state. That primitive condition can then subsist no longer; and the human race would perish unless it changed its manner of existence. . . .

This sum of forces can arise only where several persons come together: but, as the force and liberty of each man are the chief instruments of his self-preservation, how can he pledge them without harming his own interests, and neglecting the care he owes to himself? This difficulty, in its bearing on my present subject, may be stated in the following terms:

"The problem is to find a form of association which will defend and protect with the whole common force the person and goods of each associate, and in which each, while uniting himself with all, may still obey himself alone, and remain as free as before." This is the fundamental problem of which the *Social Contract* provides the solution.

In entering into the social contract, the individual surrenders his rights to the community as a whole, which governs in accordance with the general will—an underlying principle that expresses what is best for the community. The general will is a plainly visible truth that is easily discerned by reason and common sense purged of self-interest and unworthy motives. For Rousseau, the general will by definition is always right and always works to the community's advantage. True freedom consists of obedience to laws that coincide with the general will. Obedience to the general will transforms an individual motivated by self-interest, appetites, and passions into a higher type of person—a citizen committed to the general good. What happens, however, if a person's private will—that is, expressions of particular, selfish interests—clashes with the general will? As private interests could ruin the body politic, says Rousseau, "whoever refuses to obey the general will shall be compelled to do so by the whole body." Thus Rousseau rejects entirely the Lockean principle that citizens possess rights independently of and against the state. Because Rousseau grants the sovereign (the people constituted as a corporate body) virtually unlimited authority over the citizenry, some critics view him as a precursor of modern dictatorship.

The clauses of this contract. . . . properly understood, may be reduced to one—the total alienation of each associate, together with all his rights, to the whole community; for, in the first place, as each gives himself absolutely, the conditions are the same for all; and, this being so, no one has any interest in making them burdensome to others.

Moreover, the alienation being without reserve, the union is as perfect as it can be, and no associate has anything more to demand: for, if the individuals retained certain rights, as there would be no common superior to decide between them and the public, each, being on one point his own judge, would ask to be so on all; the state of nature would thus continue, and the association would necessarily become inoperative or tyrannical.

Finally, each man, in giving himself to all, gives himself to nobody; and as there is no associate over which he does not acquire the same right as he yields others over himself, he gains an equivalent for everything he loses, and an increase of force for the preservation of what he has.

If then we discard from the social compact what is not of its essence, we shall find that it reduces itself to the following terms:

"Each of us puts his person and all his power in common under the supreme direction of the general will, and, in our corporate capacity, we receive each member as an indivisible part of the whole."

At once, in place of the individual personality of each contracting party, this act of association creates a moral and collective body, composed of as many members as the assembly contains voters, and receiving from this act its unity, its common identity, its life, and its will. . . .

In order then that the social compact may not be an empty formula, it tacitly includes the undertaking, which alone can give force to the rest, that whoever refuses to obey the general will shall be compelled to do so by the whole body. This means nothing less than that he will be forced to be free; for this is the condition which, by giving each citizen to his country, secures him against all personal dependence. In this lies the key to the working of the political machine; this alone legitimizes civil undertakings, which, without it, would be absurd, tyrannical, and liable to the most frightful abuses.

The passage from the state of nature to the civil state produces a very remarkable change in man, by substituting justice for instinct in his conduct, and giving his actions the morality they had formerly lacked. Then only, when the voice of duty takes the place of physical impulses and right of appetite, does man, who so far had considered only himself, find that he is forced to act on different principles, and to consult his reason before listening to his inclinations. Although, in this state, he deprives himself of some advantages which he got from nature, he gains in return others so great, his faculties are so stimulated and developed, his ideas so extended, his feelings so ennobled, and his whole soul so uplifted, that, did not the abuses of this new condition often degrade him below that which he left, he would be bound to bless continually the happy moment which took him from it forever, and, instead of a stupid and unimaginative animal, made him an intelligent being and a man.

Let us draw up the whole account in terms easily commensurable. What man loses by the social contract is his natural liberty and an unlimited right to everything he tries to get and succeeds in getting; what he gains is civil liberty and the proprietorship of all he possesses. If we are to avoid mistake in weighing one against the other, we must clearly distinguish by natural liberty, which is bounded only by the strength of the individual, from civil liberty, which is limited by the general will; and possession, which is merely the effect of force or the right of the first occupier, from property, which can be founded only on a positive title.

We might, over and above all this, add, to what man acquires in the civil state, moral liberty, which alone makes him truly master of himself; for the mere impulse of appetite is slavery, while obedience to a law which we prescribe to ourselves is liberty. . . .

The first and most important deduction from the principles we have so far laid down is that the general will alone can direct the State according to the object for which it was instituted, i.e. the common good: for if the clashing of particular interests made the establishment of societies necessary, the agreement of these very interests made it possible. The common element in these different interests is what forms the social tie; and, were there no point of agreement between them all, no society could exist. It is solely on the basis of this common interest that every society should be governed. . . .

It follows from what has gone before that the general will is always right and tends to the public advantage; but it does not follow that the deliberations of the people are always equally correct. Our will is always for our own good, but we do not always see what that is; the people is never corrupted, but it is often deceived, and on such occasions only does it seem to will what is bad.

There is often a great deal of difference between the will of all and the general will; the latter considers only the common interest, while the former takes private interest into account, and is no more than a sum of particular wills: but take away from these same wills the pluses and minuses that cancel one another, and the general will remains as the sum of the differences.

If, when the people, being furnished with adequate information, held its deliberations, the citizens had no communication one with another, the grand total of the small differences would always give the general will, and the decision would always be good. But when factions arise, and partial associations are formed at the expense of the great association, the will of each of these associations becomes general in relation to its members, while it remains particular in relation to the State: it may then be said that there are no longer as many votes as there are men, but only as many as there are associations. The differences become less numerous and give a less general result. Lastly, when one of these associations is so great as to prevail over all the rest, the result is no longer a sum of small differences, but a single difference; in this case there is no longer a general will, and the opinion which prevails is purely particular.

It is therefore essential, if the general will is to be able to express itself, that there should be no partial society [factions] within the State, and that each citizen should think only his own thoughts. . . . But if there are partial societies, it is best to have as many as possible and to prevent them from being unequal. . . . These precautions are the only ones that can guarantee that the general will shall be always enlightened, and that the people shall in no way deceive itself.

ALEXIS DE TOCQUEVILLE

CRITIQUE OF THE OLD REGIME

The following passage from *The Old Regime and the French Revolution*, by Alexis de Tocqueville (1805–1859), treats the role of the philosophes in undermining the Old Regime. Born of a noble family, de Tocqueville was active in French politics. After traveling in the United States, he wrote *Democracy in America* (1835), a great work of historical literature. In 1856, he published *The Old Regime and the French Revolution*, which explored the causes of the French Revolution.

France had long been the most literary of all the nations of Europe; although her literary men had never exhibited such intellectual powers as they displayed about the middle of the 18th century, or occupied such a position as that which they then assumed. Nothing of the kind had ever been seen in France, or perhaps in any other country. They were not constantly mixed up with public affairs as in England: at no period, on the contrary, had they lived more apart from them. They were invested with no authority whatever, and filled no public offices in a society crowded with public officers; yet they did not, like the greater part of their brethren in Germany, keep entirely aloof from the arena of politics and retire into the regions of pure philosophy and polite literature. They busied themselves incessantly with matters appertaining to government, and this was, in truth, their special occupation. Thus they were continually holding forth on the origin and primitive forms of society, the primary rights of the citizen and of government, the natural and artificial relations of men, the wrong or right of customary laws, and the principles of legislation. While they thus penetrated to the fundamental basis of the constitution of their time, they examined its structure with minute care and criticised its general plan.

. . . [The thinkers of the Enlightenment} all agreed that it was expedient to substitute simple and elementary rules, deduced from reason and natural law, for the complicated traditional customs which governed the society of their time. Upon a strict scrutiny it may be seen that what might be called the political philosophy of the eighteenth century consisted, properly speaking, in this one notion.

These opinions were by no means novel; for three thousand years they had unceasingly traversed the imaginations of mankind, though without being able to stamp themselves there. How came they at last to take possession of the minds of all the writers of this period? Why, instead of progressing no farther than the heads of a few philosophers, as had frequently been the case, had they at last reached the masses, and assumed the strength and the fervour of a political passion to such a degree, that general and abstract theories upon the nature of society became daily topics of conversation, and even inflamed the imaginations of women and of the peasantry? How was it that literary men, possessing neither rank, nor honours, nor fortune, nor responsibility, nor power, became, in fact, the principal political men of the day? . . .

It was not by chance that the philosophers of the 18th century . . . coincided in entertaining notions so opposed to those which still served as bases to the society of their time: these ideas had been naturally suggested to them by the aspects of the society which they had all before their eyes. The sight of so many unjust or absurd privileges, the {burden} of which was more and more felt whilst their cause was less and less understood, urged, or rather precipitated the minds of one and all to the idea of the natural equality of man's condition. Whilst they looked upon so many strange and irregular institutions, born of other times, which no one had attempted either to bring into harmony with each other or to adapt to modern wants, and which appeared likely to perpetuate their existence though they had lost their worth, they learned to abhor what was ancient and traditional, and naturally became desirous of reconstructing the social edifice of their day upon an entirely new plan—a plan which each one traced solely by the light of his reason. . . .

Had {the French} been able, like the English, gradually to modify the spirit of their ancient institutions by practical experience without destroying them, they would perhaps have been less inclined to invent new ones. But there was not a man who did not daily feel himself injured in his fortune, in his person, in his comfort, or his pride by some old law, some ancient political custom, or some other remnant of former authority, without perceiving at hand any remedy that he could himself apply to his own particular hardship. It appeared that the whole constitution of the country must either be endured or destroyed.

The French, however, had still preserved one liberty amidst the ruin of every other: they were still free to philosophize almost without restraint upon the origin of society, the essential nature of governments, and the primordial rights of mankind.

All those who felt themselves aggrieved by the daily application of existing laws were soon enamoured of these literary politics. The same taste soon reached even those who by nature or by their condition of life seemed the farthest removed from abstract speculations. Every taxpayer wronged by the unequal distribution of the *taille*1 was fired by the idea that all men ought to be equal; every little landowner devoured by the rabbits of his noble neighbour was delighted to be told that all privileges were without distinction contrary to reason. Every public passion thus assumed the disguise of philosophy; all political action was violently driven back into the domain of literature; and the writers of the day, undertaking the guidance of public opinion, found themselves at one time in that position which the heads of parties commonly hold in free countries. No one in fact was any longer in a condition to contend with them for the part they had assumed. . . .

If now it be taken into consideration that this same French nation, so ignorant of its own public affairs, so utterly devoid of experience, so hampered by its institutions, and so powerless to amend them, was also in those days the most lettered and witty nation of the earth, it may readily be understood how the writers of the time became a great political power, and ended by being the first power in the country.

Above the actual state of society—the constitution of which was still traditional, confused, and irregular, and in which the laws remained conflicting and contradictory, ranks sharply sundered, the conditions of the different classes fixed whilst their burdens were unequal—an imaginary state of society was thus springing up, in which everything appeared simple and co-ordinate, uniform, equitable, and agreeable to reason. The imagination of the people gradually deserted the former state of things in order to seek refuge in the latter. Interest was lost in what was, to foster dreams of what might be; and men thus dwelt in fancy in this ideal city, which was the work of literary invention. . . .

This circumstance, so novel in history, of the whole political education of a great people being formed by its literary men, contributed more than anything perhaps to bestow upon the French Revolution its peculiar stamp, and to cause those results which are still perceptible.

DECLARATION OF THE RIGHTS OF MAN AND OF CITIZENS

Together with John Locke's *Second Treatise on Government*, the American Declaration of Independence, and the Constitution of the United States, the Declaration of the Rights of Man and of Citizens, which follows, is a pivotal document in the development of modern liberalism.

The Representatives of the people of France, formed into a National Assembly, considering that ignorance, neglect, or contempt of human rights, are the sole causes of public misfortunes and corruptions of Government, have resolved to set forth in a solemn declaration, these natural, imprescriptible, and unalienable rights: that this declaration, being constantly present to the minds of the members of the body social, they may be ever kept attentive to their rights and their duties: that the acts of the legislative and executive powers of Government, being capable of being every moment compared with the end of political institutions, may be more respected: and also, that the future claims of the citizens, being directed by simple and incontestible principles, may always tend to the maintenance of the Constitution, and the general happiness.

For these reasons the National Assembly doth recognize and declare, in the presence of the Supreme Being, and with the hope of his blessing and favor, the following *sacred* rights of men and of citizens:

I. *Men are born, and always continue, free, and equal in respect of their rights. Civil distinctions, therefore, can be founded only on public utility.*

II. *The end of all political associations, is, the preservation of the natural and imprescriptible rights of man; and these rights are liberty, property, security, and resistance of oppression.*

III. *The nation is essentially the source of all sovereignty; nor can any* individual *or* any body of men, *be entitled to any authority which is not expressly derived from it.*

IV. Political Liberty consists in the power of doing whatever does not injure another. The exercise of the natural rights of every man, has no other limits than those which are necessary to secure to every *other* man the free exercise of the same rights; and these limits are determinable only by the law.

V. The law ought to prohibit only actions hurtful to society. What is not prohibited by the law, should not be hindered; nor should any one be compelled to that which the law does not require.

VI. The law is an expression of the will of the community. All citizens have a right to concur, either personally, or by their representatives, in its formation. It should be the same to all, whether it protects or punishes; and *all being equal in its sight, are equally eligible to all honors, places, and employments, according to their different abilities, without any other distinction than that created by their virtues and talents.*

VII. No man should be accused, arrested, or held in confinement, except in cases determined by the law, and according to the forms which it has prescribed. All who promote, solicit, execute, or cause to be executed, arbitrary orders, ought to be punished; and every citizen called upon or apprehended by virtue of the law, ought immediately to obey, and renders himself culpable by resistance.

VIII. The law ought to impose no other penalties but such as are absolutely and evidently necessary; and no one ought to be punished, but in virtue of a law promulgated before the offence, and legally applied.

IX. Every man being presumed innocent till he has been convicted, whenever his detention becomes indispensible, all rigor [harshness] to him, more than is necessary to secure his person, ought to be provided against by the law.

X. No man ought to be molested on account of his opinions, not even on account of his *religious* opinions, provided his avowal of them does not disturb the public order established by the law.

XI. The unrestrained communication of thoughts and opinions being one of the most precious rights of man, every citizen may speak, write, and publish freely, provided he is responsible for the abuse of this liberty in cases determined by the law.

XII. A public force being necessary to give security to the rights of men and of citizens, that force is instituted for the benefit of the community, and not for the particular benefit of the persons with whom it is entrusted.

XIII. A common contribution being necessary for the support of the public force, and for defraying the other expenses of government, it ought to be divided equally among the members of the community, according to their abilities.

XIV. Every citizen has a right, either by himself or his representative, to a free voice in determining the necessity of public contributions, the appropriation of them, and their amount, mode of assessment and duration.

XV. Every community has a right to demand of all its agents, an account of their conduct.

XVI. Every community in which a separation of powers and a security of rights is not provided for, wants a constitution.

XVII. The rights to property being inviolable and sacred, no one ought to be deprived of it, except in cases of evident public necessity, legally ascertained, and on condition of a previous just indemnity.

MARY WOLLSTONECRAFT

A VINDICATION OF THE RIGHTS OF WOMAN

When in 1789 the French revolutionaries issued their "Declaration of the Rights of Man," it was only a matter of time before a woman published a "Declaration of the Rights of Woman." That feat was accomplished in 1791 in France by Olympe de Gouges. In England, Mary Wollstonecraft (1759–1797), strongly influenced by her, published her own statement, *A Vindication of the Rights of Woman,* in 1792. Her protest against the prevailing submissiveness of women was reinforced by the philosophy of the Enlightenment and the ideals of the French Revolution, which she observed firsthand from 1792 to 1794. A career woman, she made her living as a prolific writer closely associated with the radicals of her time, one of whom, William Godwin, she married shortly before her death. Wollstonecraft became famous for her vigorous protests against the subjection of women. Children, husbands, and society generally, she pleaded in *A Vindication of the Rights of Woman,* were best served by well-educated, self-reliant, and strong women capable of holding their own in the world.

. . . I have turned over various books written on the subject of education, and patiently observed the conduct of parents and the management of schools; but what has been the result?—a profound conviction that the neglected education of my fellow creatures is the grand source of the misery I deplore, and that women, in particular, are rendered weak and wretched. . . . The conduct and manners of women, in fact, evidently prove that their minds are not in a healthy state. . . . One cause of this . . . I attribute to a false system of education, gathered from the books written on this subject by men who, considering females rather as women than human creatures, have been more anxious to make them alluring mistresses than affectionate wives and rational mothers. . . .

. . . A degree of physical superiority of men cannot . . . be denied, and it is a noble prerogative! But not content with this natural pre-eminence, men endeavour to sink us still lower, merely to render us alluring objects for a moment. . . .

My own sex, I hope, will excuse me, if I treat them like rational creatures, instead of flattering their *fascinating* graces, and viewing them as if they were in a state of perpetual childhood, unable to stand alone. I earnestly wish to point out in what true dignity and human happiness consists. I wish to persuade women to endeavour to acquire strength, both of mind and body. . . .

Dismissing, then, those pretty feminine phrases, which the men condescendingly use to soften our slavish dependence, and despising that weak elegancy of mind, exquisite sensibility, and sweet docility of manners, supposed to be the sexual characteristics of the weaker vessel, I wish to show that elegance is inferior to virtue, that the first object of laudable ambition is to obtain a character as a human being, regardless of the distinction of sex. . . .

The education of women has of late been more attended to than formerly; yet they are still reckoned a frivolous sex, and ridiculed or pitied by the writers who endeavour by satire or instruction to improve them. It is acknowledged that they spend many of the first years of their lives in acquiring a smattering of accomplishments; meanwhile strength of body and mind are sacrificed to libertine notions of beauty, to the desire of establishing themselves—the only way women can rise in the world—by marriage. And this desire making mere animals of them, when they marry they act as such children may be expected to act,—they dress, they paint, and nickname God's creatures. Surely these weak beings are only fit for a seraglio [harem]! Can they be expected to govern a family with judgment, or take care of the poor babes whom they bring into the world? . . .

Contending for the rights of woman, my main argument is built on this simple principle, that if she be not prepared by education to become the companion of man, she will stop the progress of knowledge and virtue; for truth must be common to all, or it will be inefficacious with respect to its influence on general practice. And how can woman be expected to co-operate unless she knows why she ought to be virtuous? unless freedom strengthens her reason till she comprehends her duty, and sees in what manner it is connected with her real good. If children are to be educated to understand the true principle of patriotism, their mother must be a patriot; and the love of mankind, from which an orderly train of virtues spring, can only be produced by considering the moral and civil interest of mankind; but the education and situation of woman at present shuts her out from such investigations. . . .

Consider—I address you as a legislator—whether, when men contend for their freedom, and to be allowed to judge for themselves respecting their own happiness, it be not inconsistent and unjust to subjugate women, even though you firmly believe that you are acting in the manner best calculated to promote their happiness? Who made man the exclusive judge, if woman partake with him of the gift of reason?

In this style argue tyrants of every denomination, from the weak king to the weak father of a family; they are all eager to crush reason, yet always assert that they usurp its throne only to be useful. Do you not act a similar part when you *force* all women, by denying them civil and political rights, to remain immured [imprisoned] in their families groping in the dark? for surely, sir, you will not assert that a duty can be binding which is not founded on reason? If, indeed, this be their destination, arguments may be drawn from reason; and thus augustly supported, the more understanding women acquire, the more they will be attached to their duty—comprehending it—for unless they comprehend it, unless their morals be fixed on the same immutable principle as those of man, no authority can make them discharge it in a virtuous manner. They may be convenient slaves, but slavery will have its constant effect, degrading the master and the abject dependent.

But if women are to be excluded, without having a voice, from a participation of the natural rights of mankind, prove first, to ward off the charge of injustice and inconsistency, that they [lack] reason, else this flaw in your new constitution will ever show that man must, in some shape, act like a tyrant, and tyranny, in whatever part of society it rears its brazen front, will ever undermine morality. . . .

In what does man's pre-eminence over the brute creation consist? The answer is as clear as that a half is less than the whole, in Reason. . . . Yet . . . deeply rooted processes have clouded reason. . . . Men, in general, seem to employ their reason to justify prejudices, which they have imbibed, they can scarcely trace how, rather than to root them out.

The power of generalising ideas, of drawing comprehensive conclusions from individual observations . . . has not only been denied to women; but writers have insisted that it is inconsistent, with a few exceptions, with their sexual character. Let men prove this, and I shall grant that woman only exists for man. I must, however, previously remark, that the power of generalising ideas, to any great extent, is not very common amongst men or women. But this exercise is the true cultivation of the understanding; and everything conspires to render the cultivation of the understanding more difficult in the female than the male world. . . .

I shall not go back to the remote annals of antiquity to trace the history of woman; it is sufficient to allow that she has always been either a slave or a despot, and to remark that each of these situations equally retards the progress of reason. The grand source of female folly and vice has ever appeared to me to arise from narrowness of mind; and the very constitution of civil governments has put almost insuperable obstacles in the way to prevent the cultivation of the female understanding; yet virtue can be built on no other foundation. . . .

When do we hear of women who, starting out of obscurity, boldly claim respect on account of their great abilities or daring virtues? Where are they to be found? . . .

With respect to women, when they receive a careful education, they are either made fine ladies, brimful of sensibility, and teeming with capricious fancies, or mere notable women. The latter are often friendly, honest creatures, and have a shrewd kind of good sense, joined with worldly prudence, that often render them more useful members of society than the fine sentimental lady, though they possess neither greatness of mind nor taste. The intellectual world is shut against them. Take them out of their family or neighbourhood, and they stand still; the mind finding no employment, for literature affords a fund of amusement which they have never sought to relish, but frequently to despise. The sentiments and taste of more cultivated minds appear ridiculous, even in those whom chance and family connections have led them to love; but in mere acquaintance they think it all affectation.

A man of sense can only love such a woman on account of her sex, and respect her because she is a trusty servant. He lets her, to preserve his own peace, scold the servants, and go to church in clothes made of the very best materials. . . . [W]omen, whose minds are not enlarged by cultivation, or . . . by reflection, are very unfit to manage a family, for, by an undue stretch of power, they are always tyrannising to support a superiority that only rests on the arbitrary distinction of fortune.

Women have seldom sufficient serious employment to silence their feelings; a round of little cares, or vain pursuits frittering away all strength of mind and organs, they become naturally only objects of sense. In short, the whole tenor of female education (the education of society) tends to render the best disposed romantic and inconstant; and the remainder vain and [contemptible]. In the present state of society this evil can scarcely be remedied, I am afraid, in the slightest degree; should a more laudable ambition ever gain ground they may be brought nearer to nature and reason, and become more virtuous and useful as they grow more respectable. . . .

Women . . . all want to be ladies. Which is simply to have nothing to do, but listlessly to go they scarcely care where, for they cannot tell what.

But what have women to do in society? I may be asked, but to loiter with easy grace. . . . Women might certainly study the art of healing, and be physicians as well as nurses. . . . They might also study politics . . . for the reading of history will scarcely be more useful than the study of romances. . . . Business of various kinds, they might likewise pursue, if they were educated in a more orderly manner, which might save many from common and legal prostitution. . . . The few employments open to a woman, so far from being liberal, are menial. . . .

Some of these women might be restrained from marrying by a proper spirit of delicacy, and others may not have had it in their power to escape in this pitiful way from servitude; is not that Government then very defective, and very unmindful of the happiness of one-half of its members, that does not provide for honest, independent women, by encouraging them to fill respectable stations? . . .

It is a melancholy truth; yet such is the blessed effect of civilisation! the most respectable women are the most oppressed; and, unless they have understandings far superior to the common run of understandings, taking in both sexes, they must, from being treated like contemptible beings, become contemptible. How many women thus waste life away the prey of discontent, who might have practised as physicians, regulated a farm, managed a shop, and stood erect, supported by their own industry, instead of hanging their heads. . . .

Would men but generously snap our chains, and be content with rational fellowship instead of slavish obedience, they would find us more observant daughters, more affectionate sisters, more faithful wives, more reasonable mothers—in a word, better citizens. We should then love them with true affection, because we should learn to respect ourselves; and the peace of mind of a worthy man would not be interrupted by the idle vanity of his wife, nor the babes sent to nestle in a strange bosom, having never found a home in their mother's. . . .

. . . The sexual distinction which men have so warmly insisted upon, is arbitrary. . . . Asserting the rights which women in common with men ought to contend for, I have not attempted to [make light of] their faults; but to prove them to be the natural consequence of their education and station in society. If so, it is reasonable to suppose that they will change their character, and correct their vices and follies, when they are allowed to be free in a physical, moral, and civil sense.

Let woman share the rights, and she will emulate the virtues of man; for she must grow more perfect when emancipated. . . .

ADAM SMITH

THE WEALTH OF NATIONS

The Wealth of Nations **carries the important message of** ***laissez faire*****, which means that the government should intervene as little as possible in economic affairs and leave the market to its own devices. It advocates the liberation of economic production from all limiting regulation in order to benefit "the people and the sovereign," not only in Great Britain but in the community of countries. Admittedly, in his advocacy of free trade Smith made allowance for the national interest, justifying "certain public works and certain public institutions," including the government and the state. He defended, for instance, the Navigation Acts, which stipulated that goods brought from its overseas colonies into England be carried in British ships. Neither did he want to ruin established industries by introducing free trade too suddenly. Adam Smith was an eighteenth-century cosmopolitan who viewed political economy as an international system. His preference was clearly for economic cooperation among nations as a source of peace. In the passage that follows, Smith argues that economic activity unrestricted by government best serves the individual and society.**

Every individual is continually exerting himself to find out the most advantageous employment for whatever capital he can command. It is his own advantage, indeed, and not that of the society, which he has in view. But the study of his own advantage, naturally, or rather necessarily, leads him to prefer that employment which is most advantageous to the society. . . .

. . . As every individual, therefore, endeavours as much as he can both to employ his capital in the support of domestic industry, and so to direct that industry that its produce may be of the greatest value, every individual necessarily labours to render the annual revenue of the society as great as he can. He generally, indeed, neither intends to promote the public interest, nor knows how much he is promoting it. By preferring the support of domestic to that of foreign industry, he intends only his own security; and by directing that industry in such a manner as its produce may be of the greatest value, he intends only his own gain, and he is in this, as in many other cases, led by an invisible hand to promote an end which was no part of his intention. Nor is it always the worse for the society that it was no part of it. By pursuing his own interest he frequently promotes that of the society more effectually than when he really intends to promote it. I have never known much good done by those who affected to trade for the public good. . . .

. . . The statesman who should attempt to direct private people in what manner they ought to employ their capitals, would not only load himself with a most unnecessary attention, but assume an authority which could safely be trusted, not only to no single person, but to no council or senate whatever, and which would nowhere be so dangerous as in the hands of a man who had folly and presumption enough to fancy himself fit to exercise it. . . .

It is thus that every system which endeavours, either by extraordinary encouragements to draw towards a particular species of industry a greater share of the capital of the society than would naturally go to it, or, by extraordinary restraints, force from a particular species of industry some share of the capital which would otherwise be employed in it, is in reality subversive to the great purpose which it means to promote. It retards, instead of accelerating, the progress of the society towards real wealth and greatness; and diminishes, instead of increasing, the real value of the annual produce of its land and labour.

All systems either of preference or of restraint, therefore, being thus completely taken away, the obvious and simple system of natural liberty establishes itself of its own accord. Every man, as long as he does not violate the laws of justice, is left perfectly free to pursue his own interest his own way, and to bring both his industry and capital into competition with those of any other man, or order of men. The sovereign is completely discharged from a duty, in the attempting to perform which he must always be exposed to innumerable delusions, and for the proper performance of which no human wisdom or knowledge could ever be sufficient; the duty of superintending the industry of private people, and of directing it towards the employments most suitable to the interest of the society. According to the system of natural liberty, the sovereign has only three duties to attend to; three duties of great importance, indeed, but plain and intelligible to common understandings: first, the duty of protecting the society from the violence and invasion of other independent societies: secondly, the duty of protecting, as far as possible, every member of the society from the injustice or oppression of every other member of it, or the duty of establishing an exact administration of justice; and, thirdly, the duty of erecting and maintaining certain public works and certain public institutions which it can never be for the interest of any individual, or small number of individuals, to erect and maintain; because the profit could never repay the expense to any individual or small number of individuals, though it may frequently do much more than repay it to a great society.

ROBERT OWEN

A NEW VIEW OF SOCIETY

In 1799, Robert Owen (1771–1858) became part owner and manager of the New Lanark cotton mills in Scotland. Distressed by the widespread mistreatment of workers, Owen resolved to improve the lives of his employees and show that it was possible to do so without destroying profits. He raised wages, upgraded working conditions, refused to hire children under ten, and provided workers with neat homes, food, and clothing, all at reasonable prices. He set up schools for children and for adults. In every way, he demonstrated his belief that healthier, happier workers produced more than the less fortunate ones. Owen believed that industry and technology could and would enrich humankind if they were organized according to the proper principles. Visitors came from all over Europe to see Owen's factories.

Just like many philosophes, Owen was convinced that the environment was the principal shaper of character—that the ignorance, alcoholism, and crime of the poor derived from bad living conditions. Public education and factory reform, said Owen, would make better citizens of the poor. Owen came to believe that the entire social and economic order must be replaced by a new system based on harmonious group living rather than on competition. He established a model community at New Harmony, Indiana, but it was short-lived.

In the following selection, Owen proposes the establishment of a model community that would ameliorate the plight of the poor and unemployed.

The immediate cause of the present distress is the depreciation of human labour. This has been occasioned by the general introduction of mechanism into the manufactures of Europe and America, but principally into those of Britain, where the change was greatly accelerated by the inventions of Arkwright and Watt.

The introduction of mechanism into the manufacture of objects of desire in society reduced their price; the reduction of price increased the demand for them, and generally to so great an extent as to occasion more human labour to be employed after the introduction of machinery than had been employed before. . . .

A little reflection will show that the working classes have now no adequate means of contending with mechanical power; one of three results must therefore ensue:—

1. The use of mechanism must be greatly diminished; or,
2. Millions of human beings must be starved, to permit its existence to the present extent; or,
3. Advantageous occupation must be found for the poor and unemployed working classes, to whose labour mechanism must be rendered subservient, instead of being applied, as at present, to supersede it. . . .

It would . . . be a . . . sign of barbarism, and an act of gross tyranny, were any government to permit mechanical power to starve millions of human beings. The thought will not admit of one moment's contemplation; it would inevitably create unheard-of misery to all ranks. . . .

Under the existing laws,[1] the unemployed working classes are maintained by, and consume part of, the property and produce of the wealthy and industrious, while their powers of body and mind remain unproductive. They frequently acquire the bad habits which ignorance and idleness never fail to produce; they amalgamate with the regular poor, and become a nuisance to society.

Most of the poor have received bad and vicious habits from their parents; and so long as their present treatment continues, those bad and vicious habits will be transmitted to their children and, through them, to succeeding generations.

[1]Poor laws

Any plan, then, to ameliorate their condition, must prevent bad and vicious habits from being taught to their children, and provide the means by which only good and useful ones may be given to them. . . .

Under this view of the subject, any plan for the amelioration of the poor should combine means to prevent their children from acquiring bad habits, and to give them good ones—to provide useful training and instruction for them—to provide proper labour for the adults—to direct their labour and expenditure so as to produce the greatest benefit to themselves and to society; and to place them under such circumstances as shall remove them from unnecessary temptations, and closely unite their interest and duty.

The plan represented is on a scale considered to be sufficient to accommodate about 1,200 persons.

And these are to be supposed men, women, and children, of all ages, capacities, and dispositions; most of them very ignorant; many with bad and vicious habits, possessing only the ordinary bodily and mental faculties of human beings, and who require to be supported out of the funds appropriated to the maintenance of the poor—individuals who are at present not only useless and a direct burthen on the public, but whose moral influence is highly pernicious, since they are the medium by which ignorance and certain classes of vicious habits and crimes are fostered and perpetuated in society.

It is evident that while the poor are suffered to remain under the circumstances in which they have hitherto existed, they and their children, with very few exceptions, will continue unaltered in succeeding generations.

In order to effect any radically beneficial change in their character, they must be removed from the influence of such circumstances, and placed under those which, being congenial to the natural constitution of man and the well-being of society, cannot fail to produce that amelioration in their condition which all classes have so great an interest in promoting.

Such circumstances, after incessant application to the subject, I have endeavoured to combine in the arrangement of the establishment represented in the drawings, so far as the present state of society will permit. These I will not attempt to explain more particularly.

Each lodging-room within the squares is to accommodate a man, his wife, and two children under three years of age; and to be such as will permit them to have much more comforts than the dwellings of the poor usually afford.

It is intended that the children above three years of age should attend the school, eat in the mess-room, and sleep in the dormitories; the parents being, of course, permitted to see and converse with them at meals and all other proper times;—that before they leave school they shall be well instructed in all necessary and useful knowledge;—that every possible means shall be adopted to prevent the acquirement of bad habits from their parents or otherwise;—that no pains shall be spared to impress upon them such habits and dispositions as may be most conductive to their happiness through life, as well as render them useful and valuable members of the community to which they belong.

It is proposed that the women should be employed—

First,—In the care of their infants, and in keeping their dwellings in the best order.

Second,—In cultivating the gardens to raise vegetables for the supply of the public kitchen.

Third,—In attending to such of the branches of the various manufactures as women can well undertake; but not to be employed in them more than four or five hours in the day.

Fourth,—In making up clothing for the inmates of the establishment.

Fifth,—In attending occasionally, and in rotation, in the public kitchen, mess-rooms, and dormitories; and, when properly instructed, in superintending some parts of the education of the children in the schools.

It is proposed that the elder children should be trained to assist in gardening and manufacturing for a portion of the day, according to their strength; and that the men should be employed, all of them, in agriculture, and also in manufactures, or in some other occupation for the benefit of the establishment.

The ignorance of the poor, their ill-training, and their want of a rational education make it necessary that those of the present generation should be actively and regularly occupied through the day in some essentially useful work; yet in such a manner as that their employment should be healthy and productive. The plan which has been described will most amply admit of this. . . .

It is impossible to find language sufficiently strong to express the inconsistency, as well as the injustice, of our present proceedings towards the poor and working classes. They are left in gross ignorance; they are permitted to be trained up in habits of vice, and in the commission of crimes; and, as if purposely to keep them in ignorance and vice, and goad them on to commit criminal acts, they are perpetually surrounded with temptations which cannot fail to produce all those effects. . . .

The poor and unemployed working classes, however, cannot, must not, be abandoned to their fate, lest the consequences entail misfortune on us all. Instead of being left, as they now are, to the dominion of ignorance, and to the influence of circumstances which are fatal to their industry and morals—a situation in which it is easy to perceive the inefficacy, or rather the injuriousness, of granting them a provision in a mere pecuniary shape—they should, on the contrary, be afforded the means of procuring a certain and comfortable subsistence by their labour, under a system which will not only direct that labour and its earnings to the best advantage, but, at the same time, place them under circumstances the most favourable to the growth of morals and of happiness. In short, instead of allowing their habits to proceed under the worst influence possible, or rather, as it were, to be left to chance, thus producing unintentionally crimes that render necessary the severities of our penal code, let a system for the prevention of pauperism and of crimes be adopted, and the operation of our penal code will soon be restricted to very narrow limits.

The outlines of such a plan, it is presumed, have been, however imperfectly, suggested and sketched in this Report. . . .

The principles and plan are now more fully before the public. If the former contain error, or the latter be impracticable, it becomes the duty of many to expose either. If, however, the plan shall prove, on investigation, to be correct in principle, to be easy of practice, and that it can relieve the poor and unemployed of the working classes from the grievous distresses and degradation under which they suffer, it becomes equally the duty of all who profess to desire the amelioration of the lower orders, to exert themselves without further delay to carry it into execution, in order that another year of extensive and unnecessary suffering and demoralization, from the want of a sufficiency of wholesome food and proper training and instruction, may not uselessly pass away.

EDMUND BURKE

REFLECTIONS ON THE REVOLUTION IN FRANCE

Burke regarded the revolutionaries as wild-eyed fanatics who had uprooted all established authority, tradition, and institutions, thereby plunging France into anarchy. Not sharing the faith of the philosophes in human goodness, Burke held that without the restraints of established authority, people revert to savagery. For Burke, monarchy, aristocracy, and Christianity represented civilizing forces that tamed the beast in human nature. By undermining venerable institutions, he said, the French revolutionaries had opened the door to anarchy and terror. Burke's *Reflections*, excerpts of which follow, was instrumental in the shaping of conservative thought.

. . . You [revolutionaries] chose to act as if you had never been moulded into civil society, and had every thing to begin anew. You began ill, because you began by despising every thing that belonged to you. . . . If the last generations of your country appeared without much lustre in your eyes, you might have passed them by, and derived your claims from a more early race of ancestors. Under a pious predilection for those ancestors, your imaginations would have realized in them a standard of virtue and wisdom, beyond the vulgar practice of the hour: and you would have risen with the example to whose imitation you aspired. Respecting your forefathers, you would have been taught to respect yourselves. You would not have chosen to consider the French as a people of yesterday, as a nation of low-born servile wretches, until the emancipating year of 1789. . . . By following wise examples you would have given new examples of wisdom to the world. You would have rendered the cause of liberty venerable in the eyes of every worthy mind in every nation. . . . You would have had a free constitution; a potent monarchy; a disciplined army; a reformed and venerated clergy; a mitigated but spirited nobility, to lead your virtue. . . .

Compute your gains: see what is got by those extravagant and presumptuous speculations which have taught your leaders to despise all their predecessors, and all their contemporaries, and even to despise themselves, until the moment in which they became truly despicable. By following those false lights, France has bought undisguised calamities at a higher price than any nation has purchased the most unequivocal blessings! . . . France, when she let loose the reins of regal authority, doubled the licence, of a ferocious dissoluteness in manners, and of an insolent irreligion in opinions and practices; and has extended through all ranks of life. . . . all the unhappy corruptions that usually were the disease of wealth and power. This is one of the new principles of equality in France. . . .

. . . The science of government being therefore so practical in itself, and intended for such practical purposes, a matter which requires experience, and even more experience than any person can gain in his whole life, however sagacious and observing he may be, it is with infinite caution that any man ought to venture upon pulling down an edifice which has answered in any tolerable degree for ages the common purposes of society, or on building it up again, without having models and patterns of approved utility before his eyes. . . .

. . . The nature of man is intricate; the objects of society are of the greatest possible complexity; and therefore no simple disposition or direction of power can be suitable either to man's nature, or to the quality of his affairs.

When ancient opinions of life are taken away, the loss cannot possibly be estimated. From that moment we have no compass to govern us; nor can we know distinctly to what port we steer. . . .

. . . Nothing is more certain than that our manners, our civilization, and all the good things which are connected with manners and with civilization have, in this European world of ours, depended for ages upon two principles and were, indeed, the result of both combined: I mean the spirit of a gentleman and the spirit of religion. . . .

Burke next compares the English people with the French revolutionaries.

. . . Thanks to our sullen resistance to innovation, thanks to the cold sluggishness of our national character, we still bear the stamp of our forefathers. . . . We are not the converts of Rousseau; we are not the disciples of Voltaire; Helvetius has made no progress amongst us.1 Atheists are not our preachers; madmen are not our lawgivers. We know that *we* have made no discoveries, and we think that no discoveries are to be made, in morality, nor many in the great principles of government. . . . We fear God; we look up with awe to kings, with affection to parliaments, with duty to magistrates, with reverence to priests, and with respect to nobility. . . .

. . . We are afraid to put men to live and trade each on his own private stock of reason, because we suspect that this stock in each man is small, and that the individuals would do better to avail themselves of the general bank and capital of nations and of ages.

KLEMENS VON METTERNICH

THE ODIOUS IDEAS OF THE PHILOSOPHES

Two decades of revolutionary warfare had shaped Metternich's political thinking. After the fall of Napoleon, Metternich worked to restore the European balance and to suppress revolutionary movements. In the following memorandum to Tsar Alexander I, dated December 15, 1820, Metternich denounces the French philosophes for their "false systems" and "fatal errors" that weakened the social fabric and gave rise to the French Revolution. In their presumption, the philosophes forsook the experience and wisdom of the past, trusting only their own thoughts and inclinations.

The progress of the human mind has been extremely rapid in the course of the last three centuries. This progress having been accelerated more rapidly than the growth of wisdom (the only counterpoise to passions and to error); a revolution prepared by the false systems . . . has at last broken out. . . .

. . . There were . . . some men [the philosophes], unhappily endowed with great talents, who felt their own strength, and . . . who had the art to prepare and conduct men's minds to the triumph of their detestable enterprise—an enterprise all the more odious as it was pursued without regard to results, simply abandoning themselves to the one feeling of hatred of God and of His immutable moral laws.

France had the misfortune to produce the greatest number of these men. It is in her midst that religion and all that she holds sacred, that morality and authority, and all connected with them, have been attacked with a steady and systematic animosity, and it is there that the weapon of ridicule has been used with the most ease and success.

Drag through the mud the name of God and the powers instituted by His divine decrees, and the revolution will be prepared! Speak of a social contract,1 and the revolution is accomplished! The revolution was already completed in the palaces of kings, in the drawing-rooms and boudoirs of certain cities, while among the great mass of the people it was still only in a state of preparation. . . .

. . . The French Revolution broke out, and has gone through a complete revolutionary cycle in a very short period, which could only have appeared long to its victims and to its contemporaries. . . .

. . . The revolutionary seed had penetrated into every country. . . . It was greatly developed under the *régime* of the military despotism of Bonaparte. His conquests displaced a number of laws, institutions, and customs; broke through bonds sacred among all nations, strong enough to resist time itself; which is more than can be said of certain benefits conferred by these innovators.

JOHN STUART MILL

ON LIBERTY

Freedom of thought and expression were principal concerns of nineteenth-century liberals. The classic defense of intellectual freedom is *On Liberty* (1859), written by John Stuart Mill (1806–1873), a prominent British philosopher. Mill argued that no individual or government has a monopoly on truth, for all human beings are fallible. Therefore, the government and the majority have no legitimate authority to suppress views, however unpopular; they have no right to interfere with a person's liberty so long as that person's actions do no injury to others. Nothing is more absolute, contended Mill, than the inviolable right of all adults to think and live as they please so long as they respect the rights of others. For Mill, toleration of opposing and unpopular viewpoints is a necessary trait in order for a person to become rational, moral, and civilized.

The object of this essay is to assert one very simple principle, as entitled to govern absolutely the dealings of society with the individual. . . . That principle is that the sole end for which mankind are warranted, individually or collectively, in interfering with the liberty of action of any of their number is self-protection. That the only purpose for which power can be rightfully exercised over any member of a civilized community, against his will, is to prevent harm to others. His own good, either physical or moral, is not a sufficient warrant. He cannot rightfully be compelled to do or forbear because it will be better for him to do so, because it will make him happier, because, in the opinions of others, to do so would be wise or even right. These are good reasons for remonstrating with him, or reasoning with him, or persuading him, or entreating him, but not for compelling him or visiting him with any evil in case he do otherwise. To justify that, the conduct from which it is desired to deter him must be calculated to produce evil to someone else. The only part of the conduct of anyone for which he is amenable to society is that which concerns others. In the part which merely concerns himself, his independence is, of right, absolute. Over himself, over his own body and mind, the individual is sovereign. . . .

. . . This, then, is the appropriate region of human liberty. It comprises, first, the inward domain of consciousness, demanding liberty of conscience in the most comprehensive sense, liberty of thought and feeling, absolute freedom of opinion and sentiment on all subjects, practical or speculative, scientific, moral, or theological. The liberty of expressing and publishing opinions may seem to fall under a different principle, since it belongs to that part of the conduct of an individual which concerns other people, but, being almost of as much importance as the liberty of thought itself and resting in great part on the same reasons, is practically inseparable from it. Secondly, the principle requires liberty of tastes and pursuits, of framing the plan of our life to suit our own character, of doing as we like, subject to such consequences as may follow, without impediment from our fellow creatures, so long as what we do does not harm them, even though they should think our conduct foolish, perverse, or wrong. Thirdly, from this liberty of each individual follows the liberty, within the same limits, of combination among individuals; freedom to unite for any purpose not involving harm to others: the persons combining being supposed to be of full age and not forced or deceived.

No society in which these liberties are not, on the whole, respected is free, whatever may be its form of government; and none is completely free in which they do not exist absolute and unqualified. The only freedom which deserves the name is that of pursuing our own good in our own way, so long as we do not attempt to deprive others of theirs or impede their efforts to obtain it. Each is the proper guardian of his own health, whether bodily *or* mental and spiritual. Mankind are greater gainers by suffering each other to live as seems good to themselves than by compelling each to live as seems good to the rest. . . .

. . . Let us suppose, therefore, that the government is entirely at one with the people, and never thinks of exerting any power of coercion unless in agreement with what it conceives to be their voice. But I deny the right of the people to exercise such coercion, either by themselves or by their government. The power itself is illegitimate. The best government has no more title to it than the worst. It is as noxious, or more noxious, when exerted in accordance with public opinion than when in opposition to it. If all mankind minus one were of one opinion, mankind would be no more justified in silencing that one person than he, if he had the power, would be justified in silencing mankind. Were an opinion a personal possession of no value except to the owner, if to be obstructed in the enjoyment of it were simply a private injury, it would make some difference whether the injury was inflicted only on a few persons or on many. But the peculiar evil of silencing the expression of an opinion is that it is robbing the human race, posterity as well as the existing generation—those who dissent from the opinion, still more than those who hold it. If the opinion is right, they are deprived of the opportunity of exchanging error for truth; if wrong, they lose, what is almost as great a benefit, the clearer perception and livelier impression of truth produced by its collision with error.

HENRIK IBSEN

A DOLL'S HOUSE

Realism was not restricted to the novel alone. The leading realist playwright, Henrik Ibsen (1828–1906), a Norwegian, examined with clinical precision the commercial and professional classes, their personal ambitions, business practices, and family relationships. In a period of less than ten years, Ibsen wrote four realist "problem plays"—*Pillars of Society* (1877), *A Doll's House* (1879), *Ghosts* (1881), and *An Enemy of the People* (1882)—that drew attention to bourgeois pretensions, hypocrisy, and social conventions that thwart individual growth. Thus, Ibsen's characters are typically torn between their sense of duty to others and their own selfish wants. Although Ibsen wrote about profound social issues, he viewed himself as a dramatist relating a piece of reality and not a social reformer agitating for reform.

In *A Doll's House*, Ibsen took up a theme that shocked late-nineteenth-century bourgeois audiences: a woman leaving her husband and children in search of self-realization. Nora Helmer resents being a submissive and dutiful wife to a husband who does not take her seriously, who treats her like a child, a doll.

In the following selection from *A Doll's House*, Nora tells her husband, Torvald, how she resents being treated like a child and why she is leaving him.

(She sits down at one side of the table.)

HELMER Nora—what is this?—this cold, set face?

NORA Sit down. It will take some time; I have a lot to talk over with you.

HELMER *(sits down at the opposite side of the table)* You alarm me, Nora!—and I don't understand you.

NORA No, that is just it. You don't understand me, and I have never understood you either—before to-night. No, you mustn't interrupt me. You must simply listen to what I say. Torvald, this is a settling of accounts.

HELMER What do you mean by that?

NORA *(after a short silence)* Isn't there one thing that strikes you as strange in our sitting here like this?

HELMER What is that?

NORA We have been married now eight years. Does it not occur to you that this is the first time we two, you and I, husband and wife, have had a serious conversation?

HELMER What do you mean by serious?

NORA In all these eight years—longer than that—from the very beginning of our acquaintance, we have never exchanged a word on any serious subject.

HELMER Was it likely that I would be continually and for ever telling you about worries that you could not help me to bear?

NORA I am not speaking about business matters. I say that we have never sat down in earnest together to try and get at the bottom of anything.

HELMER But, dearest Nora, would it have been any good to you?

NORA That is just it; you have never understood me. I have been greatly wronged, Torvald— first by papa and then by you.

HELMER What! By us two—by us two, who have loved you better than anyone else in the world?

NORA *(shaking her head)* You have never loved me. You have only thought it pleasant to be in love with me.

HELMER Nora, what do I hear you saying?

NORA It is perfectly true, Torvald. When I was at home with papa, he told me his opinion about everything, and so I had the same opinions; and if I differed from him I concealed the fact, because he would not have liked it. He called me his doll-child, and he played with me just as I used to play with my dolls. And when I came to live with you—

HELMER What sort of an expression is that to use about our marriage?

NORA *(undisturbed)* I mean that I was simply transferred from papa's hands into yours. You arranged everything according to your own taste, and so I got the same tastes as you—or else I pretended to, I am really not quite sure which—I think sometimes the one and sometimes the other. When I look back on it, it seems to me as if I had been living here like a poor woman—just from hand to mouth. I have existed merely to perform tricks for you, Torvald. But you would have it so. You and papa have committed a great sin against me. It is your fault that I have made nothing of my life.

HELMER How unreasonable and how ungrateful you are, Nora! Have you not been happy here?

NORA No. I have never been happy. I thought I was, but it has never really been so.

HELMER Not—not happy!

NORA No, only merry. And you have always been so kind to me. But our home has been nothing but a playroom. I have been your doll-wife, just as at home I was papa's doll-child; and here the children have been my dolls. I thought it great fun when you played with me, just as they thought it great fun when I played with them. That is what our marriage has been, Torvald.

HELMER There is some truth in what you say—exaggerated and strained as your view of it is. But for the future it shall be different. Playtime shall be over, and lesson-time shall begin.

NORA Whose lessons? Mine, or the children's?

HELMER Both yours and the children's, my darling Nora.

NORA Alas, Torvald, you are not the man to educate me into being a proper wife for you.

HELMER And you can say that!

NORA And I—how am I fitted to bring up the children?

HELMER Nora!

NORA Didn't you say so yourself a little while ago—that you dare not trust me to bring them up?

HELMER In a moment of anger! Why do you pay any heed to that?

NORA Indeed, you were perfectly right. I am not fit for the task. There is another task I must undertake first. I must try and educate myself—you are not the man to help me in that. I must do that for myself. And that is why I am going to leave you now.

HELMER *(springing up)* What do you say?

NORA I must stand quite alone, if I am to understand myself and everything about me. It is for that reason that I cannot remain with you any longer.

HELMER Nora! Nora!

NORA I am going away from here now, at once. I am sure Christine will take me in for the night—

HELMER You are out of your mind! I won't allow it! I forbid you!

NORA It is no use forbidding me anything any longer. I will take with me what belongs to myself. I will take nothing from you, either now or later.

HELMER What sort of madness is this!

NORA To-morrow I shall go home—I mean, to my old home. It will be easiest for me to find something to do there.

HELMER You blind, foolish woman!

NORA I must try and get some sense, Torvald.

HELMER To desert your home, your husband and your children! And you don't consider what people will say!

NORA I cannot consider that at all. I only know that it is necessary for me.

HELMER It's shocking. This is how you would neglect your most sacred duties.

NORA What do you consider my most sacred duties?

HELMER Do I need to tell you that? Are they not your duties to your husband and your children?

NORA I have other duties just as sacred.

HELMER That you have not. What duties could those be?

NORA Duties to myself.

HELMER Before all else, you are a wife and a mother.

NORA I don't believe that any longer. I believe that before all else I am a reasonable human being, just as you are—or, at all events, that I must try and become one. I know quite well, Torvald, that most people would think you right, and that views of that kind are to be found in books; but I can no longer content myself with what most people say, or with what is found in books. I must think over things for myself and get to understand them.

HELMER Can you not understand your place in your own home? Have you not a reliable guide in such matters as that?—have you no religion?

NORA I am afraid, Torvald, I do not exactly know what religion is.

HELMER What are you saying?

NORA I know nothing but what the clergyman said, when I went to be confirmed. He told us that religion was this, and that, and the other. When I am away from all this, and am alone, I will look into that matter too. I will see if what the clergyman said is true, or at all events if it is true for me.

HELMER This is unheard of in a girl of your age! But if religion cannot lead you aright, let me try and awaken your conscience. I suppose you have some moral sense? or—answer me—am I to think you have none?

NORA I assure you, Torvald, that is not an easy question to answer. I really don't know. The thing perplexes me altogether. I only know that you and I look at it in quite a different light. I am learning, too, that the law is quite another thing from what I supposed; but I find it impossible to convince myself that the law is right. According to it a woman has no right to spare her old dying father, or to save her husband's life. I can't believe that.

HELMER You talk like a child. You don't understand the conditions of the world in which you live.

NORA No, I don't. But now I am going to try. I am going to see if I can make out who is right, the world or I.

HELMER You are ill, Nora; you are delirious; I almost think you are out of your mind.

NORA I have never felt my mind so clear and certain as tonight.

HELMER And is it with a clear and certain mind that you forsake your husband and your children.

NORA Yes, it is.

HELMER Then there is only one possible explanation.

NORA What is that?

HELMER You do not love me any more.

NORA No, that is just it.

HELMER Nora!—and you can say that!

NORA It gives me great pain, Torvald, for you have always been so kind to me, but I cannot help it. I do not love you any more.

HELMER *(regaining his composure)* Is that a clear and certain conviction too?

NORA Yes, absolutely clear and certain. That is the reason I will not stay here any longer.

HELMER And can you tell me what I have done to forfeit your love?

NORA Yes, indeed I can. It was to-night, when the wonderful thing did not happen; then I saw you were not the man I had thought you.

HELMER Explain yourself better—I don't understand you.

When Nora was a young wife, Torvald became dangerously ill; doctors told her (but not him) that the only way to save her husband's life was to live in a warmer climate. Nora tried tears and entreaties with Torvald, saying that he ought to be kind to her by taking her on an extended trip to Italy, even if it meant taking a loan. Unaware of Nora's true intent—she wanted to save his life—Torvald would not hear of it. When she said her father provided the money, Torvald agreed. In reality, she borrowed the money by forging her dying father's name, something Torvald never knew. She continues to pay off the loan by carefully managing the funds alloted to her by Torvald for running the house, and Torvald does not know her secret. Recently promoted to a top position in the bank, Torvald fires Krogstad, who happened to be the person from whom Nora had borrowed the money. On news that he was fired, Krogstad delivers a letter to Torvald's home revealing the loan and the forgery. After reading the letter, Torvald hurls invectives at Nora: "miserable creature," "hypocrite," "liar," "criminal." "I shall not allow you to bring up the children; I dare not trust them to you."

NORA I have waited so patiently for eight years; for goodness knows, I knew very well that wonderful things don't happen every day. Then this horrible misfortune came upon me; and then I felt quite certain that the wonderful thing was going to happen at last. When Krogstad's letter was lying out there, never for a moment did I imagine that you would consent to accept this man's conditions. I was so absolutely certain that you would say to him: Publish the thing to the whole world. And when that was done—

HELMER Yes, what then—when I had exposed my wife to shame and disgrace?

NORA When that was done, I was so absolutely certain, you would come forward and take everything upon yourself, and say: I am the guilty one.

HELMER Nora—!

NORA You mean that I would never have accepted such a sacrifice on your part? No, of course not. But what would my assurances have been worth against yours? That was the wonderful thing which I hoped for and feared; and it was to prevent that, that I wanted to kill myself.

HELMER I would gladly work night and day for you, Nora—bear sorrow and want for your sake. But no man would sacrifice his honour for the one he loves.

NORA It is a thing hundreds of thousands of women have done.

HELMER Oh, you think and talk like a heedless child.

NORA Maybe. But you neither think nor talk like the man I could bind myself to. As soon as your fear was over—and it was not fear for what threatened me, but for what might happen to you—when the whole thing was past, as far as you were concerned it was exactly as if nothing at all had happened. Exactly as before, I was your little skylark, your doll, which you would in future treat with doubly gentle care, because it was so brittle and fragile. *(Getting up.)* Torvald—it was then it dawned upon me that for eight years I had been living here with a strange man, and had borne him three children—. Oh, I can't bear to think of it! I could tear myself into little bits!

HELMER *(sadly)* I see, I see. An abyss has opened between us—there is no denying it. But, Nora, would it not be possible to fill it up?

NORA As I am now, I am no wife for you.

HELMER I have it in me to become a different man.

NORA Perhaps—if your doll is taken away from you.

HELMER But to part!—to part from you! No, no. Nora, I can't understand that idea.

NORA *(going out to the right)* That makes it more certain that it must be done.

(She comes back with her cloak and hat and a small bag which she puts on a chair by the table)

HELMER Nora, Nora, not now! Wait till to-morrow.

NORA *(putting on her cloak)* I cannot spend the night in a strange man's room.

HELMER But can't we live here like brother and sister—?

NORA *(putting on her hat)* You know very well that would not last long. *(Puts the shawl round her.)* Good-bye, Torvald. I won't see the little ones. I know they are in better hands than mine. As I am now, I can be of no use to them.

HELMER But some day, Nora—some day?

NORA How can I tell? I have no idea what is going to become of me.

HELMER But you are my wife, whatever becomes of you.

NORA Listen, Torvald. I have heard that when a wife deserts her husband's house, as I am doing now, he is legally freed from all obligations towards her. In any case I set you free from all your obligations. You are not to feel yourself bound in the slightest way, any more than I shall. There must be perfect freedom on both sides. See, here is your ring back. Give me mine.

HELMER That too?

NORA That too.

HELMER Here it is.

NORA That's right. Now it is all over. I have put the keys here. The maids know all about everything in the house—better than I do. Tomorrow, after I have left her, Christine will come here and pack up my own things that I brought with me from home. I will have them sent after me.

HELMER All over! All over!—Nora, shall you never think of me again?

NORA I know I shall often think of you and the children and this house.

HELMER May I write to you, Nora?

NORA No—never. You must not do that.

HELMER But at least let me send you—

NORA Nothing—nothing—

HELMER Let me help you if you are in want.

NORA No. I can receive nothing from a stranger.

HELMER Nora—can I never be anything more than a stranger to you?

NORA *(taking her bag)* Ah, Torvald, the most wonderful thing of all would have to happen.

HELMER Tell me what that would be!

NORA Both you and I would have to be so changed that—Oh, Torvald, I don't believe any longer in wonderful things happening.

HELMER But I will believe in it. Tell me? So changed that—?

NORA That our life together would be a real wedlock. Good-bye.

(She goes out through the hall.)

HELMER *(sinks down on a chair at the door and buries his face in his hands)* Nora! Nora! *(looks round, and rises)* Empty. She is gone. *(A hope flashes across his mind.)* The most wonderful thing of all—?

(The sound of a door shutting is heard from below.)

KARL MARX AND FRIEDRICH ENGELS

COMMUNIST MANIFESTO

In the opening section of the *Manifesto*, the basic premise of the Marxian philosophy of history is advanced: class conflict—the idea that the social order is divided into classes based on conflicting economic interests.

BOURGEOIS AND PROLETARIANS

The history of all hitherto existing society is the history of class struggles.

Freeman and slave, patrician and plebeian [aristocrat and commoner, in the ancient world], lord and serf, guild-master [master craftsman] and journeyman [who worked for a guild-master], in a word, oppressor and oppressed, stood in constant opposition to one another, carried on an uninterrupted, now hidden, now open fight, that each time ended, either in a revolutionary reconstitution of society at large, or in the common ruin of the contending classes.

In the earlier epochs of history we find almost everywhere a complicated arrangement of society into various orders, a manifold gradation of social rank. In ancient Rome we have patricians, knights, plebeians, slaves; in the Middle Ages, feudal lords, vassals [landowners pledged to lords], guild-masters, journeymen, apprentices, serfs; in almost all of these classes, again, subordinate gradations.

The modern bourgeois society that has sprouted from the ruins of feudal society, has not done away with class antagonisms. It has but established new forms of struggle in place of the old ones.

Our epoch, the epoch of the bourgeoisie [capitalist class], possesses, however, this distinctive feature; it has simplified the class antagonisms. Society as a whole is more and more splitting up into two great hostile camps, into two great classes directly facing each other: Bourgeoisie and Proletariat [industrial workers].

From the serfs of the middle ages sprang the chartered burghers of the earliest towns. From these burgesses the first elements of the bourgeoisie were developed.

The discovery of America, the rounding of the Cape, opened up fresh ground for the rising bourgeoisie. The East-Indian and Chinese markets, the colonization of America, trade with the colonies, the increase in the means of exchange and in commodities generally, gave to commerce, to navigation, to industry, an impulse never before known, and thereby, to the revolutionary element in the tottering feudal society, a rapid development.

The feudal system of industry, under which industrial production was monopolized by closed guilds, now no longer sufficed for the growing wants of the new market. The manufacturing system took its place. The guild-masters were pushed on one side by the manufacturing middle class; division of labor between the different corporate guilds vanished in the face of division of labor in each single workshop.

Meantime the markets kept ever growing, the demand ever rising. . . . Thereupon steam and machinery revolutionized industrial production. The place of manufacture was taken by the giant, Modern Industry, the place of the industrial middle class, by industrial millionaires, the leaders of whole industrial armies, the modern bourgeois.

Modern Industry has established the world's market, for which the discovery of America paved the way. This market has given an immense development to commerce, to navigation, to communication by land. This devel-opment has, in its turn, reacted on the extension of industry; and in proportion, as industry, commerce, navigation, railways extended, in the same proportion, the bourgeoisie developed, increased its capital, and pushed into the background every class handed down from the Middle Ages.

We see, therefore, how the modern bourgeoisie is itself the product of a long course of development, of a series of revolutions in the modes of production and of exchange.

Each step in the development of the bourgeoisie was accompanied by a corresponding political advance of that class. An oppressed class under the sway of the feudal nobility, an armed and self-governing association in the mediaeval commune [town], . . . the bourgeoisie has at last, since the establishment of Modern Industry and of the world's market, conquered for itself, in the modern representative State, exclusive political sway. The executive of the modern State is but a committee for managing the common affairs of the whole bourgeoisie.

The bourgeoisie, historically, has played a most revolutionary part.

The bourgeoisie, wherever it has got the upper hand, has put an end to all feudal, patriarchal, idyllic relations. It has pitilessly torn asunder the motley feudal ties that bound man to his "natural superiors," and has left remaining no other nexus [link] between man and man than naked self-interest, than callous "cash payment." It has drowned the most heavenly ecstasies of religious fervor, of chivalrous enthusiasm, . . . in the icy water of egotistical calculation. It has resolved personal worth into exchange value, and in place of the numberless indefeasible chartered freedoms, has set up that single, unconscionable freedom—Free Trade. In one word, for exploitation, veiled by religious and political illusions, it has substituted naked, shameless, direct, brutal exploitation. . . .

The bourgeoisie, states the *Manifesto,* has subjected nature's forces to human control to an unprecedented degree and has replaced feudal organization of agriculture (serfdom) and manufacturing (guild system) with capitalist free competition. But the capitalists cannot control these "gigantic means of production and exchange." Periodically, capitalist society is burdened by severe economic crises; capitalism is afflicted with overproduction—more goods are produced than the market will absorb. In all earlier epochs, which were afflicted with scarcity, the *Manifesto* declares, such a condition "would have seemed an absurdity." To deal with the crisis, the capitalists curtail production, thereby intensifying the poverty of the proletariat, who are without work. In capitalist society, the exploited worker suffers from physical poverty—a result of low wages—and spiritual poverty—a result of the monotony, regimentation, and impersonal character of the capitalist factory system. For the proletariat, work is not the satisfaction of a need but a repulsive means for survival. The products they help make bring them no satisfaction; they are alienated from their labor.

In proportion as the bourgeoisie, *i.e.*, capital, is developed, in the same proportion is the proletariat, the modern working class, developed—a class of laborers, who live only so long as they find work, and who find work only so long as their labor increases capital. These laborers, who must sell themselves piecemeal, are a commodity, like every other article of commerce, and are consequently exposed to all the vicissitudes of competition, to all the fluctuations of the market.

Owing to the extensive use of machinery and to division of labor, the work of the proletarians has lost all individual character, and, consequently, all charm for the workman. He becomes an appendage of the machine, and it is only the most simple, most monotonous, and most easily acquired knack, that is required of him. Hence, the cost of production of a workman is restricted, almost entirely, to the means of subsistence that he requires for his maintenance, and for the propagation of his race. But the price of a commodity, and therefore also of labor, is equal to its cost of production. In proportion, therefore, as the repulsiveness of the work increases, the wage decreases. Nay more, in proportion as the use of machinery and division of labor increases, in the same proportion the burden of toil also increases, whether by prolongation of the working hours, by increase of the work exacted in a given time, or by increased speed of the machinery, etc.

Modern industry has converted the little workshop of the patriarchal master into the great factory of the industrial capitalist. Masses of laborers, crowded into the factory, are organized like soldiers. As privates of the industrial army they are placed under the command of a perfect hierarchy of officers and sergeants. Not only are they slaves of the bourgeois class, and of the bourgeois state; they are daily and hourly enslaved by the machine, by the overlooker, and, above all, by the individual bourgeois manufacturer himself. The more openly this despotism proclaims gain to be its end and aim, the more petty, the more hateful and the more embittering it is.

The less the skill and exertion of strength implied in manual labor, in other words, the more modern industry develops, the more is the labor of men superseded by that of women. Differences of age and sex have no longer any distinctive social validity for the working class. All are instruments of labor, more or less expensive to use, according to their age and sex.

No sooner has the laborer received his wages in cash, for the moment escaping exploitation by the manufacturer, than he is set upon by the other portions of the bourgeoisie, the landlord, the shopkeeper, the pawnbroker, etc. . . .

The exploited workers organize to defend their interests against the capitalist oppressors.

But with the development of industry the proletariat not only increases in number; it becomes concentrated in greater masses, its strength grows, and it feels that strength more. The various interests and conditions of life within the ranks of the proletariat are more and more equalized, in proportion as machinery obliterates all distinctions of labor and nearly everywhere reduces wages to the same low level. The growing competition among the bourgeois, and the resulting commercial crises, make the wages of the workers ever more fluctuating. The unceasing improvement of machinery, ever more rapidly developing, makes their livelihood more and more precarious: the collisions between individual workmen and individual bourgeois take more and more the character of collisions between two classes. Thereupon the workers begin to form combinations (trade unions) against the bourgeoisie; they club together in order to keep up the rate of wages; they found permanent associations in order to make provision beforehand for these occasional revolts. Here and there the contest breaks out into riots.

Now and then the workers are victorious, but only for a time. The real fruit of their battles lies, not in the immediate results, but in [their ever-expanding unity]. . . .

This organization of the proletarians into a class, and consequently into a political party, is continually being upset again by the competition between the workers themselves. But it ever rises up again, stronger, firmer, mightier. It compels legislative recognition of particular interests of the workers, by taking advantage of the divisions among the bourgeoisie itself. Thus the ten-hour bill[1] in England was carried. . . .

Increasingly, the proletariat, no longer feeling part of the old society, seeks to destroy it.

In the conditions of the proletariat, those of the old society at large are already virtually swamped. The proletarian is without property; his relation to his wife and children has no longer anything in common with the bourgeois family relations; modern industrial labor, modern subjection to capital, the same in England as in France, in America as in Germany, has stripped him of every trace of national character. Law, morality, religion, are to him so many bourgeois prejudices, behind which lurk in ambush just as many bourgeois interests.

All the preceding classes that got the upper hand sought to fortify their already acquired status by subjecting society at large to their conditions of appropriation. The proletarians cannot become masters of the productive forces of society, except by abolishing their own previous mode of appropriation, and thereby also every other previous mode of appropriation. They have nothing of their own to secure and to fortify; their mission is to destroy all previous securities for, and insurances of, individual property.

All previous historical movements were movements of minorities, or in the interest of minorities. The proletarian movement is the self-conscious, independent movement of the immense majority, in the interest of the immense majority. The proletariat, the lowest stratum of our present society, cannot stir, cannot raise itself up, without the whole super-incumbent [overlying] strata of official society being [shattered].

Though not in substance, yet in form, the struggle of the proletariat with the bourgeoisie is at first a national struggle. The proletariat of each country must, of course, first of all settle matters with its own bourgeoisie.

In depicting the most general phases of the development of the proletariat, we traced the more or less veiled civil war, raging within existing society, up to the point where that war breaks out into open revolution, and where the violent overthrow of the bourgeoisie lays the foundation for the sway of the proletariat. . . .

[1]The Ten Hours Act (1847) provided a ten and a half hour day from 6 A.M. to 6 P.M., with an hour and a half for meals for women and children.

The modern laborer . . . instead of rising with the progress of industry, sinks deeper and deeper below the conditions of existence of his own class. He becomes a pauper, and pauperism develops more rapidly than population and wealth. And here it becomes evident that the bourgeoisie is unfit any longer to be the ruling class in society and to impose its conditions of existence upon society as an overriding law. It is unfit to rule because it is incompetent to assure an existence to its slave within his slavery, because it cannot help letting him sink into such a state that it has to feed him instead of being fed by him. Society can no longer live under this bourgeoisie, in other words its existence is no longer compatible with society.

The essential condition for the existence and for the sway of the bourgeois class, is the formation and augmentation of capital; the condition for capital is wage-labor. Wage-labor rests exclusively on competition between the laborers. The advance of industry, whose involuntary promoter is the bourgeoisie, replaces the isolation of the laborers, due to competition, by their revolutionary combination, due to association. The development of modern industry, therefore, cuts from under its feet the very foundation on which the bourgeoisie produces and appropriates products. What the bourgeoisie therefore produces above all, are its own gravediggers. Its fall and the victory of the proletariat are equally inevitable. . . .

Communists, says the *Manifesto,* are the most advanced and determined members of working-class parties. Among the aims of the communists are organization of the working class into a revolutionary party; overthrow of bourgeois power and the assumption of political power by the proletariat; and an end to exploitation of one individual by another and the creation of a classless society. These aims will be achieved by the abolition of bourgeois private property (private ownership of the means of production) and the abolition of the bourgeoisie as a class.

The Communists, therefore, are on the one hand, practically, the most advanced and resolute section of the working class parties of every country, that section which pushes forward all others; on the other hand, theoretically, they have over the great mass of the proletariat the advantage of clearly understanding the line of march, the conditions, and the ultimate general results of the proletarian movement.

The immediate aim of the Communists is the same as that of all the other proletarian parties: formation of the proletariat into a class, overthrow of the bourgeois supremacy, conquest of political power by the proletariat. . . .

The distinguishing feature of Communism is not the abolition of property generally, but the abolition of bourgeois property. But modern bourgeois private property is the final and most complete expression of the system of producing and appropriating products, that is based on class antagonisms, on the exploitation of the many by the few.

In this sense the theory of the Communists may be summed up in the single sentence: Abolition of private property. . . .

One argument leveled against communists by bourgeois critics, says the *Manifesto,* is that the destruction of the bourgeoisie would lead to the disappearance of bourgeois culture, which is "identical with the disappearance of all culture," and the loss of all moral and religious truths. Marx insists that these ethical and religious ideals lauded by the bourgeoisie are not universal truths at all but are common expressions of the ruling class at a particular stage in history.

That culture, the loss of which he [the bourgeois] laments, is for the enormous majority, a mere training to act as a machine.

But don't wrangle with us so long as you [the bourgeoisie] apply to our [the communists'] intended abolition of bourgeois property, the standard of your bourgeois notions of freedom, culture, law, etc. Your very ideas are but the outgrowth of the conditions of your bourgeois production and bourgeois property, just as your jurisprudence is but the will of your class made into a law for all, a will, whose essential character and direction are determined by the economical conditions of existence of your class.

The selfish misconception that induces you to transform into eternal laws of nature and of reason, the social forms springing from your present mode of production and form of property—historical relations that rise and disappear in the progress of production—this misconception you share with every ruling class that has preceded you. What you see clearly in the case of ancient property, what you admit in the case of feudal property, you are of course forbidden to admit in the case of your own bourgeois form of property. . . .

The charges against Communism made from a religious, a philosophical, and, generally, from an ideological standpoint, are not deserving of serious examination.

Does it require deep intuition to comprehend that man's ideas, views, and conceptions, in one word, man's consciousness changes with every change in the conditions of his material existence, in his social relations and in his social life?

What else does the history of ideas prove than that intellectual production changes its character in proportion as material production is changed? The ruling ideas of each age have ever been the ideas of its ruling class. . . .

. . . The ideas of religious liberty and freedom of conscience merely gave expression to the sway of free competition within the domain of knowledge.

"Undoubtedly," it will be said, "religious, moral, philosophical, and juridical ideas have been modified in the course of historic development. But religion, morality, philosophy, political science, and law, constantly survived this change.

"There are besides, eternal truths, such as Freedom, Justice, etc., that are common to all states of society. But Communism abolishes eternal truths, it abolishes all religion and all morality, instead of constituting them on a new basis; it therefore acts as a contradiction to all past historical experience."

What does this accusation reduce itself to? The history of all past society has consisted in the development of class antagonisms, antagonisms that assumed different forms at different epochs.

But whatever form they may have taken, one fact is common to all past ages, *viz.*, the exploitation of one part of society by the other. No wonder, then, that the social consciousness of past ages, despite all the multiplicity and variety it displays, moves within certain common forms, or general ideas, which cannot completely vanish except with the total disappearance of class antagonisms.

The Communist revolution is the most radical rupture with traditional property relations; no wonder that its development involves the most radical rupture with traditional ideas.

Aroused and united by communist intellectuals, says the *Manifesto*, the proletariat will wrest power from the bourgeoisie and overthrow the capitalist system that has oppressed them. In the new society, people will be fully free.

But let us have done with the bourgeois objections to Communism.

We have seen above that the first step in the revolution by the working class is to raise the proletariat to the position of the ruling class, to win the battle of democracy.

The proletariat will use its political supremacy to wrest, by degrees, all capital from the bourgeoisie; to centralize all instruments of production in the hands of the State, *i.e.*, of the proletariat organized as the ruling class; and to increase the total of productive forces as rapidly as possible. . . .

When, in the course of development, class distinctions have disappeared and all production has been concentrated in the hands of a vast association of the whole nation, the public power will lose its political character. Political power, properly so called, is merely the organized power of one class for oppressing another. If the proletariat during its contest with the bourgeoisie is compelled, by the force of circumstances, to organize itself as a class, if, by means of a revolution, it makes itself the ruling class, and, as such, sweeps away by force the old conditions of production, then it will, along with these conditions, have swept away the conditions for the existence of class antagonism, and of classes generally, and will thereby have abolished its own supremacy as a class.

In place of the old bourgeois society with its classes and class antagonisms we shall have an association in which the free development of each is the condition for the free development of all. . . .

The Communists disdain to conceal their views and aims. They openly declare that their ends can be attained only by the forcible overthrow of all existing social conditions. Let the ruling classes tremble at a communistic revolution. The proletarians have nothing to lose but their chains. They have a world to win.

Working men of all countries, unite!

CECIL RHODES

CONFESSION OF FAITH

One ardent supporter of British expansion was Cecil Rhodes (1853–1902). Raised in a parsonage north of London, Rhodes went to southern Africa at the age of seventeen for his health and to join his brother. Within two years he had established himself in the diamond industry. In the 1870s, he divided his time between Africa and studying at Oxford University. While at Oxford he was inspired by Disraeli's Crystal Palace speech and the views of the prominent Oxford professor John Ruskin (1819–1900), who urged England "to found colonies as fast and as far as she is able, formed of the most energetic and worthiest of men." In this spirit Rhodes wrote, for his own satisfaction, a "Confession of Faith." Composed in 1877, when he was twenty-four years old, it offered a vision of racist expansionism popular before the First World War. It was not published in his lifetime.

His faith propelled him into political and financial prominence in South Africa. In 1889 he became head of the British South African Company, whose territory, twice as large as England, was named Rhodesia six years later (it was renamed Zimbabwe in 1980). He controlled 90 percent of the world's diamond production and a large share of South Africa's gold fields. Never regarding wealth as an end in itself—he endowed the Rhodes Scholarships at Oxford—he sought to extend British influence in East Africa and around the world.

In 1890 he was named prime minister of the British Cape Colony, where government forces were heavily involved in conflict with the original Dutch settlers, the Boers. Driven north by the British, the Boers had set up their own state. Rhodes died during the Boer War (1899–1902), which put the Boers under British rule.

Excerpts follow from the "Confession of Faith" of 1877, included in the appendix of John E. Flint's biography of Cecil Rhodes. Flint reproduced the document "in its original form without any editing of spelling or punctuation."

> It often strikes a man to inquire what is the chief good in life; to one the thought comes that it is a happy marriage, to another great wealth, and as each seizes on his idea, for that he more or less works for the rest of his existence. To myself thinking over the same question the wish came to render myself useful to my country. I then asked myself how could I and after reviewing the various methods I have felt that at the present day we are actually limiting our children and perhaps bringing into the world half the human beings we might owing to the lack of country for them to inhabit that if we had retained America there would at this moment be millions more of English living. I contend that we are the finest race in the world and that the more of the world we inhabit the better it is for the human race. Just fancy those parts that are at present inhabited by the most despicable specimens of human beings what an alteration there would be if they were brought under Anglo-Saxon influence, look again at the extra employment a new country added to our dominions gives. I contend that every acre added to our territory means in the future birth to some more of the English race who otherwise would not be brought into existence. Added to this the absorption of the greater portion of the world under our rule simply means the end of all wars. . . .
>
> The idea gleaming and dancing before ones eyes like a will-of-the-wisp at last frames itself into a plan. Why should we not form a secret society with but one object the furtherance of the British Empire and the bringing of the whole uncivilised world under British rule for the recovery of the United States for the making the Anglo-Saxon race but one Empire. What a dream, but yet it is probable, it is possible. I once heard it argued by a fellow in my own college, I am sorry to own it by an Englishman, that it was a good thing for us that we have lost the United States. There are some subjects on which there can be no arguments, and to an Englishman this is one of them, but even from an American's point of view just picture what they have lost, look at their government, are not the frauds that yearly come before the public view a disgrace to any country and especially their's which is the finest in the world. Would they have occurred had they remained under English rule great as they have become how infinitely greater

they would have been with the softening and elevating influences of English rule, think of those countless 000's [thousands] of Englishmen that during the last 100 years would have crossed the Atlantic and settled and populated the United States. Would they have not made without any prejudice a finer country of it than the low class Irish and German emigrants? All this we have lost and that country loses owing to whom? Owing to two or three ignorant pigheaded statesmen of the last century, at their door lies the blame. Do you ever feel mad? do you ever feel murderous. I think I do with those men. I bring facts to prove my assertion. Does an English father when his sons wish to emigrate ever think of suggesting emigration to a country under another flag, never—it would seem a disgrace to suggest such a thing I think that we all think that poverty is better under our own flag than wealth under a foreign one.

Put your mind into another train of thought. Fancy Australia discovered and colonised under the French flag. . . . We learn from having lost to cling to what we possess. We know the size of the world we know the total extent. Africa is still lying ready for us it is our duty to take it. It is our duty to seize every opportunity of acquiring more territory and we should keep this one idea steadily before our eyes that more territory simply means more of the Anglo-Saxon race more of the best the most human, most honourable race the world possesses.

To forward such a scheme what a splendid help a secret society would be a society not openly acknowledged but who would work in secret for such an object.

I contend that there are at the present moment numbers of the ablest men in the world who would devote their whole lives to it. . . . What has been the main cause of the success of the Romish Church? The fact that every enthusiast, call it if you like every madman finds employment in it. Let us form the same kind of society a Church for the extension of the British Empire. A society which should have its members in every part of the British Empire working with one object and one idea. . . .

(In every Colonial legislature the Society should attempt to have its members prepared at all times to vote or speak and advocate the closer union of England and the colonies, to crush all disloyalty and every movement for the severance of our Empire. The Society should inspire and even own portions of the press for the press rules the mind of the people. The Society should always be searching for members who might by their position in the world by their energies or character forward the object but the ballot and test for admittance should be severe). . . .[1]

For fear that death might cut me off before the time for attempting its development I leave all my worldly goods in trust to S. G. Shippard and the Secretary for the Colonies at the time of my death to try to form such a Society with such an object.

[1]It is not clear why Rhodes placed this paragraph inparentheses.

JOSEPH CHAMBERLAIN

THE BRITISH EMPIRE: COLONIAL COMMERCE AND "THE WHITE MAN'S BURDEN"

British imperialists like Joseph Chamberlain (1836–1914) argued that the welfare of Britain depended upon the preservation and extension of the empire, for colonies fostered trade and served as a source of raw materials. In addition, Chamberlain asserted that the British Empire had a sacred duty to carry civilization, Christianity, and British law to the "backward" peoples of Africa and Asia. As a leading statesman, Chamberlain made many speeches, both in Parliament and before local political groups, that endorsed imperialist ventures. Excerpts from these speeches, later collected and published under the title *Foreign and Colonial Speeches* (1897), follow.

June 10, 1896

. . . The Empire, to parody a celebrated expression, is commerce. It was created by commerce, it is founded on commerce, and it could not exist a day without commerce. (Cheers). . . . The fact is history teaches us that no nation has ever achieved real greatness without the aid of commerce, and the greatness of no nation has survived the decay of its trade. Well, then, gentlemen, we have reason to be proud of our commerce and to be resolved to guard it from attack. (Cheers.). . . .

March 31, 1897

. . . We have suffered much in this country from depression of trade. We know how many of our fellow-subjects are at this moment unemployed. Is there any man in his senses who believes that the crowded population of these islands could exist for a single day if we were to cut adrift from us the great dependencies which now look to us for protection and assistance, and which are the natural markets for our trade? (Cheers.) The area of the United Kingdom is only 120,000 miles; the area of the British Empire is over 9,000,000 square miles, of which nearly 500,000 are to be found in the portion of Africa with which we have been dealing. If tomorrow it were possible, as some people apparently desire, to reduce by a stroke of the pen the British Empire to the dimensions of the United Kingdom, half at least of our population would be starved (cheers). . . .

January 22, 1894

We must look this matter in the face, and must recognise that in order that we may have more employment to give we must create more demand. (Hear, hear.) Give me the demand for more goods and then I will undertake to give plenty of employment in making the goods; and the only thing, in my opinion, that the Government can do in order to meet this great difficulty that we are considering, is so to arrange its policy that every inducement shall be given to the demand; that new markets shall be created, and that old markets shall be effectually developed. (Cheers.) . . . I am convinced that it is a necessity as well as a duty for us to uphold the dominion and empire which we now possess. (Loud cheers.) . . . I would never lose the hold which we now have over our great Indian dependency—(hear, hear)—by far the greatest and most valuable of all the customers we have or ever shall have in this country. For the same reasons I approve of the continued occupation of Egypt; and for the same reasons I have urged upon this Government, and upon previous Governments, the necessity for using every legitimate opportunity to extend our influence and control in that great African continent which is now being opened up to civilisation and to commerce; and, lastly, it is for the same reasons that I hold that our navy should be strengthened—(loud cheers)—until its supremacy is so assured that we cannot be shaken in any of the possessions which we hold or may hold hereafter.

Believe me, if in any one of the places to which I have referred any change took place which deprived us of that control and influence of which I have been speaking, the first to suffer would be the working-men of this country. Then, indeed, we should see a distress which would not be temporary, but which would be chronic, and we should find that England was entirely unable to support the enormous population which is now maintained by the aid of her foreign trade. If the working-men of this country understand, as I believe they do—I am one of those who have had good reason through my life to rely upon their intelligence and shrewdness—if they understand their own interests, they will never lend any countenance to the doctrines of those politicians who never lose an opportunity of pouring contempt and abuse upon the brave Englishmen, who, even at this moment, in all parts of the world are carving out new dominions for Britain, and are opening up fresh markets for British commerce, and laying out fresh fields for British labour. (Applause.) . . .

March 31, 1897

. . . We feel now that our rule over these territories can only be justified if we can show that it adds to the happiness and prosperity of the people—(cheers)—and I maintain that our rule does, and has, brought security and peace and comparative prosperity to countries that never knew these blessings before. (Cheers.)

In carrying out this work of civilisation we are fulfilling what I believe to be our national mission, and we are finding scope for the exercise of those faculties and qualities which have made of us a great governing race. (Cheers.) I do not say that our success has been perfect in every case, I do not say that all our methods have been beyond reproach; but I do say that in almost every instance in which the rule of the Queen has been established and the great *Pax Britannica*[1] has been enforced, there has come with it greater security to life and property, and a material improvement in the condition of the bulk of the population. (Cheers.) No doubt, in the first instance, when these conquests have been made, there has been bloodshed, there has been loss of life among the native populations, loss of still more precious lives among those who have been sent out to bring these countries into some kind of disciplined order, but it must be remembered that this is the condition of the mission we have to fulfil. . . .

. . . You cannot have omelettes without breaking eggs; you cannot destroy the practices of barbarism, of slavery, of superstition, which for centuries have desolated the interior of Africa, without the use of force; but if you will fairly contrast the gain to humanity with the price which we are bound to pay for it, I think you may well rejoice in the result of such expeditions as those which have recently been conducted with such signal success—(cheers)—in Nyassaland, Ashanti, Benin, and Nupé [regions in Africa]—expeditions which may have, and indeed have, cost valuable lives, but as to which we may rest assured that for one life lost a hundred will be gained, and the cause of civilisation and the prosperity of the people will in the long run be eminently advanced. (Cheers.) But no doubt such a state of things, such a mission as I have described, involve heavy responsibility. . . . and it is a gigantic task that we have undertaken when we have determined to wield the sceptre of empire. Great is the task, great is the responsibility, but great is the honour—(cheers); and I am convinced that the conscience and the spirit of the country will rise to the height of its obligations, and that we shall have the strength to fulfil the mission which our history and our national character have imposed upon us. (Cheers.)

[1]Pax Britannica means "British Peace" in the tradition of the Pax Romana—the peace, stability, and prosperity that characterized the Roman Empire at its height in the first two centuries A.D.

KARL PEARSON

SOCIAL DARWINISM: IMPERIALISM JUSTIFIED BY NATURE

In the last part of the nineteenth century, the spirit of expansionism was buttressed by application of Darwin's theory of evolution to human society. Theorists called Social Darwinists argued that nations and races, like the species of animals, were locked in a struggle for existence in which only the fittest survived and deserved to survive. British and American imperialists employed the language of Social Darwinism to promote and justify Anglo-Saxon expansion and domination of other peoples. Social Darwinist ideas spread to Germany, which was inspired by the examples of British and American expansion. In a lecture given in 1900 and titled "National Life from the Standpoint of Science," Karl Pearson (1857–1936), a British professor of mathematics, expressed the beliefs of Social Darwinists.

What I have said about bad stock seems to me to hold for the lower races of man. How many centuries, how many thousands of years, have the Kaffir [a tribe in southern Africa] or the negro held large districts in Africa undisturbed by the white man? Yet their intertribal struggles have not yet produced a civilization in the least comparable with the Aryan[1] [western European]. Educate and nurture them as you will, I do not believe that you will succeed in modifying the stock. History shows me one way, and one way only, in which a high state of civilization has been produced, namely, the struggle of race with race, and the survival of the physically and mentally fitter race. . . .

. . . Let us suppose we could prevent the white man, if we liked, from going to lands of which the agricultural and mineral resources are not worked to the full; then I should say a thousand times better for him that he should not go than that he should settle down and live alongside the inferior race. The only healthy alternative is that he should go and completely drive out the inferior race. That is practically what the white man has done in North America. . . . But I venture to say that no man calmly judging will wish either that the whites had never gone to America, or would desire that whites and Red Indians were to-day living alongside each other as negro and white in the Southern States, as Kaffir and European in South Africa, still less that they had mixed their blood as Spaniard and Indian in South America. . . . I venture to assert, then, that the struggle for existence between white and red man, painful and even terrible as it was in its details, has given us a good far outbalancing its immediate evil. In place of the red man, contributing practically nothing to the work and thought of the world, we have a great nation, mistress of many arts, and able, with its youthful imagination and fresh, untrammelled impulses, to contribute much to the common stock of civilized man. . . .

But America is but one case in which we have to mark a masterful human progress following an inter-racial struggle. The Australian nation is another case of great civilization supplanting a lower race unable to work to the full the land and its resources. . . . The struggle means suffering, intense suffering, while it is in progress; but that struggle and that suffering have been the stages by which the white man has reached his present stage of development, and they account for the fact that he no longer lives in caves and feeds on roots and nuts. This dependence of progress on the survival of the fitter race, terribly black as it may seem to some of you, gives the struggle for existence its redeeming features; it is the fiery crucible out of which comes the finer metal. You may hope for a time when the sword shall be turned into the ploughshare, when American and German and English traders shall no longer compete in the markets of the world for their raw material and for their food supply, when the white man and the dark shall share the soil between them, and each till it as he lists [pleases]. But, believe me, when that day comes mankind will no longer progress; there will be nothing to check the fertility of inferior

[1]Most European languages derive from the Aryan language spoken by people who lived thousands of years ago in the region from the Caspian Sea to the Hindu Kush Mountains. Around 2000 B.C., some Aryan-speaking people migrated to Europe and India. Nineteenth-century racialist thinkers held that Europeans, descendants of the ancient Aryans, were racially superior to other peoples.

stock; the relentless law of heredity will not be controlled and guided by natural selection. Man will stagnate. . . .

The . . . great function of science in national life . . . is to show us what national life means, and how the nation is a vast organism subject . . . to the great forces of evolution. . . . There is a struggle of race against race and of nation against nation. In the early days of that struggle it was a blind, unconscious struggle of barbaric tribes. At the present day, in the case of the civilized white man, it has become more and more the conscious, carefully directed attempt of the nation to fit itself to a continuously changing environment. The nation has to foresee how and where the struggle will be carried on; the maintenance of national position is becoming more and more a conscious preparation for changing conditions, an insight into the needs of coming environments. . . .

. . . If a nation is to maintain its position in this struggle, it must be fully provided with trained brains in every department of national activity, from the government to the factory, and have, if possible, a *reserve of brain and physique* to fall back upon in times of national crisis. . . .

You will see that my view—and I think it may be called the scientific view of a nation—is that of an organized whole, kept up to a high pitch of internal efficiency by insuring that its numbers are substantially recruited from the better stocks, and kept up to a high pitch of external efficiency by contest, chiefly by way of war with inferior races, and with equal races by the struggle for trade-routes and for the sources of raw material and of food supply. This is the natural history view of mankind, and I do not think you can in its main features subvert it. . . .

. . . Is it not a fact that the daily bread of our millions of workers depends on their having somebody to work for? that if we give up the contest for trade-routes and for free markets and for waste lands, we indirectly give up our food-supply? Is it not a fact that our strength depends on these and upon our colonies, and that our colonies have been won by the ejection of inferior races, and are maintained against equal races only by respect for the present power of our empire? . . .

. . . We find that the law of the survival of the fitter is true of mankind, but that the struggle is that of the gregarious animal. A community not knit together by strong social instincts, by sympathy between man and man, and class and class, cannot face the external contest, the competition with other nations, by peace or by war, for the raw material of production and for its food supply. This struggle of tribe with tribe, and nation with nation, may have its mournful side; but we see as a result of it the gradual progress of mankind to higher intellectual and physical efficiency. It is idle to condemn it; we can only see that it exists and recognise what we have gained by it—civilization and social sympathy. But while the statesman has to watch this external struggle, . . . he must be very cautious that the nation is not silently rotting at its core. He must insure that the fertility of the inferior stocks is checked, and that of the superior stocks encouraged; he must regard with suspicion anything that tempts the physically and mentally fitter men and women to remain childless. . . .

. . . The path of progress is strewn with the wrecks of nations; traces are everywhere to be seen of the hecatombs [slaughtered remains] of inferior races, and of victims who found not the narrow way to perfection. Yet these dead people are, in very truth, the stepping stones on which mankind has arisen to the higher intellectual and deeper emotional life of today.

JOHN ATKINSON HOBSON

AN EARLY CRITIQUE OF IMPERIALISM

One of the early English critics of imperialism was the social reformer and economist John Atkinson Hobson (1858–1940). Hobson's primary interest was social reform, and he turned to economics to try to solve the problem of poverty. Like Rhodes, he was influenced by Ruskin's ideas, but his interpretation of them led him to a diametrically opposed view of colonialism. As an economist, he argued that the unequal distribution of income made capitalism unproductive and unstable. It could not maintain itself except through investing in less developed countries on an increasing scale, thus fostering colonial expansion. Lenin, leader of the Russian Revolution, later adopted this thesis. Hobson's stress upon the economic causes of imperialism has been disputed by some historians who see the desire for national power and glory as a far more important cause. Hobson attacked imperialism in the following passages from his book *Imperialism* (1902).

. . . The decades of Imperialism have been prolific in wars; most of these wars have been directly motivated by aggression of white races upon "lower races," and have issued in the forcible seizure of territory. Every one of the steps of expansion in Africa, Asia, and the Pacific has been accompanied by bloodshed; each imperialist Power keeps an increasing army available for foreign service; rectification of frontiers, punitive expeditions, and other euphemisms for war are in incessant progress. The *pax Britannica*, always an impudent falsehood, has become of recent years a grotesque monster of hypocrisy; along our Indian frontiers, in West Africa, in the Soudan, in Uganda, in Rhodesia fighting has been well-nigh incessant. Although the great imperialist Powers have kept their hands off one another, save where the rising empire of the United States has found its opportunity in the falling empire of Spain, the self-restraint has been costly and precarious. Peace as a national policy is antagonised not merely by war, but by militarism, an even graver injury. Apart from the enmity of France and Germany, the main cause of the vast armaments which are draining the resources of most European countries is their conflicting interests in territorial and commercial expansion. Where thirty years ago there existed one sensitive spot in our relations with France, or Germany, or Russia, there are a dozen now; diplomatic strains are of almost monthly occurrence between Powers with African or Chinese interests, and the chiefly business nature of the national antagonisms renders them more dangerous, inasmuch as the policy of Governments passes more under the influence of distinctively financial juntos [cliques]. . . .

Our economic analysis has disclosed the fact that it is only the interests of competing cliques of business men—investors, contractors, export manufacturers, and certain professional classes—that are antagonistic; that these cliques, usurping the authority and voice of the people, use the public resources to push their private businesses, and spend the blood and money of the people in this vast and disastrous military game, feigning national antagonisms which have no basis in reality. It is not to the interest of the British people, either as producers of wealth or as tax-payers, to risk a war with Russia and France in order to join Japan in preventing Russia from seizing [K]orea; but it may serve the interests of a group of commercial politicians to promote this dangerous policy. The South African war [the Boer War, 1899–1902], openly fomented by gold speculators for their private purposes, will rank in history as a leading case of this usurpation of nationalism. . . .

. . . So long as this competitive expansion for territory and foreign markets is permitted to misrepresent itself as "national policy" the antagonism of interests seems real, and the peoples must sweat and bleed and toil to keep up an ever more expensive machinery of war. . . .

. . . The industrial and financial forces of Imperialism, operating through the party, the press, the church, the school, mould public opinion and public policy by the false idealisation of those primitive lusts of struggle, domination, and acquisitiveness which have survived throughout the eras of peaceful industrial order and whose stimulation is needed once again for the work of imperial aggression, expansion, and the forceful exploitation of lower races. For these business politicians biology and sociology weave thin convenient theories of a race struggle for the subjugation of the inferior peoples, in order that we, the Anglo-Saxon, may take their lands and live upon their labours; while economics buttresses the argument by representing our work in conquering and ruling them as our share in the division of labour among nations, and history devises reasons why the lessons of past empire do not apply to ours, while social ethics paints the motive of "Imperialism" as the desire to bear the "burden" of educating and elevating races of "children." Thus are the "cultured" or semi-cultured classes indoctrinated with the intellectual and moral grandeur of Imperialism. For the masses there is a cruder appeal to hero-worship and sensational glory, adventure and the sporting spirit: current history falsified in coarse flaring colours, for the direct stimulation of the combative instincts. But while various methods are employed, some delicate and indirect, others coarse and flamboyant, the operation everywhere resolves itself into an incitation and direction of the brute lusts of human domination which are everywhere latent in civilised humanity, for the pursuance of a policy fraught with material gain to a minority of co-operative vested interests which usurp the title of the commonwealth. . . .

. . . The presence of a scattering of white officials, missionaries, traders, mining or plantation overseers, a dominant male caste with little knowledge of or sympathy for the institutions of the people, is ill-calculated to give to these lower races even such gains as Western civilisation might be capable of giving.

The condition of the white rulers of these lower races is distinctively parasitic; they live upon these natives, their chief work being that of organising native labour for their support. The normal state of such a country is one in which the most fertile lands and the mineral resources are owned by white aliens and worked by natives under their direction, primarily for their gain: they do not identify themselves with the interests of the nation or its people, but remain an alien body of sojourners, a "parasite" upon the carcass of its "host," destined to extract wealth from the country and retire to consume it at home. All the hard manual or other severe routine work is done by natives. . . .

Nowhere under such conditions is the theory of white government as a trust for civilisation made valid; nowhere is there any pro-vision to secure the predominance of the interests, either of the world at large or of the governed people, over those of the encroaching nation, or more commonly a section of that nation. The relations subsisting between the superior and the inferior nations, commonly established by pure force, and resting on that basis, are such as preclude the genuine sympathy essential to the operation of the best civilising influences, and usually resolve themselves into the maintenance of external good order so as to forward the profitable development of certain natural resources of the land, under "forced" native labour, primarily for the benefit of white traders and investors, and secondarily for the benefit of the world of white Western consumers.

This failure to justify by results the forcible rule over alien peoples is attributable to no special defect of the British or other modern European nations. It is inherent in the nature of such domination. . . .

FRIEDRICH NIETZSCHE

THE WILL TO POWER AND THE ANTICHRIST

Two of Nietzsche's works—*The Will to Power* and *The Antichrist*—are represented in the following readings. First published in 1901, one year after Nietzsche's death, *The Will to Power* consists of the author's notes written in the years 1883 to 1888. The following passages from this work show Nietzsche's contempt for democracy and socialism and proclaim the will to power.

THE WILL TO POWER

720 (1886–1887)

The most fearful and fundamental desire in man, his drive for power—this drive is called "freedom"—must be held in check the longest. This is why ethics . . . has hitherto aimed at holding the desire for power in check: it disparages the tyrannical individual and with its glorification of social welfare and patriotism emphasizes the power-instinct of the herd.

728 (March–June 1888)

. . . A society that definitely and *instinctively* gives up war and conquest is in decline: it is ripe for democracy and the rule of shopkeepers—In most cases, to be sure, assurances of peace are merely narcotics.

751 (March–June 1888)

"The will to power" is so hated in democratic ages that their entire psychology seems directed toward belittling and defaming it. . . .

752 (1884)

. . . Democracy represents the disbelief in great human beings and an elite society: "Everyone is equal to everyone else." "At bottom we are one and all self-seeking cattle and mob."

753 (1885)

I am opposed to 1. socialism, because it dreams quite naively of "the good, true, and beautiful" and of "equal rights" (— anarchism also desires the same ideal, but in a more brutal fashion); 2. parliamentary government and the press, because these are the means by which the herd animal becomes master.

762 (1885)

European democracy represents a release of forces only to a very small degree. It is above all a release of laziness, of weariness, of *weakness.*

765 (Jan.–Fall 1888)

. . . Another Christian concept, no less crazy, has passed even more deeply into the tissue of modernity: the concept of the "equality of souls before God." This concept furnishes the prototype of all theories of equal rights: mankind was first taught to stammer the proposition of equality in a religious context, and only later was it made into morality: no wonder that man ended by taking it seriously, taking it practically!—that is to say, politically, democratically, socialistically, in the spirit of the pessimism of indignation.

854 (1884)

In the age of *suffrage universel,* i.e., when everyone may sit in judgment on everyone and everything, I feel impelled to reestablish *order of rank.*

855 (Spring–Fall 1887)

What determines rank, sets off rank, is only quanta of power, and nothing else.

857 (Jan.–Fall 1888)

I distinguish between a type of ascending life and another type of decay, disintegration, weakness. Is it credible that the question of the relative rank of these two types still needs to be posed?

858 (Nov. 1887–March 1888)

What determines your rank is the quantum of power you are: the rest is cowardice.

861 (1884)

A declaration of war on the masses by *higher men* is needed! Everywhere the mediocre are combining in order to make themselves master! Everything that makes soft and effeminate, that serves the ends of the "people" or the "feminine," works in favor of *suffrage universel*, i.e., the dominion of *inferior* men. But we should take reprisal and bring this whole affair (which in Europe commenced with Christianity) to light and to the bar of judgment.

862 (1884)

A doctrine is needed powerful enough to work as a breeding agent: strengthening the strong, paralyzing and destructive for the world-weary.

The annihilation of the decaying races. Decay of Europe.—The annihilation of slavish evaluations.—Dominion over the earth as a means of producing a higher type.—The annihilation of the tartuffery [hypocrisy] called "morality." . . . The annihilation of *suffrage universel*; i.e., the system through which the lowest natures prescribe themselves as laws for the higher.—The annihilation of mediocrity and its acceptance. (The onesided, individuals—peoples; to strive for fullness of nature through the pairing of opposites: race mixture to this end).—The new courage—no *a priori* [innate and universal] truths (such truths were sought by those accustomed to faith!), but a *free* subordination to a ruling idea that has its time: e.g., time as a property of space, etc.

870 (1884)

The root of all evil: that the slavish morality of meekness, chastity, selflessness, absolute obedience, has triumphed—ruling natures were thus condemned (1) to hypocrisy, (2) to torments of conscience—creative natures felt like rebels against God, uncertain and inhibited by eternal values. . . .

In summa: the best things have been slandered because the weak or the immoderate swine have cast a bad light on them—and the best men have remained hidden—and have often misunderstood themselves.

874 (1884)

The degeneration of the rulers and the ruling classes has been the cause of the greatest mischief in history! Without the Roman Caesars and Roman society, the insanity of Christianity would never have come to power.

When lesser men begin to doubt whether higher men exist, then the danger is great! And one ends by discovering that there is *virtue* also among the lowly and subjugated, the poor in spirit, and that *before God* men are equal—which has so far been the . . . [height] of nonsense on earth! For ultimately, the higher men measured themselves according to the standard of virtue of slaves—found they were "proud," etc., found all their higher qualities reprehensible.

997 (1884)

I teach: that there are higher and lower men, and that a single individual can under certain circumstances justify the existence of whole millennia—that is, a full, rich, great, whole human being in relation to countless incomplete fragmentary men.

998 (1884)

The highest men live beyond the rulers, freed from all bonds; and in the rulers they have their instruments.

999 (1884)

Order of rank: He who *determines* values and directs the will of millennia by giving direction to the highest natures is the *highest* man.

1001 (1884)

Not "mankind" but *overman* is the goal!

1067 (1885)

. . . *This world is the will to power—and nothing besides!* And you yourselves are also this will to power—and nothing besides!

Nietzsche regarded Christianity as a life-denying religion that appeals to the masses. Fearful and resentful of their betters, he said, the masses espouse a faith that preaches equality and compassion. He maintained that Christianity has "waged a war to the death against (the) higher type of man." The following passages are from *The Antichrist*, written in 1888.

THE ANTICHRIST

2. What is good?—All that heightens the feeling of power, the will to power, power itself in man.

What is bad?—All that proceeds from weakness.

What is happiness?—The feeling that power *increases*—that a resistance is overcome.

Not contentment, but more power; *not* peace at all, but war; *not* virtue, but proficiency (virtue in the Renaissance style, *virtù*, virtue free of moralic acid).

The weak and ill-constituted shall perish: first principle of *our* philanthropy. And one shall help them to do so.

What is more harmful than any vice?—Active sympathy for the ill-constituted and weak—Christianity. . . .

3. The problem I raise here is not what ought to succeed mankind in the sequence of species (—the human being is an *end*—): but what type of human being one ought to *breed*, ought to *will*, as more valuable, more worthy of life, more certain of the future.

This more valuable type has existed often enough already: but as a lucky accident, as an exception, never as *willed*. He has rather been the most feared, he has hitherto been virtually *the* thing to be feared—and out of fear the reverse type has been willed, bred, *achieved*: the domestic animal, the herd animal, the sick animal man—the Christian. . . .

5. One should not embellish or dress up Christianity: it has waged *a war to the death* against this *higher* type of man, it has excommunicated all the fundamental instincts of this type, it has distilled evil, the *Evil One*, out of these instincts—the strong human being as the type of reprehensibility, as the "outcast." Christianity has taken the side of everything weak, base, ill-constituted, it has made an ideal out of *opposition* to the preservative instincts of strong life; it has depraved the reason even of the intellectually strongest natures by teaching men to feel the supreme values of intellectuality as sinful,

as misleading, as *temptations*. The most deplorable example: the depraving of Pascal,[1] who believed his reason had been depraved by original sin while it had only been depraved by his Christianity!. . .

7. Christianity is called the religion of *pity*.—Pity stands in antithesis to the tonic emotions which enhance the energy of the feeling of life: it has a depressive effect. One loses force when one pities. . . .

15. In Christianity neither morality nor religion come into contact with reality at any point. Nothing but imaginary *causes* ("God," "soul," "ego," "spirit," "free will"—or "unfree will"): nothing but imaginary *effects* ("sin," "redemption," "grace," "punishment," "forgiveness of sins"). . . .

18. The Christian conception of God—God as God of the sick, God as spider, God as spirit—is one of the most corrupt conceptions of God arrived at on earth: perhaps it even represents the low-water mark in the descending development of the God type. God degenerated to the *contradiction of life*, instead of being its transfiguration and eternal *Yes!* In God a declaration of hostility towards life, nature, the will to life! God the formula for every calumny of "this world," for every lie about "the next world"! In God, nothingness deified, the will to nothingness sanctified! . . .

21. In Christianity the instincts of the subjugated and oppressed come into the foreground: it is the lowest classes which seek their salvation in it. . . .

43. The poison of the doctrine "*equal* rights for all"—this has been more thoroughly sowed by Christianity than by anything else; from the most secret recesses of base instincts, Christianity has waged a war to the death against every feeling of reverence and distance between man and man, against, that is, the *precondition* of every elevation, every increase in culture—it has forged out of the [resentment] of the masses its *chief weapon* against *us*, against everything noble, joyful, high-spirited on earth, against our happiness on earth. . . . "Immortality" granted to every Peter and Paul has been the greatest and most malicious outrage on *noble* mankind ever committed.—*And* let us not underestimate the fatality that has crept out of Christianity even into politics! No one any longer possesses today the courage to claim special privileges or the right to rule, the courage to feel a sense of reverence towards himself and towards his equals—the courage for a *pathos of distance*. . . . Our politics is *morbid* from this lack of courage!—The aristocratic outlook has been undermined most deeply by the lie of equality of souls; and if the belief in the "prerogative of the majority" makes revolutions and *will continue to make them*—it is Christianity, let there be no doubt about it, *Christian* value judgement which translates every revolution into mere blood and crime! Christianity is a revolt of everything that crawls along the ground directed against that which is *elevated*: the Gospel of the "lowly" *makes* low. . . .

[1]Blaise Pascal (1623–1662) was a French mathematician, philosopher, and eloquent defender of the Christian faith.

SIGMUND FREUD

THE UNCONSCIOUS AND *CIVILIZATION AND ITS DISCONTENTS*

Readings from two works of Freud are included: *A Note on the Unconscious in Psychoanalysis* (1912) and *Civilization and Its Discontents* (1930). Freud's scientific investigation of psychic development led him to conclude that powerful mental processes hidden from consciousness govern human behavior more than reason does. His exploration of the unconscious produced a new image of the human being that has had a profound impact on twentieth-century thought and beyond. In the following excerpt from *A Note on the Unconscious in Psychoanalysis*, Freud defined the term *unconscious*.

A NOTE ON THE UNCONSCIOUS IN PSYCHOANALYSIS

I wish to expound in a few words and as plainly as possible what the term "unconscious" has come to mean in psychoanalysis and in psychoanalysis alone. . . .

. . . The well-known experiment, . . . of the "post-hypnotic suggestion" teaches us to insist upon the importance of the distinction between *conscious* and *unconscious* and seems to increase its value.

In this experiment, as performed by Bernheim,[1] a person is put into a hypnotic state and is subsequently aroused. While he was in the hypnotic state, under the influence of the physician, he was ordered to execute a certain action at a certain fixed moment after his awakening, say half an hour later. He awakes, and seems fully conscious and in his ordinary condition; he has no recollection of his hypnotic state, and yet at the prearranged moment there rushes into his mind the impulse to do such and such a thing, and he does it consciously, though not knowing why. It seems impossible to give any other description of the phenomenon than to say that the order has been present in the mind of the person in a condition of latency, or had been present unconsciously, until the given moment came, and then had become conscious. But not the whole of it emerged into consciousness: only the conception of the act to be executed. All the other ideas associated with this conception—the order, the influence of the physician, the recollection of the hypnotic state, remained unconscious even then. . . .

The mind of the hysterical patient is full of active yet unconscious ideas; all her symptoms proceed from such ideas. It is in fact the most striking character of the hysterical mind to be ruled by them. If the hysterical woman vomits, she may do so from the idea of being pregnant. She has, however, no knowledge of this idea, although it can easily be detected in her mind, and made conscious to her, by one of the technical procedures of psychoanalysis. If she is executing the jerks and movements constituting her "fit," she does not even consciously represent to herself the intended actions, and she may perceive those actions with the detached feelings of an onlooker. Nevertheless analysis will show that she was acting her part in the dramatic reproduction of some incident in her life, the memory of which was unconsciously active during the attack. The same preponderance of active unconscious ideas is revealed by analysis as the essential fact in the psychology of all other forms of neurosis. . . .

. . . The term *unconscious* . . . designates . . . ideas with a certain dynamic character, ideas keeping apart from consciousness in spite of their intensity and activity.

In the tradition of the Enlightenment philosophes, Freud valued reason and science, but he did not share the philosophes' confidence in human goodness and humanity's capacity for future progress. In *Civilization and Its Discontents* (1930), Freud posited the frightening theory that human beings are driven by an inherent aggressiveness that threatens civilized life—that civilization is fighting a losing battle with our aggressive instincts. Although Freud's pessimism was no doubt influenced by the tragedy of World War I, many ideas expressed in *Civilization and Its Discontents* derived from views that he had formulated decades earlier.

---

[1]Hippolyte Bernheim (1840–1919), a French physician, used hypnosis in the treatment of his patients and published a successful book on the subject.

CIVILIZATION AND ITS DISCONTENTS

The element of truth behind all this, which people are so ready to disavow, is that men are not gentle creatures who want to be loved, and who at most can defend themselves if they are attacked; they are, on the contrary, creatures among whose instinctual endowments is to be reckoned a powerful share of aggressiveness. As a result, their neighbour is for them not only a potential helper or sexual object, but also someone who tempts them to satisfy their aggressiveness on him, to exploit his capacity for work without compensation, to use him sexually without his consent, to seize his possessions, to humiliate him, to cause him pain, to torture and to kill him. *Homo homini lupus.* [Man is wolf to man.] Who, in the face of all his experience of life and of history, will have the courage to dispute this assertion? As a rule this cruel aggressiveness waits for some provocation or puts itself at the service of some other purpose, whose goal might also have been reached by milder measures. In circumstances that are favourable to it, when the mental counterforces which ordinarily inhibit it are out of action, it also manifests itself spontaneously and reveals man as a savage beast to whom consideration towards his own kind is something alien. Anyone who calls to mind the atrocities committed during the racial migrations or the invasions of the Huns, or by the people known as Mongols under Jenghiz Khan and Tamerlane, or at the capture of Jerusalem by the pious Crusaders, or even, indeed, the horrors of the recent World War—anyone who calls these things to mind will have to bow humbly before the truth of this view.

The existence of this inclination to aggression, which we can detect in ourselves and justly assume to be present in others, is the factor which disturbs our relations with our neighbour and which forces civilization into such a high expenditure [of energy]. In consequence of this primary mutual hostility of human beings, civilized society is perpetually threatened with disintegration. The interest of work in common would not hold it together; instinctual passions are stronger than reasonable interests. Civilization has to use its utmost efforts in order to set limits to man's aggressive instincts and to hold the manifestations of them in check by psychical reaction-formations. Hence, therefore, the use of methods intended to incite people into identifications and aim-inhibited relationships of love, hence the restriction upon sexual life, and hence too the ideal's commandment to love one's neighbour as oneself—a commandment which is really justified by the fact that nothing else runs so strongly counter to the original nature of man. In spite of every effort, these endeavours of civilization have not so far achieved very much. It hopes to prevent the crudest excesses of brutal violence by itself assuming the right to use violence against criminals, but the law is not able to lay hold of the more cautious and refined manifestations of human aggressiveness. The time comes when each one of us has to give up as illusions the expectations which, in his youth, he pinned upon his fellowmen, and when he may learn how much difficulty and pain has been added to his life by their ill-will. At the same time, it would be unfair to reproach civilization with trying to eliminate strife and competition from human activity. These things are undoubtedly indispensable. But opposition is not necessarily enmity; it is merely misused and made an *occasion* for enmity.

The communists believe that they have found the path to deliverance from our evils. According to them, man is wholly good and is well-disposed to his neighbour; but the institution of private property has corrupted his nature. The ownership of private wealth gives the individual power, and with it the temptation to ill-treat his neighbour; while the man who is excluded from possession is bound to rebel in hostility against his oppressor. If private property were abolished, all wealth held in common, and everyone allowed to share in the enjoyment of it, ill-will and hostility would disappear among men. Since everyone's needs would be satisfied, no one would have any reason to regard another as his enemy; all would willingly undertake the work that was necessary. I have no concern with any economic criticisms of the communist system. . . . But I am able to recognize that the psychological premises on which the system is based are an untenable illusion. In abolishing private property we deprive the human love of aggression of one of its instruments, certainly a strong one, though certainly not the strongest; but we have in no way altered the differences in power and influence which are misused by aggressiveness, nor have we altered anything in its nature. Aggressiveness was not created by property. It reigned almost without limit in primitive times, when property was still very scanty, and it already shows itself in the nursery almost before property has given up its primal, anal form; it forms the basis of every relation of affection and love among people (with the single exception, perhaps, of the mother's relation to her male child). If we do away with personal rights over material wealth, there still remains prerogative in the field of sexual relationships, which is bound to become the source of the strongest dislike and the most violent hostility among men who in other respects are on an equal footing. If we were to remove this factor, too, by allowing complete freedom of sexual life and thus abolishing the family, the germ-cell of civilization, we cannot, it is true, easily foresee what new paths the development of civilization could take; but one thing we can expect, and that is that this indestructible feature of human nature will follow it there.

It is clearly not easy for men to give up the satisfaction of this inclination to aggression. They do not feel comfortable without it. . . .

If civilization imposes such great sacrifices not only on man's sexuality but on his aggressivity, we can understand better why it is hard for him to be happy in that civilization. . . .

In all that follows I adopt the standpoint, therefore, that the inclination to aggression is an original, self-subsisting instinctual disposition in man, and I return to my view that it constitutes the greatest impediment to civilization.

ERICH MARIA REMARQUE

ALL QUIET ON THE WESTERN FRONT

The following reading is taken from Erich Maria Remarque's novel *All Quiet on the Western Front* (1929), the most famous literary work to emerge from World War I. A veteran of the trenches himself, Remarque (1898–1970) graphically described the slaughter that robbed Europe of its young men. His narrator is a young German soldier.

We wake up in the middle of the night. The earth booms. Heavy fire is falling on us. We crouch into corners. We distinguish shells of every calibre.

Each man lays hold of his things and looks again every minute to reassure himself that they are still there. The dug-out heaves, the night roars and flashes. We look at each other in the momentary flashes of light, and with pale faces and pressed lips shake our heads.

Every man is aware of the heavy shells tearing down the parapet, rooting up the embankment and demolishing the upper layers of con-crete. When a shell lands in the trench we note how the hollow, furious blast is like a blow from the paw of a raging beast of prey. Already by morning a few of the recruits are green and vomiting. They are too inexperienced. . . .

The bombardment does not diminish. It is falling in the rear too. As far as one can see spout fountains of mud and iron. A wide belt is being raked.

The attack does not come, but the bombardment continues. We are gradually benumbed. Hardly a man speaks. We cannot make ourselves understood.

Our trench is almost gone. At many places it is only eighteen inches high, it is broken by holes, and craters, and mountains of earth. A shell lands square in front of our post. At once it is dark. We are buried and must dig ourselves out. . . .

Towards morning, while it is still dark, there is some excitement. Through the entrance rushes in a swarm of fleeing rats that try to storm the walls. Torches light up the confusion. Everyone yells and curses and slaughters. The madness and despair of many hours unloads itself in this outburst. Faces are distorted, arms strike out, the beasts scream; we just stop in time to avoid attacking one another. . . .

Suddenly it howls and flashes terrifically, the dug-out cracks in all its joints under a direct hit, fortunately only a light one that the concrete blocks are able to withstand. It rings metallically, the walls reel, rifles, helmets, earth, mud, and dust fly everywhere. Sulphur fumes pour in.

If we were in one of those light dug-outs that they have been building lately instead of this deeper one, none of us would be alive.

But the effect is bad enough even so. The recruit starts to rave again and two others follow suit. One jumps up and rushes out, we have trouble with the other two. I start after the one who escapes and wonder whether to shoot him in the leg—then it shrieks again, I fling myself down and when I stand up the wall of the trench is plastered with smoking splinters, lumps of flesh, and bits of uniform. I scramble back.

The first recruit seems actually to have gone insane. He butts his head against the wall like a goat. We must try to-night to take him to the rear. Meanwhile we bind him, but in such a way that in case of attack he can be released at once. . . .

Suddenly the nearer explosions cease. The shelling continues but it has lifted and falls behind us, our trench is free. We seize the hand-grenades, pitch them out in front of the dug- out and jump after them. The bombardment has stopped and a heavy barrage now falls behind us. The attack has come.

No one would believe that in this howling waste there could still be men; but steel helmets now appear on all sides out of the trench, and fifty yards from us a machine-gun is already in position and barking.

The wire entanglements are torn to pieces. Yet they offer some obstacle. We see the storm-troops coming. Our artillery opens fire. Machine-guns rattle, rifles crack. The charge works its way across. Haie and Kropp begin with the hand-grenades. They throw as fast as they can, others pass them, the handles with the strings already pulled. Haie throws seventy-five yards, Kropp sixty, it has been measured, the distance is important. The enemy as they run cannot do much before they are within forty yards.

We recognize the smooth distorted faces, the helmets: they are French. They have already suffered heavily when they reach the remnants of the barbed wire entanglements. A whole line has gone down before our machine-guns; then we have a lot of stoppages and they come nearer.

I see one of them, his face upturned, fall into a wire cradle. His body collapses, his hands remain suspended as though he were praying. Then his body drops clean away and only his hands with the stumps of his arms, shot off, now hang in the wire.

The moment we are about to retreat three faces rise up from the ground in front of us. Under one of the helmets a dark pointed beard and two eyes that are fastened on me. I raise my hand, but I cannot throw into those strange eyes; for one mad moment the whole slaughter whirls like a circus round me, and these two eyes alone are motionless; then the head rises up, a hand, a movement, and my hand-grenade flies through the air and into him.

We make for the rear, pull wire cradles into the trench and leave bombs behind us with the strings pulled, which ensures us a fiery retreat. The machine-guns are already firing from the next position.

We have become wild beasts. We do not fight, we defend ourselves against annihilation. It is not against men that we fling our bombs, what do we know of men in this moment when Death is hunting us down—now, for the first time in three days we can see his face, now for the first time in three days we can oppose him; we feel a mad anger. No longer do we lie helpless, waiting on the scaffold, we can destroy and kill, to save ourselves, to save ourselves and to be revenged.

We crouch behind every corner, behind every barrier of barbed wire, and hurl heaps of explosives at the feet of the advancing enemy before we run. The blast of the hand-grenades impinges powerfully on our arms and legs; crouching like cats we run on, overwhelmed by this wave that bears us along, that fills us with ferocity, turns us into thugs, into murderers, into God only knows what devils; this wave that multiplies our strength with fear and madness and greed of life, seeking and fighting for nothing but our deliverance. If your own father came over with them you would not hesitate to fling a bomb at him.

The forward trenches have been abandoned. Are they still trenches? They are blown to pieces, annihilated—there are only broken bits of trenches, holes linked by cracks, nests of craters, that is all. But the enemy's casualties increase. They did not count on so much resistance.

It is nearly noon. The sun blazes hotly, the sweat stings in our eyes, we wipe it off on our sleeves and often blood with it. At last we reach a trench that is in a somewhat better condition. It is manned and ready for the counter-attack, it receives us. Our guns open in full blast and cut off the enemy attack.

The lines behind us stop. They can advance no farther. The attack is crushed by our artillery. We watch. The fire lifts a hundred yards and we break forward. Beside me a lance-corporal has his head torn off. He runs a few steps more while the blood spouts from his neck like a fountain.

It does not come quite to hand-to-hand fighting; they are driven back. We arrive once again at our shattered trench and pass on beyond it. . . .

We have lost all feeling for one another. We can hardly control ourselves when our glance lights on the form of some other man. We are insensible, dead men, who through some trick, some dreadful magic, are still able to run and to kill.

A young Frenchman lags behind, he is overtaken, he puts up his hands, in one he still holds his revolver—does he mean to shoot or to give himself up!—a blow from a spade cleaves through his face. A second sees it and tries to run farther; a bayonet jabs into his back. He leaps in the air, his arms thrown wide, his mouth wide open, yelling; he staggers, in his back the bayonet quivers. A third throws away his rifle, cowers down with his hands before his eyes. He is left behind with a few other prisoners to carry off the wounded.

Suddenly in the pursuit we reach the enemy line.

We are so close on the heels of our retreating enemies that we reach it almost at the same time as they. In this way we suffer few casualties. A machine-gun barks, but is silenced with a bomb. Nevertheless, the couple of seconds has sufficed to give us five stomach wounds. With the butt of his rifle Kat smashes to pulp the face of one of the unwounded machine-gunners. We bayonet the others before they have time to get out their bombs. Then thirstily we drink the water they have for cooling the gun.

Everywhere wire-cutters are snapping, planks are thrown across the entanglements, we jump through the narrow entrances into the trenches. Haie strikes his spade into the neck of a gigantic Frenchman and throws the first hand-grenade; we duck behind a breastwork for a few seconds, then the straight bit of trench ahead of us is empty. The next throw whizzes obliquely over the corner and clears a passage; as we run past we toss handfuls down into the dug-outs, the earth shudders, it crashes, smokes and groans, we stumble over slippery lumps of flesh, over yielding bodies; I fall into an open belly on which lies a clean, new officer's cap.

The fight ceases. We lose touch with the enemy. We cannot stay here long but must retire under cover of our artillery to our own position. No sooner do we know this than we dive into the nearest dug-outs, and with the utmost haste seize on whatever provisions we can see, especially the tins of corned beef and butter, before we clear out.

We get back pretty well. There is no further attack by the enemy. We lie for an hour panting and resting before anyone speaks. We are so completely played out that in spite of our great hunger we do not think of the provisions. Then gradually we become something like men again.

SIEGFRIED SASSOON

BASE DETAILS

Front-line soldiers often looked with contempt on generals who, from a safe distance, ordered massive assaults against enemy lines protected by barbed wire and machine guns. Such attacks could cost the lives of tens of thousands of soldiers in just a few days. Siegfried Sassoon (1886–1967), a British poet who served at the front for much of the war and earned a Military Cross for bravery, showed his disdain for coldhearted officers in the following poem, composed in 1917.

If I were fierce, and bald, and short of breath,
I'd live with scarlet Majors at the Base,
And speed glum heroes up the line to death.
You'd see me with my puffy petulant face,
Guzzling and gulping in the best hotel,
Reading the Roll of Honour. "Poor young chap,"
I'd say—"I used to know his father well;
Yes, we've lost heavily in this last scrap."
And when the war is done and youth stone dead,
I'd toddle safely home and die—in bed.

WILFRED OWEN

DISABLED

Wilfred Owen (1893–1918), another British poet, volunteered for duty in 1915. At the Battle of the Somme he sustained shell shock, and he was sent to a hospital in Britain. In 1918 he returned to the front and was awarded the Military Cross; he died one week before the Armistice. In the following poem, "Disabled," Owen portrays the enduring misery of war.

He sat in a wheeled chair, waiting for dark,
And shivered in his ghastly suit of gray,
Legless, sewn short at elbow. Through the park
Voices of boys rang saddening like a hymn,
Voices of play and pleasure after day,
Till gathering sleep mothered them from him.
About this time Town used to swing so gay
When glow-lamps budded in the light blue trees,
And girls glanced lovelier as the air grew dim,—
In the old times, before he threw away his knees. . . .
He asked to join. He didn't have to beg;
Smiling they wrote his lie: aged nineteen years.
Germans he scarcely thought of; all their guilt,
And Austria's, did not move him. And no fears
Of Fear came yet. He thought of jeweled hilts
For daggers in plaid socks; of smart salutes;
And care of arms; and leave; and pay arrears;
Esprit de corps,[1] and hints for young recruits.
And soon, he was drafted out with drums and cheers. . . .
Now, he will spend a few sick years in Institutes,
And do what things the rules consider wise,
And take whatever pity they may dole.
Tonight he noticed how the women's eyes
Passed from him to the strong men that were whole.
How cold and late it is! Why don't they come
And put him into bed? Why don't they come?

[1]*Esprit de corps:* group spirit.

WOODROW WILSON

THE IDEALISTIC VIEW

Wilson sought a peace of justice and reconciliation, one based on democratic and Christian ideals, as the following excerpts from his speeches illustrate.

(May 26, 1917)

We are fighting for the liberty, the self-government, and the undictated development of all peoples, and every feature of the settlement that concludes this war must be conceived and executed for that purpose. Wrongs must first be righted and then adequate safeguards must be created to prevent their being committed again. . . .

. . . No people must be forced under sovereignty under which it does not wish to live. No territory must change hands except for the purpose of securing those who inhabit it a fair chance of life and liberty. No indemnities must be insisted on except those that constitute payment for manifest wrongs done. No readjustments of power must be made except such as will tend to secure the future peace of the world and the future welfare and happiness of its peoples.

And then the free peoples of the world must draw together in some common covenant, some genuine and practical co-öperation that will in effect combine their force to secure peace and justice in the dealings of nations with one another.

The following are excerpts from the Fourteen Points, the plan for peace that Wilson announced on January 8, 1918.

IV. Adequate guarantees given and taken that national armaments will be reduced to the lowest point consistent with domestic safety.

V. A free, open-minded, and absolutely impartial adjustment of all colonial claims, based upon a strict observance of the principle that in determining all such questions of sovereignty the interests of the populations concerned must have equal weight with the equitable claims of the government whose title is to be determined. . . .

VIII. All French territory should be freed and the invaded portions restored, and the wrong done to France by Prussia in 1871 in the matter of Alsace-Lorraine, which has unsettled the peace of the world for nearly fifty years, should be righted, in order that peace may once more be made secure in the interest of all.

IX. A readjustment of the frontiers of Italy should be effected along clearly recognizable lines of nationality.

X. The peoples of Austria-Hungary, whose place among the nations we wish to see safeguarded and assured, should be accorded the freest opportunity of autonomous development. . . .

XII. The Turkish portions of the present Ottoman Empire should be assured a secure sovereignty, but the other nationalities which are now under Turkish rule should be assured an undoubted security of life and an absolutely unmolested opportunity of autonomous development, and the Dardanelles should be permanently opened as a free passage to the ships and commerce of all nations under international guarantees.

XIII. An independent Polish state should be erected which should include the territories inhabited by indisputably Polish populations, which should be assured a free and secure access to the sea, and whose political and economic independence and territorial integrity should be guaranteed by international covenant.

XIV. A general association of nations must be formed under specific covenants for the purpose of affording mutual guarantees of political independence and territorial integrity to great and small states alike.

(February 11, 1918)

. . . The principles to be applied [in the peace settlement] are these:

First, that each part of the final settlement must be based upon the essential justice of that particular case and upon such adjustments as are most likely to bring a peace that will be permanent;

Second, that peoples and provinces are not to be bartered about from sovereignty tosovereignty as if they were mere chattels and pawns in a game, even the great game, now forever discredited, of the balance of power; but that

Third, every territorial settlement involved in this war must be made in the interest and for the benefit of the populations concerned, and not as a part of any mere adjustment or compromise of claims amongst rival states; and

Fourth, that all well-defined national aspiration shall be accorded the utmost satisfaction that can be accorded them without introducing new or perpetuating old elements of discord and antagonism that would be likely in time to break the peace of Europe and consequently of the world.

(April 6, 1918)

. . . We are ready, whenever the final reckoning is made, to be just to the German people, deal fairly with the German power, as with all others. There can be no difference between peoples in the final judgment, if it is indeed to be a righteous judgment. To propose anything but justice, even-handed and dispassionate justice, to Germany at any time, whatever the outcome of the war, would be to renounce and dishonor our own cause. For we ask nothing that we are not willing to accord.

(December 16, 1918)

. . . The war through which we have just passed has illustrated in a way which never can be forgotten the extraordinary wrongs which can be perpetrated by arbitrary and irresponsible power.

It is not possible to secure the happiness and prosperity of the world, to establish an enduring peace, unless the repetition of such wrongs is rendered impossible. This has indeed been a people's war. It has been waged against absolutism and militarism, and these enemies of liberty must from this time forth be shut out from the possibility of working their cruel will upon mankind.

(January 3, 1919)

. . . Our task at Paris is to organize the friendship of the world, to see to it that all the moral forces that make for right and justice and liberty are united and are given a vital organization to which the peoples of the world will readily and gladly respond. In other words, our task is no less colossal than this, to set up a new international psychology, to have a new atmosphere.

(January 25, 1919)

. . . We are . . . here to see that every people in the world shall choose its own masters and govern its own destinies, not as we wish, but as it wishes. We are here to see, in short, that the very foundations of this war are swept away. Those foundations were the private choice of small coteries of civil rulers and military staffs. Those foundations were the aggression of great powers upon the small. Those foundations were the holding together of empires of unwilling subjects by the duress of arms. Those foundations were the power of small bodies of men to work their will upon mankind and use them as pawns in a game. And nothing less than the emancipation of the world from these things will accomplish peace.

GEORGES CLEMENCEAU

FRENCH DEMANDS FOR SECURITY AND REVENGE

Wilson's promised new world clashed with French demands for security and revenge. Almost all the fighting on the war's western front had taken place in France; its industries and farmlands lay in ruins, and many of its young men had perished. France had been invaded by Germany in 1870 as well as in 1914, so the French believed that only by crippling Germany could they gain security. Premier Georges Clemenceau, who was called "the Tiger," dismissed Wilson's vision of a new world as mere noble sentiment divorced from reality, and he fought tenaciously to gain security for France. Clemenceau's profound hatred and mistrust of Germany are revealed in his book *Grandeur and Misery of Victory* (1930), written a decade after the Paris Peace Conference.

For the catastrophe of 1914 the Germans are responsible. Only a professional liar would deny this. . . .

What after all is this war, prepared, undertaken, and waged by the German people, who flung aside every scruple of conscience to let it loose, hoping for a peace of enslavement under the yoke of a militarism destructive of all human dignity? It is simply the continuance, the recrudescence, of those never-ending acts of violence by which the first savage tribes carried out their depredations with all the resources of barbarism. The means improve with the ages. The ends remain the same. . . .

Germany, in this matter, was unfortunate enough to allow herself (in spite of her skill at dissimulation) to be betrayed into an excess of candour by her characteristic tendency to go to extremes. *Deutschland über alles. Germany above everything!* That, and nothing less, is what she asks, and when once her demand is satisfied she will let you enjoy a peace under the yoke. Not only does she make no secret of her aim, but the intolerable arrogance of the German aristocracy, the servile good nature of the intellectual and the scholar, the gross vanity of the most competent leaders in industry, and the wide-spread influence of a violent popular poetry conspire to shatter throughout the world all the time-honoured traditions of individual, as well as international, dignity. . . .

On November 11, 1918, the fighting ceased.

It is not I who will dispute the German soldier's qualities of endurance. But he had been promised a *fresh and frolicsome war*, and for four years he had been pinned down between the anvil and the hammer. . . . Our defeat would have resulted in a relapse of human civilization into violence and bloodshed. . . .

Outrages against human civilization are in the long run defeated by their own excess, and thus I discern in the peculiar mentality of the German soldier, with his "*Deutschland über alles*," the cause of the premature exhaustion that brought him to beg for an armistice before the French soldier, who was fighting for his independence. . . .

And what is this "Germanic civilization," this monstrous explosion of the will to power, which threatens openly to do away entirely with the diversities established by many evolutions, to set in their place the implacable mastery of a race whose lordly part would be to substitute itself, by force of arms, for all national developments? We need only read [General Friedrich von] Bernhardi's famous pamphlet *Our Future*, in which it is alleged that Germany sums up within herself, as the historian Treitschke asserts, the greatest manifestation of human supremacy, and finds herself condemned, by her very greatness, either to absorb all nations in herself or to return to nothingness. . . . Ought we not all to feel menaced in our very vitals by this mad doctrine of universal Germanic supremacy over England, France, America, and every other country?. . .

What document more suitable to reveal the direction of "German culture" than the famous manifesto of the ninety-three super-intellectuals of Germany,[1] issued to justify the bloodiest and the least excusable of military aggressions against the great centres of civilization? At the moment . . . violated Belgium lay beneath the heel of the malefactor (October 1914) . . . [and German troops were] razing . . . great historical buildings to the ground [and] burning down . . . libraries. It would need a whole book to tell of the infamous treatment inflicted upon noncombatants, to reckon up those who were shot down, or put to death, or deported, or condemned to forced labour. . . .

Well, this was the hour chosen by German intellectuals to make themselves heard. Let all the nations give ear!. . .

. . . Their learning made of them merely Germans better than all others qualified to formulate, on their own account, the extravagances of Germanic arrogance. The only difference is that they speak louder than the common people, those docile automatons. The fact is that they really believe themselves to be the representatives of a privileged "*culture*" that sets them above the errors of the human race, and confers on them the prerogative of a superior power. . . .

The whole document is nothing but denials without the support of a single proof. "*It is not true* that Germany wanted the War." [Kaiser] William II had for years been "*mocked at by his adversaries of today on account of his unshakable love of peace.*" They neglect to tell us whence they got this lie. They forget that from 1871 till 1914 we received from Germany a series of war threats in the course of which Queen Victoria and also the Czar had to intervene with the *Kaiser* direct for the maintenance of peace.

I have already recalled how our German intellectuals account for the violation of the Belgian frontier:

> *It is not true that we criminally violated Belgian neutrality. It can be proved that France and England had made up their minds to violate it. It can be proved that Belgium was willing. It would have been suicide not to forestall them. . . .*

. . . And when a great chemist such as Ostwald tells us, with his colleagues, that our struggle "*against the so-called German militarism*" is really directed "*against German culture,*" we must remember that *this same savant published a history of chemistry* in which the name of [eighteenth-century French chemist Antoine] Lavoisier was not mentioned.

The "intellectuals" take their place in public opinion as the most ardent propagandists of the thesis which makes Germany the very model of the "*chosen people.*" The same Professor Ostwald had already written, "*Germany has reached a higher stage of civilization than the other peoples, and the result of the War will be an organization of Europe under German leadership.*" Professor Haeckel had demanded *the conquest of London, the division of Belgium between Germany and Holland, the annexation of North-east France, of Poland, the Baltic Provinces, the Congo, and a great part of the English colonies.* Professor Lasson went further still:

> *We are morally and intellectually superior to all men. We are peerless. So too are our organizations and our institutions. Germany is the most perfect creation known in history, and the Imperial Chancellor, Herr von Bethmann-Hollweg, is the most eminent of living men.*

Ordinary laymen who talked in this strain would be taken off to some safe asylum. Coming from duly hallmarked professors, such statements explain all German warfare by alleging that Germany's destiny is universal domination, and that for this very reason she is bound either to disappear altogether or to exercise violence on all nations with a view to their own betterment. . . .

May I further recall, since we have to emphasize the point, that on September 17, 1914, Erzberger, the well-known German statesman, an eminent member of the Catholic Party, wrote to the Minister of War, General von Falkenhayn, "*We must not worry about committing an offence against the rights of nations nor about violating the laws of humanity. Such feelings today are of secondary importance*"? A month

[1]Shortly after the outbreak of war, ninety-three leading German scholars and scientists addressed a letter to the world, defending Germany's actions.

later, on October 21, 1914, he wrote in *Der Tag*, "*If a way was found of entirely wiping out the whole of London it would be more humane to employ it* than to allow the blood of a single German soldier to be shed on the battlefield!". . .

. . . General von Bernhardi himself, the best pupil, as I have already said, of the historian Treitschke, whose ideas are law in Germany, has just preached the doctrine of "World power or Downfall" at us. So there is nothing left for other nations, as a way of salvation, but to be conquered by Germany. . . .

I have sometimes penetrated into the sacred cave of the Germanic cult, which is, as every one knows, the *Bierhaus* [beer hall]. A great aisle of massive humanity where there accumulate, amid the fumes of tobacco and beer, the popular rumblings of a nationalism upheld by the sonorous brasses blaring to the heavens the supreme voice of Germany, "*Deutschland über alles!*" Men, women, and children, all petrified in reverence before the divine stoneware pot, brows furrowed with irrepressible power, eyes lost in a dream of infinity, mouths twisted by the intensity of will-power, drink in long draughts the celestial hope of vague expectations. These only remain to be realized presently when the chief marked out by Destiny shall have given the word. There you have the ultimate framework of an old but childish race.

ERICH MARIA REMARQUE

THE LOST GENERATION

In Erich Maria Remarque's *All Quiet on the Western Front*, a wounded German soldier reflects on the war and his future. He sees himself as part of a lost generation.
(See also page 313.)

Gradually a few of us are allowed to get up. And I am given crutches to hobble around on. But I do not make much use of them; I cannot bear Albert's gaze as I move about the room. His eyes always follow me with such a strange look. So I sometimes escape to the corridor;—there I can move about more freely.

On the next floor below are the abdominal and spine cases, head wounds and double amputations. On the right side of the wing are the jaw wounds, gas cases, nose, ear, and neck wounds. On the left the blind and the lung wounds, pelvis wounds, wounds in the joints, wounds in the kidneys, wounds in the testicles, wounds in the intestines. Here a man realizes for the first time in how many places a man can get hit.

Two fellows die of tetanus. Their skin turns pale, their limbs stiffen, at last only their eyes live—stubbornly. Many of the wounded have their shattered limbs hanging free in the air from a gallows; underneath the wound a basin is placed into which drips the pus. Every two or three hours the vessel is emptied. Other men lie in stretching bandages with heavy weights hanging from the end of the bed. I see intestine wounds that are constantly full of excreta. The surgeon's clerk shows me X-ray photographs of completely smashed hip-bones, knees, and shoulders.

A man cannot realize that above such shattered bodies there are still human faces in which life goes its daily round. And this is only one hospital, one single station; there are hundreds of thousands in Germany, hundreds of thousands in France, hundreds of thousands in Russia. How senseless is everything that can ever be written, done, or thought, when such things are possible. It must be all lies and of no account when the culture of a thousand years could not prevent this stream of blood being poured out, these torture-chambers in their hundreds of thousands. A hospital alone shows what war is.

I am young, I am twenty years old; yet I know nothing of life but despair, death, fear, and fatuous superficiality cast over an abyss of sorrow. I see how peoples are set against one another, and in silence, unknowingly, foolishly, obediently, innocently slay one another. I see that the keenest brains of the world invent weapons and words to make it yet more refined and enduring. And all men of my age, here and over there, throughout the whole world see these things; all my generation is experiencing these things with me. What would our fathers do if we suddenly stood up and came before them and proffered our account? What do they expect of us if a time ever comes when the war is over? Through the years our business has been killing;—it was our first calling in life. Our knowledge of life is limited to death. What will happen afterwards? And what shall come out of us?

JOSEPH STALIN

THE HARD LINE

Firmly entrenched in power by 1929, Stalin started a second revolution (called the Stalin revolution), mobilizing at top speed the economic potential of the country, however limited the human and material resources available, whatever the obstacles, and whatever the human price. The alternative, he was sure, was foreign domination that would totally destroy his country's independence. In this spirit, he addressed a gathering of industrial managers in 1931, talking to them not in Marxist-Leninist jargon, but in terms of hard-line Russian nationalism.

It is sometimes asked whether it is not possible to slow down the tempo a bit, to put a check on the movement. No, comrades, it is not possible! The tempo must not be reduced! On the contrary, we must increase it as much as is within our powers and possibilities. This is dictated to us by our obligations to the workers and peasants of the U.S.S.R. This is dictated to us by our obligations to the working class of the whole world.

To slacken the tempo would mean falling behind. And those who fall behind get beaten. But we do not want to be beaten. No, we refuse to be beaten! One feature of the history of old Russia was the continual beatings she suffered for falling behind, for her backwardness. She was beaten by the Mongol Khans. She was beaten by the Turkish beys. She was beaten by the Swedish feudal lords. She was beaten by the Polish and Lithuanian gentry. She was beaten by the British and French capitalists. She was beaten by the Japanese barons. All beat her—for her backwardness: for military backwardness, for cultural backwardness, for political backwardness, for industrial backwardness, for agricultural backwardness. She was beaten because to do so was profitable and could be done with impunity. Do you remember the words of the pre-revolutionary poet [Nikolai Nekrassov]: "You are poor and abundant, mighty and impotent, Mother Russia." These words of the old poet were well learned by those gentlemen. They beat her, saying: "You are abundant," so one can enrich oneself at your expense. They beat her, saying: "You are poor and impotent," so you can be beaten and plundered with impunity. Such is the law of the exploiters—to beat the backward and the weak. It is the jungle law of capitalism. You are backward, you are weak—therefore you are wrong; hence, you can be beaten and enslaved. You are mighty—therefore you are right; hence, we must be wary of you.

That is why we must no longer lag behind.

In the past we had no fatherland, nor could we have one. But now that we have overthrown capitalism and power is in the hands of the working class, we have a fatherland, and we will defend its independence. Do you want our socialist fatherland to be beaten and to lose its independence? If you do not want this you must put an end to its backwardness in the shortest possible time and develop genuine Bolshevik tempo in building up its socialist system of economy. There is no other way. That is why Lenin said during the October Revolution: "Either perish, or overtake and outstrip the advanced capitalist countries."

We are fifty or a hundred years behind the advanced countries. We must make good this distance in ten years. Either we do it, or they crush us.

This is what our obligations to the workers and peasants of the U.S.S.R. dictate to us.

JOSEPH STALIN

LIQUIDATION OF THE KULAKS

Collectivization, not surprisingly, met with fierce resistance, especially from the more successful peasants called kulaks, who were averse to surrendering their private plots and their freedom in running their households. Their resistance therefore had to be broken, and the Communist party fomented a rural class struggle, seeking help from the poorer peasants. Sometimes, however, even the poorest peasants sided with the local kulaks. Under these conditions, Stalin did not shrink from unleashing violence in the countryside aimed at the "liquidation of the kulaks as a class." For Stalin the collectivization drive meant an all-out war on what was for him the citadel of backwardness: the peasant tradition and rebelliousness so prominent under the tsars. The following reading—Stalin's address to the Conference of Marxist Students of the Agrarian Question, December 1929—conveys his intentions. It is a good example of Stalin's rhetoric; he drives home his point by continually restating his argument.

The characteristic feature of our work during the past year is: (a) that we, the party and the Soviet government, have developed an offensive on the whole front against the capitalist elements in the countryside; and (b) that this offensive, as you know, has brought about and is bringing about very palpable, *positive* results.

What does this mean? It means that we have passed from the policy of *restricting* the exploiting proclivities of the kulaks to the policy of *eliminating* the kulaks as a class. This means that we have made, and are still making, one of the most decisive turns in our whole policy.

. . . Could we have undertaken such an offensive against the kulaks five years or three years ago? Could we then have counted on success in such an offensive? No, we could not. That would have been the most dangerous adventurism! That would have been playing a very dangerous game at offensive. We would certainly have come to grief and, once we had come to grief, we would have strengthened the position of the kulaks. Why? Because we did not yet have strongholds in the rural districts in the shape of a wide network of state farms and collective farms upon which to rely in a determined offensive against the kulaks. Because at that time we were not yet able to *substitute* for the capitalist production of the kulaks socialist production in the shape of the collective farms and state farms. . . .

But today? What is the position? Today, we have an adequate material base which enables us to strike at the kulaks, to break their resistance, to eliminate them as a class, and to *substitute* for their output the output of the collective farms and state farms. . . .

Now, as you see, we have the material base which enables us to *substitute* for kulak output the output of the collective farms and state farms. That is why our offensive against the kulaks is now meeting with undeniable success. That is how the offensive against the kulaks must be carried on, if we mean a real offensive and not futile declamations against the kulaks.

That is why we have recently passed from the policy of *restricting* the exploiting *proclivities* of the kulaks to the policy of *eliminating the kulaks as a class. . . .* Now we are able to carry on a determined offensive against the kulaks, to break their resistance, to eliminate them as a class and substitute for their output the output of the collective farms and state farms. Now, the kulaks are being expropriated by the masses of poor and middle peasants themselves, by the masses who are putting solid collectivization into practice. Now the expropriation of the kulaks in the regions of solid collectivization is no longer just an administrative measure. Now, the expropriation of the kulaks is an integral part of the formation and development of the collective farms. . . .

. . . [Should] the kulak . . . be permitted to join the collective farms[?] Of course not, for he is a sworn enemy of the collective farm movement. Clear, one would think.

LEV KOPELEV

TERROR IN THE COUNTRYSIDE

The liquidation of the kulaks began in late 1929, extending through the length and breadth of the country during the winter. The confiscation of kulak property, the deportations, and the killing rose to a brutal climax in the following spring and continued for another two years, by which time the bulk of the private farms had been eliminated. By some estimates, almost five million people were liquidated. Some were driven from their huts, deprived of all possessions, and left destitute in the dead of winter; the men were sent to forced labor and their families left abandoned. Others killed themselves or were killed outright, sometimes in pitched battles involving a whole village—men, women, and children.

The upheaval destroyed agricultural production in these years; farm animals died or were killed in huge numbers; fields lay barren. In 1932 and 1933, famine stalked the south and southeast, killing additional millions. The vast tragedy caused by collectivization did not deter Stalin from pursuing his goals: the establishment of state farms run like factories and the subordination of the rebellious and willful peasantry to state authority.

Here a militant participant in the collectivization drive, Lev Kopelev, recalls some of his experiences. These passages are from his memoirs published in 1978. Kopelev (1912–1997), raised in a Ukrainian middle-class Jewish family, evolved from a youthful Stalinist into a tolerant, gentle person in later years. After trying to keep Russian soldiers from raping and pillaging in German territory in 1945, he was given a ten-year sentence for antistate crimes. Subsequently out of favor because of his literary protests against the inhumanities of the Soviet system, he was exiled from the Soviet Union to West Germany in 1980.

The grain front! Stalin said the struggle for grain was the struggle for socialism. I was convinced that we were warriors on an invisible front, fighting against kulak sabotage for the grain which was needed by the country, by the five-year plan. Above all, for the grain, but also for the souls of these peasants who were mired in unconscientiousness, in ignorance, who succumbed to enemy agitation, who did not understand the great truth of communism. . . .

The highest measure of coercion on the hard-core holdouts was "undisputed confiscation."

A team consisting of several young kolkhozniks [collective farmers] and members of the village soviet . . . would search the hut, barn, yard, and take away all the stores of seed, lead away the cow, the horse, the pigs.

In some cases they would be merciful and leave some potatoes, peas, corn for feeding the family. But the stricter ones would make a clean sweep. They would take not only the food and livestock, but also "all valuables and surpluses of clothing," including icons in their frames, samovars, painted carpets and even metal kitchen utensils which might be silver. And any money they found stashed away. Special instructions ordered the removal of gold, silver and currency. . . .

Several times Volodya and I were present at such plundering raids. We even took part: we were entrusted to draw up inventories of the confiscated goods. . . . The women howled hysterically, clinging to the bags.

"Oy, that's the last thing we have! That was for the children's kasha [cereal]! Honest to God, the children will starve!"

They wailed, falling on their trunks:

"Oy, that's a keepsake from my dead mama! People, come to my aid, this is my trousseau, never e'en put on!"

I heard the children echoing them with screams, choking, coughing with screams. And I saw the looks of the men: frightened, pleading, hateful, dully impassive, extinguished with despair or flaring up with half-mad, daring ferocity.

"Take it. Take it away. Take everything away. There's still a pot of borscht on the stove. It's plain, got no meat. But still it's got beets, taters 'n' cabbage. And it's salted! Better take it, comrade citizens! Here, hang on, I'll take off my shoes. They're patched and re-patched, but maybe they'll have some use for the proletariat, for our dear Soviet power."

It was excruciating to see and hear all this. And even worse to take part in it. . . . And I persuaded myself, explained to myself. I mustn't give in to debilitating pity. We were realizing historical necessity. We were performing our revolutionary duty. We were obtaining grain for the socialist fatherland. For the five-year plan. . . .

I have always remembered the winter of the last grain collections, the weeks of the great famine. And I have always told about it. But I did not begin to write it down until many years later. . . .

How could all this have happened?

Who was guilty of the famine which destroyed millions of lives?

How could I have participated in it?. . .

We were raised as the fanatical [believers] of a new creed, the only true *religion* of scientific socialism. The party became our church militant, bequeathing to all mankind eternal salvation, eternal peace and the bliss of an earthly paradise. It victoriously surmounted all other churches, schisms and heresies. The works of Marx, Engels and Lenin were accepted as holy writ, and Stalin was the infallible high priest.

. . . Stalin was the most perspicacious, the most wise (at that time they hadn't yet started calling him "great" and "brilliant"). He said: "The struggle for grain is the struggle for socialism." And we believed him unconditionally. And later we believed that unconditional collectivization was unavoidable if we were to overcome the capriciousness and uncertainty of the market and the backwardness of individual farming, to guarantee a steady supply of grain, milk and meat to the cities. And also if we were to reeducate millions of peasants, those petty landowners and hence potential bourgeoisie, potential kulaks, to transform them into laborers with a social conscience, to liberate them from "the idiocy of country life," from ignorance and prejudice, and to accustom them to culture, to all the boons of socialism. . . .

In the following passage Kopelev reflects, even more searchingly, on his own motivation and state of mind as a participant in Stalin's collectivization drive.

With the rest of my generation I firmly believed that the ends justified the means. Our great goal was the universal triumph of Communism, and for the sake of that goal everything was permissible—to lie, to steal, to destroy hundreds of thousands and even millions of people, all those who were hindering our work or could hinder it, everyone who stood in the way. And to hesitate or doubt about all this was to give in to "intellectual squeamishness" and "stupid liberalism," the attributes of people who "could not see the forest for the trees."

That was how I had reasoned, and everyone like me, even when I did have my doubts, when I saw what "total collectivization" meant—how . . . mercilessly they stripped the peasants in the winter of 1932–33. I took part in this myself, scouring the countryside, searching for hidden grain, testing the earth with an iron rod for loose spots that might lead to buried grain. With the others, I emptied out the old folks' storage chests, stopping my ears to the children's crying and the women's wails. For I was convinced that I was accomplishing the great and necessary transformation of the countryside; that in the days to come the people who lived there would be better off for it; that their distress and suffering were a result of their own ignorance or the machinations of the class enemy; that those who sent me—and I myself—knew better than the peasants how they should live, what they should sow and when they should plow.

In the terrible spring of 1933 I saw people dying from hunger. I saw women and children with distended bellies, turning blue, still breathing but with vacant, lifeless eyes. And corpses—corpses in ragged sheepskin coats and cheap felt boots; corpses in peasant huts, in the melting snow of old Vologda, under the bridges of Kharkov. . . . I saw all this and did not go out of my mind or commit suicide. Nor did I curse those who had sent me to take away the peasants' grain in the winter, and in the spring to persuade the barely walking, skeleton-thin or sickly-swollen people to go into the fields in order to "fulfill the Bolshevik sowing plan in shock-worker style."

Nor did I lose my faith. As before, I believed because I wanted to believe. Thus from time immemorial men have believed when possessed by a desire to serve powers and values above and beyond humanity: gods, emperors, states; ideals of virtue, freedom, nation, race, class, party. . . .

Any single-minded attempt to realize these ideals exacts its toll of human sacrifice. In the name of the noblest visions promising eternal happiness to their descendants, such men bring merciless ruin on their contemporaries. Bestowing paradise on the dead, they maim and destroy the living. They become unprincipled liars and unrelenting executioners, all the while seeing themselves as virtuous and honorable militants—convinced that if they are forced into villainy, it is for the sake of future good, and that if they have to lie, it is in the name of eternal truths.

. . . That was how we thought and acted—we, the fanatical disciples of the all-saving ideals of Communism. When we saw the base and cruel acts that were committed in the name of our exalted notions of good, and when we ourselves took part in those actions, what we feared most was to lose our heads, fall into doubt or heresy and forfeit our unbounded faith. . . . The concepts of conscience, honor, humaneness we dismissed as idealistic prejudices, "intellectual" or "bourgeois," and hence, perverse.

MIRON DOLOT

EXECUTION BY HUNGER

Miron Dolot witnessed the horrors of state-induced famine in Ukraine and later emigrated to the West. In *Execution by Hunger: The Hidden Holocaust* (1985), excerpted below, Dolot recounts his experiences.

The year 1932 witnessed the last battle of collectivization: the battle for bread, or to be more specific, for the crop of 1932. On the one side was the Communist government; on the other, the starving farmers. The government forces resorted to any means in getting as many agricultural products from the countryside as possible, without regard to the consequences. The farmers, already on the verge of starvation, desperately tried to keep what food they had left, and, in spite of government efforts to the contrary, tried to stay alive. . . .

The long and cold winter of 1931–1932 was slowly giving way to spring. . . .

Around this time the plight of the villagers became desperate. This was the memorable spring of 1932 when the famine broke out, and the first deaths from hunger began to occur. I remember the endless procession of beggars on roads and paths, going from house to house. They were in different stages of starvation, dirty and ragged. With outstretched hands, they begged for food, any food: a potato, a beet, or at least a kernel of corn. Those were the first victims of starvation: destitute men and women; poor widows and orphaned children who had no chance of surviving the terrible ordeal.

Some starving farmers still tried to earn their food by doing chores in or outside the village. One could see these sullen, emaciated men walking from house to house with an ax, or a shovel, in search of work. Perhaps someone might hire them to dig up the garden, or chop some firewood. They would do it for a couple of potatoes. But not many of us had a couple of potatoes to spare.

Crowds of starving wretches could be seen scattered all over the potato fields. They were looking for potatoes left over from last year's harvest. No matter what shape the potatoes were in, whether frozen or rotten, they were still edible. Others were roaming the forest in search of food; the riverbanks were crowded too; there was much new greenery around: young shoots of reed or other river plants. One might catch something, anything, in the water to eat.

But the majority of those who looked for help would go to the cities as they used to do before. it was always easier to find some work there, either gardening, cleaning backyards, or sweeping streets. But now, times had changed. It was illegal to hire farmers for any work. The purpose of the prohibition was twofold: it was done not only to stop the flow of labor from the collective farms, but also, and primarily, to prevent the farmers from receiving food rations in the cities. . . .

By this time our village was in economic ruin. Poverty was universal. We had never been rich, it is true, but economically, we had always been completely self-sufficient and had never gone hungry for so long. now starving, we were facing the spring of 1932 with great anxiety for there was no hope of relief from the outside. Deaths from starvation became daily occurrences. There was always some burial in the village cemetery. One could see strange funeral processions: children pulling homemade handwagons with the bodies of their dead parents in them or the parents carting the bodies of their children. There were no coffins; no burial ceremonies performed by priests. The bodies of the starved were just deposited in a large common grave, one upon the other; that was all there was to it. . . .

Looking back to those events now, it seems to me that I lived in some kind of a wicked fantasy world. All the events which I witnessed and experienced then and which I am now describing, seem unreal to me because of their cruelty and unspeakable horror. It is simply too difficult to associate all those happenings with real life in a normal human society. . . .

The battle for the Ukrainian wheat crop of 1932 started almost two months before the harvest.

At the end of May, some strangers appeared in our village, and little by little, we began finding out who they were. The Party had mobilized 112,000 of its most active and reliable members in order to organize a speedy harvest of the new crop, and to secure its swift and smooth requisitioning and final delivery to the State. Soon these members became known to us as the Hundred Thousanders, or just Thousanders. There were nine of them in our village. . . . In no time at all, these new Thousanders took over our entire village like tyrants, imposing their wills and their demands upon us. . . .

Comrade Thousander's announcement that in 1932 we had to deliver the same quota of grain as in 1931 was a hard blow to us. We simply could not fulfill his demands. The 1932 grain quota was not based on the actual amount of grain sown, cultivated, and har-vested; it was based upon an unrealistic government plan. . . .

Faced with starvation, the villagers tried everything possible to save themselves and their families. Some of them started eating dogs and cats. Others went hunting for birds: crows, magpies, swallows, sparrows, storks, and even nightingales. one could see starving villagers searching in the bushes along the river for birds' nests or looking for crabs and other small crustaceans in the water. Even their hard shells, though not edible, were cooked and the broth consumed as nourishment. One could see crowds of famished villagers combing the woods in search of roots or mushrooms and berries. Some tried to catch small forest animals.

Driven by hunger, people ate everything and anything: even food that had already rotted—potatoes, beets, and other root vegetables that pigs normally refused to eat. They even ate weeds, the leaves and bark of trees, insects, frogs, and snails. Nor did they shy away from eating the meat of diseased horses and cattle. Often that meat was already decaying and those who ate it died of food poisoning. . . .

One morning in late January 1933, while it was still dark, Mother and I set out along the main street through the center of the village for the county town. We followed the street to the main road which led straight into the town. . . .

Soon, however, as we slowly made our way through the snow toward the village center, graphic evidence of starvation became visible. We noticed a black object which, from afar, looked like a snow-covered tree stump. As we came near, however, we saw that it was the body of a dead man. Frozen limbs protruding from under the snow gave the body the appearance of some grotesque creature. I bent down and cleared the snow off the face. It was Ulas, our elderly neighbor whom we had last seen about a month ago.

A few steps further, we saw another frozen body. it was the corpse of a woman. As I brushed away the snow, horror made my blood turn cold: under her ragged coat, clutched tightly to her bosom with her stiff hands, was the frozen little body of her baby.

We finally left our village behind and stepped onto the open road which led to the county seat. However, another ghostly panorama now opened in front of us. Everywhere we looked dead and frozen bodies lay by the sides of the road. To our right were bodies of those villagers who apparently had tried to reach the town in search of work and food. Weakened by starvation, they were unable to make it and ended up lying or falling down by the roadside, never to rise again. The gentle snow mercifully covered their bodies with its white blanket.

One could easily imagine the fate of those people whose bodies were lying to our left. They most probably were returning from the county town, without having accomplished anything. They had tramped many kilometers in vain, only to be refused a job and a chance to stay alive. They were returning home empty-handed. Death caught up with them as they trudged homeward, resigned to dying in their village.

The wide open kolhosp[1] fields, stretching for kilometers on both sides of the main road, looked like a battlefield after a great war. Littering the fields were the bodies of the starving farmers who had been combing the potato fields over and over again in the hope of finding at least a fragment of a potato that might have been overlooked or left over from the last harvest. They died where they collapsed in

[1] 1The Ukrainian term for collective farm.

their endless search for food. Some of those frozen corpses must have been lying out there for months. Nobody seemed to be in a hurry to cart them away and bury them. . . .

. . . Dmytro had never returned home after he had been taken to the county center.[2] His young wife Solomia was left alone with their daughter. She had gone to work in the collective farm, taking her little child with her. As the wife of a banished man, she too was considered an "enemy of the people," and her child was refused admission to the nursery. Later, Solomia was expelled from the collective farm, and thus forced to seek a job in the city. That was impossible, however, because she could not show a certificate of release from the collective farm. She found herself trapped in the circle of the Communist death ring. She had to return to her village.

When winter came, Solomia went from house to house, willing to work for just a piece of bread. She was too proud to beg. People were sympathetic and helped her as much as they could. However, as the famine worsened, and the villagers were no longer able to help her, she was not seen on her rounds any more.

We found the front door of Solomia's house open, but the entrance was blocked with snowdrifts, and it was hard to get inside. When we finally reached the living room, we saw a pitiful sight: Solomia was hanging from the ceiling in the middle of the room. She was dressed in her Ukrainian national costume, and at her breast hung a large cross. It was obvious that she had made preparations before committing suicide. Her hair was combed neatly in two braids hanging over her shoulders.

Frightened, we ran to fetch Mother. We helped her take down Solomia's frozen body, and laid it on a bench, and covered it with a handmade blanket. It was only after we finished doing this that we noticed the dead body of her little daughter. The child was lying in a wooden tub in the corner under the icons, clean and dressed in her best clothes. Her little hands were folded across her chest.

On the table was a note:

> *Dear Neighbors:*
>
> *Please bury our bodies properly. I have to leave you, dear neighbors. I can bear this life no longer. There is no food in the house, and there is no sense in living without my little daughter who starved to death, or my husband. If you ever see Dmytro, tell him about us. He will understand our plight, and he will forgive me. Please tell him that I died peacefully, thinking about him and our dear daughter.*
>
> *I love you, my dear neighbors, and I wish with all my heart that you somehow recover from this disaster. Forgive me for troubling you. Thank you for everything you have done for me.*
>
> *Solomia.*

After reading the note, we stood there for a while, motionless and forlorn. Our mother tried to suppress the sound of her weeping, pressing the corner of her head scarf to her lips. Mykola gazed at the corpses in disbelief.

In my imagination I was recreating the agony of their dying: the child's hunger cries, and then the death convulsions of its exhausted little body.

How great must have been the sufferings of the mother. She had to listen helplessly to the pleas of her child for food, while she herself was near starvation. She must have felt great relief, I thought, when she saw her little daughter breathing for the last time. Then, in my imagination, I saw the mother attending to her lifeless child: dressing her in the best and cleanest clothing she had, praying on her knees near the body, and finally kissing her for the last time before her own suicide. . . .

[2]Dmytro, a neighbor and distant relative of the author, had been jailed after punching a collective farm official who accused him of sabotage.

Toward the end of March, the famine struck us with full force. Life in the village had sunk to its lowest level, an almost animallike struggle for survival of the fittest.

The village ceased to exist as a coherent community. The inhabitants who still managed to stay alive shut themselves within the walls of their houses. people became too weak even to step outside their doors. Each house became an entity in itself. Visits became a rarity. All doors were bolted and barred against any possible intruders. Even between immediate neighbors, there was little, if any, communication, and people ceased caring about one another. In fact, they avoided each other. Friends and even relatives became strangers. Mothers abandoned their children, and brother turned away from brother. . . .

One must consider the inexorable pressure of hunger under which a person can completely become bereft of his or her senses and sink to an absolute animallike level. That happened to many of our villagers. The more resistant ones who kept on living with minimal or no food at all for some time, felt no more of the initial hunger pangs. They either lapsed into comas, or existed in a semicomatose, lethargic stupor. But some reacted differently. They became like madmen. They lost all traces of compassion, honor, and morality. They suffered from hallucinations of food, of something to bite into and chew, to satisfy the gnawing pains of their empty stomachs. Intolerable cravings assailed them; they were ready to sink their teeth into anything, even into their own hands and arms, or into the flesh of others.

The first rumors of actual cannibalism were related to the mysterious and sudden disappearances of people in the village. . . .

As the cases of missing persons grew in number, an arrest was made which shook us to our souls. A woman was taken into custody, charged with killing her two children.

Another woman was found dead, her neck contorted in a crudely made noose. The neighbors who discovered the tragedy also found the reason for it. The flesh of the woman's three-year-old daughter was found in the oven.

LEV RAZGON

TRUE STORIES

"Corrective labor" was part of Stalin's efforts to terrorize the peoples of the Soviet Union into compliance with his plan to modernize the country's economy and society. All those accused of disloyalty to the party and not killed outright ended up in one of the *gulags. Gulag* is the Russian term for the Soviet forced-labor camps, scattered, like islands in an archipelago, over the entire Soviet Union. The inhabitants of that archipelago were the *zeks*, as the political prisoners were called. Their labor served a double purpose. It was designed as punishment for their alleged crimes and as a means of obtaining vital raw materials—including lumber and minerals—from areas too inhospitable for, or outright hostile to, regular labor. Forced labor also built the canal linking the Leningrad area with the White Sea in the far north.

In 1988, Lev Razgon, a survivor of Stalin's camps, published an account of his experiences, which appeared in English under the title *True Stories* in 1997. Razgon was a journalist who married the daughter of a high-ranking member of the Soviet secret police. Gaining access to the Soviet elite, in 1934 he attended the Seventeenth Party Congress. In 1937, his father-in-law was arrested for "counter-revolutionary" activities, along with many family friends; the following year the police came for Razgon and his wife. She perished in a transit prison en route to a northern camp, and Razgon spent the next seven years in a labor camp. Released in 1945, he was confined to various provincial towns, but in 1949 was rearrested and returned to the camps. Finally, he was released again in 1956 after Stalin's death.

Over the years Razgon began to write down his prison experiences for his desk drawer, with the specific intent of preserving the memory of fellow prisoners who did not survive. As the Soviet Union began to crumble, Razgon was able to publish his stories. The following extracts from *True Stories* reveal the brutality and irrationality of the Soviet prison system under Stalin. In the first selection, Razgon reproduces a discussion he had with a former prison guard, whom he met by chance in a hospital ward in 1977. The guard described to Razgon his role as an executioner of political prisoners.

THE ROUTINE OF EXECUTION

"It was like this. In the morning we'd hand everything over to the new shift and go into the guardhouse. We'd collect our weapons, and then and there they'd give us each a shot glass of vodka. After that we'd take the list and go round with the senior warder to pick them up from the cells and take them out to the truck."

"What kind of truck?"

"A closed van. Six of them and four of us in each one."

"How many trucks would leave at the same time?"

"Three or four."

"Did they know where they were going? Did someone read them their death sentence before, or what?"

"No, no sentences were announced. No one even spoke, just, 'Come out, then straight ahead, into the van—fast!'"

"Were they in handcuffs?"

"No, we didn't have any."

"How did they behave, once they were in the van?"

"The men, well, they kept quiet. But the women would start crying, they'd say: 'What are you doing, we're not guilty of anything, comrades, what are you doing?' and things like that."

"They used to take men and women together?"

"No, always separately."

"Were the women young? Were there a lot of them?"

"Not so many, about two vanloads a week. No very young ones but there were some about twenty-five or thirty. Most were older, and some even elderly."

"Did you drive them far?"

"Twelve kilometers or so, to the hill. The Distant Hill, it was called. There were hills all around and that's where we unloaded them."

"So you would unload them, and then tell them their sentence?"

"What was there to tell them?! No, we yelled, 'Out! Stand still!' They scrambled down and there was already a trench dug in front of them. They clambered down, clung together and right away we got to work. . . ."

"They didn't make any noise?"

"Some didn't, others began shouting, 'We're Communists, we are being wrongly executed,' that type of thing. But the women would only cry and cling to each other. So we just got on with it. . . ."

"Did you have a doctor with you?"

"What for? We would shoot them, and those still wriggling got another bullet and then we were off back to the van. The work team from the Dalag camps was already nearby, waiting."

"What work team was that?"

"There was a team of criminal inmates from Dalag who lived in a separate compound. They were the trusties[1] at Bikin and they also had to dig and fill in the pits. As soon as we left they would fill in that pit and dig a new one for the next day. When they finished their work, they went back to the compound. They got time off their sentence for it and were well fed. It was easy work, not like felling timber."

"And what about you?"

"We would arrive back at the camp, hand in our weapons at the guardhouse and then we could have as much to drink as we wanted. The others used to lap it up—it didn't cost them a kopeck. I always had my shot, went off to the canteen for a hot meal, and then back to sleep in the barracks."

"And did you sleep well? Didn't you feel bad or anything?"

"Why should I?"

"Well, that you had just killed other people. Didn't you feel sorry for them?"

"No, not at all. I didn't give it a thought. No, I slept well and then I'd go for a walk outside the camp. There's some beautiful places around there. Boring, though, with no women."

"Were any of you married?"

"No, they didn't take married men. Of course, the bosses made out all right. There were some real lookers on the Dalag work team! Your head would spin! Cooks, dishwashers, floor cleaners—the bosses had them all. We went without. It was better not to even think about it . . . ."

"Grigory Ivanovich, did you know that the people you were shooting were not guilty at all, that they hadn't done anything wrong?"

"Well, we didn't think about that then. Later, yes. We were summoned to the procurators [officials] and they asked us questions. They explained that those had been innocent people. There had been mistakes, they said, and—what was the word?—excesses. But they told us that it was nothing to do with us, we were not guilty of anything."

"Well, I understand, then you were under orders and you shot people. But when you learned that you had been killing men and women who were not guilty at all, didn't your conscience begin to bother you?"

"Conscience? No, Naum'ich, it didn't bother me. I never think about all that now, and when I do remember something. . . . no, nothing at all, as if nothing had happened. You know, I've become so soft-hearted that one look at an old man suffering today and I feel so much pity that I even cry sometimes. But those ones, no, I'm not sorry for them. Not at all, it's just like they never existed. . . ."

The "special operation" at Bikin existed for almost three years. Well, two and a half, to be more exact. It also probably had its holidays and weekends—perhaps no one was shot on Sundays, May Day, Revolution Day and the Day of the Soviet Constitution. Even so, that means that it functioned for a total of

[1] Trusties were convicts regarded as trustworthy, who were given special duties and privileges

770 days. Every morning on each of those days four trucks set out from Bikin compound for the Distant Hill. Six people in each truck, a total of 24. It took 25–30 minutes for them to reach the waiting pit. The "special operation" thus disposed of 15,000 to 18,000 people during its existence. Yet it was of a standard design, just like any transit camp. The well-tried, well-planned machinery operated without interruption, functioning regularly and efficiently, filling the ready-made pits with bodies—in the hills of the Far East, in the Siberian forests, and in the glades of the Tambov woods or the Meshchera nature reserve. They existed everywhere, yet nothing remains of them now. There are no terrible museums as there are today at Auschwitz, or at Mauthausen in Austria. There are no solemn and funereal memorials like those that testify to the Nazi atrocities at Khatyn[2]. . . . or Lidice.[3] Thousands of unnamed graves, in which there lie mingled the bones of hundreds of thousands of victims, have now been overgrown by bushes, thick luxuriant grass and young new forest. Not exactly the same as the Germans, it must be admitted. The men and women were buried separately here. Our regime made sure that even at that point no moral laxity might occur.

And the murderers? They are still alive.

. . . There were a great many, of course, who took part in these shootings. There were yet more, however, who never made the regular journey to the Distant Hill or the other killing grounds. Only in bourgeois society are the procurator and others obliged to attend an execution. Under our regime, thank God, that was not necessary. There were many, many more involved in these murders than those who simply pulled the trigger. For them a university degree, often in the "humanities," was more common than the rudimentary education of the Niyazovs [the former guard Razgon questioned]. They drafted the instructions and decisions; they signed beneath the words "agreed," "confirmed," "to be sentenced to . . ." Today they are all retired and most of them receive large individual pensions. They sit in the squares and enjoy watching the children play. They go to concerts and are moved by the music. We meet them when we attend a meeting, visit friends, or find ourselves sitting at the same table, celebrating with our common acquaintances. They are alive, and there are many of them.

COLLECTIVE GUILT

In the most general terms, paragraph 17 [of the Soviet criminal code] said that each member of a criminal group (and membership in that group was expressed by knowledge of its existence and failure to report it) was responsible not only for his own individual criminal deeds but also for the deeds of the criminal group as a whole and for each of its individual members, taken separately. It did not matter that the individual in question might not know the other members of the group, might be unaware what they were up to, and might not have any idea at all what the group he belonged to was doing. The purpose of the "doctrine of complicity" was to alleviate the exhausting labors of the interrogators. Undoubtedly, however, it also lightened the burden of those under investigation. The techniques of cross-examination became far simpler. Several dozen people were linked together in a group and then one of them, the weakest, was beaten almost to death in order to obtain confessions of espionage, sabotage, subversion and, of course, attempts on the life of "one of the leaders of the Party and the government." The others could be more gently treated, only requiring beating until they admitted they knew the individual who had given a "complete and full confession." Then the same crimes, in accordance with paragraph 17, were automatically attributed to them as well. What this sounded like during a court hearing I can describe from the words of a man I came to know in the camps.

Yefim Shatalov was a very high-ranking manager and for years he headed the State Cement Administration. Why they needed to send him to prison, God only knows! He had no political interests

[2]In 1942 German forces massacred all the inhabitants of the Belorussian village of Khatyn. (Not to be confused with Katyn . . . where in 1940 23,500 Polish officers were murdered by the [Soviet] NKVD.)

[3]After Czech resistance fighters assassinated Richard Heydrich, Chief of the Security Police, the Germans took savage revenge on the little Czech village of Lidice. They massacred all the men and deported the women and children to concentration camps (some children with suitable "Aryan features" were sent to live with German families and to be reared as Germans). The Nazis then burned, dynamited, and levelled the village.

or involvements and did not wish to have any, since he was always prepared to serve his immediate superior faithfully and truthfully, and was unquestionably loyal to his ultimate chief, Comrade Stalin. Furthermore, he was incredibly circumspect and every step he took was protected by an entire system of safety measures. When he was baldly accused of sabotage he conducted himself so aggressively in court that the judge, in panic, deferred the hearing of his case. Some time after, Shatalov was presented with a new charge sheet and within an hour he was summoned to appear before a new sitting of the Military Tribunal. The chairman now was Ulrich himself. For the defendant Vasya Ulrich was an old, dear and kind acquaintance. For many years they had always sat at the same table at the Party elite's sanatorium, The Pines; they went for walks together, shared a drink or two, and exchanged men's jokes. Evidently the chairman was observing the old principles that justice must be rapid, fair and clement in his conduct of this hearing. What follows includes almost everything that was said, as recalled by Yefim Shatalov.

Ulrich (in a business-like, quiet, and jaded voice): Defendant! you have read the charge sheet? Do you recognize your guilt?

Shatalov (with all the force of his love and loyalty to the judge): No! I am not guilty in any respect!

Ulrich: Did you know that there was a counter-revolutionary Right-Trotskyist organization in the People's Commissariat of Heavy Industry?

Shatalov (throwing up his arms): I had no idea whatsoever. I had no suspicion there was such a hostile gang of saboteurs and terrorists there.

Ulrich (gazing with affectionate attention at his former drinking companion): You were not in prison during the last trial of the Right-Trotskyist center, were you?

Shatalov: No, I was not.

Ulrich: You were reading the newspapers then?

Shatalov (slowly, trying to grasp the purpose of such a strange question): I did. . . .

Ulrich: So you read Pyatakov's testimony that there was a counter-revolutionary organization in the People's Commissariat of Heavy Industry?

Shatalov (uncertainly): Of course, of course.

Ulrich (triumphantly): Well, there we are! So you knew there was a counter-revolutionary organization in the People's Commissariat of Heavy Industry. (Turning to the secretary of the court.) Write down: the defendant acknowledges that he knew about the existence of Pyatakov's organization. . . .

Shatalov (shouts passionately, stuttering from horror): But it was from the newspapers, the newspapers, that I learnt there was an organ-ization there!

Ulrich (calm and satisfied): But to the court it is not important where you found out. You knew! (Hurriedly, like a priest at a poorly-paid funeral.) Any questions? No. You want to say a last word? No need for repetition, we've heard it already! (Nodding right and left at his assessors.) I pronounce sentence. Mmmh . . . 15 years . . .

I shall not insist that this trial strictly met the requirement for fairness. Yet compared to others it was clement, leaving Shatalov among the living. And it was indisputably rapid. Evidently the speed was typical. In the late 1950s I attended a memorial evening at the Museum of the Revolution for Kosarev, the 1930s Komsomol leader executed by Stalin. The head of the Central Committee administrative department told me that Khrushchev had entrusted him to re-examine Kosarev's case: "The hearing began at 11.00 a.m.," read the record of the trial, "and ended at 11.10 a.m."

THE HEARTLESS BUREAUCRACY

Auntie Pasha, a kindly middle-aged woman, washed the floors in the camp office. She pitied the office workers because they were so helpless and impractical: and she darned and sewed patches on the trousers and quilt jackets of the "trusties" who were not yet privileged to wear first-hand clothing. The story of her life was simple. Auntie Pasha came from Zlatoust in the Urals. Her husband, a furnace man, died during an accident at work and she was left with two teenage sons. Their life was predictably hard. Someone taught Auntie Pasha to go to Chelyabinsk to buy stockings and then sell them (naturally, at a suitably higher price) in Zlatoust where they were not to be found. The rest was recorded in the charge sheet and the sentence passed by the court. "For the purposes of speculation" she had "obtained 72 pairs of knitted stockings in Chelyabinsk which she then tried to resell at the market in Zlatoust." Auntie Pasha was reported, arrested, tried and sentenced to seven years imprisonment with confiscation of all her property. The children were taken in by acquaintances and, besides, they were almost old enough to take up any profession at the trade school. Five years passed, the war began, and Auntie Pasha's boys had reached the age when they could defend the Motherland. So off they went to fight. First Auntie Pasha was informed that her younger son had been killed. Staying behind in the office at night to wash the floors, she moaned and beat her head against the table.

Then one evening she came up to me with a glassy-eyed expression and handed over a thick package which she had been given in Records and Distribution. This contained several medical reports and the decisions of various commissions. To these was added a letter to Auntie Pasha from the hospital administrator. It concerned her elder son. He had been severely wounded and was in the hospital. The doctors had done all within their power and he was, as they put it in his medical history, "fit, to all intents and purposes"—apart, that is, from having lost both arms and one leg. He could be discharged from the hospital if there was some close relation to look after him. Evidently the son had explained where she was because the administrator advised the mother of this wounded soldier to send an appeal to the USSR Procurator General's Office, including the enclosed documents, after which they would release her and she could come and fetch him.

"Manuilich, dear heart," Auntie Pasha said, starting to cry, "You write for me."

So I wrote, and very persuasively. I attached all the documents and handed in the letter. Two or three months passed, and each day I reassured Auntie Pasha: they received a great many such appeals, I told her, and it would take time to process her release. I described in detail the lengthy procedures as her application passed from one level to another. Auntie Pasha wept, but believed me and each day I gave her paper on which to write her son a letter.

One day I went into Records and Distribution myself. A great pile of mail lay on the table, already sorted out to be handed over, or its contents communicated, to the prisoners. Auntie Pasha's surname caught my eye. I picked up the flimsy sheet of headed paper from the USSR Procurator General's Office and read it through. A public procurator of a certain rank or class informed Auntie Pasha that her application had been examined and her request for early release turned down because there were "no grounds." I carefully placed the single sheet on the table and went out onto the verandah, terrified that I might suddenly meet Auntie Pasha. . . . Everywhere, in the barracks and in the office, there were people I did not want to see. I ran to the latrines and there, clinging to the stinking walls, started to shake uncontrollably. Only two times in my prison life did this happen. Why was I crying? Then I understood: I felt ashamed, terribly ashamed, before Auntie Pasha.

She had already served five years for 72 pairs of stockings. She had given the state her two sons. Now, there it was, there were "no grounds.". . .

ADOLF HITLER

MEIN KAMPF

In the "Beer Hall Putsch" of November 1923, Hitler attempted to overthrow the state government in Bavaria as the first step in bringing down the Weimar Republic. But the Nazis quickly scattered when the Bavarian police opened fire. Hitler was arrested and sentenced to five years' imprisonment—he served only nine months. While in prison, Hitler wrote *Mein Kampf (My Struggle)* (1925–1926), in which he presented his views. The book came to be regarded as an authoritative expression of the Nazi world-view and served as a kind of sacred writing for the Nazi movement.

Hitler's thought—a patchwork of nineteenth-century anti-Semitic, Volkish, Social Darwinist, and anti-Marxist ideas—contrasted sharply with the core values of both the Judeo-Christian and the Enlightenment traditions. Central to Hitler's world-view was racial mythology: a heroic Germanic race that was descended from the ancient Aryans, who once swept across Europe, and was battling for survival against racial inferiors. In the following passages excerpted from *Mein Kampf*, Hitler presents his views of race, of propaganda, and of National Socialist territorial goals.

THE PRIMACY OF RACE

Nature does not want a pairing of weaker individuals with stronger ones; it wants even less a mating of a higher race with a weaker one. Otherwise its routine labors of promoting a higher breed lasting perhaps over hundreds of thousands of years would be wiped out.

History offers much evidence for this process. It proves with terrifying clarity that any genetic mixture of Aryan blood with people of a lower quality undermines the culturally superior people. The population of North America consists to a large extent of Germanic elements, which have mixed very little with inferior people of color. Central and South America shows a different humanity and culture; here Latin immigrants mixed with the aborigines, sometimes on a large scale. This example alone allows a clear recognition of the effects of racial mixtures. Remaining racially pure the Germans of North America rose to be masters of their continent; they will remain masters as long as they do not defile their blood.

The result of mixing races in short is: a) lowering the cultural level of the higher race; b) physical and spiritual retrogression and thus the beginning of a slow but progressive decline.

To promote such a development means no less than committing sin against the will of the eternal creator. . . .

Everything that we admire on earth—science, technology, invention—is the creative product of only a few people, and perhaps originally of only *one* race; our whole culture depends upon them. If they perish, the beauties of the earth will be buried. . . .

All great cultures of the past perished because the original creative race was destroyed by the poisoning of its blood.

Such collapse always happened because people forgot that all cultures depend on human beings. In order to preserve a given culture it is necessary to preserve the human beings who created it. Cultural preservation in this world is tied to the iron law of necessity and the right to victory of the stronger and better. . . .

If we divide humanity into three categories: into founders of culture, bearers of culture, and destroyers of culture, the Aryan would undoubtedly rate first. He established the foundations and walls of all human progress. . . .

The mixing of blood and the resulting lowering of racial cohesion is the sole reason why cultures perish. People do not perish by defeat in war, but by losing the power of resistance inherent in pure blood.

All that is not pure race in this world is chaff. . . .

A state which in the age of racial poisoning dedicates itself to the cultivation of its best racial elements will one day become master of the world.

Modern anti-Semitism was a powerful legacy of the Middle Ages and the unsettling changes brought about by rapid industrialization; it was linked to racist doctrines that asserted the Jews were inherently wicked and bore dangerous racial qualities. Hitler grasped the political potential of anti-Semitism: by concentrating all evil in one enemy, he could provide non-Jews with an emotionally satisfying explanation for all their misfortunes and thus manipulate and unify the German people.

ANTI-SEMITISM

The Jew offers the most powerful contrast to the Aryan. . . . Despite all their seemingly intellectual qualities the Jewish people are without true culture, and especially without a culture of their own. What Jews seem to possess as culture is the property of others, for the most part corrupted in their hands.

In judging the Jewish position in regard to human culture, we have to keep in mind their essential characteristics. There never was—and still is no—Jewish art. The Jewish people made no original contribution to the two queen goddesses of all arts: architecture and music. What they have contributed is bowdlerization or spiritual theft. Which proves that Jews lack the very qualities distinguishing creative and culturally blessed races. . . .

The first and biggest lie of Jews is that Jewishness is not a matter of race but of religion, from which inevitably follow even more lies. One of them refers to the language of Jews. It is not a means of expressing their thoughts, but of hiding them. While speaking French a Jew thinks Jewish, and while he cobbles together some German verse, he merely expresses the mentality of his people.

As long as the Jew is not master of other peoples, he must for better or worse speak their languages. Yet as soon as the others have become his servants, then all should learn a universal language (Esperanto for instance), so that by these means the Jews can rule more easily. . . .

For hours the blackhaired Jewish boy lies in wait, with satanic joy on his face, for the unsuspecting girl whom he disgraces with his blood and thereby robs her from her people. He tries by all means possible to destroy the racial foundations of the people he wants to subjugate.

But a people of pure race conscious of its blood can never be enslaved by the Jew; he remains forever a ruler of bastards.

Thus he systematically attempts to lower racial purity by racially poisoning individuals.

In politics he begins to replace the idea of democracy with the idea of the dictatorship of the proletariat.

He found his weapon in the organized Marxist masses, which avoid democracy and instead help him to subjugate and govern people dictatorially with his brutal fists.

Systematically he works toward a double revolution, in economics and politics.

With the help of his international contacts he enmeshes people who effectively resist his attacks from within in a net of external enemies whom he incites to war, and, if necessary, goes on to unfurling the red flag of revolution over the battlefield.

He batters the national economies until the ruined state enterprises are privatized and subject to his financial control.

In politics he refuses to give the state the means for its self-preservation, destroys the bases of any national self-determination and defense, wipes out the faith in leadership, denigrates the historic past, and pulls everything truly great into the gutter.

In cultural affairs he pollutes art, literature, theatre, befuddles national sentiment, subverts all concepts of beauty and grandeur, of nobleness and goodness, and reduces people to their lowest nature.

Religion is made ridiculous, custom and morals are declared outdated, until the last props of national character in the battle for survival have collapsed. . . .

Thus the Jew is the big rabble-rouser for the complete destruction of Germany. Wherever in the world we read about attacks on Germany, Jews are the source, just as in peace and during the war the newspapers of both the Jewish stock market and the Marxists systematically incited hatred against Germany. Country after country gave up its neutrality and joined the world war coalition in disregard of the true interest of the people.

Jewish thinking in all this is clear. The Bolshevization of Germany, i.e., the destruction of the German national people-oriented intelligentsia and thereby the exploitation of German labor under the yoke of Jewish global finance are but the prelude for the expansion of the Jewish tendency to conquer the world. As so often in history, Germany is the turning point in this mighty struggle. If our people and our state become the victims of blood-thirsty and money-thirsty Jewish tyrants, the whole world will be enmeshed in the tentacles of this octopus. If, however, Germany liberates itself from this yoke, we can be sure that the greatest threat to all humanity has been broken. . . .

Hitler was a master propagandist and advanced his ideas on propaganda techniques in *Mein Kampf.* He mocked the learned and book-oriented German liberals and socialists who he felt were entirely unsuited for modern mass politics. The successful leader, he said, must win over the masses through the use of simple ideas and images, constantly repeated, to control the mind by evoking primitive feelings. Hitler contended that mass meetings were the most effective means of winning followers. What counted most at these demonstrations, he said, was will power, strength, and unflagging determination radiating from the speaker to every single individual in the crowd.

PROPAGANDA AND MASS RALLIES

The task of propaganda does not lie in the scientific training of individuals, but in directing the masses toward certain facts, events, necessities, etc., whose significance is to be brought to their attention.

The essential skill consists in doing this so well that you convince people about the reality of a fact, about the necessity of an event, about the correctness of something necessary, etc. . . . You always have to appeal to the emotions and far less to the so-called intellect. . . .

The art of propaganda lies in sensing the emotional temper of the broad masses, so that you, in psychologically effective form, can catch their attention and move their hearts. . . .

The attention span of the masses is very short, their understanding limited; they easily forget. For that reason all effective propaganda has to concentrate on very few points and drive them home through simple slogans, until even the simplest can grasp what you have in mind. As soon as you give up this principle and become too complex, you will lose your effectiveness, because the masses cannot digest and retain what you have offered. You thereby weaken your case and in the end lose it altogether.

The larger the scope of your case, the more psychologically correct must be the method of your presentation. . . .

The task of propaganda lies not in weighing right and wrong, but in driving home your own point of view. You cannot objectively explore the facts that favor others and present them in doctrinaire sincerity to the masses. You have to push relentlessly your own case. . . .

Even the most brilliant propaganda will not produce the desired results unless it follows this fundamental rule: You must stick to limiting yourself to essentials and repeat them endlessly. Persistence on this point, as in so many other cases in the world, is the first and most important precondition for success. . . .

Propaganda does not exist to furnish interesting diversions to blasé young dandies, but to convince above all the masses. In their clumsiness they always require a long lead before they are ready to take notice. Only by thousandfold repetition will the simplest concepts stick in their memories.

No variation of your presentation should change the content of your propaganda; you always have to come to the same conclusion. You may want to highlight your slogans from various sides, but at the end you always have to reaffirm it. Only consistent and uniform propaganda will succeed. . . .

Every advertisement, whether in business or politics, derives its success from its persistence and uniformity. . . .

The mass meeting is . . . necessary because an incipient supporter of a new political movement will feel lonely and anxiously isolated. He needs at the start a sense of a larger community which among most people produces vitality and courage. The same man as member of a military company or battalion and surrounded by his comrades will more lightheartedly join an attack than if he were all by himself. In a crowd he feels more sheltered, even if reality were a thousandfold against him.

The sense of community in a mass demonstration not only empowers the individual, but also promotes an esprit de corps. The person who in his business or workshop is the first to represent a new political creed is likely to be exposed to heavy discrimination. He needs the reassurance that comes from the conviction of being a member and a fighter in a large comprehensive organization. The sense of this organization comes first to him in a mass demonstration. When he for the first time goes from a petty workshop or from a large factory, where he feels insignificant, to a mass demonstration surrounded by thousands and thousands of like-minded fellows—when he as a seeker is gripped by the intoxicating surge of enthusiasm among three or four thousand others—when the visible success and the consensus of thousands of others prove the correctness of his new political creed and for the first time arouse doubts about his previous political convictions—then he submits to the miraculous influence of what we call "mass suggestion." The will, the yearning, and also the power of thousands of fellow citizens now fill every individual. The man who full of doubts and uncertain enters such a gathering, leaves it inwardly strengthened; he has become a member of a community. . . .

Hitler was an extreme nationalist who wanted a reawakened, racially united Germany to expand eastward at the expense of the Slavs, whom he viewed as racially inferior.

LEBENSRAUM

A people gains its freedom of existence only by occupying a sufficiently large space on earth. . . .

If the National Socialist movement really wants to achieve a hallowed mission in history for our people, it must, in painful awareness of its position in the world, boldly and methodically fight against the aimlessness and incapacity which have hitherto guided the foreign policy of the German people. It must then, without respect for "tradition" and prejudice, find the courage to rally the German people to a forceful advance on the road which leads from their present cramped living space to new territories. In this manner they will be liberated from the danger of perishing or being enslaved in service to others.

The National Socialist movement must try to end the disproportion between our numerous population and its limited living space, the source of our food as well as the base of our power—between our historic past and the hopelessness of our present impotence. . . .

The demand for restoring the boundaries of 1914 is a political nonsense with consequences so huge as to make it appear a crime—quite apart from the fact that our pre-war boundaries were anything but logical. They neither united all people of German nationality nor served strategic-political necessity. . . .

In the light of this fact we National Socialists must resolutely stick to our foreign policy goals, namely *to secure for the German people the territorial base to which they are entitled.* This is the only goal which before God and our German posterity justifies shedding our blood. . . . Just as our forebears did not receive the soil on which we live as a gift from heaven—they had to risk their lives for it—so in future we will not secure the living space for our people by divine grace, but by the might of the victorious sword.

However much all of us recognize the necessity of a reckoning with France, it would remain ineffectual if we thereby limited the scope of our foreign policy. It makes sense only if we consider it as a rear-guard action for expanding our living space elsewhere in Europe. . . .

If we speak today about gaining territory in Europe, we think primarily of Russia and its border states. . . .

DAVID H. BUFFUM

NIGHT OF THE BROKEN GLASS *(KRISTALLNACHT)*

The Nazi press depicted the terrible events of *Kristallnacht*—the burning and vandalizing of thousands of Jewish synagogues, homes, and businesses throughout Germany and the killing and maiming of Jews—as a "spontaneous wave of righteous indignation" directed at enemies of Germany. In reality the violence was planned and coordinated by the government, and many Germans were horrified by the destruction of property and the abuse inflicted on helpless people. The following account of the vicious onslaught in Leipzig was prepared by David H. Buffum, the American consul.

At 3 a.m. November 10, 1938 was unleashed a barrage of Nazi ferocity as had had no equal hitherto in Germany, or very likely anywhere else in the world since savagery, if ever. Jewish dwellings were smashed into and contents demolished or looted. In one of the Jewish sections an eighteen year old boy was hurled from a three story window to land with both legs broken on a street littered with burning beds and other household furniture and effects from his family's and other apartments. This information was supplied by an attending physician. It is reported from another quarter that among domestic effects thrown out of a Jewish dwelling, a small dog descended four flights to a broken spine on a cluttered street. Although apparently centered in poor districts, the raid was not confined to the humble classes. One apartment of exceptionally refined occupants known to this office, was violently ransacked, presumably in a search for valuables that was not in vain, and one of the marauders thrust a cane through a priceless medieval painting portraying a biblical scene. Another apartment of the same category is known to have been turned upside down in the frenzied course of whatever the invaders were after. Reported loss of looting of cash, silver, jewelry, and otherwise easily convertible articles, have been frequent.

Jewish shop windows by the hundreds were systematically and wantonly smashed throughout the entire city at a loss estimated at several millions of marks. There are reports that substantial losses have been sustained on the famous Leipzig "Bruhl," as many of the shop windows at the time of the demolition were filled with costly furs that were seized before the windows could be boarded up. In proportion to the general destruction of real estate, however, losses of goods are felt to have been relatively small. The spectators who viewed the wreckage when daylight had arrived were mostly in such a bewildered mood, that there was no danger of impulsive acts, and the perpetrators probably were too busy in carrying out their schedule to take off a whole lot of time for personal profit. At all events, the main streets of the city were a positive litter of shattered plate glass. According to reliable testimony, the debacle was executed by S. S. men and Storm Troopers not in uniform, each group having been provided with hammers, axes, crowbars and incendiary bombs.

Three synagogues in Leipzig were fired simultaneously by incendiary bombs and all sacred objects and records desecrated or destroyed, in most instances hurled through the windows and burned in the streets. No attempts whatsoever were made to quench the fires, functions of the fire brigade having been confined to playing water on adjoining buildings. All of the synagogues were irreparably gutted by flames, and the walls of the two that are in the close proximity of the consulate are now being razed. The blackened frames have been centers of attraction during the past week of terror for eloquently silent and bewildered crowds. One of the largest clothing stores in the heart of the city was destroyed by flames from incendiary bombs, only the charred walls and gutted roof having been left standing. As was the case with the synagogues, no attempts on the part of the fire brigade were made to extinguish the fire, although apparently there was a certain amount of apprehension for adjacent property, for the walls of a coffee house next door were covered with asbestos and sprayed by the doughty firemen. It is extremely difficult to believe, but the owners of the clothing store were actually charged with setting the fire and on that basis were dragged from their beds at 6 a.m. and clapped into prison.

Tactics which closely approached the ghoulish took place at the Jewish cemetery where the temple was fired together with a building occupied by caretakers, tombstones uprooted and graves violated. Eye witnesses considered reliable report that ten corpses were left unburied at this cemetery for a week's time because all grave diggers and cemetery attendants had been arrested.

Ferocious as was the violation of property, the most hideous phase of the so-called "spontaneous" action, has been the wholesale arrest and transportation to concentration camps of male German Jews between the ages of sixteen and sixty, as well as Jewish men without citizenship. This has been taking place daily since the night of horror. This office has no way of accurately checking the numbers of such arrests, but there is very little question that they have gone into several thousands in Leipzig alone. Having demolished dwellings and hurled most of the moveable effects to the streets, the insatiably sadistic perpetrators threw many of the trembling inmates into a small stream that flows through the Zoological Park, commanding horrified spectators to spit at them, defile them with mud and jeer at their plight. The latter incident has been repeatedly corroborated by German witnesses who were nauseated in telling the tale. The slightest manifestation of sympathy evoked a positive fury on the part of the perpetrators, and the crowd was powerless to do anything but turn horror-stricken eyes from the scene of abuse, or leave the vicinity. These tactics were carried out the entire morning of November 10th without police intervention and they were applied to men, women and children.

There is much evidence of physical violence, including several deaths. At least half a dozen cases have been personally observed, victims with bloody, badly bruised faces having fled to this office, believing that as refugees their desire to emigrate could be expedited here. As a matter of fact this consulate has been a bedlam of humanity for the past ten days, most of these visitors being desperate women, as their husbands and sons had been taken off to concentration camps.

Similarly violent procedure was applied throughout this consular district, the amount of havoc wrought depending upon the number of Jewish establishments or persons involved. It is understood that in many of the smaller communities even more relentless methods were employed than was the case in the cities. Reports have been received from Weissenfels to the effect that the few Jewish families there are experiencing great difficulty in purchasing food. It is reported that three Aryan professors of the University of Jena have been arrested and taken off to concentration camps because they had voiced disapproval of this insidious drive against mankind.

STEFAN ZWEIG

THE WORLD OF YESTERDAY

One of modern German-speaking Europe's most important authors, Stefan Zweig (see page 309) was born into a well-to-do Viennese Jewish household, came of age during the waning years of the monarchy, and witnessed both the devastation of World War I and the chaos of the interwar years. A passionate European and a convinced Austrian patriot, Zweig was disgusted by national chauvinisms, particularly the virulent German nationalism clearly discernible in Austria after the collapse of the Habsburg monarchy. His *World of Yesterday* (1943) both laments the loss of European cosmopolitanism and offers biting criticism of the inability, or unwillingness, of many Austrians to come to terms with the violent intolerance in their own society and the spreading danger of Nazism. Zweig's despair was all-consuming; he took his own life in South American exile, unable to reconcile himself to the changes in his beloved Europe and his Austrian homeland.

In the following selection from his autobiography, Zweig describes the orgy of hate that engulfed Vienna immediately after the Anschluss.

I thought that I had foreboded all the terror that would come to pass when Hitler's dream of hate would come true and he would triumphantly occupy Vienna, the city which had turned him off, poor and a failure, in his youth. But how timid, how petty, how lamentable my imagination, all human imagination, in the light of the inhumanity which discharged itself on that March 13, 1938, that day when Austria and Europe with it fell prey to sheer violence! The mask was off. The other States having plainly shown their fear, there was no further need to check moral inhibitions or to employ hypocritical pretexts about "Marxists" having to be politically liquidated. Who cared for England, France, for the whole world! Now there was no longer mere robbery and theft, but every private lust for revenge was given free rein. University professors were obliged to scrub the streets with their naked hands, pious white-bearded Jews were dragged into the synagogue by hooting youths and forced to do knee-exercises and to shout "Heil Hitler" in chorus. Innocent people in the streets were trapped like rabbits and herded off to clean the latrines in the S. A. barracks. All the sickly, unclean fantasies of hate that had been conceived in many orgiastic nights found raging expression in bright daylight. Breaking into homes and tearing earrings from trembling women may well have happened in the looting of cities, hundreds of years ago during medieval wars; what was new, however, was the shameless delight in public tortures, in spiritual martyrization, in the refinements of humiliation. All this has been recorded not by one but by thousands who suffered it; and a more peaceful day—not one already morally fatigued as ours is—will shudder to read what a single hate-crazed man perpetrated in that city of culture in the twentieth century. For amidst his military and political victories Hitler's most diabolic triumph was that he succeeded through progressive excesses in blunting every sense of law and order. Before this "New Order," the murder of a single man without legal process and without apparent reason would have shocked the world; torture was considered unthinkable in the twentieth century, expropriations were known by the old names, theft and robbery. But now after successive [murderous] nights the daily mortal tortures in the S. A. prisons and behind barbed wire, what did a single injustice or earthly suffering signify? In 1938, after Austria, our universe had become accustomed to inhumanity, to lawlessness, and brutality as never in centuries before. In a former day the occurrences in unhappy Vienna alone would have been sufficient to cause international proscription, but in 1938 the world conscience was silent or merely muttered surlily before it forgot and forgave.

Those days, marked by daily cries for help from the homeland when one knew close friends to be kidnapped and humiliated and one trembled helplessly for every loved one, were among the most terrible of my life. These times have so perverted our hearts that I am not ashamed to say that I was not shocked and did not mourn upon learning of the death of my mother in Vienna; on the contrary, I even felt something like composure in the knowledge that she was now safe from suffering and danger. Eighty-four years old, almost completely deaf, she occupied rooms in our old home and thus could not, even under the new "Aryan" code, be evicted for the time being and we had hoped somehow to get her abroad after a while. One of the first Viennese ordinances had hit her hard. At her advanced age she was a little shaky on her legs and was accustomed, when on her daily laborious walk, to rest on a bench in the Ringstrasse or in the park, every five or ten minutes. Hitler had not been master of the city for a week when the bestial order forbidding Jews to sit on public benches was issued—one of those orders obviously thought up only for the sadistic purpose of malicious torture. There was logic and reason in robbing Jews for with the booty from factories, the home furnishings, the villas, and the jobs compulsorily vacated they could feather their followers' nests, reward their satellites; after all, Goering's picture-gallery owes its splendor mainly to this generously exercised practice. But to deny an aged woman or an exhausted old man a few minutes on a park bench to catch his breath—this remained reserved to the twentieth century and to the man whom millions worshipped as the greatest in our day.

Fortunately, my mother was spared suffering such brutality and humiliation for long. She died a few months after the occupation of Vienna and I cannot forbear to write about an episode in connection with her passing; it seems important to me to record just such details for a time in which such things will again seem impossible.

One morning the eighty-four-year-old woman suddenly lost consciousness. The doctor who was called declared that she could hardly live through the night and engaged a nurse, a woman of about forty, to attend her deathbed. Neither my brother nor I, her only children, was there nor could we have come back, because a return to the deathbed of a mother would have been counted a misdeed by the representatives of German culture. A cousin of ours undertook to spend the night in the apartment so that at least one of the family might be present at her death. He was then a man of sixty, and in poor health; in fact he too died about a year later. As he was uncovering his bed in an adjoining room the nurse appeared and declared her regret that because of the new National-Socialist laws it was impossible for her to stay overnight with the dying woman. To her credit be it said that she was rather shamefaced about it. My cousin being a Jew and she a woman under fifty, she was not permitted to spend a night under the same roof with him, even at a deathbed, because according to the [vile Nazi] mentality, it must be a Jew's first thought to practice race defilement upon her. Of course the regulation was extremely embarrassing, but she would have to obey the law. So my sixty-year-old cousin had to leave the house in the evening so that the nurse could stay with my dying mother; it will be intelligible, then, why I considered her almost lucky not to have to live on among such people.

ADOLF HITLER

"POLAND WILL BE DEPOPULATED AND SETTLED WITH GERMANS"

An American journalist was given a copy of Hitler's speech to his generals at the August 22 conference. Probably the supplier was an official close to Admiral Canaris, an opponent of Hitler who had attended the conference. The journalist then gave it to the British ambassador. The speech is reproduced below.

Decision to attack Poland was arrived at in spring. Originally there was fear that because of the political constellation we would have to strike at the same time against England, France, Russia and Poland. This risk too we should have had to take. Göring had demonstrated to us that his Four-Year Plan is a failure and that we are at the end of our strength, if we do not achieve victory in a coming war.

Since the autumn of 1938 and since I have realised that Japan will not go with us unconditionally and that Mussolini is endangered by that nitwit of a King and the treacherous scoundrel of a Crown Prince, I decided to go with Stalin. After all there are only three great statesmen in the world, Stalin, I and Mussolini. Mussolini is the weakest, for he has been able to break the power neither of the crown nor of the Church. Stalin and I are the only ones who visualise the future. So in a few weeks hence I shall stretch out my hand to Stalin at the common German-Russian frontier and with him undertake to re-distribute the world.

Our strength lies in our quickness and in our brutality; Genghis Khan has sent millions of women and children into death knowingly and with a light heart. History sees in him only the great founder of States. As to what the weak Western European civilisation asserts about me, that is of no account. I have given the command and I shall shoot everyone who utters one word of criticism, for the goal to be obtained in the war is not that of reaching certain lines but of physically demolishing the opponent. And so for the present only in the East I have put my death-head formations[1] in place with the command relentlessly and without compassion to send into death many women and children of Polish origin and language. Only thus we can gain the living space that we need. Who after all is today speaking about the destruction of the Armenians?

Colonel-General von Brauchitsch has promised me to bring the war against Poland to a close within a few weeks. Had he reported to me that he needs two years or even only one year, I should not have given the command to march and should have allied myself temporarily with England instead of Russia for we cannot conduct a long war. To be sure a new situation has arisen. I experienced those poor worms Daladier and Chamberlain in Munich. They will be too cowardly to attack. They won't go beyond a blockade. Against that we have our autarchy and the Russian raw materials.

Poland will be depopulated and settled with Germans. My pact with the Poles was merely conceived of as a gaining of time. As for the rest, gentlemen, the fate of Russia will be exactly the same as I am now going through with in the case of Poland. After Stalin's death—he is a very sick man—we will break the Soviet Union. Then there will begin the dawn of the German rule of the earth. . . .

The opportunity is as favourable as never before. I have but one worry, namely that Chamberlain or some other such pig of a fellow ("Saukerl") will come at the last moment with proposals or with ratting ("Umfall"). He will fly down the stairs, even if I shall personally have to trample on his belly in the eyes of the photographers.

No, it is too late for this. The attack upon and the destruction of Poland begins Saturday[2] early. I shall let a few companies in Polish uniform attack in Upper Silesia or in the Protectorate. Whether the world believes it is quite indifferent ("Scheissegal"). The world believes only in success.

[1] 1The S.S. Death's Head formations were principally employed in peacetime in guarding concentration camps. With the S.S. Verfügungstruppen they formed the nucleus of the Waffen S.S.

[2] August 26.

For you, gentlemen, fame and honour are beginning as they have not since centuries. Be hard, be without mercy, act more quickly and brutally than the others. The citizens of Western Europe must tremble with horror. That is the most human way of conducting a war. For it scares the others off.

The new method of conducting war corresponds to the new drawing of the frontiers. A war extending from Reval, Lublin, Kaschau to the mouth of the Danube. The rest will be given to the Russians. Ribbentrop has orders to make every offer and to accept every demand. In the West I reserve to myself the right to determine the strategically best line. Here one will be able to work with Protectorate regions, such as Holland, Belgium and French Lorraine.

And now, on to the enemy, in Warsaw we will celebrate our reunion.

The speech was received with enthusiasm. Göring jumped on a table, thanked blood-thirstily and made bloodthirsty promises. He danced like a wild man. The few that had misgivings remained quiet. (Here a line of the memorandum is missing in order no doubt to protect the source of information.)[3]

During the meal which followed Hitler said he must act this year as he was not likely to live very long. His successor however would no longer be able to carry this out. Besides, the situation would be a hopeless one in two years at the most.

[3]This sentence in parentheses forms part of the original typescript.

THE INDOCTRINATION OF THE GERMAN SOLDIER

The following excerpts from German army propaganda and letters written by soldiers show how Nazi ideology influenced ordinary German troops. The first is a news-sheet published by the High Command of the Armed Forces in the spring of 1940, and distributed to all army units, which expressed quasi-religious fervor for the Führer.

THE FÜHRER AS SAVIOR

Behind the battle of annihilation of May 1940 stands in lone greatness the name of the Führer.

All that has been accomplished since he has taken the fate of our people into his strong hands!

. . . He gave the people back its unity, smashed the parties and destroyed the hydra of the organizations . . . he decontaminated the body of our people from the Jewish subversion, created a stock-proud, race-conscious *Volk*, which had overcome the racial death of diminishing births and was granted renewed [abundance of childbirths] as a carrier of the great future of the Fatherland. He subdued the terrible plight of unemployment and granted to millions of people who had already despaired of the *Volk* a new belief in the *Volksgemeinschaft* [community of the people] and happiness in a new Fatherland. . . .

His genius, in which the whole strength of Germandom is embodied with ancient powers, has animated the souls of 80,000,000 Germans, has filled them with strength and will, with the storm and stress *[Sturm und Drang]* of a renewed young people; and, himself the first soldier of Germany, he has entered the name of the German soldier into the book of immortality.

All this we were allowed to experience. Our great duty in this year of decision is that we do not accept it as observers, but that we, enchanted, and with all the passion of which we are capable, sacrifice ourselves to this Führer and strive to be worthy of the historical epoch molded by a heaven-storming will.

This same religious devotion to Hitler and Nazi ideology was expressed in literature given to company commanders to assist them in indoctrinating their troops.

Only the Führer could carry out what had not been achieved for a thousand years. . . . [He has] brought together all the German stock . . . for the struggle for freedom and living space . . . [and] directed all his thoughts and efforts toward the National Socialist education of the *Volk*, the inner cohesion of the state, the armament and offensive capability of the Wehrmacht. . . . When the German Eastern Armies fought an unparalleled battle during the winter of 1941– 42 in the snow and ice of the Russian winter, he said: "Any weakling can put up with victories. Only the strong can stand firm in battles of destiny. But heaven gives the ultimate and highest prize only to those who are capable of withstanding battles of destiny." In the difficult winter of 1942–43 the strength of the Führer was demonstrated once more, when . . . he called upon the German *Volk* at the front and in the homeland to stand firm and make the supreme effort. The Führer . . . clearly sees the goal ahead: a strong German Reich as the power of order in Europe and a firm root of the German *Lebensraum.* This goal will be achieved if the whole *Volk* remains loyal to him even in difficult times and as long as we soldiers do our duty.

Such words were not without their impact on German soldiers. In November 1940, one soldier expressed his feelings about Hitler in a letter home.

The last words of the Führer's radio address are over and a new strength streams through our veins. It is as if he spoke to each individual, to everyone of us, as if he wanted to give everyone new strength. With loyalty and a sense of duty, we must fight for our principles and endure to the end. Our Führer represents our united German Fatherland. . . . What we do for him, we do for all of you; what we sacrifice in foreign lands, we sacrifice for our loved ones. When the Führer speaks on these festive occasions, I feel deep in my soul that you at home also feel that we must be ready to make all sacrifices. . . . German victory is as certain as our love for each other. Just as we believe in our love, so we believe in our final victory and in the future of our people and our Fatherland.

Similar sentiments were voiced by a private in a letter to his brother.

The Führer has grown into the greatest figure of the century, in his hand lies the destiny of the world and of culturally-perceptive humanity. May his pure sword strike down the Satanic monster. Yes, the blows are still hard, but the horror will be forced into the shadows through the inexorable Need, through the command which derives from our National Socialist idea. This [battle] is for a new ideology, a new belief, a new life! I am glad that I can participate, even if as a tiny cog, in this war of light against darkness.

BOLSHEVIKS AND JEWS AS DEVILS

German propaganda described Jews and Russian communists in racial and religious terms, calling them a morally depraved form of humanity in the service of Satan. A tract from SS headquarters illustrates the mythical nature of Nazi ideology.

Just as night rises up against the day, just as light and darkness are eternal enemies, so the greatest enemy of world-dominating man is man himself. The sub-man—that creature which looks as though biologically it were of absolutely the same kind, endowed by Nature with hands, feet and a sort of brain, with eyes and mouth—is nevertheless a totally different, a fearful creature, is only an attempt at a human being, with a quasi-human face, yet in mind and spirit lower than any animal. Inside this being a cruel chaos of wild, unchecked passions: a nameless will to destruction, the most primitive lusts, the most undisguised vileness. A sub-man—nothing else! . . . Never has the sub-man granted peace, never has he permitted rest. . . . To preserve himself he needed mud, he needed hell, but not the sun. And this underworld of sub-men found its leader: the eternal Jew!

The news-sheet distributed to regular army units used similar language.

Anyone who has ever looked at the face of a red commissar knows what the Bolsheviks are like. Here there is no need for theoretical expressions. We would insult the animals if we described these mostly Jewish men as beasts. They are the embodiment of the Satanic and insane hatred against the whole of noble humanity. The shape of these commissars reveals to us the rebellion of the *Untermenschen* [sub-men] against noble blood. The masses, whom they have sent to their deaths [in this war against Germany] by making use of all means at their disposal such as ice-cold terror and insane incitement, would have brought an end to all meaningful life, had this eruption not been dammed at the last moment.

In October 1941, Walter von Reichenau, commander of the sixth army, appealed to his men in the language of Nazi racial ideology.

The essential goal of the campaign against the Jewish-Bolshevik system is the complete destruction of its power instruments and the eradication of the Asiatic influence on the European cultural sphere. . . . Therefore the soldier must have *complete* understanding for the necessity of the harsh, but just atonement of Jewish subhumanity.

In November 1941, General von Manstein, commander of the eleventh army, used much the same language.

Since 22 June the German *Volk* is in the midst of a battle for life and death against the Bolshevik system. This battle is conducted against the Soviet army not only in a conventional manner according to the rules of European warfare. . . .

Judaism constitutes the mediator between the enemy in the rear and the still fighting remnants of the Red Army and the Red leadership. It has a stronger hold than in Europe on all key positions of the political leadership and administration, it occupies commerce and trade and further forms cells for all the disturbances and possible rebellions.

The Jewish-Bolshevik system must be eradicated once and for all. Never again may it interfere in our European living space.

The German soldier is therefore not only charged with the task of destroying the power instrument of this system. He marches forth also as a carrier of a racial conception and as an avenger of all the atrocities which have been committed against him and the German people.

The soldier must show understanding for the harsh atonement of Judaism, the spiritual carrier of the Bolshevik terror.

And in that same month, Colonel-General Hoth also interpreted the war as a struggle between racial superiors and inferiors.

It has become increasingly clear to us this summer, that here in the East spiritually unbridgeable conceptions are fighting each other: German sense of honor and race, and a soldierly tradition of many centuries, against an Asiatic mode of thinking and primitive instincts, whipped up by a small number of mostly Jewish intellectuals: fear of the knout [whip used for flogging], disregard of moral values, levelling down, throwing away of one's worthless life.

More than ever we are filled with the thought of a new era, in which the strength of the German people's racial superiority and achievements entrust it with the leadership of Europe. We clearly recognize our mission to save European culture from the advancing Asiatic barbarism. We now know that we have to fight against an incensed and tough opponent. This battle can only end with the destruction of one or the other; a compromise is out of the question.

The front-line soldier was affected by ideological propaganda.

I have received the "Stürmer" [a notoriously anti-Semitic newspaper] now for the third time. It makes me happy with all my heart. . . . You could not have made me happier. . . . I recognized the Jewish poison in our people long ago; how far it might have gone with us, this we see only now in this campaign. What the Jewish-regime has done in Russia, we see every day, and even the last doubters are cured here in view of the facts. We must and we will liberate the world from this plague, this is why the German soldier protects the Eastern Front, and we shall not return before we have uprooted all evil and destroyed the center of the Jewish-Bolshevik "world-do-gooders."

ANTON KUZMICH DRAGAN

A SOVIET VETERAN RECALLS

Anton Kuzmich Dragan, a Russian soldier, describes the vicious street fighting in Stalingrad during late September 1942.

"The Germans had cut us off from our neighbours. The supply of ammunition had been cut off; every bullet was worth its weight in gold. I gave the order to economize on ammunition, to collect the cartridge-pouches of the dead and all captured weapons. In the evening the enemy again tried to break our resistance, coming up close to our positions. As our numbers grew smaller, we shortened our line of defence. We began to move back slowly towards the Volga, drawing the enemy after us, and the ground we occupied was invariably too small for the Germans to be able easily to use artillery and aircraft.

"We moved back, occupying one building after another, turning them into strongholds. A soldier would crawl out of an occupied position only when the ground was on fire under him and his clothes were smouldering. During the day the Germans managed to occupy only two blocks.

"At the crossroads of Krasnopiterskaya and Komsomolskaya Streets we occupied a three-storey building on the corner. This was a good position from which to fire on all comers and it became our last defence. I ordered all entrances to be barricaded, and windows and embrasures to be adapted so that we could fire through them with all our remaining weapons.

"At a narrow window of the semi-basement we placed the heavy machine-gun with our emergency supply of ammunition—the last belt of cartridges. I had decided to use it at the most critical moment.

"Two groups, six in each, went up to the third floor and the garret. Their job was to break down walls, and prepare lumps of stone and beams to throw at the Germans when they came up close. A place for the seriously wounded was set aside in the basement. Our garrison consisted of forty men. Difficult days began. Attack after attack broke unendingly like waves against us. After each attack was beaten off we felt it was impossible to hold off the onslaught any longer, but when the Germans launched a fresh attack, we managed to find means and strength. This lasted five days and nights.

"The basement was full of wounded; only twelve men were still able to fight. There was no water. All we had left in the way of food was a few pounds of scorched grain; the Germans decided to beat us with starvation. Their attacks stopped, but they kept up the fire from their heavy-calibre machine-guns all the time.

"We did not think about escape, but only about how to sell our lives most dearly—we had no other way out. . . .

"The Germans attacked again. I ran upstairs with my men and could see their thin, blackened and strained faces, the bandages on their wounds, dirty and clotted with blood, their guns held firmly in their hands. There was no fear in their eyes. Lyuba Nesterenko, a nurse, was dying, with blood flowing from a wound in her chest. She had a bandage in her hand. Before she died she wanted to help to bind someone's wound, but she failed . . .

"The German attack was beaten off. In the silence that gathered around us we could hear the bitter fighting going on for Mameyev Kurgan and in the factory area of the city.

"How could we help the men defending the city? How could we divert from over there even a part of the enemy forces, which had stopped attacking our building?

"We decided to raise a red flag over the building, so that the Nazis would not think we had given up. But we had no red material. Understanding what we wanted to do, one of the men who was severely wounded took off his bloody vest and, after wiping the blood off his wound with it, handed it over to me.

"The Germans shouted through a megaphone: 'Russians! Surrender! You'll die just the same!'

"At that moment a red flag rose over our building.

"'Bark, you dogs! We've still got a long time to live!' shouted my orderly, Kozhushko.

"We beat off the next attack with stones, firing occasionally and throwing our last grenades. Suddenly from behind a blank wall, from the rear, came the grind of a tank's caterpillar tracks. We had no anti-tank grenades. All we had left was one anti-tank rifle with three rounds. I handed this rifle to an anti-tank man, Berdyshev, and sent him out through the back to fire at the tank point-blank. But before he could get into position he was captured by German tommy-gunners. What Berdyshev told the Germans I don't know, but I can guess that he led them up the garden path, because an hour later they started to attack at precisely that point where I had put my machine-gun with its emergency belt of cartridges.

"This time, reckoning that we had run out of ammunition, they came impudently out of their shelter, standing up and shouting. They came down the street in a column.

"I put the last belt in the heavy machine-gun at the semi-basement window and sent the whole of the 250 bullets into the yelling, dirty-grey Nazi mob. I was wounded in the hand but did not leave go of the machine-gun. Heaps of bodies littered the ground. The Germans still alive ran for cover in panic. An hour later they led our anti-tank rifleman on to a heap of ruins and shot him in front of our eyes, for having shown them the way to my machine-gun.

"There were no more attacks. An avalanche of shells fell on the building. The Germans stormed at us with every possible kind of weapon. We couldn't raise our heads.

"Again we heard the ominous sound of tanks. From behind a neighbouring block stocky German tanks began to crawl out. This, clearly, was the end. The guardsmen said good-bye to one another. With a dagger my orderly scratched on a brick wall: 'Rodimtsev's guardsmen fought and died for their country here.' The battalion's documents and a map case containing the Party and Komsomol cards of the defenders of the building had been put in a hole in a corner of the basement. The first salvo shattered the silence. There were a series of blows, and the building rocked and collapsed. How much later it was when I opened my eyes, I don't know. It was dark. The air was full of acrid brickdust. I could hear muffled groans around me. Kozhushko, the orderly, was pulling at me:

"'You're alive . . .'

"On the floor of the basement lay a number of other stunned and injured soldiers. We had been buried alive under the ruins of the three-storey building. We could scarcely breathe. We had no thought for food or water—it was air that had become most important for survival. I spoke to the soldiers:

"'Men! We did not flinch in battle, we fought even when resistance seemed impossible, and we have to get out of this tomb so that we can live and avenge the death of our comrades!'

"Even in pitch darkness you can see somebody else's face, feel other people close to you.

"With great difficulty we began to pick our way out of the tomb. We worked in silence, our bodies covered with cold, clammy sweat, our badly-bound wounds ached, our teeth were covered with brickdust, it became more and more difficult to breathe, but there were no groans or complaints.

"A few hours later, through the hole we had made, we could see the stars and breathe the fresh September air.

"Utterly exhausted, the men crowded round the hole, greedily gulping in the autumn air. Soon the opening was wide enough for a man to crawl through. Kozhushko, being only relatively slightly injured, went off to reconnoitre. An hour later he came back and reported:

"'Comrade Lieutenant, there are Germans all round us; along the Volga they are mining the bank; there are German patrols nearby . . .'

"We took the decision to fight our way through to our own lines."

RUDOLF HOESS

COMMANDANT OF AUSCHWITZ

To speed up the "final solution of the Jewish problem," the SS established death camps in Poland. Jews from all over Europe were crammed into cattle cars and shipped to these camps to be gassed or worked to death. At Auschwitz, the most notorious of the concentration camps, the SS used five gas chambers to kill as many as 9,000 people a day. Special squads of prisoners, called *Sonderkommandos*, were forced to pick over the corpses for gold teeth, jewelry, and anything else of value for the German war effort. Some 1.3 million Jews perished at Auschwitz. In the following passage from *Commandant of Auschwitz*, Rudolf Hoess (1900–1947), who commanded the camp and was executed by Poland after the war, recalled the murder process when he was in a Polish prison.

In the spring of 1942 the first transports of Jews, all earmarked for extermination, arrived from Upper Silesia.

They were taken from the detraining platform to the "cottage"—to bunker I—across the meadows where later building site II was located. The transport was conducted by Aumeier and Palitzsch and some of the block leaders. They talked with the Jews about general topics, inquiring concerning their qualifications and trades, with a view to misleading them. On arrival at the "cottage," they were told to undress. At first they went calmly into the rooms where they were supposed to be disinfected. But some of them showed signs of alarm, and spoke of death by suffocation and of annihilation. A sort of panic set in at once. Immediately all the Jews still outside were pushed into the chambers, and the doors were screwed shut. With subsequent transports the difficult individuals were picked out early and most carefully supervised. At the first signs of unrest, those responsible were unobtrusively led behind the building and killed with a small-caliber gun, that was inaudible to the others. The presence and calm behavior of the Special Detachment [of *Sonderkommandos*] served to reassure those who were worried or who suspected what was about to happen. A further calming effect was obtained by members of the Special Detachment accompanying them into the rooms and remaining with them until the last moment, while an SS man also stood in the doorway until the end.

It was most important that the whole business of arriving and undressing should take place in an atmosphere of the greatest possible calm. People reluctant to take off their clothes had to be helped by those of their companions who had already undressed, or by men of the Special Detachment.

The refractory ones were calmed down and encouraged to undress. The prisoners of the Special Detachment also saw to it that the process of undressing was carried out quickly, so that the victims would have little time to wonder what was happening. . . .

Many of the women hid their babies among the piles of clothing. The men of the Special Detachment were particularly on the lookout for this, and would speak words of encouragement to the woman until they had persuaded her to take the child with her. The women believed that the disinfectant might be bad for their smaller children, hence their efforts to conceal them.

The smaller children usually cried because of the strangeness of being undressed in this fashion, but when their mothers or members of the Special Detachment comforted them, they became calm and entered the gas chambers, playing or joking with one another and carrying their toys.

I noticed that women who either guessed or knew what awaited them nevertheless found the courage to joke with the children to encourage them, despite the mortal terror visible in their own eyes.

One woman approached me as she walked past and, pointing to her four children who were manfully helping the smallest ones over the rough ground, whispered:

"How can you bring yourself to kill such beautiful, darling children? Have you no heart at all?"

One old man, as he passed by me, hissed:

"Germany will pay a heavy penance for this mass murder of the Jews."

His eyes glowed with hatred as he said this. Nevertheless he walked calmly into the gas chamber, without worrying about the others.

One young woman caught my attention particularly as she ran busily hither and thither, helping the smallest children and the old women to undress. During the selection she had had two small children with her, and her agitated behavior and appearance had brought her to my notice at once. She did not look in the least like a Jewess. Now her children were no longer with her. She waited until the end, helping the women who were not undressed and who had several children with them, encouraging them and calming the children. She went with the very last ones into the gas chamber. Standing in the doorway, she said:

"I knew all the time that we were being brought to Auschwitz to be gassed. When the selection took place I avoided being put with the able-bodied ones, as I wished to look after the children. I wanted to go through it all, fully conscious of what was happening. I hope that it will be quick. Goodbye!"

From time to time women would suddenly give the most terrible shrieks while undressing, or tear their hair, or scream like maniacs. These were immediately led away behind the building and shot in the back of the neck with a small-caliber weapon.

It sometimes happened that, as the men of the Special Detachment left the gas chamber, the women would suddenly realize what was happening, and would call down every imaginable curse upon our heads.

I remember, too, a woman who tried to throw her children out of the gas chamber, just as the door was closing. Weeping, she called out:

"At least let my precious children live."

There were many such shattering scenes, which affected all who witnessed them.

During the spring of 1942 hundreds of vigorous men and women walked all unsuspecting to their death in the gas chambers, under the blossom-laden fruit trees of the "cottage" orchard. This picture of death in the midst of life remains with me to this day.

The process of selection, which took place on the unloading platforms, was in itself rich in incident.

The breaking up of families, and the separation of the men from the women and children, caused much agitation and spread anxiety throughout the whole transport. This was increased by the further separation from the others of those capable of work. Families wished at all costs to remain together. Those who had been selected ran back to rejoin their relations. Mothers with children tried to join their husbands, or old people attempted to find those of their children who had been selected for work, and who had been led away.

Often the confusion was so great that the selections had to be begun all over again. The limited area of standing room did not permit better sorting arrangements. All attempts to pacify these agitated mobs were useless. It was often necessary to use force to restore order.

As I have already frequently said, the Jews have strongly developed family feelings. They stick together like limpets. . . .

Then the bodies had to be taken from the gas chambers, and after the gold teeth had been extracted, and the hair cut off, they had to be dragged to the pits or to the crematoria. Then the fires in the pits had to be stoked, the surplus fat drained off, and the mountain of burning corpses constantly turned over so that the draught might fan the flames. . . .

It happened repeatedly that Jews of the Special Detachment would come upon the bodies of close relatives among the corpses, and even among the living as they entered the gas chambers. They were obviously affected by this, but it never led to any incident.[1]

[1]On October 7, 1944, the Sonderkommandos attacked the SS. Some SS guards were killed, and one crematorium was burned. Most of the prisoners who escaped were caught and killed.

Y. PFEFFER

CONCENTRATION CAMP LIFE AND DEATH

Jews not immediately selected for extermination faced a living death in the concentration camp, which also included non-Jewish inmates, many of them opponents of the Nazi regime. The SS, who ran the camps, took sadistic pleasure in humiliating and brutalizing their helpless Jewish victims. In 1946, Y. Pfeffer, a Jewish survivor of Majdanek concentration camp in Poland, described the world created by the SS and Nazi ideology.

You get up at 3 a.m. You have to dress quickly, and make the "bed" so that it looks like a matchbox. For the slightest irregularity in bed-making the punishment was 25 lashes, after which it was impossible to lie or sit for a whole month.

Everyone had to leave the barracks immediately. Outside it is still dark—or else the moon is shining. People are trembling because of lack of sleep and the cold. In order to warm up a bit, groups of ten to twenty people stand together, back to back so as to rub against each other.

There was what was called a wash-room, where everyone in the camp was supposed to wash—there were only a few faucets—and we were 4,500 people in that section (no. 3). Of course there was neither soap nor towel or even a handkerchief, so that washing was theoretical rather than practical. . . . In one day, a person there [be]came a lowly person indeed.

At 5 a.m. we used to get half a litre of black, bitter coffee. That was all we got for what was called "breakfast." At 6 a.m.—a headcount (*Appell* in German). We all had to stand at attention, in fives, according to the barracks, of which there were 22 in each section. We stood there until the SS men had satisfied their game-playing instincts by "humorous" orders to take off and put on caps. Then they received their report, and counted us. After the headcount—work.

We went in groups—some to build railway tracks or a road, some to the quarries to carry stones or coal, some to take out manure, or for potato-digging, latrine-cleaning, barracks—or sewer—repairs. All this took place inside the camp enclosure. During work the SS men beat up the prisoners mercilessly, inhumanly and for no reason.

They were like wild beasts and, having found their victim, ordered him to present his backside, and beat him with a stick or a whip, usually until the stick broke.

The victim screamed only after the first blows, afterwards he fell unconscious and the SS man then kicked at the ribs, the face, at the most sensitive parts of a man's body, and then, finally convinced that the victim was at the end of his strength, he ordered another Jew to pour one pail of water after the other over the beaten person until he woke and got up.

A favorite sport of the SS men was to make a "boxing sack" out of a Jew. This was done in the following way: Two Jews were stood up, one being forced to hold the other by the collar, and an SS man trained giving him a knock-out. Of course, after the first blow, the poor victim was likely to fall, and this was prevented by the other Jew holding him up. After the fat, Hitlerite murderer had "trained" in this way for 15 minutes, and only after the poor victim was completely shattered, covered in blood, his teeth knocked out, his nose broken, his eyes hit, they released him and ordered a doctor to treat his wounds. That was their way of taking care and being generous.

Another customary SS habit was to kick a Jew with a heavy boot. The Jew was forced to stand to attention, and all the while the SS man kicked him until he broke some bones. People who stood near enough to such a victim, often heard the breaking of the bones. The pain was so terrible that people, having undergone that treatment, died in agony.

Apart from the SS men there were other expert hangmen. These were the so-called Capos. The name was an abbreviation for "barracks police." The Capos were German criminals who were also camp inmates. However, although they belonged to "us," they were privileged. They had a special, better barracks of their own, they had better food, better, almost normal clothes, they wore special red or green riding pants, high leather boots, and fulfilled the functions of camp guards. They were worse even than the SS men. One of them, older than the others and the worst murderer of them all, when he descended on a victim, would not revive him later with water but would choke him to death. Once, this murderer caught a boy of 13 (in the presence of his father) and hit his head so that the poor child died instantly. This "camp elder" later boasted in front of his peers, with a smile on his beast's face and with pride, that he managed to kill a Jew with one blow.

In each section stood a gallows. For being late for the headcount, or similar crimes, the "camp elder" hanged the offenders.

Work was actually unproductive, and its purpose was exhaustion and torture.

At 12 noon there was a break for a meal. Standing in line, we received half a litre of soup each. Usually it was cabbage soup, or some other watery liquid, without fats, tasteless. That was lunch. It was eaten—in all weather—under the open sky, never in the barracks. No spoons were allowed, though wooden spoons lay on each bunk—probably for show, for Red Cross committees. One had to drink the soup out of the bowl and lick it like a dog.

From 1 p.m. till 6 p.m. there was work again. I must emphasize that if we were lucky we got a 12 o'clock meal. There were "days of punishment"—when lunch was given together with the evening meal, and it was cold and sour, so that our stomach was empty for a whole day.

Afternoon work was the same: blows, and blows again. Until 6 p.m.

At 6 there was the evening headcount. Again we were forced to stand at attention. Counting, receiving the report. Usually we were left standing at attention for an hour or two, while some prisoners were called up for "punishment parade"—they were those who in the Germans' eyes had transgressed in some way during the day, or had not been punctilious in their performance. They were stripped naked publicly, laid out on specially constructed benches, and whipped with 25 or 50 lashes.

The brutal beating and the heart-rending cries—all this the prisoners had to watch and hear.

MARIE NEUMANN

"WE'RE IN THE HANDS OF A MOB, NOT SOLDIERS, AND THEY'RE ALL DRUNK OUT OF THEIR MINDS"

As Russian troops advanced into Germany, many terrified German civilians fled westward, and not without reason. The invading Russians, seeking vengeance for the misery and ruin the Nazis had inflicted on their homeland and kinfolk, committed numerous atrocities against the conquered enemy. It quickly became official Soviet policy to prevent the perpetration of such personal acts of revenge and mayhem.

Marie Neumann of Baerwalde in Pomerania was one of the victims of this "terrible revenge." She put her nightmare in writing in 1948. Thirty years later, after reading *Nemesis at Potsdam* by Alfred-Maurice de Zayas, she sent the author her story. Following an exchange of letters and two personal visits, de Zayas was convinced she was telling the truth and later incorporated her testimony into a book about the postwar fate of Germans in Eastern Europe. Frau Neumann eventually left the Soviet zone of occupation and began a new life in West Germany. Unlike many others, she survived the acts of cruelty carried out against her and her family, described in the following passages from her 1948 account.

. . . My sister was on one side of the house with her seven-year-old daughter, and I was on the other side with her two other children and my husband. Someone had pressed a burning candle into his hand. My sister and I were raped again and again. The beasts lined up for us. During this time one of the military policemen held the door shut. I saw this because I was finally left alone before my sister was. Once she and her daughter both screamed in a most unnatural way, so that I thought they were being killed; and I wanted to go over to them when the policeman standing guard burst into our room and knocked my husband to the ground with his rifle. My niece Ilschen was crying and threw herself on my husband while the boy and I held the policeman's arm crying loudly, otherwise he would probably have killed my husband.

When we were finally granted a little peace and my husband had regained his senses, my sister came over to us and begged my husband to help her, asking, "Karl, what's going to happen to us?" My husband said, "I can't help any of you; we're in the hands of a mob, not soldiers, and they're all drunk out of their minds." I said, "Karl has to hide himself or they'll beat him to death; they've already beaten him half to death." My husband agreed with me and wanted to hide, but Grete held him back and begged him to think of her poor children. My husband then answered: "Grete, I just can't help anybody, but I'll stay with you; all we can do is hide, all of us, out in the hayloft." No sooner said than done. But just as we were climbing up into the loft, three men appeared; since there was snow outside, they had seen our tracks. We had to climb down; the two little girls were kissed and their mother raped again. She and her children cried so that it broke my heart. She cried out desperately: "O God, O God, why is this happening?" The men left, and my husband said: "They're going to kill me, they're going to kill all of you, and what they'll do to the children you can well imagine." My husband said that hiding now made no sense, we don't have any time to do it. I said: "Everybody get up there. I'll lock all the doors and they'll have to break them down first," hoping that it would give us the time to hide ourselves. But I had forgotten in the excitement that the yard gates had been broken down already because we had been closing them whenever we could. We had just gotten into the loft when there came a howling and yelling of rabble in our yard, shooting like crazy into the ground, and then they came after us. It had gotten dark in the meantime and they had flashlights. They were civilians and some military wearing cornered hats with pompoms. What happened next I can barely write down, the pen sticks in my hand. They hanged us all in that hayloft, from the rafters, except for the children. The mob strangled them by hand with a rope.

Later I was told by the people who had taken shelter in the Hackbarth family's cellar on Polziner Street that they had heard our unnatural screams, even down in the cellar; but no one had the courage to come for us, they were all fighting for their own lives at the time. I came to on the floor, lying next to my loved ones. I didn't know yet what had happened to them, although I had a good idea, it was the details I lacked. Because I was first thrown to the floor when the mob caught us, hit on the head and raped, after which I was hanged. I had lost consciousness immediately. Later I heard voices. I was lying on the floor, four men kneeling around me. They said, "Frau komm," and when I tried to stand, I fell down at once. Later I found myself in the yard being held up by two men. They took me inside and laid me on a bed. One of the four men, a civilian, a Pole, stayed by me and asked: "Frau, who did?" I said: "The Russians." Then he hit me and said: "Russians, good soldiers. German SS, pigs, hang women and children." I fell into a fit of crying; it was impossible to stop. Then the other three came back in, but when they saw me, they left my apartment. Shortly thereafter a Russian came in carrying a whip, constantly yelling at me. Apparently he wanted me to be still, but I just couldn't. So he hit me once with the whip, then kept hitting the side of the bed. When that didn't work, he gave up and left my house. Then I heard voices in front of the house and got more scared than I was ever before or since. Seized by a cold panic I ran out to the little creek next to our garden, where the geese used to swim. I wanted to drown myself and tried for a long time until I was faint. But even that didn't bring my life to an end.

How I got through all this I don't know to this day. In any case someone had hauled me out of the creek. When I regained my senses I made my way to Fraulein Bauch's room on the ground floor of Schmechel's, the shopkeeper. Dear God how I was freezing because there were no windows or doors left in the place, and my clothes were wet; it was the night of March 4th to 5th and there was still snow and ice about. After a while I saw there was a bed in the room, so I laid down thinking I was alone in the place. But I quickly saw that someone had been sitting at the table and was now standing up, coming over to my bed, and, oh no, it was a Russian. Suddenly my whole miserable plight came before my eyes. I cried again and begged him if he wouldn't please shoot me. He shined a flashlight into my face, took off his coat and showed me his medals, saying that he was a first lieutenant and that I need not be afraid. He took a hand towel down from the wall and began to rub me dry. When he saw my throat, he asked: "Who did?" I said, "the Russians." "Yes, yes," he said, "Was the Bolsheviks, but now not Bolsheviks, now White Russians; White Russians good." He then took his bayonet and cut off my panties, whereupon I again was ready to die, for I didn't know what to expect anymore. He rubbed my legs dry; but I was still freezing and didn't know what I should do if I had frostbite. But then he took off my wedding ring and put it in his pocket. He asked me where my husband was, and then raped me in spite of my miserable condition. Afterwards he promised to send me to a German doctor. I was happy about that, but then I remembered there were no more German doctors in our area.

Shortly after he left four 18- to 20-year-old Russians appeared. Totally drunk, they pulled me out of bed and raped me in an unnatural way. In my condition I wasn't able to do more and fell beside the bed, so they kicked me with their boots, getting me just in the worst spot. I fainted again. When I came to, I crawled back into the bed. Then two more such bums showed up, but they left me alone as I was more dead than alive. I learned back then how much a human being can endure; I couldn't talk, couldn't cry, couldn't even utter a sound. They hit me a bit, which didn't matter to me since I couldn't feel anything, and then left me alone. I fell asleep out of sheer exhaustion.

When I awoke very early next morning, I realized again where I was. I quickly noticed an open wardrobe door, and inside was a dress. There was also a shirt and some underwear. So even though the things were much too small, I put them on; what was left of my clothes was still wet. I had to put the dress on leaving the back unfastened, to make it fit. There were no stockings to be found; mine had been wound up so tight they were like bones. Then I was visited by the Russians again. First one who apparently thought the room was empty, because when he saw me in bed, he left the room immediately. He came back with three more men; that first one wanted to hit me, but the officer wouldn't let him. So the first man pointed to the Hitler portrait on the wall which was full of bullet holes, and he said I was a Hitler fascist. I said, "No! This isn't my house." He said, "Come! Go your house!" I had to walk ahead of them to my house and must have been a pretty sight. When I got there I saw a truck parked in front, and Russian soldiers were loading my slaughtered livestock into a car. The soldiers almost laughed themselves to death when they saw me. They indicated to their officer, their fingers tapping their heads, that I was probably crazy, and when four female soldiers appeared, they wanted to shoot me. But the officer didn't permit it. He asked about my neck, and I said, "Russian soldiers; my husband, sister, children, too." When he heard the word children, he was shocked. I asked him to come to the barn with me but he didn't want to, and I wasn't allowed to go back either. So I asked to go to the commandant. He agreed at once with that and sent a soldier with me. But when we got to the corner by Kollatz, he indicated to me that I should continue along Neustettiner Street by myself. There were several men already in the marketplace, clearing things away. When I got to the butcher, Albert Nass's place, a Russian soldier told me to go in: Commander's Headquarters.

Inside the courtyard. . . .

[A] Russian soldier said, "German woman! Stairs there, go up." I was immediately made a prisoner for my effort, locked into a room with others.

When evening arrived, it was hell itself. One woman after another in our group was hauled out. The shoemaker's wife, Frau Graf, who was in her last month of pregnancy, was taken, also a woman from Wusterhausen, and the Peters' daughter Frau Schmidt. They were driven away by some soldier. The women screamed as they were being forced into the car, and the prisoners' room was full of screaming. Our nerves were raw. Then we heard the motor revving up, the Russians shone searchlights into the room through the window, so bright that several women screamed out that they were using flame throwers against us. The children cried miserably; it was horrible. Toward morning the women came back. Two came into the room and collapsed; the other woman was raped once more by the door before they let her in. They came to get me once during the night. I was taken into the slaughterhouse and assaulted on a feather bed right on the soil. When I came to, my neighbor Herr Held was crying over me. My neck had swollen so much over the past hours that I had trouble moving my mouth, and I was spitting blood.

FAREED ZAKARIA

"DEMOCRACY HAS ITS DARK SIDES"

In the following selection from his book *The Future of Freedom* (2003), Fareed Zakaria, editor of *Newsweek International*, discusses the implications of the spread of democracy throughout much of the globe. In many countries, he observes, the adoption of democratic procedures—parliaments and the ballot—has enabled dictators to gain and retain power.

We live in a democratic age. Over the last century the world has been shaped by one trend above all others—the rise of democracy. In 1900 not a single country had what we would today consider democracy: a government created by elections in which every adult citizen could vote. Today 119 do, comprising 62 percent of all countries in the world. What was once a peculiar practice of a handful of states around the North Atlantic has become the standard form of government for humankind. Monarchies are antique, fascism and communism utterly discredited. Even Islamic theocracy appeals only to a fanatical few. For the vast majority of the world, democracy is the sole surviving source of political legitimacy. Dictators such as Egypt's Hosni Mubarak and Zimbabwe's Robert Mugabe go to great effort and expense to organize national elections—which, of course, they win handily. When the enemies of democracy mouth its rhetoric and ape its rituals, you know it has won the war.

We live in a democratic age in an even broader sense. From its Greek root, "democracy" means "the rule of the people." And everywhere we are witnessing the shift of power downward. I call this "democratization," even though it goes far beyond politics, because the process is similar: hierarchies are breaking down, closed systems are opening up, and pressures from the masses are now the primary engine of social change. Democracy has gone from being a form of government to a way of life.

Consider the economic realm. What is truly distinctive and new about today's capitalism is not that it is global or information-rich or technologically driven—all that has been true at earlier points in history—but rather that it is *democratic.* Over the last half-century economic growth has enriched hundreds of millions in the industrial world, turning consumption, saving, and investing into a mass phenomenon. This has forced the social structures of societies to adapt. Economic power, which was for centuries held by small groups of businessmen, bankers, and bureaucrats has, as a result, been shifting downward. Today most companies—indeed most countries—woo not the handful that are rich but the many that are middle class. And rightly so, for the assets of the most exclusive investment group are dwarfed by those of a fund of workers' pensions.

Culture has also been democratized. What was once called "high culture" continues to flourish, of course, but as a niche product for the elderly set, no longer at the center of society's cultural life, which is now defined and dominated by popular music, blockbuster movies, and prime-time television. Those three make up the canon of the modern age, the set of cultural references with which everyone in society is familiar. The democratic revolution coursing through society has changed our very definiton of culture. The key to the reputation of, say, a singer in an old order would have been *who* liked her. The key to fame today is *how many* like her. And by that yardstick Madonna will always trump Jessye Norman. Quantity has become quality.

What has produced this dramatic shift? As with any large-scale social phenomenon, many forces have helped produce the democratic wave—a technological revolution, growing middle-class wealth, and the collapse of alternative systems and ideologies that organized society. To these grand systemic causes add another: America. The rise and dominance of America—a country whose politics and culture are deeply democratic—has made democratization seem inevitable. Whatever its causes, the democratic wave is having predictable effects in every area. It is breaking down hierarchies, empowering individuals, and transforming societies well beyond their politics. Indeed much of what is distinctive about the world we live in is a consequence of the demo-cratic idea.

We often read during the roaring 1990s that technology and information had been democratized. This is a relatively new phenomenon. In the past, technology helped reinforce centralization and hierarchy. For example, the last great information revolution—in the 1920s involving radio, television, movies, megaphones—had a centralizing effect. It gave the person or group with access to that technology the power to reach the rest of society. That's why the first step in a twentieth-century coup or revolution was always to take control of the country's television or radio station. But today's information revolution has produced thousands of outlets for news that make central control impossible and dissent easy. The Internet has taken this process another huge step forward, being a system where, in the columnist Thomas Friedman's words, "everyone is connected but no one is in control."

The democratization of technology and information means that most anyone can get his hands on anything. Like weapons of mass destruction. We now know that Osama bin Laden was working on a serious biological-weapon program during the 1990s. But what is most astonishing is that the scientific information and manuals found in Al Qaeda's Kabul safe houses were not secrets stolen from government laboratories. They were documents downloaded from the Internet. Today if you want to find sources for anthrax, recipes for poison, or methods to weaponize chemicals, all you need is a good search engine. These same open sources will, unfortunately, soon help someone build a dirty bomb. The components are easier to get than ever before. Mostly what you need is knowledge, and that has been widely disseminated over the last decade. Even nuclear technology is now commonly available. It is, after all, fifty-year-old know-how, part of the world of am radios and black-and-white television. Call it the democratization of violence.

It's more than a catchy phrase. The democratization of violence is one of the fundamental— and terrifying—features of the world today. For centuries the state has had a monopoly over the legitimate use of force in human societies. This inequality of power between the state and the citizen created order and was part of the glue that held modern civilization together. But over the last few decades the state's advantage has been weakened; now small groups of people can do dreadful things. And while terrorism is the most serious blow to state authority, central governments have been under siege in other ways as well. Capital markets, private businesses, local governments, nongovernmental organizations have all been gaining strength, sapping the authority of the state. The illegal flow of people, drugs, money, and weapons rising around the world attests to its weakness. This diffusion of power will continue because it is fueled by broad technological, social, and economic changes. In the post–September 11 world the state has returned, with renewed power and legitimacy. This too will endure. The age of terror will thus be marked by a tension, between the forces that drive the democratization of authority on the one hand and the state on the other.

To discuss these problems is not to say that democracy is a bad thing. Overwhelmingly it has had wonderful consequences. Who among us would want to go back to an age with fewer choices and less individual power and autonomy? But like any broad transformation, democracy has its dark sides. Yet we rarely speak about them. To do so would be to provoke instant criticism that you are "out of sync" with the times. But this means that we never really stop to understand these times. Silenced by fears of being branded "antidemocratic" we have no way to understand what might be troubling about the ever-increasing democratization of our lives. We asssume that no problem could ever be caused by democracy, so when we see social, political, and economic maladies we shift blame here and there, deflecting problems, avoiding answers, but never talking about the great transformation that is at the center of our political, economic, and social lives.

DEMOCRACY AND LIBERTY

"Suppose elections are free and fair and those elected are racists, fascists, separatists," said the American diplomat Richard Holbrooke about Yugoslavia in the 1990s. "That is the dilemma." Indeed it is, and not merely in Yugoslavia's past but in the world's present. Consider, for example, the challenge we face across the Islamic world. We recognize the need for democracy in those often-repressive countries. But what if democracy produces an Islamic theocracy or something like it? It is not an idle concern. Across the globe, democratically elected regimes, often ones that have been re-elected or reaffirmed through referenda, are routinely ignoring constitutional limits on their power and depriving their citizens of basic rights. This disturbing phenomenon—visible from Peru to the Palestinian territories, from Ghana to Venezuela—could be called "illiberal democracy."

For people in the West, democracy means "liberal domocracy": a political system marked not only by free and fair elections but also by the rule of law, a separation of powers, and the protection of basic liberties of speech, assembly, religion, and property. But this bundle of freedoms—what might be termed "constitutional liberalism"—has nothing intrinsically to do with democracy and the two have not always gone together, even in the West. After all, Adolf Hitler became chancellor of Germany via free elections. Over the last half-century in the West, democracy and liberty have merged. But today the two strands of liberal democracy, interwoven in the Western political fabric, are coming apart across the globe. Democracy is flourishing; liberty is not.

In some places, such as Central Asia, elections have paved the way for dictatorships. In others, they have exacerbated group conflict and ethnic tensions. Both Yugoslavia and Indonesia, for example, were far more tolerant and secular when they were ruled by strongmen (Tito and Suharto, respectively) than they are now as democracies. And in many nondemocracies, elections would not improve matters much. Across the Arab world elections held tomorrow would probably bring to power regimes that are more intolerant, reactionary, anti-Western, and anti-Semitic than the dictatorships currently in place.

In a world that is increasingly democratic, regimes that resist the trend produce dysfunctional societies—as in the Arab world. Their people sense the deprivation of liberty more strongly than ever before because they know the alternatives; they can see them on CNN, BBC, and Al-Jazeera. But yet, newly democratic countries too often become sham democracies, which produces disenchantment, disarray, violence, and new forms of tyranny. Look at Iran and Venezuela. This is not a reason to stop holding elections, of course, but surely it should make us ask, What is at the root of this troubling development? Why do so many developing countries have so much difficulty creating stable, genuinely democratic societies? Were we to embark on the vast challenge of building democracy in Iraq, how would we make sure that we succeed?

AMY CHUA

"FREE MARKET DEMOCRACY BREEDS ETHNIC HATRED AND GLOBAL INSTABILITY"

In *World on Fire* (2003), Yale law school professor Amy Chua reveals a troubling consequence of globalization: the spread of free markets and democracy, which enables a better prepared ethnic minority within a given country to amass disproportionate wealth, has exploded into ethnic hatred and violence. In the following selection, Chua states her thesis.

This book is about a phenomenon—pervasive outside the West yet rarely acknowledged, indeed often viewed as taboo—that turns free market democracy into an engine of ethnic conflagration. The phenomenon I refer to is that of *market-dominant minorities*: ethnic minorities who, for widely varying reasons, tend under market conditions to dominate economically, often to a startling extent, the "indigenous" majorities around them.

Market-dominant minorities can be found in every corner of the world. The Chinese are a market-dominant minority not just in the Philippines but throughout Southeast Asia. In 1998, Chinese Indonesians, only 3 percent of the population, controlled roughly 70 percent of Indonesia's private economy, including all of the country's largest conglomerates. More recently, in Burma, entrepreneurial Chinese have literally taken over the economies of Mandalay and Rangoon. Whites are a market-dominant minority in South Africa—and, in a more complicated sense, in Brazil, Ecuador, Guatemala, and much of Latin America. Lebanese are a market-dominant minority in West Africa. Ibo are a market-dominant minority in Nigeria. Croats were a market-dominant minority in the former Yugoslavia. And Jews are almost certainly a market-dominant minority in post-Communist Russia.

Market-dominant minorities are the Achilles' heel of free market democracy. In societies with a market-dominant ethnic minority, markets and democracy favor not just different people, or different classes, but different ethnic groups. Markets concentrate wealth, often spectacular wealth, in the hands of the market-dominant minority, while democracy increases the political power of the impoverished majority. In these circumstances the pursuit of free market democracy becomes an engine of potentially catastrophic ethnonationalism, pitting a frustated "indigenous" majority, easily aroused by opportunistic vote-seeking politicians, against a resented, wealthy ethnic minority. This confrontation is playing out in country after country today, from Indonesia to Sierra Leone, from Zimbabwe to Venezuela, from Russia to the Middle East.

Since September 11, 2001, this confrontation has also been playing out in the United States. Americans are not an ethnic minority (although we are a national-origin minority, a close cousin). Nor is there democracy at the global level. Nevertheless, Americans today are everywhere perceived as the world's market-dominant minority, wielding outrageously disproportionate economic power relative to our size and numbers. As a result, we have become the object of mass, popular resentment and hatred of the same kind that is directed at so many other market-dominant minorities around the world.

Global anti-Americanism has many causes. One of them, ironically, is the global spread of free markets and democracy. Throughout the world, global markets are bitterly perceived as reinforcing American wealth and dominance. At the same time, global populist and demo-cratic movements give strength, legitimacy, and voice to the impoverished, frustrated, excluded masses of the world—precisely the people, in other words, most susceptible to anti-American demagoguery. In more non-Western countries than Americans would care to admit, free and fair elections would bring to power anti-market, anti-American leaders. For the last twenty years Americans have been grandly promoting both marketization and democratization throughout the world. In the process we have directed at ourselves the anger of the damned.

The relationship between free market democracy and ethnic violence around the world is inextricably bound up with globalization. But the phenomenon of market-dominant minorities introduces complications that have escaped the view of both globalization's enthusiasts and its critics.

To a great extent, globalization consists of, and is fueled by, the unprecedented worldwide spread of markets and democracy. For over two decades now, the American government, along with American consultants, business interests, and foundations, has been vigorously promoting free market democracy throughout the developing and post-socialist worlds. . . .

The fact is that in the last two decades, the American-led global spread of markets and democracy has radically transformed the world. Both directly and through powerful international institutions like the World Bank, International Monetary Fund, and World Trade Organization (WTO), the United States government has helped bring capitalism and democratic elections to literally billions of people. At the same time, American multinationals, foundations, and nongovernmental organizations (NGOs) have swept the world, bringing with them ballot boxes and Burger Kings, hip-hop and Hollywood, banking codes and American-drafted constitutions.

The prevailing view among globalization's supporters is that markets and democracy are a kind of universal prescription for the multiple ills of underdevelopment. Market capitalism is the most efficient economic system the world has ever known. Democracy is the fairest political system the world has ever known and the one most respectful of individual liberty. Working hand in hand, markets and democracy will gradually transform the world into a community of prosperous, war-shunning nations, and individuals into liberal, civic-minded citizens and consumers. In the process, ethnic hatred, religious zealotry, and other "backward" aspects of underdevelopment will be swept away.

Thomas Friedman has been a brilliant proponent of this dominant view. In his best-selling book *The Lexus and the Olive Tree*, he reproduced a Merrill Lynch ad that said "The spread of free markets and democracy around the world is permitting more people everywhere to turn their aspirations into achievements," erasing "not just geographical borders but also human ones." Globalization, Friedman elaborated, "tends to turn all friends and enemies into 'competitors.'" Friedman also proposed his "Golden Arches Theory of Conflict Prevention" which claims that "no two countries that both have McDonald's have ever fought a war against each other. . . ." (Unfortunately, notes Yale history professor John Gaddis, "the United States and its NATO allies chose just that inauspicious moment to begin bombing Belgrade, where there was an embarrassing number of golden arches.")

For globalization's enthusiasts, the cure for group hatred and ethnic violence around the world is straightforward: more markets and more democracy. Thus after the September 11 attacks, Friedman published an op-ed piece pointing to India and Bangladesh as good "role models" for the Middle East and arguing that the solution to terrorism and militant Islam is: "Hello? Hello? There's a message here. It's democracy, stupid!"—"{m}ulti-ethnic, pluralistic, free-market democracy."

By contrast, the sobering thesis of this book is that the global spread of markets and democracy is a principal, aggravating cause of group hatred and ethnic violence throughout the non-Western world. In the numerous societies around the world that have a market-dominant minority, markets and democracy are not mutually reinforcing. Because markets and democracy benefit different ethnic groups in such societies, the pursuit of free market democracy produces highly unstable and combustible conditions. Markets concentrate enormous wealth in the hands of an "outsider" minority, fomenting ethnic envy and hatred among often chronically poor majorities. In absolute terms the majority may or may not be better off—a dispute that much of the globalization debate fixates on—but any sense of improvement is overwhelmed by their continuing poverty and the hated minority's extraordinary economic success. More humiliating still, market-dominant minorities, along with their foreign-investor partners, invariably come to control the crown jewels of the economy, often symbolic of the nation's patrimony and identity—oil in Russia and Venezuela, diamonds in South Africa, silver and tin in Bolivia, jade, teak, and rubies in Burma.

Introducing democracy in these circumstances does not tranform voters into open-minded cocitizens in a national community. Rather, the competition for votes fosters the emergence of demagogues who scapegoat the resented minority and foment active ethnonationalist movements demanding that the country's wealth and identity be reclaimed by the "true owners of the nation." As America celebrated the global spread of democracy in the 1990s, ethnicized political slogans proliferated: "Georgia for the Georgians," "Eritreans Out of Ethiopia," "Kenya for Kenyans," "Whites should leave Bolivia," "Kazakhstan for Kazakhs," "Serbia for Serbs," "Croatia for Croats," "Hutu Power," "Assam for Assamese," "Jews Out of Russia." Romania's 2001 presidential candidate Vladim Tudor was not quite so pithy. "I'm Vlad the Impaler," he campaigned; referring to the historically economically dominant Hungarian minority, he promised: "We will hang them directly by their Hungarian tongue!"'

When free market democracy is pursued in the presence of a market-dominant minority, the almost invariable result is backlash. This backlash typically takes one of three forms. The first is a backlash against markets, targeting the market-dominant minority's wealth. The second is a backlash against democracy by forces favorable to the market-dominant minority. The third is violence, sometimes genocidal, directed against the market-dominant minority itself.

Zimbabwe today is a vivid illustration of the first kind of backlash—an ethnically targeted anti-market backlash. For several years now President Robert Mugabe has encouraged the violent seizure of 10 million acres of white-owned commercial farmland. As one Zimbabwean explained, "The land belongs to us. The foreigners should not own land here. There is no black Zimbabwean who owns land in England. Why should any European own land here?" Mugabe himself was more explicit: "Strike fear in the heart of the white man, our real enemy!" Most of the country's white "foreigners" are third-generation Zimbabweans. Just 1 percent of the population, they have for generations controlled 70 percent of the country's best land, largely in the form of highly productive three-thousand-acre tobacco and sugar farms.

Watching Zimbabwe's economy take a free fall as a result of the mass land grab, the United States and United Kingdom together with dozens of human rights groups urged President Mugabe to step down, calling resoundingly for "free and fair elections." But the idea that *democracy* is the answer to Zimbabwe's problems is breathtakingly naive. Perhaps Mugabe would have lost the 2002 elections in the absence of foul play. Even if so, it is important to remember that Mugabe himself is a product of democracy. The hero of Zimbabwe's black liberation movement and a master manipulator of masses, he swept to victory in the closely monitored elections of 1980, promising to expropriate "stolen" white land. Repeating that promise has helped him win every election since. Moreover, Mugabe's land-seizure campaign was another product of the democratic process. It was deftly timed in anticipation of the 2000 and 2002 elections, and deliberately calculated to mobilize popular support of Mugabe's teetering regime.

In the contest between an economically powerful ethnic minority and a numerically powerful impoverished majority, the majority does not always prevail. Instead of a backlash against the market, another likely outcome is a backlash against democracy, favoring the market-dominant minority at the expense of majority will. Examples of this dynamic are extremely common. Indeed, . . . the world's most notorious cases of "crony capitalism" all involve a market-dominant ethnic minority—from Ferdinand Marcos's Chinese-protective dictatorship in the Philippines to President Siaka Stevens's shadow alliance with five Lebanese diamond dealers in Sierra Leone to President Daniel Arap Moi's "business arrangements" with a handful of Indian tycoons in Kenya today,

The third and most ferocious kind of backlash is majority-supported violence aimed at eliminating a market-dominant minority. Two recent examples are the ethnic cleansing of Croats in the former Yugoslavia and the mass slaughter of Tutsi in Rwanda. In both cases a resented and disproportionately prosperous ethnic minority was attacked by members of a relatively impoverished majority, incited by an ethnonationalist government. In other words, markets and democracy were among the causes of both the Rwandian and Yugoslavian genocides. This is a large claim, but one that [we] will try to defend.

ABBAS AMANAT

"EMPOWERED THROUGH VIOLENCE: THE REINVENTION OF ISLAMIC EXTREMISM"

Bin Laden and his followers view their struggle against the United States as a holy war against the infidel. Their goal is the creation of an Islamic world-state governed by Islamic law, a revival of the medieval caliphate. A religious fanatic and absolutist who cannot tolerate pluralism, bin Laden wants to drive westerners and Western values out of Islamic lands; he is also a theocrat who would use the state's power to impose a narrow, intolerant version of Islam on the Muslim world. He and his followers are zealots who are convinced that they are doing God's will. Recruits for suicide missions are equally convinced that they are waging holy war against the enemies of God and their centers of evil, for which they will be richly rewarded in Paradise. The hatred of radical Muslims for the West shows that in an age of globalism the world is still divided by strong cultural traditons. In the following selection, Abbas Amanat, specialist in Middle East history, analyzes the roots of Islamic radicalism, focusing on the resentment many Muslims have against the West.

To this author, a historian of the Middle East who grew up in that part of the world, bin Laden's message of violence comes as a sobering reminder of what has become of the Middle East. This is not only because an outrage of unprecedented magnitude has been committed by some Middle Easterners against the U.S., which is both demonized in that region and seductive to many who live there. Nor is it because such an act confirmed the worst stereotypes of violence and fanaticism long associated with Islam and the Middle East. It was also because the outrage revealed much about the undeniable and alarming growth of religious extremism in the Muslim world, a trend that has been deeply intertwined with the tortured historical experience of becoming modern. . . .

1.

The emergence of the construct we call Islamic extremism, with its penchant for defiance, resentment, and violence, has its roots in the history of the Muslim sense of decline and its unhappy encounter with the dominant West. It is sobering to remind ourselves how frequently the Middle East, as one part of the Muslim world, has been visited by waves of violence in its recent history. Since the end of the Second World War, the area extending from Egypt and Turkey in the west to Afghanistan in the northwest and Yemen in the south has suffered at least ten major wars—and that's not counting the U.S. engagement in Afghanistan after September 11. Casualties have run into millions. Populations have been uprooted, societies torn up by their roots, political structures demolished—all on a massive scale. Three of the region's wars were fought with Western powers (Britain's and France's attacks on Egypt during the Suez crisis in 1956; the Soviet Union's long, losing effort to subjugate Afghanistan in the 1980s; the American-led campaign to liberate Kuwait from Iraq in 1990–91); Israel and its Arab neighbors waged five wars (1948, 1956, 1967, 1973 and 1982); Yemen and Lebanon have suffered prolonged civil wars; and Iraq and Iran fought for eight years. The transforming effects of these crises haunted the last several generations in the Middle East. Throughout the region people have become ever more disillusioned with the deeply-entrenched dictatorships in their own countries, with the collapse of democratic institutions, hollow nationalistic rhetoric, and with their failing economies.

In the minds of many, Western powers shared the blame, both directly and indirectly. Whether based on historical reality or faulty perception, holding the Western powers responsible made special sense against the backdrop of a powerful West and a powerless Middle East. From the days of the European colonial powers in the 19th century to the more recent interventions of the superpowers, there has been a pattern of diplomatic, military and economic presence tying the fate of the Middle East and its resources to the West. Whether motivated by oil, grand strategy or support for Israel, the Western powers were either involved in, or perceived to be behind, most of the region's political crises.

As a result, for new generations of Middle Easterners perceptions of the West, and particularly of the U.S., dramatically changed for the worse. Long gone were the images of well-wishing Yankees who established schools, universities and hospitals, distributed food, and supported nationalist endeavors. Instead, fascination with a luster of American popular culture was only heightened thanks to Hollywood and American high tech—computers, video games, and satellite dishes. Yet in a paradoxical turn, as the lines of visa-seekers in front of U.S. consulates grew longer, a cloud of mistrust and resentment against the U.S. also settled over the region. The people in the Middle East began to view American society through the lenses of sitcoms and softwares. To many unaccustomed eyes, the U.S. seemed like the center of a greedy, materialistic and uncaring world obsessed with violence and promiscuity. The U.S.'s unreserved support for Israel, its backing of unpopular regimes, and its fighter jets over Middle Eastern skies only added to anti-American feelings.

2.

Mistrust toward the West deepened as a result of the problematic way the Middle East improvised its own version of modernity. Since the beginning of the 20th century, Westernization has transformed lifestyles and expectations. Yet, despite an undeniable measure of growth and material improvement, today's Middle East by most economic indicators is still one of the least developed regions in the world. It is grappling endlessly with failed centralized planning, high birthrates, lopsided distribution of wealth, high unemployment, widespread corruption, inefficient bureaucracies, and environmental and health problems. The frustration endemic among the young urban classes—often the children of rural migrants who came to the cities in search of a better life and a higher income—is a response to these conundrums.

For the population of the Middle East, progressively younger because of high birthrates, uprooted from their traditional setting, and deprived of illusive privileges that they can see around them and on television screens but cannot have, the familiar and comforting space of Islam offers a welcoming alternative. Daily prayers, Friday sermons, Koranic study groups, Islamic charities—these are all part of that space. But so are the street demonstrations and the clandestine pamphlets, with their fiery anti-establishment, anti-secular, and anti-Zionist message.

In dealing with these restive multitudes, the governments of the Middle East and their associated ruling elites have little to offer. They are themselves part of the problem as they contribute to the public perception of powerlessness. In the period right after World War II, nationalist ideologies were highly effective in mobilizing the public against the European colonial presence. But over time they often hindered the growth of democratic institutions and the emergence of an enduring civil society. The army officers who came to power in Egypt, Syria, Iraq, and elsewhere through military coups, and prolonged their leadership through repressive means, invested heavily in anti-Western rhetoric. Yet facing the erosion of their own legitimacy, they learned to pay a lip service to the rising Islamic sentiments in their societies, exploiting them as a cushion between the elite and the masses and to suppress individual freedoms.

The predictable victims of this appeasement were the modernizing urban middle classes of the Middle East. Though small and vulnerable, these middle classes were crucial conduits for modernizing even as they preserved a sense of national culture. Egypt, Iraq, Syria, Turkey, and Iran, in their rush for an illusive economic growth, and greater equity, purposely undermined the economic bases of their middle classes. They did so through heavy-handed state planning and the mindless nationalization programs. The middle classes in the Middle East today, besieged and intimidated, are no longer willing or able to take up the cause of demo-cratic reforms. They have instead given rise to a spoiled crust of the politically silenced and submissive class whose voice of protest is heard, increasingly, through extremist causes.

Out of this milieu came Mohamed Atta [who crashed one of the hijacked planes into the World Trade Center], a failed son of an affluent Egyptian lawyer. Another example is bin Laden's chief lieutenant, Ayman al-Zawahiri, a physician from a celebrated Egyptian family.

This staggering reorientation toward radical Islam needs to be understood in light of a deeper crisis of identity in the Arab world. In the post-colonial period, most nation-states in that region had to improvise their own ideologies of territorial nationalism in order to hold together what were often disjointed local and ethnic identities. At the same time they had to remain loyal to the ideology of pan-Arabism—the notion, or dream, that all Arab peoples make up one supernation—a project that was destined to fail dismally. Egypt came out of the colonial experience with what might have been the basis for its own Egyptian nationalism, but under Gamal Abdel Nasser, it traded that away for leadership of the pan-Arab cause. Yet the experiences of secular pan-Arabism, whether that of the Nasser era in the 1950s and 60s or the Ba'thist regimes of Iraq and Syria in the 1960s and 1970s, proved illusory to the intellectuals who championed it. It was even more unrewarding to the Arab masses who for decades were exposed to the state-run propaganda machines and to the often demagogic street politics. The harsh realities of the military and paramilitary regimes of the Arab world sobered even the most ardent supporters of Arab nationalism.

It was in this environment of despair that the disempowered Arab masses came to share the common cause of confronting Zionism. Resistance to the establishment of the Jewish homeland since the end of World War I and to the creation of the state of Israel in 1947 offered the Arab world a rallying point of great symbolic power. The subsequent experiences of multiple defeats in wars against Israel revived in the Arab psyche memories of prolonged colonial domination. From the Arab nationalist perspective, Zionism was not merely another form of imagined nationalism rooted in the 19th century, but a project designed by the West to perpetuate its imperial presence and protect its vested interests in the region—the latest manifestation of centuries of enmity against the Muslim peoples. For many in the Arab world it was comforting to believe that the reason why hundreds of millions of Arabs could not defeat Israel was because Western powers were protecting it. And more often than not there was ample evidence to convince them of the validity of their claim.

3.

Not surprisingly, the sense of despair toward repressive regimes at home and helplessness against the consolidation of the neighboring Zionist state engendered a new spirit of Islamic solidarity. It was radical in its politics, monolithic in its approach, and defiant toward the West.

The decisive shift came not inside the Arab world but with the 1979 revolution in Iran. The establishment of an Islamic republic under the leadership of the uncompromising Ayatollah Khomeini evoked throughout the Muslim world the long-cherished desire for creating a genuine Islamic regime. Even though it was preached by a radical Shi'a clergy who committed enormous atrocities against his own people, the Iranian model of revolutionary Islam was viewed as pointing the way to an "authentic" and universalist Islam. Through cassette tapes and demonstrations, Iranian revolutionaries managed to topple the Shah and the mighty Pahlavi regime despite its vast military arsenal, secularizing program, and Western backing. Even more empowering was the revolution's anti-imperialist rhetoric.

After his followers besieged the American embassy and held its staff hostage in 1980–81, Khomeini labeled the U.S. as the Great Satan for backing the "Pharaonic" powers—a label for the shah and conservative rulers elsewhere in the region—and for repressing the "disinherited" of the earth.

The Iraq–Iran War of 1980–88 further established the appeal of the paradigm of martyrdom that had long been deeply rooted in Shi'a Islam. That conflict was portrayed as an apocalyptic jihad between the forces of truth and falsehood. In addition to defending their own nation, the Iranians believed they were exporting their revolution. As the slogan on the banners declared and as the battle cries of many teenage volunteers confirmed, the path of Islamic liberation stretched across the battlefields to the Shi'a holy cities of Karbala' and Najaf in Iraq all the way to Jerusalem.

Even if the Iranian revolution failed to take root elsewhere, the celebration of martyrdom found resonance far and wide. The revolutionary Shiites of Lebanon's Hezbollah, and later the young Palestinians who eagerly volunteered for suicide bombings on behalf of the Hamas and Islamic Jihad, saw martyrdom as a way of empowerment. It is not difficult to see the same traits among the hijackers of September 11.

The accelerated pace of Islamic radicalism in the early 1980s, whether inspired by the Iranian revolution or reacting to it, helped shape the outlook of a generation from which came the extremism of Osama bin Laden himself. In his twenties, he was a pious, though uninspiring, student in Jidda University in Saudi Arabia. He came from a superrich family with close connections to the Saudi royalty. In November 1979, he must have witnessed the siege of the Grand Mosque of Mecca and the revolt under the leadership of a messianic figure who claimed to have received direct authority from the Prophet to render justice. The quick suppression of this revolt by the Saudi authorities came only a month after the signing of the Camp David peace agreement between Israel and Egypt. The treaty was received by the Islamic activists throughout the Arab world as a betrayal to the Arab and Islamic causes. Only a year later, in October 1980, the Egyptian president, Anwar al-Sadat, was assassinated by a splinter group of the Muslim Brothers with which Ayman al-Zawahiri, bin Laden's future lieutenant, was associated.

The Mecca uprising and Sadat's assassination were both inspired by a tradition of religious radicalism going back to the Society of the Muslim Brothers in the 1920s and 30s and before that to the Wahhabi movement that began in the late 18th century. The central doctrine of Wahhabism was a return to the way of "virtuous ancestors," a highly regressive, monolithic interpretation of Islam known as Salafiyya, a doctrinal propensity that for centuries encouraged strict adherence to puritanical principles.

In the early 20th century, the Salafiyya played a central part in the shaping of Saudi Arabia as an Islamic state. It also served as the guiding doctrine for the Muslim Brothers' goal of moral and political reconstruction. Inspired by the ideas of Sayyid Qutb, a leader of the Muslim Brothers—who was executed in 1966 by the Nasser regime—this ideology received a new lease on life. A true believer was required to "renounce" the dark sacrilege of his secular surroundings. The primary targets were the regimes of the Arab world, whose secularism was labeled a return to the "paganism" of pre-Islamic times. . .

The doctrine of Salafiyya and its articulation by Sayyid Qutb gained an overwhelming currency among Islamic radicals in the early 1980s. But the wilderness that might serve as a refuge for them could not be recreated in the oil-rich Saudi Arabia of bin Laden or in the tourist-infested Egypt of al-Zawahiri. Instead, Afghanistan beckoned. The burgeoning resistance movement against the occupying Soviet forces there was highly appealing to radical and moderate sentiments alike. It could unite activists of all Islamic persuasions for a common cause of fighting the spread of the godless communism.

Amanat then discusses how Osama bin Laden and other Arabs from Morocco to Yemen devoted to militant Wahhabism fought in Afghanistan where they came to be known as Arab Afghans. In Afghanistan, bin Laden and his cohorts drew up plans for the creation of a world Islamic state governed by Islamic law, a revival of the medieval caliphate. After the defeat of the Soviets, bin Laden returned to Saudi Arabia and then went to Sudan, now ruled by a militant Islamic regime. The Gulf War fueled his anti-Americanism, for he regarded as an affront to Wahhabi Islam the stationing of infidel American troops in Saudi Arabia, the home of Islam's holiest shrines.

4.

. . . Bin Laden's personal odyssey further affirmed his anti-American resolve. In 1994, under American pressure, the Saudi authorities revoked his passport and froze his assets. Two years later Washington succeeded in pressuring Sudan to deny him the safe haven he had enjoyed there. As a last resort he sought refuge with the Taliban, who had taken control of Kabul in 1996, in exchange for his financial and logistic support.

The Taliban was the other side of the al Qaeda coin. The Wahhabi propaganda campaign, which went on under Saudi auspices for at least two decades, was the chief factor behind the emergence of this militant student movement that eventually took over Afghanistan. In the 1980s and 90s through patronage and missionary work, financing the construction of new communal mosques from Indonesia and the Philippines to sub-Saharan Africa and Central Asia, training young students of many nationalities in pro-Wahhabi subsidized seminaries, making available to the public the Wahhabi literature, establishing interest-free charity and scholarships for the poor, facilitating the transfer of the Hajj pilgrims, and backing conservative clerical elements with Wahhabi proclivities, the Saudi establishment built a strong and growing network that is now changing the face of Islam throughout the towns and villages of the Muslim world. Inadvertently, this network proved to be a fertile ground for garnering support for bin Laden from Pakistan and southern Afghanistan to Central Asia, Africa and Southeast Asia.

The Taliban movement took root among the dislocated and deprived children of the Afghan refugees trained in the religious schools of Pakistan financed by private Saudi funding. Armed with Wahhabi fervor for jihad and little else, under the auspices of the Pakistani army intelligence these seminarians were organized into a fighting force. The political lacuna that came about as a result of the devastating Afghan civil war opened the way for the Taliban's gradual advance and eventual takeover. The regime they established embodied all the neo-Wahhabi zeal that was preached in the Peshawar schools. It revived and imposed a strict patriarchal order deeply hostile to women and their education and public presence. It allowed battering, even killing, of women by their male relatives, enforced facial veiling, and closed most girls schools. It displayed extraordinary intolerance toward Shiites and other minorities, obliterated even the most primitive symbols of a modern culture, and undermined all human and individual rights. In the name of purging Afghanistan of factionalism and ending the civil war, the Taliban turned it into a miserable fortress whose people suffered from starvation and isolation.

In the year that bin Laden arrived in Afghanistan, he issued a fatwa, or religious ruling, that called upon all Muslims to kill Americans as a religious duty. The 1998 bombing of the American embassies in Nairobi and Dar es Salaam was, as far as we know, his first attempt to put his own ruling into practice. This came at the time when al Qaeda's merger with Egyptian Islamic Jihad—led by Ayman al-Zawahiri, who had recently masterminded the killing of fifty-eight tourists in Luxor, Egypt—and other terrorist organizations drastically increased bin Laden's capacity to wreak havoc. The U.S. tried to punish him for the embassy bombings by firing missiles into his camps. His emerging unscathed gave him greater confidence and enhanced his reputation for invincibility in the eyes of his followers.

For bin Laden and his al Qaeda associates, the terrorist war against the U.S. was a struggle rooted in Islam's noble past and ensured of victory by God. In this context, the attack on giant structures representing American economic and military might was a largely symbolic act that would, they hoped, miraculously subdue their enemies, just as the infidels of early Islam eventually succumbed to the Prophet's attacks on their caravans. This theory of terror, violent and indiscriminate, though utterly against the mainstream interpretation of Islam, attracted a small but committed group of devotees who also saw self-sacrifice as a permissible avenue toward symbolic achievement of their goals.

In several respects, however, bin Laden's apocalyptic vision was grounded in reality and geared to the possible. He and his associates were men of worldly capabilities who could employ business administration models to generate revenue, invest capital in the market, create a disciplined leadership, recruit volunteers, incorporate other extremist groups, organize and maintain new cells, issue orders and communicate through a franchised network of semi-autonomous units on a global scale. This mix of the messianic and the pragmatic allowed al Qaeda to tailor its rhetoric to the grievances of its growing audience and to carry out recruitment and indoctrination on a wider scale.

The vast majority of Muslims do not approve of bin Laden's terrorism, nor do they share his ambition to build a monolithic community based on a pan-Islamic order. Yet there is an undeniable sympathy for the way he has manipulated grievances and symbols. The contrasting images of the "pagan" America and the "authentic" Islam find currency in wide and diverse quarters. One example is the young boys among Afghan and Pakistani refugees who were brainwashed in the Saudi-funded Wahhabi seminaries of Peshawar—and from whose ranks rose the Taliban (the word itself means "students"). Another is the new generation of Western-educated Arab middle classes who were recruited to the al Qaeda's suicide cells in Europe.

We can read in the testament of Mohamed Atta, the Egyptian ringleader of the September 11 attacks, the typical obsessive enthusiasm of a born-again Muslim. As a reward for his resort to massive terror and destruction, which he carried out with resolve and precision, Atta seeks the Koranic promise of heavenly recompense especially reserved for martyrs. His literal reading of the sacred text is imbued with sexual references. "Know," he promises his accomplices, "that the gardens of paradise are waiting for you in all their beauty. And the women of paradise are waiting, calling out, 'Come hither, friends of God.' They are dressed in their most beautiful clothing." This is all the more glaring, and perversely pathetic, when contrasted with Atta's final encounters in a Florida strip club. One can only imagine that he was gazing at the barely-clad strippers of this world in anticipation of the houris—beautiful maidens awaiting the brave and virtuous—in paradise. This was the reward he expected for his martyrdom in the "battle for the sake of God," which he was waging, as he himself reminded us, in the "way of the pious forefathers." This surreal mix of the pious and the profane, backed by a litany of Koranic verses, reveals a discomfiting pseudomodern crust over the hard core of extremism.

As for bin Laden himself, he came into the spotlight after September 11 having shrouded himself and his cause in an apocalyptic aura. His October 7 statement broadcast on television, both in tone and content, alluded to a seminal narrative of Islam. Above all, he said, he placed his total trust in God as he waged the struggle of true believers against infidels, confident of the ultimate reward of martyrdom. His references to the impending fall of the "hypocrites"—those Muslim individuals and governments who were not supportive of his cause—and to the sure victory of the righteous on horseback and armed with swords—presumably in contrast to the sophisticated weaponry of his enemies—all have resonance in the encoded story of early Islam. In a statement at the same time, bin Laden's chief lieutenant, al-Zawahiri, referred to the catastrophic loss of Muslim Spain at the end of the 15th century. This, too, was meant to remind Muslims of the greater days of Islam before its defeat by Christianity, hence complementing bin Laden's vision of the glorious past.

5.

That al-Qaeda effectively communicates to a wide audience far beyond its own extremist circle there can be no doubt. In doing so, it has found abundant opportunities, thanks to the global media, and thanks to complacency and ignorance of Western intelligence services and law enforcement agencies. The dilemmas and inconsistencies of U.S. foreign policy in the region also provided al Qaeda with its weapons of choice to appeal to the frustration and anger of the mainstream Muslims worldwide.

At the core of the resentment so widespread in the Arab and Islamic world is Israel and its treatment of the Palestinians in the occupied territories. Hundreds of millions of Arabs, and increasingly other Muslims as well, are now more then ever informed through media about the Palestinians' unending confrontations with the Israeli security forces. . . .

Broadcast through the Arab networks, and more recently on the global al-Jazeerah television network based in Qatar—the outlet of choice for bin Laden himself—these tragic depictions are increasingly intermingled with symbols of Islamic defiance: the suicidal missions of Hamas and Islamic Jihad against Israeli targets, the fiery anti-American and anti-Israeli slogans and sermons in Friday congregations. Added to this is the enormous level of Islamic radical pamphleteering with anti-American and anti-Zionist content, not infrequently laced in the Arabic textbooks with flagrant anti-Jewish racial references.

The politically repressive regimes of most Arab countries permit anti-Zionist (and even anti-Jewish) expressions as a safety valve. This further adds to the symbolic value of the Palestinian cause as a powerful expression of Arab unity with growing Islamic coloring. Since the Intifada of 1986 and the 1993 Oslo Peace Accord, the thrust of Arab public opinion has been directed toward the fate of the Palestinians in the occupied territories rather than against the very existence of Israel. Yet the oppressive Arab regimes still use the hypocritical rhetoric of national security as an impediment to the growth of democracy in their own countries. In such a repressive environment the mosque often functions as a political forum. There the differentiation between Israeli conduct and American foreign policy fades. Arab public opinion widely believes that the Jewish lobby in the U.S. is the sole determinant of American policy in the region and therefore makes little distinction between U.S. foreign policy and Israeli abuse of the Palestinians.

Proponents of Muslim piety also hold American "corrupting influences" responsible for the erosion of the assumed "authentic" mores of Islamic austerity and devotion. These influences are widely associated with the worst clichés of American popular culture and lifestyle. In this world of misperceptions, the globally permeating images of promiscuity, ostentatious wealth, organized crime, random violence, drug use, gluttony and wastefulness contrast sharply with the idealized Islamic virtues of moral outrage, self-sacrifice, other- worldliness, brotherhood, and piety. The extremists eagerly and skillfully sell these contrasts to the ill-informed Muslim masses, who more than ever now rely on visual images thanks to the power of the electronic media.

To Muslim viewers around the world these exaggerated contrasts offer an elusive comfort, since they seem to explain the root cause of the perceived malfunction of their own government and societies. They are all the more suggestive because they are shrewdly tied up with the story of sufferings of the Palestinian people at the hands of the Israelis and those of the Iraqi people under U.S.-upheld sanctions. On top of that, they are constantly reminded of the "defiling" of the Islamic holy lands by the presence of American troops in Saudi Arabia.

Bin Laden is a master at exploiting these symbolic references. The U.S. and its Western allies have tried to convince the world, and especially the Muslim world, that the campaign against bin Laden and al Qaeda is not directed at Islam but at terrorism. However, that differentiation won't carry much weight in the minds of many Muslims so long as bin Laden, "dead or alive," has at his disposal such potent propaganda weapons. The issue is not only the danger that he or people like him will turn their extremist dream into a religious war between Islam and the West. Equally important is that they will provoke an escalating conflict between militant neo-Wahhabi Islam and the retreating forces and quavering voices of moderation and tolerance in the Muslim world. Bin Laden presents to much of his audience the image of a messianic prophet. Even if he is killed for his cause, he will, in their eyes, have died a martyr's death.

MARY HABECK

JIHADIST IDEOLOGY

For some analysts September 11 demonstrated that after the defeat of the Nazis in World War II and the collapse of the Soviet Union, the West is now confronted with another ominous threat: Islamism or, as some prefer, Islamofascism. Islamists or jihadists, best represented by Osama bin Laden and Al Qaeda, regard terrorism, the deliberate targeting of civilian life, as a legitimate means of fulfilling their sacred mission: ending the humiliation of Muslims by the West; restoring the caliphate and Muslim hegemony over all lands where Islam once prevailed and even beyond; and imposing a strict interpretation of Islamic law throughout the Muslim world. Jihadists, a number of whom have lived in Europe, loathe Western civilization, which they view as materialistic, hedonistic, and sacrilegious; they are repelled by secular democracies, which draw a line between church and state, promote female equality, and tolerate homosexuality. In their eyes, the United States, the leading Western power, constitutes Islam's major enemy. They believed that striking at the World Trade Center and the Pentagon, symbols of American power, was fitting retaliation for American aggression against Muslims and that their act would demonstrate American weakness and the jihadists' resolve to destroy the infidels. Jihadists expected that the suicide bombers would be seen by their coreligionists as martyrs and the ensuing publicity would incite and mobilize the Muslim masses throughout the world to their cause. Al Qaeda, they thought, would be recognized as the vanguard of the global struggle against the enemies of Islam.

In the following selection, Mary Habeck, a student of international relations, analyzes the jihadist ideology that led to 9/11.

It should now be obvious why the United States had to be attacked on September 11. Inspired by their distinctive ideology, certain extremists decided that the United States had to be destroyed. There are two central innovations in the ideology that allow—even demand—the destruction of the United States and the murder of thousands of innocents: an aberrant definition of tawhid[1] and a concentration on violence as the core of their religion. Unlike the vast majority of the Islamic world, the extremists give tawhid political implications and use it to justify all their violent acts. They assert that tawhid means God alone has sovereignty and His laws alone—as laid out in the Qur'an and hadith[2] and by certain traditional jurists—are normative. Thus the only acceptable society for the jihadis is a government that applies the tenets of Islamic law in a way that they believe is correct. Based on this definition of tawhid, the extremists argue that democracy, liberalism, human rights, personal freedom, international law, and international institutions are illegal, illegitimate, and sinful. Because it grants sovereignty to the people and allows them to make laws for their society rather than depending entirely on the God-given legal system of Islam, democracy is the focus for jihadist critiques. The United States is recognized by the jihadis as the center of liberalism and democracy, a center that is willing to spread its ideas and challenge other ways of organizing society, and thus must be destroyed along with democracy itself. The anti-democratic rhetoric of Zarqawi and bin Ladin is not, then, just a reaction to U.S. policies, but rather a reflection of their own most deeply held religio-political views of the world.

Violence also permeates jihadist thought. In their reading of history, the confict between the United States and Islam is part of a universal struggle between good and evil, truth and falsehood, belief and infidelity, that began with the first human beings and will continue until the end of time. A literal clash of civilizations is taking place around the world and, in the end, only one system can survive: Muslims must rid the earth of democracy or else the supporters of democracy (especially the United States, but the entire "West" as well) will destroy true Islam. Jihadis do not believe that this is a theoretical or ideological struggle that can be played out peacefully; rather, the existence of a political or legal system

[1]Tawhid: The Muslim belief that there is one omnipotent God all of whose laws are binding and that God's laws are superior to all human-made injunctions.

[2]Hadith: Traditions about Muhammad's life that are an integral part of Islamic law.

with provisions that transgress the bounds of the shari'a is an act of aggression against Islam that must be dealt with through revolutionary force.

Because history is dominated by the struggle between good and evil, jihadis assert that all Muslims are called by God to participate in the fight—physically if at all possible, or at least by word or financially—acting as God's sword on earth to deal with the evildoers and their wicked way of life. Muslims who answer the call to fight must do so solely to win God's pleasure so that, in the end, it does not matter if the holy warrior accomplishes anything positive through his violence and incitement to violence: intentions alone count. If a *mujahid* is killed while slaughtering innocent civilians or soldiers on the field of battle, and he acted with pure intentions, he will be guaranteed a welcome into a paradise of unimaginable delights. At the end of time the jihadis envision a world ruled solely by their version of Islam, a world in which "the religion will be for God alone." Thus the jihadis believe that they are more than small groups of violent people who have murdered thousands of men, women, and children. Instead they are honored participants in a cosmic drama, one that will decide the fate of the world and that will ultimately end with the victory of the good, the virtuous, and the true believers.

In addition to fighting evil for God's pleasure, al-Qaida had more mundane short and long-term objectives for the 9/11 assault, objectives that have been articulated by its leaders and that they have lived out. In the short term, al-Qaida wanted to energize a war effort that they began during the early nineties, convince a larger number of Muslims to join their cause, and frighten the United States into leaving all Islamic lands. Al-Qaida's longer term goals included converting all Muslims to their version of Islam, expanding the only legitimate Islamic state (Afghanistan) until it contained any lands that had ever been ruled by Islamic law, and, finally, taking the war beyond the borders of even this expansive state until the entire world was ruled by their extremist Islam. In pursuit of these ends, they believed that the murder of thousands of innocent civilians—including Muslims—was not only legally justified but commanded by God Himself. The jihadist war is thus, in many ways, a struggle over who will control the future of Islam: will this ancient religion become associated with the hatred and violence of the jihadis, or the more tolerant vision proposed by moderate, liberal, and traditional Muslims? . . .

LEONARDO BRUNI

STUDY OF GREEK LITERATURE AND A HUMANIST EDUCATIONAL PROGRAM

Leonardo Bruni (1374-1444) was a Florentine humanist who extolled both intellectual study and active involvement in public affairs, an outlook called civic humanism. In the first reading from his History of His Own Times in Italy, Bruni expresses the humanist's love for ancient Greek literature and language.

In a treatise, De Studiis et Literis (On Learning and Literature), addressed to the noble lady Baptista di Montefeltro (1383-1450), daughter of the Count of Urbino, Bruni outlines the basic course of studies that the humanists recommended as the best preparation for a life of wisdom and virtue. In addition to the study of Christian literature, Bruni encourages a wide familiarity with the best minds and stylists of ancient Greek and Latin cultures.

LOVE FOR GREEK LITERATURE

Then first came a knowledge of Greek, which had not been in use among us for seven hundred years. Chrysoloras the Byzantine,[1] a man of noble birth and well versed in Greek letters, brought Greek learning to us. When his country was invaded by the Turks, he came by sea, first to Venice. The report of him soon spread, and he was cordially invited and besought and promised a public stipend, to come to Florence and open his store of riches to the youth. I was then studying Civil Law,[2] but ... I burned with love of academic studies, and had spent no little pains on dialectic and rhetoric. At the coming of Chrysoloras I was torn in mind, deeming it shameful to desert the law, and yet a crime to lose such a chance of studying Greek literature; and often with youthful impulse I would say to myself: "Thou, when it is permitted thee to gaze on Homer, Plato and Demosthenes,[3] and the other [Greek] poets, philosophers, orators, of whom such glorious things are spread abroad, and speak with them and be instructed in their admirable teaching, wilt thou desert and rob thyself? Wilt thou neglect this opportunity so divinely offered? For seven hundred years, no one in Italy has possessed Greek letters; and yet we confess that all knowledge is derived from them. How great advantage to your knowledge, enhancement of your fame, increase of your pleasure, will come from an understanding of this tongue? There are doctors of civil law everywhere; and the chance of learning will not fail thee. But if this one and only doctor of Greek letters disappears, no one can be found to teach thee." Overcome at length by these reasons, I gave myself to Chrysoloras, with such zeal to learn, that what through the wakeful day I gathered, I followed after in the night, even when asleep.

ON LEARNING AND LITERATURE

. . . The foundations of all true learning must be laid in the sound and thorough knowledge of Latin: which implies study marked by a broad spirit, accurate scholarship, and careful attention to details. Unless this solid basis be secured it is useless to attempt to rear an enduring edifice. Without it the great monuments of literature are unintelligible, and the art of composition impossible. To attain this essential knowledge we must never relax our careful attention to the grammar of the language, but perpetually confirm and extend our acquaintance with it until it is thoroughly our own. ... To this end we must be supremely careful in our choice of authors, lest an inartistic and debased style infect our own writing and degrade our taste; which danger is best avoided by bringing a keen, critical sense to bear upon select works, observing the sense of each passage, the structure of the sentence, the force of every word down to the least important particle. In this way our reading reacts directly upon our style. . . .

[1] Chrysoloras (c. 1355-1415), a Byzantine writer and teacher, introduced the study of Greek literature to the Italians, helping to open a new age of Western humanistic learning.

[2] Civil Law refers to the Roman law as codified by Emperor Justinian in the early sixth century a.d. and studied in medieval law schools.

[3] Demosthenes (384-322 b.c.) was an Athenian statesman and orator whose oratorical style was much admired by Renaissance humanists.

But we must not forget that true distinction is to be gained by a wide and varied range of such studies as conduce to the profitable enjoyment of life, in which, however, we must observe due proportion in the attention and time we devote to them.

First amongst such studies I place History: a subject which must not on any account be neglected by one who aspires to true cultivation. For it is our duty to understand the origins of our own history and its development; and the achievements of Peoples and of Kings.

For the careful study of the past enlarges our foresight in contemporary affairs and affords to citizens and to monarchs lessons of incitement or warning in the ordering of public policy. From History, also, we draw our store of examples of moral precepts.

In the monuments of ancient literature which have come down to us History holds a position of great distinction. We specially prize such [Roman] authors as Livy, Sallust and Curtius;[4] and, perhaps even above these, Julius Caesar; the style of whose Commentaries, so elegant and so limpid, entitles them to our warm admiration. . . .

The great Orators of antiquity must by all means be included. Nowhere do we find the virtues more warmly extolled, the vices so fiercely decried. From them we may learn, also, how to express consolation, encouragement, dissuasion or advice. If the principles which orators set forth are portrayed for us by philosophers, it is from the former that we learn how to employ the emotions—such as indignation, or pity—in driving home their application in individual cases. Further, from oratory we derive our store of those elegant or striking turns of expression which are used with so much effect in literary compositions. Lastly, in oratory we find that wealth of vocabulary, that clear easy-flowing style, that verve and force, which are invaluable to us both in writing and in conversation.

I come now to Poetry and the Poets. . . . For we cannot point to any great mind of the past for whom the Poets had not a powerful attraction. Aristotle, in constantly quoting Homer, Hesiod, Pindar, Euripides and other [Greek] poets, proves that he knew their works hardly less intimately than those of the philosophers. Plato, also, frequently appeals to them, and in this way covers them with his approval. If we turn to Cicero, we find him not content with quoting En- nius, Accius,[5] and others of the Latins, but rendering poems from the Greek and employing them habitually. . . . Hence my view that familiarity with the great poets of antiquity is essential to any claim to true education. For in their writings we find deep speculations upon Nature, and upon the Causes and Origins of things, which must carry weight with us both from their antiquity and from their authorship. Besides these, many important truths upon matters of daily life are suggested or illustrated. All this is expressed with such grace and dignity as demands our admiration. ... To sum up what I have endeavoured to set forth. That high standard of education to which I referred at the outset is only to be reached by one who has seen many things and read much. Poet, Orator, Historian, and the rest, all must be studied, each must contribute a share. Our learning thus becomes full, ready, varied and elegant, available for action or for discourse in all subjects. But to enable us to make effectual use of what we know we must add to our knowledge the power of expression. These two sides of learning, indeed, should not be separated: they afford mutual aid and distinction. Proficiency in literary form, not accompanied by broad acquaintance with facts and truths, is a barren attainment; whilst information, however vast, which lacks all grace of expression, would seem to be put under a bushel or partly thrown away. Indeed, one may fairly ask what advantage it is to possess profound and varied learning if one cannot convey it in language worthy of the subject. Where, however, this double capacity exists— breadth of learning and grace of style—we allow the highest title to distinction and to abiding fame. If we review the great names of ancient [Greek and Roman} literature, Plato, Democritus, Aristotle, Theophrastus, Varro, Cicero, Seneca, Augustine, Jerome, Lactantius, we shall find it hard to say whether we admire more their attainments or their literary power.

[4] Q. Curtius Rufus, a Roman historian and rhetorician of the mid-first century a.d., composed a biography of Alexander the Great.

[5] Q. Curtius Rufus, a Roman historian and rhetorician of the mid-first century a.d., composed a biography of Alexander the Great.

PICO DELLA MIRANDOLA

ORATION ON THE DIGNITY OF MAN

In the opening section of the *Oration*, Pico declares that unlike other creatures, human beings have not been assigned a fixed place in the universe. Our destiny is not determined by anything outside us. Rather, God has bestowed upon us a unique distinction: the liberty to determine the form and value our lives shall acquire. The notion that people have the power to shape their own lives is a key element in the emergence of the modern outlook.

I have read in the records of the Arabians, reverend Fathers, that Abdala the Saracen,[1] when questioned as to what on this stage of the world, as it were, could be seen most worthy of wonder, replied: "There is nothing to be seen more wonderful than man." In agreement with this opinion is the saying of Hermes Trismegistus: "A great miracle, Asclepius, is man."[2] But when I weighed the reason for these maxims, the many grounds for the excellence of human nature reported by many men failed to satisfy me—that man is the intermediary between creatures, the intimate of the gods, the king of the lower beings, by the acuteness of his senses, by the discernment of his reason, and by the light of his intelligence the interpreter of nature, the interval between fixed eternity and fleeting time, and (as the Persians say) the bond, nay, rather, the marriage song of the world, on David's [biblical king] testimony but little lower than the angels. Admittedly great though these reasons be, they are not the principal grounds, that is, those which may rightfully claim for themselves the privilege of the highest admiration. For why should we not admire more the angels themselves and the blessed choirs of heaven? At last it seems to me I have come to understand why man is the most fortunate of creatures and consequently worthy of all admiration and what precisely is that rank which is his lot in the universal chain of Being—a rank to be envied not only by brutes but even by the stars and by minds beyond this world. It is a matter past faith and a wondrous one. Why should it not be? For it is on this very account that man is rightly called and judged a great miracle and a wonderful creature indeed. . . .

. . . God the Father, the supreme Architect, had already built this cosmic home we behold, the most sacred temple of His godhead, by the laws of His mysterious wisdom. The region above the heavens He had adorned with Intelligences, the heavenly spheres He had quickened with eternal souls, and the excrementary and filthy parts of the lower world He had filled with a multitude of animals of every kind. But, when the work was finished, the Craftsman kept wishing that there were someone to ponder the plan of so great a work, to love its beauty, and to wonder at its vastness. Therefore, when everything was done (as Moses and Timaeus[3] bear witness), He finally took thought concerning the creation of man. But there was not among His archetypes that from which He could fashion a new offspring, nor was there in His treasurehouses anything which He might bestow on His new son as an inheritance, nor was there in the seats of all the world a place where the latter might sit to contemplate the universe. All was now complete; all things had been assigned to the highest, the middle, and the lowest orders. But in its final creation it was not the part of the Father's power to fail as though exhausted. It was not the part of His wisdom to waver in a needful matter through poverty of counsel. It was not the part of His kindly love that he who was to praise God's divine generosity in regard to others should be compelled to condemn it in regard to himself.

At last the best of artisans [God] ordained that that creature to whom He had been able to give nothing proper to himself should have joint possession of whatever had been peculiar to each of the different kinds of being. He therefore took man as a creature of indeterminate nature and, assigning him a place

[1]Abdala the Saracen possibly refers to the eighth-century a.d. writer Abd-Allah Ibn al-Muqaffa.

[2]Ancient writings dealing with magic, alchemy, astrology, and occult philosophy were erroneously attributed to an assumed Egyptian priest, Hermes Trismegistus. Asclepius was a Greek god of healing.

[3] Timaeus, a Greek Pythagorean philosopher, was a central character in Plato's famous dialogue Timaeus.

in the middle of the world, addressed him thus: "Neither a fixed abode nor a form that is thine alone nor any function peculiar to thyself have we given thee, Adam, to the end that according to thy longing and according to thy judgment thou mayest have and possess what abode, what form, and what functions thou thyself shalt desire. The nature of all other beings is limited and constrained within the bounds of laws prescribed by Us. Thou, constrained by no limits, in accordance with thine own free will, in whose hand We have placed thee, shalt ordain for thyself the limits of thy nature. We have set thee at the world's center that thou mayest from thence more easily observe whatever is in the world. We have made thee neither of heaven nor of earth, neither mortal nor immortal, so that with freedom of choice and with honor, as though the maker and molder of thyself, thou mayest fashion thyself in whatever shape thou shalt prefer. Thou shalt have the power to degenerate into the lower forms of life, which are brutish. Thou shalt have the power, out of thy soul's judgment, to be reborn into the higher forms, which are divine."

O supreme generosity of God the Father, O highest and most marvelous felicity of man! To him it is granted to have whatever he chooses, to be whatever he wills. Beasts as soon as they are born (so says Lucilius[4] bring with them from their mother's womb all they will ever possess. Spiritual beings [angels], either from the beginning or soon thereafter, become what they are to be for ever and ever. On man when he came into life the Father conferred the seeds of all kinds and the germs of every way of life. Whatever seeds each man cultivates will grow to maturity and bear in him their own fruit. If they be vegetative, he will be like a plant. If sensitive, he will become brutish. If rational, he will grow into a heavenly being. If intellectual, he will be an angel and the son of God. And if, happy in the lot of no created thing, he withdraws into the center of his own unity, his spirit, made one with God, in the solitary darkness of God, who is set above all things, shall surpass them all.

[4] Lucilius, a first-century a.d. Roman poet and Stoic philosopher, was a close friend of Seneca, the philosopher-dramatist.

NICCOLÒ MACHIAVELLI

THE PRINCE

In contrast to medieval thinkers, Machiavelli did not seek to construct an ideal Christian community but to discover how politics was *really* conducted. He studied politics in the cold light of reason, as the following passage from *The Prince* illustrates.

It now remains to be seen what are the methods and rules for a prince as regards his subjects and friends. And as I know that many have written of this, I fear that my writing about it may be deemed presumptuous, differing as I do, especially in this matter, from the opinions of others. But my intention being to write something of use to those who understand, it appears to me more proper to go to the real truth of the matter than to its imagination; and many have imagined republics and principalities which have never been seen or known to exist in reality; for how we live is so far removed from how we ought to live, that he who abandons what is done for what ought to be done, will rather learn to bring about his own ruin than his preservation.

Machiavelli removed ethics from political thinking. A successful ruler, he contended, is indifferent to moral and religious considerations. But will not the prince be punished on the Day of Judgment for violating Christian teachings? In startling contrast to medieval theorists, Machiavelli simply ignored the question. The action of a prince, he said, should be governed solely by necessity.

A man who wishes to make a profession of goodness in everything must necessarily come to grief among so many who are not good. Therefore it is necessary for a prince, who wishes to maintain himself, to learn how not to be good, and to use this knowledge and not use it, according to the necessity of the case.

Leaving on one side, then, those things which concern only an imaginary prince, and speaking of those that are real, I state that all men, and especially princes, who are placed at a greater height, are reputed for certain qualities which bring them either praise or blame. Thus one is considered liberal, another . . . miserly; . . . one a free giver, another rapacious; one cruel, another merciful; one a breaker of his word, another trustworthy; one effeminate and pusillanimous, another fierce and high-spirited; one humane, another haughty; one lascivious, another chaste; one frank, another astute; one hard, another easy; one serious, another frivolous; one religious, another an unbeliever, and so on. I know that every one will admit that it would be highly praiseworthy in a prince to possess all the above-named qualities that are reputed good, but as they cannot all be possessed or observed, human conditions not permitting of it, it is necessary that he should be prudent enough to avoid the scandal of those vices which would lose him the state, and guard himself if possible against those which will not lose it [for] him, but if not able to, he can indulge them with less scruple. And yet he must not mind incurring the scandal of those vices, without which it would be difficult to save the state, for if one considers well, it will be found that some things which seem virtues would, if followed, lead to one's ruin, and some others which appear vices result in one's greater security and wellbeing. . . .

... I say that every prince must desire to be considered merciful and not cruel. He must, however, take care not to misuse this mercifulness. Cesare Borgia was considered cruel, but his cruelty had brought order to the Romagna,[1] united it, and reduced it to peace and fealty. If this is considered well, it will be seen that he was really much more merciful than the Florentine people, who, to avoid the name of

---

[1] Cesare Borgia (c. 1476-1507) was the bastard son of Rodrigo Borgia, then a Spanish cardinal, and later Pope Alexander VI (1492-1503). With his father's aid he attempted to carve out for himself an independent duchy in north-central Italy, with Romagna as its heart. Through cruelty, violence, and treachery, he succeeded at first in his ambition, but ultimately his principality collapsed. Romagna was eventually incorporated into the Papal State under Pope Julius II (1503-1513).

cruelty, allowed Pistoia[2] to be destroyed. A prince, therefore, must not mind incurring the charge of cruelty for the purpose of keeping his subjects united and faithful; for, with a very few examples, he will be more merciful than those who, from excess of tenderness, allow disorders to arise, from whence spring bloodshed and rapine; for these as a rule injure the whole community, while the executions carried out by the prince injure only individuals. . . .

Machiavelli's rigorous investigation of politics led him to view human nature from the standpoint of its limitations and imperfections. The astute prince, he said, recognizes that human beings are by nature selfish, cowardly, and dishonest, and regulates his political strategy accordingly.

From this arises the question whether it is better to be loved more than feared, or feared more than loved. The reply is, that one ought to be both feared and loved, but as it is difficult for the two to go together, it is much safer to be feared than loved, if one of the two has to be wanting. For it may be said of men in general that they are ungrateful, voluble, dissemblers, anxious to avoid danger, and covetous of gain; as long as you benefit them, they are entirely yours; they offer you their blood, their goods, their life, and their children, as I have before said, when the necessity is remote; but when it approaches, they revolt. And the prince who has relied solely on their words, without making other preparations, is ruined; for the friendship which is gained by purchase and not through grandeur and nobility of spirit is bought but not secured, and at a pinch is not to be expended in your service. And men have less scruple in offending one who makes himself loved than one who makes himself feared; for love is held by a chain of obligation which, men being selfish, is broken whenever it serves their purpose; but fear is maintained by a dread of punishment which never fails.

Still, a prince should make himself feared in such a way that if he does not gain love, he at any rate avoids hatred; for fear and the absence of hatred may well go together, and will be always attained by one who abstains from interfering with the property of his citizens and subjects or with their women. And when he is obliged to take the life of any one, let him do so when there is a proper justification and manifest reason for it; but above all he must abstain from taking the property of others, for men forget more easily the death of their father than the loss of their patrimony. Then also pretexts for seizing property are never wanting, and one who begins to live by rapine will always find some reason for taking the goods of others, whereas causes for taking life are rarer and more fleeting.

But when the prince is with his army and has a large number of soldiers under his control, then it is extremely necessary that he should not mind being thought cruel; for without this reputation he could not keep an army united or disposed to any duty. Among the noteworthy actions of Hannibal[3] is numbered this, that although he had an enormous army, composed of men of all nations and fighting in foreign countries, there never arose any dissension either among them or against the prince, either in good fortune or in bad. This could not be due to anything but his inhuman cruelty, which together with his infinite other virtues, made him always venerated and terrible in the sight of his soldiers, and without it his other virtues would not have sufficed to produce that effect. Thoughtless writers admire on the one hand his actions, and on the other blame the principal cause of them. . . .

Again in marked contrast to the teachings of Christian (and ancient) moralists, Machiavelli said that the successful prince will use any means to achieve and sustain political power. If the end is desirable, all means are justified.

How laudable it is for a prince to keep good faith and live with integrity, and not with astuteness, every one knows. Still the experience of our times shows those princes to have done great things who have had little regard for good faith, and have been able by astuteness to confuse men's brains, and who have ultimately overcome those who have made loyalty their foundation.

You must know, then, that there are two methods of fighting, the one by law, the other by force: the first method is that of men, the second of beasts; but as the first method is often insufficient, one must

[2]Pistoia, a small Italian city in Tuscany, came under the control of Florence in the fourteenth century.
[3] Hannibal (247-182 B.C.) was a brilliant Carthaginian general whose military victories almost destroyed Roman power. He was finally defeated at the battle of Zama in 202 B.C. by the Roman general Scipio Africanus.

have recourse to the second. It is therefore necessary for a prince to know well how to use both the beast and the man. . . .

A prince being thus obliged to know well how to act as a beast must imitate the fox and the lion, for the lion cannot protect himself from traps, and the fox cannot defend himself from wolves. One must therefore be a fox to recognise traps, and a lion to frighten wolves. Those that wish to be only lions do not understand this. Therefore, a prudent ruler ought not to keep faith when by so doing it would be against his interest, and when the reasons which made him bind himself no longer exist. If men were all good, this precept would not be a good one; but as they are bad, and would not observe their faith with you, so you are not bound to keep faith with them. Nor have legitimate grounds ever failed a prince who wished to show [plausible] excuse for the non-fulfilment of his promise. Of this one could furnish an infinite number of modern examples, and show how many times peace has been broken, and how many promises rendered worthless, by the faithlessness of princes, and those that have been best able to imitate the fox have succeeded best. But it is necessary to be able to disguise this character well, and to be a great feigner and dissembler; and men are so simple and so ready to obey present necessities, that one who deceives will always find those who allow themselves to be deceived. . . .

. . . Thus it is well to seem merciful, faithful, humane, sincere, religious, and also to be so; but you must have the mind so disposed that when it is needful to be otherwise you may be able to change to the opposite qualities. And it must be understood that a prince, and especially a new prince, cannot observe all those things which are considered good in men, being often obliged, in order to maintain the state, to act against faith, against charity, against humanity, and against religion. And, therefore, he must have a mind disposed to adapt itself according to the wind, and as the variations of fortune dictate, and, as I said before, not deviate from what is good, if possible, but be able to do evil if constrained.

A prince must take great care that nothing goes out of his mouth which is not full of the above-named five qualities, and, to see and hear him, he should seem to be all mercy, faith, integrity, humanity, and religion. And nothing is more necessary than to seem to have this last quality, for men in general judge more by the eyes than by the hands, for every one can see, but very few have to feel. Everybody sees what you appear to be, few feel what you are, and those few will not dare to oppose themselves to the many, who have the majesty of the state to defend them; and in the actions of men, and especially of princes, from which there is no appeal, the end justifies the means. Let a prince therefore aim at conquering and maintaining the state, and the means will always be judged honourable and praised by every one, for the vulgar is always taken by appearances and the issue of the event; and the world consists only of the vulgar, and the few who are not vulgar are isolated when the many have a rallying point in the prince. A certain prince of the present time, whom it is well not to name, never does anything but preach peace and good faith, but he is really a great enemy to both, and either of them, had he observed them, would have lost him state or repuation on many occasions.

BALDASSARE CASTIGLIONE

THE BOOK OF THE COURTIER

Castiglione chose the court of Urbino as the setting for his Book of the Courtier; which he wrote in the form of a conversation among the courtiers and ladies of the court. The participants—such as Guidobaldo, Duke of Urbino; the Duchess, Elisabetta Gonzaga; Count Ludovico da Canossa; and Cardinal Pietro Bembo— were all real people who in Castiglione s day had actual conversations at the court. In the first two books of The Courtier, Castiglione describes the ideal courtier as an example of the Renaissance "universal man," a well-rounded person with breadth of interest and versatility of accomplishment. In the following excerpt, Count Ludovico describes the courtier as a person of noble birth, a man who is skilled in weaponry, an expert horseman, and adept at all sorts of games.

"Thus, I would have our Courtier born of a noble and genteel family; because it is far less becoming for one of low birth to fail to do virtuous things than for one of noble birth, who, should he stray from the path of his forebears, stains the family name, and not only fails to achieve anything but loses what has been achieved already. For noble birth is like a bright lamp that makes manifest and visible deeds both good and bad, kindling and spurring on to virtue as much for fear of dishonor as for hope of praise. And since this luster of nobility does not shine forth in the deeds of the lowly born, they lack that spur, as well as that fear of dishonor, nor do they think themselves obliged to go beyond what was done by their forebears; whereas to the wellborn it seems a reproach not to attain at least to the mark set them by their ancestors. Hence, it almost always happens that, in the profession of arms as well as in other worthy pursuits, those who are most distinguished are men of noble birth, because nature has implanted in everything that hidden seed which gives a certain force and quality of its own essence to all that springs from it, making it like itself: as we can see not only in breeds of horses and other animals, but in trees as well, the shoots of which nearly always resemble the trunk; and if they sometimes degenerate, the fault lies with the husbandman. And so it happens with men, who, if they are tended in the right way, are almost always like those from whom they spring, and often are better; but if they lack someone to tend them properly, they grow wild and never attain their full growth. . . .

"[B]esides his noble birth, I would wish the Courtier favored in this other respect, and endowed by nature not only with talent and with beauty of countenance and person, but with that certain grace which we call an 'air,' which shall make him at first sight pleasing and lovable to all who see him; and let this be an adornment informing and attending all his actions, giving the promise outwardly that such a one is worthy of the company and the favor of every great lord. . . .

"But to come to some particulars: I hold that the principal and true profession of the Courtier must be that of arms; which I wish him to exercise with vigor; and let him be known among the others as bold, energetic, and faithful to whomever he serves. And the repute of these good qualities will be earned by exercising them in every time and place, inasmuch as one may not ever fail therein without great blame. And, just as among women the name of purity, once stained, is never restored, so the reputation of a gentleman whose profession is arms, if ever in the least way he sullies himself through cowardice or other disgrace, always remains defiled before the world and covered with ignominy. Therefore, the more our Courtier excels in this art, the more will he merit praise. . . .

"Then, coming to bodily frame, I say it is enough that it be neither extremely small nor big, because either of these conditions causes a certain contemptuous wonder, and men of either sort are gazed at in much the same way that we gaze at monstrous things. And yet, if one must sin in one or the other of these two extremes, it is less bad to be on the small side than to be excessively big; because men who are so huge of body are often not only obtuse of spirit, but are also unfit for every agile exercise, which is something I very much desire in the Courtier. And hence I would have him well built and shapely of limb, and would have him show strength and lightness and suppleness, and know all the bodily exercises that befit a warrior. And in this I judge it his first duty to know how to handle every kind of weapon, both on foot and on horse, and know the advantages of each kind; and be especially acquainted with those arms that are ordinarily used among gentlemen, because, apart from using them in war (where perhaps so many fine points are not necessary), there often arise differences between one gentleman and another, resulting in duels, and quite often those weapons are used which happen to be at hand. Hence, knowledge of them is a very safe thing. Nor am I one of those who say that skill is forgotten in the hour of need; for he who loses his skill at such times shows that out of fear he has already lost his heart and head. . . .

"Weapons are also often used in various exercises in time of peace, and gentlemen are seen in public spectacles before the people and before ladies and great lords. Therefore I wish our Courtier to be a perfect horseman in every kind of saddle; and, in addition to having a knowledge of horses and what pertains to riding, let him put every effort and diligence into outstripping others in everything a little, so that he may be always recognized as better than the rest. . . .

"I have this Courtier of ours excel all others in what is the special profession of each. And as it is the peculiar excellence of the Italians to ride well with the rein, to manage wild horses especially with great skill, to tilt and joust, let him be among the best of the Italians in this. In tourneys, in holding a pass, in attacking a fortified position, let him be among the best of the French. In stick-throwing, bullfighting, in casting spears and darts, let him be outstanding among the Spaniards. But, above all, let him temper his every action with a certain good judgment and grace, if he would deserve that universal favor which is so greatly prized.

"There are also other exercises which, although not immediately dependent upon arms, still have much in common therewith and demand much manly vigor; and chief among these is the hunt, it seems to me, because it has a certain resemblance to war. It is a true pastime for great lords, it befits a Courtier, and one understands why it was so much practiced among the ancients. He should also know how to swim, jump, run, throw stones; for, besides their usefulness in war, it is frequently necessary to show one's prowess in such things, whereby a good name is to be won, especially with the crowd (with whom one must reckon after all). Another noble exercise and most suitable for a man at court is the game of tennis which shows off the disposition of body, the quickness and litheness of every member, and all the qualities that are brought out by almost every other exercise. Nor do I deem vaulting on horseback to be less worthy, which, though it is tiring and difficult, serves more than anything else to make a man agile and dexterous; and besides its usefulness, if such agility is accompanied by grace, in my opinion it makes a finer show than any other." . . .

Not only should the courtier be physically gifted, but he should be well educated. In the following passages, Count Ludovico declares that he should be learned in the humanities, the new educational curriculum of the Renaissance humanists. Moreover, in the spirit of the "universal man/' he should be a musician, and he should display a knowledge of drawing and painting.

"I would have him more than passably learned in letters, at least in those studies which we call the humanities. Let him be conversant not only with the Latin language, but with Greek as well, because of the abundance and variety of things that are so divinely written therein. Let him be versed in the poets, as well as in the orators and historians, and let him be practiced also in writing verse and prose, especially in our own vernacular; for, besides the personal satisfaction he will take in this, in this way he will never want for pleasant entertainment with the ladies, who are usually fond of such things. And if, because of other occupations or lack of study, he does not attain to such a perfection that his writings should merit great praise, let him take care to keep them under cover so that others will not laugh at him, and let him show them only to a friend who can be trusted; because at least they will be of profit to him in that, through such exercise, he will be capable of judging the writing of others. For it very rarely happens that a man who is un- practiced in writing, however learned he may be, can ever wholly understand the toils and industry of writers, or taste the sweetness and excellence of styles, and those intrinsic niceties that are often found in the ancients. . . .

"Gentlemen, you must know that I am not satisfied with our Courtier unless he be also a musician, and unless, besides understanding and being able to read music, he can play various instruments. For, if we rightly consider, no rest from toil and no medicine for ailing spirits can be found more decorous or praiseworthy in time of leisure than this; and especially in courts where, besides the release from vexations which music gives to all, many things are done to please the ladies, whose tender and delicate spirits are readily penetrated with harmony and filled with sweetness. Hence, it is no wonder that in both ancient and modern times they have always been particularly fond of musicians, finding music a most welcome food for the spirit." . . .

Then the Count said: "Before we enter upon that subject, I would discuss another matter which I consider to be of great importance and which I think must therefore, in no way be neglected by our Courtier: and this is a knowledge of how to draw and an acquaintance with the art of painting itself."

Castiglione also portrays the ideal court lady. She should have many of the same attributes as the courtier, and, in addition, she should be able to manage her house and her children, as well as being able to provide gracious entertainment for the men at court. In the following passage, the speaker is the Magnifico Giuliano de' Medici.

". . .1 hold that many virtues of the mind are as necessary to a woman as to a man; also, gentle birth; to avoid affectation, to be naturally graceful in all her actions, to be mannerly, clever, prudent, not arrogant, not envious, not slanderous, not vain, not contentious, not inept, to know how to gain and hold the favor of her mistress and of all others, to perform well and gracefully the exercises that are suitable for women. And I do think that beauty is more necessary to her than to the Courtier, for truly that woman lacks much who lacks beauty. Also she must be more circumspect, and more careful not to give occasion for evil being said of her, and conduct herself so that she may not only escape being sullied by guilt but even by the suspicion of it, for a woman has not so many ways of defending herself against false calumnies as a man has. But since Count Ludovico has set forth in great detail the chief profession of the Courtier, and has insisted that this be arms, I think it is also fitting to state what I judge that of the Court Lady to be, and when I have done this I shall think to have discharged the greater part of my assignment.

"Leaving aside, then, those virtues of the mind which she is to have in common with the Courtier (such as prudence, magnanimity, continence, and many others), as well as those qualities that befit all (such as kindness, discretion, ability to manage her husband's property and house and children, if she is married, and all qualities that are requisite in a good mother), I say that, in my opinion, in a Lady who lives at court a certain pleasing affability is becoming above all else, whereby she will be able to entertain graciously every kind of man with agreeable and comely conversation suited to the time and place and to the station of the person with whom she speaks, joining to serene and modest manners, and that to comeliness that ought to inform all her actions, a quick vivacity of spirit whereby she will show herself a stranger to all boorishness; but with such a kind manner as to cause her to be thought no less chaste, prudent, and gentle than she is agreeable, witty, and discreet: thus, she must observe a certain mean (difficult to achieve and, as it were, composed of contraries) and must strictly observe certain limits and not exceed them. . . .

"And since words that have no subject matter of importance are vain and puerile, the Court Lady must have not only the good judgment to recognize the kind of person with whom she is speaking, but must have knowledge of many things, in order to entertain that person graciously; and let her know how in her talk to choose those things that are suited to the kind of person with whom she is speaking, and be careful lest, unintentionally, she might sometimes utter words that could offend him. Let her take care not to disgust him by indiscreet praise of herself or by being too prolix [verbose]. Let her not proceed to mingle serious matters with playful or humorous discourse, or mix jests and jokes with serious talk. Let her not show ineptitude in pretending to know what she does not know, but let her seek modestly to do herself credit in what she does know—in all things avoiding affectation, as has been said. In this way she will be adorned with good manners; she will perform with surpassing grace the bodily exercises that are proper to women; her discourse will be fluent and most prudent virtuous, and pleasant; thus, she will be not only loved but revered by everyone, and perhaps worthy of being considered the equal of this great Courtier, both in qualities of mind and of body."

WILLIAM SHAKESPEARE

THE TRAGEDY OF HAMLET, PRINCE OF DENMARK

The main characters of Hamlet are Hamlet himself; Queen Gertrude, Hamlet's mother; Claudius, Hamlet's uncle; Horatio, Hamlet's loyal friend; Ophelia, an innocent young woman whom Hamlet loves; Ophelia's father, Polonius; and her brother, Laertes. The intrigue of Hamlet centers on the death of the king of Denmark—Hamlet's father—who was the victim of a conspiracy between the adulterous Queen Gertrude and Claudius, now the new king. Vowing to avenge his father's death, Hamlet feigns madness to discover the truth. Hamlet is known for its soliloquies—lengthy monologues that expose Hamlet's inner torment and allow us to think about our own struggle to exist in a world which often seems to conspire against us. One of the most famous soliloquies is excerpted below, where Hamlet reflects on the place of human beings in the Great Chain of Being, questions the optimistic outlook of the Renaissance humanists, and reveals the melancholy he has felt since learning of his father's death.

I have of late—but wherefore I know not—lost all my mirth, forgone all custom of exercises[1]; and indeed it goes so heavily with my disposition, that this goodly frame, the earth, seems to me a sterile promontory; this most excellent canopy, the air, look you, this brave[2] o'erhanging firmament, this majestical roof fretted[3] with golden fire, why, it appeareth nothing to me but a foul and pestilent congregation of vapors. What [a] piece of work[4] is a man, how noble in reason, how infinite in faculties, in form and moving, how express[5] and admirable in action, how like an angel in apprehension, how like a god! the beauty of the world; the paragon of animals; and yet to me what is this quintessence[6] of dust? Man delights not me— nor women neither. . . .

(ACT 2, SCENE 2, LINES 295-309)

The timelessness of Shakespeare's masterpiece is largely due to his ability to portray the struggle waged within Hamlet's soul—his dream of revenge and the forces that deprive him of it, including his own indecisiveness. In the scene below, which contains Shakespeare's most famous soliloquy, Hamlet's madness seems apparent as he considers suicide, tells Ophelia that he does not love her, and orders her to enter a monastery.

HAM.
To be, or not to be, that is the question: Whether 'tis nobler in the mind to suffer
The slings and arrows of outrageous fortune,
Or to take arms against a sea of troubles,
And by opposing, end them. To die, to sleep—
No more, and by a sleep to say we end
The heart-ache and the thousand natural shocks
That flesh is heir to; 'tis a consummation[7]
Devoutly to be wish'd. To die, to sleep—
To sleep, perchance to dream—ay, there's the rub,[8]
For in that sleep of death what dreams may come,

[1] **custom of exercises:** my usual athletic activities.
[2] **brave:** splendid.
[3] **fretted:** ornamented as with fretwork.
[4] **piece of work:** masterpiece.
[5] **express:** exact.
[6] **quintessence:** finest and purest extract.
[7] **consummation:** completion, end.
[8] **rub:** obstacle (a term from the game of bowls).

When we have shuffled off[9] this mortal coil,[10]
Must give us pause; there's the respect[11]
That makes calamity of so long life[12]
For who would bear the whips and scorns of time,[13]
Th' oppressor's wrong, the proud man's contumely, [[**contumely:** scorn]]
The pangs of despis'd love, the law's delay,
The insolence of office, and the spurns
That patient merit of th' unworthy takes,
When he himself might his quietus make[14]
With a bare bodkin[15]; who would fardels[16] bear,
To grunt and sweat under a weary life,
But that the dread of something after death,
The undiscover'd country, from whose bourn[17]
No traveller returns, puzzles[18] the will,
And makes us rather bear those ills we have,
Than fly to others that we know not of?
Thus conscience[19] does make cowards [of us all],
And thus the native hue[20] of resolution
Is sicklied o'er with the pale cast[21] of thought,[22]
And enterprises of great pitch[23] and moment
With this regard their currents turn awry,
And lose the name of action.—Soft you now,
The fair Ophelia. Nymph, in thy orisons[24]
Be all my sins remem'bred.

OPH.

Good my lord,
How does your honor for this many a day?

HAM.

I humbly thank you, well, [well, well].

OPH.

My lord, I have remembrances of yours
That I have longed long to redeliver.
I pray you now receive them.

HAM.

No, not I,
I never gave you aught.

---

[9] **shuffled off:** freed ourselves from.
[10] **this mortal coil:** the turmoil of this mortal life.
[11] **respect:** consideration.
[12] **of... life:** so long-lived.
[13] **time:** the world.
[14] **his quietus make:** write paid to his account.
[15] **bare bodkin:** mere dagger.
[16] **fardels:** burdens
[17] **bourn:** boundary, i.e. region.
[18] **puzzles:** paralyzes.
[19] **conscience:** reflection (but with some of the modern sense, too)
[20] **native hue:** natural (ruddy) complexion.
[21] **pale cast:** pallor.
[22] **thought:** i.e. melancholy thought, brooding.
[23] **pitch:** loftiness (a term from falconry, signifying the highest point of a hawk's flight).
[24] **orisons:** prayers.

OPH.

My honor'd lord, you know right well you did,
And with them words of so sweet breath compos'd
As made these things more rich.
Their perfume lost,
Take these again, for to the noble mind
Rich gifts wax poor when givers prove unkind.
There, my lord.

HAM.

Ha, ha! are you honest?[25]

OPH.

My lord?

HAM. Are you fair?

OPH.

What means your lordship?

HAM.

That if you be honest and fair, [your honesty] should admit no discourse to your beauty.

OPH.

Could beauty, my lord, have better commerce than with honesty?

HAM.

Ay, truly, for the power of beauty will sooner transform honesty from what it is to a bawd than the force of honesty can translate beauty into his likeness. This was sometime[26] a paradox,[27] but now the time gives it proof. I did love you once.

OPH.

Indeed, my lord, you made me believe so.

HAM.

You should not have believ'd me, for virtue cannot so [inoculate] our old stock but we shall relish of it.[28] I lov'd you not.

OPH.

I was the more deceiv'd.

HAM.

Get thee [to] a nunn'ry, why wouldst thou be a breeder of sinners? I am myself indifferent honest,[29] but yet I could accuse me of such things that it were better my mother had not borne me: I am very proud, revengeful, ambitious, with more offenses at my beck than I have thoughts to put them in, imagination to give them shape, or time to act them in. What should such fellows as I do crawling between earth and heaven? We are arrant knaves, believe none of us. Go thy ways to a nunn'ry. Where's your father?

OPH.

At home, my lord.

HAM.

Let the doors be shut upon him, that he may play the fool no where but in's own house. Farewell.

OPH.

O, help him, you sweet heavens!

---

[25] **honest:** chaste.

[26] sometime: formerly.

[27] paradox: tenet contrary to accepted belief.

[28] **virtue ... it:** virtue, engrafted on our old stock (of viciousness),cannot so change the nature of the plant that no trace of the original will remain.

[29] **indifferent honest:** tolerably virtuous.

HAM.

If thou dost marry, I'll give thee this plague for thy dowry: be thou chaste as ice, as pure as snow, thou shalt not escape calumny. Get thee to a nunn'ry, farewell. Or if you wilt needs marry, marry a fool, for wise men know well enough what monsters[30] you[31] make of them. To a nunn'ry, go, and quickly too. Farewell.

OPH.

Heavenly powers, restore him!

HAM.

I have heard of your paintings, well enough. God hath given you one face, and you make yourselves another. You jig and amble, and you [lisp,] you nick-name God's creatures[32] and make your wantonness [your] ignorance.[33] Go to, I'll no more on't, it hath made me mad. I say we will have no moe[34] marriages. Those that are married already (all but one) shall live, the rest shall keep as they are. To a nunn'ry, go.

Exit.

OPH.

O, what a noble mind is here o'erthrown!
The courtier's, soldier's, scholar's, eye, tongue, sword,
Th' expectation[35] and rose[36] of the fair[37] state,
The glass[38] of fashion and the mould of form,[39]
Th' observ'd of all observers,[40] quite, quite down!
And I, of ladies most deject and wretched,
That suck'd the honey of his [music] vows,
Now see [that] noble and most sovereign reason
Like sweet bells jangled out of time, and harsh;
That unmatch'd form and statue of blown[41] youth
Blasted[42] with ecstasy.[43] O, woe is me
T' have seen what I have seen, see what I see!

(ACT 3, SCENE 1, LINES 55-161)

[Ophelia withdraws.]

When Ophelia learns that Hamlet has accidentally killed her father (when he stabbed a person hiding behind a curtain thinking it was his Uncle Claudius), she goes mad with grief and dies by drowning. In the following scene, a grieving Laertes leaps into his sister's grave. Hamlet then attacks Laertes, declaring that he had always loved Ophelia.

LAER.

Lay her i' th' earth,
And from her fair and unpolluted flesh
May violets spring! I tell thee, churlish priest,

---

[30] **monsters.** Alluding to the notion that the husbands of unfaithful wives grew horns.
[31]31. **you:** you women.
[32] **You . . . creatures:** i.e. you walk and talk affectedly.
[33] **make . . . ignorance**: excuse your affectation as ignorance.
[34] **moe:** more.
[35] **expectation:** hope.
[36] **rose:** ornament.
[37] **fair.** Probably propleptic: "(the kingdom) made fair by his presence."
[38] **glass:** mirror
[39] **mould of form:** pattern of (courtly) behavior
[40] **observ"d . . . observers:** Shakespeare uses *observe* to mean not only "behold, mark attentively" but also "pay honor to."
[41] **blown:** in full bloom.
[42] **Blasted:** withered.
[43] **ecstasy:** madness.

A minist'ring angel shall my sister be
When thou liest howling.

HAM.
What, the fair Ophelia!

QUEEN.
[Scattering flowers.] Sweets[44] to the sweet, farewell!
I hop'd thou shouldst have been my Hamlet's wife.
I thought thy bride-bed to have deck'd, sweet maid,
And not have strew'd thy grave.

LAER.
O, treble woe
Fall ten times [treble] on that cursed head
Whose wicked deed thy most ingenious[45] sense
Depriv'd thee of! Hold off the earth a while,
Till I have caught her once more in mine arms.
[Leaps in the grave.]
Now pile your dust upon the quick and dead,
Till of this flat a mountain you have made
T' o'ertop old Pelion,[46] or the skyish head
Of blue Olympus.

HAM.
[Coming forward.] What is he whose grief
Bears such an emphasis, whose phrase[47] of sorrow
Conjures[48] the wand'ring stars[49] and makes them stand
Like wonder-wounded hearers?
This is I, Hamlet the Dane! [50] *[Hamlet leaps in after Laertes.]*

LAER.
The devil take thy soul! *[Grappling with him.]*

HAM.
Thou pray'st not well. I prithee take thy fingers from my throat.
For though I am not splenitive[51] [and] rash,
Yet have I in me something dangerous,
Which let thy wisdom fear.
Hold off thy hand!

KING.
Pluck them asunder.

QUEEN.
Hamlet, Hamlet!

All. Gentlemen!

HOR.
Good my lord, be quiet.
[The Attendants part them, and they come out of the grave.]

---

[44] **Sweets**: flowers.
[45] **ingenious:** intelligent.
[46] **Pelion, Olympus:** mountains in northeastern Greece.
[47] **emphasis, phrase.** Rhetorical terms, here used in disparaging reference to Laertes' inflated language.
[48] **Conjures:** puts a spell upon.
[49] **wand'ring stars:** planets.
[50] **the Dane.** This title normally signifies the KING.
[51] **splenitive:** impetuous.

HAM.
Why, I will fight with him upon this theme
Until my eyelids will no longer wag.
QUEEN.
O my son, what theme?
HAM.
I lov'd Ophelia. Forty thousand brothers
Could not with all their quantity of love
Make up my sum. What wilt thou do for her?
KING.
O, he is mad, Laertes.
QUEEN.
For love of God, forbear him.
HAM.
'Swounds, show me what thou't[52] do.
Woo't[53] weep, woo't fight, woo't fast, woo't tear thy self?
Woo't drink up eisel[54], eat a crocadile?[55]
I'll do't. Dust [thou] come here to whine?
To outface me with leaping in her grave?
Be buried quick with her, and so will I.
And if thou prate of mountains,[56] let them throw
Millions of acres on us, till our ground,
Singeing his pate against the burning zone,[57]
Make Ossa[58] like a wart! Nay, and thou'lt mouth,
I'll rant as well as thou.
QUEEN.
This is mere[59] madness,
And {thus] a while the fit will work on him;
Anon, as patient[60] as the female dove,
When that her golden couplets[61] are disclosed,[62]
His silence will sit drooping.
HAM.
Hear you, sir,
What is the reason that you use me thus?
I lov'd you ever. But it is no matter.
Let Hercules himself do what he may,
The cat will mew, and dog will have his day.[63]
Exit Hamlet.

[52] **thou't:** thou wilt.
[53] **Woo't:** wilt thou
[54] **eisel:** vinegar.
[55] **crocadile:** crocodile.
[56] **if. . . mountains.** Referring to lines 251-54.
[57] **burning zone:** sphere of the sun.
[58] **Ossa:** another mountain in Greece, near Pelion and Olympus, mouth: talk bombast (synonymous with rant in the next line).
[59] **mere:** utter.
[60] **patient:** calm.
[61] **golden couplets:** pair of baby birds, covered with yellow down.
[62] **disclosed:** hatched.
[63] **Let. . . day:** i.e. nobody can prevent another from making the scenes he feels he has a right to.

(ACT 5, SCENE 1, LINES 238-292)

Knowing that Hamlet plans to kill him, Claudius concocts a plan to use Laertes to kill Hamlet. He tells Osric, a young courtier, to arrange a fencing match. Claudius poisons Laertes' blade so that Hamlet will die if Laertes wounds him. Then the king prepares a poisoned drink which he will give to Hamlet if it appears that Hamlet is winning the match. In the following selection, from the final scene of the play, the match has just begun, Hamlet has made a hit, and Claudius has just offered him a drink of wine.

HAM.
I'll play this bout first, set it by a while.
Come. *[They play again.]* Another hit; what say you?
LAER.
[A touch, a touch,] I do confess't.
KING.
Our son shall win.
QUEEN.
He's fat,[64] and scant of breath.
Here, Hamlet, take my napkin, rub thy brows.
The Queen carouses[65] to thy fortune, Hamlet.
HAM.
Good madam!
KING.
Gertrude, do not drink.
QUEEN.
I will, my lord, I pray you pardon me.
KING.
[Aside.] It is the pois'ned cup, it is too late.
HAM.
I dare not drink yet, madam; by and by.
QUEEN.
Come, let me wipe thy face.
LAER.
My lord, I'll hit him now.
KING.
I do not think't.
LAER.
[Aside.] And yet it is almost against my conscience.
HAM.
Come, for the third, Laertes, you do but dally.
I pray you pass with your best violence;
I am sure you make a wanton of me.[66]
LAER.
Say you so? Come on. *[They play.]*
OSR.
Nothing, neither way.
LAER.
Have at you now!
[Laertes wounds Hamlet; then, in scuffling, they change rapiers.]

[64] **fat:** sweaty.
[65] **carouses:** drinks a toast.
[66] **make . . . me:** i.e. are holding back in order to let me win, as one does with a spoiled child {wanton).

KING.
Part them, they are incens'd

HAM.
Nay, come again.
[Hamlet wounds Laertes. The Queen falls.]

OSR.
Look to the Queen there ho!

HOR.
They bleed on both sides. How is it, my lord?

OSR.
How is't, Laertes?

LAER.
Why, as a woodcock to mine own springe,[67] Osric:
I am justly kill'd with mine own treachery.

HAM.
How does the Queen?

KING.
She sounds[68] to see them bleed.

QUEEN.
No, no, the drink, the drink—O my dear Hamlet—
The drink, the drink! I am pois'ned. [Dies.]

HAM.
O villainy! Ho, let the door be lock'd!
Treachery! Seek it out.

LAER.
It is here, Hamlet. [Hamlet,] thou art slain.
No med'cine in the world can do thee good;
In thee there is not half an hour's life.
The treacherous instrument is in [thy] hand,
Unbated[69] and envenom'd. The foul practice[70]
Hath turn'd itself on me. Lo here I lie,
Never to rise again, Thy mother's pois'ned.
I can no more—the King, the King's to blame.

HAM.
The point envenom'd too!
Then, venom, to thy work. *[Hurts71 the King.]*

ALL.
Treason! treason!

KING.
O, yet defend me, friends, I am but hurt.

HAM.
Here, thou incestious, [murd'rous], damned Dane,
Drink [off] this potion! Is [thy union] here? Follow my mother! *[King dies.]*

LAER.
He is justly served, It is a poison temper'd[72] by himself.

---

[67] **springe:** snare.
[68] **sounds:** swoons
[69] **Unbated:** not blunted.
[70] **foul practice:** vile plot.
[71] s.d. **Hurts:** wounds.
[72] **temper'd:** mixed.

Exchange forgiveness with me, noble Hamlet.
Mine and my father's death come not upon thee
Nor thine on me! *[Dies.]*

HAM.

Heaven make thee free of it! I follow thee.
I am dead, Horatio. Wretched queen, adieu!
You that look pale, and tremble at this chance,
That are but mutes or audience[73] to this act,
Had I but time—as this fell[74] sergeant,[75] Death,
Is strict in his arrest—O, I could tell you—
But let it be. Horatio, I am dead, Thou livest.
Report me and my cause aright
To the unsatisfied.

HOR.

Never believe it;
I am more an antique Roman[76] than a Dane.
Here's yet some liquor left.

HAM.

As th' art a man,
Give me the cup. Let go! By heaven, I'll ha't!
O God, Horatio, what a wounded name,
Things standing thus unknown, shall I leave behind me!
If thou didst ever hold me in thy heart,
Absent thee from felicity a while,
And in this harsh world draw thy breath in pain
To tell my story. *[A march afar off and a shot within].*
What warlike noise is this? *[Osric goes to the door and returns.]*

OSR.

Young Fortinbras, with conquest come from Poland,
To th' embassadors of England gives
This warlike volley.

HAM.

O, I die, Horatio,
The potent poison quite o'er-crows[77] my spirit.[78]
I cannot live to hear the news from England,
But I do prophesy th' election lights
On Fortinbras, he has my dying voice.[79]
So tell him, with th' occurrents[80] more and less
Which have solicited[81]—the rest is silence. *[Dies.]*

HOR.

Now cracks a noble heart. Good night, sweet prince,
And flights of angels sing thee to thy rest! *[March within.]*

---

[73] **mutes or audience:** silent spectators.
[74] **fell:** cruel.
[75] **sergeant:** sheriff's officer.
[76] **antique Roman:** i.e. one who will commit suicide on such an occasion.
[77] **o'er-crows:** triumphs over (a term derived from cockfighting).
[78] **spirit:** vital energy.
[79] **voice:** vote.
[80] **occurrents:** occurrences.
[81] **solicited:** instigated.

MIGUEL DE CERVANTES

DON QUIXOTE OF LA MANCHA

Cervantes' *Don Quixote of La Mancha* is a parody of the popular romances of the day that glorified medieval chivalry. The style of *Don Quixote* draws on the picaresque narrative form which developed in Spain during the sixteenth century. A picaresque narrative involves a *picaro*—a knave or rogue—who gallivants from one escapade to another, and it also has a narrator who, on the surface, appears to be relating his own autobiography. In the first chapter, the reader is introduced to Don Quixote who devotes all his time to reading books about knighthood and chivalry. The following excerpt relates how he begins to imagine himself to be a gallant knight.

In resolution, he plunged himself so deeply in his reading of these books, as he spent many times in the lecture of them whole days and nights; and in the end, through his little sleep and much reading, he dried up his brains in such sort as he lost wholly his judgment. His fantasy was filled with those things that he read, of enchantments, quarrels, battles, challenges, wounds, wooings, loves, tempests, and other impossible follies. And these toys did so firmly possess his imagination with an infallible opinion that all that *machina* of dreamed inventions which he' read was true, as he accounted no history in the world to be so certain and sincere as they were. He was wont to say, that the Cid Ruy Diaz was a very good knight, but not to be compared to the Knight of the Burning Sword, which, with one thwart blow, cut asunder two fierce and mighty giants. He agreed better with Bernardo del Carpio, because he slew the enchanted Roland in Roncesvalles. He likewise liked of the shift Hercules used when he smothered Anteon, the son of the earth, between his arms. He praised the giant Morgant marvellously, because, though he was of that monstrous progeny, who are commonly all of them proud and rude, yet he was affable and courteous. But he agreed best of all with Reinauld of Mount Alban; and most of all then, when he saw him sally out of his castle to rob as many as ever he could meet; and when, moreover, he robbed the idol of Mahomet, made all of gold, as his history recounts, and would be content to give his old woman, yea, and his niece also, for a good opportunity on the traitor Galalon, that he might lamb-skin and trample him into powder.

Finally, his wit being wholly extinguished, he fell into one of the strangest conceits that ever madman stumbled on in this world; to wit, it seemed unto him very requisite and behooveful, as well for the augmentation of his honour as also for the benefit of the commonwealth, that he himself should become a knight-errant, and go throughout the world, with his horse and armour, to seek adventures, and practise in person all that he had read was used by knights of yore; revenging of all kinds of injuries, and offering himself to occasions and dangers, which, being once happily achieved, might gain him eternal renown. The poor soul did already figure himself crowned, through the valour of his arm, at least Emperor of Trapisonda; and led thus by these soothing thoughts, and borne away with the exceeding delight he found in them, he hastened all that he might, to effect his urging desires.

Subsequently, Don Quixote polishes his armor, renames his worn-out barn horse Rozinante, and selects Dulcinea as his lady-love—a peasant woman who does not know that he loves her and who never makes an actual appearance in the novel. Then he ventures forth seeking knightly glory. Along the way, he chooses a simple peasant, Sancho Panza, to be his squire, promising to make him governor of an island. Part of the pleasure that is derived from reading Don Quixote comes from Cervantes[1] treatment of the relationship between Don Quixote and Sancho. Rather than creating stock characters patterned after a chivalric code that formally defined the interaction between a high-born knight and his underling squire, Cervantes deals with their relationship as friends, especially as the strengths of one complement the other's weaknesses. The following excerpt relates one of Don Quixote's most famous adventures—his battle with giants, which were, in reality, windmills.

As they discoursed, they discovered some thirty or forty windmills, that are in that field; and as soon as Don Quixote espied them, he said to his squire, "Fortune doth address our affairs better than we ourselves could desire; for behold there, friend Sancho Panza, how there appears thirty or forty monstrous giants, with whom I mean to fight, and deprive them all of their lives, with whose spoils we will begin to be rich; for this is a good war, and a great service unto God, to take away so bad a seed from the face of the earth." "What giants?" quoth Sancho Panza. "Those that thou seest there," quoth his lord, "with the long arms; and some there are of that race whose arms are almost two leagues long." "I pray you understand," quoth Sancho Panza, "that those which appear there are no giants, but windmills; and that which seems in them to be arms, are their sails, that, swung about by the wind, do also make the mill go." "It seems well," quoth Don Quixote, "that thou art not yet acquainted with matter of adventures. They are giants; and, if thou beest afraid, go aside and pray, whilst I enter into cruel and unequal battle with them." And, saying so, he spurred his horse Rozinante, without taking heed to his squire Sancho's cries, advertising him how they were doubtless windmills that he did assault, and no giants; but he went so fully persuaded that they were giants as he neither heard his squire's outcries, nor did discern what they were, although he drew very near to them, but rather said, as loud as he could, "Fly not, ye cowards and vile creatures! for it is only one knight that assaults you."

With this the wind increased, and the mill sails began to turn about; which Don Quixote espying, said, "Although thou movest more arms than the giant Briareus thou shalt stoop to me." And, after saying this, and commending himself most devoutly to his Lady Dulcinea, desiring her to succor him in that trance, covering himself well with his buckler, and setting his lance on his rest, he spurred on Roz- inante, and encountered with the first mill that was before him, and, striking his lance into the sail, the wind swung it about with such fury, that it broke his lance into shivers, carrying him and his horse after it, and finally tumbled him a good way off from it on the field in evil plight. Sancho Panza repaired presently to succor him as fast as his ass could drive; and when he arrived, he found him not able to stir, he had gotten such a crush with Rozinante. "Good God!" quoth Sancho, "did I not foretell unto you that you should look well what you did, for they were none other than windmills? nor could any think otherwise, unless he had also windmills in his brains."

Ever since, "tilting at windmills" has referred to nonsensical, often delusional, encounters with imaginary rivals. Another disastrous incident, when Don Quixote mistakes two flocks of sheep for two armies about to go into battle, is excerpted below.

In these discourses Don Quixote and his squire rode; when Don Quixote, perceiving a great and thick dust to arise in the way wherein he travelled, turning to Sancho, said, "This is, Sancho, the day wherein shall be manifest the good which fortune hath reserved for me. This is the day wherein the force of mine arm must be shown as much as in any other whatsoever; and in it I will do such feats as shall for ever remain recorded in the books of fame. Dost thou see, Sancho, the dust which ariseth there? Know that it is caused by a mighty army, and sundry and innumerable nations, which come marching there." "If that be so," quoth Sancho, "then must there be two armies; for on this other side is raised as great a dust." Don Quixote turned back to behold it, and seeing it was so indeed, he was marvellous glad, thinking that they were doubtlessly two armies, which came to fight one with another in the midst of that spacious plain; for he had his fantasy ever replenished with these battles, enchantments, successes, ravings, loves, and challenges which are rehearsed in books of knighthood, and all that ever he spoke, thought, or did, was addressed and applied to the like things. And the dust which he had seen was raised by two great flocks of sheep, that came through the same field by two different ways, and could not be discerned, by reason of the dust, until they were very near. Don Quixote did affirm that they were two armies with so very good earnest as Sancho believed it, and demanded of him, "Sir, what then shall we two do?" "What shall we do," quoth Don Quixote, "but assist the needful and weaker side? For thou shalt know, Sancho, that he who comes towards us is the great emperor Alifamfaron, lord of the great island of Trapobana; the other, who marcheth at our back, is his enemy, the king of the Garamantes, Pentapolin of the naked arm, so called because he still entereth in battle with his right arm naked." "I pray you, good sir," quoth Sancho, "to tell me why these two princes hate one another so much?" "They are enemies," replied Don Quixote, "because that this Alifamfaron is a furious pagan, and is enamoured of Pentapolin's daughter, who is a very beautiful and gracious princess, and, moreover, a Christian; and her father refuseth to give her to the pagan king, until first he abandon Mahomet's false sect, and become one of his religion." "By my beard," quoth Sancho, "Pen- tapolin hath reason, and I will help him all that I may." "By doing so," quoth Don Quixote, "thou performest thy duty; for it is not requisite that one be a knight to the end he may enter into such battles." "I do apprehend that myself," quoth Sancho, "very well; but where shall we leave this ass in the meantime, that we may be sure to find him again after the conflict?—for I think it is not the custom to enter into battle mounted on such a beast." "It is true," quoth Don Quixote; "that which thou mayst do is to leave him to his adventures, and care not whether he be lost or found; for we shall have so many horses, after coming out of this battle victors, that very Rozinante himself is in danger to be changed for another. But be attentive; for I mean to describe unto thee the principal knights of both the armies; and to the end thou mayst the better see and note all things, let us retire ourselves there to that little hillock, from whence both armies may easily be descried." . . .

Good God! how many provinces repeated he at that time! and how many nations did he name, giving to every one of them, with marvellous celerity and briefness, their proper attributes, being swallowed up and engulfed in those things which he had read in his lying books! Sancho Panza stood suspended at his speech, and spoke not a word, but only would now and then turn his head, to see whether he could mark those knights and giants which his lord had named; and, by reason he could not discover any, he said, "Sir, I give to the devil any man, giant, or knight, of all those you said, that ap- peareth; at least, I cannot discern them. Perhaps all is but enchantment, like that of the ghosts of yesternight." "How sayst thou so?" quoth Don Quixote. "Dost not thou hear the horses neigh, the trumpets sound, and the noise of the drums?" "I hear nothing else," said Sancho, "but the great bleating of many sheep." And so it was, indeed; for by this time the two flocks did approach them very near. "The fear that thou con- ceivest, Sancho," quoth Don Quixote, "maketh thee that thou canst neither hear nor see aright; for one of the effects of fear is to trouble the senses, and make things appear otherwise than they are; and, seeing thou fearest so much, retire thyself out of the way; for I alone am sufficient to give the victory to that part which I shall assist." And, having ended his speech, he set spurs to Rozinante, and, setting his lance in the rest, he flung down from the hillock like a thunderbolt. Sancho cried to him as loud as he could, saying, "Return, good sir Don Quixote! for I vow unto God, that all those which you go to charge are but sheep and muttons; return, I say. Alas that ever I was born! what madness is this? Look; for there is neither giant nor knight, nor cats, nor arms, nor shields parted nor whole, nor pure azures nor devilish. What is it you do? wretch that I am!" For all this Don Quixote did not return, but rather rode, saying with a loud voice, "On, on, knights! all you that serve and march under the banners of the valorous emperor Pentapolin of the naked arm; follow me, all of you, and you shall see how easily I will revenge him on his enemy, Alifarmfaron of Trapobana." And, saying so, he entered into the midst of the flock of sheep, and began to lance them with such courage and fury as if he did in good earnest encounter his mortal enemies.

The shepherds that came with the flock, cried to him to leave off; but, seeing their words took no effect, they unloosed their slings, and began to salute his pate with stones as great as one's fist. But Don Quixote made no account of their stones, and did fling up and down among the sheep, saying, "Where art thou, proud Alifamfaron? where art thou? come to me; for I am but one knight alone, who desire to prove my force with thee man to man, and deprive thee of thy life, in pain of the wrong thou dost to the valiant Pentapolin, the Garamante." At that instant a stone gave him such a blow on one of his sides, as did bury two of his ribs in his body. He beholding himself so ill dight [treated}, did presently believe that he was either slain or sorely wounded; and, remembering himself of his liquor, he took out his oil- pot, and set it to his mouth to drink; but ere he could take as much as he thought requisite to cure his hurts, there cometh another almond, which struck him so full upon the hand and oil-pot, as it broke it into pieces, and carried away with it besides three or four of his cheek teeth, and did more- over bruise very sorely two of his fingers. Such was the first and the second blow, as the poor knight was constrained to fall down off his horse. And the shepherds arriving, did verily believe they had slain him; and therefore, gathering their flock together with all speed, and carrying away their dead muttons, which were more than seven, they went away without verifying the matter any further.

At the end of the novel, after many other such adventures, Don Quixote and Sancho return home. The legacy of Cervantes' novel is most evident in the widespread use of the term "quixotic" to refer to a person who is foolishly impractical, particularly in pursuit of some kind of lofty, romantic ideals or goals.

ERASMUS

IN PRAISE OF FOLLY

One of Erasmus' most famous works was *In Praise of Folly,* written in 1509, before Luther's challenge to the church. In the following passages, speaking through the voice of Folly, Erasmus castigates monks, theologians, and other Christians for failing to discern the true purpose of the Christian life: the imitation of Christ.

As for the theologians, perhaps it would be better to pass them over in silence, "*not stirring up the hornets' nest*" and "not laying a finger on the stinkweed," since this race of men is incredibly arrogant and touchy. For they might rise up en masse and march in ranks against me with six hundred conclusions and force me to recant. And if I should refuse, they would immediately shout "heretic." For this is the thunderbolt they always keep ready at a moment's notice to terrify anyone to whom they are not very favorably inclined. . . .

. . . They are so blessed by their Selflove as to be fully persuaded that they themselves dwell in the third heaven, looking down from high above on all other mortals as if they were earth-creeping vermin almost worthy of their pity. They are so closely hedged in by rows of magistral definitions, conclusions, corollaries, explicit and implicit propositions, they have so many "*holes they can run to,*" that Vulcan [Roman god of fire] himself couldn't net them tightly enough to keep them from escaping by means of distinctions, with which they cut all knots as cleanly as the fine-honed edge of "the headsman's axe"—so many new terms have they thought up and such monstrous jargon have they coined. . . .

In all of these there is so much erudition, so much difficulty, that I think the apostles themselves would need to be inspired by a different spirit if they were forced to match wits on such points with this new breed of theologians. Paul could provide a living example of faith, but when he said "Faith is the substance of things to be hoped for and the evidence of things not seen," his definition was not sufficiently magisterial. So too, he lived a life of perfect charity, but he neither distinguished it nor defined it with sufficient dialectical precision in the first epistle to the Corinthians, chapter 13. . . .

. . . But Christ, interrupting their boasts (which would otherwise never come to an end), will say, "Where did this new race of Jews [quibbling theologians] come from? The only law I recognize as truly mine is the only one I hear nothing about. Long ago, not speaking obliquely in parables but quite openly, I promised my Father's inheritance not to hoods [worn by monks}, or trifling prayers, or fasts, but rather deeds of faith and charity. Nor do I acknowledge those who too readily acknowledge their own deeds: those who want to appear even holier than I am can go dwell in the heavens of the Abraxasians[1] if they like, or they can order that a new heaven be built for them by the men whose petty traditions they have placed before my precepts." When they hear this and see sailors and teamsters chosen in preference to them, how do you suppose their faces will look as they stare at each other? . . .

Almost as happy as the theologians are those men who are commonly called "religious" and "monks"—though both names are quite incorrect, since a good part of them are very far removed from religion and no one is encountered more frequently everywhere you go. I cannot imagine how anything could be more wretched than these men. . . . For even though everyone despises this breed of men so thoroughly that even a chance meeting with one of them is considered unlucky, still they maintain a splendid opinion of themselves. First of all, they consider it the very height of piety to have so little to do with literature as not even to be able to read. Moreover, when they roar out their psalms in church like braying asses (counting their prayers indeed, but understanding them not at all), then (of all things!) they imagine that the listening saints are soothed and caressed with manifold delight. Among them are some who make a great thing out of their squalor and beggary, who stand at the door bawling out their demands for bread—(indeed there is no inn or coach or ship where they do not make a disturbance),

[1]A heretical sect that believed there were 365 "heavens."

depriving other beggars of no small share of their income. And in this manner these most agreeable fellows, with their filth, ignorance, coarseness, impudence, recreate for us, as they say, an image of the apostles. . . .

Closely related to such men are those who have adopted the very foolish (but nevertheless quite agreeable) belief that if they look at a painting or statue of that huge . . . Christopher, they will not die on that day; or, if they address a statue of Barbara with the prescribed words, they will return from battle unharmed, or, if they accost Erasmus on certain days, with certain wax tapers, and in certain little formulas of prayer, they will soon become rich.[2] Moreover, in George they have discovered a new Hercules. . . .[3] They all but worship George's horse, most religiously decked out in breastplates and bosses [ornaments], and from time to time oblige him with some little gift. To swear by his bronze helmet is thought to be an oath fit for a king.

Now what shall I [Folly] say about those who find great comfort in soothing self-delusions about fictitious pardons for their sins, measuring out the times in purgatory down to the droplets of a water-clock, parceling out centuries, years, months, days, hours, as if they were using mathematical tables. Or what about those who rely on certain little magical tokens and prayers thought up by some pious impostor for his own amusement or profit? They promise themselves anything and everything: wealth, honor, pleasure, an abundance of everything, perpetual health, a long life, flourishing old age, and finally a seat next to Christ among the saints, though this last they don't want for quite a while yet—that is, when the pleasures of this life, to which they cling with all their might, have finally slipped through their fingers, then it will be soon enough to enter into the joys of the saints. Imagine here, if you please, some businessman or soldier or judge who thinks that if he throws into the collection basket one coin from all his plunder, the whole cesspool of his sinful life will be immediately wiped out. He thinks all his acts of perjury, lust, drunkenness, quarreling, murder, deception, dishonesty, betrayal are paid off like a mortgage, and paid off in such a way that he can start off once more on a whole new round of sinful pleasures.

Now who could be more foolish—rather, who could be happier—than those who assure themselves they will have the very ultimate felicity because they have recited daily those seven little verses from the holy psalms? A certain devil—certainly a merry one, but too loose-lipped to be very clever—is believed to have mentioned them to St. Bernard,[4] but the poor devil was cheated by a clever trick. Such absurdities are so foolish that even I am almost ashamed of them, but still they are approved not only by the common people but even by learned teachers of religion. . . .

But why have I embarked on this vast sea of superstitions?

Not if I had a hundred tongues, a hundred mouths,
A voice of iron, could I survey all kinds
Of fools, or run through all the forms of folly.[5]

So rife, so teeming with such delusions is the entire life of all Christians everywhere. And yet priests are not unwilling to allow and even foster such delusions because they are not unaware of how many emoluments accumulate from this source. In the midst of all this, if some odious wiseman should stand up and sing out the true state of affairs: "You will not die badly if you live well. You redeem your sins if to the coin you add a hatred of evil deeds, then tears, vigils, prayers, fasts, and if you change your whole way of life. This saint will help you if you imitate his life"—if that wiseman were to growl out such assertions and more like them, look how much happiness he would immediately take away from the minds of mortals, look at the confusion he would throw them into!

---

[2] Christopher refers to Saint Christopher, a popular legendary giant and the patron saint of travelers. Barbara was a widely venerated but legendary early Christian martyr and saint. Erasmus, an Italian bishop and also a saint, was martyred in about **A.D.** 303.

[3] George, the patron saint of England and of the Crusaders, was believed to have been martyred in about **A.D.** 300. Saint George's battle with a dragon was a popular legend. Hercules, a Greek hero, performed twelve difficult tasks that won him immortality as a gift of the gods. He was himself worshiped as a god by later Greeks and Romans.

[4] Saint Bernard (1091-1153) was a leading theologian, Cistercian monk, and preacher.

[5] Virgil's Aeneid 6.625-627.

MARTIN LUTHER

ADDRESS TO THE CHRISTIAN NOBILITY THE BABYLONIAN CAPTIVITY OF THE CHURCH, AND *THE FREEDOM OF THE CHRISTIAN CHALLENGING THE CHURCH*

Due to his father's wishes, Luther entered law school, but he soon dropped out because of a deep-seated spiritual despondency. Like many of his contemporaries, Luther sought to save his soul from the temptations of the flesh, the devil, and the world. He often tormented himself with the question: Why would a righteous God choose a sinner like me to be saved? In 1505, Luther entered the Augustinian monastery at Erfurt, but although he was a fastidiously conscientious monk, he did not find the spiritual solace he was seeking. Nonetheless, he persevered as a monk, was ordained into the priesthood in 1507, went on to study theology, and became a professor and preacher in Wittenberg.

In 1507, Pope Julius II proclaimed an indulgence[1] to finance the construction of the new Saint Peter's basilica in Rome. The indulgence promised Christians, living or dead, the remission of ecclesiastical penalties for sin and thus the possibility of avoiding purgatory. By April 1517, John Tetzel, a Dominican monk, was preaching the indulgence near Wittenberg, but he preached that the indulgence was itself a means to salvation, which could easily be purchased. Tetzel, playing on the emotions of those who had lost loved ones, reputedly said, "As soon as the coin in the box rings, the soul from purgatory to heaven springs." To sincere Christians it seemed as if the church was espousing an abhorrent idea— that people could buy their way into heaven. That same year, Luther denounced the abuses connected with the preaching of the indulgence in his *Ninety-Five Theses Concerning the Efficacy of Indulgences,* written in Latin, which he posted on the north door of the Castle Church on All Saints' Eve (October 31). This quarrel led quickly to other and more profound theological issues.

In August 1520, Luther attacked the whole system of papal governance in the following selection taken from his *Address to the Christian Nobility of the German Nation Concerning the Reform of the Christian Estate,* the first of his so- called "Reformation tracts," written in German. He argues that the Romanists (traditional Catholics loyal to the papacy) have built "three walls" that effectively block any reform of the church. Consequently, Luther appeals to the nobility and the leaders of the imperial cities in Germany to intervene by summoning a "free council" to reform the church.

ADDRESS TO THE CHRISTIAN NOBILITY

The Romanists, have very cleverly built three walls around themselves. Hitherto they have protected themselves by these walls in such a way that no one has been able to reform them. As a result, the whole of Christendom has fallen abominably.

In the first place, when pressed by the temporal power they have made decrees and declared that the temporal power had no jurisdiction over them, but that, on the contrary, the spiritual power is above the temporal. In the second place, when the attempt is made to reprove them with the Scriptures, they raise the objection that only the pope may interpret the Scriptures. In the third place, if threatened with a council, their story is that no one may summon a council but the pope.

In this way they have cunningly stolen our three rods from us, that they may go unpunished. They have ensconced themselves within the sage stronghold of these three walls so that they can practice all the knavery and wickedness which we see today. Even when they have been compelled to hold a council

[1] According to the Roman Catholic teaching concerning the sacrament of penance, the priest absolved the truly contrite sinner from the guilt of sin but gave the sinner a temporal penalty, or penance, to fulfill. If the penance was either insufficient or not completed before one's death, the remainder would be fulfilled in purgatory—the place where sinners made recompense for their sins before being allowed into heaven. In theory, an indulgence allowed a sinner to draw upon the treasury of merit accrued by Christ, the Virgin Mary, and the saints to remit the temporal punishment for sins.

they have weakened its power in advance by putting the prince under oath to let them remain as they were. In addition, they have given the pope full authority over all decisions of a council, so that it is all the same whether there are many councils or no councils. They only deceive us with puppet shows and sham fights. They fear terribly for their skin in a really free council! They have so intimidated kings and princes with this technique that they believe it would be an offense against God not to be obedient to the Romanists in all their knavish and ghoulish deceits. . . .

The second wall is still more loosely built and less substantial. The Romanists want to be the only masters of Holy Scripture, although they never learn a thing from the Bible all their life long. They assume the sole authority for themselves, and quite unashamed, they play about with words before our very eyes, trying to persuade us that the pope cannot err in matters of faith, regarding less of whether he is righteous or wicked. Yet they cannot point to a single letter. This is why so many heretical and un-Christian, even unnatural, ordinances stand in the canon law. But there is no need to talk about these ordinances at present. Since these Romanists think the Holy Spirit never leaves them, no matter how ignorant and wicked they are, they become bold and decree only what they want. . . .

But so as not to fight them with mere words, we will quote the Scriptures. St. Paul says in Corinthians 14 [:30], "If something better is revealed to anyone, though he is already sitting and listening to another in God's word, then the one who is speaking shall hold his peace and give place." What would be the point of this commandment if we were compelled to believe only the man who does the talking or the man who is at the top? Even Christ said in John 6 [:45] that all Christians shall be taught by God. If it were to happen that the pope and his cohorts were wicked and not true Christians, were not taught by God and were without understanding, why should the pope not follow the obscure man? Has the pope not erred many times? Who would help Christendom when the pope erred if we did not have somebody who had the Scriptures on his side?

Therefore, their claim that only the pope may interpret Scripture is an outrageous fancied fable. They cannot produce a single letter [of Scripture] to maintain that the interpretation of Scripture or the confirmation of its interpretation belongs to the pope alone. They themselves have usurped this power. . . .

The third wall falls of itself when the first two are down. When the pope acts contrary to the Scriptures, it is our duty to stand by the Scriptures, to reprove him and to constrain him, according to the word of Christ, Matthew 18 f: 15—17}, "If your brother sins against you, go and tell it to him, between you and him alone; if he does not listen to you, then take one or two others with you; if he does not listen to them, tell it to the church; if he does not listen to the church, consider him a heathen." Here every member is commanded to care for every other. How much more should we do this when the member that does evil is responsible for the government of the church, and by his evil-doing is the cause of much harm and offense to the rest! But if I am to accuse him before the church, I must naturally call the church together.

The Romanists have no basis in Scripture for their claim that the pope alone has the right to call or confirm a council. This is just their own ruling, and it is only valid as long it is not harmful to Christendom or contrary to the laws of God. Now when the pope deserves punishment, this ruling no longer obtains, for not to punish him by authority of a council is harmful to Christendom.

Luther believed that the only authority for the Christian is holy Scripture, God's word to men and women, and he viewed Christianity as a personal relationship between the individual and God. Whereas the Roman Catholic Church taught that the clergy were intermediaries between human beings and God, that a person reached God by going through the clergy, as for example, when confessing to a priest, Luther asserted that the clergy were no different from and possessed no more power than the laity. In effect, all believers are priests. This means that the Christian's path to God is direct; no clerical intermediary is required. Luther also dismissed the authority of canon law, ecclesiastical courts, and the exclusive power of the clergy to interpret the Scriptures. Luther likened the situation of Christians during his own age to that of the Jews who were forcibly taken into captivity by the Babylonians in 586 b.c. in the second of his "Reformation tracts," *The Babylonian Captivity of the Church.* In the following passage, he speaks on behalf of Christian liberty, and not only refers to the "tyranny of the pope" but equates him with the Antichrist—a secular king who is to rule the world in the years immediately prior to Christ's Second Coming before the Last Judgment and the end of the world.

THE BABYLONIAN CAPTIVITY OF THE CHURCH

I lift my voice simply on behalf of liberty and I confidently cry: No law, whether of man or of angels, may rightfully be imposed upon Christians without their consent, for we are free of all laws. And if any laws are imposed upon us, we must bear them in such a way as to preserve that sense of freedom which knows and affirms with certainty that an injustice is being done to it, even though it glories in bearing this injustice—so taking care neither to justify the tyrant nor to murmur against his tyranny. . . .

Nevertheless, since but few know . . . the blessedness of Christian liberty, and cannot know them because of the tyranny of the pope, I for one will disengage myself, and keep my conscience free by bringing this charge against the pope and all his papists: Unless they will abolish their laws and ordinances, and restore to Christ's churches their liberty and have it taught among them, they are guilty of all the souls that perish under this miserable captivity, the papacy is truly the kingdom of Babylon and of the very Antichrist. For who is "the man of sin" and "the son of perdition" [II Thess. 2:3] but he who with his doctrines and his laws increases the sins and perdition of souls in the church, while sitting in the church as if he were God? [II Thess. 2:4]. All this the papal tyranny has fulfilled, and more than fulfilled, these many centuries. It has extinguished faith, obscured the sacraments and oppressed the gospel; but its own laws, which are not only impious and sacrilegious, but even barbarous and foolish, it has decreed and multiplied without end.

Luther's idea that the individual reaches God and attains salvation without clerical intermediaries diminished the importance of the institutional church and its clergy. Luther also dismissed the authority of canon law, ecclesiastical courts, and retained only two of the seven sacraments—baptism and the Eucharist. While lecturing at the university on the Apostle Paul's Epistle to the Romans, Luther formulated his distinctive teaching of *justification by faith alone, through God's grace alone*. "Justification/" a theological term, is derived from two Latin words—*iustus* (righteous) and *facere* (to make)—and means "to make a person righteous." For Luther, however, justification was a *passive righteousness*, attained by God granting an individual faith, and not through any human efforts. His new evangelical theology of *justification by faith alone through God's grace alone* brought him further conflict with the Roman Catholic Church that maintained that *both* faith, a sincere human belief in God, and good works— church attendance, acts of charity, fasting, and pilgrimages—were necessary to achieve salvation. For Luther, however, good works did not bring a person closer to salvation, for faith alone was the avenue to heaven. A person of faith, he said, does good works—for example, demonstrating active love toward one's neighbor—in thanksgiving to God, but such actions are not rewarded with eternal life. In the following selection from his final "Reformation tract"—*The Freedom of the Christian*—Luther reflects on faith, works, and what it means to be righteous in the eyes of God.

THE FREEDOM OF THE CHRISTIAN

You may ask, "What then is the Word of God, and how shall it be used, since there are so many words of God?" I answer: The Apostle explains this in Romans 1. The Word is the gospel of God concerning his Son, who was made flesh, suffered, rose from the dead, and was glorified through the Spirit who sanctifies. To preach Christ means to feed the soul, make it righteous, set it free, and save it, provided it believes the preaching. Faith alone is the saving and efficacious use of the Word of God, according to Rom. 10 (:9): "If you confess with your lips that Jesus is Lord and believe in your heart that God raised him from the dead, you will be saved." Furthermore, "Christ is the end of the law, that every one who has faith may be justified" (Rom. 10:4). Again, in Rom. 1 (:17), "He who through faith is righteous shall live." The Word of God cannot be received and cherished by any works whatever but only by faith. Therefore it is clear that, as the soul needs only the Word of God for its life and righteousness, so it is justified by faith alone and not any works; for if it could be justified by anything else, it would not need the Word, and consequently it would not need faith.

This faith cannot exist in connection with works—that is to say, if you at the same time claim to be justified by works, whatever their character—for that would be the same as "limping with two different opinions" (I Kings 18:21), as worshipping Baal and kissing one's own hand (Job 31:27— 28), which, as Job says, is a very great iniquity. Therefore the moment you begin to have faith you learn that all things in you are altogether blameworthy, sinful, and damnable, as the Apostle says in Rom. 3 (:23), "Since all have sinned and fall short of the glory of God," and, "None is righteous, no, not one; ... all have turned aside, together they have gone wrong" (Rom. 3:10—12). When you have learned this you will know that you need Christ, who suffered and rose again for you so that, if you believe in him, you may through this faith become a new man in so far as your sins are forgiven and you are justified by the merits of another, namely, of Christ alone.

Since, therefore, this faith can rule only in the inner man, as Rom. 10 (:10) says, "For man believes with his heart and so is justified," and since faith alone justifies, it is clear that the inner man cannot be justified, freed, or saved by any outer work or action at all, and that these works, whatever their character, have nothing to do with this inner man. On the other hand, only ungodliness and unbelief of heart, and no outer work, make him guilty and a damnable servant of sin. Wherefore it ought to be the first concern of every Christian to lay aside all confidence in works and increasingly to strengthen faith alone and through faith to grow in the knowledge, not of works, but of Christ Jesus, who suffered and rose for him, as Peter teaches in the last chapter of his first Epistle (1 Pet. 5:10). No other work makes a Christian. . . .

Our faith in Christ does not free us from works but from false opinions concerning works, that is, from the foolish presumption that justification is acquired by works. Faith redeems, corrects, and preserves our consciences so that we know that righteousness does not consist in works, although works neither can nor ought to be wanting; just as we cannot be without food and drink and all the works of this mortal body, yet our righteousness is not in them, but in faith; and yet those works of the body are not to be despised or neglected on that account. In this world we are bound by the needs of our bodily life, but we are not righteous because of them. "My kingship is not of this world" (John 18:36), says Christ. He does not, however, say, "My kingship is not here, that is, in this world." And Paul says, "Though we live in the world we are not carrying on a worldly war" (II Cor. 10:3), and in Gal. 2 (:20), "The life I now live in the flesh I live by faith in the Son of God." Thus what we do, live, and are in works and ceremonies, we do because of the necessities of this life and of the effort to rule our body. Nevertheless we are righteous, not in these, but in the faith of the Son of God.

JOHN CALVIN

THE INSTITUTES OF THE CHRISTIAN RELIGION

One doctrine that assumed greater and greater importance in the revised editions of Calvin's *Institutes* was predestination: the belief that each person's salvation or damnation was already decided before birth. Luther and Zwingli also taught that God had chosen those who would have faith. But they did not agree with Calvin concerning those who were to be damned, holding that those who refused to believe did so of their own volition. Calvin taught that salvation was only offered to the elect—the chosen few who were predestined to be saved by God's sovereign will—and that the reprobate (the damned) could not believe. Some argued that Calvin's doctrine implied that God was a tyrant; others said that it intimated that God was the author of sin. To many Christians, this doctrine diminished the justice and mercy of God and made meaningless the idea of freedom of choice in the matter of salvation. Calvin's answer to these criticisms was that we cannot know the mind of God—we are not able to understand why God chooses some humans and condemns others. We must trust in God's wisdom and justice.

PREDESTINATION

In actual fact, the covenant of life is not preached equally among all men, and among those to whom it is preached, it does not gain the same acceptance either constantly or in equal degree. In this diversity the wonderful depth of God's judgment is made known. For there is no doubt that this variety also serves the decision of God's eternal election. If it is plain that it comes to pass by God's bidding that salvation is freely offered to some while others are barred from access to it, at once great and difficult questions spring up, explicable only when reverent minds regard as settled what they may suitably hold concerning election and predestination. A baffling question this seems to many. For they think nothing more inconsistent than that out of the common multitude of men some should be predestined to salvation, others to destruction. But how mistakenly they entangle themselves will become clear in the following discussion. . . .

No one who wishes to be thought religious dares simply deny predestination, by which God adopts some to hope of life, and sentences others to eternal death. But our opponents, especially those who make foreknowledge its cause, envelop it in numerous petty objections. We, indeed, place both doctrines in God, but we say that subjecting one to the other is absurd.

When we attribute foreknowledge to God, we mean that all things always were, and perpetually remain, under his eyes, so that to his knowledge there is nothing future or past, but all things are present. And they are present in such a way that he not only conceives them through ideas, as we have before us those things which our minds remember, but he truly looks upon them and discerns them as things placed before him. And this foreknowledge is extended throughout the universe to every creature. We call predestination God's eternal decree, by which he determined with himself what he willed to become of each man. For all are not created in equal condition; rather, eternal life is foreordained for some, eternal damnation for others. Therefore, as any man has been created to one or the other of these ends, we speak of him as predestined to life or to death. . . .

As Scripture, then, clearly shows, we say that God once established by his eternal and unchangeable plan those whom he long before determined once for all to receive into salvation, and those whom, on the other hand, he would devote to destruction. We assert that, with respect to the elect, this plan was founded upon his freely given mercy, without regard to human worth; but by his just and irreprehensible but incomprehensible judgment he has barred the door of life to those whom he has given over to damnation. Now among the elect we regard the call as a testimony or election. Then we hold justification another sign of its manifestation, until they come into the glory in which the fulfillment of that election lies. But as the Lord seals his elect by call and justification, so, by shutting off the reprobate from knowledge of his name or from the sanctification of his Spirit, he, as it were, reveals by these marks what sort of judgment awaits them. Here I shall pass over many fictions that stupid men have invented to overthrow predestination. They need no refutation, for as soon as they are brought forth they abundantly prove their own falsity. I shall pause only over those which either are being argued by the learned or may raise difficulty for the simple, or which impiety speciously sets forth in order to assail God's righteousness.

JOHN MILTON

PARADISE LOST

The course of contemporary English history found its fullest expression in the works of the writer, John Milton (1608-1674). He demonstrated his facility for Hebrew, Greek, and Latin while in school and immersed himself in Latin verse and in classical tragedies and comedies at Christ College, Cambridge, where he received both his bachelor's and masters degrees. In his early poems, Milton showed himself to be a master of poetic image, grace, and style, but because of his scholarly gifts, his family and friends assumed he would become a minister. Instead, he retired to his family's homes at Hammersmith and Horton to cultivate the sort of humanist education he had not received at Cambridge. While at Horton, Milton wrote the poem "At a Solemn Music" which hints at the grandiose theme of good versus evil that was to culminate in his monumental poem, *Paradise Lost,* the heroic epic for which he would forever be remembered.

In 1642, when his wife left him, Milton wrote a series of pamphlets, arguing that divorce should be granted not only for adultery, but also in cases of incompatibility or a loveless marriage. He also published two of his most famous pamphlets—*On Education*, a discourse on the value of a humanistic education, and *Aeropagitica,* a plea for freedom of the press and an indictment of royal censorship. In his first political treatise, *The Tenure of Kings and Magistrates,* following the public execution of Charles I (an event that Milton reportedly attended), he asserted the right of the people to execute a tyrannical king. However, Milton's excitement at the fall of the Stuarts was tempered by the loss of his eyesight (probably from glaucoma) which left him totally blind by the age of forty-three. During the Restoration Period, Milton wrote his last political tract, *The Readie and Easie Way to Establish a Free Commonwealth,* an indictment of the English people who chose to become slaves of the monarchy. Subsequently, Royalists in Parliament issued a warrant for Milton's arrest, imprisoned him briefly, and forced him to pay an exorbitant fine.

Although the prodigious output of prose during Milton's life is four times greater than his entire poetic production, it is for his poetry that he is remembered. During his later life, Milton began to dictate *Paradise Lost,* and while he worked, he closely identified himself with the ancient poet Homer, who also was reputedly blind when he composed the *Iliad* and the *Odyssey.* Milton composed the epic in blank verse, which rarely appeared outside of drama. Blank verse is unrhymed iambic pentameter which is the most natural form of English verse. An iambic foot is an unstressed syllable followed by a stressed one, and pentameter means that there are five iambic feet per line. For example, one of the most famous lines in the poem is read as follows: "and jus/ti-fy/ the ways of God to men." The subject of *Paradise Lost* is humanity's fall from God's grace, and with a note of irony attached, Milton chose Satan as an atypical protagonist, a type of antihero, to assert Eternal Providence and justify the ways of God to men. Milton's overwhelming sense of human guilt and sinfulness is drawn directly from the Protestant reformers who viewed human nature as corrupt, but the abundance of classical allusions demonstrates his affinity for the Renaissance. Consequently, the epic not only demonstrates how Milton overcame despair and found meaning in suffering, but it also reflects the power of his Protestant faith and his humanist belief in the capacity of the human soul to prevail against adversity.

The setting of the epic poem is Paradise, and the period of time is just before The Fall, until Adam and Eve are expelled from Paradise. The plot is, however, secondary to the ruminations and reflections of Milton's characters, including Gabriel, Adam, Eve, and, most importantly, Satan. Milton's powerful characterization of Satan actually induces sympathy from readers for the wrongs he incurs following his battle against tyranny in heaven. The rhythm and tone of the epic poem causes it to be counted as one of the great masterpieces of the English language. Moreover, Milton's theme of the fall of the human race inspired the classical composer Franz Josef Haydn's (1732-1809) oratorio *The Creation* and the Romantic poem "Enydmion" by John Keats (1795-1821), as well as many other authors and composers who are indebted to Milton for their style and theme. A number of scholars and critics have also come to recognize that many people who speak about the reality of Satan—his deportment, exploits, and expressions—have drawn their understanding, not as much from the Bible, as from a cultural perception that is traceable to Milton's *Paradise Lost.*

In the following selection from Book IX, Milton states "The Argument" for this particular section of the epic poem, dealing with The Fall of the human race occasioned by Adam and Eve in the Garden of Eden, eating of the fruit of the Tree of Knowledge, following Eve's temptation by the Serpent (the incarnation of evil).

The Argument.—Satan, having compassed the Earth, with meditated guile returns as a mist by night into Paradise; enters into the Serpent sleeping. Adam and Eve in the morning go forth to their labours, which Eve proposes to divide in several places, each labouring apart: Adam consents not, alleging the danger lest that Enemy of whom they were forewarned should attempt her found alone. Eve, loth to be thought not circumspect or firm enough, urges her going apart, the rather desirous to make trial of her strength; Adam at last yields. The Serpent finds her alone: his subtle approach, first gazing, then speaking, with much flattery extolling Eve above all other creatures. Eve, wondering to hear the Serpent speak, asks how he attained to human speech and such understanding not till now; the Serpent answers that by tasting of a certain Tree in the Garden he attained both to speech and reason, till then void of both. Eve requires him to bring her to that tree, and finds it to be the Tree of Knowledge forbidden: the Serpent, now grown bolder, with many wiles and arguments induces her at length to eat. She, pleased with the taste, deliberates a while whether to impart thereof to Adam or not; at last brings him of the fruit; relates what persuaded her to eat thereof. Adam, at first amazed, but perceiving her lost, resolves, through vehemence of love, to perish with her, and, extenuating the trespass, eats also of the fruit. The effects thereof in them both; they seek to cover their nakedness; then fall to variance and accusation of one another.

In the passage that follows, Satan reveals his bitterness about being expelled from heaven (for leading a rebellion of angels) and his desire to reap vengeance on God by destroying his creation of six nights and days, particularly Adam, "this Man of Clay," whom God formed from the dust of the earth.

"O Earth, how like to Heaven, if not preferred
More justly, seat worthier of Gods, as built
With second thoughts, reforming what was old!
For what God, after better, worse would build?
Terrestrial Heaven, danced round by other Heavens,
That shine, yet bear their bright officious[1] lamps,
Light above light, for thee alone, as seems,
In thee concentring all their precious beams
Of sacred influence! As God in Heaven
Is centre, yet extends to all, so thou
Centring receiv'st from all those orbs; in thee,
Not in themselves, all their known virtue appears,
Productive in herb, plant, and nobler birth
Of creatures animate with gradual life
Of growth, sense, reason, all summed up in Man.
With what delight could I have walked thee round,
If I could joy in aught—sweet interchange
Of hill and valley, rivers, woods, and plains,
Now land, now sea, and shores with forest crowned,
Rocks, dens, and caves! But I in none of these
Find place or refuge; and the more I see
Pleasures about me, so much more I feel
Torment within me, as from the hateful siege
Of contraries; all good to me becomes

[1] *Officious* means ready to serve, or obliging.

Bane, and in Heaven much worse would be my state.
But neither here seek I, nor in Heaven,
To dwell, unless by maistring[2] Heaven's Supreme;
Nor hope to be myself less miserable
By what I seek, but others to make such
As I, though thereby worse to me redound.
For only in destroying I find ease
To my relentless thoughts; and him destroyed,
Or won to what may work his utter loss,
For whom all this was made, all this will soon
Follow, as to him linked in weal or woe:
In woe then, that destruction wide may range!
To me shall be the glory sole among
The Infernal Powers, in one day to have marred
What he, Almighty styled, six nights and days
Continued making, and who knows how long
Before had been contriving? though perhaps ·
Not longer than since I in one night freed
From servitude inglorious well nigh half
The Angelic Name, and thinner left the throng
Of his adorers. He, to be avenged,
And to repair his numbers thus impaired—
Whether such virtue, spent of old, now failed
More Angels to create (if they at least
Are his created), or to spite us more—
Determined to advance into our room
A creature formed of earth, and him endow,
Exalted from so base original,
With heavenly spoils, our spoils. What he decreed
He effected; Man he made, and for him built
Magnificent this World, and Earth his seat,
Him Lord pronounced, and, O indignity!
Subjected to his service Angel-wings
And flaming ministers, to watch and tend
Their earthly charge. Of these the vigilance
I dread, and to elude, thus wrapt in mist
Of midnight vapour, glide obscure, and pry
In every bush and brake, where hap may find
The Serpent sleeping, in whose mazy folds
To hide me, and the dark intent I bring.
O foul descent! that I, who erst contended
With Gods to sit the highest, am now constrained
Into a beast, and, mixed with bestial slime,
This essence to incarnate and imbrute,[3]
That to the highth of Deity aspired!
But what will not ambition and revenge
Descend to? Who aspires must down as low
As high he soared, obnoxious, first or last,

---

[2]Maistring means mastering.
[3] *Imbrute* means to reduce to brutality.

To basest things. Revenge, at first though sweet,
Bitter ere long back on itself recoils.
Let it; I reck[4] not, so it light well aimed,
Since higher I fall short, on him who next
Provokes my envy, this new favourite
Of Heaven, this Man of Clay, son of despite,
Whom, us the more to spite, his Maker raised
From dust: spite then with spite is best repaid."

When Adam and Eve part from one another to perform their daily tasks, the Serpent finds the opportunity to tempt Eve while she is alone. Fascinated by his ability to speak, Eve asks the serpent how he came to possess such a quality. The Serpent tells her how he ate the "fair Apples, of fairest colours mixed, ruddy and gold/' When he tells her that the tree is not far away, Eve asks the Serpent to lead her to the tree—only to discover it is the tree the fruit of which God has forbidden Adam and Eve to eat, lest they die. Undaunted, the Serpent lures Eve to eat of the forbidden fruit by telling her that she will not die, but rather, she will be like God and possess knowledge of both good and evil.

Which when she saw, thus to her guide she spake:—
"Serpent, we might have spared our coming hither,
Fruitless to me, though fruit be here to excess,
The credit of whose virtue rest with thee—
Wondrous, indeed, if cause of such effects!
But of this tree we may not taste nor touch;
God so commanded, and left that command
Sole daughter of his voice: the rest, we live
Law to ourselves; our Reason is our Law."
To whom the Tempter guilefully replied:—
"Indeed! Hath God then said that of the fruit
Of all these garden-trees ye shall not eat,
Yet lords declared of all in Earth or Air?"
To whom thus Eve, yet sinless:—
"Of the fruit Of each tree in the garden we may eat;
But of the fruit of this fair Tree, amidst
The Garden, God hath said, 'Ye shall not eat
Thereof, nor shall ye touch it, lest ye die.'"
She scarce had said, though brief, when now more bold
The Tempter, but, with shew of zeal and love
To Man, and indignation at his wrong,
New part puts on, and, as to passion moved,
Fluctuates disturbed, yet comely, and in act
Raised, as of some great matter to begin.
As when of old some orator renowned
In Athens or free Rome, where eloquence
Flourished, since mute, to some great cause addressed,
Stood in himself collected, while each part,
Motion, each act, won audience ere the tongue
Sometimes in highth began, as no delay
Of preface brooking through his zeal of right:
So standing, moving, or to highth upgrown,
The Tempter, all impassioned, thus began:—
"O sacred, wise, and wisdom-giving Plant,

[4]Reck means to have concern or care.

Mother of science! now I feel thy power
Within me clear, not only to discern
Things in their causes, but to trace the ways
Of highest agents, deemed however wise.
Queen of this Universe! do not believe
Those rigid threats of death. Ye shall not die
How should ye? By the Fruit? it gives you life
To knowledge. By the Threatener? look on me,
Me who have touched and tasted, yet both live,
And life more perfet have attained than Fate
Meant me, by venturing higher than my lot.
Shall that be shut to Man which to the Beast
Is open? or will God incense his ire
For such a petty trespass, and not praise
Rather your dauntless virtue, whom the pain
Of death denounced, whatever thing Death be,
Deterred not from achieving what might lead
To happier life, knowledge of Good and Evil?
Of good, how just! of evil—if what is evil
Be real, why not known, since easier shunned?
God, therefore, cannot hurt ye and be just;
Not just, not God; not feared then, nor obeyed:
Your fear itself of death removes the fear.
Why, then, was this forbid? Why but to awe,
Why but to keep ye low and ignorant,
His worshipers? He knows that in the day
Ye eat thereof your eyes, that seem so clear,
Yet are but dim, shall perfetly be then
Opened and cleared, and ye shall be as Gods,
Knowing both good and evil, as they know,
That ye should be as Gods, since I as Man,
Internal Man, is but proportion meet—
I, of brute, human; ye, of human, Gods.
So ye shall die perhaps, by putting off
Human, to put on Gods—death to be wished,
Though threatened, which no worse than this can bring!
And what are Gods, that Man may not become
As they, participating godlike food?
The Gods are first, and that advantage use
On our belief, that all from them proceeds.
I question it; for this fair Earth I see,
Warmed by the Sun, producing every kind;
Them nothing. If they all things, who enclosed
Knowledge of Good and Evil in this Tree,
That whoso eats thereof forthwith attains
Wisdom without their leave? and wherein lies
The offence, that Man should thus attain to know?
What can your knowledge hurt him, or this Tree
Impart against his will, if all be his?
Or is it envy? and can envy dwell

In Heavenly breasts? These, these and many more
Causes import your need of this fair Fruit,
Goddess humane, reach, then, and freely taste!" . . .

Milton recounts the effect Eve's disobedience to God had upon Adam when she tells him of her deed.

Thus Eve with countenance blithe her story told;
But in her cheek distemper flushing glowed.
On the other side, Adam, soon as he heard
The fatal trespass done by Eve, amazed,
Astonied stood and blank, while horror chill
Ran through his veins, and all his joints relaxed.
From his slack hand the garland wreathed for Eve
Down dropt, and all the faded roses shed.
Speechless he stood and pale, till thus at length
First to himself he inward silence broke:—
"O fairest of Creation, last and best
Of all God's works, creature in whom excelled
Whatever can to sight or thought be formed,
Holy, divine, good, amiable, or sweet!
How art thou lost! how on a sudden lost,
Defaced, deflowered, and now to death devote!
Rather, how hast thou yielded to transgress
The strict forbiddance, how to violate
The sacred Fruit forbidden? Some cursed fraud
Of enemy hath beguiled thee, yet unknown,
And me with thee hath ruined; for with thee
Certain my resolution is to die.
How can I live without thee? . . .

Despite his reservations, Adam, spurred on by Eve, decides to eat of the forbidden fruit, and the couple then submits to their carnal desires for each other.

He scrupled not to eat,
Against his better knowledge, not deceived,
But fondly overcome with female charm.
Earth trembled from her entrails, as again
In pangs, and Nature gave a second groan;
Sky loured, and, muttering thunder, some sad drops
Wept at completing of the mortal Sin
Original; while Adam took no thought,
Facing his fill, nor Eve to iterate
Her former trespass feared, the more to soothe
Him with her loved society; that now,
As with new wine intoxicated both,
They swim in mirth, and fancy that they feel
Divinity within them breeding wings
Wherewith to scorn the Earth.
But that false Fruit Far other operation first displayed,
Carnal desire inflaming. He on Eve
Began to cast lascivious eyes; she him
As wantonly repaid. . . .

Milton recounts their shame when they recognize what they have done, and Book IX closes with Adam blaming Eve, and she him, for their loss of innocence.

Soon as the force of that fallacious Fruit,
That with exhilarating vapour bland
About their spirits had played, and inmost powers
Made err, was now exhaled, and grosser sleep,
Bred of unkindly fumes, with conscious dreams
Incumbered, now had left them, up they rose
As from unrest, and, each the other viewing,
Soon found their eyes how opened, and their minds
How darkened. Innocence, that as a veil
Had shadowed them from knowing ill, was gone;
Just confidence, and native righteousness,
And honour, from about them, naked left
To guilty Shame: he covered, but his robe
Uncovered more. So rose the Danite strong,
Herculean Samson, from the harlot-lap
Of Philistean Dalilah,[1] and waked
Shorn of his strength; they destitute and bare
Of all their virtue. Silent, and in face
Confounded, long they sat, as strucken mute;
Till Adam, though not less than Eve abashed,
At length gave utterance to these words constrained:—
"O Eve, in evil hour thou didst give ear
To that false Worm, of whomsoever taught
To counterfeit Man's voice—true in our fall,
False in our promised rising; since our eyes
Opened we find indeed, and find we know
Both good and evil, good lost and evil got:
Bad Fruit of Knowledge, if this be to know,
Which leaves us naked thus, of honour void,
Of innocence, of faith, of purity,
Our wonted ornaments now soiled and stained,
And in our faces evident the signs
Of foul concupiscence; whence evil store,
Even shame, the last of evils; of the first
Be sure then. How shall I behold the face
Henceforth of God or Angel, erst with joy
And rapture so oft beheld? Those Heavenly Shapes
Will dazzle now this earthly with their blaze
Insufferably bright. Oh, might I here
In solitude live savage, in some glade
Obscured, where highest woods, impenetrable
To star or sunlight, spread their umbrage broad,
And brown as evening. Cover me, ye pines!
Ye cedars, with innumerable boughs
Hide me, where I may never see them more!

[1]The reference here is to the Old Testament story (Judges 16) of the Danite strong man, Samson, whose strength reputedly was in his hair, and the Philistine temptress, Deliah, who seduced him and cut his hair.

But let us now, as in bad plight, devise
What best may, for the present, serve to hide
The parts of each other that seem most
To shame obnoxious, and unseemliest seen—
Some tree, whose broad smooth leaves, together sewed,
And girded on our loins, may cover round
Those middle parts, that this new comer, Shame,
There sit not, and reproach us as unclean." . . .
To whom, soon moved with touch of blame, thus Eve:—
"What words have passed thy lips, Adam severe?
Imput st thou that to my default, or will
Of wandering, as thou call'st it, which who knows
But might as ill have happened thou being by,
Or to thyself perhaps? Hadst thou been there,
Or here the attempt, thou couldst not have discerned
Fraud in the Serpent, speaking as he spake;
No ground of enmity between us known
Why he should mean me ill or seek to harm.
Was I to have never parted from thy side?
As good have grown there still, a lifeless rib.
Being as I am, why didst not thou, the Head,
Command me absolutely not to go,
Going into such danger, as thou saidst?
Too facile then, thou didst not much gainsay,
Nay, didst permit, approve, and fair dismiss.
Hadst thou been firm and fixed in thy dissent,
Neither had I transgressed, nor thou with me."
To whom, then first incensed, Adam replied:—
"Is this the love, is this the recompense
Of mine to thee, ingrateful Eve, expressed
Immutable when thou wert lost, not I—
Who might have lived, and joyed immortal bliss,
Yet willingly chose rather death with thee?
And am I now upbraided as the cause
Of thy transgressing? not enough severe,
It seems, in thy restraint!
What could I more? I warned thee, I admonished thee, foretold
The danger, and the lurking Enemy
That lay in wait; beyond this had been force,
And force upon free will hath here no place.
But confidence then bore thee on, secure
Either to meet no danger, or to find
Matter of glorious trial; and perhaps
I also erred in overmuch admiring
What seemed in thee so perfet that I thought
No evil durst attempt thee. But I rue
That error now, which is become my crime,
And thou the accuser. Thus it shall befall
Him who, to worth in women overtrusting,
Lets her will rule: restraint she will not brook;

And, left to herself, if evil thence ensue,
She first his weak indulgence will accuse."
Thus they in mutual accusation spent
The fruitless hours, but neither self-condemning;
And of their vain contest appeared no end.

JOHN BUNYAN

THE PILGRIM'S PROGRESS

John Bunyan (1628-1688) combined everyday speech with the eloquent prose of the King James Version of the Bible into a vivid narrative style. Like Luther and Milton, he understood human nature to be corrupt, and throughout his life, he sought assurance of his salvation from sin. Bunyan had little formal education and participated in the English civil war. Although he saw little actual fighting, he suffered lifelong guilt over the death of the young man who came to replace him. After his discharge from the army, Bunyan married a fervently pious woman and entered into a period of spiritual crises which lasted about five years. During this time he often felt that he was assailed by devils, physically abused, and threatened with damnation. He recounted these painful encounters in his spiritual autobiography, *Grace Abounding to the Chief of Sinners*. Bunyan eventually recovered from his dark night of despair and became an electrifying preacher. However, when he refused to conform to the liturgy of the Church of England, Bunyan was sent to prison, where he remained for the greater part of twelve years. During his imprisonment, Bunyan preached to his fellow prisoners, studied, and supported his family by making and selling shoelaces. Most important, he began *The Pilgrim's Progress*—a book that was destined to become the most successful allegory ever written in English. Part I of *The Pilgrim's Progress* is told in the guise of a dream as it details the spiritual journey of Christian (the leading character) to the Celestial City. On his journey, Christian must overcome despair, fear, corruption, the burden of sin, "Vanity Fair," and the "Valley of the Shadow of Death" before finding Faithful, who leads him into the knowledge of Gods grace.

The following passage contains one of the most compelling images in the allegory—the loss of Christian's "burden," which he carries on his shoulders, symbolizing the burden of sin. When it falls from his shoulders into a sepulchre (symbolizing the empty tomb of Christ's resurrection), Christian leaps for joy.

Now, I saw in my dream that the highway up which Christian was to go was fenced on either side with a wall that was called Salvation.*[[Isa. 26:1]] Up this way, therefore, did burdened Christian run, but not without great difficulty, because of the load on his back.

He ran thus till he came to a place somewhat ascending; and upon that place stood a cross, and a little below, in the bottom, a sepulchre. So I saw in my dream, that just as Christian came up with the cross, his burden loosed from off his shoulders, and fell from off his back, and began to tumble, and so continued to do till it came to the mouth of the sepulchre, where it fell in, and I saw it no more.

When God releases us of our guilt and burden, we are as those that leap for joy.

Then was Christian glad and lightsome, and said with a merry heart, "He hath given me rest by His sorrow, and life by His Death." Then he stood still awhile to look and wonder; for it was very surprising to him that the sight of the cross should thus ease him of his burden. He looked, therefore, and looked again, even till the springs that were in his head sent the water down his cheeks. [[Zech.12:10]] Now, as he stood looking and weeping, behold, three Shining Ones came to him, and saluted him with "Peace be to thee." So the first said to him, "Thy sins be forgiven thee";[[Mark 2:5]] the second stripped him of his rags, and clothed him with a change of raiment,§[[Zech. 3:4]] the third also set a mark on his forehead||[[Eph. 1:13]] and gave him a roll with a seal upon it, which he bade him look on as he ran, and that he should give it in at the celestial gate: so they went their way. Then Christian gave three leaps for joy, and went on, singing:

"Thus far did I come laden with my sin;
Nor could aught ease the grief that I was in.
Till I came hither: what a place is this!
Must here be the beginning of my bliss?
Must here the burden fall from off my back?

Must here the strings that bound it to me crack?
Blest cross! blest sepulchre! blest rather be
The Man that was there put to shame for me!"

Christian then finds Hopeful, and they nearly succumb to a Flood of Temptation, before meeting the Giant Despair and his wife, Diffidence, who beat them and imprison them in Doubting Castle. Hopeful and Christian escape when Christian finds the key called Promise, which unlocks any door, including the door of the dungeon. Together, Hopeful and Christian encounter further temptation, conquer Conceit, and overcome Ignorance and Guilt before arriving at the gate of the Celestial City. They cannot enter the Celestial City, however, until they cross the River of Death—symbolizing an individual's fear of death—a river that can only be crossed by believing in Jesus Christ.

Death is not welcome to nature, though by it we pass out of this world into glory.

The pilgrims then began to inquire if there was no other way to the gate; to which they answered, "Yes; but there hath not any save two, to wit, Enoch and Elijah,[1] been permitted to tread that path since the foundation of the world, nor shall until the last trumpet shall sound." The pilgrims then, especially Christian, began to despond in his mind, and looked this way and that; but no way could be found by them by which they might escape the river. Then they asked the men if the waters were all of a depth. They said, "No"; yet they could not help them in that case; "for," said they, "you shall find it deeper or shallower as you believe in the King of the place."

They then addressed themselves to the water; and, entering, Christian began to sink, and crying out to his good friend Hopeful, he said, "I sink in deep waters; the billows go over my head; all His waves go over me. Selah."[2]

Then said the other, "Be of good cheer, my brother; I feel the bottom, and it is good." Then said Christian, "Ah! my friend, the sorrows of death have compassed me about; I shall not see the land that flows with milk and honey." And, with that, a great darkness and horror fell upon Christian, so that he could not see before him. Also here he in a great measure lost his senses, so that he could neither remember nor orderly talk of any of those sweet refreshments that he had met with in the way of his pilgrimage. But all the words that he spake still tended to discover that he had horror of mind, and heart- fears that he should die in that river, and never obtain entrance in at the gate. Here also, as they that stood by perceived, he was much in the troublesome thoughts of the sins that he had committed, both since and before he began to be a pilgrim. It was also observed that he was troubled with apparitions of hobgoblins and evil spirits; forever and anon he would intimate so much by words.

Christian delivered from his fears in death.

Hopeful, therefore, here had much ado to keep his brother's head above water; yea, sometimes he would be quite gone down, and then, ere a while, he would rise up again half dead. Hopeful would also endeavor to comfort him, saying, "Brother, I see the gate, and men standing by to receive us"; but Christian would answer, "It is you, it is you they wait for: you have been hopeful ever since I knew you." "And so have you," said he to Christian. "Ah, brother," said he, "surely, if I were right, He would now arise to help me; but for my sins He hath brought me into this snare, and hath left me." Then said Hopeful, "My brother, you have quite forgot the text where it is said of the wicked, "There are no bands in their death, but their strength is firm; they are not troubled as other men, neither are they plagued like other men."[3] These troubles and distresses that you go through in these waters are no sign that God hath forsaken you; but are sent to try you, whether you will call to mind that which hitherto you have received of His goodness, and live upon Him in your distresses."

Then I saw in my dream that Christian was in a muse[4] awhile. To whom also Hopeful added these words, "Be of good cheer, Jesus Christ maketh thee whole." And, with that, Christian brake out with a loud voice, "Oh, I see Him again; and He tells me, 'When thou passest through the waters, I will be

---

[1] Enoch and Elijah are Old Testament prophets.
[2] Selah is a word that occurs often in Psalms which probably is a musical term.
[3] Biblical reference Psalms 73:4, 5.
[4] To muse is to reflect or to meditate in silence.

with thee; and through the rivers, they shall not overflow thee.'"[5] Then they both took courage; and the enemy was, after that, as still as a stone, until they were gone over. Christian, therefore, presently found ground to stand upon; and so it followed that the rest of the river was but shallow. Thus they got over. . . .

In a poem at the end of Part I, Bunyan admonishes the reader to interpret the metaphors of his dream correctly.

Now, reader, I have told my dream to thee,
See if thou canst interpret it to me,
Or to thyself or neighbor; but take heed
Of misinterpreting; for that, instead
Of doing good, will but thyself abuse:
By misinterpreting, evil ensues.
Put by the curtains, look within my veil,
Turn up my metaphors and do not fail,
There, if thou seekest them, such things to find
As will be helpful to an honest mind.

In 1684, Bunyan published Part II of *The Pilgrim's Progress*—detailing the journey of Christiana, Christian's wife, and their children. Written in a lighter tone than Part I, Christiana and her children meet Mr. Sagacity and the characters of Mercy and Prudence. After they pass through the Valley of Humiliation, they encounter "a sweet grace," Humility. Later, they are greeted by shepherds—Knowledge, Experience, Watchful, and Sincere—and join with Great- Heart to kill Giant Despair and to demolish Doubting Castle. Finally the pilgrims cross the River of Death and are welcomed joyfully into the Celestial City.

[5] Biblical reference Isaiah 43:2.

MOLIÈRE

TARTUFFE

Jean-Baptiste Poquelin (1622-1673), better known by his stage name Molière, brought comedy to its highest level since antiquity. Molière received his degree in law in 1642, but the very next year, he joined an acting troupe, where he developed his skills as an actor, director, and playwright. In 1658, the brother of Louis XIV became Molière's patron, and he and his company were given their own theater in Paris. Throughout his career, Molière felt the ire of the religious authorities, who viewed his plays as scandalous attacks on religion. This was particularly true of *Tartuffe, or The Imposter*—a comedy that attacks religious hypocrisy. The church was able to prevent its performance for five years, until 1669. The main character of the play is Orgon, a wealthy, middle-aged man of the bourgeoisie, who is captivated by Tartuffe, whom he sees as a holy and devout man who teaches authentic Christian beliefs. Orgon invites Tartuffe to be an esteemed guest in his home. Others in Orgon's household—his son, Damis; his brother-law, Cleante; and his wife, Elmire—try to warn him that Tartuffe is a hypocrite, but Orgon continues in his conviction that he is a devout man. In the following excerpt, Orgon extolls Tartuffe's piety to Cleante.

CLEANTE, ORGON

CLEANTE:
Well, brother, she was laughing at you to your face.
Now, don't be cross, but I believe she's got a case.
In fact, to be quite frank, I think the girl is right.
I never thought I'd ever witness such a sight:
Did he use magic to persuade you to forget
Important things, and love a person you've just met?
You've spent a fortune rescuing him from despair,
And now, it seems, you want . . .

ORGON:
Brother-in-law, stop there! You don't know anything about him.
Stop your chat.

CLEANTE:
All right, so I don't know him, I'll allow you that.
But if I'm to find out what kind of man he is . . .

ORGON:
Oh, if you knew him well, you'd be in ecstasies!
You'd never stop adoring him once you began.
He is a man . . . who ... er ... in short, a man . . . a man.
If you sat at his feet, he'd bring you peace, for sure;
The world would seem to you a great heap of manure.
I've learnt from him, the truth is clearer in my eyes.
He's taught me to reject the things I used to prize.
The people that I thought I loved, I now deny,
And I could watch my mother, children, wife all die,
And, shall I tell you what? I just couldn't care less.

CLEANTE:
What warmth, my brother, what compassion you express!

ORGON:
I wish you'd seen how it turned out when first we met!
Like me, you'd have been drawn to him from the outset.

He came to church, and every day I saw that he
Fell on his knees and bowed his head in front of me.
The congregation as a whole became aware
Of how much ardour he would pour into his prayer.
He heaved great heavy sighs, and waved his arms around,
And often he'd bend very low and kiss the ground.
When I went out, he'd always hurry on before
To offer me some holy water by the door.
He has a servant, who's under his influence,
He's told me of his station, and his indigence.
I gave him money; with becoming modesty,
He always tried to give some of it back to me.
'No, it's too much', said he, 'Oh, it's too much by half.
I don't deserve your sympathy on my behalf.'
When I refused to take it back, he would ensure,
In front of me, that it was given to the poor.
At last I was inspired by Heaven to take him in.
Since that day, we've all prospered through his discipline.
He watches everything, my honour is his life,
And he's become inseparable from my wife:
He tells me if young fellows give her the glad eye,
The man's a lot more jealous and concerned than I.
But you wouldn't believe the ardour of his zeal:
The sin that any trivial action can reveal
Disturbs him. A mere nothing shocks him to the core.
The other day, he said that he had to deplore
The fact that, when at prayer, he chanced to catch a flea,
And having caught it, killed it, much too angrily.

CLEANTE:
Good Lord! What's this I hear? Have you gone raving mad?
Or was that speech a joke, and have I just been had?
You must be teasing me.
So, what does all that mean?

ORGON:
Ugh! Brother, that's the language of the libertine.
You must work hard to keep your spirit free of crimes—
Or else, as I've explained to you a dozen times,
You may end up in dreadful trouble, very soon.

CLEANTE:
It's typical of people like you to impugn
The attitudes of others. Just because I've seen
What you can't see, you choose to call me libertine.
You say I've no respect for any sacred thing
Because I find your empty cant embarrassing.
You won't get me worked up, I take it in good part:
I know what I believe, and God sees in my heart.
A man who rules the rest by putting on such airs
Can be a hypocrite for all his fervent prayers.
When battle's joined, and men of honour come to fight,
The quiet men are brave, the boasters may take fright;

So truly pious men, whom people must admire,
Will not make such a song and dance about hell-fire.
Oh, Heavens! Can't you see there's a distinction
Between hypocrisy and true devotion?
You want the two of them to share a single space;
You can't see one's a mask, the other a true face.
You mix up artifice with real sincerity,
And try to take appearance for reality,
Respecting empty phantoms more than flesh and blood,
And bogus coinage more than currency that's good!
My fellow human beings are the strangest crew:
They can't be moderate and calm in what they do.
So, rational behaviour's not what they expect;
They set it on one side, and show it no respect.
They're all out to exaggerate and maximize,
They manage to destroy the noblest enterprise—
In passing, brother-in-law, I say this in your ear.

ORGON:
I daresay you're a doctor we should all revere:
You know the lot; in short, you're the embodiment
Of holy wisdom, and of true enlightenment.
Yes, you're an oracle, a Cato of our time.
Compared with us poor foolish dolts, Sir, you're sublime.

CLEANTE:
No, brother, no! I'm not a doctor to revere,
And all man's earthly wisdom isn't lodged up here.
No, all my learning can be summed up in a word:
I can tell truth from falsehood, see through what's absurd.
Of all my heroes, I find certain men stand out,
And I admire them: men who seem truly devout.
There's nothing nobler, nothing worthier, I feel,
Than holy fervour, genuine religious zeal.
But then, by contrast, nothing is more odious
Than all the trappings of belief that's dubious,
Those charlatans whose fervent piety's for show,
Who sacrilegiously pretend to mop and mow,
And make a mockery, with cool impertinence,
Of everything that we should hold in reverence,
Who show off their beliefs like some grotesque parade,
Who buy and sell devotion like a kind of trade,
Who strive for all the dignities that they can earn
And wink, nod, make affected gestures in return.
Those men are wildly eager to receive their pay:
They rush to make their fortunes, following God's way.
They drip with holy unction, yet they can be bought,
Extol the joys of solitude, but love the court.
They reconcile their pious notions with their vice,
They're spiteful, hasty, insincere, and cold as ice.
If they want to destroy a man, they boldly claim
That it's God's will that he's brought low, and put to shame.

They're dangerous because their anger doesn't show:
They make use of religious faith to bring us low.
They're much admired for their beliefs, and so they try
To smite us with the sword of faith and let us die.
There are a lot too many of this two-faced crew,
But it's not difficult to tell if faith is true. . . .

Orgon comes increasingly under Tartuffe's spell, so much so that he is about to break his promise to his daughter Mariane that she will marry Valere, the young man she truly loves. Instead, Orgon decides that she will marry Tartuffe. At this point, Elmire, Or- gon's wife, arranges a meeting with Tartuffe to convince him not to marry Mariane. However, when they are alone in the following scene, Tartuffe reveals his attraction to Elmire, and he tries to seduce her.

TARTUFFE, ELMIRE

TARTUFFE:
May gracious Heaven grant you true spiritual wealth,
And bring your body and your soul abundant health!
May all your days be blest! These are the true desires
Of quite the humblest mortal Heaven's grace inspires.
ELMIRE:
Thanks for that pious wish. You really are too kind.
We'll be more comfortable sitting down, you'll find.
TARTUFFE:
Now, have you quite recovered from your illness, pray?
ELMIRE:
My fever came down quickly, I feel well today.
TARTUFFE:
I've little merit, and my prayers are much too base
To bring about this evidence of Heaven's grace—
But every prayer I made to him who reigns supreme
Had your full convalescence as its only theme.
ELMIRE:
You didn't need to take such trouble, show such zeal.
TARTUFFE:
Well, your good health is dear to me.
I truly feel I'd give mine to help you in your infirmity.
ELMIRE:
Oh, what a fine display of Christian charity!
I owe you something for your kindness, now, that's true.
TARTUFFE:
But you deserve much more than I can do for you.
ELMIRE:
I've got a secret, and I'd like to sound you out.
I must say that I'm glad that nobody's about.
TARTUFFE:
I too am very glad, I too feel no regret.
Madame, I'm so delighted with our tête-à-tête.
To be alone with you has been my ardent plea,
Which till now Heaven never has accorded me.

ELMIRE:
I'd like a quiet word with you. Can I appeal
To you to be quite frank, and tell me how you feel?
TARTUFFE:
The one grace I implore, for you must know the whole,
Is humbly to expose to you my naked soul,
To swear to you that all that public fuss I made
When, drawn by your attractions, your admirers paid
Their visits, was not due to hatred of you, nay
'Twas more a holy zeal which carried me away,
Disinterested urge . . .
ELMIRE:
I take it like that too.
You want to save my soul, that governs what you do.
TARTUFFE:
(squeezing her fingers.) Oh, yes, indeed, Madame. The ardour that I feel . . .
ELMIRE:
Ouch! Don't squeeze me so hard!
TARTUFFE:
It's through excess of zeal. I never could harm you deliberately, and
In fact, I'd much prefer . . . *(Heputs his hand on her knee.)*
ELMIRE:
Monsieur, what's this? Your hand . . .
TARTUFFE:
I'm just touching your gown: the fabric is so rich.
ELMIRE:
Well, please let go of me, I'm rather ticklish.
(She pushes back her chair, and Tartuffe pushes his forward.)
TARTUFFE:
Oh, goodness, what fine lace! It's really marvellous!
This new embroidery is quite miraculous.
They never used to do this kind of thing so well.
ELMIRE:
That's so, but I think we should stick to business. Tell
Me, is it true my husband plans to break his word,
And give his daughter's hand to you? That's what I've heard.
TARTUFFE:
He's mentioned it; but, to reveal my true desires,
That's not the happiness to which my soul aspires.
A much more marvellous attraction conquers me,
Felicity for which I long most ardently.
ELMIRE:
You don't give in to earthly passions like the rest.
TARTUFFE:
A heart that's made of stone does not beat in my breast.
ELMIRE:
You care for Heaven alone, love God for all you're worth.
Your interest is fixed by nothing on this earth.
TARTUFFE: The passion for eternal beauty which I feel
Does not mean that my earthly passions are less real.

Our senses can be charmed—to us it may be given
To look on perfect beauty as a gift from Heaven.
In Heaven, a woman's beauty strikes an answering chord—
But you are the most wonderful work of the Lord.
He's taken such great pains over your countenance,
That all hearts must be won by such magnificence.
You perfect creature, every time I look at you I see
Divine Creation shining forth anew.
When I see you my heart with passion overflows—
You are a portrait for which God himself did pose.
I fought this secret love, I thought I was undone—
I feared that I was tempted by the Evil One.
I even thought it best to shun your lovely eyes,
For fear they might prevent me winning Heaven's prize.
But then, exquisite creature, I saw it would prove
That there was nothing sinful in my ardent love,
And I could reconcile it with my modesty,
And so I gave way to my feelings totally.
I do admit that it is somewhat staggering
To dare to make my heart a holy offering.
My dearest wish is that you will be well disposed,
That my infirmities will never be exposed.
In you are all my hopes, my wealth, my quietude:
On you rests my despair or my beatitude.
It all depends on you, and I can't rest until
I'm happy if you wish, or wretched if you will.

ELMIRE:
Well! That's a declaration not to be despised!
You know, to tell the truth, I am a bit surprised:
It seems to me that you should fight your instincts more,
And think what you are doing carefully, before
You say such things. You're so devout, I think you can . . .

TARTUFFE: Although I am devout, I am no less a man.
When we are faced with heavenly beauty such as yours,
Our hearts are smitten straightaway, we cannot pause.
I know that what I say sounds strange coming from me,
But then, Madame, I am no angel, as you see;
Perhaps my declaration does put me to shame,
But then, your own bewitching beauty is to blame.
The moment that I saw your lovely looks, I knew
That I had lost my heart—its queen had to be you.
Your heavenly gaze, that glows like light ineffable,
Made all resistance from my heart impossible.
I fasted, prayed, and wept, but nothing I could do
Could overcome the charms that I could see in you.
My looks, my sighs, told you my feelings were sincere;
But now I can speak out, I'll make them still more clear.
If you look kindly on me, as I humbly crave,
And pity my distress, since I'm your abject slave,
If your kind eyes can gaze on me without a frown,

And, pitying my dismal plight, deign to look down,
O marvel most delectable, you'll always be
An object of unique devotion to me.
Your honour runs no risk if you give me your heart:
You needn't fear the least exposure on my part.
Those courtiers, ladies' men whom women can't resist,
Talk all the time—no juicy gossip can be missed.
They boast of how their love affairs are getting on.
If you give in to them, it's commented upon.
You can't rely on them, their tongues are volatile;
The altar where they sacrifice they soon defile.
But men like us burn with a fire that's mote discreet.
Your secret's safe with us. We never will repeat
What's happened, for our reputation matters so,
That those we love are kept quite safe from every foe.
You'll find, if you accept the heart I offer here,
A love that's scandal-free, and pleasure without fear.

ELMIRE:

I've listened to your rhetoric, and what I hear
Has put your case. Yes, your position's very clear.
Doesn't it worry you that I might feel I ought
To tell my husband all about your paying court
To me? If I tell him about this interview.
Might it affect the way that he feels about you?

TARTUFFE:

I know that you're so full of Christian charity,
That you'll see fit to pardon my temerity.
Yes, you'll excuse the human weakness that I show,
Which brought about this outburst.
Though you're hurt, I know,
Consider your good looks, and try to bear in mind
That I'm a man of flesh and blood, and far from blind.

ELMIRE:

Another woman might perhaps decide to treat
You differently, but I intend to be discreet.
Yes, I'll make sure my husband doesn't get to learn
Of this, but let me ask a favour in return:
First, promise me your firm support in our affair,
I mean the marriage of Mariane and Valere.
Don't use the unjust power you've won as a pretence
To help you to get rich at other folks' expense. And . . .

All the while, Orgon's son, Damis, has been listening from an adjoining room. Damis denounces Tartuffe to his father but Orgon refuses to believe him. Or- gon disowns Damis, and, in order to mollify the wounded guest, gives Tartuffe all of his property. Elmire wonders if Orgon will believe Tartuffe's duplicity if he sees it with his own eyes and hears it with his own ears. She convinces Orgon to hide under a table while she meets again with Tartuffe. After Elmire pretends that she will submit to Tartuffe's advances, she asks him to check outside the door to make sure that no one is nearby. In the following scene, Tartuffe's duplicity becomes obvious to Orgon.

TARTUFFE, ELMIRE, ORGON

TARTUFFE:
So now the time has come. My rapture is profound,
Madame. I've been outside, and had a good look round.
There's nobody about, and, oh! I'm all on fire . . .

ORGON:
[interrupting}. Hold on, before surrendering to your desire.
Your promises of love have come out much too pat.
Ah, ah! An honest man, to hoodwink me like that!
It's scarcely fighting sin, the way you planned your life,
As husband to my girl, and lover to my wife!
For ages I could not believe that this was real,
I kept on hoping that you would amend your spiel.
But no—I've heard you out, and I've had quite enough.
I need no other proof, it's time to call your bluff.

ELMIRE:
[To Tartuffe]. You know, I'd really rather not have done all this.
Too bad there had to be so much unpleasantness.

TARTUFFE:
What? Can you really think? . . .

ORGON:
Oh, stop fooling about. I've had enough of this.
It's high time you got out.

TARTUFFE:
No, listen to my plan . . .

ORGON:
There's nothing to discuss.
Get out of here, and do it quick. Don't make a fuss

TARTUFFE:
No, you get out. Go on. You're not the master here.
This house belongs to me, as everyone will hear.
I've had enough. It's time to make you understand.
Don't try your dirty tricks on me—it's underhand.
You thought you could insult me, didn't realize
That I can punish you, and cut you down to size.
Now God will be avenged, and you will soon repent
The folly that led you to say it's time I went.

Soon afterword an official arrives at the house to evict Orgon and his family; then Valere informs Orgon that Tartuffe and an officer from the king are on their way to arrest him. As it turns out, however, the king has recognized Tartuffe as a criminal, so the officer arrests Tartuffe instead, and in the end, all is well for Orgon.

VOLTAIRE

CANDIDE

Several eighteenth-century thinkers, including German philosopher Gottfried Wilhelm Leibnitz (1646—1716) and English poet Alexander Pope, subscribed to the view that God had created the best of all possible worlds, that whatever evil or misfortune existed served a purpose—it contributed to the general harmony of the universe. This is the meaning of Pope's famous lines in his *Essay on Man:* "One truth is clear, WHATEVER IS IS RIGHT." This view, known as philosophical optimism implied that individuals must accept their destiny and make no attempt to change it. In *Candide* (1759), his most important work of fiction, Voltaire bitterly attacked and ridiculed philosophical optimism. In effect Voltaire asked: "In a world where we constantly experience cruelty, injustice, superstition, intolerance, and a host of other evils, how can it be said that this is the best of all possible worlds?" But Voltaire does not resign himself to despair, for he is an ardent reformer who believes that through reason human beings can improve society.

An immediate inspiration for Voltaires response to philosophical optimism was the catastrophic earthquake that struck Lisbon, Portugal, on November 1, 1755, claiming sixty thousand victims. How does such a catastrophe fit into the general harmony of things in this best of all possible worlds? Like the biblical Book of Job, *Candide* explored the question: Why do the innocent suffer? And because Voltaire delved into this mystery with wit, irony, satire, and wisdom, the work continues to be hailed as a literary masterpiece.

The illegitimate Candide (son of the sister of the baron in whose castle he lives in Westphalia) is tutored by the philosopher Pangloss, a teacher of "metaphysico- theologo-cosmolonigology," that is, a person who speaks nonsense. The naive Pangloss clings steadfastly to the belief that all that happens, even the worst misfortunes, are for the best.

Candide falls in love with Cunegund, the beautiful daughter of the baron of the castle; but the baron forcibly removes Candide from the castle when he discovers their love. Candide subsequently suffers a series of disastrous misfortunes, but he continues to adhere to the belief firmly instilled in him by Pangloss, that everything happens for the best and that this is the best of all possible worlds. Later, he meets an old beggar, who turns out to be his former teacher, Pangloss, who tells Candide that the Bulgarians have destroyed the castle and killed Cunegund and her family. Candide and Pangloss then travel together to Lisbon, where they survive the terrible earthquake, only to have Pangloss hanged (but he escapes death) by the Inquisition. Soon thereafter, Can- dide is reunited with Cunegund, who, although having been raped and sold into prostitution, had not been killed. Following further adventures and misfortunes, the lovers are again separated when Cunegund is captured by pirates.

After experiencing more episodes of human wickedness and natural disasters, Candide abandons the philosophy of optimism, declaring "that we must cultivate our gardens." By this Voltaire meant that we can never achieve Utopia, but neither should we descend to the level of brutes. Through purposeful and honest work, and the deliberate pursuit of virtue, we can improve, however modestly, the quality of human existence.

The following excerpt from *Candide* starts with Candide's first misfortune after being driven out of the castle at Westphalia. In addition to ridiculing philosophical optimism, Voltaire expresses his revulsion for militarism.

CHAPTER II

What Befell Candide Among the Bulgarians

Candide, thus driven out of this terrestrial paradise, wandered a long time, without knowing where he went; sometimes he raised his eyes, all bedewed with tears, toward Heaven, and sometimes he cast a melancholy look toward the magnificent castle where dwelt the fairest of young baronesses. He laid himself down to sleep in a furrow, heartbroken and supperless. The snow fell in great flakes, and, in the morning when he awoke, he was almost frozen to death; however, he made shift to crawl to the next town, which was called Waldberghoff- trarbk-dikdorff, without a penny in his pocket, and half dead with hunger and fatigue. He took up his stand at the door of an inn. He had not been long there before two men dressed in blue fixed their eyes steadfastly upon him.

"Faith, comrade," said one of them to the other, "yonder is a well-made young fellow, and of the right size."

Thereupon they went up to Candide, and with the greatest civility and politeness invited him to dine with them.

"Gentlemen," replied Candide, with a most engaging modesty, "you do me much honor, but, upon my word, I have no money."

"Money, sir!" said one of the men in blue to him. "Young persons of your appearance and merit never pay anything. Why, are not you five feet five inches high?"

"Yes, gentlemen, that is really my size," replied he with a low bow.

"Come then, sir, sit down along with us. We will not only pay your reckoning, but will never suffer such a clever young fellow as you to want money. Mankind were born to assist one another."

"You are perfectly right, gentlemen," said Candide; "that is precisely the doctrine of Master Pangloss; and I am convinced that everything is for the best."

His generous companions next entreated him to accept a few crowns, which he readily complied with, at the same time offering them his note for the payment, which they refused, and sat down to table.

"Have you not a great affection for—" "Oh, yes!" he replied. "I have a great affection for the lovely Miss Cunegund."

"Maybe so," replied one of the men, "but that is not the question! We are asking you whether you have not a great affection for the King of the Bulgarians?"[1]

"For the King of the Bulgarians?" said Candide. "Not at all. Why, I never saw him in my life."

"Is it possible! Oh, he is a most charming king! Come, we must drink his health."

"With all my heart, gentlemen," Candide said, and he tossed off his glass.

"Bravo!" cried the blues. "You are now the support, the defender, the hero of the Bulgarians; your fortune is made; you are on the high road to glory."

So saying, they put him in irons and carried him away to the regiment. There he was made to wheel about to the right, to the left, to draw his ramrod, to return his ramrod, to present, to fire, to march, and they gave him thirty blows with a cane. The next day he performed his exercise a little better, and they gave him but twenty. The day following he came off with ten and was looked upon as a young fellow of surprising genius by all his comrades.

Candide was struck with amazement and could not for the soul of him conceive how he came to be a hero. One fine spring morning, he took it into his head to take a walk, and he marched straight forward, conceiving it to be a privilege of the human species, as well as of the brute creation, to make use of their legs how and when they pleased. He had not gone above two leagues when he was overtaken by four other heroes, six feet high, who bound him neck and heels, and carried him to a dungeon. A court-martial sat upon him, and he was asked which he liked best, either to run the gauntlet six and thirty times through the whole regiment, or to have his brains blown out with a dozen musket balls. In vain did he remonstrate to them that the human will is free, and that he chose neither. They obliged him to make a choice, and he determined, in virtue of that divine gift called free will, to run the gauntlet six and thirty times. He had gone through his discipline twice, and the regiment being composed of two thousand men, they composed for him exactly four thousand strokes, which laid bare all his muscles and nerves, from the nape of his neck to his rump. As they were preparing to make him set out the third time, our young hero, unable to support it any longer, begged as a favor they would be so obliging as to shoot him through the head. The favor being granted, a bandage was tied over his eyes, and he was made to kneel down. At that very instant, his Bulgarian Majesty, happening to pass by, inquired into the delinquent's crime, and being a prince of great penetration, he found, from what he heard of Candide, that he was a young meta-physician, entirely ignorant of the world. And, therefore, out of his

[1] I.e., Prussians.

great clemency, he condescended to pardon him, for which his name will be celebrated in every journal, and in every age. A skillful surgeon made a cure of Candide in three weeks by means of emollient unguents prescribed by Dioscorides. His sores were now skinned over, and he was able to march when the King of the Bulgarians gave battle to the King of the Abares.[2]

CHAPTER III

How Candide Escaped from the Bulgarians, and What Befell Him Afterwards

Never was anything so gallant, so well accoutered, so brilliant, and so finely disposed as the two armies. The trumpets, fifes, oboes, drums, and cannon, made such harmony as never was heard in hell itself. The entertainment began by a discharge of cannon, which, in the twinkling of an eye, laid flat about six thousand men on each side. The musket bullets swept away, out of the best of all possible worlds, nine or ten thousand scoundrels that infested its surface. The bayonet was next the sufficient reason for the deaths of several thousands. The whole might amount to thirty thousand souls. Candide trembled like a philosopher and concealed himself as well as he could during this heroic butchery.

At length, while the two kings were causing *Te Deum* to be sung in each of their camps, Candide took a resolution to go and reason somewhere else upon causes and effects. After passing over heaps of dead or dying men, the first place he came to was a neighboring village, in the Abarian territories, which had been burned to the ground by the Bulgarians in accordance with international law. Here lay a number of old men covered with wounds, who beheld their wives dying with their throats cut, and hugging their children to their breasts all stained with blood. There several young virgins, whose bellies had been ripped open after they had satisfied the natural necessities of the Bulgarian heroes, breathed their last; while others, half burned in the flames, begged to be dispatched out of the world. The ground about them was covered with the brains, arms, and legs of dead men.

Candide made all the haste he could to another village, which belonged to the Bulgarians, and there he found that the heroic Abares had treated it in the same fashion."[3] From thence continuing to walk over palpitating limbs or through ruined buildings, at length he arrived beyond the theater of war, with a little provision in his pouch, and Miss Cune- gund's image in his heart. When he arrived in Holland his provisions failed him; but having heard that the inhabitants of that country were all rich and Christians, he made himself sure of being treated by them in the same manner as at the Baron's castle before he had been driven from thence through the power of Miss Cunegund's bright eyes.

He asked charity of several grave-looking people, who one and all answered him that if he continued to follow this trade, they would have him sent to the house of correction, where he should be taught to earn his bread.

He next addressed himself to a person who had just been haranguing a numerous assembly for a whole hour on the subject of charity. The orator, squinting at him under his broad-brimmed hat, asked him sternly what brought him thither and whether he was for the good cause.

"Sir," said Candide, in a submissive manner, "I conceive there can be no effect without a cause; everything is necessarily concatenated and arranged for the best. It was necessary that I should be banished from the presence of Miss Cunegund, that I should afterward run the gauntlet, and it is necessary I should beg my bread till I am able to earn it: all this could not have been otherwise."

"Hark you, friend," said the orator, "do you hold the Pope to be Antichrist?"

"Truly, I never heard anything about it," said Candide, "but whether he is or not, I am in want of something to eat."

"You deserve not to eat or to drink," replied the orator, "wretch, monster that you are! Hence! Avoid my sight and never come near me again while you live."

---

[2] I.e., French. The Seven Years' War had begun in 1756.

[3] Voltaire was not noted for his patriotism. His detachment enables him to flay both sides.

The orator's wife happened to put her head out of the window at that instant, when, seeing a man who doubted whether the Pope was Antichrist, she discharged upon his head a chamber pot full of __. Good heavens, to what excess does religious zeal transport the female kind!

A man who had never been christened, an honest Anabaptist*[4] named James, was witness to the cruel and ignominious treatment showed to one of his brethren, to a two-footed featherless being, who had a soul.§[5] Moved with pity, he carried him to his own house, cleaned him up, gave him meat and drink, and made him a present of two florins, at the same time proposing to instruct him in his own trade of weaving Persian silks which are fabricated in Holland. Candide threw himself at his feet, crying:

"Now I am convinced that Master Pangloss told me truth, when he said that everything was for the best in this world, for I am infinitely more affected by your extraordinary generosity than by the inhumanity of that gentleman in the black cloak and his wife."

The next day, as Candide was walking out, he met a beggar all covered with scabs, his eyes were sunk in his head, the end of his nose was eaten off, his mouth drawn on one side, his teeth as black as coal, snuffling and coughing most violently, and every time he attempted to spit, out dropped a tooth.

CHAPTER IV

How Candide Found His Old Master in Philosophy, Dr. Pangloss, Again and What Happened to Them

Candide, divided between compassion and horror, but giving way to the former, bestowed on this shocking figure the two florins which the honest Anabaptist James had just before given to him. The specter looked at him very earnestly, shed tears, and threw his arms about his neck Candide started back aghast.

"Alas!" said the one wretch to the other, "don't you know your dear Pangloss?"

"What do I hear? Is it you, my dear master! You I behold in this piteous plight? What dreadful misfortune has befallen you? What has made you leave the most magnificent and delightful of all castles? What is become of Miss Cune- gund, the mirror of young ladies and nature's masterpiece?"

"Oh, Lord!" cried Pangloss, "I am so weak I cannot stand."

Thereupon Candide instantly led him to the Anabaptist's stable, and procured him something to eat. As soon as Pangloss had a little refreshed himself, Candide began to repeat his inquiries concerning Miss Cunegund.

"She is dead," replied the other.

Candide immediately fainted away. His friend recovered him by the help of a little bad vinegar which he found by chance in the stable. Candide opened his eyes.

"Dead! Miss Cunegund dead!" he said. "Ah, where is the best of worlds now? But of what illness did she die? Was it for grief upon seeing her father kick me out of his magnificent castle?"

"No," replied Pangloss, "her belly was ripped open by the Bulgarian soldiers after they had ravished her as much as it was possible for a damsel to be ravished. They knocked the Baron her father on the head for attempting to defend her; my lady her mother was cut in pieces; my poor pupil was served just in the same manner as his sister; and as for the castle, they have not left one stone upon another; they have destroyed all the ducks, and the sheep, the barns, and the trees. But we have had our revenge, for the Abares have done the very same thing in a neighboring barony, which belonged to a Bulgarian lord."

At hearing this, Candide fainted away a second time, but having come to himself again, he said all that it became him to say. He inquired into the cause and effect, as well as into the sufficient reason, that had reduced Pangloss to so miserable a condition.

[4] Voltaire looked with favor on the sixteenth-century sect (which was persecuted by both Catholics and Protestants).

[5] §The Anabaptist adds the soul to the famous definition of man of a Greek philosopher, to whom Antisthenes, the Cynic, thereupon presented a plucked chicken.

"Alas!" replied the other. "It was love: love, the comfort of the human species; love, the preserver of the universe, the soul of all sensible beings. Love! Tender love!"

"Alas," replied Candide, "I have had some knowledge of love myself, this sovereign of hearts, this soul of souls. Yet it never cost me more than a kiss and twenty kicks on the backside. But how could this beautiful cause produce in you so hideous an effect?"

Pangloss made answer in these terms: "Oh, my dear Candide, you must remember Pacquette, that pretty wench, who waited on our noble Baroness. In her arms I tasted the pleasures of paradise, which produced these hell-torments with which you see me devoured. She was infected with the disease and perhaps is since dead of it. She received this present of a learned Franciscan monk, who derived it from the fountainhead; he was indebted for it to an old countess, who had it of a captain of horse, who had it of a marchioness, who had it of a page; the page had it of a Jesuit, who, during his novitiate, had it in a direct line from one of the fellow- adventurers of Christopher Columbus. For my part I shall give it to nobody, I am a dying man."

"Oh, Pangloss," cried Candide, "what a strange genealogy is this! Is not the devil the root of it?"

"Not at all," replied the great man. "It was a thing unavoidable, a necessary ingredient in the best of worlds,[6] for if Columbus had not, in an island of America, caught this disease, which contaminates the source of generation, and frequently impedes propagation itself, and is evidently opposite to the great end of nature, we should have had neither chocolate nor cochineal.[7] It is also to be observed that, even to the present time in this continent of ours, this malady, like our religious controversies, is peculiar to ourselves. The Turks, the Indians, the Persians, the Chinese, the Siamese, and the Japanese are entirely unacquainted with it; but there is a sufficient reason for them to know it in a few centuries. In the meantime, it is making prodigious progress among us, especially in those armies composed of well-disciplined hirelings, who determine the fate of nations; for we may safely affirm that, when an army of thirty thousand men fights another equal in number, there are about twenty thousand of them poxed on each side."

"Very surprising, indeed," said Candide. "But you must get cured."

"How can I?" said Pangloss. "My dear friend, I have not a penny in the world; and you know one cannot be bled or have a clyster [enema] without a fee."

This last speech had its effect on Candide. He flew to the charitable Anabaptist James, he flung himself at his feet, and gave him so touching a picture of the miserable situation of his friend that the good man, without any further hesitation, agreed to take Dr. Pangloss into his house and to pay for his cure. The cure was effected with only the loss of one eye and an ear. As he wrote a good hand and understood accounts tolerably well, the Anabaptist made him his bookkeeper. At the expiration of two months, being obliged to go to Lisbon about some mercantile affairs, he took the two philosophers with him in the same ship. Pangloss, during the voyage, explained to him how everything was so constituted that it could not be better. James did not quite agree with him on this point.

"Mankind," said he, "must, in some things, have deviated from their original innocence; for they were not born wolves, and yet they worry one another like those beasts of prey. God never gave them twenty-four pounders nor bayonets, and yet they have made cannon and bayonets to destroy one another. To this account I might add not only bankruptcies but the law, which seizes on the effects of bankrupts only to cheat the creditors."

"All this was indispensably necessary," replied the one- eyed doctor, "for private misfortunes are public benefits; so that the more private misfortunes there are, the greater is the general good."

While he was arguing in this manner, the sky was overcast, the winds blew from the four quarters of the compass, and the ship was assailed by a most terrible tempest, within sight of the port of Lisbon.

[6] Voltaire mocks Pope's "all partial evil, universal good."

[7] A dye made from insects indigenous to Central America.

CHAPTER VI

How the Portuguese Made a Superb Auto-Da-Fe[8] *to Prevent Any Future Earthquakes, and How Candide Underwent Public Flagellation*

After the earthquake which had destroyed three-quarters of the city of Lisbon, the sages of that country could think of no means more effectual to preserve the kingdom from utter ruin, than to entertain the people with an *auto-da-fe,* it having been decided by the University of Coimbra that burning a few people alive by a slow fire and with great ceremony is an infallible secret to prevent earthquakes.

In consequence thereof they had seized on a Biscayan for marrying his godmother,[9] and on two Portuguese for taking out the bacon of a larded pullet they were eating.[10] After dinner, they came and secured Dr. Pangloss and his pupil Candide, the one for speaking his mind and the other for seeming to approve what he had said. They were conducted to separate apartments, extremely cool, where they were never incommoded with the sun. Eight days afterward they were each dressed in a *sanbenito*and their heads were adorned with paper miters. The miter and *sanbenit*[11]*o* worn by Candide were painted with flames reversed and with devils that had neither tails nor claws; but Dr. Plangloss' devils had both tails and claws, and his flames were upright. In these habits they marched in procession, and heard a very pathetic sermon, which was followed by a chant, beautifully intoned. Candide was flogged in regular cadence while the chant was being sung. The Biscayan and the two men who would not eat bacon were burned, and Pangloss was hanged, although this is not a common custom at these solemnities. The same day there was another earthquake, which made most dreadful havoc.[12]

Candide, amazed, terrified, confounded, astonished, and trembling from head to foot, said to himself, "If this is the best of all possible worlds, what are the others? If I had only been whipped, I could have put up with it, as I did among the Bulgarians. But, O my dear Pangloss! You greatest of philosophers! That ever I should live to see you hanged, without knowing for what! O my dear Anabaptist, you best of men, that it should be your fate to be drowned in the very harbor! O Miss Cunegund, you mirror of young ladies! That it should be your fate to have your belly ripped open."

He was making the best of his way from the place where he had been preached to, whipped, absolved, and received benediction, when he was accosted by an old woman, who said to him, "Take courage, my son, and follow me."

[8] A ceremonial public execution held by the Inquisition. The one referred to here took place on June 20, 1756.
[9] This was held to contravene the established spiritual relationship.
[10] This was considered by the Inquisition to be an infallible sign of belonging to the Jewish faith.
[11] A black sackcloth garment, painted with figures of devils, etc., identifying the several crimes.
[12] "A second tremor had actually occurred on December 21, 1755. Voltaire takes poetic license with the dates.

JONATHAN SWIFT

GULLIVER'S TRAVELS

As one of the greatest satirists of the English language, Jonathan Swift (1667— 1745) is best known for *Travels into Several Remote Nations of the World,* better known as *Gulliver's Travels,* which was first published in 1726. Parodying a travelogue, the four books of Swift's masterpiece tell of the voyages of Lemuel Gulliver. His first voyage takes Gulliver to Lilliput, where the Lilliputians are only six inches tall and Gulliver is the giant; the situation is reversed, however, during Gulliver's second voyage, to Brobdingnag, a land of giants. The third voyage takes Gulliver to the floating island of Laputa, and Book IV, the most famous, describes Gulliver's voyage to the land of the Houyhnhnms (rational, virtuous horses), who tolerate and use the race of Yahoos (vicious and disgusting human beings) for menial services.

Gulliver's four voyages provided Swift with the opportunity to scrutinize the social, political, and economic institutions of his day, which seem hauntingly familiar even in today's world. In the land of the Lilliputians, Gulliver discovers that these miniature creatures by whom he is initially amused are, in reality, callous, cutthroat, back stabbing, and vengeful. Similarly, Gulliver assumes that the gigantic Brobdingnags must be contrary brutes, only to find that they live in an ideal society that is governed by a humane "philosopher-king," who places moral virtue ahead of maintaining political power. In his attack on the land of Laputa, Swift uses much of Book III to satirize the administration of Sir Robert Walpole, a Whig minister. Swift's finest satire is reserved for the Yahoos, atrocious exaggerations of the human race possessing virtually no rational sense. Today, the term *yahoo* is used as an epithet to describe any brutish, uncouth, or vicious person.

Just prior to the publication of *Gulliver's Travels,* Swift wrote a letter to Alexander Pope in which he proclaimed that in general he hated "that animal called man," although he loved individual humans. He declared that he would prove false the idea that the human being is an "*animal rationale* [rational animal]" and would, instead, show that a human being is really "only *rationis capax* [capable of reason]. Upon this great foundation of Misanthropy . . . the whole building of my Travells is erected." Therefore, on the one hand, Swift was

simply restating the age-old Christian idea of original sin—humans are yahoos. But on the other hand, he was also expressing a mitigated optimism about humans—that they are capable of being rational—an idea that blossomed during the Enlightenment.

In the following passage from *Gulliver's Travels,* Gulliver discusses with a wise Houyhnhnm how "yahoos" behave in his native England. Here Swift is at his best in exposing and lampooning the foibles of his fellow Englishmen.

He asked me what were the usual causes or motives that made one country go to war with another. I answered they were innumerable, but I should only mention a few of the chief. Sometimes the ambition of princes, who never think they have land or people enough to govern; sometimes the corruption of ministers, who engage their master in a war in order to stifle or divert the clamour of the subjects against their evil administration. Difference in opinions hath cost many millions of lives: for instance, whether flesh be bread, or bread be flesh; whether the juice of a certain berry be blood or wine; whether whistling be a vice or a virtue; whether it be better to kiss a post, or throw it into the fire; what is the best colour for a coat, whether black, white, red, or gray; and whether it should be long or short, narrow or wide, dirty or clean; with many more. Neither are any wars so furious and bloody, or of so long continuance, as those occasioned by difference in opinion, especially if it be in things indifferent.

Sometimes the quarrel between two princes is to decide which of them shall dispossess a third of his dominions, where neither of them pretend to any right. Sometimes one prince quarrelleth with another, for fear the other should quarrel with him. Sometimes a war is entered upon, because the enemy is too strong, and sometimes because he is too weak. Sometimes our neighbours want the things which we have, or have the things which we want; and we both fight, till they take ours or give us theirs. It is a very justifiable cause of a war to invade a country after the people have been wasted by famine, destroyed by pestilence, or embroiled by factions among themselves. It is justifiable to enter into war against our nearest ally, when one of his towns lies convenient for us, or a territory of land, that would render our dominions round and complete. If a prince sends forces into a nation where the people are poor and ignorant, he may lawfully put half of them to death, and make slaves of the rest, in order to civilize and reduce them from their barbarous way of living. It is a very kingly, honourable, and frequent practice, when one prince desires the assistance of another to secure him against an invasion, that the assistant, when he hath driven out the invader, should seize on the dominions himself, and kill, imprison or banish the prince he came to relieve. Alliance by blood or marriage is a frequent cause of war between princes; and the nearer the kindred is, the greater is their disposition to quarrel: poor nations are hungry, and rich nations are proud; and pride and hunger will ever be at variance. For these reasons, the trade of a soldier is held the most honourable of all others; because a soldier is a Yahoo hired to kill in cold blood as many of his own species, who have never offended him, as possibly he can.

There is likewise a kind of beggarly princes in Europe, not able to make war by themselves, who hire out their troops to richer nations, for so much a day to each man; of which they keep three fourths to themselves, and it is the best part of their maintenance; such are those in Germany and other northern parts of Europe. . . .

. . . And being no stranger to the art of war, I gave him a description of cannons, culverins, muskets, carabines, pistols, bullets, powder, swords, bayonets, battles, sieges, retreats, attacks, undermines, countermines, bombardments, sea fights; ships sunk with a thousand men, twenty thousand killed on each side; dying groans, limbs flying in the air, smoke, noise, confusion, trampling to death under horses' feet; flight, pursuit, victory; fields strewed with carcases left for food to dogs, and wolves, and birds of prey; plundering, stripping, ravishing, burning, and destroying. And to set forth the valour of my own dear countrymen, I assured him that I had seen them blow up a hundred enemies at once in a siege, and as many in a ship, and beheld the dead bodies come down in pieces from the clouds, to the great diversion of the spectators.

I was going on to more particulars, when my master commanded me silence. He said whoever understood the nature of Yahoos might easily believe it possible for so vile an animal to be capable of every action I had named, if their strength and cunning equalled their malice. But as my discourse had increased his abhorrence of the whole species, so he found it gave him a disturbance in his mind, to which he was wholly a stranger before. He thought his ears being used to such abominable words, might by degrees admit them with less detestation. That although he hated the Yahoos of this country, yet he no more blamed them for their odious qualities, than he did a *gnnayh* (a bird of prey) for its cruelty, or a sharp stone for cutting his hoof. But when a creature pretending to reason could be capable of such enormities, he dreaded lest the corruption of that faculty might be worse than brutality itself. He seemed therefore confident, that instead of reason, we were only possessed of some quality fitted to increase our natural vices; as the reflection from a troubled stream returns the image of an ill-shapen body, not only larger, but more distorted.

He added, that he had heard too much upon the subject of war, both in this and some former discourses. There was another point which a little perplexed him at present. I had informed him, that some of our crew left their country on ac count of being ruined by *Law;* that I had already explained the meaning of the word; but he was at a loss how it should come to pass, that the law which was intended for every man's preservation, should be any man's ruin. Therefore he desired to be farther satisfied what I meant by law, and the dispensers thereof, according to the present practice in my own country; because he thought nature and reason were sufficient guides for a reasonable animal, as we pretended to be, in showing us what we ought to do, and what to avoid.

I assured his Honour that law was a science wherein I had not much conversed, further than by employing advocates, in vain, upon some injustices that had been done me: however, I would give him all the satisfaction I was able.

I said there was a society of men among us, bred up from their youth in the art of proving by words multiplied for the purpose, that white is black, and black is white, according as they are paid. To this society all the rest of the people are slaves. For example, if my neighbour hath a mind to my cow, he hires a lawyer to prove that he ought to have my cow from me. I must then hire another to defend my right, it being against all rules of law that any man should be allowed to speak for himself. Now in this case I who am the right owner lie under two great disadvantages. First, my lawyer, being practised almost from his cradle in defending falsehood, is quite out of his element when he would be an advocate for justice, which as an office unnatural, he always attempts with ill-will. The second disadvantage is that my lawyer must proceed with great caution, or else he will be reprimanded by the judges, and abhorred by his brethren, as one that would lessen the practice of the law. And therefore I have but two methods to preserve my cow. The first is to gain over my adversary's lawyer with a double fee, who will then betray his client by insinuating that he hath justice on his side. The second way is for my lawyer to make my cause appear as unjust as he can, by allowing the cow to belong to my adversary: and this, if it be skillfully done, will certainly bespeak the favour of the bench.

Now, your Honour is to know that these judges are persons appointed to decide all controversies of property, as well as for the trial of criminals, and picked out from the most dexterous lawyers, who are grown old or lazy, and having been biassed all their lives against truth and equity, are under such a fatal necessity of favouring fraud, perjury, and oppression, that I have known several of them refuse a large bribe from the side where justice lay, rather than injure the faculty, by doing any thing unbecoming their nature or their office.

It is a maxim among these lawyers, that whatever hath been done before may legally be done again: and therefore they take special care to record all the decisions formerly made against common justice and the general reason of mankind. These, under the name of *precedents,* they produce as authorities, to justify the most iniquitous opinions; and the judges never fail of directing accordingly.

In pleading they studiously avoid entering into the merits of the cause, but are loud, violent, and tedious in dwelling upon all circumstances which are not to the purpose. For instance, in the case already mentioned, they never desire to know what claim or title my adversary hath to my cow; but whether the said cow were red or black, her horns long or short, whether the field I graze her in be round or square, whether she was milked at home or abroad, what diseases she is subject to, and the like; after which they consult precedents, adjourn the cause from time to time, and in ten, twenty, or thirty years, come to an issue.

It is likewise to be observed, that this society hath a peculiar cant [dialect] and jargon of their own, that no other mortal can understand, and wherein all their laws are written, which they take special care to multiply; whereby they have wholly confounded the very essence of truth and falsehood, of right and wrong; so that it will take thirty years to decide whether the field left me by my ancestors for six generations belongs to me, or to a stranger three hundred miles off.

In the trial of persons accused for crimes against the state the method is much more short and commendable: the judge first sends to sound the disposition of those in power, after which he can easily hang or save the criminal, strictly preserving all due forms of law.

Here my master interposing, said it was a pity that creatures endowed with such prodigious abilities of mind as these lawyers, by the description I gave of them, must certainly be, were not rather encouraged to be instructors of others in wisdom and knowledge. In answer to which I assured his Honour that in all points out of their own trade, they were the most ignorant and stupid generation among us, the most despicable in common conversation, avowed enemies to all knowledge and learning, and equally disposed to pervert the general reason of mankind in every other subject of discourse, as in that of their own profession.

My master was yet wholly at a loss to understand what motives could incite this race of lawyers to perplex, disquiet, and weary themselves, and engage in a confederacy of injustice, merely for the sake of injuring their fellow-animals; neither could he comprehend what I meant in saying they did it for hire. Whereupon I was at much pains to describe to him the use of money, the materials it was made of, and the value of the metals, that when a Yahoo had got a great store of this precious substance, he was able to purchase whatever he had a mind to; the finest clothing, the noblest houses, great tracts of land, the most costly meats and drinks, and have his choice of the most beautiful females. Therefore since money alone was able to perform all these feats, our Yahoos thought they could never have enough of it to spend or save, as they found themselves inclined from their natual bent either to profusion or avarice. That the rich man enjoyed the fruit of the poor man's labour, and the latter were a thousand to one in proportion to the former. That the bulk of our people were forced to live miserably, by labouring every day for small wages to make a few live plentifully.

WILLIAM WORDSWORTH

ODE: INTIMATIONS OF IMMORTALITY FROM RECOLLECTIONS OF EARLY CHILDHOOD

Much of Wordsworth's poetry is autobiographical. For example, from 1791 until 1792, Wordsworth traveled throughout France, savoring the sights and sounds of freedom. But when French radicals seized control of the government and began their Reign of Terror, Wordsworth felt betrayed and became despondent. On the verge of a total mental collapse, Wordsworth's sister, Dorothy, and Coleridge suggested that he return to the Wye River Valley (where England meets Wales) to recapture his poetic muse by communing with Nature. In 1802, Wordsworth began to compose his "Ode: Intimations of Immortality from Recollections of Early Childhood," and he wrote about the subject matter of the poem and the circumstances under which he wrote the poem:

Nothing was more difficult for me in childhood than to admit the notion of death as a state applicable to my own being. ... I used to brood over the stories of Enoch and Elijah[1] and almost to persuade myself that whatever might become of others I'd be translated in something of the same way to heaven. . . . {T]he poem rests entirely upon two recollections of childhood, one that of a splendour in the objects of sense which is passed away, and the other an indisposition to bend to the law of death as applying to our own particular case. A Reader who has not a vivid recollection of these feelings having existed in his mind cannot understand the poem.

The original title of the poem was simply "Ode" followed by an inscription from Virgil's *Ecologue IV:* "Let us sing of somewhat higher things." Today, however, the poem has a longer title and opens with three lines taken from the concluding lines of Wordsworth's poem, "My Heart Leaps Up":

The Child is father of the Man;
And I could wish my days to be
Bound each to each by natural piety.

In the quoted lines of Wordsworth's poem, he reflects on his belief (adapted from Plato) that the human soul exists independently of the body and that it preexisted before becoming incarnate in the body. Moreover, Wordsworth purported that when the soul is put in a body it gradually loses its vision of that which is immortal. Thus, he asserts "the Child is Father of the Man," and wishes that he could be in possession of the absolute truths he once possessed when he existed only as pure soul.

Like Plato, Wordsworth also believed that a human being's soul is immortal; therefore, death is nothing more than the soul's separation from the body. These reflections are at the heart of Wordsworth "Ode" which opens with him thinking about the time when everything on earth seemed completely new—Plato's concept of pure Forms. He then ponders the beauty of the cycle of Nature—how the rainbow and rose fade, the moon ceases to shine during the day, birds and lambs mature, and how Nature continually regenerates her beauties. Wordsworth then pens some of his most memorable lines pertaining to the human experience:

Not in entire forgetfulness,
And not in utter nakedness,
But trailing clouds of glory do we come
From God, who is our home . . .

[1] According to the Old Testament, Enoch, a descendant of Adam, and the prophet, Elijah, did not die a typical human death, but, rather, they were transported to heaven in some kind of miraculous way. "Enoch walked with God, and he was not; for God took him" (Genesis 5:24) and "Elijah went up by a whirlwind into heaven" (II Kings 2:11). Similarly, in the New Testament, the Apostle Paul refers to Enoch's being "taken": "and he [Enoch] was not found, because God had taken him" (Hebrews 11:5).

The lines excerpted below illustrate how human beings gradually lose their vision of immortality by becoming imprisoned in a material body ("her Inmate Man"), which causes them to forget the eternal truths of the "imperial palace" of God's heaven—similar to Plato's World of Being.

There was a time when meadow, grove, and stream,
The earth, and every common sight,
To me did seem
Apparell'd in celestial light,
The glory and the freshness of a dream.
It is not now as it has been of yore;—
Turn wheresoe'er I may,
By night or day.
The Rainbow comes and goes,
And lovely is the Rose,
The Moon doth with delight
Look round her when the heavens are bare:
Waters on a starry night
Are beautiful and fair:
The sunshine is a glorious birth;
But yet I know, where'er I go,
That there hath pass'd away a glory from the earth.
Now, while the Birds thus sing a joyous song,
And while the young Lambs bound
As to the tabor's sound,
To me alone there came a thought of grief:
A timely utterance gave that thought relief,
And I again am strong.
The Cataracts blow their trumpets from the steep,
No more shall grief of mine the season wrong;
I hear the Echoes through the mountains throng,
The Winds come to me from the fields of sleep,
And all the earth is gay,
Land and sea
Give themselves up to jollity,
And with the heart of May
Doth every Beast keep holiday,
Thou Child of Joy,
Shout round me, let me hear thy shouts, thou happy Shepherd Boy!
Ye blessed Creatures, I have heard the call
Ye to each other make; I see
The heavens laugh with you in your jubilee;
My heart is at your festival,
My head hath it's coronal,
The fullness of your bliss, I feel—I feel it all.
Oh evil day! if I were sullen
While the Earth herself is adorning,
This sweet May-morning,
And the Children are pulling,
On every side,
In a thousand vallies far and wide,
Fresh flowers; while the sun shines warm,

And the Babe leaps up on his mother's arm:—
I heal, I hear, with joy I hear!
—But there's a Tree, of many one,
A single Field which I have look'd upon,
Both of them speak of something that is gone:
The Pansy at my feet
Doth the same tale repeat:
Whither is fled the visionary gleam?
Where is it now, the glory and the dream?
Our birth is but a sleep and a forgetting:
The Soul that rises with us, our life's Star,
Hath had elsewhere it's setting,
And cometh from afar:
Not in entire forgetfulness,
And not in utter nakedness,
But trailing clouds of glory do we come
From God, who is our home:
Heaven lies about us in our infancy!
Shades of the prison-house begin to close
Upon the growing Boy,
But He beholds the light, and whence it flows,
He sees it in his joy;
The Youth, who daily farther from the East
Must travel, still is Nature's Priest,
And by the vision splendid
Is on his way attended;
At length the Man perceives it die away,
And fade into the light of common day.
Earth fills her lap with pleasures of her own;
Yearnings she hath in her own natural kind,
And, even with something of a Mother's mind,
And no unworthy aim,
The homely nurse doth all she can
To make her foster-child, her Inmate Man,
Forget the glories he hath known,
And that imperial palace whence he came.

The concluding lines from Wordsworth's "Ode" demonstrate further his affinity for Plato's philosophy and his understanding of the concept of *recollection*— whereby a soul remembers (at least in part) what it once knew so completely—particularly by pondering the beauty of the natural world. Wordsworth, however, cautions that we can never totally recapture the immortal truths we once knew, for "nothing can bring back the hour / Of splendour in the grass, or glory in the flower."

A place of thought where we in waiting lie;
Thou little Child, yet glorious in the might
Of untam'd pleasures, on thy Being's height,
Why with such earnest pains dost thou provoke
The Years to bring the inevitable yoke,
Thus blindly with thy blessedness at strife?
Full soon thy Soul shall have her earthly freight,
And custom lie upon thee with a weight,

Heavy as frost, and deep almost as life!
O joy! that in our embers
Is something that doth live,
That nature yet remembers
What was so fugitive!
The thought of our past years in me doth breed
Perpetual benedictions: not indeed
For that which is most worthy to be blest;
Delight and liberty, the simple creed
Of Childhood, whether fluttering or at rest,
With new-born hope for ever in his breast:—
Not for these I raise
The song of thanks and praise;
But for those obstinate questionings
Of sense and outward things,
Fallings from us, vanishings;
Blank misgivings of a Creature
Moving about in worlds not realiz'd,
High instincts, before which our mortal Nature
Did tremble like a guilty Thing surpriz'd:
But for those first affections,
Those shadowy recollections,
Which, be they what they may,
Are yet the fountain light of all our day,
Are yet a master light of all our seeing;
Uphold us, cherish us, and make
Our noisy years seem moments in the being
Of the eternal Silence: truths that wake,
To perish never;
Which neither listlessness, nor mad endeavour,
Nor Man nor Boy,
Nor all that is at enmity with joy,
Can utterly abolish or destroy!
Hence, in a season of calm weather,
Though inland far we be,
Our Souls have sight of that immortal sea
Which brought us hither,
Can in a moment travel thither,
And see the Children sport upon the shore,
And hear the mighty waters rolling evermore.
Then, sing ye Birds, sing, sing a joyous song!
And let the young Lambs bound
As to the tabor's sound!
We in thought will join your throng,
Ye that pipe and ye that play,
Ye that through your hearts to day
Feel the gladness of the May!
What though the radiance which was once so bright
Be now for ever taken from my sight,
Though nothing can bring back the hour

Of splendour in the grass, of glory in the flower;
We will grieve not, rather find
Strength in what remains behind.
In the primal sympathy
Which having been must ever be,
In the soothing thoughts that spring
Out of human suffering,
In the faith that looks through death,
In years that bring the philosophic mind.
And oh ye Fountains, Meadows, Hills, and Groves,
Think not of any severing of our loves!
Yet in my heart of hearts I feel your might;
I only have relinquish'd one delight
To live beneath your more habitual sway.
I love the Brooks which down their channels fret,
Even more than when I tripp'd lightly as they;
The innocent brightness of a new-born Day
Is lovely yet;
The Clouds that gather round the setting sun
Do take a sober colouring from an eye
That hath kept watch o'er man's mortality;
Another race hath been, and other palms are won.
Thanks to the human heart by which we live,
Thanks to its tenderness, its joys, and fears,
To me the meanest flower that blows can give
Thoughts that do often lie too deep for tears.

JOHN KEATS

ODE ON A GRECIAN URN

The Grecian urn of Keats' ode existed only in his imagination, but what a fascinating image it is: young lovers are seen in "mad pursuit," and although they never kiss, neither does their love ever fade; trees never lose their leaves; and musicians never tire of playing their melodies. In essence, the images on the urn reveal to Keats a sense of immortality, for the images, which would have been nothing but "fleeting moments" in the natural world, have been captured on the urn for all eternity to share. Each verse captures Keats' fascination with a different scene, and each question begs the reader to appreciate what Keats is seeing in his mind's eye. The poem is brought to a close with the dictum, "Beauty is truth, truth beauty," for Keat this eternal verity is "all ye need to know." These concluding lines are counted among some of the most famous, and oft-quoted lines, in the history of the English language.

I

Thou still unravish'd bride of quietness,
Thou foster-child of silence and slow time,
Sylvan[1] historian, who canst thus express
A flowery tale more sweetly than our rhyme:
What leaf-fring'd legend haunts about thy shape
Of deities or mortals, or of both,
In Tempe or the dales of Arcady?[2]
What men or gods are these? What maidens loth?
What mad pursuit? What struggle to escape?
What pipes and timbrels? What wild ecstasy?

II

Heard melodies are sweet, but those unheard
Are sweeter; therefore, ye soft pipes, play on;
Not to the sensual ear,[3] but, more endear'd,
Pipe to the spirit ditties of no tone:
Fair youth, beneath the trees, thou canst not leave
Thy song, nor ever can those trees be bare;
Bold Lover, never, never canst thou kiss,
Though winning near the goal—yet, do not grieve;
She cannot fade, though thou hast not thy bliss,
For ever wilt thou love, and she be fair!

III

Ah, happy, happy boughs! that cannot shed
Your leaves, nor ever bid the Spring adieu:
And, happy melodist, unwearied,
For ever piping songs for ever new;

---

[1] *Sylvan* references that which is rustic, representing a forest or woodland.
[2] *Tempe* is a lush valley in Greece that often is used to mean sylvan beauty, and *Arcady* refers to the place in ancient Greece that was associated with pastoral perfection.
[3] *Sensual ear* refers to the physical sense of hearing, rather than the "spiritual ear" which is the essence of much of the music Keats imagines when contemplating the urn.

More happy love! more happy, happy love!
For ever warm and still to be enjoy'd,
For ever panting, and for ever young;
All breathing human passion far above,
That leaves a heart high-sorrowful and cloy'd,
A burning forehead, and a parching tongue.

IV

Who are these coming to the sacrifice?
To what green altar, O mysterious priest,
Lead'st thou that heifer lowing at the skies,
And all her silken flanks with garlands drest?
What little town by river or sea shore,
Or mountain-built with peaceful citadel,
Is emptied of this folk, this pious morn?
And, little town, thy streets for evermore
Will silent be; and not a soul to tell
Why thou art desolate, can e'er return.

V

O Attic[4] shape! Fair attitude! with brede
Of marble men and maidens overwrought,[5]
With forest branches and the trodden weed;
Thou, silent form, dost tease us out of thought
As doth eternity: Cold Pastoral!
When old age shall this generation waste,
Thou shalt remain, in midst of other woe
Than ours, a friend to man, to whom thou sayst,
"Beauty is truth, truth beauty,"[6]—that is all
Ye know on earth, and all ye need to know.

[4] *Attic* refers to the region in Greece where its capital, Athens, is located.
[5] *Overwrought* in this verse refers to the ornamentation of the urn, including its interwoven patterns called "brede."
[6] "Beauty is truth, truth beauty" are lines found in a volume of Keats poetry from 1820, *Annals of the Vine Arts*.

VICTOR HUGO

LES MISÉRABLES

Les Misérables **is a story that displays Hugo s commitment to political and economic reform in France. The novel not only reflects Hugo s passion for social justice, but it also reveals his concern for the wretched victims of the Industrial Revolution—the *misérables.* During the twentieth century, the novel inspired the long-running Broadway musical, as well as a number of motion pictures. The setting of the novel is the Parisian underworld between the years 1815 and 1832. The protagonist is the ex-convict, Jean Valjean, who has spent nineteen years in prison for stealing a loaf of bread and for attempting several times to escape. After his release, Valjean commits a minor crime, for which he is hunted by Inspector Javert. Valjean finally leaves his life of crime, and, under the assumed name of Madeleine, becomes financially successful as a factory owner. Some time after Valjean becomes mayor of the town, Javert is appointed police inspector there. In the following passage, Javert tells the mayor that another man has been arrested as Jean Valjean.**

"Well, what is the matter, Javert?"

Jarvert remained silent for a moment, as if reflecting, and then raised his voice with a sad solemnity, which, however, did not exclude simplicity.

"A culpable deed has been committed, sir."

"What deed?"

"An inferior agent of authority has failed in his respect to a magistrate in the gravest manner. I have come, as is my duty, to bring the fact to your knowledge." "Who is this agent?" M. Madeleine asked.

"Myself."

"And who is the magistrate who has cause to complain of the agent?"

"You, Monsieur le Maire."

M. Madeleine sat up, and Javert continued, with a stern air and still looking down:

"Monsieur le Maire, I have come to request that you will procure my dismissal from service."

M. Madeleine in his stupefaction opened his mouth, but Javert interrupted him:

"You will say that I could have sent in my resignation, but that is not enough. Such a course is honorable, but I have done wrong, and deserve punishment. I must be dismissed."

And after a pause he added:

"Monsieur le Marie, you were severe to me the other day unjustly, be so to-day justly."

"What is the meaning of all this nonsense?" M. Madeleine exclaimed. "What is the culpable act you have committed? What have you done to me? You accuse yourself; you wish to be removed—"

"Dismissed," said Javert.

"Very good, dismissed. I do not understand it."

"You shall do so, sir."

Javert heaved a deep sigh and continued, still coldly and sadly:

"Six weeks ago, M. le Maire, after the scene about that girl, I was furious, and denounced you."

"Denounced me?"

"To the prefect of police at Paris."

M. Madeleine, who did not laugh much oftener than Javert, burst into a laugh.

"As a mayor who had encroached on the police?"

"As an ex-galley-slave."

The mayor turned livid, but Javert, who had not raised his eyes, continued:

"I thought you were so, and have had these notions for a long time. A resemblance, information you sought at Faverolles, the strength of your loins, the adventure with old Fauchelevent, your skill with firearms, your leg which halts a little—and so on. It was very absurd, but I took you for a man of the name of Jean Valjean."

"What name did you say?"

"Jean Valjean; he is a convict I saw twenty years ago when I was assistant keeper at the Toulon bagne. On leaving the galley, this Valjean, as it appears, robbed a bishop, and then committed a highway robbery on a little Savoyard. For eight years he has been out of the way and could not be found, and I imagined—in a word, I did as I said. Passion decided me, and I denounced you to the prefect."

M. Madeline, who had taken up the charge book again, said with a careless accent:

"And what was the answer you received?"

"That I was mad!"

"Well?"

"They were right."

"It is fortunate that you allow it."

"I must do so, for the real Jean Valjean has been found." The book M. Madeleine was holding fell from his grasp; he raised his head, looked searchingly at Javert, and said with an indescribable accent: "Oh!"

His conscience tormented that another man would suffer for his crime, Valjean decides to confess his past, and he is arrested by Javert. He escapes from the town ¡ail, but he must continuously evade Javert, a believer in the harsh penal codes of France who sees Valjean's escape as an insult to justice. Valjean adopts Cosette, an illegitimate child, who grows up to be a beautiful woman. Cosette meets Marius, a former monarchist whose views change so much that he fights in the streets on the barricades during an insurrection in Paris. After the two young people fall in love, Marius thinks about how much he loves Cosette.

For six weeks past Marius had slowly and gradually taken possession of Cosette; it was a perfectly ideal, but profound, possession. As we have explained, in first love men take the soul long before the body; a later date they take the body before the soul, and at times they do not take the soul at all,— the Faublas and Prudhommes add, because there is no such thing, but the sarcasm is fortunately a blasphemy Marius, then, possessed Cosette in the way that minds possess; but he enveloped her with his entire soul, and jealousy seized her with an incredible conviction. He possessed her touch, her breath, her perfume, the deep flash of her blue eyes, the softness of her skin when he touched her hand, the charming mark which she had on her neck, and all her thoughts. They had agreed never to sleep without dreaming of each other, and had kept their word. He, therefore, possessed all Cosette's dreams. He looked at her incessantly, and sometimes breathed on the short hairs which she had on her neck, and said to himself that there was not one of those hairs which did not belong to him. He contemplated and adored the things she wore, her bows, her cuffs, her gloves, and slippers, like sacred objects of which he was the master. He thought that he was the lord of the small tortoise-shell combs which she had in her hair, and he said to himself, in the confused stammering of dawning voluptuousness, that there was not a seam of her dress, not a mesh of her stockings, not a wrinkle in her bodice, which was not his. By the side of Cosette he felt close to his property, near his creature, who was at once his despot and his slave. It seemed that they had so blended their souls that, if they had wished to take them back, it would have been impossible for them to recognize them. This is mine— no, it is mine—I assure you that you are mistaken. This is really I—what you take for yourself is myself; Marius was something which formed part of Cosette, and Cosette was something that formed part of Marius. Marius felt Cosette live in him; to have Cosette, to possess Cosette, was to him not different from breathing.

When Marius thinks that he has lost Cosette, he joins his radical student friends in an insurrection in Paris. Valjean joins the students, discovers that they have captured Javert, and offers to execute him. Instead, he allows Javert to escape. When Marius is wounded, Valjean saves him by carrying him through the sewers of Paris, only to be arrested by Javert as he emerges from the sewer. Javert, experiencing a change of heart, allows Valjean to go free, then commits suicide for breaching his duty.

Javert retired slowly from the Rue de l'Homme Armé. He walked with drooping head for the first time in his life, and, equally for the first time in his life, with his hands behind his back. Up to that day Javert had only assumed, of Napoleon's two attitudes, the one which expresses resolution, the arms folded on the chest; the one indicating uncertainty, the arms behind the back, was unknown to him. Now a change had taken place, and his whole person, slow and somber, was stamped with anxiety. He buried himself in the silent streets, but followed a certain direction; he went by the shortest road to the Seine, reached the Quai des Ormes, walked along it, passed the Grève, and stopped, a little distance from the Châtelet Square, at the corner of the Pont Notre Dame. The Seine makes there, between that bridge and the Pont au Change on one side, and the Quai de la Mégisserie and the Quai aux Fleurs on the other, a species of square lake traversed by a rapid. This point on the Seine is feared by boatmen; nothing can be more dangerous than this rapid, which just then was contracted and irritated by the stakes of the mill-bridge, since demolished. The two bridges, so close to each other, heighten the danger, for the water hurries formidably through the arches. It rolls in large folds, it is heaped up and piled up; the stream strives to pull away the piles of the bridge with its strong liquid cords. Men who fall in there do not re-appear, and the best swimmers are drowned.

Javert leaned his elbows on the parapet, his chin on his hand, and while his hands mechanically closed on his thick whiskers, he reflected. . . .

One thing had astonished him—Jean Valjean had shown him mercy; and one thing had petrified him—that he, Javert, had shown mercy to Jean Valjean. . . .

Nothing could be seen, but the hostile coldness of the water and the sickly smell of the damp stones could be felt. A ferocious breath rose from this abyss, and the swelling of the river, divined rather than perceived, the tragic muttering of the water, the mournful vastness of the bridge arches, a possible fall into this gloomy vacuum—all this shadow was full of horror.

Javert remained for some moments motionless, gazing at this opening of the darkness, and considered the invisible with an intentness which resembled attention. All at once he took off his hat and placed it on the brink of the quay. A moment after a tall, black figure, which any belated passer-by might have taken at a distance for a ghost, appeared standing on the parapet, stooped toward the Seine, then drew itself up, and fell straight into the darkness. There was a dull plash [splatter], and the shadows alone were in the secret of this obscure form which had appeared beneath the waters.

At the end of the novel, as he lies on his deathbed, Valjean comforts Marius and Cosette.

His face grew pale, and at the same time smiling; life was no longer there, but there was something else. His breath stopped, but his glance expanded; he was a corpse on whom wings could be seen. He made Cosette a sign to approach, and then Marius; it was evidently the last minute of the last hour, and he began speaking to them in so faint a voice that it seemed to come from a distance, and it was as if there were henceforth a wall between them and him.

"Come hither, both of you; I love you dearly. Oh! how pleasant it is to die like this! You, too, love me, my Cosette; I felt certain that you had always a fondness for the poor old man. How kind it was of you to place that pillow at my back! You will weep for me a little, will you not? but not too much, for I do not wish you to feel real sorrow. . . .

Do not weep, my children; I am not going very far; and I shall see you from there; you will only have to look when it is dark, and you will see me smile. . . .

[God] is above. He sees us all, and He knows all that He does amid his great stars. I am going away, my children. Love each other dearly and always, There is no other thing in the world but that; love one another. You will sometimes think of the poor old man who died here. Ah, my Cosette, it is not my fault that I did not see you every day, for it broke my heart. I went as far as the corner of the street, and must have produced a strange effect on the people who saw me pass, for

I was like a madman, and even went out without my hat. My children, I can no longer see very clearly. I had several things to say to you, but no matter. Think of me a little. You are blessed beings. I know not what is the matter with me, but I see light. Come hither. I die happy. Let me lay my hands on your beloved heads."

Cosette and Marius fell on their knees, heart-broken and choked with sobs, each under one of Jean Valjean's hands. These august hands did not move again.

He had fallen back, and the light from the two candles illumined him; his white face looked up to heaven, and he let Cosette and Marius cover his hands with kisses.

He was dead.

The night was starless and intensely dark; doubtless some immense angel was standing in the gloom, with outstretched wings, waiting for the soul.

EMILY BRONTE

WUTHERING HEIGHTS

Three novels published in 1847 by the Bronte sisters—Charlotte (1816-1855), *Jane Eyre;* Emily (1818-1848), *Wuthering Heights;* and Anne (1820-1849), *Agnes Grey*—exemplify the English Gothic romance novel. Like many of their female contemporaries, the Bronte sisters published under a pseudonym, namely, Cur- rer, Ellis, and Acton Bell. Of the three, *Wuthering Heights,* the only novel Emily Bronte ever published, is arguably the most famous. It is written as a full-blown Gothic Romance—replete with unearthly phantoms and graveyards, but ever- mindful that they represent a transcendent world filled with spiritual meaning. The plot focuses on the disparate pair of Heathcliff, an adopted member of the aristocratic Earnshaw family, and the wildly passionate and headstrong Catherine Earnshaw, who, although attracted to Heathcliff, believes that it would be beneath her to marry an orphaned commoner. Knowing this, Heathcliff departs Wuthering Heights ("wuthering" itself means "stormy") but returns three years later, only to discover that Catherine's brother, Hindley, is now in charge of the estate and that Catherine has married Edgar Linton, an aristocratic gentleman who is deeply dedicated to her. The now successful Heathcliff, driven by vengeance for his perceived mistreatment at the hands of the Earnshaws, seeks to ruin them first by financially ruining Hindley. Through Heathcliff, Bronte creates her own version of the Byronic hero—uncultivated, driven, passionate, and tormented. For example, Nelly Dean (a maid-servant to Catherine) relates how Heathcliff convinces her to carry a letter to Catherine, who is dying from a fever while pregnant with Edgar's child. While Edgar is attending services at the Gimmerton Church, Nelly reads the letter to Catherine just before Heathcliff bursts into her room. The following selection, narrated by Nelly, is drawn from this encounter. It is one of the most memorable scenes in the novel, because it epitomizes Heathcliff's fiery temperament and Catherine's bittersweet love for him.

In the evening, she said, the evening of my visit to the Heights, I knew, as well as if I saw him, that Mr. Heathcliff was about the place; and I shunned going out, because I still carried his letter in my pocket, and didn't want to be threatened or teased any more. I had made up my mind not to give it till my master went somewhere, as I could not guess how its receipt would affect Catherine. The consequence was that it did not reach her before the lapse of three days. The fourth was Sunday, and I brought it into her room after the family were gone to church. There was a man servant left to keep the house with me, and we generally made a practice of locking the doors during the hours of service; but on that occasion the weather was so warm and pleasant that I set them wide open, and, to fulfill my engagement, as I knew who would be coming, I told my companion that the mistress wished very much for some oranges, and he must run over to the village and get a few, to be paid for on the morrow. He departed, and I went upstairs.

Mrs. Linton sat in a loose, white dress, with a light shawl over her shoulders, in the recess of the open window, as usual. Her thick, long hair had been partly removed at the beginning of her illness, and now she wore it simply combed in its natural tresses over her temples and neck. Her appearance was altered, as I had told Heathcliff; but when she was calm, there seemed unearthly beauty in the change. The flash of her eyes had been succeeded by a dreamy and melancholy softness; they no longer gave the impression of looking at the objects around her: they appeared always to gaze beyond, and far beyond—you would have said out of this world. Then the paleness of her face—its haggard aspect having vanished as she recovered flesh—and the peculiar expression arising from her mental state, though painfully suggestive of their causes, added to the touching interest which she awakened; and— invariably to me, I know, and to any person who saw her, I should think—refuted more tangible proofs of convalescence, and stamped her as one doomed to decay.

A book lay spread on the sill before her, and the scarcely perceptible wind fluttered its leaves at intervals. I believe Linton had laid it there: for she never endeavored to divert herself with reading, or occupation of any kind, and he would spend many an hour in trying to entice her attention to some subject which had formerly been her amusement. She was conscious of his aim, and in her better moods endured his efforts placidly, only showing their uselessness by now and then suppressing a wearied sigh, and checking him at last with the saddest of smiles and kisses. At other times, she would turn petulantly away, and hide her face in her hands, or even push him off angrily; and then he took care to let her alone, for he was certain of doing no good.

Gimmerton chapel bells were still ringing; and the full, mellow flow of the beck in the valley came soothingly on the ear. It was a sweet substitute for the yet absent murmur of the summer foliage, which drowned that music about the Grange when the trees were in leaf. At Wuthering Heights it always sounded on quiet days following a great thaw or a season of steady rain. And of Wuthering Heights Catherine was thinking as she listened: that is, if she thought or listened at all; but she had the vague, distant look I mentioned before, which expressed no recognition of material things either by ear or eye.

"There's a letter for you, Mrs. Linton," I said, gently inserting it in one hand that rested on her knee. "You must read it immediately, because it wants an answer. Shall I break the seal?" "Yes," she answered, without altering the direction of her eyes. I opened it—it was very short. "Now," I continued, "read it." She drew away her hand, and let it fall. I replaced it in her lap, and stood waiting till it should please her to glance down; but that movement was so long delayed that at last I resumed:

"Must I read it, ma'am? It is from Mr. Heathcliff."

There was a start and a troubled gleam of recollection, and a struggle to arrange her ideas. She lifted the letter, and seemed to peruse it; and when she came to the signature she sighed; yet still I found she had not gathered its import, for, upon my desiring to hear her reply, she merely pointed to the name, and gazed at me with mournful and questioning eagerness.

"Well, he wishes to see you," said I, guessing her need of an interpreter. "He's in the garden by this time, and impatient to know what answer I shall bring."

As I spoke, I observed a large dog lying on the sunny grass beneath raise its ears as if about to bark, and then smoothing them back, announce, by a wag of the tail, that someone approached whom it did not consider a stranger. Mrs. Linton bent forward, and listened breathlessly. The minute after, a step traversed the hall; the open house was too tempting for Heathcliff to resit *[sic]* walking in: most likely he supposed that I was inclined to shirk my promise, and so resolved to trust to his own audacity. With straining eagerness Catherine gazed towards the entrance of her chamber. He did not hit the right room directly, she motioned me to admit him, but he found it out ere I could reach the door, and in a stride or two was at her side, and had her grasped in his arms.

He neither spoke nor loosed his hold for some five minutes, during which period he bestowed more kisses than ever he gave in his life before, I daresay: but then my mistress had kissed him first, and I plainly saw that he could hardly bear, for downright agony, to look into her face! The same conviction had stricken him as me, from the instant he beheld her, that there was no prospect of ultimate recovery there—she was fated, sure to die.

"Oh, Cathy! Oh, my life! how can I bear it?" was the first sentence he uttered, in a tone that did not seek to disguise his despair. And now he stared at her so earnestly that I thought the very intensity of his gaze would bring tears into his eyes; but they burned with anguish: they did not melt.

"What now?" said Catherine, leaning back and returning his look with a suddenly clouded brow: her humor was a mere vane for constantly varying caprices. "You and Edgar have broken my heart, Heathcliff! And you both came to bewail the deed to me, as if *you* were the people to be pitied! I shall not pity you, not I. You have killed me—and thriven on it, I think. How strong you are! How many years do you mean to live after I am gone?"

Heathcliff had knelt on one knee to embrace her; he attempted to rise, but she seized his hair, and kept him down.

"I wish I could hold you," she continued bitterly, "till we were both dead! I shouldn't care what you suffered. I care nothing for your sufferings. Why shouldn't *you* suffer? I do! Will you forget me? Will you be happy when I am in the earth? Will you say twenty years hence, 'That's the grave of Catherine Earnshaw. I loved her long ago, and was wretched to lose her; but it is past. I've loved many others since: my children are dearer to me than she was; and a death, I shall not rejoice that I am going to her; I shall be sorry that I must leave them!' Will you say so, Heathcliff?"

"Don't torture me till I am as mad as yourself," cried he, wrenching his head free, and grinding his teeth.

The two, to a cool spectator, made a strange and fearful picture. Well might Catherine deem that heaven would be a land of exile to her, unless with her mortal body she cast away her mortal character also. Her present countenance had a wild vindictiveness in its white cheek, and a bloodless lip and scintillating eye; and she retained in her closed fingers a portion of the locks she had been grasping. As to her companion, while raising himself with one hand, he had taken her arm with the other; and so inadequate was his stock of gentleness to the requirements of her condition, that on his letting go I saw four distinct impressions left blue in the colorless skin.

"Are you possessed with a devil," he pursued savagely, "to talk in that manner to me when you are dying? Do you reflect that all those words will be branded on my memory, and eating deeper eternally after you have left me? You know you lie to say I have killed you: and, Catherine, you know that I could as soon forget you as my existence! Is it not sufficient for your infernal selfishness that, while you are at peace, I shall writhe in the torments of hell?"

"I shall not be at peace," moaned Catherine, recalled to a sense of physical weakness by the violent, unequal throbbing of her heart, which beat visibly and audibly under this excess of agitation. She said nothing further till the paroxysm was over; then she continued, more kindly—

"I'm not wishing you greater torment than I have, Heathcliff. I only wish us never to be parted: and should a word of mine distress you hereafter, think I feel the same distress underground, and for my own sake, forgive me! Come here and kneel down again! You never harmed me in your life. Nay, if you nurse anger, that will be worse to remember than my harsh words! Won't you come here again? Do!"

Heathcliff went to the back of her chair, and leaned over, but not so far as to let her see his face, which was livid with emotion. She bent round to look at him; he would not permit it: turning abruptly, he walked to the fireplace, where he stood, silent, with his back towards us. Mrs. Linton's glance followed him suspiciously: every movement woke a new sentiment in her. After a pause and a prolonged gaze, she resumed; addressing me in accents of indignant disappointment—

"Oh, you see, Nelly, he would not relent a moment to keep me out of the grave. *That* is how I'm loved! Well, never mind. That is not *my* Heathcliff. I shall love mine yet; and take him with me: he's in my soul. And," added she, musingly, "the thing that irks me most is this shattered prison, after all. I'm tired of being enclosed here. I'm wearying to escape into that glorious world, and to be always there: not seeing it dimly through tears, and yearning for it through the walls of an aching heart; but really with it, and in it. Nelly, you think you are better and more fortunate than I; in full health and strength: you are sorry for me—very soon that will be altered. I shall be sorry for *you*. I shall be incomparably beyond and above you all. I *wonder* he won't be near me!" She went on to herself. "I thought he wished it. Heathcliff, dear! you should not be sullen now. Do come to me, Heathcliff."

In her eagerness she rose and supported herself on the arm of the chair. At that earnest appeal he turned to her, looking absolutely desperate. His eyes, wide and wet, at last flashed fiercely on her; his breast heaved convulsively. An instant they held asunder, and then how they met I hardly saw, but Catherine made a spring, and he caught her, and they were locked in an embrace from which I thought my mistress would never be released alive: in fact, to my eyes, she seemed directly insensible. He flung himself into the nearest seat, and on my approaching hurriedly to ascertain if she had fainted, he gnashed at me, and foamed like a mad dog, and gathered her to him with greedy jealousy. I did not feel as if I were in the company of a creature of my own species: it appeared that he would not understand, though I spoke to him; so I stood off, and held my tongue, in great perplexity.

A movement of Catherine's relieved me a little presently: she put up her hand to clasp his neck, and bring her cheek to his as he held her; while he, in return, covering her with frantic caresses, said wildly—

"You teach me now how cruel you've been—cruel and false. *Why* did you despise me? *Why* did you betray your own heart, Cathy? I have not one word of comfort. You deserve this. You have killed yourself. Yes, you may kiss me, and cry; and wring out my kisses and tears: they'll blight you—they'll damn me? What right—answer me—for the poor fancy you felt for Linton? Because misery and degradation, and death, and nothing that God or Satan could inflict would have parted us, *you,* of your own will, did it. I have not broken your heart—*you* have broken it; and in breaking it, you have broken mine. So much the worse for me, that I am strong. Do I want to live? What kind of living will it be when you—oh, God! would *you* like to live with your soul in the grave?"

"Let me alone. Let me alone," sobbed Catherine. "If I have done wrong, I'm dying for it. It is enough! You left me too: but I won't upbraid you! I forgive you. Forgive me!"

"It is hard to forgive, and to look at those eyes, and feel those wasted hands," he answered. "Kiss me again; and don't let me see your eyes! I forgive what you have done to me. I love *my* murderer—but *yours!* How can I?"

They were silent—their faces hid against each other, and washed by each other's tears. At least, I suppose the weeping was on both sides; as it seemed Heathcliff *could* weep on a great occasion like this.

I grew very uncomfortable, meanwhile; for the afternoon wore fast away, the man whom I had sent off returned from his errand, and I could distinguish, by the shine of the western sun up the valley, a concourse thickening outside Gimmerton chapel porch.

"Service is over," I announced. "My master will be here in half an hour."

Heathcliff groaned a curse, and strained Catherine closer: she never moved.

Ere long I perceived a group of the servants passing up the road towards the kitchen wing. Mr. Linton was not far behind; he opened the gate himself and sauntered slowly up, probably enjoying the lovely afternoon that breathed as soft as summer.

"Now he is here," I exclaimed. "For Heaven's sake, hurry down! You'll not meet anyone on the front stairs. Do be quick; and stay among the trees till he is fairly in."

"I must go, Cathy," said Heathcliff, seeking to extricate himself from his companion's arms. "But if I live, I'll see you again before you are asleep. I won't stray five yards from your window."

"You must not go!" she answered, holding him as firmly as her strength allowed. "You *shall* not, I tell you."

"For one hour," he pleaded earnestly.

"Not for one minute," she replied.

"I *must*—Linton will be up immediately," persisted the alarmed intruder.

He would have risen, and unfixed her fingers by the act— she clung fast, grasping: there was mad resolution in her face.

"No!" she shrieked. "Oh, don't, don't go. It is the last time! Edgar will not hurt us. Heathcliff, I shall die! I shall die!"

"Damn the fool! There he is," cried Heathcliff, sinking back into his seat. "Hush, my darling! Hush, hush, Catherine! I'll stay. If he shot me so, I'd expire with a blessing on my lips."

And there they were fast again. I heard my master mounting the stairs—the cold sweat ran from my forehead: I was horrified.

"Are you going to listen to her ravings?" I said passionately. "She does not know what she says. Will you ruin her, because she has not wit to help herself? Get up! You could be free instantly. That is the most diabolical deed that ever you did. We are all done for—master, mistress, and servant."

I wrung my hands, and cried out; and Mr. Linton hastened his step at the noise. In the midst of my agitation, I was sincerely glad to observe that Catherine's arms had fallen relaxed and her head hung down.

"She's fainted or dead," I thought: "so much the better.

Far better that she should be dead, than lingering a burden and a misery maker to all about her."

Edgar sprang to his unbidden guest, blanched with astonishment and rage. What he meant to do, I cannot tell; however, the other stopped all demonstrations, at once, by placing the lifeless-looking form in his arms.

"Look, there!" he said; "unless you be a fiend, help her first—then you shall speak to me!"

He walked into the parlor, and sat down. Mr. Linton summoned me, and with great difficulty, and after resorting to many means, we managed to restore her to sensation; but she was all bewildered; she sighed, and moaned, and knew nobody. Edgar, in his anxiety for her, forgot her hated friend. I did not. I went, at the earliest opportunity, and besought him to depart; affirming that Catherine was better, and he should hear from me in the morning how she passed the night.

"I shall not refuse to go out of doors," he answered; "but I shall stay in the garden: and, Nelly, mind you keep your word tomorrow. I shall be under those larch trees. Mind! or I pay another visit, whether Linton be in or not."

He sent a rapid glance through the half-open door of the chamber, and, ascertaining that what I stated was apparently true, delivered the house of his luckless presence.

Even after Catherine's death (due to fever and giving premature birth to her daughter Cathy), Heathcliff's vengeance on the Earnshaws has yet to run its course. To ruin Edgar Linton, he marries his sister, Isabella, and makes her completely miserable, even referring to her as "a mere slut/7 Heathcliff then forces Cathy to marry Linton (his son with Isabella) just so he can gain complete control of Thrushcross Grange—the Linton estate. Having nearly exhausted himself in reaping vengeance on the Earnshaws, Heathcliff begins to have supernatural visions about reconciling with Catherine. The Yorkshire settings, which have paralleled the tempestuous relationship between Heathcliff and Catherine throughout, once again serve to enhance the scenes of Heathcliff's visionary ruminations. The brutal, impassioned action of the novel (which astonished Emily's contemporaries) finally ceases with the death of Heathcliff on a *stormy* night in his own room.

HERMAN MELVILLE

MOBY DICK

Herman Melville (1819-1891) was born in New York City and led a comfortable life until his father died in 1832. His mother then became a domineering force in his life as did the dogmatic form of Calvinism she practiced, which Melville was compelled to endure. Throughout his life, Melville was skeptical about organized religion but uncomfortable with the prospect of atheism. In 1839, he enlisted as a deck hand on a merchant ship, and for the next five years, Melville traversed the world; later, he signed on as a seaman on the warship the *United States.* These adventures gave rise to his most famous book—*Moby Dick; or; The Whale*—which many critics argue is the best American novel of the era. As Melville worked and reworked his story of a whaling adventure, he credited Nathaniel Hawthorne for its actual transformation into a compelling masterpiece and dedicated it to him when it appeared in 1851. Melville's rebellion against what he perceives to be a false idea of God is symbolized by Captain Ahab and his quest for "The White Whale." Ahab believes that if he can only "strike through the mask"—penetrate the physical reality of the whale and thus get beyond the superficial—he can know the truth about the whale which leads to truth about God. In his "Cetology [the study of whales] Chapters," Melville meticulously details the attack, death, and processing of each whale—piece by piece—with the hope of discovering some ultimate meaning and truth.

The novel is laden with mystical images of both the demonic and the heavenly. For example, the three chief shipmates represent various opinions about religion and the capacity of human beings. The first mate, Starbuck, is a Christian idealist who bucks the course that Ahab has laid out for his ship. In contrast, Stubb is a self-professed fatalist, who accepts life without critically questioning it. He is cheerful and optimistic, but he fails to grasp the seriousness of Ahab's quest for the White Whale, and it is Stubb who dispassionately abandons the cabin-boy, Pip, at sea, when he is washed overboard. Finally, Flask represents the materialist dolt who never thinks critically about anything, except the task immediately in front of him. Later, when Ahab nails a gold Spanish doubloon to the main mast as a reward for whomever sights the White Whale, Flask can only contemplate buying expensive cigars with it.

The images of evil, however, are less clear-cut. Consider, for example, three of the crew: Queequeg, the Manxman, and Fedallah. Queequeg, a Muslim, is covered in mystical tatoos, and he fashions his own coffin, which ultimately serves as the life raft for the ship's only survivor, Ishmael. The Manxman, from the Isle of Man and hence his name, serves as a prophet figure, much like the biblical prophet Elijah. He interprets omens, which Ahab consistently ignores, that foretell doom for the *Pequod.* Fedallah—a Parsee from India who believes in coequal, coeternal gods of good and evil—is a quiet, obscure figure whom some critics interpret to be the Devil Incarnate, whereas others view him as a disembodied soul.

The symbolic significance of Ahab, and his relationship to the White Whale, is very complex. In a very real sense, Moby Dick represents evil for Ahab, because it is he who is responsible for Ahab's physical deformity—the loss of a leg. Melville, nonetheless, consistently represents Moby Dick as "the White Whale," with the whiteness representing The Good, The True, and The Beautiful of Greek philosophy. If such is the case, then it is Ahab who represents evil, and Moby Dick becomes God's agent of divine vengeance on a sinful humanity when he causes Ahab's death at the end of the novel.

All these symbols come into play in the following chapter, "The Quarter- Deck," narrated by Ishmael. In it, Melville demonstrates Ahab's single-minded- ness in pursuing Moby Dick and his ability to motivate everyone in the crew, except Starbuck, to participate in a ritualistic toast (reminiscent of the drinking of the cup in the Christian Eucharist) vowing death to Moby Dick.

CHAPTER 36

The Quarter-Deck

(Enter Ahab: Then, all.)

It was not a great while after the affair of the pipe,[1] that one morning shortly after breakfast, Ahab, as was his wont, ascended the cabin-gangway to the deck. There most sea- captains usually walk at that hour, as country gentlemen, after the same meal, take a few turns in the garden.

Soon his steady, ivory stride was heard, as to and fro he paced his old rounds, upon planks so familiar to his tread, that they were all over dented, like geological stones, with the peculiar mark of his walk. Did you fixedly gaze, too, upon that ribbed and dented brow, there also, you would see still stranger foot-prints—the foot prints of his one unsleeping, ever-pacing thought.

But on the occasion in question, those dents looked deeper, even as his nervous step that morning left a deeper mark. And, so full of his thought was Ahab, that at every uniform turn that he made, now at the main-mast and now at the binnacle, you could almost see that thought turn in him as he turned, and pace in him as he paced; so completely possessing him, indeed, that it all but seemed the inward mould of every outer movement.

"D'ye mark him, Flask?" whispered Stubb; "the chick that's in him pecks the shell. 'Twill soon be out."

The hours wore on;—Ahab now shut up within his cabin; anon, pacing the deck, with the same intense bigotry of purpose[2] in his aspect.

It drew near the close of day. Suddenly he came to a halt by the bulwarks, and inserting his bone leg into the auger- hole there, and with one hand grasping a shroud, he ordered Starbuck to send everybody aft.

"Sir!" said the mate, astonished at an order seldom or never given on ship-board except in some extraordinary case.

"Send everybody aft," repeated Ahab. "Mast-heads, there! come down!"

When the entire ship's company were assembled, and with curious and not wholly unapprehensive faces, were eyeing him, for he looked not unlike the weather horizon when a storm is coming up, Ahab, after rapidly glancing over the bulwarks, and then darting his eyes among the crew, started from his stand-point; and as though not a soul were nigh him resumed his heavy turns upon the deck. With bent head and half-slouched hat he continued to pace, unmindful of the wondering whispering among the men; till Stubb cautiously whispered to Flask, that Ahab must have summoned them there for the purpose of witnessing a pedestrian feat. But this did not last long. Vehemently pausing, he cried:—

"What do ye do when ye see a whale, men?"

"Sing out for him!" was the impulsive rejoinder from a score of clubbed voices.

"Good!" cried Ahab, with a wild approval in his tones; observing the hearty animation into which his unexpected question had so magnetically thrown them.

"And what do ye next, men?"

"Lower away, and after him!"

"And what tune is it ye pull to, men?"

"A dead whale or a stove boat!"[3]

More and more strangely and fiercely glad and approving, grew the countenance of the old man at every shout; while the mariners began to gaze curiously at each other, as if marvelling how it was that they themselves became so excited at such seemingly purposeless questions.

---

[1] Affair of the pipe refers to an incident in Chapter 30 in which Ahab throws his smoking pipe into the ocean, because he realizes that he no longer enjoys it. This small incident is but one symbol for Ahab's rejection of his connection to the human race. Before the end of the novel, Ahab will throw more objects overboard.

[2]Bigotry of purpose means being intent on only one thing.

[3] *Stove boat* is a reference to a boat with a hole in it.

But, they were all eagerness again, as Ahab, now half- revolving in his pivot-hole, with one band reaching high up a shroud, and tightly, almost convulsively grasping it, addressed them thus:—

"All ye mast-headers have before now heard me give orders about a white whale. Look ye! d'ye see this Spanish ounce of gold?"—holding up a broad bright coin to the sun—"it is a sixteen dollar piece, men,—a doubloon. D'ye see it? Mr. Starbuck, hand me yon top-maul."

While the mate was getting the hammer, Ahab, without speaking, was slowly rubbing the gold piece against the skirts of his jacket, as if to heighten its lustre, and without using any words was meanwhile lowly humming to himself, producing a sound so strangely muffled and inarticulate that it seemed the mechanical humming of the wheels of his vitality in him.

Receiving the top-maul from Starbuck, he advanced towards the main-mast with the hammer uplifted in one hand, exhibiting the gold with the other, and with a high raised voice exclaiming: "Whosoever of ye raises me a white- headed whale with a wrinkled brow and a crooked jaw; whosoever of ye raises me that white-headed whale, with three holes punctured in his starboard fluke—look ye, whosoever of ye raises me that same white whale, he shall have this gold ounce, my boys!"

"Huzza! Huzza![4]" cried the seamen, as with swinging tarpaulins they hailed the act of nailing the gold to the mast.

"It's a white whale, I say," resumed Ahab, as he threw down the top-maul; "a white whale. Skin your eyes for him, men; look sharp for white water; if ye see but a bubble, sing out."

All this while Tashtego,[5] Daggoo, and Queequeg had looked on with even more intense interest and surprise than the rest, and at the mention of the wrinkled brow and crooked jaw they had started as if each was separately touched by some specific recollection.

"Captain Ahab," said Tashtego, "that white whale must be the same that some call Moby Dick."

"Moby Dick?" shouted Ahab. "Do ye know the white whale then, Tash?"

"Does he fan-tail a little curious, sir, before he goes down?" said the Gay-Header deliberately.

"And has he a curious spout, too," said Daggoo, "very bushy, even for a parmacetty, and mighty quick, Captain Ahab?"

"And he have one, two, tree—oh! good many iron in him hide, too, Captain," cried Queequeg disjointedly, "all twiske-tee betwisk, like him—him—" faltering hard for a word, and screwing his hand round and round as though uncorking a bottle—"like him—him—"

"Corkscrew!" cried Ahab, "aye, Queequeg, the harpoons lie all twisted and wrenched in him; aye, Daggoo, his spout is a big one, like a whole shock of wheat, and white as a pile of our Nantucket wool after the great annual sheep-shearing; aye, Tashtego, and he fan-tails like a split jib in a squall. Death and devils! men, it is Moby Dick ye have seen—Moby Dick—Moby Dick!"

"Captain Ahab," said Starbuck, who, with Stubb and Flask, had thus far been eyeing his superior with increasing surprise, but at last seemed struck with a thought which somewhat explained all the wonder. "Captain Ahab, I have heard of Moby Dick—but it was not Moby Dick that took off thy leg?"

"Who told thee that?" cried Ahab; then pausing, "Aye, Starbuck; aye, my hearties all round; it was Moby Dick that dismasted me; Moby Dick that brought me to this dead stump I stand on now. Aye, aye," he shouted with a terrific, loud, animal sob, like that of a heart-stricken moose; "Aye, aye! it was that accursed white whale that razeed me; made a poor pegging lubber of me for ever and a day!" Then tossing both arms, with measureless imprecations he shouted out: "Aye, aye! and I'll chase him round Good Hope, and round the Horn, and round the Norway Maelstrom, and round perdition's flames before I give him up. And this is what ye have shipped for, men! to chase that white whale on both sides of land, and over all sides of earth, till he spouts black blood and rolls fin out. What say ye, men, will ye splice hands on it, now? I think ye do look brave."

"Aye, aye!" shouted the harpooneers and seamen, running closer to the excited old man: "A sharp eye for the White Whale; a sharp lance for Moby Dick!"

---

[4] Huzza is an expression of joy.

[5] Tashtego is an American Indian who serves as Stubb's harpooner, and Daggoo, an African, is Flask's harpooner.

"God bless ye," he seemed to half sob and half shout. "God bless ye, men. Steward! go draw the great measure of grog. But what's this long face about, Mr. Starbuck; wilt thou not chase the white whale? art not game for Moby Dick?"

"I am game for his crooked jaw, and for the jaws of Death too, Captain Ahab, if it fairly comes in the way of the business we follow; but I came here to hunt whales, not my commander's vengeance. How many barrels will thy vengeance yield thee even if thou gettest it, Captain Ahab? it will not fetch thee much in our Nantucket market."

"Nantucket market! Hoot! But come closer, Starbuck; thou requirest a little lower layer. If money's to be the measurer, man, and the accountants have computed their great counting-house the globe, by girdling it with guineas, one to every three parts of an inch; then, let me tell thee, that my vengeance will fetch a great premium *here!*"

"He smites his chest," whispered Stubb, "what's that for? methinks it rings most vast, but hollow."

"Vengeance on a dumb brute!" cried Starbuck, "that simply smote thee from blindest instinct! Madness! To be enraged with a dumb thing, Captain Ahab, seems blasphemous."

"Hark ye yet again,—the little lower layer. All visible objects, man, are but as pasteboard masks. But in each event—in the living act, the undoubted deed—there, some unknown but still reasoning thing puts forth the mouldings of its features from behind the unreasoning mask. If man will strike, strike through the mask! How can the prisoner reach outside except by thrusting through the wall? To me, the white whale is that wall, shoved near to me. Sometimes I think there's naught beyond. But 'tis enough. He tasks me; he heaps me; I see in him outrageous strength, with an inscrutable malice sinewing it. That inscrutable thing is chiefly what I hate; and be the white whale agent, or be the white whale principal, I will wreak that hate upon him. Talk not to me of blasphemy, man; I'd strike the sun if it insulted me. For could the sun do that, then could I do the other; since there is ever a sort of fair play herein, jealousy presiding over all creations. But not my master, man, is even that fair play. Who's over me? Truth hath no confines. Take off thine eye! more intolerable than fiends' glarings is a doltish stare! So, so; thou reddenest and palest; my heat has melted thee to anger-glow. But look ye, Starbuck, what is said in heat, that thing unsays itself. There are men from whom warm words are small indignity. I meant not to incense thee. Let it go. Look! see yonder Turkish cheeks of spotted tawn—living, breathing pictures painted by the sun. The Pagan leopards— the unrecking and unworshipping things, that live; and seek, and give no reasons for the torrid life they feel! The crew,

man, the crew! Are they not one and all with Ahab, in this matter of the whale? See Stubb! he laughs! See yonder Chilean! he snorts to think of it. Stand up amid the general hurricane, thy one tost sapling cannot, Starbuck! And what is it? Reckon it. 'Tis but to help strike a fin; no wondrous feat for Starbuck. What is it more? From this one poor hunt, then, the best lance out of all Nantucket, surely he will not hang back, when every foremast-hand has clutched a whetstone? Ah! constrainings seize thee; I see! the billow lifts thee! Speak, but speak!—Aye, aye! thy silence, then, *that* voices thee. *{Aside)* Something shot from my dilated nostrils, he has inhaled it in his lungs. Starbuck now is mine; cannot oppose me now, without rebellion."

"God keep me!—keep us all!" murmured Starbuck, lowly.

But in his joy at the enchanted, tacit acquiescence of the mate, Ahab did not hear his foreboding invocation; nor yet the low laugh from the hold; nor yet the presaging vibrations of the winds in the cordage; nor yet the hollow flap of the sails against the masts, as for a moment their hearts sank in. For again Starbucks downcast eyes lighted up with the stubbornness of life; the subterranean laugh died away; the winds blew on; the sails filled out; the ship heaved and rolled as before. Ah, ye admonitions and warnings! why stay ye not when ye come? But rather are ye predictions than warnings, ye shadows! Yet not so much predictions from without, as verifications of the foregoing things within. For with little external to constrain us, the innermost necessities in our being, these still drive us on,

"The measure! the measure!" cried Ahab.

Receiving the brimming pewter, and turning to the har- pooneers, he ordered them to produce their weapons. Then ranging them before him near the capstan, with their harpoons in their hands, while his three mates stood at his side with their lances, and the rest of the ship's company formed a circle round the group; he stood for an instant searchingly eyeing every man of his crew. But those wild eyes met his, as the bloodshot eyes of the prairie wolves meet the eye of their leader, ere he rushes on at their head in the trail of the bison; but, alas! only to fall into the hidden snare of the Indian.

"Drink and pass!" he cried, handing the heavy charged flagon to the nearest seaman. "The crew alone now drink. Round with it, round! Short draughts—long swallows, men; 'tis hot as Satan's[6] hoof. So, so; it goes round excellently. It spiralizes in ye; forks out at the serpent-snapping eye. Well done; almost drained. That way it went, this way it comes. Hand it me—here's a hollow! Men, ye seem the years; so brimming life is gulped and gone. Steward, refill!

"Attend now, my braves. I have mustered ye all round this capstan; and ye mates, flank me with your lances; and ye harpooneers, stand there with your irons; and ye, stout mariners, ring me in, that I may in some sort revive a noble custom of my fisherman fathers before me. O men, you will yet see that—Ha! boy, come back? bad pennies come not sooner. Hand it me. Why, now, this pewter had run brimming again, wert not thou St. Vitus'[7] imp—away, thou ague!

"Advance, ye mates! Cross your lances full before me. Well done! Let me touch the axis." So saying, with extended arm, he grasped the three level, radiating lances at their crossed centre; while so doing, suddenly and nervously twitched them; meanwhile, glancing intently from Starbuck to Stubb; from Stubb to Flask. It seemed as though, by some nameless, interior volition, he would fain have shocked into them the same fiery emotion accumulated within the Leyden jar[8] of his own magnetic life. The three mates quailed before his strong, sustained, and mystic aspect. Stubb and Flask looked sideways from him; the honest eye of Starbuck fell downright.

"In vain!" cried Ahab; "but, maybe, 'tis well. For did ye three but once take the full-forced shock, then mine own electric thing, *that* had perhaps expired from out me. Perchance, too, it would have dropped ye dead. Perchance ye need it not. Down lances! And now, ye mates, I do appoint ye three cup-bearers to my three pagan kinsmen there—yon three most honorable gentlemen and noblemen, my valiant harpooneers. Disdain the task? What, when the great Pope washes the feet of beggars, using his tiara for ewer? Oh, my sweet cardinals! your own condescension, *that* shall bend ye to it. I do not order ye; ye will it. Cut your seizings and draw the poles, ye harpooneers!"

Silently obeying the order, the three harpooneers now stood with the detached iron part of their harpoons, some three feet long, held, barbs up, before him.

"Stab me not with that keen steel! Cant them; cant them over! know ye not the goblet end? Turn up the socket! So, so; now, ye cup-bearers, advance. The irons! take them; hold them while I fill!" Forthwith, slowly going from one officer to the other, he brimmed the harpoon sockets with the fiery waters from the pewter.

"Now, three to three, ye stand. Commend the murderous chalices! Bestow them, ye who are now made parties to this indissoluble league. Ha! Starbuck! but the deed is done! Yon ratifying sun now waits to sit upon it. Drink, ye harpooneers! drink and swear, ye men that man the deathful whaleboat's bow—Death to Moby Dick! God hunt us all, if we do not hunt Moby Dick to his death!" The long, barbed steel goblets were lifted; and to cries and maledictions against the white whale, the spirits were simultaneously quaffed down with a hiss. Starbuck paled, and turned, and shivered. Once more, and finally, the replenished pewter went the rounds among the frantic crew; when, waving his free hand to them, they all dispersed; and Ahab retired within his cabin.

---

[6] *Satan's hoof* refers to the common understanding that Satan had a cloven foot (like a goat or a deer) as well as horns.

[7] St. Vitus' imp refers to a supposed small demon associated with the patron saint who protects sailors from storms.

[8] Leyden jar refers to an antiquated device used to store electric energy. Today it is called a capacitor.

CHARLES DICKENS

NICHOLAS NICKLEBY

Dickens skillfully creates characters who are concerned only with safeguarding their privileged way of life and ignoring the misery of the working class. These people run the prisons, schools, law courts, and other agencies, both private and governmental, that oppress the poor. In *Nicholas Nickleby,* young Nicholas Nickleby, an idealistic nineteen year old, who, through the efforts of his miserly and conniving uncle, Ralph Nickleby, secures a teaching position at Dotheboys Hall, a dreadful boarding school in Yorkshire. The school is operated by Wack- ford Squeers who, aided by his heartless wife, tries to squeeze as much profit as he can from the school by depriving the boys of basic necessities. A cruel tyrant, he also brutalizes his charges. In the following passage, Squeers takes Nicholas into the classroom for the first time.

And yet this scene, painful as it was, had its grotesque features, which, in a less interested observer than Nicholas, might have provoked a smile. Mrs. Squeers stood at one of the desks, presiding over an immense basin of brimstone and treacle, of which delicious compound she administered a large instalment to each boy in succession: using for the purpose a common wooden spoon, which might have been originally manufactured for some gigantic top, and which widened every young gentleman's mouth considerably: they being all obliged, under heavy corporal penalties, to take in the whole of the bowl at a gasp. In another corner, huddled together for companionship, were the little boys who had arrived on the preceding night, three of them in very large leather breeches, and two in old trousers, a something tighter fit than drawers are usually worn; at no great distance from these was seated the juvenile son and heir of Mr. Squeers—a striking likeness of his father—kicking, with great vigour, under the hands of Smike, who was fitting upon him a pair of new boots that bore a most suspicious resemblance to those which the least of the little boys had worn on the journey down—as the little boy himself seemed to think, for he was regarding the appropriation with a look of most rueful amazement. Besides these, there was a long row of boys waiting, with countenances of no pleasant anticipation, to be treacled; and another file, who had just escaped from the infliction, making a variety of wry mouths indicative of anything but satisfaction. The whole were attired in such motley, ill-sorted, extraordinary garments, as would have been irresistibly ridiculous, but for the foul appearance of dirt, and disease, with which they were associated.

"Now," said Squeers, giving the desk a great rap with his cane, which made half the little boys nearly jump out of their boots, "is that physicking over?"

"Just over," said Mrs. Squeers, choking the last boy in her hurry, and tapping the crown of his head with the wooden spoon to restore him. "Here, you Smike; take away now. Look sharp!"

Smike shuffled out with the basin, and Mrs. Squeers having called up a little boy with a curly head and wiped her hands upon it, hurried out after him into a species of wash- house, where there was a small fire and a large kettle, together with a number of little wooden bowls which were arranged upon a board.

Into these bowls, Mrs. Squeers, assisted by the hungry servant, poured a brown composition which looked like diluted pincushions without the covers, and was called porridge. A minute wedge of brown bread was inserted in each bowl, and when they had eaten their porridge by means of the bread, the boys ate the bread itself, and had finished their breakfast; whereupon Mr. Squeers said, in a solemn voice, "For what we have received, may the Lord make us truly thankful!"—and went away to his own.

Nicholas distended his stomach with a bowl of porridge, for much the same reason which induces some savages to swallow earth—lest they should be inconveniently hungry when there is nothing to eat. Having further disposed of a slice of bread and butter, allotted to him in virtue of his office, he sat himself down to wait for school-time.

He could not but observe how silent and sad the boys all seemed to be. There was none of the noise and clamour of a school-room; none of its boisterous play, or hearty mirth. The children sat crouching and shivering together, and seemed to lack the spirit to move about. The only pupil who evinced the slightest tendency towards locomotion or playfulness was Master Squeers, and as his chief amusement was to tread upon the other boys' toes in his new boots, his flow of spirits was rather disagreeable than otherwise.

After some half-hour's delay, Mr. Squeers reappeared, and the boys took their places and their books, of which latter commodity the average might be about one to eight learners. A few minutes having elapsed, during which Mr. Squeers looked very profound, as if he had a perfect apprehension of what was inside all the books, and could say every word of their contents by heart if he only chose to take the trouble, that gentleman called up the first class.

Obedient to this summons there ranged themselves in front of the schoolmaster's desk, half-a-dozen scarecrows, out at knees and elbows, one of whom placed a torn and filthy book beneath his learned eye.

"This is the first class in English spelling and philosophy, Nickleby," said Squeers, beckoning Nicholas to stand beside him. "We'll get up a Latin one, and hand that over to you. Now then, where's the first boy?"

"Please, sir, he's cleaning the back parlour window," said the temporary head of the philosophical class.

"So he is, to be sure," rejoined Squeers. "We go upon the practical mode of teaching, Nickleby; the regular education system. C-l-e-a-n, clean, verb active, to make bright, to scour. W-i-n, win, d-e-r, der, winder, a casement. When the boy knows this out of the book, he goes and does it. It's just the same principle as the use of the globes. Where's the second boy?"

"Please, sir, he's weeding the garden," replied a small voice.

"To be sure," said Squeers, by no means disconcerted. "So he is. B-o-t, bot, t-i-n, bottin, n-e-y, ney, bottinney, noun substantive, a knowledge of plants. When he has learned that bottinney means a knowledge of plants, he goes and knows 'em. That's our system, Nickleby; what do you think of it?"

"It's a very useful one, at any rate," answered Nicholas.

"I believe you," rejoined Squeers, not remarking the emphasis of his usher. "Third boy, what's a horse?"

"A beast sir," replied the boy.

"So it is," said Squeers. "Ain't it, Nickleby?"

"I believe there is no doubt of that, sir," answered Nicholas.

"Of course there isn't," said Squeers. "A horse is a quadruped, and quadruped's Latin for beast, as every body that's gone through the grammar, knows, or else where's the use of having grammars at all?"

"Where, indeed!" said Nicholas abstractedly.

"As you're perfect in that," resumed Squeers, turning to the boy, "go and look after *my* horse, and rub him down well, or I'll rub you down. The rest of the class go and draw water up, till somebody tells you to leave off, for it's washing-day tomorrow, and they want the coppers filled."

So saying, he dismissed the first class to their experiments in practical philosophy, and eyed Nicholas with a look, half cunning and half doubtful, as if he were not altogether certain what he might think of him by this time.

"That's the way we do it, Nickleby," he said, after a pause.

Nicholas shrugged his shoulders in a manner that was scarcely perceptible, and said he saw it was.

"And a very good way it is, too," said Squeers. "Now, just take them fourteen little boys and hear them some reading, because, you know, you must begin to be useful. Idling about here, won't do."

Mr. Squeers said this, as if it had suddenly occurred to him, either that he must not say too much to his assistant, or that his assistant did not say enough to him in praise of the establishment. The children were arranged in a semicircle round the new master, and he was soon listening to their dull, drawling, hesitating recital of those stories of engrossing interest which are to be found in the more antiquated spelling books.

In this exciting occupation, the morning lagged heavily on. At one o'clock, the boys, having previously had their appetites thoroughly taken away by stir-about and potatoes, sat down in the kitchen to some hard salt beef, of which Nicholas was graciously permitted to take his portion to his own solitary desk, to eat it there in peace. After this, there was another hour of crouching in the school-room and shivering with cold, and then school began again.

It was Mr. Squeers's custom to call the boys together and make a sort of report, after every half-yearly visit to the metropolis, regarding the relations and friends he had seen, the news he had heard, the letters he had brought down, the bills which had been paid, the accounts which had been left unpaid, and so forth. This solemn proceeding always took place in the afternoon of the day succeeding his return; perhaps, because the boys acquired strength of mind from the suspense of the morning, or, possibly, because Mr. Squeers himself acquired greater sternness and inflexibility from certain warm potations in which he was wont to indulge after his early dinner. Be this as it may, the boys were recalled from house-window, garden, stable, and cow-yard, and the school were assembled in full conclave, when Mr. Squeers, with a small bundle of papers in his hand, and Mrs. S. following with a pair of canes, entered the room and proclaimed silence.

"Let any boy speak a word without leave," said Mr. Squeers mildly, "and I'll take the skin off his back."

This special proclamation had the desired effect, and a death-like silence immediately prevailed, in the midst of which Mr. Squeers went on to say:

"Boys, I've been to London, and have returned to my family and you, as strong and well as ever."

According to half-yearly custom, the boys gave three feeble cheers at this refreshing intelligence. Such cheers! Sighs of extra strength with the chill on.

"I have seen the parents of some boys," continued Squeers, turning over his papers, "and they're so glad to hear how their sons are getting on, that there's no prospect at all of their going away, which of course is a very pleasant thing to reflect upon, for all parties."

Two or three hands went to two or three eyes when Squeers said this, but the greater part of the young gentlemen having no particular parents to speak of, were wholly uninterested in the thing one way or other.

"I have had disappointments to contend against," said Squeers, looking very grim; "Bolder's father was two pound ten short. Where is Bolder?"

"Here he is, please sir," rejoined twenty officious voices. Boys are very like men to be sure.

"Come here, Bolder," said Squeers.

An unhealthy-looking boy, with warts all over his hands, stepped from his place to the master's desk, and raised his eyes imploringly to Squeers's face; his own, quite white from the rapid beating of his heart.

"Bolder," said Squeers, speaking very slowly, for he was considering, as the saying goes, where to have him. "Bolder, if your father thinks that because—why, what's this, sir?"

As Squeers spoke, he caught up the boy's hand by the cuff of his jacket, and surveyed it with an edifying aspect of horror and disgust.

"What do you call this, sir?" demanded the schoolmaster, administering a cut with the cane to expedite the reply.

"I can't help it, indeed, sir," rejoined the boy, crying. "They will come; it's the dirty work I think, sir—at least I don't know what it is, sir, but it's not my fault."

"Bolder," said Squeers, tucking up his wristbands, and moistening the palm of his right hand to get a good grip of the cane, "you are an incorrigible young scoundrel, and as the last thrashing did you no good, we must see what another will do towards beating it out of you."

With this, and wholly disregarding a piteous cry for mercy, Mr. Squeers fell upon the boy and caned him soundly: not leaving off indeed, until his arm was tired out.

"There," said Squeers, when he had quite done; "rub away hard as you like, you won't rub that off in a hurry. Oh! you won't hold that noise, won't you? Put him out, Smike."

The drudge knew better from long experience, than to hesitate about obeying, so he bundled the victim out by a side door, and Mr. Squeers perched himself again on his own stool, supported by Mrs. Squeers, who occupied another at his side.

"Now let us see," said Squeers. "A letter for Cobbey. Stand up, Cobbey."

Another boy stood up, and eyed the letter very hard while Squeers made a mental abstract of the same.

"Oh!" said Squeers: "Cobbey's grandmother is dead, and his uncle John has took to drinking, which is all the news his sister sends, except eighteenpence, which will just pay for that broken square of glass. Mrs. Squeers, my dear, will you take the money?"

The worthy lady pocketed the eighteenpence with a most business-like air, and Squeers passed on to the next boy, as coolly as possible.

"Graymarsh," said Squeers, "he's the next. Stand up, Gray marsh."

Another boy stood up, and the schoolmaster looked over the letter as before.

"Graymarsh's maternal aunt," said Squeers, when he had possessed himself of the contents, "is very glad to hear he's so well and happy, and sends her respectful compliments to Mrs. Squeers, and thinks she must be an angel. She likewise thinks Mr. Squeers is too good for this world; but hopes he may long be spared to carry on the business. Would have sent the two pair of stockings as desired, but is short of money, so forwards a tract instead, and hopes Graymarsh will put his trust in Providence. Hopes, above all, that he will study in everything to please Mr. and Mrs. Squeers, and look upon them as his only friends; and that he will love Master Squeers; and not object to sleeping five in a bed, which no Christian should. Ah!" said Squeers, folding it up, "a delightful letter. Very affecting indeed."

It was affecting in one sense, for Graymarsh's maternal aunt was strongly supposed, by her more intimate friends, to be no other than his maternal parent; Squeers, however, without alluding to this part of the story (which would have sounded immoral before boys), proceeded with the business by calling out "Mobbs," whereupon another boy rose, and Graymarsh resumed his seat.

"Mobbs's step-mother," said Squeers, "took to her bed on hearing that he wouldn't eat fat, and has been very ill ever since. She wishes to know, by an early post, where he expects to go to if he quarrels with his vittles; and with what feelings he could turn up his nose at the cow's liver broth, after his good master had asked a blessing on it. This was told her in the London newspapers—not by Mr. Squeers, for he is too kind and too good to set anybody against anybody—and it has vexed her so much, Mobbs can't think. She is sorry to find he is discontented, which is sinful and horrid, and hopes Mr. Squeers will flog him into a happier state of mind; with this view, she has also stopped his half-penny a week pocket-money, and given a double-bladed knife with a corkscrew in it to the Missionaries, which she had bought on purpose for him."

"A sulky state of feeling," said Squeers, after a terrible pause, during which he had moistened the palm of his right hand again, "won't do. Cheerfulness and contentment must be kept up. Mobbs, come to me!"

Mobbs moved slowly towards the desk, rubbing his eyes in anticipation of good cause for doing so; and he soon afterwards retired by the side door, with as good cause as a boy need have.

Mr. Squeers then proceeded to open a miscellaneous collection of letters; some enclosing money, which Mrs. Squeers "took care of;" and others referring to small articles of apparel, as caps and so forth, all of which the same lady stated to be too large, or too small, and calculated for nobody but young Squeers, who would appear indeed to have had most accommodating limbs, since everything that came into the school fitted him to a nicety. His head, in particular, must have been singularly elastic, for hats and caps of all dimensions were alike to him.

This business despatched, a few slovenly lessons were performed, and Squeers retired to his fireside, leaving Nicholas to take care of the boys in the school-room, which was very cold, and where a meal of bread and cheese was served out shortly after dark.

There was a small stove at that corner of the room which was nearest to the master's desk, and by it Nicholas sat down, so depressed and self-degraded by the consciousness of his position, that if death could have come upon him at that time he would have been almost happy to meet it. The cruelty of which he had been an unwilling witness, the coarse and ruffianly behaviour of Squeers even in his best moods, the filthy place, the sights and sounds about him, all contributed to this state of feeling; but when he recollected that, being there as an assistant, he actually seemed—no matter what unhappy train of circumstances had brought him to that pass—to be the aider and abettor of a system which filled him with honest disgust and indignation, he loathed himself, and felt, for the moment, as though the mere consciousness of his present situation must, through all time to come, prevent his raising his head again.

But, for the present, his resolve was taken, and the resolution he had formed on the preceding night remained undisturbed. He had written to his mother and sister, announcing the safe conclusion of his journey, and saying as little about Dotheboys Hall, and saying that little as cheerfully, as he possibly could. He hoped that by remaining where he was, he might do some good, even there; at all events, others depended too much on his uncle's favour to admit of his awakening his wrath just then.

One reflection disturbed him far more than any selfish considerations arising out of his own position. This was the probable destination of his sister Kate. His uncle had deceived him, and might he not consign her to some miserable place where her youth and beauty would prove a far greater curse than ugliness and decrepitude? To a caged man, bound hand and foot, this was a terrible idea; but no, he thought, his mother was by; there was the portrait-painter, too—simple enough, but still living in the world, and of it. He was willing to believe that Ralph Nickleby had conceived a personal dislike to himself. Having pretty good reason, by this time, to reciprocate it, he had no great difficulty in arriving at this conclusion, and tried to persuade himself that the feeling extended no farther than between them.

As he was absorbed in these meditations, he all at once encountered the upturned face of Smike, who was on his knees before the stove, picking a few stray cinders from the hearth and planting them on the fire. He had paused to steal a look at Nicholas, and when he saw that he was observed, shrunk back, as if expecting a blow.

"You need not fear me," said Nicholas kindly. "Are you cold?"

"N-n-o."

"You are shivering."

"I am not cold," replied Smike quickly. "I am used to it."

There was such an obvious fear of giving offence in his manner, and he was such a timid, broken-spirited creature, that Nicholas could not help exclaiming, "Poor fellow!"

If he had struck the drudge, he would have slunk away without a word. But, now, he burst into tears.

"Oh dear, oh dear!" he cried, covering his face with his cracked and horny hands. "My heart will break. It will, it will."

"Hush!" said Nicholas, laying his hand upon his shoulder. "Be a man; you are nearly one by years, God help you."

"By years!" cried Smike. "Oh dear, dear, how many of them! How many of them since I was a little child, younger than any that are here now! Where are they all?"

"Whom do you speak of?" inquired Nicholas, wishing to rouse the poor half-witted creature to reason. "Tell me."

"My friends," he replied, "myself—my—oh! what sufferings mine have been!"

"There is always hope," said Nicholas; he knew not what to say.

"No," rejoined the other, "no; none for me. Do you remember the boy that died here?"

"I was not here, you know," said Nicholas gently; "but what of him?"

"Why," replied the youth, drawing closer to his questioners side, "I was with him at night, and when it was all silent he cried no more for friends he wished to come and sit with him, but began to see faces round his bed that came from home; he said they smiled, and talked to him; and he died at last lifting his head to kiss them. Do you hear?"

"Yes, yes," rejoined Nicholas.

"What faces will smile on me when I die!" cried his companion, shivering. "Who will talk to me in those long nights! They cannot come from home; they would frighten me, if they did, for I don't know what it is, and shouldn't know them. Pain and fear, pain and fear for me, alive or dead. No hope, no hope!"

The bell rang to bed: and the boy, subsiding at the sound into his usual listless state, crept away as if anxious to avoid notice. It was with a heavy heart that Nicholas soon afterwards—no, not retired; there was no retirement there—followed—to his dirty and crowded dormitory.

For years the Squeers have starved and whipped Smike who is really the abandoned son of Ralph Nickleby, Nicholas' uncle, a fact not discovered until after Smike's death. Painfully thin and broken in spirit, Smike flees from the abusive Squeers, but is caught.

Another day came, and Nicholas was scarcely awake when he heard the wheels of a chaise approaching the house. It stopped. The voice of Mrs. Squeers was heard, and in exultation, ordering a glass of spirits for somebody, which was in itself a sufficient sign that something extraordinary had happened. Nicholas hardly dared to look out of the window; but he did so, and the very first object that met his eyes was the wretched Smike: so bedabbled with mud and rain, so haggard and worn and wild, that, but for his garments being such as no scarecrow was ever to wear, he might have been doubtful, even then, of his identity.

"Lift him out," said Squeers, after he had literally feasted his eyes, in silence, upon the culprit. "Bring him in; bring him in!"

"Take care," cried Mrs. Squeers, as her husband proffered his assistance. "We tied his legs under the apron and made 'em fast to the chaise, to prevent his giving us the slip again."

With hands trembling with delight, Squeers unloosened the cord; and Smike, to all appearance more dead than alive, was brought into the house and securely locked up in a cellar, until such time as Mr. Squeers should deem it expedient to operate upon him, in presence of the assembled school.

Upon a hasty consideration of the circumstances, it may be matter of surprise to some persons, that Mr. and Mrs. Squeers should have taken so much trouble to repossess themselves of an incumbrance of which it was their wont to complain so loudly; but their surprise will cease when they are informed that the manifold services of the drudge, if performed by anybody else, would have cost the establishment some ten or twelve shillings per week in the shape of wages; and furthermore, that all runaways were, as a matter of policy, made severe examples of, at Dotheboys Hall, inasmuch as, in consequence of the limited extent of its attractions, there was but little inducement, beyond the powerful impulse of fear, for any pupil, provided with the usual number of legs and the power of using them, to remain.

The news that Smike had been caught and brought back in triumph, ran like wild-fire through the hungry community, and expectation was on tiptoe all the morning. On tiptoe it was destined to remain, however, until afternoon; when Squeers, having refreshed himself with his dinner, and further strengthened himself by an extra libation or so, made his appearance (accompanied by his amiable partner) with a countenance of portentous import, and a fearful instrument of flagellation, strong, supple, wax-ended, and new,—in short, purchased that morning, expressly for the occasion.

"Is every boy here?" asked Squeers, in a tremendous voice.

Every boy was there, but every boy was afraid to speak; so Squeers glared along the lines to assure himself; and every eye drooped, and every head cowered down, as he did so.

"Each boy keep his place," said Squeers, administering his favourite blow to the desk, and regarding with gloomy satisfaction the universal start which it never failed to occasion. "Nickleby! to your desk, sir."

It was remarked by more than one small observer, that there was a very curious and unusual expression in the usher's face; but he took his seat, without opening his lips in reply. Squeers, casting a triumphant glance at his assistant and a look of most comprehensive despotism on the boys, left the room, and shortly afterwards returned, dragging Smike by the collar—or rather by that fragment of his jacket which was nearest the place where his collar would have been, had he boasted such a decoration.

In any other place, the appearance of the wretched, jaded, spiritless object would have occasioned a murmur of compassion and remonstrance. It had some effect, even there; for the lookers-on moved uneasily in their seats; and a few of the boldest ventured to steal looks at each other, expressive of indignation and pity.

They were lost on Squeers, however, whose gaze was fastened on the luckless Smike, as he inquired, according to custom in such cases, whether he had anything to say for himself.

"Nothing, I suppose?" said Squeers, with a diabolical grin.

Smike glanced round, and his eye rested, for an instant, on Nicholas, as if he had expected him to intercede; but his look was riveted on his desk.

"Have you anything to say?" demanded Squeers again: giving his right arm two or three flourishes to try its power and suppleness. "Stand a little out of the way, Mrs. Squeers, my dear; I've hardly got room enough."

"Spare me, sir!" cried Smike.

"Oh! that's all, is it?' said Squeers. "Yes, I'll flog you within an inch of your life, and spare you that."

"Ha, ha, ha," laughed Mrs. Squeers, "that's a good un!"

"I was driven to do it," said Smike faintly; and casting another imploring look about him.

"Driven to do it, were you?" said Squeers. "Oh! it wasn't your fault; it was mine, I suppose—eh?"

"A nasty, ungrateful, pig-headed, brutish, obstinate, sneaking dog," exclaimed Mrs. Squeers, taking Smike's head under her arm, and administering a cuff at every epithet; "what does he mean by that?"

"Stand aside, my dear," replied Squeers. "We'll try and find out."

Mrs. Squeers being out of breath with her exertions, complied. Squeers caught the boy firmly in his grip; one desperate cut had fallen on his body—he was wincing from the lash and uttering a scream of pain—it was raised again, and again about to fall—when Nicholas Nickleby suddenly starting up, cried "Stop!" in a voice that made the rafters ring.

"Who cried stop?" said Squeers, turning savagely round.

"I," said Nicholas, stepping forward. "This must not go on."

"Must not go on!" cried Squeers, almost in a shriek.

"No!" thundered Nicholas.

Aghast and stupefied by the boldness of the interference, Squeers released his hold of Smike, and, falling back a pace or two, gazed upon Nicholas with looks that were positively frightful.

"I say must not," repeated Nicholas, nothing daunted; "shall not. I will prevent it."

Squeers continued to gaze upon him, with his eyes starting out of his head; but astonishment had actually, for the moment, bereft him of speech.

"You have disregarded all my quiet interference in the miserable lad's behalf," said Nicholas; "you have returned no answer to the letter in which I begged forgiveness for him, and offered to be responsible that he would remain quietly here. Don't blame me for this public interference. You have brought it upon yourself; not I."

"Sit down, beggar!" screamed Squeers, almost beside himself with rage, and seizing Smike as he spoke.

"Wretch," rejoined Nicholas, fiercely, "touch him at your peril! I will not stand by, and see it done. My blood is up, and I have the strength of ten such men as you. Look to yourself, for by Heaven I will not spare you, if you drive me on!"

"Stand back" cried Squeers, brandishing his weapon.

"I have a long series of insults to avenge," said Nicholas, flushed with passion; "and my indignation is aggravated by the dastardly cruelties practised on helpless infancy in this foul den. Have a care; for if you do raise the devil within me, the consequences shall fall heavily upon your own head!"

He had scarcely spoken, when Squeers, in a violent outbreak of wrath, and with a cry like the howl of a wild beast, spat upon him, and struck him a blow across the face with his instrument of toruture, which raised up a bar of livid flesh as it was inflicted. Smarting with the agony of the blow, and concentrating into that one moment all his feelings of rage, scorn, and indignation, Nicholas spring upon him, wrested the weapon from his hand, and pinning him by the throat, beat the ruffian till he roared for mercy.

The boys—with the exception of Master Squeers, who, coming to his father's assistance harassed the enemy in the rear—moved not, hand or foot; but Mrs. Squeers, with many shrieks for aid, hung on to the tail of her partner's coat, and endeavoured to drag him from his infuriated adversary; while Miss Squeers, who had been peeping through the key-hole in expectation of a very different scene, darted in at the very beginning of the attack, and after launching a shower of inkstands at the usher's head, beat Nicholas to her heart's content: animating herself at every blow, with the recollection of his having refused her proffered love, and thus imparting additional strength to an arm which (as she took after her mother in this respect) was, at no time, one of the weakest.

Nicholas, in the full torrent of his violence, felt the blows no more than if they had been dealt with feathers; but, becoming tired of the noise and uproar, and feeling that his arm grew weak besides, he threw all his remaining strength into half-a-dozen finishing cuts, and flung Squeers from him, with all the force he could muster. The violence of his fall precipitated Mrs. Squeers completely over an adjacent form; and Squeers striking his head against it in his descent, lay at his full length on the ground, stunned and motionless.

Having brought affairs to this happy termination, and ascertained, to his thorough satisfaction, that Squeers was only stunned, and not dead (upon which point he had had some unpleasant doubts at first), Nicholas left his family to restore him, and retired to consider what course he had better adopt. He looked anxiously round for Smike, as he left the room, but he was nowhere to be seen.

After a brief consideration, he packed up a few clothes in a small leathern valise, and, finding that nobody offered to oppose his progress, marched boldly out by the front door, and shortly afterwards, struck into the road which led to Greta Bridge.

HENRIK IBSEN

A DOLL'S HOUSE

In *A Doll's House,* Ibsen took up a theme that shocked late nineteenth-century bourgeois audiences: a woman leaving her husband and children in search of self-realization. Nora Helmer resents being a submissive and dutiful wife to a husband who does not take her seriously, who treats her like a child, a doll.

In the following selection from A Doll's House, Nora tells her husband, Torvald, how she resents being treated like a child and why she is leaving him.

(She sits down at one side of the table.)

HELMER Nora—what is this?—this cold, set face?

NORA Sit down. It will take some time; I have a lot to talk over with you.

HELMER *(sits down at the opposite side of the table)* You alarm me, Nora!—and I don't understand you.

NORA No, that is just it. You don't understand me, and I have never understood you either—before to-night. No, you mustn't interrupt me. You must simply listen to what I say. Torvald, this is a settling of accounts.

HELMER What do you mean by that?

NORA *(after a short silence).* Isn't there one thing that strikes you as strange in our sitting here like this?

HELMER What is that?

NORA We have been married now eight years. Does it not occur to you that this is the first time we two, you and I, husband and wife, have had a serious conversation?

HELMER What do you mean by serious?

NORA In all these eight years—longer than that—from the very beginning of our acquaintance, we have never exchanged a word on any serious subject.

HELMER Was it likely that I would be continually and for ever telling you about worries that you could not help me to bear?

NORA I am not speaking about business matters. I say that we have never sat down in earnest together to try and get at the bottom of anything.

HELMER But, dearest Nora, would it have been any good to you?

NORA That is just it; you have never understood me. I have been greatly wronged, Torvald—first by papa and then by you.

HELMER What! By us two—by us two, who have loved you better than anyone else in the world?

NORA *(shaking her head)* You have never loved me. You have only thought it pleasant to be in love with me.

HELMER Nora, what do I hear you saying?

NORA It is perfectly true, Torvald. When I was at home with papa, he told me his opinion about everything, and so I had the same opinions; and if I differed from him I concealed the fact, because he would not have liked it. He called me his doll-child, and he played with me just as I used to play with my dolls. And when I came to live with you—

HELMER What sort of an expression is that to use about our marriage?

NORA *(undisturbed)* I mean that I was simply transferred from papa's hands into yours. You arranged everything according to your own taste, and so I got the same tastes as you—or else I pretended to, I am really not quite sure which—I think sometimes the one and sometimes the other. When I look back on it, it seems to me as if I had been living here like a poor woman—just from hand to mouth. I have existed merely to perform tricks for you Torvald. But you would have it so. You and papa have committed a great sin against me. It is your fault that I have made nothing of my life.

HELMER How unreasonable and how ungrateful you are, Nora! Have you not been happy here?

Nora No, I have never been happy. I thought I was, but it has never really been so.

Helmer Not—not happy!

Nora No, only merry. And you have always been so kind to me. But our home has been nothing but a playroom. I have been your doll-wife, just as at home I was papa's doll- child; and here the children have been my dolls. I thought it great fun when you played with me, just as they thought it great fun when I played with them. That is what our marriage has been, Torvald.

Helmer There is some truth in what you say—exaggerated and strained as your view of it is. But for the future it shall be different. Playtime shall be over, and lesson-time shall begin.

Nora Whose lessons? Mine, or the children's?

Helmer Both yours and the children's, my darling Nora.

Nora Alas, Torvald, you are not the man to educate me into being a proper wife for you.

Helmer And you can say that!

Nora And I—how am I fitted to bring up the children?

Helmer Nora!

Nora Didn't you say so yourself a little while ago—that you dare not trust me to bring them up?

Helmer In a moment of anger! Why do you pay any heed to that?

Nora Indeed, you were perfectly right. I am not fit for the task. There is another task I must undertake first. I must try and educate myself—you are not the man to help me in that. I must do that for myself. And that is why I am going to leave you now.

Helmer *(springing up)* What do you say?

Nora I must stand quite alone, if I am to understand myself and everything about me. It is for that reason that I cannot remain with you any longer.

Helmer Nora! Nora!

Nora I am going away from here now, at once. I am sure Christine will take me in for the night—

Helmer You are out of your mind! I won't allow it! I forbid you!

Nora It is no use forbidding me anything any longer. I will take with me what belongs to myself. I will take nothing from you, either now or later.

Helmer What sort of madness is this!

Nora To-morrow I shall go home—I mean, to my old home. It will be easiest for me to find something to do there.

Helmer You blind, foolish woman!

Nora I must try and get some sense, Torvald.

Helmer To desert your home, your husband and your children! And you don't consider what people will say!

Nora I cannot consider that at all. I only know that it is necessary for me.

Helmer It's shocking. This is how you would neglect your most sacred duties.

Nora What do you consider my most sacred duties?

Helmer Do I need to tell you that? Are they not your duties to your husband and your children?

Nora I have other duties just as sacred.

Helmer That you have not. What duties could those be?

Nora Duties to myself.

Helmer Before all else, you are a wife and a mother.

Nora I don't believe that any longer. I believe that before all else I am a reasonable human being, just as you are— or, at all events, that I must try and become one. I know quite well, Torvald, that most people would think you right, and that views of that kind are to be found in books; but I can no longer content myself with what most people say, or with what is found in books. I must think over things for myself and get to understand them.

Helmer Can you not understand your place in your own home? Have you not a reliable guide in such matters as that?—have you no religion?

Nora I am afraid, Torvald, I do not exactly know what religion is.

HELMER What are you saying?

NORA I know nothing but what the clergyman said, when I went to be confirmed. He told us that religion was this, and that, and the other. When I am away from all this, and am alone, I will look into that matter too. I will see if what the clergyman said is true, or at all events if it is true for me.

HELMER This is unheard of in a girl of your age! But if religion cannot lead you aright, let me try and awaken your conscience. I suppose you have some moral sense? Or—answer me—am I to think you have none?

NORA I assure you, Torvald, that is not an easy question to answer. I really don't know. The thing perplexes me altogether. I only know that you and I look at it in quite a different light. I am learning, too, that the law is quite another thing from what I supposed; but I find it impossible to convince myself that the law is right. According to it a woman has no right to spare her old dying father, or to save her husband's life. I can't believe that.

HELMER You talk like a child. You don't understand the conditions of the world in which you live.

NORA No, I don't. But now I am going to try. I am going to see if I can make out who is right, the world or I.

HELMER You are ill, Nora; you are delirious; I almost think you are out of your mind.

NORA I have never felt my mind so clear and certain as tonight.

HELMER And is it with a clear and certain mind that you forsake your husband and your children?

NORA Yes, it is.

HELMER Then there is only one possible explanation.

NORA What is that?

HELMER You do not love me any more.

NORA No, that is just it.

HELMER Nora!—and you can say that?

NORA It gives me great pain, Torvald, for you have always been so kind to me, but I cannot help it. I do not love you any more.

HELMER *(regaining his composure)* Is that a clear and certain conviction too?

NORA Yes, absolutely clear and certain. That is the reason I will not stay here any longer.

HELMER And can you tell me what I have done to forfeit your love?

NORA Yes, indeed I can. It was to-night, when the wonderful thing did not happen; then I saw you were not the man I had thought you.

HELMER Explain yourself better—I don't understand you.

NORA I have waited so patiently for eight years; for goodness knows, I knew very well that wonderful things don't happen everyday. Then this horrible misfortune came upon me; and then I felt quite certain that the wonderful thing was going to happen at last. When Krogstad's letter was lying out there, never for a moment did I imagine that you would consent to accept this man's conditions. I was so absolutely certain that you would say to him: Publish the thing to the whole world. And when that was done—

HELMER Yes, what then?—when I had exposed my wife to shame and disgrace?

NORA When that was done, I was so absolutely certain, you would come forward and take everything upon yourself, and say: I am the guilty one.

HELMER Nora !

NORA You mean that I would never have accepted such a sacrifice on your part? No, of course not. But what would my assurances have been worth against yours? That was the wonderful thing which I hoped for and feared; and it was to prevent that, that I wanted to kill myself.

HELMER I would gladly work night and day for you, Nora— bear sorrow and want for your sake. But no man would sacrifice his honour for the one he loves.

NORA It is a thing hundreds of thousands of women have done.

HELMER Oh, you think and talk like a heedless child.

NORA Maybe. But you neither think nor talk like the man I could bind myself to. As soon as your fear was over—and it was not fear for what threatened me, but for what might happen to you—when the whole thing was past, as far as you were concerned it was exactly as if nothing at all had happened. Exactly as before, I was your little skylark, your doll, which you would in future treat with doubly gentle care, because it was so brittle and fragile. *(Getting up.)* Torvald—it was then it dawned upon me that for eight years I had been living here with a strange man, and had borne him three children. Oh, I can't bear to think of it! I could tear myself into little bits!

HELMER *(sadly)* I see, I see. An abyss has opened between us—there is no denying it. But, Nora, would it not be possible to fill it up?

NORA As I am now, I am no wife for you

HELMER I have it in me to become a different man.

NORA Perhaps—if your doll is taken away from you.

HELMER But to part!—to part from you! No, no. Nora, I can't understand that idea.

NORA *(going out to the right)* That makes it more certain that it must be done. *(She comes back with her cloak and hat and a small bag which she puts on a chair by the table.)*

HELMER Nora, Nora, not now! Wait till to-morrow.

NORA *(putting on her cloak)* I cannot spend the night in a strange man's room.

HELMER But can't we live here like brother and sister ?

NORA *(putting on her hat)* You know very well that would not last long. *(Puts the shawl round her.)* Good-bye, Torvald. I won't see the little ones. I know they are in better hands than mine. As I am now, I can be of no use to them.

HELMER But some day, Nora—some day?

NORA How can I tell? I have no idea what is going to become of me.

HELMER But you are my wife, whatever becomes of you.

NORA Listen, Torvald. I have heard that when a wife deserts her husband's house, as I am doing now, he is legally freed from all obligations towards her. In any case I set you free from all your obligations. You are not to feel yourself bound in the slightest way, any more than I shall. There must be perfect freedom on both sides. See here is your ring back. Give me mine.

HELMER That too?

NORA That too.

HELMER Here it is.

NORA That's right. Now it is all over. I have put the keys here. The maids know all about everything in the house— better than I do. To-morrow, after I have left her, Christine will come here and pack up my own things that I brought with me from home. I will have them sent after me.

HELMER All over! All over!—Nora, shall you never think of me again?

NORA I know I shall often think of you and the children and this house.

HELMER May I write to you, Nora?

NORA No—never. You must not do that.

HELMER But at least let me send you

NORA Nothing—nothing

HELMER Let me help you if you are in want.

NORA No. I can receive nothing from a stranger.

HELMER Nora—can I never be anything more than a stranger to you?

NORA *(taking her bag)* Ah, Torvald, the most wonderful thing of all would have to happen.

HELMER Tell me what that would be!

NORA Both you and I would have to be so changed that .

OH, Torvald, I don't believe any longer in wonderful things happening.

HELMER But I will believe in it. Tell me? So changed that ?

NORA That our life together would be a real wedlock. Good-bye.

(She goes out through the hall.)

HELMER *(sinks down on a chair at the door and buries his face in his hands)* Nora! Nora! *(looks round, and rises.)* Empty. She is gone. *(A hope flashes across his mind.)* The most wonderful thing of all? *(The sound of a door shutting is heard from below.)*

LEO TOLSTOY

ANNA KARENINA

No Russian writer has greater fame outside of his homeland than Leo Tolstoy who is renown, not only as an author, but also as a reformer and religious philosopher. Tolstoy was an aristocrat and former soldier who believed that for a work of literature to be good it must come "singing from the author's soul" and make commonplace feelings procurable by all people. This was what he called "universal art." During his many travels throughout Europe, Tolstoy witnessed the problems that freed serfs faced, and, following their liberation in 1861, he worked actively to set up schools for peasants patterned after those he had encountered during his travels. In 1862, he married Sophie Andreyevna Behrs with whom he had fifteen children. But throughout much of his life, Tolstoy suffered from an inner conflict—he was torn between his natural instincts and his zest for life and his moral responsibility to make life better for those who had less than he did. But by 1877, his inner torment was resolved through a religious conversion. The centerpiece of Tolstoy's faith was not dogma but morality. For him, Jesus was not divine but a genuine ethical person and teacher who set a noble example of loving humanity and repudiating violence and hate, and following Jesus' path was the avenue to personal happiness.

The novel that many critics regard as one of the finest novels ever written is Tolstoy's *Anna Karenina* (1874-1876), his classic story of love and adultery in Russian high society. In it, Tolstoy probes the complexities of marital relationships, including a wife's adultery, the lure of illicit passion, and a woman's place in society. The Russian aristocracy may have had a casual attitude toward marital fidelity, but for Tolstoy a violation of the sacred bond of marriage was a crime that incurred severe punishment. Anna Arkadyevna Karenina is a beautiful woman of the social elite who is married to Alexey Alexandrovich Karenin, an influential governmental official who obsesses over both his money and his social position. The fact that he cares little for Anna's sexual passion or her personal happiness makes her susceptible to the social graces of Count Alexey Kirilich Vronsky—who epitomizes high society on a grand scale. Vronsky loves women and loves flaunting his money. In contrast to the torrid love affair of Anna and Vronsky is the relationship of Princess Catherine Alexandrovna Shtcherbatskaya (known as Kitty) with Konstantin Dmitrich Levin, a man who recognizes (as did Tolstoy) that land is the tie that binds families and societies one to another. It is Levin who serves as Tolstoy's mouthpiece in asserting the simplicity of the pastoral life and his appreciation for the work of the peasants on the land. Tolstoy had no love for industrialization and capitalism, hallmarks of the modern age, and on nearly every page, he provides the reader with illuminating descriptions of the upper classes of Russian society. Much of this is evident in the following passage—an argument between Kitty's parents (Prince and Princess Shtcherbatskaya) over whether she should pin her hopes on Levin (her father's choice) or follow her passion for Vronsky, with whom she is completely enamored (her mother's preference). Moreover, Tolstoy uses the encounter to contrast the marriage customs in England, where free choice was generally favored, and the arranged marriages which predominated in France.

The young Princess Kitty Shtcherbatskaya was eighteen. It was the first winter that she had been out in the world. Her success in society had been greater than that of either of her elder sisters, and greater even than her mother had anticipated. To say nothing of the young men who danced at the Moscow balls being almost all in love with Kitty, two serious suitors had already this first winter made their appearance: Levin, and immediately after his departure, Count Vronsky.

Levin's appearance at the beginning of the winter, his frequent visits, and evident love for Kitty, had led to the first serious conversations between Kitty's parents as to her future, and to disputes between them. The prince was on Levin's side; he said he wished for nothing better for Kitty. The princess for her part, going round the question in the manner peculiar to women, maintained that Kitty was too young, that Levin had done nothing to prove that he had serious intentions, that Kitty felt no great attraction to him, and other side issues; but she did not state the principal point, which was that she looked for a better match for her daughter, and that Levin was not to her liking, and she did not understand him. When Levin had abruptly departed, the princess was delighted, and said to her husband triumphantly: "You see I was right." When Vronsky appeared on the scene, she was still more delighted, confirmed in her opinion that Kitty was to make not simply a good, but a brilliant match.

In the mother's eyes there could be no comparison between Vronsky and Levin. She disliked in Levin his strange and uncompromising opinions and his shyness in society, founded, as she supposed, on his pride and his queer sort of life, as she considered it, absorbed in cattle and peasants. She did not very much like it that he, who was in love with her daughter, had kept coming to the house for six weeks, as though he were waiting for something, inspecting, as though he were afraid he might be doing them too great an honor by making an offer, and did not realize that a man, who continually visits at a house where there is a young unmarried girl, is bound to make his intentions clear. And suddenly, without doing so, he disappeared. "It's as well he's not attractive enough for Kitty to have fallen in love with him," thought the mother.

Vronsky satisfied all the mother's desires. Very wealthy, clever, of aristocratic family, on the highroad to a brilliant career in the army and at court, and a fascinating man. Nothing better could be wished for.

Vronsky openly flirted with Kitty at balls, danced with her and came continually to the house; consequently there could be no doubt of the seriousness of his intentions. But, in spite of that the mother had spent the whole of that winter in a state of terrible anxiety and agitation.

Princess Shtcherbatskaya had herself been married thirty years ago, her aunt arranging the match. Her husband, about whom everything was well known beforehand, had come, looked at his future bride, and been looked at. The matchmaking aunt had ascertained and communicated their mutual impression. That impression had been favorable. Afterwards, on a day fixed beforehand, the expected offer was made to her parents, and accepted. All had passed very simply and easily. So it seemed, at least, to the princess. But over her own daughters she had felt how far from simple and easy is the business, apparently so commonplace, of marrying off one's daughters. The panics that had been lived through, the thoughts that had been brooded over, the money that had been wasted, and the disputes with her husband over marrying the two older girls, Darya and Natalia! Now, since the youngest had come out, she was going through the same terrors, the same doubts, and still more violent quarrels with her husband than she had over the elder girls. The old prince, like all fathers indeed, was exceedingly punctilious on the score of the honor and reputation of his daughters. He was ir rationally jealous over his daughters, especially over Kitty, who was his favorite. At every turn he had scenes with the princess for compromising her daughter. The princess had grown accustomed to this already with her other daughters, but now she felt that there was more ground for the prince's touchiness. She saw that of late years much was changed in the manners of society, that a mother's duties had become still more difficult. She saw that girls of Kitty's age formed some sort of clubs, went to some sort of lectures, mixed freely in men's society; drove about the streets alone, many of them did not curtsey, and, what was the most important thing, all the girls were firmly convinced that to choose their husbands was their own affair, and not their parents'. "Marriages aren't made nowadays as they used to be," was thought and said by all these young girls, and even by their elders. But how marriages were made now, the princess could not learn from any one. The French fashion—of the parents arranging their children's future—was not accepted; it was condemned. The English fashion of the complete independence of girls was also not accepted, and not possible in Russian society. The Russian fashion of matchmaking by the offices of intermediate persons was for some reason considered unseemly; it was ridiculed by every one and by the princess herself. But how girls were to be married, and how parents were to marry them, no one knew. Every one with whom the princess had chanced to discuss the matter said the same thing: "Mercy on us, it's high time in our day to cast off all that old-fashioned business. It's the young people have to marry, and not their parents; and so we ought to leave the young people to arrange it as they choose." It was very easy for any one to say that who had no daughters, but the princess realized that in the process of getting to know each other, her daughter might fall in love, and fall in love with some one who did not care to marry her or who was quite unfit to be her husband. And, however much it was instilled into the princess that in our times young people ought to arrange their lives for themselves, she was unable to believe it, just as she would have been unable to believe that, at any time whatever, the most suitable playthings for children five years old ought to be loaded pistols. And so the princess was more uneasy over Kitty than she had been over her elder sisters.

Although Anno is married to Karenin and has a son with him, she leaves both of them for Vronsky with whom she later has a child. While Vronsky is still able to participate in the social life he has always savored, Anna finds herself shunned by the society that once adored her, and she is jealous of Vronsky's social freedom. This is evident in the following selection in which the aristocratic couple, the Kartasovs, refuse to sit next to the couple—Anna and Yashvin, Anna's escort for the evening—in the adjoining box at the theater. Even though Vronsky goes to Anna following her "hideous" treatment, he begins to feel the pressure of such chronic societal wariness, which compromises his social standing, and his love for Anna begins to wane.

Vronsky for the first time, experienced a feeling of anger against Anna, almost a hatred for her willfully refusing to understand her own position. This feeling was aggravated by his being unable to tell her plainly the cause of his anger. If he had told her directly what he was thinking, he would have said:

"In that dress, with a princess only too well known to every one, to show yourself at the theater is equivalent not merely to acknowledging your position as a fallen woman, but is flinging down a challenge to society, that is to say, cutting yourself off from it forever."

He could not say that to her. "But how can she fail to see it, and what is going on in her?" he said to himself. He felt at the same time that his respect for her was diminished while his sense of her beauty was intensified. . . .

Vronsky went into the theater at half-past eight. The performance was in full swing. The little old box-keeper, recognizing Vronsky as he helped him off with his fur coat, called him "Your Excellency," and suggested he should not take a number but should simply call Fyodor. In the brightly lighted corridor there was no one but the box-opener and two attendants with fur cloaks on their arms listening at the doors. Through the closed doors came the sounds of the discreet *staccato* accompaniment of the orchestra, and a single female voice rendering distinctly a musical phrase. The door opened to let the box-opener slip through, and the phrase, drawing to the end reached Vronsky's hearing clearly. But the doors were closed again at once, and Vronsky did not hear the end of the phrase and the cadence of the accompaniment, though he knew from the thunder of applause that it was over. When he entered the hall, brilliantly lighted with chandeliers and gas jets, the noise was still going on. On the stage the singer, bowing and smiling, with bare shoulders flashing with diamonds, was, with the help of the tenor who had given her his arm, gathering up the bouquets that were flying awkwardly over the footlights. Then she went up to a gentleman with glossy pomaded hair parted down the center, who was stretching across the footlights holding out something to her, and all the public in the stalls as well as in the boxes was in excitement, craning forward, shouting and clapping. The conductor in his high chair assisted in passing the offering, and straightened his white tie. Vronsky walked into the middle of the stalls, and, standing still, began looking about him. That day less than ever was his attention turned upon the familiar, habitual surroundings, the stage, the noise, all the familiar, uninteresting, parti-colored herd of spectators in the packed theater.

There were, as always, the same ladies of some sort with officers of some sort in the back of the boxes; the same gaily dressed women—God knows who—and uniforms and black coats; the same dirty crowd in the upper gallery; and among the crowd, in the boxes and in the front rows, were some forty of the *real* people. And to those oases Vronsky at once directed his attention, and with them he entered at once into relation. . . .

Vronsky had not yet seen Anna. He purposely avoided looking in her direction. But he knew by the direction of people's eyes where she was. . . .

{Vronsky} moved his opera-glass from the stalls and scanned the boxes. Near a lady in a turban and a bald old man, who seemed to wave angrily in the moving opera glass, Vronsky suddenly caught sight of Anna's head, proud, strikingly beautiful, and smiling in the frame of lace. She was in the fifth box, twenty paces from him. She was sitting in front, and slightly turning, was saying something to Yashvin. The setting of her head on her handsome, broad shoulders, and the restrained excitement and brilliance of her eyes and her whole face reminded him of her just as he had seen her at the ball in Moscow. But he felt utterly different towards her beauty now. In his feeling for her now there was no element of mystery, and so her beauty, though it attracted him even more intensely than before, gave him now a sense of injury. She was not looking in his direction, but Vronsky felt that she had seen him already. . . .

In that box on the left were the Kartasovs. Vronsky knew them, and knew that Anna was acquainted with them. Madame Kartasova, a thin little woman, was standing up in her box, and, her back turned upon Anna, she was putting on a mantle that her husband was holding for her. Her face was pale and angry, and she was talking excitedly. Kartasov, a fat, bald man, was continually looking round at Anna, while he attempted to soothe his wife. When the wife had gone out, the husband lingered a long while, and tried to catch Anna's eye, obviously anxious to bow to her. But Anna, with unmistakable intention, avoided noticing him, and talked to Yashvin, whose cropped head was bent down to her. Kartasov went out without making his salutation, and the box was left empty.

Vronsky could not understand exactly what had passed between the Kartasovs and Anna, but he saw that something humiliating for Anna had happened. He knew this both from what he had seen, and most of all from the face of Anna, who, he could see, was taxing every nerve to carry through the part she had taken up. And in maintaining this attitude of external composure she was completely successful. Any one who did not know her and her circle, who had not heard all the utterances of the women expressive of commiseration, indignation, and amazement, that she should show herself in society, and show herself so conspicuously with her lace and her beauty, would have admired the serenity and loveliness of this woman without a suspicion that she was undergoing the sensations of a man in the stocks.

Knowing that something had happened, but not knowing precisely what, Vronsky felt a thrill of agonizing anxiety, and hoping to find out something, he went towards his brother's box. . . .

. . . With rapid steps he went downstairs; he felt that he must do something, but he did not know what. Anger with her for having put herself and him in such a false position, together with pity for her suffering, filled his heart. . . .

Noticing in the next act that her box was empty, Vronsky, rousing indignant "hushes" in the silent audience, went out in the middle of a solo and drove home.

Anna was already at home. When Vronsky went up to her, she was in the same dress as she had worn at the theater. She was sitting in the first armchair against the wall, looking straight before her. She looked at him, and at once resumed her former position.

"Anna," he said.

"You, you are to blame for everything!" she cried, with tears of despair and hatred in her voice, getting up.

"I begged, I implored you not to go; I knew it would be unpleasant. ..."

"Unpleasant!" she cried— "hideous! As long as I live I shall never forget it. She said it was a disgrace to sit beside me."

"A silly woman's chatter," he said: "but why risk it, why provoke? ..."

"I hate your calm. You ought not to have brought me to this. If you had loved me ..."

"Anna! How does the question of my love come in?"

"Oh, if you loved me, as I love, if you were tortured as I am! ..." she said, looking at him with an expression of terror.

He was sorry for her, and angry notwithstanding. He assured her of his love because he saw that this was the only means of soothing her, and he did not reproach her in words, but in his heart he reproached her.

And the asseverations of his love, which seemed to him so vulgar that he was ashamed to utter them, she drank in eagerly, and gradually became calmer. The next day, completely reconciled, they left for the country.

Anna's deceitful relationship with Count Vronsky ends in the loss of everything Anna cherishes, causing her to commit suicide by throwing herself under a train. Unlike Anna, who seeks life's purpose totally through romantic love, Levin's concern for spiritual development—by discovering "one should live for the soul"— provides him with a vehicle for meaning and happiness, and it enhances his marriage to Kitty.

FYODOR DOSTOYEVSKY

NOTES FROM UNDERGROUND

Because he perceived human beings as inherently depraved, irrational, and rebellious and probed the unconscious mind, Dostoevsky was also a forerunner of the modernist movement in thought and culture (see Chapter 16). The work that best links Dostoevsky to the modernist movement is *Notes from Underground* (1864). In this work, the narrator (the Underground Man) rebels against the efforts of rationalists, humanists, liberals, and socialists to define human nature according to universal principles and to reform society so as to promote greater happiness. He rebels against science and reason, against the entire liberal and socialist vision. He does so in the name of human subjectivity: the uncontain- able, irrepressible, whimsical, and foolish human will. Human nature, says the Underground Man, is too volatile, too diversified to be schematized by the theoretical mind.

For the Underground Man, there are no absolute and timeless truths that precede the individual and to which the individual should conform. There is only a terrifying world of naked wills vying with one another. In such a world, people do not necessarily seek happiness, prosperity, and peace—all that is good for them, according to "enlightened" thinkers. To the rationalist who aims to eliminate suffering and deprivation, Dostoevsky replies that some people freely choose suffering and depravity because it gratifies them—for some, "even in a toothache there is enjoyment"—and they are repelled by wealth, peace, security, and happiness. If Dostoevsky is right, if individuals do not act out of enlightened self-interest, if they are driven by instinctual cravings that resist reasons appeals, then what hope is there for a social planner wishing to create the "good" society?

In rejecting external security and liberal and socialist concepts of progress—in aspiring to assert his own individuality even if this means acting against his own best interests—the Underground Man demonstrates that a powerful element of irrationality underlies human nature, an element that reason can neither understand nor justify. In succeeding decades, philosophers, social theorists, and literary figures would become preoccupied with this theme.

In the first part of *Notes from Underground,* the Underground Man addresses an imaginary audience. In a long monologue, he expresses a revulsion for the liberal-rationalist assertion that with increased enlightenment, people would "become good and noble," that they would realize it was to their advantage to pursue "prosperity, wealth, [political] freedom, peace." The Underground Man argues that the individuals principal concern is not happiness or security but a free and unfettered will.

. . . Oh, tell me, who first declared, who first proclaimed, that man only does nasty things because he does not know his own real interests; and that if he were enlightened, if his eyes were opened to his real normal interests, man would at once cease to do nasty things, would at once become good and noble because, being enlightened and understanding his real advantage, he would see his own advantage in the good and nothing else, and we all know that not a single man can knowingly act to his own disadvantage. Consequently, so to say, he would begin doing good through necessity. Oh! the babe! Oh, the pure, innocent child! Why, in the first place, when in all these thousands of years has there ever been a time when man has acted only for his own advantage? What is to be done with the millions of facts that bear witness that men, *knowingly,* that is, fully understanding their real advantages, have left them in the background and have rushed headlong on another path, to risk, to chance, compelled to this course by nobody and by nothing, but, as it were, precisely because they did not want the beaten track, and stubbornly, willfully, went off on another difficult, absurd way seeking it almost in the darkness. After all, it means that this stubbornness and willfulness were more pleasant to them than any advantage. Advantage! What is advantage? And will you take it upon yourself to define with perfect accuracy in exactly what the advantage of man consists of? And what if it so happens that a man's advantage *sometimes* not only may, but even must, consist exactly in his desiring under certain conditions what is harmful to himself and not what is advantageous. . . . After all, you, [imaginary] gentlemen, so far as

I know, have taken your whole register of human advantages from the average of statistical figures and scientific-economic formulas. After all, your advantages are prosperity, wealth, freedom, peace—and so on, and so on. So that a man who, for instance, would openly and knowingly oppose that whole list would, to your thinking, and indeed to mine too, of course, be an obscurantist [one who prevents enlightenment] or an absolute madman, would he not? But, after all, here is something amazing: why does it happen that all these statisticians, sages and lovers of humanity, when they calculate human advantages invariably leave one out! . . .

. . . The fact is, gentlemen, it seems that something that is dearer to almost every man than his greatest advantages must really exist, or (not to be illogical) there is one most advantageous advantage (the very one omitted of which we spoke just now) which is more important and more advantageous than all other advantages, for which, if necessary, a man is ready to act in opposition to all laws, that is, in opposition to reason, honor, peace, prosperity—in short, in opposition to all those wonderful and useful things if only he can attain that fundamental, most advantageous advantage which is dearer to him than all. . . .

. . . Why, one may choose what is contrary to one's own interests, and sometimes one *positively ought* (that is my idea). One's own free unfettered choice, one's own fancy, however wild it may be, one's own fancy worked up at times to frenzy—why that is that very "most advantageous advantage" which we have overlooked, which comes under no classification and through which all systems and theories are continually being sent to the devil. And how do these sages know that man must necessarily need a rationally advantageous choice? What man needs is simply *independent* choice, whatever that independence may cost and wherever it may lead. Well, choice, after all, the devil only knows. . . .

Life is more than reasoning, more than "simply extracting square roots," declares the Underground Man. The will, which is "a manifestation of all life," is more precious than reason. Simply to have their own way, human beings will do something stupid, self-destructive, irrational. Reason constitutes only a small part of the human personality.

. . . You see, gentlemen, reason, gentlemen, is an excellent thing, there is no disputing that, but reason is only reason and can only satisfy man's rational faculty, while will is a manifestation of all life, that is, of all human life including reason as well as all impulses. And although our life, in this manifestation of it, is often worthless, yet it is life nevertheless and not simply extracting square roots. After all, here I, for instance, quite naturally want to live, in order to satisfy all my faculties for life, and not simply my rational faculty, that is, not simply one-twentieth of all my faculties for life. What does reason know? Reason only knows what it has succeeded in learning (some things it will perhaps never learn; while this is nevertheless no comfort, why not say so frankly?) and human nature acts as a whole, with everything that is in it, consciously or unconsciously, and, even if it goes wrong, it lives. I suspect, gentlemen, that you are looking at me with compassion; you repeat to me that an enlightened and developed man, such, in short, as the future man will be, cannot knowingly desire anything disadvantageous to himself, that this can be proved mathematically. I thoroughly agree, it really can—by mathematics. But I repeat for the hundredth time, there is one case, one only, when man may purposely, consciously, desire what is injurious to himself, what is stupid, very stupid—simply in order *to have the right* to desire for himself even what is very stupid and not to be bound by an obligation to desire only what is rational. After all, this very stupid thing, after all, this caprice of ours, may really be more advantageous for us, gentlemen, than anything else on earth, especially in some cases. And in particular it may be more advantageous than any advantages even when it does us obvious harm, and contradicts the soundest conclusions of our reason about our advantage—because in any case it preserves for us what is most precious and most important—that is, our personality, our individuality. Some, you see, maintain that this really is the most precious thing for man; desire can, of course, if it desires, be in agreement with reason; particularly if it does not abuse this practice but does so in moderation, it is both useful and sometimes even praiseworthy. But very of ten, and even most often, desire completely and stubbornly opposes reason, and . . . and . . . and do you know that that, too, is useful and sometimes even praiseworthy?

To intellectuals who want to "cure men of their old habits and reform their will in accordance with science and common sense," the Underground Man asks: Is it possible or even desirable to reform human beings? Perhaps they prefer uncertainty and caprice, chaos and destruction, or just living in their own way. How else do they preserve their uniqueness?

... In short, one may say anything about the history of the world—anything that might enter the most disordered imagination. The only thing one cannot say is that it is rational. The very word sticks in one's throat. And, indeed, this is even the kind of thing that continually happens. After all, there are continually turning up in life moral and rational people, sages, and lovers of humanity, who make it their goal for life to live as morally and rationally as possible, to be, so to speak, a light to their neighbors, simply in order to show them that it is really possible to live morally and rationally in this world. And so what? We all know that those very people sooner or later toward the end of their lives have been false to themselves, playing some trick, often a most indecent one. Now I ask you: What can one expect from man since he is a creature endowed with such strange qualities? Shower upon him every earthly blessing, drown him in bliss so that nothing but bubbles would dance on the surface of his bliss, as on a sea; give him such economic prosperity that he would have nothing else to do but sleep, eat cakes and busy himself with ensuring the continuation of world history and even then man, out of sheer ingratitude, sheer libel, would play you some loathsome trick. He would even risk his cakes and would deliberately desire the most fatal rubbish, the most uneconomical absurdity, simply to introduce into all this positive rationality his fatal fantastic element. It is just his fantastic dreams, his vulgar folly, that he will desire to retain, simply in order to prove to himself (as though that were so necessary) that men still are men and not piano keys, which even if played by the laws of nature themselves threaten to be controlled so completely that soon one will be able to desire nothing but by the calendar. And, after all, that is not all: even if man really were nothing but a piano key, even if this were proved to him by natural science and mathematics, even then he would not become reasonable, but would purposely do something perverse out of sheer ingratitude, simply to have his own way. And if he does not find any means he will devise destruction and chaos, will devise sufferings of all sorts, and will thereby have his own way. He will launch a curse upon the world . . . [to] convince himself that he is a man and not a piano key! If you say that all this, too, can be calculated and tabulated, chaos and darkness and curses, so that the mere possibility of calculating it all beforehand would stop it all, and reason would reassert itself—then man would purposely go mad in order to be rid of reason and have his own way! I believe in that, I vouch for it, because, after all, the whole work of man seems really to consist in nothing but proving to himself continually that he is a man and not an organ stop. It may be at the cost of his skin! But he has proved it; he may become a caveman, but he will have proved it. And after that can one help sinning, rejoicing that it has not yet come, and that desire still depends on the devil knows what! . . .

. . . Gentlemen, I am tormented by questions; answer them for me. Now you, for instance, want to cure men of their old habits and reform their will in accordance with science and common sense. But how do you know, not only that it is possible, but also that it is *desirable,* to reform man in that way? And what leads you to the conclusion that it is so *necessary* to reform man's desires? In short, how do you know that such a reformation will really be advantageous to man? And go to the heart of the matter, why are you *so sure* of your conviction that not to act against his real normal advantages guaranteed by the conclusions of reason and arithmetic is always advantageous for man and must be a law for all mankind? . . .

And why are you so firmly, so triumphantly convinced that only the normal and the positive—in short, only prosperity—is to the advantage of man? Is not reason mistaken about advantage? After all, perhaps man likes something besides prosperity? Perhaps he likes suffering just as much? Perhaps suffering is just as great an advantage to him as prosperity. Man is sometimes fearfully, passionately in love with suffering and that is a fact. There is no need to appeal to universal history to prove that; only ask yourself, if only you are a man and have lived at all. As far as my own personal opinion is concerned, to care only for prosperity seems to me somehow even ill-bred. Whether its good or bad, it is sometimes very pleasant to smash things, too. After all, I do not really insist on suffering or on prosperity either.

I insist on my caprice, and its being guaranteed to me when necessary. Suffering would be out of place in vaudevilles, for instance; I know that. In the crystal palace [utopia] it is even unthinkable; suffering means doubt, means negation, and what would be the good of a crystal palace if there could be any doubt about it? And yet I am sure man will never renounce real suffering, that is, destruction and chaos.

MARK TWAIN

THE ADVENTURES OF HUCKLEBERRY FINN

Portraying true-to-life characters, situations, and dialogue, the journalist, philosopher, humorist, and novelist Samuel Langhorne Clemens (1835-1910), better known as Mark Twain (a term used by riverboat pilots meaning "two fathoms"), exemplified American Realism. Twain's boyhood in Hannibal, Missouri, on the Mississippi River, is evident in his most famous novel—*The Adventures of Huckleberry Finn* (1884). Following the Civil War, Southerners introduced "Jim Crow" laws that curtailed the freedom of former slaves and legalized new forms of oppression. Twain chose to write an antislavery novel twenty years after the Civil War had ended, because in his eyes, Jim Crow was as insidious as slavery. Racism and slavery are the dominant themes of *Huck Finn,* which centers on the relationship between Huck Finn and the runaway slave Jim. Their adventures together and with young Tom Sawyer, the principal character in Twain's previous novel, allow Twain to explore the issue of child abuse and the social and moral development of two young boys. On March 17, 1885, *Huck Finn* was banned from the Concord, Massachusetts, public library. The directors of the library declared that the book was better suited for the slums than for intelligent, respectable people. They based their decision primarily on the dialect that Huck employs throughout his narration, but they also considered Huck Finn and Tom Sawyer to be unsatisfactory role models. Twain, nonetheless, predicted that his banned book would sell an additional twenty-five thousand copies (he was right).

Huck Finn, the protagonist and narrator of the novel, is the thirteen-year- old son of Pap, the town drunk, who beats him regularly. Huck, therefore, is compelled to survive by his own initiative. When Huck goes to live with the Widow Douglas and her sister Miss Watson, they effectively "civilize" him by teaching him manners and cleanliness and by sending him to church and to school. Pap, however, kidnaps Huck, and imprisons him in a cabin on the Mississippi River. To free himself from Pap, Huck escapes and fakes his own death. But while he is hiding out waiting for the commotion over his death to subside, he meets Jim, one of Miss Watson's slaves, who is fleeing the plantation, because he has overheard her say that she intends to sell him. Huck and Jim live contentedly on an island in the river, until Huck learns that people on shore believe that Jim is holed up on the island, and they issue a reward for his capture. Jim and Huck then decide to flee up the Ohio River and into the "free states" of the North where slavery is illegal. Throughout their adventures together, Huck is continually faced with the moral choice of whether to hand Jim over to the authorities because he is someone else's "property."

Jim and Huck subsequently team up with a pair of con artists, the Duke and the Dauphin (who calls himself "king"), pretenders to the French throne. In the chapter that follows, "You Can't Pray a Lie," Huck reflects on the southern scene, as well as the deceptions played out by the Duke and the Dauphin, including fake dance lessons and elocution studies. When Huck learns that they have sold Jim to a local farmer named Silas Phelps, he reflects on the moral consequences of both his actions and those of the Duke and the Dauphin. Ultimately, Huck makes the conscientious choice to free his friend Jim with the help of Tom Sawyer.

YOU CAN'T PRAY A LIE

We dasn't stop again at any town for days and days; kept right along down the river. We was down south in the warm weather now, and a mighty long ways from home. We begun to come to trees with Spanish moss on them, hanging down from the limbs like long, gray beards. It was the first I ever see it growing, and it made the woods look solemn and dismal. So now the frauds reckoned they was out of danger, and they begun to work the villages again.

First they done a lecture on temperance; but they didn't make enough for them both to get drunk on. Then in another village they started a dancing school; but they didn't know no more how to dance than a kangaroo does; so the first prance they made the general public jumped in and pranced them out of town. Another time they tried to go at yellocu- tion; but they didn't yellocute long till the audience got up and give them a solid good cussing, and made them skip out. They tackled missionarying, and mesmerizing, and doctoring, and telling fortunes, and a little of everything; but they couldn't seem to have no luck. So at last they got just about dead broke, and laid around the raft as she floated along, thinking and thinking, and never saying nothing, by the half a day at a time, and dreadful blue and desperate.

And at last they took a change and begun to lay their heads together in the wigwam and talk low and confidential two or three hours at a time. Jim and me got uneasy. We didn't like the look of it. We judged they was studying up some kind of worse deviltry than ever. We turned it over and over, and at last we made up our minds they was going to break into somebody's house or store, or was going into the counterfeit-money business, or something. So then we was pretty scared, and made up an agreement that we wouldn't have nothing in the world to do with such actions, and if we ever got the least show we would give them the cold shake and clear out and leave them behind. Well, early one morning we hid the raft in a good, safe place about two mile below a little bit of a shabby village named Pikesville, and the king he went ashore and told us all to stay hid whilst he went up to town and smelt around to see if anybody had got any wind of the "Royal Nonesuch" there yet. ("House to rob, you *mean,*" says I to myself; "and when you get through robbing it you'll come back here and wonder what has become of me and Jim and the raft—and you'll have to take it out in wondering.") And he said if he warn't back by midday the duke and me would know it was all right, and we was to come along.

So we stayed where we was. The duke he fretted and sweated around, and was in a mighty sour way. He scolded us for everything, and we couldn't seem to do nothing right; he found fault with every little thing. Something was a-brewing, sure. I was good and glad when midday come and no king; we could have a change, anyway—and maybe a chance for *the* chance on top of it. So me and the duke went up to the village, and hunted around there for the king, and by and by we found him in the back room of a little low doggery, very tight, and a lot of loafers bullyragging him for sport, and he a-cussing and a-threatening with all his might and so tight he couldn't walk, and couldn't do nothing to them. The duke he begun to abuse him for an old fool, and the king begun to sass back, and the minute they was fairly at it I lit out and shook the reefs out of my hind legs, and spun down the river road like a deer, for I see our chance; and I made up my mind that it would be a long day before they ever see me and Jim again. I got down there all out of breath but loaded up with joy, and sung out:

"Set her loose, Jim; we're all right now!"

But there warn't no answer, and nobody come out of the wigwam. Jim was gone! I set up a shout—and then another—and then another one; and run this way and that in the woods, whooping and screeching; but it warn't no use— old Jim was gone. Then I set down and cried; I couldn't help it. but I couldn't set still long. Pretty soon I went out on the road, trying to think what I better do, and I run across a boy walking, and asked him if he'd seen a strange nigger dressed so and so, and he says:

"Yes."

"Whereabouts?" says I.

"Down to Silas Phelps's place, two mile below here. He's a runaway nigger, and they've got him. Was you looking for him?"

"You bet I ain't! I run across him in the woods about an hour or two ago, and he said if I hollered he'd cut my livers out—and told me to lay down and stay where I was; and I done it. Been there ever since; afeared to come out."

"Well," he says, "you needn't be afeared no more, becuz they've got him. He run off f'm down South, som'ers."

"It's a good job they got him."

"Well, I *reckon!* There's two hundred dollars' reward on him. Its like picking up money out'n the road."

"Yes, it is—and I could 'a' had it if I'd been big enough; I see him first. Who nailed him?"

"It was an old fellow—a stranger—and he sold out his chance in him for forty dollars, becuz he's got to go up the river and can't wait. Think o' that, now! You bet *Yd* wait, if it was seven year."

"That's me, every time," says I. "But maybe his chance ain't worth no more than that, if he'll sell it so cheap. Maybe, there's something ain't straight about it."

"But it *is,* though—straight as a string. I see the handbill myself. It tells all about him, to a dot—paints him like a picture, and tells the plantation he's frum, below Newr*leans.* No-sirree-^, they ain't no trouble 'bout *that* speculation, you bet you. Say, gimme a chaw tobacker, won't ye?"

I didn't have none, so he left. I went to the raft, and set down in the wigwam to think. But I couldn't come to nothing. I thought till I wore my head sore, but I couldn't see no way out of the trouble. After all this long journey, and after all we'd done for them scoundrels, here it was all come to nothing, everything all busted up and ruined, because they could have the heart to serve Jim such a trick as that, and make him a slave again all his life, and amongst strangers, too, for forty dirty dollars.

Once I said to myself it would be a thousand times better for Jim to be a slave at home where his family was, as long as he'd *got* to be a slave, and so I'd better write a letter to Tom Sawyer and tell him to tell Miss Watson where he was. But I soon give up that notion for two things: she'd be mad and disgusted at his rascality and ungratefulness for leaving her, and so she'd sell him straight down the river again; and if she didn't, everybody naturally despises an ungrateful nigger, and they'd make Jim feel it all the time, and so he'd feel ornery and disgraced. And then think of *me!* It would get all around that Huck Finn helped a nigger to get his freedom; and if I was ever to see anybody from that town again I'd be ready to get down and lick his boots for shame. That's just the way: a person does a low-down thing, and then he don't want to take no consequences of it. Thinks as long as he can hide, it ain't no disgrace. That was my fix exactly. The more I studied about this the more my conscience went to grinding me, and the more wicked and low-down and ornery I got to feeling. And at last, when it hit me all of a sudden that here was the plain hand of Providence slapping me in the face and letting me know my wickedness was being watched all the time from up there in heaven, whilst I was stealing a poor old woman's nigger that hadn't ever done me no harm, and now was showing me there's One that's always on the lookout, and ain't a-going to allow no such miserable doings to go only just so fur and no further, I most dropped in my tracks I was so scared. Well, I tried the best I could to kinder soften it up somehow for myself by saying I was brung up wicked, and so I warn't so much to blame; but something inside of me kept saying, "There was the Sunday school, you could 'a' gone to it; and if you'd 'a' done it they'd 'a' learnt you there that people that acts as I'd been acting about that nigger goes to everlasting fire."

It made me shiver. And I about made up my mind to pray, and see if I couldn't try to quit being the kind of a boy I was and be better. So I kneeled down. But the words wouldn't come. Why wouldn't they? It warn't no use to try and hide it from Him. Nor from *me,* neither. I knowed very well why they wouldn't come. It was because my heart warn't right; it was because I warn't square; it was because I was playing double. I was letting *on* to give up sin, but away inside of me I was holding on to the biggest one of all. I was trying to make my mouth *say* I would do the right thing and the clean thing, and go and write to that nigger's owner and tell where he was; but deep down in me I knowed it was a lie, and He knowed it. You can't pray a lie—I found that out.

So I was full of trouble, full as I could be; and didn't know what to do. At last I had an idea; and I says, I'll go and write the letter—and *then* see if I can pray. Why, it was astonishing, the way I felt as light as a feather right straight off, and my troubles all gone. So I got a piece of paper and a pencil, all glad and excited, and set down and wrote:

Miss Watson, your runaway nigger Jim is down here two mile below Pikesville, and Mr. Phelps has got him and he will give him up for the reward if you send.

HUCK FINN

I felt good and all washed clean of sin for the first time I had ever felt so in my life, and I knowed I could pray now. But I didn't do it straight off, but laid the paper down and set there thinking—thinking how good it was all this happened so, and how near I come to being lost and going to hell. And went on thinking. And got to thinking over our trip down the river; and I see Jim before me all the time: in the day and in the nighttime, sometimes moonlight, sometimes storms, and we a-floating along, talking and singing and laughing. But somehow I couldn't seem to strike no places to harden me against him, but only the other kind. I'd see him standing my watch on top of his'n, 'stead of calling me, so I could go on sleeping; and see him how glad he was when I come back out of the fog; and when I come to him again in the swamp, up there where the feud was; and such-like times; and would always call me honey, and pet me, and do everything he could think of for me, and how good he always was; and at last I struck the time I saved him by telling the men we had smallpox aboard, and he was so grateful, and said I was the best friend old Jim ever had in the world, and the *only* one he's got now; and then I happened to look around and see that paper.

It was a close place. I took it up, and held it in my hand. I was a-trembling, because I'd got to decide, forever, betwixt two things, and I knowed it. I studied a minute, sort of holding my breath, and then says to myself:

"All right, then, I'll *go* to hell"—and tore it up.

It was awful thoughts and awful words, but they was said. And I let them stay said; and never thought no more about reforming. I shoved the whole thing out of my head, and said I would take up wickedness again, which was in my line, being brung up to it, and the other warn't. And for a starter I would go to work and steal Jim out of slavery again; and if I could think up anything worse, I would do that, too; because as long as I was in, and in for good, I might as well go the whole hog.

Then I set to thinking over how to get at it, and turned over some considerable many ways in my mind; and at last fixed up a plan that suited me. So then I took the bearings of a woody island that was down the river a piece, and as soon as it was fairly dark I crept out with my raft and went for it, and hid it there, and then turned in. I slept the night through, and got up before it was light, and had my breakfast, and put on my store clothes, and tied up some others and one thing or another in a bundle, and took the canoe and cleared for shore. I landed below where I judged was Phelps's place, and hid my bundle in the woods, and then filled up the canoe with water, and loaded rocks into her and sunk her where I could find her again when I wanted her, about a quarter of a mile below a little steam sawmill that was on the bank.

Then I struck up the road, and when I passed the mill I see a sign on it, "Phelps's Sawmill," and when I come to the farm houses, two or three hundred yards further along, I kept my eyes peeled, but didn't see nobody around, though it was good daylight now. Bui: I didn't mind, because I didn't want to see nobody just yet—I only wanted to get the lay of the land. According to my plan, I was going to turn up there from the village, not from below. So I just took a look, and shoved along, straight for town. Well, the very first man I see when I got there was the duke. He was sticking up a bill for the "Royal Nonesuch"—three-night performance—like that other time. *They* had the cheek, them frauds! I was right on him before I could shirk. He looked astonished, and says;

"Hel-*lo!* Where'd *you* come from?" Then he says, kind of glad and eager, "Where's the raft?—got her in a good place?"

I says:

"Why, that's just what I was going to ask your grace."

Then he didn't look so joyful, and says:

"What was your idea for asking *me?*" he says.

"Well," I says, "when I see the king in that doggery yesterday I says to myself, we can't get him home for hours, till he's soberer; so I went a-loafing around town to put in the time and wait. A man up and offered me ten cents to help him pull a skiff over the river and back to fetch a sheep, and so I went along; but when we was dragging him to the boat, and the man left me a-holt of the rope and went behind him to shove him along, he was too strong for me and jerked loose and ran, and we after him. We didn't have no dog, and so we had to chase him all over the country till we tired him out. We never got him till dark; then we fetched him over, and I started down for the raft. When I got there and see it was gone, I says to myself, 'They've got into trouble and had to leave; and they've took my nigger, which is the only nigger I've got in the world, and now I'm in a strange country, and ain't got no property no more, nor nothing, and no way to make my living'; so I set down and cried. I slept in the woods all night. But what *did* become of the raft, then?—and Jim—poor Jim!"

"Blamed if I know—that is, what's become of the raft. That old fool had made a trade and got forty dollars, and when we found him in the doggery the loafers had matched half-dollars with him and got every cent but what he'd spent for whisky; and when I got him home late last night and found the raft gone, we said, 'That little rascal has stole our raft and shook us, and run off down the river.'"

"I wouldn't shake my *nigger,* would I?—the only nigger I had in the world, and the only property."

"We never thought of that. Fact is, I reckon we'd come to consider him *our* nigger; yes, we did consider him so— goodness knows we had trouble enough for him. So when we see the raft was gone and we flat broke, there warn't anything for it but to try the 'Royal Nonesuch' another shake. And I've pegged along ever since, dry as a powder-horn. Where's that ten cents? Give it here."

I had considerable money, so I give him ten cents, but begged him to spend it for something to eat, and give me some, because it was all the money I had, and I hadn't had nothing to eat since yesterday. He never said nothing. The next minute he whirls on me and says:

"Do you reckon that nigger would blow on us? We'd skin him if he done that!"

"How can he blow? Hain't he run off?" "No! That old fool sold him, and never divided with me, and the moneys gone."

"*Sold* him?" I says, and begun to cry; "why, he was *my* nigger, and that was my money. Where is he?—I want my nigger."

"Well, you can't *get* your nigger, that's all—so dry up your blubbering. Looky here—do you think *you'd* venture to blow on us? Blamed if I think I'd trust you—"

He stopped, but I never see the duke look so ugly out of his eyes before. I went on a-whimpering, and says:

"I don't want to blow on nobody; and I ain't got no time to blow, nohow; I got to turn out and find my nigger."

He looked kinder bothered, and stood there with his bills fluttering on his arm, thinking, and wrinkling up his forehead. At last he says:

"I'll tell you something. We got to be here three days. If you'll promise you won't blow, and won't let the nigger blow, I'll tell you where to find him." So I promised, and he says:

"A farmer by the name of Silas Ph—" and then he stopped. You see, he started to tell me the truth; but when he stopped that way, and begun to study and think again, I reckoned he was changing his mind. And so he was. He wouldn't trust me; he wanted to make sure of having me out of the way the whole three days. So pretty soon he says:

"The man that bought him is named Abram Foster— Abram G. Foster—and he lives forty mile back here in the country, on the road to Lafayette."

"All right," I says, "I can walk it in three days. And I'll start this very afternoon."

"No you won't, you'll start *now;* and don't you lose any time about it, neither, nor do any gabbling by the way. Just keep a tight tongue in your head and move right along, and then you won't get into trouble with *us,* d'ye hear?"

That was the order I wanted, and that was the one I played for. I wanted to be left free to work my plans.

"So clear out," he says; "and you can tell Mr. Foster whatever you want to. Maybe you can get him to believe that Jim *is* your nigger—some idiots don't require documents—leastways I've heard there's such down South here. And when you tell him the handbill and the reward's bogus, maybe he'll believe you when you explain to him what the idea was for getting 'em out. Go 'long now, and tell him anything you want to; but mind you don't work your jaw *between* here and there."

So I left, and struck for the back country. I didn't look around, but I kinder felt like he was watching me. But I knowed I could tire him out at that. I went straight out in the country as much as a mile before I stopped; then I doubled back through the woods towards Phelps's. I reckoned I better start in on my plan straight off without fooling around, because I wanted to stop Jim's mouth till these fellows could get away. I didn't want no trouble with their kind. I'd seen all I wanted to of them, and wanted to get entirely shut of them.

In executing Tom's elaborate scheme to free Jim, Tom is shot in the leg, and Jim sacrifices his own freedom to help Tom. The novel ends with the discovery of the deaths of Pap and Miss Watson who, two months before her death, made an amendment to her will legally freeing Jim.

WALT WHITMAN

LEAVES OF GRASS

In his book of poetry called *Leaves of Grass,* first published in 1855, Walt Whitman (1819-1892) expressed himself on many issues, sometimes using complex extended metaphors (such as the sea or ocean). Whitman was a multifarious, free-spirited individual. He loved democracy, nature, metaphysics, and philosophy, and he was an advocate of toleration, proportion, and moderation—all of which is evident somewhere in the wide-ranging subject matter of the poems contained in *Leaves of Grass.* Upon receiving a copy of *Leaves of Grass* from Whitman, Ralph Waldo Emerson—poet, philosopher, and essayist—wrote to him, saying, "I greet you at the beginning of a great career." Whitman, however, never wrote another book and struggled to support himself throughout most of his life. In 1881, James R. Osgood (1836-1892),[1] Whitmans publisher, released the sixth edition of *Leaves of Grass,* but he was compelled to withdraw it a year later, because Boston's district attorney claimed that it violated the city's statutes regarding obscene literature. However, when a Philadelphia publisher issued the book, sales soared, and Whitman's fame grew. Thus, the term "banned in Boston" became an emblem of distinction, instead of a mark of shame, virtually ensuring that a book would have huge sales.

Distressed by the loss of 600,000 lives during the Civil War (1861-1865), during which Whitman served as a nurse, he published a series of poems called *Drum-Taps,* including the one that follows—"Beat! Beat! Drums!"—that deals with the chaos caused by war. This poem, and the others comprising *Drum- Taps,* were included in later editions of *Leaves of Grass.*

BEAT! BEAT! DRUMS!

Beat! beat! drums!—blow! bugles! blow!
Through the windows—through doors—burst like a ruthless force,
Into the solemn church, and scatter the congregation,
Into the school where the scholar is studying,
Leave not the bridegroom quiet—no happiness must he have now with his bride,
Nor the peaceful farmer any peace, ploughing his field or gathering his grain,
So fierce you whirr and pound you drums—so shrill you bugles blow.
Beat! beat! drums!—blow! bugles! blow!
Over the traffic of cities—over the rumble of wheels in the streets;
Are beds prepared for sleepers at night in the houses?
no sleepers must sleep in those beds,
No bargainers' bargains by day—no brokers or speculators—would they continue?
Would the talkers be talking? would the singer attempt to sing?
Would the lawyer rise in the court to state his case before the judge?
Then rattle quicker, heavier drums—you bugles wilder blow.
Beat! beat! drums!—blow! bugles! blow!
Make no parley—stop for no expostulation,
Mind not the timid—mind not the weeper or prayer,
Mind not the old man beseeching the young man,
Let not the child's voice be heard, nor the mother's entreaties,
Make even the trestles to shake the dead where they lie awaiting the hearses,
So strong you thump O terrible drums—so loud you bugles blow.

---

[1] In 1880, Osgood dissolved his partnership with Henry Oscar Houghton (1823-1895). Most of Osgood's titles were appropriated by the newly formed Houghton Mifflin & Company—the publishers of this literary reader.

O CAPTAIN! MY CAPTAIN!

Following the assassination of the sixteenth president of the United States, Abraham Lincoln (1 809-1 865), Whitman composed a series of poems called *Memories of President Lincoln,* which were later included in *Leaves of Grass.* One of the most poignant— "O Captain, My Captain!"—soon became a mainstay for memorization by schoolchildren.

O Captain! my Captain! our fearful trip is done,
The ship has weather'd every rack, the prize we sought is won,
The port is near, the bells I hear, the people all exulting,
While follow eyes the steady keel, the vessel grim and daring:
But O heart! heart! heart! O the bleeding drops of red,
Where on the deck my Captain lies, Fallen cold and dead.
O Captain! my Captain! rise up and hear the bells;
Rise up—for you the flag is flung—for you the bugle trills,
For you bouquets and ribbon'd wreaths—for you the shores a-crowding,
For you they call, the swaying mass, their eager faces turning;
Here Captain! dear father! The arm beneath your head!
It is some dream that on the deck, You've fallen cold and dead.
My Captain does not answer, his lips are pale and still,
My father does not feel my arm, he has no pulse nor will,
The ship is anchor'd safe and sound, its voyage closed and done,
From fearful trip the victor ship comes in with object won;
Exult O shores, and ring O bells! But I with mournful tread,
Walk the deck my Captain lies, Fallen cold and dead.

JOSEPH CONRAD

HEART OF DARKNESS

Behavior driven by the unconscious and the human beings capacity to act irrationally and cruelly—the dark side of human nature, which was the subject of Freud's investigations—intrigued many modernist writers, including British novelist Joseph Conrad (1857-1924), born Jozel Tendor Konrad Korzeniowski. In 1862, when Conrad was not yet five years old, his father, who had participated in an insurrection to liberate Poland from Russian rule, was exiled to northern Russia. In this harsh environment, his mother died of tuberculosis in 1865. His father, who translated the works of French and English authors into Polish, which the precocious young Conrad read voraciously, made the difficult decision to place his only child in the care of Josephs maternal uncle in Poland, where he attended school. Joseph lost his father when he was twelve, and five years later, he left school to become an apprentice seaman on a French merchant ship. In 1878, speaking only a few words of English, he joined the British merchant navy.

During his twenty years at sea, Conrad visited exotic lands and experienced danger. These adventures found literary expression in Conrad's novels and short stories, including *An Outcast of the Islands* (1896), *Lord Jim* (1900), *Heart of Darkness* (1902), *Nostromo* (1904), and *The Secret Agent* (1907). But Conrad was far more than a masterful renderer of adventure stories. His reputation as one of England's finest novelists derives from both his compelling prose and his creative exploration of human depravity, a phenomenon to which he seemed irresistibly drawn. In 1891, after a four-month stay in the Congo Free State, a land notoriously exploited and brutalized by agents of the Belgian King Leopold, Conrad suffered psychological trauma. His experiences in the heart of Africa led him to write his most compelling work, *Heart of Darkness.*

The two principal characters in the work are Kurtz, a company agent who runs a very successful ivory trading post deep in the Congo, and Marlow, a river- boat pilot, who is repelled by the cruelty inflicted on Africans by the company's agents. Marlow, who narrates his experiences, pilots a steamer upriver to Kurtz's station. Slowly he learns about Kurtz from the other agents of the company, including those accompanying him, and from a young Russian devoted to Kurtz, whom Marlow spots on the shore near Kurtz's post. Marlow finds out that not only is Kurtz a poet, musician, and painter with politically progressive views, but that when he first came to Africa, Kurtz was imbued with humanitarian sentiments. One company employee describes him as "an emissary of pity and science and progress" who intended to bring enlightenment to "savage" Africans. But in the primeval African jungle, his other self, long repressed by European values, comes to the fore. Kurtz becomes a depraved tyrant, who decorates the fence poles around his house with human heads. The charismatic Kurtz has made disciples of the villagers, who view him as a godlike figure; they heed his every word and, at his command, launch murderous raids against nearby villages for more ivory. Kurtz engages in mysterious ceremonies—Conrad leaves the nature of these ceremonies to the reader's imagination, but it is likely that they are human sacrifices—which contribute to his uncanny power over the Africans.

Although shriveled by disease, Kurtz is reluctant to return with Marlow, but eventually relents. As the ship travels down the river, Marlow engages Kurtz in long conversations. During one of these talks, Kurtz senses that death is imminent, and suddenly gripped by "craven terror," he blurts out: "The horror! The horror!" He dies later that evening. Here, too, as in the case of the ceremonies, Conrad relies on the reader to determine the meaning of Kurtz's agonizing cry.

There now exists a rich body of commentary analyzing the layers of meaning in Conrad's work. One obvious interpretation is that Conrad intended to write an indictment of imperialism, for *Heart of Darkness* expressed his revulsion of avaricious European imperialists who, in their quest for riches, plundered and destroyed African villages and impressed the natives into forced labor. Their greed, callousness, and brutality belied the altruism that they claimed was their motivation for coming to Africa.

Most commentators also regard *Heart of Darkness* as a tale of moral deterioration: The forbidding jungle environment, far from the restraints of European civilization, and the repulsive scramble for riches disfigure Kurtz, who is

transformed into a sadist driven by dark urges no longer buried within his unconscious. The wilderness "whispered to him things about himself which he did not know, things of which he had no conception till he took counsel with this great solitude—and the whisper had proved irresistibly fascinating." When the dying Kurtz cries out: "The horror! The horror!" in "that supreme moment of complete knowledge," was he referring to his own moral collapse? Thus "darkness" refers not only to the jungle interior, but also to the destructive tendencies that are at the core of human nature. Marlow's travels into the dark interior of Africa in search of Kurtz can be seen as a descent into the dark interior of the unconscious. Civilization, as Freud maintained, is very fragile; only a thin barrier separates it from barbarism. Given the right circumstances, all human beings are capable of the moral disfigurement experienced by Kurtz.

In the following excerpt from *Heart of Darkness,* Marlow, an experienced seaman, sets out upstream on a steamer in order to relieve Kurtz at the Inner Station. The journey is filled with symbolic meaning. Marlowe is not only penetrating a primeval forest, but he is also returning to humanity's primitive, barbaric past, particularly the inner darkness of the human heart which is capable of savage behavior. Marlow, like Freud, understands the importance of resisting this descent to savagery.

. . I don't pretend to say that steamboat floated all the time. More than once she had to wade for a bit, with twenty cannibals splashing around and pushing. We had enlisted some of these chaps on the way for a crew. Fine fellows—cannibals—in their place. They were men one could work with, and I am grateful to them. And, after all, they did not eat each other before my face: they had brought along a provision of hippo meat which went rotten, and made the mystery of the wilderness stink in my nostrils. Phoo! I can sniff it now. I had the manager on board and three or four pilgrims with their staves—all complete. Sometimes we came upon a station close by the bank, clinging to the skirts of the unknown, and the white men rushing out of a tumbledown hovel, with great gestures of joy and surprise and welcome, seemed very strange—had the appearance of being held there captive by a spell. The word ivory would ring in the air for a while—and on we went again into the silence, along empty reaches, round the still bends, between the high walls of our winding way, reverberating in hollow claps the ponderous beat of the stern wheel. Trees, trees, millions of trees, massive, immense, running up high; and at their foot, hugging the bank against the stream, crept the little begrimed steamboat, like a sluggish beetle crawling on the floor of a lofty portico. It made you feel very small, very lost, and yet it was not altogether depressing, that feeling. After all, if you were small, the grimy beetle crawled on—which was just what you wanted it to do. Where the pilgrims imagined it crawled to I don't know. To some place where they expected to get something, I bet! For me it crawled towards Kurtz—exclusively; but when the steam pipes started leaking we crawled very slow. The reaches opened before us and closed behind, as if the forest had stepped leisurely across the water to bar the way for our return. We penetrated deeper and deeper into the heart of darkness. It was quiet there. At night sometimes the roll of drums behind the curtain of trees would run up the river and remain sustained faintly, as if hovering in the air high over our heads, till the first break of day. Whether it meant war, peace, or prayer we could not tell. The dawns were heralded by the descent of a chill stillness; the woodcutters slept, their fires burned low; the snapping of a twig would make you start. We were wanderers on prehistoric earth, on an earth that wore the aspect of an unknown planet. We could have fancied ourselves the first of men taking possession of an accursed inheritance, to be subdued at the cost of profound anguish and of excessive toil. But suddenly, as we struggled round a bend, there would be a glimpse of rush walls, of peaked grass roofs, a burst of yells, a whirl of black limbs, a mass of hands clapping, of feet stamping, of bodies swaying, of eyes rolling, under the droop of heavy and motionless foliage. The steamer toiled along slowly on the edge of a black and incomprehensible frenzy. The prehistoric man was cursing us, praying to us, welcoming us—who could tell? We were cut off from the comprehension of our surroundings; we glided past like phantoms, wondering and secretly appalled, as sane men would be before an enthusiastic outbreak in a madhouse. We could not understand because we were too far and could not remember, because we were traveling in the night of first ages, of those ages that are gone, leaving hardly a sign—and no memories.

"The earth seemed unearthly. We are accustomed to look upon the shackled form of a conquered monster, but there— there you could look at a thing monstrous and free. It was unearthly, and the men were—No, they were not inhuman. Well, you know, that was the worst of it—this suspicion of their not being inhuman. It would come slowly to one. They howled and leaped, and spun, and made horrid faces; but what thrilled you was just the thought of their humanity— like yours—the thought of your remote kinship with this wild and passionate uproar. Ugly. Yes, it was ugly enough; but if you were man enough you would admit to yourself that there was in you just the faintest trace of a response to the terrible frankness of that noise, a dim suspicion of there being a meaning in it which you—you so remote from the night of first ages—could comprehend. And why not? The mind of man is capable of anything—because everything is in it, all the past as well as all the future. What was there after all? Joy, fear, sorrow, devotion, valor, rage—who can tell? but truth—truth stripped of its cloak of time. Let the fool gape and shudder—the man knows, and can look on without a wink. But he must at least be as much of a man as these on the shore. He must meet that truth with his own true stuff— with his own inborn strength."

It is this lure of savage reversion, symbolized by the wilderness, which has overwhelmed Kurtz. Far from the restraints of European civilization, Kurtz is claimed by the powers of darkness. The manager of the Central Station, who is onboard the steamer, fills Marlow in on Kurtz's background and doings.

"... The wilderness had patted him on the head, and, behold, it was like a ball—an ivory ball; it had caressed him, and—lo!—he had withered; it had taken him, loved him, embraced him, got into his veins, consumed his flesh, and sealed his soul to its own by the inconceivable ceremonies of some devilish initiation. He was its spoiled and pampered favorite. Ivory? I should think so. Heaps of it, stacks of it. The old mud shanty was bursting with it. You would think there was not a single tusk left either above or below the ground in the whole country. 'Mostly fossil,' the manager had remarked, disparagingly. It was no more fossil than I am; but they call it fossil when it is dug up. It appears these niggers do bury the tusks sometimes—but evidently they couldn't bury this parcel deep enough to save the gifted Mr. Kurtz from his fate. We filled the steamboat with it, and had to pile a lot on the deck. Thus he could see and enjoy as long as he could see, because the appreciation of his favor had remained with him to the last. You should have heard him say, 'My ivory.' Oh yes, I heard him. 'My Intended, my ivory, my station, my river, my—' everything belonged to him. It made me hold my breath in expectation of hearing the wilderness burst into a prodigious peal of laughter that would shake the fixed stars in their places. Everything belonged to him—but that was a trifle. The thing was to know what he belonged to, how many powers of darkness claimed him for their own. That was the reflection that made you creepy all over. It was impossible—it was not good for one either—trying to imagine. He had taken a high seat amongst the devils of the land—I mean literally. You can't understand. How could you?—with solid pavement under your feet, surrounded by kind neighbors ready to cheer you or to fall on you, stepping delicately between the butcher and the policeman, in the holy terror of scandal and gallows and lunatic asylums—how can you imagine what particular region of the first ages a man's untrammeled feet may take him into by the way of solitude—utter solitude without a policeman—by the way of silence—utter silence, where no warning voice of a kind neighbor can be heard whispering of public opinion? These little things make all the great difference. When they are gone you must fall back upon your own innate strength, upon your own capacity for faithfulness. . . .

"... The original Kurtz had been educated partly in England, and—as he was good enough to say himself—his sympathies were in the right place. His mother was half-English, his father was half-French. All Europe contributed to the making of Kurtz; and by and by I learned that, most appropriately, the International Society for the Suppression of Savage Customs had intrusted him with the making of a report, for its future guidance. And he had written it, too. I've seen it. I've read it. It was eloquent, vibrating with eloquence, but too high-strung, I think. Seventeen pages of close writing he had found time for! But this must have been before his—let us say—nerves, went wrong, and caused him to preside at certain midnight dances ending with unspeakable rites, which—as far as I reluctantly gathered from what I heard at various times—were offered up to him—do you understand?—to Mr. Kurtz himself. But it was a beautiful piece of writing. The opening paragraph, however, in the light of later information, strikes me now as ominous. He began with the argument that we whites, from the point of development we had arrived at, 'must necessarily appear to them [savages] in the nature of supernatural beings—we approach them with the might as of a deity,' and so on, and so on. 'By the simple exercise of our will we can exert a power for good practically unbounded,' etc., etc. From that point he soared and took me with him. The peroration was magnificent, though difficult to remember, you know. It gave me the notion of an exotic Immensity ruled by an august Benevolence. It made me tingle with enthusiasm. This was the unbounded power of eloquence—of words—of burning noble words. There were no practical hints to interrupt the magic current of phrases, unless a kind of note at the foot of the last page, scrawled evidently much later, in an unsteady hand, may be regarded as the exposition of a method. It was very simple, and at the end of that moving appeal to every altruistic sentiment it blazed at you, luminous and terrifying, like a flash of lightning in a serene sky: 'Exterminate all the brutes!'"

As the steamer approaches the Inner station, Marlow spots a white man on the shore who greets them. He turns out to be a young and strange Russian adventurer very much devoted to Kurtz. Accompanied by the Russian, Marlow heads for Kurtz's house. When he is within distance, he peers into his field glasses.

"... I directed my glass to the house. There were no signs of life, but there was the ruined roof, the long mud wall peeping above the grass, with three little square window holes, no two of the same size; all this brought within reach of my hand, as it were. And then I made a brusque movement, and one of the remaining posts of that vanished fence leaped up in the field of my glass. You remember I told you I had been struck at the distance by certain attempts at ornamentation, rather remarkable in the ruinous aspect of the place. Now I had suddenly a nearer view, and its first result was to make me throw my head back as if before a blow. Then I went carefully from post to post with my glass, and I saw my mistake. These round knobs were not ornamental but symbolic; they were expressive and puzzling, striking and disturbing—food for thought and also for the vultures if there had been any looking down from the sky; but at all events for such ants as were industrious enough to ascend the pole. They would have been even more impressive, those heads on the stakes, if their faces had not been turned to the house. Only one, the first I had made out, was facing my way.

I was not so shocked as you may think. The start back I had given was really nothing but a movement of surprise. I had expected to see a knob of wood there, you know. I returned deliberately to the first I had seen—and there it was, black, dried, sunken, with closed eyelids, a head that seemed to sleep at the top of that pole, and, with the shrunken dry lips showing a narrow white line of the teeth, was smiling, too, smiling continuously at some endless and jocose dream of that eternal slumber.

"I am not disclosing any trade secrets. In fact, the manager said afterwards that Mr. Kurtz's methods had ruined the district. I have no opinion on that point, but I want you clearly to understand that there was nothing exactly profitable in these heads being there. They only showed that Mr. Kurtz lacked restraint in the gratification of his various lusts, that there was something wanting in him—some small matter which, when the pressing need arose, could not be found under his magnificent eloquence. Whether he knew of this deficiency himself I can't say. I think the knowledge came to him at last—only at the very last. But the wilderness had found him out early, and had taken on him a terrible vengeance for the fantastic invasion. I think it had whispered to him things about himself which he did not know, things of which he had no conception till he took counsel with this great solitude—and the whisper had proved irresistibly fascinating. It echoed loudly within him because he was hollow at the core. ... I put down the glass, and the head that had appeared near enough to be spoken to seemed at once to have leaped away from me into inaccessible distance.

"The admirer of Mr. Kurtz was a bit crestfallen. In a hurried, indistinct voice he began to assure me he had not dared to take these—say, symbols—down. He was not afraid of the natives; they would not stir till Mr. Kurtz gave the word. His ascendancy was extraordinary. The camps of these people surrounded the place, and the chiefs came every day to see him.

They would crawl. ... 'I don't want to know anything of the ceremonies used when approaching Mr. Kurtz,' I shouted. Curious, this feeling that came over me that such details would be more intolerable than those heads drying on the stakes under Mr. Kurtz's windows. After all, that was only a savage sight, while I seemed at one bound to have been transported into some lightless region of subtle horrors, where pure, uncomplicated savagery was a positive relief, being something that had a right to exist—obviously—in the sunshine. The young man looked at me with surprise. I suppose it did not occur to him that Mr. Kurtz was no idol of mine. He forgot I hadn't heard any of these splendid monologues on, what was it? On love, justice, conduct of life—or whatnot. If it had come to crawling before Mr. Kurtz, he crawled as much as the veriest savage of them all. I had no idea of the conditions, he said: these heads were the heads of rebels. I shocked him excessively by laughing. Rebels! What would be the next definition I was to hear? There had been enemies, criminals, workers—and these were rebels. Those rebellious heads looked very subdued to me on their sticks. 'You don't know how such a life tries a man like Kurtz,' cried Kurtz's last disciple."

FRANZ KAFKA

THE TRIAL

The Modernist concern with human irrationality was captured brilliantly by Franz Kafka (1883-1924), whose major novels, *The Trial* and *The Castle,* were published after his death and did not receive recognition until after World War II. Yet perhaps better than any other novelist of his generation, Kafka grasped the dilemma of the modern age. There is no apparent order or stability in Kafka's world. Human beings strive to make sense out of life, but everywhere ordinary occurrences thwart them. They are caught in a bureaucratic web that they cannot control; they live in a nightmare society dominated by oppressive, cruel, and corrupt officials and amoral torturers. In Kafka's world, cruelty and injustice are accepted facts of existence, power is exercised without limits, and victims cooperate in their own destruction. Traditional values and ordinary logic do not operate. Our world, thought to be secure, stale, and purposeful, easily falls apart.

Kafka understood the intense anxiety that torments modern people. In *The Trial* (1925), for example, an ordinary man who has no consciousness of wrongdoing is arrested. "K. lived in a country with a legal constitution, there was universal peace, all the laws were in force; who dared seize him in his own dwelling?" Josef K. is never told the reason for his arrest, and he is eventually executed, a victim of institutional evil that breaks and destroys him "like a dog." In these observations, Kafka anticipated the emerging totalitarian state. (Kafka's three sisters perished in the Holocaust.)

A German-speaking Jew in the alien Slav environment of Czechoslovakia, Kafka died of tuberculosis at an early age. In voicing his own deep anxieties, Kafka expressed the feelings of alienation and isolation that characterize the modern individual. He explored life's dreads and absurdities, offering no solutions or consolation. In Kafka's works, people are defeated and unable to comprehend the irrational forces that contribute to their destruction. Although the mind yearns for coherence, Kafka tells us that uncertainty, if not chaos, governs human relationships. We can be sure neither of our own identities nor of the world we encounter, for human beings are the playthings of unfathomable forces, too irrational to master.

A brooding pessimism about the human condition pervades Kafka's work. One reason for the intensified interest in Kafka after World War II, observes Angel Flores, "is that the European world of the late 30s and 40s with its betrayals and concentration camps, its resulting cruelties and indignities, bore a remarkable resemblance to the world depicted by Kafka in the opening decades of the century. History seems to have imitated the nightmarish background evoked by the dreamer of Prague."

> . . . {T}he proceedings were not only kept secret from the general public, but from the accused as well. Of course only so far as this was possible, but it had proved possible to a very great extent. For even the accused had no access to the Court records, and to guess from the course of all interrogation what documents the Court had up its sleeve was very difficult, particularly for an accused person, who was himself implicated and had all sorts of worries to distract him. Now here was where defending counsel stepped in. Generally speaking, he was not allowed to be present during the examination, consequently he had to cross-question the accused immediately after an interrogation, if possible at the very door of the Court of Inquiry, and piece together from the usually confused reports he got anything that might be of use for the Defense. But even that was not the most important thing, for one could not elicit very much in that way, though of course here as elsewhere a capable man could elicit more than others. The most important thing was counsel's personal connection with officials of the Court; in that lay the chief value of the Defense. Now K. must have discovered from experience that the very lowest grade of the Court organization was by no means perfect and contained venal and corrupt elements, whereby to some extent a breach was made in the watertight system of justice. This was where most of the petty lawyers tried to push their way in, by bribing and listening to gossip, in fact there had actually been

cases of purloining documents, at least in former times. It was not to be gainsaid that these methods could achieve for the moment surprisingly favorable results for the accused, on which the petty lawyers prided themselves, spreading them out as a lure for new clients, but they had no effect on the further progress of the case, or only a bad effect. Nothing was of any real value but respectable personal connections with the higher officials, that was to say higher officials of subordinate rank, naturally. Only through these could the course of the proceedings be influenced, imperceptibly at first, perhaps, but more and more strongly as the case went on. Of course very few lawyers had such connections, and here K.'s choice had been a very fortunate one. Perhaps only one or two other lawyers could boast of the same connections as Dr. Huld. These did not worry their heads about the mob in the lawyers' room and had nothing whatever to do with them. But their relations with the Court officials were all the more intimate. It was not even necessary that Dr. Huld should always attend the Court, wait in the Anteroom of the Examining Magistrates till they chose to appear, and be dependent on their moods for earning perhaps a delusive success or not even that. No, as K. had himself seen, the officials, and very high ones among them, visited Dr. Huld of their own accord, voluntarily providing information with great frankness or at least in broad enough hints, discussing the next turn of the various cases; more, even sometimes letting themselves be persuaded to a new point of view. Certainly one should not rely too much on their readiness to be persuaded, for definitely as they might declare themselves for a new standpoint favorable to the Defense, they might well go straight to their offices and issue a statement in the directly contrary sense, a verdict far more severe on the accused than the original intention which they claimed to have renounced completely. Against that, of course, there was no remedy, for what they said to you in private was simply said to you in private and could not be followed up in public, even if the Defense were not obliged for other reasons to do its utmost to retain the favor of these gentlemen. . . .

Dr. Huld recounts the relationship between overworked and irritated officials in the judiciary system and the lawyers for the defense. Restricted to working on only one stage of the judicial process, these officials have no comprehension of the proceedings of the court as the case unfolds. They are no more than cogs in an unfathomable bureaucratic process.

The ranks of officials in this judiciary system mounted endlessly, so that not even the initiated could survey the hierarchy as a whole. And the proceedings of the Courts were generally kept secret from subordinate officials, consequently they could hardly ever quite follow in their further progress the cases on which they had worked; any particular case thus appeared in their circle of jurisdiction often without their knowing whence it came, and passed from it they knew not whither. Thus the knowledge derived from a study of the various single stages of the case, the final verdict and the reasons for that verdict lay beyond the reach of these officials. They were forced to restrict themselves to that stage of the case which was prescribed for them by the Law, and as for what followed, in other words the results of their own work, they generally knew less about it than the Defense, which as a rule remained in touch with the accused almost to the end of the case. So in that respect, too, they could learn much that was worth knowing from the Defense. Should it surprise K., then, keeping all this in mind, to find that the officials lived in a state of irritability which sometimes expressed itself in offensive ways when they dealt with their clients? That was the universal experience. All the officials were in a constant state of irritation, even when they appeared calm. Naturally the petty lawyers were most liable to suffer from it. The following story, for example, was current, and it had all the appearance of truth. An old official, a well-meaning, quiet man, had a difficult case in hand which had been greatly complicated by the lawyer's petitions, and he had studied it continuously for a whole day and night—the officials were really more conscientious than anyone else. Well, toward morning, after twenty-four hours of work with probably very little result, he went to the entrance door, hid himself behind it, and flung down the stairs every lawyer who tried to enter. The lawyers gathered down below on the landing and took counsel what they should do; on the one hand they had no real claim to be admitted and consequently could hardly take any legal action against the official, and also, as already mentioned, they had to guard against antagonizing the body of officials. But on the other hand every day they spent away from the Court was a day lost to them, and so a great deal depended on their getting in. At last they all agreed that the best thing to do was to tire out the old gentleman. One lawyer after another was sent rushing upstairs to offer the greatest possible show of passive resistance and let himself be thrown down again into the arms of his colleagues. That lasted for about an hour, then the old gentleman—who was exhausted in any case by his work overnight—really grew tired and went back to his office. The lawyers down below would not believe it at first and sent one of their number up to peep behind the door and assure himself that the place was actually vacant. Only then were they able to enter, and probably they did not dare even to grumble. For although the pettiest lawyer might be to some extent capable of analyzing the state of things in the Court, it never occurred to the lawyers that they should suggest or insist on any improvements in the system, while—and this was very characteristic—almost every accused man, even quite simple people among them, discovered from the earliest stages a passion for suggesting reforms which often wasted time and energy that could have been better employed in other directions. The only sensible thing was to adapt oneself to existing conditions. Even if it were possible to alter a detail for the better here or there—but it was simple madness to think of it—any benefit arising from that would profit clients in the future only, while one's own interests would be immeasurably injured by attracting the attention of the ever-vengeful officials. Anything rather than that! One must lie low, no matter how much it went against the grain, and try to understand that this great organization remained, so to speak, in a state of delicate balance, and that if someone took it upon himself to alter the disposition of things around him, he ran the risk of losing his footing and falling to destruction, while the organization would simply right itself by some compensating reaction in another part of its machinery—since everything interlocked—and remain unchanged, unless, indeed, which was very probable, it became still more rigid, more vigilant, severer, and more ruthless.

K. is referred to Titorelli, on artist who paints portraits of the judges, a position that gives him access to judges and an insider's understanding of the judicial process, which Titorelli explains to K. Judicial procedures are not designed to attain justice, for "the Court procedure is impervious to proof." Innocents are swept up in a bureaucratic nightmare that dooms them.

"Are you innocent?" he asked. "Yes," said K. The answering of this question gave him a feeling of real pleasure, particularly as he was addressing a private individual and therefore need fear no consequences. Nobody else had yet asked him such a frank question. To savor his elation to the full, he added: "I am completely innocent." "I see," said the painter, bending his head as if in thought. Suddenly he raised it again and said: "If you are innocent, then the matter is quite simple." K.'s eyes darkened, this man who said he was in the confidence of the Court was talking like an ignorant child. "My innocence doesn't make the matter any simpler," said K. But after all he could not help smiling, and then he slowly shook his head. "I have to fight against countless subtleties in which the Court indulges. And in the end, out of nothing at all, an enormous fabric of guilt will be conjured up." "Yes, yes, of course," said the painter, as if K. were needlessly interrupting the thread of his ideas. "But you're innocent all the same?" "Why, yes," said K. "That's the main thing," said the painter. He was not to be moved by argument, yet in spite of his decisiveness it was not clear whether he spoke out of conviction or out of mere indifference. K. wanted first to be sure of this, so he said: "You know the Court much better than I do, I feel certain, I don't know much more about it than what I've heard from all sorts and conditions of people. But they all agree on one thing, that charges are never made frivolously, and that the Court, once it has brought a charge against someone, is firmly convinced of the guilt of the accused and can be dislodged from that conviction only with the greatest difficulty." "The greatest difficulty?" cried the painter, flinging one hand in the air. "The Court can never be dislodged from that conviction. If I were to paint all the Judges in a row on one canvas and you were to plead your case before it, you would have more hope of success than before the actual Court." "I see," said K. to himself, forgetting that he merely wished to pump the painter. . . .

"You don't seem to have any general idea of the Court yet," said the painter, stretching his legs wide in front of him and tapping with his shoes on the floor. "But since you're innocent you won't need it anyhow. I shall get you off all by myself." "How can you do that?" asked K. "For you told me yourself a few minutes ago that the Court was quite impervious to proof." "Impervious only to proof which one brings before the Court," said the painter, raising one finger as if K. had failed to perceive a fine distinction. "But it is quite a different matter with one's efforts behind the scenes; that is, in the consulting-rooms, in the lobbies or, for example, in this very studio." What the painter now said no longer seemed incredible to K., indeed it agreed in the main with what he had heard from other people. More, it was actually hopeful in a high degree. If a judge could really be so easily influenced by personal connections as the lawyer insisted, then the painter's connections with these vain functionaries were especially important and certainly not to be undervalued. That made the painter an excellent recruit to the ring of helpers which K. was gradually gathering round him. . . .

Titorelli drew his chair closer to the bed and continued in a low voice: "I forgot to ask you first what sort of acquittal you want. There are three possibilities, that is, definite acquittal, ostensible acquittal, and indefinite postponement. Definite acquittal is, of course, the best, but I haven't the slightest influence on that kind of verdict. As far as I know, there is no single person who could influence the verdict of definite acquittal. The only deciding factor seems to be the innocence of the accused. Since you're innocent, of course it would be possible for you to ground your case on your innocence alone. But then you would require neither my help nor help from anyone."

This lucid explanation took K. aback at first, but he replied in the same subdued voice as the painter: "It seems to me that you're contradicting yourself." "In what way?" asked the painter patiently, leaning back with a smile. The smile awoke in K. a suspicion that he was now about to expose contradictions not so much in the painter's statements as in the Court procedure itself. However, he did not retreat, but went on: "You made the assertion earlier that the Court is impervious to proof, later you qualified that assertion by confining it to the public sessions of the Court, and now you actually say that an innocent man requires no help before the Court. That alone implies a contradiction. But, in addition, you said at first that the Judges can be moved by personal intervention, and now you deny that definite acquittal, as you call it, can ever be achieved by personal intervention. In that lies the second contradiction!" "These contradictions are easy to explain," said the painter. "We must distinguish between two things: what is written in the Law, and what I have discovered through personal experience; you must not confuse the two. In the code of the Law, which admittedly I have not read, it is of course laid down on the one hand that the innocent shall be acquitted, but it is not stated on the other hand that the Judges are open to influence. Now, my experience is diametrically opposed to that. I have not met one case of definite acquittal, and I have met many cases of influential intervention. It is possible, of course, that in all the cases known to me there was none in which the accused was really innocent. But is not that improbable? Among so many cases no single case of innocence? Even as a child I used to listen carefully to my father when he spoke of cases he had heard about; the Judges, too, who came to his studio were always telling stories about the Court, in our circle it is in fact the sole topic of discussion; no sooner did I get the chance to attend the Court myself than I took full advantage of it; I have listened to countless cases in their most crucial stages, and followed them as far as they could be followed, and yet—I must admit it—I have never encountered one case of definite acquittal." "Not one case of acquittal, then," said K. as if he were speaking to himself and his hopes, "but that merely confirms the opinion that I have already formed of this Court. It is a pointless institution from any point of view. A single executioner could do all that is needed." "You mustn't generalize," said the painter in displeasure. "I have only quoted my own experience." "That's quite enough," said K. "Or have you ever heard of acquittals in earlier times?" "Such acquittals," replied the painter, "are said to have occurred. Only it is very difficult to prove the fact. The final decisions of the Court are never recorded, even the Judges can't get hold of them, consequently we have only legendary accounts of ancient cases. These legends certainly provide instances of acquittal; actually the majority of them are about acquittals, they can be believed, but they cannot be proved. All the same, they shouldn't be entirely left out of account, they must have an element of truth in them, and besides they are very beautiful. I myself have painted several pictures founded on such legends." "Mere legends cannot alter my opinion," said K., "and I fancy that one cannot appeal to such legends before the Court?" The painter laughed. "No, one can't do that," he said. "Then there's no use talking about them," said K., willing for the time being to accept the painter's opinions, even where they seemed improbable or contradicted other reports he had heard. He had no time now to inquire into the truth of all the painter said, much less contradict it, the utmost he could hope to do was to get the man to help him in some way, even should the help prove inconclusive. Accordingly he said: "Let us leave definite acquittal out of account, then; you mentioned two other possibilities as well." "Ostensible acquittal and postponement. These are the only possibilities," said the painter. . . .

First, then, let us take ostensible acquittal. If you decide on that, I shall write down on a sheet of paper an affidavit of innocence. The text for such an affidavit has been handed down to me by my father and is unassailable. Then with this affidavit I shall make a round of the Judges I know, beginning, let us say, with the Judge I am painting now, when he comes for his sitting tonight. I shall lay the affidavit before him, explain to him that you are innocent, and guarantee your innocence myself. And that is not merely a formal guarantee but a real and binding one." In the eyes of the painter there was a faint suggestion of reproach that K. should lay upon him the burden of such a responsibility. "That would be very kind of you," said K. "And the Judge would believe you and yet not give me a definite acquittal?" "As I have already explained," replied the painter. "Besides, it is not in the least certain that every Judge will believe me; some Judges, for instance, will ask to see you in person. And then I should have to take you with me to call on them. Though when that happens the battle is already half won, particularly as I should tell you beforehand, of course, exactly what line to take with each Judge. The real difficulty comes with the Judges who turn me away at the start—and that's sure to happen too. I shall go on petitioning them, of course, but we shall have to do without them, though one can afford to do that, since dissent by individual Judges cannot affect the result. Well then, if I get a sufficient number of Judges to subscribe to the affidavit, I shall then deliver it to the Judge who is actually conducting your trial. Possibly I may have secured his signature too, then everything will be settled fairly soon, a little sooner than usual. Generally speaking, there should be no difficulties worth mentioning after that, the accused at this stage feels supremely confident. Indeed it's remarkable, but true, that people's confidence mounts higher at this stage than after their acquittal. There's no need for them to do much more. The Judge is covered by the guarantees of the other Judges subscribing to the affidavit, and so he can grant an acquittal with an easy mind, and though some formalities will remain to be settled, he will undoubtedly grant the acquittal to please me and his other friends. Then you can walk out of the Court a free man." "So then I'm free," said K. doubtfully. "Yes," said the painter, "but only ostensibly free, or more exactly, provisionally free. For the Judges of the lowest grade, to whom my acquaintances belong, haven't the power to grant a final acquittal, that power is reserved for the highest Court of all, which is quite inaccessible to you, to me, and to all of us. What the prospects are up there we do not know and, I may say in passing, do not even want to know. The great privilege, then, of absolving from guilt our Judges do not possess, but they do have the right to take the burden of the charge off your shoulders. That is to say, when you are acquitted in this fashion the charge is lifted from your shoulders, for the time being, but it continues to hover above you and can, as soon as an order comes from on high, be laid upon you again. As my connection with the Court is such a close one, I can also tell you how in the regulations of the Law Court offices the distinction between definite and ostensible acquittal is made manifest. In definite acquittal the documents relating to the case are said to be completely annulled, they simply vanish from sight, not only the charge but also the records of the case and even the acquittal are destroyed, everything is destroyed. That's not the case with ostensible acquittal. The documents remain as they were, except that the affidavit is added to them and a record of the acquittal and the grounds for granting it. The whole dossier continues to circulate, as the regular official routine demands, passing on to the higher Courts, being referred to the lower ones again, and thus swinging backwards and forwards with greater or smaller oscillations, longer or shorter delays. These peregrinations are incalculable. A detached observer might sometimes fancy that the whole case had been forgotten, the documents lost, and the acquittal made absolute. No one really acquainted with the Court could think such a thing. No document is ever lost, the Court never forgets anything. One day—quite unexpectedly—some Judge will take up the documents and look at them attentively, recognize that in this case the charge is still valid, and order an immediate arrest. I have been speaking on the assumption that a long time elapses between the ostensible acquittal and the new arrest; that is possible and I have known of such cases, but it is just as possible for the acquitted man to go straight home from the Court and find officers already waiting to arrest him again. Then, of course, all his freedom is at an end." "And the case begins all over again?" asked K. almost incredulously. "Certainly," said the painter. "The case begins all over again, but again it is possible, just as before, to secure an ostensible acquittal. One must again apply all one's energies to the case and never give in." These last words were probably uttered because he noticed that K. was looking somewhat collapsed. "But," said K., as if he wanted to forestall any more revelations, "isn't the engineering of a second acquittal more difficult than the first?" "On that point," said the painter, "one can say nothing with certainty. You mean, I take it, that the second arrest might influence the Judges against the accused? That is not so. Even while they are pronouncing the first acquittal the Judges foresee the possibility of the new arrest. Such a consideration, therefore, hardly comes into question. But it may happen, for hundreds of reasons, that the Judges are in a different frame of mind about the case, even from a legal viewpoint, and one's efforts to obtain a second acquittal must consequently be adapted to the changed circumstances, and in general must be every whit as energetic as those that secured the first one." "But this second acquittal isn't final either," said K., turning away his head in repudiation. "Of course not," said the painter. "The second acquittal is followed by the third arrest, the third acquittal by the fourth arrest, and so on. That is implied in the very conception of ostensible acquittal." K. said nothing. "Ostensible acquittal doesn't seem to appeal to you," said the painter. "Perhaps postponement would suit you better. Shall I explain to you how postponement works?" K. nodded. The painter was lolling back in his chair, his nightshirt gaped open, he had thrust one hand inside it and was lightly fingering his breast. "Postponement," he said, gazing in front of him for a moment as if seeking a completely accurate explanation, "postponement consists in preventing the case from ever getting any further than its first stages. To achieve that it is necessary for the accused and his agent, but more particularly his agent, to remain continuously in personal touch with the Court. Let me point out again that this does not demand such intense concentration of ones energies as an ostensible acquittal, yet on the other hand it does require far greater vigilance. You daren't let the case out of your sight, you visit the Judge at regular intervals as well as in emergencies and must do all that is in your power to keep him friendly; if you don't know the Judge personally, then you must try to influence him through other Judges whom you do know, but without giving up your efforts to secure a personal interview. If you neglect none of these things, then you can assume with fair certainty that the case will never pass beyond its first stages. Not that the proceedings are quashed, but the accused is almost as likely to escape sentence as if he were free. As against ostensible acquittal postponement has this advantage, that the future of the accused is less uncertain, he is secured from the terrors of sudden arrest and doesn't need to fear having to undergo—perhaps at a most inconvenient moment—the strain and agitation which are inevitable in the achievement of ostensible acquittal. Though postponement, too, has certain drawbacks for the accused, and these must not be minimized. In saying this I am not thinking of the fact that the accused is never free; he isn't free either, in any real sense, after the ostensible acquittal. There are other drawbacks. The case can't be held up indefinitely without at least some plausible grounds being provided. So as a matter of form a certain activity must be shown from time to time, various measures have to be taken, the accused is questioned, evidence is collected, and so on. For the case must be kept going all the time, although only in the small circle to which it has been artificially restricted. This naturally involves the accused in occasional unpleasantness, but you must not think of it as being too unpleasant. For it's all a formality, the interrogations, for instance, are only short ones; if you have neither the time nor the inclination to go, you can excuse yourself; with some Judges you can even plan your interviews a long time ahead, all that it amounts to is a formal recognition of your status as an accused man by regular appearances before your Judge." Already while these last words were being spoken K. had taken his jacket across his arm and got up. . . . "Are you going already?" asked the painter, who had also got up. "I'm sure it's the air here that is driving you away. I'm sorry about it. I had a great deal more to tell you. I have had to express myself very briefly. But I hope my statements were lucid enough." "Oh, yes," said K., whose head was aching with the strain of forcing himself to listen. In spite of K.'s confirmation, the painter went on to sum up the matter again, as if to give him a last word of comfort: "Both methods have this in common, that they prevent the accused from coming up for sentence." "But they also prevent an actual acquittal," said K. in a low voice, as if embarrassed by his own perspicacity. "You have grasped the kernel of the matter," said the painter quickly.

VIRGINIA WOOLF

MRS. DALLOWAY

Virginia Woolf (1882-1941) drew heavily upon personal experience in writing her novels, particularly the emotional travail that led to at least three mental breakdowns. For her first great novel, *Mrs. Dalloway*, Woolf called upon her life experiences to give definition to the character of her protagonist—Clarissa Dalloway, the middle-aged, upper-crust wife of Richard Dalloway, a member of Parliament who is frustrated by his inability to accede to a Cabinet post. The events of Woolf s *Mrs. Dalloway* take up only one day, in the middle of June, during the 1920s.

The action centers on an evening dinner party to be hosted by Mrs. Dalloway who, as she prepares for her party, reminiscences about her past, including a lover, the commoner Peter Walsh, whom she had rejected so that she could marry Richard Dalloway, a member of the upper echelons of society. Spurned by Mrs. Dalloway, Peter travels to India, returns unexpectedly, and drops by Clarissas house. When their uneasy conversation is interrupted by Mrs. Dalloway's daughter, Peter goes to a nearby park to reflect on their past. Later that evening, he attends Mrs. Dallo way's party.

Parallel to Clarissa's interior monologue are the thoughts of Septimus Warren Smith, a World War I veteran suffering from shell shock, whose suicide has a profound effect on Clarrisa when she learns of it at her dinner party. Before the war, Septimus loved Shakespeare and wanted to be a poet; now, however, he fears that life has no meaning, and he hears voices and "talks" to his dead friend, Evans, a casualty of the war. In the following selection, while he and his wife Lucrezia stroll in a park, Septimus discusses the merits of suicide as a way to bring an end to suffering.

Lucrezia Warren Smith was saying to herself, It's wicked; why should I suffer? she was asking, as she walked down the broad path. No; I can't stand it any longer, she was saying, having left Septimus, who wasn't Septimus any longer, to say hard, cruel, wicked things, to talk to himself, to talk to a dead man [Evans], on the seat over there; when the child ran full tilt into her, fell flat, and burst out crying.

That was comforting rather. She stood her upright, dusted her frock, kissed her.

But for herself she had done nothing wrong; she had loved Septimus; she had been happy; she had had a beautiful home, and there her sisters lived still, making hats. Why should *she* suffer?

The child ran straight back to its nurse, and Rezia saw her scolded, comforted, taken up by the nurse who put down her knitting, and the kind-looking man gave her his watch to blow open to comfort her—but why should *she* be exposed? . . . Why tortured? Why? . . .

To be rocked by this malignant torturer was her lot. But why? She was like a bird sheltering under the thin hollow of a leaf, who blinks at the sun when the leaf moves; starts at the crack of a dry twig. She was exposed; she was surrounded by the enormous trees, vast clouds of an indifferent world, exposed; tortured; and why should she suffer? Why?

She frowned; she stamped her foot. She must go back again to Septimus since it was almost time for them to be going to Sir William Bradshaw. She must go back and tell him, go back to him sitting there on the green chair under the tree, talking to himself, or to that dead man Evans, whom she had only seen once for a moment in the shop. He had seemed a nice quiet man; a great friend of Septimus's, and he had been killed in the War. But such things happen to every one. Every one has friends who were killed in the War. Every one gives up something when they marry. She had given up her home. She had come to live here, in this awful city. But Septimus let himself think about horrible things, as she could too, if she tried. He had grown stranger and stranger. He said people were talking behind the bedroom walls. . . . He saw things too—he had seen an old woman's head in the middle of a fern. Yet he could be happy when he chose. They went to Hampton Court on top of a bus, and they were perfectly happy. All the little red and yellow flowers were out on the grass, like floating lamps he said, and talked and chattered and laughed, making up stories. Suddenly he said, "Now we will kill ourselves," when they were standing by the river, and he looked at it with a look which she had seen in his eyes when a train went by, or an omnibus—a look as if something fascinated him; and she felt he was going from her and she caught him by the arm. But going home he was perfectly quiet—perfectly reasonable. He would argue with her about killing themselves; and explain how wicked people were; how he could see them making up lies as they passed in the street. He knew all their thoughts, he said; he knew everything. He knew the meaning of the world, he said.

Then when they got back he could hardly walk. He lay on the sofa and made her hold his hand to prevent him from falling down, down, he cried, into the flames! and saw faces laughing at him, calling him horrible disgusting names, from the walls and hands pointing round the screen. Yet they were quite alone. But he began to talk aloud, answering people, arguing, laughing, crying, getting very excited and making her write things down. Perfect nonsense it was; about death. . . . She could stand it no longer. She would go back.

She was close to him now, could see him staring at the sky, muttering, clasping his hands. Yet Dr. Holmes said there was nothing the matter with him. What, then, had happened—why had he gone, then, why, when she sat by him, did he start, frown at her, move away, and point at her hand, take her hand, look at it terrified?

Was it that she had taken off her wedding ring? "My hand has gown so thin," she said; "I have put it in my purse," she told him.

He dropped her hand. Their marriage was over, he thought, with agony, with relief. The rope was cut; he mounted; he was free, as it was decreed that he, Septimus, the lord of men, should be free; alone (since his wife had thrown away her wedding ring; since she had left him), he, Septimus, was alone, called forth in advance of the mass of men to hear the truth, to learn the meaning, which now at last, after all the toils of civilisation—Greeks, Romans, Shakespeare, Darwin, and now himself—was to be given whole to . . . "To whom?" he asked aloud, "To the Prime Minister," the voices which rustled above his head replied. The supreme secret must be told to the Cabinet; first, that trees are alive; next, there is no crime; next, love, universal love, he muttered, gasping, trembling, painfully drawing out these profound truths which needed, so deep were they, so difficult, an immense effort to speak out, but the world was entirely changed by them for ever.

No crime; love; he repeated, fumbling for his card and pencil, when a Skye terrier sniffed his trousers and he started in an agony of fear. It was turning into a man! He could not watch it happen! It was horrible, terrible to see a dog become a man! At once the dog trotted away.

Heaven was divinely merciful, infinitely benignant. It spared him, pardoned his weakness. But what was the scientific explanation (for one must be scientific above all things)? Why could he see through bodies, see into the future, when dogs will become men? It was the heat wave presumably, operating upon a brain made sensitive by eons of evolution. Scientifically speaking, the flesh was melted off the world. His body was macerated [emaciated] until only the nerve fibres were left. It was spread like a veil upon a rock.

He lay back in his chair, exhausted but upheld. He lay resting, waiting, before he again interpreted, with effort, with agony, to mankind. He lay very high, on the back of the world. The earth thrilled beneath him. Red flowers grew through his flesh; their stiff leaves rustled by his head. Music began clanging against the rocks up here. It is a motor horn down in the street, he muttered; but up here it cautioned from rock to rock, divided, met in shocks of sound which rose in smooth columns (that music should be visible was a discovery) and became an anthem, an anthem twined round now by a shepherd boy's piping (That's an old man playing a penny whistle by the public-house, he muttered) which, as the boy stood still, came bubbling from his pipe, and then, as he climbed higher, made its exquisite plaint while the traffic passed beneath. This boy's elegy is played among the traffic, thought Septimus. Now he withdraws up into the snows, and roses hang about him—the thick red roses which grow on my bedroom wall, he reminded himself. The music stopped. He has his penny, he reasoned it out, and has gone on to the next public-house.

But he himself remained high on his rock, like a drowned sailor on a rock. I leant over the edge of the boat and fell down, he thought. I went under the sea. I have been dead, and yet am now alive, but let me rest still, he begged (he was talking to himself again—it was awful, awful!); and as, before waking, the voices of birds and the sound of wheels chime and chatter in a queer harmony, grow louder and louder, and the sleeper feels himself drawing to the shores of life, so he felt himself drawing towards life, the sun growing hotter, cries sounding louder, something tremendous about to happen.

He had only to open his eyes; but a weight was on them; a fear. He strained; he pushed; he looked; he saw Regent's Park before him. Long streamers of sunlight fawned at his feet. The trees waved, brandished. We welcome, the world seemed to say; we accept; we create. Beauty, the world seemed to say. And as if to prove it (scientifically) wherever he looked, at the houses, at the railings, at the antelopes stretching over the palings, beauty sprang instantly. To watch a leaf quivering in the rush of air was an exquisite joy. Up in the sky swallows swooping, swerving, flinging themselves in and out, round and round, yet always with perfect control as if elastics held them; and the flies rising and falling; and the sun spotting now this leaf, now that, in mockery, dazzling it with soft gold in pure good temper; and now and again some chime (it might be a motor horn) tinkling divinely on the grass stalks—all of this, calm and reasonable as it was, made out of ordinary things as it was, was the truth now; beauty, that was the truth now. Beauty was everywhere.

"It is time," said Rezia.

The word "time" split its husk; poured its riches over him; and from his lips fell like shells, like shavings from a plane, without his making them, hard, white, imperishable, words, and flew to attach themselves to their places in an ode to Time; an immortal ode to Time. He sang. Evans answered from behind the tree. The dead were in Thessaly, Evans sang, among the orchids. There they waited till the War was over, and now the dead, now Evans himself—

"For God's sake don't come!" Septimus cried out. For he could not look upon the dead.

But the branches parted. A man in grey was actually walking towards them. It was Evans! But no mud was on him; no wounds; he was not changed. I must tell the whole world, Septimus cried, raising his hand (as the dead man in the grey suit came nearer), raising his hand like some colossal figure who has lamented the fate of man for ages in the desert alone with his hands pressed to his forehead, furrows of despair on his checks, and now sees light on the desert's edge which broadens and strikes the iron-black figure (and Septimus half rose from his chair), and with legions of men prostrate behind him he, the giant mourner, receives for one moment on his face the whole—

"But I am so unhappy, Septimus," said Rezia, trying to make him sit down.

The millions lamented; for ages they had sorrowed. He would turn round, he would tell them in a few moments, only a few moments more, of this relief, of this joy, of this astonishing revelation—

"The time, Septimus," Rezia repeated. "What is the time?"

He was talking, he was starting, this man must notice him. He was looking at them.

"I will tell you the time," said Septimus, very slowly, very drowsily, smiling mysteriously at the dead man in the grey suit. As he sat smiling, the quarter struck—the quarter to twelve.

When Lucrezio can no longer withstand her husband's mental affliction, she arranges for him to visit the eminent doctor, Sir William Bradshaw, who specializes in "nerve cases/' But Dr. Bradshaw treats Septimus callously, even suggesting that his affliction is nothing more than a reflection of his inability to place things in their proper perspective. He advises Septimus to go to a sanatorium in the country to rest, but while the couple awaits the arrival of the attendants who will take him there, Septimus commits suicide by jumping out of a window. During her party later that evening, Mrs. Dalloway worries about whether everyone is having a good time. Adding to her concern is the late arrival of Sir William Bradshaw who, upon his arrival, announces that one of his patients, a young veteran, has committed suicide. In the following selection, one of the most compelling passages in the novel, Mrs. Dalloway reflects on Septimus' suicide, which she attributes to a society peopled with insensitive curs, like Bradshaw.

What business had the Bradshaws to talk of death at her party? A young man had killed himself. And they talked of it at her party—the Bradshaws talked of death. He had killed himself—but how? Always her body went through it, when she was told, first, suddenly, of an accident; her dress flamed, her body burnt. He had thrown himself from a window. Up had flashed the ground; through him, blundering, bruising, went the rusty spikes. There he lay with a thud, thud, thud in his brain, and then a suffocation of blackness. So she saw it. But why had he done it? And the Bradshaws talked of it at her party! . . .

... A thing there was that mattered; a thing, wreathed about with chatter, defaced, obscured in her own life, let drop every day in corruption, lies, chatter. This he had preserved. Death was defiance. Death was an attempt to communicate, people feeling the impossibility of reaching the centre which, mystically, evaded them; closeness drew apart; rapture faded; one was alone. There was an embrace in death.

But this young man who had killed himself—had he plunged holding his treasure? "If it were now to die, 'twere now to be most happy," she had said to herself once, coming down, in white.

Or there were the poets and thinkers. Suppose he had had that passion, and had gone to Sir William Bradshaw, a great doctor, yet to her obscurely evil, without sex or lust, extremely polite to women, but capable of some indescribable outrage—forcing your soul, that was it—if this young man had gone to him, and Sir William had impressed him, like that, with his power, might he not then have said (indeed she felt it now), Life is made intolerable; they make life intolerable, men like that?

Then (she had felt it only this morning) there was the terror; the overwhelming incapacity, one's parents giving it into one's hands, this life, to be lived to the end, to be walked with serenely; there was in the depths of her heart an awful fear. Even now, quite often if Richard had not been there reading the *Times,* so that she could crouch like a bird and gradually revive, send roaring up that immeasurable delight, rubbing stick to stick, one thing with another, she must have perished. She had escaped. But that young man had killed himself.

The novel concludes with Clarissa pondering her own "suicide" when she allowed herself to give up the possibility of a loving marriage with Peter Walsh, thus losing her unique identity as "Clarissa," only to become the snobbish "Mrs. Richard Dalloway."

D. H. LAWRENCE

LADY CHATTERLEY'S LOVER

David Herbert Lawrence (1885-1930), the son of an illiterate British coal miner whose bawdy drunkenness conflicted severely with his wife's gentility, was one of the most important, yet controversial, novelists of the twentieth century.

Lawrence was saddened and angered by the consequences of industrial society: the deterioration of nature, tedious, regimented work divorced from personal satisfaction, and a life-denying quest for wealth and possessions at the expense of humanitarian concerns. Thus, in *Women in Love* (1921), the new owner of the family coal mine, determined to utilize modern management techniques in order to extract greater wealth from the business, dismisses the human needs of the workers:

Suddenly he had conceived the pure instrumentality of mankind. There had been so much humanitarianism, so much talk of sufferings and feelings. It was ridiculous. The sufferings and feelings of individuals did not matter in the least. . . . What mattered was the pure instrumentality of the individual. As a man as of a knife: does it cut well? Nothing else mattered.

Everything in the world has its function and is good or not good in so far as it fulfills this function. . . . Was a miner a good miner? Then he was complete.

Lawrence looked back longingly on preindustrial England and wanted people to reorient their thinking away from moneymaking and suppression of the instincts.

Lawrence's affirmation of sexual passion as both necessary and beneficial for a fulfilling life led him to rail against cultural norms, including puritanical attitudes that stifled human sexuality and disfigured it with shame and guilt. His feelings about sex were poignantly expressed in his highly erotic novel, ***Lady Chatterley's Lover*** (1928). Because of its use of four-letter words and intimate descriptions of sexual activity, Lawrence was forced to publish it in Italy. An unexpurgated version was not released in Britain until I960, after a celebrated trial.

Lady Chatterley, married to Sir Clifford, who considers sex distasteful, has an affair with the gamekeeper, Mellors, a commoner who exudes sexuality and whose passionate lovemaking is deeply tender.

In the following passage from ***Lady Chatterley's Lover***, Mellors tells Lady Chatterley that modern industrial-capitalist society has taken the joy out of life, that it is necessary for human beings to rediscover the virtue of passion.

"Let's live for summat else. Let's not live ter make money, neither for us-selves not for anybody else. Now we're forced to. We're forced to make a bit for us-selves, an' a fair lot for th' bosses. Let's stop it! Bit by bit, let's stop it. We needn't rant an' rave. Bit by bit, let's drop the whole industrial life an' go back. The least little bit o' money'11 do. For everybody, me an' you, bosses an' masters, even th' king. The least little bit o' money'll really do. Just make up your mind to it, an' you've got out o' th' mess." He paused, then went on:

"An' I'd tell 'em: Look! Look at Joe! He moves lovely! Look how he moves, alive and aware. He's beautiful! An' look at Jonah! He's clumsy, he's ugly, because he's niver willin' to rouse himself. I'd tell 'em: Look! look at yourselves! one shoulder higher than t'other, legs twisted, feet all lumps! What have yer done ter yerselves, wi' the blasted work? Spoilt yerselves. No need to work that much. Take yer clothes off an' look at yourselves. Yer ought ter be alive an' beautiful, an' yer ugly an' half dead. So I'd tell 'em. An' I'd get my men to wear different clothes: 'appen close red trousers, bright red, an' little short white jackets. Why, if men had red, fine legs, that alone would change them in a month. They'd begin to be men again, to be men! An' the women could dress as they liked. Because if once the men walked with legs close bright scarlet, and buttocks nice and showing scarlet under a little white jacket: then the women 'ud begin to be women. It's because th' men *aren't* men, that th' women have to be.—An in time pull down Tevershall and build a few beautiful buildings, that would hold us all. An' clean the country up again. An' not have many children, because the world is overcrowded.

But I wouldn't preach to the men: only strip 'em an' say: "Look at yourselves! That's workin' for money!—Hark at yourselves! That's working for money. You've been working for money! Look at Tevershall! It's horrible. That's because it was built while you was working for money. Look at your girls! They don't care about you, you don't care about them. It's because you've spent your time working an' caring for money. You can't talk nor move nor live, you can't properly be with a woman. You're not alive. Look at yourselves!"

There fell a complete silence. Connie was half listening, and threading in the hair at the root of his belly a few forget- me-nots that she had gathered on the way to the hut. Outside, the world had gone still, and a little icy.

"You've got four kinds of hair," she said to him. "On your chest it's nearly black, and your hair isn't dark on your head: but your mustache is hard and dark red, and your hair here, your love-hair, is like a little bush of bright red-gold mistletoe. It's the loveliest of all!"

He looked down and saw the milky bits of forget-me- nots in the hair on his groin.

"Ay! That's where to put forget-me-nots, in the man- hair, or the maiden-hair. But don't you care about the future?"

She looked up at him.

"Oh, I do, terribly!" she said.

"Because when I feel the human world is doomed, has doomed itself by its own mingy beastliness, then I feel the Colonies aren't far enough. The moon wouldn't be far enough, because even there you could look back and see the earth, dirty, beastly, unsavory among all the stars: made foul by men. Then I feel I've swallowed gall, and it's eating my inside out, and nowhere's far enough away to get away. But when I get a turn, I forget it all again. Though it's a shame, what's been done to people these last hundred years: men turned into nothing but labour-insects, and all their manhood taken away, and all their real life. I'd wipe the machines off the face of the earth again, and end the industrial epoch absolutely, like a black mistake. But since I can't, an' nobody can, I'd better hold my peace, an' try an' live my own life: if I've got one to live, which I rather doubt."

The thunder had ceased outside, but the rain which had abated, suddenly came striking down, with a last blench of lightning and mutter of departing storm. Connie was uneasy. He had talked so long now, and he was really talking to himself, not to her. Despair seemed to come down on him completely, and she was feeling happy, she hated despair. She knew her leaving him, which he had only just realised inside himself, had plunged him back into this mood. And she triumphed a little.

She opened the door and looked at the straight heavy rain, like a steel curtain, and had a sudden desire to rush out into it, to rush away. She got up, and began swiftly pulling off her stockings, then her dress and underclothing, and he held his breath. Her pointed keen animal breasts tipped and stirred as she moved. She was ivory-coloured in the greenish light. She slipped on her rubber shoes again and ran out with a wild little laugh, holding up her breasts to the heavy rain and spreading her arms, and running blurred in the rain with the eurythmic dance-movements she had learned so long ago in Dresden. It was a strange pallid figure lifting and falling, bending so the rain beat and glistened on the full haunches, swaying up again and coming belly-forward through the rain, then stooping again so that only the full loins and buttocks were offered in a kind of homage towards him, repeating a wild obeisance.

He laughed wryly, and threw off his clothes. It was too much. He jumped out, naked and white, with a little shiver, into the hard slanting rain. Flossie sprang before him with a frantic little bark. Connie, her hair all wet and sticking to her head, turned her hot face and saw him. Her blue eyes blazed with excitement as she turned and ran fast, with a strange charging movement, out of the clearing and down the path, the wet boughs whipping her. She ran, and he saw nothing but the round wet head, the wet back leaning forward in flight, the rounded buttocks twinkling: a wonderful cowering female nakedness in flight.

She was nearly at the wide riding when he came up and flung his naked arm round her soft, naked-wet middle. She gave a shriek and straightened herself, and the heap of her soft, chill flesh came up against his body. He pressed it all up against him, madly, the heap of soft, chilled female flesh that became quickly warm as flame, in contact. The rain streamed on them till they smoked. He gathered her lovely, heavy posteriors one in each hand and pressed them in towards him in a frenzy, quivering motionless in the rain. Then suddenly he tipped her up and fell with her on the path, in the roaring silence of the rain, and short and sharp, he took her, short and sharp and finished, like an animal.

He got up in an instant, wiping the rain from his eyes.

"Come in," he said, and they started running back to the hut. He ran straight and swift: he didn't like the rain. But she came slower, gathering forget-me-nots and campion and bluebells, running a few steps and watching him fleeting away from her.

When she came with her flowers, panting to the hut, he had already started a fire, and the twigs were crackling. Her sharp breasts rose and fell, her hair was plastered down with rain, her face was flushed ruddy and her body glistened and trickled. Wide-eyed and breathless, with a small wet head and full, trickling, naive haunches, she looked another creature.

He took the old sheet and rubbed her down, she standing like a child. Then he rubbed himself, having shut the door of the hut. The fire was blazing up. She ducked her head in the other end of the sheet, and rubbed her wet hair.

"Were drying ourselves together on the same towel, we shall quarrel!" he said.

She looked up for a moment, her hair all odds and ends.

"No!" she said, her eyes wide. "It's not a towel, it's a sheet."

And she went on busily rubbing her head, while he busily rubbed his.

Still panting with their exertions, each wrapped in an army blanket, but the front of the body open to the fire, they sat on a log side by side before the blaze, to get quiet. Connie hated the feel of the blanket against her skin. But now the sheet was all wet.

She dropped her blanket and kneeled on the clay hearth, holding her head to the fire, and shaking her hair to dry it.

He watched the beautiful curving drop of her haunches. That fascinated him to-day. How it sloped with a rich down-slope to the heavy roundness of her buttocks! And in between, folded in the secret warmth, the secret entrances!

He stroked her tail with his hand, long and subtly taking in the curves and the globe-fulness.

"Tha's got such a nice tail on thee," he said, in the throaty caressive dialect. "Tha's got the nicest arse of anybody. It's the nicest, nicest woman's arse as is! An' ivry bit of it is woman, woman sure as nuts. Tha'rt not one o' them buttonarsed lasses as should be lads, are ter! Tha's got a real soft sloping bottom on thee, as a man loves in 'is guts. It's a bottom as could hold the world up, it is!"

All the while he spoke he exquisitely stroked the rounded tail, till it seem[e]d as if a slippery sort of fire came from it into his hands. And his finger-tips touched the two secret openings to her body, time after time, with a soft little brush of fire.

Sir Clifford, who is unaware of his wife's affair, tells Lady Chatterley with approval about a scientific-religious book he is reading in which the author maintains: "The universe shows us two aspects: on one side it is physically wasting, on the other it is spiritually ascending." Lady Chatterley, still fresh from her immensely satisfying lovemaking with Mellors, replies:

"What silly hocus-pocus! As if his little conceited consciousness could know what was happening as slowly as all that! It only means *he's* a physical failure on the earth, so he wants to make the whole universe a physical failure. Priggish little impertinence!"

"Oh but listen! Don't interrupt the great man's solemn words!—The present type of order in the world has risen from an unimaginable past, and will find its grave in an unimaginable future. There remains the inexhaustive realm of abstract forms, and creativity with its shifting character ever determined afresh by its own creatures, and God, upon whose wisdom all forms of order depend.—There, that's how he winds up!"

Connie sat listening contemptuously.

"He's spiritually blown out," she said. "What a lot of stuff. Unimaginables, and types of order in graves, and realms of abstract forms, and creativity with a shifty character, and God mixed up with forms of order! Why it's idiotic!"

"I must say, it is a little vaguely conglomerate, a mixture of gases, so to speak," said Clifford. "Still, I think there is something in the idea that the universe is physically wasting and spiritually ascending."

"Do you? Then let it ascend, so long as it leaves me safely and solidly physically here below."

"Do you like your physique?" he asked.

"I love it!" And through her mind went the words: It's the nicest, nicest woman's arse as is!

"But that is really rather extraordinary, because there's no denying it's an encumbrance. But then I suppose a woman doesn't take a supreme pleasure in the life of the mind."

"Supreme pleasure?" she said, looking up at him. "Is that sort of idiocy the supreme pleasure of the life of the mind? no thank you! Give me the body. I believe the life of the body is a greater reality than the life of the mind: when the body is really wakened to life. But so many people, like your famous wind-machine, have only got minds tacked on to their physical corpses."

He looked at her in wonder.

"The life of the body," he said, "is just the life of the animals."

"And that's better than the life of professional corpses. But it's not true! The human body is only just coming to real life. With the Greeks it gave a lovely flicker, then Plato and Aristotle killed it, and Jesus finished it off. But now the body is coming really to life, it is really rising from the tomb. And it will be a lovely, lovely life in the lovely universe, the life of the human body."

"My dear, you speak as if you were ushering it all in! True, you are going away on a holiday: but don't please be quite so indecently elated about it. Believe me, whatever God there is is slowly eliminating the guts and alimentary system from the human being, to evolve a higher, more spiritual being."

"Why should I believe you, Clifford, when I feel that whatever God there is has at last wakened up in my guts, as you call them, and is rippling so happily there, like dawn. Why should I believe you, when I feel so very much the contrary?"

Before departing on a vacation abroad, Lady Chatterley determines to have one more sexual encounter with Mellors.

It was a night of sensual passion, in which she was a little startled and almost unwilling: yet pierced again with piercing thrills of sensuality, different, sharper, more terrible than the thrills of tenderness, but, at the moment, more desirable. Though a little frightened, she let him have his way, and the reckless, shameless sensuality shook her to her foundations, stripped her to the very last, and made a different woman of her. It was not really love. It was not voluptuousness. It was sensuality sharp and searing as fire, burning the soul to tinder.

Burning out the shames, the deepest, oldest shames, in the most secret places. It cost her an effort to let him have his way and his will of her. She had to be a passive, consenting thing, like a slave, a physical slave. Yet the passion licked round her, consuming, and when the sensual flame of it pressed through her bowels and breast, she really thought she was dying: yet a poignant, marvellous death.

She had often wondered what Abelard meant, when he said that in their year of love he and Heloi'se had passed through all the stages and refinements of passion. The same thing, a thousand years ago: ten thousand years ago! The same on the Greek vases, everywhere! The refinements of passion, the extravagances of sensuality! And necessary, forever necessary, to burn out false shames and smelt out the heaviest ore of the body into purity. With the fire of sheer sensuality.

In the short summer night she learnt so much. She would have thought a woman would have died of shame. Instead of which, the shame died. Shame, with [which] is fear: the deep organic shame, the old, old physical fear which crouches in the bodily tools of us, and can only be eased away by the sensual fire, at last it was roused up and routed by the phallic hunt of the man, and she became to the very heart of the jungle of herself. She felt, now, she had come to the real bed-rock of her nature, and was essentially shameless. She was her sensual self, naked and unashamed. She felt a triumph, almost a vainglory. So!

That was how it was! That was life! That was how oneself really was! There was nothing left to disguise or be ashamed of. She shared her ultimate nakedness with a man, another being.

And what a reckless devil the man was! really like a devil! One had to be strong to bear him. But it took some getting at, the core of the physical jungle, the last and deepest recess of organic shame. The phallus alone could explore it. And how he had pressed in on her!

And how, in fear, she had hated it. But how she had really wanted it! She knew now. At the bottom of her soul, fundamentally, she had needed this phallic hunting out, she had secretly wanted it, and she had believed that she would never get it. Now suddenly there it was, and a man was sharing her last and final nakedness, she was shameless.

What liars poets and everybody were! They made one think one wanted sentiment. When what one supremely wanted was this piercing, consuming, rather awful sensuality. To find a man who dared do it, without shame or sin or final misgiving! If he had been ashamed afterwards, and made one feel ashamed, how awful! What a pity most men are so doggy, a bit shameful, like Clifford! Like Michaelis even! Both sensually a bit doggy and humiliating. The supreme pleasure of the mind! And what is that to a woman? What is it, really, to the man either! He becomes merely messy and doggy, even in his mind. It needs sheer sensuality even to purify and quicken the mind. Sheer fiery sensuality, not messiness.

Ah God, how rare a thing a man is! They are all dogs that trot and sniff and copulate. To have found a man who was not afraid and not ashamed! She looked at him now, sleeping so like a wild animal asleep, gone, gone in the remoteness of it. She nestled down, not to be away from him.

Till his rousing waked her completely. He was sitting up in bed, looking down at her. She saw her own nakedness in his eyes, immediate knowledge of her. And the fluid, male knowledge of herself seemed to flow to her from his eyes and wrap her voluptuously. Oh, how voluptuous and lovely it was to have limbs and body half-asleep, heavy and suffused with passion.

"Is it time to wake up?" she said.

"Half-past six." . . .

. . . He got up and threw off his pyjamas, and rubbed himself with a towel. When the human being is full of courage and full of life, how beautiful it is! So she thought, as she watched him in silence.

"Draw the curtain, will you?"

The sun was shining already on the tender green leaves of morning, and the wood stood bluey-fresh, in the nearness. She sat up in bed, looking dreamily out through the dormer window, her naked arms pushing her naked breasts together. He was dressing himself. She was half-dreaming of life, a life together with him: just a life.

He was going, fleeing from her dangerous, crouching nakedness.

"Have I lost my nightie altogether?" she said.

He pushed his hand down in the bed, and pulled out the bit of flimsy silk.

"I knowed I felt silk at my ankles," he said.

But the night-dress was slit almost in two.

"Never mind!" she said. "It belongs here, really. I'll leave it."

"Ay, leave it, I can put it between my legs at night, for company."

TRISTAN TZARA

DADA

One example of the intellectual disorientation fostered by World War I was the Dadaist Movement, which arose in 1916 in Zurich, Switzerland. The artists and writers who founded Dada intended to express their contempt for the war and the civilization that produced it. The movement spread from neutral Switzerland to Germany and Paris, attracting disillusioned intellectuals. Rejecting God, reason, and traditional standards of culture, Dadaists viewed life as absurd and nonsensical (Dada itself is a nonsense term). Tristan Tzara (1896- 1945), a Romanian-French poet and essayist, one of the founders of Dada and its chief spokesman, expressed this revulsion for the Western tradition in a series of manifestos. Below are excerpts from a lecture Tzara gave in 1922.

I know that you have come here today to hear explanations. Well, don't expect to hear any explanations about Dada. You explain to me why you exist. You haven't the faintest idea. You will say: I exist to make my children happy. But in your hearts you know that isn't so. You will say: I exist to guard my country against barbarian invasions. That's a fine reason. You will say: I exist because God wills. That's a fairy tale for children. You will never be able to tell me why you exist but you will always be ready to maintain a serious attitude about life. You will never understand that life is a pun, for you will never be alone enough to reject hatred, judgments, all these things that require such an effort, in favor of a calm and level state of mind that makes everything equal and without importance. . . .

These observations of everyday conditions have led us to a realization which constitutes our minimum basis of agreement, aside from the sympathy which binds us and which is inexplicable. It would not have been possible for us to found our agreement on principles. For everything is relative. What are the Beautiful, the Good, Art, Freedom? Words that have a different meaning for every individual. Words with the pretension of creating agreement among all, and that is why they are written with capital letters. Words which have not the moral value and objective force that people have grown accustomed to finding in them. Their meaning changes from one individual, one epoch, one country to the next. Men are different. It is diversity that makes life interesting. There is no common basis in men's minds. The unconscious is inexhaustible and uncontrollable. Its force surpasses us. It is as mysterious as the last particle of a brain cell. Even if we knew it, we could not reconstruct it.

What good did the theories of the philosophers do us? Did they help us to take a single step forward or backward? What is forward, what is backward? Did they alter our forms of contentment? We are. We argue, we dispute, we get excited. The rest is sauce. Sometimes pleasant, sometimes mixed with a limitless boredom, a swamp dotted with tufts of dying shrubs.

We have had enough of the intelligent movements that have stretched beyond measure our credulity in the benefits of science. What we want now is spontaneity. Not because it is better or more beautiful than anything else. But because everything that issues freely from ourselves, without the intervention of speculative ideas, represents us. We must intensify this quantity of life that readily spends itself in every quarter. Art is not the most precious manifestation of life. Art has not the celestial and universal value that people like to attribute to it. Life is far more interesting. Dada knows the correct measure that should be given to art: with subtle, perfidious methods, Dada introduces it into daily life. And vice versa. In art, Dada reduces everything to an initial simplicity, growing always more relative. It mingles its caprices with the chaotic wind of creation and the barbaric dances of savage tribes. It wants logic reduced to a personal minimum. . . . The absurd has no terrors for me, for from a more exalted point of view everything in life seems absurd to me. . . . The Beautiful and the True in art do not exist; what interests me is the intensity of a personality transposed directly, clearly into the work; the man and his vitality; the angle from which he regards the elements and in what manner he knows how to gather sensation, emotion, into a lacework of words and sentiments. . . .

We are often told that we are incoherent, but into this word people try to put an insult that it is rather hard for me to fathom. Everything is incoherent. The gentleman who decides to take a bath but goes to the movies instead. The one who wants to be quiet but says things that haven't even entered his head. Another who has a precise idea on some subject but succeeds only in expressing the opposite in words which for him are a poor translation. There is no logic. Only relative necessities discovered *a posteriori* [after the fact}, valid not in any exact sense but only as explanations.

The acts of life have no beginning or end. Everything happens in a completely idiotic way. That is why everything is alike. Simplicity is called Dada.

Any attempt to conciliate an inexplicable momentary state with logic strikes me as a boring kind of game. The convention of the spoken language is ample and adequate for us, but for our solitude, for our intimate games and our literature we no longer need it.

The beginnings of Dada were not the beginnings of an art, but of a disgust. Disgust with the magnificence of philosophers who for 3000 years have been explaining everything to us (what for?), disgust with the pretensions of these artists-God's-representatives-on-earth, disgust with passion and with real pathological wickedness where it was not worth the bother; disgust with a false form of domination and restriction *en masse,* that accentuates rather than appeases man's instinct of domination, disgust with all the catalogued categories, with the false prophets who are nothing but a front for the interests of money, pride disease, disgust with the lieutenants of a mercantile art made to order according to a few infantile laws, disgust with the divorce of good and evil, the beautiful and the ugly (for why is it more estimable to be red rather than green, to the left rather than the right, to be large or small?). Disgust finally with the Jesuitical dialectic which can explain everything and fill people's minds with oblique and obtuse ideas without any physiological basis or ethnic roots, all this by means of blinding artifice and ignoble charlatan's promises.

As Dada marches it continuously destroys, not in extension but in itself. From all these disgusts, may I add, it draws no conclusion, no pride, no benefit. It has even stopped combating anything, in the realization that it's no use, that all this doesn't matter. What interests a Dadaist is his own mode of life. But here we approach the great secret.

Dada is a state of mind. That is why it transforms itself according to races and events. Dada applies itself to everything, and yet it is nothing, it is the point where the yes and the no and all the opposites meet, not solemnly in the castles of human philosophies, but very simply at street corners, like dogs and grasshoppers.

Like everything in life, Dada is useless.

Dada is without pretension, as life should be.

Perhaps you will understand me better when I tell you that Dada is a virgin microbe that penetrates with the insistence of air into all the spaces that reason has not been able to fill with words or conventions.

GERTRUDE STEIN

THE AUTOBIOGRAPHY OF ALICE B. TOKLAS

In 1903, the author Gertrude Stein (1874-1946) settled in an apartment at 27 Rue de Fleurus. Stein was one of the first to collect the works of Matisse, Picasso, and Braque, and the apartment—frequented by avant-garde painters and literary figures—soon became a private art gallery. Steins secretary and companion, Alice B. Toklas, arrived in Paris in 1907. In describing her abstract style of writing, Stein declared that it was the literary equivalent of Cubism. Nonetheless, her most famous book, *The Autobiography of Alice B. Toklas* (1933), was written in a more traditional, conversational style. The voice of Toklas narrates the story, but the book actually details the life of Stein herself during the time she lived in Paris, up until 1932. The first portion of the book describes the social gatherings on Saturday evenings at 27 Rue de Fleurus, which came to be known as Gertrude Steins Salon. The following excerpt describes Stein's friendship with the artists and the beginnings of the Saturday evening gatherings.

The friendship with the Matisses grew apace. Matisse at that time was at work at his first big decoration, *Le Bonheur de Vivre* [The Joy of Life]. He was making small and larger and very large studies for it. It was in this picture that Matisse first clearly realised his intention of deforming the drawing of the human body in order to harmonise and intensify the colour values of all the simple colours mixed only with white. He used his distorted drawing as a dissonance is used in music or as vinegar or lemons are used in cooking or egg shells in coffee to clarify. I do inevitably take my comparisons from the kitchen because I like food and cooking and know something about it. However this was the idea. Cezanne had come to his unfinishedness and distortion of necessity, Matisse did it by intention.

Little by little people began to come to the rue de Fleurus to see the Matisses and the Cezannes, Matisse brought people, everybody brought somebody, and they came at any time and it began to be a nuisance, and it was in this way that Saturday evenings began. It was also at this time that Gertrude Stein got into the habit of writing at night. It was only after eleven o'clock that she could be sure that no one would knock at the studio door. She was at that time planning her long book, The Making of Americans, she was struggling with her sentences, those long sentences that had to be so exactly carried out. Sentences not only words but sentences and always sentences have been Gertrude Stein's life long passion. And so she had then and indeed it lasted pretty well to the war, which broke down so many habits, she had then the habit of beginning her work at eleven o'clock at night and working until the dawn. She said she always tried to stop before the dawn was too clear and the birds were too lively because it is a disagreeable sensation to go to bed then. There were birds in many trees behind high walls in those days, now there are fewer. But often the birds and the dawn caught her and she stood in the court waiting to get used to it before she went to bed. She had the habit then of sleeping until noon and the beating of the rugs into the court, because everybody did that in those days, even her household did, was one of her most poignant irritations.

So the Saturday evenings began.

Stein was acquainted with many of the artists who were in Paris at the time, but no friendship was closer than the one she had with Picasso. In the following excerpts, she tells how both Picasso and Matisse were influenced by African art; then she relates her belief that only Spaniards could be Cubists.

At that time negro sculpture had been well known to curio hunters but not to artists. Who first recognised its potential value for the modern artist I am sure I do not know. Perhaps it was Maillol who came from the Perpignan region and knew Matisse in the south and called his attention to it. There is a tradition that it was Derain. It is also very possible that it was Matisse himself because for many years there was a curio-dealer in the rue de Rennes who always had a great many things of this kind in his window and Matisse often went up the rue de Rennes to go to one of the sketch classes.

In any case it was Matisse who first was influenced, not so much in his painting but in his sculpture, by the african statues and it was Matisse who drew Picasso's attention to it just after Picasso had finished painting Gertrude Stein's portrait.

The effect of this african art upon Matisse and Picasso was entirely different. Matisse through it was affected more in his imagination than in his vision. Picasso more in his vision than in his imagination. Strangely enough it is only very much later in his life that this influence has affected his imagination and that may be through its having been re- enforced by the Orientalism of the russians when he came in contact with that through Diaghilev and the russian ballet.

In these early days when he created cubism the effect of the african art was purely upon his vision and his forms, his imagination remained purely spanish. The spanish quality of ritual and abstraction had been indeed stimulated by his painting the portrait of Gertrude Stein. . . .

Gertrude Stein always says that cubism is a purely spanish conception and only Spaniards can be cubists and that the only real cubism is that of Picasso and Juan Gris. Picasso created it and Juan Gris permeated it with his clarity and his exaltation. To understand this one has only to read the life and death of Juan Gris by Gertrude Stein, written upon the death of one of her two dearest friends, Picasso and Juan Gris, both Spaniards. . . .

We were very much struck, the first time Gertrude Stein and I went to Spain, which was a year or so after the beginning of cubism, to see how naturally cubism was made in Spain. In the shops in Barcelona instead of post cards they had square little frames and inside it was placed a cigar, a real one, a pipe, a bit of handkerchief etcetera, all absolutely the arrangement of many a cubist picture and helped out by cut paper representing other objects. That is the modern note that in Spain had been done for centuries.

ERNEST HEMINGWAY

THE SUN ALSO RISES

In 1921, the young Ernest Hemingway (1899-1961) and his wife Hadley Richardson traveled to Paris, where they lived for the next five years. Soon after their arrival, Hemingway met Gertrude Stein, who, in a conversation with him, coined the phrase "You are all a lost generation." Stein used the phrase to describe the generation that served in World War I, men who were unable to adjust to life after the war. Soon, however, it came to refer to all the expatriates from America, especially authors and artists. In 1926, Hemingway used Stein's sentence, along with a passage from Ecclesiastes (1:4—7), as the epigraph to his first novel. He appropriated the title of the novel, *The Sun Also Rises,* from the same Ecclesiastes passage:

One generation passeth away, and another generation cometh; but the earth abideth forever. . . . The sun also ariseth, and the sun goeth down, and hasteth to the place where he arose. . . . The wind goeth toward the south, and turneth about unto the north; it whirleth about continually, and the wind re turneth again according to his circuits. . . . All the rivers run into the sea; yet the sea is not full; unto the place from whence the rivers come, thither they return again.

***The Sun Also Rises* brought Hemingway an international reputation, Like a journalist reporting a story, Hemingway relates what he has to say as simply as possible. His writing is free of stylistic devices—metaphors, similes, image-signs—and he rarely uses adjectives and adverbs to modify his carefully chosen nouns and verbs. Hemingway's direct, clipped, bare, and hard prose style continues to exert an incalculable influence on modern writers. "Hemingway as much as any other man has put the raw language of the street, the poolroom, the barracks and the brothel into modern literature."**

The narrator of the novel is the journalist Jake Barnes, a veteran of World War I, whose unnamed injury has left him impotent. Jake is in love with Brett Ashley, whom he met in England while recovering from his war wound. Although Brett also loves Jake, she is unwilling to live without sex and plans to marry Mike Campbell, a hard-drinking Scottish war veteran. Robert Cohn, an American Jewish author who lives in Paris, also falls in love with Brett and she has an affair with him. When Bill Gorton, Jake's friend, arrives from America, he and Jake decide to travel to Spain to fish and then to attend the fiesta in Pamplona. Early their first morning in Spain, Jake goes out to dig for worms while Bill sleeps. In the following passage, he has just returned to their room.

"I saw you out of the window," he said. "Didn't want to interrupt you. What were you doing? Burying your money?"

"You lazy bum!"

"Been working for the common good? Splendid. I want you to do that every morning."

"Come on," I said. "Get up."

"What? Get up? I never get up."

He climbed into bed and pulled the sheet up to his chin.

"Try and argue me into getting up."

I went on looking for the tackle and putting it all together in the tackle-bag.

"Aren't you interested?" Bill asked.

"I'm going down and eat."

"Eat? Why didn't you say eat? I thought you just wanted me to get up for fun. Eat? Fine. Now you're reasonable. You go out and dig some more worms and I'll be right down."

"Oh, go to hell!"

"Work for the good of all." Bill stepped into his underclothes. "Show irony and pity."

I started out of the room with the tackle-bag, the nets, and the rod-case.

"Hey! come back!"

I put my head in the door.

"Aren't you going to show a little irony and pity?"

I thumbed my nose.

"That's not irony."

As I went down-stairs I heard Bill singing, "Irony and Pity. When you're feeling . . . oh, Give them Irony and Give them pity. Oh, give them Irony. When they're feeling . . . Just a little irony. Just a little pity ..." He kept on singing until he came down-stairs. The tune was: "The Bells are Ringing for Me and my Gal." I was reading a week-old Spanish paper.

"What's all this irony and pity?"

"What?" Don't you know about Irony and Pity?"

"No. Who got it up?" . . .

"There you go. And you claim you want to be a writer, too. You're only a newspaper man. An expatriated newspaper man. You ought to be ironical the minute you get out of bed. You ought to wake up with your mouth full of pity."

"Go on," I said. "Who did you get this stuff from?"

"Everybody. Don't you read? Don't you ever see anybody? You know what you are? You're an expatriate. Why don't you live in New York? Then you'd know these things. What do you want me to do? Come over here and tell you every year?"

"Take some more coffee," I said.

"Good. Coffee is good for you. It's the caffeine, in it. Caffeine, we are here. Caffeine puts a man on her horse and a woman in his grave. You know what's the trouble with you? You're an expatriate. One of the worst type. Haven't you heard that? Nobody that ever left their own country ever wrote anything worth printing. Not even in the newspapers."

He drank the coffee.

"You're an expatriate. You've lost touch with the soil. You get precious. Fake European standards have ruined you. You drink yourself to death. You become obsessed by sex. You spend all your time talking, not working. You are an expatriate, see? You hang around cafés."

"It sounds like a swell life," I said. "When do I work?"

"You don't work. One group claims women support you. Another group claims you're impotent."

"No," I said. "I just had an accident."

Alcohol had a particular allure for many of the expatriates, perhaps partially because of Prohibition at home. Some were so inclined toward self-destruction that they seemed determined to earn ownership of the label "the lost generation" as Hemingway suggests in the following passage. Jake and Bill are in a cafe in Pamplona during the evening after the bullfight at the end of the fiesta.

We had another absinthe. "When do you go back?" I asked. "To-morrow."

After a little while Bill said; "Well, it was a swell fiesta." "Yes," I said; "something doing all the time." "You wouldn't believe it. It's like a wonderful nightmare." "Sure," I said. "I'd believe anything. Including nightmares."

"What's the matter? Feel low?" "Low as hell."

"Have another absinthe. Here, waiter! Another absinthe for this señor."

"I feel like hell," I said. "Drink that," said Bill. "Drink it slow." It was beginning to get dark. The fiesta was going on. I began to feel drunk but I did not feel any better. "How do you feel?" "I feel like hell." "Have another?" "It won't do any good."

"Try it. You can't tell; maybe this is the one that gets it. Hey, waiter! Another absinthe for this señor!"

I poured the water directly into it and stirred it instead of letting it drip. Bill put in a lump of ice. I stirred the ice around with a spoon in the brownish, cloudy mixture. "How is it?" "Fine."

"Don't drink it fast that way. It will make you sick." I set down the glass. I had not meant to drink it fast. "I feel tight." "You ought to."

"That's what you wanted, wasn't it?"

"Sure. Get tight. Get over your damn depression."

"Well, I'm tight. Is that what you want?"

"Sit down."

"I won't sit down," I said. "I'm going over to the hotel." I was very drunk. I was drunker than I ever remembered having been. At the hotel I went up-stairs. Brett's door was open. I put my head in the room. Mike was sitting on the bed. He waved a bottle.

"Jake," he said. "Come in, Jake."

I went in and sat down. The room was unstable unless I looked at some fixed point.

"Brett, you know. She's gone off with the bull-fighter chap."

"No."

"Yes. She looked for you to say good-bye. They went on the seven o'clock train."

"Did they?"

"Bad thing to do," Mike said. "She shouldn't have done it."

"No."

"Have a drink? Wait while I ring for some beer."

"I'm drunk," I said. "I'm going in and lie down."

"Are you blind? I was blind myself."

"Yes," I said, "I'm blind."

"Well, bung-o." Mike said. "Get some sleep, old Jake."

I went out the door and into my own room and lay on the bed. The bed went sailing off and I sat up in bed and looked at the wall to make it stop. Outside in the square the fiesta was going on. It did not mean anything. Later Bill and Mike came in to get me to go down and eat with them. I pretended to be asleep.

"He's asleep. Better let him alone."

"He's blind as a tick," Mike said. They went out.

I got up and went to the balcony and looked out at the dancing in the square. The world was not wheeling any more. It was just very clear and bright and inclined to blur at the edges. I washed, brushed my hair. I looked strange to myself in the glass, and went down-stairs to the dining-room.

"Here he is!" said Bill. "Good old Jake! I knew you wouldn't pass out."

"Hello, you old drunk," Mike said.

"I got hungry and woke up."

"Eat some soup," Bill said.

The three of us sat at the table, and it seemed as though about six people were missing.

ADOLF HITLER

MEIN KAMPF

In the "Beer Hall Putsch" of November 1923, Hitler attempted to overthrow the state government in Bavaria as the first step in bringing down the Weimar Republic. But the Nazis quickly scattered when the Bavarian police opened fire. Hitler was arrested and sentenced to five years' imprisonment—he served only nine months. While in prison, Hitler wrote *Mein Kampf* (My Struggle), in which he presented his views. The book came to be regarded as an authoritative expression of the Nazi world-view and served as a kind of sacred writing for the Nazi movement.

Hitler's thought—a patchwork of nineteenth-century anti-Semitic, Volkish, Social Darwinist, and anti-Marxist ideas—contrasted sharply with the core values of both the Judeo-Christian and the Enlightenment traditions. Central to Hitlers world-view was racial mythology: a heroic Germanic race that was descended from the ancient Aryans, who once swept across Europe, and was battling for survival against racial inferiors. In the following passages excerpted from *Mein Kampf* Hitler presents his views of race, of propaganda, and of the National Socialist territorial goals.

THE PRIMACY OF RACE

Nature does not want a pairing of weaker individuals with stronger ones; it wants even less a mating of a higher race with a weaker one. Otherwise its routine labors of promoting a higher breed lasting perhaps over hundreds of thousands of years would be wiped out.

History offers much evidence for this process. It proves with terrifying clarity that any generic mixture of Aryan blood with people of a lower quality undermines the culturally superior people. The population of North America consists to a large extent of Germanic elements, which have mixed very little with inferior people of color. Central and South America shows a different humanity and culture; here Latin immigrants mixed with the aborigines, sometimes on a large scale. This example alone allows a clear recognition of the effects of racial mixtures. Remaining racially pure the Germans of North America rose to be masters of their continent; they will remain masters as long as they do not defile their blood.

The result of mixing races in short is: a) lowering the cultural level of the higher race; b) physical and spiritual retrogression and thus the beginning of a slow but progressive decline.

To promote such a development means no less than committing sin against the will of the eternal creator. . . .

Everything that we admire on earth—science, technology, invention—is the creative product of only a few people, and perhaps originally of only *one* race; our whole culture depends upon them. If they perish, the beauties of the earth will be buried. . . .

All great cultures of the past perished because the original creative race was destroyed by the poisoning of its blood.

Such collapse always happened because people forgot that all cultures depend on human beings. In order to preserve a given culture it is necessary to preserve the human beings who created it. Cultural preservation in this world is tied to the iron law of necessity and the fight to victory of the stronger and better. . . .

If we divide humanity into three categories: into founders of culture, bearers of culture, and destroyers of culture, the Aryan would undoubtedly rate first. He established the foundations and walls of all human progress. . . .

The mixing of blood and the resulting lowering of racial cohesion is the sole reason why cultures perish. People do not perish by defeat in war, but by losing the power of resistance inherent in pure blood.

All that is not pure race in this world is chaff. . . .

A state which in the age of racial poisoning dedicates itself to the cultivation of its best racial elements will one day become master of the world.

Modern anti-Semitism was a powerful legacy of the Middle Ages and the unsettling changes brought about by rapid industrialization; it was linked to racist doctrines that asserted the Jews were inherently wicked and bore dangerous racial qualities. Hitler grasped the political potential of anti-Semitism: by concentrating all evil in one enemy, he could provide non-Jews with an emotionally satisfying explanation for all their misfortunes and thus manipulate and unify the German people.

ANTI-SEMITISM

The Jew offers the most powerful contrast to the Aryan. . . . Despite all their seemingly intellectual qualities the Jewish people are without true culture, and especially without a culture of their own. What Jews seem to possess as culture is the property of others, for the most part corrupted in their hands.

In judging the Jewish position in regard to human culture, we have to keep in mind their essential characteristics. There never was—and still is no—Jewish art. The Jewish people made no original contribution to the two queen goddesses of all arts: architecture and music. What they have contributed is bowdlerization or spiritual theft. Which proves that Jews lack the very qualities distinguishing creative and culturally blessed races. . . .

The first and biggest lie of Jews is that Jewishness is not a matter of race but of religion, from which inevitably follow even more lies. One of them refers to the language of Jews. It is not a means of expressing their thoughts, but of hiding them. While speaking French a Jew thinks Jewish, and while he cobbles together some German verse, he merely expresses the mentality of his people.

As long as the Jew is not master of other peoples, he must for better or worse speak their languages. Yet as soon as the others have become his servants, then all should learn a universal language (Esperanto for instance), so that by these means the Jews can rule more easily. . . .

For hours the blackhaired Jewish boy lies in wait, with satanic joy on his face, for the unsuspecting girl whom he disgraces with his blood and thereby robs her from her people. He tries by all means possible to destroy the racial foundations of the people he wants to subjugate.

But a people of pure race conscious of its blood can never be enslaved by the Jew; he remains forever a ruler of bastards.

Thus he systematically attempts to lower racial purity by racially poisoning individuals.

In politics he begins to replace the idea of democracy with the idea of the dictatorship of the proletariat.

He found his weapon in the organized Marxist masses, which avoid democracy and instead help him to subjugate and govern people dictatorially with his brutal fists.

Systematically he works toward a double revolution, in economics and politics.

With the help of his international contacts he enmeshes people who effectively resist his attacks from within in a net of external enemies whom he incites to war, and, if necessary, goes on to unfurling the red flag of revolution over the battlefield.

He batters the national economies until the ruined state enterprises are privatized and subject to his financial control.

In politics he refuses to give the state the means for its self-preservation, destroys the bases of any national self- determination and defense, wipes out the faith in leadership, denigrates the historic past, and pulls everything truly great into the gutter.

In cultural affairs he pollutes art, literature, theatre, befuddles national sentiment, subverts all concepts of beauty and grandeur, of nobleness and goodness, and reduces people to their lowest nature.

Religion is made ridiculous, custom and morals are declared outdated, until the last props of national character in the battle for survival have collapsed. . . .

Thus the Jew is the big rabble-rouser for the complete destruction of Germany. Wherever in the world we read about attacks on Germany, Jews are the source, just as in peace and during the war the newspapers of both the Jewish stock market and the Marxists systematically incited hatred against Germany. Country after country gave up its neutrality and joined the world war coalition in disregard of the true interest of the people.

Jewish thinking in all this is clear. The Bolshevization of Germany, i.e., the destruction of the German national people-oriented intelligentsia and thereby the exploitation of German labor under the yoke of Jewish global finance are but the prelude for the expansion of the Jewish tendency to conquer the world. As so often in history, Germany is the turning point in this mighty struggle. If our people and our state become the victims of blood-thirsty and money-thirsty Jewish tyrants, the whole world will be enmeshed in the tentacles of this octopus. If, however, Germany liberates itself from this yoke, we can be sure that the greatest threat to all humanity has been broken. . . .

Hitler was a master propagandist and advanced his ideas on propaganda techniques in *Mein Kampf.* He mocked the learned and book-oriented German liberals and socialists who he felt were entirely unsuited for modern mass politics. The successful leader, he said, must win over the masses through the use of simple ideas and images, constantly repeated, to control the mind by evoking primitive feelings. Hitler contended that mass meetings were the most effective means of winning followers. What counted most at these demonstrations, he said, was will power, strength, and unflagging determination radiating from the speaker to every single individual in the crowd.

PROPAGANDA AND MASS RALLIES

The task of propaganda does not lie in the scientific training of individuals, but in directing the masses toward certain facts, events, necessities, etc., whose significance is to be brought to their attention.

The essential skill consists in doing this so well that you convince people about the reality of a fact, about the necessity of an event, about the correctness of something necessary, etc. . . . You always have to appeal to the emotions and far less to the so-called intellect. . . .

The art of propaganda lies in sensing the emotional temper of the broad masses, so that you, in psychologically effective form, can catch their attention and move their hearts. . . .

The attention span of the masses is very short, their understanding limited; they easily forget. For that reason all effective propaganda has to concentrate on very few points and drive them home through simple slogans, until even the simplest can grasp what you have in mind. As soon as you give up this principle and become too complex, you will lose your effectiveness, because the masses cannot digest and retain what you have offered. You thereby weaken your case and in the end lose it altogether.

The larger the scope of your case, the more psychologically correct must be the method of your presentation. . . .

The task of propaganda lies not in weighing right and wrong, but in driving home your own point of view. You cannot objectively explore the facts that favor others and present them in doctrinaire sincerity to the masses. You have to push relentlessly your own case. . . .

Even the most brilliant propaganda will not produce the desired results unless it follows this fundamental rule: You must stick to limiting yourself to essentials and repeat them endlessly. Persistence on this point, as in so many other cases in the world, is the first and most important precondition for success. . . .

Propaganda does not exist to furnish interesting diversions to blasé young dandies, but to convince above all the masses. In their clumsiness they always require a long lead before they are ready to take notice. Only by thousandfold repetition will the simplest concepts stick in their memories.

No variation of your presentation should change the content of your propaganda; you always have to come to the same conclusion. You may want to highlight your slogans from various sides, but at the end you always have to reaffirm it. Only consistent and uniform propaganda will succeed. . . .

Every advertisement, whether in business or politics, derives its success from its persistence and uniformity. . . .

The mass meeting is. . . necessary because an incipient supporter of a new political movement will feel lonely and anxiously isolated. He needs at the start a sense of a larger community which among most people produces vitality and courage. The same man as member of a military company or battalion and surrounded by his comrades will more lightheartedly join an attack than if he were all by himself. In a crowd he feels more sheltered, even if reality were a thousandfold against him.

The sense of community in a mass demonstration not only empowers the individual, but also promotes an esprit de corps. The person who in his business or workshop is the first to represent a new political creed is likely to be exposed to heavy discrimination. He needs the reassurance that comes from the conviction of being a member and a fighter in a large comprehensive organization. The sense of this organization comes first to him in a mass demonstration. When he for the first time goes from a petty workshop or from a large factory, where he feels insignificant, to a mass demonstration surrounded by thousands and thousands of like- minded fellows—when he as a seeker is gripped by the intoxicating surge of enthusiasm among three or four thousand others—when the visible success and the consensus of thousands of others prove the correctness of his new political creed and for the first time arouse doubts about his previous political convictions—then he submits to the miraculous influence of what we call "mass suggestion." The will, the yearning, and also the power of thousands of fellow citizens now fill every individual. The man who full of doubts and uncertain enters such a gathering, leaves it inwardly strengthened; he has become a member of a community. . . .

Hitler was an extreme nationalist who wanted a reawakened, racially united Germany to expand eastward at the expense of the Slavs, whom he viewed as racially inferior.

LEBENSRAUM

A people gains its freedom of existence only by occupying a sufficiently large space on earth. . . .

If the National Socialist movement really wants to achieve a hallowed mission in history for our people, it must, in painful awareness of its position in the world, boldly and methodically fight against the aimlessness and incapacity which have hitherto guided the foreign policy of the German people. It must then, without respect for "tradition" and prejudice, find the courage to rally the German people to a forceful advance on the road which leads from their present cramped living space to new territories. In this manner they will be liberated from the danger of perishing or being enslaved in service to others.

The National Socialist movement must try to end the disproportion between our numerous population and its limited living space, the source of our food as well as the base of our power—between our historic past and the hopelessness of our present impotence. . . .

The demand for restoring the boundaries of 1914 is apolitical nonsense with consequences so huge as to make it appear a crime— quite apart from the fact that our pre-war boundaries were anything but logical. They neither united all people of German nationality nor served strategic-political necessity. . . .

In the light of this fact we National Socialists must resolutely stick to our foreign policy goals, namely *to secure for the German people the territorial base to which they are entitled.* This is the only goal which before God and our German posterity justifies shedding our blood. . . .

Just as our forebears did not receive the soil on which we live as a gift from heaven—they had to risk their lives for it—so in future we will not secure the living space for our people by divine grace, but by the might of the victorious sword.

However much all of us recognize the necessity of a reckoning with France, it would remain ineffectual if we thereby limited the scope of our foreign policy. It makes sense only if we consider it as a rear-guard action for expanding our living space elsewhere in Europe. . . .

If we speak today about gaining territory in Europe, we think primarily of Russia and its border states. . . .

JOHN STEINBECK

THE GRAPES OF WRATH

The Grapes of Wrath **movingly described the ordeal of the Joad family, downtrodden Oklahoma farmers who headed to California to find work as farm laborers after being driven off their land. On the long journey west, the Joads suffer hardships: Grampa Joad, who did not want to leave his home, immediately suffers a fatal stroke; when Granma Joad dies, the family does not have the money for a proper burial.**

When the Joads arrive in California, they stay at a squatters' camp where conditions are deplorable; California is not the "Promised Land" they had expected when they began their arduous journey. The migrants have to cope with filth, chaos, and abuse by brutal police and their deputies. The Joads move to another camp set up by the government. Because of effective management, including the active participation of the migrants themselves on committees, the camp is orderly and clean, a sign that common folk, organized and working together, can improve the conditions under which they live.

Knowing that the migrants are desperate for work, greedy orchard owners cut their pay and use the police to squash strikers, "them goddam reds," as they are referred to. Eight members of the Joad family—four men, two women, and two children—work all day picking peaches. At five cents a box, they earn only a dollar or so and are overcharged for food at the company store. Outside the orchards are pickets protesting that their pay had been slashed to two and one half cents a box. Tom Joad speaks with Jim Casy, who leads the pickets. Casy is an ex- preacher whose spiritual nature and humanitarian feelings draw him into fellowship with others. Casy tells Tom how the orchard owners have deceived and exploited the migrants.

"Lookie, Tom," he said at last. "We come to work there. They says it's gonna be fi' cents. They was a hell of a lot of us. We got there an' they says they're payin' two an' a half cents. A fella can't even eat on that, an' if he got kids— So we says we won't take it. So they druv us off. An' all the cops in the worl' come down on us. Now they're payin' you five. When they bust this here strike—ya think they'll pay five?"

"I dunno," Tom said. "Payin' five now."

"Lookie," said Casy. "We tried to camp together, an' they druv us like pigs. Scattered us. Beat the hell outa fellas. Druv us like pigs. They run you in like pigs, too. We can't las' much longer. Some people ain't et for two days. You goin' back tonight?"

"Aim to," said Tom.

"Well—tell the folks in there how it is, Tom. Tell 'em they're starvin' us an' stabbin' theirself in the back. 'Cause sure as cowflops she'll drop to two an' a half jus' as soon as they clear us out."

"I'll tell em," said Tom. "I don' know how. Never seen so many guys with guns. Don' know if they'll even let a fella talk. An' folks don' pass no time of day. They jus' hang down their heads an' won't even give a fella a howdy."

"Try an' tell 'em, Tom. They'll get two an' a half, jus' the minute we're gone. You know what two an' a half is—that's one ton of peaches picked an' carried for a dollar." He dropped his head. "No—you can't do it. You can't get your food for that. Can't eat for that."

"I'll try to get to tell the folks."

"How's your ma?"

"Purty good. She liked that gov'ment camp. Baths an' hot water."

"Yeah—I heard."

"It was pretty nice there. Couldn' find no work, though. Had a leave."

"I'd like to go to one," said Casy. "Like to see it. Fella says they ain't no cops."

"Folks is their own cops."

Casy looked up excitedly. "An' was they any trouble? Fightin', stealin', drinkin'?"

"No," said Tom.

"Well, if a fella went bad—what then? What'd they do?"

"Put 'im outa the camp."

"But they wasn' many?"

"Hell, no," said Tom. "We was there a month, an' on'y one."

Casy's eyes shone with excitement. He turned to the other men. "Ya see?" he cried. "I tol' you. Cops cause more trouble than they stop. Look, Tom. Try an' get the folks in there to come on out. They can do it in a couple days. Them peaches is ripe. Tell 'em."

"They won't," said Tom. "They're a-gettin' five, an' they don' give a damn about nothin' else."

"But jus' the minute they ain't strikebreakin' they won't get no five."

"I don' think they'll swalla that. Five they're a-gettin'. Tha's all they care about."

"Well, tell 'em anyways."

"Pa wouldn' do it," Tom said. "I know 'im. He'd say it wasn't none of his business."

"Yes," Casy said disconsolately. "I guess that's right. Have to take a beatin' 'fore he'll know."

"We was outa food," Tom said. "Tonight we had meat. Not much, but we had it. Think Pa's gonna give up his meat on account a other fellas? An' Rosaharn oughta get milk. Think Ma's gonna wanta starve that baby jus' 'cause a bunch a fellas is yellin' outside a gate?"

Casy said sadly, "I wisht they could see it. I wisht they could see the on'y way they can depen' on their meat— Oh, the hell! Get tar'd sometimes. God-awful tar'd. I knowed a fella. Brang 'im in while I was in the jail house. Been tryin' to start a union. Got one started. An' then them vigilantes bust it up. An' know what? Them very folks he been tryin' to help tossed him out. Wouldn' have nothin' to do with 'im. Scared they'd get saw in his comp'ny. Says, 'Git out. You're a danger on us.' Well, sir, it hurt his feelin's purty bad. But then he says, 'It ain't so bad if you know.' He says, 'French Revolution—all them fellas that figgered her out got their heads chopped off. Always that way,' he says. Jus' as natural as rain. You didn' do it for fun no way. Doin' it 'cause you have to. 'Cause it's you. Look a Washington,' he says. 'Fit the Revolution, an' after, them sons-a-bitches turned on him. An' Lincoln the same. Same folks yellin' to kill 'em. Natural as rain.'"

"Don't soun' like no fun," said Tom.

"No, it don't. This fella in jail, he says, 'Anyways, you do what you can. An',' he says, 'the on'y thing you got to look at is that ever' time they's a little step fo'ward, she may slip back a little, but she never slips clear back. You can prove that,' he says, 'an' that makes the whole thing right. An' that means they wasn't no waste even if it seemed like they was.'"

"Talkin'," said Tom. "Always talkin'. Take my brother Al. He's out lookin' for a girl. He don't care 'bout nothin' else. Couple days he'll get him a girl. Think about it all day an' do it all night. He don't give a damn 'bout steps up or down or sideways."

"Sure," said Casy. "Sure. He's jus' doin' what he's got to do. All of us like that."

The man seated outside pulled the tent flap wide. "Goddamn it, I don' like it," he said.

Casy looked out at him. "What's the matter?"

"I don' know. I jus' itch all over. Nervous as a cat."

"Well, what's the matter?"

"I don' know. Seems like I hear somepin, an' then I listen an' they ain't nothin' to hear."

"You're jus' jumpy," the wizened man said. He got up and went outside. And in a second he looked into the tent. "They's a great big ol' black cloud a-sailin' over. Bet she's got thunder. That's what's itchin' him—'lectricity." He ducked out again. The other two men stood up from the ground and went outside.

Casy said softly, "All of 'em's itchy. Them cops been sayin' how they're gonna beat the hell outa us an' run us outa the county. They figger I'm a leader 'cause I talk so much."

The wizened face looked in again. "Casy, turn out that lantern an' come outside. They's somepin."

Casy turned the screw. The flame drew down into the slots and popped and went out. Casy groped outside and Tom followed him. "What is it?" Casy asked softly.

"I dunno. Listen!"

There was a wall of frog sounds that merged with silence. A high, shrill whistle of crickets. But through this background came other sounds—faint footsteps from the road, a crunch of clods up on the bank, a little swish of brush down the stream.

"Can't really tell if you hear it. Fools you. Get nervous," Casy reassured them. "We're all nervous. Can't really tell. You hear it, Tom?"

"I hear it," said Tom. "Yeah, I hear it. I think they's guys comin' from ever' which way. We better get outa here."

The wizened man whispered, "Under the bridge span— out that way. Hate to leave my tent."

"Le's go," said Casy.

They moved quietly along the edge of the stream. The black span was a cave before them. Casy bent over and moved through. Tom behind. Their feet slipped into the water. Thirty feet they moved, and their breathing echoed from the curved ceiling. Then they came out on the other side and straightened up.

A sharp call, "There they are!" Two flashlight beams fell on the men, caught them, blinded them. "Stand where you are." The voices came out of the darkness. "That's him. That shiny bastard. That's him."

Casy stared blindly at the light. He breathed heavily. "Listen," he said. "You fellas don' know what you're doin'. You're helpin' to starve kids."

"Shut up, you red son-of-a-bitch."

A short heavy man stepped into the light. He carried a new white pick handle.

Casy went on, "You don' know what you're a-doin'."

The heavy man swung with the pick handle. Casy dodged down into the swing. The heavy club crashed into the side of his head with a dull crunch of bone, and Casy fell sideways out of the light.

"Jesus, George. I think you killed him."

"Put the light on him," said George. "Serve the son-of-a- bitch right." The flashlight beam dropped, searched and found Casy's crushed head.

Tom looked down at the preacher. The light crossed the heavy man's legs and the white new pick handle. Tom leaped silently. He wrenched the club free. The first time he knew he had missed and struck a shoulder, but the second time his crushing blow found the head, and as the heavy man sank down, three more blows found his head. The lights danced about. There were shouts, the sound of running feet, crashing through brush. Tom stood over the prostrate man. And then a club reached his head, a glancing blow. He felt the stroke like an electric shock. And then he was running along the stream, bending low. He heard the splash of footsteps following him. Suddenly he turned and squirmed up into the brush, deep into a poison-oak thicket. And he lay still. The footsteps came near, the light beams glanced along the stream bottom. Tom wriggled up through the thicket to the top. He emerged in an orchard. And still he could hear the calls, the pursuit in the stream bottom. He bent low and ran over the cultivated earth; the clods slipped and rolled under his feet. Ahead he saw the bushes that bounded the field, bushes along the edges of an irrigation ditch. He slipped through the fence, edged in among vines and blackberry bushes. And then he lay still, panting hoarsely. He felt his numb face and nose. The nose was crushed, and a trickle of blood dripped from his chin. He lay still on his stomach until his mind came back. And then he crawled slowly over the edge of the ditch. He bathed his face in the cool water, tore off the tail of his blue shirt and dipped it and held it against his torn cheek and nose. The water stung and burned.

The black cloud had crossed the sky, a blob of dark against the stars. The night was quiet again.

Tom stepped into the water and felt the bottom drop from under his feet. He threshed the two strokes across the ditch and pulled himself heavily up the other bank. His clothes clung to him. He moved and made a slopping noise; his shoes squished. Then he sat down, took off his shoes and emptied them. He wrung the bottoms of his trousers, took off his coat and squeezed the water from it.

Along the highway he saw the dancing beams of the flashlights, searching the ditches. Tom put on his shoes and moved cautiously across the stubble field. The squishing noise no longer came from his shoes. He went by instinct toward the other side of the stubble field, and at last he came to the road. Very cautiously he approached the square of houses.

Once a guard, thinking he heard a noise, called, "Who's there?"

Tom dropped and froze to the ground, and the flashlight beam passed over him. He crept silently to the door of the Joad house. The door squalled on its hinges. And Ma's voice, calm and steady and wide awake:

"What's that?"

"Me. Tom."

"Well, you better get some sleep. A1 ain't in yet."

"He must a foun' a girl."

"Go on to sleep," she said softly. "Over under the window."

He found his place and took off his clothes to the skin. He lay shivering under his blanket. And his torn face awakened from its numbness, and his whole head throbbed.

It was an hour more before A1 came in. He moved cautiously near and stepped on Tom's wet clothes.

"Sh!" said Tom.

A1 whispered, "You awake? How'd you get wet?"

"Sh," said Tom. "Tell you in the mornin'."

Pa turned on his back, and his snoring filled the room with gasps and snorts.

"You're col'," A1 said.

"Sh. Go to sleep." The little square of the window showed gray against the black of the room.

Tom did not sleep. The nerves of his wounded face came back to life and throbbed, and his cheek bone ached, and his broken nose bulged and pulsed with pain that seemed to toss him about, to shake him. He watched the little square window, saw the stars slide down over it and drop from sight. At intervals he heard the footsteps of the watchmen.

At last the roosters crowed, far away, and gradually the window lightened. Tom touched his swollen face with his fingertips, and at his movement Al groaned and murmured in his sleep.

In the morning Ma sees Tom's battered face.

"Tom," she whispered, "what's the matter?"

"Sh!" he said. "Don't talk loud. I got in a fight."

"Tom!"

"I couldn' help it, Ma."

She knelt down beside him. "You in trouble?"

He was a long time answering. "Yeah," he said. "In trouble. I can't go out to work. I got to hide."

The children crawled near on their hands and knees, staring greedily. "What's the matter'th him, Ma?"

"Hush!" Ma said. "Go wash up."

"We got no soap."

"Well, use water."

"What's the matter'th Tom?"

"Now you hush. An' don't you tell nobody."

They backed away and squatted down against the far wall, knowing they would not be inspected.

Ma asked, "Is it bad?"

"Nose busted."

"I mean the trouble?"

"Yeah. Bad!"

A1 opened his eyes and looked at Tom. "Well, for Chris' sake! What was you in?"

"What's a matter?" Uncle John asked. . . .

Pa clumped in. "[The store] was open all right." He put a tiny bag of flour and his package of lard on the floor beside the stove. " 'S'a matter?" he asked.

Tom braced himself on one elbow for a moment, and then he lay back. "Jesus, I'm weak. I'm gonna tell ya once. So I'll tell all of ya. How 'bout the kids?"

Ma looked at them, huddled against the wall. "Go wash ya face."

"No," Tom said. "They got to hear. They got to know. They might blab if they don' know."

"What the hell is this?" Pa demanded.

"I'm a-gonna tell. Las' night I went out to see what all the yellin' was about. An' I come on Casy."

"The preacher?"

"Yeah, Pa. The preacher, on'y he was a-leadin' the strike. They come for him."

Pa demanded, "Who come for him?"

"I dunno. Same kinda guys that turned us back on the road that night. Had pick handles." He paused. "They killed 'im. Busted his head. I was standin' there. I went nuts. Grabbed the pick handle." He looked bleakly back at the night, the darkness, the flashlights, as he spoke. "I—I clubbed a guy."

Ma's breath caught in her throat. Pa stiffened. "Kill 'im?" he asked softly.

"I—don't know. I was nuts. Tried to."

Ma asked, "Was you saw?"

"I dunno. I dunno. I guess so. They had the lights on us."

For a moment Ma stared into his eyes. "Pa," she said, "break up some boxes. We got to get breakfas'. You got to go to work. Ruthie, Winfiel'. If anybody asts you—Tom is sick— you hear? If you tell—he'll—get sent to jail. You hear?"

"Yes, ma'am."

"Keep your eye on 'em, John. Don' let 'em talk to nobody." She built the fire as Pa broke the boxes that had held the goods. She made her dough, put a pot of coffee to boil. The light wood caught and roared its flame in the chimney.

Pa finished breaking the boxes. He came near to Tom. "Casy—he was a good man. What'd he wanta mess with that stuff for?"

Tom said dully, "They come to work for fi' cents a box."

"That's what we're a-gettin'."

"Yeah. What we was a-doin' was breakin' strike. They give them fellas two an' a half cents."

"You can't eat on that."

"I know," Tom said wearily. "That's why they struck. Well, I think they bust that strike las' night. We'll maybe be gettin' two an' a half cents today."

"Why, the sons-a-bitches "

"Yeah! Pa. You see? Casy was still a—good man. Goddamn it, I can't get that pitcher outa my head. Him layin' there—head jus' crushed flat an' oozin'. Jesus!" He covered his eyes with his hand.

"Well, what we gonna do?" Uncle John asked.

A1 was standing up now. "Well, by God, I know what I'm gonna do. I'm gonna get out of it."

"No, you ain't, Al," Tom said. "We need you now. I'm the one. I'm a danger now. Soon's I get on my feet I got to go·"

Ma worked at the stove. Her head was half turned to hear. She put grease in the frying pan, and when it whispered with heat, she spooned the dough into it.

Tom went on, "You got to stay, Al. You got to take care a the truck."

"Well, I don' like it."

"Can't help it, Al. It's your folks. You can help 'em. I'm a danger to 'em."

Al grumbled angrily. "I don' know why I ain't let to get me a job in a garage."

"Later, maybe." Tom looked past him, and he saw Rose of Sharon [who is pregnant] lying on the mattress. Her eyes were huge—opened wide. "Don't worry," he called to her. "Don't you worry. Gonna get you some milk today." She blinked slowly, and didn't answer him.

Pa said, "We got to know, Tom. Think ya killed this fella?"

"I don' know. It was dark. An' somebody smacked me. I don' know. I hope so. I hope I killed the bastard."

"Tom!" Ma called. "Don' talk like that."

From the street came the sound of many cars moving slowly. Pa stepped to the window and looked out. "They's a whole slew a new people comin' in," he said.

"I guess they bust the strike, awright," said Tom. "I guess you'll start at two an' a half cents."

"But a fella could work at a run, an' still he couldn' eat."

"I know," said Tom. "Eat win'fall peaches. That'll keep ya up."

Ma turned the dough and stirred the coffee. "Listen to me," she said. "I'm gettin' cornmeal today. We're a-gonna eat cornmeal mush. An' soon's we get enough for gas, we're movin' away. This ain't a good place. An' I ain't gonna have Tom out alone. No, sir."

"Ya can't do that, Ma. I tell you I'm jus' a danger to ya."

Her chin was set. "That's what we'll do. Here, come eat this here, an' then get out to work. I'll come out soon's I get washed up. We got to make some money." . . .

Ma took a plate and a cup to Tom. "Better eat a little somepin."

"I can't, Ma. I'm so darn sore I couldn' chew."

"You better try."

"No, I can't, Ma,"

She sat down on the edge of his mattress. "You got to tell me," she said. "I got to figger how it was. I got to keep straight. What was Casy a-doin'? Why'd they kill 'im?"

"He was jus' standin' there with the lights on' 'im."

"What'd he say? Can ya 'member what he says?"

Tom said, "Sure. Casy said, 'You got no right to starve people.' An' then this heavy fella called him a red son-of-a- bitch. An' Casy says, 'You don' know what you're a-doin'.' An' then this guy smashed 'im."

Ma looked down. She twisted her hands together. "Tha's what he said—'You don' know what you're doin"?"

"Yeah!"

Ma said, "I wisht Granma could a heard."

"Ma—I didn' know what I was a-doin', no more'n when you take a breath. I didn' even know I was gonna do it."

"It's awright. I wisht you didn' do it. I wisht you wasn' there. But you done what you had to do. I can't read no fault on you." She went to the stove and dipped a cloth in the heating dishwater. "Here," she said. "Put that there on your face."

He laid the warm cloth over his nose and cheek, and winced at the heat. "Ma, I'm a-gonna go away tonight. I can't go puttin' this on you folks."

Ma said angrily, "Tom! They's a whole lot I don' un'er- stan'. But goin' away ain't gonna ease us. It's gonna bear us down." And she went on, "They was the time when we was on the lan'. They was a boundary to us then. Ol' folks died off, an' little fellas come, an' we was always one thing—we was the fambly—kinda whole and clear. An' now we ain't clear no more. I can't get straight. They ain't nothin' keeps us clear. Al—he's a-hankerin' an' a-jibbitin' to go off on his own. An' Uncle John is jus' a-draggin' along. Pa's lost his place. He ain't the head no more. We're crackin' up, Tom. There ain't no fambly now. An' Rosasharn—" She looked around and found the girl's wide eyes. "She gonna have her baby an' they won't be no fambly. I don' know. I been a-tryin' to keep her goin'. Winfiel'—what's he gonna be, this-a-way? Gettin' wild, an' Ruthie too—like animals. Got nothin' to trus'. Don' go, Tom. Stay an' help."

"O.K.," he said tiredly. "O.K. I shouldn', though. I know it."

Ma went to her dishpan and washed the tin plates and dried them. "You didn' sleep."

"No."

"Well, you sleep. I seen your clothes was wet. I'll hang 'em by the stove to dry." She finished her work. "I'm goin' now. I'll pick. Rosasharn, if anybody comes, Tom sick, you hear? Don' let nobody in. You hear?" Rose of Sharon nodded. "We'll come back at noon. Get some sleep, Tom. Maybe we can get outa here tonight." She moved swiftly to him. "Tom, you ain't gonna slip out?"

"No, Ma."

"You sure? You won't go?"

"No, Ma. I'll be here."

"Awright. 'Member, Rosasharn." She went out and closed the door firmly behind her.

Tom lay still—and then a wave of sleep lifted him to the edge of unconsciousness and dropped him slowly back and lifted him again.

"You—Tom!"

"Huh? Yeah!" He started awake. He looked over at Rose of Sharon. Her eyes were blazing with resentment. "What you want?"

"You killed a fella!"

"Yeah. Not so loud! You wanta rouse somebody?"

"What da I care?" she cried. "That lady tol' me. She says what sin's gonna do. She tol' me. What chance I got to have a nice baby? ... I ain't gettin' good food. I ain't gettin' milk." Her voice rose hysterically. "An' now you kill a fella. What chance that baby got to get bore right? I know— gonna be a freak—a freak! I never done no dancin'."

Tom got up. "Sh!" he said. "You're gonna get folks in here."

"I don' care. I'll have a freak! I didn' dance no hug- dance."

He went near to her. "Be quiet."

"You get away from me. It ain't the first fella you killed, neither." Her face was growing red with hysteria. Her words blurred. "I don' wanta look at you." She covered her head with her blanket.

Tom heard the choked, smothered cries. He bit his lower lip and studied the floor. And then he went to Pa's bed. Under the edge of the mattress the rifle lay, a lever-action Winchester .38, long and heavy. Tom picked it up and dropped the lever to see that a cartridge was in the chamber. He tested the hammer on half-cock. And then he went back to his mattress. He laid the rifle on the floor beside him, stock up and barrel pointing down. Rose of Sharon's voice thinned to a whimper. Tom lay down again and covered himself, covered his bruised cheek with the blanket and made a little tunnel to breathe through. He sighed, "Jesus, oh, Jesus!"

Outside, a group of cars went by, and voices sounded.

"How many men?"

"Jes' us—three. Whatcha payin'?"

"You go to house twenty-five. Number's right on the door."

"O.K., mister. Whatcha payin'?"

"Two and a half cents."

"Why, goddamn it, a man can't make his dinner!"

"That's what we're payin'. There's two hundred men coming from the South that'll be glad to get it."

"But, Jesus, mister!"

"Go on now. Either take it or go on along. I got no time to argue."

"But "

"Look. I didn' set the price. I'm just checking you in. If you want it, take it. If you don't, turn right around and go along."

"Twenty-five, you say?"

"Yes, twenty-five."

At the book's end, the Joads and the other migrants, hungry, some to the point of starvation, penniless, and ill, have hit bottom. Yet the novel ends on a hopeful note. One of the Joads, Rose of Sharon, who has just given birth to a stillborn baby, offers her life- sustaining mother's milk to a starving stranger. Written during hard times, *The Grapes of Wrath* was both a cry of pain and an affirmation of life that urges people to be more humane, to be more compassionate, and to recognize their moral obligation to care about others, particularly the downtrodden, with whom they share a common humanity.

ELIE WIESEL

NIGHT

The Holocaust has given rise to a vast and growing body of literature. During the war, Jews in the ghettos, concentration camps, or hiding, virtually all of whom eventually perished, wrote poems and kept diaries so that the world, which they felt had forsaken them, would know of their ordeal. These writings were also a means of spiritual sustenance and defiance during dark times. Anne Frank, a young girl who lived in a secret annex in Amsterdam, kept a diary of her experience that survived her capture and death in the notorious Bergen Belsen concentration camp. First published in 1947 and translated into many languages, *The Diary of a Young Girl,* has become a modern classic. Made into a play, in 1956 it was performed simultaneously in seven German cities before audiences that sat in stunned silence.

After liberation, survivors felt a compulsion to bear witness to the willful extermination of a people and a culture. One such survivor, Elie Wiesel (1928-), who received instant acclaim with the French publication of *Night* in 1958, has since become a distinguished man of letters. Among his many honors is the Nobel Peace Prize awarded in 1986. Born in a small village in Romania, which was ceded to Hungary in 1940, Wiesel was deported with his family to Auschwitz in May 1944. His mother and sister were gassed on arrival; his father, weakened by the death journey from Auschwitz to Buchenwald, much of it by foot in freezing weather and with little food, died in early 1945, shortly before the liberation. In this passage from *Night,* which has the quality of sacred poetry, Wiesel describes his entry into another planet—Auschwitz.

. . . We pressed against the windows. The convoy was moving slowly. A quarter of an hour later, it slowed down again. Through the windows we could see barbed wire; we realized that this must be the camp.

We had forgotten the existence of Madame Schachter. Suddenly, we heard terrible screams:

"Jews, look! Look through the window! Flames! Look!"

And as the train stopped, we saw this time that flames were gushing out of a tall chimney into the black sky.

Madame Schachter was silent herself. Once more she had become dumb, indifferent, absent, and had gone back to her corner.

We looked at the flames in the darkness. There was an abominable odor floating in the air. Suddenly, our doors opened. Some odd-looking characters, dressed in striped shirts and black trousers leapt into the wagon. They held electric torches and truncheons. They began to strike out to right and left, shouting:

"Everybody get out! Everyone out of the wagon! Quickly!"

We jumped out. I threw a last glance toward Madame Schachter. Her little boy was holding her hand.

In front of us flames. In the air that smell of burning flesh. It must have been about midnight. We had arrived—at Birkenau, reception center for Auschwitz. . . .

The cherished objects we had brought with us thus far were left behind in the train, and with them, at last, our illusions.

Every two yards or so an SS man held his tommy gun trained on us. Hand in hand we followed the crowd.

An SS noncommissioned officer came to meet us, a truncheon in his hand. He gave the order:

"Men to the left! Women to the right!"

Eight words spoken quietly, indifferently, without emotion. Eight short, simple words. Yet that was the moment when I parted from my mother. I had not had time to think, but already I felt the pressure of my father's hand: we were alone. For a part of a second I glimpsed my mother and my sisters moving away to the right. Tzipora held Mother's hand. I saw them disappear into the distance; my mother was stroking my sister's fair hair, as though to protect her, while I walked on with my father and the other men. And I did not know that in that place, at that moment, I was parting from my mother and Tzipora forever. I went on walking. My father held onto my hand.

Behind me, an old man fell to the ground. Near him was an SS man putting his revolver back in its holster.

My hand shifted on my father's arm. I had one thought—not to lose him. Not to be left alone.

The SS officers gave the order:

"Form fives!"

Commotion. At all costs we must keep together.

"Here, kid, how old are you?"

It was one of the prisoners who asked me this. I could not see his face, but his voice was tense and weary.

"I'm not quite fifteen yet."

"No. Eighteen."

"But I'm not," I said. "Fifteen."

"Fool. Listen to what I say."

Then he questioned my father, who replied:

"Fifty."

The other grew more furious than ever.

"No, not fifty. Forty. Do you understand? Eighteen and forty."

He disappeared into the night shadows. A second man came up, spitting oaths at us.

"What have you come here for, you sons of bitches? What are you doing here, eh?"

Someone dared to answer him.

"What do you think? Do you suppose we've come here for our own pleasure? Do you think we asked to come?"

A little more, and the man would have killed him.

"You shut your trap, you filthy swine, or I'll squash you right now! You'd have done better to have hanged yourselves where you were than to come here. Didn't you know what was in store for you at Auschwitz? Haven't you heard about it? In 1944?"

No, we had not heard. No one had told us. He could not believe his ears. His tone of voice became increasingly brutal.

"Do you see that chimney over there? See it? Do you see those flames? (Yes, we did see the flames.) Over there—that's where you're going to be taken. That's your grave, over there. Haven't you realized it yet? You dumb bastards, don't you understand anything? You're going to be burned. Frizzled away. Turned into ashes."

He was growing hysterical in his fury. We stayed motionless, petrified. Surely it was all a nightmare? An unimaginable nightmare?

I heard murmurs around me.

"We've got to do something. We can't let ourselves be killed. We can't go like beasts to the slaughter. We've got to revolt."

There were a few sturdy young fellows among us. They had knives on them, and they tried to incite the others to throw themselves on the armed guards.

One of the young men cried:

"Let the world learn of the existence of Auschwitz. Let everybody hear about it, while they can still escape. ..."

But the, older ones begged their children not to do anything foolish:

"You must never lose faith, even when the sword hangs over your head. That's the teaching of our sages. ..."

The wind of revolt died down. We continued our march toward the square. In the middle stood the notorious Dr. Men- gele (a typical SS officer: a cruel face, but not devoid of intelligence, and wearing a monocle); a conductor's baton in his hand, he was standing among the other officers. The baton moved unremittingly, sometimes to the right, sometimes to the left.

I was already in front of him:

"How old are you?" he asked, in an attempt at a paternal tone of voice.

"Eighteen." My voice was shaking.

"Are you in good health?"

"Yes."

"What's your occupation?"

Should I say that I was a student?

"Farmer," I heard myself say.

This conversation cannot have lasted more than a few seconds. It had seemed like an eternity to me.

The baton moved to the left. I took half a step forward. I wanted to see first where they were sending my father. If he went to the right, I would go after him.

The baton once again pointed to the left for him too. A weight was lifted from my heart.

We did not yet know which was the better side, right or left; which road led to prison and which to the crematory. But for the moment I was happy; I was near my father. Our procession continued to move slowly forward.

Another prisoner came up to us:

"Satisfied?"

"Yes," someone replied.

"Poor devils, you're going to the crematory."

He seemed to be telling the truth. Not far from us, flames were leaping up from a ditch, gigantic flames. They were burning something. A lorry drew up at the pit and delivered its load—little children. Babies! Yes, I saw it—saw it with my own eyes . . . those children in the flames. (Is it surprising that I could not sleep after that? Sleep had fled from my eyes.)

So this was where we were going. A little farther on was another and larger ditch for adults.

I pinched my face. Was I still alive? Was I awake? I could not believe it. How could it be possible for them to burn people, children, and for the world to keep silent? No, none of this could be true. It was a nightmare. . . . Soon I should wake with a start, my heart pounding, and find myself back in the bedroom of my childhood, among my books. . . .

My father's voice drew me from my thoughts:

"It's a shame ... a shame that you couldn't have gone with your mother. ... I saw several boys of your age going with their mothers. ..."

His voice was terribly sad. I realized that he did not want to see what they were going to do to me. He did not want to see the burning of his only son.

My forehead was bathed in cold sweat. But I told him that I did not believe that they could burn people in our age, that humanity would never tolerate it. . . .

"Humanity? Humanity is not concerned with us. Today anything is allowed. Anything is possible, even these crematories. ..."

His voice was choking.

"Father," I said, "if that is so, I don't want to wait here. I'm going to run to the electric wire. That would be better than slow agony in the flames."

He did not answer. He was weeping. His body was shaken convulsively. Around us, everyone was weeping. Someone began to recite the Kaddish, the prayer for the dead. I do not know if it has ever happened before, in the long history of the Jews, that people have ever recited the prayer for the dead for themselves.

"Yitgadal veyitkadach shme raba. . . . May His Name be blessed and magnified. ..." whispered my father.

For the first time, I felt revolt rise up in me. Why should I bless His name? The Eternal, Lord of the Universe, the All-Powerful and Terrible, was silent. What had I to thank Him for?

We continued our march. We were gradually drawing closer to the ditch, from which an internal heat was rising. Still twenty steps to go. If I wanted to bring about my own death, this was the moment. Our line had now only fifteen paces to cover. I bit my lips so that my father would not hear my teeth chattering. Ten steps still. Eight. Seven. We marched slowly on, as though following a hearse at our own funeral. Four steps more. Three steps. There it was now, right in front of us, the pit and its flames. I gathered all that was left of my strength, so that I could break from the ranks and throw myself upon the barbed wire. In the depths of my heart, I bade farewell to my father, to the whole universe; and, in spite of myself, the words formed themselves and issued in a whisper from my lips: *Yitgadal veyitkadach shme raba. . . .* May His name be blessed and magnified. . . . My heart was bursting. The moment had come. I was face to face with the Angel of Death. . . .

No. Two steps from the pit we were ordered to turn to the left and made to go into a barracks.

I pressed my father's hand. He said:

"Do you remember Madame Schachter, in the train?"

Never shall I forget that night, the first night in camp, which has turned my life into one long night, seven times cursed and seven times sealed. Never shall I forget that smoke. Never shall I forget the little faces of the children, whose bodies I saw turned into wreaths of smoke beneath a silent blue sky.

Never shall I forget those flames which consumed my faith forever.

Never shall I forget that nocturnal silence which deprived me, for all eternity, of the desire to live. Never shall I forget those moments which murdered my God and my soul and turned my dreams to dust. Never shall I forget these things, even if I am condemned to live as long as God Himself. Never.

Wiesel describes the execution by hanging of a young boy and the reaction among the inmates.

I witnessed other hangings. I never saw a single one of the victims weep. For a long time those dried-up bodies had forgotten the bitter taste of tears.

Except once. The Oberkapo of the fifty-second cable unit was a Dutchman, a giant, well over six feet. Seven hundred prisoners worked under his orders, and they all loved him like a brother. No one had ever received a blow at his hands, nor an insult from his lips.

He had a young boy under him, a *pipel,* as they were called—a child with a refined and beautiful face, unheard of in this camp.

(At Buna, the *pipel* were loathed; they were often crueller than adults. I once saw one of thirteen beating his father because the latter had not made his bed properly. The old man was crying softly while the boy shouted: "If you don't stop crying at once I shan't bring you any more bread. Do you understand?" But the Dutchman's little servant was loved by all. He had the face of a sad angel.)

One day, the electric power station at Buna was blown up. The Gestapo, summoned to the spot, suspected sabotage. They found a trail. It eventually led to the Dutch Oberkapo. And there, after a search, they found an important stock of arms.

The Oberkapo was arrested immediately. He was tortured for a period of weeks, but in vain. He would not give a single name. He was transferred to Auschwitz. We never heard of him again.

But his little servant had been left behind in the camp in prison. Also put to torture, he too would not speak. Then the SS sentenced him to death, with two other prisoners who had been discovered with arms.

One day when we came back from work we saw three gallows rearing up in the assembly place, three black crows. Roll call. SS all round us, machine guns trained: the traditional ceremony. Three victims in chains—and one of them, the little servant, the sad-eyed angel.

The SS seemed more preoccupied, more disturbed than usual. To hang a young boy in front of thousands of spectators was no light matter. The head of the camp read the verdict. All eyes were on the child. He was lividly pale, almost calm, biting his lips. The gallows threw its shadow over him.

This time the Lagerkapo refused to act as executioner. Three SS replaced him.

The three victims mounted together onto the chairs.

The three necks were placed at the same moment within the nooses.

"Long live liberty!" cried the two adults.

But the child was silent.

"Where is God? Where is He?" someone behind me asked.

At a sign from the head of the camp, the three chairs tipped over.

Total silence throughout the camp. On the horizon, the sun was setting.

"Bare your heads!" yelled the head of the camp. His voice was raucous. We were weeping.

"Cover your heads!"

Then the march past began. The two adults were no longer alive. Their tongues hung swollen, blue-tinged. But the third rope was still moving; being so light, the child was still alive. . . .

For more than half an hour he stayed there, struggling between life and death, dying in slow agony under our eyes. And we had to look him full in the face. He was still alive when I passed in front of him. His tongue was still red, his eyes not yet glazed.

Behind me, I heard the same man asking:

"Where is God now?"

And I heard a voice within me answer him:

"Where is He? Here He is—He is hanging here on this gallows. ..."

That night the soup tasted of corpses.

At the end of the Jewish High Holy Days introducing the New Year, the Germans engage in a dreaded selection in which those deemed unfit for work are sent to the gas chambers.

YOM KIPPUR. THE DAY OF ATONEMENT.

Should we fast? The question was hotly debated. To fast would mean a surer, swifter death. We fasted here the whole year round. The whole year was Yom Kippur. But others said that we should fast simply because it was dangerous to do so. We should show God that even here, in this enclosed hell, we were capable of singing His praises.

I did not fast, mainly to please my father, who had forbidden me to do so. But further, there was no longer any reason why I should fast. I no longer accepted God's silence. As I swallowed my bowl of soup, I saw in the gesture an act of rebellion and protest against Him.

And I nibbled my crust of bread.

In the depths of my heart, I felt a great void.

The SS gave us a fine New Year's gift.

We had just come back from work. As soon as we had passed through the door of the camp, we sensed something different in the air. Roll call did not take so long as usual. The evening soup was given out with great speed and swallowed down at once in anguish.

I was no longer in the same block as my father. I had been transferred to another unit, the building one, where, twelve hours a day, I had to drag heavy blocks of stone about. The head of my new block was a German Jew, small of stature, with piercing eyes. He told us that evening that no one would be allowed to go out after the evening soup. And soon a terrible word was circulating—selection.

We knew what that meant. An SS man would examine us. Whenever he found a weak one, a *musulman* as we called them, he would write his number down: good for the crematory.

After soup, we gathered together between the beds. The veterans said:

"You're lucky to have been brought here so late. This camp is paradise today, compared with what it was like two years ago. Buna was a real hell then. There was no water, no blankets, less soup and bread. At night we slept almost naked, and it was below thirty degrees. The corpses were collected in hundreds every day. The work was hard. Today, this is a little paradise. The Kapos had orders to kill a certain number of prisoners every day. And every week—selection. A merciless selection. . . . Yes, you're lucky."

"Stop it! Be quiet!" I begged. "You can tell your stories tomorrow or on some other day."

They burst out laughing. They were not veterans for nothing.

"Are you scared? So were we scared. And there was plenty to be scared of in those days."

The old men stayed in their corner, dumb, motionless, hunted. Some were praying.

An hour's delay. In an hour, we should know the verdict—death or a reprieve.

And my father? Suddenly I remembered him. How would he pass the selection? He had aged so much. . . .

The head of our block had never been outside concentration camps since 1933. He had already been through all the slaughterhouses, all the factories of death. At about nine o'clock, he took up his position in our midst:

"Achtung!"

There was instant silence.

"Listen carefully to what I am going to say." (For the first time, I heard his voice quiver.) "In a few moments the selection will begin. You must get completely undressed. Then one by one you go before the SS doctors. I hope you will all succeed in getting through. But you must help your own chances. Before you go into the next room, move about in some way so that you give yourselves a little color. Don't walk slowly, run! Run as if the devil were after you! Don't look at the SS. Run, straight in front of you!"

He broke off for a moment, then added:

"And, the essential thing, don't be afraid!"

Here was a piece of advice we should have liked very much to be able to follow.

I got undressed, leaving my clothes on the bed. There was no danger of anyone stealing them this evening.

Tibi and Yossi, who had changed their unit at the same time as I had, came up to me and said:

"Let's keep together. We shall be stronger."

Yossi was murmuring something between his teeth. He must have been praying. I had never realized that Yossi was a believer. I had even always thought the reverse. Tibi was silent, very pale. All the prisoners in the block stood naked between the beds. This must be how one stands at the last judgment.

"They're coming!"

There were three SS officers standing round the notorious Dr. Mengele, who had received us at Birkenau. The head of the block, with an attempt at a smile, asked us:

"Ready?"

Yes, we were ready. So were the SS doctors. Dr. Mengele was holding a list in his hand: our numbers. He made a sign to the head of the block, "We can begin!" As if this were a game!

The first to go by were the "officials" of the block: *Stube- naelteste,* Kapos, foremen, all in perfect physical condition of course! Then came the ordinary prisoners' turn. Dr. Mengele took stock of them from head to foot. Every now and then, he wrote a number down. One single thought filled my mind: not to let my number be taken; not to show my left arm.

There were only Tibi and Yossi in front of me. They passed. I had time to notice that Mengele had not written their numbers down. Someone pushed me. It was my turn. I ran without looking back. My head was spinning: you're too thin, you're weak, you're too thin, you're good for the furnace. . . . The race seemed interminable. I thought I had been running for years. . . . You're too thin, you're too weak. ... At last I had arrived exhausted. When I regained my breath, I questioned Yossi and Tibi:

"Was I written down?"

"No," said Yossi. He added, smiling: "In any case, he couldn't have written you down, you were running too fast. ..."

I began to laugh. I was glad. I would have liked to kiss him. At that moment, what did the others matter! I hadn't been written down.

Those whose numbers had been noted stood apart, abandoned by the whole world. Some were weeping in silence. The SS officers went away. The head of the block appeared, his face reflecting the general weariness.

"Everything went off all right. Don't worry. Nothing is going to happen to anyone. To anyone."

Again he tried to smile. A poor, emaciated, dried-up Jew questioned him avidly in a trembling voice:

"But . . . but, *Blockaelteste,* they did write me down!"

The head of the block let his anger break out. What! Did someone refuse to believe him!

"What's the matter now? Am I telling lies then? I tell you once and for all, nothing's going to happen to you! To anyone! You're wallowing in your own despair, you fool!"

The bell rang, a signal that the selection had been completed throughout the camp. . . .

Several days had elapsed. We no longer thought about the selection. We went to work as usual, loading heavy stones into railway wagons. Rations had become more meager: this was the only change.

We had risen before dawn, as on every day. We had received the black coffee, the ration of bread. We were about to set out for the yard as usual. The head of the block arrived, running.

"Silence for a moment. I have a list of numbers here. I'm going to read them to you. Those whose numbers I call won't be going to work this morning; they'll stay behind in the camp."

And, in a soft voice, he read out about ten numbers. We had understood. These were numbers chosen at the selection. Dr. Mengele had not forgotten.

The head of the block went toward his room. Ten prisoners surrounded him, hanging onto his clothes:

"Save us! You promised . . . ! We want to go to the yard. We're strong enough to work. We're good workers. We can ... we will. . . ."

He tried to calm them, to reassure them about their fate, to explain to them that the fact that they were staying behind in the camp did not mean much, had no tragic significance. "After all, I stay here myself every day," he added. It was a somewhat feeble argument. He realized it, and without another word went and shut himself up in his room.